D1482296

STRATEGIC LOGISTICS MANAGEMENT

About the Authors

Douglas M. Lambert is the Prime F. Osborn III Eminent Scholar Chair in Transportation, Professor of Marketing and Logistics, and Director of The International Center for Competitive Excellence at the College of Business Administration, University of North Florida. From 1983 to 1985 he was PepsiCo Professor of Marketing at Michigan State University. Dr. Lambert has served as a faculty member for over 250 executive development programs in North America, Europe, and Asia. He is the author of *The Development of an Inventory Costing Methodology, The Distribution Channels Decision, The Product Abandonment Decision* and co-author of *Management in Marketing Channels* and *Strategic Logistics Management.* His publications include more than 100 articles and conference proceedings. In 1986 Dr. Lambert received the Council of Logistics Management's Distinguished Service Award, "the highest honor that can be bestowed on an individual for achievement in the physical distribution/logistics industry," for his contributions to logistics management. He holds an honors BA and MBA from the University of Western Ontario and a Ph.D. from The Ohio State University. Dr. Lambert is co-editor of *The International Journal of Logistics Management.*

James R. Stock is Professor of Marketing and Logistics at the College of Business Administration, University of South Florida. Dr. Stock held previous faculty appointments at Michigan State University, the University of Oklahoma and the University of Notre Dame. From 1986 to 1988 he held the position of Distinguished Visiting Professor of Logistics Management, School of Systems and Logistics, at the Air Force Institute of Technology, Wright-Patterson Air Force Base. Dr. Stock is the author or co-author of over 80 publications including books, monographs, articles, and proceedings papers. He is author of *Reverse Logistics;* co-author of *Distribution Consultants: A Managerial Guide to Their Identification, Selection, and Use;* and co-author of *Strategic Logistics Management.* He currently serves as editor of the *International Journal of Physical Distribution and Logistics Management* and the managing editor of *Logistics Spectrum.* He received the Armitage Medal (1988) from the Society of Logistics Engineers in recognition of his scholarly contributions to the discipline of logistics. Dr. Stock holds B.S. and MBA degrees from the University of Miami (Florida) and the Ph.D. from The Ohio State University.

STRATEGIC LOGISTICS MANAGEMENT

Third Edition

Douglas M. Lambert
Prime F. Osborn III Eminent Scholar
and Professor of Marketing and Logistics
College of Business Administration
University of North Florida

James R. Stock
Professor of Marketing and Logistics
Department of Marketing
College of Business Administration
University of South Florida

IRWIN

Chicago • Bogota • Boston • Buenos Aires • Caracas
London • Madrid • Mexico City • Sydney • Toronto

This symbol indicates that the paper in this book is made of recycled paper. Its fiber content exceeds the recommended minimum of 50% waste paper fibers as specified by the EPA.

Senior sponsoring editor:	Stephen Patterson
Developmental editor:	Andy Winston
Marketing manager:	Kurt Messersmith
Project editor:	Karen Smith
Production manager:	Diane Palmer
Designer:	Tara Bazata
Compositor:	Graphic Composition, Inc.
Typeface:	10/12 Baskerville
Printer:	R. R. Donnelley & Sons Company

Library of Congress Cataloging-in-Publication Data

Lambert, Douglas M.
Strategic logistics management / Douglas M. Lambert, James R. Stock.—3rd ed.
p. cm.—(The Irwin series in marketing)
Stock's name appears first on the earlier edition.
Includes bibliographical references and index.
ISBN 0-256-08838-1
1. Business logistics. 2. Physical distribution of goods—Management. I. Stock, James R. II. Title. III. Series.
HF5415.7.S86 1992
658.5—dc20 91–32656

Printed in the United States of America
6 7 8 9 0 DOC 8 7 6

To Bernard J. LaLonde
Teacher, Mentor, Colleague, and Friend

The Irwin Series in Marketing

Consulting Editor *Gilbert A. Churchill, Jr.*
University of Wisconsin—Madison

Alreck & Settle
The Survey Research Handbook
Second Edition

Belch & Belch
Introduction to Advertising and Promotion
Second Edition

Berkowitz, Kerin, Hartley, & Rudelius
Marketing
Third Edition

Bernhardt & Kinnear
Cases in Marketing Management
Fifth Edition

Bingham & Raffield
Business to Business Marketing Management
First Edition

Bovee & Arens
Contemporary Advertising
Fourth Edition

Boyd & Walker
Marketing Management: A Strategic Approach
First Edition

Boyd, Westfall, & Stasch
Marketing Research: Text and Cases
Seventh Edition

Burstiner
Basic Retailing
Second Edition

Cadotte
The Market Place: A Stratetic Marketing Simulation
First Edition

Cateora
International Marketing
Eighth Edition

Churchill, Ford, & Walker
Sales Force Management
Fourth Edition

Cole
Consumer and Commercial Credit Management
Ninth Edition

Cravens
Strategic Marketing
Third Edition

Cravens & Lamb
Strategic Marketing Management Cases
Fourth Edition

Crawford
New Products Management
Third Edition

Dillon, Madden, & Firtle
Essentials of Marketing Research
First Edition

Dillon, Madden, & Firtle
Marketing Research in a Marketing Environment
Second Edition

Engel, Warshaw, & Kinnear
Promotional Strategy
Seventh Edition

Faria, Nulsen, & Roussos
Compete
Fourth Edition

Futrell
ABC's of Selling
Third Edition

Futrell
Fundamentals of Selling
Fourth Edition

Hawkins, Best, & Coney
Consumer Behavior
Fifth Edition

Kurtz & Dodge
Professional Selling
Sixth Edition

Lambert & Stock
Strategic Logistics Management
Third Edition

Lehmann & Winer
Analysis for Marketing Planning
Second Edition

Lehmann
Marketing Research and Analysis
Fourth Edition

Levy & Weitz
Retailing Management
First Edition

Mason, Mayer, & Wilkinson
Modern Retailing
Sixth Edition

Mason, Mayer, & Ezell
Retailing
Fourth Edition

Mason & Perreault
The Marketing Game!
Second Edition

McCarthy & Perreault
Basic Marketing: A Global-Managerial Approach
Eleventh Edition

McCarthy & Perreault
Essentials of Marketing
Fifth Edition

Peter & Olson
Consumer Behavior and Marketing Strategy
Third Edition

Peter & Donnelly
A Preface to Marketing Management
Fifth Edition

Peter & Donnelly
Marketing Management: Knowledge and Skills
Third Edition

Quelch & Farris
Cases in Advertising and Promotion Management
Third Edition

Quelch, Dolan, & Kosnik
Marketing Management: Text and Cases
First Edition

Smith & Quelch
Ethics in Marketing
First Edition

Stanton, Spiro, & Buskirk
Management of a Sales Force
Eighth Edition

Thompson & Stappenbeck
The Marketing Strategy Game
First Edition

Walker, Boyd, & Larreche
Marketing Strategy: Planning and Implementation
First Edition

Weitz, Castleberry, & Tanner
Selling: Building Partnerships
First Edition

Preface

Notable changes occurring in the global marketplace since the publication of the first two editions of this book (1982 and 1987) have been the restructuring of international political boundaries, the creation of one of the world's largest consumer markets as a result of Europe 1992, a continued explosion of computer and information technology worldwide, the further development of global markets resulting in of a larger number of companies with operations worldwide, and a corporate emphasis on quality and customer satisfaction.

The third edition of *Strategic Logistics Management* has been significantly expanded to reflect these and the many other changes that have occurred, as well as to include state-of-the-art logistics information and technology. The basic tenets of the previous editions have been retained, but new material has been added to make the book more managerial, integrative, and "cutting edge." *Strategic Logistics Management* is still the only text that takes a marketing orientation and views the subject from a customer satisfaction perspective. While emphasizing the marketing aspects of logistics, it integrates all of the functional areas of the business as well as incorporating logistics into corporate strategy.

Logistics is big business. Its consumption of land, labor, capital, and information—coupled with its impact on the world's standard of living—is enormous. Curiously, it has only been within the past 30 years that the business community has taken a real interest in logistics. However, during that period logistics has increased in importance from a function that was perceived as barely necessary to (1) an activity where significant cost savings could be generated; (2) an activity that had enormous potential to impact customer satisfaction and hence increase sales; and (3) a marketing weapon that could be effectively utilized to gain a sustainable competitive advantage.

Strategic Logistics Management approaches the topic from a managerial perspective. Each chapter introduces basic logistics concepts in a format that is useful for management decision making. Of course, the basics—terms, concepts, and principles—are covered, but they are examined in light of how they interrelate and interface with other functions of the firm. In each chapter we have included examples of corporate applications of these concepts to illustrate how logistics activities can be managed to properly implement the marketing concept.

This book includes a good balance of theory and practical application. All the traditional logistics functions have been included. However, there are several important topics that are unique to this text or are approached in a different way. For example, the financial control of logistics is discussed in a separate chapter, as well as being interwoven throughout all chapters. We have purposely taken this approach because of the impact of logistics on the firm's profitability. Because logistics ultimately affects marketing's ability to generate and satisfy demand—and thus create customer satisfaction—the customer service activity is emphasized early in the book. Customer service can be considered the output of the logistics function. For this reason, customer service provides a focal point for the entire book, and customer service implications are considered in each of the 18 chapters.

A number of important topics not covered in many other logistics texts are covered in this book: order processing and management information systems; materials flow; financial control of logistics performance; logistics organizations; global logistics; decision support systems; channels of distribution; and the strategic logistics plan. Our goal in covering these topics in addition to the traditional activities is to provide readers with a grasp of the total picture of the logistics process.

There are a number of worthwhile improvements in the third edition. We have included many more references and examples from general management literature. This edition covers the academic and trade literature in the area of logistics extensively, and includes the most up-to-date information and examples. We have retained those elements that are "timeless" and those that made the previous editions successful.

There are several new and expanded features in this edition. We have added to and updated the Suggested Readings at the end of each chapter. Margin notes have been increased, and charts, figures, and graphs have been updated and revised where necessary. We believe that this edition is more readable for both the instructor and student. New and/or expanded topics include strategic alliances and partnerships, green marketing, decision support systems, channels of distribution, computer technology, globalization of markets, warehouse location, strategic planning, information systems, and customer service. This edition includes 12 cases, 6 more than in the previous edition. Six of these cases are new, and three have been updated and/or modified. Our aim has been to present instructors and students with the best textbook on the market. We believe we have succeeded.

The book is divided into three major sections. The first section, Chapters 1–3, provides an introduction to the logistics process by examining logistics' role in the economy and the firm and introducing the concept of integrated logistics management. The second section, Chapters 4–13, presents the functional areas of logistics from a customer service perspective, emphasizing the financial implications throughout. The topics of customer service, transportation, warehousing, inventory management, order processing and information systems, materials flow, and purchasing are discussed in detail, always with a view toward how they can be effectively managed. The third section, Chapters 14–18, emphasizes the strategic aspects of logistics management from both domestic and international perspectives. Chapter topics include decision support systems, financial control of logistics performance, logistics organizations, global logistics, and the strategic logistics plan.

The pragmatic, applied nature of the book, its managerial orientation, and its how-to appendixes make it a must-have reference book for present and future logistics professionals. The end-of-the-chapter questions and the case material help readers apply the material presented in each chapter. The questions, problems, and cases are structured to challenge readers' managerial skills. They are integrative in nature and examine issues that are important to today's logistics executive.

Douglas M. Lambert
James R. Stock

Acknowledgments

Any work of this magnitude is seldom the exclusive work of one or two individuals. A number of persons from the business and academic sectors have provided invaluable input. Several individuals from industry made helpful comments and/or provided material for this edition of the textbook including: Robert V. Delaney, executive vice president, Cass Logistics, Inc.: George A. Gecowets, executive vice president, Council of Logistics Management; Richard T. Skillinger, president, Smalley Transportation Company; and Douglas E. Zemke, senior vice president, sales and marketing, Cincinnati Bell Telephone Company. Many of our academic colleagues were extremely helpful in suggesting changes and providing input to the text, including: Professors Jay U. Sterling of the University of Alabama; David J. Bloomberg of Western Illinois University, B. Jay Coleman, University of North Florida; Robert L. Cook of Central Michigan University, William A. Cunningham of the University of South Alabama; Larry W. Emmelhainz of the Air Force Institute of Technology; Margaret A. Emmelhainz of the University of Dayton; M. Christine Lewis of Wayne State University; Robert R. Piper of the Naval Postgraduate School; A. Clyde Vollmers of Moorhead State University; and Kenneth C. Williamson of James Madison University.

Special thanks must go to colleagues at the University of North Florida including Dean Edward A. Johnson of the College of Business Administration, Associate Deans Earl Traynham and Frank McLaughlan, and Professor Robert Pickhardt, Chairman, Department of Management, Marketing and Logistics for providing a most supportive and colleagial environment that fosters faculty productivity. We are indebted to Gretchen Kabler and Gregory Peek for their research assistance in developing certain materials for this edition of the text and to Mary Lou Barr for thoroughly reading the page proofs with us and making some helpful suggestions. Also, the assistance of Andy Winston and Karen Smith at Richard D. Irwin is very much appreciated.

We are grateful to the following persons and companies for graciously providing us with exhibits, case materials, and other assistance: American Telephone and Telegraph; William C. Copacino, partner-in-charge, Logistics Strategy Group, Andersen Consulting; Martin G. Christopher, Cranfield School of Management, U.K.; Donald J. Bowersox, Michigan State University; Robert Lorin Cook, Central Michigan University; Cincinnati Bell Telephone Company; Rajiv P. Dant, Boston University; Alan Ginsberg, Manager of order-to-delivery forecasting, AT&T Consumer Products; Edgar M. Guertin, staff vice president, 3M Company; Donald R. Heide, senior vice president distribution, Target Stores; Herbert Hodus, senior vice president distribution, Child World; Ronald M. Jacobson, manager of material management systems, Rohm and Haas Company; Michiel R. Leenders, University of Western Ontario; Philip B. Schary, Oregon State University; Jay U. Sterling, University of Alabama; Frederick W. Westfall, formerly of the Air Force Institute of Technology; and Elaine M. Winter, director of communications and research, Council of Logistics Management. Our students at the University of North Florida and the University of South Florida and former students at Michigan State University, Air Force Institute of Technology, and University of Oklahoma, as well as the thousands of business executives with whom we have interacted on executive development programs, have had a strong influence on the contents of this book.

Without the support of our families, the task of writing a text would be impossible. The first author wishes to thank his parents, John and Mary Lambert, who have always been a source of love and encouragement. Their many positive influences have contributed significantly to whatever success he has enjoyed thus far in life. His wife, Lynne, was a steadfast source of love and friendship. She also provided assistance in preparation of the manuscript, encouragement to get the job done, and welcome diversions.

The second author wishes to thank his parents, William and Frances Stock, who have been a constant source of inspiration and encouragement over the years. They instilled in him the notion that of the two ways to accomplish a task—the easy way and the right way—it is always best to do it right the first time. Appreciation is also given to Herbert and Bettye Townsend, the parents of his wife, Katheryn, who during their lives, provided testimonies of hardwork and a concern for others. Their continual support will be sorely missed, but their daughter will carry on their proud tradition. Katheryn has been a constant companion, providing love and encouragement, as well as moral support and manuscript assistance. Special thanks go to his daughter, Elizabeth, and his son, Matthew, for giving up so many hours of time with their daddy so that he could write.

Finally, we wish to express our warmest appreciation to Bernard J. LaLonde, Mason Professor of Transportation and Logistics, College of Business, The Ohio State University. It was his love for the discipline of logistics and his leadership during and since our doctoral programs at The

Ohio State University that have made this text a reality. For those who know "Bud," no explanation is necessary. For those who have missed the experience, no words can explain it. We are most fortunate to be able to call him our teacher, mentor, colleague, and friend.

To all those persons who provided assistance and to the publishers and authors who graciously granted permission to use their material, we are indeed grateful. Of course, responsibility for any errors or omissions rests with the authors.

D. M. L.
J. R. S.

Contents

STRATEGIC LOGISTICS MANAGEMENT

Chapter 1

Logistics' Role in the Economy and the Firm

Objectives of This Chapter

To identify where logistics activities interface with the economic system at the macro (society) and micro (firm) levels

To identify the relationship between logistics and marketing

To explore the historical development of the logistics function

To examine the strategic function of logistics management in the modern corporation

INTRODUCTION

Few areas of study have as significant an impact on a society's standard of living as logistics. Almost every sphere of human activity is affected, directly or indirectly, by the logistics process.

Logistics Can Impact Many Activities

How often have you gone to a retail store to buy an advertised product and not found what you wanted on the shelf?

Have you ever placed an order through the mail, over the telephone, or in person, and received the wrong merchandise?

Have you ever shipped a package to a customer in the same city or across the country and had the item arrive damaged, or perhaps not arrive at all?

Have suppliers in your just-in-time system ever let you down, causing you to curtail or shut down your manufacturing operations?

When was the last time you were promised delivery of an item within a few days and it took a few weeks?

Why does it seem that packages shipped overseas always take so much longer to arrive than domestic shipments?

We often don't think of the role logistics plays in our lives until a problem occurs. Fortunately, we usually find the items we want in the store, receive the correct order, undamaged, and at the time it was promised.

Regardless of our vocation as consumers, businesspeople, educators, or government workers, it is important that we understand the logistics process. This chapter shows where logistics activities interface with the economic system at the macro (society) and micro (firm) levels. It shows the relationship between logistics and marketing. The historical development of the logistics function is presented to help the reader understand its strategic role in the modern corporation.

DEFINITION OF LOGISTICS MANAGEMENT

Since logistics is a significant component of a country's economy it is important to define, specifically, what the term means. In the past, the trade and academic press has given logistics a variety of names:

Physical distribution	Materials management
Distribution	Materials logistics management
Distribution engineering	Logistics
Business logistics	Quick-response systems
Marketing logistics	Supply chain management
Distribution logistics	Industrial logistics

At one time or another, all of these terms have referred to essentially the same thing: the management of the flow of goods from point-of-origin to point-of-consumption. But *logistics management* is the most widely accepted term among logistics professionals. One of the largest and most prestigious groups of logistics professionals, the Council of Logistics Management (formerly the National Council of Physical Distribution Management), uses the term *logistics management.*

We have used *Strategic Logistics Management* as the title of this book and accept this definition by the Council of Logistics Management:

Logistics Management Defined

> the process of planning, implementing and controlling the efficient, cost-effective flow and storage of raw materials, in-process inventory, finished goods, and related information from point-of-origin to point-of-consumption for the purpose of conforming to customer requirements.[1]

Included within this definition are customer service, traffic and transportation, warehousing and storage, plant and warehouse site selection, inventory control, order processing, distribution communications, procurement, material handling, parts and service support, salvage and scrap disposal, packaging, return goods handling, and demand forecasting. Figure 1–1 illustrates the components of logistics management.

Some have argued that logistics is only important to manufacturing firms. However, logistics is an important component of the operation of all companies, including retailers, wholesalers, and other service providers. Logistics costs are included in lawn care, financial services, and diaper delivery. Even Merrill Lynch, the stock brokerage firm, has $130 million of logistics costs supporting its financial services business.[2]

Efficient management of the flow of goods from point-of-origin to point-of-consumption at the macro (society) or micro (firm) levels requires successfully planning, implementation, and control of a multitude of logistics activities. The activities shown in Figure 1–1 may involve raw materials (subassemblies, manufactured parts, packing materials, basic commodities); in-process inventory (product partially completed and not yet ready for sale); and finished goods (completed products ready for sale to intermediate or final customers).

---

[1] Definition provided by the Council of Logistics Management, 1986.

[2] Robert V. Delaney, "CLI's 'State of Logistics' Annual Report," press conference remarks to the National Press Club, Washington, D.C. (June 7, 1991), p. 3.

FIGURE 1–1 Components of Logistics Management

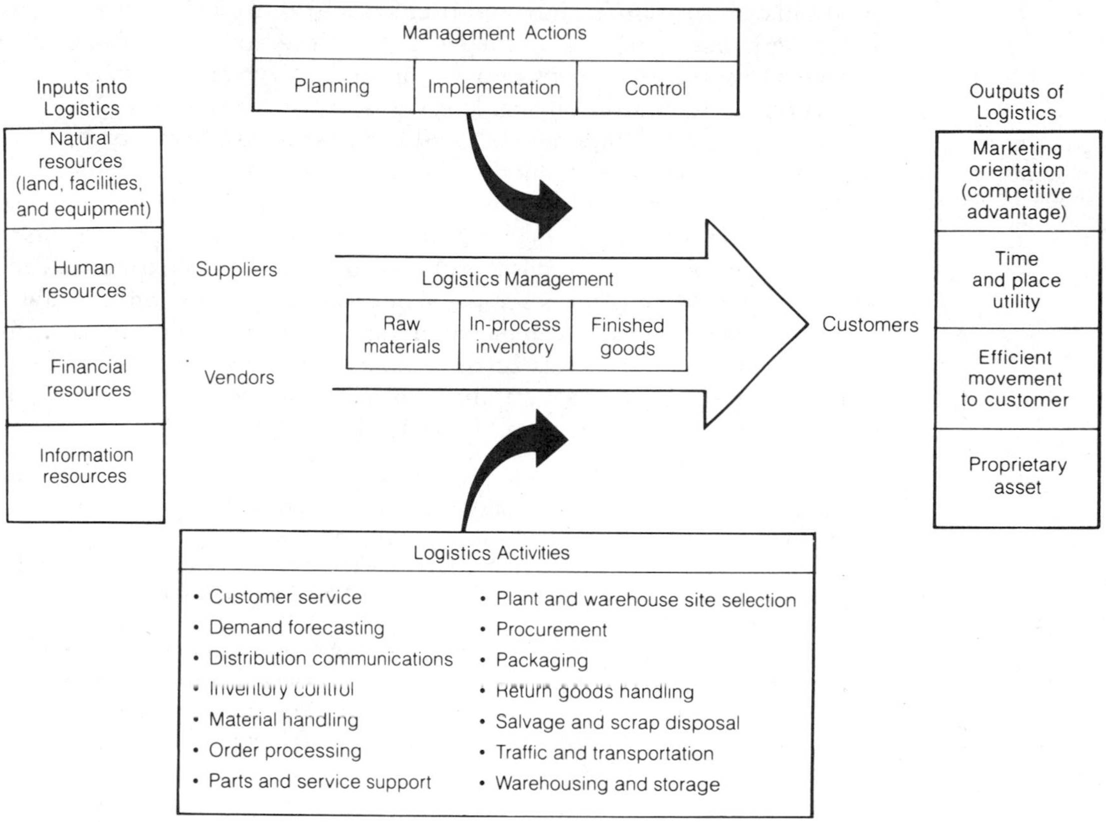

LOGISTICS' ROLE IN THE ECONOMY

The rising affluence of consumers has led to increased national and international markets for goods and services. Thousands of new products and services have been introduced in this century and are sold and distributed to customers in every corner of the world. Business firms have increased in size and complexity to meet the challenges of expanded markets and the proliferation of new products and services. Multiple-plant operations have replaced single-plant production. The distribution of products from point-of-origin to point-of-consumption has become an enormously important component of the gross national product (GNP) of industrialized nations.

In the United States, for example, logistics now contributes approximately 11 percent of GNP. U.S. industry in 1990 spent an estimated $352 billion on freight transportation; more than $221 billion on warehousing, and storage and inventory carrying costs; and more than $27 billion to administer, communicate, and manage the logistics process—a total of $600 billion.[3] Investment in transportation and distribution facilities, not including public sources, is estimated to be in the hundreds of billions of dollars. Considering its consumption of land, labor, and capital, and its impact on the standard of living, logistics is clearly big business.

Logistics Is a Significant Component of GNP

As a significant component of GNP, logistics affects the rate of inflation, interest rates, productivity, energy costs and availability, and other aspects of the economy. One study reported that the average U.S. company could improve its logistics productivity by 20 percent or more.[4] Improvements in a nation's productivity have positive effects on the prices paid for goods and services, the balance of national payments, currency valuation, the ability to compete more effectively in global markets, industry profits (higher productivity implies lower costs of operation to produce and distribute an equivalent amount of product), the availability of investment capital, and economic growth—leading to a higher level of employment.

> There has been an increase in productivity over the past two decades for the United States and her major partners. It is based on data supplied by the Bureau of Labor Statistics. Productivity has been improving at the rate of 9 percent per year in Japan and more than 5 percent per year in Germany and in France. Even in the United Kingdom, it has been improving at a rate of more than 3 percent per year.[5]
>
> Perhaps the best way to illustrate the role of logistics in the U.S. economy is to compare logistical expenditures with other societal activities. Business logistics costs are ten times that of advertising, twice the amount spent on national defense, and equal to the cost of medical care.[6] [Examples of components are shown in Table 1–1.]

LOGISTICS' ROLE IN THE FIRM

Effective logistics management enhances the marketing effort of the firm (which can create differential advantage in the marketplace) by providing efficient movement of products to customers and time and place utility to products. It can be treated, in accounting terms, as a proprietary asset of the company.

---

[3] Ibid., p. 25. Various sources estimated logistics' contributions to GNP differently. Although there is disagreement as to the exact percentage, all sources agree that the level of contribution is significant.

[4] A. T. Kearney, Inc., *Measuring and Improving Productivity in Physical Distribution Management* (Oak Brook, Ill.: National Council of Physical Distribution Management, 1984), p. 12.

[5] Robert V. Delaney, "Distribution Productivity: Old Myths and New Realities," speech presented to the Western New York Roundtable of the National Council of Physical Distribution Management, Rochester, N.Y., 1984.

[6] Robert V. Delaney, "CLI's 'State of Logistics' Annual Report," press conference remarks to the National Press Club, Washington, D.C. (June 15, 1990), p. 4.

TABLE 1–1 Components of 1990 Logistics Cost

	$ (billions)
Inventory carrying costs	
Interest	$ 66
Taxes, obsolescence, depreciation	84
Warehousing	61
Subtotal	$211
Transportation costs	
Motor carriers:	
Public and for hire	$ 77
Private and for own account	87
Local freight sources	113
Subtotal	$277
Other carriers:	
Railroads	$ 32
Water carriers	21
Oil pipelines	9
Air carriers	13
Subtotal	$ 75
Shipper related costs	4
Distribution related costs	23
Total logistics cost	$600

SOURCE: Robert V. Delaney, "CLI's 'State of Logistics' Annual Report," press conference remarks to the National Press Club, Washington, D.C. (June 7, 1991), p. 25.

Logistics Is Marketing Oriented

The Marketing Concept

During the 1950s a number of successful companies formulated and adopted the *marketing concept,* including General Electric, Procter & Gamble, IBM, McDonald's, Quaker Oats, General Foods, United Airlines, and Whirlpool Corporation. The marketing concept is the "marketing management philosophy that holds that achieving organizational goals depends on determining the needs and wants of target markets and delivering the desired satisfactions more effectively and efficiently than competitors."[7] In other words, the customer is the boss!

The Three Components of the Marketing Concept

As part of the company's marketing effort, logistics plays a key role in satisfying the firm's customers and achieving a profit for the company as a whole. Figure 1–2 represents the marketing concept from the perspective of logistics management. *Customer satisfaction* involves maximizing time and place utility to the firm's suppliers, intermediate customers, and final customers. Logistics' ability to provide customer service, coupled with marketing's skill in generating and completing sales, create an acceptable level of customer satisfaction, which can lead to a differential advantage in the marketplace. *Integrated effort* requires that the company coordinate its marketing activities (product, price, promotion, and distribution) to achieve

[7]Phillip Kotler and Gary Armstrong, *Principles of Marketing,* 4th ed. (Englewood Cliffs, N.J.: Prentice Hall, 1989), p. 22.

FIGURE 1–2 Marketing/Logistics Management Concept

Customer satisfaction
- Suppliers
- Intermediate customers
- Final customers

Integrated effort
- Product
- Price
- Promotion
- Place (distribution)

Company profit
- Maximize long-term profitability
- Lowest total costs given an acceptable level of customer service

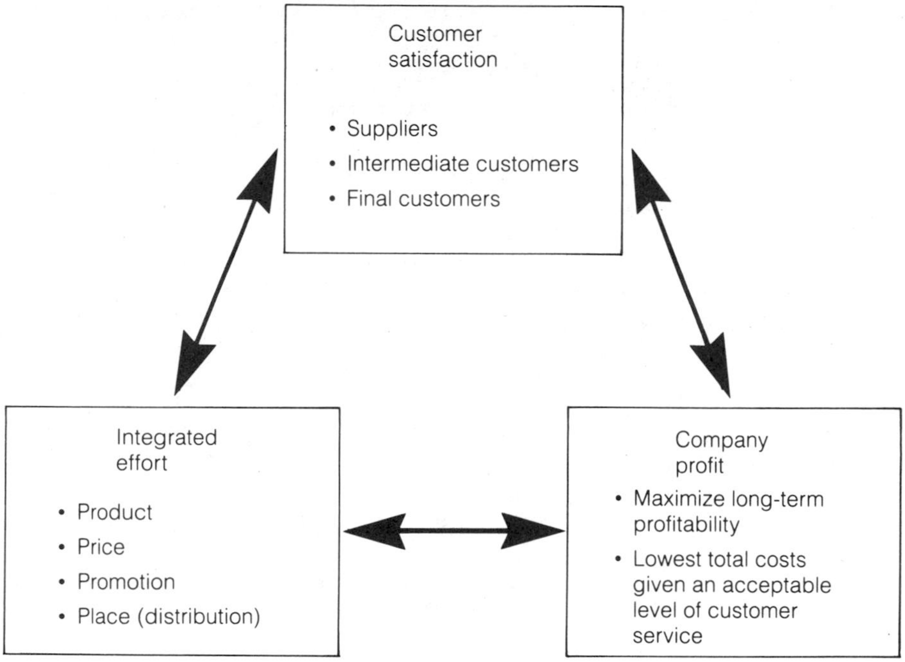

synergistic results; the total should be greater than the sum of its parts. The key to true integration is the "total cost concept," which examines the cost trade-offs that occur between and within the marketing and logistics activities. We will present a comprehensive treatment of this important issue in Chapter 2. The final component of the marketing/logistics management concept—*company profit*—recognizes the need to achieve an acceptable level of long-term profits. From a financial perspective, the optimal means of achieving this profitability may be to minimize total logistics costs while providing the level of customer service dictated by the firm's overall marketing strategy and the expectations of customers.

Logistics Adds Time and Place Utility

Manufactured products possess some value or utility because an assembled item is worth more than its unassembled components or raw materials. A completed automobile, for example, is much more valuable to a consumer than its unassembled parts. The value, or utility, of making materials available in a completed state is called *form utility.* To the consumer, however, the product not only must have form utility, but it also must be in the right place, at the right time, and be available to purchase. The value added to products beyond that added by manufacturing (form utility), is called *place, time,* and *possession utility.*[8] The logistics activity provides place and time utility, while marketing provides possession utility.[9]

Logistics Adds Value to Products

Management is quite concerned with the "value added" by logistics, because improvements in place and time utility are ultimately reflected in the firm's profits. Cost savings in logistics or a stronger marketing position due to an improved logistics system can both cause improved bottom line performance. In firms where logistics contributes a significant portion of the "value added" to a product, logistics management is particularly important. Figure 1–3 illustrates that importance in several industries.

Place utility is the value created or added to a product by making it available for purchase or consumption in the right place. Logistics is directly responsible for adding place utility to products as it efficiently moves raw materials, in-process inventory, and finished goods from point-of-origin to point-of-consumption. *Time utility* is the value created by making something available at the right time. Products are not as valuable to customers if they are not available precisely when they are needed. For example, a food processing company must have raw materials (food items), packaging materials, and other items available before the production process begins—or, if already begun, before existing supplies run out. Failure to receive these items at the proper time can cause costly production shutdowns and place the firm in a disadvantageous competitive position. As the remaining chapters of this book will show, logistics activities combine to add place and time utility to products.

Possession utility is the value added to a product by allowing the customer to take ownership of the item. Possession utility is not a result of logistics, but the offering of credit, quantity discounts, and delayed payments which enable the customer to assume possession of the product. The logistics and marketing processes culminate in possession utility.

Logistics Allows Efficient Movement to the Customer

E. Grosvenor Plowman referred to the "five rights" of a logistics system as supplying the *right product* at the *right place* at the *right time* in the *right condition* for the *right cost* to those customers consuming the product.[10]

---

[8] See L. D. H. Weld, *The Marketing of Farm Products* (New York: Macmillan, 1916).

[9] The official definition of marketing by the American Marketing Association is "the process of planning and executing the conception, pricing, promotion, and distribution of ideas, goods, and services to create exchanges that satisfy individual and organizational objectives." See "AMA Board Approves New Marketing Definition," *Marketing News* 19, no. 5 (March 1, 1985), p. 1.

[10] George A. Gecowets, "Physical Distribution Management," *Defense Transportation Journal* 35, no. 4 (August 1979), p. 5.

FIGURE 1–3 The Importance of Logistics

Logistics costs as a percent of value added

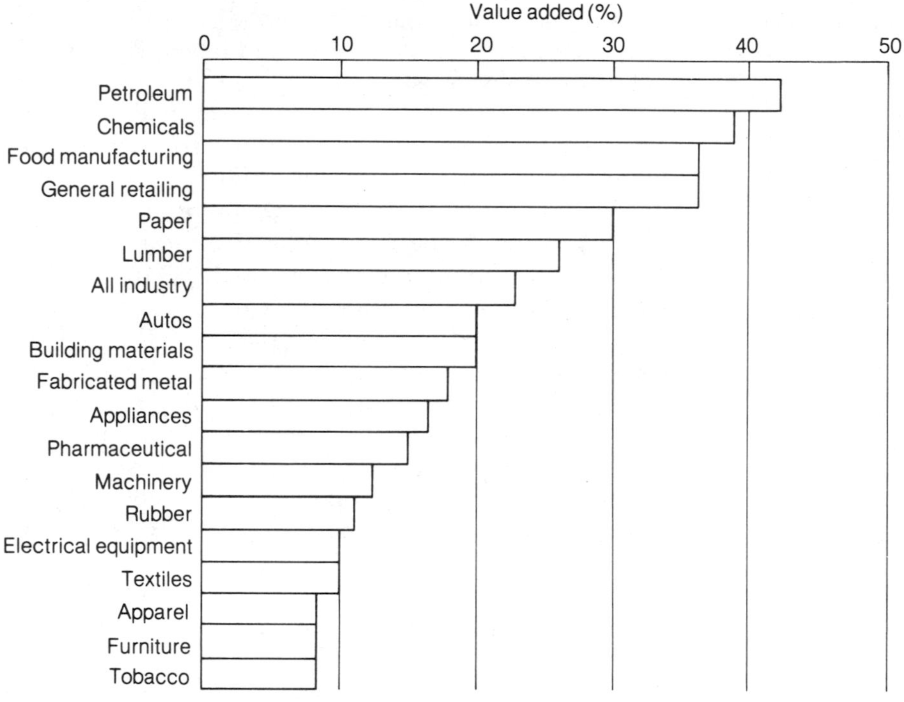

SOURCE: James E. Morehouse, "Improving Productivity in Logistics," *Handling & Shipping Management,* 1984–85 Presidential Issue 25, no. 10 (September 1984), p. 12. Reprinted with permission from *Handling & Shipping Management,* 1984–85 Presidential Issue. Copyright © 1984, Penton Publishing Inc., Cleveland, Ohio.

The term *right cost* deserves consideration. While Plowman's first four rights are analogous to the form, time, place, and possession utilities created by manufacturing and marketing, the addition of the cost component is immensely important to the logistics process. The significance of the cost aspect was voiced by Donald Parker and Peter Drucker more than two decades ago. Parker stated:

> Improvements in marketing efficiency and reductions in marketing costs still lie in the future, representing a major frontier for cost economies. . . . There is room for substantial improvement, particularly in the performance of the physical distribution functions of marketing which constitute a major part of the total marketing costs.[11]

[11] Donald D. Parker, "Improved Efficiency and Reduced Cost in Marketing," *Journal of Marketing* 26, no. 2 (April 1962), p. 16.

In a similar fashion, Drucker said:

> Almost 50 cents of each dollar the American spends for goods goes for activities that occur after the goods are made, that is, after they have come in finished form. . . . Economically . . . distribution is the process in which physical properties of matter are converted into economic value; it brings the customer to the product.[12]

While some might disagree with Drucker's 50-cent estimate, the cost involved in adding time and place utility is substantial. Figure 1–4 provides another estimate of the distribution cost component. The figure implies that logistics is the third-largest cost of doing business for a typical firm. Although the figure is somewhat simplistic and there may be difficulties in allocating and distinguishing between manufacturing, marketing, and logistics costs, it does illustrate that logistics is an important component of business that must be managed effectively. Because the control of costs is one of top management's most significant concerns for the remainder of the 1990s, efficient and effective control of the logistics function can have a substantial impact.[13] The cost of performing the logistics function has led companies such as I-T-E Electrical Products (a division of Siemens-Allis, Inc.) to examine their logistics activities with the intent of reducing costs, improving profitability, and increasing the level of service to their customers. By implementing a total logistics strategy, I-T-E was able to realize the following benefits between 1978 and 1983:

I-T-E Electrical Products Improves Its Logistics Activities

Total number of warehouses reduced from 13 to 6;
Number of direct hourly personnel reduced from 108 to 54;
Warehouse productivity increased from 430 pounds/workerhour to 810;
Inventory control accuracy increased from 97.5 percent and erratic to 99.6 percent and consistent;
Service levels improved from the 70s to the high 80s;
Expenses (as a percentage of) sales reduced from 6.8 to 4.9; and
Material replenishment time reduced from 9.6 days to 3.8 days.[14]

Welch Foods Benefits from Integrated Logistics

Welch Foods recognized the importance of logistics by fully integrating purchasing, inventory management, customer service, transportation, and public warehousing. The results included productivity, cost, and service improvements. For example, order cycle times were reduced, trans-

---

[12] Peter F. Drucker, "The Economy's Dark Continent," *Fortune* 65, no. 4 (April 1962), p. 103.

[13] See Joseph W. Duncan, "Business' Top Concern: Cost Control," *Dun's Business Month* 124, no. 6 (December 1984), p. 62. A survey of *Dun's 5000* found that 70 percent of all firms identified "controlling costs" as a major concern.

[14] James M. Ruetten, "Developing, Articulating and Implementing a Physical Distribution Strategy," *Proceedings of the Twenty-First Annual Conference of the National Council of Physical Distribution Management,* 1983, pp. 501–8.

FIGURE 1–4 One Way of Viewing the Major Costs of Doing Business

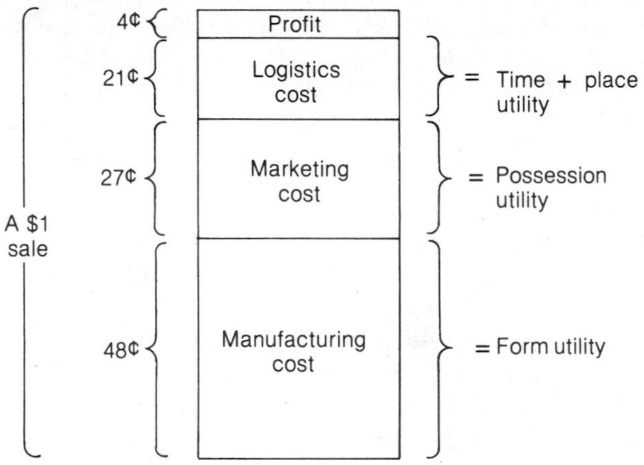

SOURCE: Adapted from Bernard J. LaLonde, John R. Grabner, and James F. Robeson, "Integrated Distribution Systems: A Management Perspective," *International Journal of Physical Distribution* 1, no. 1, October 1970, p. 36.

portation costs as a percentage of sales declined every year beginning in 1981, and the level of damaged products was reduced to less than 6 cases per 10,000 cases shipped.[15]

Logistics Is a Proprietary Asset

An efficient and economical logistics system is similar to a tangible asset on a corporation's books. It cannot be readily duplicated by the firm's competitors. If a company can provide its customers with products quickly and at low cost, it can gain market share advantages over its competitors. It might be able to sell its product at a lower cost as a result of logistics efficiencies, or provide a higher level of customer service, thereby creating goodwill. Although no firms presently identify this "asset" in their balance sheets, it theoretically could be shown as an *intangible asset,* a category that includes such items as patents, copyrights, and trademarks.

Activities Included in Logistics Management

The following variety of activities are involved in the flow of product from point-of-origin to point-of-consumption (each will be discussed at length in subsequent chapters):

[15] Everett N. Baldwin, "Jam, Jelly, Juice and Integration," *Handling & Shipping Management, 1986–87 Presidential Issue* 27, no. 10 (September 1986), pp. 38–44.

1. Customer service
2. Order processing
3. Distribution communications
4. Inventory control
5. Demand forecasting
6. Traffic and transportation
7. Warehousing and storage
8. Plant and warehouse site selection
9. Material handling
10. Procurement
11. Parts and service support
12. Packaging
13. Salvage and scrap disposal
14. Return goods handling

Customer Satisfaction Is Important to the Firm

1. *Customer service.* A pioneering study that examined the state of the art of customer service in major corporations defined customer service as "a customer-oriented philosophy which integrates and manages all of the elements of the customer interface within a predetermined optimum cost-service mix."[16] Customer service acts as the binding and unifying force for all of the logistics management activities. (See Chapter 4.) Customer satisfaction, of which customer service is an integral part, occurs if the firm's overall marketing effort is successful. Each element of a firm's logistics system can affect whether a customer receives the right product at the right place in the right condition for the right cost at the right time. Thus customer service involves successful implementation of the integrated logistics management concept in order to provide the necessary level of customer satisfaction at the lowest possible total cost.

The Firm's Central Nervous System

2. *Order processing.* "Order processing may be compared to the human body's central nervous system, triggering the distribution process and directing the actions to be taken in satisfying order demand."[17] The components of the order processing activity may be broken down into three groups: (1) *operational elements,* such as order entry/editing, scheduling, order-shipping set preparation, and invoicing; (2) *communication elements,* such as order modification, order status inquiries, tracing and expediting, error correction, and product information requests; and (3) *credit and collection elements,* including credit checking and accounts receivable processing/collecting.[18] The speed and accuracy of a firm's order processing has a great deal to do with the level of customer service the company provides.

---

[16] Bernard J. LaLonde and Paul H. Zinszer, *Customer Service: Meaning and Measurement* (Chicago: National Council of Physical Distribution Management, 1976), p. iv.

[17] A. T. Kearney, Inc., *Measuring Productivity in Physical Distribution* (Chicago: National Council of Physical Distribution Management, 1978), p. 186.

[18] Ibid., p. 191.

Advanced systems can reduce the time between order placement and shipment from a warehouse or storage facility. In many cases orders are transmitted from the buyer's computer to the vendor's computer. Advanced systems, although initially expensive to the company, can substantially improve both order processing accuracy and order response time. Often, savings in other logistics expenses (such as inventory, transportation, and/or warehousing) or increased sales from improved customer service will justify the cost of the system (see Chapter 13).

Effective Communication Is Vital

3. *Distribution communications.* Success in today's business environment requires the management of a complex communications system. Effective communication must take place between: *(a)* the firm, its customers, and its suppliers; *(b)* the major functional components of the company—marketing, manufacturing, logistics, and finance/accounting; *(c)* the various logistics-related activities such as customer service, traffic and transportation, warehousing and storage, order processing, and inventory control; and *(d)* the various components of each logistics activity. (Within inventory control, for example, would be in-plant inventory, inventory in transit, and inventory in field warehouses.) Communication is the vital link between the entire logistics process and the firm's customers. Accurate and timely communication is the cornerstone of successful logistics management.

> Benetton, a major Italian sportswear company with over 5,000 stores in 60 countries . . . has redesigned its apparel operations to rapidly meet local market needs. One automated manufacturing and distribution complex in Italy produces and ships over 50 million garments per year. Worldwide in-stock delivery standards are one week (if in stock) or four weeks (including manufacturing). Orders go directly from stores to computerized knitting machines that produce exact styles and colors on demand. Gray goods (uncolored) are held in process waiting for final color/style orders from stores. The operations feature a complete EDI link between stores, carriers, third parties, warehouses, and plants to guarantee delivery of the right goods to the right store at the right time.[19]

A firm's communications system may be as sophisticated as a computerized management information system (MIS) or as simple as word-of-mouth communication between individuals. Whatever the system, vital information must be available and communicated to individuals who "need to know." Information systems will be discussed in Chapter 13.

The Financial Impact of Inventory

4. *Inventory control.* The inventory control activity is critical because of the financial necessity of maintaining a sufficient supply of product to meet both customers' needs and manufacturing requirements. Maintaining raw materials, parts, and finished goods inventory consumes both space and capital. Money tied up in inventory is not available for use elsewhere.

---

[19] David L. Anderson, Douglas Boike, and Robert J. Quinn, "Integrated Operations: Redefining the Corporation," *Proceedings of the Annual Conference of the Council of Logistics Management,* vol. I, 1989, p. 238.

Chapter 9 examines the financial aspects of inventory control in detail; here it is sufficient to note that inventory carrying costs can range from 14 to over 50 percent, depending on the product.[20] Successful inventory control involves determining the level of inventory necessary to achieve the desired level of customer service while considering the cost of performing other logistics activities.

The Importance of Demand Forecasting

5. *Demand forecasting.* Demand forecasting involves determining the amount of product and accompanying service that customers will require at some point in the future. The need to know precisely how much product will be demanded is important to all facets of the firm's operations—marketing, manufacturing, and logistics. Marketing forecasts of future demand determine promotional strategies, allocation of sales force effort, pricing strategies, and market research activities. Manufacturing forecasts determine production schedules, purchasing and acquisition strategies, and in-plant inventory decisions.

Logistics management forecasts of demand determine how much of each item produced by the company must be transported to the various markets the firm serves. Also, logistics management must know where the demand will originate so that the proper amount of product can be placed or stored in each market area. Knowledge of future demand levels enables logistics managers to allocate their resources (budgets) to activities that will service that demand. Decision making under uncertainty is less than optimal in most cases because it is extremely difficult to allocate resources among logistics activities without knowing what products and services will be needed. Therefore it is imperative that the firm undertake some type of demand forecasting and communicate the results to the marketing, manufacturing, and logistics departments. Sophisticated computer models, trend analysis, sales force estimates, or other methods can help develop such forecasts. We will examine various types of forecasting approaches and techniques in Chapter 14.

Transportation Is an Important Component of Logistics

6. *Traffic and transportation.* One major component of the logistics process is the movement or flow of goods from point-of-origin to point-of-consumption—and perhaps their return as well. The traffic and transportation activity refers to managing the movement of products and includes activities such as selecting the method of shipment (air, rail, water, pipeline, truck); choosing the specific path (routing); complying with various local, state, and federal transportation regulations; and being aware of both domestic and international shipping requirements (see Chapters 5 and 6).

Many examples can be given to illustrate the broad utilization made of transportation. One is the Ford Motor Company. On any given day, Ford has in

[20]See Douglas M. Lambert, *The Development of an Inventory Costing Methodology: A Study of the Costs Associated with Holding Inventory* (Chicago: National Council of Physical Distribution Management, 1976).

> transit up to 50,000 finished vehicles and almost 1 billion finished parts bound for assembly plants and parts depots. In addition, over 14 million tons of raw materials and semifinished parts are transported each year.[21]

Transportation is often the single largest cost in the logistics process. Therefore, it is an important component that must be managed effectively.

Products Must Be Stored

7. *Warehousing and storage.* Products must be stored at the plant or in the field for later sale and consumption unless customers need them the instant they are produced. Generally, the greater the time lag between production and consumption, the larger the level or amount of inventory required. Warehousing and storage are activities that manage the space needed to hold or maintain inventories. Specific storage activities include decisions as to whether the storage facility should be owned, leased, or rented; warehouse layout and design; product mix considerations; safety and maintenance; security systems; personnel training; and productivity measurement. These issues will be examined in Chapters 7 and 8.

Where Should Facilities Be Located?

8. *Plant and warehouse site selection.* Whether facilities are owned, leased, or rented, the location of plants and/or warehouses (storage facilities) is extremely important. The strategic placement of plants and warehouses near the company's markets can improve the firm's customer service levels. Proper facility location can also allow lower volume-related transportation rates in moving product from plant to warehouse, plant to plant, or warehouse to customer (see Chapter 8).

The first consideration in selecting a site is the location of the firm's various markets. The needs of the customers and the location of raw materials, component parts, and subassemblies are also major considerations, for the company must be concerned with inbound movement and storage of materials in addition to outbound flows. Other important factors include labor rates; transportation services; city, county, and state taxes; security; legal concerns; local factors, such as the attitude of the community toward new industry; land cost; and availability of utilities.

9. *Material handling.* Material handling is concerned with every aspect of the movement or flow of raw materials, in-process inventory, and finished goods within a plant or warehouse (see Chapter 7). The objectives of material handling are as follows:

Objectives of Material Handling

To eliminate handling wherever possible;
To minimize travel distance;
To minimize goods in process;
To provide uniform flow free of bottlenecks; and
To minimize losses from waste, breakage, spoilage, and theft.[22]

---

[21] Charles A. Taff, *Management of Physical Distribution and Transportation,* 7th ed. (Homewood, Ill.: Richard D. Irwin, 1984), p. 17.

[22] Richard J. Tersine, *Production/Operations Management: Concepts, Structure, and Analysis,* 2nd ed. (New York: Elsevier Science Publishing, 1985), p. 382.

A firm incurs costs every time an item is handled. Since handling generally adds no value to a product, these operations should be kept to a minimum. For items with low unit value, the proportion of material handling costs to total product cost can be significant. "Poor material handling can lead directly to lost or damaged products, customer dissatisfaction, production delays, and idle employees and equipment. [Material handling] plays a vital role in reducing inventory, lowering costs, and increasing productivity."[23]

Procurement—A $1.3 Trillion Business

10. *Procurement.* Every company relies to some extent on materials and services supplied by other firms. The great majority of U.S. industries spend from 40 to 60 percent of their revenues for materials and services from outside sources.[24] *Procurement* is the acquisition of materials and services to ensure the operating effectiveness of the firm's manufacturing and logistics processes. The procurement function includes the selection of supply source locations, determination of the form in which the material is to be acquired, timing of purchases, price determination, quality control, and many other activities (see Chapter 12). The changing economic environment of recent years, marked by wide variations in availability and cost of materials, has made procurement even more important in the logistics process.

After-the-Sale Service

11. *Parts and service support.* In addition to the movement of raw materials, in-process inventory, and finished goods, logistics must be concerned with the many activities involved in repair and servicing of products. Logistics' responsibility does not end when the product is delivered to the customer. Part of the firm's marketing activity is to provide the customer with service after the sale. This involves providing replacement parts when products break down or malfunction. Automobile dealerships, for example, must have efficient service departments that offer complete servicing and auto repair. Adequate supplies of spare and replacement parts are vital to the service and repair activity—and logistics is responsible for making sure those parts are available when and where the customer needs them. In the industrial marketplace, where the product may be a piece of manufacturing equipment, downtime can be extremely costly to the customer if product failure results in a production-line slowdown or shutdown. The firm supplying the spare or replacement part must be able to respond quickly and decisively. Adequate parts and service support is extremely important whenever post-sale support is part of the firm's marketing effort.

12. *Packaging.* Packaging performs two basic functions—marketing and logistics. In a marketing sense the package acts as a form of promotion or advertising. Its size, weight, color, and printed information attract

---

[23] Ibid.

[24] Richard J. Tersine and John H. Campbell, *Modern Materials Management* (New York: Elsevier North-Holland, 1977), p. 82.

customers and convey knowledge about the product. From a logistics perspective, packaging serves a dual role. First, the package protects the product from damage while it is being stored or transported. Second, packaging can make it easier to store and move products by reducing handling and thereby material handling costs. When firms are involved in international marketing, packaging becomes even more important. Products marketed in foreign countries travel greater distances and undergo more handling operations—and handlings may occur under conditions much less favorable than in the United States. In many countries, management must deal with a lack of adequate material handling equipment and must rely on poorly trained personnel. In general, domestic packaging is not strong enough to withstand the rigors of export shipment.[25]

Packaging Serves a Dual Role

Waste Disposal

13. *Salvage and scrap disposal.* One by-product of the manufacturing and logistics process is waste material. If this material cannot be used to produce other products, it must be disposed of in some manner. Whatever the by-product, the logistics process must effectively and efficiently handle, transport, and store it. If the by-products are reusable or recyclable, logistics manages their transportation to remanufacturing or reprocessing locations.

Reverse Logistics

14. *Return goods handling.* The handling of return goods, often referred to as *reverse logistics,* is an important part of the logistics process. Buyers may return items to the seller due to product defects, overages, incorrect items received, or other reasons. Reverse logistics has been likened to going the wrong way on a one-way street because the great majority of product shipments flow in one direction. Most logistics systems are ill-equipped to handle product movement in a reverse channel. In many industries in which consumers return products for warranty repair, replacement, or recycling, reverse logistics costs may be high. The cost of moving a product back through the system from the consumer to producer may be as much as nine times the cost of moving the same product from producer to consumer. Often the returned goods cannot be transported, stored, and/or handled as easily, resulting in higher logistics costs. Reverse logistics promises to become even more important as customers demand more flexible and lenient return policies and as recycling and other environmental issues become more significant.

DEVELOPMENT OF LOGISTICS MANAGEMENT

To understand the important role of logistics management in today's business enterprise, it is worthwhile to examine the historical development of the discipline.

[25] Taff, *Management of Physical Distribution and Transportation,* p. 322.

Historical Development

Logistics in the Early 1900s

Logistics was first examined in scholarly writing in the early 1900s, although as a human activity it is centuries old. John Crowell (1901) discussed the costs and factors affecting the distribution of farm products in the U.S. government's *Report of the Industrial Commission on the Distribution of Farm Products.*[26] Later, in his *An Approach to Business Problems* (1916), Arch Shaw discussed the strategic aspects of logistics.[27] During that same year, L. D. H. Weld introduced the concepts of marketing utilities (time, place, possession) and channels of distribution.[28] In 1922, Fred Clark identified the role of logistics in marketing.[29] And in 1927 the term *logistics* was defined in a way similar to its use today.

> There are two uses of the word distribution which must be clearly differentiated . . . first, the use of the word to describe physical distribution such as transportation and storage; second, the use of word distribution to describe what is better termed marketing.[30]

With the onset of World War II, logistics was further developed and refined. Used in conjunction with a new corporate philosophy that originated in the 1950s—"the marketing concept"—logistics came to be associated to an even greater degree with the customer service and cost components of a firm's marketing efforts.

"Total Cost Analysis" Concept Is Introduced

A 1956 study of the economics of air freight added an additional dimension to the field of logistics.[31] The study introduced the concept of *total cost analysis.* Air freight is a high-cost form of transportation. However, air freight, when used instead of other modes of transportation, could result in lower inventory and warehousing costs because a firm distributes directly to its customers.

The 1960s saw a number of developments in logistics. In 1961 Edward Smykay, Donald Bowersox, and Frank Mossman wrote one of the first texts on logistics management.[32] The book examined logistics from a systems or companywide perspective and discussed the total cost concept. The Council of Logistics Management (formerly the National Council of Physical Distribution Management) was formed in 1963 "to develop the theory

---

[26] John F. Crowell, *Report of the Industrial Commission on the Distribution of Farm Products,* vol. 6 (Washington, D.C.: U.S. Government Printing Office, 1901).

[27] Arch W. Shaw, *An Approach to Business Problems* (Cambridge, Mass.: Harvard University Press, 1916).

[28] Weld, *The Marketing of Farm Products.*

[29] Fred E. Clark, *Principles of Marketing* (New York: Macmillan, 1922).

[30] Ralph Borsodi, *The Distribution Age* (New York: D. Appleton, 1927), p. 19.

[31] Howard T. Lewis, James W. Culliton, and Jack D. Steele, *The Role of Air Freight in Physical Distribution* (Boston: Harvard Business School, 1956).

[32] Edward W. Smykay, Donald J. Bowersox, and Frank H. Mossman, *Physical Distribution Management* (New York: Macmillan, 1961).

and understanding of the [logistics] process, promote the art and science of managing [logistics] systems and to foster professional dialogue and development in the field operating exclusively without profit and in cooperation with other organizations and institutions."[33]

Pioneering Research

During the remainder of the 1960s and on into the 1980s, a multitude of textbooks, articles, monographs, journals, and conferences were devoted to the subject of logistics management. One of the earliest writings to examine the connection between accounting and logistics was Michael Schiff's *Accounting and Control in Physical Distribution Management,* published in 1972.[34] The study was instrumental in creating an awareness that accounting and financial information are vital to the logistics activity. In 1976, LaLonde and Zinszer published their landmark study, *Customer Service: Meaning and Measurement,* the first detailed exploration of the topic of customer service. As part of the marketing concept, customer satisfaction requires a complete understanding of customer service. Two years later, in 1978, A. T. Kearney, Inc., under the sponsorship of the Council of Logistics Management, examined logistics productivity. The state-of-the-art appraisal of this important aspect of logistics was entitled *Measuring Productivity in Physical Distribution.* These studies continue to influence the logistics profession.

Deregulation

Beginning in the late 1970s and continuing throughout the 1980s, logistics management was significantly affected by deregulation of the transportation industry. The Airline Deregulation Acts of 1977 and 1978, Staggers Rail Act of 1980, Motor Carrier Act of 1980, and Shipping Act of 1984 removed or modified the existing economic sanctions on air, rail, motor, and ocean transport, respectively. The impact on carriers and shippers has been profound. In the case of carriers, deregulation has resulted in increased competition; greater pricing freedom (i.e., establishing and modifying rates); more flexibility in routing and scheduling; an increased need to become marketing oriented; and a need to be creative in terms of marketing mix offerings. Shippers have more carriers from which to choose. New and varied types of services are now available. Most rates are now negotiated and involve long-term agreements. Service levels provided by carriers vary widely depending on the origin/destination combination.

The Computer's Impact on Logistics

Computer technology and distribution software are two other factors that have caused businesses to become more interested in logistics management. The development of computer technology, particularly the microcomputer, has allowed executives to manage and implement logistics management much more effectively and efficiently. Firms can become much

---

[33] Information supplied by the Council of Logistics Management indicates a 1992 membership of over 6,600 logistics practitioners, consultants, and academicians.

[34] Michael Schiff, *Accounting and Control in Physical Distribution Management* (Chicago: National Council of Physical Distribution Management, 1972).

more cost efficient because of the speed and accuracy of the computer; they can use sophisticated techniques (e.g., MRP, MRPII, DRP, DRPII, Kanban, and Just-in-Time) to manage and control activities such as production scheduling, inventory control, order processing, and others. In fact, such advances, and the resulting impact on the firm's marketing, production, and financial activities, have been instrumental in creating top management awareness of logistics.[35] Beginning in the 1970s and accelerating in the 1990s has been the development and expansion of global competition. Firms have increasingly become more international, as evidenced by the increase in foreign sourcing of raw materials, component parts, subassemblies, and labor.[36] Companies have penetrated new markets throughout the world. For example, the United States became an attractive marketing opportunity for many Asian and European firms producing automobiles, electronics, and computers in the 1970s and 1980s. Similarly, markets in Western Europe (as a result of Europe 1992), China, the Soviet Union, and Eastern Europe are increasingly becoming significant markets for companies producing a variety of goods and services. Enterprising firms throughout the world have recognized the need to become more globally oriented. In many instances, companies have discovered that their international markets exhibit higher growth rates and sales volumes than domestic markets. Table 1–2 identifies some of the most important events in the development of logistics management.

International Marketing and Logistics

Factors Underlying the Development of Interest in Logistics Management

A number of factors underlie the recognition of the importance of logistics management. Among the most important factors are advances in computer technology and quantitative techniques; development of the systems approach and total cost analysis concept; recognition of logistics' role in the firm's customer service program; erosion of many firms' profits because of their failure to examine functional areas where cost savings might be realized; profit leverage resulting from increased logistics efficiency; general economic conditions since the 1950s; and recognition that logistics can help create a competitive advantage in the marketplace.

Undoubtedly, many factors operating independently (yet having joint and synergistic effects) helped bring about interest in logistics management. Certainly, recognizing the cost and service impact of the logistics pro-

---

[35] Graham Sharman, "The Rediscovery of Logistics," *Harvard Business Review* 62, no. 5 (September-October 1984), pp. 71–79.

[36] For example, the United States and Mexico have cooperated economically by allowing U.S. firms to invest directly in Mexican facilities and utilize cheaper labor than that available in the United States. Manufacturing equipment subassemblies and raw materials are not assessed duties when they are used in such facilities, referred to as Maquiladora operations.

TABLE 1–2 Historical Development of Logistics Management

Date(s)	*Event*	*Significance*
1901	John F. Crowell, *Report of the Industrial Commission on the Distribution of Farm Products*, vol. 6 (Washington D.C.: Government Printing Office)	The first text to deal with the costs and factors affecting the distribution of farm products.
1916	Arch W. Shaw, *An Approach to Business Problems* (Cambridge, Mass.: Harvard University Press)	The text discussed the strategic aspects of logistics.
1916	L. D. H. Weld, *The Marketing of Farm Products* (New York: Macmillan)	Introduced the concepts of marketing utilities and channels of distribution.
1922	Fred E. Clark, *Principles of Marketing* (New York: Macmillan)	The text defined marketing as those efforts which affect transfers in the ownership of goods and care of their physical distribution.
1927	Ralph Borsodi, *The Distribution Age* (New York: D. Appleton)	One of the first texts to define the term logistics as it is presently used.
1941–45	World War II	Military logistics operations demonstrated how distribution activities could be integrated into a single system.
1950s	Development of the marketing concept	Corporations began to emphasize customer satisfaction at a profit. Customer service later became the cornerstone of logistics management.
1954	Paul D. Converse, "The Other Half of Marketing," *Twenty-Sixth Boston Conference on Distribution* (Boston: Boston Trade Board)	A leading business and educational authority pointed out the need for academicians and practitioners to examine the physical distribution side of marketing.
1956	Howard T. Lewis, James W. Culliton, and Jack D. Steele, *The Role of Air Freight in Physical Distribution* (Boston: Harvard Business School)	Introduced the concept of total cost analysis to the area of logistics.
Early 1960s	Introduction of Raytheon Company's "unimarket" concept	Earliest reported company effort to adopt and implement logistics management concept. Raytheon utilized one distribution center for U.S. market in combination with an air freight transportation system.
Early 1960s	Michigan State University and The Ohio State University institute undergraduate and graduate programs in logistics	The first formal educational programs developed to train logistics practitioners and educators.
1961	Edward W. Smykay, Donald J. Bowersox, and Frank H. Mossman, *Physical Distribution Management* (New York: Macmillan)	One of the first texts on physical distribution. Discussed the systems approach to physical distribution management and the total cost concept in detail.
1962	Peter F. Drucker, "The Economy's Dark Continent," *Fortune* 65, no. 4 (April 1962)	A leading business and educational authority recognized the importance of distribution in the United States. Many scholars believe this article had significant impact on practitioners.
1963	National Council of Physical Distribution Management founded. In 1985 the name was changed to Council of Logistics Management	The first organization to bring together professionals in all areas of logistics for the purpose of education and training.
1969	Donald J. Bowersox, "Physical Distribution Development, Current Status, and Potential," *Journal of Marketing* 33, no. 1 (January 1969)	Integrated logistics management concept examined from a historical (past, present, and future) perspective.

TABLE 1–2 *(continued)*

Date(s)	*Event*	*Significance*
1972	Michael Schiff, *Accounting and Control in Physical Distribution Management* (Chicago: National Council of Physical Distribution Management)	Created an awareness of the importance of accounting and financial information to successful logistics management.
1976	Douglas M. Lambert, *The Development of an Inventory Costing Methodology: A Study of the Costs Associated with Holding Inventory* (Chicago: National Council of Physical Distribution Management)	Identified the cost components of one of the largest logistics expense items and developed a methodology whereby firms could calculate their inventory carrying costs.
1976	Bernard J. LaLonde and Paul H. Zinszer, *Customer Service: Meaning and Measurement* (Chicago: National Council of Physical Distribution Management)	The first comprehensive state-of-the-art appraisal of the customer service activity in major U.S. corporations.
1978	A. T. Kearney, Inc., *Measuring Productivity in Physical Distribution* (Chicago: National Council of Physical Distribution Management)	The first comprehensive state-of-the-art appraisal of productivity measurement in logistics.
1970s and 80s	Development and implementation of techniques in logistics such as MRP, MRPII, DRP, DRPII, Kanban, and Just-in-Time	Widespread implementation of these techniques highlighted the need for integrating logistics activities and maximizing their effectiveness. The techniques also pointed out the relationships between logistics and manufacturing, marketing, and other business functions.
Late 1970s and early 1980s	Deregulation of U.S. airlines, motor carriers, railroads, and ocean shipping	Significantly reduced the economic regulation of the transportation industry in the U.S. Increased competition and had substantial impact on prices and service levels of carriers. Made the transportation aspect of logistics much more important. Provided a model for other countries in their deregulation activities.
1980s	Use of computers in logistics management increases dramatically	Provided the capability of truly integrating logistics activities. Allowed cost tradeoff decisions to be made quickly and optimally. Improved logistics efficiency and productivity.
1984	Graham Sharman, "The Rediscovery of Logistics," *Harvard Business Review* 62, no. 5 (September-October 1984)	Identified the need for top management to recognize the importance of logistics to the corporation. Provided evidence of the increasing role of logistics in business strategy and planning.
1985	Michael E. Porter, *Competitive Advantage* (New York: The Free Press)	Introduced the "value-chain" concept to aid management in developing a competitive advantage in the marketplace. Primary activities of the value-chain included inbound logistics, operations, outbound logistics, marketing and sales, and service. Created major awareness that logistics can help firms create and maintain a competitive advantage.
1987	Malcolm Baldrige National Quality Award established by the U.S. Congress	Promoted quality awareness, recognized quality achievements of U.S. companies and publicized successful quality strategies. Thirty percent of the points used to grant the award

TABLE 1–2 *(concluded)*

Date(s)	*Event*	*Significance*
		is based on customer satisfaction, which includes a firm's knowledge of its customers, overall customer service systems, responsiveness, and an ability to meet customer requirements and expectations.
1993	Creation of one of the largest global markets through European economic unification on January 1, 1993.	International marketing and distribution patterns will be significantly affected. Global logistics will increase in importance.

Logistics—A Significant Cost to the Firm

cess was an important step. For example, logistics costs can be a significant portion of a typical firm's sales dollar, as we saw in Figure 1–4. For firms in some industries, the impact can be even more pronounced. Logistics costs as a percent of product value for a producer of industrial nondurable goods (e.g., chemicals, fuel) can be much higher than logistics costs for a pharmaceutical company. Generally, the product value (measured in dollars per pound) is much higher for pharmaceuticals than for industrial nondurables (raw materials and industrial products used in the manufacture of end products). As a result, logistics costs will be a smaller percentage of a firm's sales dollar for the pharmaceutical company. To illustrate, suppose a product shipment is valued at $10,000 for the pharmaceutical company and $2,000 for the industrial nondurables company. Because of factors such as market conditions, level of competition, transportation modes used, product perishability (damageability and shelf life), inventory carrying costs, and handling characteristics, the pharmaceutical company pays $500 to distribute its product while the industrial nondurable goods firm pays $250. In absolute terms the pharmaceutical company pays more, but as a percentage of product value or sales it pays only 5 percent, as opposed to 12.5 percent paid by the industrial nondurable goods firm.

In addition to the logistics expense of the firm, the profit squeeze and potential profit leverage that can result from increased efficiency in logistics have contributed significantly to the development of interest in logistics management. During the 1970s and 1980s many firms found it increasingly difficult to maintain traditional profit levels and growth rates because of increasing domestic and foreign competition, saturated markets, government regulation, and other factors.

The Profit Squeeze and its Causes

A company can pursue three basic strategies in a "profit squeeze" situation. First, it can attempt to generate additional sales volume through increased marketing efforts. For many firms, however, this may be very difficult and costly. Incremental sales increases in saturated or highly competitive markets are hard to achieve. In low-growth markets, the rate of growth may be less than the firm needs to generate additional sales. Even in high-growth market situations, a firm may be unable to achieve desired sales increases because of resource problems, competition, and other market conditions. A second way to improve profitability may be to increase prices of the firm's products. Again, such increases may not be possible given market conditions. Depending on price elasticity of demand, price increases may not have the desired impact on sales. Typically firms hesitate to increase prices unless higher costs of materials, production, or labor make those increases unavoidable. Therefore a third strategy, that of reducing the firm's costs of doing business, has been the one most companies have had to follow.

As firms looked inward, they attempted to identify areas for cost savings and/or productivity increases. Figure 1–4 identified three basic areas of a firm's operations—manufacturing, marketing, and logistics.[37] Many companies find it difficult to reduce costs in manufacturing and marketing. However, many firms engaged in manufacturing are already mechanized and highly efficient. They can increase productivity to reduce the cost of manufacturing, but the incremental costs of this approach can be quite high. There are some industries where significant production efficiencies are being achieved, but this is not the case in many others. In the marketing area, there are often elements management can reduce and/or make more cost-effective. However, many firms are unwilling to reduce marketing activities, especially advertising, fearing an adverse reaction in the marketplace. Companies that market consumer products in highly competitive industries (e.g., Procter & Gamble, Lever Brothers, General Motors, Ford, McDonald's, and Burger King) typically hesitate to reduce marketing expenditures. In fact, they usually increase the size of their gross marketing budgets each year.

Profit Leverage from Logistics

In most firms, logistics is the most promising area in which to achieve significant cost savings. And in some instances, such cost savings can have a far greater impact on the firm's profitability than increasing sales volume. Suppose, for example, that a firm's net profit on a sales dollar is 2 percent, as shown in Table 1–3. In a simplified sense, a sales increase of $1.00 would be equivalent to a cost savings of $.02. At such a small scale the numbers seem rather insignificant, but the ratio is the important factor. As the cost savings become larger, the commensurate sales increase becomes increasingly larger. An actual case helps illustrate this concept.

During the 1960s a large appliance firm found that its logistics activities were not integrated under a single logistics executive, but were dispersed throughout the organization. Some logistics elements fell under the jurisdiction of manufacturing, others under marketing or finance. Top management discovered that the company was spending almost $20 million on

[37] Conceptually, logistics is part of marketing and is included in the "place" component of the marketing mix. Organizationally, logistics is often a separate functional activity.

TABLE 1–3 Profit Leverage Provided by Logistics Cost Reduction

If Net Profit on the Sales Dollar Is 2.0 Percent, Then. . .

A Saving of	Is Equivalent to a Sales Increase of
$ 0.02	$ 1.00
2.00	100.00
200.00	10,000.00
2,000.00	100,000.00
20,000.00	1,000,000.00

SOURCE: Bernard J. LaLonde, John R. Grabner, and James F. Robeson, "Integrated Distribution Systems: A Management Perspective," *International Journal of Physical Distribution Management*, October 1970, p. 46.

logistics activities, yet no one was managing it as a major cost center. The firm created a senior-level logistics executive position and placed all logistics activities under that individual. The elimination of duplicate activities, better control, and increased management attention to the logistics activity resulted in a cost savings of approximately $10 million dollars during the first year of full implementation. The savings had a sizable impact on profitability—one that the firm could not have achieved by an equivalent level of additional sales. Factors such as competition, market growth rates, and company resources would have precluded any significant sales increases. "The profit leverage argument makes a persuasive argument to management for reviewing cost reduction opportunities available from integrated [logistics] management."[38]

Operationalizing a Logistics Management System

Logistics management approaches will vary depending on the specific characteristics of the company and its products. In Chapter 16, we will explore the question of how a firm can organize its logistics system. While the exact organizational structure will differ by company, it is important that the logistics system be as efficient as possible from a cost and service perspective.

In the face of higher costs of operation and increasing pressures from customers for better service, the logistics organization must evolve and change to meet the challenge. An understanding of the factors that make organizations effective and a knowledge of how those factors interrelate are the first steps toward developing an optimal logistics system in a company.

[38] Bernard J. LaLonde, John R. Grabner, and James F. Robeson, "Integrated Distribution Systems: A Management Perspective," *International Journal of Physical Distribution Management* 1, no. 1, October 1970, p. 46.

Whatever logistical system is selected by a firm—and there are many as we will see in Chapter 16—the system must be flexible; that is, can the system handle the non-ordinary? A study of major U.S. manufacturers, wholesalers, and retailers revealed that logistics system flexibility was extremely important to customers. Those firms considered by the industry to be logistics leaders, referred to as "leading edge" companies, place a premium on flexibility. Areas or activities where logistics flexibility is most important include special customer service requests, product introductions and phase-outs, supply disruptions, computer breakdowns, product recalls, and customization of service levels to specific markets or customers.[39]

FUTURE CHALLENGES

Logistics professionals will face many complex challenges in the next decade. Future challenges will be significant in the areas of strategic planning, the use of logistics as an offensive marketing weapon, distribution accounting, the need for broader-based management skills, use of third parties, global logistics, strategic alliances and partnerships, and technology.

Strategic Planning

Table 1–4 indicates the rising importance of logistics in competitive strategy. Between 1964 and 1987, marketing executives placed a much greater emphasis on logistics activities.

Activities such as customer service, budgeting and control of the logistics function, inventory control, and positioning of inventories have become important components of a firm's strategic planning process. Many companies, such as Ford, Quaker Oats, Whirlpool, Nabisco Brands, and Fleming Companies, have realized that a good logistics system can result in improved market share, higher levels of profitability, and competitive advantage.

The Impact of a Good Logistics System

Charles W. Smith, a marketing consultant, past president of the American Marketing Association, and former director of distribution planning and research for Nabisco, has commented:

> Today, many people in top marketing management are asking questions directed not so much at the level of distribution costs, but towards strategies for providing the kind of delivery service and market coverage that is needed to maintain and increase market share profitability. This new attitude towards

[39] Donald J. Bowersox, Patricia J. Daugherty, Cornelia L. Dröge, Dale S. Rogers, and Daniel L. Wardlow, *Leading Edge Logistics: Competitive Positioning for the 1990s* (Oak Brook, Ill.: Council of Logistics Management, 1989), p. 54.

TABLE 1–4 The Increasing Importance of Logistics

Marketing Activity	*Rank Order of Importance*		
	1964	*1975*	*1984*
Pricing	6	1	2
CUSTOMER SERVICES	5	2	1
Sales personnel management	3	3	9
Product research and development	1	4	3
MARKETING COST BUDGETING AND CONTROL	9	5	*
PHYSICAL DISTRIBUTION	11	6	8
Market research	2	7	6
Marketing organization structure	7	8	*
Advertising and sales promotion planning	4	9	7
DISTRIBUTION CHANNEL CONTROL	8	10	*
Extending customer credit	10	11	*
Public relations	12	12	10

*Not rated in the study.

SOURCES: The 1984 study was conducted by Stephen W. McDaniel and Richard T. Hise, "Shaping the Marketing Curriculum: The CEO Perspective," *Journal of Marketing Education* 6, no. 2 (Summer 1984), pp. 27–32. The 1975 study was conducted by Robert A. Robicheaux, "How Important Is Pricing in Competitive Strategy?" *Proceedings: Southern Marketing Association*, ed. Henry W. Nash and Donald P. Robin (January 1976), pp. 55–57. The 1964 study was conducted by Jon G. Udell, "How Important Is Pricing in Competitive Strategy?" *Journal of Marketing* 28, no. 1 (January 1964), pp. 44–48.

distribution reflects growing awareness on the part of top management that what is done to strengthen a company's distribution system may well determine not only its profitability but its very survival.[40]

An example of a firm that has successfully integrated logistics into the strategic planning process is 3M Canada. In 1987, the president challenged the logistics function to more fully participate in helping the firm achieve its corporate profitability objectives. As a result, a new logistics mission statement was developed; more complete integration of activities was established between logistics, marketing, and manufacturing; and higher levels of productivity were achieved.[41]

Indeed, the future success of a company will be affected by the degree to which logistics becomes integrated into the firm's strategic planning process.[42]

---

[40] Charles W. Smith, "The Road to New Profits," *Marketing Communications,* June 1984, p. 35.

[41] See Martha C. Cooper, Richard H. Goodspeed, and Charles B. Lounsbury, "Logistics as an Element of Marketing Strategy Both Inside and Outside the Firm," *Proceedings of the Annual Conference of the Council of Logistics Management,* vol. I, 1988, pp. 51–71.

[42] See David B. Livingston, "Logistics as a Competitive Weapon, Part II: Total Logistics Cost and Corporate Strategy," *Proceedings of the Annual Conference of the Council of Logistics Management,* vol. I, 1989, pp. 375–98. The importance of logistics management in strategic planning has been identified as a major trend of the 1990s by the Council of Logistics Management in an unpublished report to members entitled "Distribution in the 1990s and the National Council of Physical Distribution Management Planning Process," 1984.

Malcolm Baldrige National Quality Award

As an example, logistics has become a very important part of the strategic planning process for U.S. firms applying for the prestigious Malcolm Baldrige National Quality Award. The award, managed by the U.S. Department of Commerce, recognizes companies that have attained a high level of excellence and competitive advantage in domestic and world marketplaces.

Logistics plays a pivotal role in a firm's "winning" the Baldrige award. Thirty percent of the points used in granting the award is based on customer satisfaction. Logistics, through creation of customer service, contributes significantly to marketing's ability to satisfy customers. Without a good logistics system, it is unlikely that a firm could satisfy customers sufficiently enough to win a Baldrige award. The "Customer Focus and Satisfaction" category examines the company's knowledge of the customer, overall customer service systems, responsiveness, and ability to meet requirements and expectations.[43] Without a good logistics system, coupled with the inclusion of logistics in the strategic planning process, a firm cannot hope to score well in this important area.

Logistics as an Offensive Marketing Weapon

Logistics can be a source of competitive advantage for a firm just like a good product, promotion, and pricing strategy. "Distribution can be used as the primary reason why the target market will purchase, and distribution can be designed as a unique offering not duplicated by competition."[44]

Logistics Can Provide a Competitive Advantage

Several high-ranking logistics executives concurred that never before had logistics been in a better position to build profits for companies. As stated by C. Lee Johnson, president of Limited Distribution Services (formerly senior vice president of operations for Beatrice Foods Company): "Although the distribution function over the years has proven that it can reduce costs, it can also produce revenues. . . . We're working on the theory that effective distribution can provide us with a competitive advantage."[45]

In 1990, 3M surveyed 18,000 European customers in 16 countries. Respondents agreed that on-time delivery, short lead times, product delivered in good condition, and effective handling of problems were important to a firm attempting to increase customer satisfaction and sales.[46] "Today, in an era of shrinking product life cycles, proliferating product lines, shifting

---

[43] *1992 Application Guidelines: Malcolm Baldrige National Quality Award* (Gaithersburg, Md: National Institute of Standards and Technology, 1992), p. 25.

[44] For an interesting discussion of this topic, see Jay U. Sterling, "Integrating Customer Service and Marketing Strategies in a Channel of Distribution: An Empirical Study," unpublished Ph.D. dissertation, Michigan State University, 1985.

[45] Jack W. Farrell, "Distribution Outlook: The Time Is Right," *Traffic Management* 23, no. 9 (September 1984), p. 47.

[46] Eric N. Berkowitz, Roger A. Kerin, Steven W. Hartley, and William Rudelius, *Marketing*, 3d ed. (Homewood, Ill.: Richard D. Irwin, 1992), p. 411.

distribution chains, and changing technology, mastery of [logistics management] has become an essential ingredient of competitive success."[47] Companies that view logistics as an offensive marketing weapon will likely make logistics an integral part of their business strategy.

Distribution Accounting

The Challenge to Improve Accounting Systems

Integrated logistics management is based on total cost analysis. That is, at a given customer service level management should minimize total logistics costs rather than attempt to minimize the cost of individual activities.

In general, accountants have not kept pace with developments in logistics and have shown relatively little interest in the area. Consequently, the necessary cost data have not been available, and the lack of data has prevented firms from achieving least total cost logistics. The availability of logistics cost information should be a primary concern of management. Developing logistics cost information for decision making and control is one of the most critical tasks many firms face.

Full implementation of integrated logistics is based on total cost analysis, and the true potential will not be reached until the required cost information is made available to decision makers. As we will see in Chapter 15, there is a considerable gap between the amount of cost information required and its availability in most firms. Overcoming these limitations will be a significant challenge. The future potential of the integrated logistics management concept depends on the ability to obtain the necessary accounting information.[48] Additionally, while many firms are utilizing profitability (full cost) and contribution reports, the quality of those reports varies widely. In a study of manufacturing companies it was reported that 84 percent of the firms generated reports of questionable accuracy.[49] It is not sufficient merely to have distribution accounting systems in place; rather, accurate and timely reports must be generated from such information and given to executives who have a "need to know." Only then can the optimal logistics cost trade-offs be made.

The Need for Broader-Based Management Skills

As rising costs increase the percentage of each sales dollar that firms spend for logistics activities, the logistics function will continue to gain visibility within the organization. In fact, surveys of senior logistics executives who were members of the Council of Logistics Management found that approx-

---

[47] Ibid., p. 71.

[48] Douglas M. Lambert and Howard M. Armitage, "Distribution Costs: The Challenge," *Management Accounting,* May 1979, pp. 33–37, 45.

[49] See Douglas M. Lambert and Jay U. Sterling, "What Types of Profitability Reports Do Marketing Managers Receive?" *Industrial Marketing Management* 16, no. 4 (1987), pp. 295–303.

Logistics Professionals Will Need to Broaden Their Skills

imately 27 percent of the executives had the title of vice president and 45 percent held the position of director.[50] The reported salaries of these executives, shown in Table 1–5, show that the logistics executive has gained a position of substantial importance within the firm.

The studies also revealed broad ranges of responsibility. Vice presidents, directors, and managers spent a significant portion of their time outside the logistics function, often involved in packaging, product planning and sales forecasting.[51] With this responsibility has come the need for academic training in finance, computers, international issues, general management, human resources, and marketing (see Table 1–6). Respondents were also asked: "Identify the two major factors which will, in your judgement, influence the growth and development of the corporate distribution function during the next decade." Twenty-six percent of the executives identified logistics costs, and 24 percent mentioned customer service. The complete responses are summarized in Table 1–7. The data in Tables 1–6 and 1–7 suggest that logistics executives will increasingly be concerned with developing broad-based management skills.

Global Logistics

More Firms Enter International Markets

An increasing number of companies are becoming involved in international markets through exporting, licensing, joint ventures, and ownership. This trend should continue. With this expansion into global marketing comes a need to develop worldwide logistics networks. The international logistics executive will have to acquire a wide range of skills not needed in domestic logistics—skills in areas such as international finance, documentation, political science, and foreign business practices and customs. As the firm expands internationally, the concepts of integrated logistics management and total cost trade-off analysis become even more complex and difficult to manage.

In the future, several trends or events are expected to occur that will have an impact on those firms already involved in international logistics or those companies anticipating such involvement.[52] These items include the following:

1. An increasing number of logistics executives with international responsibility and authority.

---

[50] Bernard J. LaLonde, James M. Masters, and Terrance L. Pohlen, "The 1991 Ohio State University Survey of Career Patterns in Logistics," *Proceedings of the Annual Conference of the Council of Logistics Management,* vol. I, 1991, p. 53.

[51] Ibid.

[52] For an interesting discussion of future trends that will impact global logistics, see Andrew Kupfer, "How American Industry Stacks Up," *Fortune* 125, no. 5 (March 9, 1992), pp. 30–46.

TABLE 1–5 Average Compensation for Logistics Professionals (salary plus bonus)

	Manager	*Director*	*Vice President*
Highest third	$99,000	$115,000	$195,000
Middle third	66,000	90,000	136,000
Lowest third	53,000	68,000	105,000

SOURCE: Bernard J. LaLonde, James M. Masters, and Terrance L. Pohlen, "The 1991 Ohio State University Survey of Career Patterns in Logistics," *Proceedings of the Annual Conference of the Council of Logistics Management,* vol. I, 1991, p. 58.

TABLE 1–6 Perceived Educational Needs (1991)

Area	*Response Percentage*
Finance	20%
International business/Logistics	15
Logistics	14
Computer science	10
Marketing/Sales	7
General business/Management	6
Personnel/Human resources	5
Legal/Environment	5

NOTE: Executives were asked: "If you were offered an opportunity to return to school in the near future for three months and could take a custom-designed curriculum of your choosing, what kinds of things would you study?"

SOURCE: Bernard J. LaLonde, James M. Masters, and Terrance L. Pohlen, "The 1991 Ohio State University Survey of Career Patterns in Logistics," *Proceedings of the Annual Conference of the Council of Logistics Management,* vol. I, 1991, p. 58.

TABLE 1–7 Factors that Will Influence the Growth and Development of the Corporate Logistics Function during the Next Decade (1990s)

Factor	*Response Percentage*
Logistics cost	26%
Customer service	24
Quick response/Just-in-Time/Decision support systems	8
Electronic data interchange/Information systems	8
Competitive advantage	6
Integration	6
Globalization	5
Technology	5
Third party issues	4
Quality performance	3
Legal/Environment	2

SOURCE: Bernard J. LaLonde, James M. Masters, and Terrance L. Pohlen, "The 1991 Ohio State University Survey of Career Patterns in Logistics," *Proceedings of the Annual Conference of the Council of Logistics Management,* vol. I, 1991, p. 60.

2. Expansion of the number and size of foreign trade zones.
3. Reduction in the amount and increased standardization of international paperwork and documentation, especially the bill of lading.
4. Increasing utilization of foreign warehousing owned and controlled by the exporting firm.
5. Increasing number of smaller firms engaging in exporting with larger firms utilizing licensing, joint venture, or direct ownership in lieu of exporting to foreign markets.
6. Domestically, especially in the United States, a trend toward foreign ownership of logistics service firms, for example, public warehousing and transportation carriers.
7. Increasing vertical integration of the channel of distribution, including channel members from several different countries (especially in the acquisition of foreign sources of supply for certain raw materials).

As firms identify customer markets in foreign countries, they must establish logistics systems to provide the products and services demanded. The single most significant development in international logistics will be the increasing sophistication and expertise of global logistics executives and departments.

Strategic Alliances and Partnerships

During the decade of the 1980s, many firms began to examine the viability of developing strategic alliances and partnerships with logistics service providers. Stated simply, they were exploring the "make or buy" decision within logistics rather than manufacturing. As companies have been confronted with competitive pressures, shrinking budgets, transportation deregulation, and a need to improve customer service levels, they have been contracting some portion of their logistics activities out to third parties.[53]

At times, it may be advantageous for a firm to contract with a specific transportation carrier to service a particular market segment, even though the company has a large private motor carrier fleet. Some customers may be located in remote areas where servicing them with the firm's private fleet may be too costly. In such a case, it would be more beneficial for the firm to have a common or contract carrier service those customers rather than to do it itself.

Traditional relationships between shippers and logistics service providers have been "arm's length" transactions; that is, each entity has attempted to maximize its own interests with little regard for how the relationship

---

[53] See Yosef Sheffi, "Third Party Logistics: Present and Future Prospects," *Journal of Business Logistics* 11, no. 2 (1990), pp. 27–39.

might benefit or penalize the other party. Recently, however, firms and logistics service providers have begun to recognize the benefits that can result from developing partnerships or alliances with each other for the purpose of mutually benefiting both parties. In science, such a relationship is termed *symbiosis* because both parties benefit from the relationship.

The number of alliances or partnerships is increasing each year, as firms recognize the mutual benefits that can arise from working in concert rather than independently. All indications point toward the continuation of this trend in the foreseeable future.

Technology

Technology has had an impact on all facets of business, but in the logistics area the impact has truly been significant. The diffusion of technology is changing the way companies do business and the way firms relate to customers and suppliers.[54] Computers, information systems, and communication systems are being increasingly used in transportation, warehousing, order processing, materials management, purchasing, and procurement. Literally, every area of logistics has been affected by the technological revolution and the developments in computers and information and communication systems.

Traditional methods of managing logistics activities are proving inadequate in today's fast-paced economy, and executives have been forced to innovate. If firms do not respond appropriately, they may face losses in market share, creating for themselves positions of competitive disadvantage. Fortunately, assistance is available due to recent innovations and developments in technology.

Logistics 1995

In a Council of Logistics Management study of senior executives in manufacturing, merchandising, and logistics service organizations, "Logistics 1995," several trends occurring in logistics were identified. The top three trends were all directly related to the use of computers, communications systems, and information systems:

1. The rapid proliferation of data processing systems enables the distribution or logistics organization to handle and control information in ways that will change the traditional methods of servicing customers and supplying products.

2. Advances in computer technology will allow electronic data interchange to be pervasive by 1995. All phases of logistics will be involved, and communication technology will create opportunities for large savings.

---

[54] See Catherine L. Harris, "Information Power: How Companies Are Using New Technology to Gain Competitive Edge," *Business Week* no. 2916 (October 14, 1985), p. 108.

3. The major difference between the logistics operating environment of 1995 and that of today will be the improvement in the timeliness and completeness of the exchange of information between channel members.[55]

Toys "Я" Us Utilizes High Technology in Logistics

Numerous companies in manufacturing and merchandising have employed new technology to reap financial and customer service benefits. One such firm has been Toys "Я" Us, one of the largest toy retailers in the world. The firm has utilized the latest technology available in its newest distribution center located in California. At a cost of over $40 million, the 612,000-square-foot facility can house over 80,000 pallets, or stage bins, by stacking them 50 feet high. The venture has been very successful, as evidenced by comments of the Toys "Я" Us president at the firm's annual stockholders' meeting:

> Operators get the goods with cherry picker-type trucks guided by wires in the floor and use laser scanners to identify the cartons. The [distribution] center holds 45% more merchandise than the company's existing warehouses and takes up two-thirds the space. It lets the company get toys out of the warehouse and onto store shelves faster, keeping handling costs low and enabling Toys "Я" Us consistently to beat anyone else's prices.[56]

Similarly, J. C. Penney uses satellite transmissions to interface with its stores and its customers. Buyers can place orders with company headquarters or directly with suppliers who are linked to Penney via an electronic ordering system. "These satellite feeds allow the retailer not only to cut travel time among buyers but also to react faster to changes in styles and give each store an individual look."[57]

The use of technology in logistics offers significant potential. A firm can create a competitive advantage by adopting a strategic perspective with respect to computers, communication, and information technology.

SUMMARY

In this chapter we have seen how logistics activities interface with the economic system at the macro (society) and micro (firm) levels. We viewed logistics management as the integration of several activities for the purpose of planning, implementing, and controlling the efficient flow of raw materials, in-process inventory, and finished goods from point-of-origin to point-of-consumption. We examined the relationship between

---

[55] James F. Robeson, "Logistics 1995: 10 Top Trends," presentation given at the Seventeenth Annual Transportation Logistics Educators' Conference, September 27, 1987.

[56] Susan Caminiti, "The New Champs of Retailing," *Fortune* 122, no. 7 (September 24, 1990), p. 94.

[57] Ibid., pp. 94, 98.

logistics and marketing, especially noting the creation of time and place utility. We also looked at logistics' importance from a cost standpoint.

Examples of logistics activities included customer service, traffic and transportation, warehousing and storage, plant and warehouse site selection, inventory control, order processing, distribution communications, procurement, material handling, parts and service support, salvage and scrap disposal, packaging, return goods handling, and demand forecasting. Finally, we examined the historical development of logistics management in light of its strategic function in the modern corporation. With this as background, the reader is prepared to examine the integrated logistics management concept, the total cost concept, and the marketing and logistics audit. These are the subjects of Chapter 2.

SUGGESTED READINGS

BANKS, HOWARD. "The World's Most Competitive Economy." *Forbes* 149, no. 7 (March 30, 1992), pp. 84–88.

BOWERSOX, DONALD J. "The Strategic Benefits of Logistics Alliances." *Harvard Business Review* 68, no. 4 (July-August 1990), pp. 36–42.

———. Patricia J. Daugherty, Cornelia L. Dröge, Richard N. Germain, and Dale S. Rogers. *Logistical Excellence: It's Not Business as Usual.* Burlington, Mass.: Digital Press, 1992.

GATTORNA, JOHN, Abby Day, and John Hargreaves. "Effective Logistics Management." *Logistics Information Management* 4, no. 2 (1991), pp. 1–86.

"The Gurus of Quality." *Traffic Management* 29, no. 7 (July 1990), pp. 34–39.

LAHOWCHIC, NICHOLAS H. "Merging the Distribution Operations of Nabisco and Standard Brands, and Customer Service." *Proceedings of the Twenty-Second Annual Conference of the National Council of Physical Distribution Management,* 1984, pp. 179–96.

LANGLEY, C. JOHN, JR. "Strategic Management in Transportation and Physical Distribution." *Transportation Journal* 23, no. 3 (Spring 1983), pp. 71–78.

LANGLEY, C. JOHN, JR., AND WILLIAM D. MORICE. "Strategies for Logistics Management: Reactions to a Changing Environment." *Journal of Business Logistics* 3, no. 1 (1982), pp. 1–18.

MOREHOUSE, JAMES E. "Operating in the New Logistics Era." *Harvard Business Review* 61, no. 5 (September-October 1983), pp. 18–19.

PORTER, MICHAEL E. *Competitive Advantage.* New York: The Free Press, 1985.

PETERS, TOM, AND NANCY AUSTIN. *A Passion for Excellence.* New York: Random House, 1985.

SMITH, PETER A., ET AL. *Logistics in Service Industries.* Oak Brook, Ill.: Council of Logistics Management, 1991.

STOCK, JAMES R. "Logistics Thought and Practice: A Perspective." *International Journal of Physical Distribution and Logistics Management* 20, no. 1 (1990), pp. 3–6.

STOCK, JAMES R. *Reverse Logistics.* Oak Brook, Ill.: Council of Logistics Management, 1992.

QUESTIONS AND PROBLEMS

1. Explain how improvements in logistics productivity can influence the economic position of individual consumers and the population as a whole.
2. Briefly describe the relationship between logistics and the marketing concept. Include discussion of customer satisfaction, integrated effort, and company profit.
3. Logistics has been described as an activity that adds time and place utility to products. Indicate how logistics affects time and place utility.
4. What factors have helped business to recognize that logistics management is important to society and the firm?
5. Logistics cost reductions can provide significant profit leverage. If a firm has a net profit on its sales of 5 percent, how much would sales have to increase to match a logistics cost reduction of $500,000? In what areas of logistics would the cost reduction be most likely to occur?
6. Which of the challenges facing the logistics professional in the coming years do you believe will be the most significant? Why?
7. Briefly discuss the relationship between logistics and technology. Why is it likely that the relationship will become more important in the future?

Chapter 2

The Integrated Logistics Management Concept

Objectives of This Chapter

To show how logistics influences economic and corporate performance

To show how to implement the integrated logistics management concept using total cost analysis

To show how to conduct a marketing and logistics audit

To show how to recognize areas in which logistics performance can be improved

INTRODUCTION

Our uncertain economy is marked by mature markets, the globalization of industry, high energy costs, potential energy and material shortages, high interest rates and capital rationing, a low growth rate in productivity, and the threat of inflation. In this context, maintaining corporate profit growth and return on investment is becoming increasingly difficult. It has become necessary for management to investigate alternative methods of generating revenue and reducing costs. Few areas offer the potential for profit improvement that can be found in the logistics function. This is because logistics costs can exceed 25 percent of each sales dollar at the manufacturing level.[1]

The Foundation of Integrated Logistics Is Total Cost Analysis

Many companies have not managed logistics as an integrated system; for them, successful implementation of the integrated logistics management concept can lead to significant improvements in profitability.[2] The foundation of the integrated logistics management concept is *total cost analysis,* which we have defined as minimizing the total cost of transportation, warehousing, inventory, order processing and information systems, and lot quantity cost, while achieving a desired customer service level.

WHY SHOULD LOGISTICS ACTIVITIES BE INTEGRATED?

During the past 30 years, logistics has emerged as a separate and dynamic discipline. Many major corporations have acknowledged the importance of logistics by placing responsibility for this function at the vice presidential level.[3] Basically, the integrated logistics management concept refers to administering the various activities as an integrated system. In firms that

---

[1]Bernard J. LaLonde, John R. Grabner, and James F. Robeson, "Integrated Distribution Systems: A Management Perspective," *International Journal of Physical Distribution,* October 1970, p. 134.

[2]Roy D. Shapiro, "Get Leverage from Logistics," *Harvard Business Review* 62, no. 1 (1984), pp. 119–26; and A. T. Kearney Inc., *Measuring and Improving Productivity in Physical Distribution* (Chicago: National Council of Physical Distribution Management, 1984).

[3]A quick scan of the membership roster of the Council of Logistics Management (formerly the National Council of Physical Distribution Management) confirms this. See also Bernard J. LaLonde, James M. Masters, and Terrance L. Pohlen, "The 1991 Ohio State University Survey of Career Patterns in Logistics," *Annual Conference Proceedings of the Annual Conference of the Council of Logistics Management,* vol. 1, 1991), pp. 43–64.

have not adopted a systems integrative approach, logistics is a fragmented and often uncoordinated set of activities spread throughout various organizational functions with each individual function having its own budget and set of priorities and measurements.[4] A number of firms, including Herman Miller, Quaker Oats, and Whirlpool Corporation, have found that total distribution costs can be reduced by integrating such distribution-related activities as customer service, transportation, warehousing, inventory management, order processing and information systems, and production planning and purchasing. Without this integrated approach, inventory tends to build up at the following critical business interfaces:

Integration of Logistics Activities Smooths Corporate Interfaces

- Supplier-purchasing
- Purchasing-production
- Production-marketing
- Marketing-distribution
- Distribution-intermediary (wholesaler and/or retailer)
- Intermediary-consumer/user

In a manufacturing environment inventory commonly builds up at these interfaces for the following reasons:

Five Reasons for Large Inventories

1. Purchasing management is often rewarded for achieving low per-unit costs for raw materials and supplies.
2. Production management is usually compensated for achieving the lowest possible per-unit production costs.
3. Salespeople like to have market presence by positioning large inventories of product in the field and as close to the customer as possible. This makes it possible for salespeople to offer the fastest possible order cycle time and to minimize the difficulties associated with forecasting customers' needs.
4. In some companies transportation is the only logistics cost that is closely monitored. With transportation rates rising because of higher energy costs, higher labor costs, and higher rates for small shipments due to deregulation, transportation managers have more incentive to ship products by truckload or by railcar in order to obtain lower rates. Generally, these large shipments of products require increased inventories at both the origin and destination—for example, at the manufacturer and at the wholesaler/retailer.
5. Both consumers/users and intermediaries may attempt to reduce their inventories by purchasing more frequently, thereby forcing inventories and the associated carrying costs back toward the manufacturer. This is particularly true in times when intermediaries are concerned with cash flow management.

---

[4] Alan H. Gepfert, "Business Logistics for Better Profit Performance," *Harvard Business Review,* November-December, 1968, pp. 75–84; and Jack Farrell, *Physical Distribution Case Studies* (Boston: Cahners Books International, 1973).

In addition to improving the flow of inventory, integration improves transport asset utilization and warehouse asset utilization, and eliminates the duplication of departmental efforts. For example, rather than having the purchasing department negotiate with inbound carriers and the distribution department negotiate with outbound carriers, one organization can negotiate for both inbound and outbound transportation and plan the shipments to offset high-volume inbound shipments with high-volume outbound shipments to the same geographic areas. The central coordination of the various logistics activities forces cost trade-offs to be made between and among customer service levels, transportation, warehousing, inventory management, order processing, and production planning and/or purchasing.

LOGISTICS AND THE MARKETING FUNCTION

The importance of a marketing orientation for business success has been well documented.[5] How management allocates scarce resources to the components of the marketing mix—product, price, promotion, and place—will determine a company's market share and profitability.[6] Management can improve a firm's competitive position by spending more dollars on the marketing mix, by allocating resources more effectively and efficiently to the individual components of the marketing mix, and/or by making changes within a component that will increase effectiveness and/or efficiency.[7] Figure 2–1 summarizes the cost trade-offs that management must make. The objective is to allocate resources to the product, price, promotion, and place components of the marketing mix in a manner that will lead to the greatest long-run profits.

Product

Product is the bundle of attributes the customer receives from the purchase. Management may allocate resources to product development to bring new products to market or to improve the quality of existing products. The quality of the product influences demand in the marketplace and the price the company can charge. Reducing quality lowers manufacturing costs and

---

[5] See, for example, Thomas J. Peters and Robert H. Waterman, Jr., *In Search of Excellence* (New York: Harper & Row, 1982).

[6] This material is taken from Douglas M. Lambert, "Improving Profitability by Managing Marketing Costs," paper presented at the American Marketing Association Accounting/Marketing Conference, 1981; and Douglas M. Lambert and Douglas E. Zemke, "The Customer Service Component of the Marketing Mix," *Proceedings of the Twentieth Annual Conference of the National Council of Physical Distribution Management,* 1982, pp. 1–24.

[7] See Jay U. Sterling and Douglas M. Lambert, "Establishing Customer Service Strategies Within the Marketing Mix," *Journal of Business Logistics* 8, no. 1 (1987), pp. 1–30.

FIGURE 2–1 Cost Trade-Offs Required in Marketing and Logistics

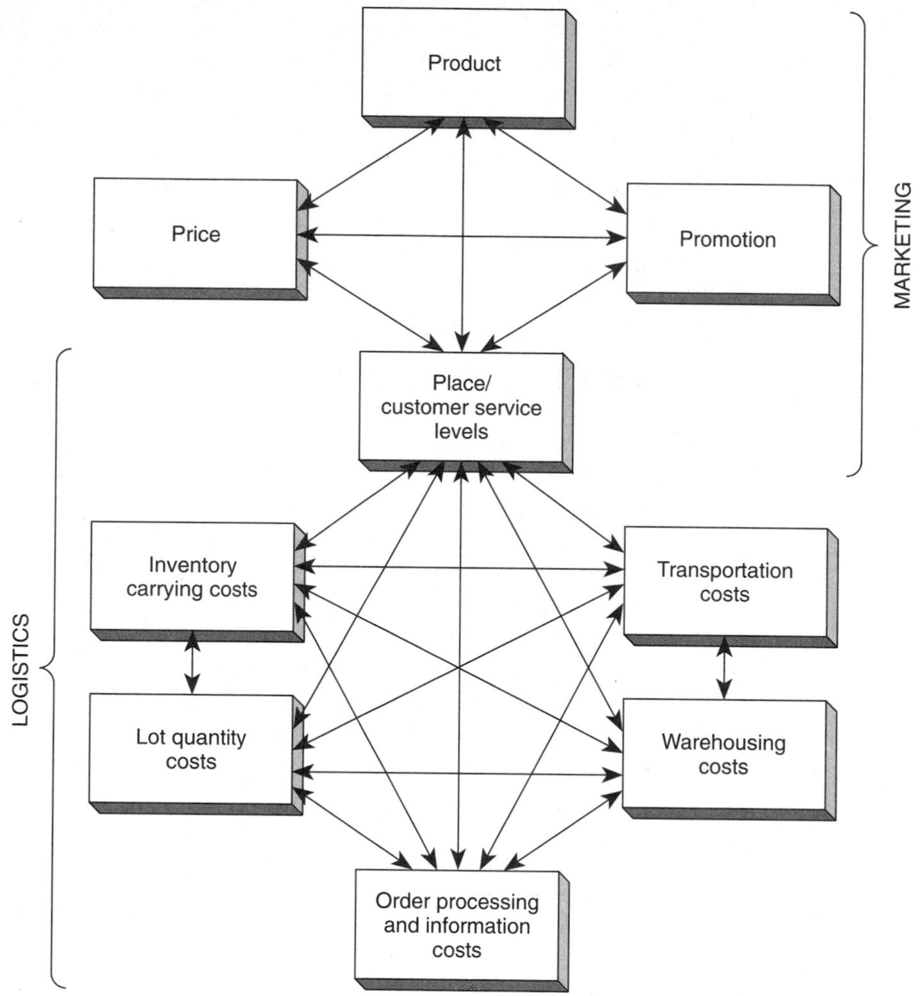

Marketing objective: Allocate resources to the marketing mix to maximize the long-run profitability of the firm.
Logistics objective: Minimize total costs given the customer service objective where: Total costs = Transportation costs + Warehousing costs + Order processing and information costs + Lot quantity costs + Inventory carrying costs.

SOURCE: Adapted from Douglas M. Lambert, *The Development of an Inventory Costing Methodology: A Study of the Cost Associated with Holding Inventory* (Chicago: National Council of Physical Distribution Management, 1976), p. 7.

It Is Increasingly Difficult to Differentiate the Firm with the Product

increases short-run profits but may erode long-run profitability. In the global marketplace, all major competitors will be required to have high-quality products. To quote a senior vice president of a Fortune 500 firm: "A high-quality product is simply the price of admission; the Japanese competitors all have high-quality innovative products. It is very difficult if not impossible to differentiate firms based on the product."

In some industries, success depends on spending substantial sums on research and development to bring a continuous stream of new products to the marketplace. However, many new products are nothing more than product line extensions that do little to increase total market size but do increase the cost of doing business. In these situations, the market is simply carved up into smaller and less profitable pieces. Management must carefully consider the profit impact of changes in the product offering.

Price

Price is the amount of money the manufacturer receives for its product. Management must determine how changes in price will affect the purchase behavior of intermediaries and ultimate consumers. Price changes are not limited to changes in a product's list price. When a manufacturer demands faster payment of accounts receivable, provides a discount for early payment, or otherwise changes the financial terms of sale, it is changing the price of its products, and such changes may affect demand. The price that the manufacturer receives for its products differs depending on the channel of distribution used.

Price Reductions

Management may attempt to increase sales and profitability by reducing prices. However, in mature industries this is a questionable strategy. For example, if a firm's net profit after taxes is 4 percent of sales, a 2 percent price reduction will lower net profit after taxes from 4 percent to 3 percent in the absence of an increase in sales. A substantial sales increase is required just to break even and maintain the 4 percent profit.[8] Achieving the necessary sales increase in a mature market is very difficult. Typically, competitors will match price reductions, and every firm will then make less profit because industry sales increase very little or not at all.

---

[8]This example assumes a 50 percent tax rate. The actual percentage sales increase required to break even is equal to:

$$\frac{\text{Percentage price reduction before taxes}}{\text{Contribution margin} - \text{Price reduction}} \times 100\%$$

For example, if the price reduction is 5 percent and the contribution margin is 20 percent, the percentage increase required is:

$$\frac{5\%}{20\% - 5\%} \times 100\% = 33\%$$

Promotion

Promotion refers to both advertising and personal selling. Increasing expenditures for advertising will increase sales, but at some point additional advertising expenditures will not increase sales enough to justify the expenditure. The amount of sales support required depends on the channel of distribution used. For example, manufacturers that use direct sales have to spend more on salespeople. The size of the sales force influences the size of the potential market and the manufacturer's market share. To justify the additional expense, however, increased expenditures for promotion must lead to an equal or greater increase in contribution as a result of increased sales.[9] In many industries there is an opportunity to use personal selling more effectively by training salespeople to sell the value-added that is provided by excellent logistics.

Personal Selling Represents an Opportunity

Place

The *place* component represents the manufacturer's expenditure for *customer service,* which can be thought of as the output of the logistics system.[10] Customer service is the interface of logistics with marketing. While customer service is the output of the logistics system, *customer satisfaction* results when the company performs well on all components of the marketing mix. Product availability and order cycle time can be used to differentiate the product and may influence the market price if customers are willing to pay more for better service. In addition, manufacturers add logistics costs to product costs, so logistics costs may affect the market price set by the company.

Customer Service Is Critical for Successful Marketing

For many firms customer service may be the best method of gaining a competitive advantage.[11] The firm may be able to significantly improve its market share and profitability by spending more than competitors on customer service/logistics. By systematically adjusting the customer service package, however, the firm may improve service and reduce the total costs of logistics. When evaluating alternative customer service strategies, management's goal should be to maximize the firm's long-run profitability.

---

[9] Contribution is equal to the selling price minus the variable costs of production, marketing, and logistics. We will discuss the contribution approach in detail in Chapter 3.

[10] The place component also considers the firm's channels of distribution. The channels used affect the level of customer service required as well as total logistics costs. Consequently, logistics system costs will influence channel design. We will deal with these relationships in the next chapter.

[11] Jay U. Sterling and Douglas M. Lambert, "Establishing Customer Service Strategies Within the Marketing Mix," *Journal of Business Logistics* 8, no. 1 (1987), pp. 1–30.

Increases in expenditures for the various components of the marketing mix require sales increases just to recover the additional costs. Most companies have limited resources and therefore must allocate these resources in a manner that will increase market share and profitability. Shifting marketing mix dollars to customer service from areas in which the money is not achieving sufficient sales may result in cost savings as well as improved customer service. The advantage of this method is that the contribution margin on resulting sales increases goes directly to the bottom line of the profit and loss statement. The impact on net profit is substantial because cost reductions in other components of the marketing mix offset the increased cost of customer service and it is not necessary to deduct the incremental service costs from the incremental contribution generated. Also, customer service improvements are not as easily duplicated by competitors as are changes in product, price, and promotion.

Customer Service Is Not Easily Duplicated by Competitors

Figure 2–1 illustrates the cost trade-offs necessary to successfully implement the integrated logistics management concept. The figure will be used throughout this text as the financial model for making logistics decisions.

THE TOTAL COST CONCEPT

Total cost analysis is the key to managing the logistics function.[12] Management should strive to minimize the *total* cost of logistics rather than the cost of each activity. Attempts to reduce the cost of individual activities may lead to increased total costs.[13] For example, consolidating finished goods inventory in a small number of distribution centers will reduce inventory carrying costs and warehousing costs but may lead to a substantial increase in freight expense or a lower sales volume as a result of reduced levels of customer service. Similarly, savings associated with large volume purchases may be less than the associated increase in inventory carrying costs.

Management must consider the total of all of the logistics costs described in Figure 2–1. Reductions in one cost invariably lead to increases in the costs of other components. Effective management and real cost savings can be accomplished only by viewing logistics as an integrated system and minimizing its total cost given the firm's customer service objectives. The cost categories introduced in Figure 2–1 are customer service levels

Logistics Must Be Viewed as an Integrated System

---

[12] This section draws heavily from Douglas M. Lambert, *The Development of an Inventory Costing Methodology: A Study of the Costs Associated with Holding Inventory* (Chicago: National Council of Physical Distribution Management, 1976), pp. 5–15, 59–67.

[13] See Marvin Flaks, "Total Cost Approach to Physical Distribution," *Business Management* 24 (August 1963), pp. 55–61; and Raymond LeKashman and John F. Stolle, "The Total Cost Approach to Distribution," *Business Horizons* 8 (Winter 1965), pp. 33–46.

(the cost of lost sales), transportation costs, warehousing costs, order processing and information costs, lot quantity costs, and inventory carrying costs.

Customer Service Levels

The cost associated with alternative customer service levels is the cost of lost sales (not only the margin lost by not meeting current sales demand, but the present value of all future contributions to profit forfeited when a customer is lost due to poor availability, long lead times, or other service failures). Most businesspeople find it difficult, if not impossible, to measure this cost. For this reason, management should strive to minimize the total of the remaining five cost components, given a desired level of customer service. By comparing total logistics system costs, management can make a knowledgeable judgment about the likelihood of recovering, through increased sales, the increase in total system costs brought about by an increase in customer service levels. Of course, management could also reduce spending in some other component of the marketing mix—promotion, for example—in order to maintain profits with a similar sales volume. Likewise, with decreases in customer service levels, management can improve profitability or increase expenditures for other components of the marketing mix in an effort to maintain or improve market position.

Customer Service Levels Should Be Based on Customer Needs and Marketing Strategy

Though the cost of lost sales associated with a particular level of customer service is elusive, better decisions are possible if management determines customer service levels based on customer needs and an understanding of the interaction between customer service and the other marketing mix components. The goal is to determine the least total cost method of logistics while keeping customer service objectives in mind. This requires that good cost data be available for the other five cost categories in Figure 2–1. With this approach, the cost of achieving a specific customer service objective is the total cost of the logistics system that provides the desired level of customer service.

Transportation Costs

Costs associated with the transportation function can be identified in total and by segments (i.e., inbound, outbound, by vendor, by customer, by mode, by carrier, by product, or by channel). This detail is necessary to determine the incremental costs associated with changes in the logistics system. If transportation costs are not currently available in any other form, management can determine them at a relatively low cost by sampling product flows and auditing freight bills (for common carriers) or corporate accounting records (for private fleets).[14] We will deal in depth with transportation costs and how to collect them in Chapter 6.

Warehousing Costs

Warehousing costs are all the expenses that can be eliminated or that must be increased as a result of a change in the number of warehousing facilities. There has been a great deal of confusion in the literature about these costs. Many authors have included all warehousing costs in inventory carrying costs.[15] This is a misconception, however, since most warehousing costs will not change with the level of inventory stocked, but rather with the number of stocking locations. However, the number of warehouses used in the logistics system will have an impact on the levels of inventory.

In the case of leased or owned facilities, the costs associated with storage are primarily fixed and take the form of step functions. Management would have to close the warehouse to eliminate the fixed costs. Costs such as labor have a fixed and a variable component. For example, a company may need one warehouse manager, an office worker, security guards, and a warehouse crew of four to maintain one warehouse location. If the volume of product moving into and out of the warehouse increases beyond a certain level, existing employees will be required to work overtime or additional employees will be hired. But these labor costs vary with the amount of product moving into and out of the warehouse and not with inventory levels. Sales volume will affect these variable costs, but inventory levels will have little or no effect.

Two Distinct Categories of Warehousing Costs

Warehousing costs should be separated into two distinct categories: those related to throughput and those related to storage. *Throughput costs* are the costs associated with selling product in a given market by moving it into and out of a warehouse in that market, and the fixed costs associated with the facility. Examples of throughput costs are the charges that public warehousers assess for moving product into and out of their facilities, and the costs of leased and owned facilities that we discussed earlier. Warehousing costs related to *inventory storage* should be included in inventory carrying costs. These warehousing costs change with the *level* of inventory held in a specific warehouse and tend to be negligible in a company-owned

---

[14]See Jay U. Sterling and Douglas M. Lambert, "A Methodology for Identifying Potential Cost Reductions in Transportation and Warehousing," *Journal of Business Logistics* 5, no. 2 (1984), pp. 1–18; and Douglas M. Lambert and Jay U. Sterling, "Managing Inbound Transportation: A Case Study," *Journal of Purchasing and Materials Management* 20, no. 2 (Summer 1984), pp. 22–29.

[15]This will be documented in Chapter 9.

or leased warehouse. In the case of public warehouses, handling charges reflect the amount of product sold in the market served by the warehouse and are distinct from storage space costs, which public warehousers bill to their customers based on the amount of inventory stored in the facility. The inclusion of throughput warehousing costs in inventory carrying costs is a mistake since they will not be reduced by cutting inventory levels. Throughput costs should be included instead in warehousing costs so that the increments can be easily added or subtracted when the logistics system configuration changes.

Order Processing and Information Costs

Only Include Costs that Will Change with the Decision

Order processing and information costs include the cost of order transmittal, order entry, order processing, related handling costs, and associated internal and external communication costs. When establishing these costs, management must remember to include in the analysis only those costs that will change with the decision being made. We will take a detailed look at order processing and information systems and their associated costs in Chapter 13.

Lot Quantity Costs

Lot quantity costs are those production-related or purchasing/acquisition costs that will change as a result of a change in the logistics system. Usually production lot quantity costs will include some or all of the following:

1. Production preparation costs.
   a. Setup time.
   b. Inspection.
   c. Setup scrap.
   d. Inefficiency of beginning operation.
2. Capacity lost due to changeover.
3. Materials handling, scheduling, and expediting.

The production preparation costs and lost capacity costs are available in most manufacturing firms since they are used as inputs to production planning. A firm can approximate the other costs by dividing the incremental total costs incurred for two different levels of activity by the change in volume. The company can also use regression analysis to isolate fixed and variable cost components. The numbers obtained can be used for logistics system planning. The lot quantity costs associated with purchasing are the costs of buying in various quantities. We will discuss these in Chapter 12.

Inventory Carrying Costs

Components of Inventory Carrying Costs

Conceptually, inventory carrying costs are the most difficult costs to determine next to the costs of lost sales. Inventory carrying costs should include only those costs that vary with the level of inventory stored and that can be categorized into the following groups: (1) *capital costs,* which is the company's opportunity cost of capital multiplied by the variable out-of-pocket investment in inventory; (2) *inventory service costs,* such as insurance and taxes on the inventory; (3) *storage space costs;* and (4) *inventory risk costs,* including obsolescence, damage, pilferage, and relocation costs. We will discuss these expenses in great detail in Chapter 9.

LOGISTICS AND CORPORATE PROFIT PERFORMANCE

Inventories and Accounts Receivable Are a Major Portion of Corporate Assets

In an uncertain economic environment, top management will be interested in asset management and cash flow management. The two most common strategies used to improve cash flow and return on assets are (1) reducing accounts receivable and (2) reducing the investment in inventory. Table 2–1, which contains selected financial data for 15 manufacturers and 10 wholesalers and retailers, provides insight into why this is so. It shows that accounts receivable ranged from 5.1 to 25.9 percent of total assets for manufacturers and from 1.6 to 31.4 percent of total assets for wholesalers and retailers. Inventories ranged from 4.4 to 21.7 percent of total assets for manufacturers and from 16.0 to 54.0 percent of total assets for wholesalers and retailers. Together, accounts receivable and inventories ranged from 9.5 to 43.3 percent and from 17.6 to 61.5 percent of total assets, respectively.

When top management mandates a reduction in accounts receivable and/or inventories, its objective is to improve cash flow and reduce the company's investment in assets. Usually, management assumes that revenues and other costs will remain the same. But reduction in the terms of sale, or even enforcement of the stated terms of sale, in effect changes the price component of the firm's marketing mix. In addition, simply reducing the level of inventory can significantly increase the cost of logistics if current inventories have been set at a level that allows the firm to achieve least total cost logistics for a desired level of customer service.

The arbitrary reduction of accounts receivable and/or inventories in the absence of technological change or changes in the logistics system can have a devastating impact on corporate profit performance. If a manufacturer changes its terms of sale, for example, the effect on wholesalers and retailers will be twofold. First, the change alters the manufacturer's price and therefore the competitive position of its products, which may lead to decreased sales. Second, it further complicates the cash flow problems of the manufacturer's customers. Forcing faster payment of invoices causes

TABLE 2–1 Selected Financial Data for Manufacturers, Wholesalers, and Retailers ($ millions)

Manufacturers	*Sales*	*Net Profits*	*Net Profits as a Percent of Sales*	*Total Assets*	*Accounts Receivable*	*Inventory Investment*	*Accounts Receivable as a Percent of Assets*	*Inventories as a Percent of Assets*
Abbott Laboratories	$ 6,158.7	$ 965.8	15.7%	$ 5,563.2	$1,070.2	$ 777.6	19.2%	14.0%
Borden, Inc.	7,632.8	363.6	4.8	5,284.3	919.8	665.5	17.4	12.6
The Clorox Company	1,484.0	153.6	10.4	1,137.7	151.5	128.1	13.3	11.3
Dresser Industries, Inc.	4,480.3	184.4	4.1	3,309.0	761.2	526.4	23.0	15.9
Ford Motor Company	81,844.0	98.7	0.1	50,823.4	3,537.0	7,115.4	7.0	14.0
General Electric Company	58,414.0	4,303.0	7.4	153,884.0	7,806.0	6,707.0	5.1	4.4
General Mills	6,448.3	381.4	5.9	3,289.5	258.7	394.4	7.9	12.0
Goodyear Tire & Rubber Co.	11,272.5	−38.3	−0.3	8,963.6	1,495.0	1,346.0	16.7	15.0
Harris Corp.	3,052.7	130.7	4.3	2,625.1	679.2	426.6	25.9	16.3
Honeywell	6,309.1	381.9	6.1	4,746.2	1,083.5	972.3	22.8	20.5
NCR Corp.	6,285.0	369.0	5.9	4,547.0	1,123.0	499.0	24.7	11.0
Newell Co.	1,072.6	101.4	9.4	870.9	111.3	177.8	12.8	20.4
Pfizer, Inc.	6,406.0	801.2	12.5	9,052.0	1,377.2	1,142.6	15.2	12.6
Sara Lee Corp.	11,605.9	470.3	4.1	7,636.4	922.2	1,653.7	12.1	21.7
Xerox Corp.	16,951.0	605.0	3.6	31,495.0	3,521.0	2,148.0	11.2	6.8
Wholesalers and Retailers								
Baxter	8,100.0	40.0	0.5	8,517.0	1,518.0	1,532.0	17.8	18.0
Bergen Brunswig Corp.	4,442.3	66.1	1.5	1,238.1	330.1	418.2	26.7	33.8
Dayton Hudson Corp.	13,644.0	410.0	3.0	6.684.0	1,138.0	1,827.0	17.0	27.3
Fleming Cos., Inc.	11,932.8	97.3	0.8	2,767.7	257.8	884.9	9.3	32.0
Kmart Corporation	29,793.0	323.0	1.1	13,145.0	698.0	6,933.0	5.3	52.7
Nordstrom	2,671.1	114.9	4.3	1,707.4	536.3	420.0	31.4	24.6
Sears, Roebuck & Company	28,958.8	257.4	0.9	25,539.0	416.5	4,074,0	1.6	16.0
Super Valu Stores, Inc.	11,136.0	147.7	1.3	2,428.9	219.2	833.2	9.0	34.3
Wal-Mart Stores, Inc.	25,810.7	1,075.9	4.2	8,198.5	155.8	4,428.1	1.9	54.0
Winn-Dixie	9,744.5	152.5	1.6	1,732.7	69.7	848.4	4.0	49.0

SOURCES: Ford Motor Co. figures are for its automotive division only. General Electric figures are from its consolidated balance sheet. Pfizer, Inc., figures are from its consolidated balance sheet. Xerox Corp. figures are from its consolidated balance sheet. Sears, Roebuck & Co. figures are for its Merchandise Group only. All figures are for 1990.

channel members to improve their cash flow by reducing their inventories of the manufacturer's products. They do so by placing smaller, more frequent orders, which may increase total logistics costs for both the manufacturer and its customers. This situation may also result in stockouts of the manufacturer's products at the wholesale or retail level of the channel, further reducing sales volume.

Arbitrary Inventory Reductions May Increase Total Costs

Similarly, a manufacturer's policy of arbitrarily reducing inventory levels to increase inventory turns, in the absence of a system change, may escalate transportation costs and/or production setup costs as the logistics system scrambles to achieve the specified customer service levels with lower inventories (assuming the company was efficiently and effectively distributing its product prior to the policy change). Alternatively, pressure to reduce expenses may preclude the use of premium transportation or increased production setups to achieve the desired customer service levels with less inventory. In this case, customer service levels would be eroded, and a decrease in market share might result. In either set of circumstances, the increased cost of transportation and/or production, or the lost sales contribution, could far exceed the savings in inventory carrying costs.

However, if management concentrates on systems changes that improve logistics efficiency and/or effectiveness, it may be able to satisfy all of the firm's objectives. For example, many companies have not kept pace with the new technology in order processing. By replacing an outdated order processing and information system, a firm may be able to achieve some or all of the following: (1) increased customer service levels; (2) lower inventories; (3) speedier collections; (4) fewer split shipments of orders; (5) decreased transportation costs as a result of freight consolidation; (6) lower warehousing costs; (7) improved forecasting accuracy and production planning; and (8) improvements in cash flow and return on assets.

The Strategic Profit Model

Return on Net Worth Is a Function of Three Controllable Factors

One useful way to determine how a proposed systems change will influence profit performance and return on assets is by using the strategic profit model (see Figure 2–2). The strategic profit model demonstrates that return on net worth, that is, the return on shareholders' investment plus retained earnings, is a function of three factors management can control: net profit, asset turnover, and financial leverage.

Net Profit. Net profit as a percent of sales is a measure of how efficiently and effectively products are manufactured and sold. However, net profit alone is not a satisfactory measure of performance. For example, would it be better to purchase stock in a company with a 2 percent net profit or one with a 10 percent net profit? In order to answer this question, one would need to know the firms' sales volumes as well as the investment required to achieve that level of sales. How efficiently management utilizes its assets should also be measured.

Asset Turnover. Asset turnover, sales divided by total assets, shows how efficiently assets are employed in order to generate a level of sales.

Return on Assets. Return on assets, which is determined by multiplying the net profit margin by asset turnover, relates profitability to the value of the assets employed. For this reason, it is the best single measure of corporate performance. This yardstick allows the comparison of alternatives, whether they are similar or different projects/companies. However, as with any measure of performance, return on assets should not be used in isolation, since it may vary considerably by industry as a result of industry conditions or the level of capital investment.

A firm can improve its return on assets by increasing net profit and/or reducing the assets it employs. In other words, increasing either net profit

FIGURE 2–2 The Strategic Profit Model

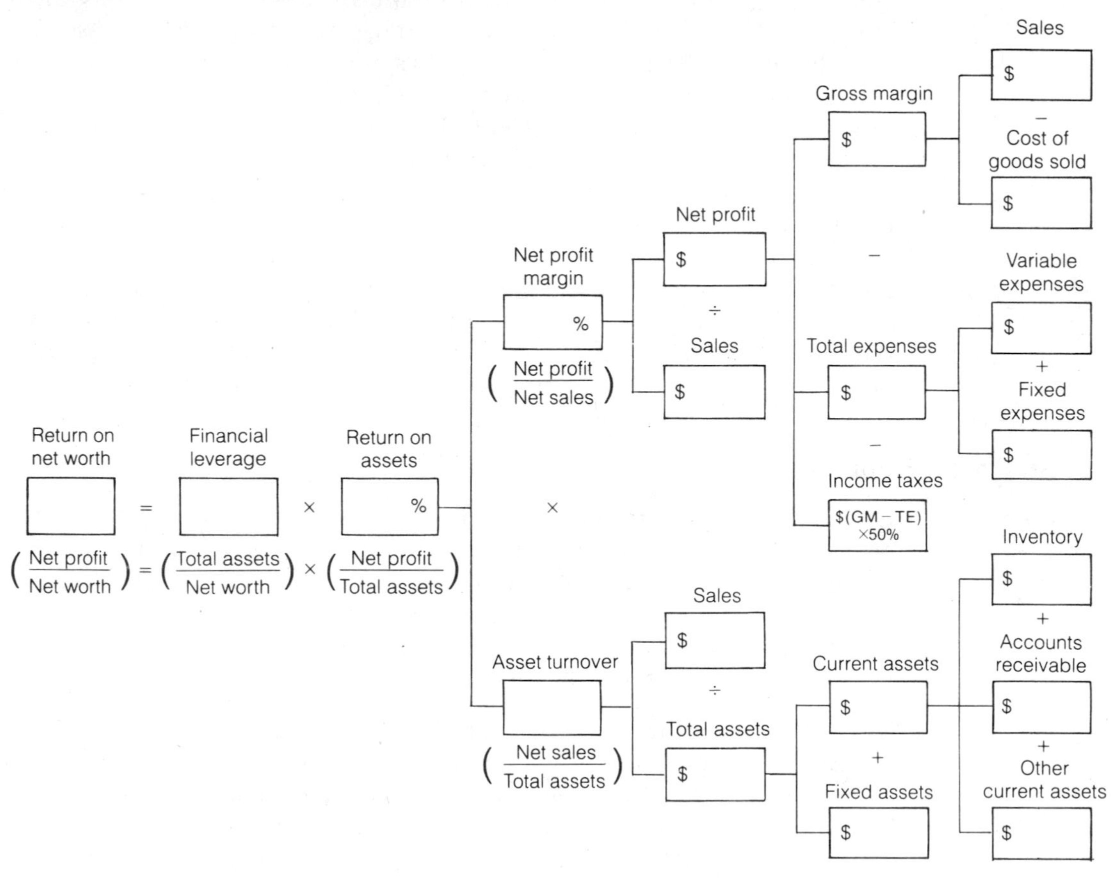

margins or asset turnover without changing the other will lead to higher return on assets.

Financial Leverage. Financial leverage is calculated by dividing total assets by the firm's net worth. It measures how management uses outside financing to increase the firm's return on net worth. Net worth or shareholders' equity equals the shareholders' investment in capital stock plus retained earnings. Simply stated, if a company can borrow money at a cost of 10 percent before taxes and 5 percent after taxes, and can invest the funds in assets that provide a return of 15 percent after taxes, earnings per share will be larger if the firm finances its growth by borrowing money and using cash from operations rather than by selling more shares. It should be noted, however, that it is possible for management to use too much financial leverage (borrow too much money) and create cash flow problems for the firm if sales decline.

Return on Net Worth. The important measure for shareholders is return on net worth, which equals net profit divided by shareholders' equity. It can be determined by multiplying the return on assets by the financial leverage ratio.

Using the Strategic Profit Model: An Example

The following example illustrates how the strategic profit model can be used. Table 2–2 contains a simplified income statement and balance sheet for L and S Incorporated. Figure 2–3 shows how the pertinent data from these financial statements can be transferred to the strategic profit model. The top portion of the model contains information from the income statement, and the bottom portion contains data from the asset side of the balance sheet.

Two Methods of Increasing Return on Assets

Since financial leverage is a strategic decision that is made by top management, most operations managers must improve return on assets to increase return on net worth. This they can accomplish by (1) increasing net profit margin or (2) increasing asset turnover. Net profit is a function of the sales volume achieved and expenses incurred to obtain that level of sales. Asset turnover is a function of sales volume and the level of assets employed. In other words, management can improve return on assets by accomplishing one of the following objectives while holding the others constant: (1) increasing sales, (2) reducing expenses, or (3) reducing the level of assets employed.

Figure 2–3 shows that return on assets for L and S Incorporated is 10 percent. If management wants to increase this figure to 12 percent, how can it do so? One method would be to increase sales by 7 percent to $107 million. This would result in a corresponding 7 percent increase in cost of goods sold and variable expenses, but net profit after taxes would increase to $6.05 million from $5.0 million (see Figure 2–4). The net profit margin would increase to 5.65 percent from 5.0 percent, and asset turnover would increase to 2.14 from 2.0. The result would be a 12 percent return on assets. Since financial leverage would remain the same, return on net worth would increase to 24 percent.

The second method of achieving the 24 percent return on net worth would be for management to reduce one or more of the following expenses by $2 million:

- Cost of goods sold
- Variable expenses
- Fixed expenses

The $2 million reduction in expenses would increase net profit after taxes by $1 million to $6 million. Since asset turnover would not change, return

TABLE 2–2 Income Statement and Balance Sheet for L and S Incorporated

L AND S INCORPORATED
Income Statement
For the Year Ended December 31, 1986
(000s)

Sales revenues		$100,000
Cost of goods sold		55,000
Gross margin on sales		45,000
Operating expenses:		
Variable expenses	$15,000	
Fixed expenses	20,000	35,000
Net profit before taxes		10,000
Income taxes		5,000
Net profit		$ 5,000

L AND S INCORPORPATED
Balance Sheet
As of December 31, 1986
(000s)

Assets			**Liabilities and Stockholders' Equity**		
Current assets:			Liabilities:		
Cash		$ 1,000	Accounts payable		$ 8,000
Accounts receivable		8,000	Notes payable, current		2,000
Inventories		15,000	Total current liabilities		$10,000
Other current assets		1,000	Long-term notes		15,000
Total current assets		$25,000	Total liabilities		$25,000
Fixed assets:					
Land		$ 4,000			
Plant and equipment		$25,000			
Less:			Stockholders' equity:		
Accumulated			Capital stock	$ 5,000	
depreciation	10,000	15,000	Retained earnings	20,000	25,000
Other fixed assets (net)		6,000	Total liabilities and stockholders' equity		$50,000
Total assets		$50,000			

on assets would be increased to 12 percent. Financial leverage would not change, and return on net worth would be 24 percent.

The third way to achieve the desired rate of return on assets would be to reduce assets by $6 million. Assume that this could be accomplished by reducing inventories by $4 million and accounts receivable by $2 million. Also assume that the proceeds would be used to retire $6 million of debt bearing an interest rate of 12 percent. The result would be to increase return on assets to 12.17 percent (see Figure 2–5). However, paying off loans of $6 million would reduce financial leverage to 1.76 (44 ÷ 25) and would result in a return on net worth of 21.4 percent. Typically, it is better to invest in more productive assets than to retire debt.

Of course, management could use any combination of the three methods above to achieve the desired 12 percent figure. Since logistics costs may represent 25 percent of the cost of doing business and 30 percent of a manufacturer's assets, better management of the logistics function offers significant potential for improving a firm's return on net worth.

FIGURE 2–3 The Strategic Profit Model with Financial Data for L and S Incorporated ($millions)

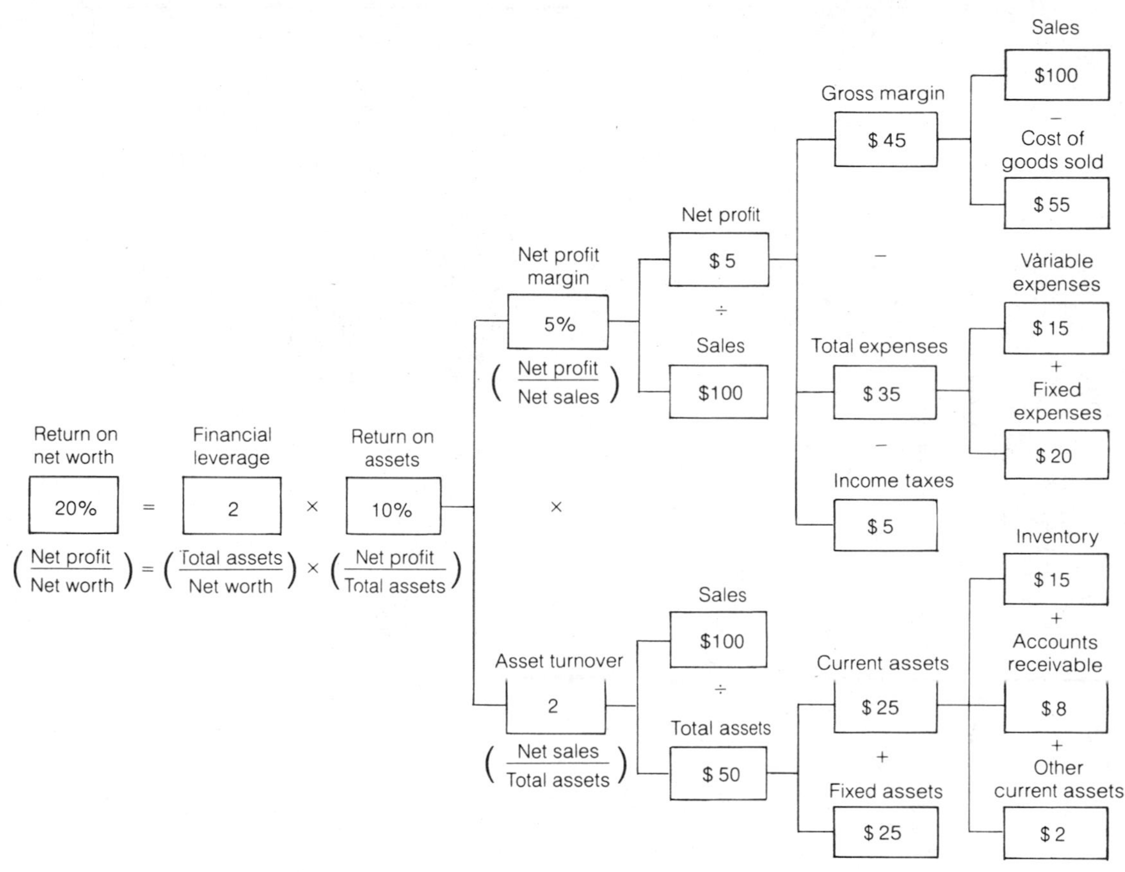

THE FINANCIAL IMPACT OF LOGISTICS DECISIONS

Cost Justification of an Improved Logistics System

Table 2–1 gave financial data for Sara Lee Corporation. In 1990 the company had a net profit of $470.3 million on sales of $11.6 billion, which represented a net profit on sales of about 4.1 percent. Total assets were $7,636.4 million, and return on assets was 6.16 percent. If an advanced order transmittal, order entry, and processing system would allow the company to reduce its annual out-of-pocket costs for transportation, warehousing, and inventory by about $43 million before income taxes, and the annual cost of such a system was $3 million before taxes, the cost would be more than recovered. If the company's effective tax rate was 50 percent, the after-tax saving would be $20 million [($43 million − $3 million) × 50 percent]. In addition, if such a system made it possible to reduce accounts receivable by as much as $50 million and inventories by $150 million, the

FIGURE 2–4 The Strategic Profit Model with Financial Data for L and S Incorporated after a Sales Increase of 7 Percent ($ millions)

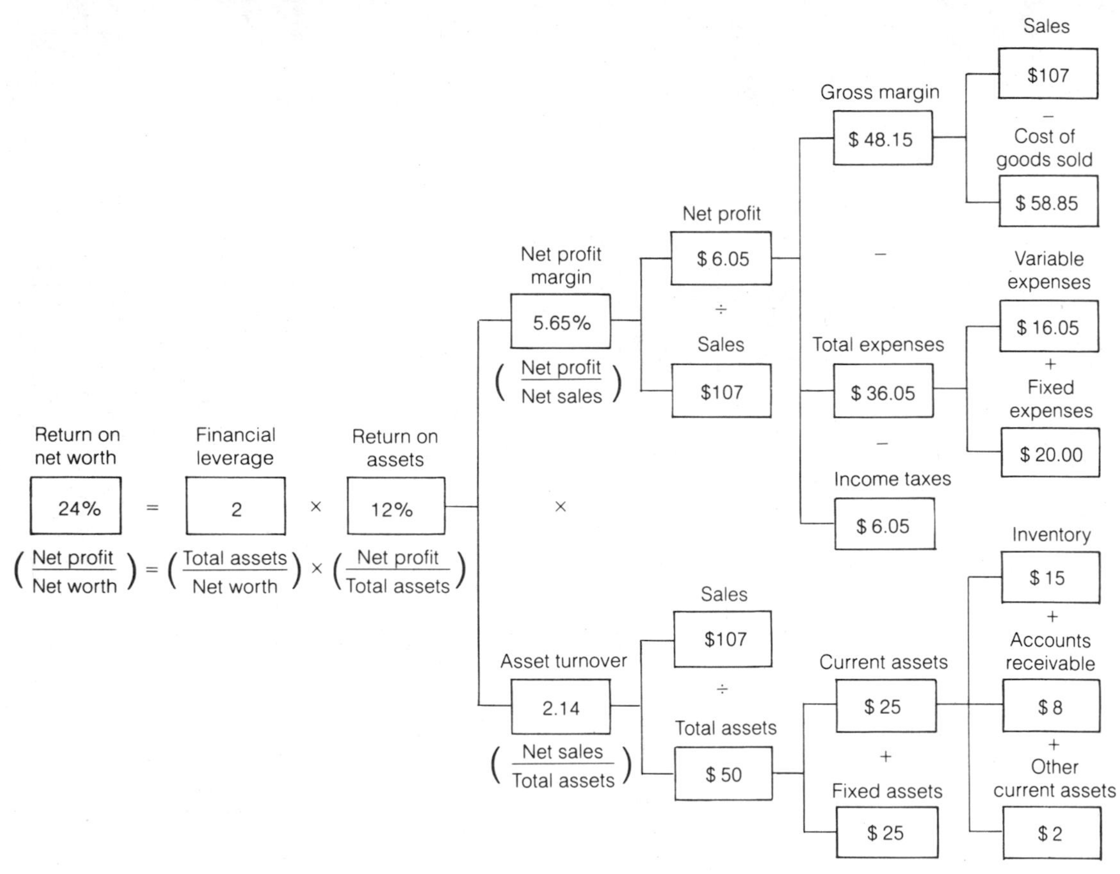

company would enjoy improvements in both cash management and return on assets.

If the $200 million could be invested at a 15 percent rate of return after taxes, the firm would realize the following benefits:

1. Net profit would increase by $50 million ($200 million at 15 percent plus $20 million) to 4.5 percent of sales.
2. Return on assets would increase from 6.16 percent to 6.81 percent.

In order for sales to have a similar impact on return on assets, sales would have to increase approximately $1,220 million, or 10.5 percent.

Improvements in return on assets and cash flow achieved through increased productivity have an additional benefit: They do not force other

FIGURE 2–5 The Strategic Profit Model with Financial Data for L and S Incorporated after Reducing Current Assets by $6 Million and Paying Off Debt at 12 Percent Interest ($ millions)

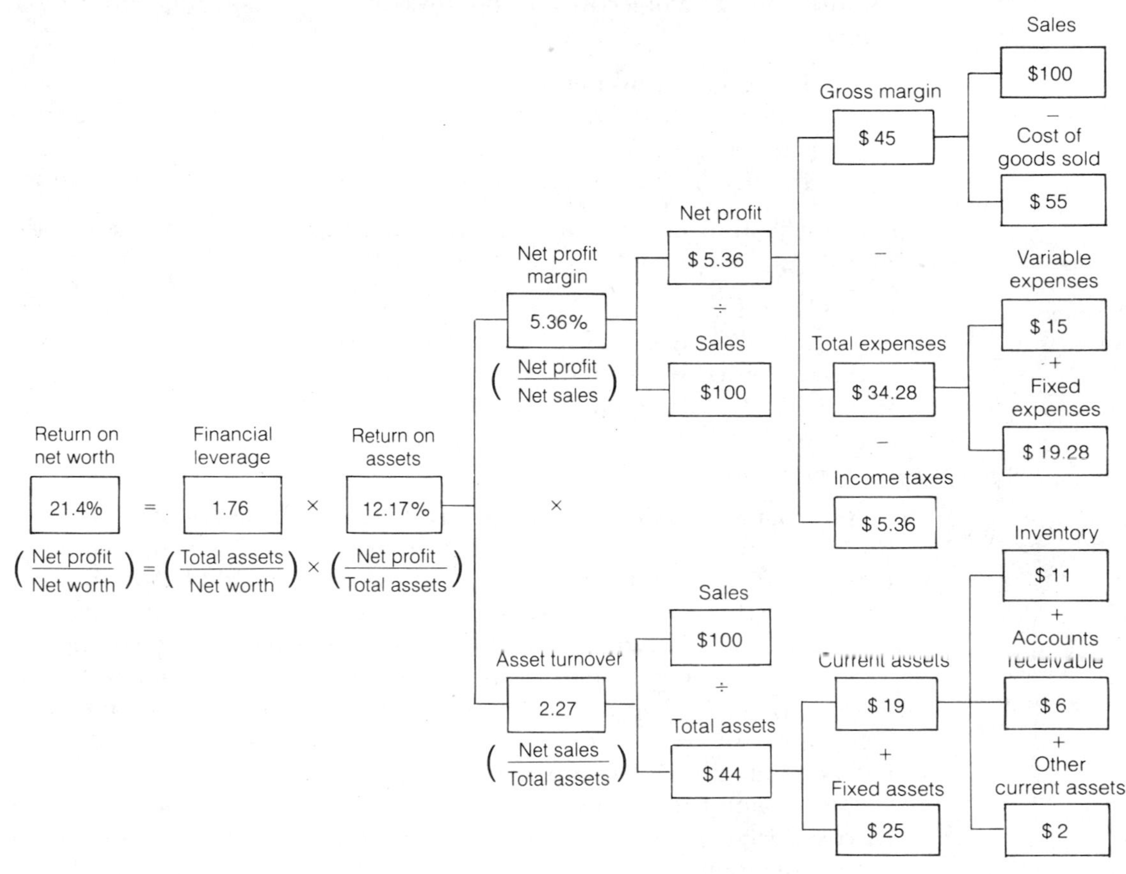

channel members to react in a way that would have a negative impact on channel efficiency. Of course, the primary benefit to the manufacturer's own operation is that the cost savings associated with a reduction in accounts receivable or inventory are not offset by the costs of reduced service levels or increased transportation costs.

TWO EXAMPLES OF INTEGRATED LOGISTICS MANAGEMENT

In the late 1960s a major manufacturer of consumer durable goods established a physical distribution function in order to "merge areas formerly independent of each other into a unified system which controlled the destiny of all finished product from its production scheduling through

Major Manufacturer of Consumer Durable Goods

shipment to its distributors."[16] In the 1980s the manufacturer expanded the function to include inbound materials flows, making it a true logistics organization. The objectives of the physical distribution function were as follows:

1. To design an overall distribution system concept to effectively and economically distribute the corporation's merchandise now and in the future.
2. To consider all elements of distribution to achieve these objectives.

The distribution task was defined as embracing or closely related to the following:

Organizes Distribution Task Force

- Physical distribution including transportation, order processing, inventory control, and warehousing.
- Data processing and data communications.
- Sales forecasting and retail feedback.
- Production planning and scheduling.
- Accounting.

Integrates Distribution Activities

One of the first things the company did upon formation of the physical distribution function was to completely restructure its system of accounting for distribution costs. It transferred the payment of freight bills on finished product, formerly the responsibility of individual manufacturing divisions, to corporate headquarters, and it established a series of prepaid expense accounts. The company also switched responsibility for payment of warehouse bills on finished product stored at field warehouses from manufacturing divisions to corporate headquarters, and it created a series of prepaid accounts similar to prepaid freight.

Since one of the major benefits of integrating the logistics function is the cost savings possible, management developed reports to document the costs of the total system and each logistics activity. Management primarily wanted to use this information to stimulate cost savings in order to improve the company's procedures and operations.

Annual Savings of $15 Million

By 1970 the physical distribution function was the largest cost savings area within the firm, with annual savings approaching $15 million. This figure included a $9 million savings in operating expenses and a $6 million reduction in inventory carrying costs as a result of lower inventories. A member of the firm's management made the following statement in a presentation:

> For a physical distribution function to truly succeed we must discard the idea that former tools of measuring costs and performance levels can be transferred to a PD concept. No longer can we talk of:

[16]This material was provided by Professor Jay U. Sterling, Graduate School of Business, University of Alabama.

> 1. Freight costs for the traffic department.
> 2. Warehousing costs for the warehouse function.
> 3. Operating costs for each individual department, such as order processing or EDP.
>
> The least expensive way to distribute a product does *not* necessarily result in the lowest possible cost in freight, warehousing, administration, or data processing areas as individual functions. Therefore, financial control with respect to physical distribution equals the effective management of the total system of distributing a company's product to the retailer or ultimate consumer.
>
> We refer to this objective as *maximum product availability at minimum overall cost.*[17]

Includes Inbound Logistics

By the mid-1980s the company expanded its physical distribution function to include purchasing and inbound materials flow, making it an integrated logistics organization. The firm initiated a program of focused purchasing[18] and reduced the number of vendors by more than 50 percent. It established stronger ties with the selected vendors and improved its information systems.

Channel Members Benefit

The system had evolved to include a total channels-of-distribution perspective. As a result, direct shipments to dealers increased fourfold. Inventory turns at the wholesale level increased from 4.3 to 10.8 times. Finally, the firm had invested heavily in new production technology that made short production runs much less costly in terms of changeover costs. This made it possible to produce slow-moving products on a weekly rather than monthly basis, thus reducing forecasting error and the levels of inventory (safety stocks and cycle stocks) required.

Abbott Canada provides another example of an integrated logistics system.[19] The system, implemented in 1984, integrated order entry, inventory management, invoicing, warehouse management, order processing, and accounts receivable functions and interfaced with the firm's Distribution Resource Planning system.[20]

Abbott Canada Provides Another Example

Abbott Canada distributed throughout Canada a wide variety of hospital equipment and medical supplies, pharmaceutical products, agricultural chemicals, vitamins and other nutritional products, and other medically related items. In order to provide a high level of customer service, Abbott operated regional distribution centers in Vancouver, Edmonton, Winnipeg, Toronto, Montreal, and Halifax. In addition, the firm maintained inventories in public warehouses in St. John's, Newfoundland; North Bay, Ontario; and Regina, Saskatchewan. A central replenishment

---

[17] Ibid.

[18] We will deal in depth with this approach in Chapter 12.

[19] Adapted from Alan M. Danse, "Integrated Distribution/Logistics Management System—A View from the Post-1982 World," *Journal of Business Logistics* 6, no. 2 (1985), pp. 80–87.

[20] We will cover DRP systems and MRP systems in Chapter 11.

inventory center in Montreal served as the hub of the distribution network and as a regional distribution center. The company stored regional and central replenishment inventories together in the same building but segregated them within the inventory management module of the new on-line system.

Order Processing System Inefficient

Before implementation of the new system, customers telephoned orders to regional centers, where order takers wrote them on a single-sheet order form that listed all of the products carried by that center. The order takers gave the order forms to pricing and inventory control clerks, who performed a manual credit check and added unit prices. Next, orders were entered and stored on a disk and transmitted at the end of the day to the data center in Montreal. Picking and shipping documents were delivered to the warehouse area, where the orders were filled. Central inventory records were updated each day to reflect order data transmitted from the regional centers. A central pricing department reviewed all prices assigned to products by the regional centers and noted errors on copies of the orders, which it then delivered to the central billing department for preparation and mailing of customer invoices. Customers seldom received invoices until a week or so after their orders had been shipped, and prices on invoices frequently differed from those quoted. In addition, the inventory records at both the regional centers and the Montreal center were not accurate. Other problems included an excessive amount of out-of-date stock, inefficient picking and putaway, and shipping errors. In addition, sales had increased very rapidly during the late 1970s and early 1980s and threatened to overwhelm the regional order entry systems.

In 1981 management decided to develop and install an entirely new order entry, pricing, inventory management, and invoicing and accounts receivable system. The firm established a project team and developed a list of 100 major shortcomings of the existing system. Before system development began, the head of MIS and the project leader reviewed an on-line distribution and warehouse management software package available from an outside vendor. Since the capabilities of the software package covered at least 80 of the 100 shortcomings of the existing system, the company purchased it. Modifications and additions to the software took about a year to complete. By August 1983 the company had installed the new invoicing and accounts receivable applications at headquarters, and the order entry, credit checking, pricing, inventory control, and warehouse management applications were on-line at the company's Winnipeg and Toronto distribution centers. After adjusting its data communications network, the company implemented the system at all of its regional centers and public warehouses by the spring of 1984.

New On-Line System

The new on-line system provided each of the regional distribution centers with one or more terminals and printers. The company equipped its public warehouses with terminals to confirm receipts and shipments and enter variances. Dedicated telephone lines connected the company's headquarters to all of the distribution centers and public warehouses.

As Orders Are Entered, Product Is Reserved

At each of the regional order entry points, customers phone in orders, and order takers equipped with display terminals enter order data into the on-line Montreal computer system. As they enter the orders, product is immediately reserved in the company's central inventory records. A multilevel pricing module automatically calculates the prices on each line item based on such factors as the total value of the order, the value of certain groups of items, and special contractual arrangements. If any item is out of stock, the system immediately alerts the order taker while the customer is still on the phone. If the customer agrees, the order taker creates a back order for the items that cannot be delivered with the initial order. If the customer wishes to know when the back ordered item(s) will be available, the order taker can access a replenishment order file that indicates the expected delivery date.

After the order taker enters each order, the system automatically checks the customer's credit. If there are no credit problems, the order is placed into an open order file that can be accessed on-line by regional distribution, customer service, and warehouse managers, as well as by company headquarters. Warehouse personnel can review open orders on their terminals and select the most efficient method of picking and shipping. One of the most significant benefits of the new system is reduced transportation expense, made possible by reductions in carrier delays, misdirected shipments, and small and less-than-truckload shipments.

Once the warehouse picking order has been established, the system prints out the required picking, packing, and shipping documentation in the order selected. When the orders have been picked, workers enter any variances encountered during the picking process into the system. Customer invoices are printed and delivered to the shipping dock to be packed with the order.

As each distribution center receives new inventory, the system creates instructions to put the incoming items in a specific location. As the new inventory is put away that information is transmitted to Montreal, where the company's central inventory records are updated to reflect the additions to inventory and the exact warehouse location of the new items. Similarly, as orders are picked, that information is communicated to the inventory management module when it is sent to the invoicing module. The new system has greatly reduced the amount of out-of-date stock.

Benefits of the New System

The new system's order entry module provides the highly accurate data required for forecasting and distribution planning. Updating inventory records on-line has improved the accuracy of inventory records. The increased accuracy in monitoring customer demand and inventory levels has resulted in lower inventories (safety stocks). Another benefit of the on-line, integrated system is "the improvement in overall management performance that results when all levels and areas of management, including purchasing, manufacturing, marketing, and distribution, are using the same timely and accurate data when dealing with problems and making decisions."[21]

CONDUCTING A MARKETING AND LOGISTICS AUDIT

An important prerequisite to successful implementation of integrated logistics management is a marketing and logistics audit. Management should conduct an audit program routinely, although the length of time between audits may vary among firms. In many cases, management will become involved in special studies that include an audit, but these should not substitute for regularly scheduled audits.

Audits of current practices and performance are required if the firm is to successfully adapt to the changing business environment. Knowledge of past behavior and current policies and practices, as well as of competitive and environmental behavior, is important for future planning. Management can accomplish this by evaluating corporate objectives and plans, given the audit results. A good audit should include evaluation of the external market as well as internal operations.

The External Market Audit

Items that should be included in the external market audit are customer service levels demanded in the marketplace, market requirements, and competition.

1. In the category of *customer service* it is important to determine *out-of-stock/order completeness,* the percentage of items ordered that can be shipped on the initial shipment; *order cycle time/variability,* the time that the customer expects to wait after placing an order before receiving the products, as well as the accepted ranges of variability in this time; *system accuracy,* the ability to ship the ordered products and invoice correctly; and *information capabilities,* which may include ability to determine product availability at the time of order placement, order status, advance information on price changes, and shipping data.

2. In the *market requirements* category it is important to determine the level of product quality and the breadth of the product line; whether there are new potential markets for the products and the location of such markets; the price and promotion policies that should be considered; whether there are identifiable market segments for the company's products; how market needs differ by such business segments as geographic area, customer, and product; and demand elasticity with regard to various marketing mix strategies.

---

[21] Danse, "Integrated Distribution/Logistics Management System," p. 87.

3. Finally, it is necessary to obtain information about the *competition,* including company-specific data such as the competing firms' customer service levels, their strengths and weaknesses, and their distribution policies/patterns.

Figure 2–6 summarizes the elements of the external market audit. We will discuss the external audit—and how to conduct it—in Chapter 4.

The Internal Operations Audit

Once the company has completed the external market audit, its next step is to perform an internal operations audit. The internal audit should include investigation of existing customer service levels, transportation, warehousing operations, the order processing system, lot quantity considerations, and inventory management (see Figure 2–7). Each of these areas will be the subject of subsequent chapters, and Chapter 18 will offer a detailed audit procedure.

DEVELOPING A LOGISTICS STRATEGY

Once the firm has completed a marketing and logistics audit, identified the strengths and weaknesses of the current operations, and recognized market opportunities, it must formulate objectives for the logistics function. To achieve those objectives, the company should develop a logistics strategy. At this point, management must consider various alternatives. For example, it may be possible to achieve the desired objectives—perhaps a 95 percent in-stock product availability and 72-hour delivery[22]—with a motor carrier-based system and few field warehouses, or with a rail and motor carrier combination, which would require more field warehouses and increased levels of inventory. When management has established the costs of various structural alternatives, it must select the structure that is the most likely to accomplish the specified objectives at the least total cost. It is important to recognize that vendor-related policies and procedures often differ depending on the structural alternatives being considered.

With the logistics structure determined, management must establish criteria for evaluating and selecting individual channel members, and methods of evaluating their performance. Then it should select individual channel members and measure their performance. In instances where performance is not adequate, management should ask the following questions:

1. Can performance be improved?
2. Would a change of intermediaries and/or vendors improve performance and solve the problem?
3. Is a change of channel structure required?

---

[22] That is, on the average, 95 percent of the items ordered by a customer will be delivered within three days after the manufacturer has received the order.

FIGURE 2–6 Elements of the External Market Audit

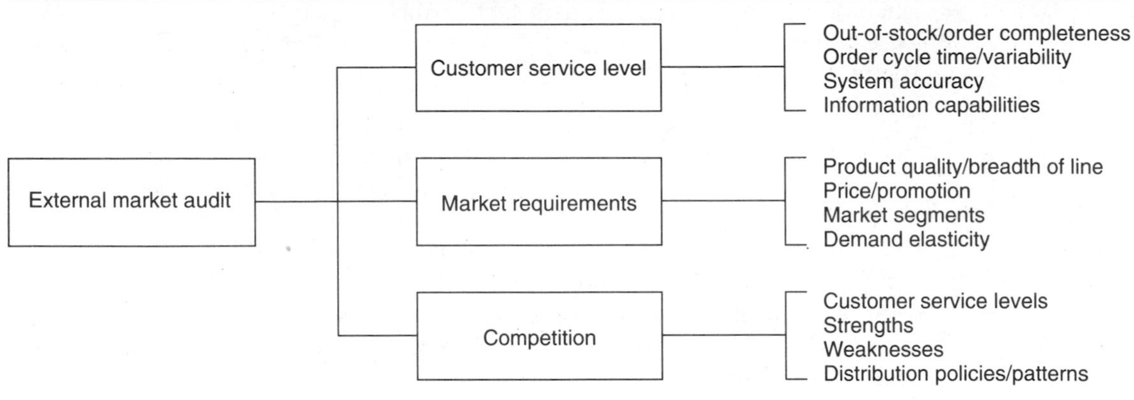

SOURCE: Douglas M. Lambert and Robert L. Cook, "Integrating Marketing and Logistics for Increased Profit," *Business* 40, no. 3 (July-August-September 1990), p. 26. Published by Georgia State University Business Press.

If the answer to the first question is yes, then management should take corrective action. Otherwise, the second question must be asked. If changing a particular channel member such as a distributor, warehouser, carrier, or vendor will not suffice, it may be necessary to change the system. This entire procedure should be repeated as a routine part of the planning process that begins with the marketing and logistics audit. We will take a detailed look at the strategic planning process in Chapter 18.

AREAS IN WHICH LOGISTICS PERFORMANCE CAN BE IMPROVED

A number of areas offer particularly good opportunities to improve logistics productivity. These include (1) customer service, (2) transportation, (3) warehousing, (4) inventory management, (5) order processing and information systems, (6) forecasting, and (7) production planning and purchasing.

Customer Service

In today's highly competitive business environment, customer service is a critical component of the marketing mix. An important element of customer service is the communication that takes place between the vendor and customer. Customer service levels can also be improved by inventory management techniques that increase product availability, as well as by order communications and transportation systems that provide more consistent and/or shorter order cycle times. Chapter 4 covers the customer service activity and how it should be managed.

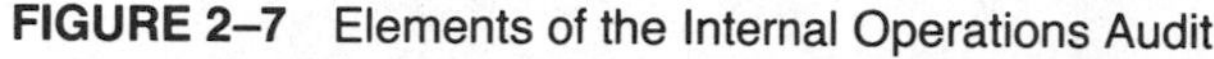

FIGURE 2–7 Elements of the Internal Operations Audit

Internal operations audit

- Customer service levels
  - Out of stock/order completeness
  - Order cycle time/variability
  - System accuracy
  - Information capabilities
- Transportation
  - Modes and number of carriers used
  - Number and size of shipments by traffic lane
  - Vehicle utilization
  - Cost
  - Refusals and returns/errors
- Warehousing operations
  - Productivity
  - Degree of automation/systems used
  - Picking errors/damage
  - Shipping and receiving accuracy
- Order processing
  - Degree of automation
  - Time to complete various tasks
  - Order cost
  - Order delays/errors
- Lot quantity considerations
  - Number of vendors
  - Size of orders
  - Forecasting accuracy
  - Number/cost of production changeovers
  - Identification of production problems
- Inventory management
  - Inventory investment
  - Inventory turnover
  - Inventory balance/age/shortages
  - Inventory management systems

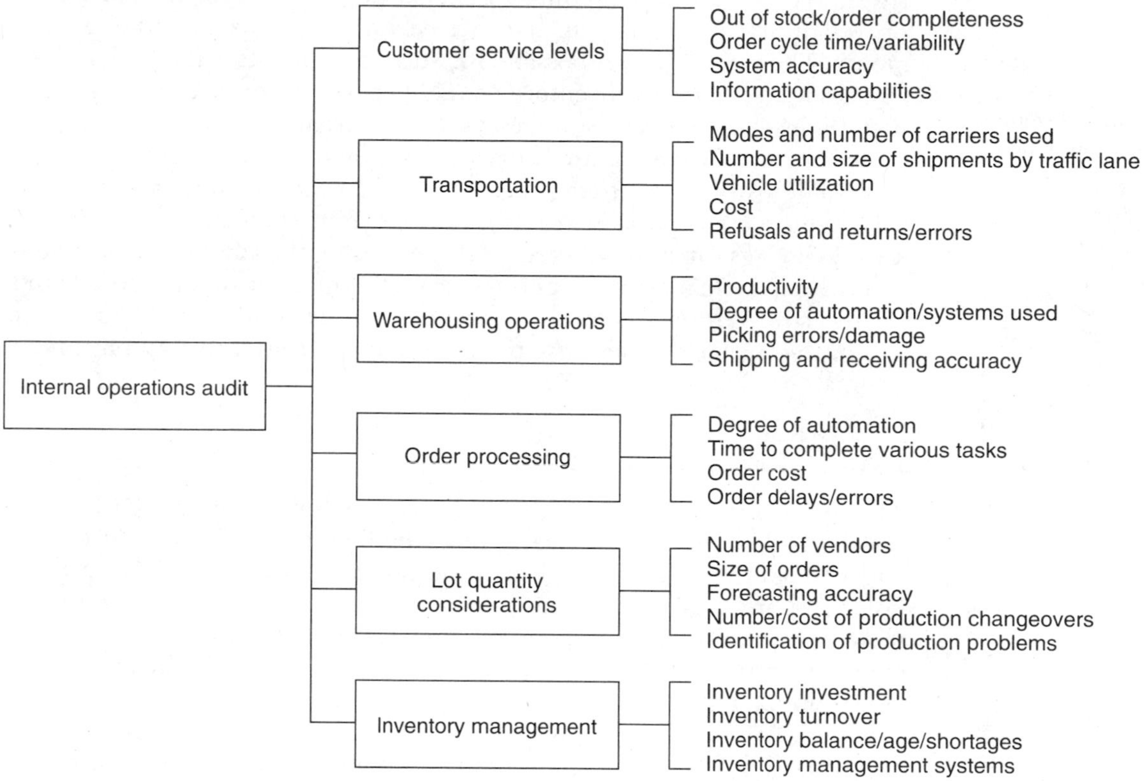

SOURCE: Douglas M. Lambert and Robert L. Cook, "Integrating Marketing and Logistics for Increased Profit," *Business* 40, no. 3 (July-August-September 1990), p. 27. Published by Georgia State University Business Press.

Transportation

Large Savings Are Possible from Transportation Consolidation

Transportation usually represents the largest single logistics expense. The company that embarks on a program of transportation consolidation can realize substantial savings. If it also implements an advanced order processing system, as much as three or four days may be made available for planning more efficient and less costly movement of products. Chapter 6 explores methods of improving management of the transportation activity.

Warehousing

Many of the management accounting techniques developed for manufacturing operations (e.g., standard costs and flexible budgets) are applicable to warehousing. Warehouse management systems can also improve warehousing performance significantly. We will discuss the productivity improvements that are possible in warehousing in Chapter 8.

Inventory Management

Inventory Competes with Other Investment Opportunities

Inventory can account for more than 35 percent of a firm's assets. Improved inventory management can free capital for use in other investments. The rate of return possible for such investments is the opportunity cost associated with the inventory. In addition, out-of-pocket carrying costs, such as insurance, taxes, storage costs, and inventory risk costs, can raise the total cost of carrying inventory to more than 40 percent of the inventory value. Advanced order processing systems and computerized inventory management packages are just two ways inventory levels can be reduced. Savings can also be obtained by decreasing the labor costs associated with inventory management and reducing the number of back orders and related costs. Firms back order when they cannot completely fill an order within the specified order cycle time. We will cover inventory management in detail in Chapters 9 and 10.

Order Processing and Information Systems

No Products Flow until Information Flows

The order is the device that sets the logistics system in motion. Order processing is the nerve center that guides the flow of products to customers and cash to the firm. Many firms have not capitalized on the latest technology in order processing and information systems. The implementation of an advanced order processing system can lead to significant productivity gains by improving customer service, reducing costs by eliminating errors and redundancy, and improving cash flow by making the order flow more efficient. The order processing systems that link the firm with its vendors also offer significant opportunities for profit improvement. Order processing and information systems are the topic of Chapter 13.

Forecasting

Forecasting product demand is necessary to schedule production and to ensure that required inventories are made available at reasonable cost where customers expect to make the purchase. If logistics is to successfully provide time and place utility, management must be able to forecast each item by market area for a specific period. In recent years, forecasting has been studied extensively and methods have been developed to make predictions more objective and reliable.[23] However, many companies are still relatively unsophisticated in their approach to this very important logistics activity. Consequently, improved forecasting procedures offer significant potential for increasing productivity. We will look at forecasting techniques in Chapter 14.

---

[23] Those interested in an in-depth review of forecasting techniques should refer to Steven C. Wheelwright and Spyros Makridakis, *Forecasting Methods for Management* (New York: John Wiley & Sons, 1973).

Production Planning and Purchasing

Production planning and purchasing represent the two major components of lot quantity costs. Production planning, which determines when products should be produced and in what quantities, is becoming an important part of the logistics function in many firms. We will discuss production planning in Chapter 11.

Purchasing Should Be Part of the Logistics Function

Purchasing is another activity that firms have successfully included in the logistics function. A major reason for doing so is to offset high-volume outbound transportation lanes with inbound shipments, in order to obtain backhauls (return loads) for the private fleet or contract carriage operations. In addition, purchasing policies and procedures influence inventories of raw materials, as well as production planning and finished product availability, if the purchased materials are not in stock when required for production. Purchasing is the topic of Chapter 12.

SUMMARY

In this chapter we examined the importance of the integrated logistics management concept and the reasons for its growth. We saw how a firm can implement integrated logistics management using total cost analysis and how it can measure the impact of logistics decisions on corporate profit performance. Examples showed how two firms have implemented logistics management. We took a look at the marketing and logistics audit—the basis for developing a strategic logistics plan. Finally, the chapter closed with a description of areas that offer significant potential for improving logistics performance. In the next chapter, we will see how integrated logistics can increase the profitability of each level of the channel of distribution.

SUGGESTED READINGS

A. T. Kearney, Inc. *Measuring and Improving Productivity in Physical Distribution Management—1984.* Oak Brook, Ill.: National Council of Physical Distribution Management, 1984.

Bowersox, Donald J., Patricia J. Daugherty, Cornelia L. Dröge, Dale S. Rogers, and Daniel L. Wardlow. *Leading Edge Logistics: Competitive Positioning for the 1990s.* Oak Brook, Ill.: Council of Logistics Management, 1989.

Danse, Alan M. "Integrated Distribution/Logistics Management System—A View from the Post-1982 World." *Journal of Business Logistics* 6, no. 2 (1985), pp. 63–88.

Ernst and Whinney. *Corporate Profitability and Logistics.* Oak Brook, Ill.: Council of Logistics Management, 1987.

Heskett, James L. "Sweeping Changes in Distribution." *Harvard Business Review* 51, no. 2 (March-April 1973), pp. 123–32.

LALONDE, BERNARD J., AND JAMES M. MASTERS. "Logistics: Perspectives for the 1990s." *The International Journal of Logistics Management* 1, no. 1 (1990), pp. 1–6.

LANGLEY, C. JOHN, JR., AND WILLIAM D. MORICE. "Strategies for Logistics Management: Reactions to a Changing Environment." *Journal of Business Logistics* 3, no. 1 (1982), pp. 1–16.

ROBESON, JAMES F., AND ROBERT G. HOUSE. *The Distribution Handbook.* New York: Free Press, 1985.

SHAPIRO, ROY D. "Get Leverage from Logistics." *Harvard Business Review* 62, no. 3 (May-June 1984), pp. 119–26.

QUESTIONS AND PROBLEMS

1. What factors in the business environment make logistics so important for companies in the 1990s?
2. What cost categories must be considered if integrated logistics management is to be implemented using total cost analysis?
3. The two most common management strategies that result from the desire to improve cash flow and return on assets are reducing accounts receivable and reducing the investment in inventory. What are the shortcomings associated with arbitrarily reducing accounts receivable and/or inventories without changing the firm's logistics system?
4. How can the strategic profit model be used to show the financial impact of a change in the structure of the logistics system?
5. What area or areas of logistics do you believe offer the most potential for improving performance? Explain.
6. Using the 1990 financial data for Honeywell (Table 2–1), show how return on assets would be affected if the company implemented an advanced order processing system capable of reducing accounts receivable by $50 million and inventories by $100 million. For your analysis, assume the money could be invested in other assets that would generate a return of 20 percent after taxes, and that the increased communications cost of $500,000 per year would be offset by savings of $500,000 in transportation and warehousing costs.
7. Based on your calculations in question 6, by what percentage would annual sales have to increase in order to obtain the same increase in return on net worth?

Chapter 3

Channels of Distribution

Objectives of This Chapter

To show how the distribution channel plays an integral part in a firm's marketing strategy

To familiarize the reader with the types of channel structures

To describe the factors that influence channel design, evolution, and performance

To show the role of logistics in channel management

To show how to implement logistics cost trade-offs in a channel of distribution

INTRODUCTION

The Exchange Process

In any society—industrialized or nonindustrialized—goods must be physically moved or transported between the place they are produced and the place they are consumed. Except in very primitive cultures, where each family met its own household needs, the exchange process has become the cornerstone of economic activity. Exchange takes place when there is a discrepancy between the amount, type, and timing of goods available and the goods needed. If a number of individuals or organizations within the society have a surplus of goods that someone else needs, there is a basis for exchange. Channels of distribution develop when many exchanges take place between producers and consumers.

The extent to which a channel of distribution creates an efficient flow of products from the producer to the consumer is a major concern of management. For example, manufacturers depend on the distribution channel for such functions as selling, transportation, warehousing, and physical handling. Consequently, the manufacturer's objective is to obtain optimum performance of these functions at minimum total cost. In order to successfully market its products, a manufacturer must (1) select the appropriate channel structure, (2) choose the intermediaries to be used and establish policies regarding channel members, and (3) devise information and control systems to ensure that performance objectives are met.[1] Likewise, wholesalers and retailers must select manufacturers' products in a way that will provide the best assortment for their customers and lead to the desired profitability for themselves.

Due to the dynamic nature of the business environment, management must monitor and evaluate the performance of the distribution channel regularly and frequently. When performance goals are not met, management must evaluate possible channel alternatives and implement changes. Channel management is particularly important in mature and declining markets and during periods of economic slowdown when market growth

[1] Bert C. McCammon, Jr., and Robert W. Little, "Marketing Channels: Analytical Systems and Approaches," in *Science in Marketing*, ed. George Schwartz (New York: John Wiley & Sons, 1965), p. 354.

cannot conceal inefficient practices. Nevertheless, the distribution channel has been recognized as "one of the least managed areas of marketing."[2]

WHAT IS A CHANNEL OF DISTRIBUTION?

A Channel of Distribution Defined

"A channel of distribution can be defined as the collection of organization units, either internal or external to the manufacturer, which performs the functions involved in product marketing."[3] The marketing functions are pervasive; they include buying, selling, transporting, storing, grading, financing, bearing market risk, and providing marketing information.[4] Any organizational unit, institution, or agency that performs one or more of the marketing functions is a member of the channel of distribution.

The structure of a distribution channel[5] is determined by which marketing functions are performed by specific organizations. Some channel members perform single marketing functions—carriers transport products, and public warehousers store them. Others, such as wholesalers, perform multiple functions. Channel structure affects (1) control over the performance of functions, (2) the speed of delivery and communication, and (3) the cost of operations.[6] While a direct manufacturer-to-user channel usually gives management greater control over the performance of marketing functions, distribution costs normally are higher, making it necessary for the firm to have substantial sales volume or market concentration. With indirect channels, the external institutions or agencies (warehousers, wholesalers, retailers) assume much of the cost burden and risk, but the manufacturer receives less revenue per unit.

Channel Structure Is Influenced by the Target Market and the Product

Most distribution channels are loosely structured networks of vertically aligned firms. The specific structure depends to a large extent on the nature of the product and the firm's target market. Figure 3–1 illustrates a number of possible channel structures for consumer products. Figure 3–2 depicts alternative channels for industrial products. However, the figures do not show the many forms of middlemen/intermediaries. Also, they do not include the institutions involved in transportation (carriers) and storage

[2] Revis Cox and Thomas F. Schutte, "A Look at Channel Management," in *Marketing Involvement in Society and the Economy,* ed. Philip McDonald (Chicago: American Marketing Association, 1969), p. 105.

[3] Douglas M. Lambert, *The Distribution Channels Decision* (New York: National Association of Accountants, and Hamilton, Ontario: The Society of Management Accountants of Canada, 1978), pp. 1–2.

[4] Fred E. Clark, *Principles of Marketing* (New York: Macmillan, 1922), p. 11; and Robert Bartels, *Marketing Theory and Metatheory* (Homewood, Ill.: Richard D. Irwin, 1970), pp. 166–75.

[5] Channel structure is determined by the types of middlemen the manufacturer uses. Alternative channel structures are shown in Figure 3–1.

[6] Louis W. Stern, "Channel Control and Interorganization Management," in *Marketing and Economic Development,* ed. Peter D. Bennett (Chicago: American Marketing Association, 1965), pp. 655–65.

FIGURE 3–1 Alternative Channels of Distribution for Consumer Goods

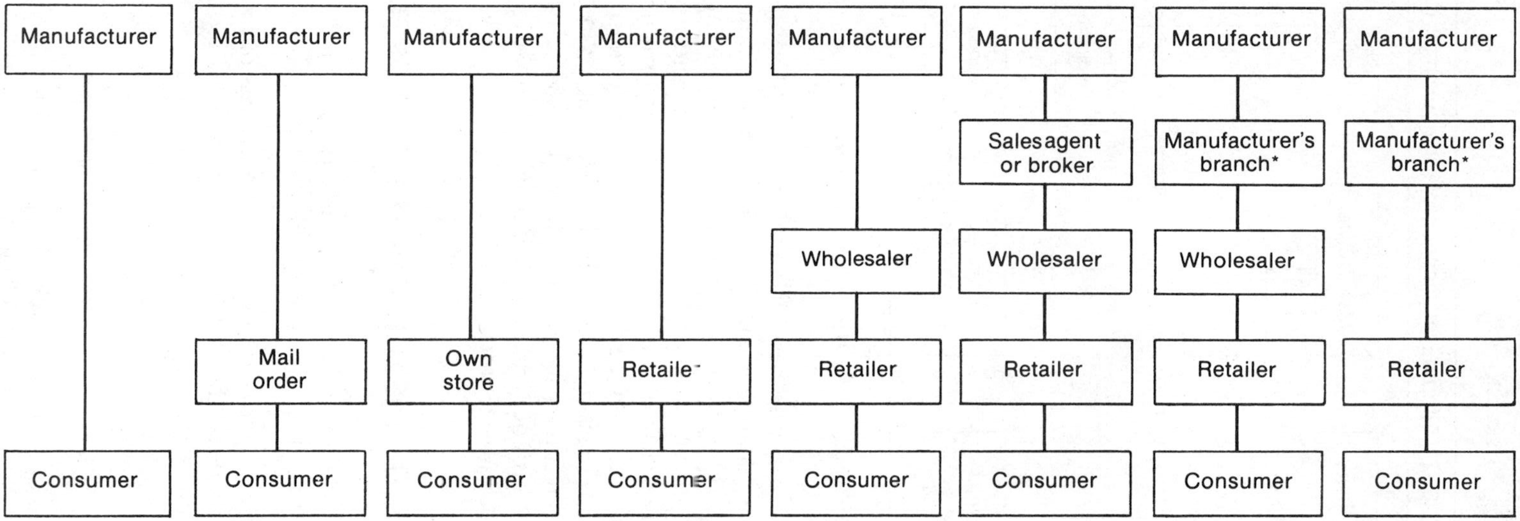

Manufacturer
Consumer

Manufacturer
Mail order
Consumer

Manufacturer
Own store
Consumer

Manufacturer
Retailer
Consumer

Manufacturer
Wholesaler
Retailer
Consumer

Manufacturer
Salesagent or broker
Wholesaler
Retailer
Consumer

Manufacturer
Manufacturer's branch*
Wholesaler
Retailer
Consumer

Manufacturer
Manufacturer's branch*
Retailer
Consumer

*A manufacturer's branch is owned by the manufacturer.

FIGURE 3–2 Alternative Channels of Distribution for Industrial Goods

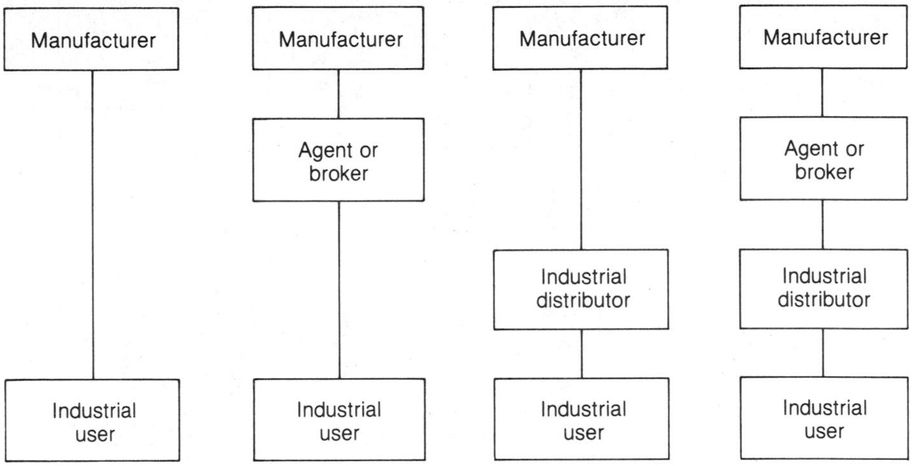

(warehousers), even though these, too, are basic and necessary marketing functions.

No "Best" Channel Exists for All Firms

There is no "best" channel structure for all firms producing similar products. Management must determine channel structure within the framework of the firm's corporate and marketing objectives, its operating philosophy, its strengths and weaknesses, and its infrastructure of manufacturing facilities and warehouses. If the firm has targeted multiple market segments, management may have to develop multiple channels to service these markets efficiently. For example, Whirlpool Corporation sells a major portion of its product through Sears, uses distributors and dealers for its Whirlpool brand line, and also sells to original equipment manufacturers (OEM accounts).

WHY DO CHANNELS OF DISTRIBUTION DEVELOP?[7]

Wroe Alderson explained the emergence of channels of distribution in terms of the following factors:[8]

1. Intermediaries evolve in the process of exchange because they can increase the efficiency of the process by creating time, place, and possession utility.

---

[7] This section is adapted from Douglas M. Lambert, *The Distribution Channels Decision,* pp. 12–19.

[8] Wroe Alderson, "Factors Governing the Development of Marketing Channels," in *Marketing Channels for Manufactured Products,* ed. R. M. Clewett (Homewood, Ill.: Richard D. Irwin, 1954), pp. 8–16.

2. Channel intermediaries enable the adjustment of the discrepancy of assortments by performing the functions of sorting and assorting.
3. Marketing agencies form channel arrangements to make possible the routinization of transactions.
4. Finally, channels facilitate the searching process by consumers.

The Evolution of Marketing Channels

Intermediaries Reduce Market Contacts

Marketing channels develop because intermediaries (wholesalers and retailers) make the marketing process more efficient by reducing the number of market contacts. For example, in primitive cultures most household needs are met by family members. However, many household needs can be met more efficiently by exchange. Specialization in production creates efficiency and for this reason has become a way of life. A household must exchange goods and services in order to provide for all of its needs.

Consider a community in which there are five households specializing in the production of one product per family. The number of transactions necessary for decentralized exchange among these households is 10.[9] However, a central market operated by a dealer reduces to five the number of transactions necessary for centralized exchange.[10] In this case, the ratio of advantage of the centralized exchange through one intermediary is two. Figure 3–3 illustrates the differences between decentralized and centralized exchange.

Calculating the Advantage of an Intermediary

The advantage of an intermediary becomes more evident as the number of specialized producers increases. For example, if there are 100 specialized producers, the number of decentralized transactions becomes 4,950 and the ratio of intermediary advantage becomes 49.5. Figure 3–4 shows that 10 customers purchasing from four suppliers results in 40 market contacts. If the suppliers sell to these customers through one intermediary, the number of required contacts is 14, a 65 percent reduction. This example clearly demonstrates that a manufacturer selling to low-volume customers could substantially reduce selling and logistics costs by using a wholesaler/distributor.

The Discrepancy of Assortment and Sorting

Intermediaries Provide Utility

Intermediaries provide possession, time, and place utility. They create possession utility through the process of exchange, the result of the buying and selling functions. They provide time utility by holding inventory available for sale. And they provide place utility by physically moving goods to

---

[9] In general, the number of transactions can be determined using the formula $n(n-1)/2$ and the ratio of intermediary advantage equals $(n-1)/2$, where n is the number of specialized producers.

[10] The number of transactions in a central market operated by one intermediary is generally equal to n.

FIGURE 3–3 Decentralized versus Centralized Exchange

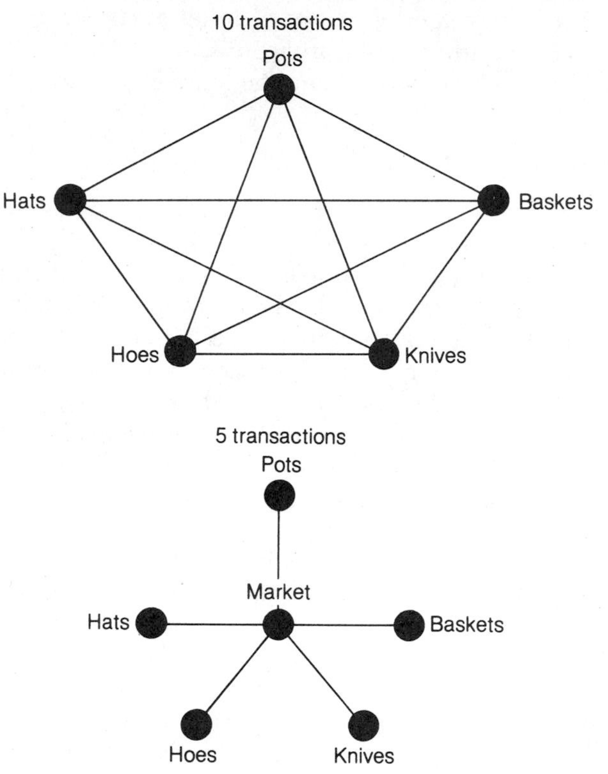

SOURCE: Wroe Alderson, "Factors Governing the Development of Marketing Channels," in *Marketing Channels for Manufactured Products*, ed. R. M. Clewett (Homewood, Ill.: Richard D. Irwin, 1954), p. 7.

the market. The assortment of goods and services held by a producer and the assortment demanded by the customer often differ. Channel intermediaries' primary function is to adjust this discrepancy by performing the following "sorting" processes:

1. *Sorting out*—breaking down a heterogeneous supply into separate stocks that are relatively homogeneous. ("Sorting out is typified by the grading of agricultural products or by pulling out rejects in some manufacturing operations.")
2. *Accumulating*—bringing similar stocks together into a larger homogeneous supply.
3. *Allocation*—breaking a homogeneous supply down into smaller and smaller lots. (Allocating at the wholesale level is referred to as "breaking bulk." Goods received in carloads are sold in case lots. A buyer in case lots in turn sells individual units.)

FIGURE 3–4 How Intermediaries Reduce the Cost of Market Contact between Supplier and Customer

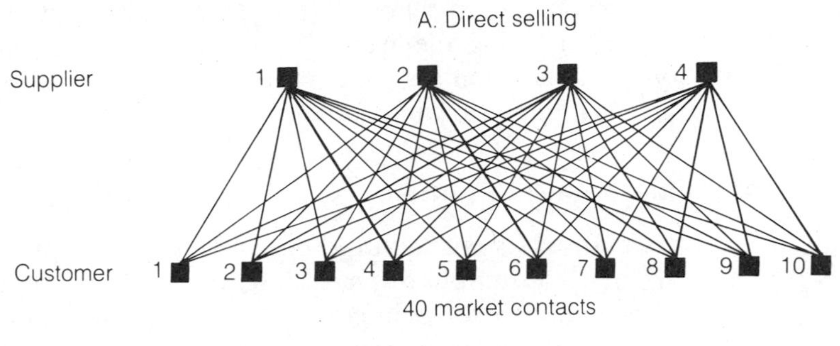

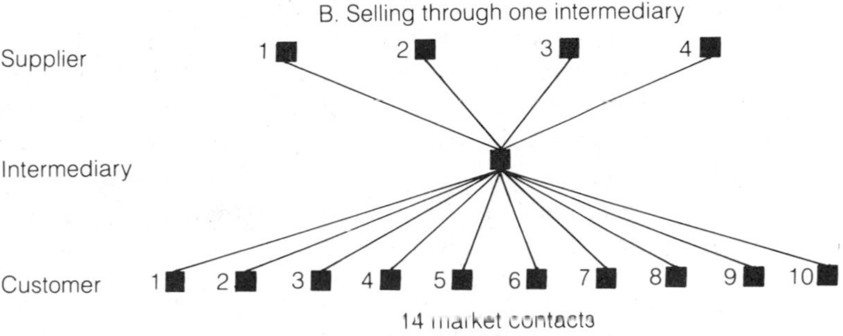

SOURCE: Douglas M. Lambert, *The Distribution Channels Decision* (New York: National Association of Accountants, and Hamilton, Ontario: The Society of Management Accountants of Canada, 1978), pp. 15–16. Reprinted with permission. Copyright © 1978 by National Association of Accountants. All rights reserved.

4. *Assorting*—building up the assortment of products for use in association with each other. (Wholesalers build assortments of goods for retailers, and retailers build assortments for their customers.)[11]

Sorting out and accumulating predominate in the marketing of agricultural and extractive products, and allocation and assorting predominate in the marketing of finished manufactured goods. Because the assortment of goods and services the customer demands may be much broader than the assortment a single manufacturer provides, specialization develops in the exchange process to reduce distribution costs. That is, the discrepancy of assortment drives the producer to use intermediaries to reach the customer because doing so leads to improved distribution efficiency.

[11] Wroe Alderson, "Factors Governing the Development of Marketing Channels," pp. 12–13.

Routinization of Transactions

Routinization Reduces Cost

The cost of distribution can be minimized if transactions are routine—that is, if every transaction is not subject to bargaining, with its resulting loss of efficiency. Marketing agencies form channel arrangements to make routinization possible. Channel cooperation and efficiency are improved by the routine handling of transactions.

Searching Through Marketing Channels

Buyers and sellers engage in a search process, in which consumers try to satisfy their consumption needs and producers attempt to predict those needs. Searching involves uncertainty because producers cannot be positive about consumers' needs and consumers cannot be sure that their consumption needs will be satisfied. Consumers also cannot be certain where to shop to satisfy these needs. If the searching process is successful, allocation and assorting will take place, and both the consumer and the producer will benefit. Marketing channels facilitate the process of searching when institutions organize by separate lines of trade and provide information to their markets.

In summary, the use of an intermediary reduces some or all of the following costs:

Costs That Are Reduced by Intermediaries

- Selling costs (because fewer market contacts are required).
- Transportation costs (because intermediaries may result in fewer but larger volume shipments).
- Inventory carrying costs (if the intermediary takes ownership).
- Storage costs.
- Order processing costs.
- Accounts receivable/bad debts (if the intermediary takes ownership).
- Customer service costs.

CHANNEL STRUCTURE[12]

Authors disagree about the importance of various factors that influence channel structure. Michman viewed channel structure as a function of product life cycle, logistics systems, and effective communication networks.[13] Aspinwall believed that channel structure was a function of product characteristics.[14] Weigand, on the other hand, found a direct relation-

---

[12] This section is adapted from Douglas M. Lambert, *The Distribution Channels Decision*, pp. 19–26.

[13] Ronald Michman, "Channel Development and Innovation," *Marquette Business Review* 15 (Spring 1971), pp. 45–49.

[14] Leo Aspinwall, "The Characteristics of Goods and Parallel Systems Theories," in *Managerial Marketing*, ed. Eugene Kelley and William Lazer (Homewood, Ill.: Richard D. Irwin, 1958), pp. 434–50.

ship between firm size and the type of distribution channel employed, with large firms more likely to be vertically integrated.[15] Vertical integration occurs when one member of a channel performs the functions of another member, thus combining one or more of the channel levels through ownership, administered power, or contractual agreements.[16]

Bucklin's Theory of Channel Structure

The most detailed theory of channel structure was developed by Bucklin.[17] He bases his theory on the economic relationships among distributive institutions and agencies. He stated that the purpose of the channel is to provide consumers with the desired combination of its outputs (lot size, delivery time, and market decentralization) at minimal cost. Consumers determine channel structure by purchasing combinations of service outputs. The best channel has formed when no other group of institutions generates more profits or more consumer satisfaction per dollar of product cost. Bucklin concluded that functions will be shifted from one channel member to another in order to achieve the most efficient and effective channel structure. Given a desired level of output by the consumer and competitive conditions, channel institutions will arrange their functional tasks in such a way as to minimize total channel costs. This shifting of specific functions may lead to addition or deletion of channel members.

Postponement and Speculation

Bucklin's theory of channel structure is based on the concepts of postponement and speculation.[18] Costs can be reduced by *(a)* postponing changes in the form and identity of a product to the last possible point in the marketing process, and *(b)* postponing inventory location to the last possible point in time, since risk and uncertainty costs increase as the product becomes more differentiated. Postponement results in savings because it moves differentiation nearer to the time of purchase, when demand is more easily forecast. This reduces risk and uncertainty costs. Logistics costs are reduced by sorting products in large lots, in relatively undifferentiated states.

Postponement

Companies can use postponement to shift the risk of owning goods from one channel member to another. That is, a manufacturer may refuse to produce until it receives firm orders; a middleman may postpone owning inventories by purchasing from sellers who offer faster delivery or by purchasing only when a sale has been made; and consumers may postpone ownership by buying from retail outlets where the products are in stock.

---

[15] Robert E. Weigand, "The Marketing Organization, Channels, and Firm Size," *Journal of Business* 36 (April 1963), pp. 228–36.

[16] H. O. Ruhuke, "Vertical Integration: Trend for the Future," *Advanced Management Journal,* January 1966, pp. 69–73.

[17] Louis P. Bucklin, *A Theory of Distribution Channel Structure* (Berkeley, Calif.: Institute of Business and Economic Research, University of California, 1966).

[18] Louis P. Bucklin, "Postponement, Speculation and the Structure of Distribution Channels," *Journal of Marketing Research* 2, no. 1 (February 1965), pp. 26–31.

Perhaps the best example of postponement is the mixing of paint colors at the retail level. Rather than having to forecast the exact colors that consumers will want to purchase, the retailer mixes paint in any color that the consumer wishes to purchase at the time of purchase. Other examples include color panels in the front of built-in kitchen appliances that enable the same unit to be any one of a number of colors; the centralization of slow-selling products in one warehouse location; and the building of slow-moving items only after orders have been received.

Speculation

Speculation is the converse of postponement: "The principle of speculation holds that changes in form, and the movement of goods to forward inventories, should be made at the earliest possible time in the marketing process in order to reduce the costs of the marketing system."[19] That is, a channel institution assumes risk rather than shifting it. Speculation can reduce marketing costs through *(a)* the economies of large-scale production; *(b)* the placement of large orders, which reduces the costs of order processing and transportation; *(c)* the reduction of stockouts and their associated cost; and *(d)* the reduction of uncertainty.

To reduce the need for speculative inventories, many firms are exploring strategies of time-based competition.[20] For example, in 1989, Northern Telecom was able to "manufacture products in about half the time it took just two or three years ago. Inventory and overhead have dropped, and quality has improved. Overall customer satisfaction has steadily risen."[21]

Postponement and speculation are concepts that allow us to understand channel structures and their evolution. The existence of speculative inventories may result in an indirect channel if the intermediary can perform the inventory risk-taking function at a lower cost than the manufacturer. Freight forwarders and agent middlemen who do not take title may reduce logistics costs in more direct channels of distribution where non-speculative inventories are present.

Functional Spin-Off within the Channel of Distribution

Functional Spin-Off: Five Key Hypotheses

Mallen's concept of functional spin-off within the distribution channel helps the marketer understand channel structure and predict structural change. His framework supports Bucklin's concepts of postponement and speculation. Mallen's work has several key hypotheses:

1. A producer will spin off a marketing function to a marketing intermediary if the latter can perform the function more efficiently than the former.

[19] Ibid., p. 27.

[20] This will be discussed at greater length in Chapter 10.

[21] Roy Merrills, "How Northern Telecom Competes on Time," *Harvard Business Review* 67, no. 4 (July-August 1989), p. 109.

2. If there are continual economies to be obtained within a wide range of volume changes, the middleman portion of the industry (and perhaps individual middlemen) will become bigger and bigger.
3. A producer will keep a marketing function if the producer can perform the function at least as efficiently as the intermediary.
4. If a producer is more efficient in one market, the producer will perform the marketing function; if in another market the middleman is more efficient, then the middleman will perform the function.
5. If there are not economies of scale in a growing market, more firms may be expected to enter the channel.[22]

These hypotheses are supported by the earlier writings of Stigler[23] and Dommermuth and Anderson.[24]

Additional factors that can influence channel structure include the following:

- Technological, cultural, physical, social, and political factors.
- Physical factors—such as geography, size of market area, location of production centers, and concentration of population.
- Local, state, and federal laws.
- Social and behavioral variables.

Reasons for Uneconomic Channels

Due to the influence of social, cultural, political, and economic variables, channels may not necessarily be as efficient or effective as they should be. McCammon gave the following reasons for the existence of uneconomic channels:[25]

1. *Reseller solidarity.* Resellers in many lines of trade function as groups that tend to support traditional trade practices and long-established institutional relationships. The presence of a strong professional or trade association tends to reinforce conservative group behavior and inhibit innovation within the channel.
2. *Entrepreneurial values.* The large reseller, given sufficient time to adjust, tends to be responsive to innovation, but smaller resellers tend to have relatively static expectations.

---

[22] Bruce Mallen, "Functional Spin-Off: A Key to Anticipating Change in Distribution Structure," *Journal of Marketing* 37, no. 3 (July 1973), p. 24.

[23] George Stigler, "The Division of Labor Is Limited by the Extent of the Market," *Journal of Political Economy* 59 (June 1951), pp. 185–93.

[24] William Dommermuth and R. Clifton Anderson, "Distribution Systems—Firms, Functions, and Efficiencies," *Business Topics* 17 (Spring 1969), pp. 51–56.

[25] Bert C. McCammon, Jr., "Alternative Explanations of Institutional Change and Channel Evolution," in *Marketing Channels,* ed. William G. Moller, Jr. and David L. Wilemon (Homewood, Ill.: Richard D. Irwin, 1971), pp. 136–41.

3. *Organizational rigidity.* A firm, because of organizational rigidities, prefers to respond incrementally to innovation. It gradually will imitate the innovating firm or develop counterstrategies over an extended period of time. If the innovator has penetrated the firm's core market, however, it must respond quickly to this challenge in order to ensure continued operation.
4. *The firm's channel position.* Firms operating as members of the dominant channel are either unwilling or unable to develop an entirely new method of distribution. Thus, a firm completely outside the system is most likely to introduce basic innovations.
5. *Market segmentation.* Innovative methods of operation appeal to a limited number of market segments, and conventional institutions are not compelled to change.

FLOWS IN THE CHANNEL OF DISTRIBUTION

Typical channels of distribution are illustrated in Figures 3–5 to 3–7.[26] Figure 3–5 shows the distribution channels of a grocery products manufacturer that sells its products to wholesalers, chain stores, cooperatives, and the military. The wholesalers and co-ops service retail accounts. Accounts are serviced by a national sales force.

Figure 3–6 illustrates the channels of distribution of a footwear retailer. The company-owned retail outlets also sell the products of other domestic and foreign manufacturers.

Figure 3–7 shows the distribution channels of an industrial goods manufacturer that sells a wide assortment of heavy durable goods to five nonconsumer markets. The primary channel of distribution is composed of independent dealers who serve as sales intermediaries. For one product line, company-owned and independent dealers are used. Generally, dealers are limited to one product line, but there are exceptions. The manufacturer also sells directly to governments and to certain national accounts. In such cases the manufacturer pays the local dealer to service the account. If the dealer has a good relationship with a government customer, the dealer controls the account. Products are transported to dealers for predelivery service in virtually all cases. Although the firm ships most products directly to dealers, for some product lines it uses consolidation depots or distribution centers as warehousing locations. The company uses three parts depots.

Information Flows Precede Product Flows

These figures illustrate the product flows and information flows that take place in each channel. Remember that product flows take place only after information flows are initiated. In addition to product and informa-

[26]These exampes are adapted from Douglas M. Lambert, *The Distribution Channels Decision,* pp. 150–67.

FIGURE 3–5 Distribution Channels—Grocery Products Manufacturer

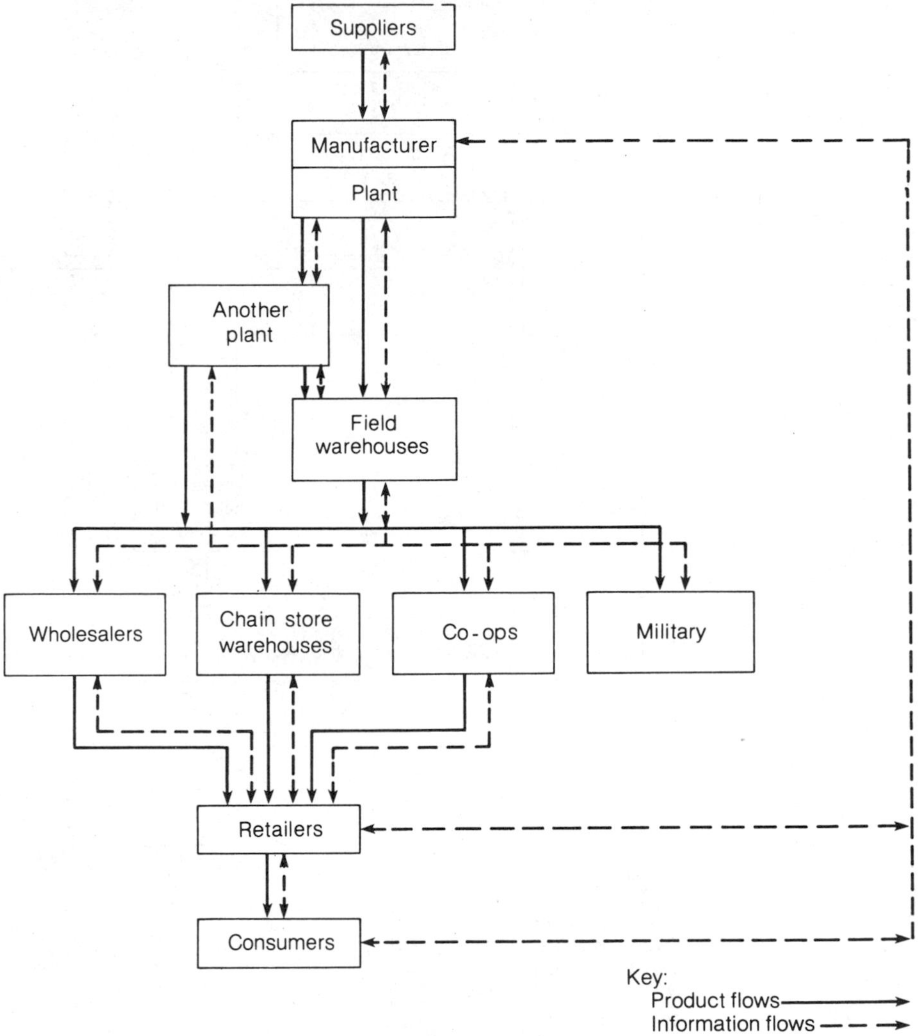

SOURCE: Adapted from Douglas M. Lambert, *The Distribution Channels Decision* (New York: National Association of Accountants, and Hamilton, Ontario: The Society of Management Accountants of Canada, 1978), p. 151. Reprinted with permission. Copyright 1978 by the National Association of Accountants. All rights reserved.

tion flows, payments for the merchandise and promotional materials also move through the system. The manufacturer may send salespeople to call on wholesalers and retailers, reach them by telephone using an inside sales force, or use some combination of these approaches. Sales data and market research data also flow from customers to the manufacturer. Such data help the manufacturer determine whether its products are selling, to whom they

FIGURE 3–6 Distribution Channels—Footwear Retailer

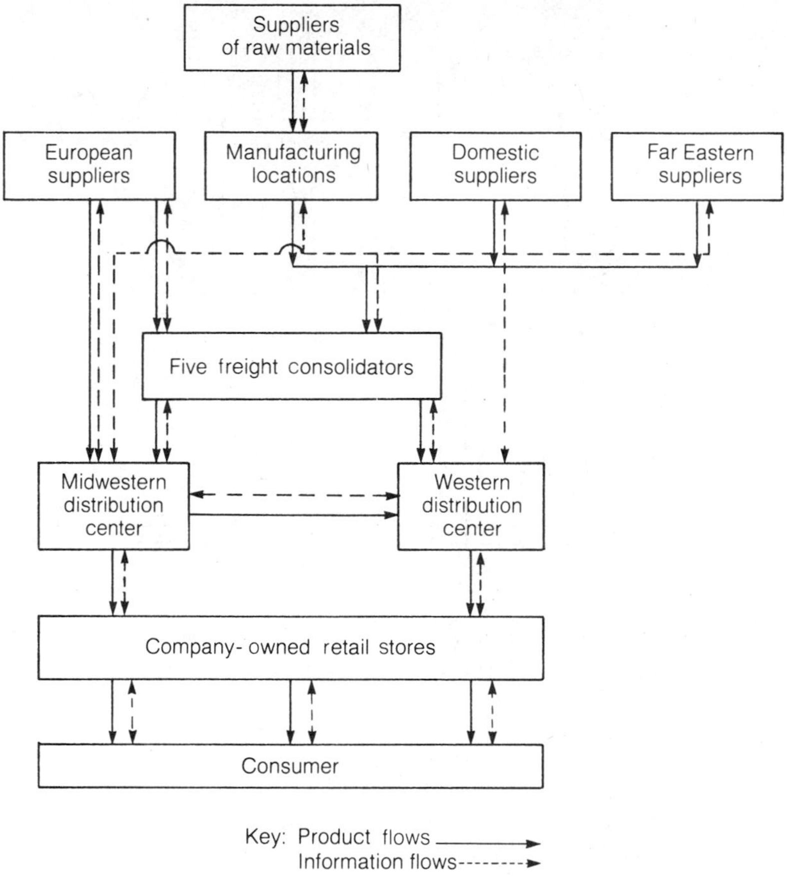

SOURCE: Adapted from Douglas M. Lambert, *The Distribution Channels Decision* (New York: National Association of Accountants, and Hamilton, Ontario: The Society of Management Accountants of Canada, 1978), p. 163. Reprinted with permission. Copyright 1978 by National Association of Accountants. All rights reserved.

are selling, and possibly why they are selling. Other types of information continually flowing between channel members include the quantity of inventory at each point in the channel, future production runs, service requirements, and delivery schedules.

Information Flows Affect Inventory Levels

In order to maximize profitability the manufacturer wants wholesalers and retailers to hold large inventories. Similarly, wholesalers and retailers want to shift responsibility to other channel members. The quality and speed of the information flows determine inventory size at each level of the channel. These inventories are referred to as *safety stocks*. We will discuss them in detail in Chapter 10.

FIGURE 3–7 Distribution Channels—Industrial Goods Manufacturer

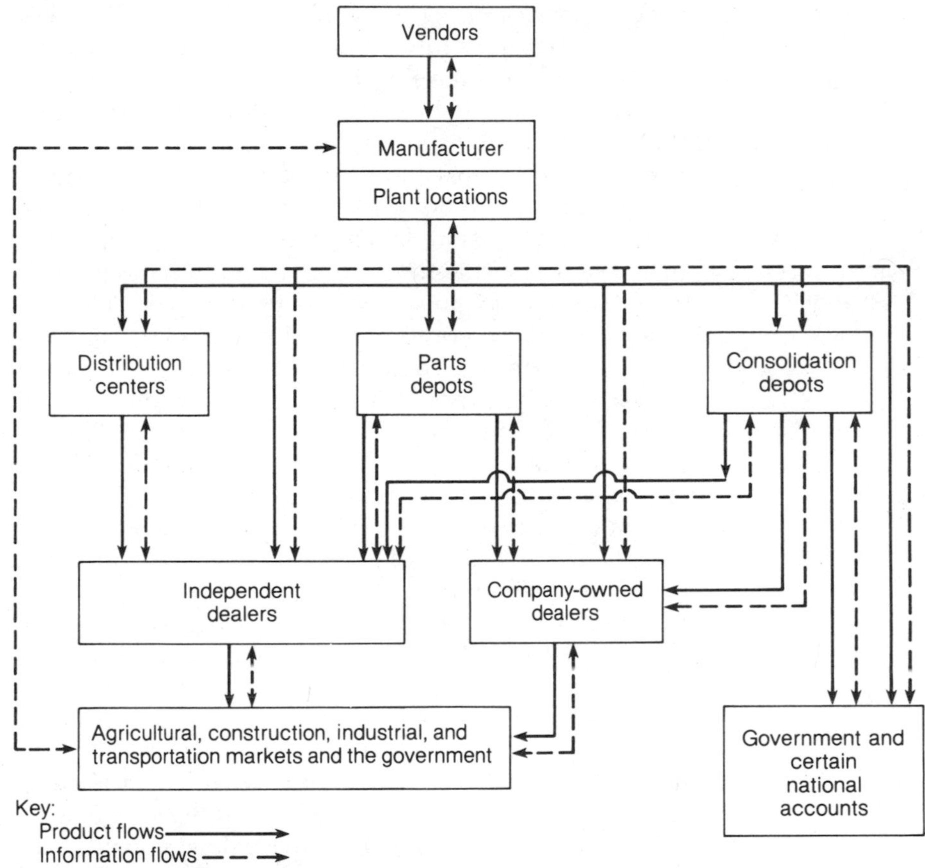

SOURCE: Adapted from Douglas M. Lambert, *The Distribution Channels Decision* (New York: National Association of Accountants, and Hamilton, Ontario: The Society of Management Accountants of Canada, 1978), p. 167. Reprinted with permission. Copyright 1978 by National Association of Accountants. All rights reserved.

Firms Need a Communications Link with Consumers

In many cases manufacturers need to include a direct communication link between the consumer and the firm, because product problems often do not become apparent until the product is in the hands of the end user. Given no direct method of communicating with the manufacturer, the consumer may take a course of action that is costly to the manufacturer as well as to other users. For instance, the unhappy consumer may tell a government agency or consumer advocate group about the product problem. This could prompt costly government regulation or even result in a direct reprimand, monetary or otherwise, for the firm. The consumer is likely to share his or her dissatisfaction with friends, neighbors, and family. Such unfavorable word-of-mouth advertising may hurt sales. The consumer may also write to the manufacturer. However, letter writing takes time and effort and therefore is the least likely course of action. In addition, the defective product may cause serious and costly liabilities that could significantly alter the manufacturer's future success in the marketplace.

If consumers have a direct and convenient way to communicate with the firm, there is less potential for large liabilities; the system can provide the firm with early warning of product defects, as well as advertising and promotion problems and product availability. A formal consumer response department can alert the manufacturer of a need to recall a product early—before major liabilities occur. Just as inventory acts as a buffer throughout the channel, so does communications.

Communications Act as a Buffer

Management must coordinate the firm's logistics strategy with the other components of the marketing mix to successfully implement overall marketing strategy. In some cases, existing channels of distribution may dictate what types of products the firm sells and how it prices and promotes them. For example, General Mills and Procter & Gamble make excellent products that are well advertised and competitively priced. One of the most important factors that separates these companies from their smaller competitors, however, is the size and effectiveness of their distribution channels. Generally, management expects new products to be compatible with current distribution channels.

The physical flow of products (logistics channel) and the legal exchange of ownership (transaction channel) must both take place for the channel of distribution to be successful. But a product may change ownership without physically moving, and it may be transported from one location to another without changing ownership. Because transaction channel activities are not directly related to physical movement, there is no reason for both to occur at the same time. One major manufacturer's distributors sell home appliances to dealers, but the manufacturer bypasses the distributors and ships large orders directly to the dealers. By 1985 the "dealer direct" program accounted for approximately 50 percent of the firm's sales volume. Although ownership passes from the manufacturer to the distributor to the dealer, the product flows directly from the manufacturer to the dealer, resulting in greater logistics efficiency. This is referred to as channel separation. Successful channel separation requires (1) a fast, reliable transportation system; (2) an on-line, interactive order processing system; and (3) swift, efficient information flows, such as inward Wide Area Telephone Service (WATS) lines or computer-to-computer transmission of orders and other information. While both the logistics channel and transaction channel must function in order to achieve a profitable sale, the firm should use channel separation if it results in improved performance.

Channel Separation

CHANNEL DESIGN

Considerable evidence suggests that the majority of channels are not designed but evolve over time.[27] An in-depth study of 18 manufacturers supports this conclusion. When executives were asked, "How was your current channel structure determined?" typical responses were:

> "This channel has been in use for as long as our product has been distributed nationally."
>
> "Our distribution channels have never changed at least as far as I'm aware of."
>
> "Hit and miss . . . trial and error. It is the kind of thing that happened over time."
>
> "Do not know for sure but the channel we are using now is the one that we have always used."
>
> "The current channel has evolved over time."
>
> "Changes in physical distribution have been in response to competition."
>
> "The company's major channel has been using company-owned retail outlets and this policy was adopted many years ago."
>
> "There was a time when every salesman had a warehouse. We had to show sales how we could reduce total costs and provide the desired service without the facility."
>
> "Basically when we started some 70 years ago we chose to sell through the five-and-dime stores. We have never totally moved away from being a direct house. How was it selected? It started that way and I think that it kind of happened. I think that we might be victims of one of those situations where business has run us and maybe we didn't run it."[28]

Most Channels of Distribution Are Not Planned

Current practice reveals a lack of planning. Better management of distribution channels can create many benefits. For example, in many cases not all channel alternatives were known when structural arrangements were negotiated; these decisions may later prove to be less than optimal. Identifying suboptimal channel arrangements and making structural changes will lead to increased profitability.

Even if the best channel is selected, unanticipated environmental changes may make it necessary to reconsider the channels of distribution. Environmental factors may include changes in consumer needs, markets, products and product lines, the competitive situation, the economic environment, and government regulation and incentives. In response to any one of these factors, the channel leader (manufacturer, wholesaler, or re-

---

[27] Phillip McVey, "Are Channels of Distribution What the Textbooks Say?" *Journal of Marketing* 24, no. 1 (January 1960), pp. 61–65.

[28] Douglas M. Lambert, *The Distribution Channels Decision,* pp. 56–59. Reprinted with permission. Copyright 1978 by National Association of Accountants. All rights reserved.

tailer) may decide to replace the existing channel, modify it by replacing only a part of the channel, or develop a multichannel system.[29]

Channel strategy must be based on overall corporate and marketing objectives. Channel performance goals must be stated in operational terms, such as projected market coverage, sales and service support, sales volume, profitability, and return on investment. The channel strategy includes decisions regarding intensity of distribution, use of direct or indirect channels, the services of intermediaries in each geographic area, and implementation plans.

A firm must become involved in the channel design process when it is considering entering the market with a new product or when existing channels are falling short of performance objectives. The channel design process consists of the following steps:[30]

Steps in the Channel Design Process

1. Establish channel objectives.
2. Formulate a channel strategy.
3. Determine channel structure alternatives.
4. Evaluate channel structure alternatives.
5. Select channel structure.
6. Determine alternatives for individual channel members.
7. Evaluate and select individual channel members.
8. Measure and evaluate channel performance.
9. Evaluate channel alternatives when performance objectives are not met.

The manufacturer, wholesaler, or retailer may lead the channel design process, depending on the relative market power, financial strength, and availability of desired channel members.

The Manufacturer's Perspective

A manufacturer has market power when customers demand its product. When consumers demand a manufacturer's brand, retailers and consequently wholesalers are anxious to market its existing and new products because such products are profitable. However, a small manufacturer of a little-known brand may find it difficult to attract channel members for its existing products or new product offerings. Such a manufacturer lacks market power when entering channel negotiations. Financial resources determine a manufacturer's ability to perform marketing functions internally. Small manufacturers usually cannot afford to distribute directly to retailers and must rely on wholesalers. Furthermore, in some locations acceptable middlemen may not be available in every line of trade.

---

[29] See A. L. McDonald, Jr., "Do Your Distribution Channels Need Reshaping?" *Business Horizons* 7, no. 3 (Summer 1964), pp. 29–38.

[30] Adapted from Douglas M. Lambert, *The Distribution Channels Decision,* pp. 44, 45.

In industrial markets, when deciding between a direct or indirect channel of distribution, the manufacturer must consider the customer and the customer's needs, the product line, the size of the geographic area to be covered, the number of customers, the nature of the selling job, and the projected profitability of each option. For a small manufacturer with geographically dispersed customers, the cost of a direct channel may be prohibitive. Firms in this situation include some manufacturers of electrical supplies and small hand and machine tools. Even the manufacturer of a full line of products who has geographically concentrated customers may find direct channels less profitable than indirect channels for some of the products and customers. For example, many pharmaceutical companies have increased their use of wholesalers, even in concentrated market areas, because of the high customer service levels required.

The Wholesaler's Perspective

Wholesalers make it possible to efficiently provide possession, time, and place utility. Wholesalers are economically justified because they improve distribution efficiency by "breaking bulk," building assortments of goods, and providing financing for retailers or industrial customers.

Wholesalers' market power is greatest when retailers order a small amount of each manufacturer's products, or when the manufacturers involved have limited financial resources. For some products, such as Maytag appliances and some lines of jewelry and fashion apparel, per-unit prices and margins may be large enough to enable the manufacturer to sell directly to retailers, even when the number of items sold to each retailer is small. But manufacturers of low-value or low-margin items such as cigarettes and some food items may find it profitable to sell only through wholesalers, even though each retailer may order in relatively large quantities.

Wholesalers' and distributors' financial strength determines the number of marketing functions they can perform. Each function represents a profit opportunity as well as an associated risk and cost. The presence or absence of other firms offering comparable services influences the market power of individual wholesalers. Traditionally wholesalers have been regional in scope. In some industries like pharmaceuticals, wholesaler mergers have occurred. Foremost-McKesson and Bergen Brunswig are large pharmaceutical wholesalers that have become national in scope.

The Retailer's Perspective

Retailers exist in the channel of distribution when they provide convenient product assortment, availability, price, and image within the geographic market served. The degree of customer preference (loyalty due to customer service and price/value performance) that a retailer enjoys in a specific area directly affects its ability to negotiate channel relationships. The retailer's financial capability and size also determine its degree of influence over other channel members.

CHANNEL DESIGN CONSIDERATIONS

Among the factors management must consider when establishing a channel of distribution are market coverage objectives, product characteristics, customer service objectives, and profitability.[31]

Market Coverage Objectives

In order to establish market coverage objectives, management must consider customer buying behavior, the type of distribution required, channel structure, and the degree of control necessary for success.

Customer Buying Behavior. The patronage motives of potential customer segments must be determined in order to select intermediaries who can perform the selling function most efficiently and effectively. Figure 3–8 summarizes the nine types of behavior that may characterize a target market's purchase behavior. Three or four cells usually represent the behavior of a specific target group, with the remaining left empty. This analysis enables the channel designer to determine the retail segment or segments most capable of reaching the target market or markets. Industrial marketers also must identify potential users and determine how these consumers will make the purchase decision. The industrial purchaser's decision-making process depends on whether the firm is a user, an OEM, or a distributor.

Type of Distribution. There are basically three types of distribution that can be used to make product available to consumers: intensive distribution, exclusive distribution, and selective distribution. In *intensive distribution,* the product is sold to as many appropriate retailers or wholesalers as possible. Intensive distribution is appropriate for products such as chewing gum, candy bars, soft drinks, bread, film, and cigarettes where the primary factor influencing the purchase decision is convenience. All of these items fall into the convenience goods/convenience stores category in the product-patronage matrix (Figure 3–8). Industrial products that may require intensive distribution include pencils, paper clips, transparent tape, file folders, typing paper, transparency masters, screws, and nails.

Intensive Distribution

[31]The material in this section is adapted from Donald J. Bowersox, M. Bixby Cooper, Douglas M. Lambert, and Donald A. Taylor, *Management in Marketing Channels* (New York: McGraw-Hill, 1980), chap. 7, pp. 201–9.

FIGURE 3–8 Identifying Potential Channel Members Based on Consumer Buying Behavior

Categorization of Stores	*Categorization of Products*		
	Convenience Goods	*Shopping Goods*	*Specialty Goods*
Convenience stores (7-Eleven)	Consumer buys the most readily available brand of product at the most accessible store	Consumer selects product from the assortment carried by the closest store	Consumer purchases favorite brand from the closest store that has the item in stock
Shopping stores (Kmart, Kroger, Macy's)	Consumer is indifferent to the brand of product but shops among different stores for better service and/or lower prices	Consumer compares brands and retail stores	Consumer has a strong preference for a particular brand but compares stores for the best service and/or price
Specialty stores (Tiffany's)	Consumer prefers a specific store but is indifferent to the brand of product	Consumer prefers a certain store but examines the store's assortment for the best buy	Consumer has a strong preference for both a particular store and a specific brand

SOURCE: Adapted from Louis P. Bucklin, "Retail Strategy and the Classification of Consumer Goods," *Journal of Marketing*, January 1963, pp. 53–54.

Exclusive Distribution

When a single outlet is given an exclusive franchise to sell the product in a geographic area, the arrangement is referred to as *exclusive distribution*. Products such as specialty automobiles, some major appliances, some brands of furniture, and certain lines of clothing that enjoy a high degree of brand loyalty are likely to be distributed on an exclusive basis. This is particularly true if the consumer is willing to overcome the inconvenience of traveling some distance to obtain the product. Usually, exclusive distribution is undertaken when the manufacturer desires more aggressive selling on the part of the wholesaler or retailer, or when channel control is important. Exclusive distribution may enhance the product's image and enable the firm to charge higher retail prices. The specialty goods/specialty store combination is the ultimate form of exclusive distribution. However, management sometimes chooses exclusive dealing for shopping goods, such as certain brands or lines of clothing, shoes, or stereo equipment, if sales to specialty stores or shopping stores enhance the product's image and provide sufficient margins to retailers.

Sometimes manufacturers use multiple brands in order to offer exclusive distribution to more than one retailer or distributor. Exclusive distribution occurs more frequently at the wholesale level than at the retail level. Anheuser-Busch, for example, offers exclusive rights to distributors, who in turn use intensive distribution at the retail level (in states such as Florida where this is allowed).

Selective Distribution

In *selective distribution,* the number of outlets that may carry a product is limited, but not to the extent of exclusive dealing. Shopping goods companies with established reputations commonly employ selective distribution, but this setup is also used by new companies or for new products as a means of gaining distribution. By carefully selecting wholesalers and/or retailers, the manufacturer can concentrate on potentially profitable accounts and develop solid working relationships to ensure that the product is properly merchandised. The producer may also restrict the number of retail outlets if the product requires specialized servicing or sales support. Selective distribution may be used for products such as clothing, appliances, televisions, stereo equipment, home furnishings, and sports equipment.

In general, exclusive distribution lends itself to direct channels (manufacturer to retailer). Intensive distribution is more likely to involve indirect channels with two or more intermediaries.

Channel Structure. With customer requirements and the type of distribution determined, management must select channel institutions. The increased use of scrambled merchandising—that is, nontraditional channels of distribution—has made this task somewhat more difficult. For example, grocery stores have added nongrocery products like pots and pans, children's toys, hardware items, and in some cases television sets in order to improve margins and profitability.

Factors Restricting Availability of Intermediaries

Other factors may restrict the availability of intermediaries. These include (1) the financial strength of the intermediaries; (2) the need for specialized facilities; (3) market coverage provided; (4) product lines carried; (5) the degree of support given to the product; (6) logistics capabilities; and (7) an intermediary's ability to grow with the business.

Control. In many cases, a firm may have to exercise some control over other channel members to ensure product quality and/or postpurchase services. The need for control stems from management's desire to protect the firm's long-range profitability. For example, a manufacturer of premium confectionery products achieves national distribution through a chain of company-owned retail outlets and selected department stores, drug stores, and specialty outlets. The marketing manager said the company does not sell to wholesalers because it wishes to avoid the mass market, fearing a loss of control over margins and product quality. If the manufacturer sold the product to a wholesaler, it could not prevent the wholesaler from selling to a mass merchant such as Kmart. A mass merchandiser would undoubtedly discount this nationally recognized brand, thus jeopardizing the very profitable company stores and other channels of distribution that rely on the substantial margins allowed by premium prices.

Product Characteristics

In addition to market coverage objectives, product characteristics are a major consideration in channel design. Nine product characteristics should be analyzed by the channel designer: (1) the product's value, (2) the technicality of the product, (3) the degree of market acceptance, (4) the degree of substitutability, (5) the product's bulk, (6) the product's perishability, (7) the degree of market concentration, (8) seasonality, and (9) the width and depth of the product line.

Value. Products with a high per-unit cost require a large inventory investment. Consequently, manufacturers with limited resources usually shift some of the burden by using intermediaries. The requirement of large inventories limits the number of available intermediaries. In some cases the large dollar-per-unit margin may cover the cost of direct sales and result in the manufacturer's selecting direct distribution. But channels tend to be indirect when the unit value is low, unless sales volume is high enough to support direct channels. In general, intensive distribution is used for low-value products.

The product's value also influences its inventory carrying cost and the desirability of premium transportation. Low-value, low-margin grocery products may be shipped by rail car and stored in field warehouses. High-value component parts and products such as high-fashion merchandise may be shipped by air freight to minimize in-transit inventories and reduce inventory carrying costs by holding inventory at a central location.

Technicality. Highly technical products usually require demonstration by a salesperson. In addition, prepurchase and postpurchase service often require that repair parts be stocked. Technical products include such items as home computers, high-priced stereo components, expensive cameras and video equipment, imported sports cars, and a multitude of industrial products. Generally, direct channels and selective or exclusive distribution policies are used for these kinds of products.

Market Acceptance. The degree of market acceptance determines the amount of selling effort required. If a leading manufacturer offers a new product and plans significant introductory advertising, customer acceptance will be high and intermediaries will want to carry the product. But new products with little market acceptance and low brand identification require aggressive selling at each level of the channel. If middlemen are reluctant to support the line, the manufacturer may have to employ "missionary salespeople" or "detail people" to promote the line to various channel members.

Substitutability. Product substitutability is closely related to brand loyalty. Brand loyalty is lowest for convenience goods and highest for specialty goods. When brand loyalty is low, product substitution is likely and intensive distribution is required. Firms place a premium on point-of-purchase displays in high-traffic areas. To gain support from wholesalers and/or retailers, the producer may offer higher than normal margins for shopping and specialty goods. Selective or exclusive distribution makes product support easier.

Bulk. Generally, low-value, high-weight products are restricted to markets close to the point of production. These products often require special materials-handling skills. With low weight and small cubes, more units can be shipped in a truck, rail car, or container, thereby reducing the per-unit cost of transportation. Tank truck shipment of orange juice concentrate from Florida to northern markets for packaging is an example of moving a product closer to the point of consumption to overcome value and bulk restrictions.

Perishability. Perishability refers to physical deterioration or to product obsolescence caused by changing customer buying patterns or technological change. Perishable products are usually sold on a direct basis in order to move product through the channel more quickly and reduce the potential for inventory loss.

Market Concentration. When the market is concentrated in a geographic area, direct channels may be the most effective and efficient method of distribution. When markets are widely dispersed, however, specialized intermediaries are necessary; they can capitalize on the efficiencies associated with moving larger quantities. Because of widely dispersed markets, many food processing companies use brokers to market their products. This factor also explains the existence of pooling agencies, such as freight forwarders and local cartage firms, which aggregate small shipments into truckload or carload units for movement to distant points.

Seasonality. Seasonality must be considered when applicable. For some products, sales volumes peak at certain times of the year (toy sales at Christmas); in other cases, raw materials, such as fresh fruits and vegetables, may only be available at specific times. Both cases require out-of-season storage. Manufacturers must invest in warehouses or provide incentives to intermediaries so that they perform the storage function. For example, manufacturers might offer a seasonal discount to wholesalers or retailers who agree to take early delivery.

Width and Depth. The width and depth of a supplier's product line influence channel design. A manufacturer of products with low per-unit values may use intensive distribution with direct sales if the product line is broad enough to result in a relatively large average sales volume. Grocery manufacturers such as Kellogg and General Foods are examples. Usually, a manufacturer of a limited line of products will use indirect channels to achieve adequate market coverage at a reasonable cost.

Customer Service Objectives

Customer service represents the place component of the marketing mix. Customer service can be used to differentiate the product or influence the market price—if customers are willing to pay more for better service. In addition, the channel of distribution selected determines the costs of providing a specified level of customer service.

Customer Service Measures

Customer service is a complex subject[32] and is usually measured in terms of (1) the level of product availability, (2) the speed and consistency of the customer's order cycle, and (3) the communication that takes place between seller and customer. Management should establish customer service levels only after carefully studying customer needs.

Availability. The most important measure of customer service is inventory availability within a specified order cycle time. Availability is usually expressed in terms of (1) the number of items out of stock compared to the total number of items in inventory, (2) the items shipped as a percentage of the number of items ordered, (3) the value of items shipped as a percentage of the value of items ordered, and/or (4) the number of orders shipped complete as a percentage of total orders received.

Measure 1 is deficient unless products are categorized based on profit contribution; a stockout on a fast-moving item would be treated the same as a stockout on a slow-moving item. The weakness of measure 2 is its failure to recognize products' importance to the customer. Furthermore, some products have higher contribution margins than others, and losing the sale of one of these will have a greater impact on corporate profits. Measure 3, based on the value of items ordered, is somewhat better than the first two measures but still does not eliminate their weaknesses. Measure 4 is most likely to reflect the *customer's* view of customer service. The best measure of customer service reflects the product's importance to the customer and the customer's importance to the company.

Order Cycle. The order cycle is the time that elapses between the customer's order placement and the time he or she receives the product. The ability to consistently achieve the targeted order cycle time influences the amount of inventory held throughout the channel of distribution. Consequently, the speed and consistency of the order cycle are prime factors in channel design. Most customers prefer consistent service to fast service, since the former allows them to plan inventory levels to a greater extent than is possible with a fast but highly variable order cycle.

---

[32] We will cover customer service in detail in Chapter 4.

Communication. Communication refers to the firm's ability to supply timely information to the customer regarding such factors as order status, order tracking, back order status, order confirmation, product substitution, product shortages, and product information requests. The use of automated information systems usually results in fewer errors in shipping, picking, packing, labeling, and documentation. The ability of channel members to provide good communications systems is a major factor in channel design.

Profitability

Management Must Estimate the Profitability of Alternative Channel Structures

The profitability of various channels of distribution is the major criterion in channel design. Table 3–1 illustrates the framework for judging alternative channel structures on the basis of estimated cost and revenue analysis. Management can use market research to formulate revenue estimates for each alternative channel structure. It must estimate variable manufacturing costs for various levels of activity, and variable marketing and logistics costs, such as sales commissions, transportation, warehousing, and order processing, along with accounts receivable. Management should apply the corporate cost of money to accounts receivable. It should also add to each channel alternative assignable nonvariable costs incurred for each segment, including expenses like bad debts, sales promotion, salaries, and inventory carrying costs. Finally, management should use the corporate opportunity cost of money as a charge for all other assets required by each channel structure alternative. The size of the net segment margin will determine which structural alternative is the best option from the standpoint of financial performance. This information, combined with estimates of future growth for each structural alternative, permits the channel designer to select the most desirable alternative. The cost/revenue analysis shown in Table 3–1 also can be used to measure channel structure and channel member performance.

The following example illustrates the recommended approach. Traditional accounting data showed a net profit of $2.5 million before taxes on sales of $42.5 million. While management believed that this profit was not adequate, traditional accounting gave few clues with regard to the specific problem. However, a contribution approach to profitability analysis by type of account can be used to diagnose areas where performance is inadequate (see Table 3–2). In this example, sales to drugstores were the largest of the four channels used by the manufacturer, but the segment controllable margin-to-sales ratio was the lowest; it was less than one-half that of the second most profitable segment, and only 37 percent of the most profitable segment. Nevertheless, at $3.1 million the segment controllable margin is substantial, and it is doubtful that elimination of drugstores would be a wise decision. A product-channel matrix analysis showed that product mix was not the source of the problem. Further segmentation of the drugstore

TABLE 3–1 Channel Cost/Revenue Analysis—Contribution Approach with a Charge for Assets Employed

	Channel Alternative				
	1	*2*	*3*	*4*	*5*
Net Sales					
Cost of goods sold (variable manufacturing cost)					
Manufacturing contribution					
Marketing and logistics costs					
Variable costs:					
Sales commissions					
Transportation					
Warehousing (handling in and out)					
Order processing					
Charge for investment in accounts receivable					
Segment contribution margin					
Assignable nonvariable costs (costs incurred specifically for the segment during the period):					
Bad debts					
Display racks					
Sales promotion					
Salaries					
Segment related advertising					
Inventory carrying costs					
Other					
Segment controllable margin					
Charge for assets used by segment					
Net segment margin					

Assumption: Public warehouses are used for field inventories.

channel revealed that national drugstore chains had a segment controllable margin-to-sales ratio almost as large as that of the grocery chains and somewhat better than discount stores, that regional drugstore chains were almost as profitable as discount stores, and that small independent pharmacies were losing money (see Table 3–3). With this information, management could determine the impact on corporate profitability if the independent pharmacies were served by drug wholesalers or by field warehouses supported by telemarketing and scheduled deliveries. The alternative that would lead to the greatest improvement in long-term profitability should be selected.

Rather than contribution reports, most firms use a full costing system, which assigns fixed costs to individual segments.[33] However, this system provides incorrect information because costs "common" to multiple segments are allocated to segments according to some arbitrary measure of activity. Vital information about the controllability and behavior of segment

[33] Douglas M. Lambert and Jay U. Sterling, "What Types of Profitability Reports Do Marketing Managers Receive?" *Industrial Marketing Management* 16, no. 4 (1987), pp. 295–303.

TABLE 3–2 Profitability by Type of Account: A Contribution Approach ($ thousands)

		Type of Account			
	Total Company	*Department Stores*	*Grocery Chains*	*Drug stores*	*Discount Stores*
Sales	$42,500	$6,250	$10,500	$19,750	$6,000
Less discounts, returns, and allowances	2,500	250	500	1,750	—
Net sales	40,000	6,000	10,000	18,000	6,000
Cost of goods sold (variable manufacturing costs)	20,000	2,500	4,800	9,200	3,500
Manufacturing contribution	20,000	3,500	5,200	8,800	2,500
Variable selling and distribution costs:					
Sales commissions	800	120	200	360	120
Transportation costs	2,500	310	225	1,795	170
Warehouse handling	600	150	—	450	—
Order-processing costs	400	60	35	280	25
Charge for investment in accounts receivable	700	20	50	615	15
Contribution margin	15,000	2,840	4,690	5,300	2,170
Assignable nonvariable costs (costs incurred specifically for the segment during the period):					
Sales promotion and slotting allowances	1,250	60	620	400	170
Advertising	500	—	—	500	—
Bad debts	300	—	—	300	—
Display racks	200	—	—	200	—
Inventory carrying costs	1,250	150	200	800	100
Segment controllable margin	$11,500	$2,630	$3,870	$3,100	$1,900
Segment controllable margin-to-sales ratio	27.1%	42.1%	36.9%	15.7%	31.7%

NOTE: This approach could be modified to include a charge for the assets employed by each of the segments, as well as a deduction for the change in market value of these assets. The result would be referred to as the net segment margin (residual income).

SOURCE: Douglas M. Lambert and Jay U. Sterling, "Educators Are Contributing to Major Deficiencies in Marketing Profitability Reports," *Journal of Marketing Education* 12, no. 3 (Fall, 1990), pp. 43–44.

costs is lost. For example, if a segment is found to be unprofitable under a full costing approach and as a result is discontinued, the fixed costs will simply be reallocated to the remaining segments.

Research has identified the following shortcomings of the profitability reports used by executives in major corporations:

Shortcomings of Corporate Profitability Reports

1. Full manufactured costs (which sometimes included a profit for the plant) were used in calculating costs of goods sold.
2. Operating costs such as development, selling, and administration were fully allocated to products often on a percentage-of-sales basis.
3. Costs such as transportation, warehousing, sales commissions, and sales promotions were not reported as separate line items.
4. When marketing and logistics costs were identified explicitly as expenses, they usually were allocated to products on a percentage of sales basis.
5. Inconsistencies in terminology were common. When executives referred to contribution margins, often the numbers used were actually manufacturing contribution.

TABLE 3–3 Profitability by Type of Account: A Contribution Approach ($ thousands)

	Type of Account			
	Drugstore Channel	*National Drug Chains*	*Regional Drug Chains*	*Independent Pharmacies*
Sales	$19,750	$4,250	$5,500	$10,000
Less discounts, returns, and allowances	1,750	250	500	1,000
Net sales	18,000	4,000	5,000	9,000
Cost of goods sold (variable manufacturing costs)	9,200	2,100	2,600	4,500
Manufacturing contribution	8,800	1,900	2,400	4,500
Variable selling and distribution costs:				
Sales commissions	360	80	100	180
Transportation costs	1,795	120	200	1,475
Warehouse handling	450	—	100	350
Order-processing costs	280	25	55	200
Charge for investment in accounts receivable	615	20	35	560
Contribution margin	$5,300	$1,655	$1,910	$1,735
Assignable nonvariable costs (costs incurred specifically for the segment during the period):				
Sales promotion and slotting allowances	400	90	110	200
Advertising	500	—	—	500
Bad debts	300	—	—	300
Display racks	200	—	—	200
Inventory carrying costs	800	80	100	620
Segment controllable margin	$3,100	$1,485	$1,700	($85)
Segment controllable margin-to-sales ratio	15.7%	34.9%	30.9%	—

NOTE: This approach could be modified to include a charge for the assets employed by each of the segments, as well as a deduction for the change in market value of these assets. The result would be referred to as the net segment margin (residual income).

SOURCE: Douglas M. Lambert and Jay U. Sterling, "Educators Are Contributing to Major Deficiencies in Marketing Profitability Reports," *Journal of Marketing Education* 12, no. 3 (Fall, 1990), pp. 44–45.

6. Opportunity costs such as inventory carrying costs, a charge for accounts receivable, and a charge for other assets employed did not appear on profitability reports.
7. Reports that covered more than one year were not adjusted for inflation.
8. Reports were not adjusted to reflect replacement costs.[34]

Cost Allocations Distort Profitability

In summary, cost allocations can seriously distort a segment's profitability. "Seriously distorted product costs can lead managers to choose a losing competitive strategy by de-emphasizing and overpricing products that are highly profitable and by expanding commitments to complex, unprofitable lines. The company persists in the losing strategy because executives have no alternative sources of information to signal when product costs are distorted."[35]

[34] Ibid.

[35] Robert S. Kaplan, "One Cost System Isn't Enough," *Harvard Business Review* 66 (January–February, 1988), pp. 61–66.

TABLE 3–4 Profitability by Type of Account: A Full-Cost Approach ($ thousands)

		Type of Account			
	Total Company	*Department Stores*	*Grocery Chains*	*Drugstores*	*Discount Stores*
Net sales	$40,000	$6,000	$10,000	$18,000	$6,000
Cost of goods sold (full manufacturing costs)	25,000	3,750	6,250	11,250	3,750
Manufacturing margin	15,000	2,250	3,750	6,750	2,250
Less expenses:					
Sales commissions	800	120	200	360	120
Transportation costs ($/case)	2,500	375	625	1,125	375
Warehouse handling ($/cu. ft.)	600	90	150	270	90
Order-processing costs ($/order)	400	30	50	300	20
Sales promotion (% of sales)	1,250	187	312	563	188
Advertising (% of sales)	500	75	125	225	75
Bad debts (% of sales)	300	45	75	135	45
General overhead and administrative expense (% of sales)	6,150	922	1,538	2,768	922
Net profit (before taxes)	$2,500	$406	$675	$1,004	$415
Profit-to-sales ratio	6.3%	6.8%	6.8%	5.6%	6.9%

SOURCE: Douglas M. Lambert and Jay U. Sterling, "Educators Are Contributing to Major Deficiences in Marketing Profitability Reports," *Journal of Marketing Education* 12, no. 3 (Fall 1990), p. 49.

Table 3–4 illustrates how the channel profitability analysis contained in Table 3–2 would change if it were calculated using average costs. Drugstores would show by far the largest dollar profit. The profit-to-sales ratio for drugstores would compare favorably with that of the other channels (82 percent of the profit-to-sales ratio for grocery chains), whereas the controllable margin-to-sales ratio of the drugstore channel was less than half (43 percent) of that earned by the grocery channel. The differences in the two methods of accounting would be much greater in a product profitability analysis because manufacturing, marketing, and logistics costs would vary more across products. If the costs in Table 3–4 had been allocated on a percentage of sales basis, as is the practice in most firms, the profit-to-sales ratios for the four channels would have been equal.

CHANNEL PERFORMANCE MEASUREMENT

Marketing literature rarely focuses on measuring channel performance. There are three possible explanations for this:

1. Measuring channel performance is difficult.
2. Some aspects of channel performance may be difficult to quantify, making a unified index of performance difficult to achieve.
3. Published standards are not available for industry comparisons.[36]

---

[36] Douglas M. Lambert, *The Distribution Channels Decision*, p. 36. Reprinted with permission. Copyright 1978 by National Association of Accountants. All rights reserved.

Revzan suggested the following steps as a necessary beginning analysis on which a whole series of special studies can be built:

1. The measurement of the size of the potential trading areas.
2. The development of sales potentials for each of these trading areas.
3. The subdivision of (1) and (2) by product lines, if necessary, with accompanying measures of the estimated market penetration ratio of each line.
4. The subdivision of (1) and (2) and (3) by salesmen and salesmen's territories. This involves knowledge, by time-and-duty analyses, of how many customers a given type of salesman can adequately service per working day.
5. The calculation of the cost-of-getting ratios by product lines, salesmen, territories, etc., in terms of the direct, semidirect and indirect components based on historical and estimated future bases.
6. The alternative costs, as in (5), for substituting possible channel alternatives.
7. The subdivisions of the cost estimates in (5) and (6) by various size classes of customers.
8. Finally, a comparison of actual sales, cost, and profit results with the budgeted potentials, together with a critical explanation of the reasons why the potentials have or have not been realized.[37]

Measures of Channel Performance

One measure of channel performance is the extent to which the company's target market is being satisfied, given the firm's goals and objectives. Table 3–5 contains potential measures of channel effectiveness that consider consumer satisfaction.

Next, management must analyze channel structure to determine if the corporate channel strategy has been successfully implemented. Table 3–6 shows a number of criteria that can be used to measure the efficiency of the distribution channel structure. When management evaluates channel structure, it must compare the firm's ability to perform the marketing functions internally with the channel member's ability to perform these functions. Table 3–7 contains a number of quantitative measures of channel performance, and Table 3–8 illustrates qualitative measures that managers may use when reevaluating the channel of distribution and specific channel members. Management should set objectives for the channel, and measure actual performance against planned performance. Also, evaluation measures should be developed over time and used to isolate potential problem areas. Perhaps the best measure of channel performance is profitability as illustrated earlier in this chapter.

[37] David A. Revzan, "Evaluation of Channel Effectiveness," *Wholesaling in Marketing Organizations* (New York: John Wiley & Sons, 1961), pp. 151–55.

TABLE 3–5 Measures of Channel Effectiveness

1. Lot size: Product available in desired quantities?
2. Delivery time: Product available when needed?
3. Search: Product available in store expected, thus making search time reasonable?
4. Assortment: Product available in desired model, color, size and with desired features?
5. Customer service: Sales help adequate?
   Delivery provided if required?
   Follow-up service if required?
   Financing available?
   Warranty honored?
   Adjustment made if quality inferior (if product is defective in any way)?
6. Brand image strong?

SOURCE: Adapted from Adel I. El-Ansary and M. Bixby Cooper, "An Exploratory Framework for Examining Distribution Channel Performance," unpublished paper, Louisiana State University, 1976, pp. 6–7; reported in Douglas M. Lambert, *The Distribution Channels Decision* (New York: National Association of Accountants, and Hamilton, Ontario: The Society of Management Accountants of Canada, 1978), p. 38. Reprinted with permission.

TABLE 3–6 Measures of Channel Structure Efficiency

1. Number of channel levels
2. Number of outlets per level
3. The extent and distribution cost outcome of functional shift in the channel
4. The extent and distribution cost outcome of functional substitution in the channel
5. The extent and distribution cost outcome of functional interchange in the channel
6. The extent and distribution cost outcome of postponement in the channel
7. The extent and distribution cost outcome of speculation in the channel
8. Availability of clear channel policies on:
   a. inventory levels
   b. transportation
   c. warehousing
   d. customer service
   e. pricing and discounts
   f. promotion
9. Extent of channel member turnover
10. Market image of channel members
11. Financial strength of channel members
12. Competitive strength of channel

SOURCE: Adel I. El-Ansary and M. Bixby Cooper, "An Exploratory Framework for Examining Distribution Channel Performance," unpublished paper, Louisiana State University, 1976, pp. 8–9; reported in Douglas M. Lambert, *The Distribution Channels Decision* (New York: National Association of Accountants, and Hamilton, Ontario: The Society of Management Accountants of Canada, 1978), p. 39. Reprinted with permission.

IMPLEMENTING COST TRADE-OFFS IN A CHANNEL OF DISTRIBUTION

Channel Goal: Improve Overall Efficiency

In Chapter 2 we introduced the integrated logistics management concept and the cost trade-offs required in a logistics system (see Figure 3–9). Cost trade-off analysis can be performed either within a single firm or between different levels of the channel. For the individual firm, the goal is to find the most efficient way to offer the desired level of service. For the channel, the goal is to improve overall efficiency by reallocating functions, and therefore costs, among its members. The level of customer service offered by the manufacturer, for example, will have a significant impact on other channel members.

TABLE 3–7 Quantitative Measures of Channel or Channel Member Performance

1. Total distribution cost per unit
2. Transportation cost per unit
3. Warehousing cost per unit
4. Production cost per unit
5. Costs associated with avoiding stockouts
6. Percent of stockout units
7. Percent of obsolete inventories
8. Percent of bad debts
9. Customer service level by product and by market segment
10. Accuracy of sales forecasts
11. Number of errors in order filling
12. Number of new markets entered
13. Percent sales volume in new markets entered
14. Percent of markdown volume
15. Number and percent of discontinued channel intermediaries (distribution turnover)
16. Number and percent of new distributors
17. Percent of damaged merchandise
18. Percent of shipments astray
19. Size of orders
20. Ability to keep up with new technology—data transmission
21. Percent of shipments—less than truckload (LTL) versus truckload (TL)
    —less than carload (LCL—used with rail shipments) versus carload (CL)
22. Energy costs
23. Number of customer complaints

SOURCE: Adapted from Adel I. El-Ansary, "A Model for Evaluating Channel Performance," unpublished paper, Louisiana State University, 1975, pp. 10–11; reported in Douglas M. Lambert, *The Distribution Channels Decision* (New York: National Association of Accountants, and Hamilton, Ontario: The Society of Management Accountants of Canada, 1978), p. 40. Reprinted with permission.

A manufacturer whose product availability is poor and whose order cycle time is inconsistent may force wholesalers to carry more inventory as safety stock in order to offer an acceptable level of service to the retail level of the channel. In this case, lower logistics costs for the manufacturer were achieved at the expense of the other channel members, and the entire channel may be less efficient.

Information Technology Can Increase Channel Efficiency *and* Effectiveness

However, if management concentrates on systems changes that improve logistics efficiency or effectiveness, it may be possible to satisfy all of the firm's objectives. For example, many companies have not kept pace with technology in the area of order processing. By replacing an outdated, mail-based, order processing and information system with advanced technology, a firm may be able to achieve some or all of the following: (1) increased customer service levels, (2) lower inventories, (3) speedier collections, (4) decreased transportation costs, (5) lower warehousing costs, and (6) improvements in cash flow and return on assets.

The manufacturer has minimal additional cash invested in inventory held by the customer rather than in the manufacturer's warehouse. Furthermore, the non-cost-of-money components of inventory carrying cost are shifted to the next level of the channel. For this reason, channel efficiency may be increased if the manufacturer's terms of sale encourage other channel members to purchase larger quantities less frequently. Figure 3–10 illustrates this concept. The supplier's variable product costs are

TABLE 3–8 Qualitative Measures of Channel Performance

1. Degree of channel coordination
2. Degree of cooperation
3. Degree of conflict
4. Degree of domain consensus (role prescription and variation)
5. Recognition of superordinate goals
6. Degree of development of channel leadership
7. Degree of functional duplication
8. Degree of commitment to channel
9. Degree of power locus development
10. Degree of flexibility in functional shiftability
11. Availability of information about:
    - *a.* Physical inventory
    - *b.* Product characteristics
    - *c.* Pricing structure
    - *d.* Promotional data
        - (1) Personal selling assistance
        - (2) Advertising
        - (3) Point-of-purchase displays
        - (4) Special promotions
    - *e.* Market conditions
    - *f.* Services available
    - *g.* Organizational changes
12. Assimilation of new technology
13. Innovation in distribution generated within the channel
14. Extent of intrabrand competition
15. Extent of routinization of channel tasks
16. Extent of use of optimal inventory standards
17. Relations with trade associations
18. Relations with consumer groups

SOURCE: Adapted from Adel I. El-Ansary, "A Model for Evaluating Channel Performance," unpublished paper, Louisiana State University, 1975, pp. 10–11; reported in Douglas M. Lambert, *The Distribution Channels Decision* (New York: National Association of Accountants, and Hamilton, Ontario: The Society of Management Accountants of Canada, 1978), p. 41. Reprinted with permission.

\$5, but the manufacturer's are \$11. The manufacturer's variable manufactured cost—that is, out-of-pocket cash invested in inventory—is \$25, but the wholesaler's investment is \$62. Similarly, the retailer's cost is \$82. Financial ratios will be different when a manufacturer holds an account receivable rather than inventory. However, minimal additional out-of-pocket costs are incurred, and the non-cost-of-money components of inventory carrying costs are shifted.

Inventory Location Affects Total Channel Costs

Location of inventory within the channel of distribution affects total channel costs and customer service significantly. Generally, the closer to the consumer the product is held, the higher the inventory carrying cost. If extending the terms of sale encourages other channel members to purchase larger quantities or accept a longer order cycle, or if increased sales result from the higher service levels, the entire channel of distribution may be more profitable. Firms that respond to a market's challenges with innovative new strategies reap the rewards.

In addition to rethinking traditional strategies for improving cash flow and return on assets, channel leaders may wish to consider automating and integrating the order processing and information systems within the channel. This can reduce lead time variability and create time for planning. The latest communications technology offers a unique opportunity for improv-

FIGURE 3–9 Cost Trade-Offs Required in a Logistics System

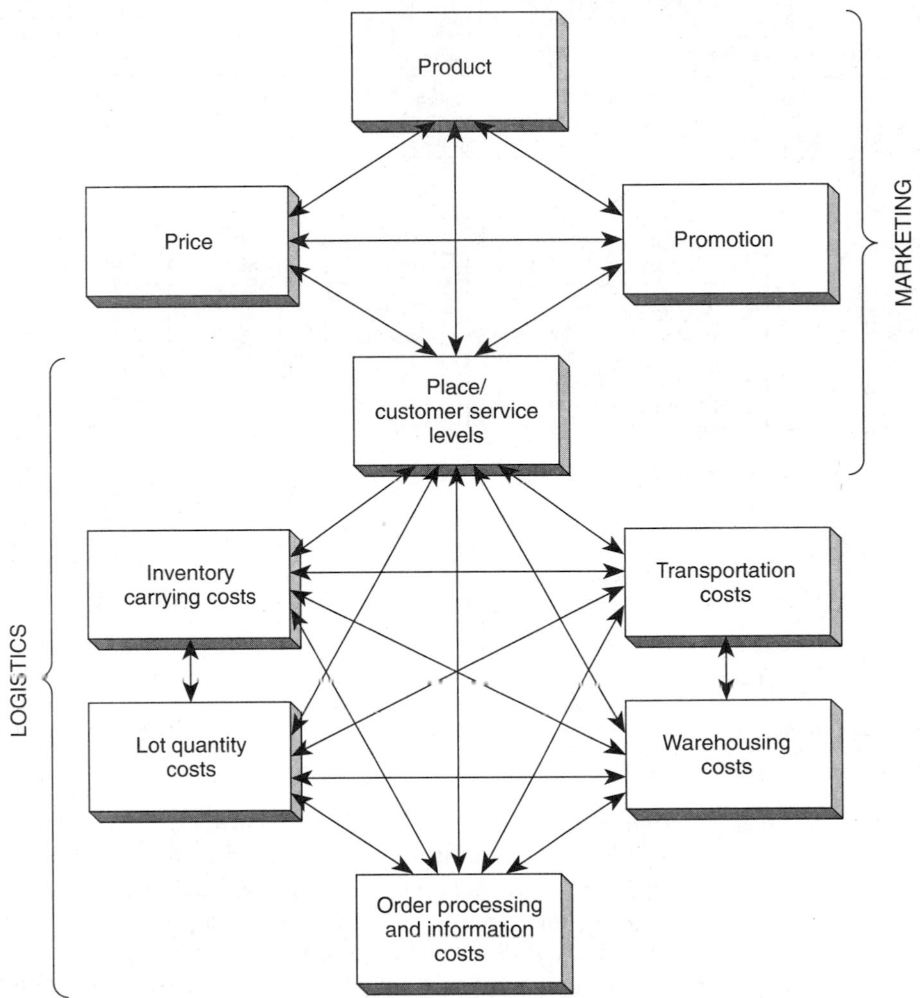

Marketing objective: Allocate resources to the marketing mix to maximize the long-run profitability of the firm.
Logistics objective: Minimize total costs given the customer service objective where: total costs = Transportation costs + Warehousing costs + Order processing and information costs + Lot quantity costs + Inventory carrying costs.

SOURCE: Adapted from Douglas M. Lambert, *The Development of an Inventory Costing Methodology: A Study of the Costs Associated with Holding Inventory* (Chicago: National Council of Physical Distribution Management, 1976), p. 7.

FIGURE 3–10 Inventory Positions and Major Flows in a Channel of Distribution

Suppliers — Manufacturer — Wholesalers — Retailers

Orders, Payments (flow from retailers back toward suppliers); Information (two-way); Product (flow from suppliers toward retailers)

Suppliers		Manufacturer		Wholesalers		Retailers	
Variable cost of product	$5	Variable cost of material	$10	Variable cost of product	$60	Variable cost of product	$80
Full manufactured cost	$7	Acquisition costs	$1	Other acquisition costs	$2	Other acquisition costs	$2
Selling price	$10	Other variable costs	$14	Selling price	$80	Selling price	$150
		Total variable cost of product	$25				
		Full manufactured cost	$40				
		Selling price	$60				

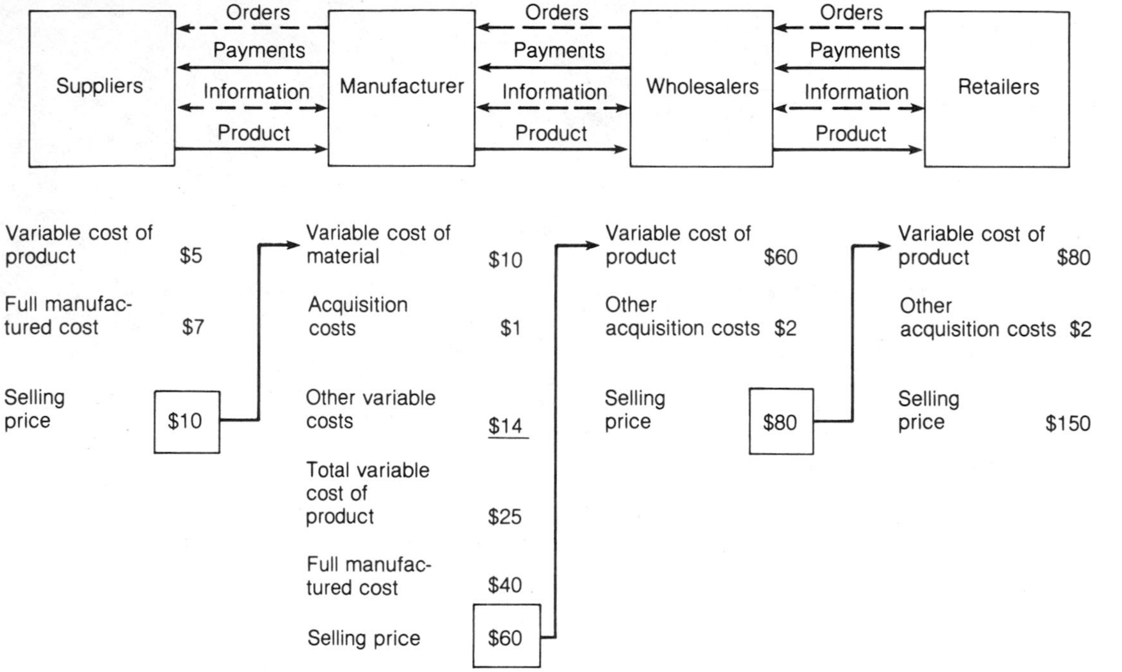

SOURCE: Douglas M. Lambert and Mark L. Bennion, "New Channel Strategies for the 1980's," in *Marketing Channels: Domestic and International Perspectives,* ed. Michael G. Harvey and Robert F. Lusch (Norman: Center for Economic and Management Research, School of Business Administration, University of Oklahoma, 1982), p. 127.

ing the efficiency and effectiveness of the channel of distribution. If communications flows throughout the channel are improved, all members will be able to reduce inventories while improving customer service. In addition, the planning time that results will allow freight consolidations, warehousing cost savings, and lower lot quantity costs. We will cover the benefits of automated order processing and information systems in detail in subsequent chapters.

Usually, increased customer service levels create increased expenses, and sales must increase just to break even on the service improvement. However, by improving communications, customer service levels can be improved and total operating costs reduced—truly a unique opportunity.

While many firms have achieved significant success implementing the integrated logistics management concept within their own organizations, the next level of integration, extending the integrated logistics concept across the channel offers the greatest potential.

> Logic will tell you that this focus on optimizing the entire channel has to yield better performance than the sum of optimized parts. It does not make economic sense for a manufacturer and distributor to duplicate inventory in warehouses next to each other. If they jointly manage it, they have to be able to

achieve better performance. Similarly, if a supplier and a manufacturer jointly manage transportation to take advantage of backhauls and reduce empty miles, they will both be better off. Also, if a manufacturer can gain insight into the actual sales rate at the end of the channel (at the retailer) and obtain information on pipeline inventories as well, he has to be able to do a better job of forecasting and production planning.[38]

Procter & Gamble Company known for years as perhaps the best example of a "power marketer" (large expenditures to develop consumer pull for its products) has more recently focused considerable attention on building channel partnerships with key customers. For example, in an effort to build linkages with Wal-Mart, Procter & Gamble Company (P&G) sent a 12 person task force to Bentonville, Arkansas, to develop a joint strategy. The results are remarkable support for the benefits of integrating logistics into the firm's marketing strategy as well as the benefits of integrated channel management: "P&G now receives daily data by satellite on Wal-Mart's Pampers sales and forecasts and ships orders automatically. As a result, Wal-Mart can maintain smaller inventories and still cut the number of times it runs out of Pampers. And P&G has gone from a vendor that was maybe the least desirable to deal with to the most desirable to deal with," says a now-retired former president of Wal-Mart. The results have been astonishing. Procter's volume at Wal-Mart grew by more than 40%, or by more than $200 million.[39]

Supply Chain Management

Quick Response

Although a number of terms have been used to describe channel integration including pipeline management, supply chain management, intercorporate logistics, the total systems approach and quick response, supply chain management is typically the preferred term in manufacturing and quick response is the term of choice in retailing. "Quick Response seeks to maximize customer satisfaction by having the right inventory in the right place at the right time, without incurring the expenses associated with excess inventory. To maintain this balance, information on supply and demand needs to be available in real time."[40]

Many Quick Response programs only link the manufacturer and the retailer, but in the apparel industry linkages extend from the retail store to the apparel manufacturer to the fabric manufacturer to the fiber producer. Implementation of Quick Response had reduced the traditional nine month fashion cycle to six weeks and the goal is to further reduce the cycle to two weeks.[41] Channel integration strategies will be discussed further in Chapters 13 and 18.

[38] William C. Copacino and Frank F. Britt, "Perspectives on Global Logistics," *The International Journal of Logistics Management,* Vol. 2, No. 1, 1991, p. 38.

[39] Sachary Schiller, "Stalking the New Consumer," *Business Week,* 28 August 1989, 62.

[40] "QR Requires Streamlined Data Collection Methods," *Chain Store Age Executive,* September, 1990, p. 80.

[41] "Quick Response in The Apparel Industry," Harvard Business School, 1990, 18p.

SUMMARY

In this chapter we saw (1) that the distribution channel plays an integral part in a firm's marketing strategy; (2) the types of channel structures that are used; (3) the factors that influence channel design, evolution, and performance; and (4) how communications can improve the efficiency and effectiveness of distribution channels. Now that we have established the necessary background, we will discuss the major logistics activities in depth, beginning with customer service, the subject of Chapter 4.

SUGGESTED READINGS

Bowersox, Donald J., M. Bixby Cooper, Douglas M. Lambert, and Donald A. Taylor. *Management in Marketing Channels.* New York: McGraw-Hill, 1980.

Bucklin, Louis P. *A Theory of Distribution Channel Structure.* Berkeley: Institute of Business and Economic Research, University of California, 1966.

Ellram, Lisa M. "Supply Chain Management: The Industrial Organization Perspective." *International Journal of Physical Distribution and Logistics Management* 21, no. 1 (1991), pp. 13–22.

Ellram, Lisa M., and Martha C. Cooper, "Supply Chain Management, Partnerships , and the Shipper-Third Party Relationship," *The International Journal of Logistics Management* 1, no. 2 (1990), pp. 1–10.

Hlavacek, James D., and Tommy J. McCuistion. "Industrial Distributors—When, Who and How?" *Harvard Business Review* 61, no. 2 (March–April 1983), pp. 96–101.

Horscroft, Peter, and Alan Braithwaite. "Enhancing Supply Chain Efficiency: The Strategic Lead Time Approach." *The International Journal of Logistics Management* 1, no. 2 (1990), pp. 47–52.

Kelly, Kevin. "A Bean-Counter's Best Friend." *Business Week*/Quality, 1991, pp. 42–43.

Lambert, Douglas M. *The Distribution Channels Decision.* New York: National Association of Accountants, and Hamilton, Ontario: The Society of Management Accountants of Canada, 1978.

Mallen, Bruce. "Functional Spin-Off: A Key to Anticipating Change in Distribution Structure." *Journal of Marketing* 37, no. 3 (July 1973), pp. 18–25.

Mallen, Bruce. *Principles of Marketing Channel Management.* Lexington, Mass.: Lexington Books, 1977.

Stern, Louis W., and Adel I. El-Ansary. *Marketing Channels,* 2nd ed. Englewood Cliffs, N.J.: Prentice Hall, 1982.

QUESTIONS AND PROBLEMS

1. Why do channels of distribution develop?
2. In this chapter, we discussed the responses of businesspeople to the question, "How was your current channel structure determined?" Would you have anticipated the responses given? Explain.
3. Give an example of (*a*) a firm that uses postponement and (*b*) a firm that uses speculation in the channel of distribution.
4. Explain the concept of structural separation and its implications for channel design.
5. What is meant by intensive, exclusive, and selective distribution? Give examples illustrating when each of these forms of distribution would be an acceptable strategy.
6. Explain how product characteristics influence channel design.
7. How can communications technology be used to improve channel efficiency and effectiveness?

Chapter 4

Customer Service

Objectives of This Chapter

To define customer service

To show the importance of the customer service function to a firm's marketing and logistics efforts

To show how to calculate cost/revenue trade-offs

To show how to conduct a customer service audit

To identify opportunities for improving customer service performance

INTRODUCTION

Customer service represents the output of the logistics system and the place component of the firm's marketing mix. It is a measure of the effectiveness of the logistics system in creating time and place utility for a product. The level of customer service not only determines whether existing customers will remain customers, but how many potential customers will become customers. Thus the customer service level a firm provides has a direct impact on its market share;[1] its total logistics costs; and ultimately, its profitability. For this reason, it is imperative that customer service be an integral part of the design and operation of any logistics system.

WHAT IS CUSTOMER SERVICE?

The meaning of *customer service* varies from one company to the next. Furthermore, vendors and their customers often view the concept quite differently. In broad terms, customer service can be considered the measure of how well the logistics system is performing in creating time and place utility for a product, including postsale support.

Customer Service Is Defined Three Ways

In most corporations customer service is defined in one of three ways: as an *activity* that has to be managed, such as order processing, invoicing, or handling customer complaints; as *performance measures,* such as the ability to ship 95 percent of the orders received complete within 48 hours; or, as an element in the total *corporate philosophy* rather than as an activity or a set of performance measures.[2]

---

[1]The relationship between customer service and market share has been documented in Jay U. Sterling, "Integrating Customer Service and Marketing Strategies in a Channel of Distribution: An Empirical Study," unpublished Ph.D. dissertation, Michigan State University, 1985.

[2]Bernard J. LaLonde and Paul H. Zinszer, *Customer Service: Meaning and Measurement* (Chicago: National Council of Physical Distribution Management, 1976), pp. 156–59.

Definitions of Customer Service

In a landmark study of customer service, corporate executives were asked to define customer service as it applied to logistics in their companies.[3] The following responses were typical:

Activity Related. "Order entry, tracing, proof of delivery, invoicing, order processing, broker contact."—Food manufacturer.

"All of the activities required to accept, process, deliver and bill customer orders and to follow up on any activity that erred."—Chemicals and plastics manufacturer.

Performance Related. "Make shipments to customers of product ordered within 10 days of receipt of order."—Food manufacturer.

"Percent of orders received and processed in 48 hours with no back orders."—Pharmaceuticals manufacturer.

Corporate Philosophy Related. "A complex of activities involving all areas of the business which combine to deliver and invoice the company's products in a fashion that is perceived as satisfactory by the customer and which advance our company's objectives."—Food manufacturer.

A more recent definition views customer service

> . . . as a process which takes place between buyer, seller, and third party. The process results in a value added to the product or service exchanged. This value added in the exchange process might be short term as in a single transaction or longer term as in a contractual relationship. The value added is also shared, in that each of the parties to the transaction or contract are better off at the completion of the transaction than they were before the transaction took place. Thus, in a process view: Customer service is a process for providing significant value-added benefits to the supply chain in a cost effective way.[4]

Customer Service Can Impact Demand

Successful implementation of the marketing concept requires both obtaining customers and keeping them, while satisfying the firm's long-range profit and return on investment objectives. Creating demand—obtaining customers—is often thought of solely in terms of promotion (selling and advertising), product, and price, but customer service can have a significant impact on demand.[5] In addition, customer service determines whether customers will remain customers.

---

[3] The responses listed are drawn from LaLonde and Zinszer, *Customer Service,* pp. 203–17.

[4] Bernard J. LaLonde, Martha C. Cooper, and Thomas G. Noordewier, *Customer Service: A Management Perspective* (Chicago: Council of Logistics Management, 1988), p. 5.

[5] Jay U. Sterling and Douglas M. Lambert, "Establishing Customer Service Strategies Within the Marketing Mix," *Journal of Business Logistics* 8, no. 1 (1987), pp. 1–30.

Elements of Customer Service

A number of elements are commonly associated with customer service, although the degree of importance attached to any of them varies from company to company depending on customer needs. For example, Peter Gilmour developed the following list of customer service elements:

1. *Availability of item* represents the ability of the supplier to satisfy customers' orders within a time limit generally accepted by the industry for the particular item (e.g., a chemical from stock; an expensive piece of equipment in six weeks).
2. *After-sales service and backup* includes speedy and ready replacement of defective or damaged items; commissioning of equipment if the customer experiences difficulties; subsequent follow-up to ascertain if user is happy with the purchase.
3. *Efficient telephone handling of orders and queries* includes the availability of personnel within the organization who can be quickly accessed for intelligent handling of customer queries, whether of a technical nature or about availability, price, or status of an earlier order. It also includes the training of operator/receptionist to immediately recognize the right contact to best handle the customer's call.
4. *Order convenience* represents the efficiency, accuracy, and simplicity of paperwork necessary to conform to legal requirements and interface with the firm's and the customer's business systems.
5. *Competent technical representatives* involves training, background knowledge, and the presentation of representatives calling on customers.
6. *Delivery time* is the elapsed time for the normal ordering procedure between receipt by the supplier of a firm commitment for an order and receipt of the goods by the customer. Naturally only ex-stock items are included here.
7. *Reliability* means the supplier's commitment to maintain a promised delivery schedule and to advise customers if such deliveries subsequently cannot be made on time.
8. *Demonstration of equipment* represents willingness of the supplier to allow a prospective customer to examine a particular piece of equipment on his own premises prior to signing a purchase contract. Also includes the willingness and competence of the supplier's staff to demonstrate equipment without any purchase commitment.
9. *Availability of published material.*[6]

---

[6] Peter Gilmour, "Customer Service: Differentiating by Marketing Segment," *International Journal of Physical Distribution and Materials Management* 7, no. 3 (1977), p. 145.

Three Groups of Customer Service Elements

Bernard J. LaLonde and Paul Zinszer categorized the elements of customer service into three groups—pretransaction, transaction, and post-transaction.[7] Figure 4-1 summarizes the customer service elements identified by LaLonde and Zinszer.

Pretransaction Elements. The pretransaction elements of customer service tend to be nonroutine and policy related, and they require management input. These activities, although not specifically involved with logistics, have a significant impact on product sales. The specific elements of pretransaction customer service include the following:

1. *A written statement of customer service policy.* The customer service policy statement would be based on customer needs, define service standards, determine who reports the performance measurements to whom and with what frequency, and be operational.
2. *Provide customers with a written statement of service policy.* It makes little sense to provide a level of service designed to improve market penetration and then fail to inform the customer of what is being provided. A written statement reduces the likelihood that the customer will have unrealistic expectations of performance. It also provides the customer with information on how to communicate with the firm if specified performance levels are not attained.
3. *Organization structure.* Although there is no organization structure best suited to successful implementation of a customer service policy, the structure selected should facilitate communication and cooperation between and among those functions involved in implementing the customer service policy. In addition, the firm should provide customers with the name and phone number of a specific individual who can satisfy their need for information. The individuals who manage the customer service components must have the appropriate responsibility and authority, and must be rewarded in a manner that encourages them to interface with other corporate functions.

Achieving Customer Service Objectives Should Be a High-Level Responsibility

4. *System flexibility.* Flexibility is required for the system to effectively respond to unplanned events, such as snowstorms, shortages of raw materials or energy, and strikes.
5. *Management services.* Training manuals and seminars designed to help the customer improve inventory management, ordering, or merchandising are elements of customer service.

All of the above pretransaction elements of customer service are essential components of a successful marketing strategy.

[7] LaLonde and Zinszer, *Customer Service*, pp. 272–82.

FIGURE 4–1 Elements of Customer Service

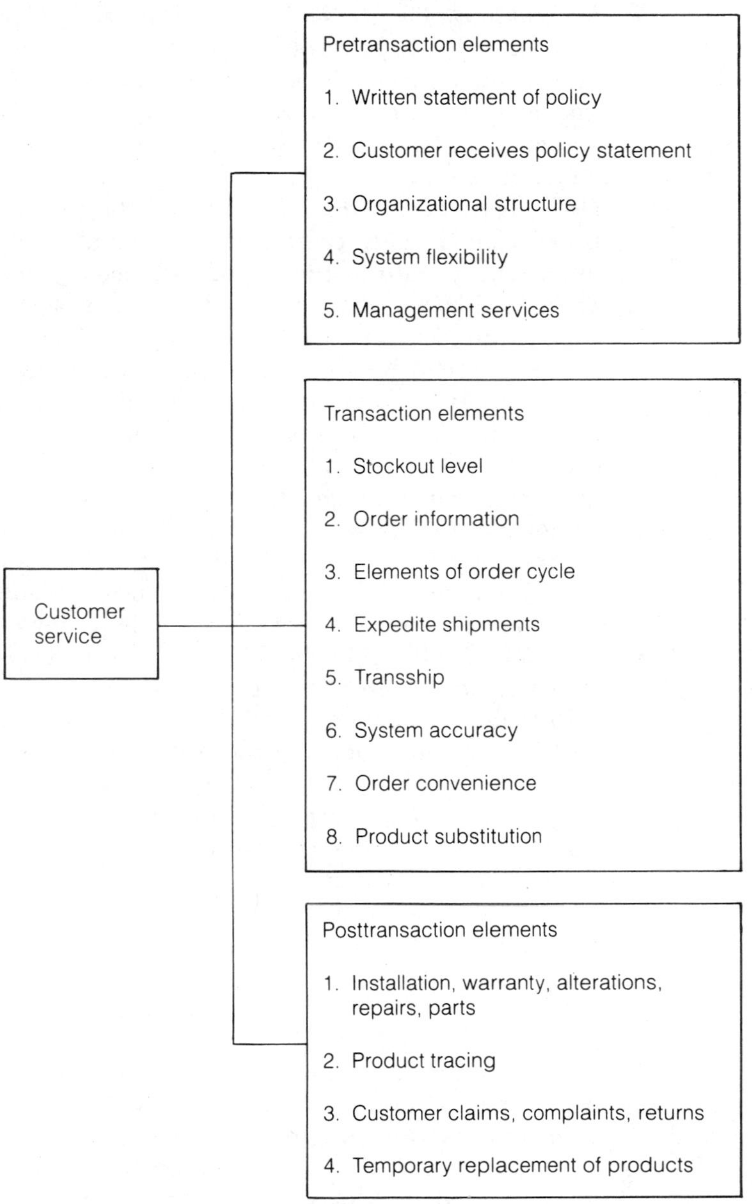

SOURCE: Bernard J. LaLonde and Paul H. Zinszer, *Customer Service: Meaning and Measurement* (Chicago: National Council of Physical Distribution Management, 1976), p. 281.

Transaction Elements. Transaction elements are the activities normally associated with customer service, including the following:

1. *Stockout level.* The stockout level is a measure of product availability. Stockouts should be recorded by product and by customer in order to determine where problems exist. When stockouts occur, customer goodwill can be maintained by arranging for suitable product substitution and/or expediting the shipment when the product is received in stock.
2. *Order information.* Order information is the ability to provide the customer with fast and accurate information about such considerations as inventory status, order status, expected shipping and delivery dates, and back-order status. A back-order capability allows orders that require immediate attention to be identified and expedited. The number of back orders and their associated order cycle times can be used to measure system performance. The ability to back order is important because the alternative may be to force a stockout. The number of back-orders should be recorded by customer and by product categories to identify and correct poor system performance.

The Order Cycle Defined

3. *Elements of the order cycle.* The order cycle is the total elapsed time from initiation of the order by the customer until delivery to the customer. Individual components of the order cycle include order communication, order entry, order processing, order picking and packing, and delivery. Because customers are mainly concerned with total order cycle time, it is important to monitor and manage each of the components of the order cycle to determine the cause of variations.
4. *Expedite shipments.* Expedited shipments are those that receive special handling in order to reduce the normal order cycle time. Although expediting costs considerably more than standard handling, the cost of a lost customer may be even higher. It is important for management to determine which customers qualify for expedited shipments and which do not. Presumably, such a policy would be based on how much individual customers contribute to the manufacturer's profitability.
5. *Transshipments.* Transshipments are the transporting of product between field locations to avoid stockouts. They are often made in anticipation of customer demand.
6. *System accuracy.* Mistakes in system accuracy—the accuracy of quantities ordered, products ordered, and billing—are costly to both manufacturer and the customer. Errors should be recorded and reported as a percentage of the number of orders handled by the system.
7. *Order convenience.* Order convenience refers to the degree of difficulty that a customer experiences when placing an order. Problems

FIGURE 4–2 Impact of Substitution on Service Level

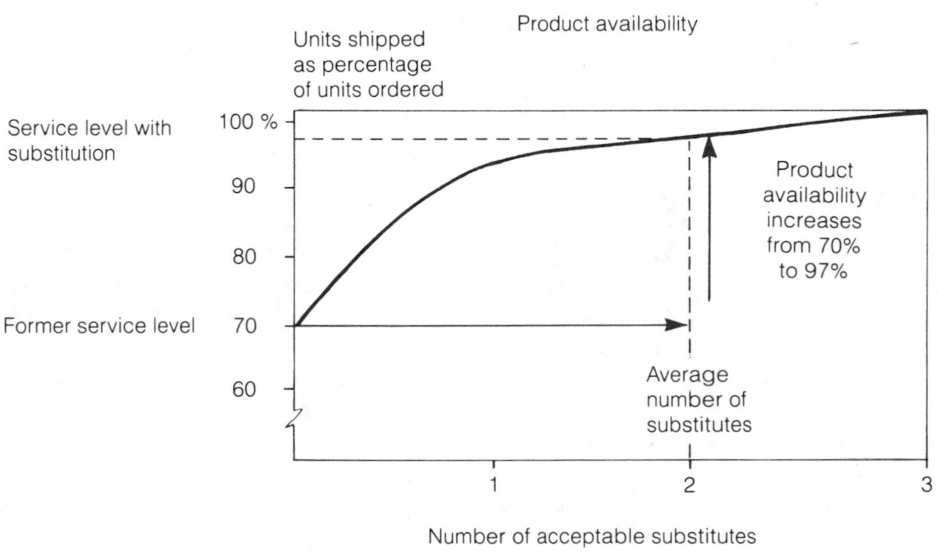

may result from confusing order forms or using nonstandard terminology; both can lead to errors and poor customer relations. An appropriate performance measurement is the number of errors as a percentage of the number of orders. These problems can be identified and reduced or eliminated by conducting field interviews with customers.

Substitution Can Improve Customer Service

8. *Product substitution.* Substitution occurs when the product ordered is replaced by the same item in a different size or with another product that will perform as well or better. For example, a customer may order a case of Ivory shampoo for normal hair in 15-ounce bottles. If the customer is willing to accept 8-ounce bottles or 20-ounce bottles during a stockout, the manufacturer can increase the customer service level as measured by product availability within some specified time period. Two product substitutions allow the manufacturer to increase the customer service level from 70 percent to 97 percent with no change in inventory (see Figure 4–2). If the firm attained a 97 percent customer service level without product substitution, two product substitutions would enable it to maintain the same service level with a 28 percent reduction in inventory.

   In order to develop an appropriate product substitution policy, the manufacturer should work closely with customers to inform them or gain their consent. It should also keep product substitution records to monitor performance. A successful product substitution program requires good communication between the manufacturer and customers.

The transaction elements of customer service are the most visible because of the direct impact they have on sales.

Posttransaction Elements. The posttransaction elements of customer service support the product after it has been sold. The specific posttransaction elements include:

1. *Installation, warranty, alterations, repairs, parts.* These elements of customer service can be a significant factor in the decision to purchase; they should be evaluated in a manner similar to the transaction elements. To perform these functions, the following are necessary: (1) assistance in seeing that the product is functioning as expected when the consumer begins using it; (2) availability of parts and/or repairmen; (3) documentation support for the field force to assist in performing their jobs, as well as accessibility to a supply of parts; and (4) an administrative function that validates warranties.[8]
2. *Product tracing.* Product tracing is another necessary component of customer service. In order to avoid litigation, firms must be able to recall potentially dangerous products from the marketplace as soon as problems are identified.

Reverse Logistics

3. *Customer claims, complaints, and returns.* Usually, logistics systems are designed to move products in one direction—toward the customer. Nevertheless, almost every manufacturer has some goods returned, and the nonroutine handling of these items is expensive. A corporate policy should specify how to handle claims, complaints, and returns. The company should maintain data on claims, complaints, and returns in order to provide valuable consumer information to product development, marketing, logistics, and other corporate functions.
4. *Product replacement.* Temporary placement of product with customers waiting for receipt of a purchased item or waiting for a previously purchased product to be repaired is an element of customer service.

METHODS OF ESTABLISHING A CUSTOMER SERVICE STRATEGY

Poor Service Negates Marketing Programs

A firm's entire marketing effort can be rendered ineffective by poorly conceived customer service policies. Yet customer service is often a forgotten component of the marketing mix, and the level of customer service is often based on industry norms, management judgment, or past practices—not on what the customer wants, or what would maximize corporate profit-

[8] LaLonde and Zinszer, *Customer Service,* p. 278.

ability.[9] What is the advantage of having a well-researched and needed product, priced to sell and promoted well, if customers cannot find it on the shelf at the retail level? However, *too much* customer service will needlessly reduce corporate profits. It is essential that a firm adopt a customer service policy that is based on customer needs, is consistent with overall marketing strategy, and advances the corporation's long-range profit objectives.

Four Methods of Developing a Customer Service Strategy

A number of methods have been proposed to aid in establishing a profitable customer service strategy. But the following four methods have the most merit: (1) determining channel service levels based on knowledge of consumer reactions to stockouts; (2) cost/revenue trade-offs; (3) ABC analysis of customer service; and (4) the customer service audit.

Consumer Reactions to Stockouts

In consumer goods companies, customer service levels are measured between the manufacturer and its intermediaries. These measures exclude the consumer—the person who purchases the product at the retail level. However, a stockout at the manufacturer-wholesaler interface does not always result in the wholesaler's stocking out the retail accounts it services—depending on the amount of safety stock the wholesaler carries. The retailer's inventories also may prevent the consumer from facing a stockout at that level.

One way to establish the level of customer service that should be provided to wholesalers and retailers is to determine what the consumer is likely to do in the event of a stockout. Figure 4–3 illustrates consumers' possible reactions when they are faced with a stockout at the retail level. For example, a consumer enters a retail store to purchase Ivory shampoo for normal hair in a 15-ounce bottle. If the item is unavailable, the customer can go to another store to purchase the product. Such inconvenience may not be worth it for a bottle of shampoo, but there are a number of products for which customers are willing to switch stores.[10]

For Some Products Consumers Are Willing to Switch Stores

Most manufacturers of infant formula do not advertise their products to consumers in national media. They spend the bulk of their advertising dollars giving the product to hospitals and doctors who, in turn, give it to new mothers. Because of the high perceived risk associated with the purchase of a nutritional product for a baby, the mother will request the brand given to her by the doctor or used while she and the baby were at the hospital.[11] Although the two leading brands of products may have identical ingredients, the consumer would rather switch stores than switch brands.

---

[9] Harvey M. Shycon and Christopher R. Sprague, "Put a Price Tag on Your Customer Service Levels," *Harvard Business Review* 53, no. 4 (July-August 1975), pp. 71–78.

[10] Consumers may be quite willing to switch stores for a shampoo with special properties. For example, it may be the only shampoo that will solve a person's dandruff problem.

[11] In fact, many doctors further reduce the likelihood of brand switching by telling the mother not to switch the brand of formula.

FIGURE 4–3 Model of Consumer Reaction to a Repeated Stockout

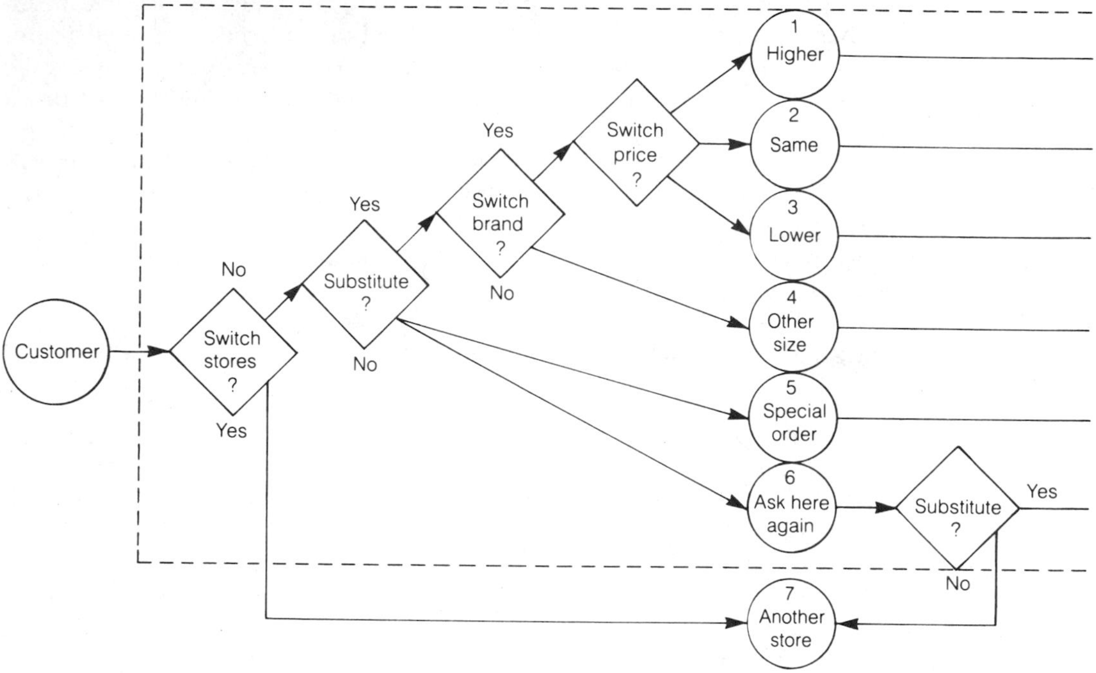

SOURCE: Clyde K. Walter, "An Empirical Analysis of Two Stockout Models," unpublished Ph.D. dissertation, Ohio State University, 1971.

This information is critical when formulating a customer service strategy. While the penalty for stocking out the retailer may be very low, the manufacturer will incur a high cost if it stocks out a doctor or a hospital. If a service failure causes a doctor to switch from Ross Laboratories' product, Similac, to Mead Johnson's product, Enfamil, Ross Laboratories will lose the business of all future mothers that doctor treats. Similarly, if a hospital stops stocking a brand as a result of poor product availability or any other problem with customer service, the firm will lose future contributions to profit from mothers who give birth at that hospital and use an infant formula. While it may be difficult to determine the exact cost of losing the business of a doctor or hospital, the customer service implications are clear. Hospitals and doctors require a high level of customer service, which may include lead times of 48 hours and 99 percent in-stock availability.

Retailers, on the other hand, will most likely lose the sale if they experience a stockout on Similac. Since retail management must be conscious of how its store is positioned compared to competitors, it must be concerned about the frequency of stockouts on items for which consumers are willing to switch stores. Frequent stockouts on such items could cause consumers to permanently switch their shopping loyalties to another store.[12] With this information, the manufacturer could set a longer order cycle for retailers, but use the additional time to reduce variability in lead times and provide high levels of in-stock availability. While the retailers would be required to adjust to longer lead times, the greater stability and high levels of in-stock availability would enable them to satisfy their customers without maintaining excessive inventories.

In Most Stockout Situations Consumers Will Not Switch Stores

In most stockout situations, consumers are not willing to accept the inconvenience of switching retail outlets. This brings us to the second decision point in Figure 4–3, substitution. At this point, the consumer must decide if substitution is acceptable. The consumer who wanted to purchase Ivory shampoo may be willing to postpone the purchase until the next shopping trip if he or she still has some shampoo left at home. If not, the consumer may substitute another brand. It is unlikely that consumers would place special orders for products like shampoo.

Whirlpool and Sears Study Consumer Needs

For some items, however, the majority of consumers are willing and may even expect to place a special order. In the early 1970s, Whirlpool and Sears, in a study of consumer purchase behavior, found that the majority of consumers did not expect to take delivery of major appliances the same day. In fact, most consumers were willing to wait from five to seven days for delivery. This study had significant implications for the companies' logistical systems. First, only floor models of appliances were necessary at the retail level. Second, retail distribution centers needed to carry only fast-moving standard items.

All other products were manufactured and/or shipped from the manufacturer's mixing warehouse only when the manufacturer received orders from retailers. Once manufactured, the product was shipped to the manufacturer's mixing warehouse, from there to a Sears distribution center, and from the distribution center to the consumer. All of this took place within the required five to seven days.

Implementation of this system substantially reduced system-wide inventories without sacrificing the necessary customer service. Sears no longer had to predict the color, size, and features desired by consumers at each retail outlet. By 1984 the system had undergone a number of refinements, and in major U.S. markets, Sears customers received 48- to 72-hour delivery on Kenmore appliances. In addition, Sears established similar programs with vendors of other products. While this type of system may not be possible for all consumer products, it illustrates how consumer research can be used to establish customer service strategy.

---

[12] A study of 7,189 shoppers found that those experiencing stockouts left the store with a lower image of the store and less satisfaction and purchase intentions. See Paul H. Zinszer and Jack A. Lesser, "An Empirical Evaluation of the Role of Stockout on Shopper Patronage Process," *1980 Educators' Conference Proceedings* (Chicago: American Marketing Association, 1980), pp. 221–24.

Usually, consumers will switch stores when they experience a stockout on an item with a high level of brand preference. But for other products, consumers will substitute size or brand. Figure 4–2 showed how customer service levels could be increased from 70 percent to 97 percent with no corresponding increase in inventories if customers were willing to accept two product substitutions. When this is the case, customer service levels should not be measured based on each stock-keeping unit (such as the 15-ounce bottle of Ivory shampoo for normal hair), but on all units of that product (all sizes of Ivory shampoo for normal hair).[13]

Increasingly, Consumers Are Willing to Switch Brands when Faced with a Stockout

The final option for consumers who face a retail stockout is to switch brands. They may switch to a same-price, higher-price, or lower-price brand. When substitution takes place, the retailer does not lose a sale. Depending on the substitution strategy the consumer employs, the seller may not experience any negative impact on either sales or profits; for instance, the consumer may substitute an item that sells for a higher price or may buy one national brand instead of another. If the manufacturer knows that consumers are willing to substitute size, it should use this information to convince retailers and wholesalers that they too should accept these substitutes.[14]

If brand switching takes place, however, the manufacturer definitely loses at least the contribution to profit from this one purchase. By stocking out and putting the consumer in the position of switching brands, the manufacturer is allowing the competitor to conduct product sampling and receive compensation for it. In addition, the substituted brand may become the consumer's first choice in the future. If this happens, the manufacturer loses the present value of all future contributions to profit that it would have realized had the consumer not changed his or her purchase behavior. These amounts are difficult, or impossible, to determine.[15]

Cost/Revenue Trade-Offs

The sum of the expenditures for such logistics activities as transportation, warehousing, order processing and information systems, production setups and purchasing, and inventory management can be viewed as the company's expenditure for customer service. Figure 4–4 illustrates the cost trade-offs required to implement an integrated logistics management con-

---

[13] Stock-keeping units are individual units of product that differ from others in shape, size, color, or some other characteristic.

[14] For a review of the literature on consumer response to stockouts as well as a proposed research methodology, see W. E. Miklas, "Measuring Customer Response to Stockouts," *International Journal of Physical Distribution and Materials Management* 9, no. 5 (1979), pp. 213–42.

[15] For an example of how 1,182 consumers responded when faced with stockouts of products they had intended to buy, see Larry W. Emmelhainz, James R. Stock, and Margaret A. Emmelhainz, "Retail Stockouts: Now What?" *Annual Conference Proceedings* (Oak Brook, Ill.: Council of Logistics Management, 1989), pp. 71–79.

FIGURE 4–4 Cost Trade-Offs Required in a Logistics System

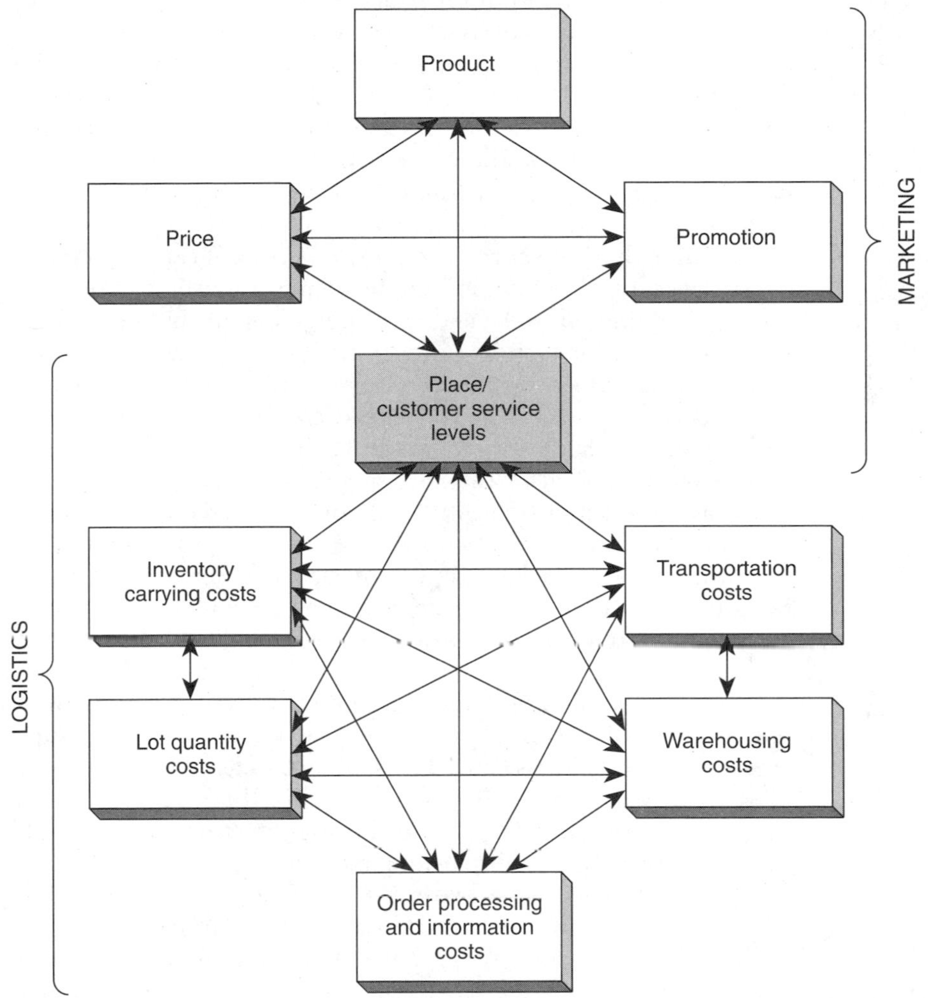

Marketing objective: Allocate resources to the marketing mix to maximize the long-run profitability of the firm.
Logistics objective: Minimize total costs given the customer service objective where: Total costs = Transportation costs + Warehousing costs + Order processing and information costs + Lot quantity costs + Inventory carrying costs.

SOURCE: Adapted from Douglas M. Lambert, *The Development of an Inventory Costing Methodology: A Study of the Costs Associated with Holding Inventory* (Chicago: National Council of Physical Distribution Management, 1976), p. 7.

cept. In order to achieve least-cost logistics, management must minimize total logistics costs, given a specified level of customer service. Consequently, the costs associated with improving the level of service can be compared to the increase in sales required to recover the additional costs. For example, a company is currently offering a 95 percent customer service level—by its own measures—at least total cost. If sales management insists that service levels be increased to 98 percent to achieve the company's market-penetration objectives, the cost of the most efficient logistics method can be calculated for the new service objective and compared to the current cost.

What Increase in Sales Volume Is Required to Break Even on the Customer Service Improvement?

Assume that the cost of the most efficient logistics system for a 98 percent service goal is $2 million higher than the existing system's cost. If each dollar of additional sales yields a 25 percent contribution to fixed costs and profit—that is, for each $1 in revenue, the company incurs 75 cents in out-of-pocket manufacturing, marketing, and logistics costs—what additional sales volume will the company need to recover the increase in logistics costs? We can calculate the point at which the company breaks even on the service improvement by dividing the $2 million increase in costs by the 25 percent contribution margin. The company needs a sales increase of $8 million per year. We can estimate the likelihood that this will occur by determining what $8 million represents as a percentage increase in sales. A 2 percent increase in sales volume might be viewed as likely, whereas a 20 percent sales increase might be considered unlikely, given the competitive situation.

Another method of determining the cost/revenue implications of alternative levels of customer service is to take advantage of unplanned decreases in service levels caused by such events as strikes, snowstorms, shortages, or products failing quality inspection. "Before," "during," and "after" measures of retail sales provide the manufacturer with valuable insights into the impact of various customer service levels on retail sales.

It Is Also Important to Determine How Intermediaries React to Service Failures

Although the manufacturer's ultimate goal should be to provide needed products to the ultimate consumer, manufacturers rarely engage in direct transactions with consumers. Usually manufacturers reach consumers through intermediaries such as wholesalers and retailers. For this reason, it is important to determine how retailers or wholesalers will react to service failures. In case studies of six wholesaling institutions, all with annual sales exceeding $500 million, Marcus Bennion found that a number of short-run and long-run reactions were possible when buyers encountered a stockout (see Figure 4–5).[16] In order to evaluate the costs and benefits of various service policies, the manufacturer must determine its customers' reactions.

[16] Marcus Lyndsay Bennion, "An Investigation of Wholesale Buyer Reaction to Manufacturer Customer Service Failures in the Grocery Channel," unpublished Ph.D. dissertation, Michigan State University, 1980.

FIGURE 4–5 Generalized Model of Reactions to Customer Service Failures

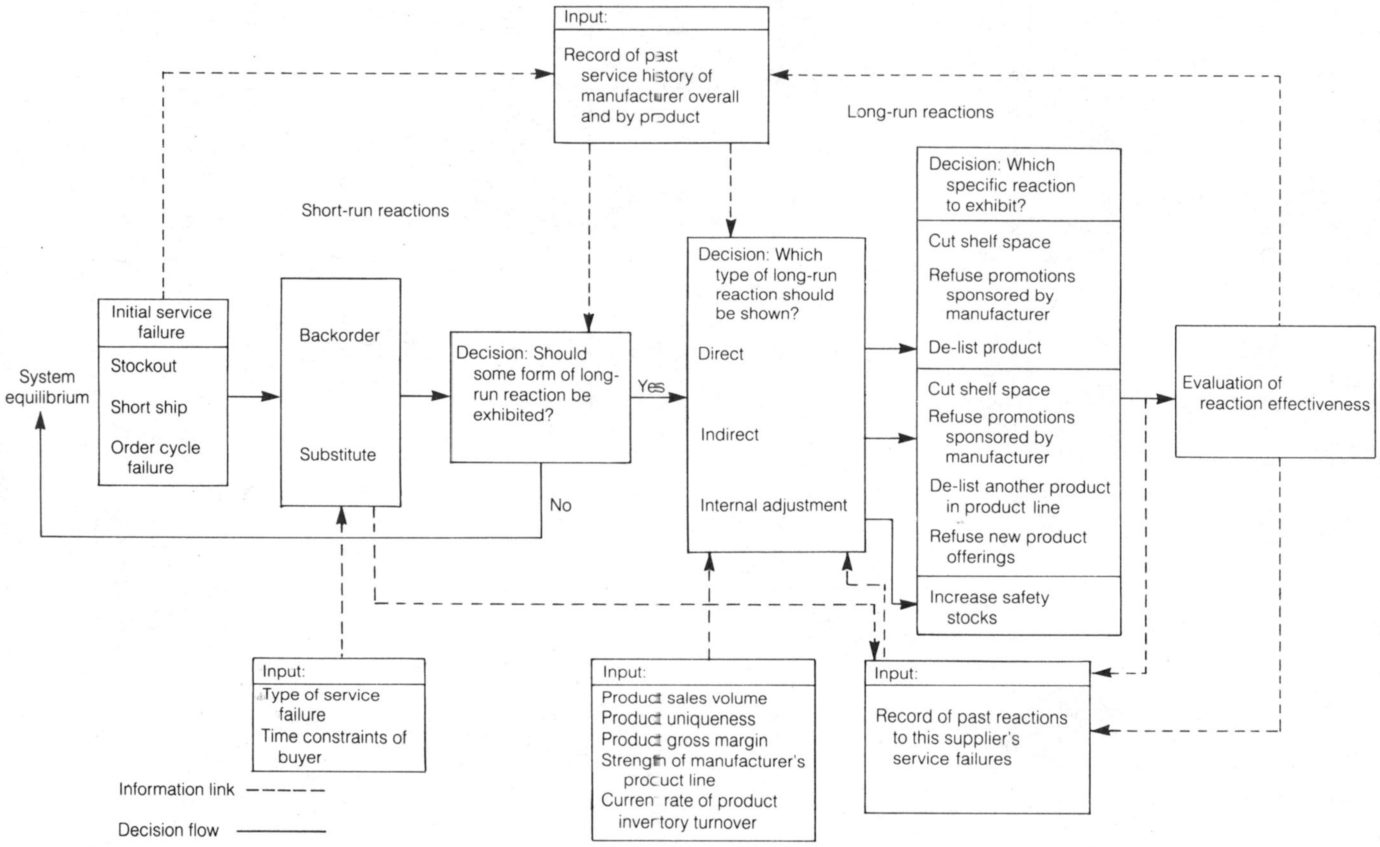

SOURCE: Marcus Lyndsay Bennion, "An Investigation of Wholesale Buyer Reaction to Manufacturer Customer Service Failures in the Grocery Channel," unpublished Ph.D. dissertation, Michigan State University, 1980, p. 163.

TABLE 4–1 A Customer-Product Contribution Matrix

Customer Classification	*Product*			
	A	*B*	*C*	*D*
I	1	2	6	10
II	3	4	7	12
III	5	8	13	16
IV	9	14	15	19
V	11	17	18	20

SOURCE: Bernard J. LaLonde and Paul H. Zinszer, *Customer Service: Meaning and Measurement* (Chicago: National Council of Physical Distribution Management, 1976), p. 181.

ABC Analysis

The ABC analysis used to improve customer service efficiency is similar to the ABC analysis used for inventory planning.[17] The logic behind this approach is that some customers and products are more profitable than others. Thus a company should maintain higher levels of customer service for the most profitable customer-product combinations. Profitability should be measured on a contribution basis, excluding joint costs and fixed overhead allocations.[18] Trends in profitability also should be measured/estimated so that potential growth is considered.

Table 4–1 illustrates a customer-product contribution matrix that can be used to classify customers and products according to their impact on the manufacturer's profit performance. It is interpreted as follows:

Customer-Product Contribution Matrix

1. Products in Category A are the firm's most profitable products, followed by Categories B, C, and D. The products in Category A represent a small percentage of the total product line.
2. Products in Category D represent the firm's least profitable products. Typically, 80 percent of the product line falls into this category.
3. Customers in Category I are the most profitable for the manufacturer and may number no more than 5 or 10.
4. Customers in Category V are the least profitable customers because they purchase in small quantities or generate small annual sales volume. The price and service concessions they receive could total hundreds or thousands of dollars. Category V usually contains the majority of customers.
5. The most profitable customer-product combination occurs when products in Category A are sold to customers in Category I (priority

[17] We will discuss ABC analysis for inventory planning in Chapter 10.

[18] We will a discuss a method for obtaining profitability on a segmental basis in Chapter 13.

TABLE 4–2 Making the Customer-Product Contribution Matrix Operational

Priority Range	*In-Stock Standard*	*Delivery Standard (hours)*	*Order Completeness Standard*
1–5	100.0%	48	99%
6–10	97.5	72	97
11–15	95.0	96	95
16–20	90.0	120	93

SOURCE: Bernard J. LaLonde and Paul H. Zinszer, *Customer Service Meaning and Measurement* (Chicago: National Council of Physical Distribution Management, 1976), p. 182.

number 1). The next most profitable combination occurs when products in Category B are sold to customers in Category I. The next most profitable are products in Category A sold to customers in Category II, and so on until the least profitable customer-product relationship—when products in Category D are sold to customers in Category V (priority number 20).

The customer-product contribution matrix is put into operation in a manner similar to that shown in Table 4–2. Priority range 1 to 5 is assigned an in-stock standard of 100 percent and a delivery standard of 48 hours, and orders are shipped complete 99 percent of the time. The reason the order completeness standard is not 100 percent when the in-stock standard is 100 percent, is that customers in Category I also order products in priority range 6 to 10.

The lowest priority range, 16 to 20, has an in-stock standard of 90 percent, a delivery standard of 120 hours, and an order completeness standard of 93 percent. This method recognizes the need to provide the most profitable customers with service levels that encourage repeat business. A firm does not want to stock out its most profitable customers on its most profitable products. Less profitable accounts can be made more valuable by reducing the costs of servicing them. For example, one method of making unprofitable accounts profitable is to limit the time when orders can be placed and then consolidate them for shipment to customers. By requiring that small customers in a specific geographic area place their orders biweekly on Mondays for delivery the following Friday, a firm can increase its profitability. Benefits to the customer include reduced order cycle variability; higher levels of in-stock availability; and, if the customer pays the freight, reduced transportation costs.

Servicing Less Profitable Customers

The Customer Service Audit

The customer service audit is used to evaluate the level of service a company is providing and as a benchmark for appraising the impact of changes in customer service policy. The audit is designed to identify the important elements of customer service, the manner in which performance is con-

Four Stages of a Customer Service Audit

trolled, and the internal communication system. Audit procedures should comprise four distinct stages: an external customer service audit, an internal customer service audit, the identification of potential solutions, and the establishment of customer service levels.[19]

The External Customer Service Audit. The starting point in any thorough study of customer service is the external audit. The key objectives of an external audit are (1) to identify the elements of customer service that customers believe to be important when making the decision to buy, and (2) to determine how customers perceive the service being offered by each of the major vendors in the market.

Objectives of the External Customer Service Audit

The first step of an external audit is the identification of the customer service variables that are most important to the firm's customers. For a consumer packaged-goods firm, the relevant customer service variables might include some or all of the following: average order cycle time, order cycle variability, orders shipped complete, in-stock variability, accuracy in filling orders, order status information, action on complaints, returns policy, remote order transmission (computer-to-computer order entry), ability to expedite emergency orders, billing procedure, palletized and unitized loads for handling efficiency, speed and accuracy in billing, handling of claims, availability of inventory status, freight pickup allowances for distributors wishing to pick up freight at the manufacturers warehouses, backhaul policy, and ability to select the carrier.

It is important to develop the list of variables based on interviews with the firm's customers. A list such as the one above, or one created by management, might serve as a useful starting point in discussions with customers. If marketing executives are involved, the list could be expanded to include other marketing mix components, such as product quality, price, terms of sale, quantity discount structure, number of sales calls, cooperative advertising, and national advertising support for the product.

Advantages of Including the Marketing Function

There are three advantages to including the marketing function. First, marketing involvement facilitates the implementation of trade-offs within the marketing mix. Second, marketing often has considerable expertise in questionnaire design, which is the next step in the process. Third, marketing's involvement adds credibility to the research findings, which increases acceptance and facilitates successful implementation.

Alternatives to using the corporate market research department include an outside market research firm, a local university where the research might be conducted by an MBA class, a doctoral student and/or a professor, or a consulting firm or vendor with specific expertise. The advantages of using one of these alternatives are that the company sponsoring the re-

[19]The following material is adapted from Douglas M. Lambert and Douglas E. Zemke, "The Customer Service Component of the Marketing Mix," *Proceedings of the Twentieth Annual Conference of the National Council of Physical Distribution Management,* 1982, pp. 1–24.

search does not have to be identified, and assistance is available for developing the questionnaires. Identifying the sponsoring firm may bias responses, and questionnaire length and clarity will influence the response rate.

Identifying the Research Sponsor May Bias Responses

It should be emphasized that the variables used in the external audit must be specifically tailored to the industry under study. Using variables from past research instruments as survey questions leads to misinterpretation and nonresponse when applied to different industries and channel structures.[20] In addition, the quantity and type of variables used to select and evaluate vendors is both complex and not subject to simple replication of previous research endeavors.

For example, in a comprehensive study in the plastics industry, the 110 variables used were categorized by marketing mix components as follows: product (21), price (14), promotion (29), and customer service (46). Similar research in the office systems industry was conducted prior to the plastics industry research. However, only 34 variables were the same as those used in the office systems industry, 12 were revised from variables in the office systems research, and 64 were specific to the plastics industry. While almost one-half of the price, promotion, and customer service variables were similar to those used in the office systems industry, 17 of the 21 product variables were different.[21]

Variables Are Industry Specific

When the relevant customer service elements have been determined, the second step in the external audit procedure is to design a questionnaire to gain feedback from a statistically valid sample of customers. The appendix to this chapter contains an example of a questionnaire format designed to determine the importance customers attach to marketing variables. Customers were asked to circle, on a scale of 1 to 7, the number that best expressed the importance they attached to each variable. The survey defined an *important* variable as possessing significant weight in the evaluation of suppliers, whereas an *unimportant* variable did not.[22]

Competitive Performance Ratings Are Important

An important consideration in the external audit is determining competitive performance ratings for major vendors. This can be accomplished by asking respondents to evaluate major vendors' performance on each of

---

[20] Jay U. Sterling and Douglas M. Lambert, "Establishing Customer Service Strategies Within the Marketing Mix," *Journal of Business Logistics* 8, no. 1 (1987), pp. 1–30.

[21] Douglas M. Lambert and Thomas C. Harrington, "Establishing Customer Service Strategies Within the Marketing Mix: More Empirical Evidence," *Journal of Business Logistics* 10, no. 2 (1989).

[22] Although a considerable body of research in service quality in service industries uses expectations scales with strongly agree and strongly disagree as the anchor points, research has shown that results obtained are the same as those obtained using importance scales. See Douglas M. Lambert and M. Christine Lewis, "A Comparison of Attribute Importance and Expectation Scales for Measuring Service Quality," in *Enhancing Knowledge Development in Marketing,* ed. William Bearden et al. (Chicago, Ill.: American Marketing Association, 1990), p. 291.

the variables. (See Part A of the questionnaire in the appendix.) Responses to these questions help the firm compare customers' perceptions of vendor performance. Obviously vendors want to score high on variables that are highest in importance to customers.

The questionnaire should include questions that require respondents to rate their overall satisfaction with each vendor and indicate the percentage of business they allocate to each vendor (see Part B of the questionnaire). Also, Part C of the questionnaire seeks to obtain specific levels of expected performance for key variables, such as the number of sales calls.

Overall Satisfaction with Vendors Should Be Determined

Finally, the questionnaire also should include demographic information that will enable the firm to determine if there are significant differences in response by such variables as type of account (wholesaler, retailer, etc.); market served (national versus regional); specific geographic location; sales volume; sales growth; profit as a percent of sales; and sales volume of each vendor's products.

Pretesting Is a Must

Before mailing the questionnaire, it should be pretested with a small group of customers to ensure that the questions are understandable and that important variables have not been ignored. The mailing list can be developed from an accounts receivable list; a sales/marketing department list of prospects; or lists of contracts, projects, bids lost, or inactive accounts. The accounts receivable list enables stratification of the sample to achieve an adequate number of large, medium, and small customers. If management wants an analysis of inactive accounts, it can send color-coded questionnaires to identify these accounts.

External Audit Enables Management to Identify Problems and Opportunities

The results of the customer service survey used in the external audit enable management to identify problems and opportunities. Table 4–3 illustrates the type of information that can be provided. This survey evaluated both customer service and other marketing mix variables. The two columns on the left side of Table 4–3 show that the ranking of the variables was not influenced by the order in which the questions appeared on the questionnaire.

In this example, 7 of the 12 variables with the highest mean customer importance scores were customer service variables. This result highlights the importance of customer service within the firm's marketing mix. A small standard deviation in customer importance ratings means that there was little variation in the respondents' individual evaluations of a variable's importance. For variables with a large standard deviation, however, it is important to use the demographic information (see Part D of the questionnaire) to determine which customers want which services. The same argument holds for the last variable, "Store layout planning assistance from manufacturer." For example, do large-volume, high-growth customers rate this higher in importance and small customers rate it lower in importance?

The previously described study in the plastics industry revealed similar results regarding the importance of customer service. The 18 variables rated as most important by the respondents (those with a mean score of

TABLE 4–3 Overall Importance Compared to Selected Performance of Major Manufacturers as Evaluated by Dealers

Rank		Variable Description	Overall Importance—All Dealers		Dealer Evaluations of Manufacturers									
					Mfr. 1		Mfr. 2		Mfr. 3		Mfr. 4		Mfr. 5	
			Mean	Std. Dev.	Mean	Std. Dev.	Mean	Std. Dev.	Mean	Std. Dev.	Mean	Std. Dev.	Mean	Std. Dev.
1	9	Ability of manufacturer to meet promised delivery date (on-time shipments)	6.4	.8	5.9	1.0	4.1	1.6	4.7	1.6	6.6	.6	3.3	1.6
2	39	Accuracy in filling orders (correct product is shipped)	6.4	.8	5.6	1.1	4.7	1.4	5.0	1.3	5.8	1.1	4.4	1.5
3	90	*Competitiveness* of price	6.3	1.0	5.1	1.2	4.9	1.4	4.5	1.5	5.4	1.3	3.6	1.8
4	40	Advance notice on shipping delays	6.1	.9	4.6	1.9	3.0	1.6	3.7	1.7	5.1	1.7	3.1	1.7
5	94	Special pricing discounts available on contract/project quotes	6.1	1.1	5.4	1.3	4.0	1.7	4.1	1.6	6.0	1.2	4.5	1.8
6	3	Overall manufacturing and design *quality* of product relative to the price range involved	6.0	.9	6.0	1.0	5.3	1.3	5.1	1.2	6.5	.8	4.8	1.5
7	16	Updated and current price data, specifications, and promotion materials provided by manufacturer	6.0	.9	5.7	1.3	4.1	1.5	4.8	1.4	6.3	.9	4.3	1.9
8	47	*Timely* response to requests for assistance from manufacturer's sales representative	6.0	.9	5.2	1.7	4.6	1.6	4.4	1.6	5.4	1.6	4.3	1.7
9	14	Order cycle consistency (small variability in promised versus actual delivery, i.e., vendor consistently meets expected date)	6.0	.9	5.8	1.0	4.1	1.5	4.8	1.4	6.3	.9	4.4	1.7
10	4b	Length of promised order cycle (lead) times (from order submission to delivery) for base line/in-stock (quick ship) product	6.0	1.0	6.1	1.1	4.5	1.4	4.9	1.5	6.2	1.1	3.7	2.0
11	54	Accuracy of manufacturer in forecasting and committing to estimated shipping dates on contract/project orders	6.0	1.0	5.5	1.2	4.0	1.6	4.3	1.4	6.3	1.1	3.5	1.6
12	49a	Completeness of order (% of line items eventually shipped complete)—made to order product (contract orders)	6.0	1.0	5.5	1.2	4.3	1.2	4.7	1.3	6.0	1.1	4.0	1.6
50	33a	Price *range* of product line offering (e.g., low, medium, high price levels) for major vendor	5.0	1.3	4.4	1.5	4.6	1.6	5.1	1.5	5.2	1.4	3.9	1.6
101	77	Store layout planning assistance from manufacturer	2.9	1.6	4.2	1.7	3.0	1.5	3.4	1.6	4.7	1.6	3.4	1.2

Note: Mean (average score) is based on a scale of 1 (not important) through 7 (very important).

SOURCE: Douglas M. Lambert and Jay U. Sterling, "Developing Customer Service Strategy," unpublished manuscript, University of South Florida, March 1986.

Logistics Dominates the List of Most Important Variables

6.0 or more on a scale of 1 to 7) were comprised of nine logistics/customer service variables (accuracy in filling orders, consistent lead times, ability to expedite emergency orders in a fast responsive manner, information provided when order is placed—projected shipping date, advance notice of shipping delays, information provided when order is placed—projected delivery date, action on complaints, length of promised lead times, and information provided when order is placed—inventory availability); five product quality variables (supplier's resins are of consistent quality, processability of the resin, supplier's resins are of consistent color, supplier's resins are of consistent melt flow, and overall quality of resin relative to price); two price variables (competitiveness of price and adequate advance notice of price changes); and two promotion related variables (quality of the sales force—honesty and quality of the sales force—prompt follow-up).[23]

It should be noted that the honesty of the sales force variable was to a large extent a logistics variable. The in-depth interviews revealed that the honesty variable was related to the degree of accurate information about product availability and delivery provided by the sales force. Because inventory records were not on-line and real-time, customers would be told that inventory was available when in fact it had been sold, and the batch process system had not updated the inventory levels. Customers did not realize that there was a problem until the product did not arrive.

Although the mix of most important attributes is somewhat different for the two industries, a review of Table 4–3 reveals that the following variables were the same: ability to meet promised delivery date, accuracy in filling orders, advance notice of shipping delays, consistent lead times (order cycle consistency), shipping date information, length of lead time, overall product quality relative to price, competitiveness of price, and prompt follow-up from the sales force. These variables have also been identified as the most important attributes in other industries.

Importance Ratings Cannot Be Used Alone

Most customer service studies emphasize the importance ratings of the variables being researched, which assumes that the variables rated the highest in importance determine the share of business given to each vendor. But this may not be true, for one or more of the following reasons:

- All of an industry's major suppliers may be performing at "threshold" levels, or at approximately equal levels, which makes it difficult to distinguish between suppliers.
- Variables for which there are significant variances in vendor performance may be better predictors of market share than the variables described above.
- Customers may rate a variable as extremely important, but there may be few or no suppliers who are providing satisfactory levels of service

[23] Lambert and Harrington, p. 50.

for that variable. Such variables offer opportunities to provide differential service in the marketplace.

- A variable may be rated low in importance with a low variance in response. In addition, there may be no single supplier providing adequate service levels. Therefore, customers do not recognize the advantages of superior service for that variable. If one vendor improved performance, it could lead to gains in market share.[24]

Both Importance Measures and Performance Measures Are Required

In order to determine what variables represent the best opportunity for increasing market share and/or profitability, both importance and performance measures are necessary. For this reason, Table 4–3 contains customer evaluations of perceived performance for the firm being researched and its four major competitors. This gives management some insight into the relative competitive position of each vendor, as viewed by the firm's customers. It is important that management determine what it is that the top-rated vendor is doing to create this perception. Management also must consider what actions it can take to improve customer perceptions of its service.

The company must compare customer perceptions of service to internal measures of performance. This may show that the customer is not aware of the service being provided or that management is measuring service performance incorrectly.

The Internal Customer Service Audit. The internal audit requires a review of the firm's current practices. This will provide a benchmark for appraising the impact of changes in customer service strategy.[25] The internal customer service audit should provide answers to the following questions:

Internal Audit Questions

- How is customer service currently measured within the firm?
- What are the units of measurement?
- What are the performance standards or objectives?
- What is the current level of attainment—results versus objectives?
- How are these measures derived from corporate information flows and the order processing system?
- What is the internal customer service reporting system?
- How do each of the functional areas of the business (e.g., logistics, marketing) perceive customer service?
- What is the relation between these functional areas in terms of communications and control?[26]

---

[24] Jay U. Sterling and Douglas M. Lambert, "Establishing Customer Service Strategies Within the Marketing Mix," *Journal of Business Logistics* 8, no. 1 (1987), pp. 1–30.

[25] This section is adapted from Douglas M. Lambert and M. Christine Lewis, "Managing Customer Service to Build Market Share and Increase Profit," *Business Quarterly* 48, no. 3 (Autumn 1983), pp. 50–57.

[26] Ibid., p. 52.

Purpose of Internal Audit

The overall purpose of the internal audit is to identify inconsistencies between the firm's practices and its customers' expectations. It is also important to verify customer perceptions, since customers may perceive service performance to be worse than it really is. In such a situation, the firm should change customer perceptions rather than the level of service provided.

The communications system largely determines the sophistication and control of customer service within a company. As LaLonde and Zinszer stated, "Without good control of information flow within the firm and between the firm and its customers, the customer service function is usually relegated to reporting performance level statistics and reacting to special problems."[27] That is why an internal audit must evaluate the communications flow from customers to the company and the communications flow within the company, and must review the customer service measurement and reporting system. The internal audit should give top management a clear understanding of the firm's communications with customers.

Most communications between customer and firm can be grouped into the following eight categories relating to the ordering-shipping-billing cycle: order entry; postorder entry inquiries/changes; delivery; postdelivery reports of damages, shortages, or overages; billing; postbilling dispute; payment delay; and payment.[28] The extent to which these communications are organized and managed can significantly affect both market share and profitability. The audit will help assess the effectiveness and cost of these communications.

Interviews with Management Are a Good Source of Data

Management interviews are another way to gather data. Interviews should be conducted with managers responsible for order processing, inventory management, warehousing, transportation, customer service, accounting/finance, production, materials management, and sales/marketing. Such interviews help determine how managers of each of these functions perceive customer service, communicate with customers, and interface with other functional areas. Specifically, the interviews address:

- Definition of responsibilities.
- Size and organizational structure.
- Decision-making authority and processes.
- Performance measurements and results.
- Definition of customer service.
- Management's perception of how customers define customer service.
- Plans to alter or improve customer service.
- Intrafunctional communications.
- Interfunctional communications.
- Communications with key contacts such as consumers, customers, common carriers, and suppliers.

---

[27] LaLonde and Zinszer, *Customer Service*, p. 168.

[28] Lambert and Lewis, "Managing Customer Service," p. 53.

Management must also evaluate the customer service measurement and reporting system in order to determine how customer service is measured, the units of measurement, performance standards employed, current results, the corporate function controlling each activity, sources of data, reporting formats and compilation methods, reporting frequency, distribution of reports, and transmission methods. It is equally important to understand how customers obtain information from the company. Thus, the internal audit should determine the types of information available to customers, the person in the company who provides each type of information, the way in which customers reach these departments, the average time taken to respond to customer inquiries, and the accessibility of needed information to the person(s) responsible for answering the inquiry. Appendix A of Chapter 18 provides an example of the questions that can be asked during an internal customer service audit.

Identifying Potential Solutions. The external audit enables management to identify problems with the firm's customer service and marketing strategies. Used in combination with the internal audit, it may help management adjust these strategies and vary them by segment in order to increase profitability. But if management wants to use such information to develop customer service and marketing strategies for optimal profitability, it must use these data to benchmark against its competitors.

The most meaningful competitive benchmarking occurs when customer evaluations of competitors' performance are compared to each other and to customers' evaluations of the importance of vendor attributes.[29] Once management has used this type of analysis to determine opportunities for gaining a competitive advantage, every effort should be made to identify best practice, that is, the most cost-effective use of technology and systems, regardless of the industry in which it has been successfully implemented. Noncompetitors are much more likely to share their knowledge and it is possible to uncover opportunities for significant competitive advantage over industry rivals.

A Methodology for Competitive Benchmarking

A methodology for competitive benchmarking is presented with data collected from a segment of the chemical industry. The analysis involves a comparison of the performance of two major vendors in the industry. The products marketed by these firms were considered to be commodities. In this example only two firms are analyzed, but the analysis can be expanded to more than one competitor or more than one segment.

The first step is to generate a table with importance evaluations for each of the variables as well as the performance evaluations of the firm and its major competitor (see Table 4–4). To simplify the data for this example only customer service attributes are considered and only 10 of them are

[29]The material in this section is taken from Douglas M. Lambert and Arun Sharma, "A Customer-Based Competitive Analysis for Logistics Decisions," *International Journal of Physical Distribution and Logistics Management* 20, no. 1 (1990), pp. 17–24.

TABLE 4–4 Importance and Performance Evaluations for Selected Customer Service Attributes

			Performance Evaluation		
No.	*Attribute*	*Importance*	*Company A*	*Company B*	*Relative Performance*
1	Accuracy in filling orders	6.42	5.54	5.65	−0.11
2	Ability to expedite emergency orders in a fast, responsive manner	6.25	4.98	5.23	−0.25
3	Action on complaints (e.g., order servicing, shipping, product, etc.)	6.07	4.82	5.18	−0.36†
4	Accuracy of supplier in forecasting and committing to shipping date for custom-made products	5.92	4.53	4.73	−0.20
5	Completeness rate (percentage of order eventually shipped)	5.69	5.29	5.27	+0.02
6	Rapid adjustment of billing and shipping errors	5.34	4.64	4.90	−0.24
7	Availability of blanket orders	4.55	5.03	4.15	+0.88*
8	Frequency of deliveries (supplier consolidates multiple/split shipments into one larger, less frequent shipment)	4.29	5.07	5.03	+0.04
9	Order processing personnel located in your market area	3.58	5.33	5.21	+0.12
10	Computer-to-computer order entry	2.30	4.07	3.53	+0.54*

*Performance evaluations of A and B are significantly different at $p \leq 0.01$.

†Performance evaluations of A and B are significantly different at $p \leq 0.05$.

SOURCE: Douglas M. Lambert and Arun Sharma, "A Customer-Based Competitive Analysis for Logistics Decisions," *International Journal of Physical Distribution and Logistics Management* 20, no. 1 (1990), p. 18.

included. Attributes were sorted by mean importance rating (to the customers) and a systematic random sample of 10 measures was selected. The attributes selected ensured that the analysis and discussion were based on a set of attributes that were representative of the full range of importance to customers.

The Competitive Position Matrix

The next step is to prepare a competitive position matrix that has two dimensions: importance and relative performance. The performance is determined by calculating the difference in the evaluation of the sponsor company less the evaluation of the major competitor. There are nine cells in the matrix which can be grouped into three broad categories:

1. Competitive advantage.
   a. Major strength (high importance, high relative performance).
   b. Minor strength (low importance, high relative performance).
2. Competitive parity.
3. Competitive disadvantage.
   a. Major weakness (high importance, low relative performance).
   b. Minor weakness (low importance, low relative performance).

The first and most important cell represents the major strengths of the company. The attributes in this cell need to be emphasized in the communications with customers. The second most important cell represents the major weaknesses of the company. These need to be improved, or customers need to be convinced that these attributes are not important. The minor strengths cell represents those things that the firm does well but that customers believe are not important. Customers need to be convinced that these attributes are important to them, or expenditures need to be reduced.

Options for Preparing a Competitive Position Matrix

The competitive position matrix can be created in a variety of ways, based on the objectives of the manager. For example, the company can be compared to the average of all competitors for the entire industry. This matrix provides a representation of the company's competitive position in the entire market. A second option is to compare the company to the average of all competitors for each segment. This matrix provides a representation of the company's competitive position in each segment and suggests segment-specific strategies. A third option is to compare the company to the average of all competitors for any major account. This matrix provides a representation of the company's competitive position for a single account and suggests account-specific strategies. These analyses can be extended to study the firm's competitive position relative to specific competitors in the industry or within market segments. Performing the analysis using specific competitors will allow management to target the primary customers of those competitors when the firm is the second or third source of supply. It also provides information that can be used to design strategies to protect the firm's primary customers from competitive threats.

The relative performance of Company A when compared to Company B is presented in Table 4–4. As can be seen from the table, firms A and B are very similar in performance evaluations, the maximum and minimum differences being 0.88 and 0.02, respectively, on a seven-point scale. The evaluations are statistically different for three of the attributes. The competitive position matrix is presented in Figure 4–6, which shows that the performance of the major competitors was viewed as virtually identical by customers. In addition, no managerially useful differences in performance evaluations could be found based on geography, customer type, or sales volume.

The top cell in the competitive parity column suggests that performance improvements should be made on attributes 1, 2, 3, 4, 5, and 6 as long as the incremental costs associated with achieving these improvements are not greater than the incremental revenues earned by doing so. For example, implementation of a service quality program in the distribution center may result in a significant improvement in the accuracy in filling orders, and this achievement may be at a relatively low cost or no net cost to the firm. On the other hand, accuracy in forecasting and committing to shipping date for custom-made products may require a new forecasting package and/or production planning model. Also, improving the order completeness rate may require new computer systems or significant increases in inventory. In summary, there are two variables that can be ma-

FIGURE 4–6 Competitive Position Matrix

Competitive disadvantage
Competitive parity
Competitive advantage
Major weakness
Major strength
Minor weakness
Minor strength
1* 2* 3* 4* *5 6* 7* *8 *9 *10
IMPORTANCE
7 5 3 1
HIGH
MEDIUM
LOW
–3.0 –1.0 +1.0 +3.0
Relative performance
*denotes attribute number

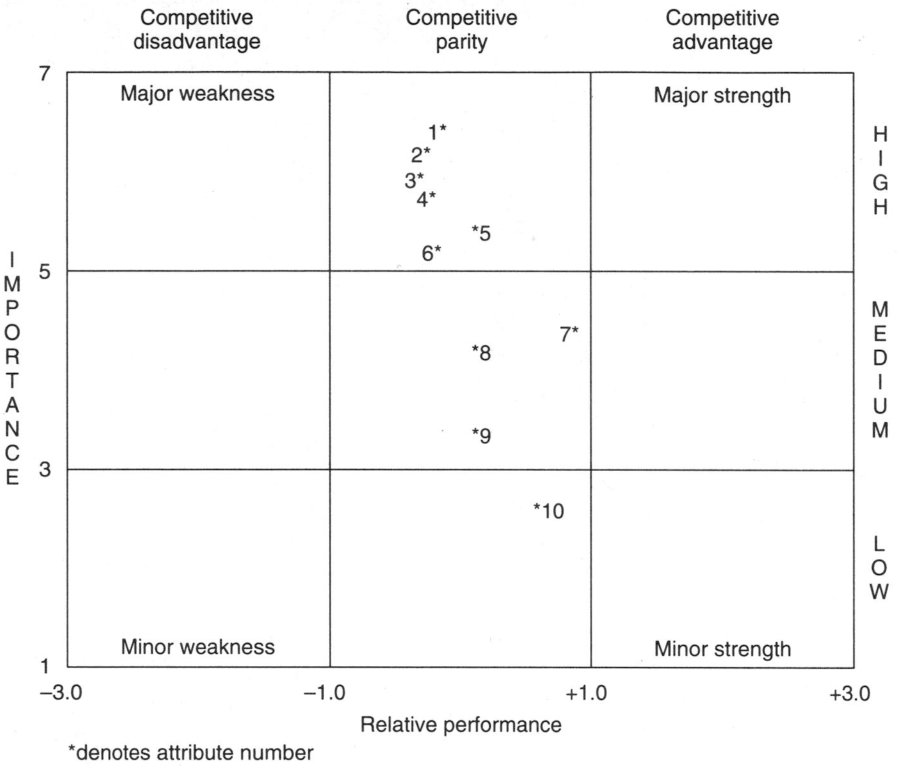

SOURCE: Douglas M. Lambert and Arun Sharma, "A Customer-Based Competitive Analysis for Logistics Decisions," *International Journal of Physical Distribution and Logistics Management* 20, no. 1 (1990), p. 21.

nipulated. First, the preference can be improved by actually performing better or by changing the buyers' perceptions regarding the firm's performance, if their perceptions can be shown to be incorrect using the firm's internal performance data. Second, the importance of an attribute can be changed by proving to the customer why it should be more or less important than the customer perceives it to be.

As will be shown, there is a danger to using the competitive position matrix by itself to identify strategic opportunities for gaining a competitive advantage. It is necessary to develop a performance evaluation matrix to be used in conjunction with the competitive position matrix. The performance evaluation matrix is obtained by creating a three-by-three matrix with the importance of each attribute and evaluation of the performance of the company as two dimensions. The matrix is divided into nine cells as follows:

FIGURE 4–7 Performance Evaluation Matrix

IMPORTANCE	1–3	3–5	5–7	
5–7	Definitely improve	Improve 2* *3 *4 *6	Maintain/improve *1 *5	HIGH
3–5	Improve	Maintain	Reduce/maintain *7 *8 *9	MEDIUM
1–3	Maintain	Reduce/maintain *10	Reduce/maintain	LOW

Performance evaluation

*denotes attribute number

SOURCE: Douglas M. Lambert and Arun Sharma, "A Customer-Based Competitive Analysis for Logistics Decisions," *International Journal of Physical Distribution and Logistics Management* 20, no. 1 (1990), p. 21.

- Maintain/improve service (high importance, high performance).
- Improve service (high importance, medium performance).
- Definitely improve service (high importance, low performance).
- Improve service (medium importance, low performance).
- Maintain service (medium importance, medium performance).
- Maintain service (low importance, low performance).
- Reduce/maintain service (medium importance, high performance).
- Reduce/maintain service (low importance, medium performance).
- Reduce/maintain service (low importance, high performance).

The Performance Evaluation Matrix

The performance evaluation matrix presented in Figure 4–7 shows that Company A was not meeting customer expectations on four of the six variables rated highest in importance by customers and was exceeding expectations on the two least important variables (those evaluated as 2.30 and 3.58 in importance). Similar results were found for the other vendors evaluated by the respondents: No vendor was performing up to customer expectations on all of the variables rated high in importance by customers, and all were performing above expectations on the variables that were rated lowest in importance. A cautionary note is in order: High standard deviations in importance or performance evaluations make it necessary to determine if market segments exist. If segments do exist, this analysis must be performed by market segment.

Figure 4–7 implies that if marketing resources were being allocated in the most efficient and effective manner, all of the numbers should fall on the diagonal. That is, we would want to perform at a level of five or more on those variables that customers evaluated as high in importance, between three and five for those variables rated as medium in importance, and so on. However, as will be shown in step four, this may not be the ideal strategy when the information contained in Figure 4–6 is also considered.

The Two Matrixes Must Be Used Together

The two matrices (Figures 4–6 and 4–7) must be used together because the competitive position matrix by itself also may result in incorrect conclusions about areas of improvement. For example, the competitive position matrix implies that management should increase expenditures on Attributes 1, 2, 3, 4, 5, and 6 in an effort to make them major strengths. In fact, all six attributes appear to offer comparable opportunities. However, the performance evaluation matrix suggests that Attributes 2, 3, 4, and 6 offer the greatest opportunities for building a competitive advantage.

The competitors were evaluated very similarly on all of the attributes. Consequently, the performance evaluation matrix needs to be studied to identify the areas that offer the greatest opportunity for improvement. In some cases the entire industry may be performing badly on an attribute, and improving the firm's performance may represent a substantial opportunity to gain a competitive advantage. As an example, customers felt that accuracy in filling orders (Attribute 1) was one of the most important attributes of customer service (6.4 on a 7-point scale). However, the company and its major competitor were rated at virtually the same level of performance on this attribute (5.5 and 5.7 respectively), and there is a definite opportunity for improvement. When Figures 4–6 and 4–7 are considered simultaneously, it can be seen that Attribute 5 does not represent the same potential for improvement as Attributes 1, 2, 3, 4, and 6. This is because Company A is performing close to customer expectations on Attribute 5. While Figure 4–7 suggests that the firm can reduce its expenditures on Attributes 7, 8, 9, and 10, Figure 4–6 suggests that caution be exercised with Attributes 8, 9, and 10 since reductions in expenditures may result in relative competitive weaknesses. Clearly, care must be exercised in interpreting the data with respect to some attributes. For example, "computer-to-computer order entry" received a low overall importance score. However, this attribute may be of vital importance to a small number of large customers. Failure to implement computer-to-computer ordering systems might result in losing these customers. On the other hand, small moulders and extruders might view this technology as "star wars." For these customers, simply having someone at the vendor location answer the telephone

FIGURE 4–8 Strategic Opportunities for a Competitive Advantage

Competitive disadvantage
Competitive parity
Competitive advantage

Major weakness
Major strength
Minor weakness
Minor strength

1* 2* 3* 4* *5 6* *7 *8 *9 *10

IMPORTANCE: 7, 5, 3, 1

HIGH
MEDIUM
LOW

−3.0 −1.0 +1.0 +3.0

Relative performance

*denotes attribute number

→ indicates desired shift in relative performance

- -→ indicates potential opportunities that may be revealed within specific customer segments

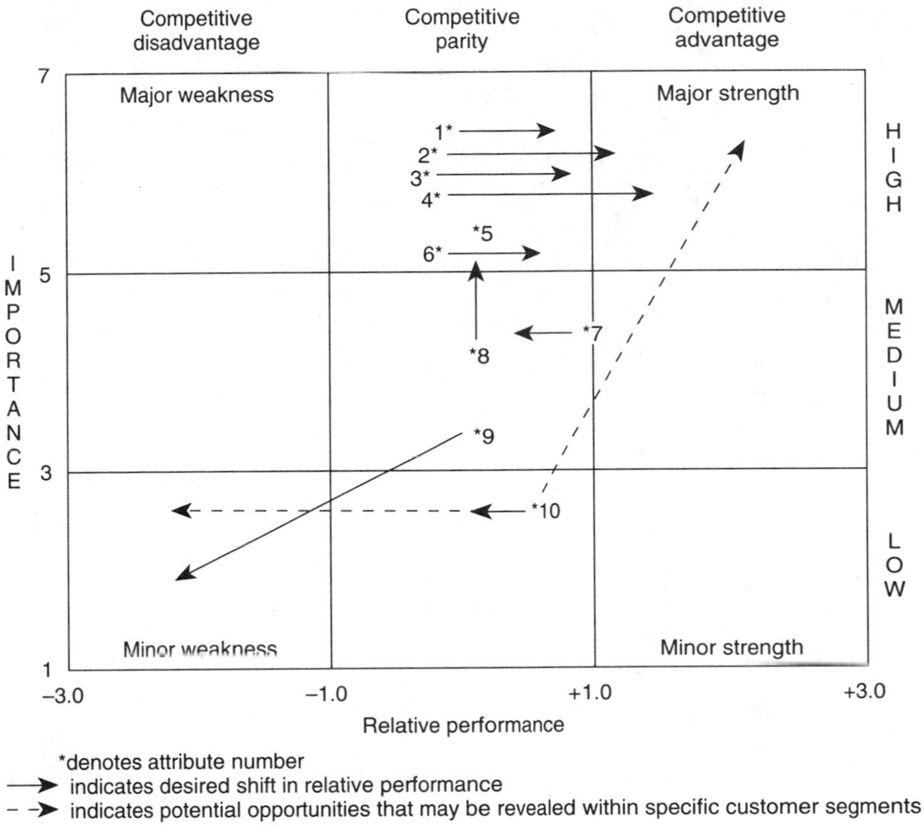

SOURCE: Douglas M. Lambert and Arun Sharma, "A Customer-Based Competitive Analysis for Logistics Decisions," *International Journal of Physical Distribution and Logistics Management* 20, no. 1 (1990), p. 23.

and input the order using a cathode-ray tube (CRT) with on-line capability is all that is necessary. More in-depth study would be required to determine if expenditures can be reduced without significantly affecting the purchase decision.

Figure 4–8 provides the greatest insight in terms of where expenditures can be changed to achieve a competitive advantage because it illustrates the strategic opportunities for gaining a competitive advantage based on the importance of the attributes to customers and the firm's performance relative to its major competitor. Figure 4–8 shows that Attributes 1, 2, 3, 4, or 6 can become relative competitive strengths and that Attributes 2 and 4 have the potential to become major strengths and a source of competitive advantage. In order to make Attributes 1, 3, 5, and 6 into major strengths, customers would have to be convinced that these attributes are more important to them. Otherwise, a relative competitive performance of more than + 1.0 would require that Company A's performance exceed customer expectations. Emphasis on Attribute 7 should be reduced for all customers unless there is a segment of profitable customers that views this attribute to be high in importance. If such a segment exists, Attribute 7 should be stressed for this segment. Customers should be shown why frequency of deliveries (Attribute 8) is more important to them than they currently believe it is. Typically, when multiple/split shipments are consolidated into a larger, less frequently scheduled delivery, customers prefer the service because of the consistency, which increases their ability to plan. Also, customers should be convinced that it is not necessary to have order processing personnel located in local markets (Attribute 9), and expenditures for local order entry should be reduced. High levels of performance with centralized order processing personnel would change customer perceptions about the need for a local presence. Analysis of segments may reveal that Attribute 10 should be moved to the major strength category for large profitable customers and that expenditures should be reduced for small moulders and extruders who rate computer-to-computer capability as low in importance.

The performance evaluation matrix and the competitive position matrix can be used together to guide the development of logistics strategy for competitive advantage. It is important to emphasize that a company's logistics strategy needs to be designed giving full consideration to the basic strategy of the company and also the costs involved in a change in strategy. Within the customer service package, it may be possible to lengthen lead times for certain customers and use the additional planning time to provide these customers with higher levels of in-stock availability and more consistent delivery. This may improve service without increasing costs and may thereby improve profitability. If the improvement in service leads to increased sales, profits will increase further.

In situations in which customers would prefer lower levels of marketing services in exchange for higher levels of customer service, the firm's marketing mix should be adjusted. Of course, the power structure within the firm determines the extent to which this is possible.

Service Performance Standards and the Measurement of Performance

Establishing Customer Service Levels. The final steps in the audit procedure are the actual establishment of service performance standards and the ongoing measurement of performance. Management must set target service levels for segments such as type of customer, geographic area, channel of distribution, and product line. It must inform all employees responsible for implementing the customer service levels and develop compensation schemes that encourage attainment of the customer service objectives. Formal reports that document performance are a necessity. Finally, management must repeat the entire procedure periodically to ensure that the customer service package reflects current customer needs. In fact,

FIGURE 4–9 Possible Measures of Customer Service Performance

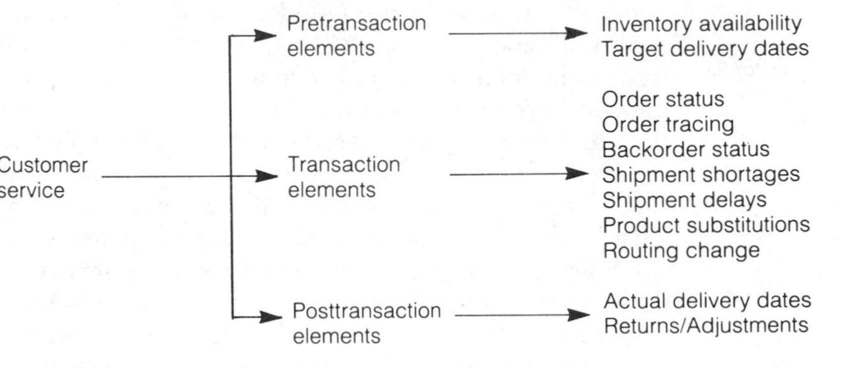

it is the collection of customer information over time that is most useful in guiding corporate strategy.

DEVELOPING AND REPORTING CUSTOMER SERVICE STANDARDS

Once management has determined which elements of customer service are most important, it must develop standards of performance. Designated employees should regularly report results to the appropriate levels of management. William Hutchinson and John Stolle offered the following four steps for measuring and controlling customer service performance:

Four Steps for Measuring and Controlling Customer Service Performance

1. Establish quantitative standards of performance for each service element.
2. Measure actual performance for each service element.
3. Analyze variance between actual services provided and the standard.
4. Take corrective action as needed to bring actual performance into line.[30]

Customer cooperation is essential for the company to obtain information about speed, dependability, and condition of the delivered product. To be effective, customers must be convinced that service measurement/monitoring will help improve future service.

Figure 4–9 contains a number of possible measures of service performance. The emphasis any manufacturer places on individual elements must be based on what that manufacturer's customers believe to be impor-

[30] William H. Hutchinson, Jr. and John F. Stolle, "How to Manage Customer Service," *Harvard Business Review,* 46, no. 6 (November-December 1968), pp. 85–96.

tant. Such service elements as inventory availability, delivery dates, order status, order tracing, and back-order status require good communications between the manufacturer and its customers. Because many companies have not kept pace with technology in order processing, this area offers significant potential for improving customer service. Consider the possibilities for improved communications if customers can either phone their orders to customer service representatives who have CRTs, or input orders on their own terminals. Immediate information on inventory availability can be provided and product substitution can be arranged in a stockout. Customers also can be given target delivery dates.

Automated Order Processing Improves Customer Service

Figure 4–10 gives examples of customer service standards. The standards chosen should be the ones that best reflect what customers need rather than what management thinks customers need. Designated employees should measure and compare performance to the standard, and report this information to the appropriate levels of management on a regular and timely basis.

The firm's order processing and accounting information systems can provide much of the information necessary for developing a customer-product contribution matrix and meaningful customer service management reports. We will discuss these important interfaces in detail in Chapters 13 and 15.

IMPEDIMENTS TO AN EFFECTIVE CUSTOMER SERVICE STRATEGY

Many companies have no effective customer service strategy. Even the best managed firms may be guilty of one of the following:

Eleven Hidden Costs of Customer Service

1. Misdefining customer service.
2. Overlooking customer profitability.
3. Using unrealistic customer service policies.
4. Failing to research.
5. Burying customer service costs.
6. Misusing customer service as a sales incentive.
7. Having blurred lines of authority.
8. Equating the number of warehouses with customer service.
9. Adding bodies rather than systems.
10. Employing undertrained, undercompensated personnel.
11. Misreading the seller's market.[31]

Failing to segment markets in terms of the service offered may be a costly mistake. Management often hesitates to offer different levels of service for

[31] Warren Blanding, "The Hidden Eleven Costs of Customer Service," *Transportation and Distribution Management* 14, no. 4 (July-August 1974), pp. 6–10.

FIGURE 4–10 Examples of Customer Service Standards

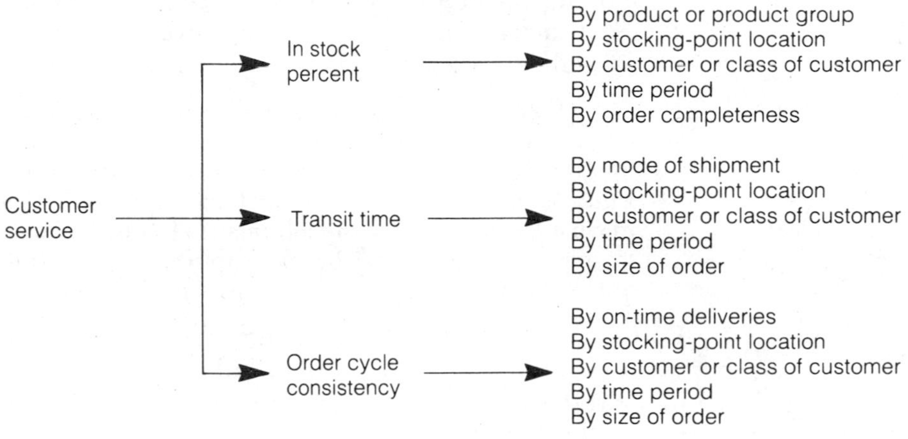

fear of violating the Robinson-Patman Act. The act requires that firms cost justify such policies. However, most firms do not have the necessary cost information.[32] Nevertheless, management can segment markets based on customers' evaluations of the importance of marketing services, and can obtain the necessary financial data using sampling techniques.

Salespeople Often Create Unrealistic Expectations

Salespeople can misuse customer service by promising faster delivery to obtain an order. But most customers value reliability and consistency in filling orders more than speed of delivery. Consequently, attempting to decrease the order cycle on an ad hoc basis increases transportation costs for the expedited shipments; order-assembly costs also rise because of the disruption of normal work flow. In addition, neither the customer nor the company has much to gain. When salespeople override customer service policies on shipping dates, lead times, shipping points, modes of transportation, and units of sale, they disrupt other customers' orders and cause an increase in logistics costs. In other situations, salespeople have been known not to "sell" the services being provided by the company.[33]

---

[32] See Douglas M. Lambert, *The Distribution Channels Decision* (New York: National Association of Accountants, and Hamilton, Ontario: The Society of Management Accountants of Canada, 1978); Douglas M. Lambert and John T. Mentzer, "Is Integrated Physical Distribution Management a Reality?" *Journal of Business Logistics* 2, no. 1 (1980), pp. 18–27; and Douglas M. Lambert and Howard M. Armitage, "Distribution Costs: The Challenge," *Management Accounting,* May 1979, pp. 33–37, 45.

[33] Douglas M. Lambert, James R. Stock, and Jay U. Sterling, "A Gap Analysis of Buyer and Seller Perceptions of the Importance of Marketing Mix Attributes," in *Enhancing Knowledge Development in Marketing,* ed. William Bearden et al. (Chicago: American Marketing Association, 1990), p. 208.

A firm's customer service standards and performance expectations are affected substantially by the competitive environment and what is perceived to be traditional industry practices. Consequently, it is imperative that management understands industry norms, expectations and the costs of providing high levels of customer service. Evidence suggests that:

> Many firms do not measure the cost effectiveness of service levels and have no effective way of determining competitive service levels. Information is fed back into the company through a sales organization that is often times concerned with raising service levels or through industry anecdotes and/or outraged customers. The net result of this information feedback is that firms may over-react to imprecise cues from the marketplace, or even from within their own organizations.[34]

Considering the vast sums of money firms spend on research and development and advertising, it makes little sense for a company not to adequately research the levels of customer service necessary for profitable long-range business development.

Finally, the economic environment since the late 1970s has caused top management to push for more inventory turns and lower accounts receivable. As we saw in Chapter 2, both of these reactions can lead to decreased levels of customer service and, eventually, lower corporate profitability.

IMPROVING CUSTOMER SERVICE PERFORMANCE

An Effective Customer Service Strategy Requires a Thorough Understanding of Customers

The levels of customer service a firm achieves can be improved by the following actions: (1) thoroughly researching customers' needs, (2) setting service levels that make realistic trade-offs between revenues and expenses, (3) making use of the latest technology in order processing systems, and (4) measuring and evaluating the performance of individual logistics activities. An effective customer service strategy *must* be based on an understanding of how customers define *service.* The customer service audit and surveys of customers are imperative:

> Many customer service surveys show that customers define service differently than suppliers and prefer a lower but more reliable service level than that currently offered. Under these circumstances, there is no reason why a firm can't improve service as the customers perceive it and at the same time cut costs. To improve service as measured by this objective standard is often less costly than to improve service as measured by arbitrary in-house standards.[35]

---

[34] Bernard J. LaLonde, Martha C. Cooper, and Thomas G. Noordewier, "*Customer Service: A Management Perspective,* (Oak Brook, Ill.: Council of Logistics Management, 1988), p. 29.

[35] Robert E. Sabath, "How Much Service Do Customers Really Want?" *Business Horizons,* April 1978, p. 26.

Once it has determined its customers' view of service, management must select a customer service strategy that advances the firm's objectives for long-range profit and return on investment. As Sabath has said:

> It should be clear that the optimum service level is not always the lowest cost level. The optimum level is one that retains customers at the lowest possible costs—and meets the company's growth needs. Defined this way, an optimum service level may be achieved by trading off some [logistics] cost savings for more valuable marketing advantages or manufacturing efficiencies. The point is that with objective, customer-defined service levels and a good handle on costs, everyone knows exactly what is being traded and what is received in return.[36]

The optimum level of customer service is the one that retains the "right" or "desired" customers.

Planning Time Results from Automating the Order Processing System

Many firms have antiquated order processing systems. For them, automation of order processing represents a significant opportunity for improving customer service. The primary benefit of automating the order processing system is the reduction in order cycle time. Given the fact that most customers prefer a consistent delivery cycle to a shorter one, it usually is unnecessary—or unwise—to reduce the order cycle time for customers. But by using the additional time internally for planning, the company can achieve savings in transportation, warehousing, inventory carrying costs, production planning, and purchasing. Automation improves customer service by providing the following benefits to the customer: better product availability, more accurate invoices, the ability to lower safety-stock levels and the associated carrying costs, and improved access to information on order status. In short, automated order processing systems enhance the firm's ability to perform all of the transaction and posttransaction elements of customer service.

Finally, the development of an effective customer service program requires the establishment of customer service standards that do the following:

1. Reflect the customer's point of view.
2. Provide an operational and objective measure of service performance.
3. Provide management with cues for corrective action.[37]

Management should also measure and evaluate the impact of individual logistics activities—such as transportation, warehousing, inventory management, production planning/purchasing, and order processing—on the level of customer service. Designated employees should report achievements regularly to the appropriate levels of management. Management

---

[36] Ibid.

[37] LaLonde and Zinszer, *Customer Service*, p. 180.

should compare actual performance to standards and take corrective action when performance is inadequate. For management to be successful and efficient, a firm needs timely information. It also is necessary to hold individuals accountable for their performance, since information alone does not guarantee improved decision making.

SUMMARY

This chapter opened with a discussion of how to define customer service. Although the importance of the individual elements of customer service varies from company to company, we discussed the common elements that are of concern to most companies. We also saw the necessity for a customer service strategy consistent with marketing and corporate strategies. The successful implementation of the integrated logistics management concept depends on management's knowledge of the costs associated with different system designs, and of the relationship between system design and customer service levels. We saw how management can obtain better knowledge of the costs and revenues associated with different levels of customer service, and how it can implement cost/service trade-offs.

The customer service audit is a method of determining the existing service levels, determining how performance is measured and reported, and appraising the impact of changes in customer service policy. Questionnaires are a means of finding out what management and customers view as important aspects of customer service.

Although customer service may represent the best opportunity for a firm to achieve a sustainable competitive advantage, many firms implement customer service strategies that are simply duplicates of those implemented by their major competitors. The audit framework represented in this chapter can be used by management to collect and analyze customer and competitive information.

We saw that there are some common roadblocks to an effective customer service strategy—as well as some ways to improve performance. In the next chapter we will discuss the influence of transportation on the efficiency and effectiveness of the logistics function.

SUGGESTED READINGS

Christopher, Martin. "Creating Effective Policies for Customer Service." *International Journal of Physical Distribution and Materials Management* 13, no. 2 (1983), pp. 3–24.

Ellram, Lisa M., and Martha C. Cooper. "Supply Chain Management, Partnerships, and the Shipper-Third Party Relationship." *The International Journal of Logistics Management* 1, no. 2 (1990), pp. 1–10.

GILMOUR, PETER. "Customer Service: Differentiating by Market Segment." *International Journal of Physical Distribution and Materials Management* 12, no. 3 (1982), pp. 37–44.

KYJ, MYROSLAW J. "Customer Service as a Competitive Tool." *Industrial Marketing Management* 16 (1987), pp. 225–30.

LALONDE, BERNARD J., MARTHA C. COOPER, AND THOMAS G. NOORDEWIER. *Customer Service: A Management Perspective.* Chicago: Council of Logistics Management, 1988.

LALONDE, BERNARD J., AND MARTHA C. COOPER. *Partnerships in Providing Customer Service: A Third-Party Perspective.* Chicago: Council of Logistics Management, 1989.

LEVY MICHAEL. "Toward an Optimal Customer Service Package." *Journal of Business Logistics* 2, no. 2 (1981), pp. 87–109.

———. "Diminishing Returns for Customer Service." *International Journal of Physical Distribution and Materials Management* 11, no. 1 (1981), pp. 14–24.

———. "Customer Service: A Managerial Approach to Controlling Marketing Channel Conflict." *International Journal of Physical Distribution and Materials Management* 11, no. 7 (1981), pp. 38–52.

LEVY, MICHAEL, JOHN WEBSTER, AND ROGER A. KERIN. "Formulating Push Marketing Strategies: A Method and Application." *Journal of Marketing* 47, no. 1 (Winter 1983), pp. 25–34.

MATHE, HERVÉ, AND ROY D. SHAPIRO. "Managing the Service Mix: After Sale Service for Competitive Advantage." *The International Journal of Logistics Management* 1, no. 1 (1990), pp. 44–50.

OZMENT, JOHN, AND DOUGLAS N. CHARD. "Effects of Customer Service on Sales: An Analysis of Historical Data." *International Journal of Physical Distribution and Materials Management* 16, no. 3 (1986), pp. 14–28.

PERREAULT, WILLIAM D., AND FREDERICK A. RUSS. "Physical Distribution Service: A Neglected Aspect of Marketing Management." *MSU Business Topics* 22, no. 3 (Summer 1974), pp. 37–45.

———. "Physical Distribution Service in Industrial Purchase Decisions." *Journal of Marketing* 40, no. 2 (April 1976), pp. 3–10.

———. "Quantifying Marketing Trade-Offs in Physical Distribution Policy Decisions." *Decision Sciences* 7, no. 2 (1976), pp. 186–201.

———. "Improving Physical Distribution Service Decisions with Trade-Off Analysis." *International Journal of Physical Distribution and Materials Management* 7, no. 3 (1977), pp. 117–27.

STERLING, JAY U., AND DOUGLAS M. LAMBERT. "Customer Service Research: Past, Present and Future." *International Journal of Physical Distribution and Materials Management* 19, no. 2 (1989), pp. 3–23.

STERLING, JAY U., AND DOUGLAS M. LAMBERT. "Establishing Customer Service Strategies Within the Marketing Mix." *Journal of Business Logistics* 8, no. 1 (1987), pp. 1–30.

TUCKER, FRANCES GAITHER. "Creative Customer Service Management." *International Journal of Physical Distribution and Materials Management* 13, no. 3 (1983), pp. 34–50.

UHR, ERNEST B., ERNEST C. HOUCK, AND JOHN C. ROGERS. "Physical Distribution Service." *Journal of Business Logistics* 2, no. 2 (1981), pp. 158–69.

VOORHEES, ROY DALE, AND JOHN I. COPPETT. "Marketing-Logistics Opportunities for the 1990s." *Journal of Business Strategy* 7, no. 2 (Fall 1986), pp. 33–38.

QUESTIONS AND PROBLEMS

1. Customer service can be defined as an activity, a performance measure, or a corporate philosophy. What are the advantages and disadvantages of each of these types of definitions? How would you define customer service?
2. Explain the importance of the pretransaction, transaction, and posttransaction elements of customer service.
3. Explain why customer service should be integrated with other components of the marketing mix when management develops the firm's marketing strategy.
4. Explain how ABC analysis can be used to improve the efficiency of the customer service activity.
5. Why is the customer service audit important when establishing a corporation's customer service strategy?
6. Why does automation of the order processing system represent such an attractive opportunity for improving customer service? How is this service improvement accomplished?
7. How should management go about improving customer service performance?
8. Show how management can use cost/revenue trade-offs to determine if customer service levels should be increased from 95 percent to 98 percent in-stock availability, given the following information:
   a. Transportation costs would increase by $135,000.
   b. Inventory levels would increase by $3 million.
   c. Warehousing costs would increase by $15,000.
   d. Inventory carrying cost as a percentage of inventory value is 35 percent.
   e. Annual sales are currently $50 million.
   f. The contribution margin on the company's products averages 30 percent of the selling price.

APPENDIX
Customer Service Questionnaire

SURVEY OF MARKETING AND DISTRIBUTION PRACTICES IN THE BLANK VIDEO TAPE STOCK INDUSTRY

DEPARTMENT OF MARKETING, UNIVERSITY OF SOUTH FLORIDA

PART A: IMPORTANCE OF FACTORS CONSIDERED WHEN SELECTING AND EVALUATING VENDORS (MANUFACTURERS) OF BLANK VIDEO TAPE STOCK

INSTRUCTIONS

Listed on the following pages are various factors often provided by vendors **(manufacturers)** to their customers. **This Section involves two tasks.** Each task will be explained separately.

The first task involves your evaluation of the various factors that your firm might consider when you select a new blank video tape stock vendor, or when you evaluate the performance of one of your current vendors. Please circle on a scale of 1 to 7, the number which best expresses the *importance* to your firm of each of these factors. For example, if a factor *is not used* by your firm or possesses very little weight in your evaluation of vendors, please circle number 1 (not important). A rating of 7 (very important) should be reserved for those factors that would cause you to *reevaluate* the amount of business done with a vendor, or cause you to drop the vendor in the event of inadequate performance.

The second task is to *evaluate the current performance* of three major vendors. Please list below in the spaces labeled "Vendor A", "Vendor B" and "Vendor C" three major vendors of blank video cassettes. Next, using the scale labeled PERCEIVED PERFORMANCE, please insert the number between 1 and 7 which best expresses your perception of the vendor's current performance under the appropriate vendor heading. If you perceive that a vendor's performance is poor, insert a 1. Reserve a rating of 7 for excellent performance. If a service is not available from a vendor, please write NA, NOT AVAILABLE, in the appropriate space. **Please identify your major vendors below:**

VENDOR A (**the largest amount** of your blank tape purchases are from this vendor): __________

VENDOR B (**second largest amount** of your blank tape purchases are from this vendor): __________

VENDOR C (**third largest amount** of your blank tape purchases are from this vendor): __________

EXAMPLE

FACTORS CONSIDERED	IMPORTANCE: Not Important 1	2	3	4	5	6	Very Important 7	PERCEIVED PERFORMANCE OF VENDORS (Scale of 1 to 7) A	B	C
• Product Quality	1	2	3	4	5	6	(7)	7	6	6
• Average Lead Time	1	2	3	4	(5)	6	7	4	6	5

FACTORS CONSIDERED	IMPORTANCE: Not Important 1	2	3	4	5	6	Very Important 7	PERCEIVED PERFORMANCE OF VENDORS (Scale of 1 to 7) A	B	C
1. Cash discounts for early payment or prepayment	1	2	3	4	5	6	7	___	___	___
2. Vendor sponsored technical seminars: • at user's location	1	2	3	4	5	6	7	___	___	___
• at vendor's location	1	2	3	4	5	6	7	___	___	___
• at distributor's location	1	2	3	4	5	6	7	___	___	___
3. Quantity discount structure based on total annual purchases	1	2	3	4	5	6	7	___	___	___
4. If you use a distributor, they can get you technical help from the manufacturer	1	2	3	4	5	6	7	___	___	___
5. Availability of statistical process control information from vendor	1	2	3	4	5	6	7	___	___	___
6. Advance information (literature, specs, prices, etc.) on new product introductions	1	2	3	4	5	6	7	___	___	___
7. Consignment sales (vendor invoices after you have used the product)	1	2	3	4	5	6	7	___	___	___

VENDOR A = ______________________

VENDOR B = ______________________

VENDOR C = ______________________

FACTORS CONSIDERED	IMPORTANCE: Not Important 1	2	3	4	5	6	Very Important 7	PERCEIVED PERFORMANCE OF VENDORS (Scale of 1 to 7) A	B	C
8. Rapid adjustment of billing errors (due to pricing errors)	1	2	3	4	5	6	7	___	___	___
9. Ability of technical service representative to inspect and analyze equipment at my facility in order to evaluate interaction between tape and equipment	1	2	3	4	5	6	7	___	___	___
10. Vendor's policy on minimum order they will accept:										
• dollar value	1	2	3	4	5	6	7	___	___	___
• number of units	1	2	3	4	5	6	7	___	___	___
11. Vendor (manufacturer) supplies all tape formats in many lengths	1	2	3	4	5	6	7	___	___	___
12. Adequate identification/labeling of shipping carton	1	2	3	4	5	6	7	___	___	___
13. Accurate and timely billing (invoicing)	1	2	3	4	5	6	7	___	___	___
14. National trade journal advertising by the vendor	1	2	3	4	5	6	7	___	___	___
15. Extended dating programs (supplier allows more than 60 days for payment)	1	2	3	4	5	6	7	___	___	___
16. Vendor replaces entire allotment when there is evidence of defective product	1	2	3	4	5	6	7	___	___	___
17. Accuracy in filling orders (correct product is shipped)	1	2	3	4	5	6	7	___	___	___
18. Quality/cleanliness of packaging materials	1	2	3	4	5	6	7	___	___	___
19. **Level** of product performance:										
• electromagnetics	1	2	3	4	5	6	7	___	___	___
• audio playback levels (bias requirements)	1	2	3	4	5	6	7	___	___	___
• bit error rate (digital formats)	1	2	3	4	5	6	7	___	___	___
• dropouts (dropout rate)	1	2	3	4	5	6	7	___	___	___
• scratches	1	2	3	4	5	6	7	___	___	___
• edge damage	1	2	3	4	5	6	7	___	___	___
• slitting errors	1	2	3	4	5	6	7	___	___	___
• creases/cinches	1	2	3	4	5	6	7	___	___	___
• wind quality (packing consistency)	1	2	3	4	5	6	7	___	___	___
20. **Consistency** of product performance (from one batch to another):										
• electromagnetics	1	2	3	4	5	6	7	___	___	___
• audio playback levels (bias requirements)	1	2	3	4	5	6	7	___	___	___
• bit error rate (digital formats)	1	2	3	4	5	6	7	___	___	___
• dropouts (dropout rate)	1	2	3	4	5	6	7	___	___	___
• scratches	1	2	3	4	5	6	7	___	___	___
• edge damage	1	2	3	4	5	6	7	___	___	___
• slitting errors	1	2	3	4	5	6	7	___	___	___
• creases/cinches	1	2	3	4	5	6	7	___	___	___
• wind quality (packing consistency)	1	2	3	4	5	6	7	___	___	___
21. Vendor expedites emergency orders in a fast responsive manner	1	2	3	4	5	6	7	___	___	___
22. Assistance/counseling provided by vendor on:										
• credit	1	2	3	4	5	6	7	___	___	___
• inventory management	1	2	3	4	5	6	7	___	___	___
23. Vendor adequately tests new products before delivering to market	1	2	3	4	5	6	7	___	___	___
24. Low price	1	2	3	4	5	6	7	___	___	___
25. Computer-to-computer order entry	1	2	3	4	5	6	7	___	___	___
26. Durability of thin base extended-length tape stocks	1	2	3	4	5	6	7	___	___	___
27. Development of new technologies by vendor	1	2	3	4	5	6	7	___	___	___
28. Vendor's willingness to work with your firm to develop new products and accessories	1	2	3	4	5	6	7	___	___	___
29. Competitiveness of price	1	2	3	4	5	6	7	___	___	___

FACTORS CONSIDERED	IMPORTANCE							PERCEIVED PERFORMANCE OF VENDORS (Scale of 1 to 7)		
	Not Important 1	2	3	4	5	6	Very Important 7	A	B	C
30. Technical service characteristics:										
• honesty of tech service rep	1	2	3	4	5	6	7	___	___	___
• accessibility	1	2	3	4	5	6	7	___	___	___
• responsiveness	1	2	3	4	5	6	7	___	___	___
• problem-solving capability	1	2	3	4	5	6	7	___	___	___
• general industry experience	1	2	3	4	5	6	7	___	___	___
• product knowledge	1	2	3	4	5	6	7	___	___	___
31. Frequency of deliveries (vendor consolidates multiple and/or split shipments into one larger, less frequent shipment)	1	2	3	4	5	6	7	___	___	___
32. Sales force characteristics:										
• accessibility	1	2	3	4	5	6	7	___	___	___
• honesty	1	2	3	4	5	6	7	___	___	___
• product knowledge	1	2	3	4	5	6	7	___	___	___
• industry knowledge	1	2	3	4	5	6	7	___	___	___
• technical knowledge	1	2	3	4	5	6	7	___	___	___
• general industry experience	1	2	3	4	5	6	7	___	___	___
• concern/empathy	1	2	3	4	5	6	7	___	___	___
• shares information about my competitors	1	2	3	4	5	6	7	___	___	___
• follows up promptly	1	2	3	4	5	6	7	___	___	___
33. Quantity discount structure based on size of individual order	1	2	3	4	5	6	7	___	___	___
34. Damage-free shipments	1	2	3	4	5	6	7	___	___	___
35. Adequate availablity (vendor's ability to deliver) of new products at time of format introduction	1	2	3	4	5	6	7	___	___	___
36. Experience with the vendor's product	1	2	3	4	5	6	7	___	___	___
37. Vendor combines volumes of different products in order to compute volume discount	1	2	3	4	5	6	7	___	___	___
38. Order processing personnel are located in:										
• your city	1	2	3	4	5	6	7	___	___	___
• your state	1	2	3	4	5	6	7	___	___	___
• one centralized U.S. location	1	2	3	4	5	6	7	___	___	___
39. Timely response to requests for assistance from vendor's sales representative	1	2	3	4	5	6	7	___	___	___
40. Quality/durability of tape cases:										
• protects integrity of tape during shipping	1	2	3	4	5	6	7	___	___	___
• facilitates long term storage	1	2	3	4	5	6	7	___	___	___
• impact resistance	1	2	3	4	5	6	7	___	___	___
• protects tape from dirt, dust	1	2	3	4	5	6	7	___	___	___
• protects tape from exposure to moisture	1	2	3	4	5	6	7	___	___	___
• case design minimizes storage space	1	2	3	4	5	6	7	___	___	___
41. Vendor absorbs cost of expedited freight and handling when the vendor experiences a stockout	1	2	3	4	5	6	7	___	___	___
42. Vendor provides technical analysis of defective tape	1	2	3	4	5	6	7	___	___	___
43. Adequate advance notice of price changes provided	1	2	3	4	5	6	7	___	___	___
44. Consistency of vendor's delivered product after initial evaluation of samples by my facility	1	2	3	4	5	6	7	___	___	___
45. Flexibility of credit policies to meet special situations	1	2	3	4	5	6	7	___	___	___
46. Ability of vendor to provide technical assistance on projects	1	2	3	4	5	6	7	___	___	___
47. Product durability (tape continues play back without loss of video and audio quality): • after multiple passes		2	3	4	5	6	7	___	___	___
• after extensive shuttling		2	3	4	5	6	7	___	___	___
48. Advance notice of shipping delays	1	2	3	4	5	6	7	___	___	___
49. Assistance from vendor in handling carrier loss and damage claims	1	2	3	4	5	6	7	___	___	___

VENDOR A = ______________________

VENDOR B = ______________________

VENDOR C = ______________________

FACTORS CONSIDERED	IMPORTANCE: Not Important 1	2	3	4	5	6	Very Important 7	PERCEIVED PERFORMANCE OF VENDORS (Scale of 1 to 7) A	B	C
50. Sales rep will give you volume price even if you are buying less	1	2	3	4	5	6	7	___	___	___
51. Prompt handling of claims due to overages, shortages or shipping errors	1	2	3	4	5	6	7	___	___	___
52. Prompt notification of technical analysis results	1	2	3	4	5	6	7	___	___	___
53. Direct mail material available from vendor:										
• technical materials	1	2	3	4	5	6	7	___	___	___
• new product announcements	1	2	3	4	5	6	7	___	___	___
• pricing	1	2	3	4	5	6	7	___	___	___
• personnel announcements	1	2	3	4	5	6	7	___	___	___
54. Vendor provides the following volume-based promotions:										
• trips	1	2	3	4	5	6	7	___	___	___
• consumer merchandise (stereos, golf clubs)	1	2	3	4	5	6	7	___	___	___
• free product	1	2	3	4	5	6	7	___	___	___
• rebates	1	2	3	4	5	6	7	___	___	___
55. Availability of status information on orders	1	2	3	4	5	6	7	___	___	___
56. Accuracy of vendor in forecasting & committing to shipping date	1	2	3	4	5	6	7	___	___	___
57. Participation of vendor in trade shows	1	2	3	4	5	6	7	___	___	___
58. Length of promised lead times (from order submission to delivery):										
• Normal orders	1	2	3	4	5	6	7	___	___	___
• Emergency orders	1	2	3	4	5	6	7	___	___	___
59. Vendor's adherence to special shipping instructions	1	2	3	4	5	6	7	___	___	___
60. Sales representative can provide tape stock in emergencies	1	2	3	4	5	6	7	___	___	___
61. Vendor holds dedicated inventory in return for a commitment to buy	1	2	3	4	5	6	7	___	___	___
62. Vendor reacts quickly to market-driven price reductions	1	2	3	4	5	6	7	___	___	___
63. Ability to serve as a test site for the evaluation of a vendor's new product	1	2	3	4	5	6	7	___	___	___
64. Prompt and comprehensive response to competitive bid quotations	1	2	3	4	5	6	7	___	___	___
65. Vendor provides "pallet stock" tape	1	2	3	4	5	6	7	___	___	___
66. Vendor provides updated and current literature	1	2	3	4	5	6	7	___	___	___
67. Packaging: • number of units in shipping carton	1	2	3	4	5	6	7	___	___	___
• provides adequate protection from dirt, dust, etc.	1	2	3	4	5	6	7	___	___	___
68. Vendor gives you an adequate period of price protection after a price increase is announced	1	2	3	4	5	6	7	___	___	___
69. Availability of blanket purchase orders	1	2	3	4	5	6	7	___	___	___
70. Freight pickup allowances for pickup of orders at vendor's warehouse (will-calls)	1	2	3	4	5	6	7	___	___	___
71. Tape machine maintenance and wear:										
• tape causes head deposits that require increased head maintenance	1	2	3	4	5	6	7	___	___	___
• tape has abrasive properties resulting in abnormal head wear	1	2	3	4	5	6	7	___	___	___
72. Number of sales calls you personally receive per month from vendor's sales representatives	1	2	3	4	5	6	7	___	___	___
73. Consistent lead times (vendor consistently meets promised delivery date)	1	2	3	4	5	6	7	___	___	___
74. Availability of published price schedule	1	2	3	4	5	6	7	___	___	___
75. Action on complaints related to order servicing and shipping	1	2	3	4	5	6	7	___	___	___

FACTORS CONSIDERED	IMPORTANCE Not Important 1	2	3	4	5	6	Very Important 7	PERCEIVED PERFORMANCE OF VENDORS (Scale of 1 to 7) A	B	C
76. Vendor provides shipper/storage cases	1	2	3	4	5	6	7	___	___	___
77. Tape performs satisfactorily in unfavorable operating environments:										
• humidity	1	2	3	4	5	6	7	___	___	___
• temperature extremes	1	2	3	4	5	6	7	___	___	___
• dust	1	2	3	4	5	6	7	___	___	___
78. Quality of product line above minimum standard	1	2	3	4	5	6	7	___	___	___
79. Product longevity (tape plays satisfactorily after long periods of storage)	1	2	3	4	5	6	7	___	___	___
80. Sales rep has authority to negotiate special prices	1	2	3	4	5	6	7	___	___	___
81. Vendor sends you promotional gifts (t-shirts, coffee mugs, etc.)	1	2	3	4	5	6	7	___	___	___
82. Low or no minimum order requirements	1	2	3	4	5	6	7	___	___	___
83. Service backup if salesperson is not available	1	2	3	4	5	6	7	___	___	___
84. Ability of vendor to change requested delivery dates	1	2	3	4	5	6	7	___	___	___
85. Vendor sponsored entertainment	1	2	3	4	5	6	7	___	___	___
86. Realistic, consistent pricing policy by vendor over time	1	2	3	4	5	6	7	___	___	___
87. Vendor meets specific and/or unique customer service and delivery needs of individual customers	1	2	3	4	5	6	7	___	___	___
88. Vendor's warehousing facility is located in your immediate area	1	2	3	4	5	6	7	___	___	___
89. Bar coded products (type of code used):										
• UPC (Universal Product Code)	1	2	3	4	5	6	7	___	___	___
• 2 of 5	1	2	3	4	5	6	7	___	___	___
• Interleaved 2 of 5 (Codabar)	1	2	3	4	5	6	7	___	___	___
• 3 of 9 (Code 39)	1	2	3	4	5	6	7	___	___	___
• Other (specify) ______________	1	2	3	4	5	6	7	___	___	___
90. Bar code location: • outer carton	1	2	3	4	5	6	7	___	___	___
• product case	1	2	3	4	5	6	7	___	___	___
• on the product itself	1	2	3	4	5	6	7	___	___	___
91. Vendor absorbs cost of freight and handling on returns due to damage or product shipped in error	1	2	3	4	5	6	7	___	___	___
92. High fill rate (% of order included in initial shipment): % of line items	1	2	3	4	5	6	7	___	___	___
93. Long term (more than 1 year) contractural relationship available with vendor	1	2	3	4	5	6	7	___	___	___
94. Freight terms:										
• Prepaid (paid by vendor)	1	2	3	4	5	6	7	___	___	___
• Collect (paid by you)	1	2	3	4	5	6	7	___	___	___
95. Free WATS line (800 number) provided for entering orders with vendor	1	2	3	4	5	6	7	___	___	___
96. Ability to select delivering carriers	1	2	3	4	5	6	7	___	___	___
97. Palletized and utilized loads where possible for handling efficiency	1	2	3	4	5	6	7	___	___	___
98. Order processing personnel can provide information on:										
• product characteristics	1	2	3	4	5	6	7	___	___	___
• technical questions	1	2	3	4	5	6	7	___	___	___
• inventory availability	1	2	3	4	5	6	7	___	___	___
• projected shipping date	1	2	3	4	5	6	7	___	___	___
• projected delivery date	1	2	3	4	5	6	7	___	___	___
• availability of substitute products	1	2	3	4	5	6	7	___	___	___
99. Vendor's warehouse can accept will-calls	1	2	3	4	5	6	7	___	___	___

PART B: MEASUREMENT OF OVERALL PERFORMANCE

1. Please indicate the percent that each vendor currently represents of your annual purchases of blank video tape, as well as the percent that you would *prefer* to give each vendor under ideal conditions in the future. (Your totals should add to 100%).

	Current %	Ideal (Preferred) %
VENDOR A (**the largest amount** of your blank tape purchases are from this vendor):	_____%	_____ %
VENDOR B (**second largest amount** of your blank tape purchases are from this vendor):	_____%	_____ %
VENDOR C (**third largest amount** of your blank tape purchases are from this vendor):	_____%	_____ %
Other Vendors	_____%	_____ %
	100%	100%

2. Please mark a point anywhere on the lines below that best expressses your *level of satisfaction* with the above vendors. If you are extremely dissatisfied with a vendor's performance, a mark should be placed very near the left end of the line (labeled Poor). If you are exceptionally pleased with the Vendor's performance, a mark should be placed very near the right end of the line (labeled Excellent). A midpoint has been placed on the line to correspond with a "Satisfactory" performance level.

OVERALL VENDOR PERFORMANCE

	Poor	Satisfactory	Excellent
VENDOR A	├	┼	┤
VENDOR B	├	┼	┤
VENDOR C	├	┼	┤

3. Would you recommend these vendors to another firm?

VENDOR A	VENDOR B	VENDOR C
_____ Yes	_____ Yes	_____ Yes
_____ No	_____ No	_____ No

4. Have you ever reported to these vendors a problem with the service you received?

VENDOR A	VENDOR B	VENDOR C
_____ Yes	_____ Yes	_____ Yes
_____ No	_____ No	_____ No

5. Did the vendor respond adequately to the problem you reported?

VENDOR A	VENDOR B	VENDOR C
_____ Yes	_____ Yes	_____ Yes
_____ No	_____ No	_____ No

6. What percentage of on-time delivery performance do you currently receive from your major vendors during a typical month?

VENDOR A	VENDOR B	VENDOR C
_______%	_______%	_______%

7. If your major vendor is a DISTRIBUTOR, what is the major reason you buy from them? (Check only one item)

_____ faster delivery _____ price
_____ local service _____ other (please specify): ________________________________

8. For the **three vendors that you have evaluated**, please give the lowest price vendor a score of 0%. For the others, indicate the *percentage premium* that you would pay for their services. If two or more vendors offer the same price, give them the same score.

(EXAMPLE: If Vendor B was the lowest price vendor, it would be assigned a 0; if Vendor A's price was 2% higher than Vendor B's, it would be assigned a 2%; if Vendor C charged the same price as Vendor A, it would also be assigned a 2%; if Vendor C's price was 3% higher than Vendor B's, it would be assigned a 3%).

VENDOR A	VENDOR B	VENDOR C
_______%	_______%	_______%

PART C: EXPECTED PERFORMANCE LEVELS

Please provide the following information with respect to the levels of customer service that you need from your vendors of blank video tape stock. ***Vendor A** is identified as the vendor with whom you make your largest amount of blank tape purchases.*

1. How many sales contacts does your department receive from **VENDOR A** of blank video tape stock during a typical month (year)?

   ____ face to face calls per month ____ per year ____ telephone calls per month ____ per year

2. How many sales contacts would your department *prefer to receive* from **VENDOR A** of blank video tape stock during a typical month?

   ____ face to face calls per month ____ per year ____ telephone calls per month ____ per year

3. What response time do you expect from **VENDOR A**'s sales representative in:

   A. Emergency situations _______ hours b. Non-emergency situations _______ hours

4. How much advance notice do you *need* from **VENDOR A** on price changes? _______ days

5. How much advance notice do you *currently receive* from **VENDOR A** on price changes? _______ days

6. Under **normal conditions,** how frequently do you submit orders to **VENDOR A**? (Check one)

a. Several times a day	_____	d. Once a week	_____	f. Once a month	_____
b. Once a day	_____	e. Several times a month	_____	g. Other (please specify)	_____
c. Several times a week	_____				

7. Please indicate the percentage of your blank video tape orders that are initially transmitted to **VENDOR A** by each of the following means:

   a. U.S. Mail _____%
   b. TWX, FAX machine and/or other communication terminal _____%
   c. Free inward telephone line (paid by supplier) _____%
   d. Other telephone communication (paid by you) _____%
   e. Hand delivered to manufacturer's sales rep _____%
   f. Other (Specify) ______________________________ _____%
   TOTAL 100%

8. Under **normal conditions,** what is the total average lead time (from time order is placed to day received) in calendar days:
   a) that you *need* from **VENDOR A**? _____ days b) that you *actually receive* from **VENDOR A**? _____ days

9. What is the maximum number of days beyond the promised delivery date that you consider to be an acceptable delay? _____ days

10. What is the minimum acceptable order fill rate that you *need* from **VENDOR A?** (% of order included in initial shipment): _____%

11. What order fill rate (% of order included in initial shipment) do you *currently receive* from **VENDOR A?** _____%

12. Once you have placed an order, how long does it take to receive notification from **VENDOR A** as to the expected (promised) delivery date? (*Please specify the number of minutes, hours or days, if none is provided, answer "N"*)

    ___ ___ minutes ___ ___ hours ___ ___ days

13. For products that are available from more than one vendor, identify the percentage of times that the following alternatives are used in the event that your order cannot be filled by the committed and/or requested delivery date?

    a. Backorder (hold until *all product is available* and ship complete) _____%
    b. Cancel unavailable items and ship balance by committed date _____%
    c. Split ship (ship quantities as they become available) _____%
    d. Cancel order and go to another supplier _____%
    e. Purchase unavailable line items from another vendor _____%
    f. Other (please specify): ______________________________ _____%
    100%

14. How many orders do you place with **VENDOR A** in a typical month? _____ orders.

15. What percentage of your orders are "emergency" orders that require expedited service? _____%

16. What terms of payment are *offered* by your major vendors?

	Discount %	Number of days	Net No. of days
a. VENDOR A	_______%	________	________
b. VENDOR B	_______%	________	________
c. VENDOR C	_______%	________	________

17. What payment terms do you *actually receive* from **VENDOR A?:** number of days _____ % discount for early payment _____

18. What percentage premium should a vendor charge you for an emergency, expedited order? _______%

19. What is the typical dollar value of your average order of blank video tape stock from **VENDOR A?** $________________.00

20. What is the minimum dollar value order **VENDOR A** will ship? $________________.00

21. What percentage of the product is delivered by **VENDOR A**'s promised delivery date? _______%

22. What proportion of your orders do you realistically need to have within:

    same day _______%
    1 day _______%
    3 days _______%
    5 days _______%
    7 days _______%
    10 days or more _______%
    100%

23. What percentage of **VENDOR A**'s products arrive damage free? _____%

24. Do you evaluate vendors using (Please check one) a. Formal process/system _____ b. Informal process/system _____

25. How frequently do you evaluate vendor performance: (check one)
    a. constantly ___ b. weekly ___ c. monthly ___ d. quarterly ___ e. annually ___ f. never ___

26. In your evaluation of vendor performance, which of the following factors do you consider? (Please check all appropriate responses)
    a. Fill rate on first shipment ___ b. Lead time ___ c. Lead time variability ___
    d. Damage ___ e. Accuracy in invoicing ___ f. Quality of products shipped ___

27. Considering all blank video tape stock purchased by your firm, please indicate the percentage of each tape you buy. Also, please indicate the relative percentages of tape formats you expect to be purchasing in three years. *Totals should add up to 100%.*

BLANK TAPE PRODUCTS	**% of Present Purchases**	**Expected % of Purchases in 3 years**
Video cassette pancakes	____	____
1″ C format video tape	____	____
¾″ U-matic cassettes	____	____
¾″ SP U-matic cassettes	____	____
½″ VHS cassettes	____	____
½″ S-VHS cassettes	____	____
Betacam video cassettes	____	____
Betacam SP video cassettes	____	____
D - 1 component video cassettes	____	____
D - 2 composite video cassettes	____	____
8mm video cassettes	____	____
HI - 8 video cassettes	____	____
	100%	100%

PART D: DEMOGRAPHIC DATA

This information is required in order to identify major market segments and to provide more meaningful analyses of the previous sections. Please use approximate figures in the event that exact data are not readily available.

1. What has been the average rate of growth in your purchases of blank video tape stock for the company over the last five years? ________%

2. What is your approximate annual budget for blank video tape stock? $____________.00

3. How much blank video tape inventory (average number of days of supply of product) do you carry? ______ days

4. How many supply sources of blank tape products have you added and deleted during the past 12 months, 2 years and 5 years?

	Last 12 Months	Last 2 Years	Last 5 Years
Vendors added	________	________	________
Vendors deleted (dropped)	________	________	________

5. If you are an END USER, what percentage of the operating cost of your department is represented by your purchases of blank tape stock? _____%

6. If you are a DISTRIBUTOR, what percentage of your gross sales is represented by blank video tape sales? ______%

7. Please indicate your overall evaluation of each of the following vendors.

	Insufficient Information To Evaluate	**Very Unfavorable 1**	**2**	**3**	**4**	**5**	**6**	**Very Favorable 7**
Agfa/BASF	______	1	2	3	4	5	6	7
Ampex	______	1	2	3	4	5	6	7
Fuji	______	1	2	3	4	5	6	7
JVC	______	1	2	3	4	5	6	7
Maxell	______	1	2	3	4	5	6	7
Panasonic	______	1	2	3	4	5	6	7
Sony	______	1	2	3	4	5	6	7
TDK	______	1	2	3	4	5	6	7
3M	______	1	2	3	4	5	6	7
Other ____________	______	1	2	3	4	5	6	7

8. What is your position or title? ______________________

9. Please indicate that type of business that best reflects what you do: (check one)

- ___ TV broadcasting
- ___ TV program/commercial spot duplication
- ___ Video products distributor (equipment & tape)
- ___ Video tape distributor
- ___ Motion picture production/post production
- ___ TV program production/post production
- ___ Other (please specify): ______________________

10. What are the first three numbers of your zip code? ________

Thank you for your participation and cooperation in completing this survey. Your time and effort are sincerely appreciated. Please return the questionnaire in the envelope provided or mail to:

DOUGLAS M. LAMBERT, Ph.D. and JAMES R. STOCK, Ph.D.
Department of Marketing • College of Business Administration • BSN 3403 • University of South Florida • Tampa, Florida 33620-5500

Chapter 5

Transportation

- Introduction
  - Time and Place Utility
  - Transportation/Logistics/Marketing Interface
  - Factors Influencing Transportation Costs/Pricing
    - Product-Related Factors
    - Market-Related Factors
  - Transportation Service Characteristics
- The Transportation System
  - Alternative Transport Modes
    - Motor
    - Rail
    - Air
    - Water
    - Pipeline
  - Intermodal Combinations
    - Piggyback (TOFC/COFC)
    - Roadrailers
    - Transportation Companies
  - Role of Nonoperating Third Parties
    - Freight Forwarders
    - Shippers' Associations
    - Brokers
    - Shippers' Agents
- Other Transport Forms
  - Parcel Post
  - United Parcel Service (UPS)
  - Air Express Companies
- Transportation Regulation
  - Forms of Regulation
  - Regulatory History
  - Legal Forms of Transportation
  - Transportation Pricing
    - Cost-of-Service versus Value-of-Service Pricing
    - Categories of Rates
    - Rate Bureaus
- Regulatory Reforms
  - Carrier Perspectives
    - Motor
    - Rail
    - Air
    - Water
  - Shipper Perspectives
- Summary
- Suggested Readings
- Questions and Problems
- Appendix: Some Major Federal Transportation Regulatory Agencies

Objectives of This Chapter

To examine transportation's role in logistics and its relationship to the marketing activities of a firm

To consider the various alternative transport modes, intermodal combinations, and other transportation entities available to distribute products

To summarize past and present transportation regulation, with a view toward future developments

To examine various aspects of deregulation and their impact on carriers and shippers

INTRODUCTION

An industrialized society without an efficient transportation system seems a contradiction in terms. We often assume that products will move from where they are produced to where they are consumed with a minimum of difficulty—in terms of both time and cost. The transportation sector of most industrialized economies is so pervasive that we often fail to comprehend the magnitude of its impact on our way of life. Transportation expenditures constitute approximately 11 percent of U.S. expenditures for goods and services (GNP). In 1990 transportation costs amounted to $352 billion.[1] D. F. Pegrum analyzed the integral role transportation plays in the economy:

The Role of Transportation

> The unique position which transportation occupies in economic activity arises from the reduction by it of the resistances of time and space to the production of economic goods and services. The significance of this in terms of the allocation of economic resources is indicated by the fact that probably at least one third of our national wealth is directly devoted to transportation. So important is it that without it organized human activity would be impossible; complete stoppage of a community's transport services is the quickest way to assure complete paralysis of cooperative effort: economic, political and social.[2]

Since 1970 the transportation sector has grown considerably. Figure 5–1 shows how freight transportation—represented as intercity ton-miles—has grown over the years relative to GNP.

This chapter provides an overview of the transportation function and its importance to logistics. We will also examine alternative transportation modes and intermodal combinations available for product movement. We will also look at how regulation and deregulation have affected transportation—and their likely effects in the future.

---

[1] Robert V. Delaney, "CLI's 'State of Logistics' Annual Report" press conference remarks to the National Press Club, Washington, D.C. (June 7, 1991), p. 25.

[2] Dudley F. Pegrum, *Transportation Economics and Public Policy,* 3rd ed. (Homewood, Ill.: Richard D. Irwin, 1973), p. 19.

FIGURE 5–1 Freight Transportation Outlays versus GNP

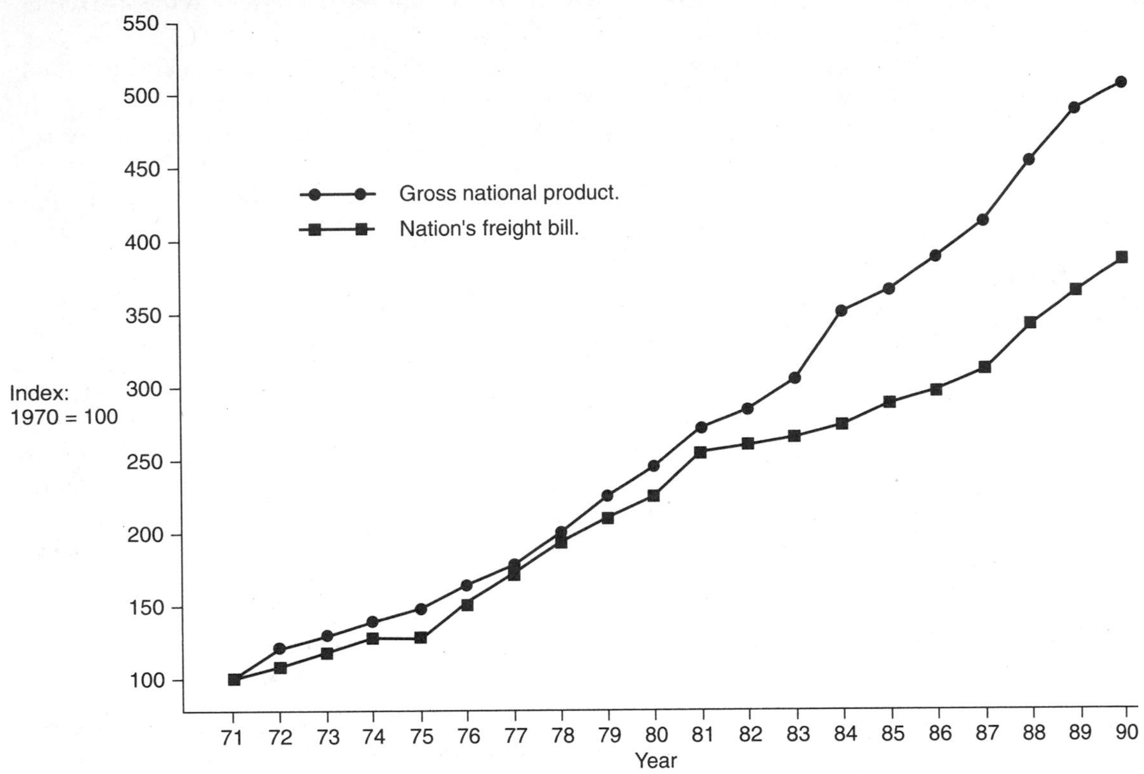

SOURCE: Robert V. Delaney, "CLI's 'State of Logistics' Annual Report," Press conference remarks to the National Press Club, Washington, D.C. (June 7, 1991), p. 35.

Time and Place Utility

Logistics involves the movement of products (raw materials, parts, supplies, finished goods) from point-of-origin to point-of-consumption. A product produced at one point has very little value to the prospective customer unless it is moved to the point where it will be consumed. Transportation achieves this movement.

Transportation Creates Utility

Movement across space or distance creates value or place utility. Time utility is mostly created or added by the warehousing and storage of product until it is needed. But transportation is also a factor in time utility; it determines how fast and how consistently a product moves from one point to another. This is known as *time-in-transit* and *consistency of service*. If a product is not available at the precise time it is needed, there may be expensive repercussions, such as lost sales, customer dissatisfaction, and production downtime. Most logistics managers are familiar with the problems created by late arrival of needed items. United Parcel Service, Federal Express,

Leaseway Transportation, CSX, and Ryder System have been successful because they are able to increase the time and place utility of their customers' products.

Transportation/Logistics/Marketing Interface

Transportation moves a firm's products to markets that are often geographically separated by great distances. By doing so, it adds to the customer's general level of satisfaction, because he or she has access to the products. Customer satisfaction is an important component of the marketing concept.

Because transportation creates place utility and contributes to time utility—both of which are necessary for successful marketing—its availability, adequacy, and cost affect business decisions seemingly unrelated to managing the transportation function itself. Harper summarized the major business decisions affected by transportation as follows:

The Major Business Decisions Affected by Transportation

Product Decisions. For those firms that deal in tangible products, one such decision is the product decision, or the decision as to what product or products to produce. The transportability of a product in terms of its physical attributes, and the cost, availability, and adequacy of transportation, should enter into any product decision.

Market Area Decisions. Closely related to the product decision for firms dealing in tangible products is the decision relative to where the product(s) should be sold. This can be affected by transportation availability, adequacy, and cost, plus the physical characteristics of the product itself.

Purchasing Decisions. What to purchase can be affected greatly by transportation considerations, regardless of the nature of the firm, whether it be a manufacturer, wholesaler, retailer, service organization, mining company, or whatever. The goods involved may be parts, raw materials, supplies, or finished goods for resale. The availability, adequacy, and cost of transportation, plus the transportation characteristics of the goods involved, have a bearing on the "what, where, and when" decision.

Location Decisions. Although decisions relative to where plants, warehouses, offices, stores, and other business facilities should be located are influenced by many factors, transportation availability, adequacy, and cost can be extremely important in such decision making. The significance of the transportation factor varies from industry to industry and from firm to firm, but transportation usually is worthy of some consideration in making location decisions.

Pricing Decisions. Since transportation is a cost factor in business operations, it can have a bearing on the pricing decisions made by business firms, especially those firms that have a cost-oriented pricing policy. In

> fact, because transportation is one of the nation's "basic" economic activities, price changes in transportation can have a serious effect on the prices of industry in general. This does not mean that in any individual firm there is an automatic cause-and-effect relationship between transportation cost changes and the firm's prices, but transportation cost is one of the factors that usually should be considered in pricing decisions.[3]

Transportation can account for 50 percent or more of the cost of basic raw materials such as sand and coal. Transportation costs for such items as computers, business machines, and electronic components may be less than 1 percent. Generally, the effective and efficient management of transportation becomes more important to a firm as transportation's share of product cost increases. The management of all aspects of transportation is affected, including inbound costs for acquisition of raw materials, parts, and supplies, and outbound costs of shipping finished goods to customers.

Factors Influencing Transportation Costs/Pricing

In general, factors influencing transportation costs/pricing can be grouped into two major categories—product-related factors and market-related factors.

Product-Related Factors. Many factors related to a product's characteristics influence the cost/pricing of transportation. A company can use these factors to determine product classifications for rate-making purposes; they can be grouped into the following categories: (1) density, (2) stowability, (3) ease or difficulty of handling, and (4) liability. *Density* refers to a product's weight-to-volume ratio. Items such as steel, canned foods, building products, and paper goods have high weight-to-volume ratios; that is, they are relatively heavy given their size. On the other hand, products such as electronics, clothing, luggage, and toys have low weight-to-volume ratios and thus are relatively lightweight given their size. In general, low-density products—those with low weight-to-volume ratios—tend to cost more to transport, on a per-pound (kilo) basis than high-density products. *Stowability* is the degree to which a product can fill the available space in a transport vehicle. For example, grain, ore, and petroleum products in bulk have excellent stowability because they can completely fill the container (e.g., rail car, tank truck, pipeline) in which they are transported. Other items, such as automobiles, machinery, livestock, and people, do not have good stowa-

Density

Stowability

[3] Donald V. Harper, *Transportation in America: Users, Carriers, Government,* 2nd ed. (Englewood Cliffs, N.J.: Prentice Hall, 1982), pp. 15–16. Reprinted by permission of Prentice Hall, Inc., Englewood Cliffs, N.J.

bility, or cube utilization. A product's stowability depends on its size, shape, fragility, and other physical characteristics.

Handling

Related to stowability is the *ease or difficulty of handling* the product. Items that are not easily handled are more costly to transport. Products that are uniform in their physical characteristics (e.g., raw materials and items in cartons, cans, or drums), or products that can be manipulated with materials-handling equipment, require less handling expense and are therefore less costly to transport. *Liability* is an important concern. Products with high value-to-weight ratios, those that are easily damaged, and those that are subject to higher rates of theft or pilferage cost more to transport. In cases where the transportation carrier assumes greater liability (e.g., with computer, jewelry, and home entertainment products), a higher price will be charged to transport the product.

Liability

Other factors, which vary in importance depending on the product category, are the product's hazardous characteristics and the need for strong and rigid protective packaging. Such factors are particularly important in the chemical and plastics industries.

Market-Related Factors. In addition to product characteristics, important market-related factors also affect transportation costs/pricing. The most significant are (1) degree of intramode and intermode competition; (2) location of markets (i.e., distance goods must be transported); (3) nature and extent of government regulation of transportation carriers; (4) balance or imbalance of freight traffic in a territory; (5) seasonality of product movements; and (6) whether the product is being transported domestically or internationally. Each of these factors, in combination, affects the costs and pricing of transportation, and we will examine each later in this chapter. In addition, however, there are also important service considerations.

Transportation Service Characteristics

Customer service is a vital component of logistics management. Each activity of logistics management contributes to the level of service a company provides to its customers, although transportation's impact on customer service is one of the most significant. The most important transportation service characteristics affecting customer service levels are dependability (consistency of service); time-in-transit; market coverage (the ability to provide door-to-door service); flexibility (with respect to the variety of products that can be handled and meeting the special needs of shippers); loss and damage performance; and the ability of the carrier to provide more than just basic transportation service (i.e., to become part of a shipper's overall marketing program).

Transportation and Customer Service

Each mode of transport—motor, rail, air, water, and pipeline—has varying service capabilities. In the next section, we will examine each mode in terms of its economic and service characteristics.

THE TRANSPORTATION SYSTEM

A variety of options is available for individuals, firms, or countries that want to move their products from one point to another. Any one or more of five transportation modes—motor, rail, air, water, or pipeline—may be selected. Figure 5–2 identifies the usage patterns of various transportation options throughout the world. Significant variations can and do exist. In addition, certain modal combinations are available, including rail-motor, motor-water, motor-air, and rail-water. Such intermodal combinations offer specialized or lower cost services not generally available when using a single transport mode. Finally, other transporters (sometimes called indirect or special carriers or nonoperating third parties) offer a variety of services to shippers. These transporters include freight forwarders, shipper cooperatives, parcel post, United Parcel Service (UPS), and other services such as Federal Express and Roadway Express. Special carriers usually act as transportation intermediaries and use one or more of the basic modes for moving their customers' products.

Alternative Transport Modes

Motor Carriage Is the Most Widely Used Mode

Motor. During the late 1960s, motor carriage replaced rail carriage as the dominant form of freight transport in the United States. Motor carriers transport over 75 percent of the tonnage of agricultural products such as fresh and frozen meats, dairy products, bakery products, confectionary items, beverages, and cigars. Many manufactured products are transported by motor carriers, including amusement, sporting, and athletic goods, toys, watches, clocks, farm machinery, radios, televisions, phonographs, records, carpets and rugs, clothing, drugs, and office and accounting machines. Most consumer goods are transported by motor carrier.

Usually, motor carriers compete with air for small shipments and rail for large shipments.[4] An efficient motor carrier can compete with an air carrier on point-to-point service for any size shipment if the distance involved is 500 miles or less. This is so because motor carriers can realize greater efficiencies in terminal, pickup, and delivery operations.

Motor carriers compete directly with railroads for truckload-size (TL-size) shipments that are transported 500 miles or more. However, rail is the dominant mode when shipment sizes exceed 100,000 pounds. Motor carriers dominate for LTL shipments. Table 5–1 shows the areas of competition between motor carriers and rail, air, and other forms of carriage.

The average length of haul for motor carriers is approximately 500 miles. Some national carriers have average hauls several times as long,

---

[4]Smaller shipments transported by motor carriers are referred to as less-than-truckload (LTL). LTL can be defined as any quantity of freight weighing less than the amount required for the application of a truckload rate.

FIGURE 5–2 International Variations in Use of Major Transport Modes (By weight)

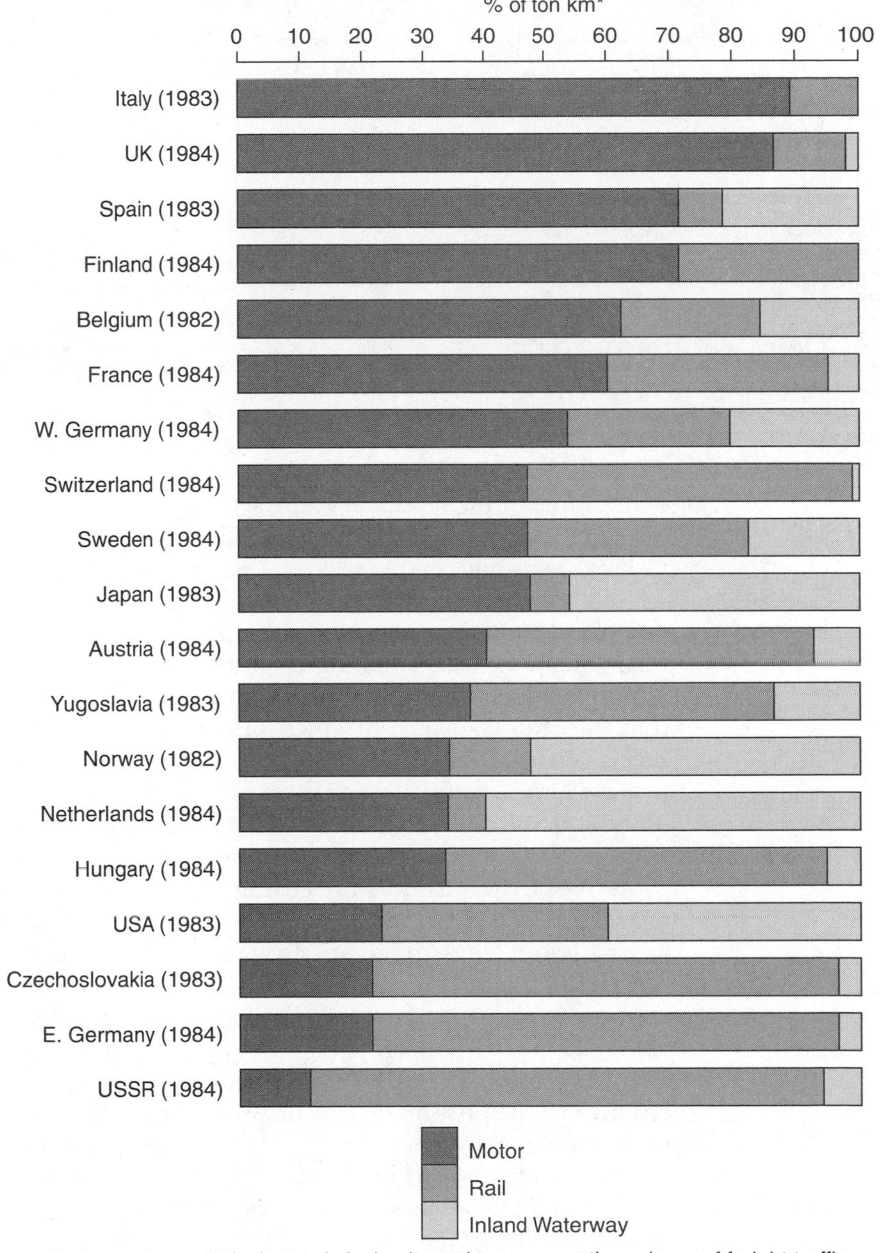

The ton-km or ton-mile is the statistical unit used to measure the volume of freight traffic moved between points. One ton of freight transported one kilometer or one mile would be equivalent to one ton-km or one ton-mile respectively.

SOURCE: Adapted from Alan C. McKinnon, *Physical Distribution Systems* (London: Routledge, 1989), p. 153.

TABLE 5–1 Competition for Intercity For-Hire Truck Service

Category	*Under 100 Pounds*	*100 to 500 Pounds*	*LTL over 500 Pounds*	*"Standby" Truckload**	*Truckload*	*Truckload Special Equipment*
General commodity carriers	X	X	X	X	X	X
Specialized commodity carriers						X
Private fleets	X	X	X	X	X	X
Contract carriers	X	X	X	X	X	X
Rail					X	X
Piggyback (trailer-on-flatcar)					X	X
Freight forwarders and shipper associations	X	X	X	X		
Specialized small shipment carriers	X	X				
Air cargo and passenger airlines	X	X	X	X		
UPS, parcel post, bus	X					

*"Standby" truckload refers to truckload service provided by general commodity carriers who offer truckload service at class or commodity rates. Typically, they carry truckloads which cannot be handled by the shipper's private fleet or specialized carriers because of balance or capacity problems, e.g., at peak periods.

SOURCE: John F. Throckmorton and Paul M. Mueller, *Motor Carrier Marketing,* Part 1 (Washington, D.C.: Sales and Marketing Council of American Trucking Associations, 1980), p. 27.

while some intracity carriers may average five miles or less.[5] LTL shipments are generally of shorter haul than TL shipments, but significant variability in lengths-of-haul exist.

Motor Carriers Offer Flexibility and Versatility

Motor carriers are more flexible and versatile than other modes. The flexibility of motor carriers is made possible by a network of over 4 million miles of roads, thus enabling them to offer point-to-point service between almost any origin-destination combination. Motor carriers are versatile in that they can transport products of varying sizes and weights over any distance. Virtually any product, including some for which equipment modifications are necessary, can be transported by motor carriers. Their flexibility and versatility have enabled them to become the dominant form of transport in the United States and in many other parts of the world.

Motor carriage offers the customer fast, reliable service with little damage or loss in transit. Motor carriers generally give much faster service than railroads and compare favorably with air carriers on short hauls. Many motor carriers, particularly those involved in "Just-in-Time" programs, operate on a scheduled timetable. This results in very short and reliable transit times. Loss and damage ratios for motor carriers are substantially lower than for most rail shipments and are slightly higher than for air freight. No other transport mode can provide the market coverage offered by motor carriers.

General Freight and Specialty Carriers

The industry can be classified into two general categories of carriers: general freight carriers and specialized motor carriers. General freight carriers generate the majority of all truck revenues and include intercity com-

[5] Roy J. Sampson, Martin T. Farris, and David L. Shrock, *Domestic Transportation: Practice, Theory, and Policy,* 5th ed. (Boston: Houghton Mifflin, 1985), p. 69.

mon carriers and other general carriers.[6] Specialized motor carriers generate the remaining revenues. These include carriers of heavy machinery, liquid petroleum, refrigerated products, agricultural commodities, motor vehicles, building materials, household goods, and other specialized items.

The amount of freight transported by motor carriers has steadily increased over the years. Motor carriage is a vital part of most firms' logistics network, because the characteristics of the motor carrier industry are more compatible with the service requirements of the firms' customers than are other transport modes. As long as it is able to provide fast, efficient service at rates between those offered by rail and air, the motor carrier industry will continue to prosper relative to other transport modes.

Rail. In some countries—for example, the People's Republic of China, the Commonwealth of Independent States (formerly the Soviet Union), Austria, and Yugoslavia—rail is the dominant transport mode. In the United States, railroads carried over 1 trillion ton-miles of freight[7] over a track network totaling approximately 233,000 miles in 1989.[8] Railroads accounted for slightly over one-third of the intercity freight traffic in ton-miles. Since World War II, when rail transported about two-thirds of the ton-mile traffic, its share of the U.S. market declined until 1986, when the downward trend was reversed. Most of the freight once shipped by rail has been shifted to motor carriers. Some traffic also has been lost to water and pipeline carriers, which generally compete with railroads for bulk commodities.

Most Rail Traffic Has Shifted to Motor Carriers

Railroads have an average length of haul of approximately 688 miles.[9] Rail service is available in almost every major metropolitan center in the world, and in many smaller communities as well. However, the rail network is not nearly as extensive as the highway network in most countries. Therefore rail transport lacks the versatility and flexibility of motor carriers because it is limited to fixed track facilities. As a result, railroads, like air, water, and pipeline transport, provide terminal-to-terminal service rather than point-to-point service for most shippers (unless they have a rail siding at their facility).

Rail Is Low Cost

Rail transport generally costs less (on a weight basis) than air and motor carriage.[10] For many shipments, rail does not compare favorably with other modes on loss and damage ratios. It has disadvantages compared to

---

[6] Carriers may be classified into one of four categories, depending on whether or not they are regulated by the government. We will discuss these categories—common, contract, exempt, and private—later in this chapter.

[7] "Rails Report 6-Month Traffic Gains," *On Track* 4, no. 14 (July 17–31, 1990), p. 2.

[8] James C. Johnson and Donald F. Wood, *Contemporary Logistics* (New York: Macmillan, 1990), p. 99.

[9] *Railroad Facts* (Washington, D.C.: Association of American Railroads, 1988), p. 31.

[10] In some transportation lanes and markets, motor carriers have been very price competitive with rail. In a few instances, motor carriers have been able to match or even undercut the rates charged by railroads.

motor carriers in terms of transit time and frequency of service, although, since deregulation of the rail industry in 1980, railroads have improved significantly in these areas. Trains travel on timetable schedules, but departures are less frequent than those of motor carriers. If a shipper has strict arrival and departure requirements, railroads are at a competitive disadvantage compared to motor carriers. Some of this disadvantage may be overcome through the use of trailer-on-flatcar (TOFC) or container-on-flatcar (COFC) service, which offer the economy of rail or water movements combined with the flexibility of trucking. Truck trailers or containers are delivered to the rail terminals, where they are loaded on flatbed railcars. At the destination terminal they are off-loaded and delivered to the consignee—the customer who receives the shipment. We will examine these services in further detail later in this chapter.

An additional area in which railroads suffer in comparison to motor carriers is equipment availability. Railroad lines use each other's cars, and at times this equipment may not be located where it is most needed. Railcars may be unavailable because they are being loaded, unloaded, moved within railroad sorting yards, or undergoing repair. Other cars may be standing idle or lost within the vast rail network.

A number of developments in the rail industry have helped to overcome some of these utilization problems. Advances have included computer routing and scheduling; the upgrading of equipment, roadbeds, and terminals; improvements in railcar identification systems; cars owned or leased by the shipper; and the use of unit trains or dedicated through-train service between major metropolitan areas (nonstop shipments of one or a few shippers' products).[11] Railroads own most of their car fleet, with the remainder either leased or owned by shippers. Shippers that own or lease cars are typically heavy users of rail and are especially sensitive to railcar shortages because of unique market or competitive conditions.

Unit Trains

During the late 1980s, railroads recaptured some of the traffic lost to trucks, pipelines, and water carriers. Improvements in equipment and facilities, upgrading of roadbeds, and better monitoring and control of rail fleets were contributing factors to the railroad's success. The relative energy-efficiency advantage railroads have over motor carriers, along with the deregulation of the rail industry, offers a promise of better things to come and perhaps a rebirth of the rail industry. The continuing trend toward consolidation through mergers and acquisitions holds promise for a brighter future for this transport mode.

Air. Domestically, air carriers transport less than 1 percent of ton-mile traffic. Revenues to air carriers from movement of freight were about $9

---

[11] Unit trains are trains of great length carrying a single product in one direction. Commodities transported by unit trains include coal, grains, U.S. mail, automobiles, fruits, and vegetables.

TABLE 5–2 The 10 Largest Airlines in the World

Rank by Revenue	*Airline*	*Country*	*1989 Revenues* (in millions)*	*Passenger Miles (in billions)*
1	AMR (American)	USA	$10,590	74
2	UAL (United)	USA	9,915	70
3	Japan	Japan	8,509	34
4	Delta	USA	8,090	56
5	British Airways	Great Britain	7,529	36
6	Lufthansa	Germany	6,941	23
7	Continental	USA	6,769	50
8	NWA (Northwest)	USA	6,554	46
9	USAir	USA	6,257	34
10	Air France	France	6,217	23

*Compiled from various airline annual reports and industry sources.

Air Freight Is a Small but Important Segment

billion in 1989, but this represented only a small percentage of the total U.S. freight bill.[12] Although increasing numbers of shippers are using air freight for regular service, most view air transport as a premium, emergency service because of its higher cost. But in instances where an item must be delivered to a distant location quickly, air freight offers the shortest time-in-transit of any transport mode. For most shippers, however, these time-sensitive shipments are relatively few in number or frequency.

Modern aircraft have cruising speeds of 500 to 600 miles per hour and are able to travel internationally. The average length of haul domestically is 793 miles, although international movements may be thousands (2,750) of miles.[13] Domestic air freight directly competes to a great extent with motor carriers, and to a much lesser degree with rail carriers. Where countries are separated by large expanses of water, the major competitor for international air freight is water carriage.

For most commercial airlines, such as those identified in Table 5–2, freight is incidental to passenger traffic. These passenger airlines carry freight on a space-available basis. But air freight companies such as UPS, Airborne, Federal Express, and Emery are classified as all-cargo carriers. These carriers transport approximately 50 percent of all domestic air freight. This percentage represents a sizable increase over 1968, when only a small percentage of air freight was handled by the all-cargo carriers.

High Cost of Air Freight

Air carriers generally handle high-value products. Air freight usually cannot be cost-justified for low-value items, because the high price of air freight would represent too much of the product cost. For example, con-

[12] *Air Transport 1990* (Washington, D.C.: Air Transport Association of America, 1990), p. 4.

[13] Ibid., p. 12.

sider an electronics component and a textbook that weigh the same but differ significantly in price. If it costs the same to air freight both of them from point A to point B, transportation charges will consume a greater portion of the textbook's total cost and a smaller portion of the electronic component's cost. Customer service considerations may influence the choice of transport mode in this situation, but only if service issues are more important than cost issues.

Air Provides Fast Time-in-Transit

Air transport provides rapid time-in-transit, but terminal and delivery delays and congestion may appreciably reduce some of this advantage. On a point-to-point basis, motor transport often matches or outperforms the total transit time of air freight:

> Surface transportation via dedicated, well-managed carriers, such as contract or private carriage, can also compete favorably with air freight on shipments up to 2,500 miles, when *total* transit time (from pickup at vendor to delivery to customer) is considered. For example, a national retailer of women's fashion apparel regularly uses its contract carrier to deliver emergency shipments to West Coast stores from its national distribution center located in the Midwest. The company found that the time air shipments spent on the ground (e.g., pickup, delivery, waiting for scheduled aircraft departures), plus transit time, exceeded the total transit time provided by motor carriage.[14]

It is the *total* transit time that is important to the shipper rather than the transit time from terminal-to-terminal. Generally, the frequency and reliability of air freight service is very good. Service coverage is usually limited to movements between major points, although there is limited service to smaller cities.

The volume of air freight has grown over the years and shows continuing growth even in the face of higher rates. Undoubtedly, as customers demand higher levels of service in the future, and as international shipments increase, air freight will continue to have a strategic role in the distribution plans of many firms.

Four Forms of Water Transportation

Water. Water transportation can be broken down into several distinct categories: (1) inland waterway such as rivers and canals, (2) lakes, (3) coastal and intercoastal ocean, and (4) international deep sea. Water carriage competes primarily with rail and pipeline, since the majority of commodities carried by water are semiprocessed or raw materials transported in bulk.

> Water carriage by nature is particularly suited for movements of heavy, bulky, low-value-per-unit commodities that can be loaded and unloaded efficiently by mechanical means in situations where speed is not of primary importance, where the commodities shipped are not particularly susceptible to shipping damage or theft, and where accompanying land movements are unnecessary.[15]

---

[14] Jay U. Sterling, "Retailing Challenges in the 1980s," paper presented to the Eighteenth Annual Conference of the National Council of Physical Distribution Management, 1980.

[15] Sampson et al., *Domestic Transportation,* p. 82.

Domestically, businesses primarily use water movements for inbound transportation. Internationally, water transport is used for both inbound and outbound product shipments. Often, water carriers transport bulk materials such as iron ore, grains, pulpwood products, coal, limestone, and petroleum internationally or domestically to points where they can be used as inputs into the manufacturing process.

Other than in international deep sea transport, water carriers are limited in their movement by the availability of lakes, rivers, canals, or intercoastal waterways. Reliance on water carriage to a greater or lesser degree is dependent on the geography of the particular location. In the United States, for example, approximately 436 billion revenue freight ton-miles, or 16 percent of the total intercity freight, is moved by water.[16] In Europe, water carriage is much more important because of the vast system of navigable waterways and the accessibility to major population centers provided by water routes. In Germany, waterways account for under 20 percent of all freight transported, and in Norway and the Netherlands, the percentage is substantially higher.[17] The average length of haul varies tremendously depending on the type of water transport. For international ocean movements, the length of haul can be many thousands of miles.

The Importance of Water Transportation Varies by Location

Water carriage is perhaps the most inexpensive method of shipping high-bulk, low-value commodities. But because of the inherent limitations of water carriers, it is unlikely that water transport will gain a larger role in domestic and international commerce, although international developments have made marine shipping increasingly important. The development of very large crude carriers (VLCCs), or supertankers, has enabled marine shipping to assume a vital role in the transport of petroleum between oil-producing and oil-consuming countries. Because of the importance of energy resources to industrialized nations, water carriage will continue to play a significant role in the transportation of energy resources. In addition, container ships have greatly expanded the use of water transport for many products.

Water Carriage Is Best Suited for High-Bulk, Low-Value Commodities

Many domestic and most international shipments involve the use of containers. The shipper in one country places cargo into an owned or leased container at its facility or at point-of-origin.[18] Then the container is transported via rail or motor carriage to a water port for loading onto a container ship. After arrival at the destination port it is unloaded and tendered to a rail or motor carrier in that country and subsequently delivered to the customer or consignee. The shipment leaves the shipper and arrives at the customer's location with minimal handling of the items within the

Containerized Shipments

---

[16] U.S. Bureau of the Census, *Statistical Abstract of the United States: 1990,* 110th ed. (Washington, D.C.: U.S. Government Printing Office, 1990), p. 597.

[17] Alan C. McKinnon, *Physical Distribution Systems* (London: Routledge, 1989), p. 153.

[18] Containers typically are eight feet high, eight feet wide, and of various lengths and are compatible conventional motor or rail equipment.

container. The use of containers in intermodal logistics reduces staffing needs, minimizes in-transit damage and pilferage, shortens time in transit because of reduced port turnaround time, and allows the shipper to take advantage of volume shipping rates.

Pipeline. Pipelines transport approximately 22 percent of all domestic intercity freight traffic measured in ton-miles.[19] Pipelines are able to transport only a limited number of products, including natural gas, crude oil, petroleum products, water, chemicals, and slurry products.[20] Natural gas and crude oil account for the majority of pipeline traffic. Slurry products, usually coal slurry, account for only a small percentage of pipeline shipments. The coal is ground into a powder, suspended in water, transported through a pipeline, and at destination is removed from the water and readied for use. Considering the world's dependence on energy products, pipelines will probably become even more important in the future. This will be particularly true for coal slurry, as some countries attempt to shift away from natural gas or petroleum-based energy systems toward coal-based systems.

Pipelines Offer High Service Levels at Low Cost

There are over 440,000 miles of intercity pipeline in the United States.[21] The average length of haul is 276 miles for crude pipelines and 343 miles for product pipelines.[22] Pipelines offer the shipper an extremely high level of service dependability at a relatively low cost. Pipelines are able to deliver their product on time because of the following factors:

The flows of products within the pipeline are monitored and controlled by computer.

Losses and damages due to pipeline leaks or breaks are extremely rare.

Climatic conditions have minimal effects on products moving in pipelines.

Pipelines are not labor-intensive; therefore, strikes or employee absences have little effect on their operations.

The cost and dependability advantages pipelines have over other transport modes has stimulated shipper interest in moving other products by pipeline. Certainly, if a product is, or can be, in liquid, gas, or slurry form, it can be transported by pipeline. As the costs of other modes increase, shippers may give additional consideration to pipelines as a mode of transport for nontraditional products.

---

[19] U.S. Bureau of the Census, *Statistical Abstract of the United States: 1990,* p. 597.

[20] Slurry is usually thought of as a solid product that is suspended in a liquid, often water, which can then be transported more easily.

[21] Donald F. Wood and James C. Johnson, *Contemporary Transportation,* 3rd. ed. (New York: Macmillan Publishing Co., 1989), p. 156.

[22] *Transportation Facts and Trends,* 15th ed. (Washington, D.C.: Transportation Association of America, 1979), p. 14.

TABLE 5–3 Estimated Distribution of Intercity Freight Ton-Miles

Mode	*1990 (billions of ton-miles)*	*Percentage of Total*			
		1990	*1980*	*1960*	*1940*
Rail	1,080	38%	38%	44%	61%
Motor carrier	735	26	22	22	10
Air	11	*	*	*	*
Inland waterway	461	16	16	17	19
Pipeline	585	20	24	17	10
Total	2,872	100	100	100	100

*Amount is less than one.

SOURCE: U.S. Bureau of the Census, *Statistical Abstract of the United States: 1990,* 110th ed. (Washington, D.C.: U.S. Government Printing Office, 1990), p. 597; and "Railroads Gain Traffic Share but Lose Dollar Market Share," *On Track* 5, no. 16 (August 21, 1991), p. 1.

TABLE 5–4 Comparison of Domestic Transportation Modes

	Motor	*Rail*	*Air*	*Water*	*Pipeline*
Economic Characteristics					
Cost	Moderate	Low	High	Low	Low
Market coverage	Point-to-point	Terminal-to-terminal	Terminal-to-terminal	Terminal-to-terminal	Terminal-to-terminal
Degree of competition (number of competitors)	Many	Moderate	Moderate	Few	Few
Predominant traffic	All types	Low-moderate value, moderate-high density	High value, low-moderate density	Low value, high density	Low value, high density
Average length of haul	515 miles	617 miles	885 miles	376–1,367 miles	276–343 miles
Equipment capacity (tons)	10–25	50–12,000	5–125	1,000–60,000	30,000–2,500,000
Service Characteristics					
Speed (time-in-transit)	Moderate	Slow	Fast	Slow	Slow
Availability	High	Moderate	Moderate	Low	Low
Consistency (delivery time variability)	High consistency	Moderate consistency	High consistency	Low-moderate consistency	High consistency
Loss and damage	Low	Moderate-high	Low	Low-moderate	Low
Flexibility (adjustment to shipper's needs)	High	Moderate	Low-moderate	Low	Low

All transport modes are viable shipping options for someone. Each mode transports a large amount of freight, as shown in Table 5–3. The particular mode(s) a shipper selects depends on the characteristics of the mode(s) and the needs of the company and its customers. Table 5–4 summarizes the economic and service characteristics of the five basic modes of transport. Sometimes, a transport mode may be used in concert or jointly with others. We will discuss these *intermodal combinations* in the next section.

Intermodal Combinations

The Advantage of Intermodalism

In addition to the five basic modes of transport, a number of intermodal combinations are available to the shipper. The more popular combinations are (1) trailer-on-flatcar (TOFC) and container-on-flatcar (COFC)—often referred to as piggyback and (2) railroaders and transportation companies. Theoretically, intermodal movements combine the cost and/or service advantages of two or more modes in a single product movement.

Piggyback (TOFC/COFC). Although technically there are differences, most logistics executives refer to TOFC and COFC as piggyback service. In piggyback service, a motor carrier trailer or a container is placed on a rail flatcar and transported from terminal to terminal. Axles can be placed under the containers so that they can be delivered by a truck or tractor. At the terminal facilities, a motor carrier performs the pickup and delivery functions. Piggyback service thus combines the low cost of long-haul rail movement with the flexibility and convenience of truck movement. A variety of piggyback services are available to shippers, and these are described in Table 5–5.

In recent years shippers have increased their usage of piggyback service. Since 1976 there has been a 200 percent increase in the use of piggyback. In 1989 there was a total of 5.9 million TOFC and COFC loadings.[23] Figure 5–3 shows the upward trend in intermodalism since 1955. While the past growth rate has not been as great as anticipated, the future bodes well for the use of TOFC/COFC. In analyzing the prospects for intermodalism, Robert V. Delaney, noted transportation consultant and author, stated:

> The opportunity for intermodal service to grow and be profitable is exciting. The U.S. surface transportation market will be $48 billion by 1994. Even if intermodal merely maintains its current market share, revenues will grow to $7 billion to $8 billion. But a commitment to improve the reliability of intermodal service can help capture a 20 percent to 30 percent share of the available market. That translates to revenues of $10 billion by 1994.[24]

A Railroad and a Trucking Company Join Forces

An interesting example of intermodalism is the partnership that began in late 1989 between the Santa Fe Railroad and J. B. Hunt Transportation Services. This combination of large railroad company with a national truckload (TL) motor carrier has provided shippers with door-to-door intermodal services between California and the Midwest. "The joint service, called 'Quantum,' offer[s] door-to-door service with unified communication and billing systems, and expedited terminal procedures. Santa Fe will carry

[23] "Management Update," *Traffic Management* 29, no. 2 (February 1990), p. 2.

[24] Robert V. Delaney, "Quoteline . . . ," *On Track* 3, no. 12 (June 16–30, 1989), p. 2.

TABLE 5–5 TOFC/COFC Plans

Plan	Type of Service	Designed for: Carriers	Designed for: Shippers
1	Ramp-to-ramp rail handling of motor carrier- and/or rail-furnished trailers in substituted rail-for-highway line-haul service. Motor carrier furnishes pickup and delivery service, charging its published tariff rates for the entire line haul.	√	
2	Complete door-to-door rail-billed freight in rail-furnished trailers, which includes pickup and delivery. Rates are generally competitive with motor carriers' and are sometimes lower.		√
2¼ (or modified Plan 2)	Similar to Plan 2 except the customer provides drayage at either origin or destination but not both. Applicable to a limited number of commodities.		√
2½	Ramp-to-ramp rail-billed freight in rail-furnished trailers. Customer provides both pickup and delivery to and from the rail ramp.	√	√
2¾	Ramp-to-ramp service with one rail-owned and one shipper-owned trailer moving at a two-trailer rate. Pickup and delivery are performed by either the customer or the shipper.	√	√
3	Ramp-to-ramp service with loaded or empty trailers furnished by the customer. Customer provides both pickup and delivery to and from the rail ramp.	√	√
4	Ramp-to-ramp rail service; either customer or railroad can provide trailers or flatcars. In either case, railroad performs only the ramp-to-ramp service. Plan 4 is applicable west of Chicago/E. St. Louis and is often in combination with another TOFC plan in the East on one bill of lading for through movement to and from the West Coast and intermediate points via rail connections.	√	√
5	Door-to-door joint motor-carrier/rail/motor-carrier truckload service in trailers furnished by the railroad or motor carrier. Rates are published in rail TOFC tariffs.		√
5¼	Similar to Plan 5 except the customer provides drayage at either origin or destination but not both.		√
5½	Ramp/terminal-to-ramp/terminal service, under which either rail or motor carrier furnishes the trailer at the railroad or motor carrier terminal location at origin. Customer provides both pickup and delivery to and from the ramp/terminal.		√
5 LTL	Door-to-door joint motor-carrier/rail/motor-carrier LTL service in trailers furnished by the railroad or motor carrier. Origin and destination motor carriers provide pickup and delivery service.		√
6	Railroad trailers are substitued for boxcars (carload) and moved on carload rates (at railroad's discretion).	√	√
7	When permitted by tariff (and subject to approval by origin rail carrier), trailers are substituted for boxcars at the boxcar rate. At destination rail ramp, customer must provide delivery to consignee's facility and return trailers to the ramp.		√
8	U.S. mail on contract rates.		

SOURCE: "Railroad Intermodal Services," *Traffic Management* 29, no. 3 (March 1990), p. 81.

FIGURE 5–3 Growth of Intermodal Transportation

Annual intermodal trailer and container loadings hit the one-million mark way back in 1962. In 1990, market projections put the volume at six million. Here's a look at the growth of intermodal shipments over the past 35 years:

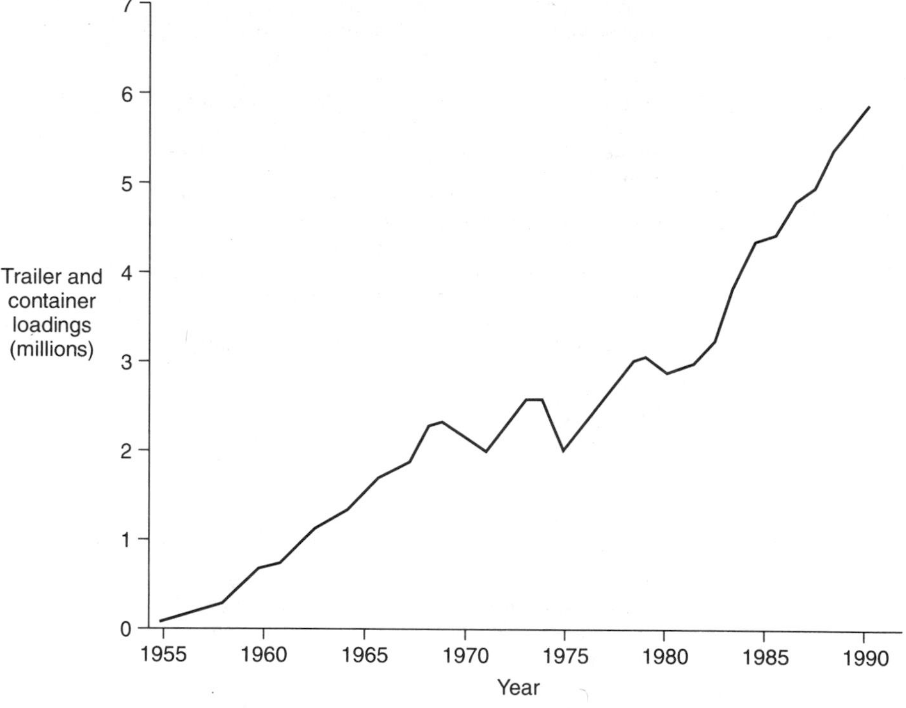

SOURCE: "TM News Capsule," *Traffic Management* 29, no. 7 (July 1990), p. 19.

freight on the long haul, and Hunt will pick up and deliver between the customer and the railhead."[25]

Roadrailers. An innovative intermodal concept was introduced in the late 1970s. Roadrailers, or trailertrains as they are sometimes called, combine motor and rail transport in a single piece of equipment. As shown in Figure 5–4, the roadrailer resembles a conventional motor carrier (truck) trailer. However, the trailer has both rubber truck tires and steel rail wheels. Over highways, tractor power units transport the trailers in the normal way. But instead of placing the trailer on a flatcar for rail movement, the wheels of the trailer are retracted and the trailer rides directly on the rail tracks.

The advantages of this intermodal form of transport are that rail flat-

[25] Mitchell E. MacDonald, "Intermodal Battles a Perception Problem," *Traffic Management* 29, no. 5 (May 1990), p. 32.

FIGURE 5–4 Selected Forms of Intermodal Transportation

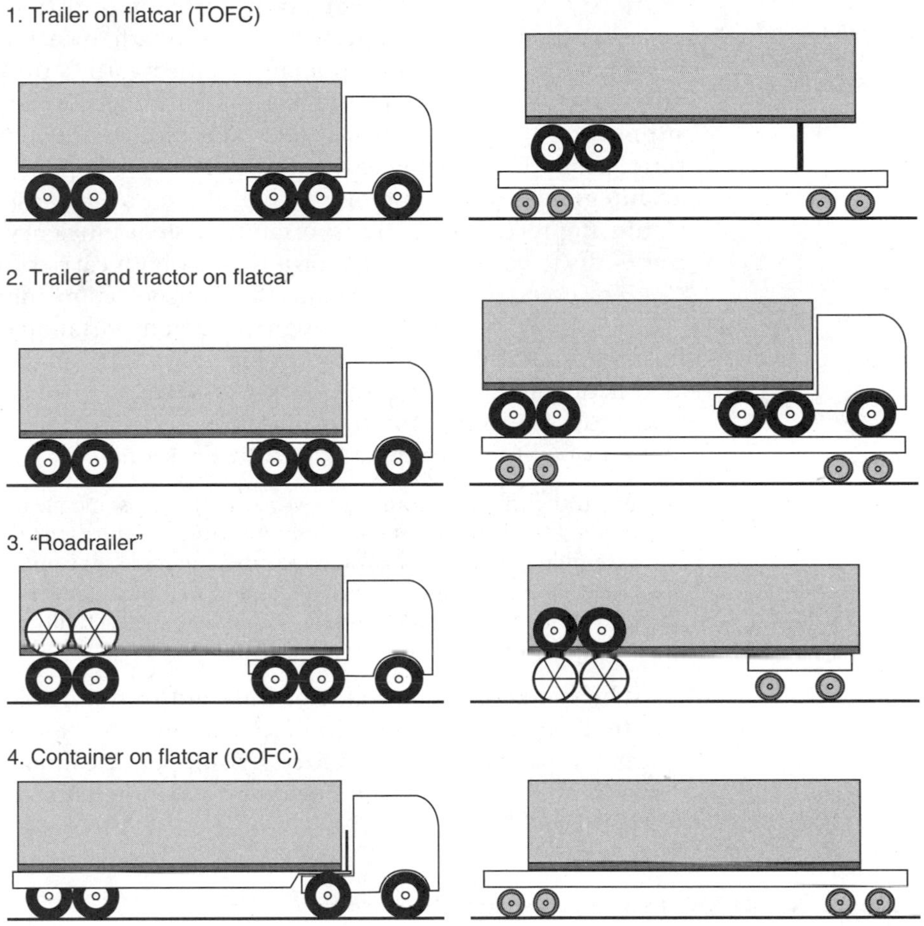

1. Trailer on flatcar (TOFC)

2. Trailer and tractor on flatcar

3. "Roadrailer"

4. Container on flatcar (COFC)

cars are not required and that the switching time to change wheels on the trailer is less than loading/unloading of the trailer from the flatcar. The major disadvantage of roadrailers has been the added weight of the rail wheels, which has reduced fuel efficiency and resulted in higher costs for the highway portion of the movement. "A more recent variation on this theme uses trailers equipped only with collapsible highway wheels. When moving by rail, the trailers sit atop removable rail wheels. The removal of those rail wheels—which would add substantial weight—subsequently increases the shipment weight that may be carried on the highway."[26]

[26]"Intermodalism—Adapting to Today," Association of American Railroads Publication no. AAR6–040187 (1987), p. 3.

True Intermodalism: The Transportation Company

Transportation Companies. An intermodal combination that, in the past, could only exist in theory, has become a legitimate reality as a result of transportation deregulation. Transportation companies—firms that control several modes of transportation through ownership—now provide shippers with "one-stop shopping." In other words, "the buyer of transportation services [is] able to purchase a full range of modal capability and supporting services from one seller and receive one invoice for the whole purchase."[27] Proponents of the transportation company concept argue that an integrated modal system like that offered by a transportation company would improve overall transportation system efficiency and allow modal trade-offs to be made, to the advantage of both carriers and shippers.

However, since deregulation, the transportation company concept has yet to be implemented. Not a single total-transportation company had been formed as of 1989. What has developed are third-party providers (known as outsourcing). From a shipper's perspective, outsourcing does provide "one-stop shopping" for transportation services, but it is not the implementation of the concept as originally envisioned.

> From the carrier's point of view . . . there are some clear differences between being a total transportation company and the third-party provider. Instead of assembling a service package that used members of one corporate family exclusively, the third-party provider may well put together a plan in which several completely independent organizations actually provide all of the transportation.[28]

The marketplace is still evolving, and transportation companies may eventually become a reality. In the meantime, the benefits of the transportation company are being realized by shippers. "Ultimately, it appears that shippers will determine the outcome . . . by the choices they make in the marketplace."[29]

Role of Nonoperating Third Parties

In addition to the intermodal combinations of piggyback, roadrailers, and transportation companies, other entities are important elements of the transportation system. They include the nonoperating third parties that may be unimodal or multimodal in scope. The major entities include freight forwarders, shippers' associations, brokers, and shippers' agents.

Freight Forwarders. Although freight forwarders are not one of the five basic modes of transport, they are a viable shipping alternative for many

---

[27] Bernard J. LaLonde, "Transportation in the 21st Century," *Handling & Shipping Presidential Issue, 1984–1985* 25, no. 10 (September 1984), p. 76.

[28] Mitchell E. MacDonald, "Total Transportation: An Unreachable Goal?" *Traffic Management* 28, no. 12 (December 1989), pp. 35–36.

[29] Ibid., p. 39.

Freight Forwarders Act as Transportation Wholesalers

companies. Forwarders act in much the same capacity as wholesalers in the marketing channel. They purchase transport services from any one or more of the five modes. They then consolidate small shipments from a number of shippers into large shipments that move at a lower rate. These companies offer shippers lower rates than the shippers could obtain directly from the carrier, because small shipments generally cost more per pound to transport than large shipments. In some instances, the freight forwarder can provide faster and more complete service than a carrier. Freight forwarders can be classified in several ways. They can be domestic and/or international (foreign) depending on whether they specialize in shipments within the country or externally to other countries. Forwarders can also be surface and/or air freight forwarders depending on mode(s) used to transport shipments. If they are involved in international shipments, forwarders will also provide documentation services, especially vital for firms with limited international marketing experience.

Shippers' Associations. Another form of transportation intermediary is the shippers' association or cooperative. In its operations, it is much like a freight forwarder, but it differs in terms of how regulatory authorities perceive it. A shippers' association can be defined as "a nonprofit cooperative that consolidates small shipments into truckload freight for member companies. It is not classified as a common carrier and has never been subject to ICC jurisdiction."[30]

Shippers' Association Defined

Shippers' associations primarily utilize motor and rail carriers for transport. They are especially important to firms that ship small quantities of product to their customers. Because small shipments are much more expensive to ship than large shipments, many companies band together to lower their transportation costs through consolidation (i.e., taking a number of small shipments and combining them into a single larger shipment). The members of the shippers' association realize service improvements. Shippers' associations can also handle truckload shipments by purchasing large blocks of flatbed rail cars at discount rates. They then fill the available cars with the truck trailers (TOFC) of member companies. Both parties benefit as a result. Shippers are charged lower rates than they could get by themselves (shipping in smaller quantities), while the railroads realize better equipment utilization and the economies of large, direct-route piggyback trains.

Brokers. Between 1935 and 1978, only 10 licenses were issued by the ICC for transportation brokers.[31] Since the initial deregulation of trans-

The Use of Brokers Is Increasing

[30] Lisa H. Harrington, "Freight Forwarders: Living with Deregulation . . . and Liking It," *Traffic Management* 23, no. 11 (November 1984), p. 59.

[31] Robert J. Walters, "Brokers," *Proceedings of the Twenty-Second Annual Conference of the National Council of Physical Distribution Management,* 1984, p. 644.

portation in 1978, the field has changed drastically. By 1987, over 5,000 licenses had been issued.[32]

What Is a Broker?

A broker is someone who arranges for the transportation of products and charges a fee to do so. Brokers are licensed by the ICC and are subject to the same rules and regulations that apply to carriers. Specifically, some of the rules that apply to brokers are as follows:

1. A broker can control any shipment. The one exception is freight that the broker owns.
2. Each party to a brokered transaction has the right to review the record of transaction, which is required by the ICC to be kept on file.
3. A broker shall not represent its operations to be that of a carrier.
4. Brokerage can be performed on behalf of a carrier, consignor, or consignee.
5. A broker can perform nonbrokerage services, that is, services other than that of arranging transportation.[33]

The majority of licensed brokers are involved in other activities in addition to being third-party agents of transportation services. For example, carriers, shippers, and warehouse firms have entered into the brokerage business. In 1982, a large railroad, Union Pacific Systems, started its own brokerage company called Union Pacific Freight Service Company.[34] That firm provides complete transportation packages (door-to-door service) to shippers.

Reasons for Using Brokers

Companies choose to utilize brokers for many reasons. Perhaps the most important has been the deregulation of the transportation sector. With deregulation, the number of options facing the logistics executive has increased substantially. For example, firms utilizing motor transport for inbound and/or outbound shipping now find themselves with a myriad of available carrier options. From 1980, when the Motor Carrier Act substantially reduced trucking regulation, to 1987, the number of ICC-regulated motor carriers rose from 18,000 to 38,000.[35] In instances in which shippers lack the necessary expertise, time, and/or personnel, brokers can be very useful.

---

[32] Alfred P. Kahn testimony in California Public Utilities Commission Case I.88–08–046 (October 27, 1988), p. 9.

[33] David L. Petri, Robert McKay Jones, Walter D. Todd, and Donald A. Wright, "Motor Carrier Transportation Costs Can Be Reduced through the Use of ICC Property/Transportation Brokers," in *Proceedings of the Twenty-First Annual Conference of the National Council of Physical Distribution Management,* 1983, p. 437.

[34] James Aaron Cooke, "Piggyback Sales: Wholesale or Retail?" *Traffic Management* 23, no. 9 (September 1984), p. 40.

[35] Jim Burnley, "Remarks Prepared for Delivery," *Proceedings of the Twenty-Second Annual Conference of the National Council of Physical Distribution Management,* 1984, p. 956; and ICC *Annual Report* (1987), p. 125.

Shippers with minimal traffic support, or no traffic department at all, can use brokers to negotiate rates, oversee shipments, and do many of the things the shipper may not be able to do because of resource constraints. In these instances the broker replaces, partially or completely, the firm's own traffic department. Typically, this occurs only with small- and medium-sized shippers.

Shippers' Agents. Shippers' agents are not licensed by the ICC and act much like shippers' associations or cooperatives. However, they specialize in providing piggyback services to shippers. They are an important intermodal link between shippers and carriers. As the use of intermodal transportation increases in the future, shippers' agents will become more important as they purchase large quantities of TOFC/COFC services at discount and resell it in smaller quantities.

Freight forwarders, shippers' associations, brokers, and shippers' agents can be viable shipping options for a firm in the same way as the five basic modes and intermodal combinations. The logistics executive must determine the optimal combination of transport alternatives that is right for his or her company.

In addition to the preceding alternatives, many companies find that other transport forms can be used to distribute their products. United Parcel Service (UPS) and parcel post are the two most dominant forms, although there are others, such as small package carriers.

Other Transport Forms

For many shippers, such as electronics firms, catalog merchandisers, cosmetic companies, and textbook distributors, parcel post, UPS, and air express companies can be very important transportation options.

Parcel Post, UPS, and Air Express Companies Are Important Transportation Options

Parcel Post. The U.S. Postal Service provides both surface and air parcel post services to companies shipping small packages. The advantages of parcel post are its low cost and wide geographical coverage, both domestically and internationally. Disadvantages include specific size and weight limitations, variability in transit time, higher loss and damage ratios than many other forms of shipment, and inconvenience, since packages must be prepaid and deposited at a postal facility. Mail-order houses are probably the most extensive users of parcel post services.

United Parcel Service (UPS). UPS is a private business which, like parcel post, transports small packages. It competes directly with parcel post and transports a majority of the small parcels shipped in the United States. The advantages of UPS include its low cost, wide geographic coverage internationally, and low variability in transit time. Its disadvantages include size and weight limitations (which are more restrictive than parcel post) and inconvenience (UPS will provide pickup for larger shippers, but smaller shippers must deposit parcels at a UPS facility).

Air Express Companies. Characterized by high levels of customer service, the air express industry has significantly expanded since its inception in 1973. The Federal Express Corporation, one of the most well-known examples of an air express company, illustrates how the concept of supplying rapid transit with very high consistency has paid off. In 1989, Federal Express had revenues of $5.2 billion (profits of $185 million),[36] exceeding those of Norfolk Southern (railroad), Trans World Airlines (airline), Consolidated Freightways (trucking), and American President Companies (water carrier). Because some firms need to transport some products quickly, the air express industry is able to offer overnight (or second day) delivery of small parcels to many locations throughout the world. Competition is fierce among the "giants" of the industry, including Federal Express, UPS, Emery, and Airborne. So long as there is a need to transport products quickly and with very high levels of consistency of service, the air express companies will continue to provide a valuable service to many shippers.

TRANSPORTATION REGULATION

There are two major areas of transportation regulation: economic and safety. All freight movements are subject to safety regulation, but not all are subject to economic regulation. The regulation of the transportation sector has had an enormous impact on the logistics activities of carriers and shippers. As a result, it requires special mention, and we will examine regulation both in portions of this chapter and in Chapter 6. We will discuss the following items in this chapter: forms of regulation (economic and safety), regulatory history, legal forms of transportation, transportation pricing, and regulatory reforms.

Forms of Regulation

Economic and Safety Regulation

Transportation regulation has historically developed along two lines. The first, and perhaps the most publicized in recent years, has been *economic* regulation. Economic regulation has affected business decisions such as mode/carrier selection, rates charged by carriers, service levels provided, and routing and scheduling. *Safety* regulation deals with labor standards, working conditions for transportation employees, hazardous materials shipments, vehicle maintenance, insurance, and other elements relating to safety of the public. Table 5–6 presents a summary of the major U.S. economic and safety legislation.

In general, economic regulation has exhibited periodic swings from

[36]"The Fifty Largest Transportation Companies," *Fortune* 121, no. 12 (June 4, 1990), pp. 328–29.

TABLE 5–6 Historical Development of U.S. Transportation Regulation

Date(s)	*Event*	*Significance*
1887	Act to Regulate Commerce [Interstate Commerce Act]	The first legislation to regulate transportation. Created the Interstate Commerce Commission (ICC)—initially to administer the railroads, and later almost all forms of transportation.
1903	Elkins Act	Known as the "anti-rebate" act. Made both the carrier and the shipper equally guilty for violations of the Act to Regulate Commerce.
1906	Hepburn Act	Allowed ICC to prescribe the maximum rates carriers could charge. Also declared oil pipelines common carriers and thus subject to regulation by the ICC.
1910	Mann-Elkins Act	Gave the ICC power to suspend proposed carrier rate changes for a limited period if it felt the rate was unreasonable.
1916	Shipping Act	Established the U.S. Shipping Board (predecessor of the Federal Maritime Commission) to regulate the ocean transportation industry.
1920	Transportation Act	Attempted to restructure the railroad industry through consolidation. Also allowed railroad pooling arrangements in certain instances. "Rule of Rate-Making" provision of Interstate Commerce Act was changed to allow railroads to earn a fair return on their investment, to give the ICC authority to establish minimum rates, and to allow the ICC to prescribe the actual rates railroads could charge if existing rates were deemed unreasonable.
1935	Motor Carrier Act	Placed motor carriers under the jurisdiction of the ICC. Established four categories of motor carriers: Common, contract, private, and exempt. Carriers were required to have certificates of authority issued by the ICC in order to operate.
1938	Civil Aeronautics Act	Created the Civil Aeronautics Board (CAB) to regulate commercial aviation in the areas of rates, routes, and market entry.
1940	Transportation Act	Placed domestic water carriers, except those with exempt status, under ICC jurisdiction. Included a statement of the National Transportation Policy.
1942	Freight Forwarders Act	Included freight forwarders in the Interstate Commerce Act and thus made them subject to ICC regulation.
1948	Reed-Bulwinkle Act	Amended Interstate Commerce Act so as to allow the establishment of rate bureaus.
1958	Transportation Act	Modified the 1940 statement of the National Transportation Policy to include the issue of "umbrella" rate making. Also eased restrictions on abandonment of rail passenger service.
1966	Department of Transportation Act	Established the Department of Transportation (DOT).
1970	Rail Passenger Service Act	Created Amtrak for intercity passenger transport. Railroads were able to turn over their passenger service to Amtrak for a fee.

TABLE 5–6 *(concluded)*

Date(s)	*Event*	*Significance*
1973	Northeast Regional Rail Reorganization Act	Created the United States Railway Association (USRA) and the Consolidated Rail Corporation (Conrail) from the bankrupt Penn Central Railroad.
1974	Hazardous Materials Transportation Act	A part of the Transportation Safety Act of 1974. Consolidated the regulation of hazardous materials under the Materials Transportation Bureau of DOT, established training requirements for firms, allowed DOT to regulate routing and loading/unloading of hazardous materials, and increased penalties for violation of the Act.
1976	Rail Revitalization and Regulatory Reform Act	Known as the "4-R Act." Provided government financial assistance to Conrail, Amtrak, and other railroads. Provided guidelines to the ICC on "just and reasonable" rates and defined "market dominance."
1977	Department of Energy Organization Act	Created the Federal Energy Regulatory Commission (FERC) to regulate oil and natural gas pipelines.
1977, 1978	Airline Deregulation Acts	Freed all-cargo aircraft operations from CAB regulations. Allowed air carriers significantly greater pricing flexibility, market entry/exit, and routing. CAB restrictions were to be gradually removed and the CAB abolished on January 1, 1985.
1978	The *Toto* Supreme Court Decision [Toto Purchasing and Supply, Common Carrier Application 128 MCC 873 (1978); Ex Parte Number MC–118]	Removed backhaul restrictions from private carriers.
1980	Motor Carrier Act	Comprehensive legislation deregulating the motor carrier industry. Major provisions allowed carriers to adjust their rates within a "zone of reasonableness" without ICC approval, reduced the authority of rate bureaus, provided greater flexibility in contract carriage, opened markets to greater competition through relaxed entry restrictions, and allowed intercorporate hauling by private carriers.
1980	Staggers Rail Act	Removed much of the ICC's authority over rail rates. Established a zone of rate flexibility. Reduced the importance of rate bureaus and authorized railroad contracts with shippers.
1980	Household Goods Transportation Act	Reduced government regulation of household movers in the areas of pricing, reporting requirements, liability (e.g., insurance), and customer payment.
1984	Shipping Act	Partially deregulated the ocean transport industry. Allowed carriers to pool or apportion traffic, allot ports and regulate sailings, publish port-to-port or point-to-point tariffs, and enter into confidential service contracts with shippers. Allowed shippers to form nonprofit groups to obtain volume rates.

regulation to deregulation and back again. The 1970s and 1980s were periods of deregulation in the United States, Canada,[37] and elsewhere throughout the world. On the other hand, safety regulation has been increasing in terms of its scope and breadth. All transport modes are regulated in the safety area by the Department of Transportation (DOT) and are subject to a variety of legislation including the Occupational Safety and Health Act (OSHA), Hazardous Materials Transportation Act, and National Environmental Policy Act.

An important part of a logistics executive's responsibility is to keep abreast of regulatory changes because of their potential impact on the firm's logistics operations. An assessment of present and future changes is often enhanced by an awareness of past regulatory activity.

Regulatory History

Governmental authorities have always viewed the transportation sector as an area that has to be maintained, protected, and promoted; hence, it has been viewed as a public utility. To achieve those objectives the government has sought to control the number of competitors, rates, and services offered.

Economic Regulation Began in 1887

American transportation regulation has developed in the last 100 years.

> It was first imposed by congressional action on railroads in 1887, on motor carriers in 1935, on U.S. flag carriers in 1936, on air carriers in 1938, on domestic water carriers in 1940, and on freight forwarders in 1942. As newer modes of transport developed, much the same type of regulation was applied to the newcomers despite quite variant economic characteristics of the modes and carriers.[38]

As Table 5–6 shows, a variety of legislation has been enacted during the past 100 years, with more likely during the remainder of the 20th century.

The major federal agencies that regulate transportation include the Interstate Commerce Commission (ICC), Department of Transportation (DOT), Federal Maritime Commission (FMC), and Federal Energy Regulatory Commission (FERC). DOT regulates the safety aspects of transport modes and the economic aspects of air carriers. The ICC, FMC, and FERC regulate economic aspects of the other modes. A summary of the major federal regulatory agencies is in the appendix to this chapter.

In recent years the role of the various federal transportation agencies in administering the regulatory environment has changed. Since the early

---

[37] See Anthony P. Ellison, "Regulatory Reforms in Transport: A Canadian Perspective," *Transportation Journal* 23, no. 4 (Summer 1984), pp. 4–19.

[38] Charles A. Taff, *Management of Physical Distribution and Transportation,* 7th ed. (Homewood, Ill.: Richard D. Irwin, 1984), p. 513.

Deregulation of Transportation

1970s, the trend has been toward decreasing economic regulation of transportation. Four of the five basic modes of transport have been deregulated. Airlines were the first, with the passage of the Airline Deregulation Acts of 1977 and 1978. Railroads and motor carriers were next, with the passage of the Staggers Rail Act (1980) and the Motor Carrier Act of 1980. In 1984, the Shipping Act partially deregulated the ocean shipping industry. We will discuss each of these acts later in the chapter when we examine the carrier perspectives of regulatory reform.

Transportation is also regulated at the state level. It is beyond the scope of this book to examine the myriad of state regulations that exist, but carriers and shippers must be familiar with all such regulations in states where they operate.

Legal Forms of Transportation

Deregulation has reshaped how logistics executives view the transport modes, particularly the legal forms of transportation. In addition to classifying alternative forms of transportation on the basis of mode, carriers can be classified on the basis of the four legal forms: common carriers, contract carriers, exempt carriers, and private carriers. The first three forms are for-hire carriers, and the last is owned by the shipper. For-hire carriers transport freight belonging to others; they are subject to various federal, state, and local statutes and regulations. For the most part, private carriers transport their own goods and supplies in their own equipment and are exempt from most regulations, with the exception of those dealing with safety and taxation. Figure 5–5 identifies the various legal forms of carriers within each of the five basic modes. While the legal distinctions still exist, transportation deregulation has blurred the lines of difference between them.

Common Carriers

Common carriers offer their services to any shipper to transport products, at published rates, between designated points. In order to legally operate, they must be granted authority from the appropriate federal regulatory agency. This authority specifies the type of commodities that can be carried and the markets the carrier can service. With the deregulation of the major transport modes in the United States during the late 1970s and early 1980s, carriers have much more flexibility with respect to market entry, routing, and rate making.

Common carriers must offer their services to the general public on a nondiscriminatory basis—that is, they must serve all shippers of the commodities they carry under their authority. A common carrier is required to publish its rates, supply adequate facilities, provide service to all points prescribed in its certificate of authority (unless withdrawal is authorized by the appropriate regulatory agency), deliver the goods entrusted to its care within a reasonable time, charge reasonable rates, and refrain from discrimination against customers. A significant problem facing common car-

FIGURE 5–5 Legal Forms of Transportation

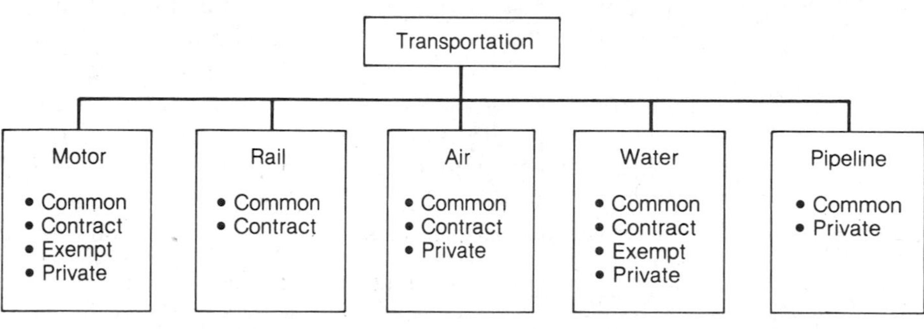

riers is that the number of customers cannot be predicted with certainty in advance, and thus future demand is uncertain.

Contract Carriers

A *contract carrier* is a for-hire carrier that does not hold itself out to serve the general public; rather it serves a limited number of shippers under specific contractual arrangements. Operating authorities, which contract carriers obtain from the federal government, authorize the carriers to serve particular areas and transport certain types of commodities. The contract between the shipper and the carrier requires that the carrier provide a specified transportation service at a specified cost. In most instances, contract-carrier rates are lower than common-carrier rates because the carrier is transporting commodities it prefers to carry. Its clients also provide it with a known, predetermined amount of traffic.

Exempt Carriers

An *exempt carrier* is a for-hire carrier that is not regulated with respect to routes, areas served, or rates. The exempt status is determined by the type of commodity hauled and the nature of the operation. Examples of exempt carriers include companies transporting unprocessed agricultural and related products such as farm supplies, livestock, fish, poultry, and agricultural seeds. Carriers of newspapers are also given exempt status. The exempt status was originally established to allow farmers to transport their products using public roads; however, it has been extended to a wider range of products. Exemptions are also provided to water carriers if their cargoes are liquids being transported in tank vessels, or if they are moving not more than three bulk commodities (such as coal, ore, and grains) in a single ship or barge. In addition, cartage firms operating locally, that is, in a municipality or a "commercial zone" surrounding a municipality, are exempt.

Generally, exempt carriers offer lower rates than common or contract carriers. However, because very few commodities are given exempt status, the exempt carrier is not a viable form of transport for most companies.

Private Carriers

A *private carrier* is not for-hire and is not subject to federal economic regulation. With private carriage, the firm is providing its own transportation. As a result, the company must own or lease the transport equipment and operate its own facilities. Until the passage of the Motor Carrier Act of 1980, it also had to be the owner of the products being transported. From a legal standpoint, the most important factor distinguishing private carriage from for-hire carriers is the restriction that the transportation activity must be incidental to the primary business of the firm. Prior to 1980, the federal government did not permit intercorporate hauling for compensation. After passage of the Motor Carrier Act of 1980, this restriction was eliminated for companies with private fleets hauling goods for wholly owned subsidiaries or backhauling products from nonaffiliated companies.

> For example, The Limited Stores, Inc., became the first private carrier to obtain authority from the ICC to secure "backhaul" business from other shippers that were located in the vicinity of its Columbus, Ohio, central distribution center (e.g., Federated Department Stores, Anchor Hocking Glass, R. G. Berry Co.). As a result, the company was able to reduce its "empty miles" from 20 percent to less than 5 percent, and generated outside revenues in excess of $500,000 per year.[39]

Advantages of Private Carriage

Private carriage traditionally had advantages over other carriers because of the flexibility and economy it offered. The major advantages of private carriage were cost- and service-related. In Chapter 6, we will examine the private versus for-hire transportation decision and discuss more fully the pros and cons of private carriage. At the present time, because of deregulation, there has been a shift from private carriage back to for-hire carriage. Due to the marketing orientation of today's motor carriers, many can offer comparable or better cost-service packages than private carriage.

Transportation Pricing

Cost-of-Service Pricing: The Lower Limit of Rates

Cost-of-Service versus Value-of-Service Pricing. Two forms or methods of transportation pricing can be utilized—cost-of-service and value-of-service. *Cost-of-service* pricing establishes transportation rates at levels that cover a carrier's fixed and variable costs, plus some profit margin. Naturally, this approach is appealing, because it establishes the lower limit of rates. It has some inherent difficulties, however. First, a carrier must be able to identify its fixed and variable costs. This involves both a recognition of the relevant cost components and an ability to measure those costs reasonably accurately. Many carrier firms are presently unable to measure those costs precisely, at least in terms of cause and effect. Second, this approach requires that fixed costs be allocated to each freight movement (shipment). As the number of shipments increase, however, the allocation of fixed costs gets spread over a larger number of movements, and thus the fixed cost-

[39] Professor Jay U. Sterling, University of Alabama, and former director of distribution for The Limited Stores, Inc.

per-unit ratio becomes smaller. As the number of shipments decreases, the ratio becomes larger. As a result, the allocation process becomes somewhat arbitrary unless exact shipment volume is known or can be accurately forecast.

Transportation costs can vary within the cost-of-service pricing approach because of two major factors: distance and volume. This is an important consideration. As distance increases, rates increase, although not as quickly. In their simplest form, distance rates are the same for all origin-destination pairs. An example of such a uniform rate is the postal rate charged for a one-ounce, first-class letter. Another distance measure is built on the tapering principle. Rates increase with distance, but not proportionally, because terminal costs and other fixed costs remain the same regardless of distance. Because of the high fixed costs of rail, railroad rates experience a greater tapering with distance than do motor carrier rates.

The second factor concerns the volume of the shipment. Economies of scale are present with large-volume shipments. The rate structure can reflect the volume in a number of ways. Rates may be based on the quantity of product shipped. Shipments above a specified volume receive truckload (TL) or carload (CL) rates, and those between these extremes receive less-than-full-vehicle-load rates. High volumes can also be used as justification for quoting a shipper special rates on particular commodities.

Value-of-Service Pricing: The Upper Limit of Rates

A second method of transportation pricing is *value-of-service.* This approach essentially charges what the market will bear, and is based on market demand for transportation service and the competitive situation. In effect, this approach establishes the upper limit on rates. Rates are set that will maximize the difference between revenues received and the variable cost incurred for carrying a shipment. For example, let's assume that two manufacturers compete for business in a market area. Manufacturer A is located in the market area, sells its product for $2.50 a unit, and earns a contribution of 50 cents per unit. If manufacturer B incurs the same costs exclusive of transportation costs but is located 400 miles from the market, 50 cents per unit represents the maximum that manufacturer B can afford to pay for transportation to the market. Also, if two forms of transportation available to manufacturer B are equal in terms of performance characteristics, the higher-priced service would have to meet the lower rate to be competitive. In most instances, competition will determine the price level when it lies between the lower and upper limits.

Line-Haul Rates and Accessorial Charges Defined

Categories of Rates. There are two types of charges assessed by carriers: line-haul rates, which are charged for the movement of goods between two points that are not in the same local pickup and delivery area, and accessorial charges, which cover all other payments made to carriers for transporting, handling, or servicing a shipment. Line-haul rates can be grouped into four types: (1) class rates, (2) exception rates, (3) commodity rates, and (4) miscellaneous rates.

Four Types of Line-Haul Rates

Class rates reduce the number of transportation rates required by grouping products into classes for pricing purposes. A product's specific classification is referred to as its class rating. A basic rate would be Class 100, with higher numbers representing more expensive rates and lower numbers less expensive rates. The charge to move a specific product classification between two locations is referred to as the *rate*. By identifying the class rating of a product, the rate per hundredweight (100 pounds) between any two points can be determined.

Exception rates, or exceptions to the classification, provide the shipper with rates lower than the published class rates. Exception rates were introduced in order to provide a special rate for a specific area, origin-destination, or commodity when competition or volume justified the lower rate. When an exception rate is published, the classification that normally applies is changed. Usually all services associated with the shipment are the same as the class rate when an exception rate is used.

Commodity rates apply when a large quantity of a product is shipped between two locations on a regular basis. These rates are published on a point-to-point basis without regard to product classification.

Since deregulation, however, carriers have been discounting many rates. In effect, the distinctions between the various types of rates have blurred as carriers actively market their services to shippers. The increasing use of negotiated rates, permitted under deregulation, has made this form of rate much more important.

FAK Rates

Miscellaneous rates include other rates that apply in special circumstances. For example, contract rates are those negotiated between a shipper and carrier. They are then formalized through a written contractual agreement between the two parties. These types of rates are increasing in usage because of the growth of contract carriage. Freight-all-kinds (FAK) rates have developed in recent years and apply to shipments rather than products. They tend to be based on the costs of providing the transportation service; the products being shipped can be of any type. The carrier provides the shipper with a rate per shipment based on the weight of the products being shipped. The FAK rates have become very popular with companies such as wholesalers and manufacturers shipping a variety of products to retail customers on a regular basis.

Rate Bureaus. Rate bureaus are organizations of common carriers within a single mode that establish and publish rates. Prior to 1980, rate bureaus established the overwhelming number of common carrier rates for motor, rail, and domestic water carriers. Since deregulation of the major transport modes, however, thc majority of rates are being established or changed by individual carriers and shippers in consort, rather than rate bureaus. Today, rate bureaus publish information on "official" rates (which are rarely the actual rates being charged). But they no longer exercise much control over the actual setting of rates.

REGULATORY REFORMS

The Trend Toward Deregulation

The degree to which the transportation sector has been regulated has varied over the years. Since 1977, the trend in the United States has been toward less regulation of transportation. The Airline Deregulation Acts of 1977 and 1978 effectively removed most airline controls, except those pertaining to safety. Nearly all of the statutes controlling airline fares, routes, and competitive practices were eliminated. Motor carriers were deregulated by the Motor Carrier Act of 1980, which eliminated many economic and service restrictions previously placed on motor carriers. Also in 1980, passage of the Railroad Transportation Policy Act (Staggers Rail Act) partially deregulated railroads. The Shipping Act of 1984 partially deregulated the ocean transport industry and allowed carriers to improve their efficiency and productivity. In the remainder of this chapter and Chapter 6, we will look at the various motor, rail, air, and water carrier reforms and their effects on carriers and shippers.

Carrier Perspectives

Deregulation of the major modes of transportation has had significant impact on motor, rail, airline, and water carriers. Freight transportation has moved into a new age. The 1990s promise to be exciting times for transportation carriers. We will begin by examining the motor carrier industry.

Motor Carrier Act of 1980

Motor. The Motor Carrier Act of 1980 had a significant impact on carriers because it substantially reduced the amount of regulation of interstate trucking by the Interstate Commerce Commission (ICC). The act specifically addressed the following:

1. *Market entry*—Restrictions on market entry were eased. The ICC would issue certificates to any motor carrier "fit, willing, and able to provide service." This eliminated a majority of protests by other carriers.
2. *Routing*—Restrictions on operating authorities were removed, resulting in the elimination of gateway and circuitous route limitations and intermediary points. The act permitted roundtrip routes.
3. *Intercorporate hauling*—Allowed private carriers to haul freight for compensation for wholly owned subsidiaries.
4. *Contract carriage*—Restrictions were eliminated on contract carrier permits, allowing for trucking firms to contract with any number of shippers in a variety of industries and geographic areas.
5. *Rates*—A "zone of rate freedom," which allowed carriers to modify their rates up or down within a specified range without obtaining prior ICC approval, was established. The zone is adjusted periodically to reflect changes in the producer price index.

6. *Brokers*—Established a new policy for licensing brokers based on the "fit, willing, and able" test.
7. *Rate bureaus*—Did not eliminate rate bureaus, but established "a number of procedural reforms that greatly limit[ed] the impact of the rate bureaus on price competition."[40]
8. *Mixed loads*—Allowed carriers to transport regulated and exempt commodities in the same vehicle. Also permitted "dual authority" (common and contract carriage) for the same carrier, and the intermixing of products from each authority in the same piece of equipment.

Increasing Competition

These provisions of the Motor Carrier Act have affected trucking firms in a variety of ways, as evidenced by events in the marketplace. Since deregulation, the number of ICC-regulated motor carriers has risen more than twofold, from 18,000 in 1980 to 40,000 in 1989.[41] Between 1980 and 1983, the ICC approved about 65,000 applications for new routes from existing carriers.[42] This trend is likely to continue in the near future, resulting in a much higher level of competition. Carriers will be under much more pressure to be cost-efficient. The shakeout of unprofitable and inefficient motor carriers that characterized the first 10 years after deregulation (1980–1989) shows little sign of abating. For example, in the LTL market, one-half of the largest motor carriers had declared bankruptcy by 1988. As shown in Table 5–7, other LTL carriers underwent mergers during the same time period. While there are major carriers, the makeup of the industry has changed significantly.

Rates and Service Offerings

As a by-product of a more competitive environment, there have been significant developments in the areas of rates and service offerings. Rates for TL and LTL have declined since 1984 as shown in Figure 5–6. Energy costs and other factors may cause these rates to increase, but the trend will likely continue downward (or perhaps stabilize) over the long term. Deregulation removed constraints on motor carriers' product, service, and price offerings, and new price/service trade-offs emerged. The following are illustrations:

In Canada, carriers offer shippers delivery in three, four, or five days for transcontinental shipments. The difference in rates for longer transit times can be 5 percent, 10 percent, or even 15 percent.[43]

---

[40] Garland Chow, "An Economic Inquiry Into the Options and Impacts of Rate Regulation on Motor Transportation Markets," in *Collective Ratemaking in the Trucking Industry,* Proceedings of the Third Annual DANA/ATA Foundation Academic Symposium, 1981 (Washington, D.C.: ATA Foundation, 1982), p. 35.

[41] Burnley, "Remarks Prepared for Delivery," p. 956.

[42] Pat Wechsler, "Trucking: A Case Study," *Dun's Business Month* 123, no. 5 (May 1984), p. 49.

[43] James E. Morehouse, "Operating in the New Logistics Era," *Harvard Business Review* 61, no. 5 (September-October 1983), p. 19.

TABLE 5–7 How the Motor Carrier Industry Has Changed Since Deregulation: Top 20 LTL Carriers, 1979 and 1988 ($ millions)

1979			*1988*	
Name	*Revenues*	*Comments*	*Name*	*Revenues*
1. Roadway Express	$1,098		1. Yellow Freight System	$1,992
2. Consolidated Freightways	849		2. Consolidated Freightways	1,749
3. Yellow Freight System	805		3. Roadway Express	1,694
4. Ryder Truck Lines	560	Merged with P.I.E.	4. Overnite Transportation	638
5. McLean Trucking	540	Bankrupt	5. ABF System	617
6. P.I.E. Nationwide	403	Merged with Ryder	6. Carolina Freight Carriers	532
7. Spector Freight System	316	Bankrupt	7. P.I.E. Nationwide*	500
8. Smith's Transfer	253	Bankrupt	8. ANR Freight System	468
9. Transcon Lines	238		9. Preston Trucking	368
10. ETMF Freight System	235†	Merged with ABF	10. Central Transport	309
11. Interstate Freight System	233	Bankrupt	11. St. Johnsbury	297
12. Overnite Transportation	229		12. Transcon Lines*	266
13. ABF System	229	Merged with ETMF	13. Central Freight Lines	211
14. American Freight System	223	Bankrupt	14. Viking	205
15. Carolina Freight Carriers	216		15. TNT Holland	182
16. Halls Motor Transit	199	Bankrupt	16. NW Transportation	172
17. Mason & Dixon Lines	184	Bankrupt	17. Watkins	172
18. Lee Way Motor Freight	172	Bankrupt	18. Churchill	140
19. T.I.M.E.-D.C.	170	Bankrupt	19. A-P-A	129
20. Wilson Freight	165	Bankrupt	20. TNT Red Star Express	127

*Declared bankruptcy in 1990.

†Estimated.

SOURCE: James Aaron Cooke, "The Shakeout Intensifies," *Traffic Management* 29, no. 5 (May 1990), p. 41.

FIGURE 5–6 How Motor Carrier Costs Have Declined Since Deregulation

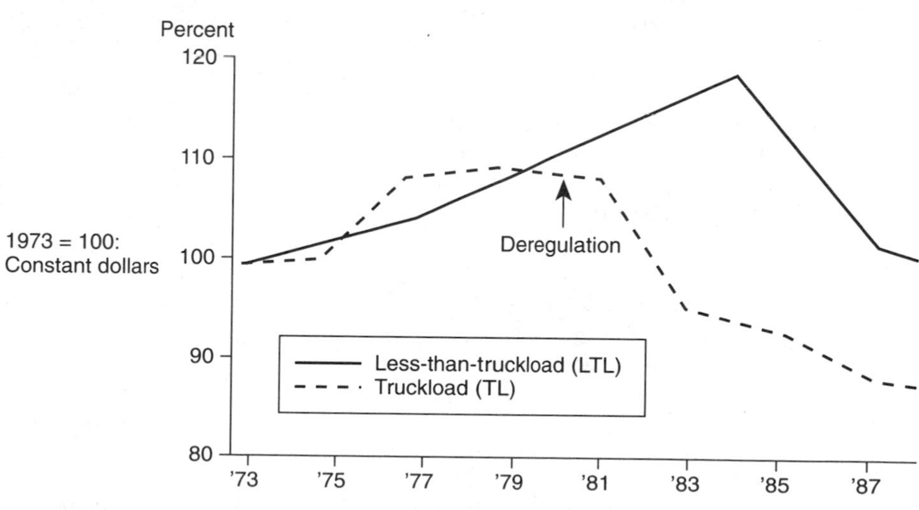

SOURCE: "Call for More Deregulation at CLM Meeting," *Traffic Management* 29, no. 11 (November 1990), p. 20.

Roadway Express and Carolina Freight Carriers instituted nationwide ZIP-code based rating systems that are easier for shippers to use and can be accessed much more quickly.[44]

ABF System developed a rate simplification program and tied it in to microcomputers.[45]

Spartan Central Express offered its customers on-time money-back guaranteed delivery. Under the terms of the program, Spartan canceled the invoice and the shipper owed nothing if the motor carrier did not deliver a shipment within the promised time period.[46] Figure 5–7 shows one of Spartan's advertisements for its overnight delivery program in which it briefly summarizes its money-back guarantee.

CF Truckload Services introduced a door-to-door service called Premium 500 that guaranteed on-time intermodal delivery or the shipper would receive a $500 refund.[47]

Leaseway Transportation expanded its contract carriage, began special warehousing programs, and offered shippers a menu approach to selecting services provided by the company.[48]

Shipper/Carrier Negotiations

Related to the offerings of new products, services, and pricing packages, carriers and shippers entered into more negotiated arrangements. According to a study by *Transportation (De)Regulation Report,* 83 percent of shippers surveyed "negotiate with truckers much more often than before 1980. . . . Twenty-four percent . . . file and maintain fewer rate bureau tariffs . . . and 22 percent don't file any."[49] The increase in the frequency of shipper/carrier negotiations is due in large part to the fact that carriers are becoming more marketing-oriented.

Toto Decision

Deregulation has also had an impact on the activities of private carriers. In 1978 the *Toto* decision of the U.S. Supreme Court [Toto Purchasing and Supply, Common Carrier Application 128 MCC 873 (1978); see also Ex Parte number MC–118] allowed private carriers to "apply for ICC rights to become a common or contract carrier and then solicit business from other shippers in order to reduce their problem of empty backhaul."[50] Private carriers are now able to expand the scope of their operations through the intercorporate hauling rights permitted under the Motor Carrier Act of 1980.

---

[44] "Trucking Execs Look at the Market," *Purchasing* 98, no. 4 (February 28, 1985), p. 53.

[45] Ibid.

[46] "Management Update," *Traffic Management* 28, no. 9 (September 1989), p. 2.

[47] "Intermodal Service Provider Put Its Money Where Its Mouth Is," *Traffic Management* 29, no. 7 (July 1990), p. 19.

[48] Ibid.

[49] "Eye These Numbers on Rate/Service Negotiations," *Purchasing* 97, no. 10 (November 15, 1984), p. 99.

[50] Wood and Johnson, *Contemporary Transportation*, p. 150.

FIGURE 5–7 Advertisement for Overnight Delivery Program with Money-Back Guarantee

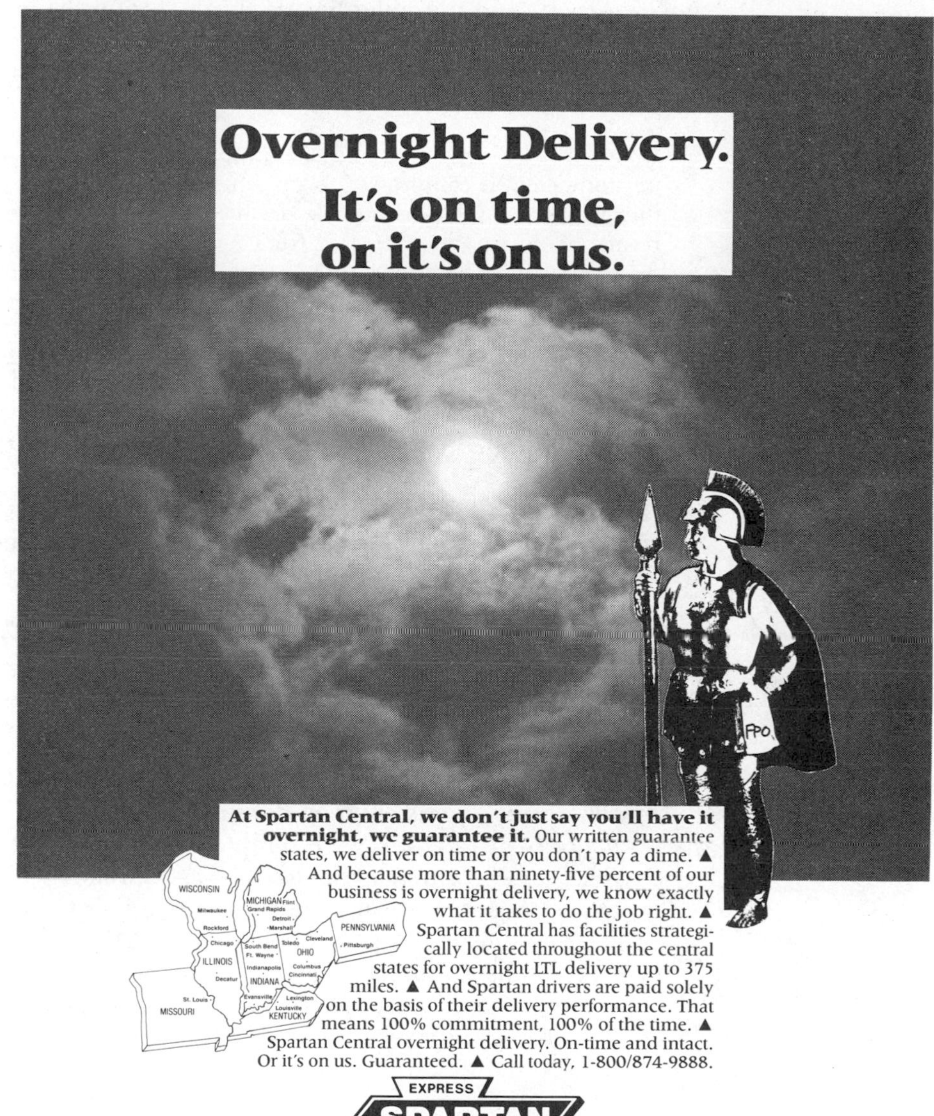

SOURCE: *Traffic Management* 29, no. 6 (June 1990). Reprinted with permission. Courtesy of Spartan Central Express, Inc.

Rail. Deregulation has had a significant impact on the railroads. Between 1975 and 1987, the number of railroad companies with operating revenues over $50 million (called Class I railroads) increased the amount of freight they transported in ton-miles by one-third. During the same period, track miles declined by 30 percent, there were 25 percent fewer freight cars and 29 percent fewer locomotives, and the number of railroad employees declined by 49 percent.[51]

> In 1981, rail revenue per ton-mile averaged 4.2 cents. By 1987, rail revenue per ton-mile was compressed to 2.6 cents per ton-mile. It is interesting to note that while revenue per ton-mile declined by one-third, the railroad industry return on investment increased from 2 to 7 percent. How did a one-third reduction in revenue lead to a threefold increase in return on investment? . . . railroads managed to reduce cost faster than declining revenues.[52]

The improvement in the rail sector was no doubt due in part to the economic recovery that the United States experienced in 1983–84. But much of the newfound prosperity for railroads must be attributed to the deregulation of the industry—specifically the passage of the Staggers Rail Act in 1980.

Staggers Rail Act of 1980

The Staggers Act was primarily concerned with improving the financial condition of the railroads. Such improvement was to be brought about primarily through rate reforms. The act appears to have accomplished that objective. Net income and rate of return on investment for the railroad industry have been positive although fluctuating since 1984.[53] The Staggers Act, more than any other single piece of legislation, reflected the wishes of the rail carriers because the legislation was initiated by the industry itself.[54] Major elements of the act included the following:

1. *Rates under open competition*—Railroads could establish any rate they wished as long as "market dominance" did not exist. In effect, the majority of rail rates were completely deregulated.
2. *Rates under "market dominance"*—For railroads with "market dominance" over their competitors, minimum and maximum rate levels were established: "As an absolute minimum, rates must exceed variable cost as a 'threshold level' in order to be reasonable and all rates below variable costs [were] declared unreasonable."[55] Maximum rates could not exceed a specified "cost recovery percentage" (reve-

---

[51] "The Staggers Rail Act: Why It Was Passed . . . What It Has Accomplished," Association of American Railroads Publication No. AAR6–040389 (1989), p. 8.

[52] Robert V. Delaney, "Logistics: A New Engine for the 1990s," *Proceedings of the Annual Conference of the Council of Logistics Management,* vol. 1 (1990), p. 6.

[53] *Railroad Facts,* pp. 20–21.

[54] "Congress Passes Rail Deregulation Bill, Sends It to President Carter," *Traffic World* 183, no. 14 (October 6, 1980), p. 27.

[55] Martin T. Farris, "The Multiple Meanings and Goals of Deregulation: A Commentary," *Transportation Journal* 20, no. 2 (Winter 1981), p. 48.

nue-variable cost ratio) established by the ICC on October 1 of each year.

3. *Zone of rate freedom*—Rail carriers were allowed to increase and decrease rates within a prescribed "zone of reasonableness." The zone was 6 percent until October 1, 1984, when it became 4 percent. After 1984 the zone of rate freedom applied only to carriers without adequate revenues.[56]
4. *Future rate increases*—Future rate increases were indexed to the inflation rate. The ICC would, on a quarterly basis, "prescribe a percentage rate increase or rate index for rail carriers in order to compensate for inflationary cost increases. Such percentage rate increase or rate index may be applicable on an industry-wide, territory-wide, or carrier-by-carrier basis."[57]
5. *Contract carriage*—Railroads were permitted to enter into long-term contracts with shippers. All contracts were to be filed with the ICC.
6. *Mergers and abandonments*—ICC standards on mergers and abandonments were relatively unchanged, but the process was speeded up.
7. *Rate bureaus*—"There can be no discussion of, or voting on, single line rates [one carrier], . . . or joint line rates [multiple carriers] unless a carrier can practically participate in the movement. . . . Discussion of joint line rates was to be limited to carriers forming part of a particular route."[58]

Cost-Service Packages

Because of their increased rate flexibility and ability to enter into long-term contracts with shippers, railroads have offered a variety of cost-service packages. In essence, railroads have custom-tailored their offerings to meet customer needs: "In this deregulated environment, the railroads have begun to adopt the techniques of industrial marketing. They are emphasizing market segmentation, bundled and unbundled services, and contracts. In addition, they . . . [have] price flexibility, particularly on seasonal and back-haul traffic."[59]

Negotiated Rates

Today, most rail rates are negotiated, and the number of rail-shipper contracts is increasing. Between 1980 and 1988, carriers and shippers negotiated more than 60,000 contracts.[60] Today contract rail carriage is the dominant method of shipping products by railroads.[61] For example, in

[56] "House-Senate Conferees in Agreement on Railroad Deregulation Language," *Traffic World* 183, no. 13 (September 29, 1980) p. 11.

[57] Public Law 96–448 (1980), Title II, Section 206.

[58] John J. Coyle, Edward J. Bardi, and Joseph L. Cavinato, *Transportation*, 2nd ed. (St. Paul, Minn.: West Publishing, 1986), p. 340.

[59] Lewis M. Schneider, "New Era in Transportation Strategy," *Harvard Business Review* 63, no. 2 (March-April 1985), p. 122.

[60] "Remember When," *On Track* 2, no. 8 (April 16–30, 1988), p. 2.

[61] For an interesting discussion of the features included in rail contracts since 1980, see C. K. Walter, "Analysis of Railroad Contract Provisions After the 1980 Staggers Act," *Journal of Business Logistics* 5, no. 1 (1984), pp. 81–91.

1989, 80 percent of Norfolk Southern's business was transported under contractual agreements.[62]

Megacarriers

Since 1980, there has been a trend toward large regional railroads, or megacarriers. In 1974, the five largest railroads accounted for about 40 percent of total industry revenues. By 1988, the top five railroads had captured approximately two-thirds of the total market.[63] In the eastern United States there are three dominant systems: CSX, Norfolk Southern, and Conrail. Burlington Northern, Union Pacific, Santa Fe, and Southern Pacific are the largest systems in the western part of the country. Figure 5–8 shows the relative size of each rail system in terms of its revenues from all sources. Mergers have allowed significant economies of scale, as well as the ability to provide single-line rates between many origin-destination pairs. At the same time that megacarriers have developed, many smaller railroad companies have emerged. Only 75 new railroads were created in the United States in the 30 years before the Staggers Rail Act of 1980 was enacted. Since its passage, however, more than 140 new regional and short-line railroads have been established. Most of these operate over lines that probably would have been abandoned were it not for the new opportunities granted railroads by the Staggers Act.[64]

Much like in the motor carrier industry, deregulation has brought a number of price and service offerings in the railroad sector. For example:

Union Pacific developed an EDI program that allowed customers to use their personal computers to access freight car movement from any major railroad.[65]

CSX Transportation established a customer service center in Jacksonville, Florida, to provide customers with a consolidated point of contact, uniform service procedures, and improved use of EDI.[66]

Conrail, Santa Fe, and the Modesto & Empire Traction Company (M&ET) cooperated to provide an expedited service for moving food products and beverages from the West Coast to the Midwest and East, using a single invoice to the customer.[67]

Air. With the passage of the Airline Deregulation Acts of 1977 and 1978, the airline industry became the first transport mode to be substantially deregulated in the United States. All-cargo aircraft operations were deregu-

---

[62] "Four Rails Termed 'Revenue Adequate'; Little Impact Foreseen," *Traffic Management* 29, no. 2 (February 1990), p. 15.

[63] "Management Update," *Traffic Management* 28, no. 12 (December 1989), p. 1.

[64] Ibid.

[65] "New EDI Program Unveiled by UP," *On Track* 4, no. 11 (June 1–15, 1990), p. 2.

[66] "Project Vision Being Developed by CSX," *On Track* 4, no. 20 (October 17–31, 1990), p. 3.

[67] "Three Roads Go After Food Business," *On Track* 4, no. 4 (February 15–28, 1990), p. 4.

FIGURE 5–8 Megacarriers: The Billion-Dollar Railroads

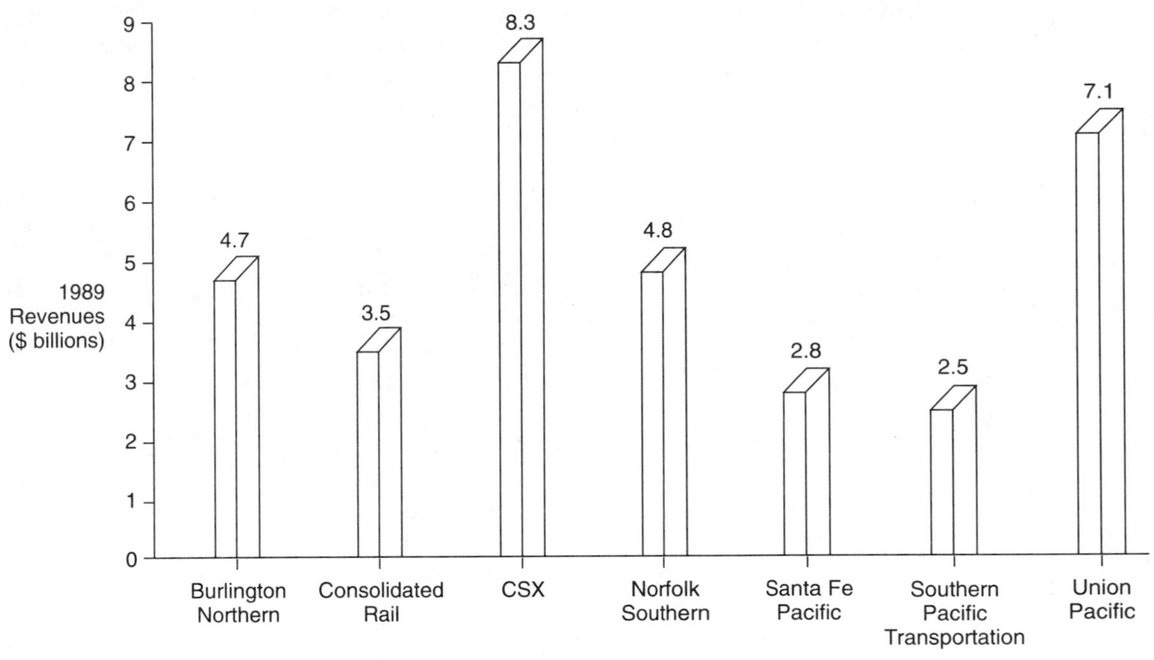

SOURCE: "The 50 Largest Transportation Companies," *Fortune* 123, no. 11 (June 3, 1991), p. 276.

lated by the 1977 act, and passenger and passenger/cargo operations were deregulated a year later by the 1978 act.

Airline Deregulation Act of 1977

The Airline Deregulation Act of 1977 removed Civil Aeronautics Board (CAB) regulations from all-cargo aircraft operations. This act affected the all-cargo airlines, Federal Express Corp., and any all-cargo operation of the regularly scheduled carriers (e.g., freighter-only aircraft). The act specifically addressed the following issues:

1. *Operating authority*—For one year after the passage of the act, any air carrier that had offered all-cargo service during 1977 could apply for the "grandfather" rights to offer all-cargo service. During the latter part of 1978 any carrier could become an all-cargo carrier.
2. *Rates*—Airlines could establish any rate for freight so long as it was not deemed discriminatory. After March 1979, carriers did not have to file freight rates with the CAB.
3. *Aircraft*—The all-cargo carriers could use any size aircraft. Previous size restrictions were eliminated.

Airline Deregulation Act of 1978

While the Airline Deregulation Act of 1978 was primarily aimed at airline passenger traffic, it also affected cargo operations of the commercial carriers. All aircraft, but especially the wide-bodied jets, are major carriers of freight in addition to passengers. So when the 1978 act passed, it had primary impact on passenger traffic and secondary impact on freight traffic. Issues addressed in the 1978 act included the following:

1. *Market entry*—All entry control was phased out on December 31, 1981. During 1979, 1980, and 1981, existing carriers could enter one new market per year and protect one route per year from outside competition.
2. *Rates*—A "zone of reasonableness" was established, which allowed carriers to raise fares as much as 5 percent or lower them up to 50 percent from the fare formula level (taking into account inflation) set by the CAB. All CAB authority over domestic fares terminated on January 1, 1983.
3. *Market coverage*—All CAB routing authority ceased in 1981. Between 1978 and 1981, airlines could apply to serve "dormant" routes where other carriers with operating authority were not operating: "Carriers were allowed to freely abandon routes from noncompensatory markets, but protection was afforded for smaller markets. A subsidy scheme was instituted to guarantee essential air transportation for 10 years into previously served points."[68]
4. *CAB*—The CAB was to be abolished on January 1, 1985. Since its termination, functions that had been under CAB control were transferred to other government agencies, including the Department of Transportation, Department of Justice, and U.S. Postal Service.

Airline Profits Are Down

For the most part, the impact of deregulation on air carriers (including passengers and freight) has been unfavorable. Operating profits of the scheduled airline industry have deteriorated from the record of $1.35 billion set in 1978. In 1979 profits began a downward trend until 1983 when airlines showed a $310 million profit after three years (1980–82) of successive losses.[69]

Since 1984, the performance of the U.S. airline industry has been erratic. Such will likely be the case well into the 1990s. The airline industry's poor financial performance is partly due to general economic conditions, industry pricing practices, fluctuations in the cost of jet fuel, and equipment updating. But deregulation itself had a largely negative effect on the airline industry.

---

[68] Martin T. Farris, "The Multiple Meanings and Goals of Deregulation: A Commentary," *Transportation Journal* 20, no. 2 (Winter 1981), p. 46.

[69] *Air Transport 1990,* p. 24.

Competition has increased, with the number of U.S. scheduled airlines rising from 23 in 1978 to 71 in 1989.[70] Expenses have increased since deregulation, but fares have gone up to a lesser degree. With respect to the transport of freight:

> In 1978, passenger (or combination) airlines controlled 84 percent of the domestic [U.S.] aircargo market, while the fledgling integrated [all-cargo] carriers handled the remaining 16 percent. By 1989, however, those numbers had reversed completely, with 84 percent of the market going to integrated carriers such as Federal Express. That reversal was accomplished by a tremendous increase in airfreight revenue.[71]

Routing and Scheduling

Significant changes have occurred in the area of routing and scheduling:

> Route consolidation appeared to be a more popular approach than route expansion. Although some carriers were able to carve out a place in a new market, the expansion process generally was a costly one. . . . Those carriers which chose to consolidate and strengthen existing routes accomplished a stronger market identity . . . at considerably lower marketing costs.[72]

"Hub-and-Spoke" System

As part of the effort to consolidate, many airlines implemented a "hub-and-spoke" routing system to replace their more traditional "point-to-point" systems. The hub-and-spoke approach is akin to organizational centralization. Traffic (passengers and freight) moves from outlying areas to a central location and then on to its final destination. The use of a major hub or mini-hub—depending on the size of the market—enables a carrier to reduce fuel and labor expenses and allows for more flexibility in scheduling flights. For example, Emery Air Freight established a major hub in Dayton, Ohio, in 1981, at a cost of $50 million. All intercity packages, regardless of size, flow through that hub.[73]

In terms of scheduling, the number of flights into and out of major cities has increased, while the number has declined for smaller cities. In cities where the number of departures have increased, service levels have shown a commensurate improvement. In locations where departures have been reduced, usually because major carriers pulled out or curtailed schedules, service levels have declined, especially in the cargo area. A reduction in the number of wide-bodied aircraft (the predominant transporter of freight) traveling into and out of an area greatly reduces the movement of

---

[70] *Air Transport 1990,* p. 19.

[71] "'Combi' Carriers Move to Recapture Domestic Market Share," *Traffic Management* 29, no. 4 (April 1990).

[72] Warren Rose, "Three Years After Airline Passenger Deregulation in the United States: A Report Card on Trunkline Carriers," *Transportation Journal* 20, no. 2 (Winter 1981), p. 52.

[73] Eleanor Johnson Tracy, "Emery Flies High Again," *Fortune* 109, no. 6 (March 19, 1984), p. 42.

air freight. Even when commuter airlines take up the slack in passenger traffic, the air freight situation is not helped, because the capacities of smaller commuter-type aircraft are much less.

Mergers

Deregulation of air carriers has affected the areas of mergers and management philosophy. Airline mergers have increased, particularly with the regional carriers, because of financial considerations regarding expansion of markets served by the airlines. And, as Rose noted, "Deregulation also brought a decided change of philosophy regarding the basis for airline competition. Historically, service was the competitive criterion. Emphasis was placed upon such factors as scheduling . . . type of aircraft, and geographical coverage. Under deregulation, however, price competition outweighed service competition."[74]

Shipping Act of 1984

Water. The final mode of transportation to be deregulated was the maritime shipping industry. The Shipping Act of 1984 was the principal vehicle for changing the regulatory environment in which ocean carriers operated. Ocean common carriers, or *liners,* are regulated by the Federal Maritime Commission (FMC). "Liners carry about 10 percent of the total tonnage, but nearly half of the total value, of U.S. oceanborne foreign trade. Regulation of ocean common carrier shipping encompasses any common carrier, U.S. flag ship or foreign flag, that moves U.S. imports or exports."[75]

Carriers have traditionally formed groups called *conferences* for the purpose of establishing rates, deciding which ports to serve, the pooling or consolidating of cargo, and allocating revenues among participating carriers. Conferences were given limited antitrust immunity under the Shipping Act of 1916. The Shipping Act of 1984 was based on that 1916 act and has had a significant impact on conferences. Specifically, the 1984 act addressed the following issues:

1. *Conferences*—Shipping conferences were maintained with greater antitrust immunity.
2. *Pooling*—Carriers were able to apportion traffic, earnings, and revenues among conference members.
3. *Ports*—Conferences could continue to allocate ports and sailings.
4. *Rates*—Conferences could establish point-to-point intermodal rates in addition to port-to-port rates. Rates could go into effect faster—within 45 days—for both conference and individual filings. Also, any carrier could deviate from its conference's rate structure with 10 days' notice.
5. *Service contracts*—Carriers could enter into service contracts, such as time/volume agreements, with shippers. Essential terms of the

[74] Rose, "Three Years After Airline Passenger Deregulation," p. 53.

[75] *U.S. Ocean Shipping . . . Congress Addresses Regulation Issues,* 98th Congress, Issue 7 (October 1984).

agreement had to be filed with the FMC and were open for public inspection

6. *Shippers' associations*—Shippers could band together to form nonprofit consolidation or distribution groups in order to obtain volume rates.[76]

The full impact of the Shipping Act of 1984 cannot yet be completely determined. It is apparent, however, that there have been several benefits to the ocean carrier, some of which were seen in 1985 and 1986. The easing of restrictions on rates, contracts, and carrier conferences has had and will continue to have far-reaching effects on ocean transport.

Effects of Rate Flexibility

Greater freedom in setting rates and an ability to obtain rate increases more quickly have enabled carriers to improve their financial condition; they can now recover their increasing operating costs more quickly. Rates can be adjusted up or down to meet shipper needs and market conditions without undue difficulty. The ability to publish point-to-point rates has facilitated intermodal movements, such as landbridge (ocean-land-ocean movement), microbridge (inland location-seaport-ocean movement), and minibridge (ocean via ship—land via rail movement).[77]

As in the rail and trucking industries, contract carriage in the ocean transport sector will continue to increase in the future. "These contracts guarantee rates for an agreed-upon period of time in exchange for committing a certain volume of cargo to [conference] member carriers. For shippers, the ability to enter into service contracts is the biggest incentive to use a conference steamship line."[78]

In addition to conferences being affected by the Shipping Act of 1984, nonvessel operating common carriers, referred to as NVOs or NVOCCs, have also been affected. NVOCCs specialize in less-than-containerload ocean shipments and perform some of the same functions as ocean freight forwarders. Figure 5–9 illustrates how NVOCCs work. They do differ, however, from forwarders in several respects.

NVOCCs

An ocean freight forwarder usually acts as an agent of the shipper and not as a carrier. Some of its principal activities include preparing and filing export and bank documentation, and negotiating freight rates on the shipper's behalf. NVOCCs, on the other hand, act as a common carrier, and freight forwarders are often their biggest customers.[79] Additionally,

---

[76] See Joseph T. Kane, "Slow Route to Reform," *Handling & Shipping Management* 25, no. 9 (September 1984), p. 36.

[77] Lisa H. Harrington, "Get Set to Join the Export Fraternity," *Traffic Management* 24, no. 2 (February 1985), p. 65.

[78] Toby B. Estis, "Are Steamship Conferences Obsolete?" *Traffic Management* 27, no. 10 (October 1988), p. 93.

[79] Toby B. Estis, "NVOCCs: A Low-Cost Alternative for LCL Shippers," *Traffic Management* 27, no. 6 (June 1988), p. 85.

FIGURE 5–9 How NVOCCs Work

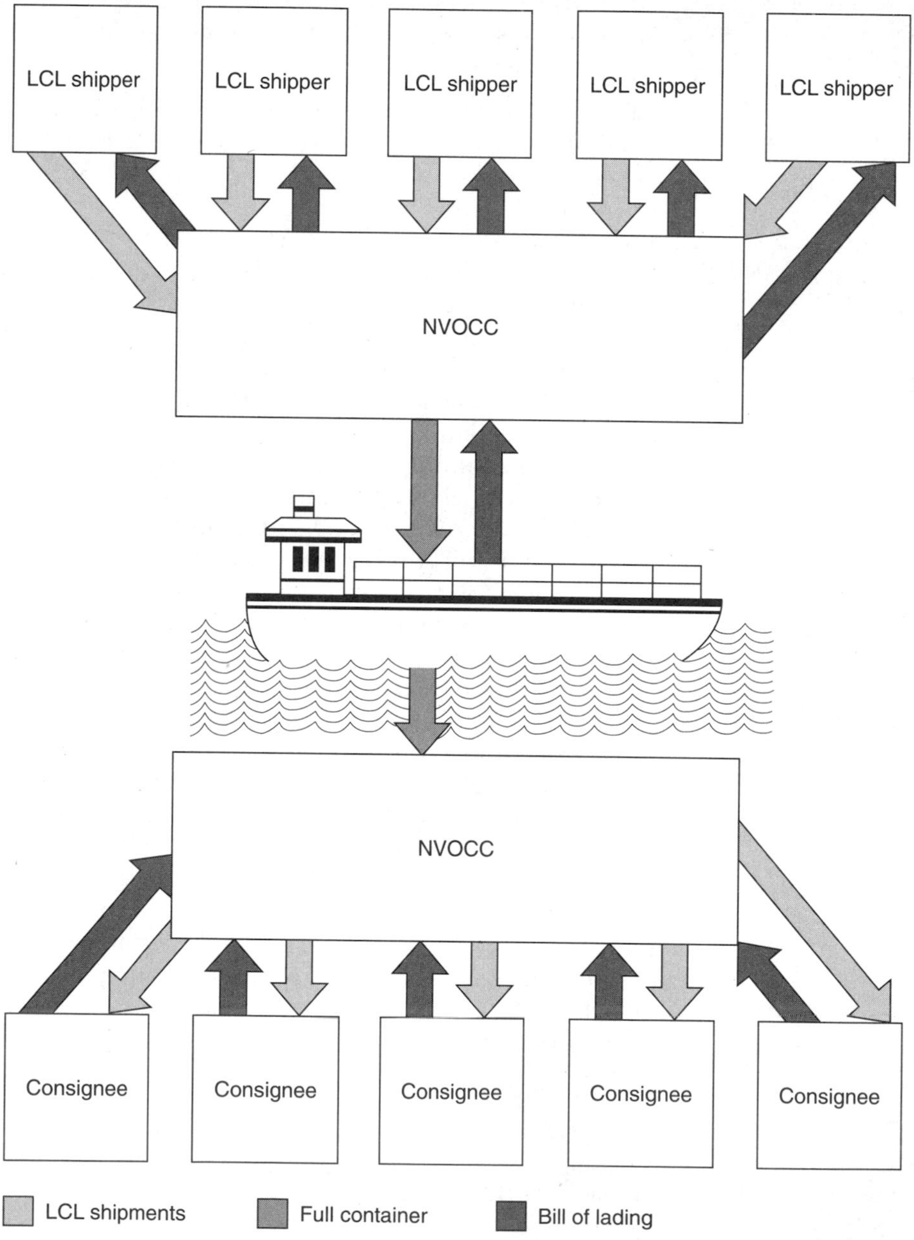

LCL shipper
LCL shipper
LCL shipper
LCL shipper
LCL shipper

NVOCC

NVOCC

Consignee
Consignee
Consignee
Consignee
Consignee

LCL shipments
Full container
Bill of lading

SOURCE: Toby B. Estis, "NVOCCs: A Low-Cost Alternative for LCL Shippers," *Traffic Management* 27, no. 6 (June 1988), p. 87.

NVOCCs are not required to be licensed by the Federal Maritime Commission (FMC) nor post a bond. Ocean freight forwarders must do both.[80]

It was initially thought that the Shipping Act of 1984 would adversely affect the NVOCCs by reducing their ability to compete with the larger and more established shipping conferences. However, it appears that they have benefited along with small, independent steamship lines and now are still an integral part of international transportation.

Shipping Conferences

Carrier conferences were strengthened by the 1984 act. Greater antitrust immunity has allowed conferences to create more innovative price/service packages and to compete more effectively with foreign vessels and others competing for U.S. imports and exports. Further deregulation of the transport modes will probably occur. Existing and future deregulation will have a dramatic affect on carrier operation and the shippers that utilize their services. In the next section, we will look at the shippers' perspective of deregulation.

Shipper Perspectives

Deregulation has affected shippers as well as carriers. Significant deregulation of the transportation sector in the span of just a few years, 1977 to 1984, has greatly influenced the traffic management decisions of today's logistics executives:

> [Companies now have an] almost endless supply of carriers to choose from, as well as new and varied types of services to transport their goods. They have access to an abundance of rate and service package plans heretofore unheard of, or permitted . . . In effect, combinations of transportation services, made possible mainly by the new laws, are limited only to a traffic executive's ingenuity.[81]

RCA and Gillette Have Benefited from Deregulation

In many instances, shippers have benefited from the deregulation of motor, rail, air, and ocean cargo carriers. For example, RCA has achieved substantial savings in transportation costs as a result of deregulation and new purchasing strategies by their traffic managers. The company estimated that yearly transportation savings from all modes (motor, rail, air, and water) exceeded $100 million.[82] Gillette has also benefited from deregulation. The firm has improved its utilization of contract carriage and its own private fleet. According to *Traffic Management,* "Gillette has saved at

---

[80] E. J. Muller, "Do NVOCCs Really Have a Global Niche?" *Distribution* 88, no. 10 (October 1989), p. 31.

[81] Steve Tinghitella, "What Transportation Deregulation Means to Shippers and Carriers," *Dun's Business Month* 123, no. 1 (January 1984), pp. 94–94.

[82] Jean Crichton, "RCA Recipe for Transportation Purchasing," *Inbound Traffic Guide* 5, no. 1 (January 1985), p. 20.

least $7 million [over the past 5 years] through improved order consolidation, more effective shipment-pooling, contract rates, and private-fleet backhauls."[83]

The Ten Areas Most Affected by Deregulation

Deregulation has affected shippers in a wide variety of ways. Ten of the most significantly affected areas are presented below:

1. *Management emphasis*—Firms are giving more authority and responsibility to traffic departments. They are doing so because of the increasing complexity of the function, and the more important role top management perceives that transportation can have in the company's marketing and strategic planning.[84]
2. *Contracts*—The number of shipper-carrier contracts has been escalating since deregulation in the motor, rail, and ocean marine carrier sectors. This trend is expected to continue over the next decade.
3. *Negotiations*—Direct negotiations with carriers have increased since deregulation. The increase in the number of carriers caused by the new freedom in market entry coupled with rate and service flexibility has fostered a new shipper-carrier "atmosphere"; that is, an across-the-table give and take between the provider and the user of transportation services.
4. *Use of brokers*—Brokers are an important option for many firms. In an increasingly complex environment, "brokers can perform the research with the suppliers, negotiate rates and discounts, and then oversee the program under [their] direction."[85]
5. *Piggyback (TOFC/COFC)*—Exemption of railroad piggyback services from ICC regulation in 1981 has enabled this intermodal form of transport to grow. This combining of the advantages of rail and truck movements with carrier pricing flexibility will allow more shippers to utilize piggyback in the future.
6. *Mode/carrier traffic shifts*—Significant shifts have already taken place among transportation carriers. As carriers have responded in different ways to deregulation, shipper firms have been reevaluating and sometimes restructuring their traditional shipping patterns among carriers. There are also mode shifts occurring, as some companies reallocate traffic to transportation modes previously used. For example, some firms are utilizing railroads to a much larger degree because of contract and pricing deregulation.
7. *Concentration of traffic*—Although shippers are reallocating traffic among carriers ("trying them out"), they are utilizing fewer carriers.

---

[83] "View from the Top," *Traffic Management* 23, no. 12 (December 1984), p. 26.

[84] See Jack W. Farrell, "The Time Is Right," *Traffic Management* 23, no. 9 (September 1984), pp. 47–52; and Frances Gaither Tucker and Seymour M. Zivan, "A Xerox Cost Center Imitates a Profit Center," *Harvard Business Review* 63, no. 3 (May-June 1985), pp. 168–76.

[85] Walters, "Brokers," p. 645.

The rise in the number of shipper-carrier contracts has resulted in more traffic being routed through fewer carriers. Carrier mergers, along with the use of contracts, have resulted in fewer choices for national and regional traffic movements.

8. *Price-service offerings*—Shippers have benefited from carrier price reductions and service improvements since deregulation. Many new and innovative services have been developed by carriers. Rewards for good service and penalties for poor service have been included in many shipper-carrier contracts. Carriers have become more marketing oriented, and both they and the shippers have reaped the benefits.
9. *Consolidation*—Consolidating shipments so as to achieve large volume-rate economies continue to be important. With deregulation, consolidation has become more desirable and easier: "First, the highly differentiated rates offered by carriers tend to be sensitive to shipment size and aggregate volume. Second, and more significant, the pricing freedom enjoyed now by all modes makes most rates negotiable."[86]
10. *Shipper-carrier partnerships/alliances*—Shippers and carriers have come to view their relationship as nonadversarial. They recognize the "win-win" relationships that can now be formed as a result of deregulation (and other factors) and have formed partnerships or strategic alliances with each other. Shippers, carriers, and consumers have benefited.

The trend for the foreseeable future is likely to be further deregulation of the transportation sector. While any projections of future deregulation will be imprecise, it is certain that shippers and carriers will work together more closely than ever before. Will the working relationship be harmonious? This will depend on the attitudes, efforts, and resources brought to bear on the opportunities created by deregulation.

SUMMARY

In this chapter we examined the role of transportation in logistics. Transportation, together with warehousing, adds time and place utility to products. It also affects many decision-making areas, including product, market area, purchasing, location, and pricing.

The five basic modes of transportation—motor, rail, air, water, and pipeline—provide movement of products between where they are produced and where they are consumed. Each mode varies in its economic

[86] Temple, Barker and Sloane, Inc., *Transportation Strategies for the 80s* (Oak Brook, Ill.: National Council of Physical Distribution Management, 1982), p. 153.

and service characteristics, and has different cost structures based on product- and market-related factors. The logistics executive must be aware of the characteristics of each mode as well as various intermodal combinations, nonoperating third parties, and auxiliary transport modes (e.g., piggyback, containers, transportation companies, freight forwarders, shippers' associations, brokers, UPS, parcel post).

We discussed transportation regulation from a historical perspective, with an examination of the forms of regulation (economic and safety); the legal forms of transport (common, contract, exempt, and private); and transportation pricing (cost-of-service versus value-of-service, and class, exception, and commodity rates). We saw that the regulatory network is an important aspect of the transportation system and one that affects the selection of a particular mode or carrier.

Deregulation of the major modes of transportation has had significant impact on motor, rail, air, and water carriers. Each piece of deregulatory legislation has had specific effects on carriers and shippers. Among the most important legislation were the Motor Carrier Act (motor), the Staggers Act (rail), the Airline Deregulation Acts (air), and the Shipping Act (water). Some of the areas most affected by deregulation were rates, market entry, the use of contracts, routing and scheduling, mergers, service levels, and the use of brokers.

The material in this chapter will form the basis for our examination in Chapter 6 of the traffic management function from a shipper and carrier perspective. In addition, we will discuss other decision strategies in the transportation area.

SUGGESTED READINGS

Bowen, Douglas John. "Ocean Freight: Outdated or Up Dated?" *Inbound Logistics* 8, no. 10 (October 1988), pp. 22–26.

Brewda, Joanne, Frank F. Britt, and Robert V. Delaney. *Intermodalism: U.S.A. Assessment, 1989–1994.* Cambridge, Mass.: Arthur D. Little, 1989.

Brown, Terence A. "Freight Brokers and General Commodity Trucking." *Transportation Journal* 24, no. 2 (Winter 1984), pp. 4–14.

Cavinato, Joseph L. *Transportation-Logistics Dictionary,* 3rd ed. Washington, D.C.: International Thomson Transport Press, 1989.

Collison, Fredrick M. "Market Segments for Marine Line Service." *Transportation Journal* 24, no. 2 (Winter 1984), pp. 40–54.

Cook, James. "Profits over Principle." *Forbes* 135, no. 6 (March 25, 1985), pp. 148–50, 154.

Cooke, James Aaron. "Piggyback Sales—Wholesale or Retail." *Traffic Management* 23, no. 9 (September 1984), pp. 39–44.

Dempsey, Paul Stephen, and William E. Thoms. *Law and Economic Regulation in Transportation.* Westport, Conn.: Quorum Books, 1986.

GLASKOWSKY, NICHOLAS A. *Effects of Deregulation on Motor Carriers.* Westport, Conn.: Eno Foundation for Transportation, Inc., 1986.

HARPER, DONALD V. "The Marketing Revolution in the Motor Trucking Industry." *Journal of Business Logistics* 4, no. 1 (1983), pp. 35–49.

HARRINGTON, LISA. "The Equipment Revolution." *Traffic Management* 26, no. 1 (January 1987), pp. 69–74.

HATMATUCK, DONALD J. "The Effects of Economic Conditions and Regulatory Changes upon Motor Carrier Tonnage and Revenues." *Transportation Journal* 24, no. 2 (Winter 1984), pp. 31–39.

LALONDE, BERNARD J. "Transportation in the 21st Century." *Handling & Shipping Presidential Issue, 1984–1985* 25, no. 10 (September 1984), pp. 76–82.

MACDONALD, MITCHELL E. "Will 'Foreign Invasion' Change U.S. Transport Scene?" *Traffic Management* 28, no. 9 (September 1989), pp. 51–59.

MAHONEY, JOHN H. *Intermodal Freight Transportation.* Westport, Conn.: Eno Foundation for Transportation Inc., 1985.

REVIS, JOSEPH S., AND CURTIS TARNOFF. "Intermodal Transportation: Past, Present, and Future." *The Private Carrier* 24, no. 9 (September 1987), pp. 10–18.

RICHARDSON, HELEN L. "Intermodal: Quality Service Door to Door." *Transportation and Distribution* 30, no. 6 (June 1989), pp. 14–18.

TEMPLE, BARKER, AND SLOANE, INC. *Creating Profitability: The Sales and Marketing Challenge.* Alexandria, Va.: Sales and Marketing Council of the American Trucking Association, 1985.

QUESTIONS AND PROBLEMS

1. Logistics management is concerned with the addition of time and place utility to products. As a component of logistics, transportation also adds utility. Explain what is meant by time and place utility, and identify how the transportation function adds utility to products.
2. Basic transportation modes can be defined and compared based on their characteristics. Briefly discuss the five transport modes, based on their economic and service characteristics.
3. Although brokers are not one of the basic modes of transportation, they are a viable shipping alternative for many companies. Discuss the role and functions of brokers in the transportation system.
4. In addition to the five basic transport modes, a number of intermodal combinations are available to a shipper. Among the most widely used are trailer-on-flatcar (TOFC) and container-on-flatcar (COFC). These combinations are referred to as piggyback movements. Describe piggyback movements from the perspectives of cost, service, and availability, and identify its major strengths and weaknesses.
5. Three types of for-hire transportation carriers exist: common, contract, and exempt. Briefly define and describe the characteristics of each carrier type. Identify the impacts, if any, that deregulation has had on each of them.

6. What is the difference between cost-of-service and value-of-service pricing in transportation? How does each one affect the rates charged by carriers?
7. Most of the modes of transportation have been deregulated since 1977. Identify the major elements of the following pieces of legislation that deregulated transportation:
   a. Airline Deregulation Acts of 1977 and 1978.
   b. Staggers Act of 1980.
   c. Motor Carrier Act of 1980.
   d. Shipping Act of 1984.

APPENDIX
Some Major Federal Transportation Regulatory Agencies*

The federal transportation regulatory agencies are arms of the legislative branch of the government. They are *not* courts. They do have recourse to the courts in order to enforce their orders, although they exercise quasi-judicial powers as well as quasi-legislative powers. Their members are appointed by the president, subject to approval by the Senate.

Interstate Commerce Commission

The ICC was created in 1887 by the Act to Regulate Commerce.

Regulates	*Major Functions*
Railroads (1887). Express companies, sleeping car companies (1906). Motor carriers (1935). (Private carriers and carriers of exclusively agricultural goods are exempt, as are motor vehicles used by farm co-ops.) Water carriers (1940). Operating coastwise, intercoastal, or on inland waters of the United States. (Carriers of liquid and/or dry bulk commodities are exempt.) Coal slurry pipelines (1906, in conjunction with oil pipelines, which have been transferred to the Federal Energy Regulatory Commission). Common carrier only. Freight forwarders (1942). (Nonprofit shippers' associations are exempt.)	Regulates, in varying degrees by mode, surface carrier operations, including rates, routes, operating rights, abandonments, and mergers. Conducts investigations and awards damages where applicable. Administers railroad bankruptcy. Prescribes uniform system of accounts and records and evaluates property owned or used by carriers subject to the act. Authorizes issuance of securities or assumption of obligations by carriers by rail and certain common and contract carriers by motor vehicle. Develops preparedness programs covering use of rail, motor, and inland waterways.

*The tables in this appendix were adapted from the Transportation Association of America, *Transportation Facts and Trends,* 15th ed. (Washington, D.C.: Transportation Association of America, 1979), p. 36.

Federal Maritime Commission

The present FMC was established by Presidential Reorganization Plan 7 of 1961, but most of its regulatory powers are similar to those granted predecessor agencies by the Shipping Acts of 1916 and 1984, and other statutes.

Regulates	*Major Functions*
All U.S.-flag and foreign-flag vessels operating in the foreign commerce of the U.S., and water common carriers operating in domestic trade to points beyond the continental United States.	Regulates services, practices, and agreements of water common carriers in international trade, and rates and practices of water common carriers operating in domestic trade to points beyond the continental United States.

Federal Energy Regulatory Commission

The FERC was created by the Department of Energy Organization Act of 1977 as a component of the Department of Energy, but with independent regulatory powers.

Regulates	*Major Functions*
Oil pipelines—common carrier only (transferred from ICC). Natural gas pipelines (transferred from Federal Power Commission).	Regulates rights, rates, abandonments, and mergers of oil and natural gas pipelines, and the charges for sale of natural gas. Establishes valuations for oil pipelines.

Chapter 6

Decision Strategies in Transportation

Objectives of This Chapter

To identify the major transportation management activities of carriers and shippers

To examine the issues of transportation costing and performance measurement within the context of transportation productivity

To identify areas of traffic management in which computer technology is important

To examine the international dimensions of transportation

To briefly describe the transportation audit

INTRODUCTION

A thorough understanding of the transportation system is a prerequisite to successful logistics decision making. Transportation is an essential part of any logistics system and must be effectively managed if the firm is to satisfy its customers and achieve an acceptable rate of return on its investment. It is integrally related to the other components of logistics, as Figure 6–1 shows.

Effective and efficient decision strategies are of paramount importance to the success of the carriers that provide transportation services and the shipper firms that use them. In the deregulated and highly competitive decade of the 1990s, transportation carriers must become experts in many areas such as marketing; understanding their customers' businesses; pricing; negotiating; routing and scheduling; and employee relations; in order to survive. At the same time, shipper firms must become aware of the opportunities—and pitfalls—in such areas as inbound and outbound transportation; mode/carrier selection; the use of contracts, brokers, and private carriage options; carrier performance evaluation; and many others.

In this chapter we will discuss some of the more important decision strategies for carriers and shippers. We will examine the issues of transportation productivity, computer technology, and strategic planning, with a view toward evaluating transportation's role in the logistics, marketing, and corporate strategies of the firm.

TRAFFIC AND TRANSPORTATION MANAGEMENT

The New Transportation Environment

The strategies of carriers and shippers are inextricably interrelated. Figure 6–2 indicates the relationship that exists between the system (carriers) and producers (manufacturers, distributors, retailers). Such an environment will require that the transportation component become an integral part of logistics strategy. Carriers must understand the role of transportation in each firm's overall logistics system. The logistics executive must be aware of how carriers aid the company in satisfying customers' needs at a profit. In many firms the traditional role of the traffic executive will have to be

FIGURE 6–1 Defining Transportation Strategy

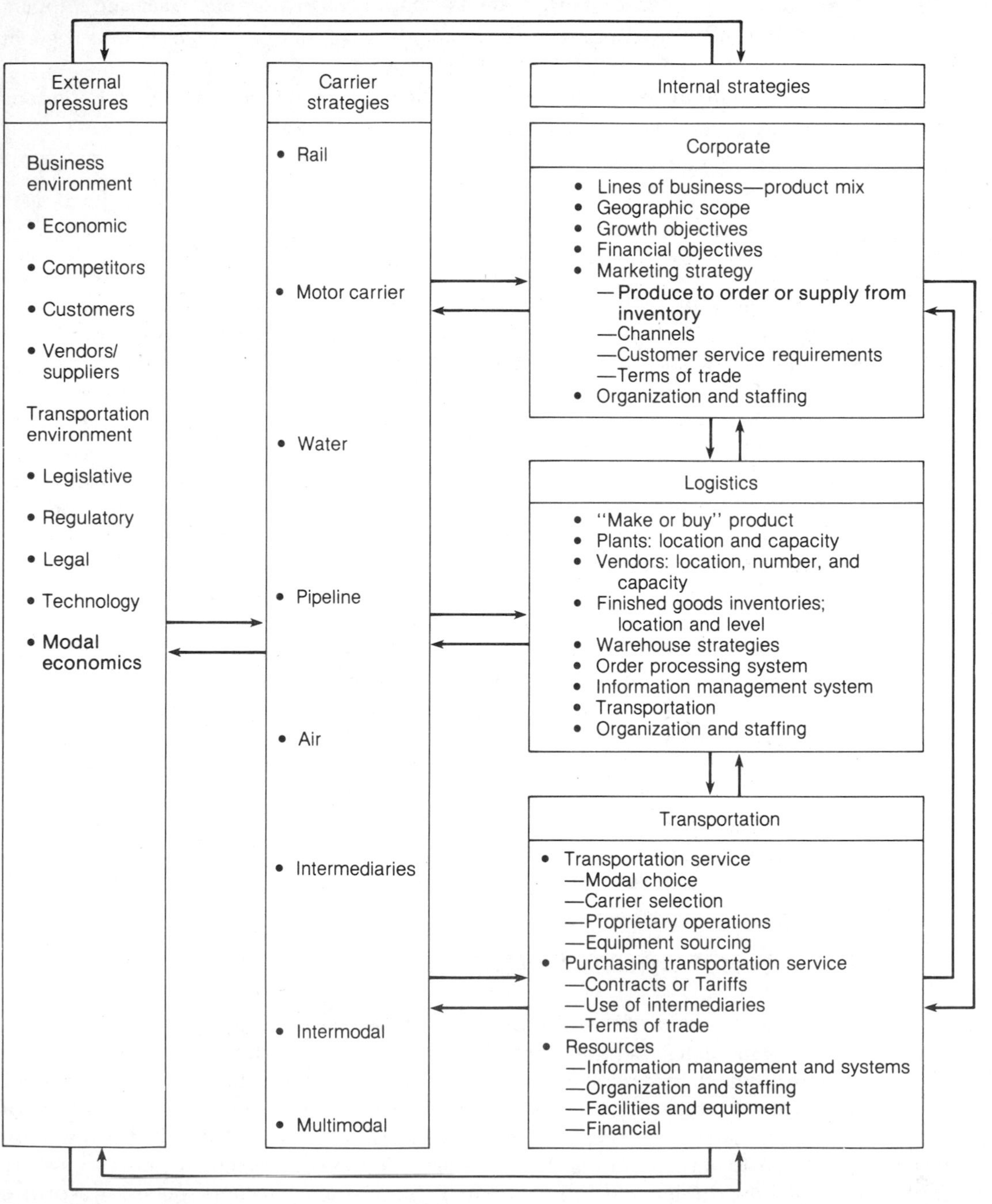

SOURCE: Temple, Barker, and Sloane, Inc., *Transportation Strategies for the Eighties* (Oak Brook, Ill.: National Council of Physical Distribution Management, 1982), p. ix.

FIGURE 6–2 Transportation in the Logistics Management Decision-Making Framework

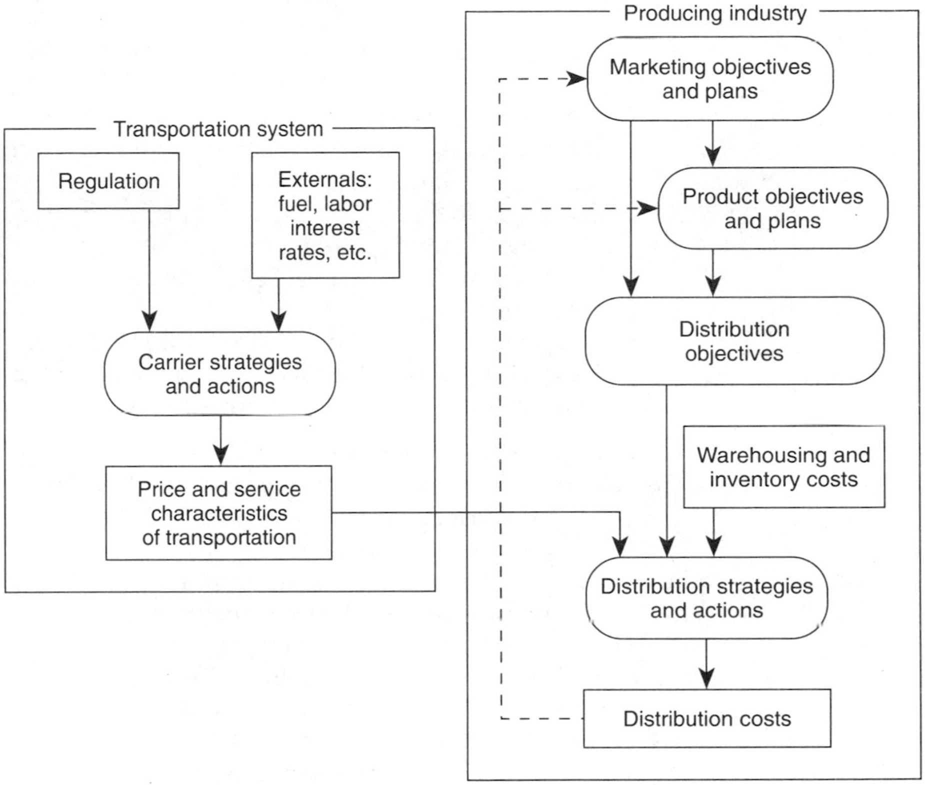

SOURCE: Peter J. Metz, "Megacarriers & Transportation Products," *Handling & Shipping Presidential Issue, 1983–84* 24, no. 10 (September 1983), p. 72. Reprinted with permission from *Handling & Shipping Management, 1983–84 Presidential Issue.* Copyright © 1983, Penton Publishing, Cleveland, Ohio.

reexamined, with greater emphasis being placed on how transportation decisions can affect the firm's marketing mix and aid in the creation of a competitive advantage for the company.

In order to be effective, the traffic function must interface with other departments within and outside of the logistics area. Examples of areas of interface include accounting (freight bills); engineering (packaging, transportation equipment); legal (warehouse and carrier contracts); manufacturing (Just-in-Time deliveries); purchasing (expediting, supplier selection); marketing/sales (customer service standards); receiving (claims, documentation); and warehousing (equipment supply, scheduling).

The transportation executive has many and varied duties; these include much more than just administering the movement of products. Specific functions of transportation management include:

Functions of Transportation Management

1. Keeping track of transportation rates and commodity classifications, and maintaining rate files.
2. Selecting the best modes of transportation—air, rail, highway, or water.
3. Choosing specific carriers or combinations of carriers, based on their financial condition, overall reputation, rates, level of service, and scope of authority.
4. Routing and tracing.
5. Consolidation and pooling orders.
6. Documenting and arranging for the paying of carriers.
7. Auditing freight bills.
8. Preparing loss and damage claim evidence, and filing claims.
9. Negotiating with carriers, carrier rate-making conferences, and regulatory bodies regarding commodity rates and classifications.[1]

Inbound Transportation

An additional activity that will become more important in the years ahead is the administration of inbound freight. Many times firms will be quoted product prices based on free on board (F.O.B.) destination. In other words, the price paid by the company for a product includes delivery to the buyer. However, the inbound transportation has not been obtained for free. The seller of the product has included the cost of transportation in its selling price. From a buyer's perspective, the seller may not be using the optimal transport mode or carrier, and thus the buyer is paying the costs of an inefficient system. What may be optimal or convenient for the seller may not be for the buyer.

The carrier/shipper relationship is an important one; it directly affects the transportation executive's ability to manage successfully. In the following sections, we will look at carriers' and shippers' perspectives of transportation management. On the carrier side, the issues we will examine include pricing/negotiation, routing and scheduling, service offerings, competition, and marketing activities. Shipper issues to be addressed include inbound and outbound transportation, mode/carrier selection, contracts, use of brokers, private carriage/leasing, and strategic partnerships/alliances.

Carrier Perspectives

Carriers and shippers are partners in the logistics process. Each must effectively and efficiently manage its operations to provide adequate levels of customer service at the least total cost. For carriers, there are many important areas that require management's attention.

---

[1] "Why the Inbound Traffic Guide," *Inbound Traffic Guide* 4, no. 1 (January/February 1984), p. 517.

Pricing/Negotiation Issues. Since deregulation, shippers have tended to use fewer carriers.[2] As shippers have utilized fewer carriers, greater emphasis has been placed on negotiated pricing. Prior to deregulation, rate negotiations typically occurred only when transportation contracts (e.g., contract carriage) were being developed. Today, most rates are the result of direct negotiation between carriers and shippers.[3]

Negotiated Pricing

Negotiation has been defined as:

> A process that attempts to maximize the value of the interaction to both buyer and seller. It recognizes the fact that the parties are in a bargaining situation and that cooperation can increase the total value of the interaction. Further, it recognizes the interdependence of buyer and seller and allows each to accept a goal of maximizing the total value of the interaction rather than trying to maximize his share. It involves a long-term view of the buyer-seller relationship.[4]

The negotiation process is a symbiotic one between carrier and shipper, and requires that carriers have fairly precise measures of their costs. There are three levels of cost for a carrier:

Carrier Costs

1. *Fully allocated cost,* which includes all costs involved in the movement of the shipment.
2. *Semivariable costs,* which are all costs involved in the movement of a shipment except overhead-related expenses.
3. *Out-of-pocket costs,* which involve only those costs requiring a direct outlay of money to perform the movement of the shipment.[5]

Before negotiations begin, carriers must establish their costs for providing specific types and levels of services. Since most negotiations are based on a "cost plus" approach, knowing the cost base is imperative. It also allows carriers and shippers to work together in an effort to reduce that carrier's cost base.

Xerox Corporation has been very aggressive in developing symbiotic relationships with its carriers. This has resulted in greater profits to the carriers and sizable cost reductions for Xerox. The combination of good negotiations and Xerox's efforts to reduce its carriers' cost bases has resulted in a reduction of empty mileage and a reduction in shipment costs.[6]

---

[2] For a discussion of this trend and other issues relating transportation to customer service, see Bernard J. LaLonde, Martha C. Cooper, and Thomas G. Noordewier, *Customer Service: A Management Perspective* (Oak Brook, Ill.: Council of Logistics Management, 1988).

[3] For a managerial discussion of carrier-shipper negotiation issues, see Jack Barry, "Advanced Negotiating: Preparation is the Key," *Distribution* 87, no. 6 (June 1988), pp. 54–56; and Joseph Cavinato, "Tips for Negotiating Rates," *Distribution* 90, no. 2 (February 1991), pp. 66–68.

[4] Donald R. Souza, "Shipper-Carrier Rate Negotiation: A New World for the Traffic Manager," *Traffic World* 197, no. 12 (March 19, 1984), p. 35.

[5] Ibid., pp. 35–36.

[6] See Peter Ketchum, "Pricing Transportation Productivity," in *Logistics: Contribution and Control,* ed. Patrick Gallagher, *Proceedings of the 1983 Logistics Resource Forum* (Cleveland: Leaseway Transportation Corp., 1983), p. 207.

In terms of carrier pricing, there is probably no one pricing program that will meet the needs of the carrier and all of its customers. Whatever the approach, however, there are certain variables that should be a part of any pricing program developed. They include the following:

Elements of a Carrier Pricing Program

1. A rating system that is simple to understand and apply.
2. Price stability for the shipper for an established period of time.
3. Volume stability for the carrier for an established period of time.
4. A rating system based on a "uniform method for all of the shipper's/receiver's locations and commodities."
5. Simplified freight bill payment.
6. Ability to integrate with electronic data interchange systems.
7. Easy conversion to computerized rating and auditing.[7]

Many carriers are introducing and/or considering some very innovative pricing programs. The Burlington Northern and Santa Fe railroads are "actively considering adopting airline-style booking techniques to manage freight car capacity and demand. . . . Under such a system, excess capacity would be made available at reduced rates and higher rates might be charged for last-minute bookings during periods of tight car supply."[8]

CSX Intermodal Pricing Program

CSX Intermodal (CSXI) introduced a pricing program for new customers. First-time intermodal shippers were given a 10 percent savings over comparable motor carrier rates. Begun in January 1991, the CSXI program exceeded company expectations during the early months of its implementation.[9]

In summary, the pricing approach must be developed based on the carrier's costs and shipper needs. Of necessity, pricing must be creative; that is, the traditional approaches of the past may not be appropriate. It will require cooperation between carriers and shippers.

Routing and Scheduling. Considering the significant capital investments in equipment and facilities, along with operating expenses, carriers have long recognized the importance of good routing and scheduling in achieving acceptable levels of company profit and customer service. In recent years, however, these areas have become much more significant because of increased levels of competition, deregulation, and economic factors (e.g., fuel, labor, equipment, and general economic activity).

What can happen in a firm when good routing and scheduling decisions are made? The case of Argyll Stores, one of the largest supermarket store groups in the United Kingdom, is illustrative. The firm implemented a computerized delivery planning system for daily route scheduling. As a

---

[7] Souza, "Shipper-Carrier Rate Negotiation," p. 36.

[8] "Two Carriers Explore Advanced Booking Plan for Freight Cars," *On Track* 5, no. 4 (March 6, 1991), p. 1.

[9] "CSXI Offering 10% Rate Reductions for New Customers," *On Track* 5, no. 5 (March 20, 1991), p. 4.

Argyll Stores Benefit from Good Routing and Scheduling

result, its vehicle fleet was reduced by 40 percent (38 to 23 trucks) over a period of time when volume increased by 20 percent.[10] Typically, even efficient operations have been able to realize 5 to 10 percent improvement in vehicle scheduling using computer-based techniques.[11]

A U.S. manufacturer of office systems and furniture products benefited significantly from improved routing and scheduling. An audit of the firm's inbound and outbound materials flows resulted in the following cost/service improvements:

1. Integration of inbound and outbound transportation.
2. Identification of inbound freight consolidation opportunities.
3. Identification of least cost transportation modes and routes.
4. Establishment of uniform shipping terms, packaging, and handling.[12]

The overall result was a transportation and handling cost savings in excess of $1.1 million annually.[13]

Ways to Achieve Benefits from Routing and Scheduling

Carriers (as well as companies operating private fleets) can achieve sizable benefits by optimizing their routing and scheduling activities. For example, by prescheduling shipments into specific market areas, while simultaneously reducing the frequency of delivery, a vehicle's load factor can be increased. The result is a cost savings to the carrier.[14] Also, a reduction in the "frequency with which pickups/deliveries are made (consistent with necessary service levels) can result in a reduction in the amount of transportation required to deliver the same amount of goods, and thus a reduction in cost of . . . transportation, and an increase in productivity."[15] Other examples include the use of fixed routes instead of variable routes,[16] for some shipments, and changing customer delivery hours. If customers can accept shipments at off-peak hours, the carrier will have a larger delivery time window and thus can improve vehicle utilization and reduce equipment cost on a per-delivery basis.[17]

---

[10] Melvyn P. Eastburn and Lawrence R. Christensen, "A Case Study Showing Dramatic Fleet Cost Reductions Through Micro-Based Vehicle Scheduling Software Package," *Proceedings of the Twenty-Second Annual Conference of the National Council of Physical Distribution Management,* 1984, p. 334.

[11] A. T. Kearney, Inc., *Measuring and Improving Productivity in Physical Distribution* (Oak Brook, Ill.: National Council of Physical Distribution Management, 1984), p. 178.

[12] See Douglas M. Lambert and Jay U. Sterling, "Managing Inbound Transportation: A Case Study," *Journal of Purchasing and Materials Management* 20, no. 2 (Summer 1984), pp. 22–29.

[13] Ibid., p. 29.

[14] A. T. Kearney, Inc., *Measuring and Improving Productivity,* p. 176.

[15] Ibid., p. 178.

[16] Fixed routes remained unchanged on a daily basis, while variable routes are changed daily in response to the specific demands on the system. Fixed routes are inherently more efficient.

[17] A. T. Kearney, Inc., *Measuring and Improving Productivity,* p. 182.

In general, the benefits to a carrier of improved routing and scheduling include "greater vehicle utilization; improved and more responsive [or consistent] customer service; reduced transportation expenses; reduced capital investment in equipment; [and] an ability to ask 'what if . . . ?' questions if a computerized system is being used."[18]

Service Offerings. One of the fundamental changes that has taken place since deregulation has been "the collaboration between carriers and shippers to develop a broad range of transportation service products tailored to the specific needs of . . . shippers."[19]

In the traditional areas of service—pickup and delivery, claims, equipment availability, time-in-transit, and consistency of service—there have been competitive pressures from the marketplace to improve service levels and consistency. Carriers have been forced to develop customer service packages that meet the needs of increasingly demanding customers. Such improvements have benefited shippers and have forced carriers to maximize their efficiency and productivity in order to remain profitable.

Transportation Services—Some Global Examples

Examples of carriers providing higher levels of traditional transportation services can be found in all modes. During 1991, A. P. Moller-Maersk Line and Sea-Land Service Inc. (international ocean marine transporters) began a vessel sharing plan for the purpose of improving service levels. Some 50 vessels were being shared in the Pacific and Intra-Asia shipping trade lanes. The plan reduced the number of ships deployed and increased the number of transpacific sailings to five per week. At the same time, Maersk and Sea-Land continued to compete against each other.[20]

In 1990, Tokyo-Jeuro Container Transport Inc., a Japanese transportation forwarder/carrier, established a joint venture with the Soviet Union's railway ministry to move container cargo between Japan and Europe. Transit times had been 25 to 40 days, but the joint venture reduced those times to 15 to 20 days. Products moving from Japan to Europe include automobile parts and components for assembly by Japanese automobile producers in Europe, common electronics, construction equipment, agricultural machinery, and chemicals.[21] The result of the carrier partnership has been improved service levels for those customers shipping products between Japan and Europe.

Carriers have begun expanding into nontraditional areas such as ware-

---

[18] Eastburn and Christensen, "A Case Study Showing Dramatic Fleet Cost Reductions," p. 343.

[19] Russell C. Cherry, Theodore V. Heuchling, Peter J. Metz, P. Ranganath Nayak, and Richard C. Norris, "Freight Transportation: A Revitalized Industry Emerges," *Forbes,* Special Advertising Supplement (1984), p. 1.

[20] Elizabeth Canna, "The Maersk/Sea-Land Deal," *American Shipper* 33, no. 5 (May 1991), p. 43.

[21] "Japanese Forwarder Teams Up with Soviet Rails," *Traffic Management* 29, no. 8 (August 1990), p. 77A.

Some Carriers Have Become Logistics Service Firms

housing, logistics consulting, import/export operations, and facility location analysis. In effect, the transportation carrier becomes a logistics service firm. For example, Ryder System, Inc., a family of companies with over $5 billion in annual revenues, provides services in truck and aviation leasing, maintenance, insurance management services, international customs brokerage operations, contract carriage, and automotive transport.[22] CSX Corporation, an $8.2 billion firm, offers one-stop shipping that includes trains, trucks, barges, ocean containers, intermodal services, and distribution warehouses.[23] Other firms that have expanded into nontraditional areas include American President Lines, Consolidated Freightways, Union Pacific, Allied Van Lines, North American Van Lines, and TNT North America.

The trend will continue over the next several years, with carriers expanding their traditional and nontraditional service offerings. In addition, competitive pressures will force overall carrier service levels to improve.

Increasing Levels of Competition

Competition. Since deregulation of the transportation industry began in the late 1970s, carrier management has faced an environment characterized by increasing levels of competition. Greater freedom of entry into the marketplace has been one of the most significant results of deregulation legislation, bringing with it sizable increases in the number of competitors in most transport modes.

Competition is also increasing between modes, as well as within them. The ability of carriers from the various transport modes to price their services more flexibly and to offer a greater number and variety of services, has created a much more competitive environment. Intermodal competition, especially between air-motor and motor-rail, has increased and will be much more intense in the future.

Competitors are also much stronger than in the past. As a result of intramode mergers and good marketing practices, many large regional and national carriers have emerged, primarily in the rail, motor, and airline industries, and have become market leaders in their respective target markets.

More Emphasis Being Placed on Marketing

Marketing Activities. Beginning in the late 1970s, carrier firms recognized the need to place greater empasis on marketing activities. Many factors contributed to that realization, including deregulation, worsening economic conditions, and increased competition. One study of motor carriers found that approximately two-thirds of the carriers had increased their expenditures on marketing, and almost as many (60 percent) had added to their marketing staffs.[24]

---

[22] Information obtained from *1990 Annual Report* of Ryder System, Inc.

[23] Information obtained from *1990 Annual Report* of CSX Corporation, p. 15.

[24] Donald V. Harper, "Consequences of Reform of Federal Economic Regulation of the Motor Trucking Industry," *Transportation Journal* 22, no. 4 (Summer 1982), p. 47.

Overall, carriers in all modes are developing marketing goals, objectives, strategies, and tactics. The more successful carriers are those that have refocused themselves from a sales-oriented to marketing-oriented firm. The former typically react to customer requests, while the latter anticipate customer needs. Sales-oriented carriers focus primarily on the transportation services they perform, with little attempt to integrate their activities with shippers' total distribution operations. Marketing-oriented carriers "view themselves as partners in the shipper's total logistics activities."[25]

Sales-Oriented versus Marketing-Oriented Carriers

Table 6–1 summarizes the distinguishing characteristics of sales- and marketing-oriented carriers, as determined by a study conducted by the University of Oklahoma. The table "shows how the two groups differ in their perceptions of the business, their strategic approaches to the business, their management policies, and their day-to-day operational approaches."[26]

Market Segmentation Strategies

Many of the marketing-oriented carrier firms are developing market segmentation strategies that will permit them to grow in size and profitability in the face of increased competition. One approach that has been used successfully by some carriers has been to segment their markets by geographic location.[27]

Some carriers have begun to segment markets based on the level of service desired by customers. Much like price elasticity of demand, where the quantity demanded will vary by price,[28] there is also service elasticity. The demand from carrier services has been shown to vary according to the level and scope of transportation services provided. For example, MS Carriers, a truckload (TL) firm located in Memphis, Tennessee, markets its services mainly to companies that have implemented a Just-In-Time (JIT) strategy and that ship in TL quantities. The carrier has been able to experience large growth rates while having one of the lowest operating ratios in the industry.[29]

---

[25] Jack W. Farrell, "Views Differ Sharply on Carrier Marketing Efforts," *Traffic Management* 23, no. 8 (August 1984), p. 45.

[26] Ibid. Also see James A. Constantin and Marie Adele Hughes, "Motor Carriers and Marketing," *Proceedings of the Twenty-Second Annual Conference of the National Council of Physical Distribution Management*, 1984, pp. 464–84.

[27] Ray A. Mundy, "Managing and Evaluating Carrier Pricing," in *Logistics: Contribution and Control*, ed. Patrick Gallagher, *Proceedings of the 1983 Logistics Research Forum* (Cleveland: Leaseway Transportation Corp., 1983), p. 127.

[28] Price elasticity of demand is defined as the ratio of the relative change in quantity to the relative change in price. A price elasticity of greater than 1 means that sales increase (decrease) by more than price decreases (increases) in percentage terms. Elasticity of less than 1 means that sales increase (decrease) by less than price decreases (increases) in percentage terms.

[29] Example provided by Dr. William A. Cunningham, Associate Professor of Marketing and Transportation and Director of the Alabama Waterways and Transportation Research Center, University of South Alabama, Mobile, Alabama.

TABLE 6–1 Sales versus Marketing-Oriented Carriers

Distinguishing Characteristics	*Sales-Oriented Carrier*	*Marketing-Oriented Carrier*
Perception of what business the carrier is in	Transportation	Marketing support
Perception of function	Main concern is the performance of transportation tasks	Main concern is the distribution environment
	Sees transportation as an end	Sees transportation as a means to an end
	Focuses on operations	Focuses on marketing
Strategic approach	Main concerns are facilities and services	Main concern is the whole marketing support system
	Emphasizes production concept	Emphasizes marketing concept
	Focuses on customers' transportation needs	Focuses on marketing and distribution needs
Management policy	Tries to fit customers' systems to its own operations	Tries to fit into its customers' distribution needs
	Reacts to customers' requests	Tries to anticipate customers' wants and needs
	Aims to sell transportation and on-time delivery	Aims to integrate customers' marketing and physical distribution needs
Operations	Aims for cost reduction and timely service	Concerns itself with cost management: the trade-offs among customer-service and distribution costs
	Concerns itself with effectiveness in operations	Concerns itself with effectiveness in customer service
	Focuses on efficiency in operations	Focuses on efficiency in operations

SOURCE: Jack W. Farrell, "Views Differ Sharply on Carrier Marketing Efforts," *Traffic Management* 23, no. 8 (August 1984), p. 46.

Carrier marketing activities will continue to gain importance, due in part to the structural changes that have taken place in the marketplace. It is likely that the remainder of the 1990s will be a "buyer's market." Opportunities for higher carrier profits and market shares will exist, but only for those firms that develop customer-focused programs. At the same time, carriers will have to train their salespeople to sell "value-added" services, an approach to selling that differs from traditional carrier sales strategies.

At the same time, many important areas will require the shippers' attention. As we discussed earlier in this chapter, carriers and shippers are partners in the logistics process. Therefore, in the following pages we will look at the shipper's perspective of traffic management.

Shipper Perspectives

The development of a strategy requires that a firm understand the important issues of transportation. While there are many items that affect the transportation component of logistics, we will examine only selected ones here. They were chosen because they affect a large number of shippers.

Transportation Cost and Service Improvements

Inbound and Outbound Transportation. Transportation is one of the most significant areas of logistics management because of its impact on customer service levels and the firm's cost structure. As Table 6–2 shows, inbound and outbound transportation costs can account for as much as 10 to 20 percent of product prices—or even more. Firms in the medium- and high-cost sectors will be especially conscious of the transportation activity. Effective management of the traffic function can result in many firms achieving significant improvements in profitability.[30]

A study of a national manufacturer of durable goods found, after a logistics audit, that the firm could reduce its annual transportation-related expenditures by 21.5 percent (equivalent to $2.9 million) by pursuing the following strategies:

1. Consolidation of outbound shipments to customers ($1.78 million savings).
2. Improved efficiency of national truck fleet ($360,000 savings).
3. Reduced local, interplant transfers ($329,000 savings).
4. Improved efficiency in receipt of less-than-truckload inbound shipments ($374,000 savings).
5. Reduced warehousing costs of $69,000.[31]

Additionally, the manufacturer improved customer service levels through reduced product loss and damage, shipment of more complete orders, lowered transit times, and offering of additional services (e.g., performance rates, contract carriage, intermodal moves).[32]

Shippers can improve their transportation systems in many ways. Areas in which cost and/or service improvements can take place include routing and scheduling of vehicles, private fleet management, shipment consolidation, contract carriage, rate negotiations, and many others.

Selecting the Right Mode and Carrier Is Critical

Mode/Carrier Selection. Economic and resource constraints mandate that each firm make the most efficient and productive mode/carrier choice decisions possible. Because of the impact on customer service, time-in-

---

[30] See E. J. Muller, "Paying the Freight," *Distribution* 87, no. 6 (June 1988), pp. 48–52.; and "Why It Pays to Manage Your Inbound Freight," *Traffic Management* 27, no. 11 (November 1988), pp. 51–55.

[31] Jay U. Sterling and Douglas M. Lambert, "A Methodology for Identifying Potential Cost Reductions in Transportation and Warehousing," *Journal of Business Logistics* 5, no. 2 (1984), p. 9.

[32] Ibid., pp. 10–11.

TABLE 6–2 Inbound and Outbound Transportation Costs as Percentages of Product Prices

Sector	*Percent*
High-cost:	
Stone, clay, and glass products	27%
Petroleum products	24
Lumber and wood products	18
Chemicals	14
Food and kindred products	13
Furniture and fixtures	12
Medium-cost:	
Paper and allied products	11
Primary metals industries	9
Textile mill products	8
Fabricated metal products	8
Miscellaneous manufacturing	8
Transportation equipment	8
Rubber and plastics products	7
Low-cost:	
Tobacco manufacturers	5
Machinery, excluding electrical instruments	5
Instruments	4
Apparel and other textiles	4
Printing and publishing	4
Electrical and electronic machinery	4
Leather and leather products	3

SOURCE: David L. Anderson, "Your Company's Logistics Management: An Asset or a Liability in the 1980s?" *Transportation Review*, Winter 1983, p. 119.

transit, consistency of service, inventories, packaging, warehousing, energy consumption, pollution caused by transportation, and other factors, transportation decision makers must develop the best possible mode/carrier strategies.

Four separate and distinct decision stages occur in the mode/carrier selection decision: (1) problem recognition, (2) search process, (3) choice process, and including (4) postchoice evaluation.

Problem Recognition Is Triggered by a Variety of Factors

Problem recognition. The problem recognition stage of the mode/carrier choice process is triggered by a variety of factors, such as customer orders, dissatisfaction with an existing mode, and changes in the distribution patterns of the firm. Table 6–3 identifies some of the most important variables that could cause a shipper to consider changing its existing mode and/or carrier mix. As the table indicates, a majority of the factors deemed most important were service-related. Once the transportation executive has reached the problem recognition stage, an order routine is followed, if appropriate, and the decision process continues to a search stage. For those cases in which the customer does not specify the mode, a search is undertaken for a feasible transportation alternative.

Information Sources for Search Process

Search process. The transportation executive scans a variety of information sources to use as inputs into the mode choice process. Possible sources include past experience, carriers sales calls, company shipping rec-

TABLE 6–3 Importance of Carrier Performance Variables in Elimination Decision

Rank	*Carrier Performance Variables*	*Mean (X)**
1.	Lack of pickup service reliability	1.37
2.	Lack of transit time reliability	1.41
3.	Lack of financial stability	1.59
4.	Quality of carrier personnel: customer services	1.76
5.	Claim settlement	1.81
6.	Lack of geographical coverage	1.84
7.	Lack of pricing flexibility	1.87
8.	Quality of carrier personnel: dispatcher	1.96
9.	Quality of carrier personnel: driver	1.99
10.	Carrier reputation	2.07
11.	Quality of carrier personnel: sales personnel	2.25
12.	Lack of capability (to handle special products, etc.)	2.48
13.	Lack of familiarity with carrier	2.61
14.	Lack of computerized billing and tracing services	2.79
15.	Lack of distribution/consolidation services:	
	Domestic	3.05
	International	3.48

*For each criterion, respondents were asked to indicate on a five-point scale how important the criterion was in the elimination decision, from 1 ("very important") to 5 ("not considered").

SOURCE: Adapted from Gwendolyn H. Baker, "The Carrier Elimination Decision: Implications for Motor Carrier Marketing," *Transportation Journal* 24, no. 1 (Fall 1984), p. 26. Reproduced with the express permission of the publisher.

ords, and present or potential customers of the firm. The extent of the search process may be minimal if the decision maker uses only past experience as an information source. As more sources of information are cited, however, the time expended in the search process may be considerable. At the point where a sufficient number of sources have been examined to satisfy the transportation executive's requirements for information, the decision becomes one of using the information obtained to select a particular mode and/or carrier alternative.

Choice process. The task facing the transportation executive at this stage is to choose a feasible alternative from among the several modes and carriers available. Using relevant and available information sources, the executive determines which of the available options can meet the requirements of shipment. Generally, service-related factors are the major determinants of mode/carrier choice. Tables 6–4, 6–5, and 6–6 identify a number of selection criteria used in the evaluation of motor, water, and air carriers, respectively. Obtaining relevant information to select and evaluate carriers is critical. The appendix of this chapter presents a possible method for gathering such data.

Selection Criteria

As the tables indicate, there are similarities across modes in terms of the most important attributes used to select and evaluate carriers. Attributes such as on-time pickups and deliveries, prompt response to customer inquiries, consistent transit times, and competitive rates seem to be important irrespective of the mode and/or carrier being considered.

In the motor carrier industry, service factors were among the most

TABLE 6–4 The Most Important Attributes Considered When Selecting and Evaluating LTL Motor Carriers

Attribute Description	*Importance Mean**
Quality of dispatch personnel (honesty)	6.5
On-time pickups	6.5
On-time deliveries	6.5
Competitive rates	6.5
Accurate billing	6.4
Assistance from carrier in handling loss and damage claims	6.4
Prompt action on complaints related to carriers service	6.4
Quality of drivers (honesty)	6.4
Prompt response to claims	6.4
Carrier's general attitude toward problems/complaint	6.3
Prompt availability of status information on delivery	6.3
Consistent (reliable) transit times	6.3
Quality of sales (honesty)	6.2
Satisfactory insurance coverage	6.2
Prompt availability of status information on shipment tracing	6.2
Ability to provide direct delivery without interlining	6.2
Quality of operating management (honesty)	6.2
Length of promised transit times (from pickup to delivery)	6.2

*Respondents were asked to indicate on a seven-point scale how important the attribute was in selecting an LTL motor carrier, from 1 (not important) to 7 (very important).

SOURCE: Douglas M. Lambert, M. Christine Lewis, and James R. Stock, "How Shippers Select and Evaluate General Commodities LTL Motor Carriers," unpublished manuscript, 1992.

highly rated factors used by logistics executives to select and evaluate carriers. As shown in Table 6–4, LTL motor carriers must be able to provide quality personnel, equipment, and service at competitive prices. Truckload carriers would be evaluated in a similar fashion.

Differences in the Characteristics of Modes and the Nature of the Product Affect the Selection Process

In comparing ocean transport to motor carriage, there are some differences in how carriers are selected and evaluated. Those differences are expected, given the characteristics of the modes and the nature of products transported by each mode. However, even though pricing issues are more important to ocean transport shippers, Table 6–5 indicates that quality issues in carrier personnel and customer services are more significant criteria in the selection and evaluation of ocean transport carriers.

Table 6–6 illustrates the importance of service factors in the air freight sector. Given the mode characteristics of air transport—such as time-in-transit speed—shippers place great emphasis on service. Price is typically not as relevant given that products being shipped by air freight are of high value and time sensitive, thus requiring very short order cycle times. Historically, shippers have been willing to pay the higher costs of air freight in return for the superior customer service levels provided by that mode.

The transportation executive then selects the mode or carrier that best satisfies the decision criteria, and the shipment is routed via that option. In cases in which a similar decision may occur in the future, such as with a repeat order from a customer, management may establish an order routine so that the same choice process will not have to be repeated. Order routines

TABLE 6–5 Importance of Ocean Shipping-Line Service Attributes

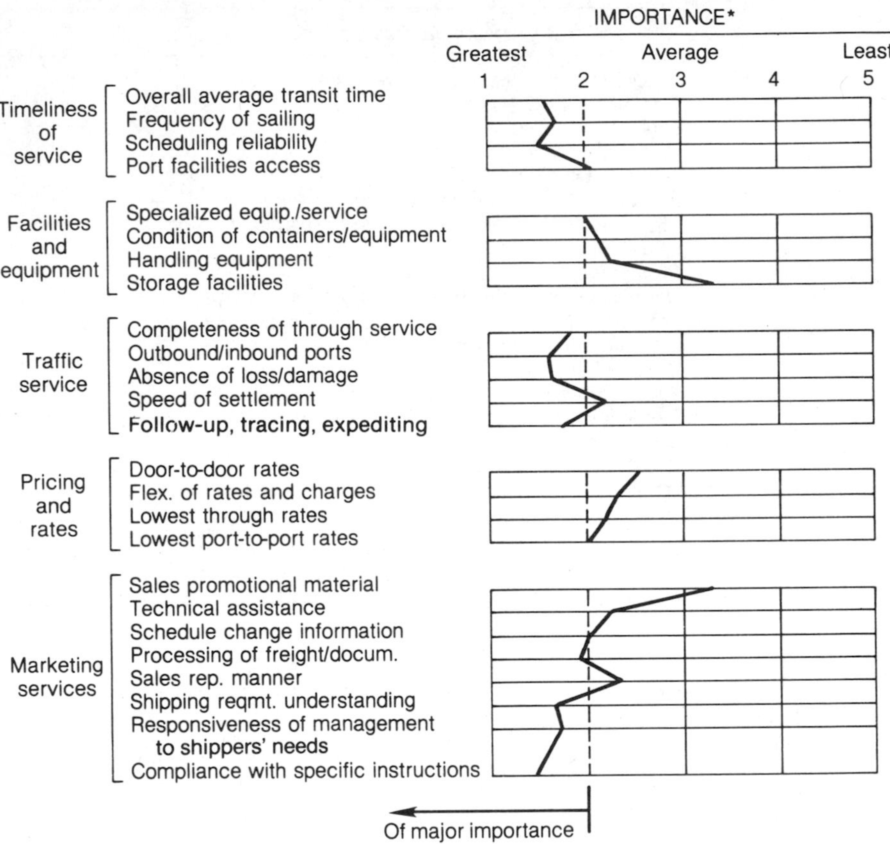

*A five-point scale was used with 1 "of greatest importance" and 5 "of least importance."

SOURCE: Fredrick M. Collison, "Market Segments for Marine Liner Service," *Transportation Journal* 24, no. 2 (Winter 1984), p. 43. Reproduced with the express permission of the publisher.

eliminate inefficiencies associated with making the same decision repeatedly.

Postchoice evaluation. Once management has made its choice of mode and carrier, it must institute some evaluation procedure to determine the performance level of the mode/carrier. Depending on the individual firm, the postchoice evaluation process may be extremely detailed, or there may be none at all. For the majority of firms, the degree of postchoice evaluation lies somewhere between the two extremes. It is rare that a company does not at least respond to customer complaints about its mode or carriers; this is one form of postchoice evaluation. Many firms use other techniques, such as cost studies, audits, reviews of on-time pickups and delivery per-

TABLE 6–6 Important Air Cargo Variables in Carrier Choice

Variable	*Mean Responses**	*Rank*
Consistent on-time delivery	1.220	1
Total time in transit	1.279	2
Carrier's ability not to lose shipments	1.300	3
Carrier's ability to minimize damage to shipments	1.578	4
Tracing capabilities	1.809	5
Pickup and delivery service	2.078	6
My ability to get flight space when needed	2.159	7
Prompt settlement of claims	2.631	8
Accurate rate information	2.978	9
Overall liability coverage	3.086	10
Low rates	3.095	11
Carrier reputation among shippers	3.183	12
Convenience of using previously used carrier	3.351	13

*The authors asked respondents to reveal the importance they placed on each of 13 variables that might be considered in the choice of an air carrier. Shippers could check one of seven responses from 1 (extremely important consideration) to 7 (not at all an important consideration).

SOURCE: Fredrick J. Stephenson and John W. Vann, "Deregulation: The Elimination of Air Cargo Tariff Filing Requirements," *Journal of Business Logistics* 3, no. 1 (1982), p. 68. Published with permission from the Council of Logistics Management, formerly the National Council of Physical Distribution Management.

formance, and damage/claims reviews. Some will statistically analyze the quality of carrier service attributes, such as on-time performance and loss/damage ratios. This has been referred to as *statistical process control.*

Procedures Used for Performance Evaluation

In some cases, these evaluative procedures may lead to the problem recognition stage if the mode and/or carrier is performing unsatisfactorily. Firms that primarily use private carriage also employed many of these procedures as part of their self-evaluation.

Information Feedback

An integral part of the mode/carrier choice model is the feedback mechanism. Information feedback can come from sources other than performance measures. The decision environment external to the selection decision also provides input into the process, such as sales personnel feedback and interdepartmental communications.

The feedback can be used as input at any point in the model. The feedback mechanism is valuable because it occurs concurrently and independently of performance measures. The mode/carrier choice decision is a universal process, in that while the factors entering into the process may vary by geographic location or industry, the basic structure of the decision remains consistent regardless of these differences.

Mode and carrier selection is becoming much more important as shippers reduce the number of carriers with whom they do business and develop core carriers. By leveraging freight volumes to get bigger discounts and higher levels of service, shippers are able to reduce their transportation costs. At the same time, carriers benefit by having to deal with fewer shippers, each shipping larger volumes of product consistently over longer periods of time.

> Square D [an electrical equipment manufacturer] reports that [it] has successfully reduced the number of carriers it uses. Five years ago as many as 1,500 carriers were involved in moving company goods. Today, 55 handle 98 percent of the freight. The savings also have been substantial. . . . The program saved $3.5 million in transportation costs when first implemented three years ago. Today, the company's annual transportation costs have stabilized at a three-year-old level, while the volume of freight moved steadily increases.[33]

The Use of Contracts Is Expanding

Contracts. The use of contracts between shippers and carriers has become widespread since deregulation of the transportation industry. Since 1980, when the Staggers Rail Act took effect, tens of thousands of rail contracts have been filed with the Interstate Commerce Commission (ICC). In the first six months after the Shipping Act of 1984 was implemented, more than 310 service contracts were filed with the Federal Maritime Commission (FMC), a "signal that the ocean shipping industry is beginning to conduct business in an entirely new way."[34] Similar results have occurred in the motor carrier industry.

The advantages of contracting are numerous. Contracts permit the shipper to exercise greater control over the transportation resource. They also assure predictability and guard against fluctuation in rates. In addition, contracting provides the shipper with service level guarantees and allows the shipper to use transportation to gain competitive advantage.[35]

Carrier-shipper contracts can prove valuable to both parties, but it is important that the contract include all of the relevant elements that apply to the shipping agreement. The transportation contract is a legal document and is therefore binding. It should not be entered into casually and should contain the items presented in Table 6–7. Except where indicated, the sample contract outline shown in the table applies to all transportation carriers. The exact format for each carrier-shipper contract will vary, depending on the mode/carrier involved, the type of shipping firm, the product(s) to be transported, the level of competition, and other factors.

Use of Brokers. Before the deregulation of the motor and rail industries, transportation brokers were concentrated in exempt agricultural and water barge transportation.[36] Since 1980, the number of brokers has expanded from less than 50 to more than 2,500.[37]

---

[33] Mitchell E. MacDonald, "Why Shippers Are Cutting Carriers," *Traffic Management* 29, no. 4 (April 1990), p. 49.

[34] John LoDico, "Service Contracts on Growth Curve in Early Months After Shipping Act," *Traffic World* 201, no. 1 (December 31, 1984), p. 40.

[35] Temple, Barker, and Sloane, *Transportation Strategies for the Eighties*, p. 154.

[36] Kevin H. Horn, "Freight Brokerage: A Model for Deregulated Transportation?" in *Logistics: Change and Synthesis*, ed. Patrick Gallagher, *Proceedings of the 1984 Logistics Resource Forum* (Cleveland: Leaseway Transportation Corp., 1984), p. 155.

[37] Francis J. Quinn, "The Broker Boom," *Traffic Management* 24, no. 2 (February 1985), p. 36.

TABLE 6–7 Does Your Transportation Contract Cover These Points?

- ☐ Rates.
- ☐ Origins and destinations to be served.
- ☐ Commodities to be transported.
- ☐ The freight documents that will govern the movement of the goods.
- ☐ The carrier's liability for bodily injury, property damage, and cargo damage.
- ☐ Indemnification (compensation) for the shipper from the carrier in the event that a third party sues the shipper for damages caused by the carrier.*
- ☐ A force majeure clause (an escape clause that voids the contract in the event of an act of God, act of war, or a strike).
- ☐ Minimum volume guarantees.
- ☐ Confirmation of the carrier's status as an independent contractor.
- ☐ Provisions for worker's compensation.*
- ☐ A schedule for payments.
- ☐ A guarantee that the contract will be confidential.
- ☐ A provision covering assignment of the contract (specifying that rights granted under the contract cannot be transferred to another party).
- ☐ A termination clause.
- ☐ Specifications for the "measure of loss" or a statement about the replacement value of damaged goods.
- ☐ Provisions stating how the agreement can be modified.
- ☐ Specifications for the carrier's equipment.
- ☐ A statement specifying which state's laws will govern the agreement.
- ☐ A severability provision (specifying that even if one clause is held invalid, the other terms of the agreement will remain in effect).
- ☐ The carrier's transit, demurrage, and terminal privileges.†

*Applies to trucking contracts only.

†Applies to rail contracts only.

SOURCE: James Aaron Cooke, "The Fine Art of Contracting," *Traffic Management* 24, no. 2 (February 1985), p. 49.

What Is a Broker?

A broker is someone who arranges for the transportation of products and charges a fee to do so. Brokers are licensed by the ICC and are subject to the same rules and regulations that apply to carriers.

Benefits of Using a Broker

There are many reasons why a shipper would use a transportation broker. Among the most important are one-stop shopping, expertise, better rates, and better service.[38] Brokers serve both large and small shippers but offer the small shipper one sizable advantage: "Small shippers . . . generally lack the transportation staff and expertise required to stay abreast of the many changes occurring in today's turbulent transportation environment. . . . A number of these shippers have turned to brokers in lieu of creating or expanding their traffic departments."[39] In many instances, a firm will use a combination of transportation options, including brokers, forwarders, common and contract carriers, and private carriage.

Private Carriage/Leasing. A private carrier is any transportation entity that moves products for the manufacturing or merchandising firm that owns it. While the equipment may transport nonowned goods in some

[38] Quinn, "The Broker Boom," p. 38.

[39] Ibid., p. 36.

cases, private carriers were primarily established to haul the products of their own companies.

The Make-or-Buy Decision in Transportation

Private carriage should not be viewed strictly as a transportation decision; rather, it is also a financial decision. There are two stages in evaluating the financial considerations of private carriage. The first involves a comparison of current cost and service data of the firm's for-hire carriers with that of a private operation, and the second is to devise a plan of implementation and a procedure for system control.

The feasibility study should begin with an evaluation of the current transportation situation, along with corporate objectives regarding potential future market expansion. Objectives should include a statement outlining past, current, and desired service levels, as well as a consideration of the business environment, such as legal restrictions and the general trend of the economy. There are 10 steps that one must follow to fully evaluate the private carriage option. These steps are discussed below.[40]

Ten Steps in the Evaluation of Private Carriage/ Leasing

Define the problem. Difficulties can originate from any one or more members of the transportation system—customer, carrier, or shipper. Does the customer receive adequate service and undamaged goods on time and at a reasonable cost? Does the carrier have the required route flexibility and operational capability to deliver the product economically? Does volume prevent delivery of the desired service level at a competitive price? Do the carrier's equipment and facilities meet the requirements of the channel members? The problem may also originate in the seller's operation; facility and dock equipment may be overburdened or underutilized, the company may be responsible for management and scheduling problems, or it may simply have a poor logistics system.

Develop transport objectives. These objectives should center on two measures. The first is the customer service level—consistent and fast delivery, as well as additional services that may be required. The second should focus on the firm's cost objectives for the total logistics process—order processing, communications, warehousing, inventory, transportation, and the return of damaged goods. The company should establish goals for each of these functions in terms of both effectiveness and efficiency.

Collect pertinent information. This requires the gathering of data that are relevant to the parties involved: inventory data, shipping procedures, product characteristics, origin and destination, volume and weight, and cost associated with the shipment of the products. Management should take the customer's viewpoint when evaluating complaints received, quantifiable service level data, and competitors' actions.

[40] See Barrie Vreeland, *Private Trucking from A to Z* (New York: Commerce and Industry Association Institute, 1968), p. 6.

Determine present cost. It is necessary to use a total cost approach that not only determines the cost of transportation but also encompasses the total distribution network. The determination of operating costs should include the cost of order processing, packaging, shipping, transportation, and the expense attributed to damaged goods and returns. In addition, the current cost of inventory investment, insurance, taxes, inventory risk, and building cost directly associated with the inventory function should be included. The determination of these current costs will serve as the point of comparison with the private trucking option and other possible alternatives.

Analyze present operations. This includes the review of both the qualitative and quantitative data the company has gathered in the attempt to uncover poor cost/service relationships. This step includes analysis of customer order patterns, transportation patterns, cyclical or seasonal variations, and potential for backhauls. Also included are evaluation of ton-mile cost and review of specific transportation costs which exceed standard.

Develop alternatives. This, the sixth step, begins with a review of cost service levels of functions in which problems have been identified; suggestions of alternative courses of action to solve those problems are then made. Three basic alternatives are almost always available in this process: (1) do nothing; (2) invest the available capital in other areas of the firm that may yield an even higher return; or (3) use funds to improve the current system.

Three Common Alternatives

The improvement of distribution operations need not include implementation of a private fleet operation. Instead, the firm may make adjustments, such as improving order processing, negotiating new carrier rates, or improving packaging—all of which may yield the same benefits as private trucking or leasing, but at a much lower cost.

Determine private fleet cost. The firm should account for all costs associated with private trucking, as well as the effects these costs will have on the firm's total costs.[41] Any added savings or costs generated in inventory, personnel, or production because of the use of private trucking should be added to or deducted from the cost of this alternative. Costs for the private trucking function include equipment, labor, and other expenses such as maintenance, insurance, and vehicle taxes.

Consider indirect factors. Many nonmonetary factors may influence the decision to switch to a private trucking operation. They include company image; advantages over competition; the advertising value of the trucks; the effects on employees and unions; the management skills required to develop and control the system; carriers' willingness to accept remaining

[41] For an interesting discussion on how Playtex Family Products Co. examined the costs of its private fleet, see Lisa H. Harrington, "How to Get the Most from Your Private Fleet Dollar," *Traffic Management* 30, no. 1 (January 1991), pp. 39–43.

freight; the potential for rate renegotiation; and corporate policy toward equipment selection, maintenance, and replacement. A wide range of factors not under the firm's control—such as the legal (ICC), economic, and technical environments—must also be considered.

Summarize alternatives. The summary should outline the cost, capital requirements, and indirect factors (advantages and disadvantages) for (1) the present method, (2) an alternative improved method that would *not* be a major change from the existing operation, and (3) a private fleet operation.[42]

Make the decision. The final step is to make a decision. It should be based on the summary and on other inputs from such sources as internal management, outside experts, and the experience of other firms that have had private fleets. Despite the quantitative information available, no decision can be cut and dried. A large number of factors must be left to judgment and the decision maker's willingness to assume some level of risk.

Cost/Benefit Analysis of Private Carriage

In our discussion of the transportation selection decision, we saw that a firm must perform a cost/benefit analysis to determine whether it should use private carriage. Any financial analysis should consider the time value of money. Table 6–8 illustrates the analysis of cash flows that must be performed. The company must calculate the net cash inflows (cash inflows minus cash outflows) for the life of the investment decision and discount them using the company's minimum acceptable rate of return on new investment. The sum of these discounted cash flows must be compared to the initial capital requirement to determine if the investment is financially sound.

If the company makes the decision to engage in private carriage, its next step is to devise a plan of implementation and a procedure for system control. Implementation begins with a review of the structure of the organization or group responsible for operating the private fleet. Management assigns the activities to be performed to groups or individuals, and formulates a timetable for phasing in the project. Because of the risk involved, most firms begin with a low level of activity, followed by intermediate reviews of results and subsequent modification of the plan. The process is repeated until the firm achieves full implementation.

Control of private carriage should center on measuring performance against standards, with the ability to identify specific problem areas. If management desires to use a total cost approach in order to charge cost against the product and customer, it can calculate a cost per mile, identifying the fixed cost associated with distribution of the product, and then adding the variable cost per mile. This information may also be useful to

---

[42] Vreeland, *Private Trucking from A to Z*, p. 7.

TABLE 6–8 Financial Consideration of the Decision to Switch to Private Carriage

	Amount	
Capital requirements:		
Cost of buying or leasing fleet	________	
Cost of maintenance facilities	________	
Cost of terminal facilities	________	
Annual cash inflows:		
Savings over using public carriers	________	
Reduction in lost sales	________	
Reduction in inventory carrying costs due to more efficient routing	________	
Total		________
Annual cash outflows:		
Fuel	________	
Labor—drivers	________	
Labor—maintenance and terminal	________	
Insurance—trucks	________	
—drivers	________	
—maintenance and terminal facilities	________	
License fees	________	
Parts supply	________	
Utilities	________	
Supervision	________	
Administrative—billing, telephone, accounting	________	
Total	________	
Annual cash inflows − annual cash outflows		________

compare budgeted to actual expenditures, or to compare the private fleet operation to common carrier statistics and industry averages. The information generated is limited, however, due to the wide variations of cost and service requirements across industries and their divisions. Since 1980, events in the business environment have significantly affected private carriage. Firms whose primary activities are not in transportation can enter into all forms of regulated trucking. The Motor Carrier Act of 1980, coupled with the ICC and court rulings, enabled private carriers to haul products for other companies on a for-hire basis, allowed intercorporate hauling, and provided freedom to lease personnel and equipment. It also allowed "one-way" leases in which "unaffiliated shippers with complementary traffic may in effect combine their private carriage operations so that the same vehicles and drivers haul one shipper's goods outbound and the other's on the backhaul."[43]

"One-Way" Leases

Leasing of equipment and/or drivers is an important consideration in private carriage. It provides ease of entry and predictable cost and service

[43] Colin Barrett, "What Future for Private Trucking?" *Distribution* 83, no. 12 (December 1984), p. 28.

Advantages of Leasing

levels. In contracting for the use of a full service fleet, even inexperienced management can know the exact cost for transportation services, and can budget accordingly.

Other advantages of leasing include the ability to adjust vehicle resources for business cycles and seasonality through special lease agreements. Also, if the fleet is to be small, the company will avoid investing in maintenance equipment and facilities. Another consideration is transportation obsolescence; new technology may render older vehicles obsolete, or the firm may outgrow its distribution and transportation system. Many firms are available to provide leased equipment, including Ryder Truck Rental, Penske Truck Leasing, and Rollins Leasing.

Private truck ownership may be preferable if capital is available and if it can be shown that vehicle investment will yield a favorable return. Other advantages might include the ability to buy needed equipment at a discount cost through reciprocity, the utilization of currently owned maintenance equipment and facilities, increased flexibility and freedom of utilization, and potential to provide special customer services that a lessor would not allow.

Leasing Options

Another form of leasing occurs when the shipper acquires both drivers and equipment from others or else leases its drivers and equipment to a for-hire carrier. Recent ICC and court rulings in 1984 have allowed private carriage operations to "single-source lease" and "trip lease." These options promise to expand the flexibility of shippers with private fleets and to provide additional opportunities to reduce operating costs. The two leasing options can be defined as follows:

Single-Source Leasing. An arrangement under which a private carrier acquires both drivers and equipment from a single source for at least 30 days.

Trip Leasing. An arrangement under which a private carrier leases its drivers and equipment to a for-hire carrier for a period of fewer than 30 days.

There is a third alternative form of equipment acquisition that is particularly appealing from a cash flow viewpoint. A firm may be able to negotiate "third-party" equity loans from a financial institution that include a "guaranteed buy-back" from the dealer at the termination of the useful life of the equipment. This type of lease is fairly common in the acquisition of computer equipment. Under this approach, monthly payments cover interest on the entire purchase price but only an amount of principal equal to the difference between the purchase price and the guaranteed buy-back. This significantly reduces a firm's cash flow outlays and results in lower interest rates if the firm has established a high credit rating with its financial institutions. By using this technique, a national clothing retailer was able to save over $250,000 in interest charges on a three-year equity loan for 22 truck tractors. In addition, the company minimized its risk by obtaining buy-back guarantees from the selected dealer equal to 58 percent of the purchase price of each tractor.[44]

The future of private trucking can hold tremendous promise for those shippers able to take advantage of its benefits. For others, for-hire carriers (common and contract) offer the most opportunities. The most likely scenario is that shippers will utilize a variety of private and for-hire options.

The Marketing Support System

Strategic Partnerships/Alliances. An effective logistics network requires a cooperative relationship between shippers and carriers. That cooperation must occur on both a strategic and an operational level. When such cooperation takes place, the shipper and carrier become part of a partnership or alliance. Companies that have implemented the concept include Black and Decker, GTE, Procter & Gamble, McKesson, Xerox, and 3M.

> In June of 1983, 3M invited senior transportation executives to its headquarters in St. Paul. The purpose of the meeting was to convey to the carriers the message that 3M wanted to become "partners in quality" with them.
>
> 3M wanted to achieve a goal of 100 percent carrier performance. To do so it had to recognize that the various institutions in the channel had a symbiotic relationship.
>
> 3M's Partners in Quality program is based on the notion of *marketing with* its carriers. By marketing with its carriers, 3M could both better serve its target markets, and 3M and its carriers could support each other's marketing efforts.[45]

3M's "Partners in Quality" Program

As stated by 3M, quality was defined as "consistent performance to customer expectations." That definition was the foundation for the "Partners in Quality" program. In materials provided to its current and prospective transportation carriers, 3M outlined the "Partners in Quality" program as follows:

> "Partners in Quality" is a communication process that unites 3M, its suppliers and customers throughout the world. It is a global process for managing transportation expectations, parts of which need to be locally administered. Managing moments of truth through the "Partners in Quality" process is outlined in the following steps:
>
> - Meet with carriers, brokers, agents and forwarders to explain the "Partners in Quality" process.
> - Explain your cost/service requirements and expectations.
> - Develop and document mutual performance standards to meet requirements and expectations.
> - Establish effective date, corrective action process to be used, and review periods.

---

[44] Material on third-party equity loans was obtained from Professor Jay U. Sterling, University of Alabama, and former director of distribution for The Limited Stores, Inc.

[45] Constantin and Hughes, "Motor Carriers and Marketing," p. 466. Emphasis in original.

TABLE 6–9 "Partners in Quality"—The Role of Carriers/Suppliers

3M is dependent upon carriers/suppliers to bring material to our plants and to deliver finished products to our customers, as well as perform other related services. We often refer to carriers/suppliers as an extension of 3M. They may be the only direct contact a customer or vendor has with 3M and, therefore, play a critical role in the 3M quality performance process.

Carriers/suppliers have the responsibility to perform in exact conformance to the agreed-upon standard. Their performance is a direct reflection upon 3M. Those who perform to 3M's expectations make an important contribution to the success of 3M. And they reap a major benefit that a partnership brings—an ongoing relationship and the opportunity for new business.

Just as we require excellence from our people, 3M expects high performance from the companies that provide materials and services. We believe carriers/suppliers need to manage quality the same as they manage people, equipment, materials, terminals or any other business facet. They must put into place a system that fosters quality awareness, individual responsibility and accountability for results. These ingredients are essential in performing transportation service that consistently meets 3M's requirement.

In total, it's just as important for carriers/suppliers to have a quality improvement process as it is for 3M. And it's equally important to make quality a way of life.

SOURCE: 3M Transportation Department. Reprinted with permission.

- Three months after implementation date, conduct a process review to assure understanding of requirements and expectations.
- Use subsequent meetings to review performance, establish future goals, and share cost/service improvement ideas.
- Establish local recognition programs for transportation excellence.

The "Partners in Quality" process provides the methods to manage the 3M transportation business strategy in a constantly changing global marketplace.[46]

From the onset of the "Partners in Quality" program in 1983 through the end of 1990, 3M was able to realize significant benefits, including:

Benefits Resulting from the "Partners in Quality Program

1. Use of fewer carriers/suppliers—a reduction in the number of carriers used from 1,240 in 1983 to 30 core carriers providing 68 percent or more of business within all modes.
2. Transportation costs down 7.5 percent.
3. Improvement in on-time delivery performance—an increase from 74 percent in 1984 to 97.5 percent at the end of 1990.
4. Freight claim amounts down 19.8 percent since 1987.
5. Productivity up 54.3 percent since 1985.
6. U.S. product sales up 17.9 percent since 1987.[47]

In many instances, shippers and carriers do not act in concert because of differences in perceptions, practice, or philosophy. Sometimes the notion that "we never did it that way before" impedes cooperation and synergism.

---

[46] As stated in "Partners in Quality . . . Worldwide," a document provided by 3M to its transportation suppliers.

[47] Information provided by Gary J. Malek, contract manager, air/truck, 3M Corporation, St. Paul, Minnesota.

Such differences result in inefficiencies in the transportation system and conflicts between shippers and carriers. As the manager of transportation for Xerox Corporation's Business System Group said, "Together implies cooperation. . . . While we are all accountable for our independent decisions, carrier-shipper cooperation is more often than not the primary ingredient to the achievement of real productivity."[48]

In essence, a successful strategic partnership or alliance is more than just a set of plans, programs, and methods. Like the marketing concept, and like customer service, partnershipping is a philosophy that permeates the entire organization. It is a way of life that becomes part of the way a firm conducts its business. Table 6–9 illustrates how 3M expresses that philosophy in its "Partners in Quality" program.

TRANSPORTATION PRODUCTIVITY

Both shippers and carriers are concerned with improving transportation productivity. Such improvements are absolutely vital to the success of the logistics system. Nishi and Gallagher argued, "There are only two ways to be productive: doing things right and doing the right things. The former is what we call efficiency, the latter, effectiveness."[49] It is primarily through improved effectiveness that significant productivity gains can be achieved by shippers and carriers.

Areas in which productivity can be improved can be categorized into three groups:

Productivity Can Be Improved in Three Areas

1. Improvements in the transportation system's design and its methods, equipment, and procedures.
2. Improvements in the utilization of labor and equipment.
3. Improvements in the performance of labor and equipment.[50]

Examples of areas within each of these groups that offer productivity improvement possibilities include: Group 1—inbound consolidation, company operated over-the-road trucking, local pickup and delivery operations, and purchased for-hire transportation; Group 2—breakbulk operations, backhaul use of fleet, routing and scheduling systems, tracing and monitoring systems, customer delivery hours, shipment consolidation/pooling, and driver utilization; and Group 3—standards for driver activity, first-line management improvements, establishment of a transportation

[48] Ketchum, "Pricing Transportation Productivity," pp. 203–9.

[49] Masao Nishi and Patrick Gallagher, "A New Focus for Transportation Management: Contribution," *Journal of Business Logistics* 5, no. 2 (1984), p. 21.

[50] A. T. Kearney, Inc., *Measuring and Improving Productivity in Physical Distribution,* p. 174.

data base, incentive compensation to encourage higher productivity and safety, and programs to increase fuel efficiency.[51]

Data Used to Evaluate Transportation Performance

From a shipper's perspective, some of the most common types of data collected that measure carrier effectiveness and efficiency include claims and/or damage ratios, transit time variability, on-time pickup and delivery percentages, cost per ton-mile, billing accuracy, customer complaint frequency, and other measures. In many firms the data do not appear on a formal report, and therefore carrier performance is examined informally. Carriers employ similar measures, although they view them from the perspective of a provider rather than a receiver of services. Additionally, some carriers measure dollar contributions by traffic lane, shipper, salesperson, and/or terminal. Those measures are used primarily for internal performance evaluations, but may be provided to customers in special situations such as rate negotiations or partnership arrangements.

The exact format for data collection is not as important as the need to have the information available in some form:

> Over the past several years, transportation measurement has evolved almost on a company-by-company basis. . . . [Figure 6–3] displays a schematic representation of the evolution of effectiveness measurement. This evolutionary process may be viewed as occurring in four separate stages.

Four Stages of Sophistication in Productivity Measurement

> Stage I is the development and use of raw data in terms of dollars. Characteristic of these data is that they are usually provided by some other functional area (e.g., sales or finance); [they are] usually financial in nature; and the time increment measured is relatively long (e.g., monthly or quarterly). At this stage, these cost data are often compared to some type of macro output such as dollar sales. Thus, a common Stage I measure might be total transportation costs as a percent of sales. Typically, outbound transportation is measured first. Only more sophisticated companies were found to be effectively capturing information about inbound freight costs and flows.
>
> In Stage II, physical measures and activity budgets are introduced for transportation activities. Units such as weight stops, orders, miles, etc., are tracked within the transportation activities over shorter time intervals, such as days or weeks. At this point, these physical units can be measured against transportation labor and nonlabor costs to track cost per pound, per mile, per stop, or per ton-mile. The introduction of time-phased activity budgets is now possible with this information.
>
> Stage III begins with the establishment of empirical or historical "goals" for the overall transportation operation. These goals could be in the form of physical units or period operational cost, but in either case can now lead to the measurement of performance (actual versus standard). . . . The development of industrial engineered standards for labor and nonlabor inputs by activity is usually the next step in further sophistication. Transportation requirements can then be converted to standard hours of work, vehicle loads, or dollars of cost, for instance. This development leads to performance measurement of labor, and nonlabor inputs by activity against variable (i.e., volume-related) bud-

[51] Ibid., pp. 174–85.

FIGURE 6–3 Evolution of Transportation Productivity Measurement

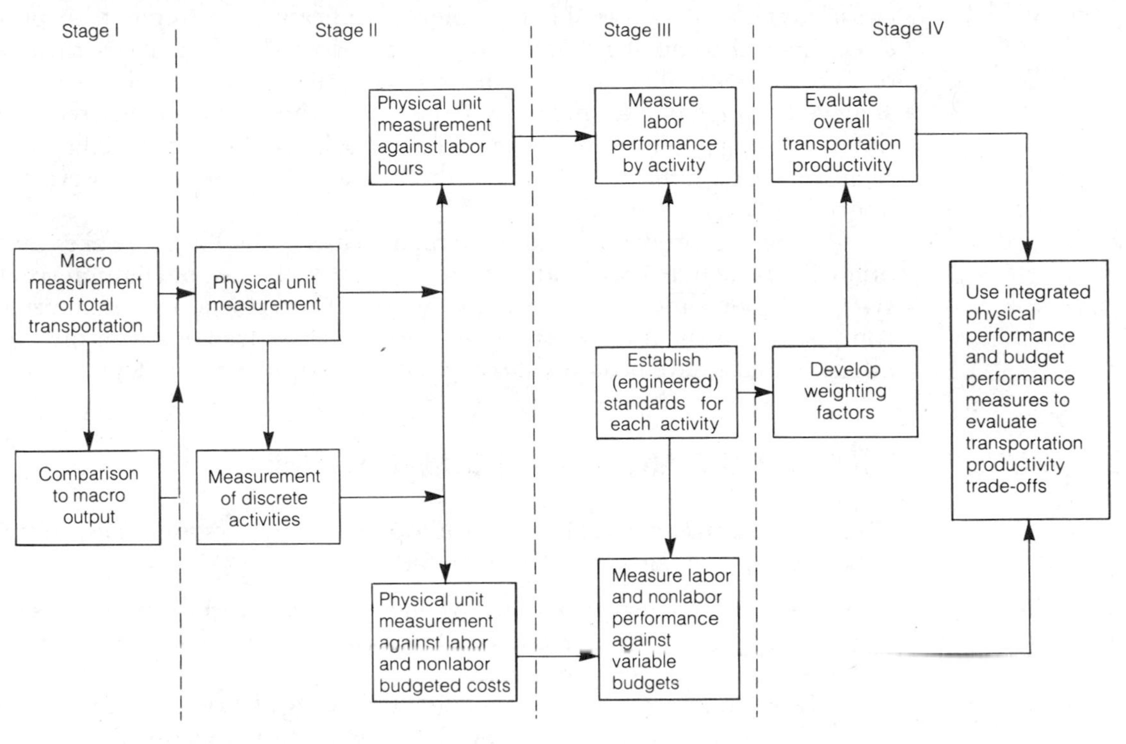

SOURCE: A. T. Kearney, Inc., *Measuring and Improving Productivity in Physical Distribution* (Oak Brook, Ill.: National Council of Physical Distribution Management, 1984), p. 173.

gets. Included here would be actual versus budgeted cost analyses as well as variance analyses highlighting the reasons for budgetary variance (e.g., standard versus actual unit cost, standard versus actual output).

Stage IV is the last step in the development of a productivity measurement system. In Stage IV, physical performance data are merged with financial data to provide management with an overall view of the transportation operation. Armed with this type of measurement system, management is in a position to control ongoing operations as well as to test alternatives and seek trade-offs to present operations.[52]

Land O'Lakes, Inc., is one example of a company that has examined the productivity of its transportation system. As a multibillion-dollar, diversified, farmer-owned cooperative specializing in agricultural services, commodities, and food products, Land O'Lakes ran a program in 1980–

[52] Ibid., pp. 171–72, 174. Published with permission from the Council of Logistics Management.

Land O'Lakes Improves Transportation Productivity

85 intended to improve transportation productivity. With the use of a policy group made up of the top-level corporate managers and an outside consultant, the firm was able to achieve significant improvements in productivity by the end of 1985. Initial projections were an annual cost savings of $2.2 to $5.5 million. For the calendar year 1983, Land O'Lakes actually achieved savings of $4.0 million.[53] At the same time the company realized the cost savings, it improved customer service, information availability, and strategic decision making. Thus, both efficiency and effectiveness were enhanced at Land O'Lakes.

Part of the productivity improvement achieved by Land O'Lakes and other firms such as FMC and Amway was due to the use of computerized systems.[54] Computers allow decision makers to perform and administer components of the transportation network better. Indeed, many of the significant results have been the direct result of computer technology.

COMPUTER TECHNOLOGY AND TRAFFIC MANAGEMENT

The use of computers has become widespread in logistics, especially in the area of traffic management. For example:

Examples of Computer Usage in Transportation

Union Camp Corporation is now able to verify freight rates in 30 seconds thanks to a computerized rating system. Annual savings amount to $1.5 million.[55]

A new computer system has enabled Ciba-Geigy Corp. to handle a 300 percent increase in imports with no increase in personnel.[56]

Leaseway Transportation Corp. offers potential customers free computer analyses of routing and scheduling, fleet sizing, mode cost-benefit trade-offs, and other transportation activities.[57]

Freight bill payment has been handled faster, better, and with fewer people at Welch Foods using the computer.[58]

Conrail provides free computer software and training to help small

---

[53] Howard S. Gochberg, "Anatomy of a Transportation Productivity Project," *Proceedings of the Twenty-Second Annual Conference of the National Council of Physical Distribution Management.* 1984, p. 893.

[54] See Patrick J. Conlon and William A. Townsend, "The 'How To' of Transportation Productivity Programs," *Proceedings of the Twenty-Second Annual Conference of the National Council of Physical Distribution Management,* 1984, pp. 53–74.

[55] Eric D. Lindeman, "Computerized Traffic Department Helps Union Camp Meet Competition," *Traffic World* 199, no. 8 (August 20, 1983), p. 46.

[56] A. M. MacKinnon, "Giving Transportation a New Look," *Handling & Shipping Presidential Issue, 1983–84* 24, no. 10 (September 1983), p. 46.

[57] "Powerful New Computer Analysis Offered Free to Shippers," *Creative Solutions* 1 (October 1983), p. 1.

[58] Jack W. Farrell, "Putting the Micro to Good Use," *Traffic Management* 24, no. 2 (February 1985), p. 55.

railroads with which it interchanges traffic establish electronic data interchange (EDI) systems.[59]

Nabisco Foods Co. developed a PC-based claims transmittal program that has dramatically reduced the number and cost of transportation claims; outstanding claims have been reduced from $2 million-plus to less than $250,000.[60]

Generally, computerized transportation activities can be categorized into four groups: transportation analysis, traffic routing and scheduling, freight rate maintenance and auditing, and vehicle maintenance. Andersen Consulting has conducted a survey of computer software for logistics since 1981 and has described the type of software available in each of the four groups as follows:

Four types of Transportation Software

1. *Transportation analysis*—This software allows management to monitor costs and service by providing historical reporting of carrier performance, shipping modes, traffic lane utilization, premium freight usage, backhauls, and so forth.
2. *Traffic routing and scheduling*—This functional area provides features such as the sequence and timing of vehicle stops, route determinations, shipping paperwork preparation, and vehicle availability.
3. *Freight rate maintenance and auditing*—These systems maintain a data base of freight rates used to rate shipments and/or to perform freight bill auditing. It compares actual freight bills with charges computed using the lowest applicable rates in the data base. It can then pay or authorize payment or report on exceptions.
4. *Vehicle maintenance*—Features commonly provided by these packages include vehicle maintenance scheduling and reporting.[61]

Schematically, a typical transportation system computer package might look like the one shown in Figure 6–4—or it might include only a portion or subset of the elements shown in the figure. The degree and scope of computer usage will vary by firm and by transportation activity. What is clear, however, is that the computer has had a significant impact on the traffic management area and will be even more important in the future.

INTERNATIONAL TRANSPORTATION

International transportation of goods can involve any of the five basic modes of transportation, although air and water carriage are perhaps the most important. Motor, rail, and water carriage are the most important freight movements *within* nations.

---

[59] "Conrail Giving Software to Small Railroads," *On Track* 4, no. 14 (July 17–31, 1990), p. 2.

[60] Francis J. Quinn, "Profile of a Partnership," *Traffic Management* 28, no. 2 (February 1989), p. 39.

[61] Richard C. Haverly, Douglas McW. Smith, and Deborah P. Steele, *Logistics Software* (Stamford, Conn.: Andersen Consulting, 1990), p. 9.

FIGURE 6–4 An Example of a Computerized Transportation Algorithm

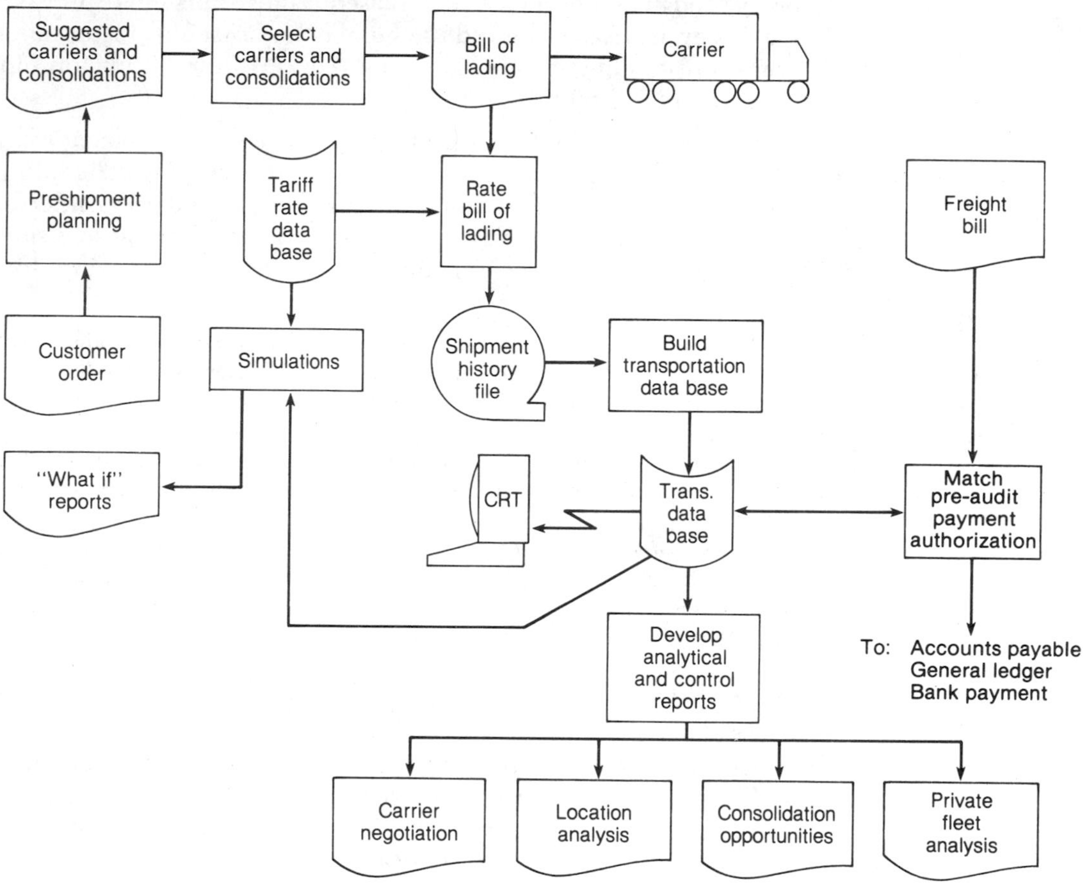

Suggested carriers and consolidations
Select carriers and consolidations
Bill of lading
Carrier
Preshipment planning
Tariff rate data base
Rate bill of lading
Freight bill
Customer order
Simulations
Shipment history file
Build transportation data base
"What if" reports
CRT
Trans. data base
Match pre-audit payment authorization
Develop analytical and control reports
To: Accounts payable General ledger Bank payment
Carrier negotiation
Location analysis
Consolidation opportunities
Private fleet analysis

SOURCE: Walter L. Weart, "The Techniques of Freight Consolidation: An Area of Increased Interest Aided by Computers," *Traffic World* 197, no. 12 (March 19, 1984), p. 54.

Traffic Management Is Different in Many Countries

There can be significant differences between the transportation infrastructure found in nations throughout the world. For example, the transportation environments of the United States and the Common Market countries differ markedly. Factors by which Common Market countries differ from the United States include:[62]

1. *Different shipper traffic structures*—Only a few of the largest companies maintain clearly identified in-house traffic units.

---

[62] Some of these differences may disappear and new ones appear as Europe 1992 becomes a reality. Europe 1992 will be discussed in Chapter 17, "Global Logistics."

2. *Different transport pricing methods*—Tariffs and classifications are simpler and smaller as well as fewer in number, [and] negotiated rates are the rule.
3. *Different modal services*—In routes, in equipment, and in the specific services they provide, carriers of Common Market freight are unlike their U.S. counterparts. Generally, their role is to provide basic transportation; paperwork, consolidation, and other services not part of the actual physical movement are performed for the shipper by others.
4. *Different forwarder duties*—Most of the work performed by shipper and carrier traffic departments in North America is handled instead by freight forwarders in Common Market countries and in all of Europe. Shippers only work directly with carriers where volume shipments move regularly; even these tend to be forwarder-processed when international through-movement and the resulting paperwork is involved.[63]

Managers of firms involved in international markets must be aware of the different transport services, costs, and availabilities of transport modes within the countries where they market their products. The differences that exist between nations can be due to taxes, subsidies, regulations, government ownership of carriers, and other factors.

One interesting example occurs in the European Economic Community (EEC): "Under EEC international rules, drivers may only work for eight hours a day. No driver may drive for more than four hours consecutively without a break of half an hour. Such regulations have vitally important implications for transport scheduling and depot locations."[64]

Transportation Modes Have Different Characteristics

Rail service in Europe is usually much better than in the United States, because equipment, track, and facilities are in better condition due to government ownership and/or subsidies of the rail system. Japan and Europe utilize water carriage to a much larger degree than the United States or Canada. Due to the length and favorable characteristics of coastlines and inland waterways, water transport is a viable alternative for many shippers. Many companies shipping between or within the borders of foreign countries need to thoroughly reevaluate transport alternatives, costs, and services. As an example, air and surface transportation directly compete for transoceanic shipments. Management must consider many factors when it compares the two alternatives. Each international shipment must be evaluated separately in order to ascertain the cost differential between air and surface transport.

Bender noted that:"International transportation costs generally represent a much higher fraction of merchandise value than is the case in

---

[63] Jack W. Farrell, "Common Market Transport: An Overview for U.S. Shippers," *Traffic Management* 16, no. 3 (March 1977), p. 36.

[64] Gordon Wills and Angela Rushton, "U.K. Progress in PDM," *International Journal of Physical Distribution and Materials Management* 12, no. 6 (1982), p. 41.

domestic transportation. The main reasons are the longer distances involved and the need to use intermodal transportation systems, with the consequent rehandling."[65] Intermodal transportation is much more common in international movements, and even though rehandling costs are higher than for single mode movements, cost savings and service improvements can result. For example, there are three basic forms of international intermodal distribution; they have been described as follows:

Forms of International Intermodalism

1. *Landbridge,* a service in which foreign cargo crosses a country en route to another country. For example, European cargo en route to Japan may be shipped by ocean to the U.S. East Coast, then moved by rail to the U.S. West Coast, and from there shipped by ocean to Japan.
2. *Minilandbridge (also called minibridge),* a special case of landbridge, where foreign cargo originates or terminates at a point within the United States.
3. *Microbridge,* a relatively new service being provided by ports on the U.S. West Coast. In contrast with minibridge, this service provides door-to-door rather than port-to-port transportation. The big advantage of microbridge is that it provides a combined rate including rail and ocean transportation in a single tariff that is lower than the sum of the separate rates.[66]

Each option is pictorially presented in Figure 6–5.

A comparison of single-mode and intermodal movements between the Far East and the U.S. East Coast demonstrates the advantages of the latter. If we compare an all-water versus minilandbridge (MLB) movement for comparable shipments, the costs are approximately the same (see Table 6–10). But MLB is significantly faster, thus offering the opportunity to reduce order-cycle times and improve customer service levels.

In making traffic and transportation decisions, the logistics manager must consider the differences between the domestic and international markets. Modal availability, rates, regulatory restrictions, service levels, and other aspects of the transportation mix may vary significantly from one market to another. It is vital that the differences be known and understood so that an optimal transportation network can be established for each international market.

---

[65] Paul S. Bender, "The International Dimension of Physical Distribution Management," in *The Distribution Handbook,* ed. James R. Robeson and Robert G. House (New York: Free Press, 1985), p. 791.

[66] Ibid., pp. 791–92.

FIGURE 6–5 International Distribution Shipping Options

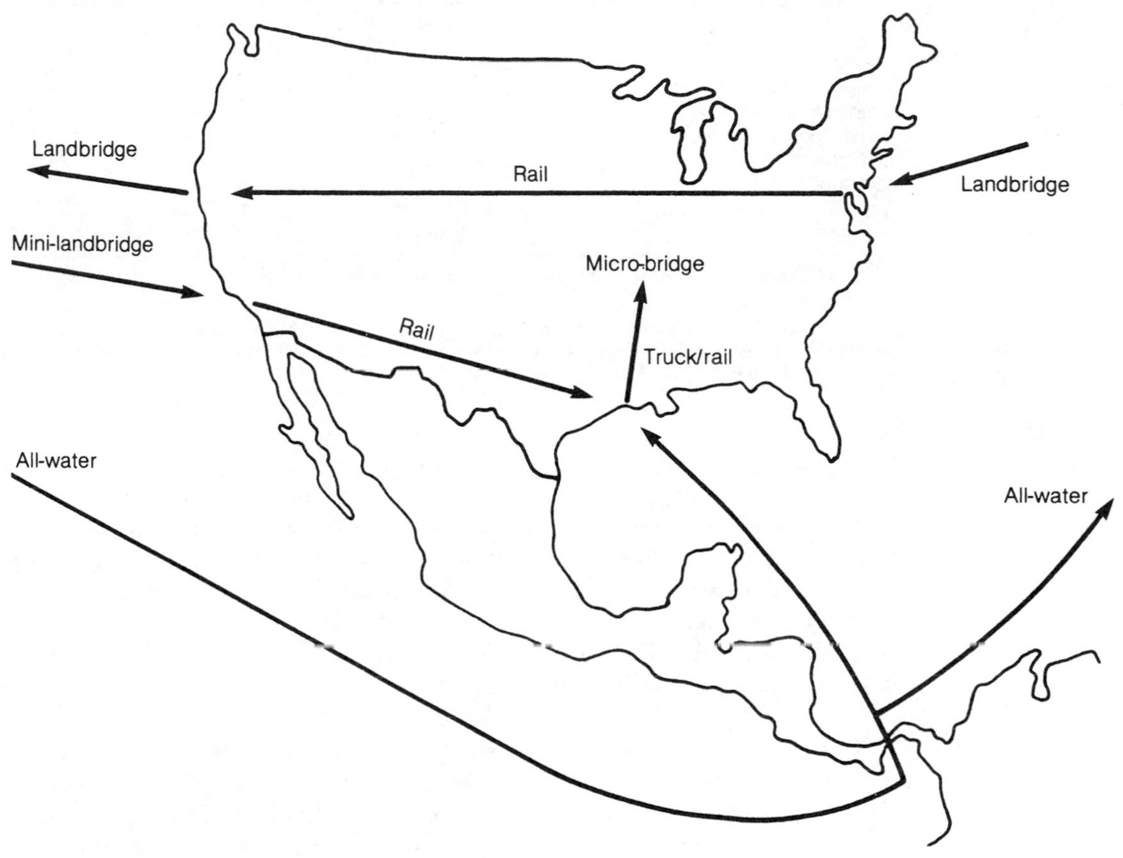

SOURCE: David L. Anderson, "International Logistics Strategies for the Eighties," *Proceedings of the Twenty-Second Annual Conference of the National Council of Physical Distribution Management,* 1984, p. 363. Used by permission of the Council of Logistics Management.

THE TRANSPORTATION AUDIT

The Transportation Audit Pinpoints Important Areas of Decision Making

No single transportation system is best for all companies, because each firm has its own unique set of products, markets, customers, and facilities. The individual company must develop a system that is both cost- and service-optimal for itself. Each component of the logistics system is capable of being audited. Such an audit should be performed periodically. A transportation system audit provides the firm with an overview of the various transportation components of their logistics network. The audit serves to identify and pinpoint the important areas of transportation decision making.

TABLE 6–10 Intermodal Distribution Economics—East Coast to Pacific Coast (per TEU)*

	All Water		
	*1,700 TEU**	*3,400 TEU**	*MLB†*
Transit time	15 days	17 days	5 days
Vessel cost (80 percent utilization)	$1,080	$ 880	—
Equipment cost	135	153	$ 45
Intermodal cost	—	—	1,300
Inventory cost to shipper	226	256	75
Totals	$1,441	$1,289	$1,420

*TEU stands for the equivalent of a 20′ × 8′ × 8′ container.

†Minilandbridge.

SOURCE: David L. Anderson, "International Logistics Strategies for the Eighties," *Proceedings of the Twenty-Second Annual Conference of the National Council of Physical Distribution Management,* 1984, p. 365. Used by permission of the Council of Logistics Management.

Conducting a Transportation Audit

In conducting the audit, the firm needs to examine the cost and service aspects of the transportation system. Theoretically, the transportation decision is fairly simple: How should products be moved from suppliers to the firm and from the firm to customers? Unfortunately, reality is more complex than theory; customers order in different quantities, they order different products, and they are geographically dispersed. Other complicating factors include multiple stocking points, inventory levels, mode and carrier characteristics, and irregular ordering patterns.

A firm must consider many factors as it plans, implements, and controls a transportation system. Product considerations affect the selection of a particular mode and carrier. Some products, because of factors such as size, weight, durability, and value, are not compatible with certain transportation modes or carriers. It is vital that the company identify the product/mode interfaces that exist in order to select the mode or carrier offering the best cost and service package.

Similarly, it is important for the firm to identify the characteristics of all potential modes and carriers. Usually there are a number of transportation options available, and it is essential that the company explore each option sufficiently to make the optimal mode/carrier choice. If there are not enough for-hire carriers available, the audit must include an examination of the private carrier option. Even when for-hire carriage is available, the firm should consider the private carrier option in case the cost-service trade-off is acceptable.

Even after a specific network is established, the system must be constantly monitored and evaluated. A thorough transportation system audit includes identification of performance standards; measurement of cost and service components; and procedures for planning, implementation, and control of the entire transportation network. Such an evaluation must take place within the context of the firm's overall logistics system. An audit provides a firm numerous opportunities to improve both the efficiency and effectiveness of the transportation operating system, including the following:

Benefits Resulting from a Transportation Audit

1. Consolidation of both inbound and outbound shipments.
2. Reductions in private fleet empty miles, and routes that maximize the cost advantage of private carriage over common carrier costs.
3. Reduction of interplant transfers.
4. Improved control over vendor transportation policies through implementation of formal vendor routing/shipping guides.
5. Implementation of outbound routing guides, by market area.
6. Elimination of multiple and inefficient channels of distribution.
7. Increased accuracy and timeliness of freight bill payments.
8. Reduction/prevention of transportation damage.
9. Reduction in transit times through consolidation of outbound LTL customer orders.
10. Reductions in freight paid to common carriers through the negotiation of commodity and/or volume discount rates.
11. More reliable and consistent delivery of customer orders (with respect to transit times and fewer split orders).
12. Reduced congestion at warehouse dock facilities due to fewer inbound and outbound trailer volumes.
13. Elimination of "shuffling" of inbound trailer loads destined for multiple plant locations.
14. Reduction of private fleet tractors and trailers due to more efficient routes, fewer empty miles, and better utilization of trailer capacities.[67]

Additionally, conducting a transportation audit will aid the shipper firm in developing a transportation business plan. Such a plan outlines an approach for conducting transportation activities between the firm, its suppliers, and customers. An example of the steps or components of a successful business plan is as follows:

- Obtain input from internal and external customers about their service expectations and cost requirements.
- Compare the customer's service and cost requirements with the carrier marketplace.
- Set goals for timely completion of the business plan process assuring conformance to cultural, environmental, and ethical observances.
- Evaluate individual carrier short-term capabilities.
- Evaluate individual carrier long-term capabilities as you would an investment.

---

[67] Sterling and Lambert, "A Methodology for Identifying Potential Cost Reductions," pp. 1–18.

- Choose carrier candidates who objectively represent the best prospects for business and who are genuinely interested in [the firm's] business.
- Make agreements with carriers needed to achieve cost and service goals.[68]

An important part of a transportation audit is the measurement of customer perceptions of carriers and the services they provide. In the appendix to this chapter, a sample transportation customer service questionnaire is presented to illustrate the kinds of information necessary to effectively select and evaluate a LTL motor carrier.[69] Certainly, variations on this survey are possible for other types of transportation modes. Whatever format is used, however, it is important to develop specific information on service attribute importance and carrier performance at regular intervals.

SUMMARY

In this chapter we examined the major transportation management strategies of carriers and shippers. Important carrier perspectives include pricing/negotiation issues, routing and scheduling, service offerings, competition, and marketing activities. From a shipper perspective, the most important considerations are inbound and outbound transportation, mode/carrier selection, contracts, use of brokers, private carriage/leasing, shipper-carrier cooperation, and transportation productivity.

We examined the transportation management activity in view of the importance of the carrier/shipper interface and discussed some of the specific functions of management. We looked at some examples of the benefits that computers have brought to the area, with a view toward computer technology's future role in traffic management. In reviewing a firm's transportation activity, we discussed the transportation audit as a useful tool.

SUGGESTED READINGS

Buffa, Frank P. "Inbound Logistics: Analyzing Inbound Consolidation Opportunities." *International Journal of Physical Distribution and Materials Management* 16, no. 4 (1986), pp. 3–32.

Cheesman, L. P. "Rural Transport: Theory into Practice." *International Journal of Physical Distribution and Logistics Management* 20, no. 5 (1990), pp. 13–19.

Coan, Peter M. "How to Control Inbound Freight Costs." *Inbound Logistics* 6, no. 1 (January 1986), pp. 25–27.

---

[68] As stated in "Transportation Business Planning," a publication of 3M, St. Paul, Minnesota (undated pamphlet).

[69] For a discussion of the methodology employed in the development of the questionnaire in the appendix, see Chapter 4, "Customer Service," and the material examining the external customer service audit.

———. "Private Fleet or Common Carrier? How Inbound Managers Decide." *Inbound Logistics* 6, no. 5 (September 1986), pp. 25–29, 48.

COOK, PETER N. C. "Value-Added Strategies in Marketing." *International Journal of Physical Distribution and Logistics Management* 20, no. 5 (1990), pp. 20–24.

DAUGHERTY, PATRICIA J., AND MICHAEL S. SPENCER. "Just-in-Time Concepts: Applicability to Logistics/Transportation." *International Journal of Physical Distribution and Logistics Management* 20, no. 7 (1990), pp. 12–18.

ERNST & WHINNEY. *Transportation Accounting and Control: Guidelines for Distribution and Financial Management* (Oak Brook, Ill.: National Council of Physical Distribution Management, 1983).

FORSYTHE, KENNETH H., JAMES C. JOHNSON, AND KENNETH C. SCHNEIDER. "Traffic Managers: Do They Get Any Respect?" *Journal of Business Logistics* 11, no. 2 (1990), pp. 87–100.

GARREAU, ALAIN, ROBERT LEIB, AND ROBERT MILLEN. "JIT and Corporate Transport: An International Comparison." *International Journal of Physical Distribution and Logistics Management* 21, no. 1 (1991), pp. 42–47.

HARRINGTON, LISA H. "Driving Down Inbound Costs." *Traffic Management* 29, no. 11 (November 1990), pp. 43–47.

HEIJMEN, JON C. M. "Transportation Cost Analysis: Techniques and Uses." In *Proceedings of the Twenty-First Annual Conference of the National Council of Physical Distribution Management,* 1983, pp. 892–938.

VAN DER HOOP, HANS. "The Transport Connection in Logistics." *International Journal of Physical Distribution and Materials Management* 14, no. 3 (1984), pp. 37–44.

"How to Get the Most for Your Transportation Dollar." *Traffic Management* 29, no. 10 (October 1990), pp. 45–48.

LALONDE, BERNARD J., JAMES M. MASTERS, ARNOLD B. MALTZ, AND LISA R. WILLIAMS. *The Evolution, Status, and Future of the Corporate Transportation Function.* Louisville, Ky.: American Society of Transportation and Logistics, Inc., 1991.

LAMBERT, DOUGLAS M., AND JAY U. STERLING. "Managing Inbound Transportation: A Case Study." *Journal of Purchasing and Materials Management* 20, no. 2 (Summer 1984), pp. 22–29.

LANGLEY, C. JOHN, JR. "Strategic Management in Transportation and Physical Distribution." *Transportation Journal* 23, no. 3 (Spring 1983), pp. 71–78.

MIN, HOKEY, AND MARTHA COOPER. "A Comparative Review of Analytical Studies on Freight Consolidation and Backhauling." *The Logistics and Transportation Review* 26, no. 2 (June 1990), pp. 149–69.

RINEHART, LLOYD M., AND DAVID J. CLOSS. "Implications of Organizational Relationships, Negotiator Personalities, and Contract Issues on Outcomes in Logistics Negotiations." *Journal of Business Logistics* 12, no. 1 (1991), pp. 123–44.

STERLING, JAY U., AND DOUGLAS M. LAMBERT. "A Methodology for Identifying Potential Cost Reductions in Transportation and Warehousing." *Journal of Business Logistics* 5, no. 2 (1984), pp. 1–18.

TEMPLE, BARKER, AND SLOANE, INC. *Creating Profitability: The Sales and Marketing Challenge.* Alexandria, Va.: Sales and Marketing Council of American Trucking Association, 1985, pp. 61–64.

TRACY, JOHN J. "How to Specify Inbound Traffic of Retail Products." *Inbound Traffic Guide* 4, no. 1 (January/February 1984), pp. 24–28.

WATERS, C. D. J. "Computer Use in the Trucking Industry." *International Journal of Physical Distribution and Logistics Management* 20, no. 9 (1990), pp. 24–31.

WELTY, GUS. "The Search for Productivity." *Railway Age* 185, no. 11 (November 1984), pp. 31–34.

QUESTIONS AND PROBLEMS

1. Indicate how the deregulation of transportation has affected carrier pricing.
2. Transportation carriers have become much more marketing-oriented. Briefly identify the major factors that caused this orientation, and describe the forms of marketing activity that have developed in the transportation industry. What would be the role of a carrier's sales force in this new marketing environment?
3. Most transportation executives believe that service factors are generally more important than cost factors in causing firms to switch from one transport mode to another. Under what circumstances would service factors be more important than cost factors?
4. In the evaluation of transportation modes, *consistency of service* is significantly more important to shippers than *time-in-transit.* Differentiate between the two terms, and identify some possible reasons why consistency of service is considered more important.
5. Private carriage should not be viewed strictly as a transportation decision—it is also a financial decision. Briefly explain the factors that underlie this statement.
6. Strategic partnerships/alliances are becoming more important as shippers and carriers increase their levels of cooperation. Using the 3M "Partners in Quality" program as an example of such a partnership/alliance, indicate some of the benefits that result for shippers and carriers entering into such arrangements.
7. Briefly distinguish between *landbridge, minilandbridge,* and *microbridge.*
8. What is the role of a transportation audit in a shipper firm? What should be the major components of that audit?

APPENDIX
Sample Transportation Service Quality Questionnaire

SURVEY OF HOW SHIPPERS SELECT AND EVALUATE GENERAL COMMODITIES LTL MOTOR CARRIERS

DEPARTMENT OF MANAGEMENT, MARKETING AND LOGISTICS, UNIVERSITY OF NORTH FLORIDA, JACKSONVILLE

PART A: FACTORS CONSIDERED WHEN SELECTING AND EVALUATING LTL MOTOR CARRIERS

INSTRUCTIONS: Listed on the following pages are various factors often provided by LTL motor carriers to their customers. **This section involves two tasks.** Each task will be explained separately. Do not evaluate small package services such as UPS or RPS.

The **first task** involves your evaluation of the various factors that your firm might consider when selecting a new LTL motor carrier, or when you evaluate the performance of one of your current carriers. Please **circle**, on a scale of 1 to 7, the number which best expresses the importance to your firm of each of these factors. If a factor is not used by your firm or has no importance in your evaluation of carriers, please circle number 1 (Not Important). If a factor is not currently provided by any of your carriers, please evaluate its importance to you if it was available. A rating of 7 (Very Important) should be reserved for those factors that would cause you to reevaluate the amount of business done with a carrier or cause you to drop a carrier in the event of inadequate performance.

The **second task** is to evaluate the current performance of three LTL motor carriers that you use. Please list below in the spaces labeled "Carrier A", "Carrier B" and "Carrier C" three *LTL motor carriers* used most frequently by your firm (if you use fewer than three LTL carriers, please evaluate those that you use). Next, using the scale labeled PERCEIVED PERFORMANCE, please **insert** the number between 1 and 7 which best expresses your perception of a carrier's current performance. If you perceive that a carrier's performance is poor, insert a 1. Reserve a rating of 7 for excellent performance. If a service is not available from a carrier, please write NA, "NOT AVAILABLE," in the appropriate space.

YOUR LTL CARRIERS:

CARRIER A (**the largest amount** of your freight is handled by this carrier) = ______________________

CARRIER B (**the second largest amount** of your freight is handled by this carrier) = ______________________

CARRIER C (**the third largest amount** of your freight is handled by this carrier) = ______________________

Example:

FACTORS CONSIDERED	IMPORTANCE							PERCEIVED PERFORMANCE OF CARRIERS (Scale of 1 to 7)		
	Not Important 1	2	3	4	5	6	Very Important 7	A	B	C
• Bar coding of shipments	1	2	(3)	4	5	6	7	NA	2	NA
• Reliability of transit times	1	2	3	4	5	(6)	7	5	7	6

FACTORS CONSIDERED	IMPORTANCE							PERCEIVED PERFORMANCE OF CARRIERS (Scale of 1 to 7)		
	Not Important 1	2	3	4	5	6	Very Important 7	A	B	C
1. Carrier's loss/damage history	1	2	3	4	5	6	7	___	___	___
2. Adequate advance notice of rate changes	1	2	3	4	5	6	7	___	___	___
3. Provides same day delivery	1	2	3	4	5	6	7	___	___	___
4. On-time deliveries	1	2	3	4	5	6	7	___	___	___
5. Prompt action on complaints related to carrier's service	1	2	3	4	5	6	7	___	___	___
6. Quality of dispatch personnel										
- knowledge of carrier's capabilities	1	2	3	4	5	6	7	___	___	___
- prompt notification of scheduling changes	1	2	3	4	5	6	7	___	___	___
- honesty	1	2	3	4	5	6	7	___	___	___
- knowledge of my business	1	2	3	4	5	6	7	___	___	___
- concern/empathy	1	2	3	4	5	6	7	___	___	___
- friendliness	1	2	3	4	5	6	7	___	___	___
7. Carrier sales rep provides assistance/counseling on:										
- transportation solutions	1	2	3	4	5	6	7	___	___	___
- inventory management	1	2	3	4	5	6	7	___	___	___
- customer reports (i.e. transit time analysis)	1	2	3	4	5	6	7	___	___	___
- inbound just-in-time systems	1	2	3	4	5	6	7	___	___	___
- rates and tariffs	1	2	3	4	5	6	7	___	___	___
- logistics training programs	1	2	3	4	5	6	7	___	___	___
- customer service problems	1	2	3	4	5	6	7	___	___	___
- EDI information systems and usage	1	2	3	4	5	6	7	___	___	___
- packaging to reduce damage	1	2	3	4	5	6	7	___	___	___
8. Competitive rates	1	2	3	4	5	6	7	___	___	___
9. Availability of rates on a diskette	1	2	3	4	5	6	7	___	___	___

FACTORS CONSIDERED	IMPORTANCE Not Important 1	2	3	4	5	6	Very Important 7	PERCEIVED PERFORMANCE OF CARRIERS (Scale of 1 to 7) A	B	C
10. Single point of contact with carrier to resolve operations problems	1	2	3	4	5	6	7	___	___	___
11. Rate structure simple and easy to understand	1	2	3	4	5	6	7	___	___	___
12. Electronic (on-line terminal) interface for:										
- pickup	1	2	3	4	5	6	7	___	___	___
- billing	1	2	3	4	5	6	7	___	___	___
- tracing	1	2	3	4	5	6	7	___	___	___
13. Frequency of sales calls you personally receive from carrier's sales representative	1	2	3	4	5	6	7	___	___	___
14. Lowest rates	1	2	3	4	5	6	7	___	___	___
15. Cash discounts for early payment or prepayment	1	2	3	4	5	6	7	___	___	___
16. Carrier has adequate interline arrangements	1	2	3	4	5	6	7	___	___	___
17. Literature/information available from carrier:										
- routing guide	1	2	3	4	5	6	7	___	___	___
- pricing	1	2	3	4	5	6	7	___	___	___
18. Availability of "released value" rates	1	2	3	4	5	6	7	___	___	___
19. Assistance from carrier in handling loss and damage claims	1	2	3	4	5	6	7	___	___	___
20. Pro number given at time of pickup	1	2	3	4	5	6	7	___	___	___
21. Quality of billing staff:										
- knowledge of carrier's billing procedures	1	2	3	4	5	6	7	___	___	___
- prompt follow-up	1	2	3	4	5	6	7	___	___	___
- honesty	1	2	3	4	5	6	7	___	___	___
- knowledge of my business	1	2	3	4	5	6	7	___	___	___
- concern/empathy	1	2	3	4	5	6	7	___	___	___
22. Ability to provide direct delivery without interlining	1	2	3	4	5	6	7	___	___	___
23. Information provided when pickup call placed:										
- projected pickup time	1	2	3	4	5	6	7	___	___	___
- projected delivery time	1	2	3	4	5	6	7	___	___	___
- rate information	1	2	3	4	5	6	7	___	___	___
24. On-time pickups	1	2	3	4	5	6	7	___	___	___
25. Bar coding to facilitate tracing	1	2	3	4	5	6	7	___	___	___
26. Carrier sponsored entertainment	1	2	3	4	5	6	7	___	___	___
27. Carrier's general attitude toward problems/complaints	1	2	3	4	5	6	7	___	___	___
28. Carrier's programs for claim prevention (i.e. truck alarms, surveillance equipment, statistical process control (SPC))	1	2	3	4	5	6	7	___	___	___
29. Prompt response to claims	1	2	3	4	5	6	7	___	___	___
30. Prompt and accurate response to billing inquiries	1	2	3	4	5	6	7	___	___	___
31. Promotional gifts (coffee mugs, golf balls, calendars, etc)	1	2	3	4	5	6	7	___	___	___
32. Sales rep available if customer service response is inadequate	1	2	3	4	5	6	7	___	___	___
33. Willingness to renegotiate rates	1	2	3	4	5	6	7	___	___	___
34. Length of promised transit times (from pickup to delivery)	1	2	3	4	5	6	7	___	___	___
35. If possible, advance notice of transit delays (e.g. weather, equipment breakdown, etc.)	1	2	3	4	5	6	7	___	___	___
36. Freight bill references your bill-of-lading or control number	1	2	3	4	5	6	7	___	___	___
37. Regular/scheduled check-in by driver for pickup	1	2	3	4	5	6	7	___	___	___
38. Single point of contact with carrier to resolve billing problems	1	2	3	4	5	6	7	___	___	___

CARRIER A = ____________________
CARRIER B = ____________________
CARRIER C = ____________________

FACTORS CONSIDERED	IMPORTANCE Not Important 1	2	3	4	5	6	Very Important 7	PERCEIVED PERFORMANCE OF CARRIERS (Scale of 1 to 7) A	B	C
39. Shipment security	1	2	3	4	5	6	7			
40. Frequency of service to key points	1	2	3	4	5	6	7			
41. Complete/understandable/legible freight bill	1	2	3	4	5	6	7			
42. Quality of drivers:										
- knowledge of carrier's capabilities	1	2	3	4	5	6	7			
- ability to handle problems	1	2	3	4	5	6	7			
- honesty	1	2	3	4	5	6	7			
- responsiveness to inquiries	1	2	3	4	5	6	7			
- helpfulness	1	2	3	4	5	6	7			
- friendliness/courtesy	1	2	3	4	5	6	7			
- willingness to make inside deliveries	1	2	3	4	5	6	7			
- appearance	1	2	3	4	5	6	7			
- uniforms	1	2	3	4	5	6	7			
43. Prompt availability of status information on:										
- shipment tracing	1	2	3	4	5	6	7			
- delivery	1	2	3	4	5	6	7			
- COD shipments	1	2	3	4	5	6	7			
44. Liftgate availability for you and your customer	1	2	3	4	5	6	7			
45. Provides new rate and discount sheets in a timely fashion	1	2	3	4	5	6	7			
46. Carrier's ability to make pickups: before noon	1	2	3	4	5	6	7			
: after 5:00 p.m.	1	2	3	4	5	6	7			
47. Quantity discount structure based on:										
- size of shipment	1	2	3	4	5	6	7			
- annual volume of shipments	1	2	3	4	5	6	7			
48. Quality of sales force:										
- knowledge of carrier's capabilities	1	2	3	4	5	6	7			
- prompt follow-up	1	2	3	4	5	6	7			
- honesty	1	2	3	4	5	6	7			
- concern/empathy	1	2	3	4	5	6	7			
- friendliness	1	2	3	4	5	6	7			
- knowledge of my business	1	2	3	4	5	6	7			
- understanding of my customer's business	1	2	3	4	5	6	7			
49. Timely response to requests for assistance from carrier's sales representative	1	2	3	4	5	6	7			
50. Adequate geographical coverage:										
- major origins/destinations of your traffic	1	2	3	4	5	6	7			
- remote regions	1	2	3	4	5	6	7			
51. Prompt and comprehensive response to competitive bid quotations (i.e., contract discounts)	1	2	3	4	5	6	7			
52. Accuracy of response to tracing inquiry (ETA)	1	2	3	4	5	6	7			
53. Cleanliness of carrier's equipment	1	2	3	4	5	6	7			
54. Carrier's reputation	1	2	3	4	5	6	7			
55. Carrier's financial condition	1	2	3	4	5	6	7			
56. Carriers ability to make deliveries: before noon	1	2	3	4	5	6	7			
: after 5:00 pm	1	2	3	4	5	6	7			
57. Ability of carrier to customize its services to meet specific and/or unique needs										
- handle emergency shipments	1	2	3	4	5	6	7			
- handle hazardous materials	1	2	3	4	5	6	7			
- adhere to special shipping instructions	1	2	3	4	5	6	7			
- handle COD shipments	1	2	3	4	5	6	7			
- rerouting/rescheduling	1	2	3	4	5	6	7			
- inside deliveries	1	2	3	4	5	6	7			
58. Carrier has satisfactory insurance coverage	1	2	3	4	5	6	7			
59. Friendships with carrier personnel	1	2	3	4	5	6	7			

FACTORS CONSIDERED	IMPORTANCE Not Important 1	2	3	4	5	6	Very Important 7	PERCEIVED PERFORMANCE OF CARRIERS (Scale of 1 to 7) A	B	C
60. Ability of carrier to deliver damage-free goods	1	2	3	4	5	6	7	___	___	___
61. Accurate billing	1	2	3	4	5	6	7	___	___	___
62. Low frequency of split shipments	1	2	3	4	5	6	7	___	___	___
63. Proof-of-delivery available with freight bill	1	2	3	4	5	6	7	___	___	___
64. Prompt advance notice of pickup delays	1	2	3	4	5	6	7	___	___	___
65. Carrier's policy on COD/refused/returned/unclaimed freight	1	2	3	4	5	6	7	___	___	___
66. Consistent (reliable) transit times	1	2	3	4	5	6	7	___	___	___
67. Ability of carrier to respond to all customer inquiries with:										
- a single point of contact	1	2	3	4	5	6	7	___	___	___
- immediate response	1	2	3	4	5	6	7	___	___	___
68. Ability to make and meet appointments for delivery	1	2	3	4	5	6	7	___	___	___
69. Accurate rating	1	2	3	4	5	6	7	___	___	___
70. Ability to handle call before deliveries	1	2	3	4	5	6	7	___	___	___
71. Safety rating	1	2	3	4	5	6	7	___	___	___
72. Sales rep has authority to negotiate rates	1	2	3	4	5	6	7	___	___	___
73. Carrier's ability to provide formal reports on:										
- billing accuracy	1	2	3	4	5	6	7	___	___	___
- claims experience	1	2	3	4	5	6	7	___	___	___
- on-time deliveries	1	2	3	4	5	6	7	___	___	___
- on-time pickups	1	2	3	4	5	6	7	___	___	___
- transit times	1	2	3	4	5	6	7	___	___	___

PART B: MEASUREMENT OF OVERALL PERFORMANCE

1. Please indicate the percent that each carrier currently represents of your annual requirements as well as the percent that you would prefer to give each carrier under ideal conditions in the future. (Your totals should add to 100%)

	Current %	Ideal (preferred) %
CARRIER A (the largest amount of your freight is handled by this carrier)	________ %	________ %
CARRIER B (the second largest amount of your freight is handled by this carrier)	________ %	________ %
CARRIER C (the third largest amount of your freight is handled by this carrier)	________ %	________ %
Other Carriers	________ %	________ %
	100 %	100 %

2. Please mark a point anywhere on the lines below that best expresses your level of satisfaction with the above carriers. If you are extremely dissatisfied with a carrier's performance, a mark should be placed very near the left end of the line (labeled Poor). If you are exceptionally pleased with the carrier's performance, a mark should be placed very near the right end of the line (labeled Excellent). A midpoint has been placed on the line to correspond with a "Satisfactory" performance level.

OVERALL CARRIER PERFORMANCE

	Poor	Satisfactory	Excellent
CARRIER A	|————	——+——	————|
CARRIER B	|————	——+——	————|
CARRIER C	|————	——+——	————|

3. Would you recommend these carriers to another shipper?

CARRIER A	**CARRIER B**	**CARRIER C**
________ Yes	________ Yes	________ Yes
________ No	________ No	________ No

4. Have you ever reported to these carriers a problem with the service you received?

CARRIER A	**CARRIER B**	**CARRIER C**
________ Yes	________ Yes	________ Yes
________ No	________ No	________ No

5. What percentage of on-time performance do you currently receive from your major LTL carriers during a typical month?

CARRIER A: pickups ________% deliveries ________%
CARRIER B: pickups ________% deliveries ________%
CARRIER C: pickups ________% deliveries ________%

6. For the three carriers that you have evaluated, please give the lowest price carrier a score of 0%. For the others, indicate the percentage premium that you pay for their service. If two or more carriers have the same rates, please give them the same score.

CARRIER A: ________%
CARRIER B: ________%
CARRIER C: ________%

PART C: EXPECTED PERFORMANCE LEVELS OF LTL MOTOR CARRIERS

Please provide the following information with respect to the levels of customer service that you need from your LTL carriers.

1. How many contacts does your department receive from your major LTL carrier's sales rep during a typical month?
   _______ face to face calls per month _______ telephone calls per month

2. How many contacts would your department prefer to receive from your major LTL carrier's sales rep during a typical month?
   _______ face to face calls per month _______ telephone calls per month

3. What is the minimum number of contacts that your department would accept from your major LTL carrier's sales rep during a typical month?
   _______ face to face calls per month _______ telephone calls per month

4. What response time do you rexpect from a carrier's sales representative in:
   a. Emergency situations _______ minutes b. Non-emergency situations _______ hours

5. How much advance notice do you need from your carriers on price changes? _______ days

6. On the average, how soon do you expect a carrier to pick up your shipment after they have been notified? _______ hours

7. What is the maximum number of hours beyond the promised delivery date that you consider to be an acceptable delay? _______ hours

8. What terms of payment are offered by your major LTL carriers?
   _______ % cash discount for early payment
   _______ % discount

9. What percentage of shipments is delivered by the carrier's promised delivery date? _______%

10. What percentage of your products arrive damage free? _______%

11. What percentage of damage free service can be reasonably expected? _______%

12. Do you evaluate carriers using a: (Please check one)
    a. Formal process/system _______ b. Informal process/system _______

13. How frequently do you evaluate carrier performance (please check one):
    constantly _______ weekly _______ monthly _______ quarterly _______ annually _______ never _______

14. On-time delivery to your firm means plus-or-minus (please indicate the specific number of minutes, hours or days):
    _______ minutes _______ hours _______ days

15. What is the percentage of on-time performance that you want from your major LTL carrier during a typical month?
    pickups _______% deliveries _______%

16. What is the minimum percentage of on-time performance that you would accept from your major LTL carrier during a typical month?
    pickups _______% deliveries _______%

17. What percentage increase in rates would you be willing to pay if a carrier was able to meet your service expectations? _______%

	Strongly Disagree 1	2	3	4	5	6	Strongly Agree 7
18. In the next five years, bar coding is going to become much more important in my selection of a LTL carrier	1	2	3	4	5	6	7
19. I require written service standards from my carrier(s)	1	2	3	4	5	6	7
20. Within the next 3 years I will not give business to a carrier that does not use Statistical Process Control (SPC) and provide me with performance reports	1	2	3	4	5	6	7

PART D: DEMOGRAPHIC DATA

This information is required in order to identify major market segments and to provide more meaningful analyses of the previous sections. Please use approximate figures in the event that exact data are not readily available.

1. What is your firm's approximate annual gross sales volume? $__________

2. How long has your firm (division) been in business? (If your answer is 4 years or less, please omit answering question 3). _______ years

3. What was the average rate of growth in gross sales for the company over the last five years? _______%

4. What are your approximate annual freight bills: Corporate? $__________ At this location? $__________

5. How many manufacturing locations does your firm operate? __________

6. For what percentage of inbound shipments is the carrier specified by suppliers? _______%

7. For what percentage of outbound shipments is the carrier specified by customers? _______%

8. Please indicate the percentage of your organization's product or raw material moved via:

	Inbound % of Tonnage Today	Inbound % of Tonnage 1995	Outbound %of Tonnage Today	Outbound %of Tonnage 1995
LTL Motor Carrier	______	______	______	______

9. How many total LTL shipments do you have in a typical month?
______________ inbound shipments ______________ outbound shipments

10. What percentage of your LTL shipments are "emergency" orders that require expedited service?
inbound _______% outbound _______%

11. What is the weight of your typical LTL shipment? ___________ lbs.

12. What is the average value of your typical LTL shipment? $___________

13. Please indicate your overall evaluation of each of the following carriers.

CARRIERS:	Insufficient Information To Evaluate	Very Unfavorable 1	2	3	4	5	6	Very Favorable 7
AAA Cooper	______	1	2	3	4	5	6	7
Alterman	______	1	2	3	4	5	6	7
Benton Bros.	______	1	2	3	4	5	6	7
Carolina	______	1	2	3	4	5	6	7
Consolidated	______	1	2	3	4	5	6	7
Estes	______	1	2	3	4	5	6	7
Gator	______	1	2	3	4	5	6	7
Old Dominion	______	1	2	3	4	5	6	7
Overnite	______	1	2	3	4	5	6	7
Roadway	______	1	2	3	4	5	6	7
Smalley	______	1	2	3	4	5	6	7
Southeastern	______	1	2	3	4	5	6	7
Southern Freight	______	1	2	3	4	5	6	7
Super Transport	______	1	2	3	4	5	6	7
Transus	______	1	2	3	4	5	6	7
Watkins	______	1	2	3	4	5	6	7
Yellow	______	1	2	3	4	5	6	7
Other (please specify) ______________	______	1	2	3	4	5	6	7

14. What industries do you serve? (Please indicate the percentage of your business represented by each of the following)

Automotive	_______%	Medical equipment	_______%
Chemicals/Plastics	_______%	Military	_______%
Computer	_______%	Paper Products	_______%
Construction	_______%	Petroleum	_______%
Consumer products	_______%	Pharmaceutical	_______%
Educational/Universities	_______%	Retail	_______%
Food products	_______%	Telecommunications	_______%
Industrial equipment	_______%	________________	_______%
Instrumentation	_______%		100 %

15. What is your position or title? ____

16. Please indicate your responsiblities (check all those that apply).

_______ Accounts receivable	_______ International traffic	_______ Purchasing
_______ Customer service	_______ Inventory control	_______ Shipping—Receiving
_______ Distribution	_______ Materials management	_______ Traffic
_______ Inbound carrier selection	_______ Outbound carrier selection	_______ Warehousing

17. What are the first three numbers of your zip code? ________________

Thank you for your participation and cooperation in completing this survey. Your time and effort are sincerely appreciated. Please return the questionnaire in the envelope provided or mail to:

DOUGLAS M. LAMBERT, Ph.D. and JAMES R. STOCK, Ph.D.
Department of Management, Marketing and Logistics • College of Business Administration,
University of North Florida • 4567 St. Johns Bluff Road, South, Jacksonville, Florida 32216-6699

Chapter 7

Warehousing

Objectives of This Chapter

To show why warehousing is important in the logistics system

To identify the types of warehousing facilities that exist

To examine the primary functions of warehousing: movement, storage, and information transfer

To provide an overview of the various types of automated and nonautomated material handling systems utilized in warehousing

To examine the role of warehousing in a Just-in-Time (JIT) environment

INTRODUCTION

Warehousing is an integral part of every logistics system. It plays a vital role in providing a desired level of customer service at the lowest possible total cost (see Figure 7–1). The warehousing activity is the link between the producer and the customer. Over the years, warehousing has evolved from a relatively minor facet of a firm's logistics system to one of its most important functions. We can define warehousing as that part of a firm's logistics system that stores products (raw materials, parts, goods-in-process, finished goods) at and between point-of-origin and point-of-consumption, and provides information to management on the status, condition, and disposition of items being stored. The term *distribution center* is also used. However, *warehouse* is the more generic term. The *Transportation-Logistics Dictionary* defines a distribution center as "a warehouse of finished goods; also applied to the facility from which wholesale and retail orders may be filled; a materials warehouse would also be distribution center for the buyers of its stock."[1]

Warehousing Defined

Nature and Importance of Warehousing

Warehousing is used for the storage of inventories during all phases of the logistics process. Two basic types of inventories can be placed into storage: (1) raw materials, components, and parts (physical supply); and (2) finished goods (physical distribution). Also, there may be inventories of goods-in-process, although in most firms, goods-in-process constitute only a small portion of a company's total inventories. Why is it necessary to hold inventories in storage? In general, the warehousing of inventories is necessary for the following reasons:

Reasons for Using Warehousing

1. To achieve transportation economies.
2. To achieve production economies.

[1] Joseph L. Cavinato, ed., *Transportation-Logistics Dictionary,* 3rd ed. (Washington, D.C.: International Thomson Transport Press, 1989), p. 72.

FIGURE 7–1 Cost Trade-Offs Required in a Logistics System

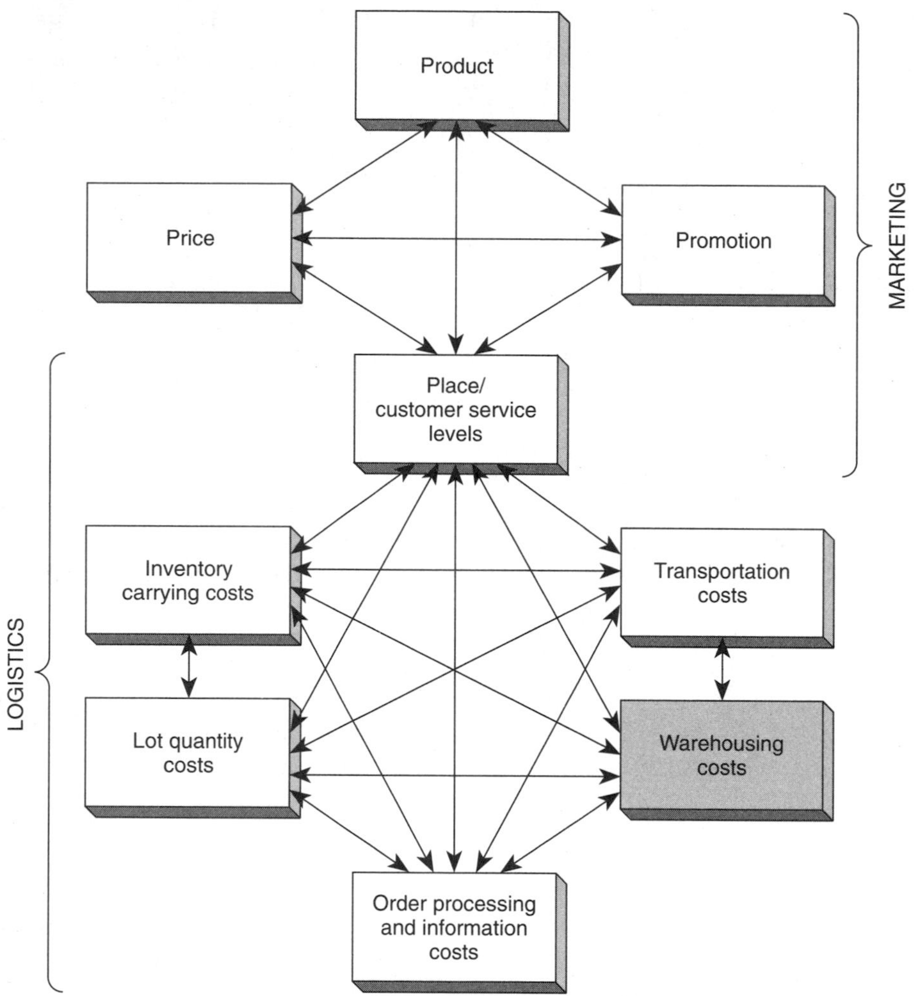

Marketing objective: Allocate resources to the marketing mix to maximize the long-run profitability of the firm.

Logistics objective: Minimize total costs given the customer service objective where: Total costs = Transportation costs + Warehousing costs + Order processing and information costs + Lot quantity costs + Inventory carrying costs.

SOURCE: Adapted from Douglas M. Lambert, *The Development of an Inventory Costing Methodology: A Study of the Costs Associated with Holding Inventory* (Chicago: National Council of Physical Distribution Management, 1976), p. 7.

3. To take advantage of quantity purchase discounts and forward buys.
4. To maintain a source of supply.
5. To support the firm's customer service policies.
6. To meet changing market conditions (e.g., seasonality, demand fluctuations, competition).
7. To overcome the time and space differentials that exist between producers and consumers.
8. To accomplish least total cost logistics commensurate with a desired level of customer service.
9. To support the Just-in-Time programs of suppliers, vendors, and customers.

Figure 7–2 identifies some of the uses of warehousing in both the physical supply and physical distribution systems. Warehouses can be used to support manufacturing, to mix products from multiple production facilities for shipment to a single customer, to breakbulk or subdivide a large shipment of product into many smaller shipments to satisfy the needs of many customers, and to combine or consolidate smaller shipments of products into a higher-volume shipment.[2]

Warehousing Used for Inbound Consolidation

In supporting manufacturing operations, warehouses often function as inbound consolidation points for the receipt of materials shipments from suppliers. As shown in Figure 7–2A, firms order raw materials, parts, components, or supplies from various suppliers, who ship large (TL or CL) quantities to a warehouse located in close proximity to the plant. Items are then transferred from the warehouse to the manufacturing plant(s).

Product Mixing

From a physical distribution or outbound perspective, warehouses can be used for product mixing, outbound consolidation, and/or breakbulk. Product mixing (Figure 7–2B) often involves multiple plant locations (e.g., Plant A, Plant B, and Plant C) that ship products (e.g., Product A, Product B, and Product C) to a central warehouse. Each plant manufactures only a portion of the total product offering of the firm. Shipments are usually made in large quantities (TL or CL) to the central warehouse, where customer orders for multiple products are combined or mixed for shipment.

Outbound Consolidation

When a warehouse is used for outbound consolidation (Figure 7–2C), TL or CL shipments are made to a central facility from a number of manufacturing locations. The warehouse then consolidates or combines products from the various plants into a single shipment to the customer.

Breakbulk

Breakbulk warehouses (Figure 7–2D) are facilities that receive large shipments of product from a manufacturing plant. Several customer orders are combined into a single shipment from the plant to the breakbulk warehouse. When the shipment is received by the warehouse, it is subdi-

[2]For an exhaustive listing of logistics definitions, see Cavinato, *Transportation-Logistics Dictionary*.

FIGURE 7–2 Uses of Warehousing in Physical Supply and Physical Distribution

A. Manufacturing Support

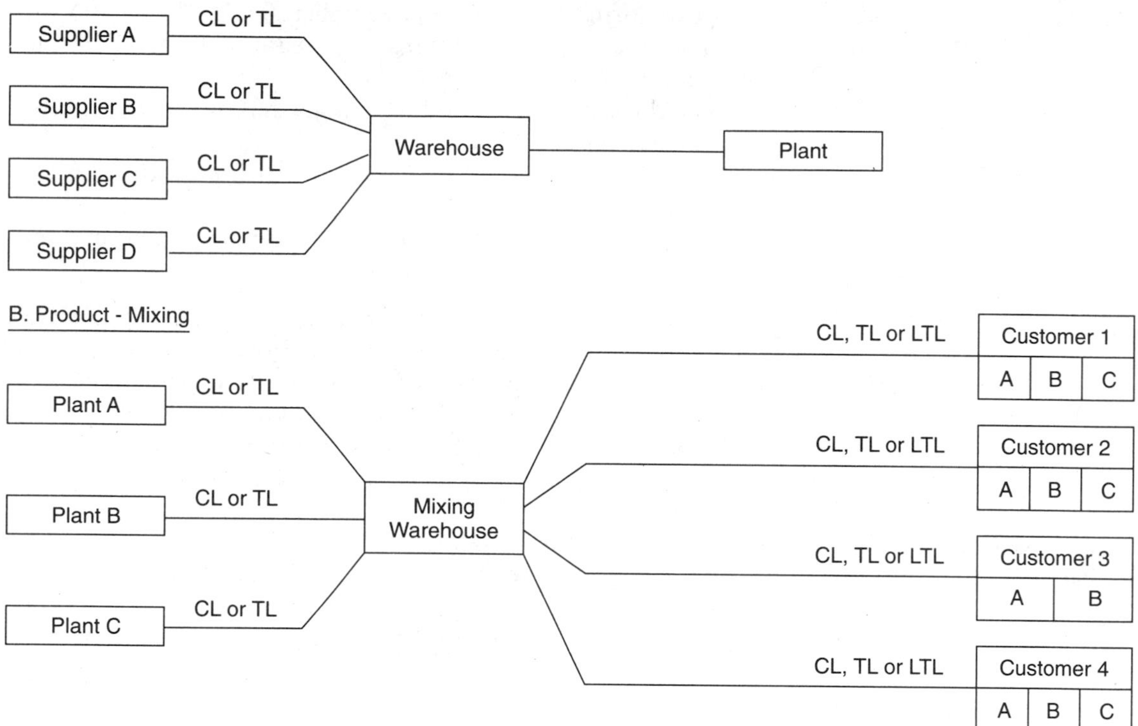

C. Consolidation

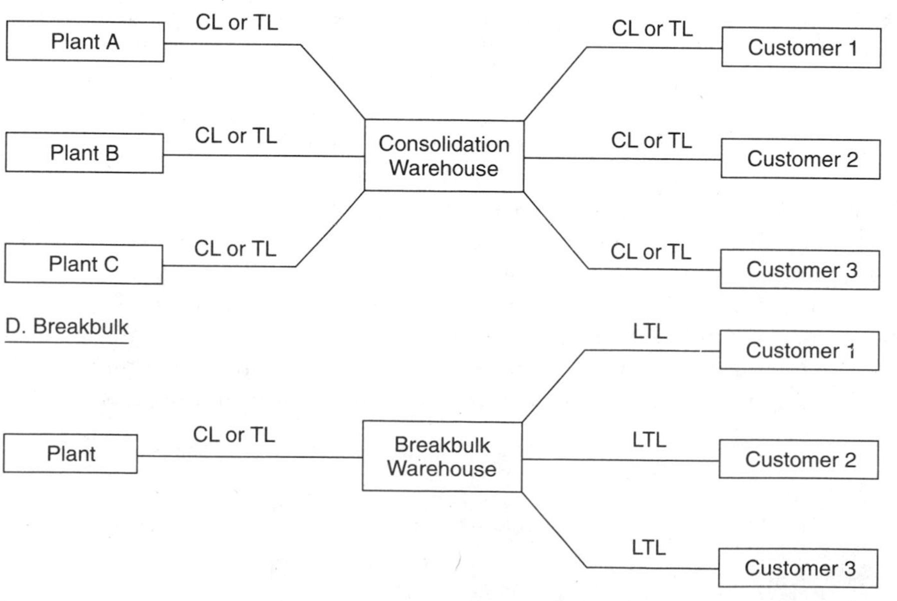

vided or broken down into smaller LTL shipments, which are sent to customers in the geographical area served by the warehouse.

Transportation Economies Are Possible with Warehousing

Transportation economies are possible for both the physical supply system and the physical distribution system. In the case of physical supply, small orders from a number of suppliers may be shipped to a consolidation warehouse near the source of supply; in this way the producer can achieve a truckload or carload shipment to the plant, which is normally a considerably greater distance from the warehouse. The warehouse is located near the sources of supply so that the LTL rates apply only to a short haul, and the volume rate is used for the long haul from the warehouse to the plant.

Warehouses are used to achieve similar transportation savings in the physical distribution system. In the packaged goods industry, manufacturers often have multiple plant locations, with each plant manufacturing only a portion of the company's product line.[3] Usually, these companies also maintain a number of field warehouse locations from which mixed shipments of the entire product line can be made to customers. Shipments from plants to field warehouses are frequently made by rail in full carload quantities of the products manufactured at each plant. Orders from customers, comprised of various items in the product line, are shipped by truck at truckload or LTL rates. The use of field warehouses results in lower transportation costs than direct shipments to customers. Savings are often significantly larger than the increased costs resulting from warehousing and the associated increase in inventory carrying costs.

Warehousing and Manufacturing Are Related

Short production runs minimize the amount of inventory held throughout the logistics system by producing quantities near to current demand. But there are increased costs of setups and line changes associated with short production runs. Also, if a plant is operating near or at capacity, frequent line changes may leave the manufacturer unable to meet product demand. If so, the cost of lost sales—the lost contribution to profit on sales that cannot be made—could be substantial.

On the other hand, the production of large quantities of product for each line change results in a lower per-unit cost on a full-cost basis, as well as more units for a given plant capacity. However, long production runs lead to larger inventories and increased warehouse requirements. Consequently, production cost savings must be balanced with increased logistics costs in order to achieve least total cost.

Warehousing is also necessary if a company is to take advantage of quantity purchase discounts on raw materials or other products. Not only is the per-unit price lower as a result of the discount, but if the company pays the freight, transportation costs will be less on a volume purchase because of transportation economies. Similar discounts and savings can accrue to manufacturers, retailers, and wholesalers. Once again, however,

[3] Such plants are often referred to as "focused factories."

those savings must be weighed against the added inventory costs that will be incurred as a result of larger inventories.

Holding inventories in warehouses may be necessary in order to maintain a source of supply. For example, the timing and quantity of purchases is important in retaining suppliers, especially during periods of shortages. It also may be necessary to hold an inventory of items that may be in short supply as the result of damage in transit, vendor stockouts, or a strike against one of the company's suppliers.

Customer service policies, such as a 24-hour delivery standard, may require a number of field warehouses in order to minimize total costs while achieving the standard. Changing market conditions may also make it necessary to warehouse product in the field, primarily because companies are unable to accurately predict consumer demand and the timing of retailer and wholesaler orders. By keeping some excess inventory in field warehouse locations, companies can respond quickly to meet unexpected demand. In addition, excess inventory allows manufacturers to fill customer orders when shipments to restock the field warehouses arrive late.

The majority of firms utilize warehousing in order to accomplish least total cost logistics at some prescribed level of customer service. The use of warehousing enables management to select the transport modes and inventory levels that, when combined with communication and order processing systems and production alternatives, minimize total costs while providing a desired level of customer service.

Factors that influence a firm's warehousing policies include the industry; the firm's philosophy; capital availability; product characteristics, such as size, perishability, product lines, substitutability, and obsolescence rate; economic conditions; competition; seasonality of demand; use of Just-in-Time programs; and the production process being used.

Types of Warehousing

In general, firms have several warehousing alternatives. Some companies may market products directly to customers (called *direct store delivery*) and thereby eliminate warehousing in the field. Mail-order catalog companies are one example of an industry that utilizes warehousing only at a point-of-origin, such as sales headquarters or plant. Most firms, however, warehouse products at some intermediate point between plant(s) and customers. When a firm decides to store product in the field, it faces two warehousing options: rented facilities, called *public warehousing,* or owned or leased facilities, called *private warehousing.*

Public and Private Warehousing

Another option also exists, termed *contract warehousing,* which is a variation of public warehousing. Contract warehousing is a partnership arrangement between the user and provider of the warehousing service. "In a contract warehouse storage space, software systems, labor and manage-

Contract Warehousing

ment are dedicated to a specific shipper's logistics system. Resources provided by the contract warehouse firm can be customized to satisfy a specific client's requirements."[4]

Firms must examine important customer service and financial considerations to choose between public and private warehousing. For example, operating costs for a public warehouse tend to be higher because the warehouse will attempt to operate at a profit; it will also have selling and advertising costs. However, there is no initial investment in facilities required when a firm uses public warehousing. From a customer service perspective, private warehousing can generally provide higher service levels because of its more specialized facilities and equipment, and better familiarity with the firm's products, customers, and markets. The two options must be examined very closely, however. In some instances, very innovative public warehouses can provide higher levels of service due to their expertise.

Types of Public Warehouses

There are six types of public warehouses: (1) general merchandise warehouses for manufactured goods, (2) refrigerated or cold storage warehouses, (3) bonded warehouses, (4) household goods and furniture warehouses, (5) special commodity warehouses, and (6) bulk storage warehouses. Each type provides users with a broad range of specialized services.

The *general merchandise warehouse* is probably the most common form. It is designed to be used by manufacturers, distributors, and customers for storing practically any kind of product.

Refrigerated or cold storage warehouses provide a temperature-controlled storage environment. Usually, they are used for preserving perishable items such as fruits and vegetables. However, a number of other items—such as frozen food products, some pharmaceuticals, photographic paper and film, and furs—require this type of facility.

Some general merchandise or special commodity warehouses are known as *bonded warehouses*. These warehouses undertake surety bonds from the U.S. Treasury and place their premises under the custody of an agent of the Treasury. Goods such as imported tobacco and alcoholic beverages are stored in this type of warehouse, although the government retains control of the goods until they are distributed to the marketplace. At that time, the importer must pay customs duties to the Internal Revenue Service. The advantage of the bonded warehouse is that import duties and excise taxes need not be paid until the merchandise is sold.

Household goods warehouses are used for storage of personal property rather than merchandise. The property is typically stored for an extended

---

[4] See William G. Sheehan, "Contract Warehousing: The Evolution of an Industry," *Journal of Business Logistics* 10, no. 1 (1989), p. 31.

warehouses as a temporary layover option. Within this category of warehouses, there are several types of storage alternatives. One is the open storage concept. The goods are stored on a cubic-foot basis per month on the open floor of the warehouse. Household goods are typically confined to this type of storage. A second kind of storage is private room or vault storage, where users are provided with a private room or vault to lock in and secure goods. A third kind, container storage, provides users with a container into which they can pack goods. Container storage affords better protection of the product than does open storage.[5]

Special commodity warehouses are used for particular agricultural products, such as grains, wool, and cotton. Ordinarily each of these warehouses handles one kind of product and offers special services particular to that product. Some of the characteristics of commodity warehouses are listed below.

They are warehouses used for products that originate from a number of scattered points and are gathered for sale in a particular market area.

The items themselves are stored in the terminal points for a considerable length of time.

The commodities are stored in bulk on an interchangeable basis; that is, commodities of the same quality and grade are considered equal to any other units.

Frequently the commodity warehouse provides services such as cleaning grain, compressing cotton, etc.[6]

Bulk storage warehouses provide tank storage of liquids and open or sheltered storage of dry products such as coal, sand, and chemicals. The services provided by such warehouses may include filling drums from bulk or mixing various types of chemicals with others to produce new compounds or mixtures.[7]

A COMPARISON OF PUBLIC AND PRIVATE WAREHOUSING

Both public and private warehouses have important characteristics. In the section that follows, we will discuss the advantages and disadvantages of each alternative.

---

[5] William J. Schultz, *American Marketing* (Belmont, Calif.: Wadsworth, 1962), p. 367.
[6] John H. Fredrick, *Using Public Warehouses* (Philadelphia: Chilton, 1957), pp. 15–17.
[7] Ibid., p. 17.

Advantages and Disadvantages of Public Warehousing

The benefits that may be realized if a firm uses public warehouses rather than privately owned or leased warehouses include: (1) conservation of capital; (2) the ability to increase warehouse space to cover peak requirements; (3) reduced risk; (4) economies of scale; (5) flexibility; (6) tax advantages; (7) knowledge of costs for storage and handling; and (8) minimization of labor disputes.

Conservation of Capital

One of the major advantages of public warehouses is that they require *no capital investment* on the part of the user. The user avoids the investment in buildings, land, and material handling equipment, as well as the costs associated with starting up the operation and hiring and training personnel.

Adjusts for Seasonality

If a firm's operations are subject to seasonality, the public warehouse option allows the user to contract for as much storage space as needed to *meet peak requirements.* A private warehouse, on the other hand, has a constraint on the maximum amount of product that can be stored and is likely to be underutilized during a portion of each year. Since most firms experience substantial variations in inventory levels due to seasonality in demand or production, sales promotions, or other factors, public warehousing offers the distinct advantage of allowing storage costs to vary directly with volume.

Reduced Risk

Companies normally plan for a distribution facility to have a lifespan of 20 to 40 years. Consequently, by investing in a private warehouse, management assumes the *risk* that the facility will become obsolete due to changes in technology or changes in the volume of business.

Economies of Scale

Public warehouses are able to achieve *economies of scale* that may not be possible for a small firm. Public warehouses handle the warehousing requirements of a number of firms, and their volume allows the employment of a full-time warehousing staff. In addition, building costs are nonlinear, and a firm pays a premium to build a small facility. Additional economies of scale can be provided by using more expensive, but more efficient, material-handling equipment, and by providing administrative and other expertise.

Public warehouses are often able to offer a number of specialized services more economically than a private warehouse. These specialized services include the following:

Broken-case handling, which is breaking down manufacturers' case quantities to enable orders for less-than-full case quantities to be filled.

Packaging of manufacturers' products for shipping. Exel Logistics, formerly Distribution Centers, Inc., a public warehousing and logistics services firm, has performed a variation of this service for the California Growers Association. Product was shipped to the Atlanta distribution center in "brights"—cans without labels—and the labels were put on the product at the warehouse as orders were received from customers.

Consolidation of damaged product and product being recalled by the manufacturer for shipment to the manufacturer in carload or truckload quantities. In addition to the documentation and prepacking that may be necessary, the public warehouse frequently performs the rework of damaged product.

Equipment maintenance and service.

Stock spotting of product for manufacturers with limited or highly seasonal product lines. Stock spotting involves shipping a consolidated carload of inventory to a public warehouse just prior to a period of maximum seasonal sales.

A break-bulk service whereby the manufacturer combines the orders of different customers located in a market and ships them at the carload or truckload rate to the public warehouse where the individual orders are separated and local delivery is provided.

Finally, economies of scale result from the consolidation of small shipments with other noncompetitors using the same public warehouse. The public warehouse consolidates orders of specific customers from the products of a number of different manufacturers on a single shipment. This results in lower shipping costs, as well as reduced congestion at the customer's receiving dock. Also, customers who pick up their orders at the public warehouse are able to obtain the products of several manufacturers with one stop, if the manufacturers all use the same facility.

Flexibility

Another major advantage offered by public warehouses is *flexibility*. Owning or holding a long-term lease on a warehouse can become a burden if business conditions necessitate changes in locations. Public warehouses require only a short-term contract, and thus short-term commitments. Short-term contracts available from public warehouses make it easy for firms to change field warehouse locations due to changes in the marketplace (e.g., population shifts), the relative cost of various transport modes, volume of a product sold, or the company's financial position.

In addition, a firm that uses public warehouses does not have to hire or lay off employees as the volume of business changes. A public warehouse provides the personnel required for extra services when they are necessary, without having to hire them on a full-time basis.

Finally, public warehousing makes it possible for the manufacturer to experiment with a warehouse location to determine its contribution to the firm's logistics system, and to discontinue the operation with relative ease if cost savings or performance objectives are not realized.

Tax Advantages

In most states a firm is at a definite advantage if it does not own property in the state, because such ownership means that the firm is doing business in the state and is thus subject to various state *taxes*. These taxes can be substantial. Consequently, if the company does not currently own property in a state, it may be advantageous to use a public warehouse. In addition, certain states do not charge property taxes on inventories in public warehouses; this tax shelter applies to both regular warehouse inventories and storage-in-transit inventories. A *free-port* provision enacted in some states allows inventory to be held for up to one year, tax-free. Finally the manufacturer pays no real estate tax. Of course, the public warehouse pays real estate tax and includes this cost in its warehouse rates, but the cost is smaller on a per-unit throughput basis because of the significantly larger volume of business possible.

Knowledge of Costs

When a manufacturer uses a public warehouse, it *knows its exact storage and handling costs* because it receives a bill each month. The manufacturer can also forecast costs for different levels of activity because the costs are known in advance. Firms that operate their own facilities often find it very difficult to determine the fixed and variable costs and the basis for variability.

Minimizes Labor Disputes

The courts have ruled that a labor union does not have the right to picket a public warehouse when the union is involved in a labor dispute with one of the customers of that public warehouse. Thus, using a public warehouse has the advantage of *insulating the manufacturer's distribution system from a labor dispute.*

Communication Problems

However, there are a number of disadvantages associated with the use of public warehousing. *Effective communication may be a problem* with public warehouses, because all computer terminals and systems are not compatible. A warehouse operator may hesitate to add another terminal for just one customer. In addition, the lack of standardization in contractual agreements makes communication regarding contractual obligations difficult.

Lack of Specialized Services

The space or *specialized services desired may not always be available* in a specific location. Many public warehouse facilities only provide local service and are of limited use to a firm that distributes regionally or nationally. Consequently, a manufacturer that wants to use public warehouses for national distribution may find it necessary to deal with several different operators and monitor several contractual agreements.

Availability of Space

Finally, public warehousing *space may not be available* when and where a firm wants it. Shortages of space do occur periodically in selected markets, and this can adversely affect the logistics and marketing strategies of a firm.

Advantages and Disadvantages of Private Warehousing

Degree of Control

In private warehousing, the company that owns the goods can exercise a greater degree of *control.* The firm has direct control of, and responsibility for, the product until the customer takes possession or delivery. This greater degree of control allows the firm to integrate the warehousing function more easily into the company's total logistics system.

Flexibility

With this warehouse control comes a greater degree of *flexibility*. Not flexibility to reduce or increase storage space quickly, but flexibility to design and operate the warehouse to fit the needs of customers and the characteristics of the product. Companies with highly specialized products requiring special handling and/or storage may not find public warehousing feasible. In such instances the firm must utilize private warehousing or ship direct to customers. The warehouse can also be modified through expansion or renovation to facilitate product changes, or it can be converted to a manufacturing plant or branch office location.

Less Costly

Another prominent advantage of private warehousing is that it can be *less costly* over the long term than public warehousing. Operating costs can be 15 to 25 percent lower if the company achieves sufficient throughput or utilization. The generally accepted industry norm for the utilization rate of a private warehouse is 75 to 80 percent. If a firm cannot achieve at least 75 percent utilization, it would generally be more appropriate to use public warehousing. Of course, good management control is a prerequisite to keeping private warehousing costs at a minimum.

Use of Human Resources

By employing private warehousing, a firm can make greater use of its present *human resources*. It can utilize the expertise of its technical specialists. In addition, the individuals working in the warehouse are company employees. Generally, there is greater care in handling and storage when the firm's own work force operates the warehouse. On the other hand, some public warehouses allow a firm to use its own employees in the handling and storage of products within the confines of the public warehouse.

Tax Benefits

A company can also realize *tax benefits* when it owns its warehouses. Depreciation allowances on buildings and equipment can substantially reduce the cost of a structure or apparatus over its life.

Intangible Benefits

Finally, there may be certain *intangible benefits* associated with warehouse ownership. When a firm distributes its products through a private warehouse, it can give the customer a sense of permanence and continuity of business operations. The customer sees the company as a stable, dependable, and lasting supplier of products. This can give the firm marketing advantages.

Lack of Flexibility

Many experts feel that the major drawback of private warehousing is the same as one of its main advantages—*flexibility*. A private warehouse may be too costly because of its fixed size and costs. Irrespective of the level of demand the firm experiences, the size of the private warehouse is restricted in the short term. A private facility cannot expand and contract to meet increases or decreases in demand. When demand is low the firm must still assume the fixed cost expense, as well as the lower productivity associated with unused warehouse space. (This disadvantage can be minimized, however, if the firm is able to rent out part of its space like a public warehouse.)

If a firm uses only private warehouses, it also loses flexibility in its strategic location options. Changes in market size, location, and preferences are often swift and unpredictable. If a company can not adapt to these changes in its warehouse structure, it may lose a valuable business opportunity. Customer service and sales could also fall if a private warehouse can not adapt to changes in the firm's product mix.

Financial Constraints

Because of the prohibitive costs involved, many firms are simply unable to generate enough *capital* to build or buy a warehouse. A warehouse is a long-term, often risky investment (which may be difficult to sell because of its customized design). Start-up is a costly and time-consuming process due to the hiring and training of employees, as well as the purchase of material handling equipment. And depending on the nature of the firm, return on investment may be greater if funds are channeled into other profit-generating opportunities.

WAREHOUSING OPERATIONS

Warehousing serves an important role in a firm's logistics system. In combination with other activities, it provides the firm's customers with an acceptable level of service. The obvious role of warehousing is to store products. However, warehousing provides breakbulk, consolidation, and information services as well. These activities emphasize product flow rather than storage. Fast and efficient movement of large quantities of raw materials, component parts, and finished goods through the warehouse, coupled with timely and accurate information about the products being stored, is the goal of every logistics system.

Functions of Warehousing

Movement

Warehousing has three basic functions: movement, storage, and information transfer. The *movement* function can be further divided into four handling activities: receiving, transfer, order selection, and shipping.[8] The *receiving* activity includes the physical unloading of products from the transportation carrier. It also includes the updating of warehouse inventory records, inspection for damage, and verification of the merchandise count against orders and shipping records. *Transfer* involves the physical movement of the product into the warehouse for storage, movement to areas for specialized services such as consolidation, and movement to outbound shipment. Customer *order selection* is the major movement activity and involves regrouping products into the assortments customers desire. Packing slips are also made up at this point. The last movement activity, *shipping*, consists of product staging and physically moving the assembled orders into carrier equipment, adjusting inventory records, and checking on orders to be shipped.

[8] Donald J. Bowersox, *Logistical Management* (New York: Macmillan, 1974), p. 212.

Storage

The second function of warehousing—*storage*—can be performed on a temporary or a semipermanent basis. *Temporary* storage emphasizes the movement function of the warehouse and includes only the storage of product necessary for basic inventory replenishment. Temporary storage is required regardless of the actual inventory turnover. The extent of temporary inventory storage depends on the design of the logistics system and the variability experienced in lead time and demand. *Semipermanent* storage is the storage of inventory in excess of that required for normal replenishment. It can also be referred to as buffer or safety stock. The most common conditions leading to semipermanent storage are (1) seasonal demand; (2) erratic demand; (3) conditioning of products such as fruits and meats; (4) speculation or forward buying; and (5) special deals, such as quantity discounts.

Information Transfer

Information transfer, the third major function of warehousing, occurs simultaneously with the movement and storage functions. Management always needs timely and accurate information as it attempts to administer the warehousing activity. Information on inventory levels, throughput levels, stockkeeping locations, inbound and outbound shipments, customer data, facility space utilization, and personnel is vital to the successful operation of a warehouse.

Activities Performed in a Warehouse

In summary, a warehouse will perform these activities:

1. Receiving and unloading trailers or box cars.
2. Put-away.
3. Storage.
4. Replenishment of order-picking locations.
5. Order selection (picking).
6. Checking.
7. Packaging and marking.
8. Staging and consolidation.
9. Loading and shipping.
10. Clerical/administrative.
11. Housekeeping.
12. Maintenance of material handling equipment.[9]

Receiving is the first stage of the warehousing process. It includes "physically accepting material, unloading that material from the inbound transportation mode, staging, verifying quantity and condition of the material, and documenting this information as required."[10] *Put-away* is the physical process of taking goods received and placing them within the warehouse in the locations where they are to be stored.

[9] A. T. Kearney, Inc., *Measuring and Improving Productivity in Physical Distribution* (Oak Brook, Ill.: National Council of Physical Distribution Management, 1984), p. 189.

[10] Ibid., p. 191.

Storage is the most basic warehousing activity. It is defined as the depositing of goods in a facility for safekeeping. *Replenishment* is the process of relocating goods from a bulk storage area to an order-pick storage area. An important warehousing task is to keep track of inventory levels efficiently so that replacement stocks can be obtained. *Order selection* is also called order picking. It involves the accurate and timely selection of product for shipment from the warehouse. Successful completion of all of the warehousing activities already mentioned eliminates the need for *checking*. However, errors and mistakes do occur within any warehouse operation, and it is usually necessary to conduct a check of previous activities. This function is analogous to the quality-control function in manufacturing.

Packaging and marking involves the preparation of the goods for shipment. Products are placed in boxes, cartons, or other containers, placed on pallets, and/or stretch-wrapped (the process of wrapping products in a plastic film), and are marked with information necessary for shipment, such as origin, destination, shipper, consignee, and package contents. *Staging and consolidation* is concerned with preparing the goods for shipment and usually takes place on the loading dock or staging area of the warehouse. The actual loading and movement of the product occurs in the *shipping* activity.

The final function, *clerical/administrative,* occurs in conjunction with all warehousing activities. Each activity must be administered effectively and efficiently. In addition, a large number of clerical duties must be performed in conjunction with each warehouse activity. In spite of numerous attempts by firms to reduce the paperwork flow involved in the logistics process, the amount of paperwork is still significant. For this reason, and many others, firms have attempted to automate the clerical function whenever possible. During all phases, housekeeping chores as well as equipment maintenance will take place.

Figure 7–3 displays most of the activities typically performed in a warehouse. The numbers in the figure correspond to the preceding list of items.

Within the warehouse it is important to eliminate any inefficiencies in movement, storage, and information transfer. These can occur in a variety of forms, such as:

Examples of Warehousing Inefficiencies

Excessive material handling labor.
Poor utilization of space and cube.
Excessive maintenance costs due to obsolete equipment.
Antiquated receiving and shipping dock conditions.[11]

Today's competitive marketplace demands more precise and accurate handling, storage, and retrieval systems, as well as improved packaging and

[11] "Where Material Handling Stands Now," *Material Handling Engineering, 1985 Handbook and Directory* 39, no. 13 (December 1984), p. A18.

FIGURE 7–3 Typical Activities Performed in a Warehouse

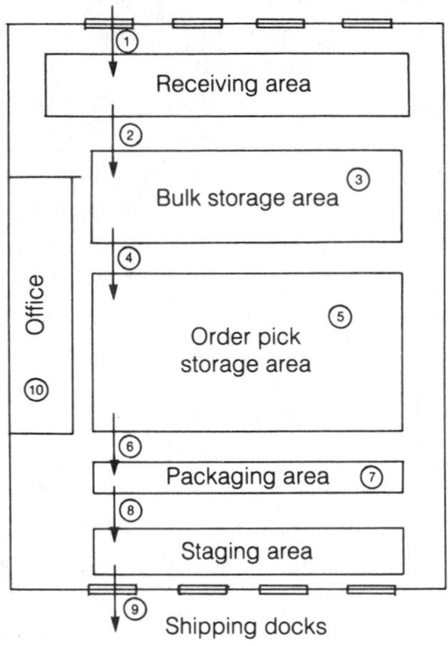

SOURCE: A. T. Kearney, Inc., *Measuring and Improving Productivity in Physical Distribution Management* (Oak Brook, Ill.: National Council of Physical Distribution Management, 1984), p. 190. Published with permission from the Council of Logistics Management, formerly the National Council of Physical Distribution Management.

shipping systems. It is therefore vital for a warehouse operation to have the optimal mix of manual (nonautomated) and automated handling systems.

Selection of an Appropriate Handling System

The specific type of equipment a firm selects depends on many factors. Some of the more pertinent questions a firm should ask itself are the following:

1. Is there excessive manual handling by employees?
2. Is high storage space being wasted?
3. Is present equipment antiquated and in need of repair?
4. Do forklifts require excessively wide aisles to swing palletized loads?
5. Is there congestion in material-staging areas?
6. Are labor costs higher than those for other warehouses in the same line of business?
7. Is equipment flexible enough to handle changes in operating procedures?
8. What are the maintenance requirements and costs of the various handling systems?

9. Can acquisition of the handling system be economically justified?
10. Are spare parts and service available?[12]

Manual or Nonautomated Warehouse Handling Systems

Manual or nonautomated handling equipment has been the mainstay of the traditional warehouse and will likely continue to be important even with the move toward automated warehouses. Equipment can be categorized according to functions performed: (1) storage and order-picking, (2) transportation and sorting, and (3) shipping.

Storage and Order-Picking Equipment

Storage and order-picking equipment includes racks, shelving, drawers, and operator controlled devices (e.g., forklift trucks).

> Generally speaking, manual storage systems do the job best when there is either very high or very low throughput for the parts stored within. Manual systems provide a great deal of flexibility in order picking, since they use the most flexible handling system around: a person.[13]

Table 7–1 details several types of racks, shelving, and drawers most often used in a warehouse. Storage racks normally store palletized or unitized loads. In most instances, some type of operator-controlled device places the load into the storage rack. Table 7–1 presents the type of materials stored, the benefits, and other information about each item. Figures 7–4 through 7–8 picture some of the more commonly used storage and order-picking equipment.

Storage Racks

The storage racks illustrated in Figure 7–4 are found in most warehouse facilities. They may be permanent or temporary and are placed within a warehouse for storage of products. They would be considered "standard" or "basic" components of a warehouse. All these storage racks are easily accessible by material handling equipment such as forklift trucks.

Gravity Flow Racks

Gravity flow storage racks, shown in Figure 7–5, are often used to store high-demand items. Products that are of uniform size and shape are well suited for this type of storage system. Items are loaded into the racks from the back, flow to the front of the racks because they are sloped forward, and then are picked from the front of the system by order-picking personnel.

Bin Shelving Systems

For small parts, bin shelving systems are useful. Figure 7–6 illustrates a typical bin configuration. Items are hand picked, so the height of the system must be within the physical reach of employees. The full cube of

---

[12] Mike Shumey, "Ways to Improve Productivity in a Physical Distribution Warehouse," *Proceedings of the Sixteenth Annual Conference of the National Council of Physical Distribution Management,* 1978, pp. 140–41.

[13] "Storage Equipment for the Warehouse," *Modern Materials Handling, 1985 Warehousing Guidebook* 40, no. 4 (Spring 1985), p. 51.

TABLE 7–1 Storage Guidelines for the Warehouse

	Equipment	*Type of Materials*	*Benefits*	*Other Considerations*
MANUAL	**Racking: Conventional pallet rack**	Pallet loads	Good storage density, good product security	Storage density can be increased further by storing loads two deep
	Drive-in racks	Pallet loads	Fork trucks can access loads, good storage density	Fork truck access is from one direction only
	Drive-through racks	Pallet loads	Same as above	Fork truck access is from two directions
	High-rise racks	Pallet loads	Very high storage density	Often used in AS/R systems, may offer tax advantages when used in rack-supported building
	Cantilever racks	Long loads or rolls	Designed to store difficult shapes	Each different SKU can be stored on a separate shelf
	Pallet stacking frames	Odd-shaped or crushable parts	Allow otherwise unstackable loads to be stacked, saving floor space	Can be disassembled when not in use
	Stacking racks	Odd-shaped or crushable parts	Same as above	Can be stacked flat when not in use
	Gravity-flow racks	Unit loads	High density storage, gravity moves loads	FIFO or LIFO flow of loads
	Shelving	Small, loose loads and cases	Inexpensive	Can be combined with drawers for flexibility
	Drawers	Small parts and tools	All parts are easily accessed, good security	Can be compartmentalized for many SKUs
	Mobile racking or shelving	Pallet loads, loose materials, and cases	Can reduce required floor space by half	Come equipped with safety devices
AUTOMATED	**Unit load AS/RS**	Pallet loads, and a wide variety of sizes and shapes	Very high storage density, computer controlled	May offer tax advantages when rack-supported
	Car-in-lane	Pallet loads, other unit loads	High storage density	Best used where there are large quantities of only a few SKUs
	Mini-load AS/RS	Small parts	High storage density, computer controlled	For flexibility, can be installed in several different configurations
	Horizontal carousels	Small parts	Easy access to parts, relatively inexpensive	Can be stacked on top of each other
	Vertical carousels	Small parts and tools	High storage density	Can serve dual role as storage and delivery system in multifloor facilities
	Man-ride machines	Small parts	Very flexible	Can be used with high-rise shelving or modular drawers

This table is a general guide to the types of available storage equipment, and where each is best used in the warehouse. Each individual storage application should be studied in detail with the equipment supplier before any equipment is specified.

SOURCE: "Storage Equipment for the Warehouse," *Modern Materials Handling, 1985 Warehousing Guidebook* 40, no. 4 (Spring 1985), p. 53. *Modern Materials Handling,* Copyright 1985 by Cahners Publishing Company, Division of Reed Holdings, Inc.

FIGURE 7–4 Nonautomated Storage Units—Storage Racks

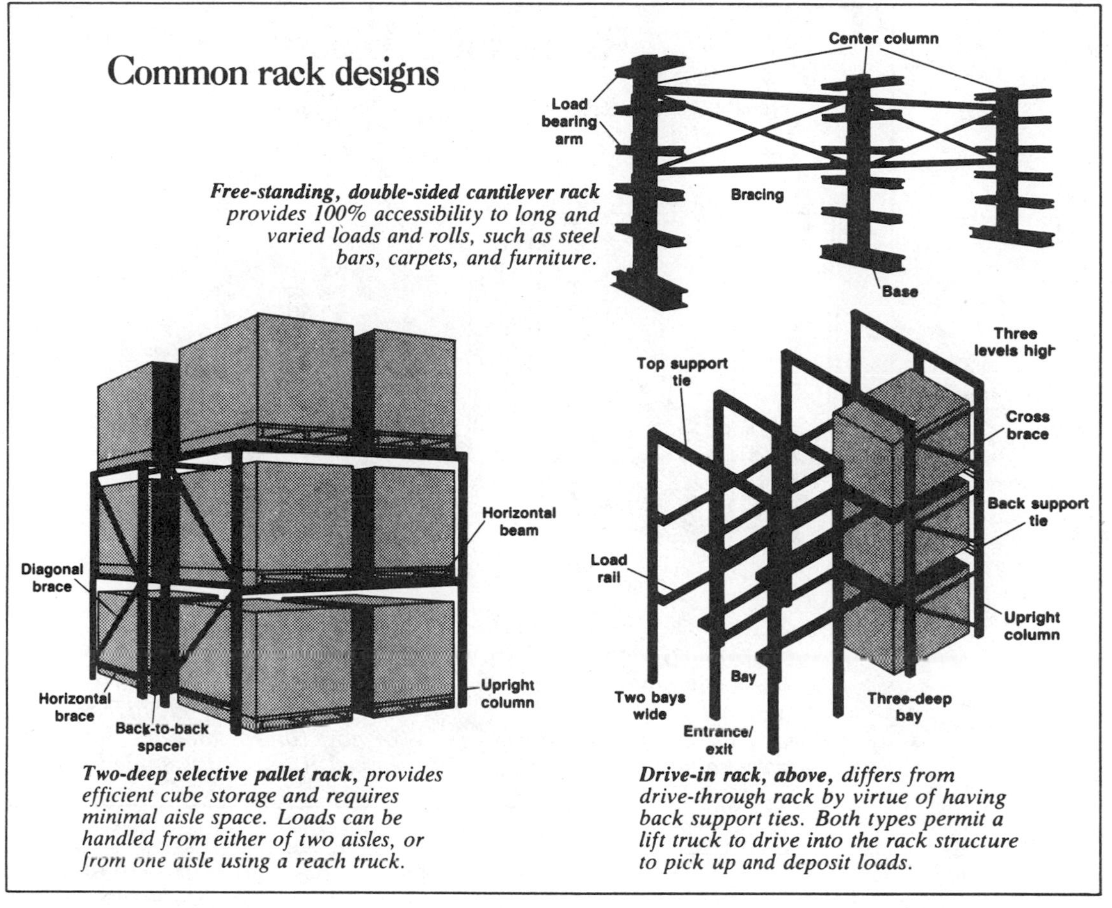

each bin can not typically be used, so some wasted space exists. Bin shelving systems are relatively inexpensive compared to other storage systems, but they have limited usefulness beyond small parts storage.

Modular Storage Drawers and Cabinets

The modular storage drawers and cabinets shown in Figure 7–7 are used for small parts. They are similar in function to bin shelving systems, but they require less physical space and allow items to be concentrated into areas that are easily accessed by employees. The drawers are pulled out and items are then picked. By design, modular storage drawers must be low to the floor, often under five feet in height, to allow access by employees picking items from the drawers.

The previously described storage systems are classified as "fixed" systems because they are stationary. Others can be classified as "movable" be-

FIGURE 7–4 (*concluded*)

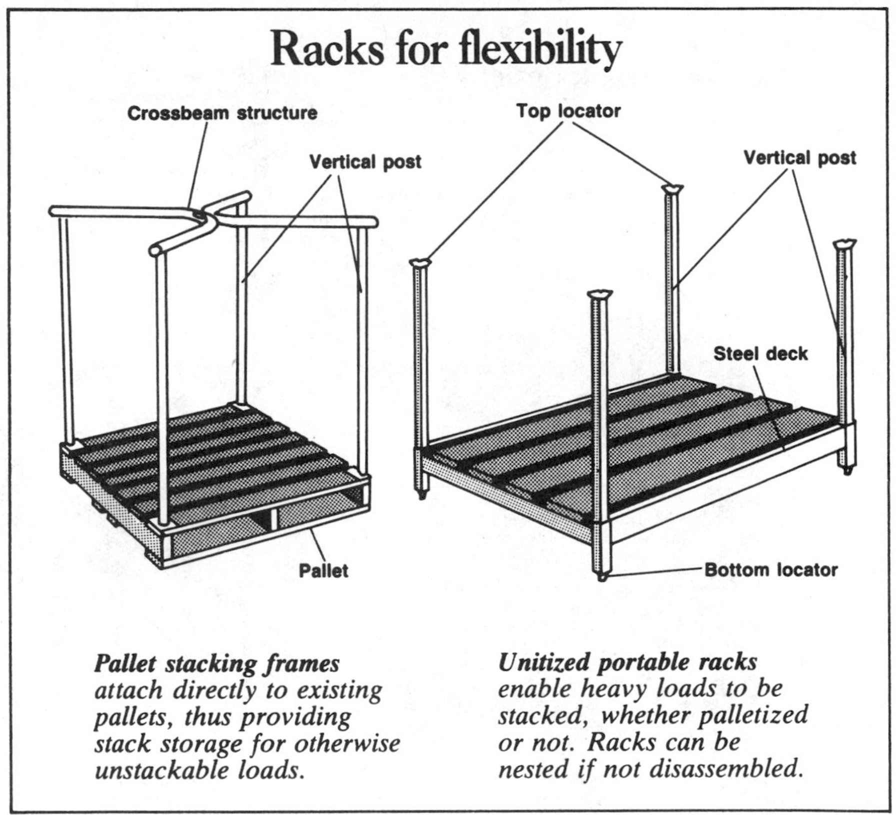

SOURCE: "The Trends Keep Coming in Industrial Storage Racks," *Modern Materials Handling* 40, no. 9 (August 1985), pp. 54–55. *Modern Materials Handling,* Copyright 1985 by Cahners Publishing Company, Division of Reed Holdings, Inc.

Bin Shelving Systems

cause they are not in fixed positions. The bin shelving systems shown in Figure 7–6 can be transformed from a fixed to a movable system as illustrated in Figure 7–8. In the bin shelving mezzanine, wheels on the bottom of the bins follow tracks in the floors, allowing the bins to be moved and stacked together when not being accessed. This allows maximum utilization of space, because full-width aisles are not needed between each bin.

Products are picked from the various storage systems using some order-picking approach. In a manual system, the personnel doing the order picking go to stock: "They either walk and pick, or they use mechanized equipment to carry them to stock locations."[14] In many cases, the

[14] "Orderpicking Systems to Boost Productivity," *Modern Materials Handling, 1985 Warehousing Guidebook* 40, no. 4 (Spring 1985), p. 56.

FIGURE 7–5 Gravity Flow Rack

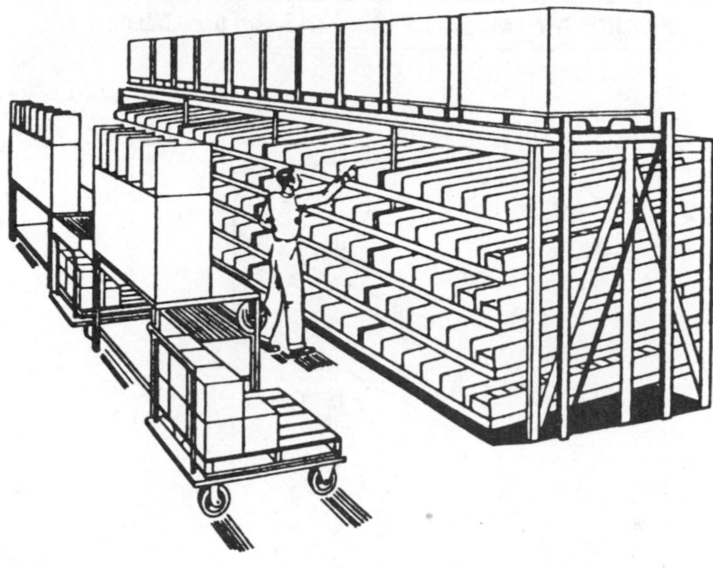

SOURCE: Department of the Navy, Naval Supply Systems Command, Publication 529. From Edward H. Frazelle, *Small Parts Order Picking: Equipment and Strategy* (Oak Brook, Ill.: Warehousing Education and Research Council, 1988), p. 3. Reprinted with permission.

FIGURE 7–6 Bin Shelving Systems

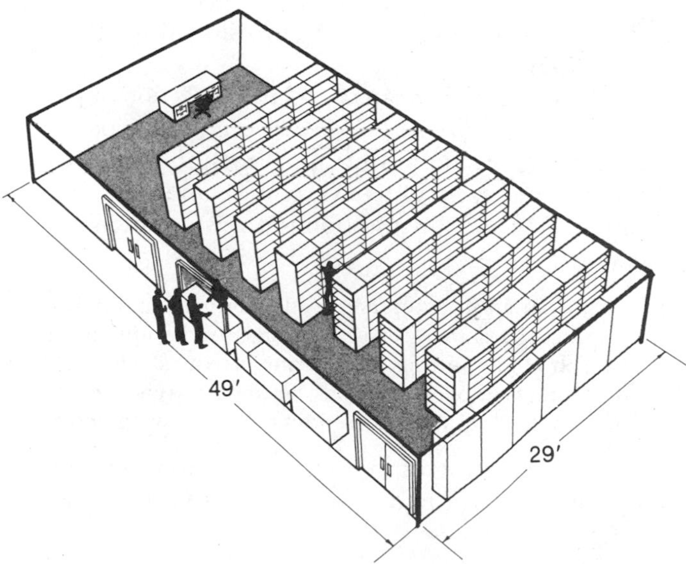

SOURCE: Courtesy of Stanley-Vidmer. From Edward H. Frazelle, *Small Parts Order Picking: Equipment and Strategy* (Oak Brook, Ill.: Warehousing Education and Research Council, 1988), p. 1. Reprinted with permission.

FIGURE 7–7 Modular Storage Drawers and Cabinets

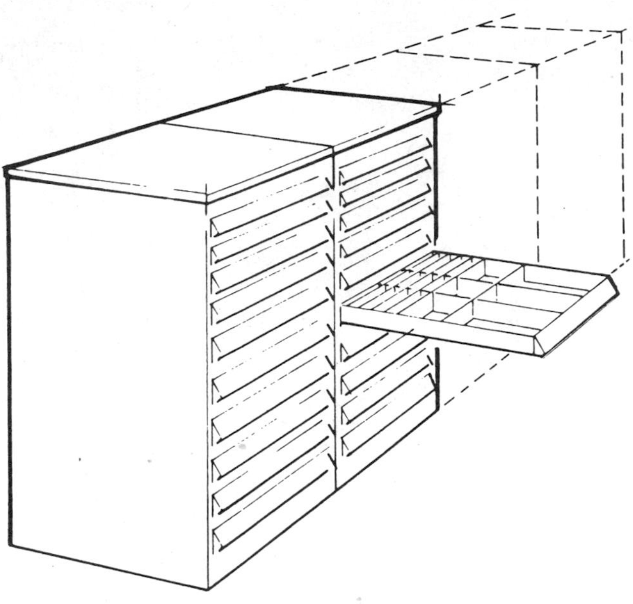

SOURCE: Department of the Navy, Naval Supply Systems Command, Publication 529. From Edward H. Frazelle, *Small Parts Order Picking: Equipment and Strategy* (Oak Brook, Ill.: Warehousing Education and Research Council, 1988), p. 2. Reprinted with permission.

order picker retrieves items from a flow-through gravity storage rack. (see Figure 7–5).

Equipment for Transporting and Sorting

The order picker can use a large selection of powered and nonpowered equipment for *transporting and sorting* items located in the racks, shelves, and drawers. Examples of apparatus of this type include forklift trucks, platform trucks, hand trucks, cranes, and carts. This equipment performs multiple functions in addition to transportation and sorting, such as order picking:

> Transportation equipment is the connecting link between all major warehousing activities, in receiving, storage, and shipping areas. It can also integrate warehousing and manufacturing activities. The right choice of transportation equipment moves materials between warehouse areas at least cost, and integrates the operations at sending and receiving destinations.[15]

Manual sorting of items is a very labor-intensive part of warehousing. It involves separating and regrouping picked items into customer orders.

[15] "Transportation and Sorting—Keys to Throughput," *Modern Materials Handling, 1985 Warehousing Guidebook* 40, no. 4 (Spring 1985), p. 73.

FIGURE 7–8 Bin Shelving Mezzanine

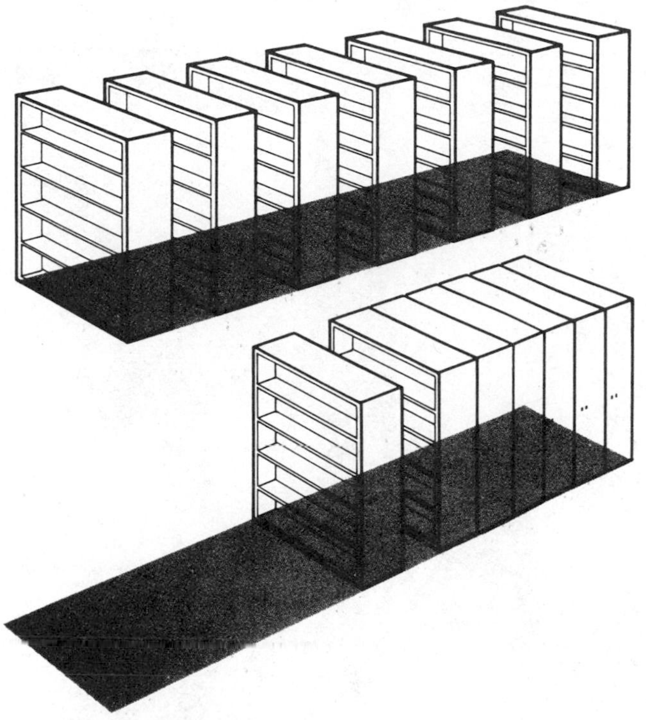

SOURCE: Courtesy of White Storage & Retrieval Systems. From Edward H. Frazelle, *Small Parts Order Picking: Equipment and Strategy* (Oak Brook, Ill.: Warehousing Education and Research Council, 1988), p. 8. Reprinted with permission.

Personnel physically examine items and place them onto pallets or slip-sheets, or into containers for shipment to customers. This is a time-consuming process subject to human error. As a result, most firms attempt to minimize manual sorting.

Product Shipment

Shipping of products to customers involves preparing items for shipment and loading them onto the transport vehicle. The powered and non-powered equipment previously discussed are used here. But, in addition, equipment such as pallets, palletizers, strapping machines, and stretch wrappers are important.

In addition, the shipping and receiving activity requires equipment for handling outbound and inbound transportation vehicles. Therefore, shipping and receiving docks are important elements of the material handling process. For example, new highway regulations increasing the amount of weight a truck trailer can haul, along with regulations allowing wider and longer trailers, have placed new demands on docks. Illustrative of some of the changes taking place are those shown in Figure 7–9, which represents

FIGURE 7–9 How Docks and Receiving Equipment Are Changing

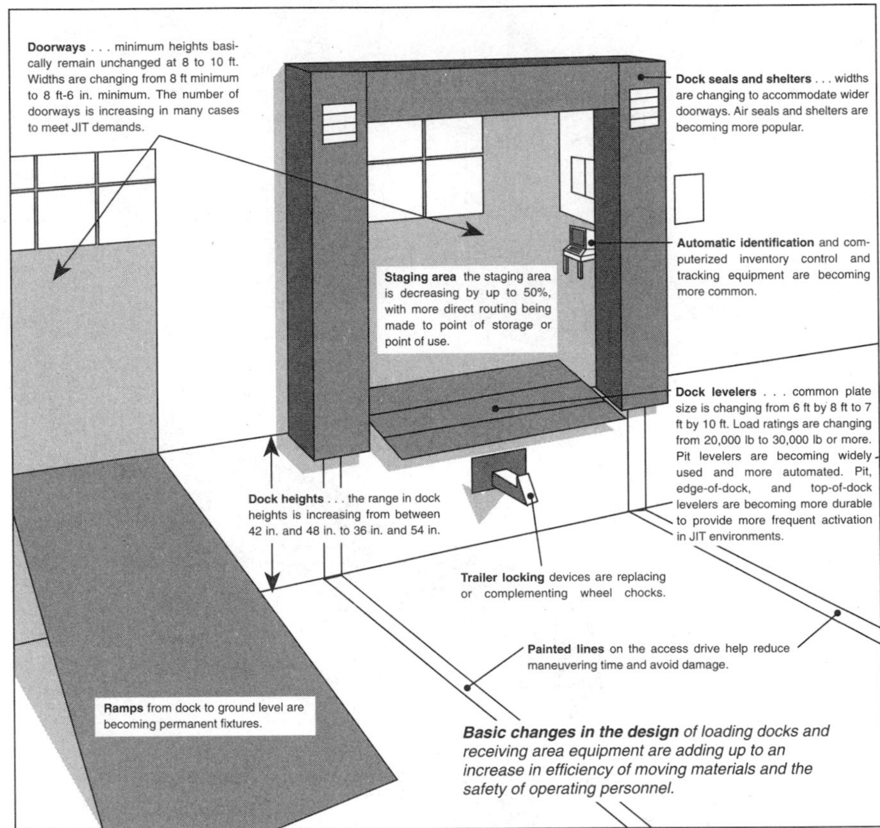

SOURCE: "Docks and Receiving—Where It All Begins," *Modern Materials Handling, 1985 Warehousing Guidebook* 40, no. 4 (Spring 1985), p. 36. *Modern Materials Handling,* Copyright 1985 by Cahners Publishing Company, Division of Reed Holdings, Inc.

a modern shipping/receiving dock. As stated previously, manual or nonautomated equipment is often used in combination with automated equipment.

Automated Warehouse Handling Systems

Automated storage and retrieval systems (AS/RS), carousels, case-picking and item-picking equipment, conveyors, robots, and scanning systems have become commonplace in all types of warehouses. As a result, many firms have been able to achieve improvements in efficiency and productivity. For example, IBM was able to combine four separate warehouses into one large distribution center through the use of automated material handling equipment. Benefits to IBM included:

1. Increasing productivity 20 to 25 percent in areas affected by mechanization.
2. Improving inventory accuracy 9 percent.
3. Boosting the accuracy of filled orders to greater than 99 percent.[16]

Automated equipment can be grouped into the same categories used to discuss nonautomated equipment—storage and order-picking, transportation and sorting, and shipping. Table 7–1 listed examples of automated *storage and order-picking* equipment. General Electric, Bausch & Lomb, Fleming Companies, Consolidated Diesel, Apple Computers, Toyota and Georgetown Manufacturing have employed automated systems with great success.

The Toyota Marketing Company's Parts Distribution Center in South Africa was partially automated between 1984 and 1991 at a cost of $5.6 million. Additional storage and handling facilities were added; new receiving, binning, and order processing systems were introduced; and a high-rise bulk warehouse was constructed. The benefits were significant and included:

1. Order processing productivity increased 300 percent.
2. Product damage rates declined by 50 percent.
3. Stock accuracy and service rates improved by 65 percent.
4. The work of three clerks was eliminated and an additional three clerks were reassigned to more essential tasks.[17]

Automated Storage and Retrieval Systems (AS/RS)

Among the most important *storage and order-picking* equipment are automated storage and retrieval systems (AS/RS):

> Automated storage and retrieval systems offer increased inventory accuracy, reduced labor costs, savings of floor space, and other advantages when compared to most manual systems. And these benefits apply when using AS/RS to store a wide variety of parts and materials—small or large parts, odd shapes such as rolls of steel, raw materials, work-in-process, or finished goods.[18]

AS/RS equipment is computer-controlled and can provide very high storage density of products of many sizes and shapes. The system at Georgetown Manufacturing Corp. "serves storage racks and machine tools, unaided by intermediate handling systems; all handling, except the setup of

---

[16] "Automated Systems Lets Us Centralize Warehousing," *Modern Materials Handling* 39, no. 17 (November 19, 1984), p. 64.

[17] C. M. Baker, "Case Study: Development of National Parts Distribution Center," *Proceedings of the Conference on the Total Logistics Concept,* Pretoria, Republic of South Africa, June 4–5, 1991, unnumbered.

[18] "How to Get Results from a AS/RS," *Modern Materials Handling* 40, no. 5 (April 1985), p. 66.

TABLE 7–2 Perceived Advantages or Benefits of Warehouse Automation Systems

Advantage/Benefit	*Percent Mentioning**
Labor cost reduction	98.8%
Ability to increase output rate	95.2
Improvement in consistency of service	92.1
Reduction in materials handling	92.1
Increased accuracy level	89.5
Service availability	87.0
Improvement in speed of service	81.0
Compatibility with existing values, past experience, and needs	77.6
Ease of understanding and operation	76.1
Capital cost reduction	73.5
Reduction in materials wastage	69.4
Increased safety levels	59.4

*Percent of respondents indicating "strongly agree" or "agree" to the statement.

SOURCE: Adapted from Kofi Q. Dadzie and Wesley J. Johnston, "Innovative Automation Technology in Corporate Warehousing Logistics," *Journal of Business Logistics* 12, no. 1 (1991), p. 76.

parts on machining pallets, requires no manual intervention; and computer control ensures the most efficient production schedules possible."[19] The firm has benefited in several ways, including a reduction in labor (40 percent fewer operators), a savings of 7,700 square feet in floor space, and reductions in lot quantity costs.

Advantages of Automated Systems

Automated systems can provide several benefits for warehouse operations. Table 7–2 identifies some of the most important benefits as identified by users of automated systems. Generally, the benefits identified can be categorized into operating cost savings, improved service levels, and increased control through more and better information.

Disadvantages of Automated Systems

However, automated systems are not without disadvantages. As shown in Table 7–3, users perceived the most significant drawback to such systems to be the initial capital cost. For example, a miniload AS/RS (see Figure 7–10), where a storage/retrieval (s/r) machine travels horizontally and vertically simultaneously in a storage aisle transporting containers to and from an order-picking station at one end of the system, generally costs between $150,000 and $300,000 per aisle.[20] Other disadvantages include the costs of maintenance, system downtime, and a lack of flexibility (i.e., modifying the system at a later date).

Some other examples of AS/RSs at Priam Corp. (a manufacturer of disc drives), IBM, and Apple Computer are illustrated in Figures 7–11, 7–12,

---

[19] "S/R Machine Delivers Directly to Machine Tools," *Modern Materials Handling* 40, no. 2 (February 1985), p. 56.

[20] Edward H. Frazelle, *Small Parts Order Picking: Equipment and Strategy* (Oak Brook, Ill.: Warehousing Education and Research Council, 1988), p. 6.

TABLE 7–3 Operational and Implementation Problems with Warehouse Automation Systems

Problem Area	*Percent Mentioning*
1. Cost of equipment/financial justification	19.0%
2. Downtime or reliability of equipment/maintenance interruptions	10.0
3. Software related problems, such as poor documentation, incompatibility, failure, or modification	8.0
4. Capacity problems, such as limited applications/integration of equipment into existing system	8.0
5. Lack of flexibility to respond to changing environment/not suitable for high degree of seasonality in business	6.0
6. Maintenance cost/maintenance parts	5.0
7. User interface/training to operate system/transition from manual to automated procedure	5.0
8. Worker acceptance of automation	4.0
9. No problems/we are adapting well	4.0
10. Lack of top management commitment	3.0
11. Obsolescence/need more up-to-date automation/need more automation	3.0

SOURCE: Kofi Q. Dadzie and Wesley J. Johnston, "Innovative Automation Technology in Corporate Warehousing Logistics," *Journal of Business Logistics* 12, no. 1 (1991), p. 72.

FIGURE 7–10 Miniload AS/RS

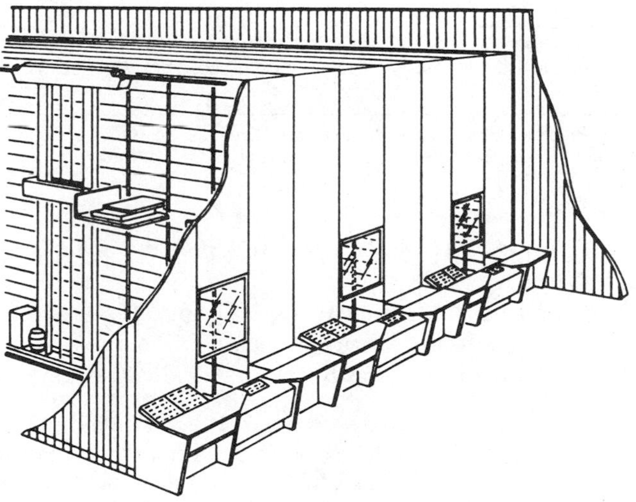

SOURCE: Department of the Navy, Naval Supply Systems Command, Publication 529. From Edward H. Frazelle, *Small Parts Order Picking: Equipment and Strategy* (Oak Brook, Ill.: Warehousing Education and Research Council, 1988), p. 6. Reprinted with permission.

FIGURE 7–11 Priam's New Facility—A Showcase of Flexible Assembly Systems

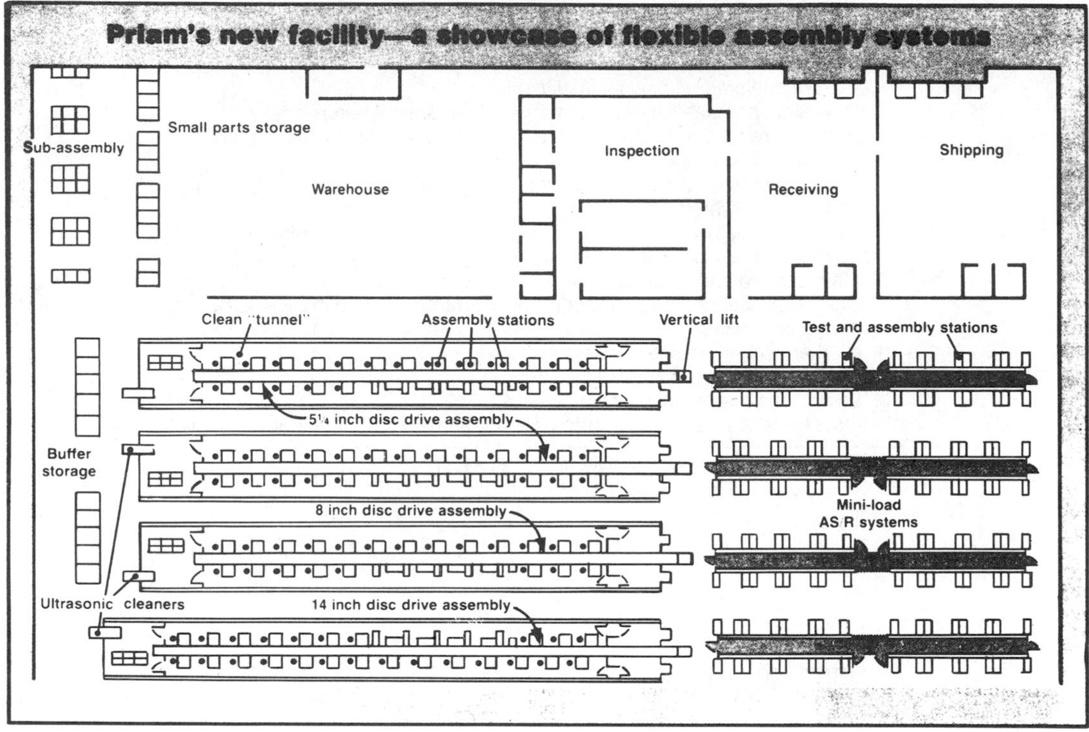

Initial assembly is done at work stations set up along the four transporter conveyors. Final assembly and testing is done at stations set up at openings in the mini-load AS/RS storage racks. Then the disc drives are packaged and shipped to customers.

SOURCE:"Our Flexible Systems Help Us Make a Better Product," *Modern Materials Handling* 39, no. 10 (July 6, 1984), p. 48. *Modern Materials Handling,* Copyright 1984 by Cahners Publishing Company, Division of Reed Holdings, Inc.

and 7–13, respectively. Each uses an AS/RS in a unique and highly successful manner.

A form of AS/RS is the carousel. Carousels are mechanical devices that house and rotate items for order-picking. The most frequently utilized carousel configurations are the horizontal and vertical systems.

Horizontal Carousels A horizontal carousel [see Figure 7–14] is a linked series of rotating bins of adjustable shelves driven on the top or bottom by a drive motor. Rotation takes place on an axis perpendicular to the floor at approximately 80 feet per minute.

Vertical Carousels A vertical carousel [see Figure 7–15] is a horizontal carousel turned on its end and enclosed in sheet metal. As with horizontal carousels, an order picker operates one or multiple carousels. The carousels are indexed either automat-

FIGURE 7–12 Maximizing Warehouse Productivity at IBM

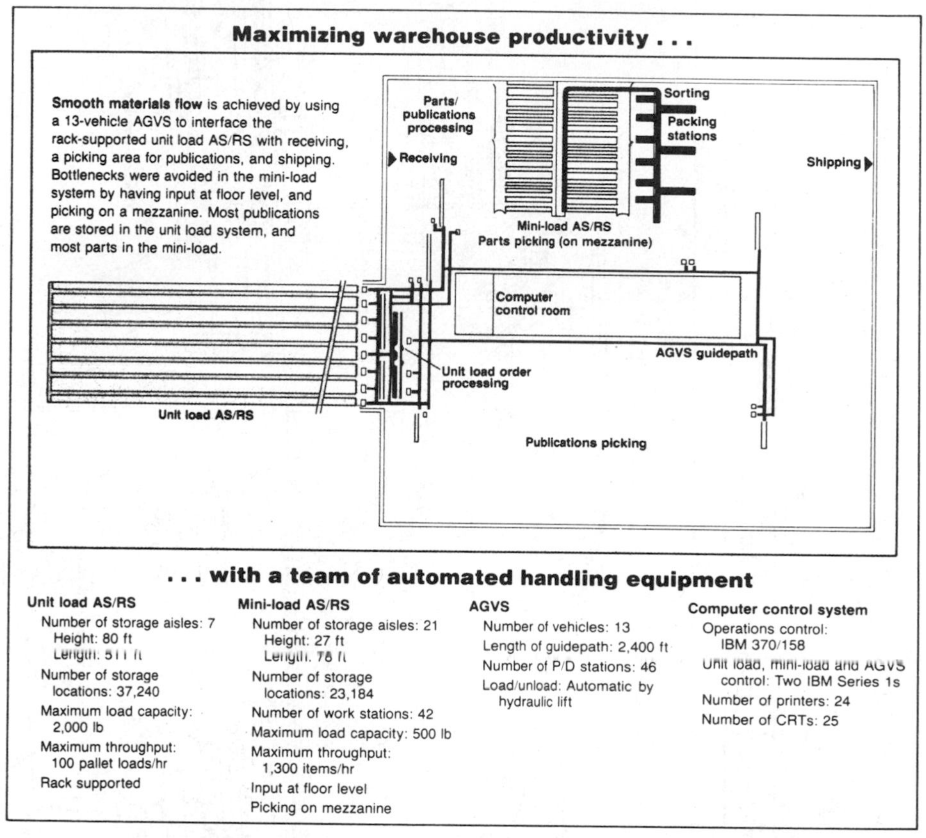

SOURCE: "Automated Systems Lets Us Centralize Warehousing," *Modern Materials Handling* 39, no. 17 (November 19, 1984), p. 66. *Modern Materials Handling*, Copyright 1984 by Cahners Publishing Company, Division of Reed Holdings, Inc.

ically via computer control, or manually by the order picker operating a keypad on the carousel's work surface.[21]

Raytheon Company's Electromagnetic Systems Division (ESD) installed a horizontal carousel system with dramatic results. Productivity at the ESD facility increased 60 percent and inventory accuracy rose from 85 percent to almost 98 percent.[22] Schematically, the ESD system is illustrated in Fig-

[21] Ibid., pp. 4–5.

[22] "Carousels Boost Productivity by 60%," *Modern Materials Handling* 42, no. 2 (February 1987), p. 59.

FIGURE 7–13 Minimizing Inventory at Apple Computer with a Flexible Mini-Load AS/RS

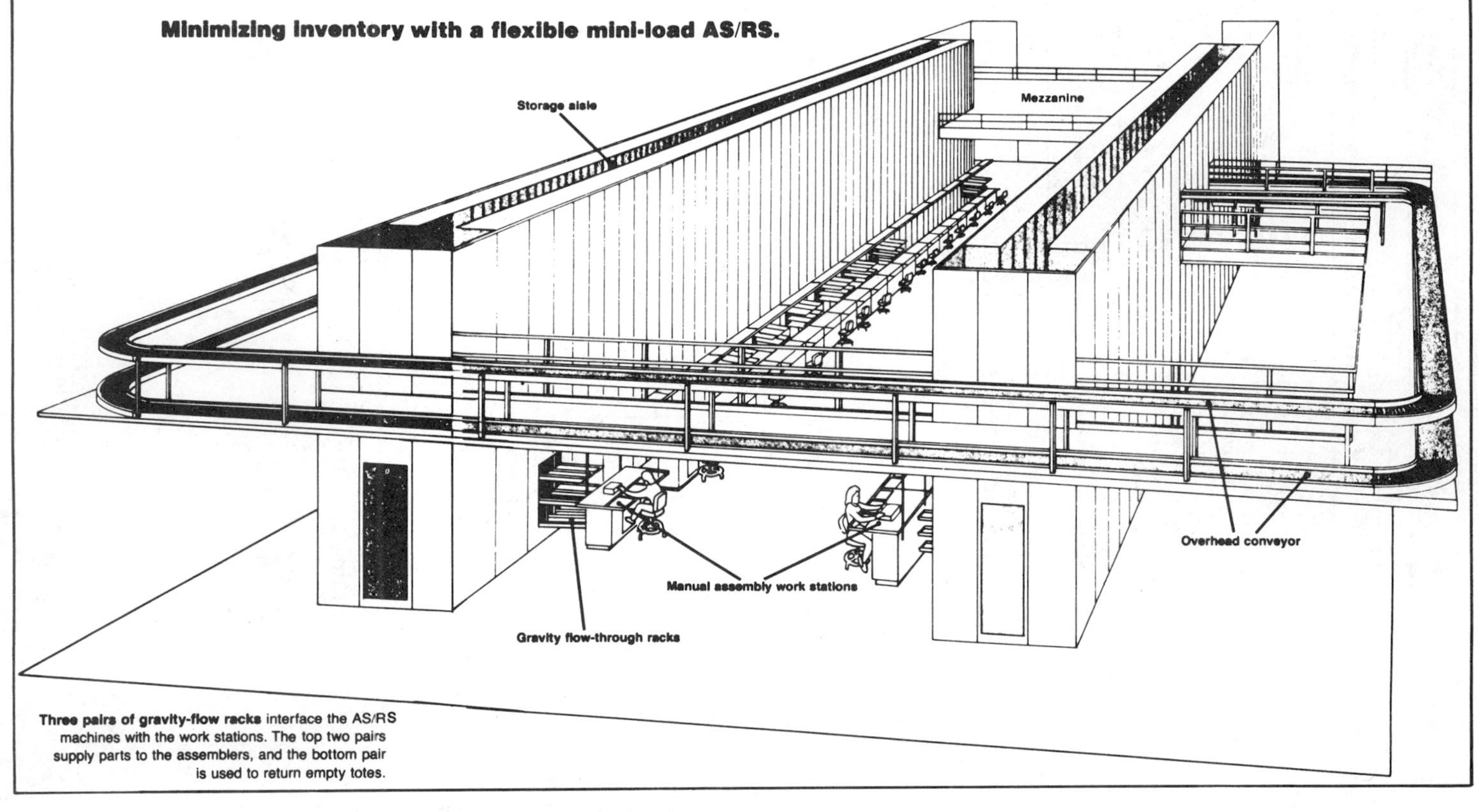

SOURCE: "Mini-Load AS/RS Trims Inventory, Speeds Assembly," *Modern Materials Handling* 39, no. 13 (September 21, 1984), pp. 48–49. *Modern Materials Handling*, Copyright 1984 by Cahners Publishing Company, Division of Reed Holdings, Inc.

FIGURE 7–14 Horizontal Carousels

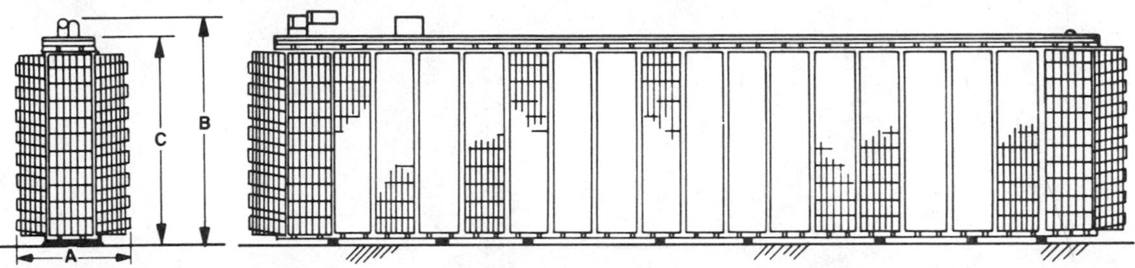

A. END ELEVATION

B. SIDE ELEVATION

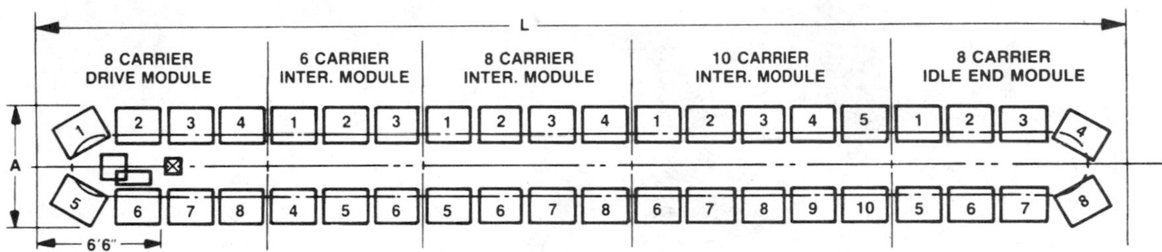

C. PLAN VIEW

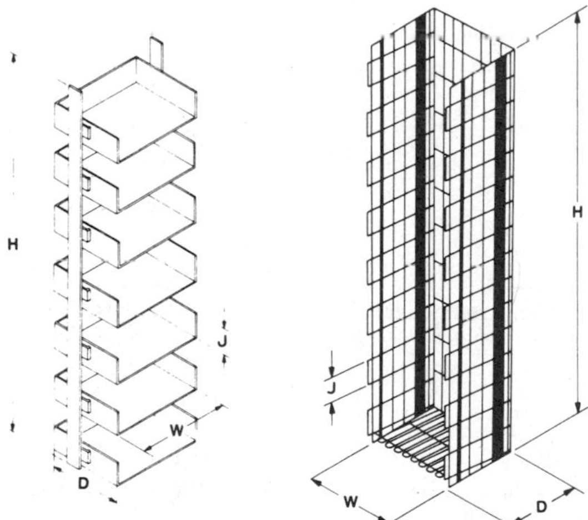

D. SHEET METAL CARRIER AND SHELVES

E. WIRE CARRIER AND SHELVES

SOURCE: Courtesy of SPS Technologies, Inc. From Edward H. Frazelle, *Small Parts Order Picking: Equipment and Strategy* (Oak Brook, Ill.: Warehousing Education and Research Council, 1988), p. 4.

FIGURE 7–15 Vertical Carousel

SOURCE: Courtesy of Kardex Systems, Inc. From Edward H. Frazelle, *Small Parts Order Picking: Equipment and Strategy* (Oak Brook, Ill.: Warehousing Education and Research Council, 1988), p. 5. Reprinted with permission.

ure 7–16. A vertical carousel system was installed by Camco, Inc., Canada's largest producer of major appliances. An improvement of 200 percent was realized in the productivity of its small parts and order-picking operation.[23]

The *transportation and sorting* activities are typically performed in combination with storage and order picking. The three most often used pieces of transportation equipment are conveyors, automatic guided vehicle sys-

[23] "Appliance Maker Gets Higher Warehouse Productivity," *Material Handling Engineering* 42, no. 7 (July 1987), p. 50.

FIGURE 7–16 Raytheon's New Automated Storeroom

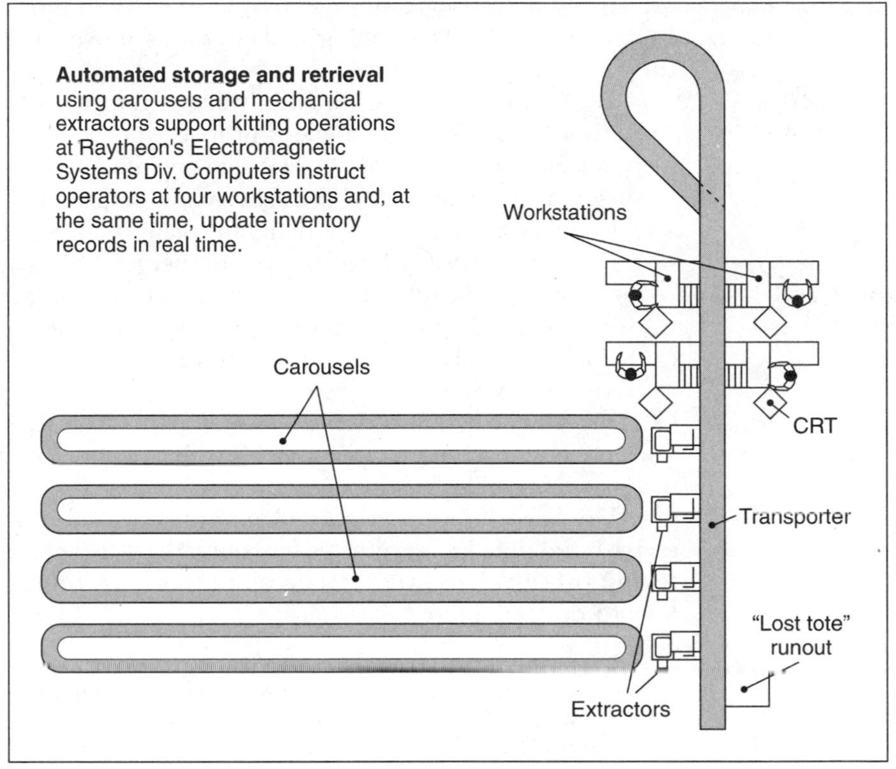

SOURCE: "Carousels Boost Productivity by 60%," *Modern Materials Handling* 42, no. 2 (February 1987), p. 59. Reprinted with permission.

tems (AGVS), and operator-controlled trucks or tractors. Sorting equipment can be specialized, such as a tilt-tray sorter with built-in diverting mechanisms, or it can be assembled from other components, such as conveyors and diverters.[24]

Conveyor Systems at Pic 'N' Save Corporation

Pic 'N' Save Corporation has developed a conveyor sorting system that handles over 100 cases per minute. The company has shipped up to 68,000 cases in one working day—a high level of productivity under normal conditions, but even more outstanding for Pic 'N' Save because the firm rarely has the same item in stock more than once. The company buys closeout

[24] "Transportation and Sorting," p. 75.

goods (overruns, discontinued items, style changes) from manufacturers and therefore has a wide variety of merchandise in inventory. Case goods are stored in a reserve storage area and are then moved to a picking area four levels high. After being picked, items move to a merge area where they are sorted and shipped.[25]

Automatic Guided Vehicle Systems (AGVS)

"AGVS in warehouses include tractors that haul one or more trailers, carts that hold cases or a single unit load, and pallet trucks that carry one or two unit loads at a time."[26] The Oldsmobile Division of General Motors has used a 185-vehicle AGVS in the manufacture of Oldsmobiles, Buicks, and Pontiacs at its Lansing, Michigan, plant. Guided vehicles in combination with an overhead conveyor system merge engines and chassis.[27]

"Man-Ride Machines"

Operator-controlled trucks or tractors can be of several types, but the most widely used approach is the "man-ride machine." This method utilizes both labor and automation in a combination that optimizes each entity. "There are two basic designs of man-ride machines. One has an operator cab and storage compartments for small parts. The second design is similar . . . except the cab is equipped with a shuttle table for manual handling or order picking of unit loads."[28]

Robots

The robot is another type of equipment used in many phases of material handling. For several years robots have been used in the manufacturing process. However, advances in robotics technology have enabled robots to be used almost anywhere:

> Robots are being applied to machine tool loading and palletizing jobs not able to be automated before. They have come into their own as a separate technology similar to machine tools. But users are finding that robots do not stand alone: They must be engineered to do a job—most of which [is] handling, with parts brought to them and removed by other handling systems. This is why they are increasingly being applied as flexible handling devices and being considered as extensions of flexible handling systems.[29]

It is likely that material handling robots will have steady growth in many application areas (see Figure 7–17).

Automation in the *shipping* area has also occurred. The two aspects of the shipping activity that have been most affected by automation are packaging and optical scanning. We have previously discussed packaging by

[25] "How We Sort Up to 135 Cases per Minute," *Modern Materials Handling* 40, no. 6 (May 1985), pp. 60–63.

[26] "Transportation and Sorting," p. 74.

[27] "Automatic Guided Vehicles Move into the Assembly Line," *Modern Materials Handling* 40, no. 1 (January 1984), pp. 78–83. See also "Overhead Handling Systems—How They Boost Productivity," *Modern Materials Handling* 40, no. 7 (June 1985), pp. 64–69.

[28] "AS/RS and Just-in-Time: Partners in Manufacturing," *Modern Materials Handling* 39, no. 11 (August 6, 1984), p. 62.

[29] "Where Material Handling Stands Now," p. A20. See also "Where Robots Are Headed in Material Handling," *Modern Materials Handling* 40, no. 6 (May 1985), pp. 68–73.

FIGURE 7–17 Robots in the Warehouse

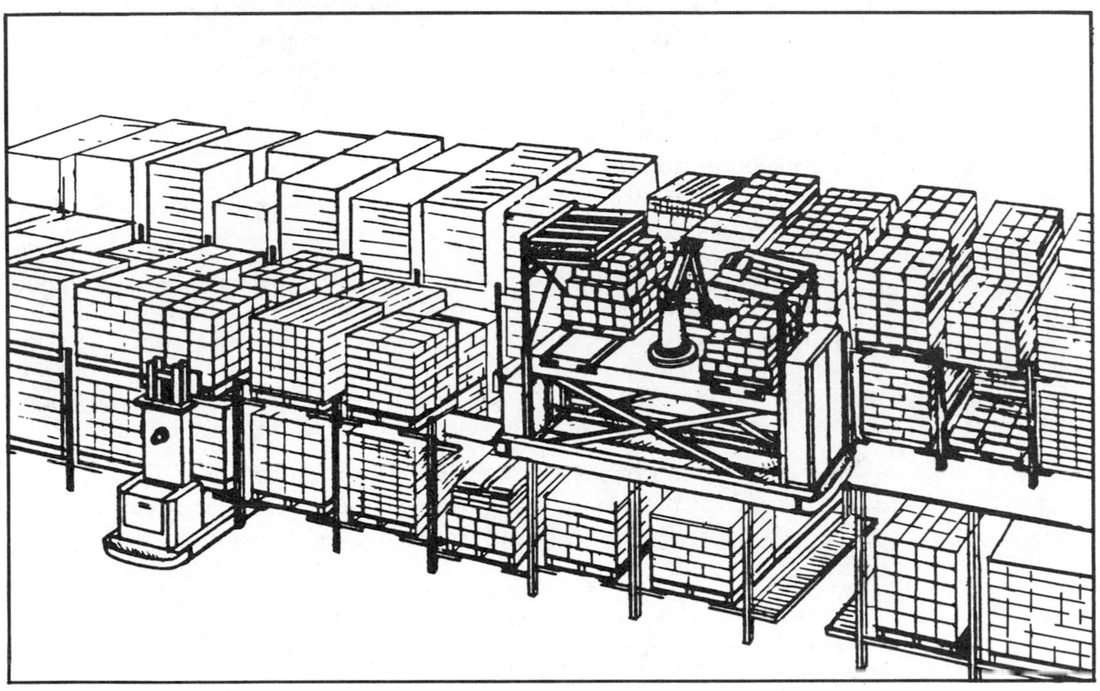

Artist's conception of guided vehicles and robotics in the warehouse. Automatically guided and programmed lift truck is shown stacking a load into a pallet rack. The robot is shown on a floor-supported vehicle capable of raising and lowering; the robot is picking from gravity flow racks and building pallet loads.

SOURCE: "Warehousing Flexibility Aided by Robots," *Material Handling Engineering* 40, no. 9 (September 1985), p. 103. Reproduced with permission of The St. Onge Company, York, Penn.

pass-through and rotary stretch-wrapping machines. We will further address the area of packaging in Chapter 8.

Optical Scanners

Another aspect of shipping automation is documentation. As other components of the warehouse become automated, firms need to computerize their tracking and information systems. Spiegel, Inc., a mail-order retailer, had to address this issue in 1985. An expected jump in customer orders of nearly 67 percent between 1984 (9 million orders) and 1988 (15 million orders) spurred Spiegel to install a "high-speed identification system that tracks orders in-house to ready them for shipping."[30] A bar code reader diverts items to the proper shipping lane for transport by private carrier, UPS, or parcel post. In addition, shipping documents, customer

[30]"Bar Codes + Sortation = Higher Throughput," *Modern Materials Handling* 40, no. 7 (June 1985), p. 62.

bills, and other business-related documentation are prepared after the order passes the optical scanner.

Fleming Companies, one of the nation's largest food wholesalers, also uses optical scanners to read computer-generated package labels. By using the scanners along with a conveyor system that connects the order-picking, sorting, and shipping areas, Fleming is able to maintain one of the most efficient food wholesale operations in the United States. The firm ships about 200,000 items each day.

In summary, the warehousing activity is rapidly automating, although most warehouses are far from being fully automated.

> True automation in every sense of the word in a distribution center would involve automatic control of warehousing functions, from automated unloading of goods at the receiving dock, to identification and sortation, storing, picking, packing, and finally loading completed orders into the delivery trucks. In actual practice . . . most 'automated' distribution warehouses have integrated some computer-controlled equipment with the manually controlled functions.[31]

Warehouse handling systems, whether automated or manual, are an important part of the firm's total logistics system. A company can realize a number of benefits by utilizing good material handling equipment, including:

Benefits from Utilizing Material Handling Equipment

1. Increased productivity per employee through increased output.
2. Reduced operating expenses.
3. Optimized machine utilization.
4. Increased space utilization.
5. Reduced damage to inventory.
6. Increased customer service levels.
7. Reduced employee fatigue.
8. Reduced accidents.
9. Improved flow of material.[32]

The type and scope of benefits a company receives will vary depending on such factors as product characteristics, existing customer service levels, and present level of company expertise.

Warehousing in a Just-in-Time (JIT) Environment

As manufacturing and merchandising firms adopt and implement Just-in-Time (JIT) programs, logistics functions such as warehousing will be directly affected. Because JIT stresses reduced inventory levels and more responsive logistics systems, greater demands are placed on warehousing to

[31] Ibid., p. 141.

[32] Shumey, "Ways to Improve Productivity," p. 140.

maximize both efficiency and effectiveness. Some examples of these demands include the following:[33]

Demands Placed on Warehousing by JIT

1. *A total commitment to quality*—Warehouse employees must perform their tasks at levels specified by customers (inbound and outbound).
2. *Reduced production lot sizes*—Items are packaged in smaller lots, and warehouse deliveries are smaller and in mixed pallet quantities.
3. *Elimination of non-value-added activities*—Nonessential and inefficient physical movement and handling activities are identified and eliminated, resulting in improved facilities layout and warehouse operating efficiencies.

How Zytec Utilizes Warehousing to Support JIT

Zytec Corporation, a manufacturer of power supplies for computers and medical equipment, successfully utilized its warehousing operations to support a JIT manufacturing system. Prior to implementing JIT, the firm's warehousing situation was described as follows:

> In January, 1985, the raw materials and purchased parts warehouse at Zytec was out of control. Boxes of parts clogged every aisle and spilled into two additional buildings. The computer on-hand balances were seldom correct, destroying MRP credibility. Unable to trust the system, purchasing agents bought excess inventory to protect against stockouts. Lines were shut down due to parts "lost in the crib" and then worked overtime when hot parts were expedited. Three inventory analysts worked 13-hour days to correct on-hand balances verified by two full-time cycle counters, yet no improvements were visible.[34]

After identifying the problems and causes of the warehousing inefficiencies, process and procedure changes were implemented that resulted in a raw materials inventory reduction of $5 million ($8.8 million to $3.8 million) and an increase in inventory accuracy from 98.5 to 99.6 percent. Only one facility was needed rather than the three that had been required before.

SUMMARY

In this chapter we discussed the importance of warehousing in the logistics system. Economies of scale, cost considerations, and customer service are the most important considerations. The types of options available to a firm include public (rented) and private (owned or leased) warehousing.

The major functions of warehousing are movement, storage, and information transfer. Movement consists of receiving, transfer, order selec-

---

[33] See Robin G. Stenger and Robert E. Murray, "Using Warehousing Operations to Support a Just-In-Time Manufacturing Program," *WERC Technical Paper No. 20* (Oak Brook, Ill.: Warehousing Education and Research Council, 1987), pp. 1–2.

[34] Ibid., p. 2.

tion, and shipping. Storage can be temporary or semipermanent. Information transfer is the link between all of the activities that take place in the warehouse.

Within a warehouse, manual (nonautomated) or automated material-handling equipment can be employed. Standard equipment can be categorized by the function it performs: storage and order-picking, transportation and sorting, or shipping. Automated equipment includes items such as automated storage and retrieval systems (AS/RS), carousels, conveyors, robots, and scanning systems.

We are now ready to examine some of the major warehouse decision strategies in Chapter 8.

SUGGESTED READINGS

ACKERMAN, KENNETH B. *Practical Handbook of Warehousing.* 3d ed. New York: Van Nostrand. Reinhold, 1990, 645 pages.

———. "Whither Warehousing?" *Warehousing Forum* 5, no. 12 (November 1990), pp. 1–2.

ANDEL, TOM. "Pallets Take New Directions." *Transportation & Distribution* 33, no. 1 (January 1992), pp. 32–34.

"Do You Use Public Warehousing . . . Why or Why Not?" *Traffic Management* 22, no. 6 (June 1983), pp. 92–94.

FILLEY, RICHARD D. "International Conference on Automation in Warehousing." *Industrial Engineering* 16, no. 2 (February 1984), pp. 39–42.

FITZGERALD, KEVIN R. "Gravity-Flow Storage Doubles Productivity." *Modern Materials Handling* 41, no. 1 (January 1986), pp. 75–77.

"IBM's Automated Factory—A Giant Step Forward." *Modern Materials Handling* 40, no. 3 (March 1985), pp. 58–65.

"Integrated Systems Double Warehouse Productivity." *Modern Materials Handling* 39, no. 7 (May 7, 1984), pp. 44–48.

"Logistics in the Warehouse." *Industrial Distribution* 73, no. 2 (September 1984), pp. 39–42.

MCGINNIS, MICHAEL A., AND LISA A. FORRY. "Changing Missions in Warehousing." *WERC Research Report* (Oak Brook, Ill.: Warehousing Education and Research Council, 1986), 35 pages.

O'DONNELL, JOAN PREVETE. "Automated Warehouse Readies Central Paper for the Future." *National Paper Trade Association (NPTA) Management News* (July 1990), pp. 22–24.

"Operating the Warehouse of the Future." *Distribution Center Management* 26, no. 2 (February 1991), pp. 1–4.

SCHWIND, GENE. "Automated Storage and Retrieval Plays in a Faster League." *Material Handling Engineering* 41, no. 10 (October 1986), pp. 79–84.

Traveling the Road of Logistics: The Evolution of Warehousing and Distribution (Chicago: American Warehousemen's Association, 1991), 106 pp.

"Warehousing: A Review for Management." *Distribution* 90, no. 3 (March 1991), pp. 90–100.

WHITE, JOHN A. "Dimensions of World-Class Warehousing." *Proceedings of the Annual Conference of the Council of Logistics Management,* 1989, pp. 215–27.

WITT, CLYDE E. "IBM's Manufacturing Gets High-Powered Material Handling Support." *Material Handling Engineering* 40, no. 3 (March 1985), pp. 58–60, 65.

QUESTIONS AND PROBLEMS

1. Warehousing is used for the storage of inventories during all phases of the logistics process. Why is it necessary for a firm to store inventories of any kind, since inventory carrying costs can be very high?
2. Distinguish between *private* and *public* warehousing. What are the advantages and disadvantages of each type?
3. Discuss what is meant by cost trade-off analysis within the context of warehousing. Give at least two examples of the cost trade-offs involved in a firm's decision to use a combination of public and private warehousing rather than public or private warehousing alone.
4. Briefly describe the three basic functions of warehousing: movement, storage, and information transfer.
5. Identify some of the advantages and benefits of automated material handling systems as opposed to the use of manual systems.

Chapter 8

Decision Strategies in Warehousing

Objectives of This Chapter

To compare public and private warehousing from a financial perspective

To identify the factors that affect the size and number of warehouses

To examine the warehouse site selection decision from macro and micro perspectives

To examine the factors that affect warehouse layout and design

To identify the role of packaging in the warehouse operation

To present examples of the use of computer technology in warehouse management

To examine various global warehousing issues

To overview the importance of productivity and accounting/control issues in warehouse management

INTRODUCTION

The importance of warehousing in marketing and logistics strategies is increasing. "Productivity in manufacturing gets the headlines because it's the key to . . . competitiveness in world markets. Productivity in warehousing doesn't get as many headlines; but it has the same overall mission."[1] If one views warehousing as a means of achieving a competitive advantage, the traditional perspective of warehousing as basically concerned with managing inventories becomes one of managing both inventories and information flows (see Figure 8–1). In the new mission of warehousing, computerization and automation become essential ingredients to logistics success.

In addition, effective warehouse management involves a thorough understanding of the functions of warehousing, the merits of public versus private warehousing, and the financial and service aspects of warehousing decisions. Companies also need knowledge of the methods that can improve warehousing performance and a strategy for locating warehousing facilities at the most optimal locations.

Strategic Decisions

Warehousing decisions may be strategic or operational. *Strategic* decisions deal with the allocation of logistics resources over an extended time in a manner that is consistent and supportive of overall enterprise policies and objectives. They can take two forms: long-range or project-type. An example of a long-range strategic decision is the choice of a logistics system design. A project-type decision might deal with consolidation of branch warehouses into a regional distribution center. Other examples of typical strategic questions include the following:

---

[1] Gene F. Schwind, "Warehousing 87: Redefining the Role," *Material Handling Engineering* 42, no. 3 (March 1987), p. 58.

FIGURE 8–1 The New Mission of Warehousing

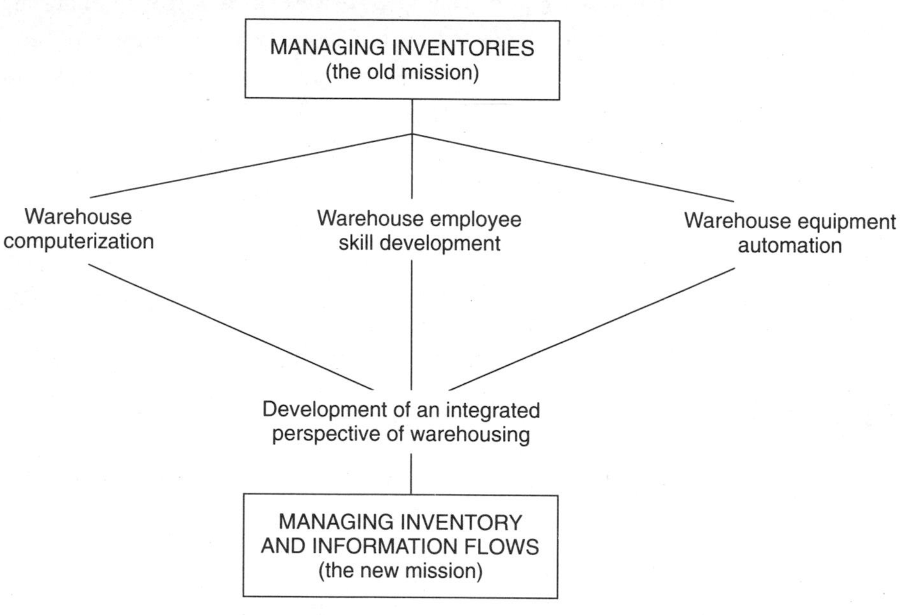

SOURCE: Reprinted with permission from *Changing Missions in Warehousing,* Michael A. McGinnis and Lisa A. Forry. © 1986, Warehousing Education and Research Council, 1100 Jorie Blvd., Oak Brook, IL 60521.

Should warehousing be owned, leased, rented, or some combination of these?

Should the warehousing functions be "spun off," that is, contracted out to a third-party provider?

Should the company install new material handling equipment or continue to hire more labor?

Operational Decisions

Operational decisions are decisions used to manage or control logistics performance. Typically, these decisions are routine in nature and involve time spans of one year or less. Due to the short time horizon involved, these decisions have more certainty than strategic decisions. They also relate to the coordination and performance of the logistics system. For example, a warehouse manager would be concerned with increasing costs and/or declining productivity in the shipping department.

PUBLIC VERSUS PRIVATE WAREHOUSING

One of the most important warehousing decisions is whether public or private facilities should be used. In order to make the proper decision from a cost and service standpoint, the logistics executive must understand the advantages and disadvantages, as well as the financial implications, of each alternative.

A Financial Perspective

Each company must consider the factors previously discussed in Chapter 7 in light of the firm's specific characteristics. A further consideration in the decision is the rate of return that the private warehouse alternative will provide. The investment in a corporate-owned warehouse should generate the same rate of return as other investments made by the firm. Appendix A to this chapter illustrates the type of financial analysis that must be performed.

Many companies find it advantageous to use some combination of public and private warehousing. The private warehouses are used to handle the basic inventory levels required for least cost logistics in markets where the volume justifies ownership. Public warehouses are used in those areas where volume is not sufficient to justify ownership and/or to store peak requirements. Public warehouses typically charge on the basis of case or hundredweight stored or handled. Consequently, when the volume of activity is sufficiently large, public warehousing charges exceed the cost of a private facility, making ownership more attractive.[2]

FACILITY DEVELOPMENT

One of the more important decisions a logistics executive faces is how to develop an optimal warehousing network for the firm's products and customers. Such a decision encompasses a number of significant elements. Management must determine the size and number of warehouses, and must also ascertain their location. Finally, each warehouse must be laid out and designed properly in order to maximize efficiency and productivity. An example of how to address some of these issues is presented in Appendix B of this chapter.

Size and Number of Warehouses

Two issues that must be addressed are the size and number of warehouse facilities. These are interrelated decisions in that they typically have an in-

[2] For a discussion of these and other public versus private warehousing issues, see William G. Sheehan, "Public vs. Contract Warehousing," *Warehousing Forum* 4, no. 5 (April 1989), pp. 1–3.

verse relationship; i.e., as the number of warehouses increases, the average size of a warehouse decreases.

Many factors influence how large a warehouse should be, although it is first necessary to define how size is measured. In general, size can be defined in terms of square footage or cubic space. Most public warehouses still use square footage dimensions in their advertising and promotional efforts. Unfortunately, square footage measures ignore the capability of modern warehouses to store merchandise vertically. Hence, the cubic space measure was developed. Cubic space refers to the amount of volume available within a facility. It is a much more realistic size estimate because it considers more of the available usable space in a warehouse. Some of the most important factors affecting the size of a warehouse are:

Factors Affecting Warehouse Size

1. Customer service levels.
2. Size of market(s) served.
3. Number of products marketed.
4. Size of the product(s).
5. Material handling system used.
6. Throughput rate.
7. Production lead time.
8. Economies of scale.
9. Stock layout.
10. Aisle requirements.
11. Office area in warehouse.
12. Types of racks and shelves used.
13. Level and pattern of demand.

Space Requirement Determination

Typically, as a company's service levels increase, it requires more warehousing space to provide storage for higher levels of inventory. As the market(s) served by a warehouse increase in number or size, additional space is also required. When a firm has multiple products or product groupings, especially if they are diverse, it needs larger warehouses in order to maintain at least minimal inventory levels of all products. In general, greater space requirements are necessary when products are large; a high throughput rate exists; production lead time is long; manual material handling systems are used; the warehouse contains office, sales, or computer activities; or demand is erratic and unpredictable.

Warehouse Size Is Related to Material Handling Equipment Used

To illustrate, consider the relation of warehouse size to the type of material handling equipment used.[3] As Figure 8–2 shows, the type of forklift truck a warehouse employs can significantly affect the amount of storage area necessary to store product. Because of different capabilities of lift

---

[3] Examples can be found in Clyde E. Witt, "Multi-Million Dollar Facelift for Exchange Service," *Material Handling Engineering* 43, no. 8 (August 1988), pp. 47–53; "How to Implement Robotic Palletizing," *Material Handling Engineering* 43, no. 7 (July 1988), pp. 61–64; and Clyde E. Witt, "Publisher Creates Textbook Case for Distribution," *Material Handling Engineering* 43, no. 3 (March 1988), pp. 41–47.

FIGURE 8–2 Narrow-Aisle Trucks Can Reduce Floor Space

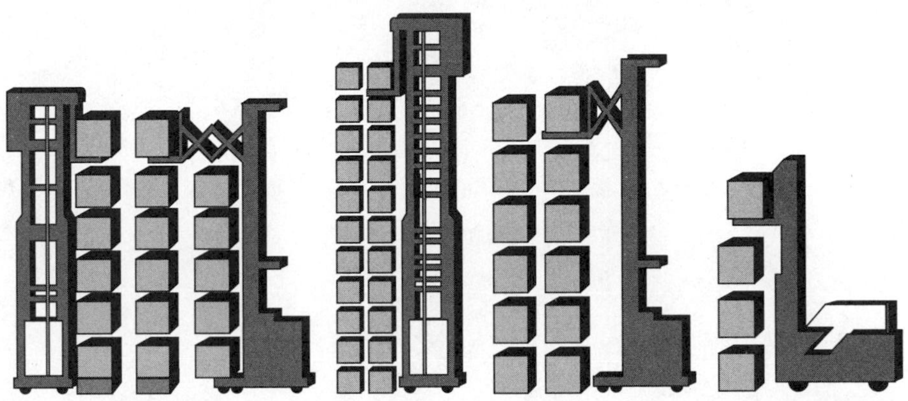

TYPE OF TRUCK	DEEP REACH	TURRET	REACH-FORK	COUNTER-BALANCED
Area required	5,550 sq. ft.	3,070 sq. ft.	6,470 sq. ft.	10,000 sq. ft.
Aisle width	102 inches	66 inches	96 inches	144 inches
Floor space saved	45%	70%	33%	———

SOURCE: James Aaron Cooke, "When to Choose a Narrow-Aisle Lift Truck," *Traffic Management* 28, no. 12 (December 1989), p. 55.

trucks, a firm can justify the acquisition of more expensive units when they are able to bring about more effective utilization of space. The four examples in Figure 8–2 illustrate the fact that warehouse layout and warehouse handling systems are integrally intertwined. The simplest type of forklift truck, the counterbalanced truck, requires 10,000 square feet of area and aisles that are 144 inches wide. At $20,000, it is the least expensive forklift. The turret truck requires only 3,070 square feet to handle the same amount of product but costs $100,000 or more.[4] The warehouse decision maker must examine the cost trade-offs involved for each of the variety of available systems, and determine which alternative is most advantageous from a cost/service perspective.

Impact of Demand on Warehouse Size

Demand also has an impact on warehouse size. Whenever demand fluctuates significantly or is unpredictable, inventory levels must be higher. This results in a need for more space and thus a larger warehouse. The

[4]See James Aaron Cooke, "When to Choose a Narrow-Aisle Lift Truck," *Traffic Management* 28, no. 12 (December 1989), p. 55.

FIGURE 8–3 The Relationship of Demand to Warehouse Size

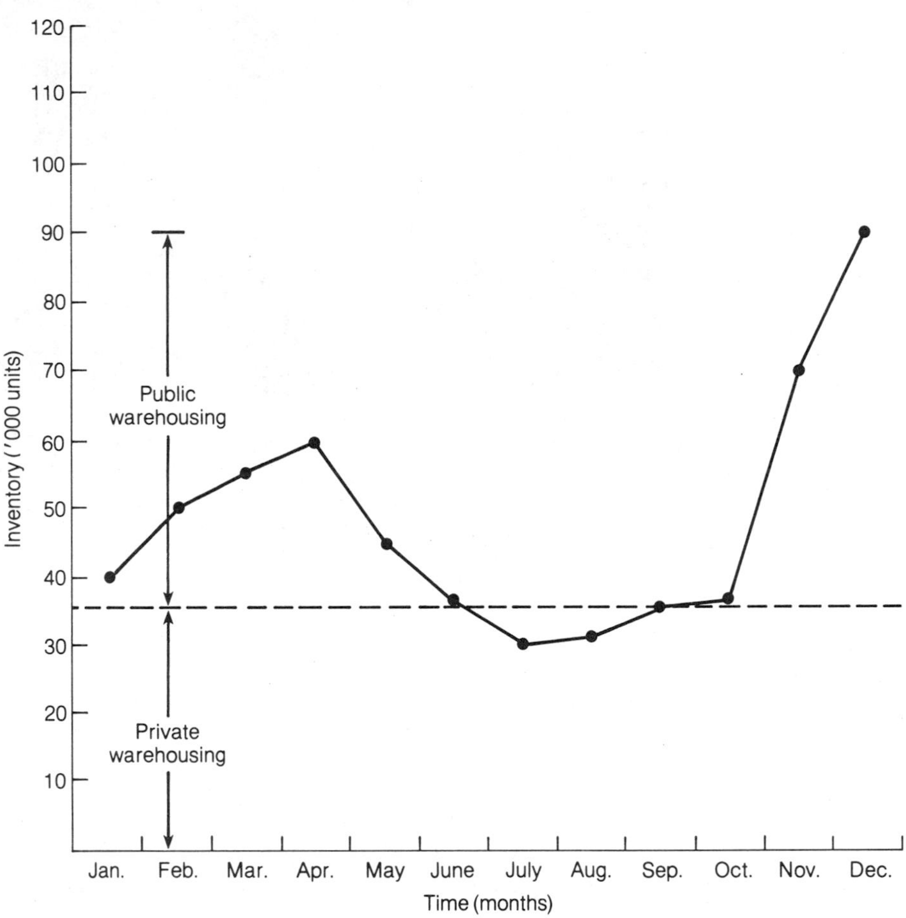

warehousing space need not all be private, however. Many firms utilize a combination of private and public warehousing. Figure 8–3 shows the relationship between demand and warehouse size. The hypothetical firm depicted in the figure utilizes private warehousing to store 36,000 units of inventory. This results in full utilization of its facilities all year, with the exception of July and August. For months in which inventory requirements exceed private warehousing space, the firm rents short-term storage from one or more public warehouses. In essence, the firm develops private facilities to accommodate a maximum level of inventory of 36,000 units.

Inventory velocity (as measured by turnover) and the maximization of "direct deliveries" to customers (bypassing a regional or wholesaler's warehouse) can also have great impact on the size of a warehouse. Whirlpool Corporation developed a computer program to simulate these two characteristics, as well as the warehousing space requirements (cube) of its total channel network (including wholesale distributors). The company calculated the square footage required for each of its factory-controlled and/or wholesale warehouses. It added space to the base requirements of each of its major product categories in order to provide for aisles and docks, as well as unused (empty) vertical and horizontal storage bays. By manipulating planned sales volumes, inventory turns, and bypassed orders shipped directly to dealers, it was able to accurately project future warehousing needs.[5]

A final illustration is the relationship of storage options (rack or floor storage) to warehouse size. Rack storage requires a smaller facility to store the same amount of product. A study of a wholesale drug operation found that rack storage was 10 percent more space-efficient and 7 percent cheaper than floor storage.[6]

Four Factors Affecting the Number of Warehouses

In deciding on the number of warehousing facilities, four factors are significant: cost of lost sales, inventory costs, warehousing costs, and transportation costs. Figure 8–4 depicts these cost areas, with the exception of cost of lost sales. Although lost sales are extremely important to a firm, they are the most difficult to calculate and predict, and they vary by company and industry. If the *cost of lost sales* appeared in Figure 8–4, it would generally slope down and to the right. The degree of slope, however, would vary.

The remaining components of the figure are more consistent across firms and industries. *Inventory costs* increase with the number of facilities, due to the fact that firms usually stock a minimum amount (safety stock) of all products at every location (although some companies have specific warehouses dedicated to a particular product or product grouping). This means that both slow and fast turnover items are stocked, and thus more total space is required. *Warehousing costs* also increase, because more warehouses mean more space to be owned, leased, or rented. The costs tend to increase at a decreasing rate after a number of warehouses are brought online, particularly if the firm leases or rents space. Public and contract warehouses often offer quantity discounts when firms acquire space in multiple locations.

Transportation costs initially decline as the number of warehouses increase. But they eventually curve upward if too many facilities are employed due to the combination of inbound and outbound transportation

---

[5]Illustration provided by Professor Jay U. Sterling, University of Alabama, and former director of logistics planning for Whirlpool Corporation.

[6]Krishan Kumar, "Warehouse Planning With or Without a Computer," *Industrial Engineering* 11, no. 8 (August 1979), p. 45; also see "Ingenious Rack Configuration Increases Storage," *Material Handling Engineering* 42, no. 7 (July 1987), p. 76.

FIGURE 8–4 Relationship between Total Logistics Cost and the Number of Warehouses

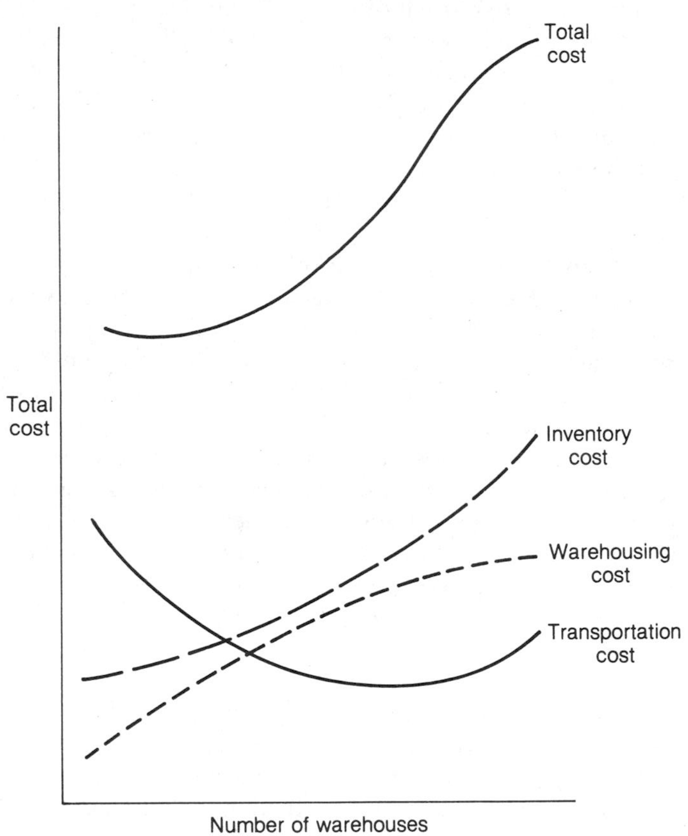

costs. A firm must be concerned with the total delivered cost of its products and not just the cost of moving products to warehouse locations. In general, the use of fewer facilities means bulk shipments from the manufacturer or supplier. The shipments typically are rated on a truckload (TL) or carload (CL) basis, which provide a lower cost per hundredweight. When customer orders arrive, products are then shipped out of the warehouse on a LTL (less-than-truckload) basis, but are rated higher. After the number of warehouses increases to a certain point, the firm may not be able to ship their products in such large quantities and may have to pay a higher rate to the transportation carrier. Local transportation costs for delivery of products from warehouses to customers may also increase because of minimum charges that apply to local cartage.

Customer Service Is the Most Important Component of the Marketing Mix

If the cost of lost sales is not included, the slopes of Figure 8–4, taken together, indicate that fewer warehouses are more optimal than many warehouses. However, customer service is perhaps the most important component of a firm's marketing and logistics systems. If the cost of lost sales is very high, a firm may wish to expand its number of warehouses. There are always cost/service trade-offs. Management must determine what level of customer service it desires and *only then* develop the optimal number of warehouses to service those customers.[7]

Other factors affecting the number of warehouses are the purchasing patterns of customers, the competitive environment, and the use of computers. If customers order small quantities on a frequent basis, the firm will sometimes need more warehouses located closer to the marketplace. A firm will usually also have more warehouses if the level of competition is high. When competitors offer rapid delivery to customers, a firm may be forced to match the service level unless it possesses some other differential advantage. If fast and efficient transportation and order communication are not available or are uncertain, then the only alternative might be additional warehouses. Computers can help minimize the firm's number of warehouses by improving warehouse layout and design, inventory control, shipping and receiving, and the dissemination of information. The substitution of information for inventories, coupled with more efficient warehouses, tends to reduce the number of warehouses needed to service a firm's customers.

Location Analysis

The site selection decision can be approached from macro and micro perspectives. The macro perspective examines the issue of where to locate warehouses geographically (in a general area) to improve the sourcing of materials and the firm's market offering (improve service and/or reduce cost). The micro perspective examines factors that pinpoint specific locations within the larger geographic areas.

In his macro approach, Edgar Hoover identified three types of location strategies: (1) market positioned, (2) production positioned, and (3) intermediately positioned.[8] The *market positioned* strategy locates warehouses nearest to the final customer. This maximizes customer service levels and enables the firm to utilize transportation economies—TL and CL shipments—from plants or sources to each warehouse location. The factors that influence the placement of warehouses near the market areas served include transportation costs, order cycle time, the sensitivity of the product,

Market Positioned Warehouses

[7]The reader may wish to refer back to Chapter 4 and review the discussion on cost/service trade-offs and the customer-product contribution matrix.

[8]Edgar M. Hoover, *The Location of Economic Activity* (New York: McGraw-Hill, 1948), p. 11.

order size, local transportation availability, and customer service levels offered.

Production Positioned Warehouses

Production positioned warehouses are located in close proximity to sources of supply or production facilities. These warehouses generally cannot provide the same level of customer service as that offered by market positioned warehouses; instead, they serve as collection points or mixing facilities for products manufactured at a number of different plants. For multiproduct companies, transportation economies result from consolidation of shipments into TL or CL quantities. The factors that influence the placement of warehouses close to the point of production are perishability of raw materials, number of products in the firm's product mix, assortment of products ordered by customers, and transportation consolidation rates.

Intermediately Positioned Warehouses

The final location strategy places warehouses at a midpoint between the final customer and the producer. Customer service levels for the *intermediately positioned* warehouses are typically higher than for the production positioned facilities and lower than market positioned facilities. A firm often follows this strategy if it must offer high customer service levels and if it has a varied product offering being produced at several plant locations.

Another macro approach is to locate facilities using one of three strategies:[9]

1. Product warehouse strategy.
2. Market area warehouse strategy.
3. General purpose warehouse strategy.

Product Warehouse Strategy

Under the *product warehouse strategy*, the firm places only one product or product grouping in a warehouse. Each warehouse will therefore have a lot of one type of product, but little or no inventory of other products. This can be a useful strategy when a firm has only a few products or product groupings that are high turnover items. If the company has important customers that demand a specific product in the market area being served by the warehouse, or if it manufactures products that have distinctly different transportation freight classifications and size/weight/loadability characteristics, it may also consider the product warehouse strategy. This strategy has also been used for new product introductions. Industries that employ this strategy include the farm equipment, appliance, electronics, apparel, and textile industries.

Market Area Warehouse Strategy

A *market area warehouse strategy* positions full line warehouses in specific market territories. Each facility stocks all the firm's products so that customers can receive complete orders from a single warehouse. Industries using this strategy include the beverage, food, paper products, glass, chemical, and furniture industries.

---

[9]This discussion is based on a manufacturing plant location strategy proposed in Roger W. Schmenner, *Making Business Location Decisions* (Englewood Cliffs, N.J.: Prentice Hall, 1982), pp. 11–15.

General Purpose Warehouse Strategy

The *general purpose warehouse strategy* is similar to the previous approach in that facilities carry a full line of products. It differs however, in that each warehouse serves all markets within a geographical market. Manufacturers of consumer packaged goods often employ this strategy.

A final macro approach includes the combined theories of a number of economic geographers. Many of these theories are based on distance and cost considerations. Von Thunen called for a strategy of facility location based on cost minimization.[10] Specifically, he argued, when locating points of agricultural production, transportation costs should be minimized to result in maximum profits for farmers. His model assumed that market price and production costs would be identical (or nearly so) for any point of production. Since farmer profits equal market price minus production costs and transportation costs, the optimal location would have to be the one that minimized transportation expenditures.

Von Thunen's Model

Weber's Model

Weber also developed a model of facility location based on cost minimization.[11] According to Weber, the optimal site was the location that minimized "total transportation costs—the costs of transferring raw materials to the plant and finished goods to the market."[12] Weber classified raw materials into two categories according to how they affected transportation costs: location and processing characteristics. Location referred to the geographical availability of the raw materials. For items with very wide availability, few constraints on facility locations would exist. Processing characteristics were concerned with whether the raw material increased, remained the same, or decreased in weight as it was processed. If it decreased, facilities would best be located near the raw material source because transportation costs of finished goods would be less with lower weights. Conversely, if processing resulted in heavier finished goods, facilities would be best located near final customers. If processing resulted in no change in weight, locating at raw material sources or markets for finished goods would be equivalent.

Hoover's Model

Other geographers included the factors of demand and profitability in the location decision. Hoover examined both cost and demand elements of location analysis.[13] Once again, his approach stressed cost minimization in determining an optimal location. Additionally, Hoover identified that transportation rates and distance were not linearly related; that is, rates increased with distance but at a decreasing rate. The tapering of rates over greater distances supported the placement of warehouses at the end points

[10] See *Von Thunen's Isolated State,* trans. C. M. Warnenburg and ed. Peter Hall (Oxford, Eng.: Pergamon Press, 1966).

[11] See *Alfred Weber's Theory of the Location of Industries,* trans. Carl J. Friedrich (Chicago: University of Chicago Press, 1929).

[12] John J. Coyle, Edward J. Bardi, and C. John Langley, Jr., *The Management of Business Logistics,* 5th ed. (St. Paul, Minn.: West Publishing, 1992) p. 448.

[13] See Hoover, *The Location of Economic Activity.*

of the channel of distribution rather that at some intermediate location. In that regard, Hoover did not fully agree with Weber's location choices.

Greenhut's Model

Greenhut expanded the work of his predecessors by including factors specific to the company (e.g., environment, security) and profitability elements in the location choice. According to Greenhut, the optimal facility location was the one that maximized profits.[14]

Another approach, simplistic in scope, locates facilities based on transportation costs. Termed the *center-of-gravity* approach, it locates a warehouse or distribution center at a point that minimizes transportation costs for products moving between a manufacturing plant and the market(s). This approach can be viewed rather simply. Envision two pieces of rope being tied together with a knot and stretched across a circular piece of board, with unequal weights attached to each end of the rope. Initially, the knot would be located in the center of the circle. Upon the release of weights, the rope would shift to the point where the weights would be in balance. Adding additional ropes with varying weights would result in the same shifting of the knot (assuming the knots were all in the same place). If the weights represented transportation costs, then the position where the knot would come to rest after releasing the weights would represent the center-of-gravity or position where transportation costs would be minimized.[15]
The approach provides general answers to the warehouse location problem, but it must be modified to take into account such factors as geography, time, and customer service levels.[16]

A Micro View of Location Analysis

From a micro perspective, more specific factors must be examined. If a firm wants to use private warehousing, it must consider:

- Quality and variety of transportation carriers serving the site.
- Quality and quantity of available labor.
- Labor rates.
- Cost and quality of industrial land.
- Potential for expansion.
- Tax structure.
- Building codes.
- Nature of the community environment.
- Costs of construction.
- Cost and availability of utilities.
- Cost of money locally.
- Local government tax allowances.

---

[14] See Melvin L. Greenhut, *Plant Location in Theory and in Practice* (Chapel Hill: University of North Carolina Press, 1956).

[15] For a similar discussion of the center-of-gravity approach, see Philip B. Schary, *Logistics Decisions* (Chicago, Ill.: Dryden Press, 1984), p. 423.

[16] See ibid., pp. 423–27.

If the firm wants to use public warehousing, it will be necessary to consider:

- Facility characteristics.
- Warehouse services provided.
- Availability and proximity to motor carrier terminals.
- Availability of local cartage.
- Other companies using the facility.
- Availability of computer services and communications.
- Type and frequency of inventory reports.

Benchmarks for Site Selection

Distribution Worldwide (now *Distribution*) magazine published one of the most comprehensive overviews of the warehouse site selection decision. The publication identified three primary considerations that needed to be examined when determining warehouse sites: (1) marketing aspects, (2) traffic (transportation economics), and (3) location or consolidation objectives.[17]

Schmenner proposed an eight-step approach to a business location search that we can apply to the warehouse site selection decision (see Figure 8–5).[18] It has been used to select a site or location for a facility. The process includes the following steps:

Schmenner's Eight-Step Approach to Site Selection

1. After the firm has made the initial decision to establish a facility at a new location (not yet determined), it solicits input from those persons in the company affected by the decision.
2. Management designates a corporate team to examine potential sites and to collect information on selected attributes, such as land availability, labor requirements, transportation options, utilities, environmental factors, and products to be stored.
3. The firm establishes a separate engineering team to examine potential sites in terms of topography, geology, and facility design.
4. Thc corporate team develops a list of key criteria for the new location. Such criteria take into account the needs of all functional areas of the business.
5. Geographic regions are evaluated in view of the key criteria established; potential regional sites are identified.
6. Specific sites within acceptable regional areas are identified. Typically, 10 or fewer sites are selected for in-depth investigation.
7. The corporate team examines each prospective site, using the set of factors deemed to be important. The team makes frequent site visits and creates a ranking of potential locations.

[17] "Benchmarks for Site Selection," *Distribution Worldwide* 75, no. 12 (December 1976), p. 36; also see "Basic Tools for Locating a Site," *Plants, Sites and Parks* (September/October 1989), pp. 46–63.

[18] Adapted from Schmenner, *Making Business Location Decisions,* pp. 16–21.

FIGURE 8–5 Approach to Site Selection*

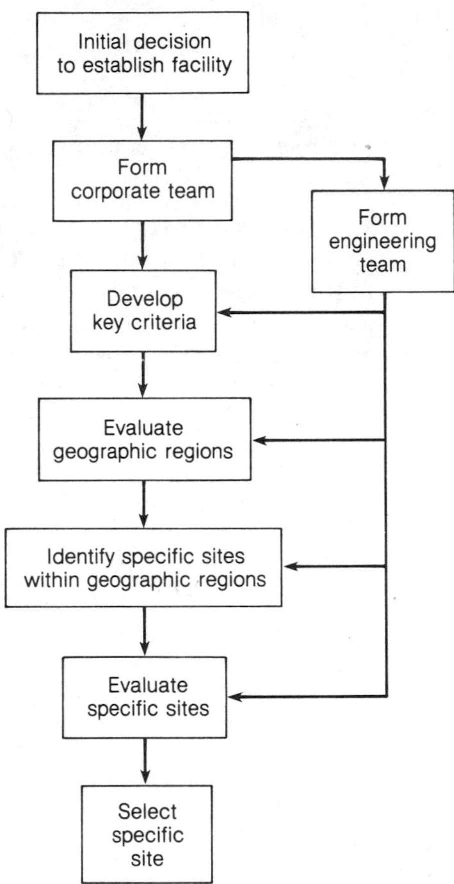

*Based on the site selection approach suggested by Schmenner.

8. A specific site is selected from the recommended locations. This decision is often made by the person most directly affected, normally the senior logistics executive.

Each step in the process is interactive, progressing from the "general" to the "specific." It may be a highly formalized or a very informal process. The process can also be centralized at the corporate level, decentralized at the divisional or functional level, or some combination of each. What is important, however, is that even with the differences that exist among companies, most firms follow some type of logical process when making a location decision.

Computer Modeling Approaches

In some cases, firms use computer modeling approaches. Computerized location models can be classified into four categories: planar models, warehousing models, network models, and discrete or mixed-integer programming models.[19]

Planar Models

Planar models are the simplest. They are optimization models in that they attempt to identify the best locations for the facilities:

> Typically a planar location problem involves the location of one or more new facilities in the plane, with costs incurred which depend upon an appropriately chosen "planar" distance (e.g., Euclidean distance) between the new facilities and existing facilities which have known planar locations. The new facilities are to be located so as to minimize an appropriately chosen total cost expression.[20]

Planar models can be very useful in identifying general locations for facilities and are widely used for this purpose. Identification of more specific locations usually involves more sophisticated modeling procedures.

Warehousing Models

Warehousing models are classified into two types: external location and internal location. External location models examine the issue of where to actually locate warehouses. Internal location models address the location of items inside the warehouse, that is, layout and design considerations (to be discussed in the next section of this chapter). The external models are often discrete or mixed-integer models, although they are often discussed separately.

Network Models

Network models are similar to planar models, with one important exception: Possible locations are constrained in that they must be on or near a transport network. While planar models identify optimal facility locations anywhere in the plane, network models only locate facilities on various transport networks such as roads, shipping lanes, rail lines, and air corridors. Therefore, the number of potential sites is more limited, although the sites determined by the model are much more realistic.

Discrete Models

Discrete models are the most realistic, but also the most complex, location models. They incorporate fixed and variable costs:

> To set up and operate a warehouse usually involves significant fixed costs that are not directly proportional to the level of activity. In many cases, the potential warehouse locations are limited to a few specific sites due to availability, capability, etc., and these sites each may have differing costs for acquiring the warehouse, differing costs for operating the warehouse, differing shipping costs, and differing capabilities. . . . With discrete location problems, we are not so much moving specified facilities about to find their best locations . . . as we are selecting a few facilities from a finite set of candidate facilities.[21]

---

[19] Richard L. Francis, Leon F. McGinnis, and John A. White, "Location Analysis," *European Journal of Operational Research* 12, no. 3 (March 1983), p. 220.

[20] Ibid., p. 222.

[21] Ibid., p. 240.

Because of their complexity and large data requirements, discrete models must employ a computer. They are, however, being used more frequently, as computers find widespread deployment in logistics.[22]

Related to the location of facilities is the decision to design an optimal structure that maximizes efficiency and effectiveness. This is the warehouse layout and design decision.

Warehouse Layout and Design

The Benefits of Good Warehouse Layout

Where should things be located in the logistics system—and more particularly, in the warehouse(s)? This consideration has a critical effect on system efficiency and productivity. A good warehouse layout can (1) increase output, (2) improve product flow, (3) reduce costs, (4) improve service to customers, and (5) provide better employee working conditions.[23] The following examples illustrate some of the considerations involved in effective warehouse layout:

A liquid and powdered bleach manufacturer is expanding a regional plant and warehouse by 50,000 square feet. *The problem:* What is the best location for the palletizers for each of the three primary products, and what is the best layout for the warehouse?

A multiproduct warehouse is served by numerous truck and rail docks. *The problem:* How to revise the layout to minimize the handling needed for storage and retrieval.

A paint manufacturer is planning a new warehouse for over 600 stockkeeping units (SKUs) of finished goods, with block storage for fastmovers plus racks and shelves for the rest. *The problem:* How to create a layout and handling system for two-year demand projections, and do it quickly, while also considering requirements for five years out.[24]

The optimal warehouse layout and design for a firm will vary by the type of product being stored, the company's financial resources, competitive environment, and needs of customers. In addition, the warehouse manager must consider the various trade-offs between labor costs, equip-

[22] Additional approaches to facility location are also being employed with the aid of computers, including linear programming (LP) methods, transshipment models, simulation, and dynamic programming. For an overview of many of these approaches, see Schary, *Logistics Decisions* (New York: Dryden Press, 1984), chap. 14.

[23] Mike Shumey, "Ways to Improve Productivity in a Physical Distribution Warehouse," in *Proceedings of the Sixteenth Annual Conference of the National Council of Physical Distribution Management,* 1978, p. 138; also see "Layout Principles that Upgrade Materials Flow," *Modern Materials Handling* 41, no. 13 (Fall 1986), pp. 25–27.

[24] James A. Tompkins and John A. White, "Location Analysis—More than Just Plant Layout!" *Modern Materials Handling* 32, no. 9 (September 1977), p. 64. *Modern Materials Handling,* copyright 1977 by Cahners Publishing Company, Division of Reed Holdings, Inc.

ment costs, space costs, and information costs. For example, as previously shown in Figure 8–2, the purchase of more expensive, yet more efficient, material handling equipment can affect the optimal size of a warehouse facility. Installation of an expensive conveyor system to reduce labor costs and raise productivity can affect the configuration of a warehouse. Considering all of the possible factors and their combinations, it is imperative that the firm develop an optimal warehousing system for itself using a logical and consistent decision strategy.

Warehouse Layout at Bergen Brunswig Corporation

Bergen Brunswig Corporation, a large U.S. firm distributing pharmaceuticals and hospital supplies, developed a seven-step approach to organized warehouse layout planning:

1. Obtain at least a five-year projection of product-line growth, or longer if available.
2. Analyze the product line, quantities moved, flow of material, and space required.
3. Analyze material handling equipment requirements.
4. Establish space requirements, including five-year projections when possible.
5. Establish relationships and closeness of all functions—shipping, receiving, order picking, packing, inventory storage, returned goods, and so forth.
6. Draw several overall alternative layouts.
7. Select the best layout and provide detailed layout.[25]

It is important that a firm establish some procedure, manual or computerized, to develop an effective and efficient warehouse layout.

Whatever layout the company finally selects for its warehouse, it is vital that all available space be utilized as fully and efficiently as possible. "Good space utilization practices begin with a layout design to provide the optimum balance between space utilization and handling efficiency."[26] Bergen Brunswig developed some useful guidelines, appropriate for all types of firms:

1. Space requirements for all products should be carefully calculated.
2. Make use of high-level storage, where practical.
3. Aisle dimensions are important. Aisles too narrow restrict flow of material and effective use of equipment. Aisles too wide simply waste space.
4. Make use of vertical overhead space for conveying material from one area to another.
5. Use mezzanines for order picking, or other warehousing functions.

---

[25] Shumey, "Ways to Improve Productivity," pp. 138–39.

[26] Ibid., p. 143.

6. Use space utilization standards to evaluate amount of space actually needed, amount of space used, and as a guide in evaluating expansion requirements.
7. Standards may be expressed as the ratio of cubic feet occupied to net usable storage space, or as percent of usable square feet to total space.[27]

Randomized Storage

Randomized and dedicated storage are two examples of how products can be located and arranged. *Randomized,* or floating slot storage, places items in the closest available slot, bin, or rack. They are then retrieved on a first-in, first-out (FIFO) basis. This approach maximizes space utilization, although it necessitates longer travel times between order-picking locations.[28] Randomized systems often employ a computerized AS/RS, which minimizes labor and handling costs.

Dedicated Storage

Another example is *dedicated* or fixed slot storage. In this approach, products are stored in permanent locations within the warehouse. Three methods can be used to implement the dedicated storage approach including storing items by (*a*) part number sequence, (*b*) usage rates, or (*c*) activity levels (e.g., "class-based storage by grouping products into classes or families based on activity levels, assigning fixed slot or dedicated storage zones for classes, and using floating slot or randomized storage within a zone").[29]

Compatibility

In terms of overall warehouse layout, products may be grouped according to their compatibility, complementarity, or popularity. *Compatibility* refers to how well products may be stored together. For example, pharmaceuticals cannot be stored with bagged agricultural chemicals because of U.S. Food and Drug Administration regulations. And many years ago, before the development of newer paints, it was discovered that automobile tires and consumer appliances could not be stored together. Apparently, chemical vapors given off by the tires reacted with the pigments in the appliance paint, resulting in slight color changes. Appliances then had to be repainted or sold at a discount.

Complementarity

Complementarity refers to how often products are ordered together and therefore stored together. Computer disc drives and monitors, pens and pencils, and desks and chairs are examples of complementary products that are usually stored in close proximity to each other.

Popularity

Popularity relates to the fact that products have different inventory turnover rates or demand rates. Another term used for this turnover rate is *velocity.* Therefore, items that are in greatest demand should be stored closest to shipping/receiving docks. Slow-moving items should be stored

---

[27] Ibid.

[28] For a discussion of random slotting techniques, see W. B. Semco, "Some Random Slotting Techniques to Consider," *Technical Paper No. 17,* Warehousing Education and Research Council (November 1984).

[29] Francis et al., "Location Analysis," p. 230.

elsewhere. For example, in a food wholesaler's warehouse, basic food items are stored close to the outbound shipping area, whereas slow movers are located in more remote areas of the warehouse.

Using the computer, it is possible to group products within a warehouse so that the following objectives are met:

Fast movers are placed nearest the outbound truck docks. This minimizes the distances traveled daily by material handling equipment.

Slow movers are located at points furthest from outbound shipping docks. This insures that lengthy horizontal moves by material handling equipment are minimized.

The middle area of the warehouse is reserved for products received in periodic batches, those requiring rework before shipping, those that are compatible with fast-moving products, and back-up overflow from fast moving areas.

Aisles are redesigned to facilitate the most efficient flow of product to and from dock areas.

Storage areas are configured to match the velocity and dimensions of each major product, rather than designing all storage bins, racks and floor storage areas in the same dimensions. This facilitates the maximum use of available cubic space, because products are not only matched to the width of each slot, but also the depth and height of each storage slot.

An Example of Warehouse Redesign

Figure 8–6 depicts a 40′ × 40′ storage area before and after redesign. In order to complete this warehouse interior redesign, all individual products (SKUs) were analyzed for a 12-month period. The following data were collected: total number of receipts and shipments; average size and frequency of receipts and shipments per day, week, and month; number of line items received and picked daily, weekly, and monthly; dimensions of the product; and material handling capacity.

Using this technique, a major manufacturer of consumer durable goods was able to increase the effective capacity of its major distribution center by 20 percent, and thereby forestall a planned expansion for several years. The firm also saved $200,000 per year in reduced labor and outside overflow warehousing.[30]

External Warehouse Layout

In addition to internal space layout, it is also important to analyze a warehouse's external configuration. Four aspects of external layout are critical: truck docks, rail requirements, external security measures, and physical features such as roof and windows.[31] Table 8–1 provides an example of

[30] Illustration provided by Professor Jay U. Sterling, University of Alabama, and former director of logistics planning for Whirlpool Corporation.

[31] Howard P. Weisz, "Analyzing Your Warehouse's External Layout," *WERC Memo No. 4*, March 1985, p. 1.

FIGURE 8–6 Two Warehouse Configurations

Before: Standard openings and depths are used for all products.

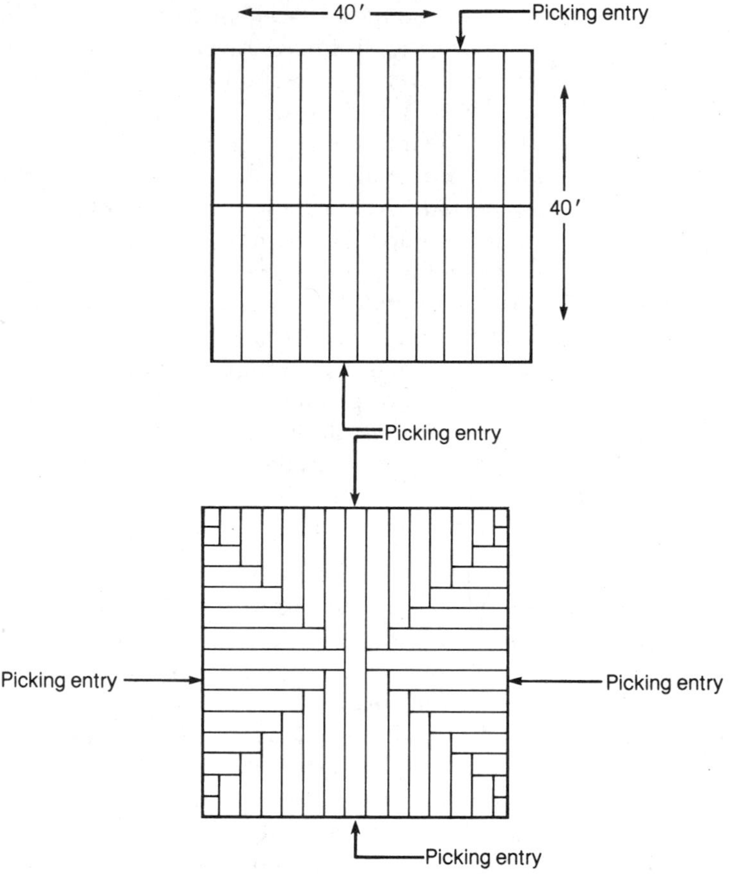

After: Both store widths and depths vary according to the volume (size) of receipts, velocity (frequency and size) of order pickups, and dimensions (widths) of the product.

SOURCE: Professor Jay U. Sterling, University of Alabama, and former director of logistics planning for Whirlpool Corporation.

TABLE 8–1 An Example of External Warehouse Layout Analysis: Truck Doors

Let's take a look at a hypothetical warehouse which handles 6,000,000 cases per year. This warehouse operates two shifts a day, five days a week. Seventy percent of inbound shipments are via truck; 90 percent of outbound shipments are via truck.

Trucks are unloaded at a rate of 200 cases per worker-hour for inbound shipments, and loaded at a rate of 175 cases per worker-hour for outbound shipments. Both inbound and outbound trucks are loaded with 500 cases. A 25 percent safety factor is desired due to the fact that the flow of trucks throughout the month is apt not to be uniform.

To determine the number of truck doors, you can work through the following calculations:

Step I: Determine Inbound Requirements

a. Percent inbound via truck × total inbound
   70 percent × 6,000,000 = 4,200,000 cases
b. Inbound cases/cases per truck
   4,200,000/500 = 8,400 inbound trucks
c. Hours per truck
   Cases per truck/inbound productivity
   500/200 = 2.5 hours per inbound truck
d. Total inbound truck hours (b × c)
   8,400 × 2.5 = 21,000 hours/year

Step II: Determine Outbound Requirements

a. Percent outbound via truck × total outbound
   90 percent × 6,000,000 = 5,400,000
b. Outbound cases/cases per truck
   5,400,000/500 = 10,800 trucks
c. Hours per truck
   Cases per truck/outbound productivity
   500/175 = 2.85 hours per outbound truck
d. Total outbound truck hours (b × c)
   10,800 × 2.85 = 30,780 hours/year

Step III: Total Hours Required

Inbound hours	21,000 hours
Outbound hours	30,780 hours
Subtotal	51,780 hours
Safety factor for peaking (25 percent)	21,945 hours
Total hours	64,725 hours

Step IV: Hours Available per Year

52 Weeks × hours per day × days per week
52 × 16 (2 shifts) × 5 = 4,160

Step V: Doors Required

Truck hours required/annual hours available
64,725 hours/4,160 hours = 15.5 or 16 doors

SOURCE: Howard P. Weisz, "Analyzing Your Warehouse's External Layout," *WERC Memo No. 4*, March 1985, pp. 1–2. Used with permission of Warehousing Education and Research Council, Inc.

the type of analysis that must be performed to determine the optimal external layout of a warehouse. Similar analyses can be done for most facets of warehouse layout and design.

The entire area of facilities development—size and number of warehouses, location analysis, warehouse layout and design—is an important, yet complex, part of warehouse management. In recent years computers have played a much more significant role, as logistics executives attempt to optimize warehouse operations.

PACKAGING

Packaging is an important warehousing and materials management concern, one that is closely tied to warehouse efficiency and effectiveness. The best package optimizes service, cost, and convenience. Good packaging can have a positive impact on layout and design—and overall warehouse productivity.

Packaging Performs Marketing and Logistics Functions

Packaging serves two basic functions: marketing and logistics. In its marketing function, the package provides customers with information about the product and promotes the product through the use of color, sizing, and so forth. "The [package] is the 'silent sales[person],' and it is the final interface between the company and its consumers. . . . Consumers generally choose to buy from the image they perceive that a product has, and what they perceive is heavily influenced by the cues given on the product's packaging: brand name, color and display."[32]

From a logistics perspective, the function of packaging is to

> organize, protect, and identify products and materials. In performing its function it also takes up space and adds weight. Industrial users of packaging strive to gain the advantages packaging offers while minimizing the disadvantages, such as added space and weight. We are getting closer to that ideal in several types of packaging, including corrugated containers, foam-in-place packaging, stretch wrapping, and strapping.[33]

Six Functions of Packaging

More specifically, packaging performs six functions:

> Containment—Products must be contained before they can be moved from one place to another.
>
> Protection—To protect [the] contents from outside environmental effects . . . and to protect the environment from the product.
>
> Apportionment—Reducing the output from industrial production to a manageable, desirable "consumer" size.
>
> Unitization—Permitting primary packages to be unitized into secondary packages (e.g., placed inside a corrugated case) and then for these secondary packages to be unitized into a tertiary package (e.g., a stretch-wrapped pallet).
>
> Convenience—allowing products to be used conveniently.
>
> Communication—the use of unambiguous, readily understood symbols is imperative.[34]

---

[32] Rod Sara, "Packaging as a Retail Marketing Tool," *International Journal of Physical Distribution and Logistics Management* 20, no. 8 (1990), p. 30.

[33] "Packaging Trends: Higher Strength, More Performance," *Modern Materials Handling* 40, no. 3 (March 1985), p. 70.

[34] Gordon L. Robertson, "Good and Bad Packaging: Who Decides?" International *Journal of Physical Distribution and Logistics Management* 20, no. 8 (1990), pp. 38–39.

TABLE 8–2 Factors That Influence Package Design Decisions

Factor	*Percent of Firms Mentioning the Factor*
Minimize damage to package contents	77%
Minimize shipping/packaging cost	73
Design package for handling with lift trucks	63
Protect contents of package from shock, impact	63
Minimize shipping cost	55
Meet carriers' requirements	47
Identification of contents	43
Weights and shapes appropriate for manual handling	41
Column strength of package, for stacking	41
Meet needs for export	40
Meet customer's specifications	39
Compatibility with existing handling and warehousing systems	37
Protection from external moisture	36
Conform to regulations on hazardous materials	36
Dimensions for good pallet patterns	35
Protection of contents from vibration	33
Dimensions for best use of space in trucks, railcars, etc	33

SOURCE: John F. Spencer, "A Picture of Packaging in the Context of Physical Distribution," *Handling & Shipping* 18, no. 10 (October 1977), p. 47.

The package should be designed to provide the most efficient storage. Good packaging "affects materials handling in terms of load stability and compatibility with the different forms of mechanization and automation. . . . It satisfies warehousing requirements through dimension and stackability for good pallet patterns and efficient storage."[35] Spencer noted that business suffers by not giving sufficient attention to packaging issues:

> It may be that the packaging trade-offs are the least used trade-offs in [logistics]. Package an item one way and you can safely expose it to shock, vibration, weather, soiling, and no harm will be done to it—that kind of packaging can save in transportation costs. Package another way, and you save on packaging, but you must spend more for better storage conditions, vehicles that cause less shock and vibration, more careful handling; the extra costs may be offset a little by lighter weight and smaller space requirements. Does industry look at these opportunities? Or does it pass them by, satisfied with conventional acceptance of packaging as it is?[36]

Factors of Good Package Design

In a study of a variety of industries, *Handling & Shipping* magazine asked companies to identify the factors governing good package design. Table 8–2 identifies the factors business firms mentioned most frequently.

---

[35] Walter F. Friedman, "The Total Package," *Distribution Worldwide* 74, no. 2 (February 1975), p. 53.

[36] John F. Spencer, "A Picture of Packaging in the Context of Physical Distribution," *Handling & Shipping* 18, no. 10 (October 1977), p. 43.

The factors can be conveniently categorized into the following characteristics: (1) standard quantities, (2) pricing (cost), (3) product or package adaptability, (4) protective level, (5) handling ability, and (6) product packability. The importance a firm places on each of the factors in the table (as well as the cost/service trade-offs it makes) varies by industry. For example, because of the difference in products (cost and physical characteristics), a food processor is more concerned than a computer manufacturer with having a package that minimizes shipping and storage costs. A computer manufacturer emphasizes the protective aspects of packaging because of the fragile, expensive nature of computer systems.

The distribution package is the result of many components of the firm's operations (see Figure 8–7).

Developing the Optimal Distribution Package

What is involved in designing the distribution package?

The ultimate goal is to develop a package that optimizes service, cost, and convenience factors for all elements of the marketing and logistics system. In the broadest approach, distribution packaging begins with the design of the product, and it ends with the re-use or disposal of the package.

More narrowly, it concentrates on the shipping container—which might be a corrugated box, cargo cage, van container, truck, covered hopper, or tank car. It also covers any inner containers or protectors, as well as the individual consumer package.

Design of the distribution package involves proper product identification with the size, type, and location of the item code or Universal Product Code and with other package information to assure correct selection, sorting, and shipping. It relates to transportation through package density and efficient cube use; it satisfies warehousing requirements through dimension and stackability for good pallet patterns and efficient storage; it also affects materials handling in terms of load stability and compatibility with the different forms of mechanization and automation; it has impact on the customer's distribution system in terms of the ability to receive and integrate merchandise with [the] warehouse operating system, particularly with less-than-full-case order picking.

The interactions of distribution packaging become complex with product protection, which applies not only in the manufacturer warehouse but also in rail or truck or other forms of transport, in the customer warehouse with many different forms of mechanized or automated materials handling, and in the consumer outlet or other end-use environment.

Distribution packaging must also consider total distribution costs, including freight rates, handling, and storage efficiency, and end-use costs of opening and disposal of the package and assembly or other preparation of the product.

The intangibles of the distribution package are important in terms of customer convenience—those hard-to-measure end-use benefits that allow smooth interface with merchandising, production, or other aspects of the customer's distribution system.

The cost of materials and producing a package, of course, is also a prime factor in any packaging system, but the optimum system is one that considers all the requirements we have outlined at the lowest total cost. Obviously, this involves a good deal more than simple design.

FIGURE 8–7 The Distribution Package

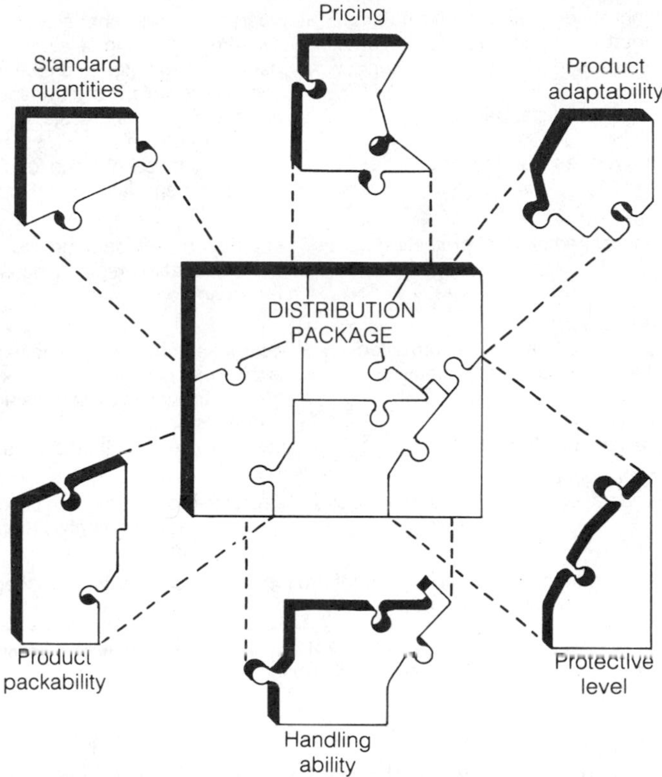

The distribution package is the result of many interactions and must be looked at in terms of the total picture for full efficiency.

SOURCE: Walter F. Friedman, "The Total Package," *Distribution Worldwide* 74, no. 2 (February 1975), p. 55.

It means that you have to mediate conflicts, evaluate trade-offs, and reach a fair balance. It means that you have to question basic manufacturing, marketing, and distribution assumptions so that invalid claims can be eliminated in favor of meaningful requirements.

It means that you have to measure warehousing and transportation and handling costs against packaging costs and all of them against product protection. And it means that you have to weigh manufacturing efficiencies and marketing decisions against distributor and retailer needs. It means that you have to be willing to pay a premium in one area in order to introduce badly needed benefits in another area—and thereby gain a very real marketing edge.[37]

[37] Ibid., p. 54. Reprinted with permission from the October 1977 issue of *Handling & Shipping*. Copyright © Penton Publishing.

TABLE 8–3 Packaging Cost Trade-Offs with Other Logistics Functions

Transportation:
- Increased package information.......decreases shipment delays.
- Increased package information.......decreases tracking of lost shipments.
- Increased package protection........decreases damage and theft in transit but increases package weight and transport cost.
- Increased standardization ....decreases handling costs, vehicle waiting time for loading/unloading.
- Increased standardization ....increases modal choices for shipper and decreases need for specialized transport equipment.

Inventory:
- Increased product protection.........decreases theft, damage, insurance; increases product availability (sales); increases product value and carrying costs.

Warehousing:
- Increased package information.......decreases order filling time, labor cost.
- Increased product protection.........increases cube utilization (stacking); but decreases cube utilization by increasing the size of the product dimensions.
- Increased standardization ....decreases material handling equipment costs.

Communications:
- Increased package information.......decreases other communications about the product such as telephone calls to track down lost shipments.

Logistics functions of packaging: Informs; protects; standardizes package dimensions; enhances handling efficiency.

SOURCE: Professor Robert L. Cook, Department of Marketing and Hospitality Services Administration, Central Michigan University, Mt. Pleasant, Mich., 1991.

Packaging and Logistics Cost Trade-Offs

Some examples of the packaging and logistics cost trade-offs are shown in Table 8–3. As identified in the table, there are many important interfaces between packaging and areas such as transportation, inventory, warehousing, and information systems.[38]

Of course, there are other factors that influence the product package, such as the channel of distribution and/or institutional requirements.

> It was required that some make-up and cosmetic products be packaged in blister containers of a certain size due to the way these products were displayed by retailers. In the oil industry there was difficulty in selling the concept of oil packaged in plastic bottles. Initially, retailers did not want to stock the product, as they felt that the old cardboard cans made better use of shelf space. Another example is that of compact discs (CDs) and how they are packaged. One of the major requirements was that the new CDs be able to utilize the old racks used by retailers for albums. In addition, there was the issue of security and anti-shoplifting. The larger packages, even though they wasted materials, were

[38] For specific company examples, see "Foam Protection Serves Electronic Parts Well," *Transportation & Distribution* 29, no. 3 (March 1989), pp. 57–58; and Helen L. Richardson, "Stop Damage at the Source," *Transportation & Distribution* 29, no. 3 (March 1989), pp. 30–32.

difficult to conceal than the bare CDs in their "jewel boxes." In these examples, least-cost packaging was traded off for other considerations.[39]

Procter & Gamble is one firm that has examined the full implications of the packaging decision. The company developed a program called "Direct Product Profitability" which examined packaging costs through the entire channel of distribution. Some of the results achieved by P&G included the following:

Packaging at Procter & Gamble

An Ivory shampoo bottle was redesigned in a squarer configuration that took up less space and saved distributors 29 cents per case.

Tide powder detergent was reformulated so that P&G was able to shrink the size of the box without reducing the number of washings per box. P&G was able to pack 14 boxes in a case instead of 12, thus reducing handling and storage.[40] During 1990, the firm introduced an even smaller package, while keeping a comparable number of wash loads yet reducing the case size.

Packaging, warehouse handling systems, and all warehousing operations are interrelated within the firm's logistics system, and all must be managed effectively.

COMPUTER TECHNOLOGY, INFORMATION, AND WAREHOUSE MANAGEMENT

We saw in Chapter 7 that the basic functions of warehousing were movement, storage, and information transfer. In each of those areas the use of computer technology has become widespread. Most warehouse activities and functions rely on computers.

Benefits of Computerization

A study of approximately 1,000 manufacturing and nonmanufacturing companies conducted by *Modern Materials Handling* found that "companies of all sizes using computers report significant gains in production planning and control and inventory management."[41] Approximately one quarter of all companies surveyed achieved gains of more than 20 percent in decreased materials cost and increased labor productivity with computerization. Between one-third and one-half of the firms achieved similar results through increased inventory turns and customer service.[42] The majority of the benefits resulted from computerization of order entry,

---

[39] Examples provided by Dr. William A. Cunningham, Associate Professor of Marketing and Transportation, and Director of the Alabama Waterways and Transportation Research Center, University of South Alabama.

[40] "Packaging/Handling Interaction Gets a Boost," *Material Handling Engineering* 40, no. 3 (March 1985), p. 48.

[41] "Computers Take Control in Manufacturing and Warehousing," *Modern Materials Handling* 39, no. 17 (November 19, 1984), p. 46.

[42] Ibid., p. 47.

FIGURE 8–8 Computers Throughout the Warehouse

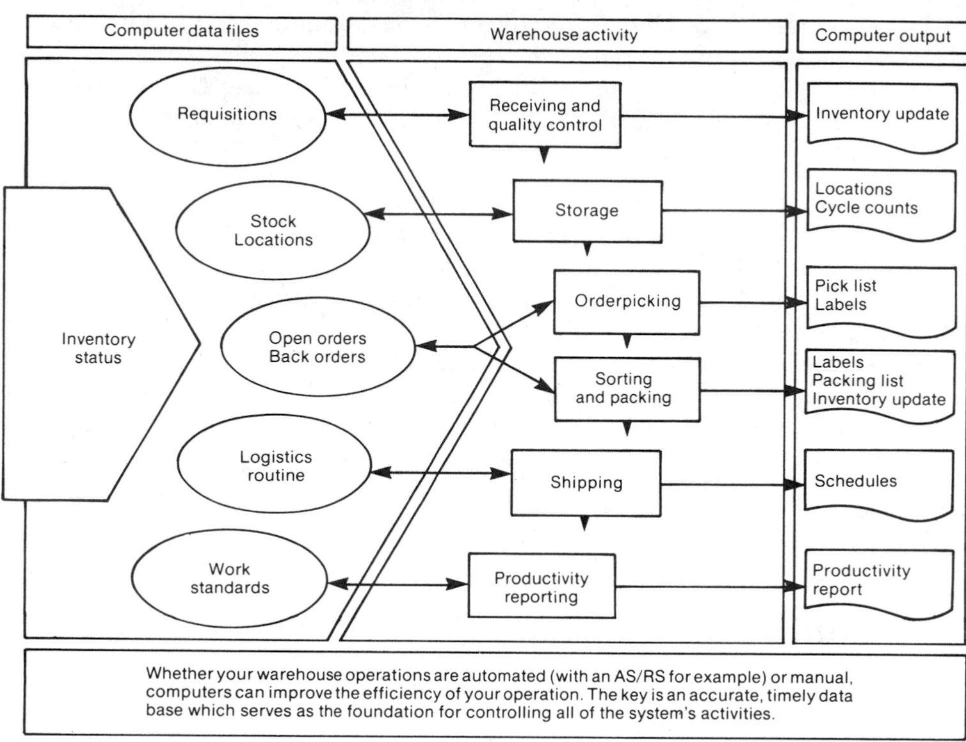

SOURCE: "Increase Productivity with Computers and Software," *Modern Materials Handling—1986 Warehousing Guidebook* 41, no. 4 (Spring 1986), p. 68. *Modern Materials Handling*, copyright 1986 by Cahners Publishing Company, Division of Reed Holdings, Inc.

inventory control, invoicing, purchasing, production planning, and stock location.

In the future, warehousing will move toward more and more computer utilization. The fully computerized warehouse will likely have a structure similar to that shown in Figure 8–8, where all activities of the warehouse interface with the system, including receiving, quality control, storage, order picking, error control, packing, and shipping.[43] Significant advantages will result, including improved customer service, lower costs, and more efficient and effective operations.

Computers at General Motors

Many firms have used computer systems to control the movement of product in the warehouse. General Motors' Warren, Michigan, Hydramatic transmission plant utilizes a network of programmable computers to op-

[43] Jerry P. Porter, "Using the Computer as an Inexpensive Tool to Improve the Warehouse System," *Industrial Engineering* 13, no. 6 (June 1981), p. 58.

erate a system that includes "2½ miles of conveyor with numerous switches and in-process queues, 22 pick-and-place robots, and 25 multistation machining centers in four interconnected production lines."[44]

Computers at Associated Grocers of Colorado

Associated Grocers of Colorado, Inc., has a computerized system that controls a variety of racking, conveyor, and automatic identification equipment in its distribution center.[45] Approximately 6,000 SKUs of dry grocery products are stored in the facility. Employees pick merchandise from a pick module (rack storage area) and physically apply bar code labels to the items. They then place the items on a belt conveyor, where they are moved to a merge and sorting area on an upper mezzanine. Bar code readers divert items to the proper conveyor lane, which transports them to floor level.[46] There they are palletized and loaded into trucks for delivery to customers. With the exception of the manual order-picking activity, almost all of the process is computer-controlled.

Computers at IBM

We discussed computer control of the storage function in Chapter 7. Most AS/RSs are controlled by some type of computer system. The IBM warehouse in North Carolina illustrates the use of a computerized AS/RS:

> At this warehouse, small parts are stored in a 25-foot high, five-aisle miniload AS/R system. Other incoming materials are stored in a high-rack system, served by counterbalanced sideloading trucks.
>
> For both storage systems, a large central computer maintains inventory records, assigns storage locations to incoming materials, and generates picking instructions. But the miniload AS/R machines are computer-controlled by a minicomputer that's off-line to the central computer. This minicomputer controls the onboard microcomputers that operate the motors on each AS/R machine.[47]

Since 1970, the most significant advances in computerization have occurred in the information transfer area. The movement and storage functions require computerization at the mechanical level—where machines and equipment are utilized. There is also an electronic level, which requires computer-to-computer interface and involves data transmission.[48]

Information is the key to successful warehouse management. However, many warehousing operations exhibit symptoms resulting from a lack of information. Not many warehouse managers operate in a total information vacuum, but many information gaps exist in warehousing operations. Fig-

---

[44] "Real-Time Monitoring at GM for Efficiency in Automation," *Modern Materials Handling* 39, no. 18 (December 10, 1984), p. 42.

[45] "How We Use Computers to Manage Distribution," *Modern Materials Handling* 40, no. 5 (April 1985), p. 78.

[46] For an interesting application of bar codes, see Gene Schwind, "Automatic Identification Gets Bottom-Line Results," *Material Handling Engineering* 40, no. 3 (March 1985), pp. 95–100.

[47] "Minicomputers as Directors of Materials Flow," *Modern Materials Handling* 35, no. 9 (September 1980), p. 78.

[48] See "Local Area Networks—The Crucial Element in Factory Automation," *Modern Materials Handling* 39, no. 7 (May 7, 1984), pp. 50–55.

ure 8–9 identifies several gaps that can occur in a typical warehouse within the areas of receiving, put-away, storage, order picking, packing and marking, staging and, shipping.[49] As indicated in the figure, a number of symptoms result from information gaps.

The Importance of Information

The importance of information in warehouse management is significant. Accurate and timely information allows a firm to minimize inventories, to improve routing and scheduling of transportation vehicles, and to generally improve customer service levels. A typical warehouse management system achieves these improvements in three ways: (1) by reducing direct labor, (2) by increasing material handling equipment efficiency, and (3) by increasing warehouse space utilization.

> This has brought about the rapid development of industrial networks—a hardware and software solution that interconnects computers, peripherals, programmable controllers, and other intelligent devices, and in effect the handling and storage equipment they control, so that they share hardware, software, and data.[50]

Networks are communications systems that allow transmission of data between a number and variety of devices such as terminals, word processors, bar code readers, robots, conveyors, automatic guided vehicles, and AS/RSs. A *local area network (LAN),* which devices are located in close proximity to one another, is typically used in warehousing.[51] Figure 8–10 shows an example of a local area network.

Local Area Network (LAN)

There are three basic ways in which devices (referred to as stations) can be attached to a LAN:

The star typology is the simplest. Every station on the network is connected directly to the central computer controller. If it breaks down, the entire network goes down.

The ring typology connects stations in a daisy chain configuration. If a single station breaks down, the entire network is liable to go down.

The bus typology consists of any number of stations connected to a single cable. This network fails only if there's a break or a short in the bus, or if an interface jams the bus by transmitting continuously.[52]

Whichever approach a firm uses, the objectives are the same—to provide better control over information flows and to allow the warehouse facility to maximize its effectiveness and efficiency. Figure 8–11 "illustrates how each warehouse activity generates documents containing data which aid in per-

---

[49] Ernst and Whinney, *Warehouse Accounting and Control: Guidelines for Distribution and Financial Managers* (Oak Brook, Ill.: National Council of Physical Distribution Management, and New York: National Association of Accountants, 1985), p. 82.

[50] "Local Area Networks," p. 50.

[51] See "A Trend to Tighter Control with Computer Networks," *Modern Materials Handling* 40, no. 1 (January 1985), pp. 74–77.

[52] "Local Area Networks," p. 53.

FIGURE 8–9 Information Gap Symptoms

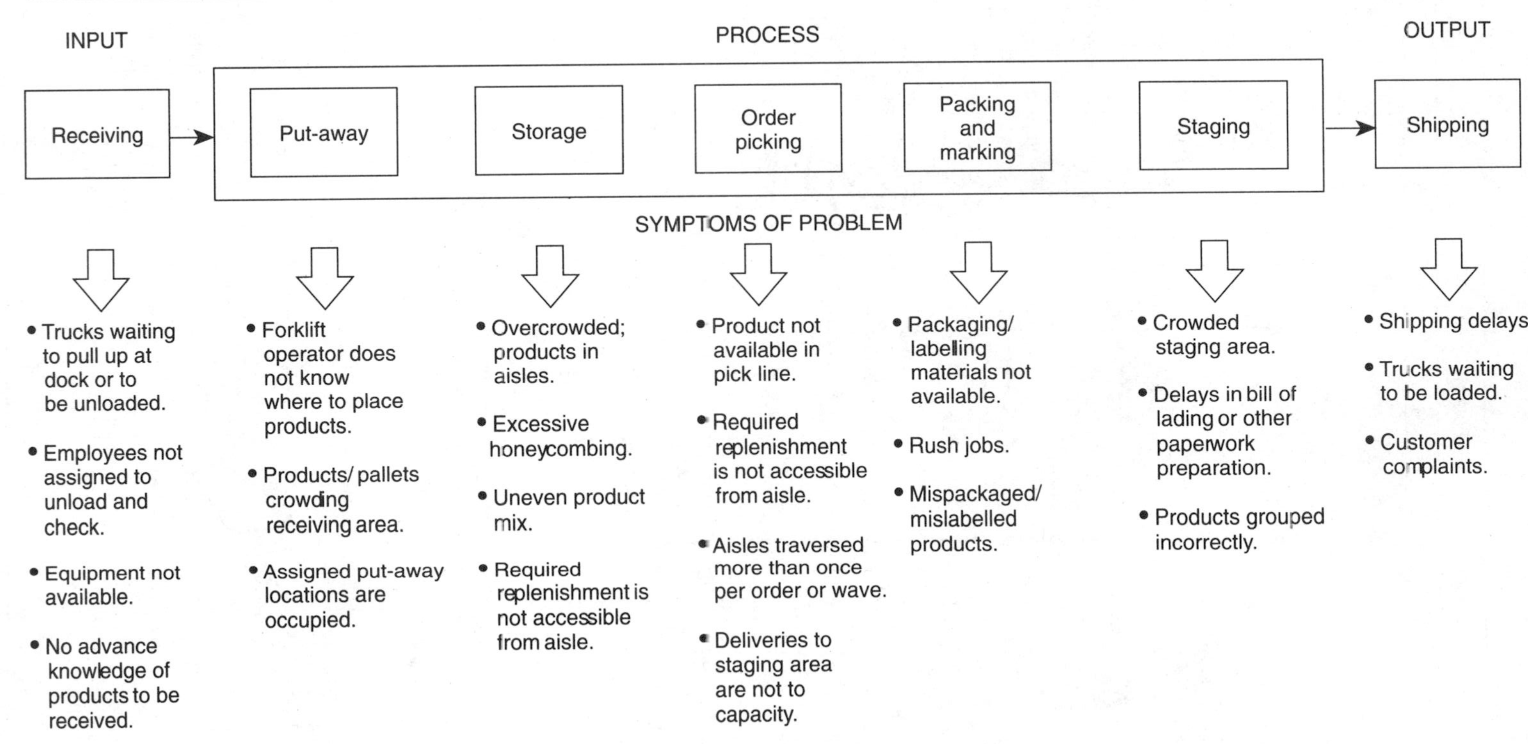

SOURCE: Ernst and Whinney, *Warehouse Accounting and Control: Guidelines for Distribution and Financial Managers* (Oak Brook, Ill.: National Council of Physical Distribution Management, and New York: National Association of Accountants, 1985), p. 82.

FIGURE 8–10 A Local Area Network (LAN) Example

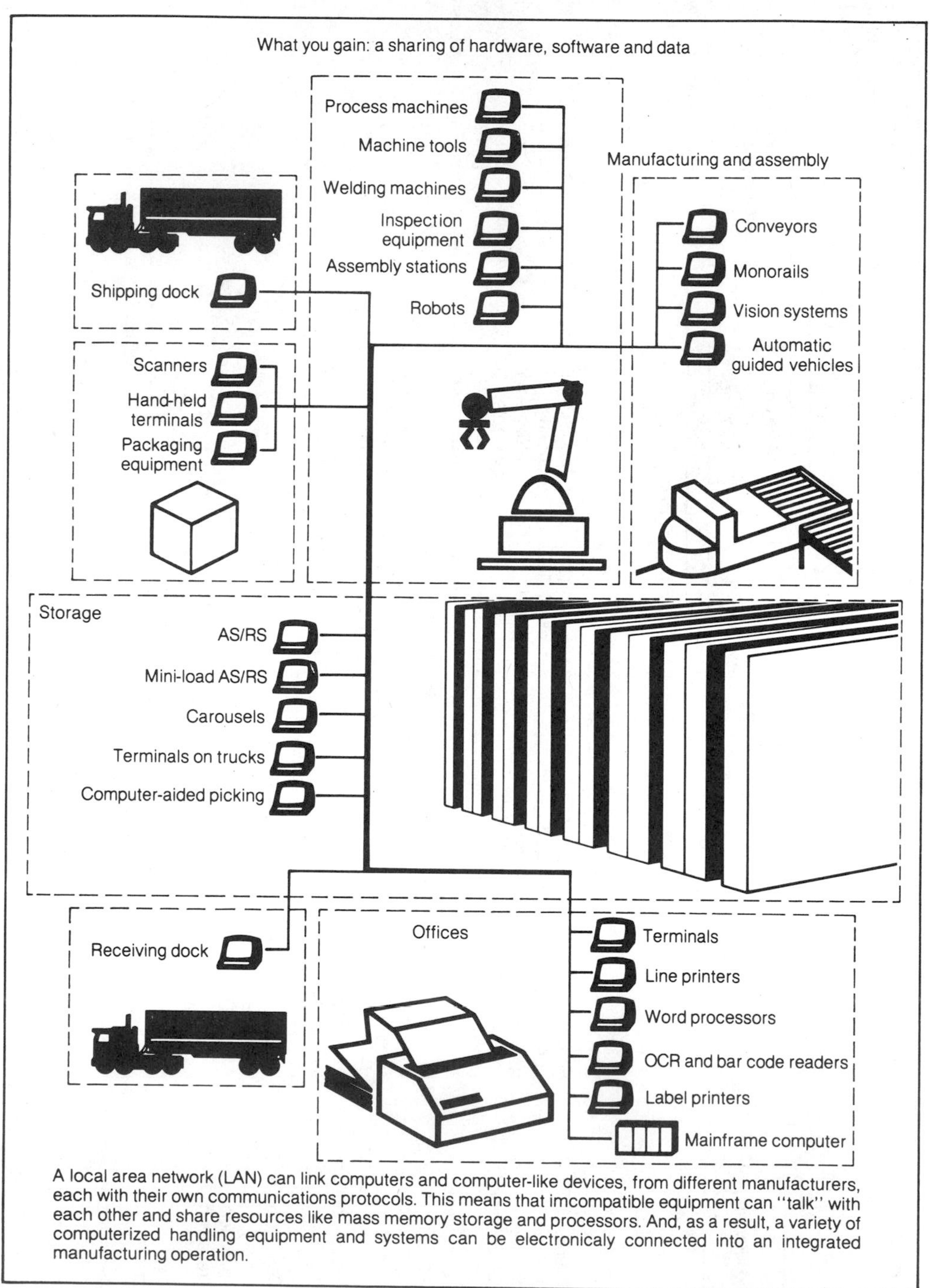

A local area network (LAN) can link computers and computer-like devices, from different manufacturers, each with their own communications protocols. This means that imcompatible equipment can "talk" with each other and share resources like mass memory storage and processors. And, as a result, a variety of computerized handling equipment and systems can be electronicaly connected into an integrated manufacturing operation.

SOURCE: "Local Area Networks—The Crucial Element in Factory Automation," *Modern Materials Handling* 39, no. 7 (May 7, 1984), p. 51. *Modern Materials Handling,* copyright 1984 by Cahners Publishing Company, Division of Reed Holdings, Inc.

FIGURE 8–11 Sample Warehouse Operations and Data Flow

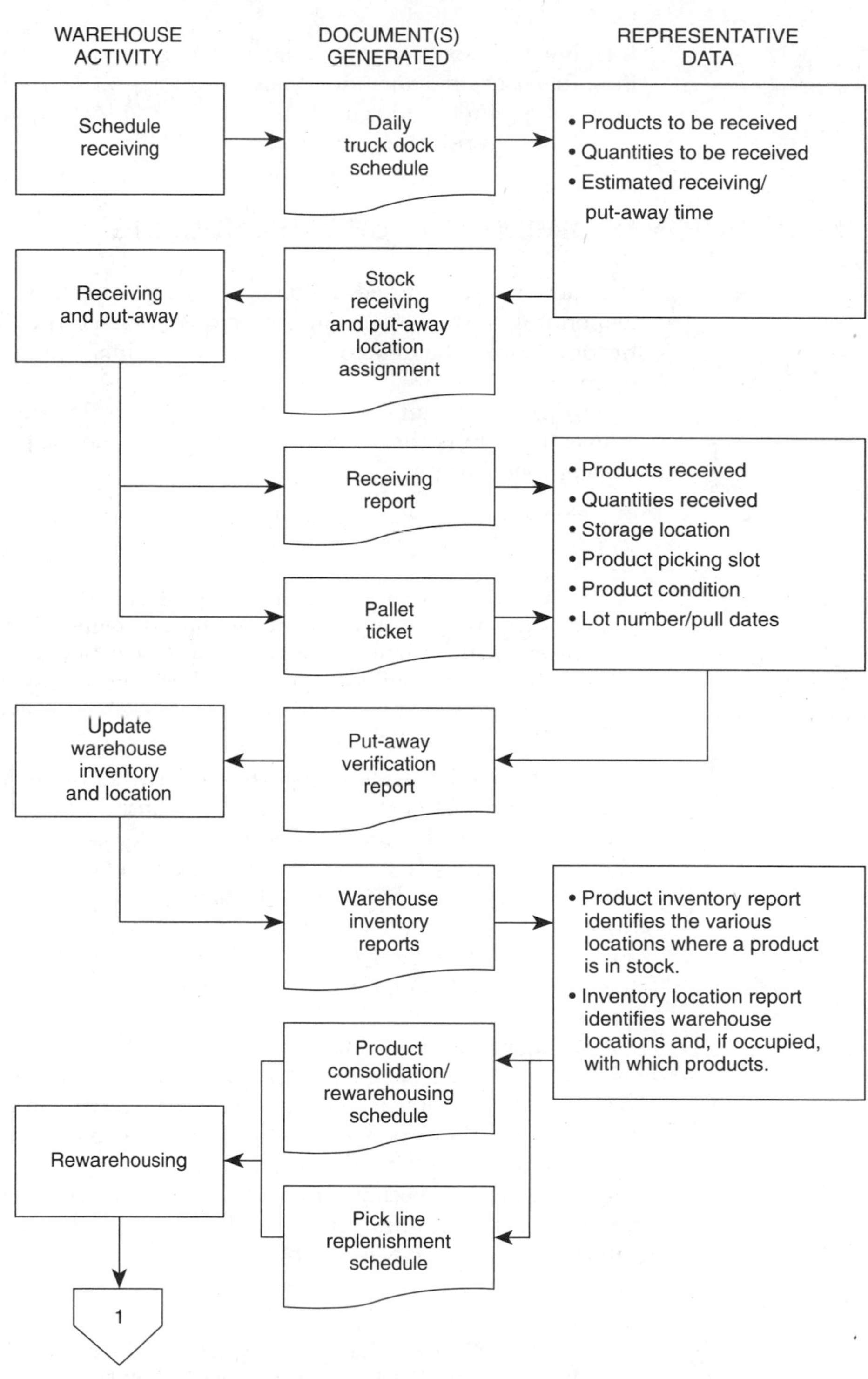

SOURCE: Ernst and Whinney, *Warehouse Accounting and Control: Guidelines for Distribution and Financial Managers* (Oak Brook, Ill.: National Council of Physical Distribution Management, and New York: National Association of Accountants, 1985), p. 85.

forming the next activity in the warehouse. Throughout the operations flow, the associated documents and their integral data elements can be used to develop timely and reliable management information . . . for recording . . . planning and scheduling operations."[53]

INTERNATIONAL DIMENSIONS OF WAREHOUSING

Products must be stored at some point prior to their final consumption. Depending on the particular conditions in effect in each foreign market, products may be stored at different points within the channel of distribution.

In the European Common Market, Philips, a large multinational electronics firm, must store and warehouse a variety of products at factories throughout Europe.

Philips Uses "Eurostores"

> Philips has poured impressive sums into the establishment of superautomated international distribution centers; or "Eurostores," for each of its product divisions.
>
> A typical Eurostore is that of Philips' Lighting Division, located in the Dutch city of Roosendaal. Its stars are an immense high-bay warehouse and an all-encompassing computer system that runs the entire operation on an "ORFO" ("ORder to FOrwarding") basis. The Eurostore is a study in quiet, rhythmic efficiency, with human management evident only at critical monitoring locations.[54]

If a firm is involved in exporting, it may store items domestically and ship them only after it receives orders. Thus, no foreign storage is necessary. However, if distributors or other types of intermediaries are used, inventories will have to be stored or warehoused at other locations within the channel. The ability of the manufacturer or supplier to push the inventory down the channel of distribution varies by each market, depending on the size of the channel intermediaries, customer inventory policies, demand for the product by final consumers, storage costs, and customer service levels necessary to serve each market.

In Japan and most European countries, the retail network is composed of a great number of small shops, each having little capacity for inventory storage. As a result, such shops order frequently from distributors, manufacturers, or other channel intermediaries. The burden of storage is carried by the manufacturer or other channel members rather than the retailer. In the United States, because there are fewer retail stores and they are much larger, the storage function is more easily shifted away from the channel intermediaries directly to the retailer.

---

[53] Ernst and Whinney, *Warehouse Accounting and Control,* p. 84.

[54] Joseph V. Barks, "Strategies for International Distribution," *Distribution* 84, no. 5 (May 1985), p. 69.

When an international firm needs warehousing facilities in a foreign market, it may find an abundance of sophisticated, modern warehouses in some industrial nations. In Japan, many companies use high-cube automated warehousing:

> The first high-cube automated warehouse was established by Fuji Heavy Industries in 1969. There are 10 aisles and 20 rows of racks, and the number of storage openings is 10,800, that is, 54 bins by 10 tiers by 20 rows. An on-line computer controls storage and retrieval by stacker cranes, and the transfer of materials from stack to conveyor system; the computer also stops and starts the conveyors, monitors pallet locations or moves, etc. Machines and equipment in this warehouse were supplied by Ishikawajimi Harima Heavy Industries and the computer by Fujitsu.[55]

The Quality and Availability of Foreign Warehousing Varies Widely

On the other hand, in many less developed countries storage facilities may be nonexistent or limited in availability or sophistication. In the latter instance, the product package or shipping container may have to serve the warehousing purpose.

In the United States, many public warehouses provide services such as consolidation and break-bulk, customer billing, traffic management, packaging, and labeling. Public warehouses in many foreign markets may also provide services in addition to storage.

> One Dutch firm . . . in addition to warehousing, offers customers brokerage, freight forwarding, packaging, insurance, and transportation service to all of Europe and the Middle East. In a product introduction for an American appliance manufacturer, it also coordinated promotional material to assure that promotional packets and displays were available for the firm's marketing teams in the target cities.[56]

Like all logistics activities, the warehousing and storage activity must be administered differently in each foreign market. It is the responsibility of the logistics executive to recognize how the storage activity differs and to adjust the firm's strategy accordingly.

WAREHOUSE PRODUCTIVITY MEASUREMENT

To obtain maximum logistics efficiency, each component of the logistics system must operate at optimal levels. This means that high levels of productivity must be achieved, especially in the warehousing area. Productivity gains in warehousing are important to the firm (in terms of reduced costs)

---

[55] Mikio Ikeda, "The Progress of PD in Japan," *Transportation and Distribution Management* 14, no. 1 (January-February 1974), p. 44.

[56] Ruel Kahler and Roland L. Kramer, *International Marketing,* 4th ed. (Cincinnati, Ohio: South-Western Publishing, 1977), p. 216.

Three Reasons Why Warehouse Productivity Is Important

and to its customers (in terms of improved customer service levels). Specifically, the firm is concerned with warehouse productivity for three reasons:

1. A typical manufacturing concern has 30 to 35 percent of its total space under roof devoted to the storage of raw material or finished goods inventory.
2. For manufacturers, warehousing costs (for both raw materials and finished goods) constitute 6 to 8 percent of the sales dollar.
3. The warehouse readily lends itself to productivity measurement and analysis.[57]

Productivity Defined

Productivity has been defined in many ways, but most definitions include the notions of real outputs and real inputs, utilization, and warehouse performance. One study defined those elements as follows:

> *Productivity is the ratio of real output to real input.* Examples are cases handled per labor-hour and lines selected per equipment-hour.
>
> *Utilization is the ratio of capacity used to available capacity.* Examples are percent of pallet spaces filled in a warehouse and employee-hours worked versus employee-hours available.
>
> *Performance is the ratio of actual output to standard output (or standard hours earned to actual hours).* Examples are cases picked per hour versus standard rate planned per hour, and actual return on assets employed versus budgeted return on assets employed.[58]

Any working definition of productivity probably includes all three components because all are interrelated.

Most firms utilize a variety of measures to examine warehouse productivity. Firms tend to evolve over time in sophistication of their productivity measures:

Four Stages in Productivity Measurement

> [Figure 8–12] displays a schematic representation of the evolution of warehouse productivity measurement. This evolutionary process may be viewed as occurring in four separate stages.
>
> Stage I pertains to the development and use of raw data in terms of dollars. Characteristic of these data is that they are usually provided by some other functional area (e.g., sales or finance); [they are] usually nonphysical in nature; and the time increment is relatively long (e.g., monthly or quarterly). At this stage, these cost data are often compared to some type of macro output, such as dollar sales. Thus, a common Stage I measure might be total warehousing costs as a percent of sales.
>
> In Stage II, physical measures and activity budgets are introduced for warehouse activities. Units such as weight, lines, orders, etc., are tracked within the warehousing activities over shorter time intervals, such as days or weeks. At this

[57] Kenneth B. Ackerman and Bernard J. LaLonde, "Making Warehousing More Efficient," *Harvard Business Review* 58, no. 2 (March-April 1980), p. 94.

[58] A. T. Kearney, Inc., *Measuring and Improving Productivity in Physical Distribution* (Oak Brook, Ill.: National Council of Physical Distribution Management, 1984), p. 188.

FIGURE 8–12 Evolution of Warehouse Productivity Measurement

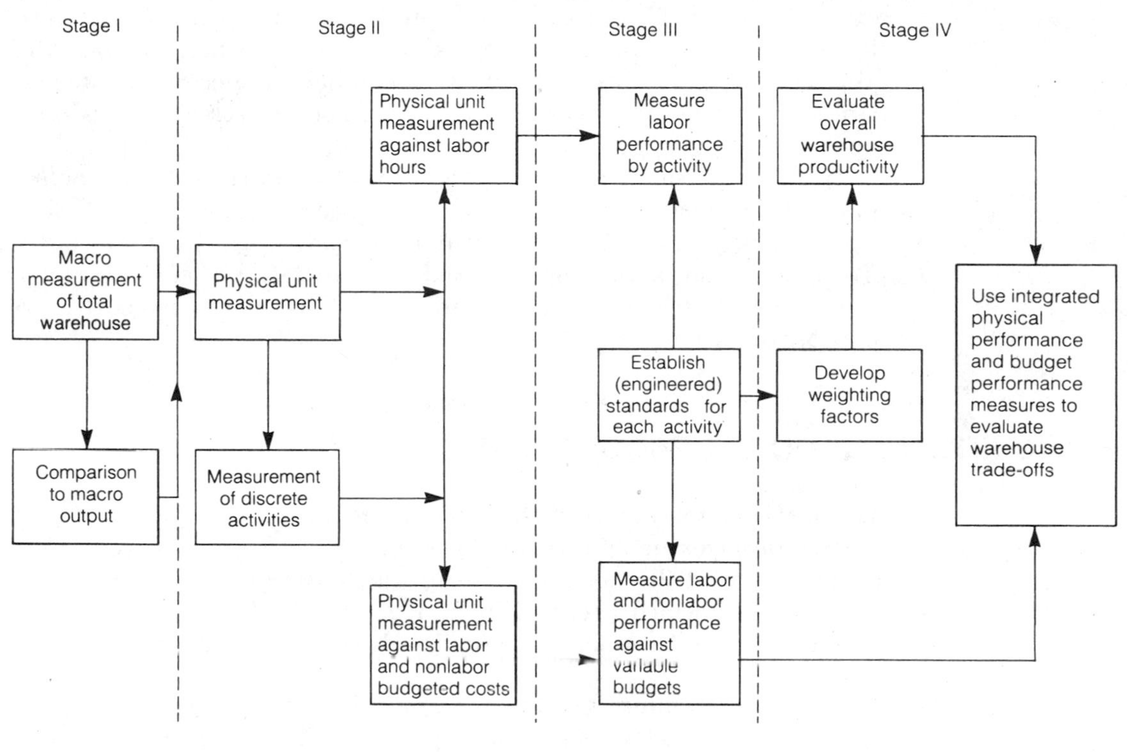

SOURCE: A. T. Kearney, Inc., *Measuring and Improving Productivity in Physical Distribution* (Oak Brook, Ill.: National Council of Physical Distribution Management, 1984), p. 226.

point these physical units can be measured against warehouse labor hours, and warehouse labor and nonlabor costs. The introduction of time-phased activity budgets is now possible with this data base.

Stage III initially sees the establishment of empirical or historical "goals" for the overall warehouse and warehouse activities. These goals could be in the form of physical units or period operating costs, but in either case can now lead to the first measurement of performance.

The development of industrial-engineered standards for labor and nonlabor inputs by activity is usually the second step in Stage III sophistication. This development leads to performance measurement . . . by activity. It should be noted that the productivity trade-offs among warehousing activities can be quantitatively gauged at this level.

Stage IV sophistication incorporates the use of physical performance and budget performance measures to evaluate trade-offs across logistics activities.[59]

[59] Ibid., pp. 225–26. Used with permission of the Council of Logistics Management, formerly the National Council of Physical Distribution Management.

A multitude of warehouse productivity measures are used. Additionally, performance data must be available and used as the basis for corrective action. It is not sufficient to merely identify problem areas; rather it is vital that the firm take appropriate actions to improve poor performance whenever possible. Therefore, a company should develop decision strategies to handle most problem areas before the problems develop. This is the essence of contingency planning.

There is no single approach that a firm can pursue. Management action is determined by a variety of factors, such as customer service levels, competition, and product mix. It is universally accepted, however, that problems should be pinpointed based on cause and effect. Once they are pinpointed, the firm can institute various controls and/or corrective actions to improve warehouse productivity.

IMPROVING WAREHOUSE PRODUCTIVITY

Because warehousing is such a significant component of the logistics process in terms of its cost and service impacts, logistics executives are acutely aware of the need to improve warehouse productivity. There are many ways in which productivity can be improved, including methods-related, equipment-related, systems-related, and training/motivation-related programs.[60]

In a study commissioned by the Council of Logistics Management and carried out by the logistics consulting firm A. T. Kearney, Inc., a number of productivity improvement programs were identified. The following discussion is based on the results of that study, entitled *Measuring and Improving Productivity in Physical Distribution.*

Methods-related programs include those involving warehouse cube utilization, warehouse layout and design, methods and procedures analysis, batch picking of small orders, combined put-away/picking, wrap packaging, unitization, inventory cycle counting, product line obsolescence, standardized packaging, and warehouse consolidation. More specifically, some of these methods-related programs were found to improve productivity:

Methods Used to Improve Warehouse Productivity

1. Expand existing warehouse storage capacity through the installation of narrow aisle equipment and racking, in lieu of standard equipment and racks.
2. Store materials more than multideep in flow bins or racks using handling equipment that reduces the number of aisles required to service a given number of storage units.

[60] This material was paraphrased from A.T. Kearney, *Measuring and Improving Productivity in Physical Distribution* (Oak Brook, Ill.: National Council of Physical Distribution, 1984), pp. 227–34. Used with permission of the Council of Logistics Management, formerly the National Council of Physical Distribution Management.

3. Use variable height storage racks to accommodate additional pallets for greater cube utilization.
4. Install mezzanines over small pick areas, which results in greater small pick capacity in the same square foot (meter) area.
5. Locate fast-moving (high-turnover) products nearest to the shipping and receiving docks to minimize travel time in the warehouse.
6. Locate products requiring similar handing in the same area so as to maximize the use of equipment and personnel.
7. Develop work simplification procedures that allow employee performance standards to be increased.
8. Utilize batch picking of infrequently picked, slow-moving items.
9. Utilize material handling equipment for both put-away and picking on a single trip, thus increasing equipment utilization.
10. Use stretch- and shrink-wrap packaging to reduce product handling requirements and shipping damage.
11. Group individual items in a shipment into larger units. Unitization can reduce handling costs by up to 90 percent.
12. Use inventory cycle counting, rather than curtailing operations for a yearly physical inventory, to improve labor costs and inventory availability.
13. Initiate programs that review product obsolescence and determine whether items can be eliminated from inventory.
14. Eliminate poorly located or uneconomic warehouses.

Equipment Used to Improve Productivity

Equipment-related programs include the use of optical scanners, automatic labeling devices, computer generated put-away and pick lists, automated material handling equipment, communications devices, computers and AS/RS, carousels, and conveyors. Specific programs include:

1. Utilize electronic scanning devices for check-in and routing cartons in an automated warehouse.
2. Use automatic labelers for put-away lists to reduce location errors and improve labor productivity.
3. Generate on-line computer sequenced put-away and pick lists that reduce "search time" for items.
4. Use automated rather than standard (nonautomated) material handling equipment.
5. Install communication devices to allow constant contact between material handlers and other warehouse personnel.
6. Use computers in all phases of warehouse operations to increase speed and accuracy of information transfer.
7. Automate or semiautomate warehouse operations to reduce labor costs and improve efficiency.

Improving Productivity with Systems

Systems-related programs include the use of router/location systems, geographic or zone picking, and random location of products in the warehouse:

1. Use computer router/location systems to improve the levels of warehouse efficiency and effectiveness.
2. Monitor labor efficiency through the use of engineered labor standards.
3. Institute programs to provide a more constant order backlog from which to work. This order backlog can be provided by lengthening the time span during which the warehouse may hold an order, thus tending to level the load, or by encouraging customers to order less frequently and in larger quantities on specified days.
4. Pick items in specified areas of the warehouse and consolidate in a centralized location.
5. Use a computer to randomly assign items to any available space to increase warehouse cube utilization.

Utilizing People to Improve Productivity

Training/motivation-related programs include employee training, management development programs, incentive systems, and awards recognition. These programs can improve warehouse productivity:

1. Conduct formal training at periodic intervals on key warehouse tasks so as to improve employee productivity and safety.
2. Conduct formal training of management personnel to improve leadership and communications skills.
3. Implement reward/incentive systems that provide bonuses or other compensation for performance above some specified standard.
4. Provide awards programs for recognizing specific individuals who perform well in their assigned task(s).

All of the preceding programs can be implemented or individually. Most firms, however, utilize several methods in combination to improve warehouse productivity.

FINANCIAL DIMENSIONS OF WAREHOUSING

The Importance of Financial Accounting and Control

Financial control of warehousing is closely tied to logistics productivity and corporate profitability.[61] Before the various activities of warehousing can be properly integrated into a single unified system, management must be aware of the cost of each activity. This is where financial accounting and control techniques become important:

In a study of 140 companies in 19 types of industries, the accounting firm of Ernst and Whinney identified five key findings related to warehouse accounting and control. They were:

---

[61] See B. J. LaLonde, "Cost Reduction in Warehouse Management," *Warehousing Forum* 1, no. 1 (December 1985), pp. 1–3.

Warehousing in Today's Corporations

1. The configuration of warehouse networks—numbers, sizes, and locations—[varies] widely between industries and often among firms in the same industry.
2. The way a company markets its products or merchandise is a major determinant of the overall warehouse network structure and function in successful companies.
3. Specific warehouse networks and the positioning of warehouse management have generally evolved in response to external developments and pressures—not as a result of strategic distribution plans.
4. The functions of individual warehouses in the distribution network fall into major categories (e.g., stockpiling, consolidation, and distribution), each of which requires different types of information to manage effectively.
5. Warehouse operations encompass discrete activities that should be analyzed separately for both operational and financial management purposes.[62]

Because of the difference among firms, even within the same industry, the study found that companies were at various levels of sophistication in terms of warehouse accounting and control. Four levels of sophistication were identified:

Levels of Sophistication in Warehouse Accounting and Control

Level I: Warehouse costs are allocated in total, using a single allocation base.

Level II: Warehouse costs are aggregated by major warehouse function (e.g., handling, storage, and administration) and are allocated using a separate allocation base for each function.

Level III: Warehouse costs are aggregated by major activity within each function (e.g., receiving, put-away, order pick, etc.) and are allocated using a separate allocation base for each activity.

Level IV: Costs are categorized in matrix form reflecting each major activity, natural expense, and cost behavior type. Separate allocations are developed for each cost category using allocation bases that reflect the key differences in warehousing characteristics among cost objectives.[63]

This is what accounting and control is all about. Simply stated, it is having the right kind of financial data available when and where they are needed, and in a form that is usable by as many functional areas of the firm as possible. Ultimately, such data are essential to making the necessary cost-

[62] Ernst and Whinney, *Warehouse Accounting and Control: Guidelines for Distribution and Financial Managers* (Oak Brook, Ill.: National Council of Physical Distribution Management, 1985), p. 22. Used with permission of the Council of Logistics Management, formerly the National Council of Physical Distribution Management.

[63] Ibid., p. 50.

service trade-offs within the warehousing activity and between other logistics functions.

SUMMARY

In this chapter we discussed some of the major decision strategies in warehousing. The decision to utilize public and/or private warehousing is important, from both a cost and service perspective. Recall the comparative analysis of the financial impact of the public versus private decision.

Facility development is a large part of warehouse management. Decisions relating to the size and number of warehouses, the location of the facilities, and layout and design issues, have significant impact on a firm's ability to satisfy its customers and make a profit. We discussed various methods, techniques, and approaches relative to each decision area.

Computer technology has had a significant impact in the warehousing area. We examined developments in the movement, storage, and information transfer aspects of warehousing. That discussion led us to explore some important management issues relating to warehouse productivity, accounting, and control.

In the next chapters we will examine the inventories that are stored in warehouses and distribution centers. With a knowledge of warehousing, it will be possible to more fully understand the role of inventory management in the logistics system.

SUGGESTED READINGS

ACKERMAN, KENNETH B. "Financial Tools—Which Ones Does the Warehouse Manager Need Most?" *Warehousing Forum* 4, no. 12 (November 1989), pp. 1–2.

———. "Leadership in the 21st Century Warehouse." *Warehousing Forum* 7, no. 6 (May 1992), pp. 1–3.

———. "Unitized Handling, the Warehouse Challenge for the 90's" *Warehousing Forum* 5, no. 9 (August 1990), pp. 1–4.

BAKER, C. M. "Case Study: Development of National Parts Distribution Center." *Proceedings of the Conference on the Total Logistics Concept,* Pretoria, Republic of South Africa, June 4–5, 1991.

BANCROFT, TONY. "Strategic Role of the Distribution Center: How to Turn Your Warehouse into a DC." *International Journal of Physical Distribution and Logistics Management* 21, no. 4 (1991), pp. 45–47.

BHARDWAJ, S. M. "The Pallet Storage System Selection Process." *WERC Research Paper* (Oak Brook, Ill.: Warehousing Education and Research Council, 1990).

BRITT, FRANK F. "A Profit Center Approach to Warehousing." *WERC Research Paper* (Oak Brook, Ill.: Warehousing Education and Research Council, 1990).

CAPACINO, WILLIAM C. "How Warehousing Provides a Competitive Edge." *Warehousing Forum* 6, no. 10 (September 1991), pp. 1–4.

GORDON, JAY. "Smart Life Truck Fleet Management." *Distribution* 91, no. 5 (May 1992), pp. 70–76.

GRAY, VICTOR, AND JOHN GUTHRIE. "Ethical Issues of Environmental Friendly Packaging." *International Journal of Physical Distribution and Logistics Management* 20, no. 8 (1990), pp. 31–36.

LANCIONI, RICHARD A., AND RAJAN CHANDRAN. "The Role of Packaging in International Logistics." *International Journal of Physical Distribution and Logistics Management* 20, no. 8 (1990), pp. 41–43.

MCGINNIS, MICHAEL A. "Basic Economic Analysis for Warehouse Decisions." *WERC Research Paper* (Oak Brook, Ill.: Warehousing Education and Research Council, 1989).

MCGINNIS, MICHAEL A., AND JONATHAN W. KOHN. "Warehousing, Competitive Advantage and Competitive Strategy." *Journal of Business Logistics* 9, no. 2 (1988), pp. 32–54.

"The Pallet Problem: Will it Be Solved in the Nineties?" *Grocery Distribution* 15, no. 3 (January/February 1990), pp. 7–9, 12–13, 40.

"Performance Management Improves Productivity." *Modern Materials Handling* 40, no. 6 (May 1985), pp. 76–78.

ROBINSON, E. POWELL, JR. "Multi-Activity Uncapacitated Facility Location Problem: A New Tool for Logistics Planning." *Journal of Business Logistics* 10, no. 2 (1989), pp. 159–79.

SCHORR, FREDRICK S. "Integrated Logistics . . . and the Role of the Third Party Warehouseman." *Warehousing Forum* 5, no. 9 (August 1990), pp. 1–4.

SPEH, THOMAS W. *How to Determine Total Warehouse Costs* (Sarasota, Fla.: DCW-USA, Inc., 1990).

SPEH, THOMAS W., AND KAY LYNNE BROWN. "A Guide for Establishing Warehouse Job Descriptions." *WERC Research Paper* (Oak Brook, Ill.: Warehousing Education and Research Council, 1989).

STOCK, JAMES R. "Managing Computer, Communication and Information Technology Strategically: Opportunities and Challenges for Warehousing." *Logistics and Transportation Review* 26, no. 2 (June 1990), pp. 32–54.

———. "Strategic Warehousing: Bringing the 'Storage Game' to Life." *WERC Research Paper* (Oak Brook, Ill.: Warehousing Education and Research Council, 1988).

QUESTIONS AND PROBLEMS

1. Identify and describe some of the more important factors that affect the specific size of a firm's warehouse(s).
2. Distinguish between the following types of facility location strategies: (*a*) market positioned, (*b*) production positioned, and (*c*) intermediately positioned.

3. Explain how layout and design can affect warehouse efficiency and productivity.
4. Packaging serves two basic functions: marketing and logistics. Identify the role of packaging in each of these functional areas.
5. Productivity has been defined as the ratio of real output to real input. In terms of the warehousing function, how could a firm measure the productivity level of its storage facilities?
6. Discuss the reasoning behind the following statement: "Financial control of warehousing is closely tied to logistics productivity and corporate profitability."

APPENDIX A
Case Study—Public versus Private Warehousing

This case highlights the comparison of leased, private warehousing to public warehousing. It also illustrates how the treatment of certain costs can influence the results of the analysis.

Synopsis

The company's warehouse facilities have reached capacity in the mid-Atlantic region. Currently, the firm owns and operates two facilities in the area and utilizes approximately 150,000 square feet of outside public warehouse space. The most pressing need is for overflow storage, which is currently being handled by the public warehouse. Overflow requirements are expected to grow substantially in the next several years.

A variety of options are considered initially by the task force charged with recommending a solution to the space requirements problem. It is estimated that approximately 210,000 square feet of space will be required in the mid-Atlantic region. The alternatives have been reduced to the following: (1) use public warehousing or (2) lease 210,000 square feet at $2.75/square foot on a five-year lease with a five year renewal option.

SOURCE: Reprinted with permission from *The Financial Evaluation of Warehousing Options: An Examination and Appraisal of Contemporary Practices,* Thomas Speh and James A. Blomquist, © 1988, Warehousing Education and Research Council, 1100 Jorie Blvd., Oak Brook, IL 60521.

Financial Analysis

Alternative 1: Public Warehousing

A. Annual cost:

Handling charges, annual	=	$ 760,723
Storage charges, annual	=	413,231
Total	=	$1,173,954

B. The public warehousing costs are based on a careful review of public operators in the area. The costs shown in the analysis above are based on the rates for the lowest cost quotation received from the vendors in the feasible set.

Alternative 2: Lease a New Facility

A. Costs are estimated on the basis of past experience and forecasted levels of expense in this specific market.

Estimated yearly operating expenses—new facility:		$ 309,914

B. Investment in the new facility.

1. Capitalized lease

a. Annual lease payment	=	$ 577,500
b. Present value of 10 annual payments of $577,500	–	$3,547,600

2. The lease is capitalized, i.e., the leased asset (building) is treated as a fixed asset, and the present value of future lease payments is treated as a debt. Capitalization of the lease is required for auditing purposes by the Financial Accounting Standards Board and is used in this type of analysis because future lease payments are as binding as if money had been borrowed by the firm to purchase the building. The net effect is to treat the lease as an asset. In this situation, the company considers their investment in the asset to be the present value of the future lease payments (as will be discussed in the commentary, not all financial analysts would agree with treating the lease in this fashion). The discount rate used to determine the present value of the lease payments is typically the firm's after-tax cost of capital, adjusted according to the risk of the project.

3. Other fixed assets required for the new facility:

Handling equipment	$ 170,800
Computer systems	26,740
Rack	252,000
Total	$ 449,540

4. Start-up costs—new facility:
   Product movement $ 10,500

5. Initial cash outlay $ 460,040

Yearly Savings, Lease versus Public

Annual Public Warehouse Cost	=	$1,173,954
Annual Private Warehouse Cost	=	309,914
Annual Total Savings	=	$ 864,040

Private cost appears understated, but the annual lease cost is not reflected in the annual operating cost because the lease is capitalized and treated as an investment).

Ten-Year Cash Flows (000s)

Year	*Initial Outlay*	*Capitalized Lease*	*Savings: Lease versus Public*	*Pre-Tax Net Cash In/Out Flow*	*Tax Depreciation**	*Savings Less Depreciation*	*Taxes 39%*	*Savings Less Depreciation and Taxes*	*Depreciation*	*After-Tax Net Cash In/Out Flow*
0	$460	$3,548	$ 0	($4,008)	0					($4,008)
1	0	0	864	864	$136	$728	$284	$444	$136	$580
2	0	0	864	864	109	755	294	461	109	570
3	0	0	864	864	71	793	309	484	71	555
4	0	0	864	864	50	814	317	497	50	547
5	0	0	864	864	45	819	319	500	45	545
6	0	0	864	864	25	839	327	512	25	537
7	0	0	864	864	22	842	328	514	22	536
8	0	0	864	864	3	861	336	525	3	528
9	0	0	864	864	0	864	337	527	0	527
10	0	0	864	864	0	864	337	527	0	527
Total	$460	$3,548	$8,640	$4,632	$461	$8,179	$3,190	$4,989	$461	$1,442

*Depreciation on rack, handling equipment, and computer hardware is factored in here to reflect the impact on cash flows as a result of the reduction of taxes.

For example:

		Year 1
Savings	=	$864,040
Depreciation	=	− 135,839
Net Profit (before tax)	=	$728,201
Federal tax (39%)	=	− 283,998
Net Profit (after tax)	=	$444,203
Depreciation	=	+ 135,839
After tax cash flow	=	$580,042

Return on Investment

Internal Rate of Return (IRR)

A. Savings stream:

Year	Savings
0	($4,007,640)
1	580,042
2	569,222
3	554,768
4	546,741
5	544,587
6	536,774
7	535,654
8	528,146
9	527,065
10	527,065

B. IRR (after taxes) + 6.13%

Net Present Value

A. Discount rate: 11% after taxes
B. NPV of the 10-year savings stream (discounted at 11%) = ($692,941)

Decision

Use Public Warehousing. IRR and NPV for the private facility do not meet company standards.

Discussion

It is interesting to note that the leased facility generates significant yearly operating savings, yet, the operating savings, as large as they are, do not generate a return on investment that exceeds the company's hurdle rate.

The cost elements included in the company's original analysis were all "hard dollars," and no incremental revenues were considered. The distribution function has its own capital "pool," but distribution projects must meet the hurdle rate that applies to all capital projects.

The lease capitalization in the case study provides an opportunity to review some fundamental financial concepts. As was described in the case, the lease is treated as an asset, and the present value of the future lease payments is shown as an asset on the balance sheet. The interesting point is that the company then treated the capitalized value of the lease as an *investment* in their cash flow analysis. That is, the capitalized lease is treated as a major cash outflow against which the cash savings will be compared to determine the rate of return.

Many managers would argue that the present value of the capitalized lease should not be treated as a lump sum cash outflow (i.e., as an investment). The present value of the annual lease payments is indeed a balance sheet item, but from a *cash flow perspective,* the annual lease payments should be treated as cash outflows in the years in which they are made. If the analysis of the leased space versus public warehousing alternative is recast to treat the lease payments as annual outflows, and the equipment outlay and start-up costs of $460,040 are treated as the initial investment, an entirely different decision would be reached. The data in the table below shows the revised analysis.

Ten-Year Cash Flow Analysis Using Annual Lease Payments ($000s)

Year	*Public Warehouse Annual Cost*	*Annual Cost of Leasing (Lease cost + Operating costs)*	*Initial Investment*	*Pretax Savings: Lease versus Public*	*After-Tax Savings (Savings, less taxes, plus depreciation)*
0			$460		
1	$1,174	$888		$286	$228
2	1,174	888		286	217
3	1,174	888		286	202
4	1,174	888		286	194
5	1,174	888		286	192
6	1,174	888		286	184
7	1,174	888		286	183
8	1,174	888		286	176
9	1,174	888		286	175
10	1,174	888		286	175

Net present value of the cash savings of lease vs. public over years 1–10 (hurdle rate of .11 after taxes) = $1,624,998

Internal rate of return (lease vs. public, after taxes) = 29.99%

Note that the net present value of the savings between leasing and public warehousing is $1.6 million compared to the negative net present value in the original analysis. The revised IRR is almost 30 percent compared to the original IRR of 6.13 percent. Clearly, this analysis would support a decision to lease the space.

This case study illustrates how the treatment of different costs affects the outcome of the financial analysis. In this instance, the way in which the lease payments are treated dramatically affects the final decision. The results suggest that all personnel involved in the warehousing analysis process must constantly challenge and carefully evaluate the way in which various cost elements are conceptualized and brought into the analysis process.

APPENDIX B

Case Study—Warehouse Consolidation

This case focuses on the reconfiguration of the firm's warehouse network. The case illustrates the conservative approach that many firms take regarding the inclusion of service and revenue impacts in the quantitative financial analysis. Interestingly, third-party warehousing is not considered, even though the firm experiences widely varying sales volumes.

Synopsis

The company's distribution centers (DCs) are near their maximum storage capacity, and sales projections suggest that volume cannot be handled with existing facilities. A recent study of customer service, conducted by a well-known consulting firm, indicated that larger customers require much less stringent order cycle times than those currently being provided by the company. Consequently, the company has the opportunity to reduce the number of distribution centers and accept a longer cycle time in order to reduce costs.

Currently, the southern region distribution center in Atlanta provides the lowest total delivered cost, and expanding the area served by the Atlanta DC would reduce total distribution costs. Savings from expanding the center's service area and the increased order cycle time could be applied to increasing the limited storage and throughput capacity at the Atlanta DC.

The Distribution Environment

The company manufactures and distributes a broad line of consumer products through grocery stores, retail drugstores, wholesalers, and mass merchandisers. Throughput is characterized by sharp peaks:

- The number of cases shipped varies from 80,000 to 740,000 per day.
- Sales peaks are reached toward the end of each quarter when volume per day increases by a factor of four.
- The number of pallets stored varies +/− 15 percent from the average.
- For five or six months during peak storage times, the distribution centers are close to maximum capacity.

Annually, more than 1.2 million orders for 1,100 products are processed by the logistics function. Transportation is primarily by truck: over 8,000 trailers are moved per year. In total, over 300 million pounds of product are shipped to more than 40,000 domestic customers.

SOURCE: Reprinted with permission from *The Financial Evaluation of Warehousing Options: An Examination and Appraisal of Contemporary Practices,* Thomas Speh and James A. Blomquist, © 1988, Warehousing Education and Research Council, 1100 Jorie Blvd., Oak Brook, IL 60521.

System Reconfiguration Analysis

The first phase of the analysis process utilized a network optimization model to evaluate two dozen network configuration alternatives. The optimal configuration had two fewer DCs than existed at the present time. The proposed alternative included:

- Closing a full-line DC in Harrisburg, Pa.
- Closing an export DC in Baltimore, Md.
- Expanding the Atlanta DC by 150,000 sq. ft. (one-third), enabling the DC to service the northeast and export customers.

The facility in Baltimore is used to handle export distribution and help achieve consolidation economies. On an annual basis, the center makes slightly more than 1,800 shipments that contain 3,000 orders and weigh 4 million pounds. Almost two-thirds of the weight originates in other company facilities. This DC's operations will be merged into the Atlanta facility under the current proposal. Total costs will be reduced by integrating international distribution into the new Atlanta facility.

The major advantages of the proposal are centered on the following:

- Expanded storage capacity to accommodate long-term growth.
- Elimination of the need to use the Atlanta plant warehouse space.
- Reduced operating costs.
- Reduced safety stock.
- Expanded capacity to handle storage and throughput peaks.
- Enhanced service due to higher fill rates and improved picking accuracy.

The final aspect of the analysis was the capital expenditure and rate of return analysis.

Financial Analysis

Project to begin in April of 1988, with an estimated completion date of June 30, 1989. The project involves the construction of a 150,000 square foot expansion to the Atlanta DC.

Cash Flows Associated with This Alternative

A. Investment (in $000s):

Expand Atlanta DC building 150,000 square feet	$4,450
Roads and truck parking	400
Drainage system	120
Architect	249
Contingency	497
Conveyor system	2,100
Total investment capital	$7,816

($4,005,000 to be spent in 1988)
($3,811,000 to be spent in 1989)

B. One-time (start-up) expenses ($000s):

Severance	$ 670
Relocation	150
Vacancy	360
Miscellaneous	400
TOTAL	$1,580

Severance expenses include the cost of settlement with employees not transferred from the old facilities to the expanded DC in Atlanta.
Relocation includes the costs of physically moving inventory from old locations to the new location.
Vacancy expenses are made up of the on-going costs of maintaining the Harrisburg facility until it is sold or subleased.

C. Annual net operating savings[1] (in $000s):

	Harrisburg	*Baltimore*	*Atlanta*	*Total*
Salaries/benefits	$463.00[2]	$ 38.60[3]	—	$ 501.60
Lease expense	490.00	124.00	—	614.00
Operating expenses	551.20	49.80	$ 60.40[4]	661.40
Transportation[5]	130.00	—	—	130.00
Net annual savings				$1,907.00

[1]These savings are "net," that is, operating costs at the new facility are subtracted from the savings at the other two facilities to arrive at a net savings figure.

[2]Includes the elimination of 23 hourly, 18 non-exempt, and 4 exempt personnel.

[3]Does not reflect a reduction in number of personnel, but includes savings due to lower pay scales in Atlanta.

[4]The plant warehouse in Atlanta would not be used for distribution.

[5]Transportation includes plant-to-DC and DC-to-customer. The $130,000 savings is a net figure reflecting the sizeable reduction in plant-to-DC transportation cost and a slight increase in DC-to-customer transportation cost associated with the new Atlanta facility.

D. Asset liquidation ($000s):

Net book value of:	
Leasehold improvements	$129.00
Machinery and equipment	478.50
Furniture and fixtures	76.20
Total book value	$683.70
Less transfers to new facility:	
Computer system	($175.40)
Racks	(67.70)
Forklift and trucks	(26.70)
Conveyors	(66.70)
Label printer	(16.20)
Total transfer	($352.70)
Value of assets to be liquidated: ($683.70 – $352.70)	$331.00
Less estimated sale proceeds:	–31.00
Net loss associated with asset liquidation	($300.00)

E. Working capital:

Reduction in inventory (safety stock)	$2,075.00

F. Annual out-of-pocket savings from inventory reduction:

Interest percentage = 13%		
Savings ($2,075 @ .13)	=	$ 270.00

The reduction of safety stock by consolidating into one DC has two effects: (1) It results in a one-time cash inflow when the inventory is reduced, and (2) It causes an annual cash inflow due to the reduction in annual interest expense.

G. Annual depreciation ($000s):

Year 1	=	$100
Years 2–9	=	$269

Calculation of Net Cash Flows, 1988–1996

A. Data ($000s):

	1988	*1989*	*1990*	*1991*	*1992*	*1993*	*1994*	*1995*	*1996*
Depreciation	$100	$269	$269	$269	$269	$269	$269	$269	$269
Tax rate*	46.6%	46.6%	48.5%	48.5%	48.5%	48.5%	48.5%	48.5%	48.5%
Deferred taxes†	($5)	$ 98	$207	$135	$ 85	$ 48	$ 48	$ 48	$ 3

*The analysis is based on pre-1987 tax rates.

†The deferred taxes shown in the third row above are a result of the tax impact from maintaining two sets of books. For internal reporting, assets are valued as close to their true value as possible. For external purposes (i.e., federal taxes), assets will be depreciated as quickly as is legally possible. If an asset is depreciated more quickly than the item actually depreciates in value, there will be a discrepancy between the two values. The deferred taxes reflect the cash flow impact of this difference.

B. Sample calculation of net cash flow:

1. Net cash flow would include:

Operating savings + Inventory savings (interest) = Total savings − Depreciation = Profit before tax − Federal tax	Calculate operating profit
= Profit after tax + Depreciation + Deferred tax = Net cash flow	Add back depreciation and deferred tax to obtain "cash flow"

2. Consider 1990 ($000s):

Operating savings	$1,907
+ Inventory savings (interest)	+ 270
= Total savings	$2,177
− Depreciation	− 269
= Profit before tax	$1,908
− Federal tax (48.5%)	− 925
= Profit after tax	$ 983
+ Depreciation	+ 269
+ Deferred tax	+ 207
= Net cash flow	$1,459

C. Total annual net cash flow ($000s), 1988–1996:

	1988	*1989*	*1990*	*1991*	*1992*	*1993*	*1994*	*1995*	*1996*
Operating savings	$0	$1,430	$1,907	$1,907	$1,907	$1,907	$1,907	$1,907	$1,907
Inventory savings (interest)	0	270	270	270	270	270	270	270	270
1-time expense	—	(1,580)	—	—	—	—	—	—	—
Asset Loss	—	(300)	—	—	—	—	—	—	—
Depreciation	(100)	(269)	(269)	(269)	(269)	(269)	(269)	(269)	(269)
Profit before tax	(100)	(449)	1,908	1,908	1,908	1,908	1,908	1,908	1,908
Federal tax	(47)	(209)	(925)	(925)	(925)	(925)	(925)	(925)	(925)
Profit after tax	(53)	(240)	983	983	983	983	983	983	983
Depreciation	100	269	269	269	269	269	269	269	269
Deferred tax	(5)	98	207	135	85	48	48	48	3
Cash Generated	42	127	1,459	1,387	1,337	1,300	1,300	1,300	1,255
Capital expense	(4,005)	(3,811)	—	—	—	—	—	—	—
Change in working capital	—	2,075	—	—	—	—	—	—	—
Net cash flow	($3,963)	($1,609)	$1,459	$1,387	$1,337	$1,300	$1,300	$1,300	$1,255

Return on Investment

Rate of Return Analysis

A. Net Present Value ($000s):

1. Net cash flow

Year	*Cash Flow*
1988	(3,963)
1989	(1,609)
1990	1,459
1991	1,387
1992	1,337
1993	1,300
1994	1,300
1995	1,300
1996	1,255

2. Hurdle rate = 14%
3. Net present value @ 14% = $1,449.8

B. Internal rate of return of the cash flow = 20.3%

C. Payback period = 5.7 years

Decision

Build the addition to the Atlanta DC as:
IRR > Hurdle rate and NPV > 0

Discussion

It is interesting to noten that the current network would not accommodate the projected growth in the firm's sales volume. Yet, there is no consideration given to including incremental revenue in the cash flow analysis. But it is possible to make a case for including incremental profits because sales presumably could not expand without an increase in the capacity of the warehousing network.

The approach shown here reflects the basic conservative stance that most firms take when analyzing warehousing capital projects. However, it could be argued that additional sales could be handled through temporary warehousing or increased productivity from the current system. The issue of incremental sales is difficult to resolve.

A significant advantage associated with the new facility is the enhancement of customer service. The new equipment to be installed in the Atlanta facility is expected to result in a higher percentage of completed orders and an increase in order picking accuracy. Order fill and order accuracy are highly regarded by customers. However, the enhancements to service are not quantified or formally recognized in the financial analysis. Again, few managers are willing to take the risk of projecting the effect of service enhancements on revenue. As is obvious in the cash flow analysis, neither increased sales nor enhanced service were needed to produce a positive net present value. However, had this been a borderline project, cash flows associated with sales and service enhancements may have pushed the project into the favorable range.

The most intriguing aspect of this analysis is the fact that third-party warehousing was not considered in the feasible set of alternatives. The situation described in the case suggests that volume is extremely volatile, resulting in the need to build substantial excess warehouse capacity to handle peak periods. It could be argued that this situation is well-suited to third-party warehousing where peak requirements for one principal can be offset with opposite requirements of another principal. It would be interesting, in this situation, to calculate a rate of return on the private facility on the basis of the savings, vis-à-vis third-party warehousing. Here, the savings may not be significant due to the excess capacity required in the private warehousing scenario. Although corporate culture may argue for private warehousing, it would have been insightful to review the financial impacts of third-party warehousing.

Chapter 9

Financial Impact of Inventory

Objectives of This Chapter

To show how inventory investment influences corporate profit performance

To show how inventory management contributes to least total cost logistics

To show how to calculate inventory carrying costs

INTRODUCTION

Inventory represents the largest single investment in assets for most manufacturers, wholesalers, and retailers. The highly competitive markets of the past 20 years have led to a proliferation of products, as companies attempt to satisfy the needs of diverse market segments. In addition, in most industries, customers have become accustomed to high levels of product availability. For many firms, the result has been higher inventory levels. Inventory investment can represent over 20 percent of manufacturers' total assets, and more than 50 percent of wholesalers' and retailers' total assets (see Table 9–1).

Inventory Must Compete with Other Investments

Because capital invested in inventories must compete with other investment opportunities available to the firm, and because of the out-of-pocket costs associated with holding inventory, inventory management is an important activity. Management must have knowledge of inventory carrying costs to make informed decisions about logistics system design, customer service levels, the number and location of distribution centers, inventory levels, where to hold inventory, transportation modes, production schedules, and minimum production runs. For example, ordering in smaller quantities on a more frequent basis will reduce inventory investment but will typically result in higher ordering costs and increased transportation costs. It is necessary to compare the savings in inventory carrying costs to the increased costs of ordering and transportation to determine how the decision to order in smaller quantities will affect profitability. A determination of inventory carrying costs is also necessary for new product evaluation, the evaluation of price deals/discounts, make versus buy decisions, and profitability reports. It is thus imperative to take a detailed look at inventory carrying costs.

FINANCIAL ASPECTS OF INVENTORY STRATEGY

The quality of inventory management and the inventory policies a firm sets can have a significant impact on corporate profitability and management's ability to implement least total cost logistics.

TABLE 9–1 Selected Financial Data for Manufacturers, Wholesalers, and Retailers, ($ Millions)

Companies	*Sales*	*Net Profits*	*Net Profits as a Percent of Sales*	*Total Assets*	*Inventory Investment*	*Inventories as a Percent of Assets*
Manufacturers						
Abbott Laboratories	$ 6,158.7	$ 965.8	15.7%	$ 5,563.2	$ 777.6	14.0%
Borden, Inc.	7,632.8	363.6	4.8%	5,284.2	665.5	12.6%
The Clorox Company	1,484.0	153.6	10.4%	1,137.7	128.1	11.3%
Dresser Industries, Inc.	4,480.3	184.4	4.1%	3,309.0	526.4	15.9%
Ford Motor Company	81,844.0	98.7	0.1%	50,823.4	7,115.4	14.0%
General Electric Company	58,414.0	4,303.0	7.4%	153,884.0	6,707.0	4.4%
General Mills	6,448.3	381.4	5.9%	3,289.5	394.4	12.0%
Goodyear Tire & Rubber Co.	11,272.5	−38.3	−0.3%	8,963.6	1,346.0	15.0%
Harris Corp.	3,052.7	130.7	4.3%	2,625.1	426.6	16.3%
Honeywell	6,309.1	381.9	6.1%	4,746.2	972.3	20.5%
NCR Corp.	6,285.0	369.0	5.9%	4,547.0	499.0	11.0%
Newell Co.	1,072.6	101.4	9.5%	870.9	177.8	20.4%
Pfizer, Inc.	6,406.0	801.2	12.5%	9,052.0	1,142.6	12.6%
Sara Lee Corp.	11,605.9	470.3	4.1%	7,636.4	1,653.7	21.7%
Xerox Corp.	16,951.0	605.0	3.6%	31,495.0	2,148.0	6.8%
Wholesalers and retailers						
Baxter International	8,100.0	40.0	0.5%	8,517.0	1,532.0	18.0%
Bergen Brunswig Corp.	4,442.3	66.1	1.5%	1,238.1	418.2	33.8%
Dayton Hudson Corp.	13,644.0	410.0	3.0%	6,684.0	1,827.0	27.3%
Fleming Companies, Inc.	11,932.8	97.3	0.8%	2,767.7	884.9	32.0%
Kmart Corporation	29,793.0	323.0	1.1%	13,145.0	6,933.0	52.7%
Nordstrom	2,671.1	114.9	4.3%	1,707.4	420.0	24.6%
Sears, Roebuck & Company	28,958.8	257.4	0.9%	25,539.0	4,074.0	16.0%
Super Valu Stores, Inc.	11,136.0	147.8	1.3%	2,428.9	833.2	34.3%
Wal-Mart Stores, Inc.	25,810.7	1,075.9	4.2%	8,198.5	4,428.1	54.0%
Winn-Dixie	9,744.5	152.5	1.6%	1,732.7	848.4	49.0%

NOTES: Ford Motor Co. figures are for its automotive division only. Pfizer, Inc. figures are from its consolidated balance sheet. Sears, Roebuck & Co. figures are for its Merchandise Group only. General Electric figures are from its consolidated balance sheet. Xerox Corp. figures are from its consolidated balance sheet. All figures are for 1990.

Inventory and Corporate Profitability

Excessive Inventories Can Lower Profitability

Inventory represents a significant portion of a firm's assets. Consequently, excessive inventory levels can lower corporate profitability in two ways: (1) net profit is reduced by out-of-pocket costs associated with holding inventory, such as insurance, taxes, storage, obsolescence, damage, and interest expense, if the firm borrows money specifically to finance inventories; and, (2) total assets are increased by the amount of the inventory investment, which decreases asset turnover. The result is a reduction in return on assets and return on net worth.

For example, ABC Company's financial data are summarized in Figure 9–1. As a result of poor forecasting, lack of attention to inventory management, and the absence of an integrated systems approach to the management of logistics, the company's inventory is $6 million too large. What would be the impact on profitability and return on net worth of a change in management practice if: (*a*) the cash made available from the $6 million

FIGURE 9–1 The Strategic Profit Model with Financial Data for ABC Company ($ millions)

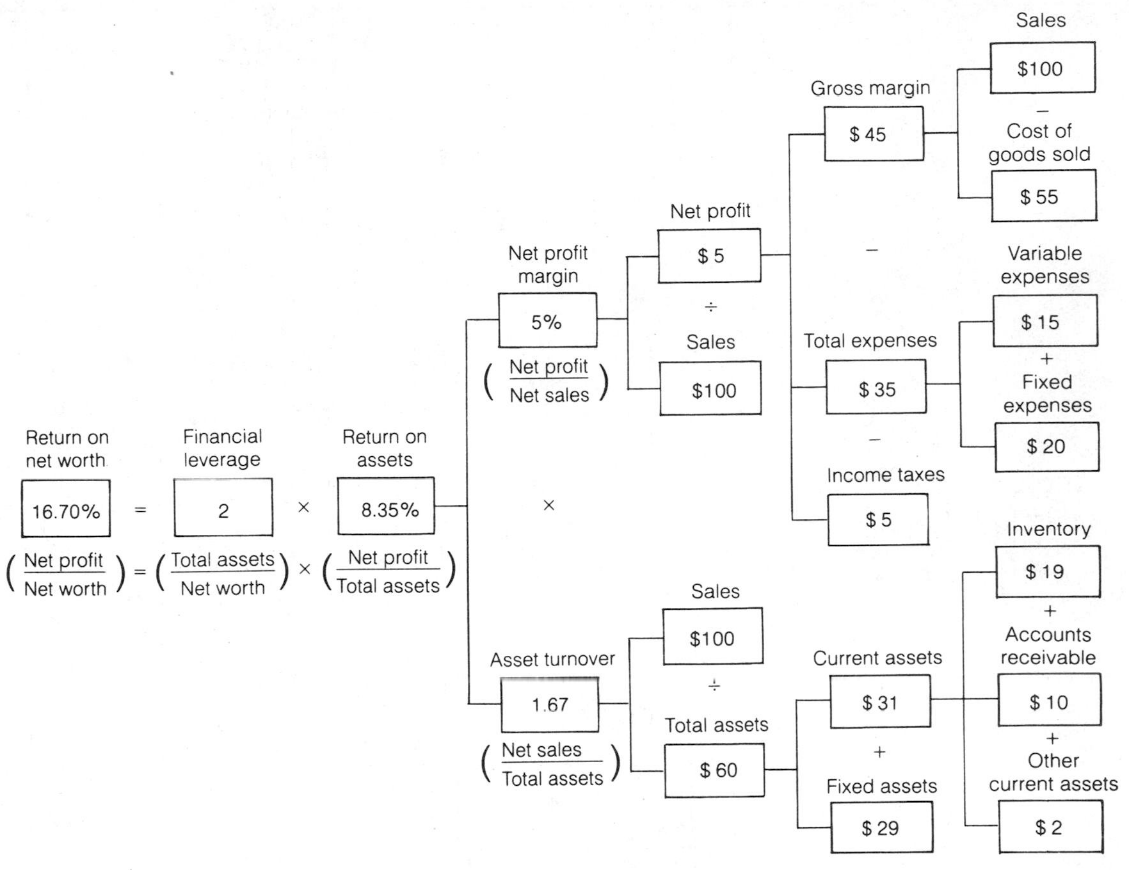

Income taxes are assumed to equal 50 percent of net profit before taxes.

reduction in inventory were used to repay a bank loan at 15 percent interest; and (*b*) the total of the other out-of-pocket costs saved by the reduction in inventory equaled 5 percent of the inventory value? Figure 9–2 gives the answer: (1) current assets and total assets are reduced by $6 million; (2) asset turnover increases from 1.67 times to 1.85 times; (3) total expenses are reduced by $1.2 million—$900,000 in fixed interest expense plus $300,000 in other fixed expenses; (4) net profit before taxes increases by $1.2 million, but income taxes increase by $600,000, resulting in an increase in after-tax net profit of $600,000; (5) net profit margin increases from 5 percent to 5.6 percent; (6) return on assets increases from 8.35 percent to 10.36 percent; (7) financial leverage declines from 2 to 1.8; and (8) return on net worth increases from 16.70 percent to 18.65 percent

FIGURE 9–2 Impact of Inventory Reduction on ABC Company's Net Worth when Bank Loan Is Repaid ($ millions)

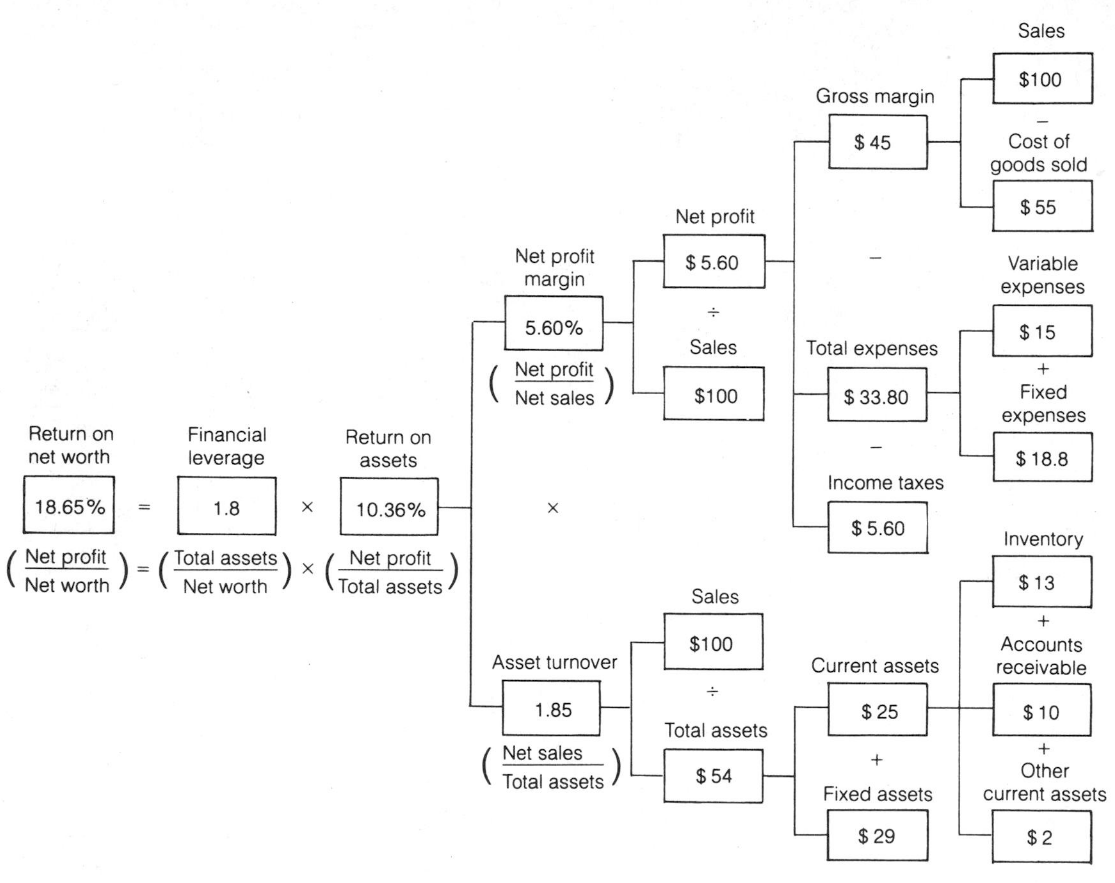

Income taxes are assumed to equal 50 percent of net profit before taxes.

Capital Rationing Raises the Cost of Carrying Inventory

If the company is experiencing capital rationing, however—that is, if there is not enough money to invest in all of the new projects available—management has to decide where to invest the money from the inventory reduction and at what rate of return. For example, if ABC were to invest the money in plant modernization that would reduce manufacturing costs and yield a 20 percent after-tax return (which equals 40 percent before tax), this *opportunity cost* should be reflected in the analysis. Excluding the cost of capital, the out-of-pocket costs associated with the inventory investment equal 5 percent of the inventory value. How will a $6 million reduction in inventory affect the company's return on net worth? Figure 9–3 shows that (1) current assets are reduced by the $6 million inventory reduction, and fixed assets are increased by $6 million, the cost of the plant

FIGURE 9–3 Impact of Inventory Reduction on ABC Company's Net Worth when Capital Rationing Exists ($ millions)

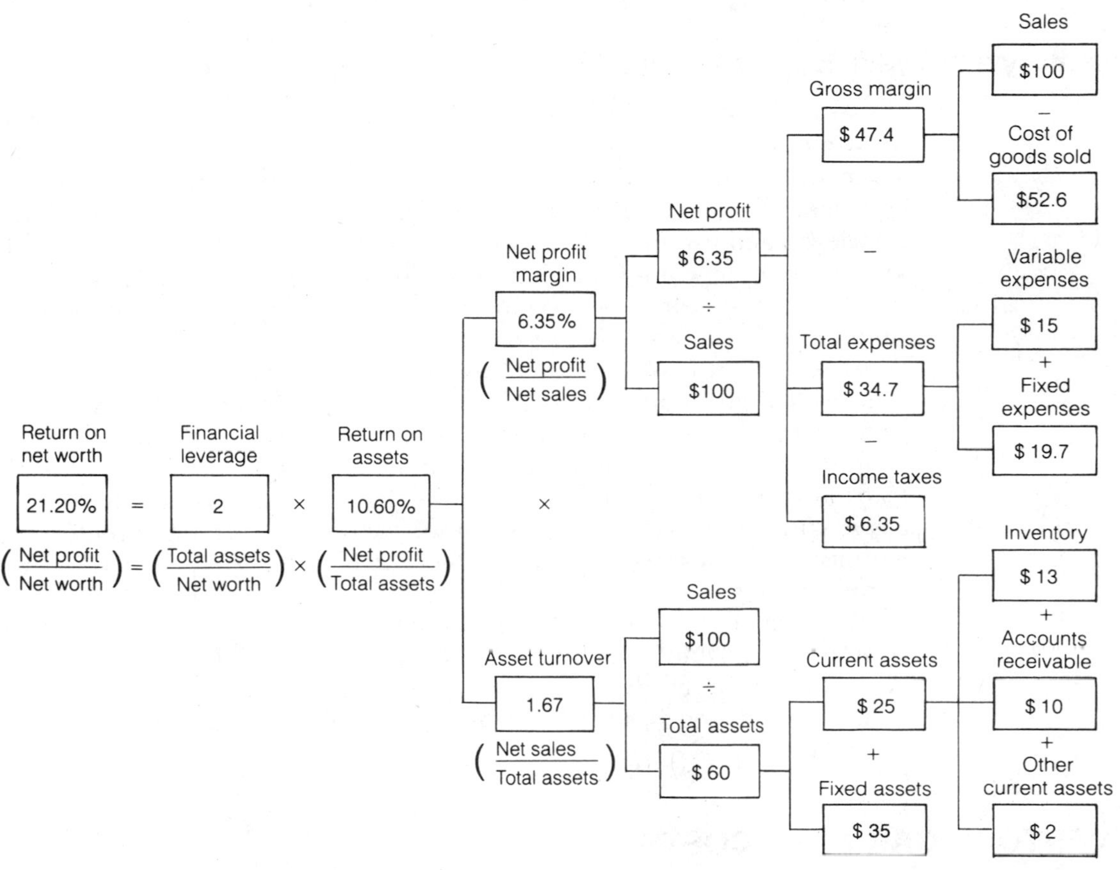

Income taxes are assumed to equal 50 percent of net profit before taxes.

modernization; (2) total assets and asset turnover remain the same; (3) as a result of improved production efficiency, the cost of goods sold is reduced by $2.4 million ($6 million × 40%) and gross margin increases from $45 million to $47.4 million; (4) fixed expenses and total expenses are reduced by $300,000 in inventory-related expenses ($6 million × 5%); (5) net profit before taxes increases by $2.7 million but income taxes increase by $1.35 million, resulting in an increase in after-tax net profit of $1.35 million; (6) net profit margin increases from 5 percent to 6.35 percent; (7) return on assets increases from 8.35 percent to 10.60 percent; (8) financial leverage remains at 2; and (9) return on net worth increases from 16.70 percent to 21.20 percent.

Both examples show that too much inventory can erode net profits and return on net worth. In order to establish the optimal inventory stocking strategy, management has to think in terms of the cost trade-offs required in a logistics system.

Inventory and Least Total Cost Logistics

Least total cost logistics is achieved by minimizing the total of the costs illustrated in Figure 9–4 for a specified level of customer service. However, successful implementation of cost trade-off analysis requires that adequate cost data be available to management. Management should not set inventory levels and inventory turnover policies arbitrarily, but instead with full knowledge of inventory carrying costs and total logistics system costs.

Inventory Carrying Costs Impact Logistics Policies

The cost of carrying inventory has a direct impact not only on the number of warehouses that a company maintains, but on all of the firm's logistics policies. Given the same customer service level, low inventory carrying costs lead to multiple warehouses and a slower mode of transportation, such as railroads. High inventory carrying costs, on the other hand, result in a limited number of stock locations and require a faster means of transportation, such as motor or air carriers, in order to minimize total costs. Without an accurate assessment of the costs of carrying inventory, it is unlikely that a company would choose the logistics policies that would minimize costs.

In addition, knowledge of the cost of carrying inventory is required to accurately determine economic manufacturing quantities, economic order quantities, and sales discounts, all of which are usually calculated on the basis of estimated costs in the majority of companies that use these formulas.[1]

INVENTORY CARRYING COSTS

Inventory carrying costs, the costs associated with the quantity of inventory stored, include a number of different cost components and generally represent one of the highest costs of logistics.[2] The magnitude of these costs and the fact that inventory levels are influenced by the configuration of the logistics system demonstrate the need for an accurate assessment of inventory carrying costs, if the appropriate trade-offs are to be made within the firm and within the channel of distribution. Nevertheless, most managers who consider the cost of holding inventory use estimates or traditional industry benchmarks.

---

[1] We will discuss these formulas in Chapter 10, Inventory Management.

[2] This section draws heavily from Douglas M. Lambert, *The Development of an Inventory Costing Methodology: A Study of the Costs Associated with Holding Inventory* (Chicago: National Council of Physical Distribution Management, 1976).

FIGURE 9–4 Cost Trade-Offs Required in a Logistics System

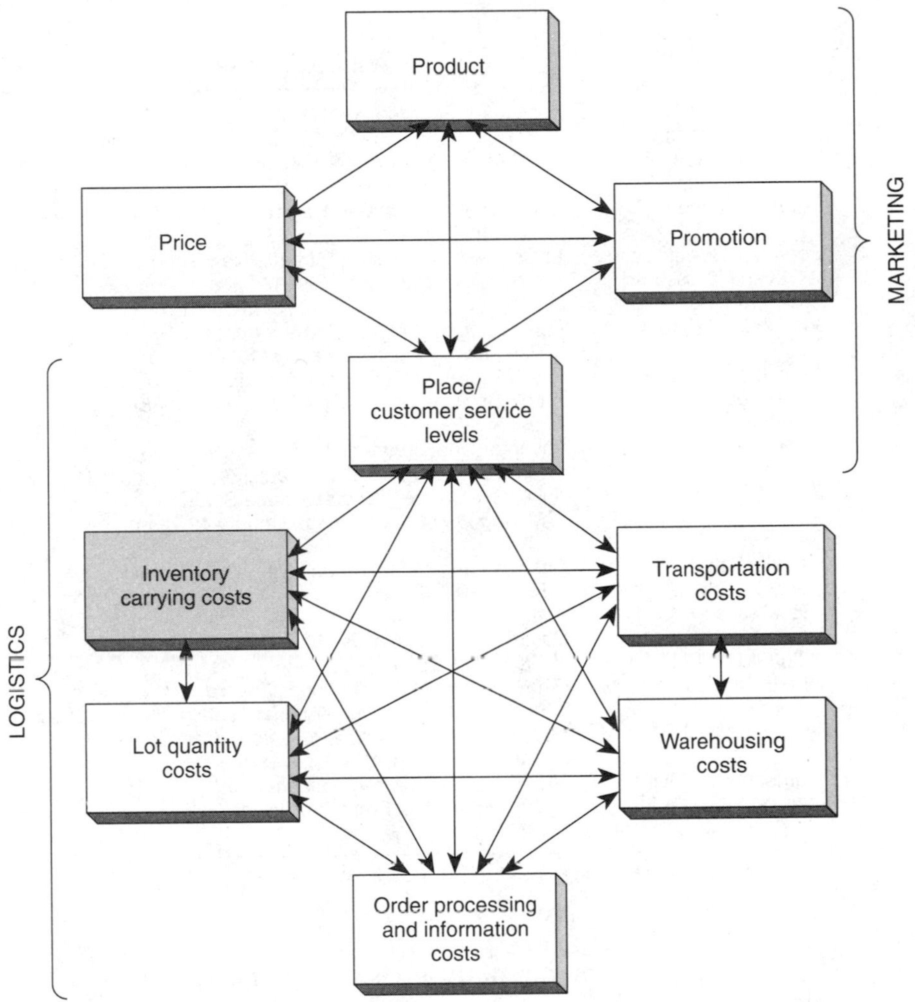

Marketing objective: Allocate resources to the marketing mix to maximize the long-run profitability of the firm.

Logistics objective: Minimize total costs, given the customer service objective, where: Total costs = Transportation costs + Warehousing costs + Order processing and information costs + Lot quantity costs + Inventory carrying costs.

SOURCE: Adapted from Douglas M. Lambert, *The Development of an Inventory Costing Methodology: A Study of the Costs Associated with Holding Inventory* (Chicago: National Council of Physical Distribution Management, 1976), p. 7.

TABLE 9–2 Estimates of Inventory Carrying Costs

Author	*Publication*	*Estimate of Carrying Costs as a Percent of Inventory Value*
L. P. Alford and John R. Bangs (eds.)	*Production Handbook* (New York: Ronald Press, 1955), p. 397.	25%
George W. Aljian	*Purchasing Handbook* (New York: McGraw-Hill, 1958), pp. 9–29.	12–34
Dean S. Ammer	*Materials Management* (Homewood, Ill.: Richard D. Irwin, 1962), p. 137.	20–25
Donald J. Bowersox, David J. Closs and Omar K. Helferich	*Logistical Management,* 3rd ed. (New York: Macmillan, 1986), pp. 189–97.	20*
Joseph L. Cavinato	*Purchasing and Materials Management* (St. Paul, Minn.: West Publishing, 1984), p. 284.	25
John J. Coyle, Edward J. Bardi, and C. John Langley, Jr.	*The Management of Business Logistics*, 4th ed. (St. Paul, Minn.: West Publishing, 1988), pp. 174–76.	25–27
Gordon T. Crook	"Inventory Management Takes Teamwork," *Purchasing,* March 26, 1962, p. 70.	25
Thomas W. Hall	"Inventory Carrying Costs: A Case Study," *Management Accounting,* January 1974, pp. 37–39.	20.4
J. L. Heskett, N. A. Glaskowsky, Jr., and R. M. Ivie	*Business Logistics,* 2nd ed. (New York: Ronald Press, 1973), p. 20.	28.7
James C. Johnson and Donald F. Wood	*Contemporary Logistics,* 4th ed. (New York: Macmillan, 1990), pp. 228–29.	25
John F. Magee	"The Logistics of Distribution," *Harvard Business Review,* July–August 1960, p. 99.	20–35
Benjamin Melnitsky	*Management of Industrial Inventory* (Conover-Mast Publication, 1951), p. 11.	25
Thomson M. Whitlin	*The Theory of Inventory Management* (Princeton, N.J.: Princeton University Press, 1957), p. 220.	25

*Not specified, although 20 percent was used in examples.

We have seen how inventory levels can affect corporate profit performance, and have discussed the need for assessment of inventory carrying costs in logistics system design. The next question might be: What inventory carrying cost percentages are managers currently using for logistics system design decisions (cost trade-off analysis) and such things as determining economic order quantities and sales discounts?

What Is the Cost of Carrying Inventory?

Unfortunately, in many companies inventory carrying costs have never been calculated, even though these costs are both real and substantial. When inventory carrying costs are calculated they often include only the current interest rate plus such expenditures as insurance and taxes. Also, many managers use traditional textbook percentages or industry averages. All of these approaches have problems.

First, there are only a few special circumstances in which the current

Textbook Carrying Costs Are Suspect

interest rate is the relevant cost of money (we will explore these shortly). Traditional textbook percentages also have serious drawbacks. Table 9–2 contains a number of estimates of inventory carrying costs that are widely referenced in logistics and inventory management literature.

The 12 to 34 percent range presented by George Aljian's *Purchasing Handbook* covers a range so large that picking a number within the range would allow a manager to cost-justify almost any inventory policy.[3] The 1960 *Harvard Business Review* article by John Magee has the same shortcoming as the Aljian publication, but Magee recognized that the cost of money should be applied only to the out-of-pocket investment in inventory.[4] In the 1974 *Management Accounting* article by Thomas Hall, carrying cost was calculated to be 20.4 percent, but Hall added an after-tax cost of capital to the other components, which were pretax numbers.[5] In addition, he included in the calculations storage costs that were not variable with the quantity of inventory held.

The time period covered by the publications listed in Table 9–2 covers the years 1951 to 1990. However, most of the carrying costs percentages used during that period were about 25 percent. If 25 percent was an accurate number in 1951, how could it be accurate in 1990, when during that period the prime interest rate fluctuated between 3 percent and 20 percent?

Inventory Carrying Costs Should Not Be Based on Industry Averages

Finally, there is the method of using inventory carrying costs that are based on industry averages. Businesspeople, for the most part, seem to find comfort in such numbers, but many problems are inherent with this practice. For example, would the logistics executive of a cosmetics manufacturer want to compare his or her firm to Avon, a company that sells its products door to door; Revlon, a company that sells its products through major department stores; or—even worse—use an average of the two companies? This latter approach, of course, would compare the executive's firm to a nonentity—no company at all. Even if two companies are very similar in terms of the manufacture and distribution of their products, the availability of capital may lead to two very different inventory strategies. That is, one firm may experience shortages of capital—capital rationing—and the other may have an abundance of cash. The former has a cost of money for inventory decisions of 40 percent pretax, which is the rate of return the company is earning on new investments. The latter has a cost of money of 10 percent pretax, which is the interest rate the company is earning on its cash. If both of these companies are well managed, which one is likely to have the most inventory? The company with the 10 percent cost of money

---

[3] George W. Aljian, *Purchasing Handbook* (New York: McGraw-Hill, 1958), pp. 9–29.

[4] John F. Magee, "The Logistics of Distribution," *Harvard Business Review* 38, no. 4, (July-August 1960), p. 99.

[5] Thomas W. Hall, "Inventory Carrying Costs: A Case Study," *Management Accounting* LV, no. 7 (January 1974), pp. 37–39.

will. Because of the lower cost of money, this company will increase inventory levels, move toward transporting carload and/or truckload quantities of its products, and have longer production runs. The company with the 40 percent cost of money will have lower inventories but will accomplish it by incurring higher production setup costs, higher transportation costs, and/or more stockouts. Each company may have what represents least total cost logistics, and yet one may turn its inventories 6 times per year and the other 12 times. Transportation costs as a percent of sales may be significantly higher for the company with the 40 percent cost of money. However, if either company were to change any component of its logistics system in order to match the other's performance, total costs could increase and return on net worth could decrease.

Calculating Inventory Carrying Costs

Four Components of Inventory Carrying Costs

Each company should determine its own logistics costs and strive to minimize the total of these costs, given its customer service objectives. Inventory carrying costs should include only those costs that vary with the quantity of inventory and that can be categorized into the following groups: (1) capital costs, (2) inventory service costs, (3) storage space costs, and (4) inventory risk costs.

Capital Costs on Inventory Investment. Holding inventory ties up money that could be used for other types of investments. This reasoning holds for internally generated funds as well as capital obtained from sources external to the firm, such as debt from banks and insurance companies or from the sale of common stock. Consequently, the company's opportunity cost of capital—the rate of return that could be realized from some other use of the money—should be used in order to accurately reflect the true cost involved. In companies experiencing capital rationing, which is the rule rather than the exception, the hurdle rate (which is the minimum rate of return on new investments) should be used as the cost of capital. When capital rationing is not in effect, it is necessary to determine where the cash from a reduction in inventory would be invested. If the money would be invested in marketable securities, then that is the rate of return for inventory carrying cost purposes. If the money would be placed in a bank account or used to reduce some form of debt, then the appropriate interest rate applies. The same logic applies for increases in inventories. What rate of return will be forgone on the cash invested in inventory?

Some companies differentiate among projects by categorizing them according to risk and looking for rates of return that reflect the perceived level of risk. For example, management could group projects into high, medium, and low categories of risk. High-risk projects might include investments in new products, since market acceptance is difficult to predict, or new equipment for the plant, if technology is changing so rapidly that the equipment could be obsolete within a short period of time. The desired rate of return on high-risk projects might be 25 percent after tax. Medium-risk projects, on the other hand, may be required to obtain an 18 percent after-tax return. Low-risk projects, which may include such investments as warehouses, private trucking, and inventory, might be expected to achieve an after-tax return of 10 percent. In such a company, corporate aversion to risk may require that cash made available by a reduction in inventory be used for another low-risk category investment. Consequently, the cost of money for inventory carrying costs would be 10 percent after taxes, which equals 20 percent before taxes (assuming a 50 percent tax rate). All inventory carrying cost components must be stated in before-tax numbers, because all of the other costs in the trade-off analysis, such as transportation and warehousing, are reported in before-tax dollars.

In some very special circumstances, such as the fruit-canning industry, short-term financing may be used to finance the seasonal buildup of inventories. The seasonal building of inventory stands in contrast to the inventories determined by the strategic deployment of product to achieve least total cost logistics. In the latter case, any change in inventory will affect the quantity of inventory carried throughout the year and usually will compete with other long-term investments for funding. In the former situation, the inventory build-up is short-term and the actual cost of borrowing is the acceptable cost of money.

Once management has established the cost of money, it must determine the out-of-pocket (cash) value of the inventory for which the inventory carrying cost is being calculated. For wholesalers or retailers, the out-of-pocket value of the inventory is the current replacement cost of the inventory, including any freight costs paid, or the current market price if the product is being phased out. In the case of manufacturers, it is necessary to know which costing alternative is being used. For example, is the company using direct costs to determine the inventory value, or is it using some form of absorption costing?

Direct versus Absorption Costing

Direct costing is a method of cost accounting based on segregating costs into fixed and variable components. For management planning and control purposes, the fixed-variable cost breakdown yields more information than that obtained from current financial statements designed for external reporting. Under direct costing, the fixed costs of production are excluded from inventory values, and therefore inventory values more closely reflect the out-of-pocket cost of their replacement. With *absorption costing* (otherwise known as full costing or full absorption costing), which is the traditional approach used by most manufacturers, fixed manufacturing overhead is included in the inventory value.

In addition to the distinction between direct costing and absorption costing, companies may value inventories based on actual costs or standard costs. There are four distinct costing alternatives:

1. *Actual absorption costing* includes actual costs for direct material and direct labor, plus predetermined variable and fixed manufacturing overhead.
2. *Standard absorption costing* includes predetermined direct material and direct labor costs, plus predetermined variable and fixed overhead.
3. *Actual direct costing* includes actual costs for direct material and direct labor, plus predetermined variable manufacturing overhead; it excludes fixed manufacturing overhead.
4. *Standard direct costing* includes predetermined costs for direct material and direct labor, plus predetermined variable manufacturing overhead; it excludes fixed manufacturing overhead.

The preceding material on methods of inventory valuation supports the conclusion that using industry averages for inventory carrying costs is not a good policy. This is because the various component percentages may not be calculated using comparable inventory valuation systems.

Three Methods of Accounting for Inventory

The situation is complicated even further if one considers the various methods of accounting for inventory. Most manufacturing companies use one of the following three methods of accounting for inventory:

1. *First-in, first-out (FIFO):* Stock acquired earliest is assumed to be sold first, leaving stock acquired more recently in inventory. Under FIFO, inventory is valued near the current replacement cost.
2. *Last-in, first-out (LIFO):* Sales are made from the most recently acquired stock, leaving items acquired in the earliest time period in inventory. This method attempts to match the most recent costs of acquiring inventory with sales. In periods of rising prices, LIFO will result in lower inventory valuation, higher cost of goods sold, and lower profits than the FIFO method. The converse is true when prices are declining.
3. *Average cost:* This method could be a moving average, in which each new purchase is averaged with the remaining inventory to obtain a new average price, or a weighted average, in which the total cost of the opening inventory plus all purchases is divided by the total number of units.

Neither FIFO nor LIFO isolates and measures the effects of cost fluctuations. However, when standard costing is used, the currently attainable standards, when compared to actual costs, provide a measure of cost variance—gains or losses—that can be reported separately.[6]

[6]Students who want to read more about direct and absorption costing and the methods of accounting for inventory should refer to Charles T. Horngren and George Foster, *Cost Accounting: A Managerial Emphasis,* 7th ed. (Englewood Cliffs, N.J.: Prentice Hall, 1991).

For the purposes of calculating inventory carrying costs, it is immaterial whether the company uses LIFO, FIFO, or average cost for inventory valuation. The value of the inventory for calculating carrying costs is determined by multiplying the number of units of each product in inventory by the standard or actual direct (variable) costs associated with manufacturing the product and moving it to the storage location. The way a manufacturer decreases its inventory investment is to sell a unit from inventory and not produce a replacement. Similarly, inventories are increased by manufacturing more product than is currently demanded. Consequently, in either case, it is the current manufacturing costs that are relevant for decision making, since these are the costs that will be incurred if inventories are increased. Likewise, if products are held in field locations, the transportation cost incurred to move them there, plus the variable costs associated with moving them into storage, are costs that are inventoried, just as are direct labor costs, direct material costs, and the variable manufacturing overhead. For example, the out-of-pocket value of a unit of product stored in a public warehouse is equal to the variable manufacturing costs, plus the transportation from the plant to the warehouse and the handling charge paid to the public warehouse.

The implicit assumption is that a reduction in finished goods inventory will lead to a corresponding reduction in inventory throughout the system (see Figure 9–5). That is, a one-time reduction in finished goods inventory results in a one-time reduction in raw materials purchases, as inventory is pushed back through the system. Similarly, a planned increase in finished goods inventory results in a one-time increase in the quantity of raw materials purchased and subsequently pushed through the system. If we multiply the one-time change in inventory value, a balance sheet account, by the opportunity cost of money, the resulting figure reflects the annual cost of having the money invested in inventory; this cost is a profit and loss statement account. All other components of the inventory carrying cost are annual costs that affect the profit and loss statement, as do the other logistics cost categories such as transportation, warehousing, lot quantity, and order processing.

Capital Costs Equal the Opportunity Cost of Money, Times the Out-of-Pocket Investment in Inventory

In summary, many businesspeople think that inventory is a relatively liquid and riskless investment. For this reason, they feel that they can justify a somewhat lower return on inventory investments. However, inventory requires capital that could be used for other corporate investments, and by having funds invested in inventory a company forgoes the rate of return that it could obtain in such investments. Therefore, the company's opportunity cost of capital should be applied to the investment in inventory. The cost of capital should be applied to the out-of-pocket investment in inventory. Although most manufacturers use some form of absorption costing for inventory, only variable (direct) manufacturing costs are relevant. That is, the company's minimum acceptable rate of return, or the appropriate opportunity cost of money, should be applied only to the variable costs

FIGURE 9–5 Inventory Positions in the Logistics System

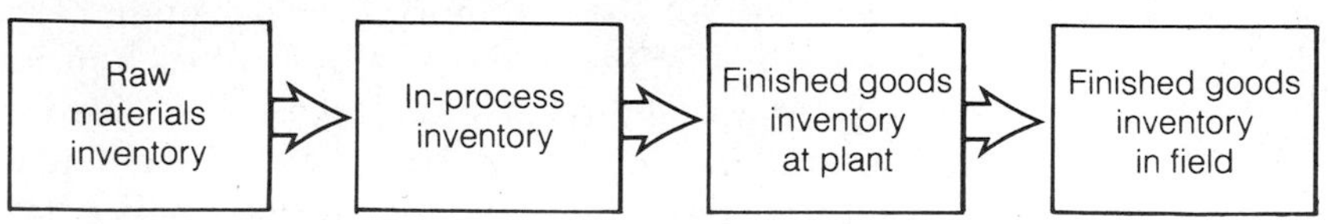

Assumption: A one-time increase (decrease) in finished goods inventory results in a one-time increase (decrease) in raw materials purchased.

directly associated with the inventory. In the case of wholesalers and retailers, the out-of-pocket investment in inventory is simply the current replacement cost plus transportation costs if they are not included in the purchase price of the products.

Inventory Service Costs. Inventory service costs are comprised of ad valorem (personal property) taxes and fire and theft insurance paid as a result of holding the inventory. Taxes vary depending on the state in which inventories are held. Tax rates can range from zero in states where inventories are exempt to as much as 20 percent of the assessed value. In general, taxes vary directly with inventory levels. Many states exempt inventories from taxation if they are placed into storage for subsequent shipment to customers in another state. Thus, with proper planning a company can minimize this component when establishing a warehousing network.

Taxes

Insurance

Insurance rates are not strictly proportional to inventory levels, since insurance is usually purchased to cover a certain value of product for a specified time period. Nevertheless, an insurance policy will be revised periodically based on expected inventory level changes. In some instances, an insurance company will issue policies in which premiums are based on the monthly amounts insured. Insurance rates depend on the materials used in the construction of the storage building, its age, and considerations such as the type of fire prevention equipment installed.

The actual dollars spent on both insurance and taxes during the past year can be calculated as a percentage of that year's inventory value and added to the cost of money component of the carrying cost. If budgeted figures are available for the coming year, they can be used as a percentage of the inventory value based on the inventory plan—the forecasted inventory level—in order to provide a future-oriented carrying cost. In most cases, there will be few if any significant changes from year to year in the tax and insurance components of the inventory carrying cost.

Storage Space Costs. We will consider four general types of facilities: (1) plant warehouses, (2) public warehouses, (3) rented or leased (contract) warehouses, and (4) company-owned (private) warehouses.

Plant Warehouses

The costs associated with *plant warehouses* are primarily fixed. If any costs are variable, they are usually variable with the amount of product that moves through the facility, throughput, and not with the quantity of inventory stored. If there are some variable costs such as the cost of taking inventory or any other expenses that would change with the level of inventory, management should include them in inventory carrying costs. Fixed charges and allocated costs are not relevant for inventory policy decisions. If the firm can rent out the warehouse space or use it for some other productive purpose instead of using it for storing inventory, and if the associated opportunity costs are not readily available to the manager, then it may make sense to substitute the appropriate fixed or allocated costs as surrogate measures. However, the best approach would be to estimate the appropriate opportunity costs.

Public Warehouses

Public warehouse charges are usually based on the amount of product moved into and out of the warehouse (handling charges) and the amount of inventory held in storage (storage charges). In most cases, handling charges are assessed when the products are moved into the warehouse and storage charges are assessed on a periodic basis, such as monthly. Sometimes, the first month's storage also must be paid when the products are moved into the facility. In effect, this makes the first month's storage a handling charge since it must be paid on every case of product regardless of how long it is held in the warehouse.

The use of public warehouses is a policy decision management makes because it is the most economical way to provide the desired level of customer service without incurring excessive transportation costs. For this reason, handling charges, which represent the majority of costs related to the use of public warehouses, should be considered as throughput costs; that is, they should be thought of as part of the warehousing cost category of the cost trade-off analysis, and not part of inventory carrying costs. Only charges for warehouse storage should be included in inventory carrying costs, since these are the public warehouse charges that will vary with the level of inventory.

In situations where a throughput rate (handling charge) is given based on the number of inventory turns, it is necessary to estimate the storage cost component by considering how the throughput costs per case will change if the number of inventory turns changes. Of course, the public warehouse fees that a company pays when its inventory is placed into field storage should be included in the value of its inventory investment.

Contract Warehouses

Rented or leased warehouse space is normally contracted for, and the contract is in force for a specified period of time. The amount of space rented is based on the maximum storage requirements during the period covered by the contract. Thus, warehouse rental charges do not fluctuate from day to day with changes in the inventory level, although rental rates can vary from month to month or year to year when a new contract is negotiated. Most costs, such as rent payment, the manager's salary, security costs, and maintenance expenses, are fixed in the short run. But some expenses, such as warehouse labor and equipment operating costs, vary with throughput.

During the term of the contract, few if any costs vary with the amount of inventory stored.

All of the costs of leased warehouses could be eliminated by not renewing the contract and are therefore a relevant input for logistics decision making. However, operating costs that are not variable with the quantity of inventory stored, such as those outlined in the preceding paragraph, should not be included in the carrying costs. Rather, these costs belong in the warehousing cost category of the cost trade-off analysis. The inclusion of fixed costs, and those that are variable with throughput in inventory carrying costs, has no conceptual basis. Such a practice is simply incorrect and will result in erroneous decisions.

Company-Owned Warehouses

The costs associated with *company-owned warehouses* are primarily fixed, although some may be variable with throughput. All operating costs that can be eliminated by closing a company-owned warehouse or the net savings resulting from a change to public warehouses should be included in warehousing costs and not in inventory carrying costs. Only those costs that vary with the quantity of inventory belong in inventory carrying costs. Typically, in company-owned warehouses, these costs will be negligible.

Inventory Risk Costs. Inventory risk costs vary from company to company, but typically include charges for (1) obsolescence, (2) damage, (3) shrinkage, and (4) relocation of inventory.

Obsolescence

The cost of *obsolescence* is the cost of each unit that must be disposed of at a loss because it can no longer be sold at regular price. Obsolescence cost is the difference between the original cost of the unit and its salvage value, or the original selling price and the reduced selling price if the price is lowered (marked down) to move the product. This figure may or may not show up on the profit and loss statement as a separate item. Usually, obsolescence costs are buried in the cost of goods manufactured account or the cost of goods sold account. Consequently, managers may have some difficulty arriving at this figure.

Damage

The cost of *damage* should be included only for the portion of damage that is variable with the amount of inventory held. Damage incurred during shipping should be considered a throughput cost, since it will continue regardless of inventory levels. Damage attributed to a public warehouse operation is usually charged to the warehouse operator if it is above some specified maximum amount. Often damage is identified as the net amount after claims.

Shrinkage

Shrinkage has become an increasingly important problem for American businesses. Many authorities think inventory theft is a more serious problem than cash embezzlement. Theft is far more common and involves far more employees, and it is hard to control. However, shrinkage costs may be more closely related to company security measures than inventory levels, even though it will definitely vary with the number of warehouse locations. Shrinkage can also result from poor record keeping, or shipping wrong products or quantities to customers. In many companies, shrinkage costs are more likely to vary with the number of warehouse locations than the amount of inventory, and management finds it more appropriate to assign some or all of these costs to the warehousing cost category.

Relocation Costs

Relocation costs are incurred when inventory is transshipped from one warehouse location to another to avoid obsolescence. For example, products that are selling well in the Midwest may not be selling on the West coast. By shipping the products to the location where they will sell, the company avoids the obsolescence cost but incurs additional transportation costs. Transshipments to avoid obsolescence or markdowns are the result of having too much inventory, and the cost should be included in inventory carrying costs. Often, transshipment costs are not reported separately, but are simply included in transportation costs. In such cases, a managerial estimate or a statistical audit of freight bills can isolate the transshipment costs. The frequency of these types of shipments will determine which approach is most practical in any given situation. That is, if such shipments are rare, the percentage component of the carrying cost will be very small and a managerial estimate should suffice.

In some cases, firms may incur transshipment costs as a result of inventory stocking policies. For example, if inventories are set too low in field locations, stockouts may occur and may be rectified by shipping product from the nearest warehouse location that has the item(s) in stock. The transportation costs associated with transshipments to avoid stockouts are a result of decisions that involve trade-offs between transportation costs, warehousing costs, inventory carrying costs, and/or stockout costs. They are transportation costs and should not be classified as inventory carrying costs.

Since managers do not always know just how much of damage, shrinkage, and relocation costs are related to the amount of inventory held, they may have to determine mathematically if a relationship exists. For example, a cost for damage may be available, but the amount of this cost due to the volume of inventory may not be known. Damage can be a function of such factors as throughput, general housekeeping, the quality and training of management and labor, the type of product, the protective packaging used, the material handling system, the number of times that the product is handled, how it is handled, and the amount of inventory (which may lead to damage as a result of overcrowding in the warehouse). To say which of these factors is most important and how much damage each one accounts for is extremely difficult. Even an elaborate reporting system may not yield the desired results, as employees may try to shift the blame for the damaged product. The quality of damage screening during the receiving func-

TABLE 9–3 Damage and Corresponding Inventory Levels at Various Points in Time

	Time Periods						
	1	*2*	*3*	*4*	*5*	*6*	*7*
Y, damage ($000)	80	100	70	60	50	70	100
X, inventory ($ millions)	11	15	13	10	7	9	13

tion, and the fact that higher inventories may hide damaged product until inventories are reduced, may contribute to the level of damage reported, regardless of the cause.

Using Regression Analysis to Determine Inventory Related Costs

To determine the portion of a cost that is variable with inventory, an analyst can use regression analysis or plot the data graphically.[7] Consider the damage rates and inventory levels shown in Table 9–3. Simple linear regression can be used as a tool for segregating the portion of a cost component that is related to the level of inventory held. The principal objective in simple linear regression analysis is to establish a quantitative relationship between two related variables. In order to establish the relationship between two variables, X and Y, a number of paired observations similar to those in Table 9–3 must be obtained.

For example, we are able to obtain the total damage figure in dollars for a number of time periods, but we do not know how much of this damage is directly related to the level of inventory. The first pair of observations ($Y = 80, X = 11$) indicates that $80,000 worth of damage occurred in the period when inventory was $11 million.

Now the data can be plotted on graph paper, with each pair of observations represented by a point on the chart (see Figure 9–6). A point is obtained by plotting the independent variable, X, along the horizontal axis and the dependent variable, Y, along the vertical axis. When all the pairs of observations have been plotted, a straight line is drawn that attempts to minimize the distance of all the points from the line (the statistical technique is referred to as least-squares regression).[8]

Once this has been done, any two points, A and B, should be selected on the estimated regression line (see Figure 9–6). The increment in the damage from A to B, and the change in the inventory from A to B should be expressed as a percentage:

[7] For more information on regression analysis, refer to any basic statistics book. For example, see Terry Sincich, *A Course in Modern Business Statistics* (San Francisco: Dellen Publishing Company, 1991), pp. 339–456.

[8] Least-squares regression minimizes the sum of the squared distances of all of the points from the line.

FIGURE 9–6 Graphing the Relationship between Damage and Inventory Levels

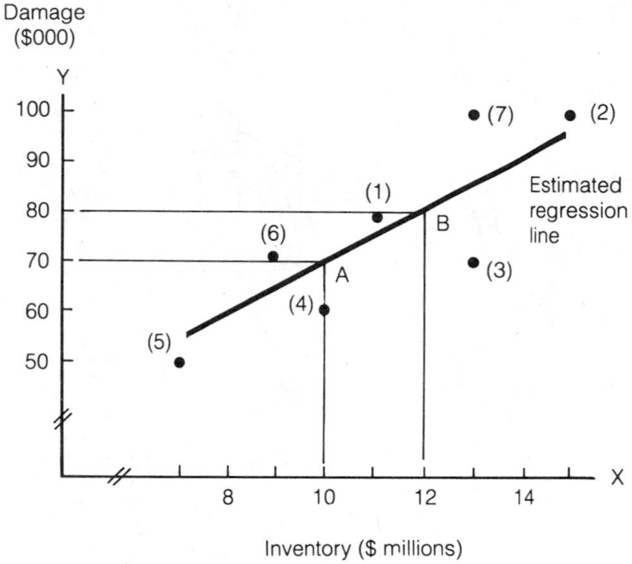

$$(\Delta D/\Delta I) \times 100\% = \frac{\$10{,}000 \times 100\%}{\$2{,}000{,}000} = 0.5\%$$

The 0.5 percent can be interpreted as the percentage of the inventory investment that is damaged because product is being held in inventory. This percentage can be added to the other cost components to determine the total carrying cost percentage. Note that if damage does in fact increase with increased levels of inventory, then the estimated regression line must move upward to the right. A line that is vertical, horizontal, or sloping downward from the left indicates that such a relationship does not exist.

The ability to successfully fit a line through the plotted points will depend on the degree of correlation, that is, the strength of the relationship present. If the points are scattered all over, this indicates that no relationship exists. A moderate correlation exists when the points are all situated relatively close to the estimated regression line. A perfect correlation exists when all of the points fall on the line. This is a correlation of 1.0. The closer the correlation is to 1.0, the stronger the relationship.

Industry Examples

Figure 9–7 summarizes the methodology that should be used to calculate inventory carrying costs. The model is *normative,* because using it will lead

FIGURE 9–7 Normative Model of Inventory Carrying Cost Methodology

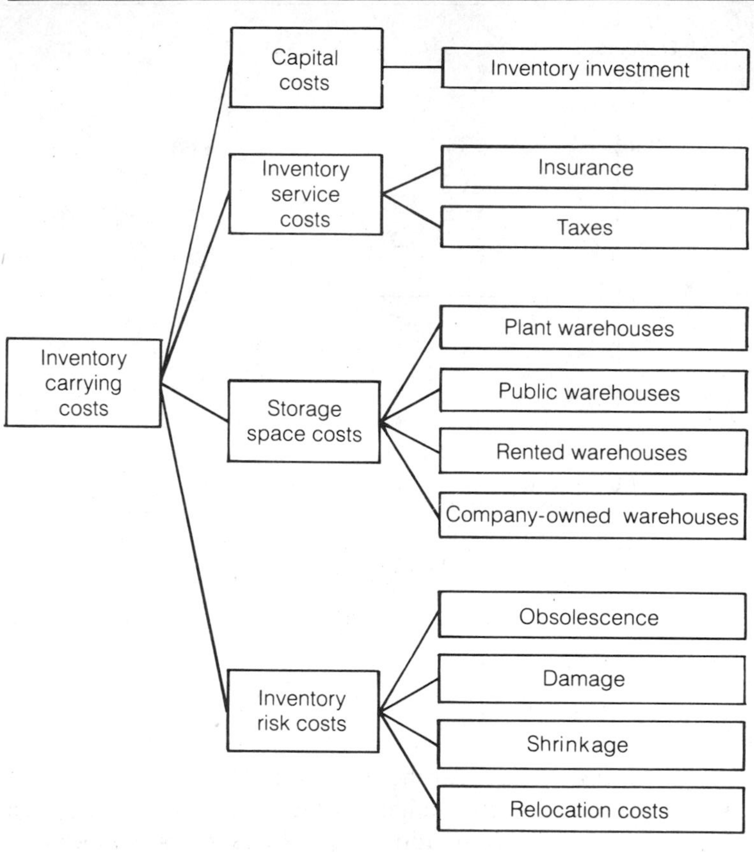

SOURCE: Douglas M. Lambert, *The Development of an Inventory Costing Methodology: A Study of the Costs Associated with Holding Inventory* (Chicago: National Council of Physical Distribution Management, 1976), p. 68.

to a carrying cost that accurately reflects a firm's costs. Now let's examine an actual application of the methodology for a manufacturer of packaged good, followed by an example from the bulk chemicals industry.

A CONSUMER PACKAGED GOODS INDUSTRY EXAMPLE

Using the methodology summarized in Figure 9–7, it was necessary to calculate costs for the following four basic categories: (1) capital costs, (2) inventory service costs, (3) storage space costs, and (4) inventory risk costs.

Capital costs. In order to establish the opportunity cost of capital—the minimum acceptable rate of return on new investments—an interview was conducted with the company's comptroller. Due to capital rationing, the current hurdle rate on new investments was 15 percent after taxes (30 percent before taxes). The company conducted a post-audit of most projects, in order to substantiate the rate of return. This was required by corporate policy, and in the majority of cases the desired rate of return was achieved, although there was considerable variability on individual marketing projects. The difficulty in estimating the rate of return on marketing projects was caused by the inability to forecast the market's acceptance of new products. Consequently, the cost of money used for inventory carrying costs was set at 30 percent before taxes. A before-tax cost of money is required, since all of the other components of inventory carrying cost and the other cost categories in logistics cost trade-off analysis, such as transportation and warehousing, are before-tax numbers.

The opportunity cost of capital should be applied only to the out-of-pocket investment in inventory. This is the direct variable expense incurred up to the point at which the inventory is held in storage. In other words, it was necessary to obtain the average variable cost of products delivered to the warehouse location. Since the company used standard fully allocated manufacturing cost for valuing inventory, it was necessary to investigate the standard cost for each product, in order to determine the variable manufactured cost per unit. Using the company's inventory plan for the coming year, it was possible to calculate the average inventory for each product. This can be determined for each storage location and for the total system.

Next, the average transportation cost per case of product was added to the variable manufactured cost. This was necessary because the transportation cost must be paid just like the manufacturing labor and raw material costs. Finally, if any warehousing costs are incurred moving product into storage in field locations, these costs should be added on a per-case basis to the standard variable manufactured cost. When public warehousing is used, any charges paid at the time products are moved into the facility should be added on a per-case basis to all products held in inventory. In the case of corporate facilities, only variable out-of-pocket costs associated with moving the products into storage should be included.

The company had $10 million in average system inventory valued at full manufactured cost. Annual sales were $175 million, or approximately $125 million at manufactured cost. The inventory value based on variable manufacturing costs and the forecasted product mix was $7 million. The $7 million was the average annual inventory held at plants and field locations in order to achieve least cost distribution. The variable costs associated with transporting the strategically deployed field inventory and moving it into public warehouses totaled $800,000. Therefore, the average system inventory was $7.8 million when valued at variable cost delivered to the storage location.

All of the remaining inventory carrying cost components should be calculated as a percentage of the variable delivered cost ($7.8 million), and added to the capital cost percentage. In some companies, however, inventory reports may value products only at full standard manufactured cost, and the cost or time involved in changing reporting practices may seem high relative to the benefits to be gained. If a firm faces this type of situation, the cost of money can be adjusted when the carrying cost is developed in order to reflect that it is being applied to a value larger than the cash generated by a reduction in inventory. Table 9–4 shows methods of adjusting the carrying cost calculation to represent only variable costs.

The assumptions are that variable costs are 80 percent of full cost and that the cost of money is 40 percent before tax or 20 percent after taxes. If the inventory shown on management reports is valued at $10 million at full cost, a

TABLE 9–4 Adjusting the Cost of Money to Fit the Method of Inventory Valuation

Method A	
Inventory at full cost	$10,000,000
Variable cost is 80 percent of full cost	×80%
Inventory at variable cost	$ 8,000,000
Cost of money before tax is 40 percent	×40%
Cost of money associated with the inventory investment	$ 3,200,000
Method B	
Cost of money before tax	40%
Variable cost is 80 percent of full cost	×80%
Adjusted cost of money	×32%
Inventory at full cost	$10,000,000
Adjusted cost of money	×32%
Cost of money associated with the inventory investment	$ 3,200,000

manager could take 80 percent of this amount and then apply the 40 percent cost of money. This would yield a capital cost of $3.2 million. Another alternative is to adjust the cost of money at the time the inventory carrying cost is developed. By taking 80 percent of the 40 percent cost of money, the *adjusted* cost of money, 32 percent, can be applied to the inventory value shown on the management reports. This method also yields a capital cost of $3.2 million. If full cost is used and the cost of money is appropriately adjusted, all remaining cost components should be calculated as a percentage of the full cost inventory value.

Inventory service costs. Return to the example of the manufacturer of packaged goods, with system inventories of $7.8 million valued at variable cost delivered to the storage location. Taxes for the year were $90,948, which is 1.166 percent of the $7.8 million inventory value; this figure was added to the 30 percent capital cost (see Table 9–5). Insurance costs covering inventory for the year were $4,524, which is 0.058 percent of the inventory value.

Storage space costs. The storage component of the *public warehousing* cost was $225,654 for the year, which equals 2.893 percent of the inventory value. Variable storage costs in *plant warehouses* should include only those costs that are variable with the amount of inventory stored. The vast majority of plant warehousing expenses were fixed in nature. Those costs that were variable fluctuated with the amount of product moved into and out of the facility (throughput) and were not variable with inventory levels. Consequently, variable storage costs were negligible in plant warehouses.

Inventory risk costs. Obsolescence cost, which is the cost of holding products in inventory beyond their useful life, was being tracked in this company and represented 0.800 percent of inventory for the past twelve months.

Shrinkage and *damage* costs were not recorded separately. Regression analysis would have been a possible means of isolating the portion of these costs that were variable with inventories. However, management was confident that no more than 10 percent of the total shrinkage and damage, $100,308, was related to inventory levels. Therefore, a managerial estimate of 10 percent was used. This was equal of 1.286 percent of the inventory value of $7.8 million.

Relocation costs, those costs incurred transporting products from one location to another to avoid obsolescence, were not available. Management said that such costs were incurred so infrequently that they were not recorded separately from ordinary transportation costs.

TABLE 9–5 Summary of Data Collection Procedure

Step No.	*Cost of Category*	*Source*	*Explanation*	*Amount (current study)*
1.	Cost of money	Comptroller	This represents the cost of having money invested in inventory and the return should be comparable to other investment opportunities	30% pretax
2.	Average monthly inventory valued at variable costs delivered to the distribution center	1. Standard cost data—comptroller's department 2. Freight rates and product specs are from distribution reports 3. Average monthly inventory in cases from printout received from sales forecasting	Only want variable costs since fixed costs go on regardless of the amount of product manufactured and stored—follow steps outlined in body of report	$7,800,000 valued at variable cost delivered to the DC. Variable manufactured cost equaled 70% of full manufactured cost. Variable cost FOB the DC averaged 78% of full manufactured cost
3.	Taxes	The Comptroller's department	Personal property taxes paid on inventory	$90,948 which equals 1.166%
4.	Insurance	The comptroller's department	Insurance rate/$100 of inventory (at variable costs)	$4,524 which equals 0.058%
5.	Recurring storage (public warehouse)	Distribution operations	This represents the portion of warehousing costs that are related to the volume of inventory stored.	$225,654 annually which equals 2.893%
6.	Variable storage (plant warehouses)	Transportation services	Only include those costs that are variable with the amount of inventory stored.	Nil
7.	Obsolescence	Distribution department reports	Cost of holding product inventory beyond its useful life	0.800 percent of inventory
8.	Shrinkage	Distribution department reports	Only include the portion attributable to inventory storage.	$100,308 which equals 1.286%
9.	Damage	Distribution department reports	Only include the portion attributable to inventory storage.	
10.	Relocation costs	Not available	Only include relocation costs incurred to avoid obsolescence.	Not available
11.	Total inventory carrying costs	Calculate the numbers generated in steps 3, 4, 5, 6, 7, 8, 9, and 10 as a percentage of average inventory valued at variable cost delivered to the distribution center, and add them to the cost of money (step 1).		36.203%

SOURCE: Douglas M. Lambert and Robert H. Quinn, "Profit Oriented Inventory Policies Require a Documented Inventory Carrying Cost," *Business Quarterly* 46, no. 3 (Autumn 1981), p. 71.

such costs were incurred so infrequently that they were not recorded separately from ordinary transportation costs.

Inventory Carrying Cost Was Calculated to Be 36 Percent

Total inventory carrying costs. When totaled, the individual percentages gave an inventory carrying cost of 36.203 percent. Thus, management would use a 36 percent inventory carrying cost when calculating cost trade-offs in the logistics system. Inventory carrying cost calculations for six additional packaged goods companies are included in the appendix to this chapter.

Table 9–5 summarizes the data collection procedure that the consumer packaged goods company used. Notice the distinction between the cost of money component of inventory carrying costs and all of the other component costs. All of the non-cost of money components (steps 3 through 10 of Table 9–5) are annual expenses. Consequently, they appear on the profit and loss statement and affect the firm's net profit. Inventory, however, is a balance sheet account. Inventory becomes an expense only when it is sold and the cost of the inventory is matched with the revenue generated by its sale. Usually, the inventory is replaced when it is sold and the inventory account on the balance sheet remains the same. If the inventory is not replaced, the cash account increases by the amount not spent on the inventory.

While cash, like inventory, is a balance sheet account, the rate of return earned on the cash does affect the profit and loss statement. Multiplying the cash value of a decrease or an increase in inventory by the opportunity cost of money presents the change in inventory as a profit and loss statement "expense"; this can be added to the other expenses, such as insurance and taxes. The out-of-pocket expenses (non-cost of money components) associated with inventory must simply be calculated as a percentage of inventory investment (cash value) and added to the cost of money to determine the total inventory carrying cost percentage.

Up to this point, we have assumed that the company has a relatively homogeneous product line, that is, that products are manufactured at each plant location, shipped in mixed quantities, and stored in the same facilities. Consequently, if the company has a 12-month inventory plan, and standard costs are available, a weighted-average inventory carrying cost can be used for all products and locations. This figure would require updating on an annual basis when the new inventory plan, updated standard costs, and the previous year's expenditures for insurance, taxes, storage, and inventory risk costs become available.

Inventory Carrying Costs May Vary by Storage Location

Management at General Mills, Inc., calculated an inventory carrying cost for each location where products were stored, and found considerable variation.[9] Since the costs have to be collected by storage location, minimal additional effort is required to "fine tune" the numbers for decisions re-

[9]William R. Steele, "Inventory Carrying Cost Identification and Accounting," *Proceedings of the Sixteenth Annual Conference of the National Council of Physical Distribution Management* (Chicago: National Council of Physical Distribution Management, 1979), pp. 75–86.

garding a specific location or type of inventory. If the differences are minimal, the weighted-average inventory carrying cost will be sufficient.

In companies with heterogeneous product lines, however, inventory carrying costs should be calculated for each individual product. For example, bulk chemical products cannot be shipped in mixed quantities or stored in the same tanks. For this reason, transportation and storage costs should be included on a specific product/location basis, rather than using an average transportation and storage cost as one would for homogeneous products. The next section contains an industry example from the bulk chemicals industry, which will clarify the distinction between homogeneous and heterogeneous products.

A BULK CHEMICALS INDUSTRY EXAMPLE

Due to the vastly different nature of bulk chemical products—in terms of storage requirements, shrinkage, and terminal locations—and because of the absence of an inventory forecast, it was necessary to determine an inventory carrying cost figure for each major product or class of products. There was an additional problem caused by the fact that the selling price per ton, the full manufactured cost, and variable costs per ton varied by plant and also varied within a plant throughout the year.

This example will focus on two products manufactured by the industrial chemicals division. One product was selected because it had a relatively low variable cost of production and the other was chosen because its variable cost of production represented a substantially higher percentage of the full manufactured cost. The two products were representative of the range of products manufactured by the company in terms of cost and shipping and storage requirements. Since the variable costs of transportation were different for each stocking point and represented a significant component of the inventory value at field terminals, inventory carrying costs were calculated for each storage location. In this example inventory carrying costs are presented for the manufacturing location and are calculated as a percentage of the variable manufactured costs.

Capital costs. An interview with the comptroller revealed that a 20 percent return after taxes was required on new investments of more than $500,000. As a result of this meeting, it was established that the opportunity cost of capital would be 20 percent after taxes or 40 percent before taxes. The opportunity cost of capital should be applied only to the out-of-pocket investment in inventory. The first step was to determine the standard variable costs of each product and to express these costs as a percentage of full manufactured costs and average net back per ton, which is the average selling price less the selling expenses per ton.[10] Since monthly reports valued inventory at average net back,

[10] During a period of shortages in the chemical industry, the firm began to value inventory investment on management reports at average net back per ton. Since the firm was able to sell the product held in inventory, holding inventory in anticipation of future orders from existing customers prevented sales to new customers. Thus average net back per ton, the selling price less the out-of-pocket costs associated with making the sale was used to represent the cash value of the inventory.

TABLE 9–6 Inventory Carrying Costs for Product LMN

	Percentage Based on Average Net Back per Ton ($393)	*Percentage Based on Budgeted Full Manufacturing Costs per Ton ($138.51)*	*Percentage Based on Variable Costs per Ton ($80.43)*
Capital costs			
Capital cost (minimum acceptable rate of return = 20% after taxes—40% before taxes)	8.188*	23.227†	40.000
Inventory service costs			
Insurance	0.265	0.752	1.295
Taxes (vary with location—average)	0.274	0.777	1.338
Storage space costs	—‡	—‡	—‡
Inventory risk costs			
Obsolescence			
Shrinkage	3.220	9.137§	15.735
Damage			
Relocation costs			
Total (before taxes)	11.947	33.893	58.368
Inventory carrying costs (per ton)	$46.95	$46.95	$46.95

*Based on variable costs of $80.43 per ton and average net back per ton of $393. Variable costs = 20.47% of average per ton net back. Therefore capital costs = 0.2047 × 40% = 8.188% of average net back per ton.

†Budgeted full manufacturing costs were $138.51. Variable costs as a percentage of full manufacturing costs = 58.068%. Therefore capital costs = .58068 × 40% = 23.227%.

‡Fixed over the relevant range of inventory levels.

§Calculated on the basis of tons of shrinkage as a percent of average inventory in tons. Applied to full manufacturing costs as a surrogate for variable manufacturing costs plus transportation, and adjusted to corresponding percentage based on net back and variable costs per ton.

SOURCE: Douglas M. Lambert, *The Development of an Inventory Costing Methodology: A Study of the Costs Associated with Holding Inventory* (Chicago: National Council of Physical Distribution Management, 1976), pp. 167–68.

all components of inventory carrying costs were expressed as a percentage of average net back per ton as well as variable costs and full manufactured costs (see Tables 9–6 and 9–7). Depending on where inventory is held, however, the variable costs as a percentage of average net back per ton may change. This is because transportation costs should be added to field inventory.

Inventory service costs. The company was self-insured for $250,000 of finished-product inventory at each warehouse location, but for inventory over $250,000 at any specific location the insurance rate was $0.2648 per $100 of average inventory. Since the cost of the insurance on the first $250,000 of inventory was not readily available, the $0.2648 per $100 figure was used in the calculation of inventory carrying costs with the realization that it may be fractionally below or above the actual figure.

Taxes paid on inventory vary depending on the state and city in which the terminal is located. The actual tax rate payable for each location should be used when determining specific sites for the terminals. In this case, management believed that tax rates would not change for the coming year, so the average tax figure for the preceding year was used. Based on average monthly inven-

TABLE 9–7 Inventory Carrying Costs for Product XYZ

	Percentage Based on Average Net Back per Ton ($50.84)	*Percentage Based on Budgeted Full Manufacturing Costs per Ton ($28.89)*	*Percentage Based on Variable Costs per Ton ($2.34)*
Capital costs			
Capital cost (minimum acceptable rate of return = 20% after taxes—40% before taxes)	1.841*	3.240	40.000
Inventory Service Costs			
Insurance	0.265	0.466	5.757†
Taxes (vary with location—average)	0.270	0.482	5.865
Storage space costs	—‡	—‡	—‡
Inventory risk costs			
Obsolescence			
Shrinkage	0.730	1.284§	15.852
Damage			
Relocation costs			
Total (before taxes)	3.106	5.472	67.474
Inventory carrying costs (per ton)	$ 1.58	$ 1.58	$ 1.58

*This depends on the percentage of average net back per ton that variable manufacturing costs plus variable transportation costs represent. For product held at the plant and based on $2.34 per ton variable cost and $50.84 average net back per ton, variable cost = 4.602% of average per ton net back. Therefore capital costs = .04602 × 40% = 1.841%. For field inventory, transportation costs would be added before calculating the variable cost percentage.

†Based on variable costs of $2.34 per ton and average net back of $50.84. Variable manufacturing costs = 4.602% of average per ton net back. Consequently, 0.265% of $50.84 = 5.757% of $2.34 and 0.270% of $50.84 = 5.865% of $2.34. Full manufacturing costs were $28.89 per ton, and percentages based on this figure were calculated in a manner similar to the percentages based on average net back per ton.

‡Fixed over the relevant range of inventory levels.

§Calculated on the basis of tons of shrinkage as a percentage of average inventory in tons. Applied to full manufacturing costs as a surrogate for variable manufacturing costs plus transportation and adjusted to corresponding percentage based on net back and variable costs per ton.

SOURCE: Douglas M. Lambert, *The Development of an Inventory Costing Methodology: A Study of the Costs Associated with Holding Inventory* (Chicago: National Council of Physical Distribution Management, 1976), pp. 165–66.

tory figures and taxes for the preceding year, this represented 0.274 percent of inventory valued at average net back. Since taxes represented such a small portion of the total carrying cost, it was unlikely that using the actual taxes for each location would significantly alter the carrying cost percentage.

Storage space costs. The costs associated with *plant storage tanks* were fixed, and therefore not relevant for decisions related to increasing the level of inventory in any particular storage tank. If an increase in inventory required additional plant storage and the installation of new tanks, a capital budgeting decision would be required. Once an additional storage tank was built, changes in the level of product held in the tank would not affect the storage costs.

A similar argument held for *rented terminal space,* since the cost of such space was fixed on an annual basis. The cost per gallon might decrease as larger quantities of storage space were contracted, but usually the total annual cost was insensitive to the quantity of product held within a given tank. Handling

TABLE 9–8 Terminal Inventory and Shrinkage for 19—

	Product XYZ			Product LMN			
	Dollars	*Tons*	*Dollars per Ton*	*Dollars*	*Tons*	*Dollars per Ton*	*Total*
January							
February							
March							
April							
May							
June							
July							
August							
September							
October							
November							
December							
Monthly average							
Annual shrinkage							
Percent shrinkage		*					*

*Best number to use since it is independent of the price per ton (since percentage can be applied to any value of inventory). However, this percentage should only be applied to out-of-pocket costs. Since variable manufacturing costs do not include transportation costs, it is recommended that this shrinkage percentage be applied to full manufacturing costs (surrogate measure for variable manufacturing cost plus transportation). From *Summary of Warehouse Valuation* report from Distribution Accounting.

SOURCE: Douglas M. Lambert, *The Development of an Inventory Costing Methodology: A Study of the Costs Associated with Holding Inventory* (Chicago: National Council of Physical Distribution Management, 1976), p. 164.

costs were related to sales (throughput), and not to the quantity of product held in storage. The manager of warehouse and terminal operations said that in some instances it was necessary to guarantee four turns of inventory per year. A logistics analyst confirmed that, although terminal lease costs were required when making a decision to locate a terminal, once the terminal was onstream its costs were considered fixed when deciding if other customers should be routed through the terminal.

Inventory risk costs. Obsolescence was not a factor, since the company was experiencing a "seller's market" for its products due to product shortages in the chemical industry. In a "buyer's market," however, the obsolescence costs should be measured.

Damage that resulted while the product was in the custody of a carrier was claimed, and was therefore not a significant cost. Managing the claims function has costs attached to it, of course. But the variable cost of making these claims against carriers should not be included in inventory carrying costs, since the majority of these claims are related to throughput and not the amount of inventory held.

All other *shrinkage* costs amounted to 1.51 percent of the average inventory for all products; however, they varied substantially by product. The wide fluctuation in the price of each product, caused by such factors as the plant in which it was produced and the supply-demand relationship, made the dollar shrinkage figure as determined by management extremely tenuous. For this reason a weighted-average cost per ton was calculated for the two products being studied (Table 9–8). However, this problem could be avoided by just considering the shrinkage in tons as a percentage of average annual inventory in tons. This yields a percentage figure that is independent of dollars.

Relocation costs, those costs incurred transporting products from one storage location to another to avoid obsolescence, were believed to be negligible and were not included.

Inventory Carrying Costs May Differ by Product

Total inventory carrying costs. The total inventory carrying cost figure to be used for decision making was 58.36 percent of variable costs before taxes for product LMN, and 67.47 percent of variable costs before taxes for product XYZ. These percentages may seem high, but they apply only to the variable costs associated with the inventory, and not to full manufacturing costs. For example, if these figures were calculated as percentages of the full manufactured costs, they would be 33.89 percent and 5.47 percent, respectively. As percentages of the average net back per ton, they would be 11.95 percent for product LMN and 3.11 percent for product XYZ, even though the inventory carrying costs, expressed in dollars, were $46.95 per ton for product LMN and $1.58 per ton for product XYZ (see Tables 9–6 and 9–7, respectively).

All of the percentages were calculated under the assumption that the inventory would be stored at the plant. However, if the inventory was located in field warehouses, the variable costs would include transportation costs plus any charges associated with moving the product into storage, and would represent a higher percentage of full manufactured cost and average net back per ton. It was recommended that the percentage based on variable costs be used when calculating inventory carrying costs.

This chemical industry example clearly illustrates why it is a mistake to use an inventory carrying cost percentage that is an industry average or textbook percentage. Not only were the inventory carrying costs significantly different for each of the products considered, but the carrying costs varied widely for each product depending on the method of inventory valuation used.

The previous examples should have clarified the methodology and how it can be applied. At this point, readers should be able to calculate an inventory carrying cost percentage for a company.

THE IMPACT OF INVENTORY TURNOVER ON INVENTORY CARRYING COSTS

Increasing Inventory Turns May Reduce Profits

In Chapter 2 we saw that, in many firms, management attempts to improve profitability by emphasizing the need to improve inventory turnover. But pushing for increased inventory turnover without considering the impact on total logistics system costs may actually lead to decreased profitability. For example, Table 9–9 illustrates the impact that increased inventory turnover has on total carrying costs.[11] For a product, product category, di-

[11] This example is adapted from Douglas M. Lambert and Robert H. Quinn, "Profit Oriented Inventory Policies Require a Documented Inventory Carrying Cost," *Business Quarterly* 46, no. 3 (Autumn 1981), pp. 64–65.

TABLE 9–9 The Impact of Inventory Turns on Inventory Carrying Costs

Inventory Turns	*Average Inventory*	*Carrying Cost at 40 Percent*	*Carrying Cost Savings*
1	$750,000	$300,000	—
2	375,000	150,000	$150,000
3	250,000	100,000	50,000
4	187,500	75,000	25,000
5	150,000	60,000	15,000
6	125,000	50,000	10,000
7	107,143	42,857	7,143
8	93,750	37,500	5,357
9	83,333	33,333	4,167
10	75,000	30,000	3,333
11	68,182	27,273	2,727
12	62,500	25,000	2,273
13	57,692	23,077	1,923
14	53,571	21,428	1,649
15	50,000	20,000	1,428

SOURCE: Douglas M. Lambert and Robert H. Quinn, "Profit Oriented Inventory Policies Require a Documented Inventory Carrying Cost," *Business Quarterly* 46, no. 3 (Autumn 1981), p. 65.

vision, or company with sales of $750,000 at cost, inventory turn would equal 1 if the average inventory were $750,000. If the inventory carrying costs were 40 percent, they would represent $300,000 on an annual basis. Increasing inventory turns from 1 to 2 times would lead to a $150,000 decrease in inventory carrying costs; this would represent a 50 percent savings. Improving turns from 6 times to 12 times also would result in a 50 percent reduction in inventory carrying costs, but it would represent a much smaller savings of $25,000. Many times management finds itself in a position where inventory turns are expected to increase each year. If the company is inefficient and has too much inventory, increasing inventory turns will lead to increased profitability. However, continued improvements in inventory turns, in the absence of a systems change, will eventually result in the firm cutting inventories below the optimal level. If a logistics system is currently efficient and the goal is to increase turns from 11 to 12, the annual savings in carrying costs would be $2,273 (see Table 9–9). Care must be taken that transportation costs, lot quantity costs, warehouse picking costs, and/or order processing and information costs do not increase by more than this amount; that lower customer service levels do not result in lost profit contribution in excess of the carrying cost savings; or that some combination of the above does not occur.

Figure 9–8 illustrates graphically the relationship between inventory carrying costs and the number of inventory turnovers, using the data that were presented in Table 9–9. The example shows that improvements in the number of inventory turns has the greatest impact if inventory is turned less than six times per year. In fact, beyond eight turns the curve becomes relatively flat. Increasing inventory turns from five to six times generates the same savings in inventory carrying costs as does improving them from 10 to 15 times. When establishing inventory turnover objectives,

FIGURE 9–8 Relationship between Inventory Turns and Inventory Carrying Costs

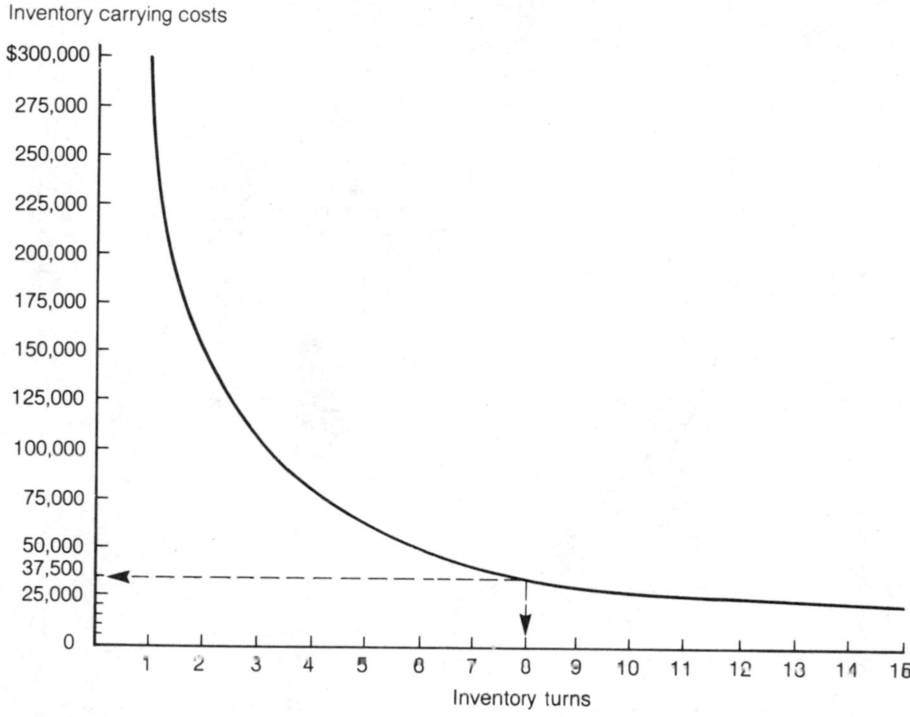

SOURCE: Douglas M. Lambert and Robert H. Quinn, "Profit Oriented Inventory Policies Require a Documented Inventory Carrying Cost," *Business Quarterly* 46, no. 3 (Autumn 1981), p. 65.

it is necessary to fully document how each alternative strategy will increase the other logistics costs and compare this to the savings in inventory carrying costs.

Inventory Carrying Costs per Unit

For a number of management decisions it may be useful to calculate inventory carrying costs on a per-unit basis. In the words of a former logistics executive:

> When managing inventories, I found it useful to calculate the average inventory carrying cost per unit shipped and compare this amount to the gross margin, contribution margin and sales price per unit for each of our SKUs. I found it much easier to convince management of the impact of their decisions by expressing the data on individual products (items) or base model groups within a given product line. It is easier to quantify trade-offs when per-unit costs are used. For example, to compare the cost of carrying an item in inventory for another three months versus transshipping it to another distribution center location versus the cost to mark it down *X* dollars to sell it at its existing location.[12]

[12] Professor Jay U. Sterling, University of Alabama, 1986.

FIGURE 9–9 Annual Inventory Carrying Costs Compared to Inventory Turnovers

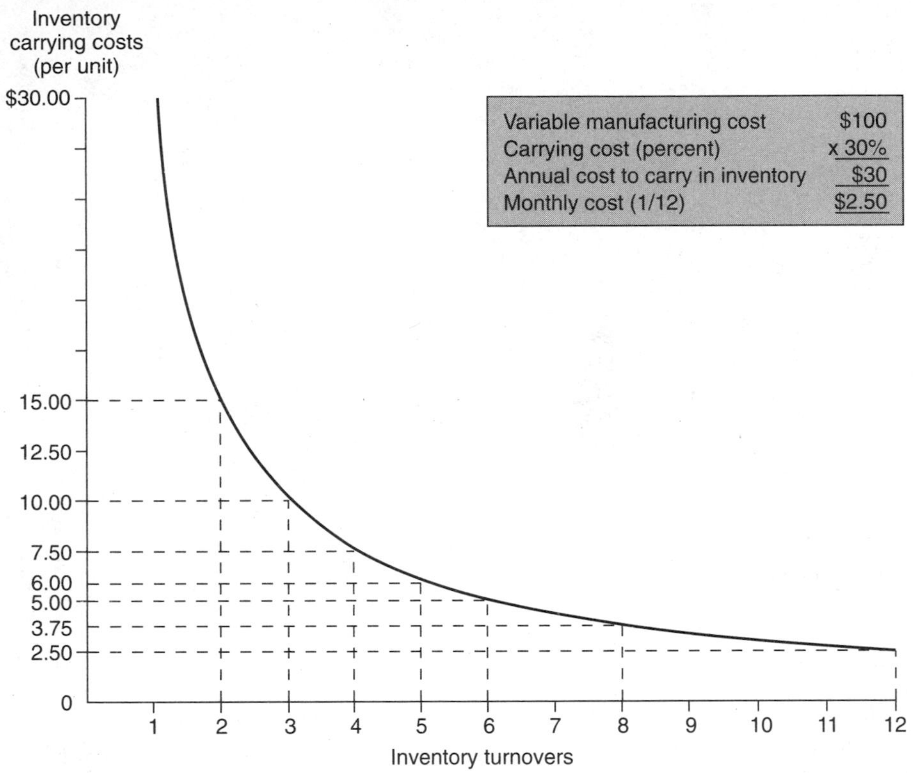

SOURCE: Jay U. Sterling and Douglas M. Lambert, "Segment Profitability Reports: You Can't Manage Your Business Without Them," unpublished manuscript, 1992.

The inventory carrying costs associated with each item sold can vary dramatically for high-turnover versus low-volume, low-turn items. The previous analysis of inventory carrying costs and inventory turns is repeated using a carrying cost per unit example in order to illustrate this point. For example, if the variable manufacturing cost of an item is $100 and the annual inventory carrying cost is 30 percent, the monthly cost to carry the item in inventory is $2.50 ($30 ÷ 12). Annual turns of 1 (12 months in inventory) would consume $30 in carrying costs, whereas 2 turns per year would cost $15, 4 turns, $7.50 and 8 turns, $3.75 (see Figure 9–9). It is not uncommon for some items in a product line to turn less than once a year. This can easily place an otherwise profitable line into a loss position. One inventory turn per year would result in a charge of $30.00 in inventory carrying costs for every unit sold. On the other hand 15 turns per year would result in a charge of only $2.00 per unit. This example should make it clear how inventory turns affect the profitability of each item sold. In the next chapter we will review methods for improving the profitability of products by better managing their inventories.

SUMMARY

In this chapter we saw how to determine the impact of inventory investment on a firm's corporate profit performance. We also examined the way in which inventory policy affects least total cost logistics, and discussed a methodology that can be used to calculate inventory carrying costs. Finally, we looked at the relationship between inventory turnover and inventory carrying costs.

By now it should be apparent that inventory is a costly investment. With an awareness of this fact, and a knowledge of the procedures used to determine inventory carrying costs, we are ready to take a detailed look at inventory management. That is the subject of Chapter 10.

SUGGESTED READINGS

LAMBERT, DOUGLAS M. *The Development of an Inventory Costing Methodology: A Study of the Costs Associated With Holding Inventory.* Chicago: National Council of Physical Distribution Management, 1976.

LAMBERT, DOUGLAS M., AND JOHN T. MENTZER. "Inventory Carrying Costs: Current Availability and Uses." *International Journal of Physical Distribution and Materials Management* 9, no. 6 (1979), pp. 256–71. Reprinted in *New Horizons in Distribution and Materials Management,* ed. Martin Christopher. *International Journal of Physical Distribution and Materials Management* 12, no. 3 (1982), pp. 56–71.

STEELE, WILLIAM R. "Inventory Carrying Cost Identification and Accounting." *Proceedings of the Sixteenth Annual Conference of the National Council of Physical Distribution.* Chicago: National Council of Physical Distribution Management, 1979, pp. 75–86.

QUESTIONS AND PROBLEMS

1. Explain how excessive inventories can erode corporate profitability.
2. Many businesspeople rely on industry averages or textbook percentages for the inventory carrying cost that they use when setting inventory levels. Why is this approach wrong?
3. Explain how you would determine the cost of capital that should be used in inventory decisions.

4. How would you determine the cash value of a manufacturer's finished goods inventory investment? How would this differ in the case of a wholesaler or retailer?
5. What is the difference between the transportation cost component of logistics cost trade-off analysis and the transportation cost included in the inventory valuation (cash value)?
6. What problems do you foresee in gathering the cost information required to calculate inventory carrying costs for a company?
7. Describe the circumstances under which inventory carrying costs can vary within a given manufacturing company. Explain why total inventory carrying costs decrease, but at an ever-slower rate, as inventory turnovers increase. Consider raw materials, goods in process, and finished goods inventories in your answer.
8. Using the following data, determine the fixed and variable warehousing costs for this plant warehouse.

Month	*Number of Loads Shipped*	*Total Plant Warehousing Cost*
January	750	$ 9,200
February	1,080	10,800
March	1,010	11,400
April	840	9,900
May	860	10,900
June	830	10,800
July	970	11,200
August	920	10,000
September	1,160	11,000
October	1,200	12,300
November	1,100	11,600
December	510	9,300

9. Calculate the inventory carrying cost percentage for XYZ Company, given the following information:
   a. Finished goods inventory is $26 million, valued at full manufactured cost.
   b. Based on the inventory plan, the weighted-average variable manufactured cost per case is 70 percent of the full manufactured cost.
   c. The transportation cost incurred by moving the inventory to field warehouse locations was $1,500,000.
   d. The variable handling cost of moving this inventory into warehouse locations was calculated to be $300,000.
   e. The company is currently experiencing capital rationing, and new investments are required to earn 15 percent after taxes.
   f. Personal property tax paid on inventory was approximately $200,000.
   g. Insurance to protect against loss of finished goods inventory was $50,000.
   h. Storage charges at public warehouses totaled $450,000.
   i. Variable plant storage was negligible.
   j. Obsolescence was $90,000.
   k. Shrinkage was $100,000.
   l. Damage related to finished goods inventory levels was $10,000.

m. Transportation costs associated with the relocation of field inventory to avoid obsolescence was $50,000.

10. ABC Company changes from a mailed-based order processing system to a system in which customers telephone in their orders. Show the impact of this change on ABC's after-tax return on net worth, given: (*a*) the financial data contained in Figure 9–1; (*b*) the annual cost of the new system is $396,000 greater than the cost of the existing system; (*c*) the inventory carrying cost is 38 percent, which includes a cost of money of 30 percent; (*d*) the estimated reduction in inventories resulting from three days of increased planning time is $6,000,000; and (*e*) the variable delivered cost of inventory (to warehouse locations) is 70 percent of full manufactured costs.

11. Using your answer from question 10, what percentage increase in sales would be necessary in order to realize a similar impact on return on net worth?

APPENDIX
Inventory Carrying Costs—Six Case Studies

In order to provide further knowledge on how to calculate inventory carrying costs, this appendix presents data from six case studies of manufacturers of packaged goods products. Although some of the companies had substantial institutional sales, most of their sales were in the household consumer market. All of the companies had sales of over $1 billion annually.

Three of the firms used public warehouses to satisfy 100 percent of their field warehousing requirements. One company used leased facilities exclusively and another used public warehouses and corporate-managed facilities on a 50–50 basis. The sixth company used private, leased, and public warehouses on a 10 percent, 40 percent, and 50 percent basis, respectively. In addition to plant warehouses, the number of field warehouses used by the respondents ranged from 5 to over 20, with two companies falling into the last category.

The data collected from the six companies are shown in Table 9A-1. The results support the contention that each company should calculate its own figure, since individual carrying cost percentages ranged from a low of 14 percent to a high of 43 percent before taxes. With few exceptions, the data were readily available in each of the companies; however, a number of minor data-collection problems were experienced:

1. One company did not have a specific hurdle rate for new investments. Another company used a hurdle rate of 20 percent but was

SOURCE: Douglas M. Lambert *The Development of an Inventory Costing Methodology: A Study of the Costs Associated with Holding Inventory* (Chicago: National Council of Physical Distribution Management, 1976), pp. 80–103.

TABLE 9A–1 Summary of Inventory Carrying Cost Data from Six Packaged Goods Companies

	Company A	*Company B*	*Company C*	*Company D*	*Company E*	*Company F*
Inventory carrying cost components						
Capital costs	40.000%	29.000%	25.500%	8.000%	30.000%	26.000%
Inventory service costs						
Insurance	0.091	0.210	1.689	0.126	0.023	4.546
Taxes	1.897	0.460	0.085	1.218	0.028	0.334
Storage space costs						
Recurring storage	0.738	—	0.573	2.681	0.456	2.925
Inventory risk costs						
Obsolescence	—	—	—	0.785	1.700	n.a.
Damage	0.233	0.398	0.500	1.393	0.124	—
Shrinkage	—	—	—	—	0.329	—
Transshipment costs	—	—	—	n.a.	0.302	—
Total inventory carrying costs (before taxes)*	42.959†	30.068	28.347	14.203‡	32.962	33.805§
Inventory carrying cost percentage used prior to this study	9.5″	15	20	8	25	15
Average inventory of division or product group studied	$10,000,000	$25,000,000	$8,000,000	$500,000	$45,000,000	$2,000,000
Method of inventory valuation	Full manufactured cost	Variable cost delivered to the customer	Actual variable costs of production	Full manufactured cost	Variable cost delivered to D.C.	Full manufactured cost
Time required for data collection	16 hours	70 hours but only 20 hours per year required for update	40 hours	30 hours	20 hours	20 hours

*As a percentage of the variable costs delivered to the distribution center (this allows a comparison to be made of all companies).

†Inventory carrying costs were 35.441 percent of the full manufactured cost.

‡Inventory carrying costs were 14.100 percent of the full manufactured cost.

§Inventory carrying costs were 27.321 percent of the full manufactured cost.

″Although 9.5 percent was the after-tax number, the company had been using it as a before-tax figure in the cost trade-off analysis.

required to pay its corporate head office only 8 percent for money that was invested in inventories or accounts receivable. Consequently, the 8 percent figure was used since it reflected the division's true cost.

2. The inventory investment data and the insurance and taxes on the inventory investment were readily available in most cases. But in one company three days work was required to determine accurately a tax calculation of 0.460 percent of the inventory value. Since a small percentage error would have little impact on a carrying cost of 30 percent, it was recommended that, in the future, the percentage of total inventory represented by each product group be applied to the

total tax figure. This procedure would require approximately 15 minutes.

3. The variable costs associated with the amount of inventory held were available in every company; however, the costs of damage and shrinkage, and to some extent the cost of obsolescence, required managerial estimates. In only one company were these costs not recorded.
4. Relocation costs, which are the costs associated with the transshipment of inventory from one stocking location to another to avoid obsolescence, were believed to be negligible.

For all six companies, the time required to calculate the carrying cost figures was minimal. However, some caution should be exercised in viewing the time required for data-collection as the absolute maximum. This is because the times reported assume a certain level of sophistication in terms of the corporate accounting system. In a less sophisticated company it is conceivable that substantial additional effort may be required in order to accurately trace some of the cost components. For example, in situations in which inventory risk costs represent a substantial proportion of the total inventory carrying costs, a managerial estimate of the proportion of these costs related to the level of inventory held would not suffice. Consequently, it would be necessary to implement a reporting system that would accurately reflect these costs, or to use regression analysis to determine the portion of these costs that were variable with the quantity of inventory.

Table 9A–2 contains a summary of *where* in each of the six organizations the individual carrying cost components were obtained. This table should be of considerable use as an indicator of where in a company one might look for specific inventory carrying cost components.

Finally, there was one minor problem in terms of using the inventory carrying cost percentage in economic order quantity (EOQ) analysis. If the quantity generated from this formula required that additional fixed storage space be added, then the EOQ should be recalculated, including an estimated annual cost for the additional facilities. Should the EOQ change appreciably, a number of additional recalculations would be necessary in order to find the best trade-off between order quantity and the additional capital costs.

TABLE 9A–2 Summary of Data Collection Procedure Showing Source of Data

Step No.	*Cost Category*	*Explanation*	*Company A*
1.	Cost of money	The cost of money invested in inventory; the return should be comparable to other investment opportunities	Corporate controller
2.	Average monthly inventory valued at variable costs delivered to the distribution center	Only want variable costs, since fixed costs remain the same regardless of inventory levels	Standard costs from accounting Inventory plan from distribution Location of inventory and freight rates from distribution
3.	Taxes	Personal property taxes paid on finished goods inventory	Manager, corporate taxes
4.	Insurance	Insurance paid on inventory investment	Budgeted figures from accounting
5.	Variable storage	Only include those costs that are variable with the amount of inventory stored	Manager, materials management
6.	Obsolescence	Obsolescence due to holding inventory	Manager, materials management planning and analysis (steps 6–9)
7.	Shrinkage	Shrinkage related to volume of inventory	
8.	Damage	Damage that is directly attributable to the level of inventory held	
9.	Relocation costs	Only relocation costs that result to avoid obsolescence	
10.	Total carrying costs percentage	Calculate the numbers generated in steps 3 to 9 as a percentage of average inventory, and add to cost of money (step 1)	

Company B	*Company C*	*Company D*	*Company E*	*Company F*
Divisional vice president and general managers	Vice president and controller	Vice president controller and treasurer	Manager, financial analysis	Vice president and controller
Monthly computer printout	Director of distribution planning from monthly inventory printout	Standard cost data from controller's dept. Freight rates and product specs from distribution reports Average monthly inventory in cases from sales forecasting	Inventory planning manager	From budget report
Property tax representative	Director, corporate insurance	Controller department	Manager, ad valorem taxes	From budget
Manager, corporate insurance	Director, corporate insurance	Controller's department	Assistant treasurer	
Warehouse managers	Director, distribution center operations	Distribution operations and transportation	Year-end summary of monthly report	Distribution report
Manager claims shrinkage and damage	Not available	From distribution department reports	Reclamation expense report	Distribution reports or knowledge of manager
			Reclamation expense report	
			Manager, materials handling systems	
Manager, distribution research	Not available	Not available	Inventory planning manager	

Chapter 10

Inventory Management

Objectives of This Chapter

To show how the basic concepts of inventory management are applied

To show how to calculate safety stocks

To show how production policies influence inventory levels

To show how inventories and customer service levels are interrelated

To show how to recognize poor inventory management

To show how to improve inventory management

To show how profit performance can be improved by systems that reduce inventories

INTRODUCTION

In the last chapter, we saw that inventory is a large and costly investment. Better management of corporate inventories can improve cash flow and return on investment. Nevertheless, most companies (retailers, wholesalers, and manufacturers) suffer through periodic inventory rituals; that is, crash inventory reduction programs are instituted every few years: "[The reduction programs] usually last two or three months and are characterized by top management edicts, middle management lip service—and insufficient knowledge of how to control inventory investment at all levels."[1]

Obviously, a more coherent program of inventory management is necessary. This chapter will provide the reader with the knowledge required to improve the practice of inventory management.

BASIC INVENTORY CONCEPTS

In this section, we will consider basic inventory concepts such as the reasons for holding inventory and the various types of inventory.

Why Hold Inventory?

Five Reasons for Holding Inventory

Formulation of an inventory policy requires an understanding of the role of inventory in manufacturing and marketing. Inventory serves five purposes within the firm: (1) It enables the firm to achieve economies of scale; (2) it balances supply and demand; (3) it enables specialization in manufacturing; (4) it provides protection from uncertainties in demand and order cycle; and (5) it acts as a buffer between critical interfaces within the channel of distribution.

[1]Jay U. Sterling, "Planning and Controlling Sales and Inventories," unpublished manuscript, University of Alabama, 1985, p. 1.

Economies of Scale. Inventory is required if a firm is to realize economies of scale in purchasing, transportation, and/or manufacturing. For example, raw materials inventory is necessary if the manufacturer is to take advantage of the per-unit price reductions associated with volume purchases. Purchased materials have a lower transportation cost per unit if ordered in larger volumes. This lower per-unit cost results because truckload and full railcar shipments receive lower transportation rates than smaller shipments of less than truckload (LTL) or less than carload (LCL) quantities.

The reasons for holding *finished goods inventory* are similar to reasons for holding raw materials inventory. Transportation economies are possible with large-volume shipments, but in order for a firm to take advantage of these more economical rates, larger quantities of finished goods inventory are required at manufacturing locations and field warehouse locations, or at customers' locations.

Finished goods inventory also makes it possible to realize manufacturing economies. Plant capacity is greater and per-unit manufacturing costs are lower if a firm schedules long production runs with few line changes. Manufacturing in small quantities leads to short production runs and high changeover costs.

The production of large quantities, however, may require that some of the items be carried in inventory for a significant period of time before they can be sold. The production of large quantities may also prevent timely and responsive recovery on items that are stocked out, since large production runs mean that items will be produced less frequently. The cost of maintaining this inventory must be compared to the production savings realized. Although frequent production changeovers reduce the quantity of inventory that must be carried, and shorten the lead time that is required in the event of a stockout, they require time that could be used for manufacturing a product. When a plant is operating at or near capacity, frequent line changes may mean that contribution to profit is lost because there is not enough product to meet demand. In such situations, the cost of lost sales plus the changeover costs must be compared to the increase in inventory carrying costs that would result from longer production runs.

Frequent Production Changeovers Reduce Manufacturing Capacity

Balancing Supply and Demand. Seasonal supply and/or demand may make it necessary for a firm to hold inventory. For example, a producer of a premium line of boxed chocolates experiences significant sales volume increases at Christmas, Valentine's Day, Easter, and Mother's Day. The cost of establishing production capacity to handle the volume at these peak periods would be substantial. In addition, substantial idle capacity and wide fluctuations in the labor force would result if the company were to produce to demand. The decision to maintain a relatively stable work force and produce at a somewhat constant level throughout the year creates significant inventory buildup at various times during the year, but at a lower total cost to the firm. The seasonal inventories are stored in a freezer warehouse that was built adjacent to the plant.

On the other hand, demand for a product may be relatively stable throughout the year, but raw materials may be available only at certain times during the year. Such is the case for producers of canned fruits and vegetables. This makes it necessary to manufacture finished products in excess of current demand and hold them in inventory.

Specialization. Inventory makes it possible for each of a firm's plants to specialize in the products that it manufactures. The finished products can be shipped to large mixing warehouses, from which customer orders and products for field warehouses can be shipped. The economies that result from the longer production runs, as well as savings in transportation costs, more than offset the costs of additional handling. Companies such as Whirlpool Corporation have found significant cost savings in the operation of consolidation warehouses that allow the firm to specialize manufacturing by plant location. The specialization by facility is known as focused factories.

Raw Materials Inventory

Protection from Uncertainties. Inventory is also held as protection from uncertainties. Raw materials inventories in excess of those required to support production can result from speculative purchases made because management expects a future price increase or future supply is in doubt due to a potential strike, for example. Other reasons include seasonal availability of supply, such as in the case of fruits or vegetables for canning, or a desire to maintain a source of supply. Regardless of the reason for maintaining a raw materials inventory, the costs of holding the inventory should be compared to the savings realized or costs avoided by holding it.

Work-in-Process Inventory

Work-in-process inventory is often maintained between manufacturing operations within a plant to avoid a shutdown if a critical piece of equipment were to break down, and to equalize flow, since not all manufacturing operations produce at the same rate. The stockpiling of work in process within the manufacturing complex permits maximum economies of production without work stoppage.

Inventory planning is critical to successful manufacturing operations since a shortage of raw materials can shut down the production line or lead to a modification of the production schedule; these events may increase expense and/or result in a shortage of finished product. While shortages of raw materials can disrupt normal manufacturing operations, excessive inventories can increase costs and reduce profitability by increasing inventory carrying costs.

Finished Goods Inventory

Finally, finished goods inventory can be used as a means of improving customer service levels by reducing the likelihood of a stockout due to unanticipated demand or variability in lead time.

If the inventory is balanced, increased inventory investment will enable the manufacturer to offer higher levels of product availability and less chance of a stockout. A balanced inventory is one that contains items in proportion to expected demand.

Inventory as a Buffer. Inventory is held throughout the channel of distribution to act as a buffer for the following critical interfaces:

- Supplier-procurement (purchasing).
- Procurement-production.
- Production-marketing.
- Marketing-distribution.
- Distribution-intermediary.
- Intermediary-consumer/user.

Because channel participants are separated geographically, it is necessary for inventory to be held throughout the channel of distribution in order to successfully achieve time and place utility.[2]

Figure 10–1 shows the typical inventory positions in a supplier-manufacturer-intermediary-consumer channel of distribution. Raw materials must be moved from a source of supply to the manufacturing location, where they will be input into the manufacturing process. In many cases this will require holding work-in-process inventory.

Once the manufacturing process has been completed, product must be moved into finished goods inventory at plant locations. The next step is the strategic deployment of finished goods inventory to field locations, which may include corporate-owned or leased distribution centers, public warehouses, wholesalers' warehouses, and/or retail chain distribution centers. Inventory is then positioned to enable customer purchase. Similarly, the customer maintains an inventory to support individual or institutional consumption.

No Product Moves Until Information Moves

All of these product flows are the result of a transaction between the manufacturer and its customer, or a decision by the ultimate consumer or user to purchase the product. The entire process depends on a communications network that moves information from the customer to the firm, through the firm back to the customer, and to the firm's suppliers. Clearly, communications is an integral part of a logistics system.

Often it is necessary to move a product backward through the channel for a variety of reasons. For example, a customer may return a product because it is damaged, or a manufacturer may need to recall a product because of defects.

Finally, another aspect that promises to become a bigger factor in the future is waste disposal. One specific example involves "bottle laws," such as those enacted in Michigan, Vermont, Oregon, and Iowa. As sensitivity to litter from packaging and concern over resource utilization increase, en-

[2] We discussed time and place utility in Chapter 1.

FIGURE 10–1 The Logistics Flow

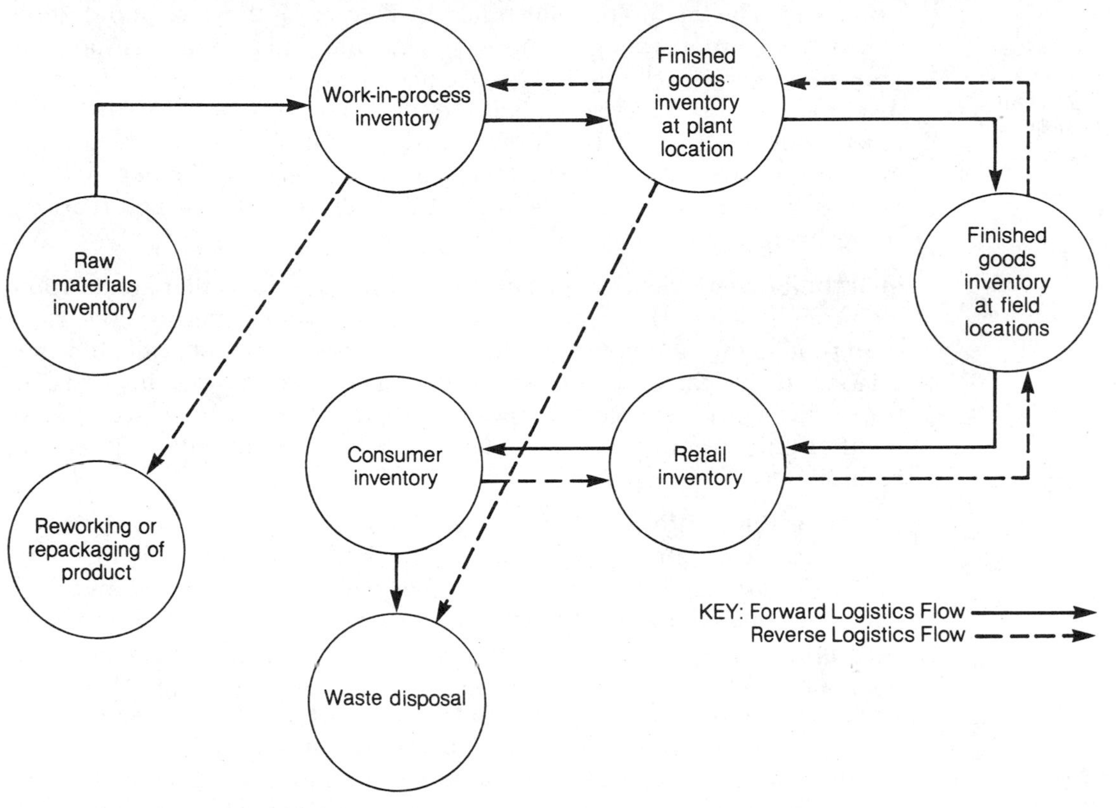

vironmentalists and concerned citizens in other states—if not nationally—are likely to push for such laws. To date, these laws have applied only to beer and soft-drink containers, but other packaging materials may become future targets.

Types of Inventory

Six Types of Inventory

Inventories can be categorized into the following types, signifying the reasons for which they are accumulated: cycle stock, in-transit inventories, safety or buffer stock, speculative stock, seasonal stock, and dead stock.

Cycle Stock. Cycle stock is inventory that results from the replenishment process and is required in order to meet demand under conditions of certainty—that is, when the firm can predict demand and replenishment times (lead times) perfectly. For example, if the rate of sales for a product is a constant 20 units per day and the lead time is always 10 days, no inventory beyond the cycle stock would be required. While assumptions of constant demand and lead time remove the complexities involved in inventory management, let's look at such an example to clarify the basic inventory principles. The example is illustrated in Figure 10–2, which shows three alternative reorder strategies. Since demand and lead time are constant and known, orders are scheduled to arrive just as the last unit is sold. Thus, no inventory beyond the cycle stock is required. The average cycle stock in all three examples is equal to half of the order quantity. However, the average cycle stock will be 200, 100, or 300 units depending on whether management orders in quantities of 400 (Part A), 200 (Part B), or 600 (Part C), respectively.

If Demand and Lead Time Are Constant, Only Cycle Stock Is Necessary

In-Transit Inventories. In-transit inventories are items that are en route from one location to another. They may be considered part of cycle stock even though they are not available for sale and/or shipment until after they arrive at the destination. For the calculation of inventory carrying costs, in-transit inventories should be considered as inventory at the place of shipment origin since the items are not available for use/sale and/or subsequent reshipment.

Safety or Buffer Stock. Safety or buffer stock is held in excess of cycle stock because of uncertainty in demand or lead time. The notion is that a portion of average inventory should be devoted to cover short-range variations in demand and lead time. Average inventory at a stock-keeping location that experiences demand and/or lead time variability, is equal to half the order quantity plus the safety stock. For example, in Figure 10–3, the average inventory would be 100 units if demand and lead time were constant. But if demand was actually 25 units per day instead of the predicted 20 units per day with a 10-day lead time, inventory would be depleted by the 8th day (200/25). Since the next order would not arrive until the 10th day (order was placed on day zero), the company would experience stockouts for two days. At 25 units of demand per day, this would be a stockout of 50 units in total. If management believed that the maximum variation in demand would be plus or minus 5 units, a safety stock of 50 units would prevent a stockout due to variation in demand. This would require holding an average inventory of 150 units.

Variability in Demand Increases Safety Stock

Now consider the case in which demand is constant but lead time can vary by plus or minus two days (Part B of Figure 10–3). If the order arrives 2 days early, the inventory on hand would be equal to a 12-day supply, or 240 units, since sales are at a rate of 20 units per day and 40 units would remain in inventory when the new order arrived. However, if the order arrived 2 days late, on day 12—which is a more likely occurrence—the firm would experience stockouts for a period of 2 days (40 units). If management believed that shipments would never arrive more than two days late, a safety stock of 40 units would ensure that a stockout due to variation in lead time would not occur if demand remained constant.

Variability in Lead Time Increases Safety Stock

In most business situations management must be able to deal with var-

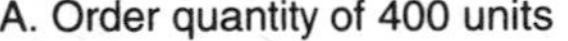

FIGURE 10–2 The Effect of Reorder Quantity on Average Inventory Investment with Constant Demand and Lead Time

A. Order quantity of 400 units

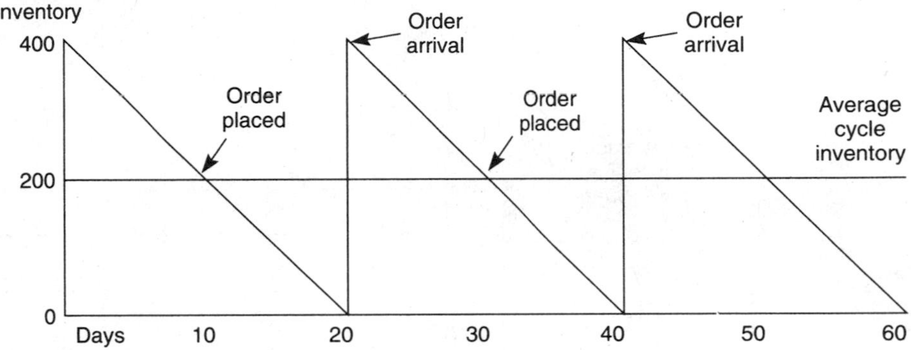

B. Order quantity of 200 units

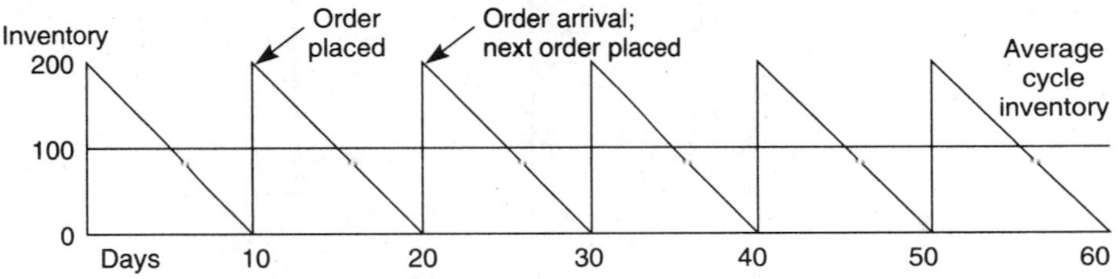

C. Order quantity of 600 units

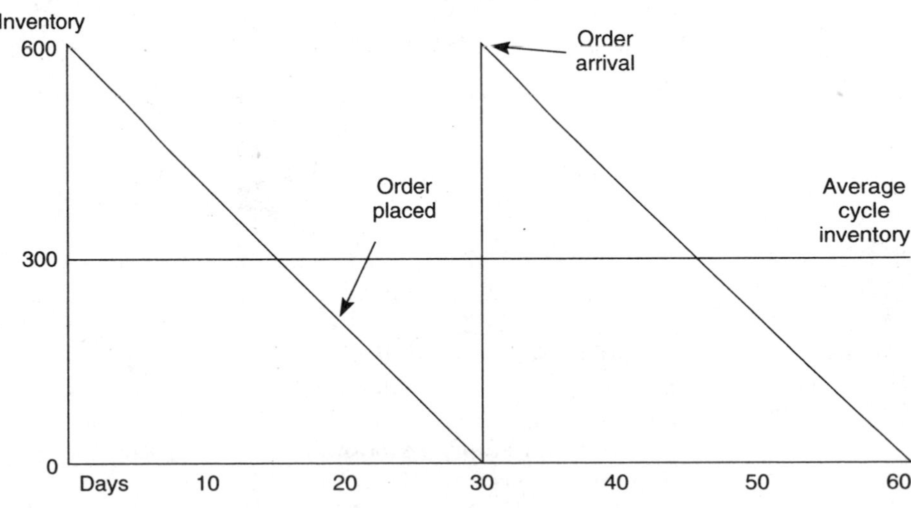

FIGURE 10–3 Average Inventory Investment under Conditions of Uncertainty

A. With variable demand

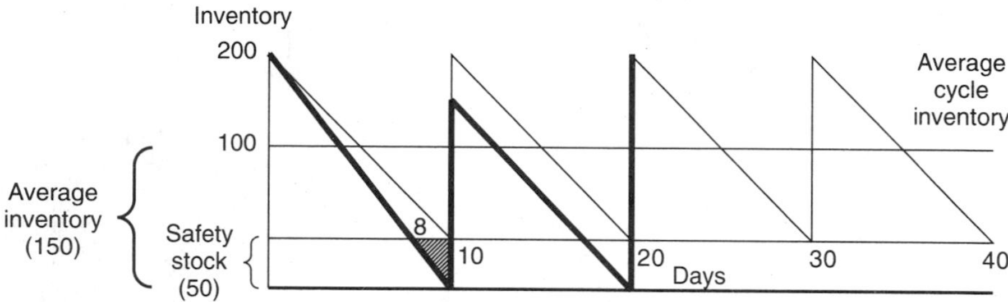

B. With variable lead time

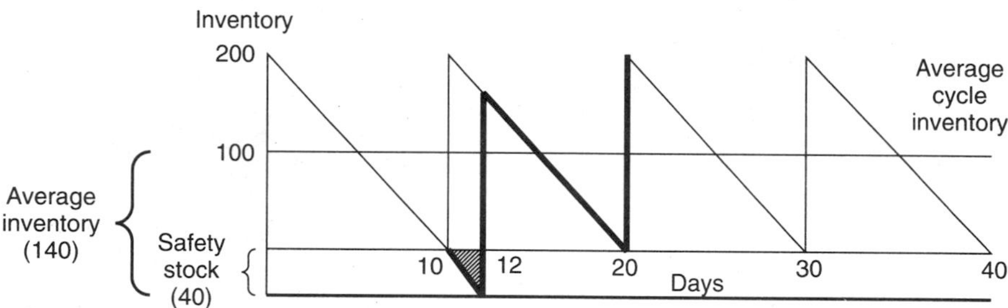

C. With variable demand and lead time

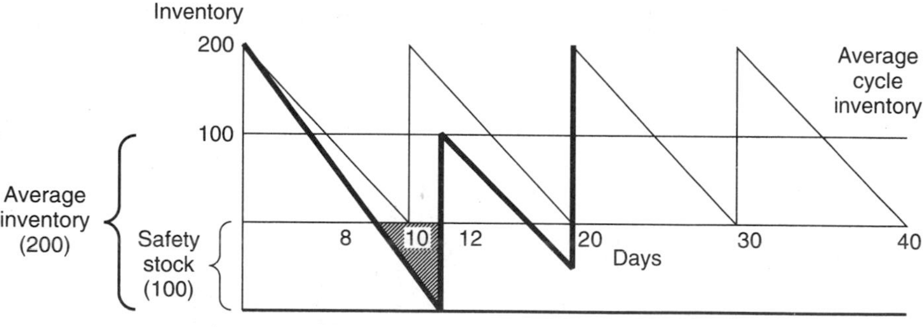

Demand and Lead Time Variability Are a Fact of Life

iability in demand and lead time. Forecasting is rarely accurate enough to predict demand, and demand is seldom, if ever, constant. In addition, transportation delays along with supplier and production problems make lead time variability a fact of life. Consider Part C of Figure 10–3, in which demand uncertainty (Part A) and lead time uncertainty (Part B) are combined. Combined uncertainty is the worst of all possible worlds. In this case demand is above forecast by the maximum, 25 units instead of 20 units per day, and the incoming order arrives two days late. The result is a stockout period of four days at 25 units per day. If management wanted to protect against the maximum variability in both demand and lead time, the firm would need a safety stock of 100 units. This policy (no stockouts) would result in an average inventory of 200 units.

Speculative Stock. Speculative stock is inventory held for reasons other than satisfying current demand. For example, materials may be purchased in volumes larger than necessary in order to receive quantity discounts, because of a forecasted price increase or materials shortage, or to protect against the possibility of a strike. Production economics may also lead to the manufacture of products at times other than when they are demanded. Finally, goods may be produced seasonally for consumption throughout the year, or at a constant level in anticipation of seasonal demand in order to maintain a stable workload and labor force.

Seasonal Stock. Seasonal stock is a form of speculative stock that involves the accumulation of inventory before a season begins in order to maintain a stable labor force and stable production runs.

Dead Stock. Dead stock is the set of items for which no demand has been registered for some specified period of time. Such stock might be obsolete on a total company basis or just at one stock-keeping location. If it is the latter, the items may be transshipped to another location to avoid the obsolescence penalty or marked down and sold at its current location.

BASIC INVENTORY MANAGEMENT

The Objectives of Inventory Management

Inventory is a major use of capital and, for this reason, the objectives of inventory management are to increase corporate profitability, to predict the impact of corporate policies on inventory levels, and to minimize the total cost of logistics activities.

Corporate profitability can be improved by increasing sales volume or cutting inventory costs. Increased sales are often possible if high levels of inventory lead to better in-stock availability and more consistent service levels. Methods of decreasing inventory-related costs include such measures as reducing the number of back orders or expedited shipments, purging obsolete or dead stock from the system, or improving the accuracy of forecasts. Transshipment of inventory between field warehouses and small-lot transfers can also be reduced or eliminated by better inventory planning. Better inventory management can increase the ability to control and predict the reaction of inventory investment to changes in management policy. For example, how will a change in the corporate hurdle rate influence the quantity of inventory held?

Finally, total cost integration should be the goal of inventory planning. That is, management must determine the inventory level required to achieve least total cost logistics, given the required customer service objectives.

Inventory managers must determine how much inventory to order and when to place the order. In order to illustrate the basic principles of reorder policy, let's consider inventory management under conditions of certainty and uncertainty. This latter case is the rule rather than the exception.

Inventory Management under Conditions of Certainty

Ordering Costs

Replenishment policy under conditions of certainty requires the balancing of ordering costs against inventory carrying costs.[3] For example, a policy of ordering large quantities infrequently may result in inventory carrying costs in excess of the savings in ordering costs. Ordering costs for products purchased from an outside supplier typically include (1) the cost of transmitting the order, (2) the cost of receiving the product, (3) the cost of placing it in storage, and (4) the cost associated with processing the invoice for payment. In the case of restocking its own field warehouses, a company's ordering costs typically include (1) the cost of transmitting and processing the inventory transfer; (2) the cost of handling the product if it is in stock, or the cost of setting up production to produce it, and the handling cost if the product is not in stock; (3) the cost of receiving at the field location; and (4) the cost of associated documentation. Remember that only direct out-of-pocket expenses should be included. These costs will be explained in detail in Chapter 13.

The EOQ Model

Economic Order Quantity. The best ordering policy can be determined by minimizing the total of inventory carrying costs and ordering costs using the economic order quantity model (EOQ).

Referring to the example given in Figure 10–2, two questions seem appropriate:

1. Should we place orders for 200, 400, or 600 units, or some other quantity?
2. What is the impact on inventory if orders are placed at 10-, 20-, or 30-day intervals, or some other time period? Assuming constant demand and lead time, sales of 20 units per day and 240 working days per year, annual sales will be 4,800 units.[4] If orders are placed every 10 days, 24 orders of 200 units will be placed. With a 20-day order interval, 12 orders of 400 units are required. If the 30-day order interval is selected, 8 orders of 600 units are necessary. The average

[3] When the supplier pays the freight cost.

[4] For this example, it was assumed that the plant was closed for four weeks during each year. In an industrial application we would use the actual number of working days for the firm in question.

inventory is 100, 200, and 300 units, respectively. Which of these policies would be best?

The cost trade-offs required to determine the most economical order quantity are shown graphically in Figure 10–4. By determining the EOQ and dividing the annual demand by it, the frequency and size of the order that will minimize the two costs are identified.

The EOQ in units can be calculated using the following formula:

$$EOQ = \sqrt{\frac{2PD}{CV}}$$

where

P = The ordering cost (dollars per order)
D = Annual demand or usage of the product (number of units)
C = Annual inventory carrying cost (as a percentage of product cost or value)
V = Average cost or value of one unit of inventory

Figure 10–5 contains the mathematical derivation of the EOQ model, which was one of the first operations research applications.

FIGURE 10–4 Cost Trade-Offs Required to Determine the Most Economical Order Quantity

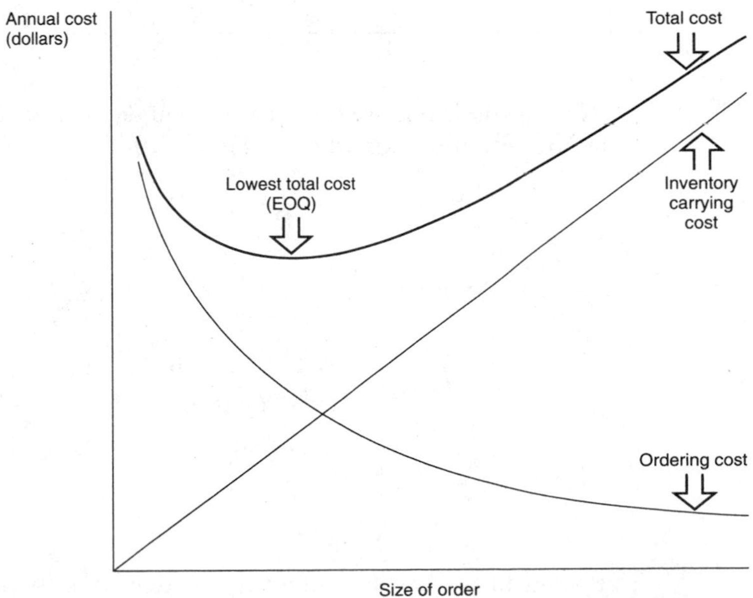

FIGURE 10–5 Mathematical Derivation of the Economic Order Quantity Model

$$\text{Total annual cost } (TAC) = \left[\frac{1}{2}(Q) \times (V) \times (C)\right] + [(P) \times (D/Q)]$$

where

Q = The average number of units in the economic order quantity during the order cycle

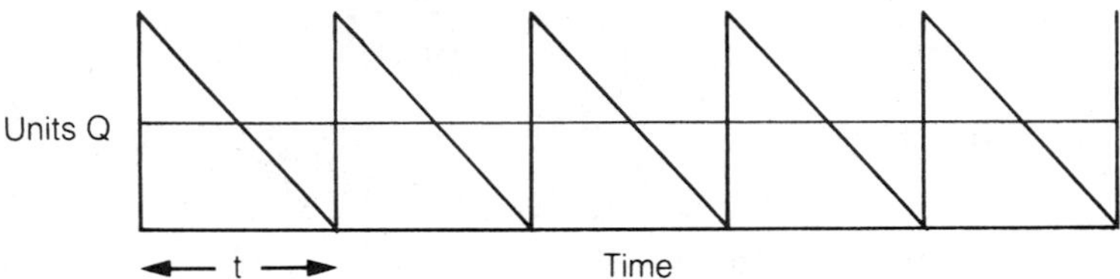

Mathematical solution

$$\frac{d\,TAC}{dQ} = \frac{VC}{2} - \frac{PD}{Q^2}$$

$$\text{Set} = \text{Zero: } \frac{VC}{2} - \frac{PD}{Q^2} = 0$$

$$\frac{VC}{2} = \frac{PD}{Q^2}$$

$$VCQ^2 = 2PD$$

$$Q^2 = \frac{2PD}{CV}$$

$$Q = \sqrt{\frac{2PD}{CV}}$$

Now, using the EOQ formula, we will determine the best ordering policy for the situation described in Figure 10–2:

V = \$100 per unit
C = 25 percent
P = \$40
D = 4,800 units

$$EOQ = \sqrt{\frac{2(\$40)(4{,}800)}{(25\%)(100)}}$$

$$= \sqrt{\frac{384{,}000}{25}}$$

$$= 124 \text{ units}$$

If 20 units fit on a pallet, then the reorder quantity of 120 units would be established. This analysis is shown in tabular form in Table 10–1.

The EOQ model has received significant attention and use in industry;

TABLE 10–1 Cost Trade-Offs Required to Determine the Most Economic Order Quantity

Order Quantity	*Number of Orders (D/Q)*	*Ordering Cost P × (D/Q)*	*Inventory Carrying Cost ½ Q × C × V*	*Total Cost*
40	120	$4,800	$ 500	$5,300
60	80	3,200	750	3,950
80	60	2,400	1,000	3,400
100	48	1,920	1,250	3,170
120	40	1,600	1,500	3,100
140	35	1,400	1,750	3,150
160	30	1,200	2,000	3,200
200	24	960	2,500	3,460
300	16	640	3,750	4,390
400	12	480	5,000	5,480

however, it is not without its limitations. The simple EOQ model is based on the following assumptions:

Assumptions of the EOQ Model

1. A continuous, constant, and known rate of demand.
2. A constant and known replenishment or lead time.
3. A constant purchase price that is independent of the order quantity or time.
4. A constant transportation cost that is independent of the order quantity or time.
5. The satisfaction of all demand (no stockouts are permitted).
6. No inventory in transit.
7. Only one item in inventory, or at least no interaction.
8. An infinite planning horizon.
9. No limit on capital availability.

It would be extremely rare to find a situation where demand is constant, lead time is constant, both are known with certainty, and costs are known precisely. However, the simplifying assumptions are of great concern only if policy decisions will change as a result of the assumptions made. The EOQ solution is relatively insensitive to small changes in the input data. Referring to Figure 10–4, one can see that the EOQ curve is relatively flat around the solution point. This is borne out in Table 10–1. Although the calculated EOQ was 124 units (rounded to 120), an EOQ variation of 20 units or even 40 units does not significantly change the total cost.

Adjusting the EOQ for Volume Discounts

Adjustments to the EOQ. Typical refinements that must be made to the EOQ model include adjustments for volume transportation rates and for quantity discounts. The simple EOQ model did not consider the impact of these two factors. The following adjustment can be made to the EOQ formula so that it will consider the impact of quantity discounts and/or freight breaks:[5]

$$Q^1 = 2\frac{rD}{C} + (1-r)\,Q^0$$

where

Q^1 = The maximum quantity that can be economically ordered to qualify for a discount on unit cost

r = The percentage of price reduction if a larger quantity is ordered

D = The annual demand in units

C = The inventory carrying cost percentage

Q^0 = The EOQ based on current price

Using the modified EOQ formula, we will determine the best ordering policy for the Johnson Manufacturing Company. Johnson Manufacturing produced and sold a complete line of industrial air-conditioning units that were marketed nationally through independent distributors. The company purchased a line of relays for use in its air conditioners from a manufacturer in the Midwest. It ordered approximately 300 cases of 24 units each, 54 times per year; the annual volume was about 16,000 cases. The purchase price was $8.00 per case, the ordering costs were $10.00 per order, and the inventory carrying cost was 25 percent. The relays weighed 25 pounds per case; Johnson Manufacturing paid the shipping costs. The freight rate was $4.00 per hundredweight (cwt.) on shipments of less than 15,000 pounds, $3.90 per cwt. on shipments of 15,000 to 39,000 pounds, and $3.64 per cwt. on orders of more than 39,000 pounds. The relays were shipped on pallets of 20 cases.

First, it is necessary to calculate the transportation cost for a case of product without discounts for volume shipments. Shipments of less than 15,000 pounds—600 cases—cost $4.00 per cwt., or $1.00 ($4.00/100 lbs. × 25 lbs.) per case.

Therefore, without transportation discounts for shipping in quantities above 15,000 pounds, the delivered cost of a case of product would be $9.00 ($8.00 plus $1.00 transportation), and the EOQ would be:

$$EOQ = \sqrt{\frac{2PD}{CV}}$$

$$= \sqrt{\frac{2(\$10)\,(16{,}000)}{.25 \times \$9.00}}$$

$$= \sqrt{\frac{320{,}000}{2.25}}$$

$$= 377, \text{ or } 380 \text{ rounded to nearest full pallet}$$

[5]See Robert G. Brown, *Decision Rules for Inventory Management* (New York: Holt, Rinehart & Winston, 1967), pp. 205–6.

If the company shipped in quantities of 40,000 pounds or more, the cost per case would be $.91 ($3.64/100 lbs. × 25 lbs). The percentage price reduction, r, made possible by shipping at the lowest freight cost is:

$$r = \frac{\$9.00 - \$8.91}{\$9.00} \times 100 = 1.0\% \text{ reduction in delivered cost}$$

The adjusted EOQ is calculated as follows:

$$\begin{aligned} Q^1 &= \frac{2(.01)\,(16{,}000)}{.25} + (1 - .01)\,(380) \\ &= 1{,}280 + 376 \\ &= 1{,}656, \text{ or } 1{,}660 \text{ rounded to the nearest full pallet} \end{aligned}$$

While the largest freight break only results in a 1 percent reduction in the delivered cost of a case of the product, the volume of annual purchases is large enough that the EOQ changes significantly, from 380 cases to 1,660 cases.

An alternative to using the above formula would be to add a column to the analysis shown in Table 10–1 and include the annual transportation cost associated with each of the order quantities, adding this amount to the total costs. The previous example is shown in tabular form in Table 10–2, which illustrates that transportation costs have a significant impact on the purchase decision. The purchase of 380 cases per order would require 43 orders per year, or the purchase of 16,340 cases in the first year. Therefore, this option is not as attractive as the 400-case order quantity, which would require 40 orders to purchase the necessary 16,000 cases and is $348 less expensive. Ten orders of 1,600 cases yields the lowest total cost.

It is also possible to include purchase discounts by adding a column, "Annual Product Cost," and appropriately adjusting the inventory carrying cost and total annual costs columns. Once again, the desired EOQ would be the order quantity that resulted in the lowest total cost.[6]

Inventory Management under Uncertainty

As we have noted, managers rarely, if ever, know for sure what demand to expect for the firm's products. Many factors including economic conditions, competitive actions, changes in government regulations, market shifts, and changes in consumer buying patterns may influence forecast accuracy. Order cycle times are also not constant. Transit times vary, it may take more time to assemble an order or wait for scheduled production on one occasion than another, supplier lead times for components and raw materials may not be consistent, and suppliers may not have the capability of responding to changes in demand.

[6] For additional examples of special purpose EOQ models, refer to Richard B. Chase and Nicholas J. Aquilano, *Production and Operations Management,* 3rd ed. (Homewood, Ill.: Richard D. Irwin, 1981), pp. 485–89.

TABLE 10–2 Cost Trade-Offs to Determine the Most Economic Order Quantity with Transportation Costs Included

A Possible Order Quantity	*B* Number of Orders per Year	*C* (*A* × $8) Purchase Price per Order	*D* Value of Orders per Year *B* × *C*	*E* Transportation Cost per Order	*F* Annual Ordering Cost	*G* Annual Transportation Cost	*H* Inventory Carrying Cost[4]	*I* Total Annual Costs[5]
300	54	$ 2,400	$129,600	$ 300[1]	$540	$16,200	$ 338	$17,078
380	43	3,040	130,720	380[1]	430	16,340	428	17,198
400	40	3,200	128,000	400[1]	400	16,000	450	16,850
800	20	6,400	128,000	780[2]	200	15,600	898	16,698
1,200	14	9,600	134,400	1,170[2]	140	16,380	1,346	17,866
1,600	10	12,800	128,000	1,456[3]	100	14,560	1,782	16,442[6]
1,800	9	14,400	129,600	1,638[3]	90	14,742	2,005	16,837
2,000	8	16,000	128,000	1,820[3]	80	14,560	2,228	16,868

[1]Orders for less than 15,000 lbs. (600 cases) have a rate of $4.00/cwt. which equals $1.00/case.

[2]Orders weighing between 15,000 lbs. and 39,000 lbs. (600 cases and 1560 cases) have a rate of $3.90/cwt. which equals 97.5¢/case.

[3]Orders weighing 40,000 lbs. or more (1600 cases) have a rate of $3.64/cwt. which equals 91¢/case.

[4]Inventory carrying cost = 1/2 (*C* + *E*) (25%).

[5]*I* = *F* + *G* + *H*.

[6]Lowest total cost.

Consequently, management has the option of either maintaining additional inventory in the form of safety stocks (as was shown in Figure 10–3) or risking a potential loss of sales revenue due to stockouts at a distribution center. We must thus consider an additional cost trade-off: inventory carrying costs versus stockout costs.

The uncertainties associated with demand and lead time cause most managers to concentrate on *when* to order rather than on the order quantity. The order quantity is important to the extent that it influences the number of orders, and consequently the number of times that the company is exposed to a potential stockout at the end of each order cycle. The point at which the order is placed is the primary determinant of the future ability to fill demand while waiting for replenishment stock.

Fixed Order Point, Fixed Order Quantity Model

One method used for inventory control under conditions of uncertainty is the *fixed order point, fixed order quantity model.* With this method, an order is placed when the inventory on hand and on order reaches a predetermined minimum level required to satisfy demand during the order cycle. The economic order quantity will be ordered whenever demand drops the inventory level to the reorder point.

Fixed Order Interval Model

In contrast, a *fixed order interval model* compares current inventory with forecast demand, and places an order for the necessary quantity at a regular, specified time. In other words, the interval between orders is fixed. This method facilitates combining orders for various items in a vendor's line, thereby qualifying for volume purchase discounts and freight consolidation savings. Figure 10–6 illustrates the two methods.

A review of Part A of Figure 10–6 shows that replenishment orders are placed on days 15, 27, and 52, respectively, under the fixed order point, fixed order quantity model. In contrast, when the fixed order interval model is used (Part B), orders are placed at 20-day intervals on days 15, 35, and 55. With the fixed order interval model it is necessary to forecast demand for days 20 through 40 on day 15, for days 40 through 60 on day 35, and so on. The fixed order interval system is more adaptive, in that management is forced to consider changes in sales activity and make a forecast for every order interval.

Calculating Safety Stock Requirements

How to Determine the Amount of Safety Stock

The amount of safety stock necessary to satisfy a given level of demand can be determined by computer simulation or statistical techniques. In this illustration we will address the use of statistical techniques. In calculating safety stock levels it is necessary to consider the joint impact of demand and replenishment cycle variability. This can be accomplished by gathering statistically valid samples of data on recent sales volumes and replenishment cycles. Once the data are gathered it is possible to determine safety stock requirements by using this formula:[7]

$$\sigma c = \sqrt{\bar{R}\,(\sigma S^2) + \bar{S}^2\,(\sigma R^2)}$$

where

σc = Units of safety stock needed to satisfy 68 percent of all probabilities (one standard deviation)
$\bar{R}$ = Average replenishment cycle
σR = Standard deviation of the replenishment cycle
$\bar{S}$ = Average daily sales
σS = Standard deviation of daily sales

Assume that the sales history contained in Table 10–3 has been developed for market area 1. The next step is to calculate the standard deviation of daily sales as shown in Table 10–4. From this sample we can calculate the standard deviation of sales. The formula is:

$$\sigma S = \sqrt{\frac{\Sigma f d^2}{n - 1}}$$

where

σS = Standard deviation of daily sales
f = Frequency of event

[7]Robert Hammond of McKinsey and Company, Inc., as reported in Robert Fetter and Winston C. Dalleck, *Decision Models for Inventory Management* (Homewood, Ill.: Richard D. Irwin, 1961), pp. 105–8. For a recent application of the formula in a simulation model, see Walter Zinn, Howard Marmorstein, and John Charnes, "The Effect of Autocorrelated Demand on Customer Service," *Journal of Business Logistics* 13, no. 1 (1992), pp. 173–92.

FIGURE 10–6 Inventory Management under Uncertainty

A. Fixed-order point, fixed-order quantity model

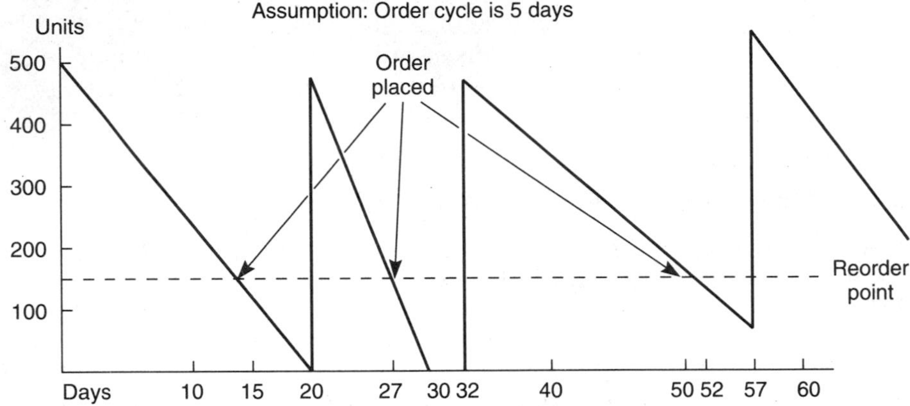

B. Fixed-order interval model

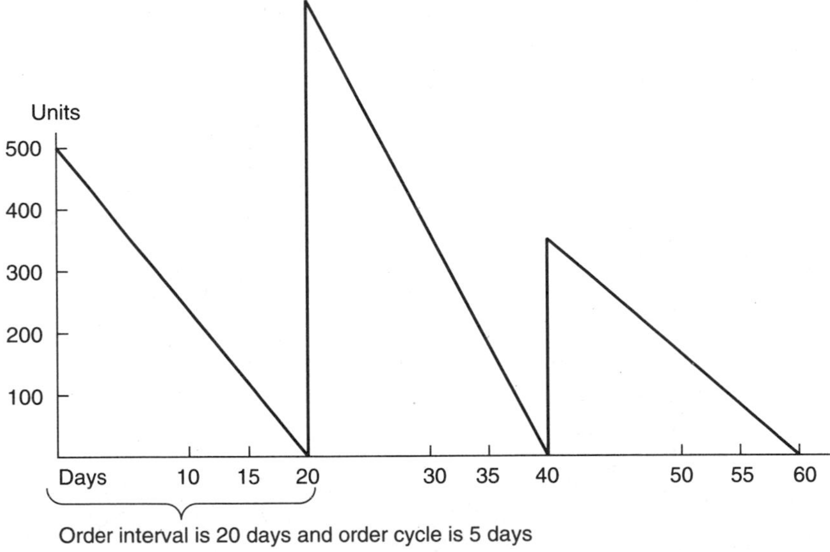

d = Deviation of event from mean
n = Total observations

Applying this formula to the data yields a standard deviation of sales approximately equal to 20 units:

$$\sigma S = \sqrt{\frac{10,000}{25 - 1}}$$
$$= 20$$

TABLE 10–3 Sales History for Market Area 1

Day	*Sales in Cases*	*Day*	*Sales in Cases*
1	100	14	80
2	80	15	90
3	70	16	90
4	60	17	100
5	80	18	140
6	90	19	110
7	120	20	120
8	110	21	70
9	100	22	100
10	110	23	130
11	130	24	110
12	120	25	90
13	100		

TABLE 10–4 Calculation of Standard Deviation of Sales

Daily Sales in Cases	*Frequency (f)*	*Deviation from Mean (d)*	*Deviation Squared (d^2)*	*fd^2*
60	1	−40	1,600	1,600
70	2	−30	900	1,800
80	3	−20	400	1,200
90	4	−10	100	400
100	5	0	0	0
110	4	+10	100	400
120	3	+20	400	1,200
130	2	+30	900	1,800
140	1	+40	1,600	1,600
$\bar{S}$ = 100	n = 25			Σfd^2 = 10,000

This means that 68 percent of the time, daily sales fall between 80 to 120 units (100 units ± 20 units). Two standard deviations' protection, or 40 units, would protect against 95 percent of all events. In setting safety stock levels, however, it is important to consider only events that exceed the mean sales volume. Thus, a safety stock level of 40 units actually affords protection against almost 98 percent of all possible events (see Figure 10–7). Given a distribution of measurements that is approximately bell-shaped, the mean, plus or minus one standard deviation, will contain approximately 68 percent of the measurements. This leaves 16 percent in each of the tails, which means that inventory sufficient to cover sales of one standard deviation in excess of mean daily sales will actually provide an 84 percent customer service level. (If the sample does not represent a normal distribution, refer to a basic statistics book for an alternative treatment.)

The same procedure can be used to arrive at the mean and standard deviation of the replenishment cycle. Once this is accomplished, the formula shown previously can be used to determine safety stock requirements

FIGURE 10–7 Area Relationships for the Normal Distribution

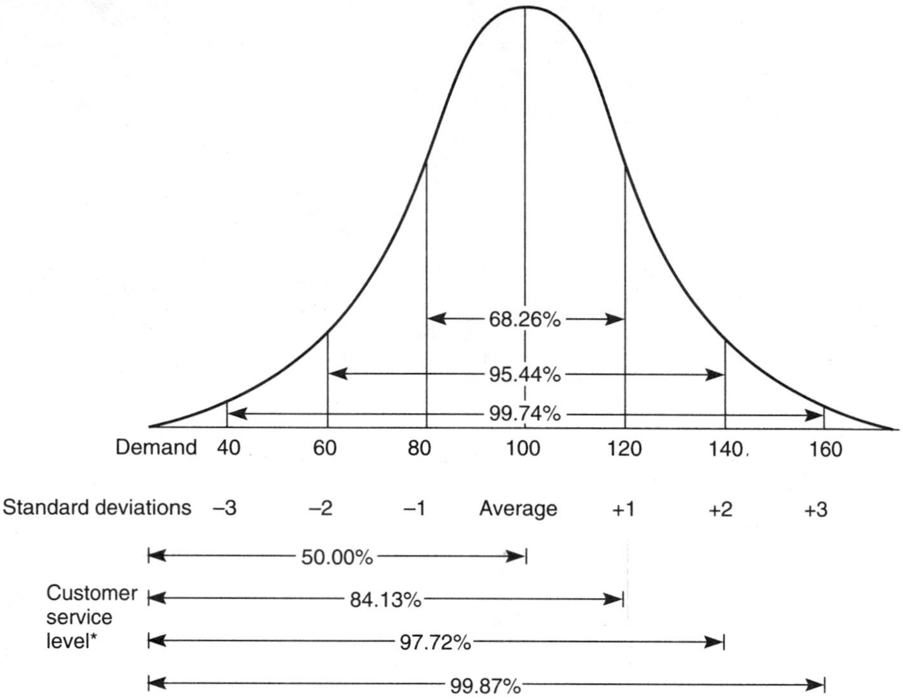

*As measured by the percentage of order cycles that will not suffer from stockouts. It is the probability that no stockout will occur during a replenishment cycle.

at a certain level of demand. For example, analysis of replenishment cycles might yield the results shown in Table 10–5. The standard deviation of the replenishment cycle is:

$$(\sigma R) = \sqrt{\frac{\Sigma f d^2}{n - 1}}$$

$$= \sqrt{2.67}$$

$$= 1.634$$

The average replenishment cycle is:

$$(\bar{R}) = 10$$

The combined safety stock required to cover variability in both demand and lead time can be found using the formula:

$$\sigma c = \sqrt{\bar{R}(\sigma S)^2 + \bar{S}^2(\sigma R)^2}$$

TABLE 10–5 Calculation of Standard Deviation of Replenishment Cycle

Lead Time in Days	*Frequency (f)*	*Deviation from Mean (d)*	*Deviation Squared (d^2)*	*fd^2*
7	1	−3	9	9
8	2	−2	4	8
9	3	−1	1	3
10	4	0	0	0
11	3	+1	1	3
12	2	+2	4	8
13	1	+3	9	9
$\bar{R} = 10$	$n = 16$			$\Sigma fd^2 = 40$

$$= \sqrt{10(20)^2 + (100^2)(1.634)^2}$$

$$= \sqrt{4{,}000 + 26{,}700}$$

$$= \sqrt{30{,}700}$$

$$= 175 \text{ cases}$$

Thus, in a situation in which daily sales vary from 60 to 140 cases and the inventory replenishment cycle varies from 7 to 13 days, a safety stock of 175 cases will allow the manufacturer to satisfy 84 percent of all possible occurrences. To protect against 98 percent of all possibilities, 350 cases of safety stock are required. Table 10–6 shows alternative customer service levels and safety stock requirements.

In order to establish the average inventory for various levels of customer service, we must first determine the EOQ. The projected yearly demand is found by multiplying the average daily demand by 250 working days,[8] which equals 25,000 cases (250 × 100). The inventory carrying cost was calculated to be 32 percent, the average value of a case of product was $4.37, and the ordering cost was $28. The average inventory required to satisfy each service level is shown in Table 10–7.

Note that the establishment of a safety stock commitment is really a policy of customer service and inventory availability. Although we have demonstrated a quantitative method of calculating safety stock requirements to protect the firm against stockouts at various levels of probability, additional calculations are necessary in order to determine the specific fill rate when stockouts occur. Fill rate represents the percentage of units demanded that are on hand to fill customer orders.

[8] For this example the average number of working days was assumed to be 250.

TABLE 10–6 Summary of Alternative Service Levels and Safety Stock Requirements

Service Level (percent)	*Number of Standard Deviations (σc) Needed*	*Safety Stock Requirements (cases)*
84.1	1.0	175
90.3	1.3	228
94.5	1.6	280
97.7	2.0	350
98.9	2.3	403
99.5	2.6	455
99.9	3.0	525

TABLE 10–7 Summary of Average Inventory Levels Given Different Service Levels

Service Levels (percent)	*Average Cycle Stock (½ × EOQ)*	*Safety Stock (units)*	*Total Average Inventory (units)*
84.1	500	175	675
90.3	500	228	728
94.5	500	280	780
97.7	500	350	850
98.9	500	403	903
99.5	500	455	955
99.9	500	525	1,025

Calculating Fill Rate

Fill rate represents the magnitude of the stockout. If a manager wants to hold 280 units as safety stock, what will the fill rate be?[9]

The fill rate can be calculated using the following formula:

$$FR = 1 - \frac{\sigma c}{EOQ}(I(K))$$

where

FR = Fill rate
σc = Combined safety stock required to consider both variability in lead time and demand (one standard deviation)
EOQ = Order quantity = 1,000 (in this example)
$I(K)$ = Service function magnitude factor (provided by Table 10–8), based on desired number of standard deviations

[9]This example was provided by Professor Robert L. Cook, Central Michigan University, Mount Pleasant, Michigan.

K (the safety factor) is the safety stock the manager decides to hold divided by σc. Returning to the question presented above, the manager's economic order quantity (EOQ) is 1,000. The safety stock determined by the manager is 280 units. Therefore, K is equal to 280 divided by 175, or 1.60. If $K = 1.60$, Table 10–8 can be used to identify $I(K) = 0.0236$ (see last column of Table 10–8).

Now the fill rate can be calculated using the formula:

$$\begin{aligned} FR &= 1 - \frac{\sigma c}{EOQ}(I(K)) \\ &= 1 - \frac{175}{1000}(0.0236) \\ &= 1 - .0041 \\ &= .9959 \end{aligned}$$

Thus, the average fill rate is 99.59 percent. That is, of every 100 units of Product A demanded, 99.59 will be on hand to be sold if the manager uses 280 units of safety stock and orders 1,000 units each time.[10]

If the manager wants to know how much safety stock of Product A to hold to attain a 95 percent fill rate, the same formula can be used:

$$\begin{aligned} FR &= 1 - \frac{\sigma c}{EOQ}(I(K)) \\ I(K) &= (1 - FR)\left(\frac{EOQ}{\sigma c}\right) \\ I(K) &= (1 - 0.95)\left(\frac{1000}{175}\right) \\ &= (0.05)(5.714) \\ &= 0.2857 \end{aligned}$$

The corresponding K value from Table 10–8 is approximately 0.25. Since K is equal to the safety stock the manager decides to hold divided by σc, the safety stock required to provide a 95 percent fill rate is 44 units (175×0.25).

Inventories and Customer Service

The establishment of a service level, and thus a safety stock policy, is really a matter of managerial judgment. Factors management should consider include customer relations and the ability of the firm to support continuous production.

In many companies, management improves customer service levels by simply adding safety stock. This is because the cost of carrying inventory

[10] If demands, lead times, order quantities, or safety stocks significantly change, the fill rate percentage will also change.

TABLE 10–8 Inventory Safety Stock Factors

σ {*Safety Factor* *K*	*Stock Protection (Single Tail σ)*	*Stockout Probability F(K)*	*Service Function (Magnitude Factor) Partial Expectation I (K)*
0.00	0.5000	0.5000	0.3989
0.10	0.5394	0.4606	0.3509
0.20	0.5785	0.4215	0.3067
0.30	0.6168	0.3832	0.2664
0.40	0.6542	0.3458	0.2299
0.50	0.6901	0.3099	0.1971
0.60	0.7244	0.2756	0.1679
0.70	0.7569	0.2431	0.1421
0.80	0.7872	0.2128	0.1194
0.90	0.8152	0.1848	0.0998
1.00	0.8409	0.1591	0.0829
1.10	0.8641	0.1359	0.0684
1.20	0.8849	0.1151	0.0561
1.30	0.9033	0.0967	0.0457
1.40	0.9194	0.0806	0.0369
1.50	0.9334	0.0666	0.0297
1.60	0.9454	0.0546	0.0236
1.70	0.9556	0.0444	0.0186
1.80	0.9642	0.0358	0.0145
1.90	0.9714	0.0286	0.0113
2.00	0.9773	0.0227	0.0086
2.10	0.9822	0.0178	0.0065
2.20	0.9861	0.0139	0.0049
2.30	0.9893	0.0107	0.0036
2.40	0.9918	0.0082	0.0027
2.50	0.9938	0.0062	0.0019
2.60	0.9953	0.0047	0.0014
2.70	0.9965	0.0035	0.0010
2.80	0.9974	0.0026	0.0007
2.90	0.9981	0.0019	0.0005
3.00	0.9984	0.0014	0.0004
3.10	0.9990	0.0010	0.0003
3.20	0.9993	0.0007	0.0002
3.30	0.9995	0.0005	0.0001
3.40	0.9997	0.0003	0.0001
3.50	0.9998	0.0002	0.0001
3.60	0.9998	0.0002	
3.70	0.9999	0.0001	
3.80	0.9999	0.0001	
3.90	0.9999	0.0001	
4.00	0.9999	0.0001	

SOURCE: Professor Jay U. Sterling, University of Alabama; adapted from Robert G. Brown, *Materials Management Systems* (New York: John Wiley & Sons, 1977), p. 429.

has often not been calculated for the firm or has been set arbitrarily at an artificially low level. Figure 10–8 graphically illustrates the relationship between customer service levels and inventory investment shown in Table 10–7. (Ignore the broken line and arrows in Figure 10–8 at this time.)

Although inventory investment figures will vary from situation to situation, relationships similar to those in the example will hold. As customer service levels move toward 100 percent, inventory levels increase disproportionately. It becomes obvious that customer service levels should not be improved solely by the addition of inventory. The need to develop an accurate inventory carrying cost for the purpose of planning should be clear.

Customer Service Should Not Be Improved Simply by Increasing Inventory

One way of resolving this problem is to substitute transportation costs for inventory carrying costs by using premium transportation to improve customer service. Another possibility is to recognize the wide differences in demand levels and demand variation associated with each product. Managers often make the mistake of treating all products the same. Generally, a more economical policy is to stock the highest volume items at retail locations, high- and moderate-volume items at field warehouse locations, and slow-moving items at centralized locations. The centralized location may be a distribution center or a plant warehouse. This type of multi-echelon stocking procedure is referred to as *ABC analysis;* we will discuss it later in this chapter. The broken line in Figure 10–8 shows how the relationship between inventory investment and customer service levels can be shifted using some of these strategies.

Production Scheduling

Earlier in this chapter, we discussed how inventory levels can be influenced by production policies. The reverse is also true. In many cases logistics policy changes—especially those that decrease inventory levels—can create significant increases in total production costs that are beyond the control of manufacturing management. For example, General Mills, Inc., had a production operations division that manufactured and distributed products for the various marketing divisions of the firm. Consequently, the logistics function received a sales forecast from marketing, and, given the divisions' inventory deployment policies and the objective to minimize total logistics costs, manufacturing was told how many units of each item to produce. Manufacturing then established a production schedule.

Logistics Policy Changes Can Increase Production Costs

The system was not without its problems, however. Manufacturing performance was judged by comparing actual production costs to the cost arrived at by multiplying the various units produced by the standard manufacturing cost for each product. The standard cost was a full cost standard comprised of (1) direct materials, (2) direct labor, (3) variable overhead, and (4) fixed overhead. The overhead costs included production setup costs that were based on a projected number of setups for each product for the year, divided by the estimated number of units produced during the year.

Logistics Decisions Can Influence Manufacturing Costs

Logistics influenced the number of setups actually incurred by manufacturing, but the standard cost was not changed during the year to reflect this. Since the number of setups incurred would influence manufacturing performance, plant management resisted policies that would change the projected number of setups. The solution was to maintain two separate standard costs for each product. One was a variable cost per unit excluding

FIGURE 10–8 Relationship between Inventory Investment and Customer Service Levels

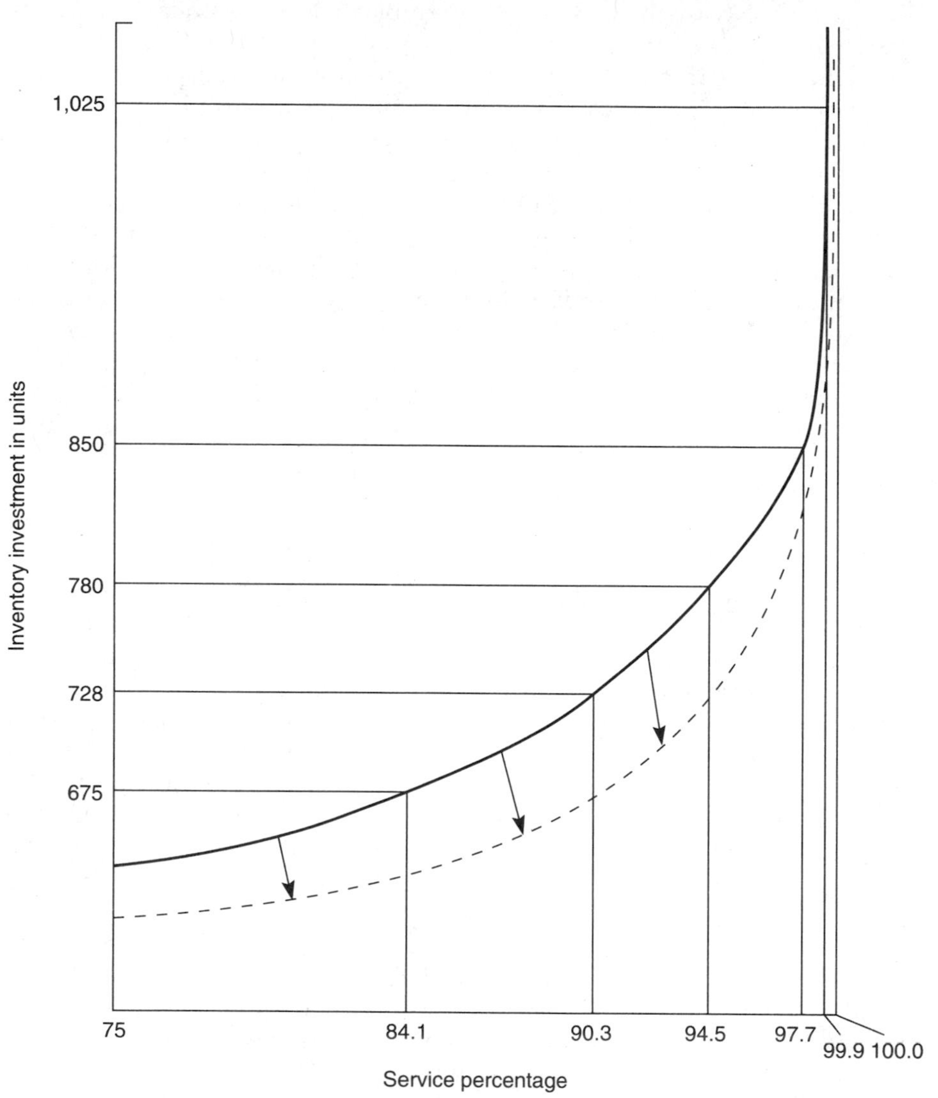

a setup component, and the other was a standard setup cost for each product. Manufacturing performance was judged on the ability to manufacture a specified quantity efficiently. Logistics was charged with the responsibility of considering setup costs in the analysis when inventory policies were determined.

An inventory policy decision that reduces logistics costs by less than the increase in production setup cost results in lower overall profit performance for the company. For this reason, logistics managers must be aware of the impact of their decisions on the efficiency of manufacturing operations and consider associated changes in manufacturing costs when establishing logistics policies.

SYMPTOMS OF POOR INVENTORY MANAGEMENT

How to Recognize Poor Inventory Management

This section deals with how to recognize situations where inventories are not being managed properly. Recognition of problem areas is the first step in determining where opportunities exist for improving logistics performance.

The following symptoms may be associated with poor inventory management:

1. Increasing numbers of back orders.
2. Increasing dollar investment in inventory with back orders remaining constant.
3. High customer turnover rate.
4. Increasing number of orders being canceled.
5. Periodic lack of sufficient storage space.
6. Wide variance in inventory turnover among distribution centers and among major inventory items.
7. Deteriorating relationships with intermediaries, as typified by dealer cancellations and declining orders.
8. Large quantities of obsolete items.

In many instances inventory levels can be reduced by one or more of the following steps:

Ways to Reduce Inventory Levels

1. Multi-echelon inventory planning. ABC analysis is an example of such planning.
2. Lead time analysis.
3. Delivery time analysis. This may lead to a change in carriers or negotiation with existing carriers.
4. Elimination of low turnover and/or obsolete items.
5. Analysis of pack size and discount structure.
6. Examination of returned goods procedures.
7. Encouragement/automation of product substitution.
8. Installation of formal reorder review systems.
9. Measurement of fill rates by stock-keeping unit (SKU).
10. Analysis of customer demand characteristics.
11. Development of a formal sales plan and source demand by a predetermined logic.

In many companies the best method of reducing inventory investment is to reduce order-cycle time by using advanced order processing systems. If the order cycle currently offered to customers is satisfactory, the time saved in order transmittal, order entry, and order processing can be used for inventory planning. The result will be a significant reduction in inventory.

IMPROVING INVENTORY MANAGEMENT

Inventory management can be improved by using one or more of the following techniques: ABC analysis, forecasting, inventory models, and advanced order processing systems.

ABC Analysis

Pareto Principal—The 80/20 Rule

> In the 18th century, Villefredo Pareto, in a study of the distribution of wealth in Milan, found that 20 percent of the people controlled 80 percent of the wealth. This logic of the few having the greatest importance and the many having little importance has been broadened to include many situations and is termed the *Pareto Principle.* This is true in our everyday lives (such as, most of the decisions we make are relatively unimportant but a few shape our future), and is certainly true in inventory systems.[11]

The logic behind ABC analysis is that 20 percent of the firm's customers or products account for 80 percent of the sales and perhaps an even larger percentage of profits. The first step in ABC analysis is to rank products by sales, or preferably by contribution to corporate profitability if such data are available. The next step is to check for differences between high-volume and low-volume items that may suggest how certain items should be managed.

Inventory levels increase with the number of stock-keeping locations.[12] By stocking low-volume items at a number of logistics centers, the national demand for these products is divided by the number of locations. Each of these locations must maintain safety stock. If one centralized location had been used for these items, the total safety stock would be much lower. For example, if only one centralized warehouse is used and sales are forecast on a national basis, a sales increase in Los Angeles may offset a sales decrease in New York. However, safety stock is required to protect against variability in demand, and there is greater variability in demand when national demand is subdivided into regions. The total system inventory will increase with the number of field warehouse locations, because the variability in demand must be covered at each location; that is, a sales increase in one market area will not be offset by a sales decrease in another market.

When a firm consolidates slow-moving items at a centralized location, transportation costs often increase. However, these costs can be offset by

---

[11]Chase and Aquilano, *Production and Operations Management,* p. 490.

lower inventory carrying costs and fewer stockout penalties. Customer service can be improved through consolidation of low-volume items by decreasing the probability of experiencing a stockout. ABC analysis is a method for deciding which items should be considered for centralized warehousing.

An Example of ABC Analysis

At this point let's consider an example of ABC analysis.[13] An analysis of sales volume by product revealed that A items accounted for 5 percent of items and contributed 70 percent of sales, B items accounted for 10 percent of items and added an additional 20 percent of sales, while C items accounted for the 65 percent of the items remaining and contributed only 10 percent of sales. The last 20 percent of the items had no sales whatsoever during the past year (see Figure 10–9)! This statistical distribution is almost always found in companies' inventories.[14] The "degree of concentration of sales among items will vary by firm, but the shape of the curve will be similar."[15]

For A items, a daily or continuous review of inventory status might be appropriate. B items might be reviewed weekly, while the C items should receive the least attention. Different customer service levels could be established for each category of inventory. An order fill rate of 98 percent might be set for A items, 90 percent for B items, and 85 percent for C items. This policy would result in an overall customer service level of 95 percent, as shown in Table 10–9. By focusing attention on the A items, management places greater emphasis on the products that contribute the most to sales and profitability.

Similarly, the amount of safety stock is less when lower volume items are stocked in fewer locations. If the firm made use of 20 distribution centers, A items might be stocked in all 20 warehouses, B items in 5 regional warehouses, and C items stocked only at the factory. Although transportation costs for B and C items are greater, the inventory reductions are usually more than enough to make a selective stocking policy worthwhile. Management can test alternative inventory policies for their impact on customer service and profitability. For example, how would the deletion of slow-moving items affect inventory? What impact would a 25 percent increase in sales have on inventory?

A Distribution-by-Value Report Forms the Basis for an ABC Analysis

A distribution-by-value report forms the basis for an ABC analysis (see Table 10–10). The report is prepared by listing annual sales for each item in descending sequence. In order to simplify this example, some items were omitted from the sequence. Distribution-by-value reports are easy to pre-

---

[12] While average inventory at each facility decreases as the number of warehouse locations increases, total system inventory (all facilities) increases.

[13] This example is adapted from Lynn E. Gill, "Inventory and Physical Distribution Management," in *The Distribution Handbook,* ed. James F. Robeson and Robert G. House (New York: The Free Press, 1985), pp. 664–67.

[14] It is referred to as *log normal distribution.*

[15] Gill, "Inventory and Physical Distribution Management," p. 664.

FIGURE 10–9 ABC Parts Classification

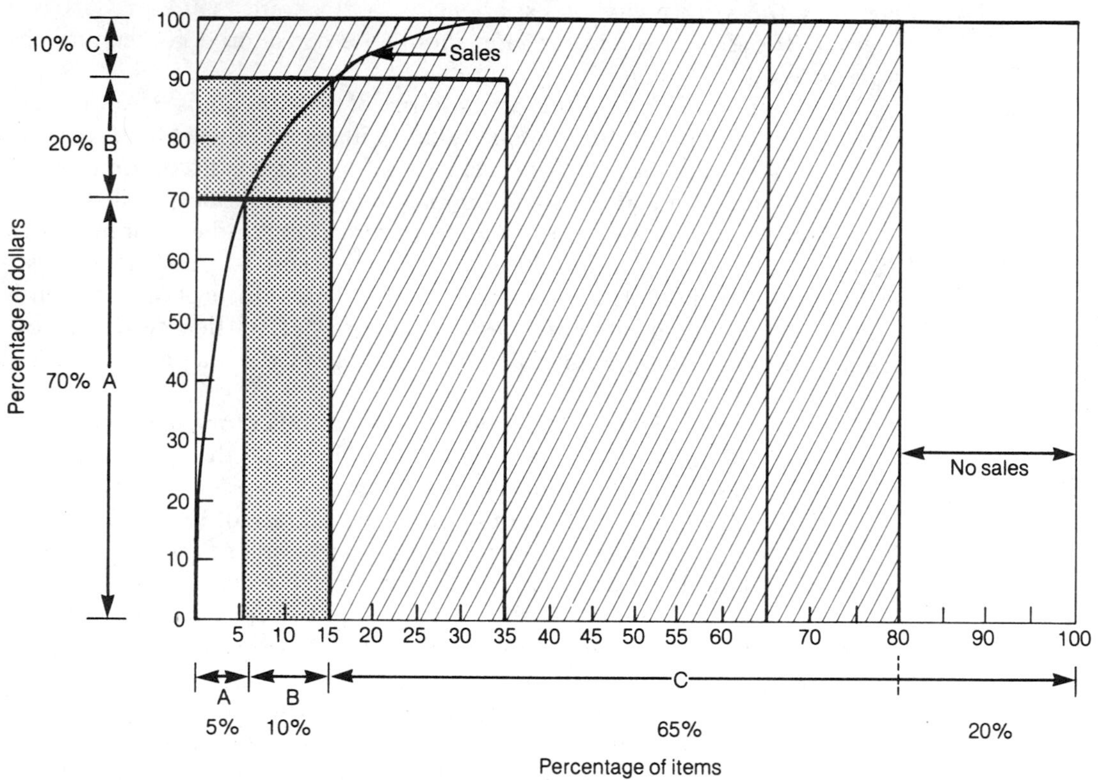

SOURCE: Lynn E. Gill, "Inventory and Physical Distribution Management," in *The Distribution Handbook,* ed. James F. Robeson, and Robert G. House (New York: The Free Press, 1985), p. 665. Copyright © 1985 by The Free Press, a Division of Macmillan, Inc. Reprinted by permission of the publisher.

TABLE 10–9 Customer Service Levels Using ABC Analysis

Category	*Percent of Sales*	*Customer Service Level (%)*	*Weighted Customer Service Level (%)*
A	70	98	68.6
B	20	90	18.0
C	10	85	8.5
	100	Overall service level	95.1

SOURCE: Lynn E. Gill, "Inventory and Physical Distribution Management," in *The Distribution Handbook,* ed. James F. Robeson and Robert G. House (New York: The Free Press, 1985), p. 664. Copyright © 1985 by The Free Press, a Division of Macmillan, Inc. Reprinted by permission of the publisher.

pare on computerized inventory systems. Each of the cumulative totals is also shown as a percent of total items and as a percent of total sales.

Forecasting

Forecasting the amount of each product that is likely to be purchased is an important aspect of inventory management. One forecasting method is to *survey buyer intentions* by mail questionnaires, telephone interviews, or personal interviews. These data can be used to develop a sales forecast. This approach is not without problems, however. It can be costly, and the accuracy of the information may be questionable.

Another approach is to solicit the opinions of salespeople or known experts in the field. This method, termed *judgment sampling*, is relatively fast and inexpensive. However, the data are subject to the personal biases of the individual salespeople or experts.

Most companies simply project future sales based on past sales data. Because most inventory systems require only a one- or two-month forecast, short-term forecasting is therefore acceptable. A number of techniques are available to aid the manager in developing a short-term sales forecast.[16] A method for developing the forecast is shown in Figure 10–10. Rather than trying to forecast at the stock-keeping unit (SKU) level, which would result in large forecast errors, management can improve forecast accuracy significantly by forecasting at a much higher level of aggregation. For example, in Figure 10–10 the forecast is developed at the total company or product line level using a forecasting model. The next step is to break that forecast down by product class and SKU, based on past sales history. The inventory is then pushed out from the central distribution center to branch/regional distribution centers using one of the following methods:

- Going rate—the rate of sales that the SKU is experiencing at each location.
- Weeks/months of supply—the number of weeks/months of sales based on expected future sales that management wishes to hold at each location.
- Available inventory—currently available inventory less back orders.

The only certainty when developing a forecast is that the forecast will not be 100 percent accurate. For this reason, many firms are developing strategies that focus on reducing the total time from sourcing of materials to delivery of the final product. The shorter this time period can be made, the less critical forecasting becomes, because the firm can respond more

[16] For excellent in-depth coverage of various forecasting methods, see Steven C. Wheelwright and Spyros Makridakas, *Forecasting Methods for Management,* 3rd. ed. (New York: John Wiley & Sons, 1980).

TABLE 10–10 Distribution-by-Value Report

Rank of Items	*Part Number*	*Annual Dollar Sales*	*Cumulative Dollar Sales*	*Cumulative Percent Items*	*Cumulative Percent Sales*	*Classification*
1	K410	$126,773	$ 126,773	0.01	1.74	A
3	9999	74,130	285,602	0.02	3.92	A
5	410	44,800	397,075	0.03	5.45	A
8	2300	32,666	510,732	0.05	7.01	A
16	K820	22,838	730,034	0.10	10.02	A
35	2601	16,899	1,158,439	0.22	15.90	A
60	K53	13,009	1,467,356	0.39	20.14	A
90	5401	10,988	1,889,201	0.58	25.93	A
126	1101	9,388	2,191,561	0.82	30.08	A
168	K860	7,879	2,610,494	1.09	35.83	A
219	1302	6,538	2,936,895	1.42	40.31	A
279	3600	5,639	3,307,741	1.81	45.40	A
321	5601	5,017	3,567,115	2.08	48.96	A
351	K350	4,619	3,642,887	2.28	50.00	A
438	1603	3,823	4,047,249	2.84	55.55	A
543	540P	3,118	4,438,494	3.52	60.92	A
674	2305	2,496	4,837,759	4.37	65.91	A
839	920L	2,000	5,231,186	5.44	70.01	A
1000	K82T	1,635	5,508,045	6.48	75.60	B
1261	1304	1,186	5,784,905	8.18	79.40	B
1394	1806	1,017	5,908,764	9.04	81.10	B
1632	5304	831	6,127,337	10.58	84.10	B
1823	2600	693	6,312,395	11.82	86.64	B
2452	3501	463	6,570,312	15.90	90.18	B
2698	4200	357	6,775,043	17.49	92.99	C
2920	460P	300	6,787,428	18.93	93.16	C
3186	131M	250	6,906,187	20.66	94.79	C
3506	4304	207	6,953,544	22.73	95.44	C
4442	410G	116	7,130,588	28.80	97.87	C
5202	3500	78	7,150,989	33.73	98.15	C
5414	K542	71	7,176,762	35.11	98.50	C
5688	3402	60	7,193,246	36.88	98.73	C
6048	110G	50	7,198,345	39.22	98.80	C
6256	1308	45	7,208,546	40.56	98.94	C
6386	110P	42	7,210,732	41.41	98.97	C
6437	2306	41	7,212,917	41.74	99.00	C
6493	920K	40	7,249,346	42.10	99.50	C
7711	83J4	8	7,261,732	50.00	99.67	C
9253	172R	6	7,266,103	60.00	99.73	C
12318	4404	1	7,285,775	79.87	100.00	C
12970	X438	0	7,285,775	84.10	100.00	C
15422	999J	0	7,285,775	100.00	100.00	C

SOURCE: Adapted from Lynn E. Gill, "Inventory and Physical Distribution Management," in *The Distribution Handbook,* ed. James F. Robeson and Robert G. House (New York: The Free Press, 1985), p. 666. Copyright © 1985 by The Free Press, a Division of Macmillan, Inc. Reprinted by permission of the publisher.

FIGURE 10–10 Building a Forecast

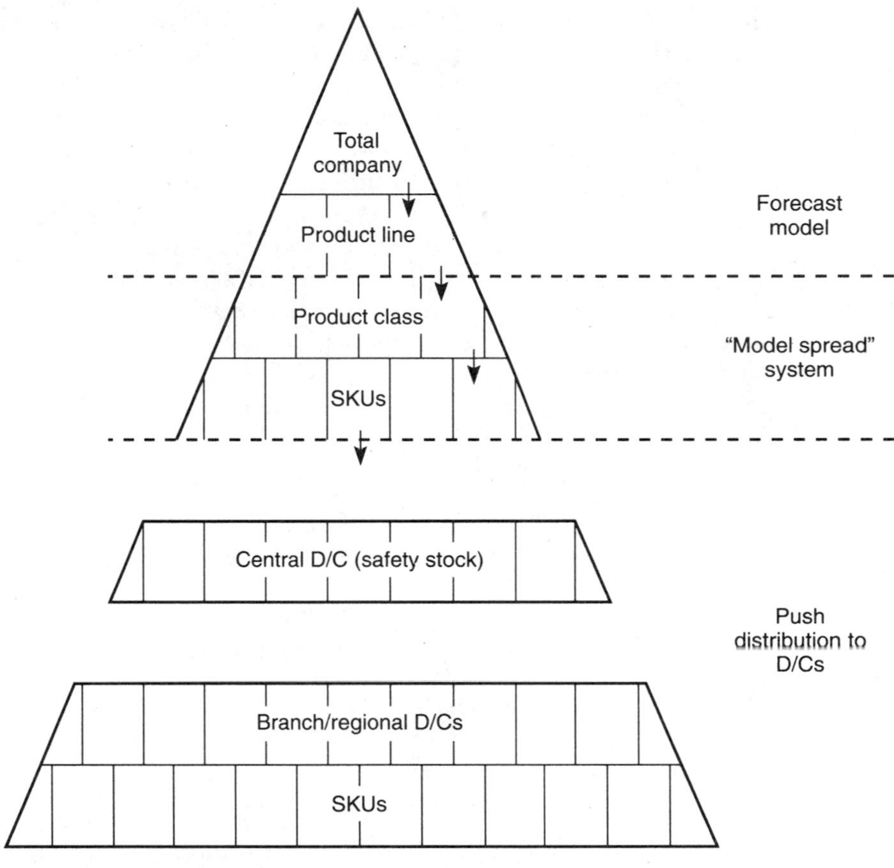

SOURCE: Professor Jay U. Sterling, University of Alabama. Used with permission.

quickly to changes in demand. Time-based competitive strategies will be discussed in detail in Chapter 18. In Chapter 14 we will examine the most frequently used forecasting techniques, along with a description of each technique and its advantages and disadvantages.

Inventory Models

A number of computerized inventory-control systems are available, including advanced versions of IBM's IMPACT[17] and COGS.[18] These systems

[17] "Inventory Management Program and Control Techniques (IMPACT)," IBM publications GE20-8105-1.

[18] "Consumer Goods System (COGS)," IBM publications DOS 5736–D31 and DOS 5736–D32.

have the ability to produce purchase orders, shipping orders, bills of lading, and invoices. Figure 10–11 illustrates the work flow and functions performed by a typical IMPACT system.

IBM's IMPACT

IBM's IMPACT was designed for firms whose main concern is the distribution phase of a production and distribution system.[19] Wholesalers, for example, are prime users. IMPACT uses "traditional" or "classical" inventory analysis. These models apply to wholesalers, retailers, or suppliers of basic materials, since most items ordered are not the result of the simultaneous order for some other item. However, there is a desire to consolidate orders where possible to save handling and shipping charges.

Five Functions Performed by IBM's IMPACT

IMPACT performs the following functions: forecasts demand; determines the safety stock required for a specified level of service; determines the order quantity and time for reorder; considers the effects of freight rates and quantity discounts; and estimates the expected results of the inventory plan. The IMPACT system does this in two phases—the initializing and estimating phase, and the operating phase. The *initializing and estimating segment,* which sets up the system and is brought into play whenever conditions or objectives change, includes the following:

1. Selection of forecasting model and ordering strategy.
2. Calculation of starting values for factors used in forecasting and ordering.
3. Estimation of the results.

On a day-to-day basis, the *operating system* does the following:

1. Decides when and how much to order.
2. Makes new forecasts of demand and forecast error.
3. Keeps records of issues, receipts, inventory status, etc.
4. Collects data to measure performance of the system.

If a fixed time period plan is used, items are reviewed each week, biweekly, or monthly. In a fixed quantity system, the inventory status is reviewed after each transaction. If the stock on hand drops to the reorder point, a new order is placed. Typically, demand forecasts are made for periods of one, two, or four weeks.

To operate the system, the users provide their own program routines for record keeping; updating the master file; forecasting; performance measurement; order follow-up (preparing purchase orders, status listings, and so forth); and linkages between their programs and IMPACT library functions. In order to gain an understanding of the detailed operations carried out by IMPACT, we will summarize the procedure it uses to determine what, when, and how much to order. This is accomplished by setting a service level and then considering inventory costs.

[19]This section, based on the following IBM publications: *Inventory Control,* 520–14491; *Introduction to IBM Wholesale IMPACT,* E20–0278–0; *Basic Principles of Wholesale IMPACT,* E20–8105–1; *Wholesale IMPACT—Advanced Principles and Implementations Manual,* E20–0174–0, is adapted from Chase and Aquilano, *Production and Operations Management,* pp. 500–506.

FIGURE 10–11 Workflow and Functions Performed in a Typical IMPACT System

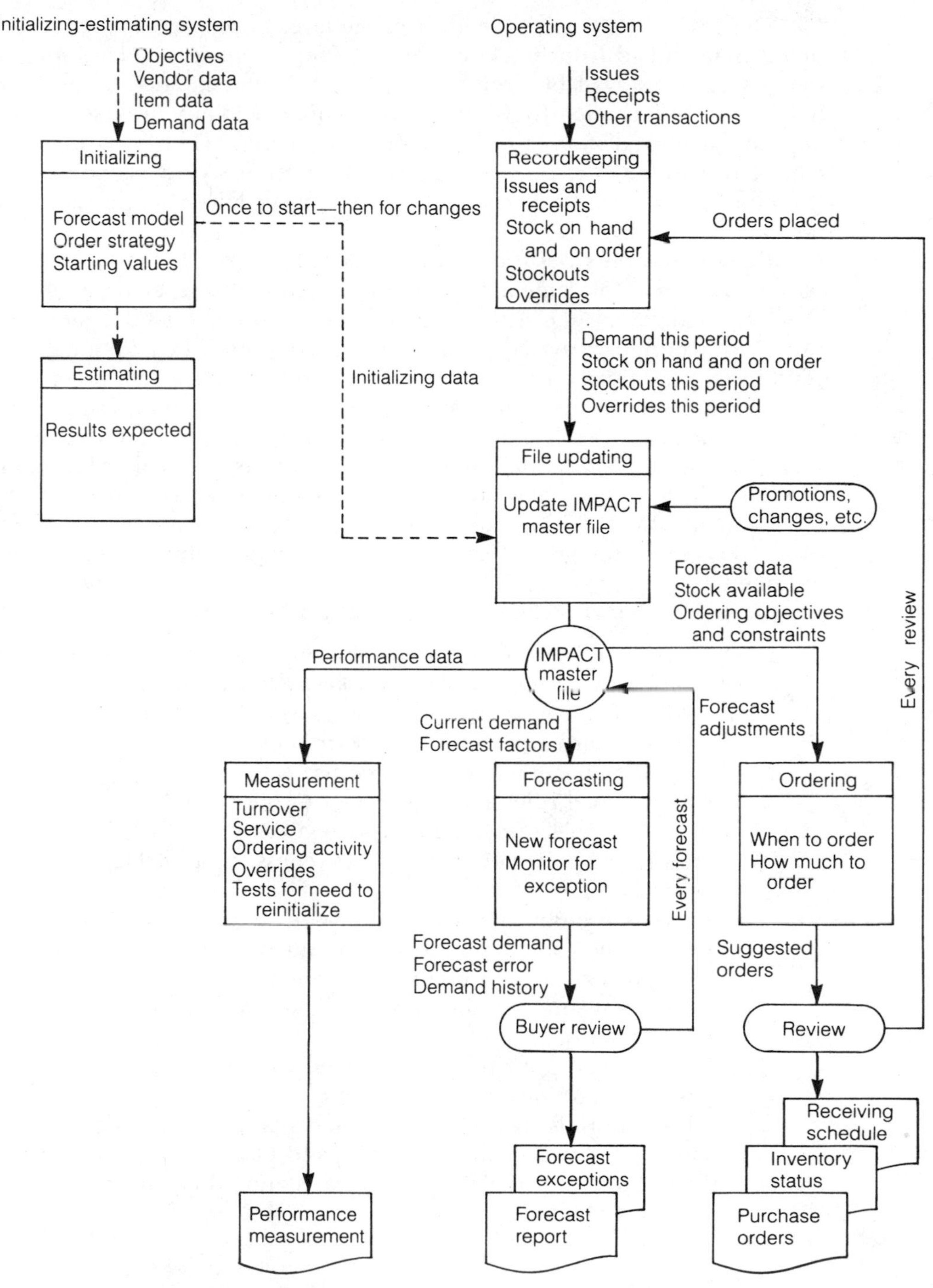

SOURCE: "Introduction to IBM Wholesale IMPACT (Inventory Management Program and Control Techniques)," GE20–0278–0, International Business Machines Corporation, Data Processing Division, White Plains, N.Y. © by International Business Machines Corporation. Reprinted by permission.

The IMPACT program defines service level as the percentage of demand that is filled from stock on hand. A 98 percent service level means that 98 units are available from stock for each 100 demanded. Items may be ordered independently (without other items) or jointly (to take advantage of quantity discounts or transportation savings). The costs that are considered are: (1) the cost of ordering, (2) inventory carrying costs, and (3) opportunity costs, such as quantity discounts or lower freight rates not taken.

The program decides the time for order placement, based on individual or joint order placement and the forecasted demand, error, and lead time. For individual items, the classic economic order quantity model is used. If discounts are available, the program computes the additional feasible order quantities and selects the lowest cost. When several items are ordered at the same time, the total must meet some quantity range (such as a truckload lot) while satisfying individual item service level requirements. It uses an "allocation" subroutine that adjusts the total order up or down, based on individual economic order quantities and customer service requirements. IMPACT also allows overrides in order placement in order to correct such things as erroneous data, or to input management judgment.

Among the benefits claimed by users of IMPACT are:

Benefits of IMPACT

1. Reduced inventory costs, because inventory size has been reduced with no loss in customer service, or service levels have increased with no additional inventory. In addition, buyers have more time to devote to problems or to develop new strategies.
2. Improved management control because:
   a. The specified rules and objectives are consistent.
   b. Rules and objectives can be easily revised.
   c. Effective measures of system effectiveness are available.
   d. Service is more stable.
   e. There is a smoother work load for personnel.
   f. There is increased awareness of inventory concepts.
   g. The process of data gathering needed to set up the program points out unprofitable product lines and abnormally slow-moving items.
   h. The costs, output from the program, are valuable for profit analysis and planning.
   i. A framework is created that can be expanded to include applications such as automatic generation and placement of orders with the vendor, and provision of forecasts and other information directly to the retailer.[20]

[20] Ibid., pp. 505–6.

Many firms use computerized inventory control systems with considerable success.[21] For example, Jefferson G. Summers, director of management information systems, Sterling Drug, Inc., reported the following success story with IBM's COGS:

Computerized Inventory Management Increased Profits at Sterling Drug

> The range of benefits from this system at Sterling Drug included cost savings in seven figures and greatly improved production and distribution operations.
>
> Some idea of the stakes for Sterling Drug can be seen in the worldwide sales figures for our divisions and subsidiaries. In 1971, they rose to $708,453,000, up from $643,873,000 in 1970, and double what they were in 1962. Sales and earnings records have been set for 21 consecutive years, and there is every expectation that this will continue.[22]

Summers went on to describe some of the other advantages of the system:

> J. D. Winig, Glenbrook Laboratories Division [of Sterling Drug] vice president—manufacturing, has expressed particular satisfaction that distribution and production managers are getting away from crisis-to-crisis operations.
>
> "The harried phone calls at four o'clock in the evening have been sharply reduced," says Mr. Winig. "Although there are still differences of opinion, our people in the plant and in management information systems are talking the same language, developing a far better common understanding of problems, and this is bound to have positive effects. We're developing an excellent aid for production management, smoothing the peaks with a sane approach to the overall problem, and have every reason to expect we will be lowering inventories."
>
> "The new system takes the hocus-pocus out of scheduling by giving us better information faster," says A. J. Freeman, Glenbrook Laboratories manager—production scheduling. "The plants and my office here in New York City now work with the same data, so that they are a party to the scheduling and adjustments made in New York. We can anticipate needs without heavy advance scheduling, and this should lead to reductions in warehouse inventories."
>
> "On the basis of experience to date, we have set a goal of rolling Glenbrook and Winthrop Division inventories back two years even as sales continue to expand. And we are confident we can do this without affecting service levels. This will mean reductions in inventory of millions of dollars. Further down the line is the potential for refining existing service levels by justifying them against experience with the new system and perhaps generating additional savings."[23]

---

[21] For a detailed summary of available inventory software see Richard C. Haverly, "Survey of Software for Physical Distribution," *Proceedings of the Twenty-Second Annual Conference of the National Council of Physical Distribution Management* (Chicago: National Council of Physical Distribution Management, 1984), pp. 717–885.

[22] Jefferson G. Summers, "A System to Roll Back Inventory Levels," *Transportation and Distribution Management* 13, no. 10 (October 1973), p. 33.

[23] Ibid., p. 35.

Order Processing Systems

Advanced Order Processing Systems Can Reduce Inventory Requirements

Many companies have not undertaken comprehensive and ongoing analysis and planning of inventory policy because of a lack of time and lack of information.[24] Many times a poor communications system is a contributing factor. A primary goal of inventory management is to achieve an optimum balance between inventory carrying costs and customer service. The essential task of determining the proper balance requires continuous and comprehensive planning. It hinges on the availability of information. Communications make information available. An automated and integrated order-processing system can reduce the time needed to perform certain elements of the order cycle, including order entry, order processing, and inventory replenishment. Time saved in the performance of these activities can be used for inventory planning, assuming the current order-cycle time is satisfactory to the manufacturer's customers. In this way, the firm can gain substantial cost savings by reducing its levels of safety stock.

In addition, an automated and integrated order processing system can reduce message errors and unexpected time delays. This facilitates better decision making and improves internal coordination in the firm. Remote terminals linked to a central processing unit can handle the most complex communications flows. The terminals can make the right data available when and where they are needed. The result is reduced inventories and faster invoicing, which improves cash flow.

With full, up-to-the-second information on orders, raw materials inventory and production scheduling can be better managed. The distribution center can meet customer commitments without increasing inventories. More accurate invoices can be prepared, customers can be invoiced sooner, and payments can be received more quickly with fewer reconciliations. When reconciliations are necessary, they can be resolved much more quickly. Reduced inventories and faster invoicing improve cash flow. Inventory management is improved by placing vital information into the hands of the decision makers and by providing them with the necessary time to use this information in planning inventory strategies.

IMPACT OF AN INVENTORY REDUCTION ON CORPORATE PROFIT PERFORMANCE

In order to illustrate the impact of an inventory reduction on corporate profit performance, consider the case of XYZ Company, whose financial data are presented in summary in Figure 10–12. The company has sales of $100 million, less $60 million cost of goods sold, yielding a gross margin

[24] Adapted from materials provided by Douglas E. Zemke, American Telephone and Telegraph Company, Business Marketing Management Division.

of $40 million. When variable expenses of $18 million, fixed expenses of $18 million, and income taxes of $2 million are deducted, the net profit is $2 million, which gives a net profit margin of 2 percent of sales.

On the balance sheet portion of the model, current assets of $22 million are comprised of inventory of $14 million, accounts receivable of $6 million, and other current assets of $2 million. The current assets plus $18 million of fixed assets result in total assets of $40 million and asset turnover of 2.5 times. The net profit of 2 percent multiplied by the asset turnover of 2.5 times equals a return on assets of 5 percent. The financial leverage of 2 to 1 boosts the return on net worth to 10 percent.

How Would a Logistics System Change Affect Corporate Return on Net Worth?

The question for consideration is: How would a change in the order processing system affect the performance of the logistics function and affect corporate return on net worth? In order to answer this question, the following information about the company is required:

1. Customers mail in orders to the company for processing; the order cycle is 10 days. That is, from the time the customer places the order in the mail until the customer receives the product, 10 days elapse, plus or minus some margin of error. (One hundred percent consistency would be unlikely.) The company's customers are satisfied with the 10-day order cycle since that is what all of the major suppliers offer to the trade.

2. The company does not calculate inventory carrying costs. If it did so, the non-cost of money components of inventory carrying costs, such as insurance, taxes, variable storage costs, obsolescence, shrinkage, and damage, would be 5 percent of the average inventory value. The fact that the company does not specifically identify inventory carrying costs does not make these costs any less real. They are still incurred.

3. The company is experiencing capital rationing. That is, there is a shortage of capital for investment in new projects, and investments promising a return of 20 percent after taxes or 40 percent before taxes cannot be undertaken. If the capital were available, management could invest up to $5 million in plant modernization, which would generate a return of 40 percent before taxes. If such an investment were made, it would be depreciated on a straight-line basis over a 10-year period ($500,000 per year if the investment were $5 million).

When the company's order processing system is subjected to further study it becomes apparent that an advanced order entry system would shorten the order cycle by four days and would offer other benefits as well. For example, customers would telephone orders to customer service representatives, who would be equipped with CRTs. With this system, the customer service representative would enter the order on a real-time inventory control system while the customer was still on the telephone. The inventory levels could be reduced by the amount of the purchase, thereby eliminating the problem of two customers being promised delivery of the same stock. If the desired product was not available, the customer service representa-

FIGURE 10–12 The Strategic Profit Model with Financial Data for XYZ Company—before System Change (Financial data in $ millions)

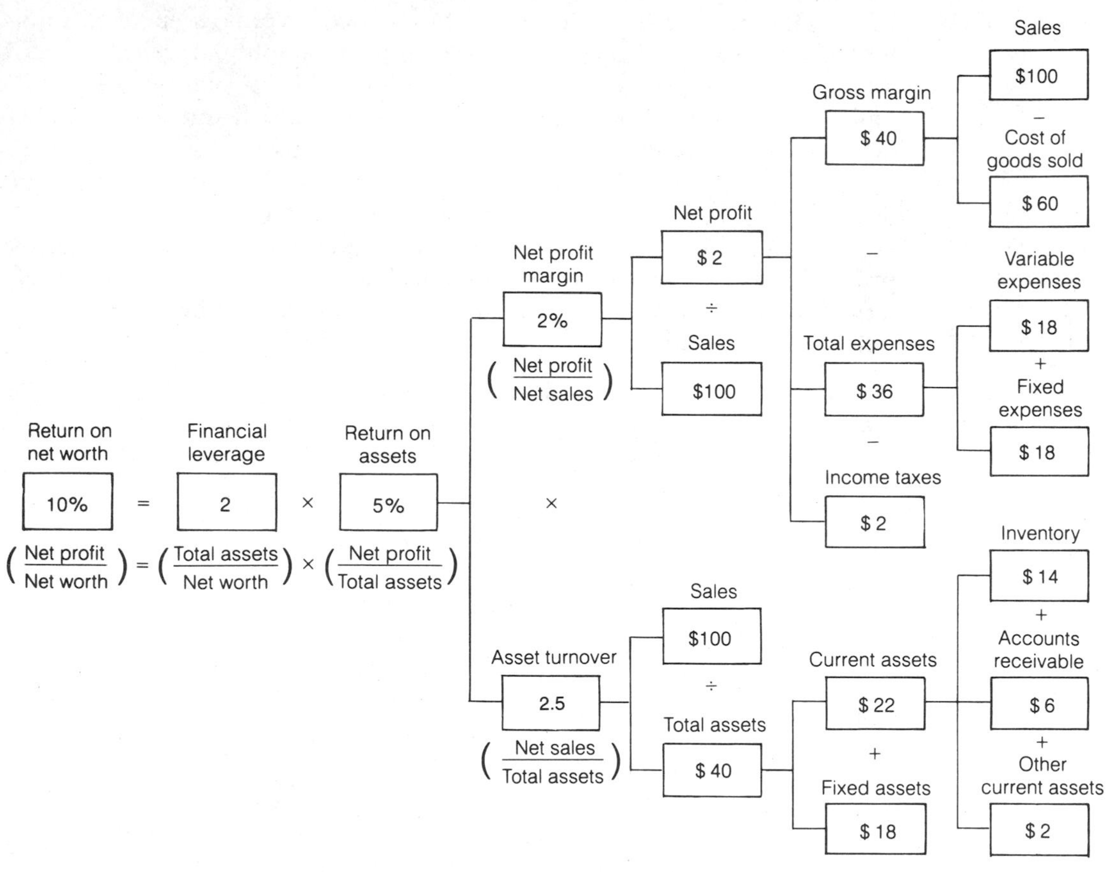

NOTE: Income taxes are assumed to equal 50 percent of net profit before taxes.

tive could arrange product substitution or schedule delivery based on planned production. Consequently, the proposed system would contribute to improved customer service.

Since customers are currently satisfied with the 10-day order cycle, the company should maintain it. Management can use the four days eliminated at the front end of the order cycle to plan production and restock field inventories, resulting in a $5 million reduction in inventories on a companywide basis. The $5 million obtained from the inventory reduction would be available for investment in the new plant equipment that was previously rejected due to the shortage of capital.

Finally, it is estimated that the annual cost of the proposed order processing system will be $750,000. What is the financial impact of the proposed system on after-tax return on net worth? Figure 10–13 provides the answer.

First, consider the impact on asset turnover. Inventory is reduced by $5 million—from $14 million to $9 million—thereby reducing current assets to $17 million. However, total assets remain unchanged at $40 million because the capital from the inventory reduction is used to buy $5 million of plant equipment; this purchase increases fixed assets by $5 million. So the asset is merely switched from a current asset to a fixed asset. Because sales and total assets are unchanged, asset turnover remains at 2.5 times.

The proposed system will affect a number of profit and loss statement accounts. The new plant equipment will reduce production costs and generate a 20 percent return after taxes, which is 40 percent before taxes, or $2 million. As a result, the cost of goods sold is reduced to $58 million from $60 million, increasing the gross margin to $42 million. Expenses that are variable with sales remain the same. But those that are variable with inventory, or with the non-cost of money, out-of-pocket costs associated with the $5 million inventory reduction, reduce fixed expenses by $250,000. However, the increased order processing expenditure of $750,000 per year, plus depreciation on the new plant equipment of $500,000 per year, raises the fixed expenses by $1.25 million, so that the fixed expenses increase to $19 million and total expenses to $37 million. Net profit before taxes is increased from $4 million to $5 million, resulting in income taxes of $2.5 million. Net profit after taxes is $2.5 million, and the net profit margin is 2.5 percent. Consequently, return on assets is increased from 5 percent to 6.25 percent. Since corporate financing is not affected, financial leverage stays at 2 to 1, and return on net worth increases from 10 percent to 12.5 percent.

The purpose of this exercise was twofold. First, it illustrated how the strategic profit model can be used to identify the impact of a change in logistics operations on return on assets and return on net worth. The example also showed that even though a firm may not calculate inventory carrying costs, the costs are indeed real. The cost of money for inventory carrying cost purposes should always reflect how the money would be used if it were not invested in inventory.

In the example, it was assumed that the money could be reinvested in a project that would yield 20 percent after taxes. Figure 10–14 shows what the return on net worth would be if the money were used to reduce bank loans by $5 million. It is assumed that the interest rate on the loan was at 10 percent. Of course, this is a pretax expense.

Since the money is being used to reduce debt, total assets decrease by $5 million, to $35 million, and asset turnover increases from 2.5 times to 2.86 times. In this example gross margin is unchanged. Fixed expenses are decreased by $750,000—a $250,000 reduction in non-cost of money,

FIGURE 10–13 The Strategic Profit Model with Financial Data for Company XYZ—after System Change (Financial data in $ millions)

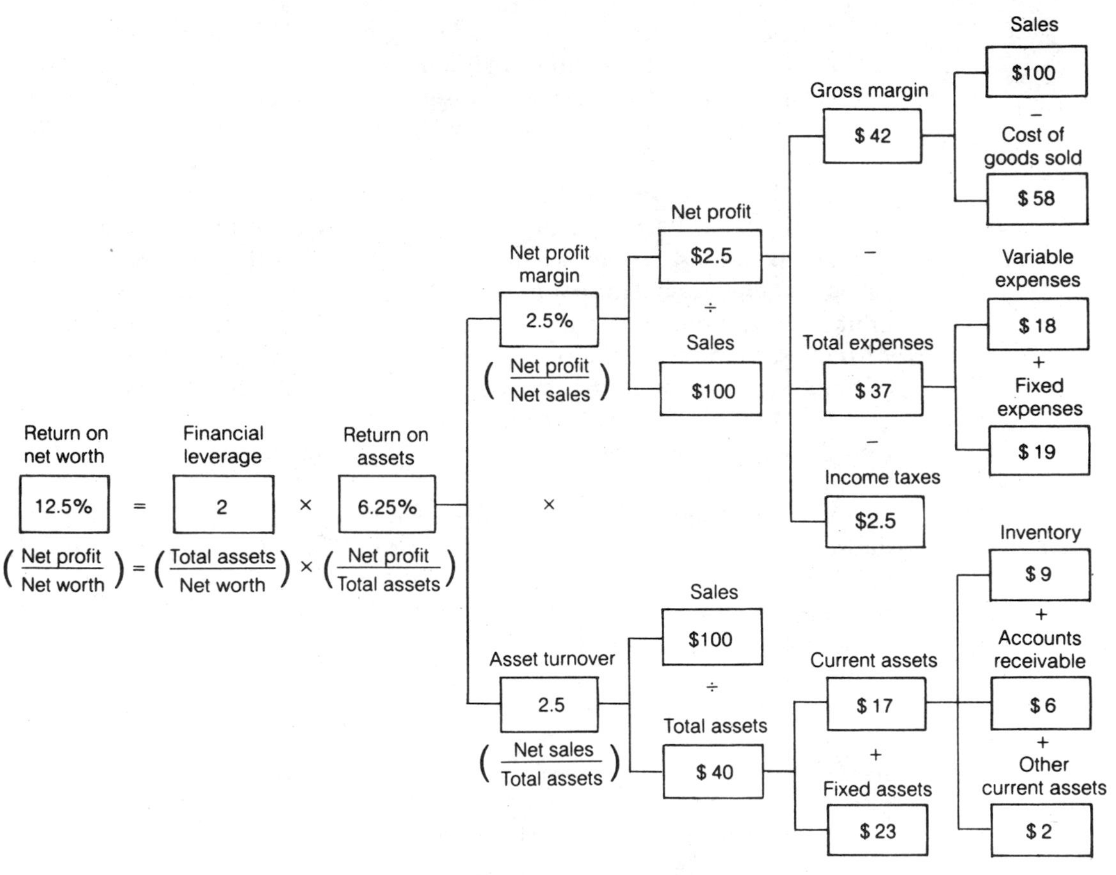

NOTE: Income taxes are assumed to equal 50 percent of net profit before taxes.

inventory-related expenses, plus a $500,000 decrease in interest expense. However, the increase in order processing and communication costs of $750,000 negates the decrease in expenses and results in no change in the total. Net profit margin remains at 2.0 percent, and return on assets becomes 5.72 percent. The reduction in debt lowers financial leverage from 2 to 1 ($40 million to $20 million) to 1.75 to 1 ($35 million to $20 million). The impact on return on net worth is a marginal increase from 10 percent to 10.01 percent.

Notice once again how changes in inventory levels, resulting from revisions in the logistics system, can influence corporate return on net worth.

FIGURE 10–14 The Strategic Profit Model for Company XYZ—after System Change, Assuming Repayment of Bank Loan (Financial data in $ millions)

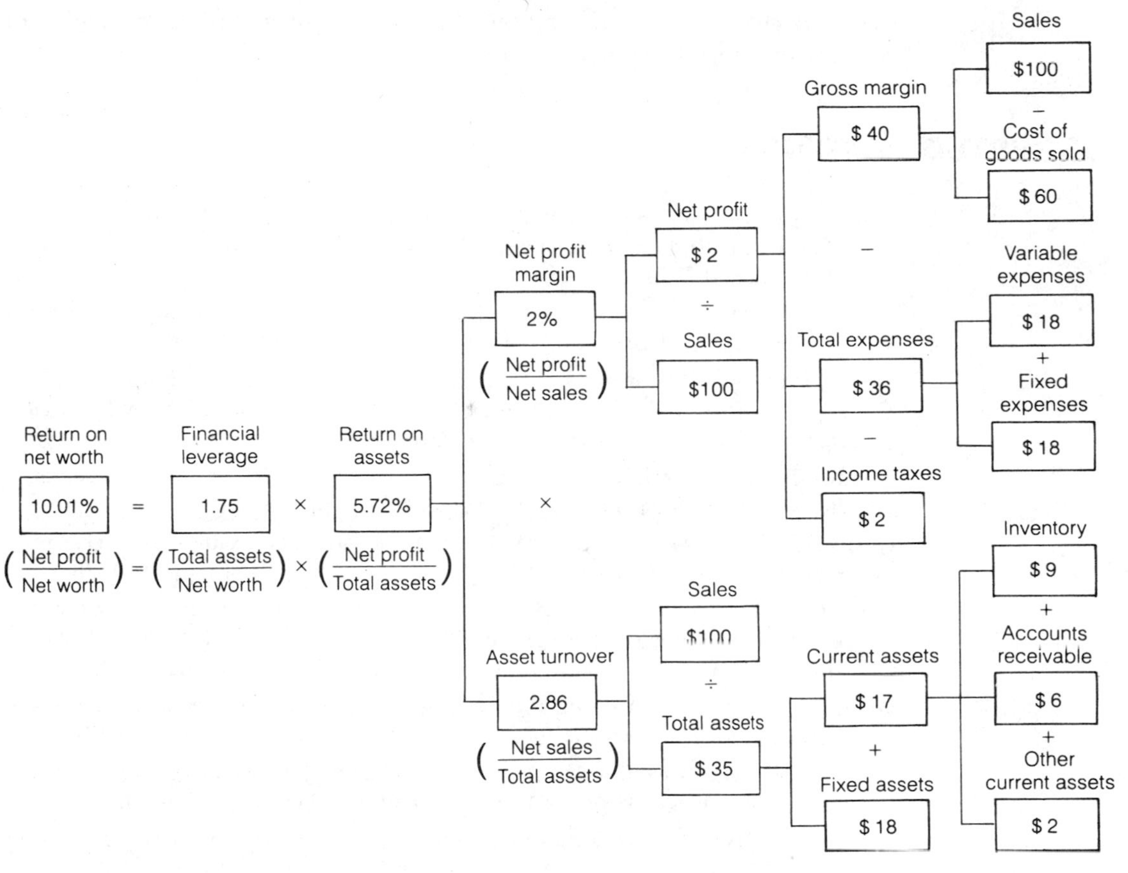

NOTE: Income taxes are assumed to equal 50 percent of net profit before taxes.

SUMMARY

In this chapter we examined the basic concepts of inventory management. The EOQ model was introduced, along with methods for adjusting it. In addition, we discussed demand and order cycle uncertainty and examined a method for considering both types of uncertainty when calculating safety stock requirements. We also saw that the traditional approach to improving customer service, increasing inventory investment, is costly and inefficient. We discussed the impact of inventory investment on production scheduling and looked at some symptoms of poor inventory management.

The chapter concluded with an explanation of techniques that can be used to improve inventory management, and a method for determining the impact of an inventory reduction on corporate profit performance. In the next chapter, we will see how a knowledge of materials management can improve logistics performance.

SUGGESTED READINGS

CHAMBERS, JOHN C., SATINDER K. MULLICK, AND DONALD D. SMITH. "How to Choose the Right Forecasting Technique." *Harvard Business Review* 49, no. 4 (July–August 1971), pp. 45–74.

CHASE, RICHARD B., AND NICHOLAS J. AQUILANO. *Production and Operations Management,* 3rd ed. Homewood, Ill.: Richard D. Irwin, 1981.

CLOSS, DAVID J. "Effectiveness of Safety Stock Decision Rules: An Empirical Investigation." *Proceedings of the Seventeenth Annual Conference of the National Council of Physical Distribution Management,* 1979, pp. 257–78.

FLORES, BENITO E., AND D. CLAY WHYBARK. "Forecasting 'Laws' for Management." *Business Horizons* 28, no. 4 (July–August 1985), pp. 48–53.

GEORGOFF, DAVID M., AND ROBERT G. MURDICK. "Managers Guide to Forecasting." *Harvard Business Review* 64, no. 1 (January–February 1986), pp. 110–20.

GILL, LYNN E., GEORGE ISOMA, AND JOEL L. SUTHERLAND. "Inventory and Physical Distribution Management." In *The Distribution Handbook,* ed. James F. Robeson and Robert G. House. New York: The Free Press, 1985, pp. 615–733.

GROSS, CHARLES W. "Bridging the Communications Gap between Managers and Forecasters." *The Journal of Business Forecasting* (Winter 1987–88), pp. 6–9.

HOWARD, KEITH. "Inventory Management in Practice." *International Journal of Physical Distribution and Materials Management* 14, no. 2 (1984), pp. 1–36.

JAIN, C. L. "Myths and Realities of Forecasting." *The Journal of Business Forecasting* (Fall 1990), pp. 18–29.

LANGLEY, C. JOHN, JR. "The Inclusion of Transportation Costs in Inventory Models: Some Considerations." *Journal of Business Logistics* 2, no. 1 (1980), pp. 106–25.

MENTZER, JOHN T., AND R. KRISHNAN. "The Effect of the Assumption of Normality on Inventory Control/Customer Service." *Journal of Business Logistics* 6, no. 1 (1985), pp. 101–20.

MERRILLS, ROY. "How Northern Telecom Competes on Time." *Harvard Business Review* 89, no. 4 (July-August 1989), pp. 108–14.

O'NEIL, BRIAN F., AND GERALD O. FAHLING. "A Liquidation Model for Excess Inventories." *Journal of Business Logistics* 3, no. 2 (1982), pp. 85–103.

TERSINE, RICHARD J., AND MICHELE G. TERSINE. "Inventory Reduction: Preventive and Corrective Strategies." *The International Journal of Logistics Management* 1, no. 2 (1990), pp. 17–24.

WILKINSON, GARY F. "Why Did You Use that Forecasting Technique?" *The Journal of Business Forecasting* (Fall 1988), pp. 2–4.

ZINN, WALTER. "Developing Heuristics to Estimate the Impact of Postponement on Safety Stock." *The International Journal of Logistics Management* 1, no. 2 (1990), pp. 11–16.

QUESTIONS AND PROBLEMS

1. Why is inventory so important to the efficient and effective management of a firm?
2. How does uncertainty in demand and lead time affect inventory levels?
3. How does the economic order quantity model mathematically select the most economical order quantity?
4. One of the product lines carried by Farha Wholesale Foods was a line of canned fruit manufactured by California Canners, Inc. Mr. Jones, the canned goods buyer, knew that the company did not reorder from its suppliers in a systematic manner and wondered if the EOQ model might be appropriate. For example, the company ordered 200 cases of fruit cocktail each week, and the annual volume was about 10,000 cases. The purchase price was $8 per case, the ordering cost was $15 per order, and the inventory carrying cost was 35 percent. California Canners, Inc., paid the transportation charges, and there were no price breaks for ordering quantities in excess of 200 cases. Does the economic order quantity model apply in this situation? If so, calculate the economic order quantity.
5. Explain the basic differences between a fixed order point, fixed order quantity model, and a fixed order interval inventory model. Which is likely to lead to the largest inventory levels?
6. Calculate the economic order quantity, the safety stock, and the average inventory necessary to achieve a 98 percent customer service level, given the following information:

   a. The average daily demand for a 25-day period was found to be:

Day	*Units Demand*	*Day*	*Units Demand*	*Day*	*Units Demand*
1	8	11	7	21	7
2	5	12	8	22	6
3	4	13	12	23	8
4	6	14	9	24	10
5	9	15	10	25	11
6	8	16	5		
7	9	17	8		
8	10	18	11		
9	7	19	9		
10	6	20	7		

   b. There is no variability in order cycle.

   c. The ordering cost is $20 per order.

d. The annual demand is 2,000.
e. The cost is $100 per unit.
f. The inventory carrying cost is 35 percent.
g. The products are purchased FOB destination.

7. Recalculate your answer to question 7 given the following sample of replenishment cycles:

Replenishment Cycle	*Lead Time in Days*	*Replenishment Cycle*	*Lead Time in Days*
1	10	10	9
2	12	11	8
3	11	12	10
4	10	13	11
5	10	14	9
6	9	15	9
7	8	16	10
8	12	17	11
9	11	18	10

8. Given your calculations in questions 6 and 7, what will the actual fill rate be if management is willing to hold inventory equal to one week's sales as safety stock?

9. What is the cost saving to the customer resulting from a manufacturer's ability to reduce variability by two days, given the following information:
a. Average sales of 40 cases per day.
b. Purchase price per case is $45.
c. Transportation cost per case is $5.
d. The order cycle is 10 days.
e. Inventory carrying cost is 40 percent.
How does this compare with the cost saving associated with a two-day reduction in the order cycle with no change in order cycle variability?

10. Using the financial data in Figure 10–12, show the impact of a $4 million reduction in inventory, given that:
a. Inventory carrying costs are 45 percent, which includes 5 percent for non-cost of money components.
b. The average variable cost of the inventory delivered to the storage location is 70 percent of full manufactured cost.
c. The inventory reduction is accomplished by eliminating rail shipments, which represent 30 percent of all shipments, and shipping all products by truck. As a result, transportation costs increase by $350,000.

11. As the inventory planning team for Cook Department Stores, one of your primary responsibilities is to aid department managers with inventory decisions. The electronics department manager has come to your group with a desire to improve department inventory planning and profitability. The department stocks a VCR brand named Super View.

Super View financial data:

Selling price/unit	$555.00
Cost of goods sold including delivery costs at current level of operations and under current inventory policies	$495.00

Super View sales data:

Representative 10 day sales (assume Cook Department Store is open 360 days/year)

Sales/Day	Number of Days (f)
1	2
2	2
6	2
10	2
16	2

Super View lead-time data:

Super View is supplied directly from Tokyo, Japan by Syonara Manufacturing.

Delivery Pattern:	Sample of 10 order cycles in days
Super View:	9, 9, 42, 13, 22, 33, 11, 18, 36, 27

Current Super View service and inventory policies:

Order policy:	EOQ: Orders are equal to the average demand that during average lead-time
Fill rate:	99 percent

The following inventory carrying cost figures were collected:

Corporate opportunity cost of capital was 37% (pre-tax).

Other costs:

Inventory taxes	1.6%
Insurance	.4%
Recurring storage	3.3%
Obsolescence	.7%
Damage	2.0%

The manager has several questions regarding inventory policy:

a. Which one of the following Super View fill rates (99%, 95%, 91%, or 87%) will result in the highest annual profit?

b. Syonara Manufacturing stated that for an additional increase in price of 1.5%, they can hire more dependable international carriers and cut the lead-time standard deviation in half. Should the electronics department manager accept or reject the offer? (Assume their current 99% fill rate and ordering policies.)

c. There are 5 Cook Department Store branches in the Detroit area. (See Table 1.) Corporate management wants to compare the annual profitability of two strategies.

(1) Provide a 99 percent fill rate for Super View by stocking the appropriate number of units of safety stock at each branch store; or

(2) Provide a 99 percent fill rate for Super View at the local area distribution center, which serves all 5 branches, and expedite safety stock when needed to each individual branch at a total expediting cost of $150.00 per week.

Which strategy will be most profitable, assuming that there will be no lost sales if the second strategy is employed?

TABLE 1 Super View Sales (per day, each branch store)

	Store				
Day	*1*	*2*	*3*	*4*	*5*
1	1	1	1	16	16
2	2	2	2	10	10
3	6	6	6	6	6
4	10	10	10	2	2
5	16	16	16	1	1
6	1	1	1	16	16
7	2	2	2	10	10
8	6	6	6	6	6
9	10	10	10	2	2
10	16	16	16	1	1
Average sales/store	7	7	7	7	7
σ s/Store	5.81	5.81	5.81	5.81	5.81

Chapter 11

Managing Materials Flow

Objectives of This Chapter

To identify the activities of materials management

To examine the concept of total quality management (TQM)

To identify and describe a variety of materials management techniques, including Kanban/Just-in-Time systems, MRP, and DRP.

INTRODUCTION

As defined in this book, logistics management is concerned with the efficient flow of raw materials, in-process inventory, and finished goods from point-of-origin to point-of-consumption.[1] An integral part of that flow, referred to as *materials management*, encompasses the administration of raw materials, subassemblies, manufactured parts, packing material, and in-process inventory.[2] In a formal sense, materials management can be defined as follows: "the single-manager organization concept embracing the planning, organizing, motivating, and controlling of all those activities and personnel principally concerned with the flow of materials into an organization."[3]

Materials Management Defined

The importance of materials management to the total logistics process cannot be overstated. Although materials management does not *directly* interface with the final customer, the degree to which raw materials, component parts, and subassemblies are made available to the production process ultimately determines the availability of products to the customer. The decisions, good or bad, made in the materials management portion of the logistics process will have a direct effect on the level of customer service offered, the ability of the firm to compete with other companies, and the level of sales and profits achieved in the marketplace.

Without efficient and effective management of inbound materials flow, the manufacturing process cannot produce products at the desired price and at the time they are required for distribution to the firm's customers. It is essential that the logistics executive understand the role of materials management and its impact on the company's cost/service mix.

In recent years, materials management has become much more important. As business enterprises have developed and matured, the role of ma-

---

[1]Some firms use the term materials management to represent logistics. While this usage of materials management is not predominant, there are a sufficient number of firms utilizing it to recognize that materials management may be used to describe the management of "materials" from point-of-origin to point-of-consumption.

[2]See Bernard J. LaLonde, John R. Grabner, and James F. Robeson, "Integrated Distribution Systems: A Management Perspective," *International Journal of Physical Distribution* 1, no. 1 (October 1970), pp. 43–49.

[3]Harold E. Fearon, "Materials Management: A Synthesis and Current View," *Journal of Purchasing* 9, no. 1 (February 1973), p. 33.

TABLE 11–1 Materials Management—Past, Present, and Future

	Past	*Present and Future*
Market:	Seller's market	Buyer's market
	Low competition	Keen competition
	Restricted export	Global-oriented
Products:	Small assortment	Wide assortments
	Long life cycle	Short life cycle
	Low technology	High technology
Production:	Full capacity load	Full capacity load
	Low flexibility	High flexibility
	Large lot sizes	Low lot sizes
	Long lead times	Short lead times
	Low costs	Low costs
	Make instead of buy	Buy instead of make
Service level:	High service level	High service level
	High inventories	Low inventories
	Slow logistics process	Quick logistics process
	Slow transport time	Quick transport time
Information technology:	Manual data processing	Electronic data processing
	Paper administration	Paperless factory
Enterprise strategy:	Production-oriented	Market-oriented

SOURCE: MCB University Press Limited, Hans F. Busch, "Integrated Materials Management," *International Journal of Physical Distribution and Materials Management* 18, no. 7 (1988), p. 28.

terials management has expanded to meet the challenges of market-driven, rather than production-driven, economies. Table 11–1 identifies some of the differences between the historical role played by materials management within firms and the present and future environments in which materials will be brought into firms' production processes.

While many things such as the need to reduce costs and provide high levels of customer service will remain important, the present and future environments are characterized by a changing set of priorities and issues—for example, global orientation, shorter product life cycles, lower levels of inventories, electronic data processing, and a market-oriented focus.

This chapter identifies the various components of materials management, and shows how to effectively manage materials flow within a manufacturing environment. We will examine specific management strategies and techniques used in the planning, implementation, and control of materials.

SCOPE OF MATERIALS MANAGEMENT ACTIVITIES

Materials Management Activities

Materials management is typically comprised of four basic activities:

1. Anticipating materials requirements.
2. Sourcing and obtaining materials.

3. Introducing materials into the organization.
4. Monitoring the status of materials as a current asset.[4]

Figure 11–1 identifies some of the functions performed by materials managers.

The definition of materials management used in this chapter views the activity as an organizational system with the various functions as subsystems: "It recognizes that the individual subsystems are all interrelated and interactive. The interfaces between the subsystems must be approached and [managed] in view of overall materials (and firm) objectives, which [and can] result in suboptimization for the firm as a whole"[5] if the proper cost-service trade-offs are not made.

The specific objectives of materials management will tie in very closely to the firm's main objectives of achieving an acceptable level of profitability and/or return on investment, and to remain competitive in a marketplace characterized by increasing competition.

Figure 11–2 highlights the major objectives of materials management: low costs, high levels of service, quality assurance, low level of tied-up capital, and support of other functions. Each objective is clearly linked to the overall corporate goals and objectives.

> The main objective—to make a substantial contribution to profit—is reached by optimising the procurement, management and allocation of material as a productive resource. Hence it is the aim of integrated materials management to achieve optimum supply by reconciling the conflicting goals of low materials costs and overhead, and to achieve a high level of customer service and a very low level of capital tied up in inventories. . . . [T]he optimisation of the supply function and, thus, the addition of intangible value are achieved by totally controlling the flow of materials and information from the supply market through the company and finally to the point of sale.[6]

Materials management encompasses a variety of logistics activities. In a manner similar to the administration of finished goods distribution, the materials manager must be concerned with purchasing and procurement, inventory control, warehousing and storage, order processing, transportation, and almost every other logistics activity. The primary differences between the materials management process and the process that distributes finished goods are that the items being handled in materials management are raw materials, component parts, and subassemblies, and the recipient of the distribution effort is the production or manufacturing group rather than the final customer.

---

[4] Ibid.

[5] Ibid.

[6] MCB University Press Limited, Yunus Kathawala and Heino H. Nauo, "Integrated Materials Management: A Conceptual Approach," *International Journal of Physical Distribution and Materials Management* 19, no. 8 (1989), p. 10.

FIGURE 11–1 Materials Managers Wear Many Hats

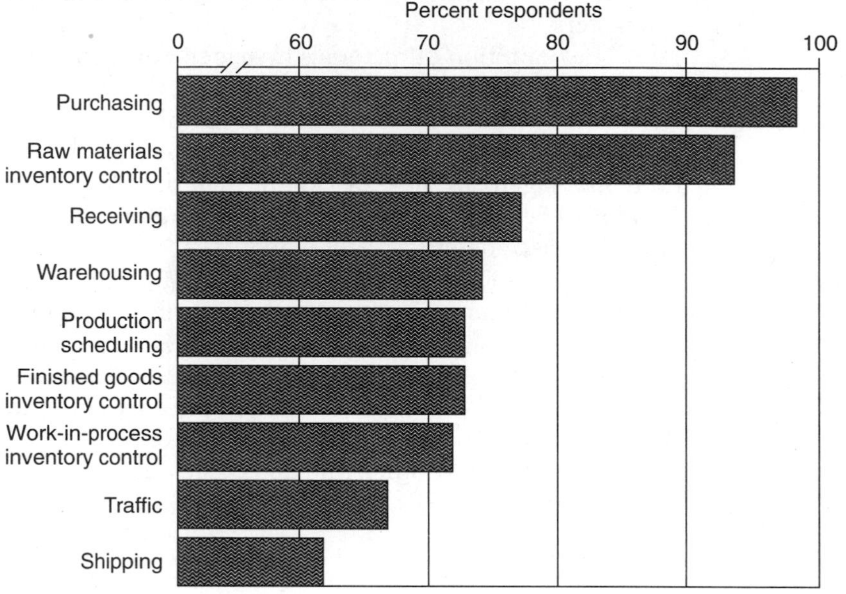

SOURCE: Rebecca Lipman, "Buyers' Goals Match Materials Managers'," *Purchasing,* August 8, 1979, p. 39. Reprinted with permission by *Purchasing* Magazine. Copyright 1979 by Cahners Publishing Company, Division of Reed Holdings, Inc.

Integral aspects of materials management include purchasing and procurement, production control, inbound traffic and transportation, warehousing and storage, MIS control, inventory planning and control, and salvage and scrap disposal.

Purchasing and Procurement

The acquisition of materials has long been an important aspect of materials management and will continue to be in the future: "The rapidly changing supply scene, with cycles of abundance and shortages, varying prices, lead times, and availabilities, provides a continuing challenge to those organizations wishing to obtain a maximum contribution from this area."[7]

Purchasing and Procurement Are Not the Same

The terms *purchasing* and *procurement* are often used interchangeably, although they do differ in scope. Purchasing generally refers to the actual buying of materials and those activities associated with the buying process. Procurement is broader in scope and includes purchasing, traffic, warehousing, and receiving inbound materials.

[7] Michiel R. Leenders, Harold E. Fearon, and Wilbur B. England, *Purchasing and Materials Management*, 9th ed. (Homewood, Ill.: Richard D. Irwin, 1989), p. 1.

FIGURE 11–2 The Objectives of Integrated Materials Management

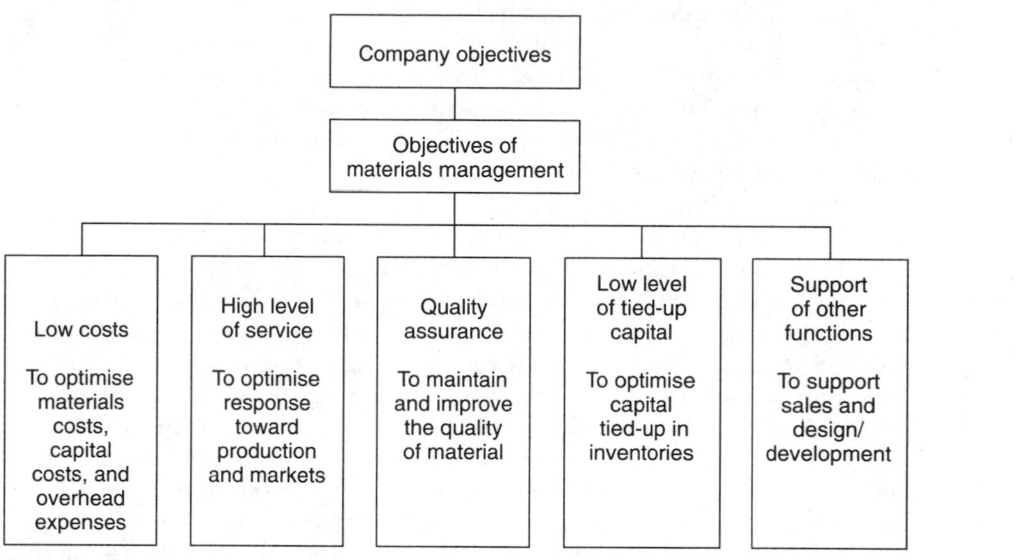

SOURCE: MCB University Press Limited, Yunus Kathawala and Heino H. Nauo, "Integrated Materials Management: A Conceptual Approach," *International Journal of Physical Distribution and Materials Management* 19, no. 8 (1989), p. 10.

Production Control

Production control is an activity traditionally positioned under manufacturing, although a few firms place it under logistics. Its position in the firm's organizational chart is probably not crucial, so long as both manufacturing and logistics have an input into the production control activity.

The role of production or manufacturing in the logistics process is twofold. First, the production activity determines how much and what kinds of finished products are produced. This, in turn, influences when and how the products are distributed to the firm's customers. Second, production directly determines the company's need for raw materials, subassemblies, and component parts that are used in the manufacturing process. Therefore, it is axiomatic that production control decisions be jointly shared by manufacturing and logistics.

Inbound Logistics

Materials management is concerned with product flows into the firm. The materials manager's customer is the manufacturing or production department rather than the intermediate or final customer in the marketplace. Much like the firm's target markets, manufacturing requires certain levels of customer service. Manufacturing depends on the ability of materials management to adequately administer a variety of functions, including traffic and transportation, warehousing and storage, and MIS control.

One of the most important activities administered by materials management is the inbound traffic and transportation function. Like their counterparts who are responsible for finished goods movement, materials managers must be aware of the various transport modes and modal combinations available to their companies, any regulations that might affect the transportation carriers their firm uses, the private versus for-hire decision, leasing, evaluating mode/carrier performance, and the cost/service trade-offs involved in the inbound movement of product.[8]

Differences between Inbound and Outbound Transportation

There are basically three major differences between the administration of inbound transportation and outbound transportation. First, the market demand that generates the need for outbound movement is generally considered to be uncertain and fluctuating. The demand that the materials manager is concerned with originates with the production activity and is much more predictable and stable. Therefore, transportation decisions made by the materials manager are not subject to the same types of problems encountered by his or her counterpart in the outbound traffic area. Second, the materials manager is more likely to be concerned with bulk movements of raw materials or large shipments of parts and subassemblies. In addition, raw materials and parts have different handling and loss and/or damage characteristics, which will affect the entire mode/carrier selection and evaluation process. Third, firms generally exercise less control over their inbound transportation because purchasing procedures tend to look at "total delivered cost." A separate analysis of inbound costs is not performed as often or in as much depth. Thus, significant cost savings are possible.

Warehousing and Storage

Firms must place raw materials, components parts, and subassemblies in storage until they need those items in the manufacturing process. Unlike the warehousing of finished goods, which often occurs in the field, items awaiting use in the production process are usually stored on-site, that is, at the point of manufacture; or else they are delivered on an "as needed" basis by a Just-in-Time (JIT) supplier. If a JIT delivery system is utilized, the need for inbound warehousing is greatly minimized or eliminated altogether. If not, and warehouses are used extensively for the storage of inbound materials, the materials manager is usually much more concerned with warehousing and inventory costs because they account for a larger

[8] For a discussion of inbound consolidation strategies as a facet of materials management activities, see Frank P. Buffa, "Inbound Consolidation Strategy: The Effect of Inventory Cost Rate Changes," *International Journal of Physical Distribution and Materials Management* 18, no. 7 (1988), pp. 3–14.

percentage of product value. Generally, finished goods are valued significantly higher than goods-in-process, raw materials, parts, or subassemblies. As a result, warehousing and storage costs are not as important, on a comparative basis, as they would be to the materials manager.

In addition, the warehousing requirements for raw materials and other items are usually quite different. For example, open or outside storage is possible with many raw materials, such as iron ore, sand and gravel, coal, and other unprocessed materials. Also, damage and/or loss due to weather, spoilage, or theft is minimal with raw materials because of their unprocessed state and/or low value per pound.

Data and Information Systems

Information Needed by the Materials Manager

The materials manager needs direct access to the firm's information system in order to properly administer materials flow into and within the organization. The types of information often needed by the materials manager include demand forecasts for production, names of suppliers and supplier characteristics, pricing data, inventory levels, production schedules, transportation routing and scheduling data, and various other financial and marketing facts. Additionally, materials management supplies input into the firm's management information system. Data on inventory levels for materials, delivery schedules, pricing, forward buys, and supplier information are examples of some of the inputs provided by materials management.

> Integrated materials management constantly has a multitude of data to process, a task that would not be possible without EDP-supported program systems. Numerous software packages for individual functional elements of integrated materials management have been developed during the last few years, packages that have been tailored for particular branches of industry and particular company sizes.[9]
>
> Thus, modern information technology will offer opportunities for the fast and safe transmission and processing of extensive amounts of data, both internally for users within the company and externally for suppliers and customers. Paperless communication is coming to the forefront whereby routine tasks in order processing and scheduling will be decisively facilitated.[10] As a result, new information technology offers great opportunities for linking the planning, control and processing functions of materials management that were hitherto performed independently, thereby creating the foundation for the establishment of integrated materials management.[11]

---

[9]See Richard C. Haverly, Douglas McW. Smith, and Deborah P. Steele, *Logistics Software* (Stamford, Conn.: Andersen Consulting, 1990).

[10]See H. J. Bocker, J. P. Daniels, J. N. Prasad, and H. M. Shane, "The Factory of Tomorrow: Challenges of the Future," *Management International Review* 26 (Fall 1986), pp. 36–50.

[11]Kathawala and Nauo, "Integrated Materials Management," p. 14.

With the proliferation of computerized information systems and data bases, coupled with electronic data interchange (EDI), this facet of materials management will become even more significant in the future.

Inventory Planning and Control

Inventory planning and control of raw materials, component parts, subassemblies, and goods-in-process are just as important as the management of finished goods inventory. Many of the concepts discussed in Chapters 9 and 10, such as ABC analysis, inventory carrying costs, and economic order quantity (EOQ), are directly applicable to materials management.

Forecasting Is an Essential Part of Materials Management

One aspect of inventory planning and control that requires further emphasis within the context of materials management is forecasting. Effective and efficient materials management requires three types of forecasts:

> *Demand Forecast.* Investigation of the firm's demand for the item, to include current and projected demand, inventory status, and lead times. Also considered are competing demands, current and projected, by industry and end-product use.
>
> *Supply Forecast.* Collection of data about current producers and suppliers, the aggregate current projected supply situation, and technological and political trends that might affect supply.
>
> *Price Forecast.* Based on information gathered and analyzed about demand and supply . . . Provides a prediction of short- and long-term prices and the underlying reasons for those trends.[12]

The firm may utilize a variety of forecasting techniques, ranging from those based on general market information (from suppliers, sales force, customers, and others) to those that are highly sophisticated computer algorithms. The specific technique or approach a firm selects should be appropriate for the unique characteristics of the company and its markets. An in-depth discussion of forecasting will be presented in Chapter 14, Decision Support Systems.

Just-in-Time systems, materials requirements planning (MRPI), manufacturing resource planning (MRPII), distribution requirements planning (DRPI), and distribution resource planning (DRPII) systems can also improve the efficiency of inventory planning and control. We will briefly discuss these systems later in this chapter.

Materials Disposal

One of the most important areas of materials management that a firm often overlooks or considers minor is the disposal of scrap, surplus, recyclable, or obsolete materials. "Originally, disposal was a scarcely recognised incidental task. During the last few years, it has gained substantial impor-

[12] Leenders, et al., *Purchasing and Materials Management,* pp. 441–42.

tance through several factors such as increased public awareness of the environment and more stringent government legislation, but also due to better recognition of the opportunities it offers in return."[13]

Many materials can be salvaged and sold to other companies. It is estimated that total annual sales of scrap and waste materials in the United States totals $billions. An illustration can highlight the profit potential: A film processing firm had been selling the residual chemicals and materials that were by-products of its operations for relatively low prices. The firm invested in a machine that could separate the waste materials into its components. While the company was still able to sell some of the components to the same salvage firm that had previously been performing the separation process, one of the residues produced was silver, which the company subsequently sold to a precious metal dealer for a handsome profit. The separator machine paid for itself in less than two years.

Why Salvage and Scrap Materials Exist

Almost all firms produce some type of surplus materials as a by-product of their operations. The existence of this material can result from overoptimistic sales forecasts, changes in product specifications, errors in estimating materials usage, losses in processing, and overbuying due to forward buys or quantity discounts on large purchases.[14]

> The basic tasks of the disposal function include a disposal classification according to whether something can be reused and what possibility of environmental pollution it bears. As a result of legal requirements and technical conditions, the hazard represented by some waste products is being met by increased awareness of the public towards a clean environment. Therefore, it is absolutely necessary to assign the responsibility for waste disposal to a central section that must report to the materials management department.[15]

This aspect of materials management will likely become much more important in the future.

TOTAL QUALITY MANAGEMENT (TQM)

Total quality management (TQM) has been defined as follows:

> TQM is both a philosophy and a set of guiding principles that represent the foundation of a continuously improving organization. TQM is the application of quantitative and human resources to improve the material services supplied to an organization, all the processes within the organization, and the degree to which the needs of the customer are met—now and in the future. TQM integrates fundamental management techniques, existing improvement efforts,

---

[13] Kathawala and Nauo, p. 12; also see E. J. Muller, "The Greening of Logistics," *Distribution* 90, no. 1 (January 1991) pp. 26–34.

[14] See Leenders et al., *Purchasing and Materials Management,* pp. 387–92.

[15] Kathawala and Nauo, "Integrated Materials Management," p. 12.

TABLE 11–2 Traditional Management and TQM Comparison

Traditional Management	*Total Quality Management*
Looks for "quick fix"	Adopts a new management philosophy
Fire-fights	Uses structured, disciplined operating methodology
Operates the same old way	Advocates "breakthrough" thinking using small innovations
Randomly adopts improvement efforts	"Sets the example" through management action
Focuses on short-term	Stresses long-term, continuous improvement
Inspects for errors	Prevents errors
Throws resources at a task	Uses people to add value
Is motivated by profit	Focuses on the customer
Relies on programs	Is a new way of life

SOURCE: James H. Saylor, "What Total Quality Management Means to the Logistician," *Logistics Spectrum* 24, no. 4 (Winter 1990), p. 20.

> and technical tools under a disciplined approach focused on continuous improvement.[16]

TQM has particular relevance and importance to materials flow within logistics. Many leading authorities have championed the importance of quality in business, including Deming and Crosby.[17] Additionally, the Malcolm Baldrige National Quality Award program of the U.S. Department of Commerce has helped shape corporate thinking on quality issues. Traditional concepts about quality have been modified and enhanced to form the TQM approach outlined in Table 11–2.

The TQM approach stresses long-term benefits resulting from continuous improvements to systems, programs, products, and people. Improvements most often result from a combination of small innovations. A structured, disciplined operating methodology is used to maximize customer service levels.

Quality Is a Philosophy of Doing Business

From a logistics perspective, Table 11–3 identifies the relationships between TQM and logistics.[18] Underlying the specific items listed in the table is the notion that quality is a philosophy of doing business. It is like the

---

[16] Office of the Deputy Assistant Secretary of Defense for TQM, *Total Quality Management: A Guide for Implementation,* DOD 5000.51–G, Washington, D.C. (Final Draft), August 23, 1989.

[17] See Howard S. Gitlow and Shelly J. Gitlow, *The Deming Guide to Quality and Competitive Position* (Englewood Cliffs, N.J.: Prentice Hall, 1987); and Philip B. Crosby, *Quality Is Free* (New York: McGraw-Hill, 1979).

[18] For a comprehensive discussion of this topic and a listing of TQM references, see Robert A. Novack, "Logistics Control: An Approach to Quality," unpublished Ph.D. dissertation, University of Tennessee, 1987.

TABLE 11–3 TQM and Logistics Direct Relationship

TQM	*Logistics*
Provides a TQM management environment	Uses systematic, integrated, consistent, organization-wide perspective for satisfying the customer
Reduces chronic waste	Emphasizes "doing it right the first time"
Involves everyone and everything	Involves almost every process
Nurtures supplier partnerships and customer relationships	Knows the importance of supply partnerships
	Key to customer relations. Customer relations are directly dependent on training, documentation, maintenance, supply support, support equipment, transportation, manpower, computer resources, and facilities
Creates a continuous improvement system	Uses logistics support analysis to continuously improve the system
Includes quality as an element of design	Influences design by emphasizing reliability, maintainability, supportability using the optimum mix of manpower and technology
Provides training constantly	Provides constant technical training for everyone
Leads long-term continuous improvement efforts geared toward prevention	Focuses on reducing life cycle costs by quality improvements geared to prevention
Encourages teamwork	Stresses the integrated efforts of everyone
Satisfies the customer (internal and external)	Places the customer first

SOURCE: James H. Saylor, "What Total Quality Management Means to the Logistician," *Logistics Spectrum* 24, no. 4 (Winter 1990), p. 22.

marketing concept, cost trade-off analysis, and the systems approach. Each is an orientation or approach to doing business that influences how individuals, departments, and companies plan, implement, and control marketing and logistics activities. Therefore, every person involved in logistics must understand his or her role in delivering a level of quality to suppliers, vendors, and final customers.

> Central to TQM success is focus on continuous improvement that leads to higher quality and better customer support whether internal or external to the organization. It normally requires a cultural change, because most organizations today focus on activities rather than process improvement.
>
> More importantly, TQM requires employee involvement to be successful. Without employee involvement, focus cannot be achieved. . . . Senior management commitment and leadership is imperative to ensure follow-through of

employee recommendations. Commitment at all levels is the "oil" that enables the organizational "engine" to work.[19]

As indicated earlier, TQM is a process. It involves almost every logistics activity and utilizes a systematic, integrated, consistent, organization-wide perspective for satisfying the customer. And, TQM emphasizes continuous improvements. As shown in Figure 11–3, the process begins with a determination of logistics requirements (e.g., customer service levels, inventory levels, transportation strategies). Those requirements are specified as a result of a logistics audit that has examined the materials management and physical distribution aspects of the total logistics system.

TQM/Logistics Process

After requirements are determined, the processes are continuously reviewed to develop ways to improve. For example, based on historical information, supplier evaluation criteria may be revised, inbound logistics strategies may be modified, or perhaps Just-in-Time relationships may be established with selected vendors or suppliers.

"An action plan . . . as well as process improvement recommendations [are] prepared. The action plan should be specified with step by step goals, completion dates, responsible personnel, and resource requirements. . . . The logistics team then acts upon the plan with progress being reviewed regularly."[20] In essence, the process resembles the spiral shown in Figure 11–3.

Benefits of a TQM Approach

Implementation of TQM within the materials management environment has resulted in significant benefits and improvements for many companies. McDonnell Douglas Corporation employed TQM concepts and reduced scrap by 58 percent. Boeing Ballistic Systems Division reduced parts and materials lead times by 30 percent and reduced material shortages from 12 percent to zero. AT&T reduced product defect rates and total process time by 30 percent and 46 percent, respectively. Hewlett Packard Company reduced scrap by 75 percent and put 60 percent of its product failure rate through TQM improvements.[21]

In summary, TQM and logistics are interrelated. The nature of the relationship was superbly stated by Kenderdine and Larson: "Managing logistics without incorporating the costs of quality is just as short-sighted as looking at the management of quality without considering the role of lo-

---

[19]Scott A. Wagoner, "Logistics and Quality Management: Leadership and the Process Improvement Link," *Logistics Spectrum* 23, no. 4 (Winter 1989), p. 13; also see Johann L. Von Flue, "Quality Management," *Logistics Spectrum* 24, no. 4 (Winter 1990), pp. 13–17.

[20]Ibid., p. 15.

[21]See Joe W. Meredith and Benjamin S. Blanchard, "Concurrent Engineering: Total Quality Management in Design," *Logistics Spectrum* 24, no. 4 (Winter 1990), pp. 31–40; and R. I. Winner, J. P. Pennell, H. E. Bertrand, and M. G. Slusarczuk, *The Role of Concurrent Engineering in Weapons System Acquisition,* IDA Report R–338 Alexandria, Va.: Institute for Defense Analyses, December 1988.

FIGURE 11–3 TQM/Logistics Process

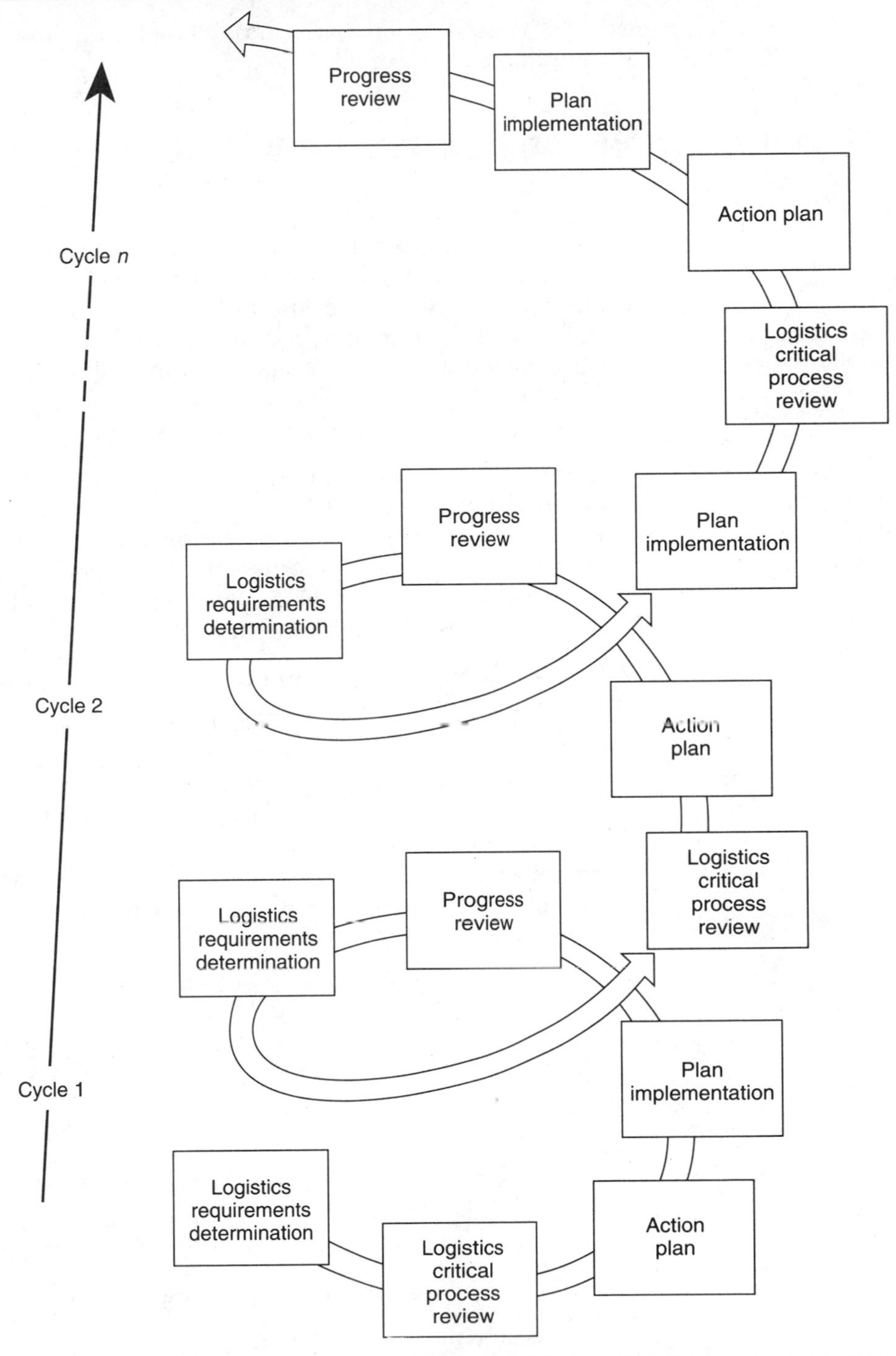

SOURCE: Scott A. Wagoner, "Logistics and Quality Management: Leadership and the Process Improvement Link," *Logistics Spectrum* 23, no. 4 (Winter 1989), p. 15.

gistics."[22] Thus, it is vital that materials flow be administered and controlled utilizing the concepts of TQM.

ADMINISTRATION AND CONTROL OF MATERIALS FLOW

Like all of the functions of logistics, materials management activities must be properly administered and controlled. Proper administration and control require some methods to identify the firm's level of performance. Specifically, the firm must be able to *measure, report,* and *improve* performance.

Measuring the Performance of Materials Management

In measuring the performance of materials management the firm should examine a number of elements, including supplier service levels, inventory, prices paid for materials, quality levels, and operating costs.[23]

Service levels can be measured using several methods, including:

Order-cycle time for each supplier.
Order fill rate for each supplier.
Percentage of orders from each supplier that are overdue.
Percentage of production orders not filled on time.
Number of stockouts resulting from late deliveries from suppliers.
Number of production delays caused by materials being out of stock.

Inventory is an important aspect of materials management and can be controlled using the following measures:

Amount of dead stock.
Comparison of actual inventory levels with targeted levels.
Comparison of inventory turnover rates with data from previous time periods.
Percentage of stockouts caused by improper purchasing decisions.
Number of production delays caused by improper purchasing decisions.

Materials *price level* measures include gains and losses resulting from forward buying, a comparison of prices paid for major items over several time periods, and a comparison of actual prices paid for materials with targeted prices.

---

[22] James M. Kenderdine and Paul D. Larson, "Quality and Logistics: A Framework for Strategic Integration," *International Journal of Physical Distribution and Materials Management* 18, no. 6 (1988), p. 9; also see S. J. Brill, "A Quality Approach to Logistics," *Proceedings of the Conference on the Total Logistics Concept,* Pretoria, Republic of South Africa, June 4–5, 1991, unnumbered.

[23] For an in-depth discussion of materials management control procedures, see Donald W. Dobler, Lamar Lee, Jr., and David N. Burt, *Purchasing and Materials Management,* 4th ed. (New York: McGraw-Hill, 1984), pp. 560–80; and A. T. Kearney, Inc., *Measuring and Improving Productivity in Physical Distribution* (Oak Brook, Ill.: National Council of Physical Distribution Management, 1984).

TABLE 11–4 Operating Reports that Should Be Developed by Purchasing and Materials Management Functions

1. Market and economic conditions and price performance.
   a. Price trends and changes for the major materials and commodities purchased. Comparisons with:
      (1) Standard costs where such accounting methods are used,
      (2) Quoted market prices, and/or
      (3) Target costs, as determined by cost analysis.
   b. Changes in demand-supply conditions for the major items purchased. Effects of labor strikes or threatened strikes.
   c. Lead time expectations for major items.
2. Inventory investment changes.
   a. Dollar investment in inventories, classified by major commodity and materials groups.
   b. Days' or months' supply, and on order, for major commodity and materials groups.
   c. Ratio of inventory dollar investment to sales dollar volume.
   d. Rates of inventory turnover for major items.
3. Purchasing operations and effectiveness.
   a. Cost reductions resulting from purchase research and value analysis studies.
   b. Quality rejection rates for major items.
   c. Percentage of on-time deliveries.
   d. Number of out-of-stock situations which caused interruption of scheduled productions.
   e. Number of change orders issued, classified by cause.
   f. Number of requisitions received and processed.
   g. Number of purchase orders issued.
   h. Employee work load and productivity.
   i. Transportation costs.
4. Operations affecting administration and financial activities.
   a. Comparison of actual departmental operating costs to budget.
   b. Cash discounts earned and cash discounts lost.
   c. Commitments to purchase, classified by types of formal contracts and by purchase orders, aged by expected delivery dates.
   d. Changes in cash discounts allowed by suppliers.

SOURCE: Michiel R. Leenders, Harold E. Fearon, and Wilbur B. England, *Purchasing and Materials Management,* 9th ed. (Homewood, Ill.: Richard D. Irwin, 1989), pp. 454–55.

In the area of *quality control,* measures that can be used are the number of product failures caused by materials defects, and the percentage of materials rejected from each shipment from each supplier.

As an overall measure of performance, management can *compare the actual budget* consumed by materials management *to the targeted budget* allocated at the beginning of the operating period.

Once the company has established performance measures for each component of the materials management process, data must be collected and results reported to those executives in decision-making positions. The major operating reports that should be developed by materials management include (1) market and economic conditions and price performance, (2) inventory investment changes, (3) purchasing operations and effectiveness, and (4) operations affecting administration and financial activities. Table 11–4 presents a summary of the reports needed.

Operating Reports Developed by Materials Management

Finally, after performance has been measured and reported, the firm must improve it whenever possible. In order to initiate improvements, the materials manager must address certain key questions. These relate to how the product is produced and how inventories are controlled. Some of the questions to be examined are the following:

Materials Managers Must Answer Many Important Questions

1. How much product is to be manufactured? What is forecasted demand? What is available capacity?
2. When are manufacturing plants to produce to meet demand? In what amount? At which facility?
3. When are raw materials to be ordered? In what quantities? From which source? With what provisions to remove shortages?
4. How large is preseason inventory buildup?
5. What are target inventory levels? Where should inventory be positioned? When should inventory be relocated?
6. How are customers allocated in periods of short supply?
7. How are backlogs managed?
8. What are information requirements? What record keeping and status reporting are needed? What cost data must be gathered?
9. When do plans and schedules get revised? What information is used? How far ahead are plans and schedules made?
10. Who sets management policy for product planning?
11. Who is responsible for planning—logistics, sales, production control?
12. Who is responsible for scheduling?[24]

Computers are also used to improve materials management performance. Systems that have gained acceptance in many firms are Kanban/Just-in-Time (JIT), MRP, and DRP.

Kanban/Just-in-Time Systems

Kanban Defined

Kanban and Just-in-Time systems have become much more important in manufacturing and logistics operations in recent years. Kanban, also known as the Toyota Production System (TPS), was developed by Toyota Motor Company during the 1950s and 1960s: "Kanban is basically the system of supplying parts and materials just at the very moment they are needed in the factory production process so those parts and materials are instantly put to use."[25] While the technique is most often associated with the automobile industry, it can apply to any manufacturing process involving repetitive operations.

An expansion of Kanban are Just-in-Time (JIT) systems. JIT links purchasing and procurement, manufacturing, and logistics. Its primary goals are to minimize inventories, improve product quality, maximize pro-

---

[24] Provided by Professor Jay U. Sterling, University of Alabama.

[25] Bruce D. Henderson, "The Logic of Kanban," *The Journal of Business Strategy* 6, no. 3 (Winter 1986), p. 6.

duction efficiency, and provide optimal customer service levels. It is basically a philosophy of doing business.

JIT Defined

JIT has been defined in several ways, including:

- A philosophy that centers on the elimination of waste in the manufacturing process.[26]
- A system that produces the required item at the time and in the quantities needed.[27]
- An inventory control philosophy whose goal is to maintain just enough material in just the right place at just the right time to make just the right amount of product.[28]
- A program which seeks to eliminate non-value-added activities from any operation with the objectives of producing high-quality products (i.e., "zero defects"), high productivity levels, lower levels of inventory, and developing long-term relationships with channel members.[29]

At the heart of the JIT system is the notion that anything over the minimum amount necessary for a task is considered wasteful: "Waste is considered anything other than the absolute minimum resources of material, machines, and manpower required to add value to the product."[30] This is in direct contrast to the traditional philosophy of "just-in-case," in which large inventories or safety stocks are held just-in-case they are needed. In JIT, the ideal lot size or EOQ is one unit, safety stock is considered unnecessary, and any inventory should be eliminated. Table 11–5 compares conventional and JIT approaches.

Toyota Develops Kanban

Perhaps the best known example of Kanban and JIT systems is the approach developed by Toyota. Through reduction of inventories, Toyota identified problems in supply and product quality, because problems were forced into the open. Safety stocks were no longer available to overcome supplier delays and faulty components, thus forcing Toyota to eliminate "hidden" production and supply problems. Figure 11–4 summarizes Toyota's Kanban system.

It is the same type of procedure that, in recent years, has been applied in many companies in the United States. The advantage of the system becomes evident when we see that "U.S. automakers carry $775 in work-in-process inventory for each car they build, while the Japanese carry only

---

[26] Roger Brooks, "MRPII: The Right Stuff for Just-in-Time," *Manufacturing Systems* 3, no. 1 (January 1985), p. 32.

[27] G. H. Manoochehri, "Suppliers and the Just-in-Time Concept," *Journal of Purchasing and Materials Management* 20, no. 4 (Winter 1984), pp. 16–21.

[28] Lee White, "JIT: What Is It and How Does It Affect DP?" *Computer World* 19, no. 24A (June 19, 1985), pp. 41–42.

[29] Larry C. Giunipero and Wai K. Law, "Organizational Support for Just-in-Time Implementation," *The International Journal of Logistics Management* 1, no. 2 (1990), pp. 35–36.

[30] Richard J. Tersine, *Production/Operations Management: Concepts, Structure, and Analysis*, 2nd ed. (New York: Elsevier Science Publishing, 1985), p. 571.

TABLE 11–5 A Comparison of Conventional and Just-in-Time Approaches

Conventional	*Just-in-Time*
Large lots are efficient (more is better)	Ideal lot size is one unit (less is better)
Faster production is more efficient	Faster production than necessary is a waste (balanced production is more efficient)
Scheduling and queues are necessary trade-offs to maximize output from equipment and personnel	Trade-offs are bad; they trade one waste for another and prevent the proper solution of problems
Inventory provides safety	Safety stock is a waste
Inventory smoothes production	Inventory is undesirable

SOURCE: Reprinted by permission of the publisher from Richard J. Tersine, *Production/Operations Management: Concepts, Structure and Analysis,* 2nd ed., p. 572. Copyright 1985 by Elsevier Science Publishing Co., Inc.

$150 per car."[31] Not every component can be handled by the Kanban or JIT approaches, but for items that are used repetitively and are not bulky or irregular in shape, the systems work very well.

Many firms have successfully adopted the JIT approach. Several large-scale studies have identified how companies in industries such as metal products, automotive and transportation, electronics, food, and beverage have implemented JIT. A study of North American manufacturers and distributors in 1988 by Touche Ross identified a number of changes and benefits that have resulted from JIT, including:

Changes and Benefits Resulting from JIT

- Ninety percent of all respondents found JIT to be strategically important to their company.
- Most firms had reduced the number of vendors and required lead times for inbound logistics.
- Two-thirds of the firms used outbound consolidation and were able to deliver daily to customers.
- Many firms had dramatically improved inventory turnover rates.
- Companies with fully operational JIT programs had reduced their average number of distribution centers and customer order lead times.[32]

In a study conducted by *Traffic Management* and Northeastern University (Boston), over 300 companies from throughout the United States reported that JIT had produced benefits for their firms in four major areas: improved inventory turns, better customer service, decreased warehouse space, and improved response time. Other benefits reported by respondents included reduced distribution costs, lower transportation costs, im-

[31] "Why Everybody Is Talking About 'Just-in-Time'," *Warehousing Review* 1, no. 1 (October 1984), p. 6.

[32] Touche Ross & Co., *Implementing Just-in-Time Logistics: Making the Right Moves to Gain Competitive Advantage* (Chicago: Touche Ross, 1988), p. 2.

FIGURE 11–4 Kanban Card Procedure

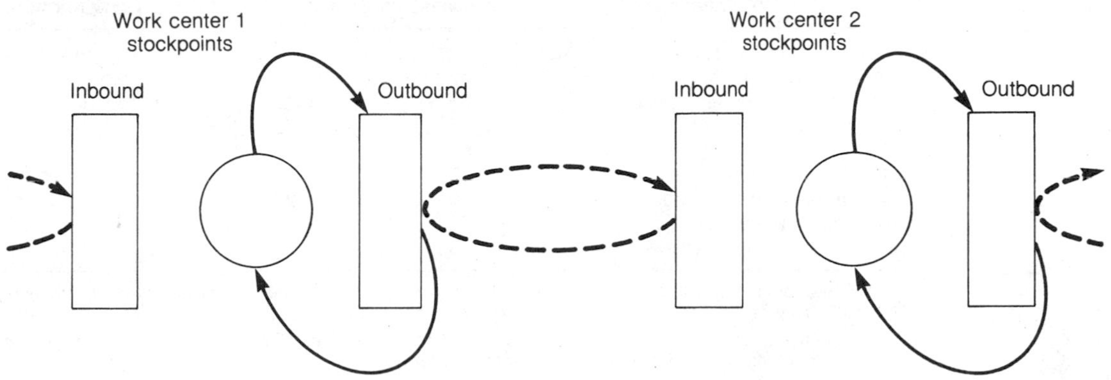

– – – Move card path. When a container of parts is selected for use from an inbound stockpoint, the move card is removed from the container and taken to the outbound stockpoint of the preceding work center as authorization to pick another container of parts.

——— Production card path. When a container of parts is picked from an outbound stockpoint, the production card is removed and left behind as authorization to make a standard container of parts to replace the one taken.

The Kanban Card System

"Kanban" literally means "signboard" in Japanese. The system involves the use of cards (called "kanbans") that are attached to containers which hold a standard quantity of a single part number. There are two types of kanban cards: "move" cards and "production" cards.

When a worker starts to use a container of parts the move card, which is attached to it, is removed and is either sent to or picked up by the preceding, or feeding work center (in many cases this is the supplier). This is the signal—or "sign"—for that work center to send another container of parts to replace the one now being used. This replacement container has a production card attached to it which is replaced by the "move" card before it is sent. The production card then authorizes the producing work center to make another container full of parts. These cards circulate respectively within or between work centers or between the supplier and the assembly plant.

In order for Kanban to work effectively, these rules must be observed:

1. There can only be one card attached to a container at any one time.
2. The using (or following) work center must initiate the movement of parts from the feeding (or preceding) work center.
3. No fabrication of parts is allowed without a kanban production card.
4. Never move or produce other than the amount indicated by the kanban card.
5. Kanban cards must be handled on a first-in, first-out (FIFO) basis.
6. Finished parts must be placed at the location point indicated on the kanban card.

Because each kanban card represents a standard number of parts being made or used within the production process, the amount of work-in-process inventory can easily be controlled by controlling the number of cards on the plant floor. Japanese managers, by simply removing a card or two, can test or strain the system and reveal bottlenecks. Then they have a problem they can address themselves to—an opportunity to improve productivity, the prime goal of Kanban.

SOURCE: "Why Everybody Is Talking About 'Just-In-Time'," *Warehousing Review* 1, no. 1 (October 1984), p. 27. Reprinted with permission from *Warehousing Review,* 1984 Charter Issue; The American Warehouse Association (publisher), 1165 N. Clark, Chicago, IL 60610.

TABLE 11–6 Attaining the JIT Objectives*

Objectives	*Achieved*	*Not Achieved*	*Don't Know Yet*
Improve inventory turns	72%	8%	20%
Improve customer service	77	7	16
Decrease warehouse space	66	17	17
Improve response time	77	9	14
Reduce distribution cost	52	16	32
Reduce transportation cost	57	12	31
Improve quality of vendor products	46	24	30
Reduce number of vendors	66	20	14
Reduce number of carriers	53	30	17

*Respondents cited these objectives (in order of importance) as the main reasons for implementing their JIT programs. Significantly, most of these goals have been achieved.

SOURCE: Francis J. Quinn, Robert C. Lieb, and Robert A. Millen, "Why U.S. Companies Are Embracing JIT," *Traffic Management* 29, no. 11 (November 1990), p. 34.

proved quality of vendor products, reduction in the number of transportation carriers, and a reduced number of vendors.[33]

Table 11–6 identifies many of the benefits of JIT. As evidenced by the table, not every firm was able to achieve all of the benefits of JIT to the same degree. In general, some firms realized greater success in achieving service-related benefits than others.

Rank Xerox Implements a JIT Program

Some specific examples of firms that have achieved success through JIT include Rank Xerox Manufacturing (Netherlands) and Ford Motor Company. As the largest Xerox company outside the United States, Rank Xerox (a joint venture between Xerox Corporation and Britain's Rank Corporation) produces and refurbishes midvolume copier equipment for distribution throughout the world. Between 1980 and 1988, Rank Xerox implemented a JIT program.

As part of the JIT program, the firm also installed an automated material handling system and information processing system. Production procedures were modified at the same time. As a result of the JIT program and other system changes, Rank Xerox realized the following benefits:

1. Its supplier base was reduced from 3,000 to 300.
2. Ninety-eight percent on-time inbound delivery was achieved, with 70 percent of materials arriving within an hour of the time they were needed.
3. Warehouse stock was reduced from a three-month to a one-half-month supply.
4. Overall material costs were reduced by more than 40 percent.

[33] Francis J. Quinn, Robert C. Lieb, and Robert A. Millen, "Why U.S. Companies Are Embracing JIT," *Traffic Management* 29, no. 11 (November 1990), p. 33.

5. Most inbound product inspection stations were eliminated because of higher quality materials from suppliers.
6. Reject levels for defective or inferior materials fell from 17 percent to 0.8 percent.
7. Positions for 40 repack people were eliminated because of standardized shipment-packaging criteria.
8. Inbound transportation costs were reduced by 40 percent.
9. On-time inbound delivery performance was improved by 28 percent.[34]

Ford Motor Co. Has Been Successful in Utilizing JIT

Ford Motor Company has also been successful in implementing JIT. At its body and assembly plant in Wixom, Michigan, Ford implemented JIT in its manufacturing and materials management activities.

> Up and running since June 1985, the Wixom operation represents phase one of a project that will put JIT programs in place at each of Ford's 17 parts and assembly plants. . . . At present, 485 suppliers are involved in the Wixom JIT operation, furnishing the plant with virtually every part necessary to assemble an automobile.
>
> Ford uses three regional motor carriers to support the . . . program. The trucking companies make daily pickups from the suppliers and deliver what amounts to a single day's supply of parts to the assembly plant. All told, 425 tons of cargo are received at Wixom each day in truckload lots.
>
> As is the case with virtually all JIT systems, there is little margin for error built into this program. Both pickups from the suppliers and deliveries to the plant must be made within certain time windows . . . [and] in-house stock has been reduced to the absolute minimum. . . . Only about an hour—two at most—passes from the time the freight arrives at the loading dock to the time it makes its way to the assembly line.
>
> For the most part, the carriers run the same route each day—from the suppliers to the plant and back again—in what's referred to as a dedicated closed-loop system. Ford believes that this setup best ensures consistent pickup and delivery.
>
> Importantly, the same drivers serve the assembly plant each and every day, thereby further ensuring service reliability. "[Ford has] received a lot of benefits from having the same driver on a particular route. That driver, in effect, has become part of [the] assembly operation."
>
> Of course, all of this wouldn't have been possible without cooperation from Ford's suppliers as well as the designated carriers. . . . Suppliers had to change their shipping procedures and become more quality conscious. And the truckers, for their part, had to interact more with suppliers than ever before. To help smooth the transition to JIT for trucker and supplier alike, Ford conducted a six-month training program with its vendors, visiting each of them for sessions that lasted between two and four hours.

[34] Lisa H. Harrington, "Why Rank Xerox Turned to Just-in-Time," *Traffic Management* 27, no. 10 (October 1988), pp. 82–87.

> To date, Ford has realized numerous benefits from the Wixom JIT program. To cite one prominent example, the company has saved more than $8 million in inventory-carrying costs. These inventory reductions, in turn, have allowed Ford to free up more space for manufacturing.[35]

Other companies that have successfully introduced JIT into their operations include Whirlpool, Textron, 3M, Brunswick, General Motors, and Cummins Engine. While the benefits arising from JIT are many, the approach may not be right for all firms, and the system has some inherent problems. These problems fall into three categories: production scheduling (plant), supplier production schedules, and supplier locations.

Problems Associated with Utilizing JIT

When leveling of the production schedule is necessary due to uneven demand, firms will require higher levels of inventory. Items can be produced during slack periods even though they may not be demanded until a later time. "The consequence will be a larger inventory of the end product because that product is not being assembled 'just-in-time' to satisfy customer demands."[36] Also, finished goods inventory has a higher value because of its form utility, and thus there is a greater financial risk resulting from product obsolescence, damage, and loss. However, higher levels of inventory, coupled with a uniform production schedule, can be more advantageous than a fluctuating schedule with less inventory. In addition, when stockout costs are great because of production slowdowns or shutdowns, JIT may not be the optimal system. JIT reduces inventory levels to the point where there is little if any safety stock, and parts shortages can adversely affect production operations.

A second problem or concern with JIT relates to supplier production schedules. Success of a JIT system depends on suppliers' ability to provide parts in accordance with the firm's production schedule. Smaller, more frequent orders can result in higher ordering costs and must be taken into account when calculating any cost savings due to reduced inventory levels. Suppliers incur higher production and setup costs due to the large number of small lot quantities produced. Generally, the result can be an increase in the cost of procuring items from suppliers, unless suppliers are able to perceive the benefits they can receive from being part of a JIT system.

Hewlett-Packard Overcomes Supplier Resistance to JIT

Hewlett-Packard's Computer Systems Division made the transition to JIT and was able to overcome supplier resistance to daily delivery of small quantities of materials. Hewlett-Packard's experience in implementing JIT with its suppliers is summarized as follows:

> Asking suppliers to make daily deliveries is a common mistake of managers who focus on the inventory-reduction benefits of JIT. Ultimately, this is the right thing to do, but it's the wrong place to start. JIT should be adopted and

---

[35] Francis J. Quinn, James J. Callari, James Aaron Cooke, and Lisa H. Harrington, "Ford Motor Company: Dedicated to Just-in-Time," *Traffic Management* 27, no. 9 (September 1988), pp. 55–56.

[36] Raymond R. Mayer, "A Critical Look at Kanban, Japan's Just-in-Time Inventory System," *Management Review* 73, no. 12 (December 1984), p. 49.

practiced inside the factory, where the company can control any problems, rather than outside, where close cooperation with another organization is necessary. Once a company begins to master JIT, it should then begin to work with suppliers to help them understand the benefits it holds for both parties.[37]

Supplier locations can be a third problem area. As distance between the firm and its suppliers increases, delivery times may become more erratic and less predictable. Shipping costs also increase as LTL movements are made. Transit time variability can cause inventory stockouts that disrupt production scheduling. When this factor is combined with higher delivery costs on a per-unit basis, total costs may be greater than savings in inventory carrying costs.

Other problem areas that can become obstacles to JIT, especially in implementation, are organizational resistance, lack of systems support, inability to define service levels, a lack of planning and inventory being shifted to suppliers.[38] Overcoming these and the previously discussed problems or obstacles requires cooperation and integration within and between companies.

JIT can be a useful and very effective method for managing a variety of functions, including production, purchasing, inventory control, warehousing, and transportation. "While JIT . . . systems should not be viewed as a panacea which will cure all the ills of . . . industry, they do offer potential benefits to those firms whose environments are suited to them."[39]

Implications of JIT for Logistics Integration

JIT has numerous implications for logistics executives. First, proper implementation of JIT requires that the firm fully integrate all logistics activities. Many trade-offs are required, but without the coordination that integrated logistics management provides, JIT systems cannot be fully implemented.

Transportation in a JIT System

Second, transportation becomes an even more vital component of logistics under a JIT system. In such an environment, the demands placed on the firm's transportation network are significant and include a need for shorter, more consistent transit times, more sophisticated communications; the use of fewer carriers with long-term relationships, a need for efficiently designed transportation and material handling equipment, and better decision-making strategies relative to when private, common, and/or contract carriage should be used.

Warehousing in a JIT System

Third, warehousing assumes an expanded role in a JIT system. A warehouse becomes more of a consolidation facility, rather than a storage facility. Since many products come into the manufacturing operation at shorter intervals, less space is required for storage, but there must be an

---

[37] Richard C. Walleigh, "What's Your Excuse for Not Using JIT?" *Harvard Business Review* 64, no. 2 (March-April 1986), p. 38.

[38] See Francis J. Quinn, James J. Callari, James Aaron Cooke, and Lisa H. Harrington, "JIT . . . Not Just a Buzzword Anymore," *Traffic Management* 27, no. 9 (September 1988), pp. 42–45.

[39] George C. Jackson, "Just-in-Time Production: Implications for Logistics Managers," *Journal of Business Logistics* 4, no. 2 (1983), p. 17.

increased capability for handling and consolidation of items. Different forms of material handling equipment may be needed to facilitate the movement of many products in smaller quantities. The location decision for warehouses serving inbound material needs may also change because suppliers are often located closer to the manufacturing facility in a JIT system.

Recently, JIT systems have also been combined with systems that plan and control material flows into, within, and out of manufacturing. These systems are typically referred to as MRP and DRP systems. They will be discussed in the following sections. Simply, "DRP manages finished product inventory in distribution; MRP manages material and in-process inventory for production. Together DRP and MRP provide precise control over material flow through the logistics system, from supplier to customer."[40]

MRP Systems

MRP has been used to signify systems called materials requirements planning (MRPI) and manufacturing resource planning (MRPII). MRPI was developed first and evolved into MRPII with the addition of financial, marketing, and purchasing aspects.

Materials requirements planning (MRPI) became a popular concept in the 1960s and 1970s. As Norman Daniel stated: "The essence of MRP[I] is that one works backward from the demand (the customer) to determine materials and other requirements."[41] From a managerial perspective, MRPI consists of (1) a computer system, (2) a manufacturing information system, and (3) a concept and philosophy of management.[42]

Managerial Components of MRPI

MRPI utilizes an array of computer hardware and software. As an information system it focuses on inventory, production scheduling, and the administration of all manufacturing resources—people, dollars, equipment, and materials. As a management philosophy MRPI is viewed as a means to an end.

MRPI Defined

Defined, MRPI is a computer-based production and inventory control system that attempts to minimize inventories yet maintain adequate materials for the production process. Specifically, MRPI attempts to:

1. Ensure the availability of materials, components, and products for planned production and for customer delivery.
2. Maintain the lowest possible level of inventory.
3. Plan manufacturing activities, delivery schedules, and purchasing activities.[43]

---

[40] Philip B. Schary, *Logistics Decisions: Text and Cases* (Chicago: Dryden Press, 1984), p. 193.

[41] Norman E. Daniel, "Distribution Requirements Planning: Problems and Promises," in *Logistics: Contribution and Control,* ed. Patrick Gallagher, *Proceedings of the 1983 Logistics Resource Forum* (Cleveland: Leaseway Transportation Corp., 1983), p. 213.

[42] John C. Anderson and Roger G. Schroeder, "Getting Results from Your MRP System," *Business Horizons* 27, no. 3 (May/June 1984), p. 59.

[43] Tersine, *Production/Operations Management,* p. 498.

The MRPI system differs from traditional inventory control systems in one fundamental way: "In a[n] MRP[I] operation, the master production schedule (as updated each week) is the force that directly initiates and drives subsequent activities of the purchasing and manufacturing functions."[44] MRPI systems are usually employed when one or more of the following conditions exist:

When Are Conditions Right for MRPI?

When usage (demand) of the material is discontinuous or highly unstable during a firm's normal operating cycle. This situation is typified by an intermittent manufacturing or job shop operation, as opposed to a continuous processing or mass-production operation.

When demand for the material is directly dependent on the production of other specific inventory items or finished products. MRP[I] can be thought of as primarily a component fabrication planning system, in which the demand for all parts (materials) is dependent on the demand (production schedule) for the parent product.

When the purchasing department and its suppliers, as well as the firm's own manufacturing units, possess the flexibility to handle order placements or delivery releases on a weekly basis.[45]

Advantages of MRPI

MRPI systems offer many advantages over traditional systems, including improved business results (return on investment, profits), improved manufacturing performance results, better manufacturing control, more accurate and timely information,[46] less inventory, time-phased ordering of materials, less material obsolescence, higher reliability, more responsiveness to market demand, and reduced production costs.

Disadvantages of MRPI

MRPI does have a number of drawbacks, and a firm considering adopting the system should examine them. First, MRPI does not tend to optimize materials acquisition costs. Because inventory levels are kept to a minimum, materials must be purchased more frequently and in smaller quantities. This results in increased ordering costs. Higher transportation bills and higher unit costs are also incurred because the firm is less likely to qualify for large volume discounts. The company must weigh the anticipated savings from reduced inventory costs against the greater acquisition costs resulting from smaller and more frequent orders. Another disadvantage of MRPI is the potential hazard of production slowdown or shutdown that may arise because of such factors as unforeseen delivery problems and materials shortages.

The availability of safety stocks gives production some protection against stockouts of essential material. As safety stocks are reduced, this level of protection is lost. A final disadvantage of MRPI arises from the use of computer software packages: "Because standardized computer programs are used, modifications to accommodate unique operating situations

[44] Dobler et al., *Purchasing and Materials Management,* p. 247.

[45] Ibid.

[46] Anderson and Schroeder, "Getting Results from Your MRP System," p. 60.

in a given firm become major factors that must be considered thoroughly and built into the system at the time it is designed. . . . Once the system is established, basic program changes cannot be made easily."[47]

Inputs to an MRPI System

Figure 11–5 portrays the MRPI system and its outputs. The master production schedule serves as the major input into the MRPI system. Other inputs include the bill of materials file and the inventory records file. The bill of materials file contains the component parts of the finished product, identified by part number. The inventory records file maintains a record of all inventory on hand and on order. It also keeps track of due dates for all component parts as well as finished goods.

Outputs of an MRPI System

Reports generated from MRPI systems include planning reports that can be used to forecast inventory and specify future requirements, performance reports for identifying and determining if actual and programmed item lead times and actual and programmed quantity usages and costs agree, and exception reports, which point out discrepancies, such as errors, late or overdue orders, excessive scrap, or nonexistent parts.[48]

Black & Decker Successfully Employs MRPI

For many companies, MRPI can be very beneficial. Black & Decker reported lead time reductions of 20 percent, 21 percent less work-in-process inventory, and a 35 percent increase in the number of jobs completed on schedule.[49] While such figures are impressive, they are more so in view of the fact that the firm increased production volume by over 10 percent per year during the same period. Other companies that have successively employed MRPI include Abbott Laboratories (Canada), Corning Glass Works, and The Stanley Works.

While MRPI is still being used by many firms, it has been updated and expanded to include financial, marketing, and logistics elements. This newer version is called manufacturing resource planning, or MRPII.

Description of an MRPII System

MRPII affects almost every major corporate function, including engineering, finance, manufacturing, logistics, and marketing. It is a set of computer modules or packages that "allows a firm to evaluate manufacturing action plans from a resource (labor, plant capacity) point of view, manage and control these plans, and review their financial implications."[50]

Manufacturing resource planning (MRPII) includes the entire set of activities involved in the planning and control of production operations. It consists of a variety of functions or modules (see Figure 11–5) and includes production planning, resource requirements planning, master production scheduling, material requirements planning (MRPI), shop floor control, and purchasing.[51]

---

[47] Dobler et al., *Purchasing and Materials Management,* p. 272.

[48] See Leenders et al., *Purchasing and Materials Management,* pp. 195–97.

[49] Ashok Rao, "Perspectives on Selecting Material Requirements Planning Features," in *Material Requirements Planning* (Pennsauken, N.J.: Auerbach Publishers, 1982), p. 3.3.1.

[50] Allan F. Ayers, "How MRP Can Add 15% to Your Bottom Line," *Canadian Transportation & Distribution Management* 86, no. 11 (November 1983), pp. 45–50.

[51] John F. Magee, William C. Copacino, and Donald B. Rosenfield, *Modern Logistics Management: Integrating Marketing, Manufacturing, and Physical Distribution* (New York: John Wiley & Sons, 1985), p. 150.

FIGURE 11–5 Elements of an MRPI System

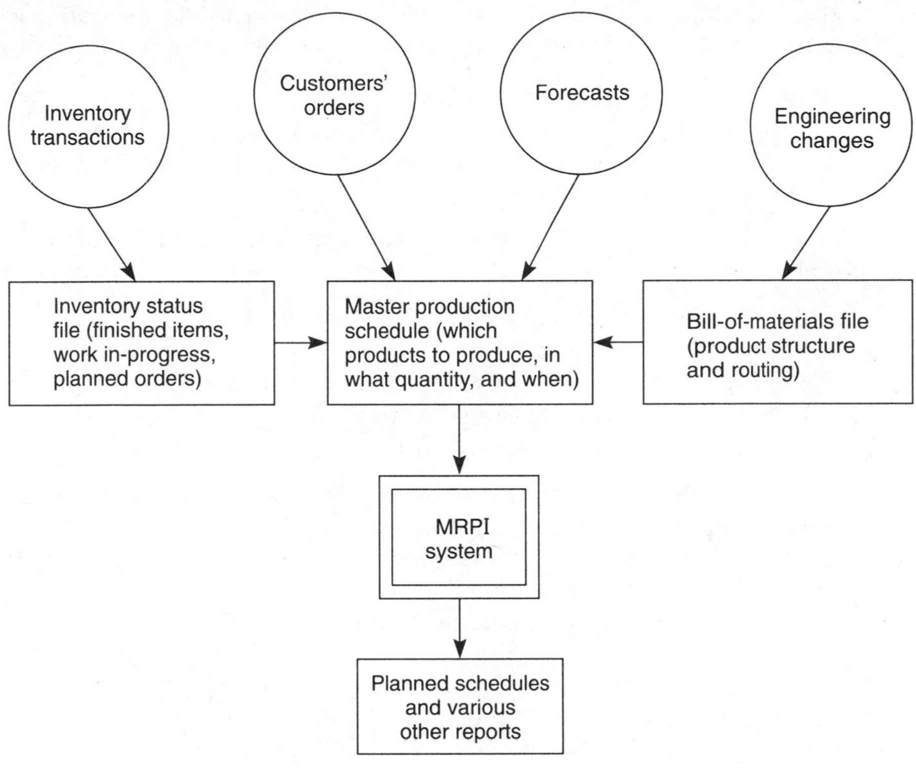

SOURCE: MCB University Press Limited, Amrik Sohal and Keith Howard, "Trends in Materials Management," *International Journal of Physical Distribution and Materials Management* 17, no. 5 (1987), p. 11.

Four Categories of MRPII Users

Users of MRPII can be classified into four categories based on the firm's level of sophistication. The categories were developed by Oliver Wight, one of the pioneers of MRPII systems. His classification scheme is widely accepted today and consists of the following four groups:

Class A:

Closed loop system, used for priority planning and capacity planning. The master production schedule is leveled and used by top management to run the business. Most deliveries are on time, inventory is under control, and little or no expediting is done.

Class B:

Closed loop system with capability for both priority planning and capacity planning. In this case, the master production schedule is somewhat inflated, top management does not give full support, some inventory reductions have been obtained, but capacity is sometimes exceeded, and some expediting is required.

Class C:

Order-launching system with priority planning only. Capacity planning is done informally with a probable inflated master production schedule. Expediting is used to control the flow of work; and modest reduction in inventory is achieved.

Class D:

The MRP[II] system exists mainly in data processing. Many records are inaccurate. The informal system is largely used to run the company. Little benefit is obtained from the MRP[II] system.[52]

Benefits of MRPII

Class A firms can expect to realize the maximum benefits of MRPII, which include:

1. Inventory reductions of one-fourth to one-third.
2. Higher inventory turnover ratio.
3. Improved consistency in on-time customer delivery.
4. Reduction in purchasing costs due to less expedited shipments.
5. Minimization of work force overtime.[53]

These benefits typically result in savings to a firm beyond the initial costs of implementing MRPII. Costs can easily exceed $750,000 during the first year of setup, although smaller companies may spend as little as $250,000. Therefore, the benefits must be tangible and sizable.

MRPII at Coppus Engineering

For example, Coppus Engineering Company, a manufacturer of turbines, blowers, and burners for the petrochemical industry, spent over $1 million for its MRPII system. A breakdown of the total cost showed that Coppus spent $280,000 for software; $280,000 on a computer; $180,000 for management and worker time; $125,000 on employee training; $110,000 for a data base; and $75,000 for vendor support.[54] The total cost was substantial; the firm's annual sales were approximately $25 million at the time the MRPII system was brought on-line. The company was able to achieve payback in only two and a half years, however, due to cost savings resulting from the following:

- Inventory accuracy surpassed 90 percent.
- On-time deliveries went from 30–40 percent to 80 percent.
- Lead time on turbine shipping was cut from 16 weeks to 10–12 weeks.
- Over $2 million was cut from raw materials inventory.
- Queues at machining stations were cut by 35 to 40 percent.
- Overtime labor was cut by over 50 percent.[55]

---

[52] Anderson and Schroeder, "Getting Results from Your MRP System," p. 60. Copyright 1984 by the Foundation for the School of Business at Indiana University. Reprinted by permission.

[53] "MRPII: A Framework for Factory Management," *Dun's Business Month Special Report* 123, no. 2 (February 1984), p. L.

[54] "MRPII Pays Off in Dollars and Sense," *Modern Materials Handling* 39, no. 10 (July 6, 1984), p. 60.

[55] Ibid.

Many Firms Report Cost Savings from MRPII Systems

Other firms have achieved equally impressive results. Warren Communications, a division of General Signal Corporation, markets power supplies used in telephone systems. The company installed an MRPII system and estimated first-year savings of $850,000, with the majority of savings coming from reductions in inventory and more efficient use of personnel and equipment.[56] Corning Glass Works achieved savings and improvements in excess of $1 million annually,[57] and companies such as Litton and SKF Industries (Roller Bearings Division) reported similar results.[58]

DRP Systems

DRPI and DRPII Defined

Distribution requirements planning (DRPI) has been defined as "a system of determining demands for inventory at distribution centers, consolidating the demand information backwards, and acting as input to the production and materials system."[59]

> Distribution resource planning (DRPII) is an extension of distribution requirements planning (DRPI). Distribution requirements planning applies the time-phased DRPI logic to replenish inventories in multiechelon warehousing systems. Distribution resource planning extends DRPI to include the planning of key resources in a distribution system—warehouse space, manpower levels, transport capacity (trucks, railcars, etc.), and financial flows.[60]

In DRPII, "Distribution needs drive the master schedule, which in turn drives the bill of materials, which controls materials requirements planning."[61] In essence, DRPI and DRPII are outgrowths of MRPI and MRPII, applied to the logistics activities of a firm. Figure 11–6 depicts the DRPII system schematically.

Although not shown in the figure, accurate forecasts are essential ingredients to successful DRPII systems. "A DRP[II] system translates the forecast of demand for each SKU [stock-keeping unit] at each warehouse and distribution center into a time-phased replenishment plan. If the SKU forecasts are not accurate, then the plan will not be accurate."[62] Because of the importance of forecasting to JIT, MRP, and DRP systems, this topic will be examined in detail in Chapter 14, "Decision Support Systems."

---

[56] "MRPII: A Framework for Factory Management," p. U.

[57] Ibid., p. O.

[58] See Nolan W. Rhea, "MRPII Integrated with AS/RS," *Material Handling Engineering* 40, no. 2 (February 1985), pp. 50–52; and "Total Commitment Makes MRPII Work," *Modern Materials Handling* 40, no. 5 (April 1985), pp. 63–65.

[59] Joseph L. Cavinato, *Transportation–Logistics Dictionary,* 3rd ed. (Washington, D.C.: International Thomson Transport Press, 1989), p. 72.

[60] Magee et al., *Modern Logistics Management,* p. 150.

[61] Perry A. Trunick, "Can Resource Planning Really Help You? Part II," *Handling & Shipping Management* 24, no. 6 (June 1983), p. 78.

[62] Mary Lou Fox, "Closing the Loop with DRPII," *Production and Inventory Management Review* 7, no. 5 (May 1987), p. 39–41.

FIGURE 11–6 Distribution Resource Planning (DRPII)

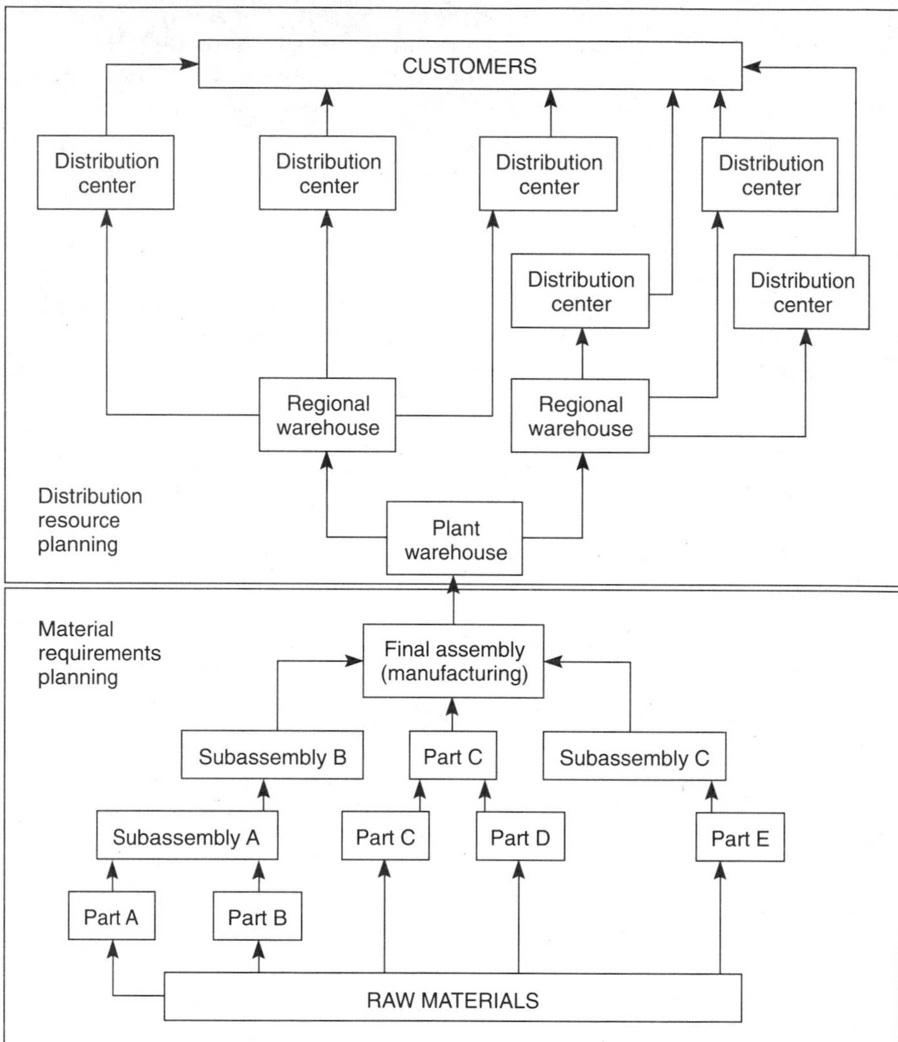

SOURCE: "How DRP Helps Warehouses Smooth Distribution," *Modern Materials Handling* 39, no. 6 (April 9, 1984), p. 53. *Modern Materials Handling,* copyright 1984 by Cahners Publishing Company, Division of Reed Holdings, Inc.

An example of how DRPII works in a hypothetical company is shown in Figure 11–7. The logic would be much the same for real firms.

There are many potential benefits associated with the use of a DRPII system, especially in the marketing and logistics areas.

FIGURE 11–7 How DRPII Forecasts Demand—A Case History

BOSTON DISTRIBUTION CENTER

On hand balance: 352 Lead Time: 2 weeks
Safety stock: 55 Order quantity: 500

	Past Due	Week 1	2	3	4	5	6	7	8
Gross requirements		50	50	60	70	80	70	60	50
Scheduled receipts						500			
Projected on hand	352	302	252	192	122	542	472	412	362
Planned orders				500					

SAN DIEGO DISTRIBUTION CENTER

On hand balance: 140 Lead Time: 2 weeks
Safety time: 2 weeks Order quantity: 150

	Past Due	Week 1	2	3	4	5	6	7	8
Gross requirements		20	25	15	20	30	25	15	30
Scheduled receipts						150			
Projected on hand	140	120	95	80	60	180	155	145	110
Planned orders				150					

CHICAGO DISTRIBUTION CENTER

On hand balance: 220 Lead Time: 2 weeks
Safety stock: 115 Order quantity: 800

	Past Due	Week 1	2	3	4	5	6	7	8
Gross requirements		115	115	120	120	125	125	125	120
Scheduled receipts		800							
Projected on hand	220	905	790	670	550	425	300	175	855
Planned orders							800		

CENTRAL SUPPLY FACILITY

On hand balance: 1250
Safety stock: 287
Lead Time: 3 weeks
Order quantity: 2200

	Past Due	Week 1	2	3	4	5	6	7	8
Gross requirements	0	0	0	650	0	0	800	0	0
Scheduled receipts									
Projected on hand	1250	1250	1250	600	600	600	2000	2000	2000
Master sched-rcpt							2200		
Master sched-start				2200					

→ to Material Requirements Planning Schedule →

MMH, Inc. has three distribution centers (DCs) located across the United States, and a central supply facility at its manufacturing plant in Quebec, Canada. Here's how their distribution resource planning (DRP[II]) system works over an eight-week period:

The Boston DC has a safety stock level set at 55 units of widgets. When stock goes below that level, the DC sends out an order for 500 more widgets. The lead time for shipment from the central facility to the Boston DC is two weeks.

The DRP display for the Boston DC shows the demand forecast, called *gross requirements,* for eight weeks. Starting with an on-hand balance of 352 widgets, the DC forecasts that it will have only 42 widgets during week five (the 122 widgets on hand minus the 80 in gross requirements).

This is below the safety stock level, so DRP initiates a planned order of 500 widgets during week three (week five minus the lead time). Stock comes, as forecasted, and the DC is back to safe operating levels.

Widgets are a high-volume seller in Chicago, so the Chicago DC has a higher gross requirement than the Boston DC. It also orders more widgets at a time.

The DRP display for the Chicago DC shows that 800 widgets are already in transit (scheduled receipts) and due to arrive in week one. They do, and the next order, for 800 widgets, is placed in week six to satisfy the upcoming below-safety stock condition in week eight.

Through experience, the San Diego DC expresses their safety stock as safety time (two weeks).

Examining the DRP display, the DC realizes that without replenishment, 30 widgets (60 minus 30) would be remaining in week five, five widgets (30 minus 25) in week six, and a negative on-hand balance of ten (5 minus 15) in week seven. So, the DC initiates a planned order for 150 widgets in week three—week seven minus the safety time minus the lead time (four weeks total).

The DRP display for the central supply facility is similar to that for the DCs; however, it displays recommendations for the master schedule in terms of the start and receipt of manufacturing orders.

The gross requirements in the facility are caused by the DCs; the Boston and San Diego DCs produced demands for a total of 650 widgets in week three, while Chicago DC produced demands for 800 widgets in week six. The facility finds it will have a negative on-hand balance in week six. Therefore it initiates a master schedule order in week three of 2,200 widgets to cover the shortage.

SOURCE: "How DRP Helps Warehouses Smooth Distribution," *Modern Materials Handling* 39, no. 6 (April 9, 1984), p. 57. *Modern Materials Handling,* copyright 1984 by Cahners Publishing Company, Division of Reed Holdings, Inc.

Marketing Benefits of DRPII Systems

Marketing benefits include:

1. Improved service levels resulting in on-time customer deliveries and fewer customer complaints. This is because one can plan what is needed and then execute this plan. Customer promises are met, and not missed.
2. The ability to plan promotions and new introductions effectively. This includes tying advertising into the planning process.
3. The ability to see in advance when a product will not be available, so that it is not being marketed aggressively when the supply is short. In most cases, using DRP means that companies can get the products they need. But even in situations where this is not possible, at least marketing people are aware of the situation in advance and can take some other action.
4. Better working relationships with the other functions of the company. This is because everyone is working with the same set of numbers, and because the causes of problems are more visible than before. With DRP, people can see why something went wrong, and they can do something about correcting it. Without such a tool, the situation is often so confused that it is never really obvious what went wrong and why.
5. The ability to offer not only a product to a customer, but also a service in helping him manage his own inventory. A firm can do this by extending its DRP system into the customer's inventories.

Logistics Benefits of DRPII Systems

Logistics benefits include:

1. Reduced freight costs to the distribution centers, due to fewer rush or premium freight shipments and better planning for loading trucks and rail cars.
2. Lower inventories. DRP can accurately tell *what* is needed and *when,* and keep this information up to date as changes occur.
3. Reduced warehouse space due to lower inventories, as mentioned above.
4. Better obsolescence control. DRP can monitor when the stock for each item in each distribution center will run out, and warn the planner of any obsolescence problems while there is still time to do something about it.
5. Reduced distribution cost from the DCs to the customers due to fewer back orders. DRP can have the right products in stock when they are needed, so they can all be shipped at the same time.
6. Better coordination and a more beneficial working relationship between distribution and manufacturing. With DRP, the people in manufacturing can truly see the needs of the distribution network, and they are kept up to date as things change. This nearly provides total communication of the distribution needs to manufacturing. In addition, the same system is used for both manufacturing and distribution. People understand one another and can work together better because they use the same system.
7. Better tools for budgeting. DRP is a very accurate simulation of distribution operation and, as such, it can be used to develop budgets.[63]

---

[63] *Distribution Resource Planning—Distribution Management's Most Powerful Tool,* by Andre J. Martin with Darryl V. Landvater, Foreword by Oliver W. Wight (Essex Junction, Vt.: 1983, Oliver Wight Limited Publications, Inc., 5 Oliver Wight Drive, Essex Junction, VT 05452), pp. 4–6.

THE LOGISTICS/MANUFACTURING INTERFACE

Systems such as Kanban, JIT, MRP, and DRP require that the logistics and manufacturing activities of a firm work together closely. Without such cooperative effort, the full advantages of systems like JIT can never be realized. Conflicts, both real and perceived, must be minimized. This requires joint logistics/manufacturing planning and decision-making. There are a number of areas in which cooperation is necessary and great improvements can be made. The following actions can be of significant benefit:

Joint Logistics/Manufacturing Planning and Decision Making Is Vital

- Logistics must support manufacturing's efforts to increase investment in equipment and computerized hardware/software that will increase manufacturing flexibility and reduce replenishment lead times.
- Manufacturing and logistics must work together in the production scheduling area to reduce production planning cycle time. Logistics can provide input into production scheduling and system requirements.
- Elimination of strictly manufacturing or production orientations. Strategies include shortening of lead times, setup times, and production run sizes, so as to minimize average inventory levels and stockouts.
- Develop strategies to reduce vendor/supplier lead times for parts and supplies.
- Adopt the philosophy that slow movers (i.e., products with low inventory turnover ratios) should be produced only after orders are received. Do not have inventories of those items available.

Many other areas of logistics/manufacturing interface exist. It is important that each functional area of the firm examine its role in the JIT, MRP, or DRP system and identify how it can work individually and jointly to optimize the firm's strategic position.

SUMMARY

This chapter examined the broad areas of materials flow. We discussed the functions of purchasing and procurement, production control, inbound logistics, warehousing and storage, data and information systems, inventory planning and control, and materials disposal. The relationships between materials management and total quality management (TQM) were identified. The TQM process was discussed and some examples of its implementation were presented.

The administration and control of materials flow requires that the firm measure, report, and improve performance. Concepts and approaches being used and/or developed include Kanban/Just-in-Time, MRP, and DRP systems. Each system has been implemented by a variety of firms, with significant results. Advantages in computer technology have enabled many of the systems to be implemented successfully in manufacturing, retailing, and service firms. The impact on logistics has been substantial.

In the next chapter we will examine one of the most significant areas within materials management—purchasing.

SUGGESTED READINGS

COLE, ROBERT E. "Target Information for Competitive Performance." *Harvard Business Review* 63, no. 3 (May-June 1985), pp. 100–109.

DAUGHERTY, PATRICIA J., AND MICHAEL S. SPENCER. "Just-in-Time Concepts: Applicability to Logistics/Transportation." *International Journal of Physical Distribution and Logistics Management* 20, no. 7 (1990), pp. 12–18.

GARREAU, ALAIN, ROBERT LIEB, AND ROBERT MILLEN. "JIT and Corporate Transport: An International Comparison." *International Journal of Physical Distribution and Logistics Management* 21, no. 1 (1991), pp. 42–47.

GOMES, ROGER, AND JOHN T. MENTZER. "A Systems Approach to the Investigation of Just-in-Time." *Journal of Business Logistics* 9, no. 2 (1988), pp. 71–88.

HENN, CARL L. "Logistics for a Better World." *Logistics Spectrum* 25, no. 3 (Fall 1991), pp. 3–9.

KARMARKAR, UDAY. "Getting Control of Just-in-Time." *Harvard Business Review* 67, no. 5 (September-October 1989), pp. 122–31.

LAM, KAREN D. "The Future of Total Quality Management (TQM)." *Logistics Spectrum* 24, no. 4 (Winter 1990), pp. 45–48.

MILLER, JEFFREY G., AND PETER GILMOUR. "Materials Managers: Who Needs Them?" *Harvard Business Review* 57, no. 4 (July-August 1979), pp. 143–53.

"MRPII and JIT Combat Waste in Manufacturing." *Modern Materials Handling* 40, no. 7 (June 1985), pp. 70–73.

NIEBUHR, ROBERT E., AND FRED P. ADAMS. "Evaluating and Developing Materials Management Personnel." *International Journal of Physical Distribution and Materials Management* 19, no. 9 (1989), pp. 31–35.

NOVACK, ROBERT A. "Quality and Control in Logistics: A Process Model." *International Journal of Physical Distribution and Materials Management* 19, no. 11 (1989), pp. 1–44.

OLIVER, NICK. "JIT: Issues and Items for the Research Agenda." *International Journal of Physical Distribution and Logistics Management* 20, no. 7 (1990), pp. 3–11.

SWENSETH, SCOTT R., AND FRANK P. BUFFA. "Just-in-Time: Some Effects on the Logistics Function." *The International Journal of Logistics Management* 1, no. 2 (1990), pp. 25–34.

VON FLUE, JOHANN L. "The Future with Total Quality Management." *Logistics Spectrum* 24, no. 1 (Spring 1990), pp. 23–27.

WIGHT, OLIVER W. *MRPII: Unlocking America's Productivity Potential.* Boston: CBI Publishing, 1981.

YAO-JUN, SUN, AND LI KENING. "Materials Distribution and its Reform in China." *Asia Pacific International Journal of Business Logistics* 1, no. 2 (1988), pp. 8–11.

ZIPKIN, PAUL H. "Does Manufacturing Need a JIT Revolution?" *Harvard Business Review* 91, no. 1 (January-February 1991), pp. 40–50.

QUESTIONS AND PROBLEMS

1. Identify how total quality management (TQM) differs from traditional management, and indicate how TQM can be applied to logistics.
2. Briefly describe the concept of Just-in-Time (JIT) and its relationship to logistics.
3. Discuss the role of vendors and suppliers in a JIT system. Identify areas where potential conflicts may occur.
4. MRP and DRP are relatively recent systems innovations in materials management and manufacturing. Describe the types of situations where MRP and DRP can be used in a firm.
5. There are many potential benefits of distribution requirements planning (DRPI) and distribution resource planning (DRPII). Briefly identify the marketing and logistics benefits that result from utilizing DRP.

Chapter 12

Purchasing

Objectives of This Chapter

To show how better management of purchasing activities can lead to increased profitability

To introduce the activities that must be performed by the purchasing function

To describe the impact of Just-in-Time production on purchasing

To show how purchasing costs can be managed

To show how to measure and evaluate purchasing performance

INTRODUCTION

In the United States, purchasing agents for manufacturing firms buy more than $1.3 trillion worth of goods each year.[1] In addition, state and federal purchases are approximately $1 trillion.[2] How well this money is spent is a question that is of considerable concern to both purchasing agents and top management. When one reflects on the fact that purchases consistently represent the largest single expense of doing business, it becomes evident that there is a pressing need for reliable measures of purchasing efficiency. Table 12–1 presents purchasing data for the entire U.S. manufacturing sector and shows that purchased materials account for 56 percent of the sales dollar on average and range from 34 percent to 90 percent. When expenditures for capital equipment are included, the average percentage increases to 60. "As firms respond to the mandate to become more efficient if they are to compete effectively with foreign manufacturers, it seems likely that additional labor costs will be designed out of the processes used; thus the material/sales ratio will further increase. Any function of the firm which accounts for well over half of its receipts certainly deserves a great deal of managerial attention."[3] In this chapter we will examine the challenges of purchasing and see how firms are dealing with this important concern.

PURCHASING ACTIVITIES

The terms *purchasing* and *procurement* are often used interchangeably, although they do differ in scope. Purchasing generally refers to the actual buying of materials and those activities associated with the buying process.

---

[1] U.S. Bureau of the Census, *1985 Annual Survey of Manufacturers* (Washington, D.C.: U.S. Government Printing Office, Statistics for Industry Groups and Industries, M85(AS)–1), pp. 1–8, 1–9, and Appendix; as reported in Michiel R. Leenders, Harold E. Fearon, and Wilbur B. England, *Purchasing and Materials Management,* 9th ed. (Homewood, Ill.: Richard D. Irwin, 1989), pp. 6–7.

[2] Leenders, Fearon, and England, *Purchasing and Materials Management,* p. 513.

[3] Ibid., pp. 8–9.

TABLE 12–1 Cost of Materials—Value of Industry Shipments Ratios for Manufacturing Firms, 1985

Standard Industrial Code	*Industry*	*Cost of Materials (millions)**	*Capital Expenditures, New (millions)†*	*Total Material and Capital Expenditures (millions)*	*Value of Industry Shipments (millions)‡*	*Material/ Sales Ratio*	*Total Purchase Sales Ratio*
20	Food and kindred products	$197,275	$7,049	$204,324	$301,562	65	68
21	Tobacco products	6,626	669	7,295	18,507	36	39
22	Textile mill products	32,258	1,863	34,121	53,277	61	64
23	Apparel and other textile products	29,130	697	29,827	56,993	51	52
24	Lumber and wood products	33,169	1,664	34,833	54,185	61	64
25	Furniture and fixtures	14,764	763	15,527	31,294	47	50
26	Paper and allied products	53,039	6,276	59,315	93,414	57	64
27	Printing and publishing	39,104	4,715	43,819	111,885	35	39
28	Chemicals, allied products	101,696	8,269	109,965	197,311	52	56
29	Petroleum and coal products	161,291	3,438	164,729	179,135	90	92
30	Rubber, miscellaneous plastics products	35,754	3,430	39,184	71,324	50	55
31	Leather, leather products	4,444	103	4,547	8,567	52	53
32	Stone, clay, glass products	26,179	2,780	28,959	55,064	48	53
33	Primary metal	70,603	4,755	75,358	110,301	64	68
34	Fabricated metal	70,490	4,346	74,836	139,580	51	54
35	Machinery, except electric	102,831	8,323	111,154	215,080	48	52
36	Electric, electronic equipment	83,079	10,471	93,550	192,732	43	49
37	Transportation equipment	180,856	10,377	191,233	301,386	60	64
38	Instruments and related products	20,982	2,581	23,563	61,008	34	39
39	Miscellaneous manufacturing	12,442	667	13,109	26,527	47	49
All Operating Manufacturing Establishments							
	1971	356,016	20,940	376,956	670,970	53	56
	1973	478,169	26,978	505,147	875,443	55	58
	1975	597,327	37,262	634,589	1,039,377	57	61
	1977	782,417	47,459	829,876	1,358,526	58	61
	1979	999,157	61,533	1,060,690	1,727,214	58	61
	1981	1,193,969	78,632	1,272,601	2,017,542	59	63
	1983	1,170,238	61,931	1,232,169	2,054,853	57	60
	1985	1,276,013	83,237	1,359,250	2,279,132	56	60

SOURCE: U.S. Bureau of the Census, *1985 Annual Survey of Manufactures* (Washington, D.C.: U.S. Government Printing Office, Statistics for Industry Groups and Industries, M85(AS)–1), pp. 1–8, 1–9, and Appendix; as reported in Michiel R. Leenders, Harold E. Fearon, and Wilbur B. England, *Purchasing and Materials Management,* 9th ed. (Homewood, Ill.: Richard D. Irwin, 1989), pp. 6–7.

*Refers to direct charges actually paid or payable for items consumed or put into production during the year, including freight charges and other direct charges incurred by the establishment in acquiring these materials. Manufacturers included the cost of materials or fuel consumed regardless of whether these items were purchased by the individual establishment from other companies, transferred to it from other establishments of the same company, or withdrawn from inventory. It excludes the cost of services used, such as advertising, insurance, telephone, etc., and research, developmental, and consulting services of other establishments. It also excludes materials, machinery, and equipment used in plant expansion or capitalized repairs which are chargeable to fixed assets accounts.

†Includes funds spent for permanent additions and major alterations to manufacturing establishments, and new machinery and equipment used for replacement purposes and additions to plant capacity if they are chargeable to a fixed asset account.

‡The received or receivable net selling values, FOB plant, after discounts and allowances, and excluding freight charges and excise taxes. However, where the products of an industry are customarily delivered by the manufacturing establishment, e.g., bakery products, the value of shipments is based on the delivered price of the goods.

Procurement has a broader meaning, and includes purchasing, traffic, warehousing, and receiving inbound materials.

The Goals of Purchasing

"The purchasing decision maker might be likened to a juggler, attempting to keep several balls in the air at the same time, for the purchaser must achieve several goals simultaneously."[4] The goals of purchasing are to:

1. Provide an uninterrupted flow of materials, supplies, and services required to operate the organization.
2. Keep inventory investment and loss at a minimum.
3. Maintain adequate quality standards.
4. Find or develop competent vendors.
5. Standardize, where possible, the items bought.
6. Purchase required items and services at the lowest ultimate price.
7. Improve the organization's competitive position.
8. Achieve harmonious, productive working relationships with other departments within the organization.
9. Accomplish the purchasing objectives at the lowest possible level of administrative costs.[5]

Among the primary purchasing activities that influence the ability of the firm to achieve its objectives are supplier selection and evaluation (sourcing), quality control, and forward buying.

Supplier Selection and Evaluation

In the acquisition process, perhaps the most important activity is selecting the best supplier from among a number of vendors that can supply the needed materials. The buying process is complex because of the variety of factors that must be considered when making such a decision. The process includes both decision makers and decision influencers, which combine to form the decision-making unit (DMU). The process has a number of stages and includes the following 12 steps: identify needs, establish specifications, search for alternatives, establish contact, set purchase and usage criteria, evaluate alternative buying actions, determine budget availability, evaluate specific alternatives, negotiate with suppliers, buy, use, and conduct post-purchase evaluation.[6] It may not be necessary to go through all 12 stages of the buying process unless the decision is a totally new one. If the decision has been made before (routine buying), then many of the steps can be bypassed.

12 Steps in the Buying Process

---

[4] Ibid., p. 24.

[5] Ibid., pp. 25–27.

[6] Yoram Wind, "The Boundaries of Buying Decision Centers," *Journal of Purchasing and Materials Management* 14, no. 2 (Summer 1978), p. 24.

Variables Used When Making the Purchasing Decision

Purchasing managers may use some or all of the following variables when making the purchasing decision:

- Lead time.
- Lead time variability.
- Percentage of on-time deliveries.
- Percentage in-stock availability.
- Convenience in ordering/communication.
- Ability to expedite.
- Downtime caused by vendor errors, partial shipments, and/or late deliveries.
- Product reliability.
- Ease of maintenance/operation.
- Product failures caused by parts/materials.
- Quality rejects.
- Technical specifications.
- Technical/training services offered.
- Competitiveness of price.
- Confidence in the sales representative.
- Past experience with vendor.
- Overall reputation of the vendor.
- Financing terms.
- Postpurchase sales service.
- Vendor's flexibility in adjusting to the buying company's needs.
- Engineering/design capabilities.

In a study of purchasing managers, White identified six major product categories that were purchased by most companies: (1) component parts, (2) raw materials, (3) process materials, (4) accessory equipment, (5) major equipment, and (6) operating supplies.[7] Each product category could be purchased in any of four buying situations:

Four Buying Situations

1. *Routine order situations*—includes situations where the product has been purchased many times previously and where order routines or procedures are generally established.
2. *Procedural problem situations*—includes purchases which are not routine and which may require that employees learn how to use the product.
3. *Performance problem situations*—includes nonroutine purchases of products which are designed to be substitutes for current products but which must be tested for performance.
4. *Political problem situations*—includes nonroutine purchases of products whose use would affect many departments of the company;

[7] Phillip D. White, "Decision Making in the Purchasing Process: A Report," *AMA Management Briefing* (New York: American Management Association, 1978), pp. 13–14.

thus, a number of individuals throughout the firm will be involved in the decision process.[8]

The Four Most Important Evaluation Criteria

When White asked purchasing managers to rank each of the 16 evaluation criteria along the dimensions of product category and buying situation, he obtained the results shown in Table 12–2. In general, the factors of quality, price, delivery, and service were consistently rated as important in almost every product category/buying situation. While many firms perform the evaluation processs informally, some companies establish formal, written procedures for the purchasing process.

In the 1980s, the increased concern for productivity improvements caused management attention to focus on the purchasing function and on the development of closer ties with a reduced number of vendors.[9] In order to determine the impact of supplier performance on productivity, performance must be measured and evaluated. Next, the data can be used to identify those suppliers with whom the firm wishes to develop long-term relationships, to identify problems so that corrective action can be taken, and to realize productivity improvements.[10]

A variety of evaluation procedures are possible; there is no best method or approach. The important thing is to make certain that some procedures are used. Table 12–3 presents an example of an evaluation procedure. The manager must identify all potential suppliers for the item(s) being purchased. The next step is to develop a list of factors by which to evaluate each supplier. Management can use the 16 factors identified by White or develop another list. Once the factors have been determined, the performance of individual suppliers should be evaluated on each factor (e.g., product reliability, price, ordering convenience). A five-point scale (1 = worst rating; 5 = highest rating) is used in the illustration, but other scales may be used.

The Performance of Individual Suppliers Should Be Evaluated

After evaluating suppliers on each factor, management must determine the importance of the factors to its particular situation. If, for example, product reliability was of paramount importance to the firm, that factor would be given the highest importance rating. If price was not as important as product reliability, management would assign price a lower importance rating. Any factor that was not important to the firm would be assigned a zero.[11]

---

[8] Reprinted by permission of the publisher from *Decision Making in the Purchasing Process: A Report,* AMA Management Briefing, by Phillip D. White, pp. 15–17, © 1978 by AMACOM, a division of American Management Association, New York. All rights reserved.

[9] Robert E. Spekman, "Strategic Supplier Selection: Understanding Long-Term Buyer Relationships," *Business Horizons* (July–August, 1988), pp. 75–81.

[10] Thomas C. Harrington, Douglas M. Lambert, and Martin Christopher, "A Methodology for Measuring Vendor Performance," *Journal of Business Logistics* 12, no. 1 (1991), p 83.

[11] Some factors may be of no importance to the firm in one type of buying situation but of moderate or high importance at other times. Therefore, it is necessary that all potential

TABLE 12–2 A Matrix for Rating Product and Supplier Attributes by Buying Situation and Product Category

	Routine Order Situations	*Procedural Problem Situations*	*Performance Problem Situations*	*Political Problem Situations*
Component parts	1. Reliabity of delivery 2. Price 3. Past experience 4. Overall supplier reputation 5. Ease of operation or use 6. Ease of maintenance	1. Ease of operation or use 2. Reliability of delivery 3. Training offered 4. Training time required 5. Technical service offered 6. Technical specifications	1. Ordering convenience 2. Supplier flexibility 3. Ease of operation or use 4. Technical service offered 5. Training offered 6. Financing terms	1. Sales service 2. Overall supplier reputation 3. Reliability of delivery 4. Training offered 5. Ease of maintenance 6. Ordering convenience
Raw materials	1. Reliability of delivery 2. Price 3. Product reliability 4. Past experience 5. Overall supplier reputation 6. Technical specifications	1. Technical service offered 2. Product reliability 3. Training offered 4. Technical specifications 5. Overall supplier reputation	1. Technical service offered 2. Product reliability 3. Ease of operation or use 4. Technical specifications 5. Reliability of delivery 6. Training offered	1. Product reliability 2. Reliability of delivery 3. Technical specifications 4. Technical service offered 5. Price 6. Overall supplier reputation
Process materials	1. Reliability of service 2. Price 3. Overall supplier reputation 4. Past experience 5. Product reliability 6. Ease of operation or use	1. Training offered 2. Ease of operation or use 3. Technical service offered 4. Technical time required 5. Reliability of delivery 6. Technical specifications	1. Ordering convenience 2. Ease of operation or use 3. Technical service offered 4. Supplier flexibility 5. Training offered 6. Financing terms	1. Overall supplier reputation 2. Sales service 3. Training offered 4. Ease of maintenance 5. Ordering convenience 6. Reliability of delivery
Accessory equipment	1. Reliability of delivery 2. Price 3. Ease of operation or use 4. Past experience 5. Overall supplier reputation 6. Ease of maintenance	1. Training offered 2. Ease of operation or use 3. Training time required 4. Technical service 5. Reliability of delivery 6. Product reliability	1. Supplier flexibility 2. Ordering convenience 3. Training offered 4. Technical specifications 5. Ease of operation or use 6. Financing terms	1. Sales service 2. Training offered 3. Reliability of delivery 4. Overall supplier reputation 5. Ease of maintenance 6. Ordering convenience
Major equipment	1. Reliability of delivery 2. Price 3. Overall supplier reputation 4. Past experience 5. Ease of maintenance 6. Sales service	1. Technical service offered 2. Training offered 3. Overall supplier reputation 4. Ease of operation or use 5. Technical specifications 6. Product reliability	1. Ease of operation or use 2. Technical service offered 3. Product reliability 4. Technical specifications 5. Ease of maintenance 6. Overall supplier reputation	1. Technical service 2. Product reliability 3. Overall supplier reputation 4. Price 5. Technical specifications 6. Ease of maintenance and ease of operation or use
Operating supplies	1. Reliability of delivery 2. Price 3. Past experience 4. Overall supplier reputation 5. Supplier flexibility 6. Ease of operation or use	1. Training offered 2. Ease of operation or use 3. Technical service offered 4. Training time required 5. Ease of maintenance 6. Product reliability	1. Product reliability 2. Technical service offered 3. Ease of operation or use 4. Technical specifications 5. Reliability of delivery 6. Ease of maintenance	1. Reliability of delivery 2. Overall supplier reputation 3. Price 4. Product reliability 5. Ease of operation 6. Technical specifications

SOURCE: Adapted, by permission of the publisher, from *Decision Making in the Purchasing Process: A Report,* AMA Management Briefing, by Phillip D. White, pp. 20–47.

TABLE 12–3 Evaluating Suppliers in a Typical Manufacturing Firm

Factor	Rating of Supplier (1 = Worst Rating; 5 = Highest Rating) 1 2 3 4 5	(×)	Importance of Factor to Your Firm (0 = No Importance; 5 = Highest Importance) 0 1 2 3 4 5	(=)	Weighted Composite Rating (0 = Minimum; 25 = Maximum)
Supplier A					
Product reliability					
Price					
Ordering convenience					
•					
•					
•					
After-sale service					
Total for supplier A					________
Supplier B					
Product reliability					
Price					
Ordering convenience					
•					
•					
•					
After-sale service					
Total for supplier B					________
Supplier C					
Product reliability					
Price					
Ordering convenience					
•					
•					
•					
After-sale service					
Total for supplier C					________

Decision rule: Select the supplier with highest composite rating.

The next step is to develop a weighted composite measure for each factor. This is done by multiplying the supplier's rating for a factor by the factor's importance. The addition of the composite scores for each supplier provides an overall rating that can be compared to other suppliers. The higher the composite score, the more closely the supplier meets the needs and specifications of the procuring company. One of the major benefits of this approach is that it forces management to formalize the important elements of the purchasing decision and to question existing methods, assumptions, and procedures.

Implementation of a vendor performance evaluation methodology in a company that assembled kits for the health-care industry resulted in a reduction in the number of vendors, closer relationships with remaining

---

factors be included in the rating form in order to eliminate the need for a different form for each buying situation.

TABLE 12–4 Sourcing Problems in International Markets

1. Lack of local technological backup.
2. License and foreign exchange difficulties.
3. Poor service from indigenous supply sources (e.g., poor delivery-schedule performance, quality failure, limited variety).
4. Political instability or risk affecting investment (either with respect to the company itself or potential suppliers).
5. Tariffs and host government pressure to buy within the country.
6. Governmental pressures regarding their own purchasing from the company.
7. Necessity for carrying higher inventories.
8. Necessity for intensifying goods-inwards [inbound] inspection activities.
9. "Home" derived specifications not available from local supply markets.
10. Quality inconsistency of certain imported components.
11. Lack of trained local staff, affecting supply department performance.

SOURCE: D. H. Farmer, "Source Decision Making in the Multinational Company Environment," *Journal of Purchasing* 8, no. 1 (February 1972), pp. 34–35.

suppliers, and a 34 percent reduction in component inventories [within the first few months].[12] After two full years of using the quarterly performance reports, buyers had reduced component inventories by more than 60 percent.

International Sourcing

The process of supplier selection is more difficult when materials are being purchased in international markets. However, more firms are buying raw materials, components, and subassemblies from foreign sources, primarily because of cost and availability. Between 1984 and 1987, the proportion of companies with corporate international procurement operations increased from 46 percent to 61 percent.[13] When a company utilizes foreign suppliers it should have an understanding of some of the problems associated with international sourcing. Table 12–4 identifies a number of potential sourcing problems that a firm should consider *before* engaging in foreign sourcing.

International sourcing requires additional expertise in many areas, for example:

> Radix Group International's Ed Salinas reports that U.S. companies exporting a wide range of products are losing hundreds of millions of dollars by paying excessive customs duties by not taking advantage of "duty drawbacks"—a little known customs law. The law provides that companies importing components assembled into finished products, with those products then exported or sent abroad under the same conditions, may apply for a refund of 99 percent of the duty paid on components. According to Mr. Salinas, less than 25 percent of the $17 billion in collected duties was returned in 1989.[14]

[12] Harrington, Lambert, and Christopher, "A Methodology for Measuring Vendor Performance," pp. 97–98.

[13] Joseph R. Carter and Ron Narasimhan, "Purchasing in the International Marketplace: Implications for Operations," *Journal of Purchasing and Materials Management* 26, no. 3 (Summer 1990), pp. 2–11.

[14] D'Ann Brosnahan, "Pointers: Duty-Drawbacks Can Pay Off," *Purchasing World* 35, no. 2 (February 1991), p. 3.

The rewards associated with the proper selection and evaluation of suppliers can be significant. As we saw in Chapter 1 (Table 1–3), logistics cost savings can be leveraged into substantial profit improvements. Similarly, purchasing activities can have positive effects on the firm's profits. Figure 12–1 shows the dramatic profit leverage that is possible from effective purchasing management. Not only will a reduction in the cost of materials increase the profit margin on every unit that is manufactured and sold, but the lower cost associated with the materials purchased will also reduce the investment in inventories. In addition, customer service improvements are possible because the manufacturing process can operate smoothly, without slowdowns or shutdowns. And since effective purchasing management results in the acquisition of high-quality materials, there is also less likelihood of customer return of finished goods due to product failure.

Quality Control

Price Is Only One Element of the Total Cost

Although cost is one of the most important considerations in materials acquisition, quality control is also vital. The initial purchase price of an item is only one element of the total cost. For example, some items are easier to work with than others and can save production costs. Materials of higher quality may require fewer fabrication processes or have a longer life span, thus resulting in lower overall product costs and/or higher prices for finished products. Companies must achieve some balance between the components of the acquisition process, namely, price, cost, and value received.[15]

After the quality level has been determined, usually by manufacturing, it becomes purchasing's responsibility to secure the proper materials. The correct quality specification must be given to suppliers. The vendor that offers the best cost/quality package should be selected. Quality level can be specified to suppliers in a variety of ways, including:

Ways of Specifying Quality

- Commercial standards.
- Design specifications.
- Engineering drawings.
- Material and method-of-manufacture specifications.
- Performance specifications.
- Function and fit specifications.
- Brand or trade names.
- Samples.
- Market grades.
- Qualified products list.
- Combination of above specifications.[16]

---

[15] Lamar Lee, Jr., David N. Burt, and Donald W. Dobler, *Purchasing and Materials Management*, 5th ed. (New York: McGraw-Hill, 1990), p. 29.

[16] Ibid., pp. 128–136. (A detailed explanation of specification is provided.)

FIGURE 12–1 Relationship of Purchasing to the Firm's Profitability

When purchasing is a high percent of controllable expenditures . . .

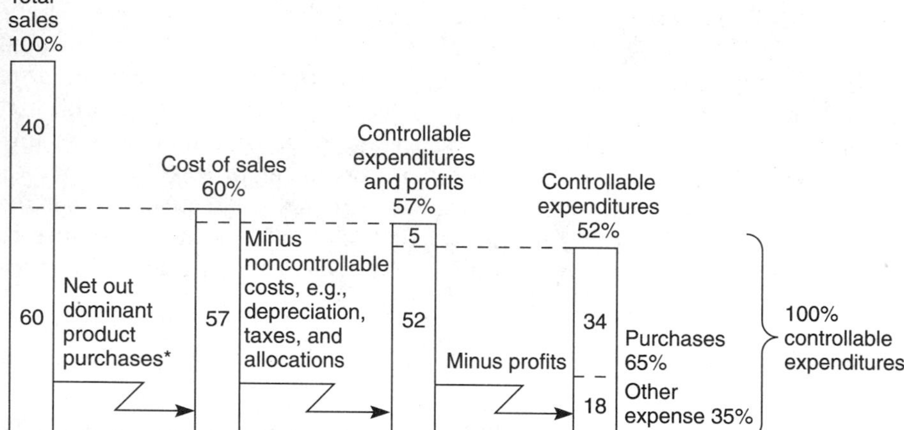

*Primary commodities of oil, grain, wood products and metals companies are not usually procured by purchasing.

Dramatic profit leverage usually is available.

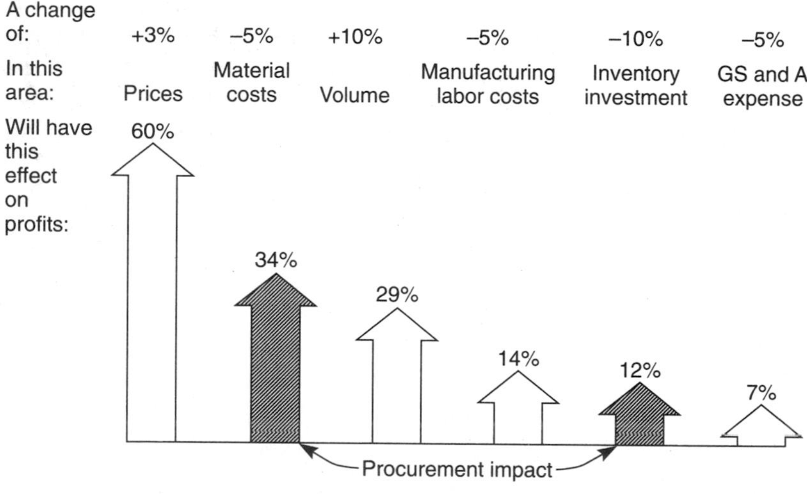

SOURCE: Frank L. Bauer, "Better Purchasing: High Rewards at Low Risk," *Journal of Purchasing and Materials Management*, 12, no. 2 (Summer 1976), p. 4.

The firm should never pay higher prices to obtain materials with higher quality levels than those specified by manufacturing, unless there are justifiable marketing or logistics reasons for doing so. Purchasing materials that needlessly exceed quality specifications adds unnecessary costs to the ultimate product.

Forward Buying

All purchasing activities, except emergency purchases, represent *forward buying* if materials, component parts, and subassemblies are available in advance of the time they are needed. More accurately, forward buying refers to the purchase of materials in quantities exceeding current requirements, well in advance of their need or use.

Tersine and Grasso stated that:

> For an organization to practice forward buying, it must be experiencing some unusual, changing, or unstable market condition. This kind of a purchase can be made because of a pending price increase, a potential supply shortage, or some unusual . . . condition. Effective forward buying can help maximize purchasing's contribution to profits.[17]

Reasons for Forward Buying

Essentially, there are two major reasons why a firm would engage in forward buying. First, forward buying minimizes the effects of rising material costs. At least for a time, until the materials are depleted from inventory, the firm is protected from price increases in the marketplace. Second, forward buying provides protection against future availability problems. As an example, firms that secured large quantities of gasoline or diesel fuel after the 1973 oil embargo, in anticipation of higher fuel costs and spot shortages, were able to carry out almost normal operations, while other companies had to curtail their activities. Forward buying is more popular among firms as availability uncertainties become more commonplace.

Disadvantages of Forward Buying

While there are benefits associated with forward buying, there are also disadvantages. Many companies make forward purchases in anticipation of price increases. There are times, however, when materials prices actually go down because of technological developments, competitive pressures, and other factors. There is a risk that the firm may purchase materials at prices higher than necessary. Another often overlooked disadvantage of forward buying is the increased inventory carrying cost incurred with holding excess inventory. The savings realized from forward buying must exceed the additional inventory carrying costs. Table 12–5 presents an example of the role of inventory carrying costs in the forward buying decision. In this example, the firm purchases $2,000 worth of an item once a month. The $2,000 purchase represents the firm's monthly usage of this

---

[17] Richard J. Tersine and Edward T. Grasso, "Forward Buying in Response to Announced Price Increases," *Journal of Purchasing and Materials Management* 14, no. 2 (Summer 1978), p. 20.

TABLE 12–5 Using Inventory Carrying Costs to Evaluate Forward Buying

					Increase In Inventory Carrying Cost			
Number of Months Supply Purchased	*Value*	*Average Inventory (½ × Order Quantity)*	*Savings in Order Processing Cost from Fewer Orders Being Placed*	*Savings in Purchase Price*	*Inventory Carrying Cost for Buy-Ahead Period 30% × Avg. Inv. × No. of Months / 12*	*Inventory Carrying Cost for Remaining Months Assuming Purchases of $2,200/Mo.*	*Less Inventory Carrying Costs if No Forward Buying Takes Place*	*Net Saving from Forward Buying*
1	$ 2,000	$ 1,000	$ —	$ —	$ 25*	$302.50†	$327.50	$ —
2	4,000	2,000	20	200	100	275.00	327.50	172.50
3	6,000	3,000	40	400	225	247.50	327.50	295.00
4	8,000	4,000	60	600	400	220.00	327.50	367.50
5	10,000	5,000	80	800	625	192.50	327.50	390.00
6	12,000	6,000	100	1,000	900	165.00	327.50	362.50
7	14,000	7,000	120	1,200	1,225	137.50	327.50	285.00
8	16,000	8,000	140	1,400	1,600	110.00	327.50	157.50
9	18,000	9,000	160	1,600	2,025	82.50	327.50	(20.00)
10	20,000	10,000	180	1,800	2,500	55.00	327.50	(247.50)
11	22,000	11,000	200	2,000	3,025	27.50	327.50	(525.00)
12	24,000	12,000	220	2,200	3,600‡	—	327.50	(852.50)

Assumptions:
1) Monthly usage = $2,000
2) Expected price increase = 10 percent
3) Inventory carrying cost = 30 percent
4) Ordering cost = $20.00
5) Vendor pays the freight

Key:
*$1,000 × 30% × 1/12 = $25

†$\frac{\$2,200}{2}$ × 30% × 11/12 = $302.50

‡$12,000 × 30% × 12/12 = $3,600

SOURCE: Douglas M. Lambert, "Purchasing Performance Measurement," unpublished manuscript, 1986.

item. The vendor's salesperson explains that the price will increase by 10 percent next month and encourages the purchasing manager to consider forward buying. If the firm buys for a period of one month, the average level of inventory would be $1,000 for the first month. But there would be no savings in the purchase price. The inventory carrying costs incurred would equal $25 for one month (30 percent of the average level of inventory, which is $1,000 divided by 12), and $302.50 for the next 11 months (30 percent × $1,100 × 11/12). Since the firm would experience a total inventory carrying cost of $327.50 with no forward buying, the net savings from continuing with the current practice is zero. However, if the purchasing manager obtains a two-month supply, the forward buy of one month's worth of product will result in a $20 savings in ordering costs and a $200 savings in purchase price, for a total savings of $220. The increase in inventory carrying cost would be $47.50 ($375.00 − $327.50), resulting in a net savings of $172.50 ($220.00 − $47.50). If the purchasing manager buys an amount equal to nine months of usage, however, the savings in purchase price and ordering costs is offset entirely by the additional inventory carrying costs.

As shown in Table 12–5, the optimal forward buy would be a five-month supply, which would result in a net savings of $390. However, if the purchasing manager is judged solely on the per-unit purchase price, he or she would purchase a 12-month supply, at a cost to the firm of $852.50. That is, purchasing a 12-month supply would result in a decrease in pretax profits of $852.50. This example illustrates that inventory carrying costs must be included in the forward buying decision. Since the funds expended for inventories are not available for other uses, the firm should anticipate future working capital needs before engaging in forward buying.

Cost trade-offs are a key to successfully managing the purchasing function. By thinking in terms of the cost trade-offs shown in Figure 12–2, management should minimize the total of these costs rather than attempt to minimize the cost of either component. This is critical, as attempts to reduce individual costs may in fact actually increase total costs.

JUST-IN-TIME PURCHASING

The Japanese Just-in-time (JIT) production concept is increasingly being recognized as a cornerstone of the Japanese success story. Most of the early U.S. interest in JIT pertained to its applications within the repetitive manufacturing plant; for example, the Japanese Kanban (card) system of providing parts just in time to go into the next higher level assembly became a popular topic at professional development conferences and workshops in 1981. More recently, JIT purchasing has begged our attentions.[18]

---

[18] Richard J. Schonberger and James P. Gilbert, "Just-in-Time Purchasing: A Challenge for U.S. Industry," *California Management Review* 26, no. 1 (Fall 1983), p. 54.

FIGURE 12–2 Cost Trade-Offs to Be Considered by the Purchasing Executive

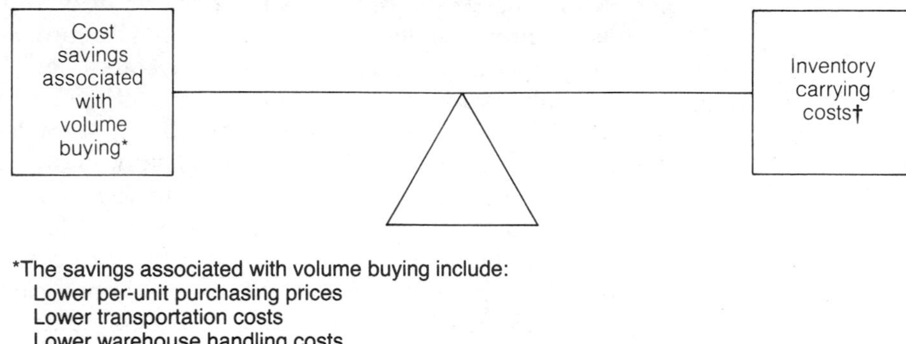

*The savings associated with volume buying include:
Lower per-unit purchasing prices
Lower transportation costs
Lower warehouse handling costs
Lower order-processing costs
Lower production lot quantity costs
Lower stockout costs

†The costs of carrying inventory include:
Capital costs associated with the inventory investment
Inventory service costs (insurance and taxes)
Storage space costs
Inventory risk costs

SOURCE: Douglas M. Lambert and Jay U. Sterling, "Measuring Purchasing Performance," *Production and Inventory Management Review* 4, no. 6 (June 1984), p. 52. Reprinted with permission from *P&IM Review,* June 1984. Copyright 1984 by T.D.A. Publications, Inc., Hollywood, FL.

In the Japanese system, the ordering costs are reduced so that the savings in inventory carrying cost gained from cutting lot sizes are not offset by increased purchase order cost. Figure 12–3 illustrates how a reduction in ordering costs shifts the total cost curve downward to the left and results in a smaller economic order quantity. In addition, every effort is made to improve vendor quality levels. Philip Crosby has estimated that 50 percent or more of a firm's quality problems are the result of defective purchased materials.[19]

Just-in-Time purchasing requires frequent releases of orders and frequent deliveries of products. For this to work, purchasers and suppliers must develop long-term relationships rather than use the multiple sourcing practices popular in the United States.

Characteristics of JIT Purchasing

Table 12–6 shows a number of characteristics of JIT purchasing. The JIT characteristics are interrelated and displayed in four groups: suppliers (number, location, longevity, and assistance/advice offered); quantities (product outputs, parts inputs, contracts administered, and purchasing paperwork); quality (specifications coordination, and control); and shipping (inbound freight and freight/storage modes).[20]

[19] Philip B. Crosby, in "How to Stem the Tide of Shoddy Materials," ed. Douglas Smock, *Purchasing* 92, no. 9 (May 13, 1982), p. 51, as reported in Schonberger and Gilbert, "Just-in-Time Purchasing," p. 55.

[20] Adapted from Schonberger and Gilbert, "Just-in-Time Purchasing," pp. 58–63.

FIGURE 12–3 Reducing Ordering Costs Results in a Smaller Economic Order Quantity

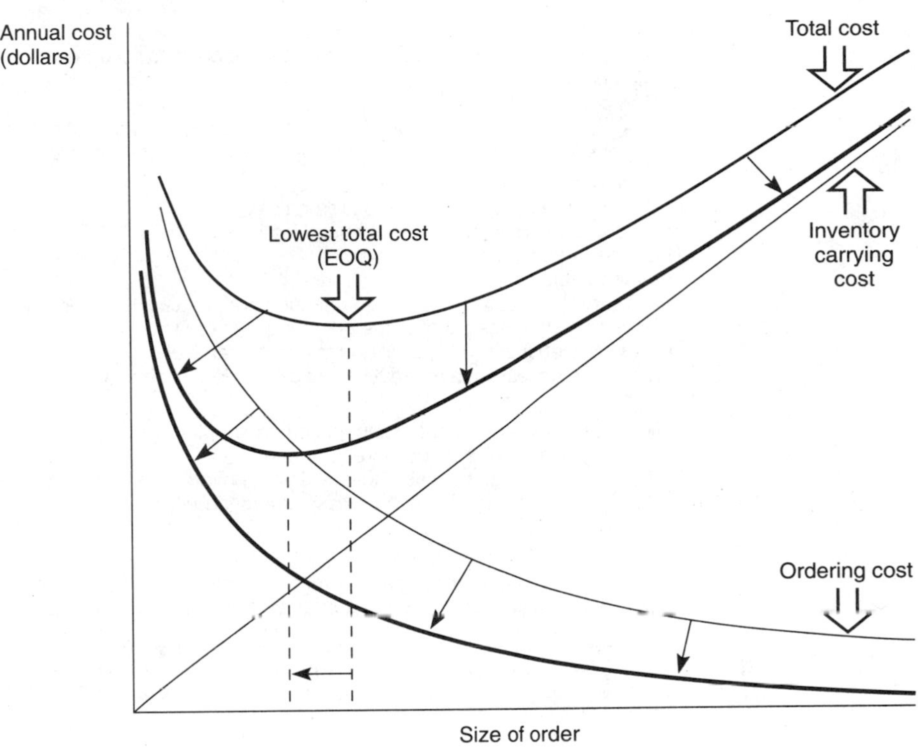

Vendor Selection

Supplier-Buyer Plant Proximity

Management can facilitate JIT purchasing by developing long-term relationships with a small number of nearby suppliers. The objective is to achieve strong, stable purchase agreements with an uninterrupted supply of materials. The closer the JIT purchasing comes to piece-by-piece delivery, the greater the contribution to productivity and avoidance of defective lots. But piece-by-piece delivery leads to higher transportation costs unless the supplier and seller are in close proximity. For example, if a manufacturer builds an assembly plant near suppliers' plants, it can supply its assembly lines with multiple deliveries per day in small vehicles, rather than infrequent deliveries in 40-foot truckloads. Thus, one way to reduce the transportation associated with small lots is to reduce the distance between supplier and buyer plants.

TABLE 12–6 Characteristics of JIT Purchasing

Suppliers
- Few suppliers
- Nearby suppliers
- Repeat business with same suppliers
- Active use of analysis to enable desirable suppliers to become/stay price competitive
- Clusters of remote suppliers
- Competitive bidding mostly limited to new part numbers
- Buyer plant resists vertical integration and subsequent wipeout of supplier business
- Suppliers are encouraged to extend JIT buying to *their* suppliers

Quantities
- Steady output rate (a desirable prerequisite)
- Frequent deliveries in small lot quantities
- Long-term contract agreements
- Minimal release paperwork
- Delivery quantities variable from release to release but fixed for whole contract term
- Little or no permissible overage or shortage of receipts
- Suppliers encouraged to package in exact quantities
- Suppliers encouraged to reduce their production lot sizes (or store unreleased material)

Quality
- Minimal product specifications imposed on supplier
- Help suppliers to meet quality requirements
- Close relationships between buyers' and suppliers' quality assurance people
- Suppliers encouraged to use process control charts instead of lot sampling inspection

Shipping
- Scheduling of inbound freight
- Gain control by use of company-owned or contract shipping, contract warehousing, and trailers for freight consolidation/storage where possible, instead of using common carriers

SOURCE: Richard J. Schonberger and James P. Gilbert, "Just-in-Time Purchasing: A Challenge for U.S. Industry," *California Management Review* 26, no. 1 (Fall 1983), p. 58. © 1983 by the Regents of the University of California. Reprinted from the *California Management Review*, vol. XXVI, no. 1. By permission of the Regents.

Focused Factories

The potential advantages of supplier-buyer proximity apply in the United States as well as in Japan. Yet most U.S. industry has considered vertical integration to be a desirable path to corporate growth and success. Nevertheless, a strong case can be made for developing special manufacturing competency in more narrowly focused areas. These smaller, "focused" plants offer significant cost savings in areas such as construction and operating costs. This approach downgrades integration in favor of a narrow base of highly competent suppliers. Japanese manufacturers tend to avoid vertical integration. Instead, they develop final assembly competency and contract out as much fabrication as possible to experts. This helps cement stable purchase agreements with reliable suppliers.

Purchase Agreements

JIT purchasing is facilitated by an even, repetitive master production schedule. Repetitive manufacture of products evens out the demand for individual parts. This steady demand for parts has an impact on shipping

JIT Purchase Agreements

quantities, containers, and purchasing paperwork. In Japan, JIT purchase agreements usually involve little paperwork. The purchase order, like a blanket order, may specify an overall quantity, but the supplier will deliver in accordance with a schedule or with daily production needs, which are telephoned from the buying plant.

Exact Quantities

U.S. suppliers generally ship the approximate quantity specified in the purchase agreement. The buyer counts the materials when they are received and may refuse the shipment if there is too large a discrepancy. An overage or shortage of 10 percent is often considered to be acceptable. The JIT purchase agreement does not permit variability. In most cases, the Japanese buyer expects and receives the exact quantity.

"Loose" Engineering Specifications

U.S. engineers tend to specify tolerances for almost every conceivable design feature for which parts are purchased. The Japanese place more importance on performance specifications and less on design specifications. The supplier is permitted to innovate on the premise that the supplier is the expert.

Benefits of Value Analysis

Value analysis is a respected U.S. purchasing practice that may receive more attention as a result of the interest in JIT purchasing. When negotiating a JIT purchase agreement, the supplier receives the buyer's specifications and provides a bid price. If the price is too high, the buyer may visit the supplier's plant to review the bid. The objective is to identify the supplier's highest costs and, if possible, to modify the minimal specifications in order to reduce the supplier's cost and the price bid.

Engineering/Quality Coordination

The benefits of closer coordination on engineering and quality matters are even more significant. Engineers and quality control people may visit a supplier's plant frequently. In this way, engineering questions and potential quality problems are quickly resolved. Potential quality concerns are identified before they become major problems, and quality control people may help the supplier establish process controls.

Control of Inbound Transportation

In the United States, inbound freight decisions such as delivery and routing are left to the supplier's traffic department. This is the case even when materials are purchased "FOB shipping point" and the buyer owns the goods and absorbs inventory carrying costs on them from the date of ship-

TABLE 12–7 Buyer Benefits of JIT Purchasing

Material Costs
- Reduced inventory carrying cost
- Reduced cost of parts via long-term learning curve effects with limited suppliers
- Reduced transportation costs with nearby suppliers
- Reduced scrap costs, since defects are detected early

Administrative Efficiency
- Few requests for bids
- Few suppliers to contract with
- Contracts negotiated infrequently
- Minimal release paperwork
- Reduced expediting
- Reduced travel and telephone distances and costs
- Encourages more frequent communication with supplier
- Simple accounting for parts received, if suppliers use standard containers
- Reliable identification of incoming orders, if suppliers use thorough container labeling

Quality
- Fast detection of defects, since deliveries are frequent
- Fast correction of defects, since supplier setups are frequent and lots small
- Less need for inspection (of lots), since process control is encouraged
- High quality of parts purchased—and of products they go into

Material Design
- Fast response to engineering changes
- Design innovations, since supplier is the expert and not hamstrung by restrictive specifications

Productivity
- Reduced material costs
- Reduced rework
- Reduced inspection
- Reduced delay because of off-specification parts, late deliveries, or delivery shortages
- Reduced purchasing, production control, inventory control, and supervision, with more reliable parts provisioning and smaller quantities carried

SOURCE: Richard J. Schonberger and James P. Gilbert, "Just-in-Time Purchasing: A Challenge for U.S. Industry," *California Management Review* 26, no. 1 (Fall 1983), p. 65. © 1983 by the Regents of the University of California. Reprinted from the *California Management Review,* vol. XXVI, no. 1. By permission of the Regents.

ment. JIT purchasing requires steady, reliable incoming deliveries. The objective is to avoid excessive inventory carrying costs for materials that arrive early and to avoid disruptions in manufacturing operations that can occur when goods arrive late. Therefore, the buying firms must become involved in selecting both the transportation mode and the specific carrier.

Benefits of JIT Purchasing

Benefits to the Buyer

Table 12–7 summarizes the benefits of JIT purchasing to the buyer. The most important benefit is the reduction in inventories that it makes possible. There are also scrap/quality and productivity benefits.

In addition, purchasing-related paperwork is reduced. Conventional lot size economics suggests that smaller lots mean more orders to process

TABLE 12–8 Supplier Benefits of JIT Purchasing

Material Costs
- Reduced finished and work-in-process inventory carrying costs
- Reduced purchased inventories if JIT is used with firm's own suppliers

Administrative Efficiency
- Encourages more frequent communication with buyer, thereby avoiding mix-ups
- Increased control of finished goods inventory because outgoing shipments are steady and predictable
- Supplier firm gains status in the eyes of the JIT buyer for higher quality and design responsiveness
- Reduced long-run risk of doing business

Quality
- Avoids production of defective large lots
- Improves coordination on quality assurance matters

Material Design
- Improves coordination on engineering related problems

Productivity
- Increases the ability to predict and share peak capacity
- Assists in the retention of a trained labor force

SOURCE: Richard J. Schonberger and James P. Gilbert, "Just-in-Time Purchasing: A Challenge for U.S. Industry," *California Management Review* 26, no. 1 (Fall 1983), p. 66. © 1983 by the Regents of the University of California. Reprinted from the *California Management Review,* vol. XXVI, no. 1. By permission of the Regents.

and therefore increased order-processing costs. But the environment in which JIT buying best functions is one in which:

> The buyer's production schedules are relatively level, so that demand for bought materials is steady and predictable;
> Larger, steadier orders are given to a smaller number of suppliers, thus encouraging excellence and loyalty;
> Purchase agreements are long-term, with minimal paperwork. They provide for frequent small-lot deliveries, thus revealing quality problems sooner; and
> Suppliers are responsive to the need for improved containers and labeling.[21]

Thus, smooth demand, few suppliers, long-term agreements, and fewer quality problems often result in lower order-processing costs.

Benefits to the Supplier

Table 12–8 shows the supplier benefits of JIT purchasing. The supplier receives a contract that is exclusive (or nearly so), long-term, and invariable, which affords the supplier the opportunity to cut peak capacity, retain a trained labor force, reduce its inventories, and implement JIT purchasing with its suppliers.

---

[21] Ibid., p. 65.

PURCHASING RESEARCH AND PLANNING

Uncertainty in the business environment is making the purchasing decisions for key items more complex and the effects of these decisions more long lasting.[22] Important environmental considerations include uncertainty of supply and dependence on foreign sources for key commodities; price increases on key commodities; extended and variable lead times; energy shortages or price increases; and, increasing worldwide competition.

Important Environmental Considerations

The changing environment makes it necessary for purchasing management to do a more effective job of researching the supply market and planning. Purchasing needs to provide information about supply conditions, such as availability, lead times, and technology, to different groups within the firm, including top management, engineering and design, and manufacturing. This information is important when formulating long-term strategy and making short-term decisions. Key materials for which availability, pricing, and quality problems may occur should be identified so that action plans can be developed before problems become critical and costly.

Strategic Planning for Purchasing

Strategic planning for purchasing involves materials screening, risk assessment, strategy development, and implementation. It is also important to determine if materials bottlenecks will jeopardize current or future production; if new products should be introduced; if materials quality may be expected to change; if prices are likely to increase or decrease; and the appropriateness of forward buying. Management should develop specific plans to ensure that the material supply chain will operate uninterrupted.

Materials screening should result in a list of critical purchased items. Typical criteria to be used for internal screening are percentage of product cost, percentage of total purchase expenditure, end item commonality, and use on high-margin end items.[23] Criteria used for external screening include number of suppliers, availability of raw materials to suppliers, supplier cost and profitability needs, supply capacity, and technological trends.[24]

Risk assessment requires that the purchaser determine the probability of best or worst conditions occurring. Supply strategies should be developed for the predicted events. Monczka and Fearon identified the following potential purchasing strategies:

Purchasing Strategies

- Evaluate supplier relations.
- Buy out supplier(s).

---

[22] This material is adapted from Robert M. Monczka, "Managing the Purchasing Function," in *The Distribution Handbook,* James F. Robeson and Robert G. House, eds. (New York: The Free Press, 1985), pp. 478–480.

[23] Ibid., p. 479.

[24] Ibid.

- Develop worldwide sources.
- Develop long-term relationship with suppliers.
- Use long-term contracts.
- Customer provision of materials supply.
- Engage in joint venture purchasing.
- Trade.
- Develop multiple sourcing.
- Centralize coordination of purchasing.
- Reduce the scrap rate.[25]

Implementation of a particular strategy requires the involvement of top management and integration with the firm's overall business plan.

PURCHASING COST MANAGEMENT

Purchasing departments, like other functional areas, must manage and reduce costs.[26] Purchasing can use a number of methods to reduce administrative costs, purchase prices, and inventory carrying costs, but the most prevalent are purchase cost reduction programs, price change management programs, volume (time and/or quantity) contracts, and systems contracts and stockless purchasing.[27]

Cost Reduction Programs

An effective purchasing cost reduction program requires top management support, definition of cost reduction or avoidances, effective goal setting, review and approval of cost reductions or avoidances, measurement of reduction to a specific goal, reporting, and making achievement in individual cost reduction or avoidance part of the performance appraisal process.[28]

For a successful cost reduction program, top management must communicate the need for cost saving accomplishments in both good and bad economic times. It must adequately define cost reduction objectives, so that accomplishments can be measured and performances evaluated. For example, in many firms a cost reduction is defined as a decrease in prior purchase price, and cost avoidance as the amount that would have been paid minus the amount actually paid. Management also has to establish programs with buyers based on opportunities for cost reduction.

---

[25] R. M. Monczka and H. E. Fearon, "Coping with Material Shortages," *Journal of Purchasing and Materials Management* 10, no. 2 (May 1974), pp. 5–19.

[26] Monczka, "Managing the Purchasing Function," pp. 480–83.

[27] Ibid., p. 480.

[28] Ibid.

Cost reduction programs should include the development of competition, a requirement of supplier cost reduction, substitution of materials, standardization, a make-or-buy analysis, value analysis, the reduction of scrap, a change in tolerances, an improvement of payment terms and conditions, volume buying, and process changes.[29]

Price Change Management

Purchasing managers must challenge vendor price increases and not treat them as pass-through costs. It is important to work with suppliers to restrict rate of price increases to a reasonable and equitable level.

Furthermore, purchasing should establish a systematic method of handling all price increase requests from suppliers. At a minimum, the system should require:

- The reason for the price change request be determined.
- The total dollar value impact on the firm be specified.
- Suppliers to justify the price change.
- Management to review the price change.
- Strategies to deal with price increases.

In order to restrict price increases, management should require price protection clauses and advance notification of price increases of 30, 60, or 90 days. As part of a program of price change management, purchasing should determine the impact of engineering changes on product costs in order to determine if engineering changes should be made.

Volume Contracts

Volume contracts combine purchase requirements over time, or different line item requirements. As a result, they can increase the purchaser's leverage with vendors and lead to reductions in purchase prices and administrative costs. A review of purchase prices for a particular item often identifies the opportunity for suppliers to provide quotes on a semiannual or contract basis. And an increase in the purchase quantity can enable suppliers to reduce their costs and prices as a result of production or purchasing economies. In addition, the vendor may be willing to accept lower per-unit margins on a higher volume of business.

Past purchase patterns should be available from buy-history cards, computer-generated requirements plans, and copies of historical purchase requisitions and orders, as well as from suppliers. Management needs to systematically and regularly review the firm's purchase history for new opportunities for volume contracting.

---

[29] Ibid., p. 481.

Systems Contracts and Stockless Purchasing

Systems contracts are a means of reducing materials-related costs such as unit purchase price, transportation, inventory, and administration. Systems contracts, or *blanket orders,* as they are sometimes called, are arranged for a given volume of purchases over a specified time period. The vendor supplies products to individual plant locations as ordered, and payment is arranged through purchasing: "While this agreed-to quantity is not legally binding, it is generally sufficient assurance for the vendor to seek volume purchases from its sources. These volume purchases help reduce the final cost to the buyer. A key advantage is that a stipulated price is fixed over the period of the contract.[30]

Systems contracts are often referred to as *stockless purchasing.* Stockless purchasing implies that the firm does not carry inventory of purchased materials. While a systems contract may or may not result in "zero" inventory, the underlying principles of systems contracting are necessary for stockless purchasing. The objectives of systems contracts and stockless purchasing are to:

Objectives of Systems Contracts and Stockless Purchasing

- Lower inventory levels.
- Reduce the number of suppliers.
- Reduce administrative cost and paperwork.
- Reduce the number of purchases of small dollar value and requisitions that purchasers have to handle (and thereby increase the amount of time available for other key activities).
- Provide the opportunity for larger dollar volumes of business to suppliers.
- Provide for timely delivery of material directly to the user.
- Standardize purchase items where possible.[31]

Systems contracts and stockless purchasing systems are best suited to frequently purchased items of low dollar value with administrative processing costs that are relatively large compared to unit prices. In many cases, the combined administrative, processing, and inventory carrying costs may exceed the item's cost. Systems contracting may lead to larger supplier discounts, reduced processing costs, and increased product availability. Both systems require the following: identification of appropriate supplies, and supplier selection; use of a standard item catalog for availability and ordering; establishment of order communication methods; identification of acceptable receipt areas (docks, warehouses, etc.); monitoring of supplier delivery performance within established delivery parameters (e.g., 4, 8, 24, or 48 hours); and established payment methods to accumu-

---

[30] Joseph L. Cavinato, *Purchasing and Materials Management* (St. Paul, Minn.: West Publishing, 1984), pp. 29–30.

[31] Monczka, "Managing the Purchasing Function," pp. 482–83.

late receipts and pay for all items received over a given time period (e.g., 30 days).[32]

Usually, the length of the contract varies from one to three years and includes price protection clauses. The purchaser should have the right to test market the items to ensure that suppliers' unit prices are reasonable.

MEASUREMENT AND EVALUATION OF PURCHASING PERFORMANCE

Management must identify the information that is required to perform purchasing activities and to measure and evaluate purchasing performance.[33] The following data should be included in the management information system in order to measure and evaluate purchasing performance:

Data for Measuring and Evaluating Purchasing Performance

- Purchase item number and description.
- Quantity required.
- Date on which item is required.
- Date on which purchase requisition is received or authorized.
- Purchase requisition or authorization number.
- Supplier(s) quoted.
- Date on which supplier(s) is quoted.
- Date on which quotes are required from supplier(s).
- Supplier quote(s).
- Supplier price discount schedule.
- Purchase order number.
- Date on which purchase order is placed.
- Purchase price per unit.
- Quantity or percent of annual requirements purchased.
- Planned purchase price per unit.
- Supplier name.
- Supplier address.
- Supplier's promised ship date.
- Supplier lead time (days or weeks for purchase item).
- Date on which purchase item is received.
- Quantity received.
- Purchase item accepted or rejected (unit/lot).
- Storage location.
- Buyer.
- Work unit.
- Requested price change.
- Effective date of requested price change.

---

[32] Ibid., p. 483.

[33] The material in this section is adapted from Robert M. Monczka, "Managing the Purchasing Function," pp. 486–92.

- Date on which price change is approved.
- Ship to location.[34]

Generally, the primary users of purchasing measurement and evaluation reports include top level managers, corporate functional managers, operating unit functional managers, and middle managers at plant and operating unit sites.

Information Needs Differ by Level of Management

The information needs of each of these groups is quite different. Top management, for example, may want to know how the firm's purchasing department compares with that of other firms, and how effective it is. Corporate functional managers, such as corporate vice president of purchasing, may want complete functional reviews; policy and procedure audits; and a review of key quantitative indicators, such as inventory, minority purchases, and administrative budget measures. The purchasing department manager of the operating unit may want to have a series of regularly reported indicators in order to monitor performance and take corrective action when necessary.

Performance Measures

Key Performance Measures

Monczka, Carter, and Hoagland found that purchasing organizations use a number of key performance measures for purchasing control, including price effectiveness; cost savings; workload; administration and control; efficiency; vendor quality and delivery; material flow control; regulatory, societal, and environmental measures; procurement planning and research; competition; inventory; and transportation.[35]

Price Effectiveness. Price effectiveness measures are used to determine (1) actual price performance against plan, (2) actual price performance against market, and (3) actual price performance among buying groups and locations. Purchase price variances from plan can be calculated for individual line items and for the total purchasing budget. Typical indicators are price variances measured in terms of (1) actual unit cost minus planned cost; (2) a price variance percentage—actual unit cost over planned cost; or (3) an extended price variance—actual unit cost minus planned cost, multiplied by an estimated annual quantity.

Cost Reduction versus Cost Avoidance

Cost Savings. Measures of cost savings include both cost reduction and cost avoidance. A *cost reduction* occurs when the new unit cost is lower than the old unit cost on a stock-keeping unit basis. *Cost avoidance* occurs when

---

[34] Ibid., pp. 486–87. From the *Distribution Handbook,* James F. Robeson and Robert G. House, eds. Copyright © 1985 by The Free Press, a Division of Macmillan, Inc. Used by permission of the publisher.

[35] R. M. Monczka, P. L. Carter, and J. H. Hoagland, *Purchasing Performance: Measurement and Control* (East Lansing: Michigan State University, Graduate School of Business Administration, Division of Research, 1979).

the new unit price is lower than the average quoted price, even when the new unit price represents an increase over the old price.

Workload. Workload can be broken down into three categories: (1) *workload in,* which is a measure of the new work coming into the purchasing department; (2) *workload current,* which is a measure of the backlog of work; and (3) *workload completed,* which is a measure of the work accomplished.[36] Measures of workload in include counts of work received, such as purchase requisitions, purchase information requests received, and the number of pricing requests received. Workload current is usually measured in terms of counts of the backlog of work, such as purchase requisitions on hand and items on hand. Measures of workload completed include purchase orders placed, line items ordered, dollars ordered, contracts written, and price proposals written.

Administration and Control. Administration and control is usually accomplished using an annual administrative budget for the purchasing function. The most common method is to start with the current budget and adjust it up or down, depending on the business forecast, the projected workload, and economic conditions.

Common Measures of Efficiency

Efficiency. Efficiency measures relate purchasing outputs to purchasing inputs. They range from two-factor measures that have one input and one output, to multifactor measures that relate several outputs to several inputs. Common two-factor measures include purchase orders per buyer, line items per buyer, dollars committed per buyer, change notices per buyer, contracts written per buyer, average open order commitment, worker hours per line item, worker hours per purchase order, worker hours per contract, administrative dollars per purchase order, administrative dollars per contract, and administrative dollars per purchase dollar.[37]

Vendor Quality and Delivery. Vendor quality measures include the percentage of items (pieces, orders, shipments, or dollar value) that are accepted or rejected; the total cost of purchasing one unit of product from a vendor; and the frequency and severity of defects. Vendor delivery is generally measured in terms of on-time, early, or late deliveries (piece, orders, shipments, or dollar value).

Material Flow Control. Reports that measure the flow of material from vendors to the buying organizations can be classified into four groups: (1) open purchase orders and their due dates, (2) past-due open orders, (3) orders that are needed immediately, and (4) ability of buyers and vendors to meet due dates.

Regulatory, Societal, and Environmental Measures. A number of measures can be used to show how a purchasing department is performing

---

[36] Ibid., p. 490.

[37] Ibid.

relative to regulatory, societal, and environmental goals. Examples include (1) purchases with small and minority-owned businesses, (2) purchases placed in labor surplus areas, and (3) number and percentage of minority employees.

Procurement Planning and Research. Generally, procurement planning and research can be evaluated on the basis of the number of procurement plans established per year (including availability and price forecasting); price forecasting accuracy (actual to forecast); lead time forecasting accuracy (actual to forecast); and the number of make-or-buy studies completed.

Competition. Competition measures the extent to which the buying organization has developed alternatives in the supply marketplace and improved purchase prices and terms. Competition measures may include annual purchase dollars, the percentage of purchases on annual contracts, and the volume of purchases placed with single source suppliers (thereby limiting competition).

Inventory. Inventory measures include inventory turnover, consignments, and inventory levels.

Transportation. Transportation measures are used to determine the expense incurred for premium transportation. Premium transportation costs are incurred when other-than-normal transportation is used.

SUMMARY

In this chapter we saw how better management of purchasing activities can lead to increased profitability. We discussed the activities that must be performed by the purchasing function and explored the implications of Just-in-Time purchasing. Because the costs of purchased materials represent a significant cost of doing business, we devoted a considerable amount of attention to the management of purchasing costs and the measurement and evaluation of purchasing performance.

In the next chapter we will see how the latest technology in order-processing and information systems can be used to improve efficiency and effectiveness throughout the logistics system, at every level of the distribution channel.

SUGGESTED READINGS

BARLOW, C. WAYNE, AND GLENN P. EISEN. *Purchasing Negotiations.* Boston, Mass.: CBI Publishing, 1983.

CAVINATO, JOSEPH L. *Purchasing and Materials Management.* St. Paul, Minn.: West Publishing, 1984.

DOBLER, DONALD W., DAVID N. BURT, AND LAMAR LEE, JR. *Purchasing and Materials Management,* 5th ed. New York: McGraw-Hill, 1990.

ELLRAM, LISA M. "The Supplier Selection Decision in Strategic Partnerships." *Journal of Purchasing and Materials Management* 26, no. 4 (Fall 1990), pp. 8–14.

GENTRY, JULIE J. *Purchasing Involvement in Transportation Decision Making.* Tempe, Ariz.: Center for Advanced Purchasing Studies/National Association of Purchasing Management, 1991.

HARRINGTON, THOMAS C., DOUGLAS M. LAMBERT, AND MARTIN CHRISTOPHER. "A Methodology for Measuring Vendor Performance," *Journal of Business Logistics* 12, no. 1 (1991), pp. 83–104.

HEINRITZ, STUART, PAUL V. FARRELL, LARRY GIUNIPERO, AND MICHAEL KOLCHIN. *Purchasing: Principles and Applications,* 8th ed. Englewood Cliffs, N.J.: Prentice Hall, 1991.

LEENDERS, MICHIEL R., HAROLD E. FEARON, AND WILBUR B. ENGLAND. *Purchasing and Materials Management,* 9th ed. Homewood, Ill.: Richard D. Irwin, 1989.

MONCZKA, ROBERT M., PHILIP L. CARTER, AND JOHN H. HOAGLAND. *Purchasing Performance: Measurement and Control. East Lansing:* Michigan State University, Graduate School of Business Administration, Division of Research, 1979.

SCHONBERGER, RICHARD J., AND JAMES P. GILBERT. "Just-in-Time Purchasing: A Challenge for U.S. Industry." *California Management Review* 26, no.1 (Fall 1983), pp. 54–68.

TERSINE, RICHARD J., AND ALBERT B. SCHWARZKOPF. "Optimal Transition Ordering Strategies with Announced Price Increases." *The International Journal of Logistics Management* 2, no. 1 (1991), pp. 26–34.

THOMPSON, KENNETH N. "Vendor Profile Analysis." *Journal of Purchasing and Materials Management* 26, no. 1 (Winter 1990), pp. 11–18.

WHITE, PHILIP D. *Decision Making in the Purchasing Process: A Report.* New York: American Management Association, 1978.

QUESTIONS AND PROBLEMS

1. Explain why supplier selection and evaluation is the most important activity in the purchasing and procurement function.
2. In a study published by the American Management Association, White discussed four buying or purchasing situations (see p. 490). How might this information be used to better manage the purchasing function?
3. International sourcing of materials is a much more difficult process than domestic sourcing. What are some of the more significant problems in international sourcing that affect the logistics manager?
4. Explain the concept of forward buying and its relationship to total cost trade-off analysis.
5. Using a format similar to that shown in Table 12–5, determine the optimal forward buy (in months) given the following information:
   a. Monthly usage is $4,000.
   b. Expected price increase is 10 percent.

c. Inventory carrying cost is 40 percent.
d. The ordering cost is $25 per order.
e. The vendor pays the freight.

6. What are the major advantages of Just-in-Time purchasing? What difficulties are possible in implementing such a system?

7. Why is cost measurement an important purchasing management activity?

8. Which of the 12 purchasing performance measures do you believe would be of the greatest use to management? Why?

Chapter 13

Order Processing and Information Systems

Objectives of This Chapter

To show how the order processing system can influence performance of the logistics function

To show how order processing systems can be used to improve customer communications and increase efficiency in many areas of logistics

To show how the order processing system can form the basis of a logistics information system

To show how the logistics information system is used for both strategic and tactical planning.

INTRODUCTION

The order processing system is the nerve center of the logistics system. A customer order serves as the communications message that sets the logistics process in motion. The speed and quality of the information flows have a direct impact on the cost and efficiency of the entire operation. Slow and erratic communications can lead to lost customers and/or excessive transportation, inventory, and warehousing costs, as well as possible production inefficiencies caused by frequent line changes. The order processing and information system forms the foundation for the logistics and corporate management information systems. It is an area that offers considerable potential for improving logistics performance.

CUSTOMER ORDER CYCLE

Six Components of the Order Cycle

The *customer order cycle* includes all of the elapsed time from the placement of the order until the product is received and placed into the customer's inventory. The typical order cycle consists of the following components: (1) order preparation and transmittal, (2) order receipt and order entry, (3) order processing, (4) warehousing picking and packing, (5) order transportation, and (6) customer delivery and unloading.

Figure 13–1 illustrates the flow associated with the order cycle. In this example, the total order cycle is eight days, from the customer's point of view. However, many manufacturers make the mistake of measuring and controlling only the portion of the order cycle that is internal to their firm. That is, they monitor only the elapsed time from receipt of the customer order until it is shipped. The shortcomings of this approach are obvious. In the example presented in Figure 13–1, the portion of the total order cycle that is internal to the manufacturer (steps 2, 3, and 4) amounts to only three of the eight days. This ratio is not unusual for companies that do not have an automated order entry and processing system. Improving the efficiency of the three-day portion of the order cycle that is "controlled"

FIGURE 13–1 Total Order Cycle: A Customer's Perspective

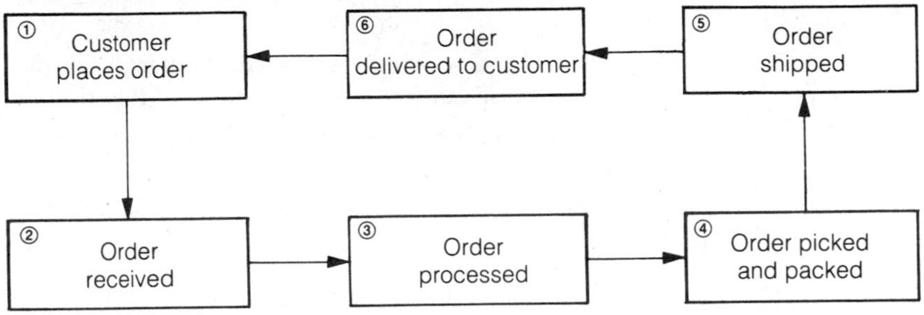

Key:

1	Order preparation and transmittal	1 day
2	Order received and entered into system	1 day
3	Order processing	1 day
4	Warehouse picking and packing	1 day
5	Transit time	3 days
6	Warehouse receiving and placing into storage	1 day
	Total order cycle time	8 days

by the manufacturer may be costly compared to eliminating a day from the five days not directly under the manufacturer's control. For example, it may be possible to reduce transit time by as much as one day by monitoring carrier performance and switching business to those carriers with the fastest and most consistent transit times.

However, a change in the method of order placement and order entry may have the potential for the most significant reduction in order cycle time. An advanced order processing system could reduce the total order cycle by as much as two days. In addition, the improved information flows could enable management to more efficiently execute the warehousing and transportation, reducing the order cycle by another one or two days.

Order Cycle Variability

In the example described in Figure 13–1, we treated the performance of order cycle components as though no variability occurred. Figure 13–2 illustrates the variability that is likely to occur for each component of the order cycle and for the total. For this illustration, we assume that each of the variable time patterns is a normal statistical distribution. However, other statistical distributions may actually be experienced. In our example, the actual order cycle could range from a low of 5 days to as many as 21 days, with the most likely length being 13 days. Variability in order cycle time is costly to the manufacturer's customer; the customer must carry safety stock to cover for possible delays or lose sales as a result of stockouts.

Return to the example in Figure 13–2. If the average order cycle time is 13 days but can be as long as 21 days, the customer must maintain additional inventory equivalent to 8 days' sales just to cover variability in lead

FIGURE 13–2 Total Order Cycle with Variability

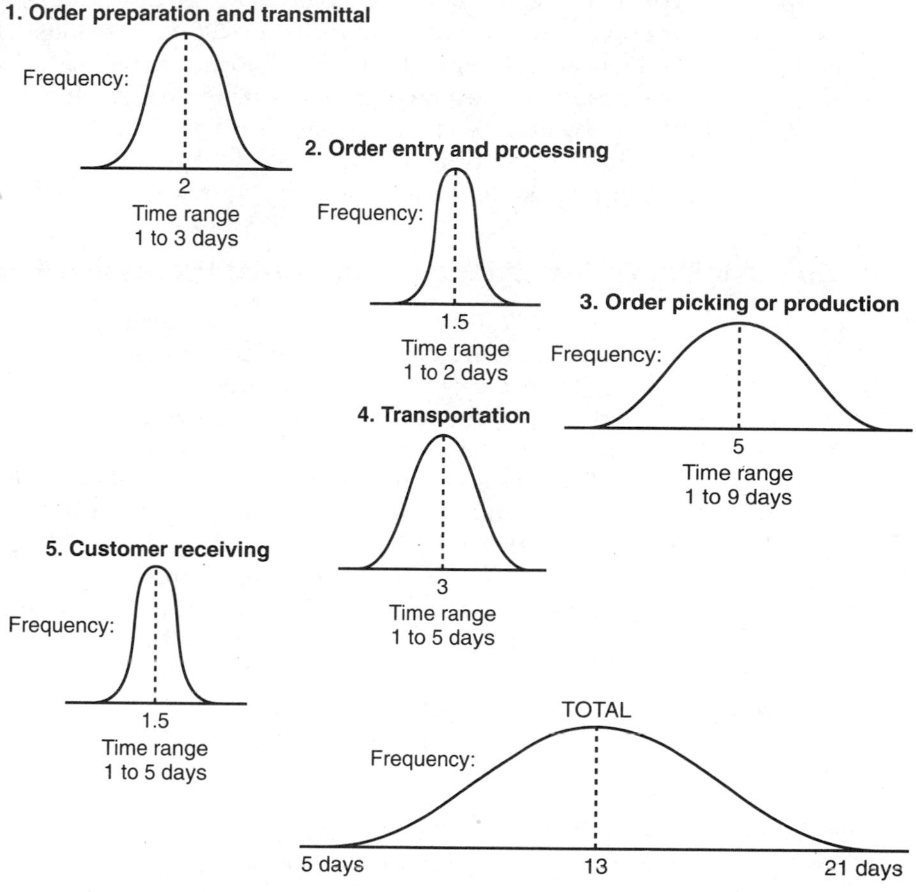

time. If daily sales equal 20 units and the company's economic order quantity is 260 units—a 13-day supply—the average cycle stock is 130 units—one-half the order quantity. The additional inventory required to cover the order cycle variability of 8 days is 160 units. Excluding demand uncertainty, average inventory will increase from 130 units to 290 units due to the variability in the order cycle.

Which has the greatest impact on the customer's inventory—a five-day reduction in the order cycle, or a five-day reduction in order cycle variability? If the customer continued to order the economic order quantity of 260 units, a five-day reduction in the order cycle would result in little or no change in inventories. The customer would simply wait five days longer before placing an order. On the other hand, if the customer ordered 160 units every time instead of 260, the average cycle stock would be 80 units rather than 130 units, but safety stock of 160 units would be required to cover the eight days of variability. The result would be a reduction in total average inventory of 50 units, from 290 to 240 units. However, a five-day reduction in order cycle variability would reduce safety stocks by 190 units and result in an average inventory of 160 units. This example should make clear why order cycle consistency is preferred to fast delivery.

In the next two sections we will look at how customer orders enter the order processing function, and the typical path taken by a customer's order.

How Do Customer Orders Enter the Firm's Order Processing Function?

Methods of Order Entry

There are a number of ways that a customer order can be placed, transmitted, and entered into a manufacturer's order processing function. Traditionally, customers wrote down orders and gave them to salespeople or mailed them to the supplier. The next level of sophistication was telephoning the order to the manufacturer's order clerk, who wrote it up. An advanced system might have customers telephoning orders to customer service representatives located at the manufacturer's headquarters and equipped with CRTs. This type of system allows the customer service representative to determine if the ordered products are available in inventory. The items are then deducted from inventory so that they are not promised to another customer. If there is a stockout on the item, the representative can arrange product substitution while the customer is still on the telephone, or can inform the customer when the product will be available. In effect, this type of system eliminates the first two days of the order cycle that is described in Figure 13–1.

Electronic Methods of Order Entry Are Becoming More Common

Electronic methods, such as an electronic terminal with information transmitted by telephone lines, and computer-to-computer hookups are becoming more widely used in order to gain the maximum speed and accuracy in order transmittal and order entry. We will discuss these types of systems in more detail later in this chapter.

Generally, rapid forms of order transmittal are more costly. However, the logistics system cannot be set in motion until the order is entered at the processing point, and an increase in order processing speed will make it possible to reduce inventories throughout the system while maintaining the desired customer service level. In addition, management can use the time it saved in order transmittal to realize opportunities in transportation consolidation. An alternative strategy is to decrease the order cycle time offered to the customer; this may allow the customer to hold less inventory.

There is a direct trade-off between inventory carrying costs and communications costs. However, the more sophisticated the communications system becomes, the more vulnerable the company becomes to any internal or external communications malfunction. This is due to the fact that, with advanced order processing systems and lower inventory levels, safety stocks

FIGURE 13–3 The Path of a Customer's Order

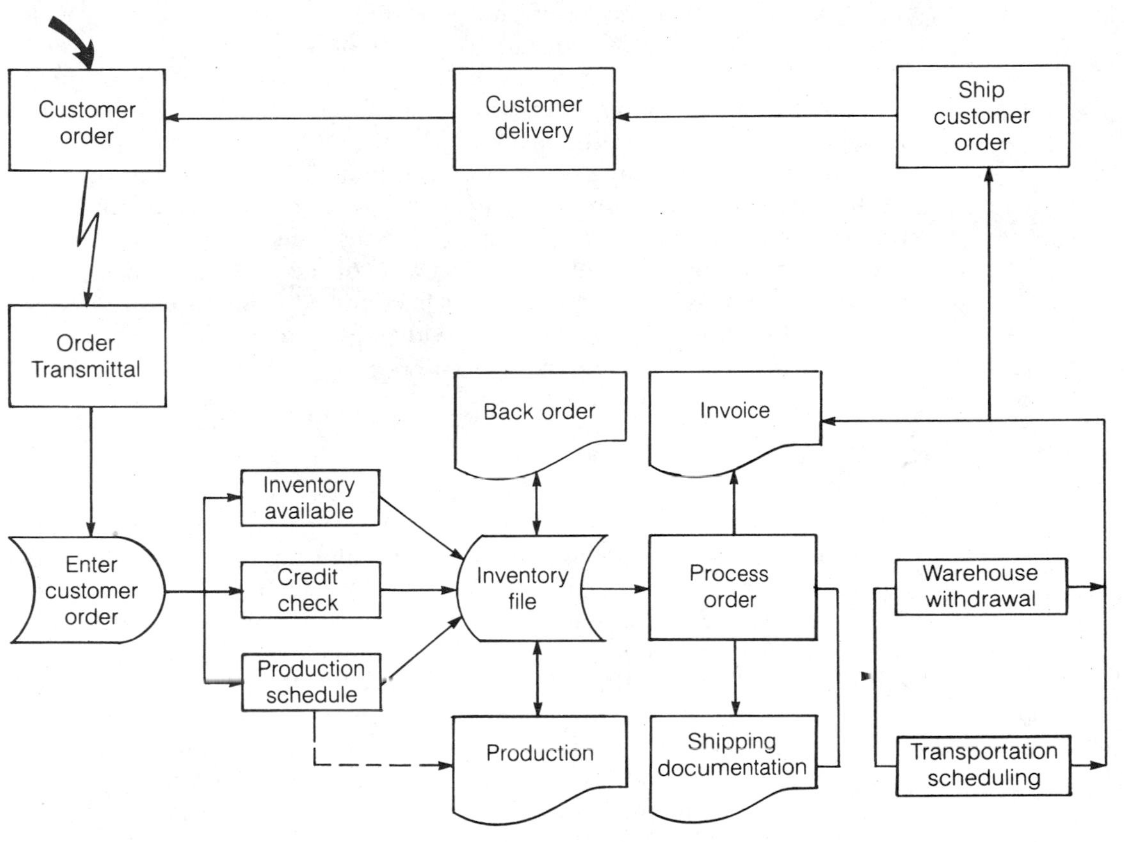

are substantially reduced, leaving the customer with minimal protection against stockouts that result from any variability in the order cycle time. In many channels of distribution, significant potential exists for using advanced order processing to improve logistics performance.

The Path of a Customer's Order

When studying a firm's order processing system, it is important to understand the information flow that begins when a customer places an order. Figure 13–3 represents one interpretation of the path that a customer's order might take. In the first step, the customer recognizes the need for certain products and transmits an order to the supplying manufacturer. We have discussed the various methods of order transmittal, and will examine them further in a later section of this chapter.

Once the manufacturer receives the order and enters it into the order processing system, it must make various checks to determine (1) if the desired product is available in inventory in the quantities ordered, (2) if the customer's credit is satisfactory to accept the order, and (3) if the product is scheduled for production if not currently in inventory. The inventory file is then updated, product is back ordered if necessary, and production is issued a report showing the inventory balance. Management can also use the information on daily sales as an input to its sales forecasting package. Order processing next provides: information to accounting for invoicing; acknowledgment of the order to send to the customer; picking and packing instructions to enable warehouse withdrawal of the product; and shipping documentation. When the product has been pulled from warehouse inventory and transportation has been scheduled, documentation is sent to accounting so that invoicing may proceed.

THE COMMUNICATIONS FUNCTION

Four Ways to Evaluate Alternative Methods of Order Transmittal

The primary function of the order processing system is to provide a communication network that links the customer and the manufacturer. Management should evaluate various methods of order transmittal for consistency of message delivery. Usually, greater inconsistency is associated with slower methods of order transmittal. Manual methods of order transmittal require more handling by individuals, and consequently there is greater chance of a communication error. Management can evaluate methods of order transmittal on the basis of speed, cost, consistency, and accuracy. Order transmittal should be as direct as possible; orders transmitted electronically rather than manually minimize the risk of human error.

In addition, the order processing system can communicate useful sales information to marketing (for market analysis and forecasting), to finance (for cash-flow planning), and to logistics or production (for production planning and scheduling—see Figure 13–4). Finally, the order processing system provides information to those employees who assign orders to warehouses, clear customer credit, update inventory files, prepare warehouse picking instructions, and prepare shipping instructions and the associated documentation. Communication is extremely important because it sets the logistics system in motion.

Advanced Order Processing Systems

Computers Have Improved Order Processing Systems

No component of the logistics function has benefited more from the application of electronic and computer technology than order entry and processing. Some advanced systems are so sophisticated that the only human effort required is to enter the order and monitor the results.

FIGURE 13–4 Management Information Provided by an Advanced Order Processing System

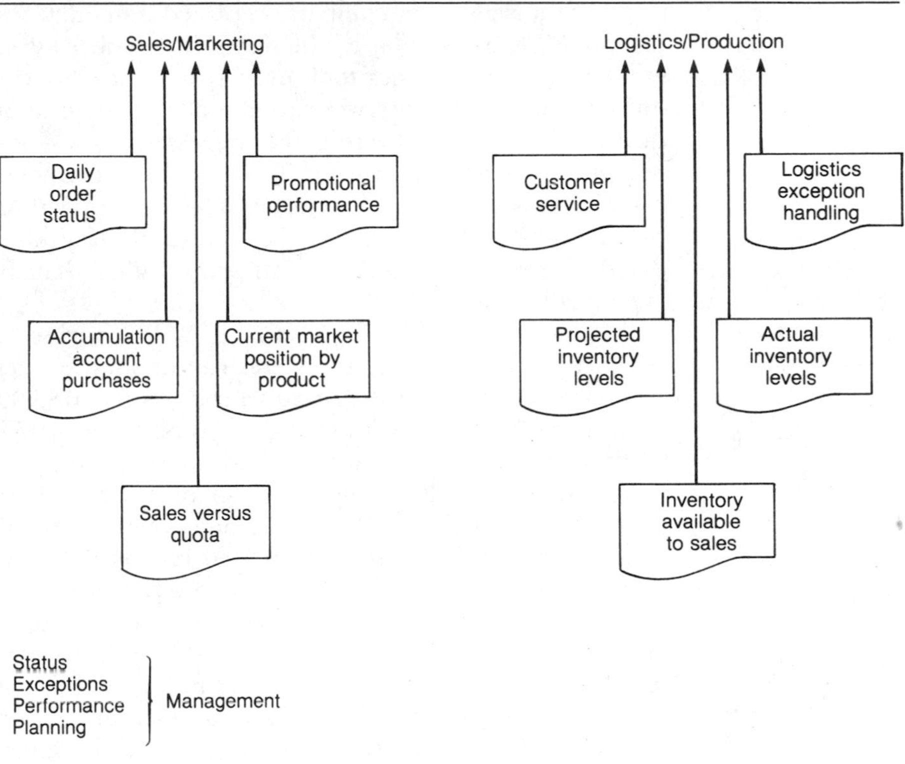

SOURCE: American Telephone and Telegraph Company, *Business Marketing,* Market Management Division.

At one level of advanced order processing systems, customers and salespeople transmit orders to distribution centers or corporate headquarters via a toll-free number. The order clerk is equipped with a data terminal and can both enter and access information on a real-time basis. As soon as the order clerk enters the customer code, the order format, including the customer's name, billing address, credit code, and shipping address, is displayed on the screen. The clerk receives the rest of the order information verbally and enters it on the terminal; it is displayed along with the header information. Deviations from standard procedure, such as products on promotion, special pricing arrangements, and allocations, may be highlighted on the CRT (also referred to as the "screen") to ensure that the order clerk grants them special attention. The system can match order quantity against a list of minimum shipment quantities to ensure that the order meets the necessary specifications. The clerk may then read the order back to the customer. When the order meets all criteria for accuracy and completeness, it is released for processing.

A major chemical company replaced a manual system with a system using CRT input similar to the one just described. Prior to the new order entry system, employees took orders over the phone and recorded them on a form. The orders were then transferred to another form for keypunching, and finally were batch-processed into the system. The CRT order entry system was cost-justified based on its savings over the manual system. As a result, sales increased by 23 percent with no increase in order processing costs. An additional benefit was that customer billing took place the day after the product was shipped, rather than five days later. This improved cash flow.

American Hospital Supply Corp. Uses Advanced Order Processing System to Increase Profits

American Hospital Supply Corp. (AHS) provides an example of how advanced order processing systems can be used to increase market share and profitability. AHS distributes products from 8,500 manufacturers to more than 100,000 health care providers. In the 1970s, the company established computer links with its customers and suppliers. Using terminals provided by AHS, hospitals can enter orders directly to an assigned AHS distribution center. In addition, customers can inquire about the availability of product and determine anticipated recovery on stockouts. As a result, hospitals are no longer required to orally communicate their orders to AHS. The technology enabled AHS to cut both customer inventories and its own, improve fill rates, reduce order cycle times, and receive better terms from suppliers for purchasing in higher volumes. In addition, the company's market share increased dramatically. Even more important, AHS often locked out rival distributors that did not have direct communications with hospitals. AHS analyzes the industry data that it collects in order to spot order trends and customer needs more quickly.[1]

Advanced Order Processing at E. R. Squibb and Sons, Inc.

E. R. Squibb and Sons, Inc., provides another example of a firm that has successfully implemented an advanced order processing system. In 1978, a decentralized, batch-oriented order entry system was replaced with an on-line, distributed computer network called SOLIDS (Squibb On-Line Inventory and Distribution System).[2]

Orders are entered on CRTs to a computerized system that integrates inventory and information management. Prior to the new system, the company's 125,000 customers, predominantly pharmacies and hospitals, mailed orders to Squibb or placed them with sales representatives who mailed or telephoned them to one of the company's nine distribution centers. The orders were accumulated in groups of 50 to 150, keypunched, and batch processed in order to price the products, sort the line items in

---

[1]Catherine L. Harris, "Information Power," *Business Week,* no. 2916 (October 14, 1985), p. 109. (Note: AHS is now part of Baxter Corp.)

[2]This example is taken from "Squibb's New Order Entry System," *Distribution* 79, no. 3 (March 1980), pp. 67–70.

optimum picking sequences, and print customer invoices. Stockouts were automatically back ordered by the computer, which transmitted the day's shipments and inventory position to the data center each evening.

The major shortcomings of the system were:

- More time elapsed between order placement and entering the order than in order processing and order picking and packing.
- Data could be transmitted only from distribution centers to the data center. Customer and product information on file at the data center had to be sent to the distribution centers by mail, telex, or telephone.
- The availability of inventory was not known when the order was accepted, and customers did not know about stockouts until they received the shipment.[3]

Squibb considered three options for the new system:

> In preparing for SOLIDS, Squibb's Planning and Systems Department ran feasibility studies on three concepts for order entry/inventory management/information management systems. The first was a decentralized system of independent batch machines (the existing concept for order entry alone). The second was a totally centralized system in which input/output terminals would be directly linked to the data center's mainframes. The third was an on-line, distributed computer network.
>
> Even if the batch computers were to be replaced with interactive systems at the distribution centers, the first alternative was relatively expensive and still lacked the desired communications capability.
>
> With the second alternative, the dedicated telephone lines would have entailed extremely high communications costs (although hardware costs would have been substantially lower), and there would have been no local storage and control of distribution information. Also, a hardware malfunction would halt the distribution system nationally.[4]

After one year of study thc company selected alternative three—a network of interactive minicomputers linked to the data center for two-way transmission, using dial-up telephone lines:

> Each satellite distribution center is a complete warehouse and shipping point. The procedure at the satellites is exactly the same as the master distribution center, even though the actual order processing is done by the master computer, which may be located as much as 1,500 miles away.
>
> The disk drives controlled by the master computer store a number of data files. Among them are the Product Information File (including for each line item its name, package, size, inventory status, price, and weight) and Customer Information File (including name, address, credit rating).
>
> The Product Information File is common to all distribution centers; the Customer Information File at the master computer contains only customers

[3] Ibid., pp. 67–68.

[4] Ibid., pp. 67–68, 70.

served by the master center and its satellite (the satellite having no data files of its own). The central product inventory and customer information files for the entire Squibb system—those that must be accessed by other data processing systems running on the mainframes—are maintained at the Data Center.

The on-line configuration of SOLIDS offers several major advantages over a batch system. Order data are verified on the CRT screen at the time of entry rather than after keypunching. Direct data entry reduces the possibility of transcription errors. (In the batch system, the order information was first recorded on a paper form and then transposed [entered] by the keypunch operator.)

Prompting from SOLIDS ensures that all data necessary to complete an order are collected from customers while they are still on the phone. In the on-line mode, order and inventory transactions update files as they are entered and all information in files is immediately available for inquiry.

The master/satellite configuration offers identical SOLIDS service at nine locations, with computers at only the five master centers. There can be as many as three satellites linked to each master, so that up to 11 or more distribution centers can be added to SOLIDS with additional investment in only the low-cost video and printing terminals and leased lines.

SOLIDS can then be easily and economically extended to new distribution centers to maintain or improve customer service as distribution patterns change. System backup has been increased, too. When a master computer temporarily shuts down, SOLIDS service can be switched over to another distribution center. (Downtime hasn't been long enough to make this necessary).[5]

First Year Benefits of the New System

The first year benefits of the new system included the following:

- *Increased same-day shipments.* These increased from 59 percent to 75 percent with all other non-back-ordered shipments leaving the following day.
- *Higher order entry productivity.* Order takers at the Metro distribution center, for example, now average one minute of video terminal time per order.
- *Improved customer relations.* Telephone customers can be given prices, special offers, stock status, and other information over the telephone during their initial call.
- *More informative invoices.* Longer descriptions of line items, itemized calculation of figures, more data for sales representatives, reference to the terminal operator who entered the order, special offer information, and time entered. (Some of the additional information, of course, is of more interest to Squibb than to its customers.)
- *More accurate orders.* This has been accomplished through on-line verification and elimination of a data entry step.
- *Lower system operating cost.* Substantial savings have been achieved through consolidation of distribution sites and order entry positions,

[5] Ibid., p. 70.

improved efficiency, and elimination of redundancy in order processing.[6]

An Advanced System at Manville Canada, Inc.

Another company that has successfully implemented an advanced order transmittal, order entry, and order processing system is Manville Canada, Inc.[7] In 1978 Manville Canada invested $750,000 in an on-line system that paid for itself in less than two years.

Prior to the implementation of the new system, a customer would telephone an order for fiberglass home insulation—one of Manville Canada's products—to one of three customer service clerks located in Toronto. One of these clerks was assigned to the telephone, while the other two were kept busy writing orders. The telephone clerk received the order and passed it on to one of the others for processing. Information required to complete the order was obtained from different files in many locations and manually filled in on each order set.

When this process was completed, the clerks sent the order to the order and billing department, where it was typed and sent to the shipping location. Once the order was shipped, shipping returned the order form and a shipping document to the customer service clerks, who verified and forwarded them to the billing department to be typed again.

The three customer service clerks could process an average of 12 orders per day, with overtime required during peak periods. This piecemeal method of handling customer orders created a considerable amount of pressure and resulted in a relatively high incidence of human error.

With the new system, customers telephone orders to customer service clerks, who enter the name of the customer on a video display screen. At this point, all pertinent customer information is displayed on the screen and applied to the order. When the product is entered, all inventory, price, and other related information about that item is displayed and applied to the order.

When all items have been added to the order, the total weights and percentages of a truckload shipment are calculated. If the order is for less than a truckload quantity, the customer is told the cost of increasing the order to truckload as well as the discount that would occur. In this way, customer service clerks provide an inside sales function. The computer also calculates the total value of the order and compares this to the credit limit that has been established for that customer. If the securement amount is greater than the credit limit, the order is placed on credit hold pending review by the credit manager.[8]

---

[6] Ibid.

[7] This example was furnished by Donald J. Allison, former vice president–corporate business logistics, Manville Canada, Inc.

Once the order is completed, the shipping documents, such as packing slips and bills of lading, are printed at the shipping locations. At each shipping location, the shipping date, along with such data as the quantity shipped, carrier, carrier number, and products substituted, is entered into a terminal. At this point inventory files are automatically updated.

The customer service clerk reviews and verifies all information on the order and releases the order for billing. The billing is then printed out automatically by the computer—in French and English—and mailed to the customer. The computer also generates accounts receivable and sales detail reports. If required, a back order is created.

Benefits associated with the new system are numerous. Edits built into the system reduced billing errors by as much as 85 percent. With a 5 percent reasonability factor built into the system, it is able to detect errors made by clerks as they are processing the order through its various stages. The system has also streamlined Manville Canada's organization by 19 people and has largely eliminated time- and space-consuming typing and filing. The level of customer service has been improved. In addition, the company's cash flow has been accelerated by several days because of the system's ability to generate customer billings the same day the shipment is made. The company has also integrated the system with its inventory management system.

As orders are placed and shipped, inventory backlogs are automatically updated. This feature provides accurate data for production scheduling and a great variety of other reports: marketing-securement and billing reports, exception reports showing beyond-normal transportation costs, and carrier revenue reports.

Interfaces are also possible between similar systems that have been set up in the Toronto-, Montreal-, and Edmondton-based operations. This allows orders to be placed from any one region to any other region in the Canadian operation. It also permits total control of the order by the customer service clerk who has responsibility for that customer regardless of where in Canada the order will be shipped. The flow of an order through the Manville Canada system is shown in Figure 13–5.

General Motors Considers an Advanced Communications System

The auto industry also realizes the advantages of advanced communications systems. General Motors' new Saturn project was designed to integrate communications from consumers to vendors (see Figure 13–6).[9] The original plan for Saturn was to have customers sit down at a computer

---

[8]The company refers to orders received as securements. As orders come in, they are accumulated, measured, and reported on securement reports. Once the customer is billed, the order is counted as a sale.

[9]This example is adapted from Eric Gelman, Richard Manning, Daniel Pedersen, and Nikki Finke Greenberg, "Wheels of the Future," *Newsweek* CV, no. 24 (June 17, 1985), pp. 69–71.

FIGURE 13–5 An Advanced Order Processing System, Implemented at Manville Canada, Inc.

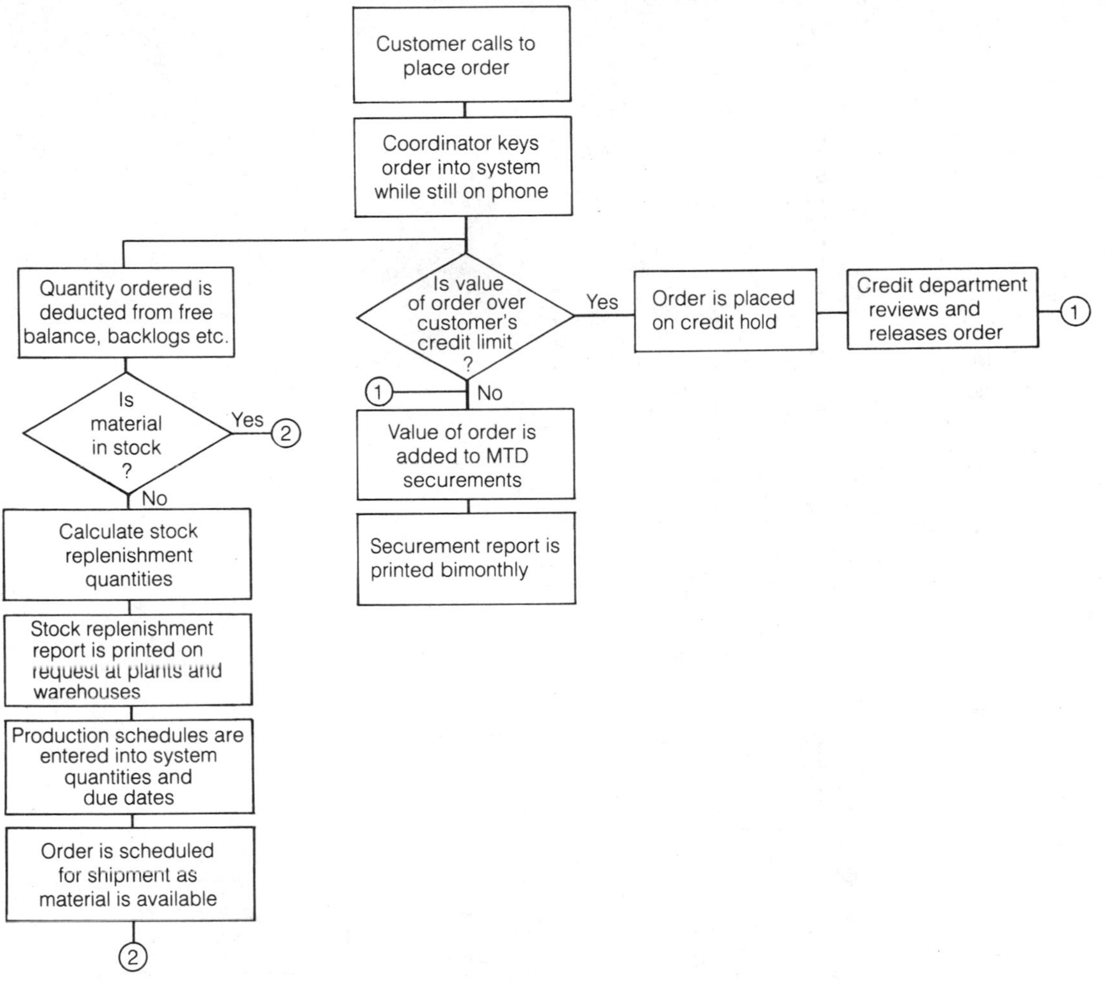

SOURCE: Donald J. Allison, former vice president–corporate business logistics, Manville Canada, Inc.

terminal in a dealer's showroom and, with a salesperson's help, select their options. If a consumer does not smoke, he or she can order a dashboard with no ashtray and no lighter. Windows can be tinted or untinted. Other choices include carpeting, radios/disc players and speaker systems, tires, colors, digital speedometer, and cruise control, to name just a few. After reviewing the choices, the consumer will press the "enter" key. Then the order will be released to the Electronic Data Systems (EDS) communications network, a vast array of computers linked by 18 Information Process-

FIGURE 13–5 *(continued)*

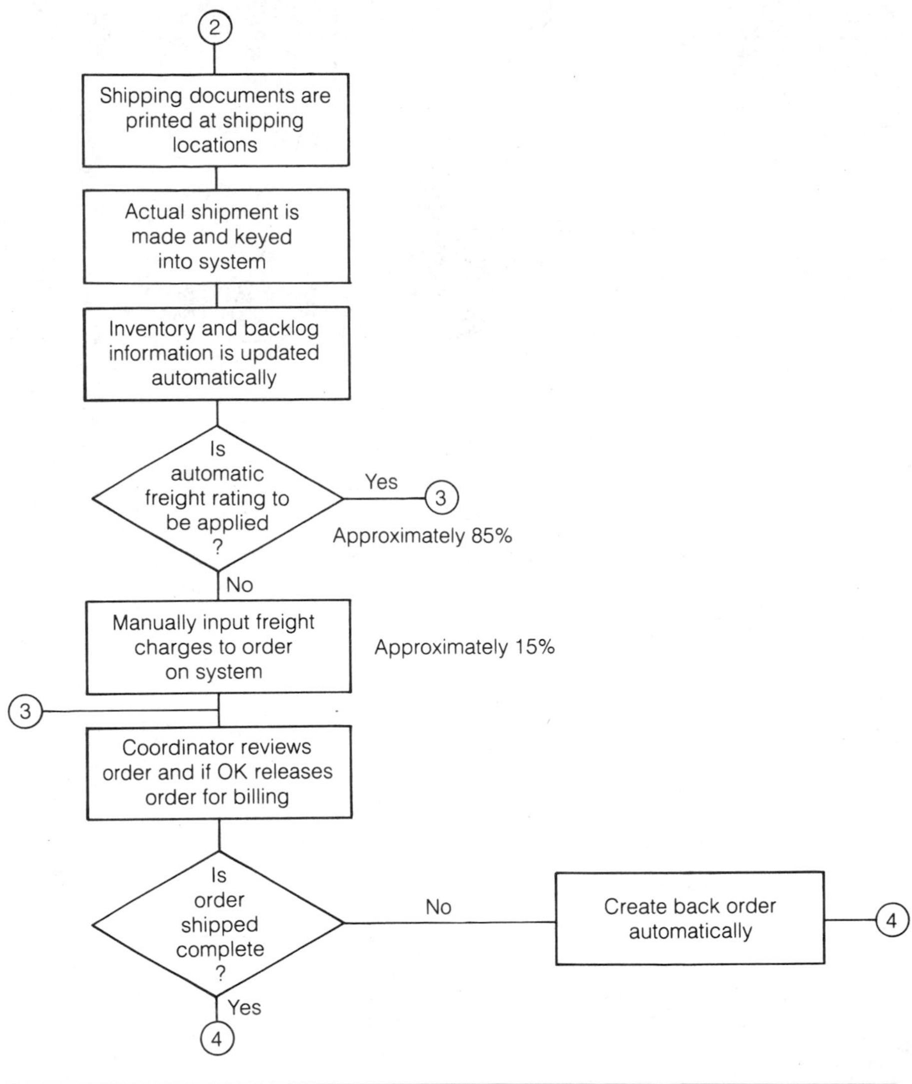

ing Centers around the United States. Computers at the Saturn plant will receive the order and give it a number and an assembly date. Then orders will be released to GM's suppliers, who will build their 15,000 parts on a no-inventory system; each is made when ordered, not before.

At the Saturn showroom, the salesperson will use the EDS network to check the consumer's credit, to arrange GMAC financing, and/or to obtain

FIGURE 13–5 *(concluded)*

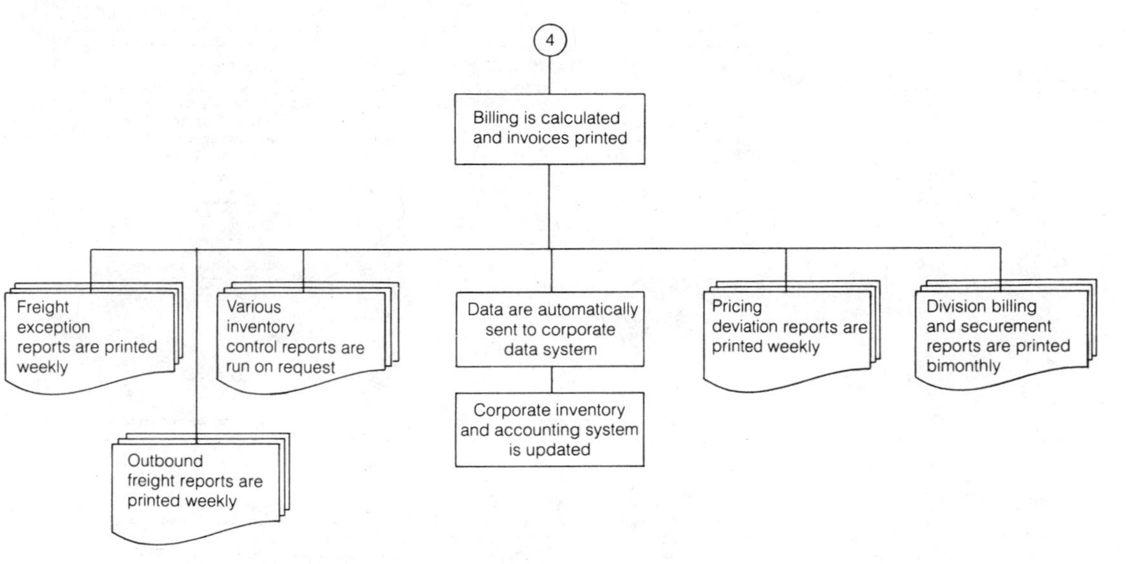

insurance from GM's insurance subsidiary (MIC). The consumer will take delivery of the car in a week.

On the Saturn assembly line, a radio transponder will be attached to the frame of each car. As the car moves down the assembly line, the transponder will signal to computers and robots: "I am job #123456 and I need a six-cylinder engine. . . . I am job #123456 and I need six spark plugs. . . . I am job #123456 and I need an untinted windshield. . . . a blue paint job. . . ."[10]

As each car is loaded onto a truck for shipment, an EDS computer will signal the dealer that the car is on the way, instruct GMAC to start finance charges, MIC to start insurance premiums, and release payments to the supplier for the parts. All of this will be accomplished at a savings to the consumer of $2,000 in the car's price.

A *Newsweek* article probed the impact of the new GM strategy:

> "Have you thought what happens if Saturn succeeds?" asks David Cole, director of the Office for the Study of Automotive Transportation at the University of Michigan. "It means it cuts 75 to 80 percent out of labor, including management. The thrust for everyone else in the industry will be to look at what EDS and GM have done and [then] make a decision as to whether to leave [the industry]—or change, the way EDS and GM have. It means that the United

[10] Ibid., p. 66.

FIGURE 13–6 GM Discovers Advanced Communications Systems

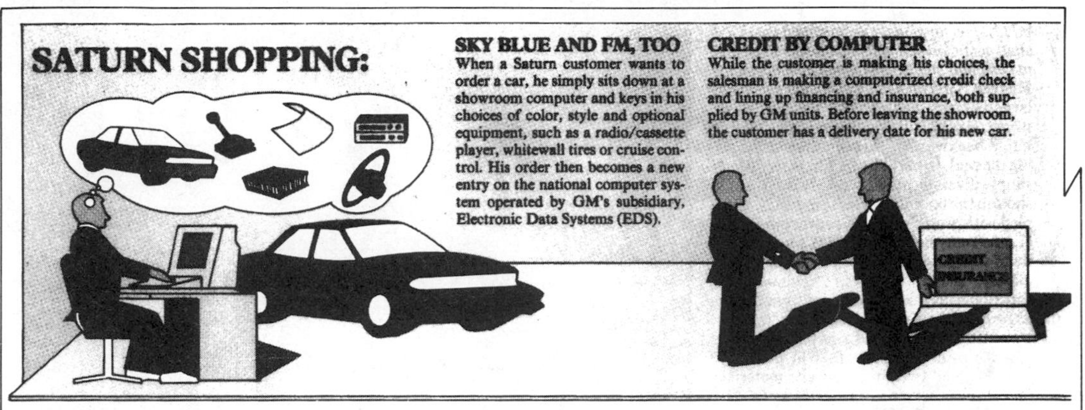

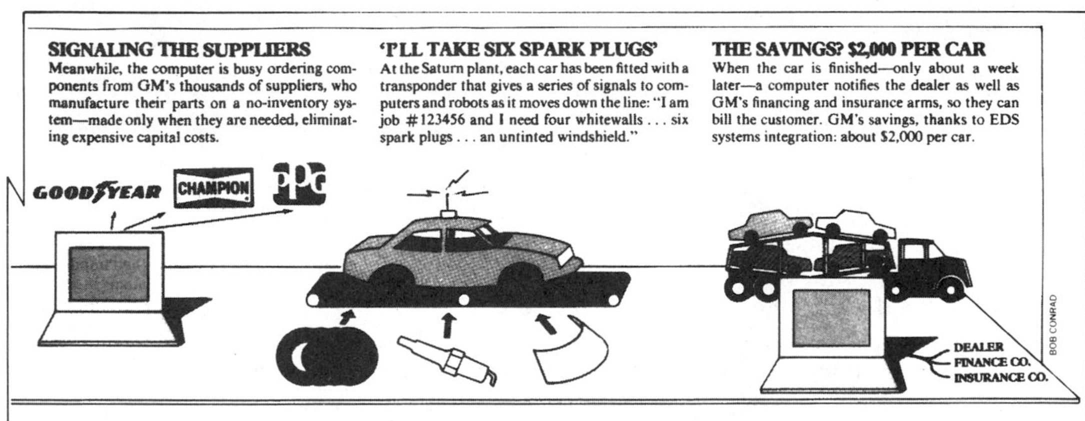

SOURCE: Eric Gelman, Richard Manning, Daniel Pedersen, and Nikki Finke Greenberg, "Wheels of the Future," *Newsweek* CV, no. 24 (June 17, 1985), pp. 66–67.

States becomes the premier technology power in the world. The only way the United States can surpass the competition, which can pay its work force one half or one tenth what we pay ours, is by out-teching them. That is what EDS and GM are working toward."

Beyond the factory floor, the flow of information will allow dinosaur GM to move in the marketplace with the agility of an athlete. "Think what access to information can do," says New York auto industry analyst Maryann Keller of Vilas-Fischer Associates. "By sitting down at a computer, people running GM will be able to see what colors are selling, what components are selling. If you want to look at the number of orders to date for two-door cars, you log into the computer. Now you've just done what it previously would have taken a market researcher three to six weeks to do. You don't end up with 20,000 unsalable cars."[11]

The Order Sets the Logistics System in Motion

Generally, the more rapid a form of order transmittal is, the more it costs. Likewise, on-line order entry may be more costly than simpler systems when viewed strictly on the basis of price. However, the logistics system cannot be set into motion until the order is entered at the processing point; an increase in order processing speed, accuracy, and consistency will make it possible to reduce inventories throughout the system while maintaining the desired customer service level. In addition, management can use the time saved in order transmittal and entry to realize transportation consolidation opportunities. As an alternative strategy, the manufacturer could decrease the order cycle time offered to the customer, which would allow the customer to hold less inventory. In addition, a reduction in the order cycle time would result in lower in-transit inventories if the customer changed the order quantity. But we have already seen that most customers prefer a consistent order cycle to a shorter one. Therefore, in the event of a decrease in lead time due to faster order transmittal and entry, a manufacturer's best strategy would be to keep the planning time made available and reduce costs by lowering inventory levels and reducing freight costs. The total reduction in the manufacturer's costs will more than offset the increased communications expenditures.

Inside Sales/Telemarketing

Benefits of Telemarketing

Inside sales/telemarketing is an extension of the automated order processing systems we have discussed. It enables the firm to maintain contact with existing customers who are not large enough to justify frequent sales visits; increase contact with large, profitable customers; and efficiently explore new market opportunities. Customer contacts made by telephone from an inside sales group will achieve the desired market coverage in an economical, cost-effective manner. In addition, the use of data terminals for direct order input integrates inside sales with logistics operations. One of the major cost advantages of inside sales/telemarketing comes from the associated logistics efficiencies.

Inside sales/telemarketing can be cost-justified on the basis of increased sales, reduced expenses, or a combination of the two. If management desires to build sales volume, it may not reduce the selling expenses associated with the existing sales force. Inside sales may simply increase the firm's total selling expenses, and increased sales volume will be required to justify the additional expense. In most cases, however, expense reductions are possible if the program is implemented correctly. One method of improving

[11] Ibid., pp. 66–67.

efficiency is to place all small customers on scheduled deliveries in order to reduce transportation costs and other logistics costs. Justifying the expenditure for inside sales solely on projected sales increases is risky, to say the least. Many factors may prevent the company from achieving the desired sales increase, which may cause management to abandon the program in periods of financial difficulty. Programs that increase profitability by reducing costs will be retained, however.

An important step in cost justification is to conduct a pilot project. In this way, management can substantiate and project the program costs, as well as the cost savings from logistics and selling efficiencies, and the profit contribution from sales increases, for the national program. States or other market areas that are comparable in past sales history, market penetration, competition, and other important variables should be selected as control markets (old system) and test markets (proposed inside sales program). Control and test markets should also reflect the firm's national business so that it can make projections based on the pilot.

Electronic Data Interchange

Sometimes information is entered directly to the computer. CPU (central processing unit) to CPU ordering systems are referred to as electronic data interchange.

Defintion of EDI

Electronic data interchange (EDI) can be defined as "the interorganizational exchange of business documentation in structured, machine-processable form,"[12] or simply, one computer communicating directly with another computer. As illustrated in Figure 13–7, EDI replaces verbal and written communications with electronic ones.

Information can be transmitted between parties in two ways. As shown in Figure 13–8, EDI communications can be direct to others ("one-to-many") or through a third party provider ("many-to-many"). An example of a "one-to-many" EDI system is as follows:

> A manufacturer writes its replenishment orders to a computer file instead of printing them. At a mutually agreed-on time, it connects this computer by telephone line—either leased or dial-up—to a processing function and then to the supplier's machine. After an initial "handshake" routine, which establishes the identities of the machines, the manufacturer's computer forwards the relevant orders to the supplier's computer.
>
> Next, the supplier processes the orders, perhaps sending an acknowledgment to the sender. At the same time, the supplier's system generates packing notes and associated documentation for the warehouse and carrier, then produces its invoices as a computer file and forwards them to the manufacturer.

---

[12] Margaret A. Emmelhainz, *Electronic Data Interchange: A Total Management Guide* (New York: Van Nostrand Reinhold, 1990), p. 4.

FIGURE 13–7 EDI versus Traditional Methods

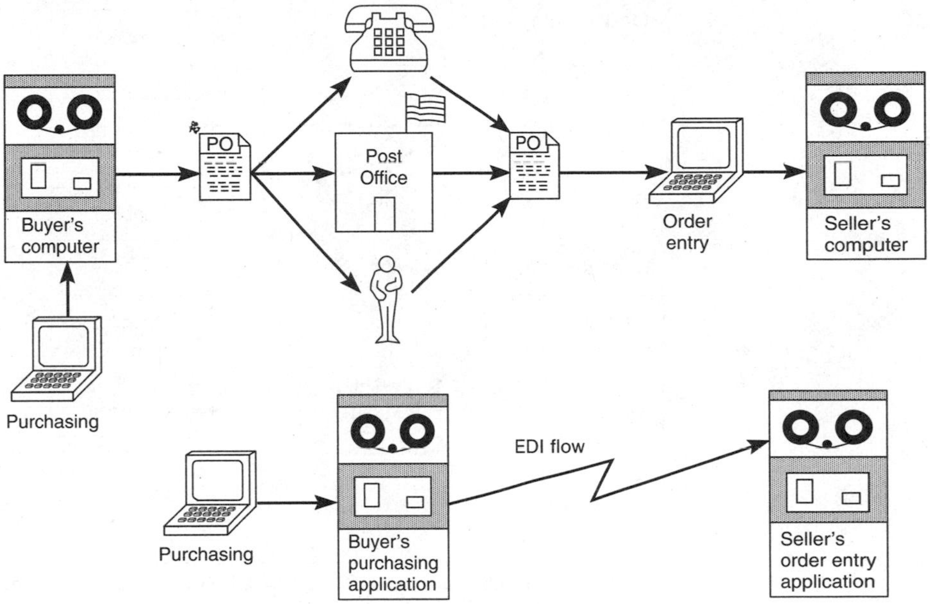

SOURCE: Margaret A. Emmelhainz, *Electronic Data Interchange: A Total Management Guide* (New York: Van Nostrand Reinhold, 1990), p. 5.

The manufacturer, in turn, sends its remittance advice electronically and may even pay the bills through a bank clearinghouse system.[13]

EDI can be combined with other computer systems such as artificial intelligence (AI):

Benetton Combines EDI with Artificial Intelligence

At the Italian clothing manufacturer Benetton, for example, computers not only determine what will be included in upcoming production runs, but also designate optimum routing for all finished goods.

At each Benetton store, the point-of-sale cash registers maintain a running inventory of item sales, which they transmit via EDI to computers in branch offices. The branch offices, in turn, transmit the data to the central office computer, which uses artificial intelligence and a modeling program to make decisions on production runs. If red sweaters are selling fast, the computer tells the manufacturing system to design and produce more red sweaters. The system then determines how the shipments will be routed to the stores, freeing the

[13]Lisa H. Harrington, "The ABCs of EDI," *Traffic Management* 29, no. 8 (August 1990), p. 51.

FIGURE 13–8 Typical EDI Configurations

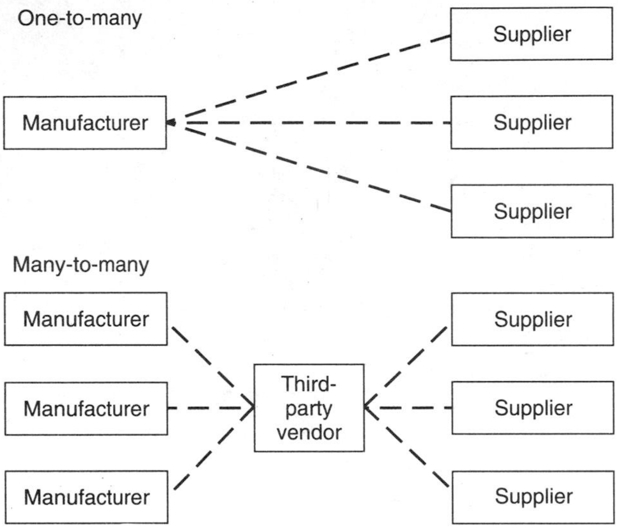

One-to-many

Manufacturer	←	Supplier
	←	Supplier
	←	Supplier

Many-to-many

Manufacturer	→	Third-party vendor	←	Supplier
Manufacturer	→		←	Supplier
Manufacturer	→		←	Supplier

SOURCE: GE Information Service, as reported in Lisa H. Harrington, "The ABCs of EDI," *Traffic Management* 29, no. 8 (August 1990), p. 51.

traffic department—which consists of only six people—to spend its time researching new routings and handling problems.[14]

EDI applications in logistics are growing among all firms but especially among *Fortune* 500 manufacturers and merchandisers. A *Traffic Management* study conducted in 1989 found that approximately one-half of a randomly selected group of its readers were utilizing EDI technology. The activities where EDI was employed most frequently included shipment tracing, purchase order transmittal, sending freight bills to customers, and obtaining transportation rates/tariffs.[15]

The many uses of EDI and the resulting benefits that arise from such systems have resulted in increased usage of EDI. As stated by John Naisbitt, the author of *Megatrends:* "The global information economy of the future will rest on a global network and EDI will be behind this."[16] Examples of EDI usage and its benefits include applications in manufacturing, merchandising, and service industries.

---

[14] Ibid.

[15] "EDI—The Wave of the Future," *Traffic Management* 28, no. 8 (August 1989), pp. 50–55.

[16] John Naisbitt, quoted in *Input EDI Reporter* (November 1988), p. 3.

Oregon Steel Mills, a small manufacturer of steel plate used in construction and military applications, implemented EDI in its traffic department. The firm, utilizing only PCs, transmitted bills of lading electronically to its major rail carriers. Errors were reduced, railcar tracing took minutes instead of hours, manpower requirements in the traffic department were reduced, and customer service levels improved.[17]

Computers have been utilized in warehouse layout and design, shipping and receiving, order picking systems, and sorting systems. In recent years, the public warehousing industry has implemented a system called Warehouse Information Network System (WINS). WINS allows direct communication between the users and providers of public warehousing services. The messages that can be transmitted directly between computers include information on shipping orders, inventory status, warehouse activity levels, warehouse stock transfer shipments, and other administrative matters.[18] Pillsbury Co., the grocery manufacturer, has employed WINS successfully. Utilizing this EDI technique, Pillsbury reduced error rates by 35 percent within its network of 75 public warehouses.[19]

In the retailing sector, EDI has proven to be extremely beneficial:

> Wal-Mart was able to increase turnover by 30 percent, reduce order cycle time by 50 percent, and increase return on investment by 30 percent through the use of electronic data interchange to coordinate with suppliers. Levi Strauss decreased fabric inventory by 67 percent on one of their lines by an EDI linkup with its suppliers. J. C. Penney's sales on certain products increased 59 percent while inventory was reduced 20 percent from customer linkups.[20]

EDI Uses in Transportation

The labor-intensive nature of the transportation sector and its heavy paperwork demands made the transport industry one of the first to turn to EDI. The following list illustrates the degree to which EDI is being used by transportation carriers:

- Union Pacific conducts 80 percent of its interline transactions electronically.
- Carolina Freight Carriers transmits approximately 1,200 customer invoices electronically each week.
- Over 70 percent of the interline waybill traffic on 13 railroads is handled electronically.
- RAILING Corp., an Association of American Railroads subsidiary, has a computer data base that contains the industry's entire inventory

[17] "EDI Proves 'Godsend' to One-Man Department," *Traffic Management* 28, no. 8 (August 1989), pp. 56–67.

[18] Gene R. Nelson, "And Now WINS!" *Warehousing Review,* October 1984, p. 11.

[19] "EDI in the Warehouse: Cutting Errors 35 Percent," *Traffic Management* 28, no. 8 (August 1989), pp. 59–60.

[20] Martha C. Cooper, Richard H. Goodspeed, and Charles B. Lounsbury, "Logistics as an Element of Marketing Strategy Both Inside and Outside the Firm," *Proceedings of the Annual Conference of the Council of Logistics Management,* vol. I (1988), pp. 69–70.

of railcars, containers, and trailers; it receives electronic reports of over 60 percent of car movements in the United States.
- A customer of Roadway Express has eliminated all paper flow between itself and the motor carrier. Roadway receives payments from the customer electronically, based on direct data transmission.[21]

EDI has become very important and widely used within the channels of distribution for consumer and industrial goods. A major discounter, Gold Circle Stores, converted to 100 percent bar code scanning.[22] Firms such as Kmart, General Motors, Ford, DuPont, Shell Oil, and Whirlpool use EDI for the majority of their products as they move within their respective channels of distribution.[23]

Electronic Mail

A variation of EDI, *electronic mail,* has also become an important form of data transmission:

> Electronic mail involves electronic transmission of a variety of data, sometimes involving a computer, but often not. EDI *always* involves one computer in contact with at least one other, usually transmitting specific documents such as invoices, waybills, or purchase orders.[24]

The electronic mail market is a multibillion dollar business that has exhibited tremendous growth during the past decade. One of the major reasons for the growth rate, in addition to the speed and accuracy of data transmission, is cost savings. United Van Lines of St. Louis has been using electronic mail for several years and has achieved significant cost savings as a result. Under its previous manual systems, United Van Lines spent several dollars to transmit a single communication. With electronic mail, the cost has been reduced to 30 cents per transmission.

Integrating Order Processing and the Company's Logistics Management Information System

The Order Processing System Initiates Many Activities

The order processing system initiates such logistics activities as:

- Determining the transportation mode, carrier, and loading sequence.
- Inventory assignment and preparing picking and packing lists.
- Warehouse picking and packing.
- Updating the inventory file, subtracting actual products picked.
- Automatically printing replenishment lists.

---

[21] Ibid., pp. 49–52.

[22] See "Discounters Commit to Bar-Code Scanning," *Chain Store Age Executive* 61, no. 9 (September 1985), pp. 49–50.

[23] Bill Maraschiello, "EDI: An End to the 'Paper Chase,'" *Handling & Shipping Management* 26, no. 11 (October 1985), p. 52.

[24] Ibid., p. 48.

- Preparing shipping documents (a bill of lading if using a common carrier).
- Shipping the product to the customer.

Other computerized order processing applications include maintaining inventory levels, and preparing productivity reports, financial reports, and special management reports.

Order Processing Provides Important Information to the MIS

Processing an order necessitates the flow of information from one department to another, as well as the referencing or accessing of several files or data bases—such as customer credit status, inventory availability, and transportation schedules. The information system may be fully automated or manual; most are somewhere in between. Depending on the sophistication of the order processing system and the corporate management information system (MIS), the quality and speed of the information flow will vary, affecting the manufacturer's ability to achieve transportation consolidations and the lowest possible inventory levels. Generally, manual systems are very slow and error prone. The time required to complete various activities tends to be quite long and variable, and information delays occur frequently. Such a system seriously restricts a company's ability to implement integrated logistics management—specifically, to reduce total costs while maintaining or improving customer service. Some common problems include the inability to detect pricing errors, access timely credit information, or determine inventory availability. Negative impacts that occur as a result include invoice errors, payment delays, and inappropriate rejection of an order due to incorrect inventory information. Lost sales and higher costs combine to reduce the manufacturer's profitability.

Indeed, timely and accurate information has value. Information delays hamper the completion of all activities that follow them in the process. Automating and integrating the order process frees time and reduces the likelihood of information delays. Automation helps managers integrate the logistics system and allows them to reduce costs through reductions in inventory and freight rates. The communications network is clearly a key factor in achieving least total cost logistics.

Basic Need for Information

Benefits of a Logistics MIS

A logistics management information system is necessary in order to provide management with the knowledge to exploit new markets; to make changes in packaging design; to choose between common, contract, or private carriage; to increase or decrease inventories; to determine the profitability of customers; to establish profitable customer service levels; to choose between public and private warehousing; and to determine the number of field warehouses and the extent to which the order processing system should be automated. To make these strategic decisions, management must know how costs and revenue will change given the alternatives being considered.

Once management has made a decision, it must evaluate performance on a routine basis in order to determine (1) if the system is operating in control and at a level consistent with original profit expectations, and (2) if current operating costs justify an examination of alternative systems. This is referred to as *operational decision making*. The order processing system can be a primary source of information for both strategic and operational decision making.

An advanced order processing system is capable of providing a wealth of information to various departments within the organization. Terminals for data access can be made available to logistics management, production management, and sales/marketing management. The system can provide a wide variety of reports on a regularly scheduled basis, as well as status reports on request. It can also accommodate requests for all current reports, as well as a variety of data including customer order history, order status, and market and inventory position.

Designing the Information System

Knowledge of Customer Needs Is the First Step in System Design

The design of a logistics management information system should begin with a survey of customer needs and a determination of standards of performance for meeting these needs. Next, customer needs must be matched with the current abilities of the firm, and current operations must be surveyed to identify areas that will require monitoring. It is important at this stage to interview various levels of management. In this way, the firm can determine what strategic and operational decisions are made, and what information is needed for decision making and in what form. Table 13–1 illustrates the various types of strategic and operational decisions that management must make within each of the functions of logistics.

A Common Data Base Is Needed

The next stage is to survey current data processing capabilities to determine what changes must be made. Finally, common data files must be created and management reports designed, considering the costs and benefits of each. Figure 13–9 identifies the basic features of an integrated information system. A good system design must support the management uses previously described, and must have the capability of moving information from locations where it is collected to the appropriate levels of management. Telephones, teletypewriters, personal conversations, and computer-to-computer linkups are just a few of the ways that information can be transferred. In addition to information processing, the computerized information system must have a storage capability in order to hold information until it is required for decision making.

Sources of Data

Data for a logistics management information system can come from many sources. The most significant sources of data for the common data base (see Figure 13–9) are (1) the order processing system, (2) company records, (3) industry data, and (4) management data.

TABLE 13–1 Typical Strategic and Operational Decisions by Logistics Function

Decision Type	*Customer Service*	*Transportation*	*Warehousing*	*Order Processing*	*Inventory*
Strategic	Setting customer service levels	Selecting transportation modes	Determination of number of warehouses and locations	Extent of mechanization	Replenishment systems
		Freight consolidation programs	Extent of warehouse automation	Centralized or decentralized	Safety stock levels
		Common carriers versus private trucking	Public versus private warehousing		
Operational	Service level measurements	Rate freight bills	Picking	Order tracking	Forecasting
		Freight bill auditing	Packing	Order validation	Inventory tracking
		Claims administration	Stores measurement	Credit checking	Carrying-cost measurements
		Vehicle scheduling	Warehouse stock transfer	Invoice reconciliation	Inventory turns
		Rate negotiation	Staffing	Performance measurements	
		Shipment planning	Warehouse layout and design		
		Railcar management	Selection of materials-handling equipment		
		Shipment routing and scheduling	Performance measurements		
		Carrier selection			
		Performance measurements			

SOURCE: American Telephone and Telegraph Company, *Business Marketing,* Market Management Division.

FIGURE 13–9 Logistics Information System

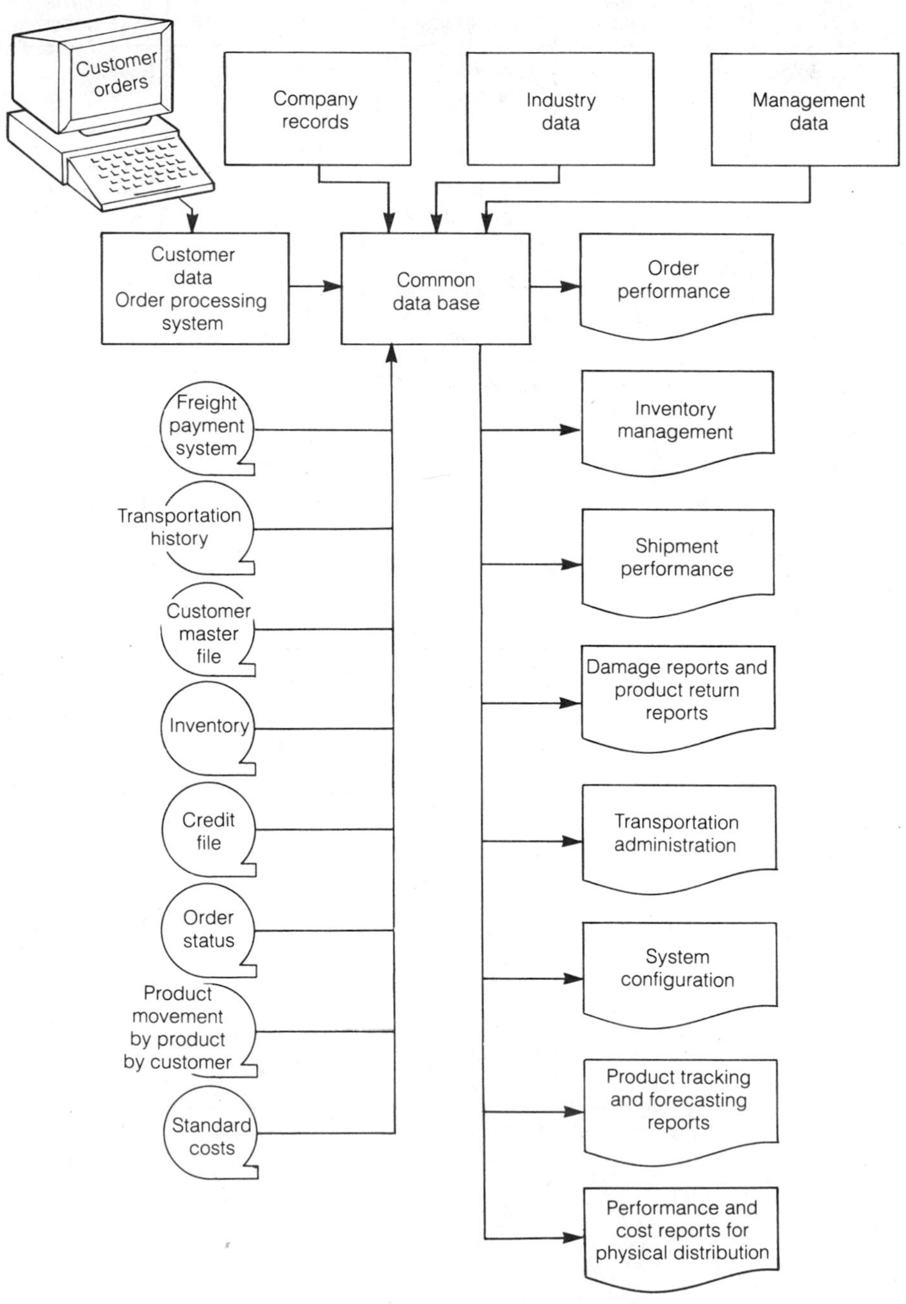

SOURCE: American Telephone and Telegraph Company, *Business Marketing,* Market Management Division.

The *order processing system* is capable of providing data such as customer locations, items demanded, revenue by customer and item, sales patterns (when items are ordered), order size, and salesperson. *Company records* can be used to provide manufacturing and logistics cost information, the cost of capital, company resources, and the amount spent on various items such as insurance, taxes, obsolescence, and damage.

Industry data can be obtained from trade and professional organizations. Firms such as A. C. Nielsen Company sell statistics on competitors and their relative market shares. Professional journals and trade publications are a useful source of data; they may report on research projects and surveys of current practices. Statistics compiled by the federal government may also be of significant value, since they report such statistics as population shifts, inventory levels, housing starts, and consumer-credit expenditures.

Management can also provide the computerized data base with useful input. This input may include likely reactions by competitors, future trends in sales, government policy, availability of supplies, and the probable success of alternative strategies.

Capabilities of a Computerized Information System

Usually, the data base contains computerized data files, such as the freight payment system, transportation history, inventory status, open orders, deleted orders, and standard costs for various logistics activities, as well as for marketing and manufacturing. The computerized information system must be capable of (1) data retrieval, (2) data processing, (3) data analysis, and (4) report generation.

Data retrieval is the capability of recalling data such as freight rates, standard warehousing costs, or the current status of a customer order. Basically, the data are still in their raw form; the computerized records allow fast and convenient access to the information.

Data processing is the capability to transform the data to a more useful form by relatively simple and straightforward conversion. Examples of data processing capability include preparation of warehousing picking instructions, preparation of bills of lading, and printing purchase orders.

Data analysis refers to taking the data from orders and providing management with information for strategic and operational decision making. A number of mathematical and statistical models are available to aid the firm's management, including linear programming and simulation models. Linear programming is probably the most widely used strategic and operational planning tool in logistics management. It is an optimization technique that subjects various possible solutions to constraints that are identified by management. Simulation is a technique used to model a situation so that management can determine how the system's performance is likely to change if various alternative strategies are chosen. The model is tested using known facts. Although simulation does not provide an optimal solution, the technique allows management to determine satisfactory solutions from a range of alternatives. A number of simulation models are available for purchase if the firm does not have the resources to develop its

FIGURE 13–10 A Modular Data Base System for Reporting Cost and Revenue Flows

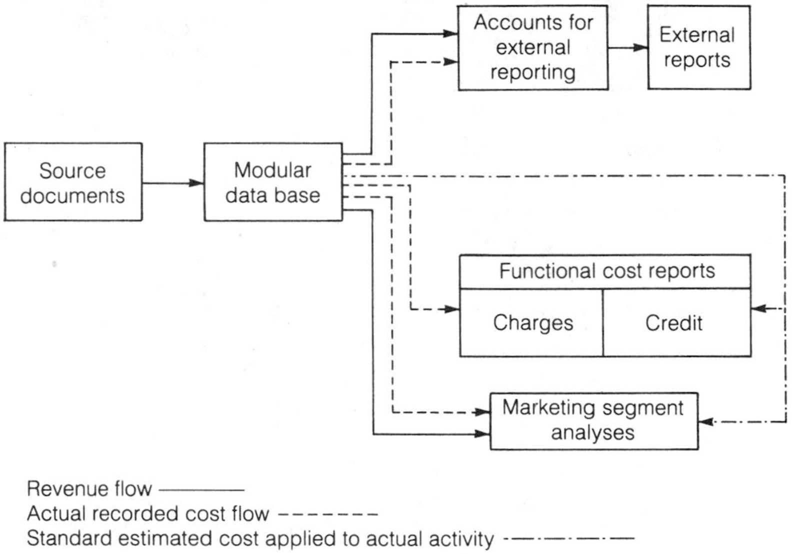

Source documents
Modular data base
Accounts for external reporting
External reports
Functional cost reports
Charges
Credit
Marketing segment analyses

Revenue flow ————
Actual recorded cost flow - - - - - - -
Standard estimated cost applied to actual activity -—-—-—

SOURCE: Frank H. Mossman, Paul M. Fischer, and W. J. E. Crissy, "New Approaches to Analyzing Marketing Profitability," *Journal of Marketing* 38, no. 2 (April 1974), p. 45.

own.[25] We will examine decision support systems for logistics in detail in Chapter 14.

The last feature of an information system is *report generation.* Typical reports that can be generated from a logistics management information system include order performance reports; inventory management reports; shipment performance reports; damage reports; transportation administration reports; system configuration reports, which may contain the results of data analysis from mathematical and statistical models; and cost reports for logistics.

A DATA BASE FOR DECISION MAKING

The Modular Data Base Concept

One of the most promising data base systems for generating logistics cost information and profit contribution performance reports is the modular data base concept (see Figure 13–10).[26] This is a central storage system

[25] See Richard C. Haverly, "Survey of Software for Physical Distribution," *Proceedings of the Twenty-Second Annual Conference of the National Council of Physical Distribution Management* (Chicago: National Council of Physical Distribution Management, 1984), pp. 717–885.

[26] See Frank H. Mossman, Paul M. Fischer, and W. J. E. Crissy, "New Approaches to Analyzing Marketing Profitability," *Journal of Marketing* 38, no. 2 (April 1974), pp. 43–48.

TABLE 13–2 Information that May Be Recorded in the Modular Data Base by Customer Order

Customer Order Data	
Customer number	Salesperson number
Customer name	Territory
Order number	Region
Previous order number	Partial ship back order number
Customer order number	Credit limit
Customer billing address	Credit outstanding
Customer shipping address	Prepaid/collect freight
Customer order date	Terms
Requested shipping date	Instructions regarding shipping and product substitutions
Date product reserved	
Date released to distribution center	Quantity, product number, price
Date picked/packed	Packing and shipping instructions
Ship date	Transportation commodity classification
Date, time, and operator	Carrier
Priority code	Bill of lading number

where source documents, such as invoices, transportation bills, and other expenses and revenue items, are fed into a data base in coded form.

Inputs can be coded at the lowest possible level of aggregation according to function, subfunction, customer territory, product, salesperson, channel of distribution, transport mode, carrier revenue, or expense, to name just a few. For example, the information that may be recorded by customer order is shown in Table 13–2. The system is capable of filing large amounts of data and allows rapid aggregation and retrieval of various modules of information for decision making or external reporting. The modular data base, combined with standard costs, is capable of generating both function cost reports and segment contribution reports.[27] The system works by charging functions, such as warehousing and transportation, with actual costs; the costs are then compared to predetermined standards. Individual segments such as customers or products are credited with segment revenues and charged the standard cost, plus controllable variances.

In addition to being able to evaluate the profitability of individual customers, product line, territories, and/or channels of distribution, the data base permits the user to simulate trade-off decisions and determine the effect of proposed system changes on total costs. Figure 13–11 summarizes the report-generating capabilities of the modular data base. In order to implement the modular data base approach, it is necessary to collect the raw cost data and break them down into fixed-variable and direct-indirect components. In other words, the data must be sufficiently refined to permit the formulation of meaningful modules. Full implementation of the integrated logistics management concept and knowledgeable decision making

[27] Segment contribution reports were described in detail in Chapter 3, pp. 96–100.

FIGURE 13–11 Report Generating Capabilities of the Modular Data Base

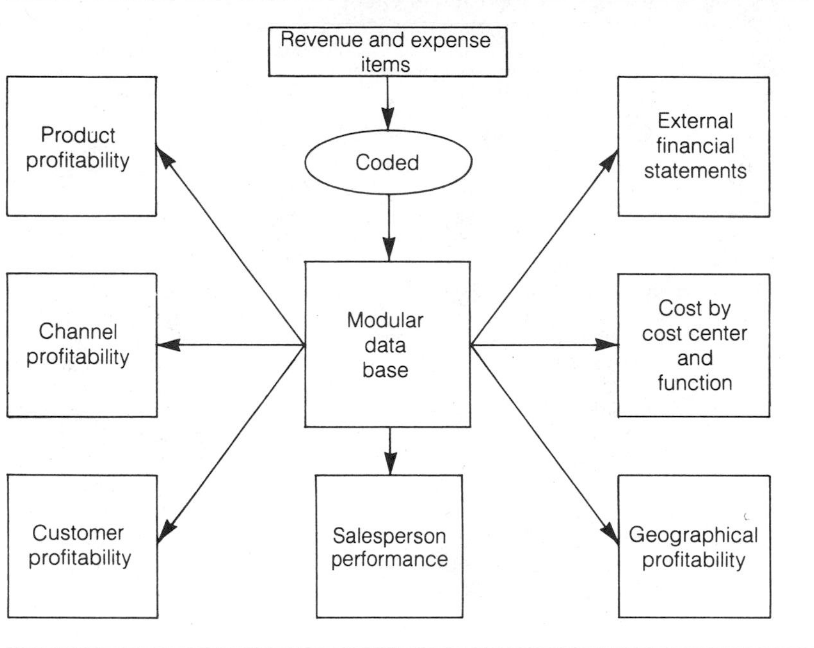

in the areas of strategic and operational planning require a sophisticated management information system.

FINANCIAL CONSIDERATIONS

Cost Justification for an Advanced Order Processing System

Of course, it will be necessary to justify an advanced order processing system in terms of a cost/benefit analysis. The costs of developing the system, *start-up costs,* can be justified by discounting the improvement in cash flows associated with the new system and comparing them to the initial investment. In most cases, cash flow will improve by changing to an advanced order processing system if the volume of orders processed is large. In smaller operations, however, this may not be true if the proposed system is more than the company needs.

In any case, the difference in cash flow that results from implementing the proposed system can be calculated using the framework shown in Figure 13–12. It is important, when the cash flow is calculated, to include in the analysis only those costs that will change with the system change. Usually, the most significant cost differences will occur in the order processing, inventory, transportation, and warehousing cost components.

Figure 13–13 illustrates how an advanced order processing system can

FIGURE 13–12 Cost Trade-Offs Required in a Logistics System

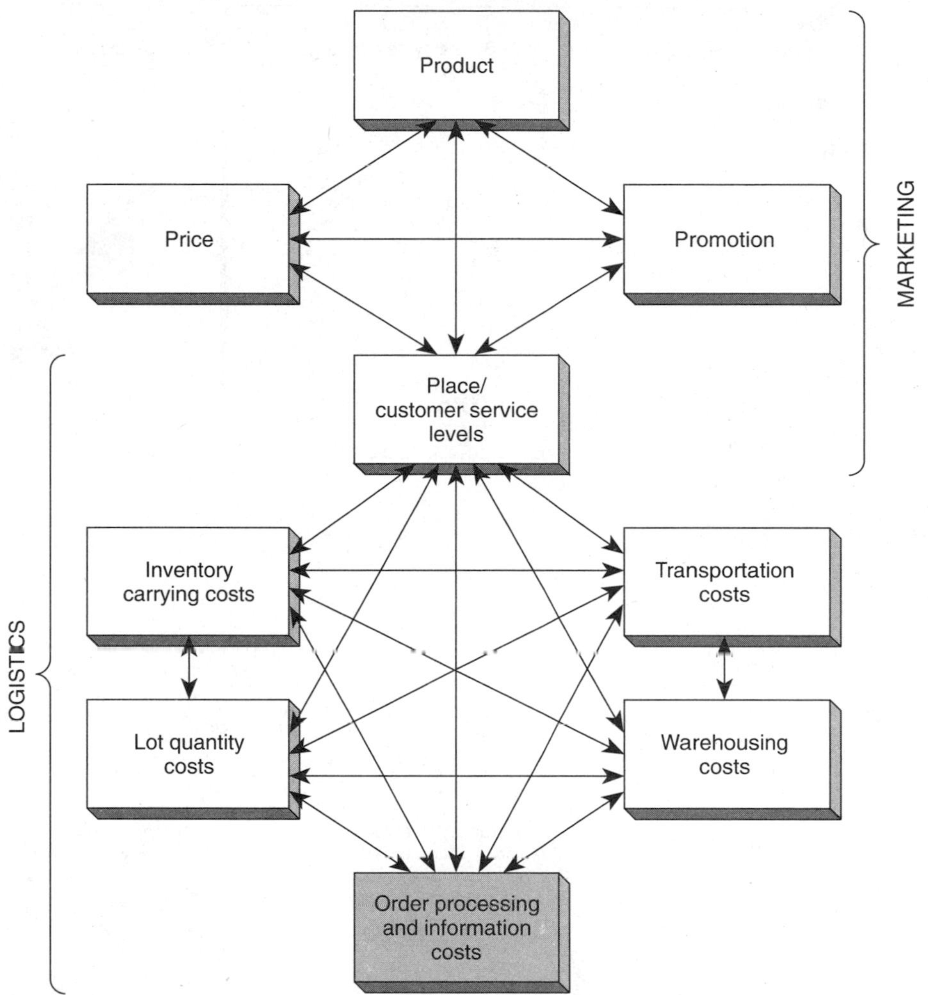

Marketing objective: Allocate resources to the marketing mix to maximize the long-run profitability of the firm.

Logistics objective: Minimize total costs, given the customer service objective where: Total costs = Transportation costs + Warehousing costs + Order processing and information costs + Lot quantity costs + Inventory carrying costs.

SOURCE: Adapted from Douglas M. Lambert, *The Development of an Inventory Costing Methodology: A Study of the Costs Associated with Holding Inventory* (Chicago: National Council of Physical Distribution Management, 1976), p. 7.

FIGURE 13–13 Total Order Cycle with Variability Both Before and After Implementing an Advanced Order Processing System

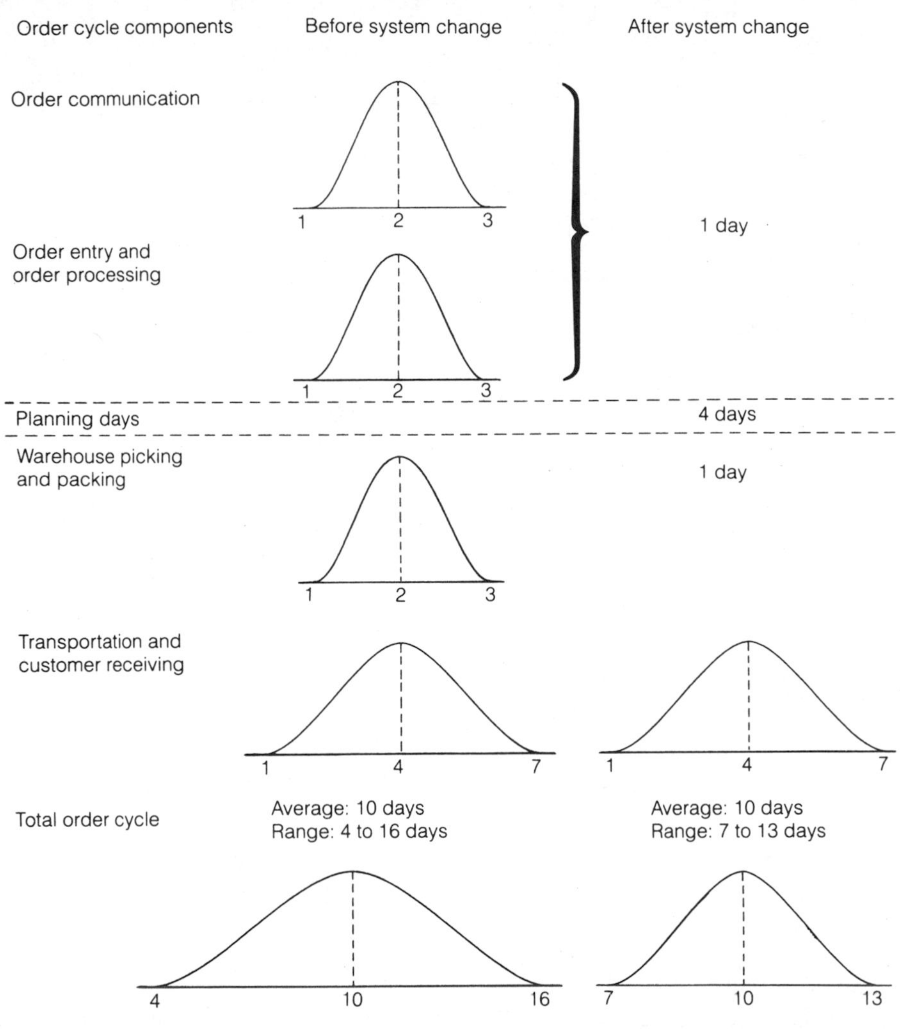

free time for planning. By reducing order communication, order entry, and order processing time from an average of four days to one day, on the average three days are made available for planning. This planning time means that sales forecasting and production scheduling receive sales information three days sooner, as do the managers of logistics activities such as warehousing, transportation, and inventory management. The advance notice at field warehouses allows the more productive allocation of orders to level volume. In any case, it is possible to plan so that all orders are shipped from warehouse locations after the sixth day. In essence, then, four days are available for planning warehouse picking and packing, transportation consolidations, and reduced levels of safety stock. This assumes, of course, that the manufacturer's customers find a 10-day order cycle acceptable, and a reduction in order cycle is not given to them. If transportation and customer receiving is the only variability remaining in the order cycle, variability in the total order cycle can be reduced from 6 days (when the order cycle ranged from 4 to 16 days) to 3 days (with the order cycle ranging from 7 to 13 days). This improvement in order cycle consistency allows the manufacturer's customers to cut their safety stocks by half. In fact, the increased planning time often results in a reduction in transit time and transit time variability. In this example, the results might be an additional day of planning time, and a customer order cycle ranging from 9 to 11 days. In any case, the entire channel of distribution becomes more efficient and realizes cost savings as a result of the advanced order processing application. In addition, the improved customer service may create increased sales and market share for the manufacturer.

Generally, the fixed costs associated with an advanced order processing system are higher than those incurred by a manual system. However, the variable costs per order are significantly less with the advanced system. We will expand this type of cost analysis in Chapter 15, which deals specifically with the calculation of logistics cost savings.

SUMMARY

In this chapter we saw how the order processing system can directly influence the performance of the logistics function. We also examined how order processing systems can be used to improve customer communications and total order cycle time, and/or lead to substantial inventory reductions and transportation efficiencies. Information is vital for the planning and control of logistics systems, and we saw how the order processing system can form the basis of a logistics information system.

Modern computer technology and communication systems make it possible for management to have the information required for strategic and operational planning of the logistics function. The order processing system can significantly improve the quality and quantity of information for decision making. The next chapter will deal with decision support systems for logistics management.

SUGGESTED READINGS

Bookbinder, James H., and David M. Dilts. "Logistics Information Systems in a Just-in-Time Environment." *Journal of Business Logistics* 10, no. 1 (1989), pp. 50–67.

EMMELHAINZ, MARGARET A. "Strategic Issues of EDI Implementation." *Journal of Business Logistics* 9, no. 2 (1988), pp. 55–70.

———. "Implementation of EDI in Logistics: An Introduction. *Annual Conference Proceedings.* Chicago: Council of Logistics Management, 1990, pp. 83–91.

GUSTIN, CRAIG M. "Trends in Computer Application in Transportation and Distribution Management." *International Journal of Physical Distribution and Materials Management* 14, no. 1 (1984), pp. 52–60.

LALONDE, BERNARD J., AND MARTHA C. COOPER. *Partnerships in Providing Customer Service: A Third-Party Perspective.* Chicago: Council of Logistics Management, 1989, pp. 79–105.

NELSON, GENE R. "Electric Data Interchange Developments in Distribution: Wins-Warehouse Information Network Standards." *Proceedings of the Twenty-Second Annual Conference of the National Council of Physical Distribution Management.* Chicago: National Council of Physical Distribution Management, 1984, pp. 427–36.

SCHARY, PHILIP B., AND JAMES COAKLEY. "Logistics Organization and the Information System." *International Journal of Logistics Management* 2, no. 2 (1991), pp. 22–29.

SHEFFI, YOSEF. "The Shipment Information Center." *International Journal of Logistics Management* 2, no. 2 (1991), pp. 1–12.

WEISS, MARTIN A. "Implications of Electronic Order Exchange Systems for Logistics Planning and Strategy." *Journal of Business Logistics* 5, no. 1 (1984), pp. 16–39.

QUESTIONS AND PROBLEMS

1. What do wholesalers and retailers perceive to be the order cycle provided to them by a manufacturer?
2. Explain the impact of order cycle variability on the inventory levels of wholesalers and retailers.
3. How is logistics performance affected by the order processing system used?
4. What are the primary advantages associated with the implementation of an integrated and automated order processing system?
5. As described in this chapter, the plan for the Saturn project was to build cars to individual customer orders. Is this indeed the case? If not, what do you believe happened in the implementation? Evaluate the worth of building cars to individual customer orders.
6. Electronic data interchange applications have experienced significant growth in recent years. Why do you believe this growth in EDI has occurred? What are the primary benefits of EDI? Do you think that the growth rate in EDI applications will be sustained? Why or why not?
7. How does the order processing system form the foundation of the logistics management information system?

8. How is the logistics management information system used to support planning of logistics operations?

9. What are the primary advantages of the modular data base system?

10. Company X operates an order processing department whose costs consist of monthly lease charges, indirect labor (customer service reps and data entry clerks), supervisory salaries, and a charge for general corporate burden. The division is treated as a cost center whose expenses are first accumulated and then allocated back to other cost and profit centers on the basis of their ability to bear such charges.

The company is currently investigating ways in which a more equitable order processing charge can be assessed to its user divisions. As a first step, you have been asked to investigate the behavior of costs in the department to determine if there is a significant relationship between volume (as measured by orders processed) and total departmental cost. You have secured the following data. Data have been adjusted for inflation.

Quarter	*Number of Orders Processed*	*Departmental Cost*
1	40,000	44,000
2	64,000	52,000
3	52,000	40,000
4	90,000	69,000
5	50,000	48,000
6	58,000	48,000
7	76,000	61,000
8	88,000	64,000
0	02,000	54,000
10	85,000	60,000
11	72,000	54,000
12	80,000	68,000

Determine the breakdown of fixed and variable expenses by:

a. Analyzing the change in costs with respect to volume changes in each year; and

b. Drawing a scatter diagram on the graph on the next page and making reasonable inferences regarding cost behavior.

Note: If you need to refresh your memory about regression analysis and scatter diagrams (graphing the data), see Chapter 9.

11. Show the impact that implementation of an automated order processing system would have on a manufacturer's return on investment, given the following information:

a. Net profit after taxes is $2 million.

b. Return on assets is currently 10 percent.

c. With the current system, customer orders are mailed, salespeople collect them and either hand carry them to sales offices (where they are telephoned or mailed to headquarters), or telephone or mail orders directly to headquarters.

d. With the proposed order processing system, customers will telephone orders to inside salespeople (customer service representatives) equipped with CRTs, who immediately input the order.

The Analysis of Costs in an Order Processing Department—Scatter Diagram Approach

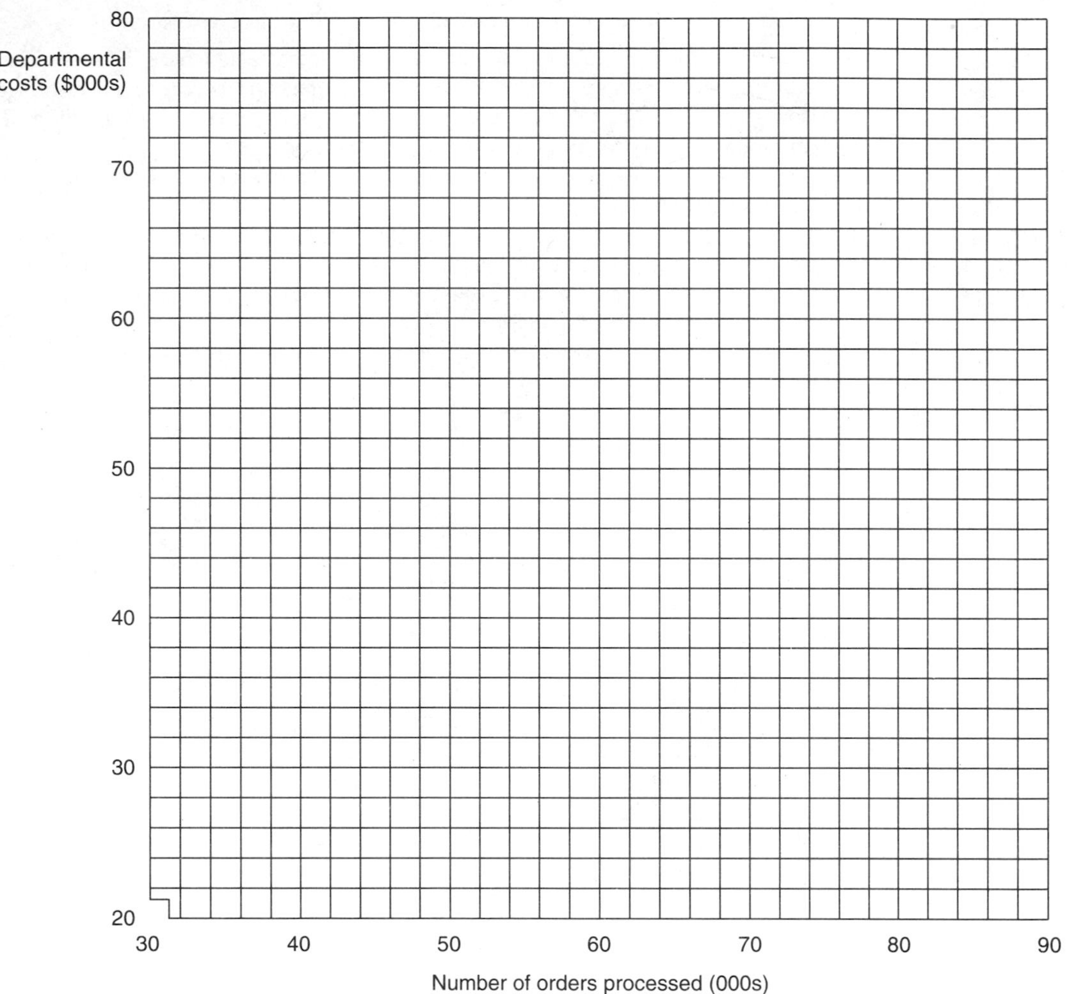

e. The proposed order processing system will provide management with four additional planning days and eliminate two days of variability in the order cycle.

f. The planning time made available by the proposed order processing system will enable management to: reduce inventories by $2 million; achieve $450,000 in transportation savings as a result of consolidations; and reduce handling charges in public warehouses by $75,000 as a result of direct plant-to-customer shipments.

g. The proposed system will increase order processing costs by $225,000 per year.
h. The non-cost of money components of inventory carrying costs are 5 percent of the inventory value.
i. The company is experiencing capital rationing and could achieve a 20 percent after-tax rate of return on additional capital if it were available.

12. Explain how the proposed order processing system described in question 11 would affect the customer service levels provided by the manufacturer.

Chapter 14

Decision Support Systems

Objectives of This Chapter

To identify the many uses of decision support systems in logistics

To provide an overview of the ways in which computers can be used in logistics operations

To identify how environmental scanning is an important element of logistics decision making

To examine the role of forecasting in logistics planning

To identify the role of artificial intelligence (AI) and expert systems (ES) in logistics operations

INTRODUCTION

In the first 13 chapters of this book, we examined a large number of logistics concepts, principles, and examples. Without help, the logistics executive faces an almost overwhelming responsibility. In recent years, that help has come from advances in computer technology and information systems.

Computer and information technology have been utilized in logistics for many years, but with the widespread introduction and development of microcomputers (PCs) around 1980, their use has increased tremendously. Evidence of that trend was provided in a Council of Logistics Management study, "Logistics 1995," which surveyed senior executives in manufacturing, merchandising, and service organizations. The top three trends identified in the study directly related to the use of computers and information technology:[1]

1. The rapid proliferation of data processing systems enables the distribution or logistics organization to handle and control information in ways which will change the traditional methods of servicing customers and supplying products.
2. Advances in computer technology will allow electronic data interchange to be pervasive by 1995. All phases of logistics will be involved, and communication technology will create opportunities for large savings.
3. The major difference between the logistics operating environment of 1995 and today will be the improvement in the timeliness and completeness of the exchange of information between channel members.

Firms of all types are utilizing computers to support logistics activities. This is especially true for companies thought to be "leading edge," that is,

[1]James F. Robeson, "Logistics 1995: 10 Top Trends," presentation at the Seventeenth Annual Transportation and Logistics Educators' Conference, Atlanta, Georgia, September 27, 1987.

leaders in their industry. Such firms are heavy users of computers in the areas of order entry, order processing, finished goods inventory control, performance measurement, freight audit/payment, and warehousing.[2]

"Until recently, the main problems organizations faced in making use of computers were to get an adequate technology for the applications they wanted, and to learn how to manage large-scale, complex projects."[3] Those and other problems have been overcome with the advent of the decision support system (DSS). Decision support systems are computer-based and support the executive decision-making process. The DSS can be defined as follows: "an integrative system of subsystems that have the purpose of providing information to aid a decision maker in making better choices than would otherwise be possible." The subsystems that are commonly associated with a DSS are the following:

Decision Support Systems Defined

- Decision-relevant models.
- Interactive computer hardware and software.
- A data base.
- A data management system.
- Graphical and other sophisticated displays.
- A modeling language that is "user friendly."[4]

A DSS can be illustrated as shown in Figure 14–1. The system is differentiated into three distinct components: data acquisition, data processing, and data presentation. *Data acquisition* involves the use of multiple sources such as user data bases, user inputs, and public data bases. Computerized company data bases are the primary information resource for the logistics executive. User inputs are also important because data files must often be manipulated. Therefore, users are frequently involved in many aspects of data base management. A third source is the various public data bases that have become available in recent years. Firms are using public data bases to supplement their own internal data bases.

Data Acquisition

Data Processing

After the data have been made available, they can be processed in a variety of ways:

> First, the data may have to be aggregated, merged, or otherwise manipulated to put it into an appropriate level of detail and configuration for analysis. This would be considered a processing step.
>
> Second, the preprocessed data will get analyzed. This may include statistical

---

[2]Jack W. Farrell, "How Top Companies View the Role of Computers," *Traffic Management* 27, no. 5 (May 1988), p. 47; also see Donald J. Bowersox, Patricia J. Daugherty, Cornelia L. Dröge, Dale S. Rogers, and Daniel L. Wardlow, *Leading Edge Logistics: Competitive Positioning for the 1990's* (Oak Brook, Ill.: Council of Logistics Management, 1989).

[3]Peter G. W. Keen, "Decision Support Systems: Translating Analytic Techniques into Useful Tools," *Sloan Management Review* 21, no. 3 (Spring 1980), p. 33

[4]William R. King, "Achieving the Potential of Decision Support Systems," *The Journal of Business Strategy* 3, no. 3 (Winter 1983), p. 84.

FIGURE 14–1 Decision Support System

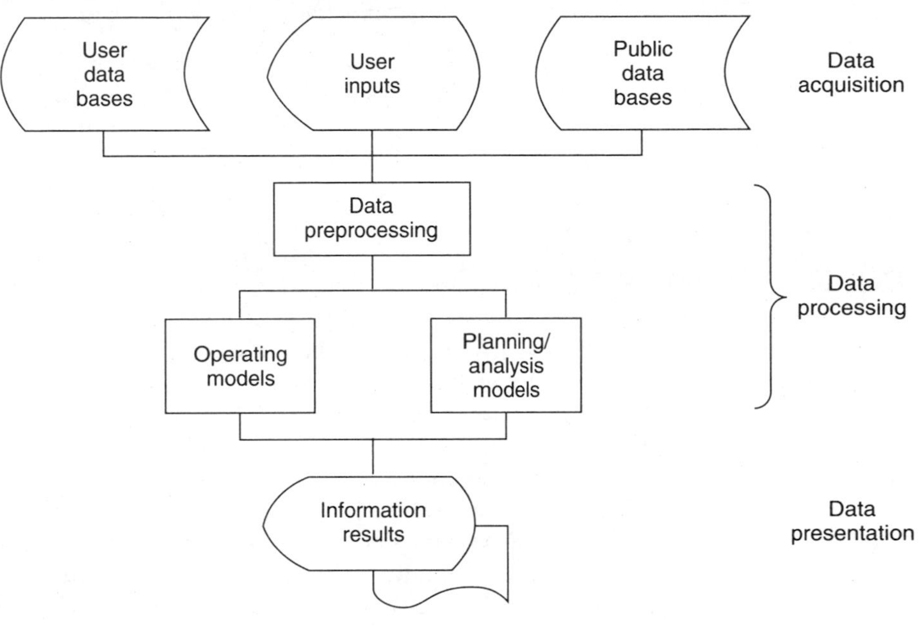

SOURCE: Allan F. Ayers, "Decision Support Systems: A Useful Tool for Manufacturing Management," paper published by K. W. Tunnell Company, Inc. (1985), p. 2.

> analysis (such as linear regression), groupings or percentages of totals, or matrix manipulation using an electronic worksheet approach.
>
> Third, all these manipulations might call for "what if" capabilities or other simulations to test results and the sensitivity of those results to changes in the data.[5]

It is in the area of *data processing* that technological change has brought about significant results: "The advent of low-cost, high-volume data processing and transmission is revolutionizing logistics control systems."[6]

Data Presentation

Finally, the DSS includes *data presentation.* The data may be presented visually (e.g., terminal display) or in hard copy (e.g., formal report). Typically, a logistics executive employs both formats.

As evidenced by the preceding discussion, a DSS incorporates many components and is applications-oriented. More specifically, a DSS has the following objectives:

---

[5] Allan F. Ayers, "Decision Support Systems—New Tool for Manufacturing," *Computerworld Focus* (June 19, 1985), p. 36.

[6] Graham Sharman, "The Rediscovery of Logistics," *Harvard Business Review* 62, no. 5 (September–October 1984), p. 72.

1. To assist logistics executives in their decision processes.
2. To support, but not replace, managerial judgment.
3. To improve the effectiveness of logistics decisions.[7]

Perhaps the most vital ingredient of a DSS is the quality of the data used as input into the system. DSSs require information about the environment, both internal and external to the firm. Thus, an important first step in DSS planning, implementation, and control is to have a good environmental scanning activity.

ENVIRONMENTAL SCANNING

A strategic logistics plan can be no better than the data on which it is based. As a result, the logistics executive must be aware of the environment in which his or her firm operates. A firm must regularly and systematically appraise its environment (environmental scanning) and determine the most optimal logistics strategies to pursue (opportunity analysis).

Environmental Scanning Defined

Environmental scanning is the process by which the firm's environments are linked to strategic decision making. Operationally, it is the process that identifies and evaluates environmental events and interrelationships for the purpose of aiding the logistics executive in the development of strategy:

> Information about the environment in which an organization operates is a vital asset and resource. Timely and reliable information about past and present conditions, constraints, and opportunities is a source of competitive power that will help an organization outperform its competitors with effective strategic decisions. Lack of information may result in great difficulties.[8]

The environments in which a firm operates, and which affect company strategies and programs, are economic, competitive, technological, social/cultural, and political/legal. For example, the bankruptcies of U.S. airlines such as Eastern, Braniff, and Pan American during the late 1980s and early 1990s had a significant impact on firms shipping products by air freight over routes once served by those carriers. In some cases, other airlines stepped in and serviced those markets. But for some shippers, air freight service, particularly container traffic, was significantly reduced, resulting in a few firms changing their method of distribution totally from airlines to trucks.

In the political and legal environment, the lifting of sanctions in 1991 from the Republic of South Africa (RSA) by most of Europe and the United States will have long-term marketing and logistics consequences. Undoubtedly, the RSA will become a significant economic trading partner with the

---

[7] Efraim Turban, *Decision Support and Expert Systems* (New York: Macmillan Publishing Co., 1988), p. 8.

[8] Jugoslav S. Milutinovich, "Business Facts for Decision Makers: Where to Find Them," *Business Horizons* 28, no. 2 (March–April 1985), p. 63.

TABLE 14–1 Three Approaches to Environmental Scanning

	Scanning Models		
	Irregular	*Regular*	*Continous*
Media for scanning activity	Ad hoc studies	Periodically updated studies	Structured data collection and processing systems
Scope of scanning	Specific events	Selected events	Broad range of environmental systems
Motivation for activity	Crisis initiated	Decision and issue oriented	Planning process oriented
Temporal nature of activity	Reactive	Proactive	Proactive
Time frame for data	Retrospective	Primarily current and retrospective	Prospective
Time frame for decision impact	Current and short-term future	Short-term	Long-term
Organizational makeup	Various staff agencies	Various staff agencies	Environmental scanning unit

SOURCE: Liam Fahey and Wililam R. King, "Environmental Scanning for Corporate Planning," *Business Horizons* 20, no. 4 (August 1977), p. 63. Copyright 1977 by the Foundation for the School of Business at Indiana University. Reprinted by permission.

major industrialized nations as well as a conduit for reaching the southern African continent. As firms worldwide choose to enter the RSA market, numerous logistical challenges will face them.

As a final example, changes taking place in the economic, competitive, and technological environments will have profound impacts on logistics. The manufacturing of computer chips and other high-technology products presently taking place in the Pacific Basin region may become less common. As manufacturing processes become more automated, the logistics disadvantages of remote locations begin to outweigh the labor cost savings that prompted the initial decisions to locate in areas where skilled labor was cheap. It is likely that some of those manufacturing facilities will relocate to more "favorable" logistics sites during the next several years.[9]

Typically, a company will employ one or more of three environmental scanning approaches (see Table 14–1):

1. Irregular scanning.
2. Regular scanning.
3. Continuous scanning.[10]

[9] Additional examples of environmental influences on logistics will be presented in Chapter 17, "Global Logistics."

[10] See Liam Fahey and William R. King, "Environmental Scanning for Corporate Planning," *Business Horizons* 20, no. 4 (August 1977), pp. 61–71.

Irregular Scanning

Irregular scanning is "reactive," that is, it is based on monitoring events that have already occurred in the environment: "The scanning focus is toward the past, and its intent is to identify the implications of an event that has already taken place. The emphasis is on immediate or short-term reactions to the crisis, and little attention is paid to identifying and evaluating future environmental trends and events."[11] Examples include motor carriers responding to increased fuel prices as a result of an oil embargo, the merger of two railroads that are a firm's competitors, or a significant price reduction by a logistics service firm in the channel of distribution.

Regular Scanning

Regular scanning is anticipatory rather than reactive. It is performed regularly and systematically. Examples include periodic surveys of customer preferences and perceptions, or evaluation of customer or product contribution margins conducted as part of a logistics audit.

Continuous Scanning

Continuous scanning is long-term in its orientation and involves a continuous monitoring of the environment. This is the best type of environmental scanning because the firm is able to identify, evaluate, and respond to forces in the environment much sooner. Examples include the regular appraisal of carrier performance, monitoring of transportation regulatory activity of the federal government, and the use of customer panels in marketing research. Fahey and King related some of the subtleties of continuous scanning:

> Perhaps most important from an operational point of view is the fact that continuous scanning must be organizationally structured. Unlike the irregular models, in which studies may be left to the appropriate staff agency, the systems-oriented approach will require, at least, a scanning agency which functions as central clearinghouse for environmental information. Computerized information systems dedicated to scanning activities may also be required.
>
> Moreover, the continuous model necessitates a planning process viewpoint that is an integration of the information processing and information utilization planning functions. While the other models provide environmental information to support specific choices, the continuous model supports the variety of choices inherent in strategic planning—from the selection of organizational missions and objectives to the choice of specific programs and funding commitments.[12]

Each of the three approaches can be useful, and most logistics executives utilize all of them as part of their environmental scanning activities. Whichever approach a firm uses, the logistics executive must follow a logical sequence of steps in order to respond to the environment in an optimal fashion. One possible sequence is the five-step approach identified below:

The Environmental Scanning Process

1. Search for information sources.
2. Select information sources to scan.

---

[11] Ibid., p. 62.

[12] Ibid., p. 63. Copyright 1977 by the Foundation for the School of Business at Indiana University. Reprinted by permission.

3. Identify criteria by which to scan.
4. Scan and establish results.
5. Determine special action based on scanning results.[13]

Information obtained from the environmental scanning activity can be used for a variety of purposes. One of the most important uses is in forecasting.

FORECASTING

Renfro and Morrison argued, "Nothing is more important to accurate forecasting than developing a logical and consistent system which is responsive to the needs of managers and capable of being attuned to a changing environment."[14] It is so important that *Fortune* 500 companies spend an average of a quarter of a million dollars on forecasting each year.[15]

Why Forecast?

The rationale for forecasting is twofold. First, proper logistics system control requires forward planning. Forward planning, in turn, requires good forecasts. The need for forward planning is great if the logistics executive wishes to keep operations running smoothly; to adequately prepare for, and meet, future conditions and challenges; and to minimize present or potential problems in the logistics system of the company.

Second, forecasting is needed if management is to be able to approximate the future with some reasonable accuracy. Forecasting can provide a fairly accurate picture of the future; it is the driving force behind all forward planning activities within the firm.

For example, Compaq Computer Corporation, manufacturer of IBM-compatible microcomputers, used forecasting in 1984 to "guess right" about its future strategy.[16] The firm faced a choice of either specializing in its existing portable computer market, or expanding into the desktop microcomputer market to compete head to head with IBM. The latter strategy would have required the company to invest heavily in product development and necessitated expansion of its organization and manufacturing capacity. Utilizing forecasts to predict the future and assess the market, in combination with top management involvement, Compaq decided to enter the desktop market. As a result, Compaq's sales rose from $111 million to $329 million during 1984, while its earnings increased from $4.7 million to $12.8 million.[17]

---

[13] William L. Renfro and James L. Morrison, "Detecting Signals of Change: The Environmental Scanning Process," *The Futurist* 18, no. 4 (August 1984), pp. 49–50.

[14] Gilbert Frisbie and Vincent A. Mabert, "Crystal Ball vs. System: The Forecasting Dilemma," *Business Horizons* 24, no. 5 (September–October 1981), p. 72.

[15] David C. Carlson, Robin T. Peterson and David J. Lill, "State of the Art Advances but Its Use Is Still Sparse," *Journal of Business Forecasting* 2, no. 2 (Summer 1983), p. 14.

[16] See David M. Georgoff and Robert G. Murdick, "Manager's Guide to Forecasting," *Harvard Business Review* 64, no. 1 (January–February 1986), pp. 110–20.

[17] Ibid., p. 111.

Selecting and Implementing a Forecasting Method

There are many forecasting techniques available. Selecting the right one involves a thorough and in-depth analysis of the available options. There are seven basic steps to follow in selecting and implementing the appropriate forecasting method:[18]

1. Identify the problem or purpose that the forecast will address.
2. Gather available factual data, both internal and external to the company. This can be accomplished through the firm's environmental scanning activity.
3. Determine which forecasting method most closely meets the objectives of the firm and the type of data available. In some instances, a new forecasting model will have to be developed.
4. Generate good assumptions for each of the forecast elements. Each element in the forecast should be as accurate as possible.
5. Compare the forecast to expectations; that is, review the initial forecast and compare its output with the results expected or with what actually occurred.
6. Analyze variance: "Most forecasts show variances of one sort or another, and these must be carefully analyzed to see if they are caused by erroneous assumptions or faults in . . . logic."[19]
7. Make adjustments in the forecast, if required, and "fine tune" it to better mirror reality.

Appropriateness, Cost, and Accuracy

Many considerations are involved in selecting a forecasting technique. Among the most important are appropriateness, cost, and accuracy:

> An appropriate method not only fits the factors thought to affect the item to be forecast but also fits the forecasting situation; e.g., a technique appropriate for one-time forecasts would not be used for inventory control.
>
> The questions of accuracy and cost involve a trade-off. It is possible to get a better forecast by spending more time and money, but it is necessary to decide if the extra accuracy is worth the extra cost.[20]

Characteristics of Good Forecasts

In addition, forecasting techniques should be capable of handling a large number of items efficiently. This is called *computational efficiency*. The technique should also be robust, that is, relatively insensitive to minor errors in the data input into the forecast. Finally, the forecasting technique needs to properly balance responsiveness and stability. It needs to take into account changes in each element of the forecast, but it must not overreact to wide variations in any one, or a few, elements.

As a *Harvard Business Review* article noted, "To handle the increasing

---

[18] Ben I. Boldt, Jr., "Sound Business Forecasting," *Today's Executive* 5, no. 1 (Spring/Summer 1982), pp. 6–11.

[19] Ibid., p. 10.

[20] Neil Seitz, *Business Forecasting: Concepts and Microcomputer Applications* (Reston, Va.: Reston Publishing, 1984), p. 6.

variety and complexity of managerial forecasting problems, many forecasting techniques have been developed in recent years. Each has its special use, and care must be taken to select the correct technique for a particular application.[21] Table 14–2 shows examples of some of the most commonly used forecasting techniques. Included in the table are moving average, exponential smoothing, adaptive filtering, and regression models.[22]

Improving Forecasting Ability

Logistics executives can use a number of strategies to improve their forecasting ability. They can combine forecasts, simulate a range of input assumptions, and use managerial judgment:

> The research on combining forecasts to achieve improvements (particularly in accuracy) is extensive, persuasive, and consistent. The results of combined forecasts greatly surpasses most individual projections, techniques, and analysis. Combining forecasts—particularly with techniques that are dissimilar—offers the manager an assured way of improving quality.[23]

By simulating a range of input assumptions, the logistics executive can perform a sensitivity analysis on the inputs and results of the forecasting technique. This will help to identify the key input variables and to examine how forecast results vary as inputs change. Finally, managerial judgment must be used. Like all quantitative techniques, a forecast is an aid to decision making, not a substitute for it. The logistics executive therefore needs to subjectively evaluate the input variables, the model, and the results produced by the forecast. Good managerial common sense is a valuable addition to a quantitative forecast.

Examples of How Forecasting Can Be Used

Forecasting is used in a variety of situations to aid logistics decision making. For example, forecasting can be used to help answer many important logistics questions such as:

1. What will be the level of future customer demand for the firm's products? Accurate predictions of demand can help determine proper inventory levels, transportation requirements, and the scheduling of production facilities.
2. Based on historical trends, what will be the levels of various logistics costs in the short- and long-term? Projections of costs for labor, equipment, acquisition of raw materials and parts, transportation charges, and other logistics activities allow management to properly plan their future logistics expenditures for important decisions such as whether to utilize public versus private warehousing, what private fleet acquisitions to make, and what types of material handling equipment to purchase.

---

[21] John C. Chambers, Satinder K. Mullick, and Donald D. Smith, "How to Choose the Right Forecasting Technique," *Harvard Business Review* 49, no. 4 (July–August 1971), p. 45.

[22] For an in-depth discussion of these and other forecasting techniques, see Spyros Makridakis and Steven C. Wheelwright, *The Handbook of Forecasting* (New York: John Wiley, 1987).

[23] Georgoff and Murdick, "Manager's Guide to Forecasting," p. 119.

TABLE 14–2 Overview of Selected Forecasting Methods

Method	*Description*	*Time Horizon*	*Computer Requirements*	*Quantitative Sophistication*	*Cost*	*Accuracy*
Sales force estimates	Compilation of estimates by sales force, channel members, or other interested parties. Estimates are usually adjusted to account for error and/or changes.	Short or medium range	Computer not necessary	Minimal	Low	Varies low to high
Delphi technique	An iterative method using experts. Estimates are obtained from each expert at each iteration. New estimates are developed by each expert after having seen a summary of the group's previous results.	Medium or long range	Computer not necessary	Minimal	Low to moderate	Low
Market surveys	Data collected from consumer and industrial customers (actual or potential) using a variety of data collection methods.	Varies	Computer is necessary	Moderate to high	High	Varies low to high

Moving average	Average of past sales or other forecasted variables. Assigns equal weight to each time period in simplest form, may weight time periods differently in more complex forms.	Varies	Computer is helpful but not necessary	Minimal	Low	Moderate to high
Exponential smoothing	Extension of moving average but assigns most importance to recent data. Trend and seasonality can be included in the model.	Short or medium range	Computer is helpful but not necessary	Minimal	Low	Moderate to high
Adaptive filtering	Uses a weighted combination of actual and estimated outcomes. Used when the data pattern changes over time.	Short or medium range	Computer is necessary	Moderate	Moderate to high	Moderate to high
Box-Jenkins	A time series projection technique. Iterative procedure that develops a moving average that is adjusted for seasonal and trend factors. It assigns smaller errors to history than any other model.	Varies	Computer is necessary	High	High	High
Regression models	Predictive equation used to produce forecast estimates. Objective is to minimize forecast error.	Varies	Computer is necessary	Moderate	Moderate	Moderate to high

3. What will be the cost and availability of various raw materials, components, parts, and supplies in the future? Forecasting can aid purchasing and procurement in making forward buy decisions if costs are expected to rise or if items are projected to be in short supply.

Forecasting is an important part of logistics decision making. It is vital that logistics executives understand and utilize good forecasting techniques to aid them in various planning, implementation, and control activities.[24]

Many of the forecasting methods require the use of a computer. The use of computers in all phases of logistics is continuing to increase. In the next section, some of the many uses of computers in logistics will be presented.

SELECTED COMPUTER APPLICATIONS IN LOGISTICS

In an industry survey of almost 1,000 logistics executives, *Modern Materials Handling* found that many firms were experiencing increases in operating efficiencies of 20 (some more than 40) percent because of their use of computers.[25] Some of the areas where improvement occurred included labor productivity, cost of materials, inventory turns, and customer service (see Figure 14–2).

Within logistics, firms are utilizing mainframe, mini- and microcomputers to plan, implement, and control activities. Andersen Consulting's survey of logistics software packages over the last decade has revealed that there has been a large increase in the number of microcomputer (PC) packages available to firms.[26] Because of the proliferation in the number of PCs since 1980, more and more PC-based software is being used in logistics.

A study of member firms of the Council of Logistics Management revealed that mainframe and PC usage were greatest in the areas of order processing, inventory control, transportation rate determination, and distribution system modeling. Table 14–3 identifies the specific applications of computers within logistics. As evidenced by the results shown in the table, firms use mainframes, PCs, or both in logistics management. As systems and software become more powerful, computer usage will increase further, especially the use of PCs.

Use of Computers at Hunt-Wesson Foods

Hunt-Wesson Foods provides a good example of the benefits of computerizing the logistics planning and control activities. Hunt-Wesson utilized a computerized logistics planning system that resulted in an ongoing

[24] For a discussion of various uses of forecasting in logistics, see Lynn E. Gill, "Demand Forecasting: A Vital Tool in Logistics Management," in *The Distribution Handbook,* eds. James F. Robeson and Robert G. House (New York: The Free Press, 1985), pp. 441–67.

[25] Ira P. Krepchin, "From Planning to Shop Floor—Computers Take Charge," *Modern Materials Handling* 40, no. 12 (October 1985), pp. 60–61.

[26] See Richard C. Haverly, Douglas McW. Smith, and Deborah P. Steele, *Logistics Software, 1990 Edition* (Stamford, Conn.: Andersen Consulting, 1990).

FIGURE 14–2 Computers Improve Operating Efficiencies

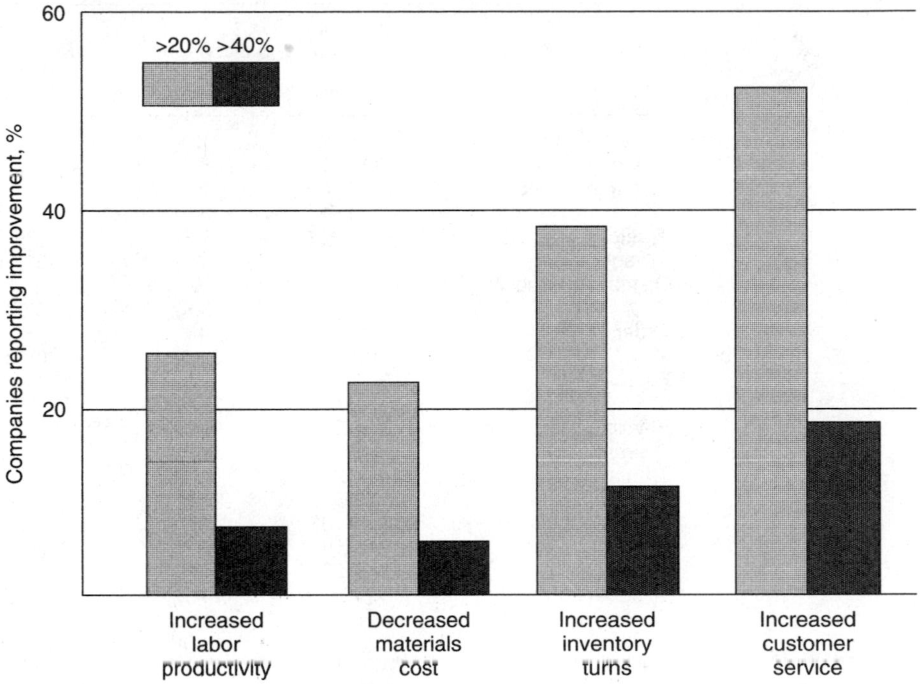

SOURCE: Ira P. Krepchin, "From Planning to Shop Floor—Computers Take Charge," *Modern Materials Handling* 40, no. 12 (October 1985), p. 60. *Modern Materials Handling,* copyright 1985 by Cahners Publishing Company, division of Reed Holdings, Inc.

annual savings of $3 million.[27] The system, which began operating in 1971, had four components:

1. *Data files*—Data are maintained on raw material sources (volumes, prices); on production plants (capacities, unit production costs); on distribution centers (capacities, costs); on customers (location, volume); and on transportation (permissible links, freight rates).
2. *Model*—Involves 34 product groups, 18 plants and refineries, 53 candidate distribution center locations, 289 zones of customer demand, and about 70,000 alternative transportation links.
3. *Solver*—Permits the calculation of optimal solutions from scratch in just a few minutes.
4. *Interface facilities*—Mechanisms for requesting computer runs, and the output reports.[28]

[27] Arthur M. Geoffrion and Richard F. Powers, "Management Support Systems," *Wharton Magazine* 5, no. 3 (Spring 1981), p. 30.

[28] Ibid., pp. 30–31.

TABLE 14–3 Importance and Use of Computers in Various Logistics Management Activities

	Average % of Time on This Activity	*Respondents Who Use Mainframe**	*Respondents Who Use PCs**	*Respondents Who Use Both**
Supervising distribution personnel	*N* = 423 (30.44%)	32 (7.6%)	88 (20.8%)	58 (13.7%)
Inventory control	*N* = 300 (14.9)	139 (46.3)	24 (8.0)	102 (34.0)
Traffic carrier selection/ negotiation	*N* = 267 (12.9)	31 (11.6)	98 (36.7)	41 (15.4)
Distribution modeling	*N* = 281 (12.0)	39 (13.9)	118 (42.0)	73 (26.0)
Order processing	*N* = 203 (11.7)	141 (69.5)	6 (2.9)	27 (13.3)
Forecasting	*N* = 342 (10.6)	91 (26.6)	92 (26.9)	104 (30.4)
Physical distribution service level analysis	*N* = 294 (10.5)	64 (21.8)	78 (26.5)	83 (28.2)
Transportation routing and scheduling	*N* = 227 (9.5)	57 (25.1)	61 (26.9)	36 (15.9)
Material handling	*N* = 183 (9.5)	27 (14.8)	37 (20.2)	26 (14.2)
Traffic rate determination	*N* = 235 (9.3)	35 (14.9)	108 (46.0)	39 (16.6)
Facility location	*N* = 215 (8.1)	28 (13.0)	76 (35.3)	47 (21.9)
Facility design	*N* = 141 (7.6)	8 (5.7)	49 (34.8)	8 (5.7)
Transportation mode selection	*N* = 187 (7.2)	29 (15.5)	54 (28.9)	20 (10.7)

*Numbers in parentheses represent the percent of respondents for that activity.

SOURCE: Adapted from John T. Mentzer, Camille P. Schuster, and David J. Roberts, "Microcomputer Versus Mainframe Usage in Logistics," *The Logistics and Transportation Review* 26, no. 2 (June 1990), p. 125.

The system at Hunt-Wesson is typical of many others in the industry. Because of the associated benefits, usage of such computer systems continues to grow.

In the supermarket sector, computers, in combination with information systems, have been used with great effect. Computers have turned traditional grocery stores into "electronic supermarkets" with the introduction of computerized checkout machines (scanners) and electronic display shelf markers for products.

Computers at Johnson Wax

Johnson Wax streamlined and computerized its finished goods and receiving/storage operations. Figure 14–3 identifies the computer system utilized by the company. The system runs 24 hours a day, seven days a week; this requires minimal computer downtime. Johnson Wax uses fault-tolerant computers that have backups in both hardware and software components. Difficulties can be corrected quickly. In addition, the utilization of

FIGURE 14–3 Fault-Tolerant Computers Control Daily Operations at Johnson Wax

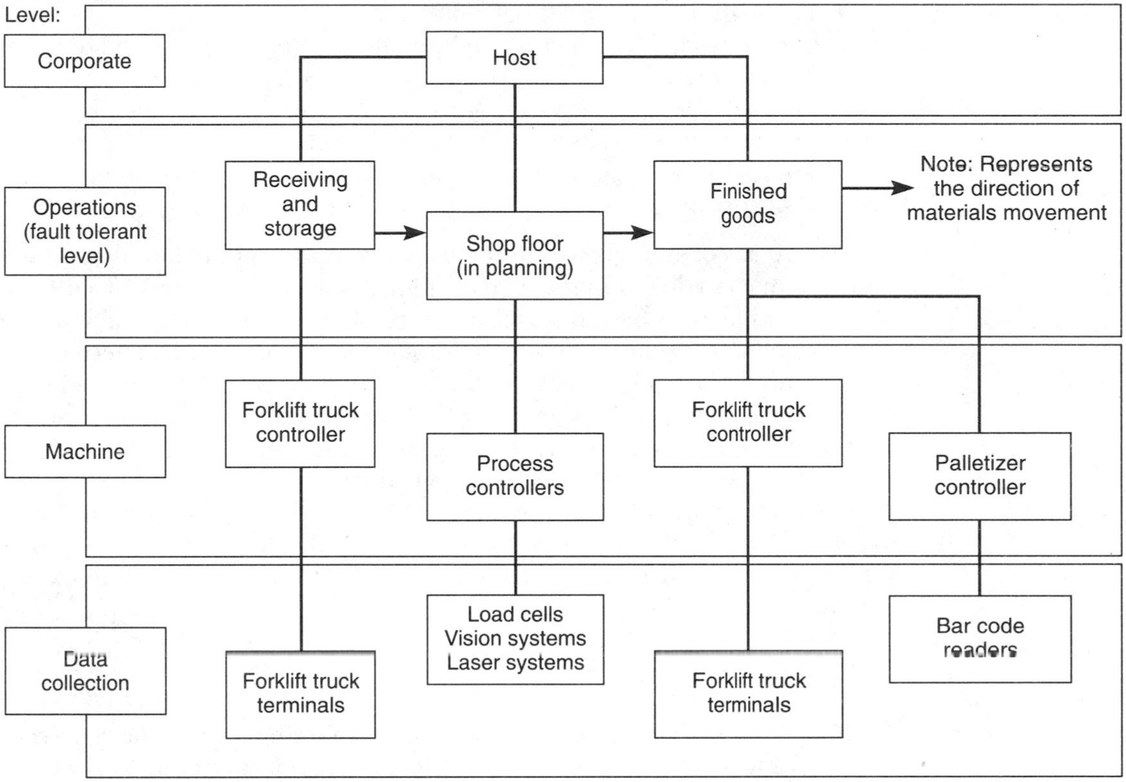

Computers in the different levels of Johnson Wax's control hierarchy have different requirements. The mainframe must be versatile enough to handle a variety of tasks, from planning to statistical analysis. The operations computers, responsible for the daily functioning of the plant, must be reliable, with fast, consistent response time, and be adaptable to a distributed approach.

SOURCE: Ira P. Krepchin, "Computer Control Saves $3.5 Million Annually," *Modern Materials Handling* 40, no. 14 (November 1985), p. 70. *Modern Materials Handling,* copyright 1985 by Cahners Publishing Company, division of Reed Holdings, Inc.

radio-controlled fork-lift trucks and bar code scanners has streamlined the process. Results were significant: "Annual savings of $3.5 million in raw materials, inventory space, personnel, freight, and distribution costs have been realized. And . . . finished goods inventory reconciliation showed an accuracy of 99.8 percent."[29]

Computers at Borg-Warner

Computerization at the Borg-Warner Central Environmental Systems plant in Norman, Oklahoma, resulted in similar benefits. A new computer

[29] Ira P. Krepchin, "Computer Control Saves $3.5 Million Annually," *Modern Materials Handling* 40, no. 14 (November 1985), p. 69.

system replaced an obsolete computer warehouse-controller system and resulted in the following benefits:

- Throughput was up 20 percent.
- Inventory accuracy increased dramatically and was projected to reach 95 percent.
- There was a large decrease in the number of overtime hours.
- The new system took up less physical space.
- There was a direct computer link between the S/R system and the MRPII system.[30]

There has been a growth in the use of computers in material handling equipment control and management. Johnson Wax and Borg-Warner Central Environmental Systems are only two of the many companies where computers have become the dominant means of controlling material handling equipment.[31] Figure 14–4 shows the degree to which material handling equipment is computer controlled. In instances in which computers were utilized, they were typically programmable controllers. This was due in part to their design for specific applications.

As mentioned previously, computers are being utilized in many areas of logistics. In the following sections, we will look at examples of how computers have been used in modeling, artificial intelligence (AI), and expert systems (ES).

Modeling

Modeling Defined

Modeling can be defined as the process of developing a symbolic representation of a total system. A model must accurately represent the "real world" and be managerially useful. The purpose of models has been described as:

> Essentially . . . to replicate reality and to assess the behavior of that reality if changes are introduced. A model supports, rather than replaces, the managerial decision-making process. By using a model, we are able to establish a current situation and then play "what if" games. This "what if" ability is significant. It allows us to quickly consider many different alternatives and test the outcome.[32]

Uses of Models

Models may also be grouped according to their use. Table 14–4 identifies three general categories of models based on how they are used: *diagnostic, tactical,* and *strategic.* Diagnostic and tactical models are used more

---

[30] Ira P. Krepchin,"Warehouse Computer Retrofit Increases Throughput 20%," *Modern Materials Handling* 40, no. 14 (November 1985), pp. 63–64.

[31] See Jerry P. Porter, "Computerized Warehouse Helps Hold Down Operating Costs," *Industrial Engineering* 13, no. 6 (June 1981), pp. 56–64.

[32] John H. Campbell, "The Manager's Guide to Computer Modeling," *Business* 32, no. 4 (October–November–December 1982), p. 11.

FIGURE 14–4 Computers Control Material Handling Equipment

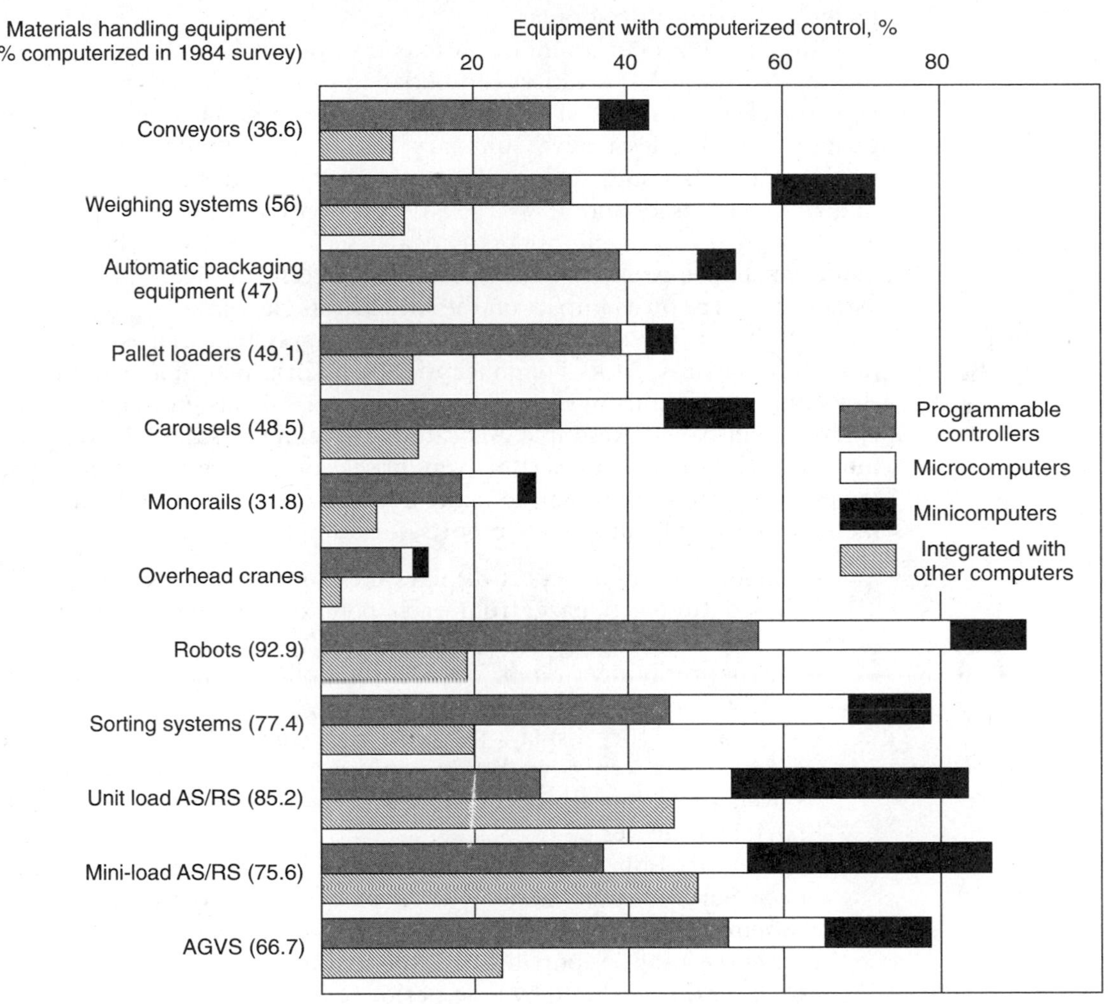

SOURCE: Ira P. Krepchin, "From Planning to Shop Floor—Computers Take Charge," *Modern Materials Handling* 40, no. 12 (October 1985), p. 61. *Modern Materials Handling,* copyright 1985 by Cahners Publishing Company, division of Reed Holdings, Inc.

TABLE 14–4 Framework of Models

Category	*Scope*	*Applications*
Diagnostic	Specific task	Business indicators
Tactical	Functional	Business activities
Strategic	General purpose	Broad economic questions

SOURCE: John H. Campbell, "The Manager's Guide to Computer Modeling," *Business* 32, no. 4 (October-November-December 1982), p. 11.

frequently in logistics because they are task and/or function specific. To illustrate the difference between the three types of models, we can examine issues in the transportation area.

A diagnostic model examines various transportation indicators, such as unit costs, freight/sales ratios, consolidation opportunity costs, or private fleet profile.[33] A model of this type analyzes data about these issues and generates some descriptive summary results about them. The tactical model examines issues such as the methods and modes of transportation that should be used, and how large a fleet a firm should have.[34] It is mostly a prescriptive model, as opposed to a descriptive model. The strategic model examines issues like transportation's role in the marketing mix efforts of the firm or its impact on the firm's strategic marketing plan.

A Computerized Modeling System at IBM

IBM has utilized a computerized modeling system that is both diagnostic and tactical. At its Poughkeepsie, New York, manufacturing facility (for computer mainframes and components), IBM has employed a modeling system called Resource Allocation Modeling System (RAMS). The model specifically examines IBM's vendor selection process. The model has generated savings equivalent to many times its cost, and provides management with valuable and timely reports, including:

A vendor utilization report displays the amounts that should be purchased for each part, from each potential vendor, in every time period.

A purchasing budget report displays the dollars to be spent with each vendor, for each part, by time period.

A shortfalls report displays the parts that cannot be procured as required, their respective short quantities, for every time period.

An average part cost report displays the average procurement cost by part, by time period.

An inventory utilization report displays the inventory cost incurred for each part, by time period, when parts are delivered earlier than required.

A resource usage report displays the amount of resources utilized at each vendor location, by time period.[35]

Whirlpool Corporation's WHAMOL Model

A classic example was the computer modeling system used by the Whirlpool Corporation called WHAMOL (Whirlpool Heuristic, Analytical Model of Logistics). WHAMOL was used to simulate potential "what if" operating environments and logistics strategies. The model had the following features:

---

[33] Ibid., p. 12.

[34] Ibid.

[35] Paul S. Bender and Michael H. Isaac, "Made to Order Computer Models Are Used—Where Else—At IBM," *Handling & Shipping Management Presidential Issue, 1984–1985* 25, no. 10 (September 1984), p. 62.

1. Accurately calculated logistic costs and investments.
2. Selected product source and mode to meet service constraints at lowest cost for different types of orders.
3. Provided a detailed evaluation of system alternatives rapidly and at low cost.
4. Provided information on product movement, costs incurred, and investments required.

During the 1970s, Whirlpool was able to apply WHAMOL to a number of important logistics decisions. The system was able to simulate the following:

Logistics costs for a proposed new product line.
Logistics costs of 10 alternative sites for a proposed new manufacturing facility.
Optimum site and size of warehousing to serve West Coast distributors.
Current versus potential logistics costs of certain selected Whirlpool brand distributors and branches.

The model was very successful in meeting the objective established by Whirlpool, namely: "to insure that Whirlpool's [logistics] strategy, which is either operating, or planned for future implementation, will in effect achieve its stated goals of minimum costs and maximum service levels."[36]

Modeling at Pet Inc.

A rather interesting example of the use of logistics modeling in a corporate merger or acquisition occurred in 1989 when Pet Inc., a manufacturer of specialty foods, acquired Van de Kamp's Frozen Seafoods. Before the acquisition was completed, Pet used its in-house logistics model to evaluate the cost and service implications. Within three days after the acquisition, all of Van de Kamp's orders were being processed on Pet systems and all products were being distributed through Pet's logistics system.

> What's the payoff from this successful integration of systems and operations? From a quantitative standpoint, monthly inventories in 1989 dropped an average of nearly $1.5 million compared to the previous year. This was achieved despite a 10-percent increase in the number of cases sold.
>
> Pet last year also realized the highest inventory turnover rate in the company's history at 5.34. And the case-fill ratio has consistently hit the target of 98 percent. Notably, the distribution department accomplished this with no increase in manpower.[37]

In the future, the company anticipates expanding its use of computer models to aid its marketing and logistics processes.

---

[36] "Physical Distribution at Whirlpool," written summary of presentation made by the now retired John Crouse, vice president for physical distribution, at a corporate quarterly review meeting, May 1976, p. 6.

[37] Francis J. Quinn, "A Model Distribution System," *Traffic Management* 29, no. 6 (June 1990), p. 34.

Artificial Intelligence

Other modeling applications are numerous.[38] Recently, the most exciting opportunities in modeling have occurred in the area of *artificial intelligence* (AI) and expert systems (ES). "Computers are now capable of simulating some of the aspects of human intelligence. The object of an expert system, for example, is to capture all the knowledge accumulated by a human who has achieved mastery in a particular domain, and to apply that knowledge to given situations in much the same ways as the human expert does."[39] Although the technology is still being developed, applications of artificial intelligence to logistics offer tremendous potential to the logistics community: "Applications stemming from AI research include expert systems (knowledge engineering), computer-aided instruction, voice synthesis and recognition, vision systems, natural language translators, game-playing systems, and robotics."[40]

Artificial Intelligence (AI) and Expert Systems (ES)

Developed out of the field of computer science, artificial intelligence (AI) is

What Is Artifical Intelligence?

> concerned with the concepts and methods of inference by a computer and the symbolic representation of the knowledge used in making inferences. The term intelligence covers many cognitive skills, including the ability to solve problems, to learn, to understand language, and in general, to behave in a way that would be considered intelligent if observed in a human.[41]

AI is a comprehensive term encompassing a number of areas, including computer-aided instruction, voice synthesis and recognition, game playing systems, natural language translators, robotics, and expert systems (ES).[42] While the number of applications of AI is limited at the present time, the potential in logistics is staggering. AI has been used to "aid in the design of automated warehousing systems, to configure computer systems and to identify material requirements, to group varied sized shipments into logical entities for easier pallet building, and to aid in short-interval scheduling of warehouse, trucking, and manufacturing operations."[43]

---

[38] See Ronald H. Ballou, "Heuristics: Rules of Thumb for Logistics Decision Making," *Journal of Business Logistics* 10, no. 1 (1989), pp. 122–32; and Richard F. Powers, "Optimization Models for Logistics Decisions," *Journal of Business Logistics* 10, no. 1 (1989), pp. 106–21.

[39] Wally Rhines, "Artificial Intelligence: Out of the Lab and Into Business," *The Journal of Business Strategy* 6, no. 1 (Summer 1985), p. 50.

[40] Omar Keith Helferich, "Computers that Mimic Human Thought: Artificial Intelligence for Materials and Logistics Management," *Journal of Business Logistics* 5, no. 2 (1984), p. 123.

[41] Mary Kay Allen and Omar Keith Helferich, *Putting Expert Systems to Work in Logistics* (Oak Brook, Ill.: Council of Logistics Management, 1990), p. A6.

[42] Omar K. Helferich, Stephen J. Schon, Mary Kay Allen, Raymond L. Rowland, and Robert L. Cook, "Applications of Artificial Intelligence—Expert Systems to Logistics," *Proceedings of the Annual Conference of the Council of Logistics Management,* vol. I (1986).

[43] John F. Magee, William C. Copacino, and Donald B. Rosenfield, *Modern Logistics Management* (New York: John Wiley, 1985), p. 150.

Of specific interest to logistics executives is the subarea of AI known as expert systems (ES). An ES is defined as:

Expert Systems Defined

> A computer program that uses knowledge and reasoning techniques to solve problems normally requiring the abilities of human experts. An expert system is an artificial intelligence (AI) program that achieves competence in performing a specialized task by reasoning with a body of knowledge about the task and the task domain.[44]

Expert systems are capable of being applied to a variety of marketing and logistics problem categories, including interpretation, monitoring, debugging, repair, instruction, and control.[45] (See Table 14–5.) More specifically, expert systems can be used in the following areas of logistics:[46]

1. *Transportation*
   Interpret economic and regulatory data and predict impact on transportation.
   Assess for-hire/owned private fleet/leased private fleet vehicle decisions and prescribe remedy.
   Design vehicle routing to aid managers in minimizing route time, and asset utilization.
   Plan shipment routing.
   Monitor carrier performance and prescribe carriers in selection process.
   Instruct traffic managers on proven carrier negotiation techniques.
2. *Warehousing/Material Handling Systems*
   Assess alternative warehouse site locations and prescribe remedy.
   Design specifications for advanced material handling systems for either a vendor or customer.
   Design warehouse layout.
   Plan and control receiving/shipping dock scheduling.
   Monitor warehouse performance and prescribe actions to improve performance.
   Instruct receiving personnel on quality control inspection procedures regarding specific vendors and products.
3. *Inventory*
   Interpret sales and environmental data and predict product demand.
   Assess inventory availability goals and uncertainty levels by location and prescribe safety stock levels.
   Control system inventory levels.
   Diagnose and debug demand forecast correction errors.

---

[44] Allen and Helferich, *Putting Expert Systems to Work in Logistics,* p. A10.

[45] See Paul Harmon and David King, *Expert Systems* (New York: John Wiley, 1985), p. 94.

[46] The listing of ES applications herein is taken from Helferich et al., "Applications of Artificial Intelligence—Expert Systems in Logistics," pp. 48–54.

TABLE 14–5 What Is an Expert System? The Case of ABC Scientific

A good way to understand expert systems is to consider the case of ABC Scientific. ABC Scientific, a hypothetical company, has problems similar to many existing wholesalers and retailers. Through a series of acquisitions and mergers, the company now maintains a vastly diversified product line of over 30,000 SKUs. The highly specialized products are documented in a catalog. The products are quite diverse in function and use, so it is difficult for any of ABC's employees to be familiar with, much less knowledgeable of, them all.

ABC Scientific has a customer base distributed throughout the United States. Over 100 order entry and customer service representatives located at the corporate headquarters handle orders and customer inquiries. The majority of the orders come in by telephone and the customer ordering the product rarely knows exactly what they want, much less the ABC catalog model or part number. For example, a school might call to order a replacement light bulb for a piece of physics laboratory equipment. In order to select exactly the right bulb several specifics must be known such as the general type, size, wattage, color, and usage. Selecting the right bulb would generally not be too difficult because light bulbs are such familiar products. With a little training on what types of light bulbs are carried, most order clerks could determine the right questions to ask to determine the right bulb for the job.

However, if the product is something completely unfamiliar, such as a complex piece of medical equipment, it would be difficult to even know what questions to ask in order to determine if ABC could satisfy the requirement. In this case, someone with specialized knowledge of medical equipment would be required. In fact for some medical items, ABC's catalog lists over 100 pages of different model numbers of the same type of item. This fact is further complicated by ABC's inventory of 30,000 stocked items.

With so many products and so many choices within product lines it is nearly impossible for the order entry personnel to possess expert knowledge of each product type. ABC would like to have an expert knowledgeable on each product readily available to answer any call so that no matter what product a customer was looking for, he would be able to receive immediate and accurate assistance. Without this expertise the customer is likely to abandon ABC for a supplier who appears more knowledgeable and can provide better service. Equally as displeasing to ABC is the likelihood that the product was available on ABC's shelves and the order clerk mistakenly told the customer it was not.

Further complicating the problem is the high turnover rate of the order clerks and customer assistance personnel. Once an order clerk becomes familiar with a number of products, he may be promoted and vital knowledge could be lost.

The ideal solution to ABC's predicament must possess several key features. First, the solution should improve the effectiveness of ABC's personnel in advising the customer about the product best suited to his needs. This feature should result in increased revenues for ABC. ABC would earn a reputation as a company a customer could rely on for quick fulfillment of his needs, even when the customer does not thoroughly understand those needs. Second, a good solution should provide assistance in training new personnel and making them proficient almost immediately. Third, the solution must be responsive to the customer—a computerized solution with a 20-minute response time would not be adequate when the customer is waiting on the phone. Fourth, the solution must be cost effective. Finally, the solution must permit the knowledge of the existing order specialists to be captured and retained.

Expert systems technology matches all the requirements for an effective solution to ABC's problem. Expert systems mimic human experts and serve as intelligent advisors on specific areas of expertise. They are designed to deal with symbolic knowledge that would be necessitated for this problem, knowledge about color, shape, and usage, among others. Further, they can reason with uncertain or conflicting information and missing details. Expert systems can store large amounts of facts and information, yet reach conclusions or provide advice by using shortcuts (referred to . . . as "heuristics") to "think" about the problem.

An ABC order clerk would probably use an expert catalog advisor on his personal computer. In order to facilitate the phone conversation with the customer, the system might even have a speech interface versus a keyboard interface. The clerk might begin an interactive consultation with the expert system by typing or saying the name of the product the customer required (e.g., light bulb). The system would then prompt the order clerk with questions that should be asked of the user to determine which of ABC's products could best satisfy the demand. The figure below depicts an interactive consultation with the expert catalog advisor. The responses

TABLE 14–5 (*concluded*)

next to the >> prompt are those that the order clerk provides to the system based upon the customer's response. Note how easy it is to use and understand this system.

A Sample Consultation with the ABC Scientific Expert Catalog Advisor

Welcome to the ABC Catalog Advisor

What product type does the customer require?
>>*light bulb*

What is the light bulb used for?
>>*a photo emitter*

Who was the original manufacturer of the photo emitter?
>>*Beckman Instruments*

What is the model number of this Beckman photo emitter?
>>*unknown*

Is the light emitter a "professional" or "series 5000" unit?
>>*unknown*

Which is the unit, a floor model or a desktop model?
>>*desktop*

Advice: Model No. 4367 best meets the customer's needs.
Unit price is $1.67.
We have 450 in stock.

Do you wish to see alternate light bulbs which can also satisfy this requirement?
>>*no*

Does the customer wish to place an order?
>>■

SOURCE: Mary Kay Allen and Omar Keith Helferich, *Putting Expert Systems to Work in Logistics* (Oak Brook, Ill.: Council of Logistics Management, 1990), pp. 22–24.

Instruct inventory personnel regarding procedures for taking physical inventory.

4. *Purchasing*
   Interpret environmental data and predict future prices of key materials.
   Control material shortages.
   Monitor material prices.
   Monitor vendor performance and prescribe vendors in vendor sourcing and selection process.
   Instruct buyers on purchasing new products/materials.
5. *Packaging*
   Assess internal packing container arrangements and prescribe best arrangement of items.
   Design product packaging given physical and element environment.
   Diagnose and debug package/carton malfunctions.

Monitor packaging department productivity/performance and prescribe improvements.

6. *Information systems*
   Assess logistics communications needs and prescribe order transmittal methods/equipment.
   Plan logistics information flow.
   Plan and control backorder processing.
   Monitor order management department performance and prescribe improvements.
   Instruct order entry personnel regarding order entry procedures.
7. *Customer service*
   Interpret customer information and prescribe future key customer service needs.
   Plan and control inventory allocations/product substitutions.
   Monitor customer service performance and prescribe actions to improve customer service.
   Instruct tracing personnel on proven tracing methods regarding the carrier, product, or country.

Expert Systems at Xerox

Xerox Corporation, the multibillion-dollar office products equipment manufacturer and winner of the Malcolm Baldrige National Quality Award in 1989, has utilized expert systems to manage its vehicle routing and scheduling. Utilizing 70 to 80 trucks assigned to Xerox from five national motor carriers, the firm moves 250 million pounds of products in 12,000 truckload shipments annually to thousands of customers being serviced from three distribution centers located in California, Texas, and New York.[47]

Expert Systems of Digital Equipment and Eastman Kodak

Digital Equipment Corporation (DEC), the computer manufacturer, has used an ES to reduce work-in-process cycle times from 35 to 5 days.[48] Eastman Kodak Company, the multinational firm that produces film and cameras, uses expert systems in its distribution centers to improve worker productivity in picking and palletizing products for shipment. For example, the training period for new employees was reduced from 6–12 weeks to 1–2 days.[49]

When to Use an Expert System

In deciding whether expert systems should be used to solve a particular logistics problem, Allen and Helferich have identified five criteria to aid decision makers. If any of the criteria are met, an ES is appropriate:

1. The task or problem solution requires the use of human knowledge, judgement, and experience.

---

[47] James Aaron Cooke, "Xerox's Drive for Logistics Quality," *Traffic Management* 29, no. 10 (October 1990), pp. 50–53.

[48] Allen and Helferich, *Putting Expert Systems to Work in Logistics*, pp. 44–45.

[49] Ibid., p. 44.

2. The task requires the use of heuristics (e.g., rules-of-thumb) or decisions based on incomplete or uncertain information.
3. The task primarily requires symbolic reasoning versus numerical computation.
4. The task is neither too easy (taking a human expert less than a few minutes) nor too difficult (requiring more than a few hours for an expert to perform).
5. Substantial variability exists in people's ability to perform the task. Novices gain competence with experience. Experts are better than novices at performing the task.[50]

If an ES is appropriate, the next decision facing the logistics executive is whether the system can be economically justified. Again, Allen and Helferich have provided guidelines to help firms make such a decision. The six criteria listed below consider both decision effectiveness and economic considerations.

How to Justify the Use of Expert Systems

1. There is a need to capture the expertise. The expertise may not be available on a continuing basis.
2. Pockets of knowledge or knowledge bottlenecks regarding the task exist.
3. Expertise on the task is needed in many locations.
4. Inadequate human resources capable of performing this task are available.
5. Conventional solutions to the task are considered to be inadequate or nonexistent.
6. The cost of developing, implementing, and maintaining the knowledge-based system is less than continuing operations in the current manner.[51]

For many firms, the use of expert systems is both appropriate and justifiable. With the number of applications increasing, the costs of computer hardware and software decreasing, and the capabilities of microcomputers expanding, more companies will find that AI, especially expert systems, will become an important and necessary component of logistics planning, implementation, and control.

SUMMARY

The use of computers in all facets of business is widespread. Computers have become an invaluable aid to the logistics executive in making various operational and strategic decisions. Decision support systems, which are computer based, provide information for the decision-making process. The DSS has three components: data acquisition, data processing, and data presentation.

The environmental scanning activity is a useful way of obtaining the

---

[50] Ibid., p. 115.

[51] Ibid., p. 117.

necessary data for decision making. It is the process that identifies and evaluates environmental events and interrelationships for the purpose of aiding the logistics executive in the development of strategy. Environmental scanning can take any of three forms: irregular scanning, regular scanning, and continuous scanning. The information obtained through environmental scanning can be used in a variety of ways, although one major use is in forecasting.

Forecasting is important because proper logistics control requires forward planning; it is therefore necessary to be able to accurately predict future circumstances and events. There are many forecasting methods, including regression analysis, trend analysis, Box-Jenkins, moving average, adaptive filtering, exponential smoothing, and simulation. Many of the forecasting methods require the use of a computer. Forecasting is only one of many logistics activities where the computer is used.

Computers are widely employed in many areas of logistics, including transportation, inventory control, warehousing, order processing, material handling, and so forth. Some of the most exciting areas of computerization are modeling, artificial intelligence (AI), and expert systems (ES).

As an aid to decision making, the computer has allowed management to make better cost trade-off decisions and improve customer service levels. It has enabled the logistics executive to analyze great volumes of data and to do it quickly. In the next chapter, we will see how the computer can be applied to the financial control of logistics performance.

SUGGESTED READINGS

ALLEN, MARY KAY. *The Development of an Artificial Intelligence System for Inventory Management.* Oak Brook, Ill.: Council of Logistics Management, 1986.

ALLEN, MARY K., AND MARGARET A. EMMELHAINZ. "Decision Support Systems: An Innovative Aid to Managers." *Journal of Business Logistics* 5, no. 2 (1984), pp. 128–42.

ALLEN, MARY K., AND OMAR KEITH HELFERICH. *Putting Expert Systems to Work in Logistics.* Oak Brook, Ill.: Council of Logistics Management, 1990.

ANDRIOLE, STEPHEN J. "The Promise of Artificial Intelligence." *Journal of Systems Management* 36, no. 7 (July 1985), pp. 8–17.

BENDER, PAUL S. "Logistics System Design." In *The Distribution Handbook,* eds. James F. Robeson and Robert G. House, New York: Free Press, 1985, pp. 143–224.

BOWMAN ROBERT. "A Computerized Route to Better Decisions." *Distribution* 91, no. 5 (May 1992), pp. 28–34.

CALANTONE, ROGER J., AND MICHAEL H. MORRIS. "The Utilization of Computer-Based Decision Support Systems in Transportation." *International Journal of Physical Distribution and Materials Management* 15, no. 7 (1985), pp. 5–18.

COOKE, JAMES AARON. "Computers Lead the Way to Total Inbound Control." *Traffic Management* 29, no. 1 (January 1990), pp. 50–53.

COPACINO, WILLIAM, AND DONALD B. ROSENFIELD. "Analytical Tools for Strategic Planning." *International Journal of Physical Distribution and Materials Management* 15, no. 3 (1985), pp. 47–61.

CURRY, BRUCE, AND LUIZ MOUTINHO. "Expert Systems for Site Location Decisions." *Logistics Information Management* 4, no. 4 (1991), pp. 19–27.

DE LEEUW, KEES. "Computers in the 1990s and the Impact on Logistics." *Asia Pacific International Journal of Business Logistics* 1, no. 2 (1988), pp. 21–29.

DIEBOLD, JOHN. "Taking Stock of the Information Age." *Management Review* 74, no. 9 (September 1985), pp. 18–21.

FLORES, BENITO E., AND D. CLAY WHYBARK. "Forecasting 'Laws' for Management." *Business Horizons* 28, no. 4 (July–August 1985), pp. 48–53.

GIBSON, CYRUS F., AND PATRICIA T. KOSINAR. "Meeting the Need for Information Technology Literacy." *Management Review* 74, no. 9 (September 1985), pp. 24–27.

HALEY, GEORGE T., AND R. KRISHNAN. "It's Time for CALM: Computer-Aided Logistics Management." *International Journal of Physical Distribution and Materials Management* 15, no. 7 (1985), pp. 19–32.

KIESLER, SARA. "The Hidden Messages in Computer Networks." *Harvard Business Review* 64, no. 1 (January–February 1986), pp. 46–60.

LANGLEY, C. JOHN, JR. "Information-Based Decision Making in Logistics Management." *International Journal of Physical Distribution and Materials Management* 15, no. 7 (1985), pp. 41–55.

LE MAY, STEPHEN A., AND WALLACE R. WOOD. "Developing Logistics Decision Support Systems." *Journal of Business Logistics* 10, no. 2 (1989), pp. 1–23.

LOCKLIN, RONALD M. "Choosing a Data Communications Network." *The Journal of Business Strategy* 6, no. 3 (Winter 1986), pp. 14–26.

MAGNET, MYRON. "Who Needs a Trend-Spotter?" *Fortune* 112, no. 13 (December 9, 1985), pp. 51–56.

MENTZER, JOHN T., AND JAMES E. COX, JR. "A Model of the Determinants of Achieved Forecast Accuracy." *Journal of Business Logistics* 5, no. 2 (1984), pp. 143–55.

MENTZER, JOHN T., CAMILLE P. SCHUSTER, AND DAVID J. ROBERTS. "Microcomputer versus Mainframe Usage in Logistics." *The Logistics and Transportation Review* 26, no. 2 (June 1990). pp. 115–32.

POWERS, RICHARD F. "Optimization Models for Logistics Decisions." *Journal of Business Logistics* 10, no. 1 (1989), pp. 106–21.

RHEA, NOLAN W. "Think About Artificial Intelligence." *Material Handling Engineer* 42, no. 6 (June 1987), pp. 71–79.

SHAPIRO, JEREMY F. "Quantitative Methods in Distribution." In *The Distribution Handbook,* eds. James F. Robeson and Robert G. House. New York: Free Press, 1985, pp. 373–409.

VAN DER MUELEN, P. R. H., AND G. SPIJKERMAN. "The Logistics Input-Output Model and Its Application." *International Journal of Physical Distribution and Materials Management* 15, no. 3 (1985), pp. 17–25.

QUESTIONS AND PROBLEMS

1. Briefly describe the role of decision support systems in logistics decision making.
2. Define environmental scanning. Identify the roles that irregular, regular, and continuous scanning have in logistics.
3. Discuss the importance of appropriateness, cost, and accuracy in forecasting.
4. Identify areas of logistics where expert systems (ES) and artificial intelligence (AI) are being used to improve efficiency and effectiveness.
5. A survey conducted by *Modern Materials Handling* found that computer usage was most common in the order entry, order processing, and inventory control activities. Explain why you think these activities have utilized computers to a larger degree than other areas of logistics.

Chapter 15

Financial Control of Logistics Performance

Objectives of This Chapter

To show how to use logistics costs for decision making

To show how to measure and control performance of the logistics function

To show how to cost-justify changes in logistics structure

INTRODUCTION

In Chapter 2 we saw that logistics costs can exceed 25 percent of the cost of doing business at the manufacturing level. For this reason, better management of the logistics function offers the potential for large savings, which can contribute to improved corporate profitability. In mature markets—in which large sales increases are difficult to achieve and corporate profitability is continuously being eroded by increasing costs and competition—it is necessary to look for ways to improve productivity.

In many firms logistics has not been managed as an integrated system. Even in those firms that have accepted the integrated logistics management concept, evidence suggests that the required cost data are not available.[1] The accurate measurement and control of logistics costs offers significant potential for improving cash flow and return on assets. In this chapter we will concentrate on financial control of logistics performance.

THE IMPORTANCE OF ACCURATE COST DATA

Prior to 1960, logistics was viewed as a fragmented and often uncoordinated set of activities spread throughout various organizational functions. However, over the past three decades, the notion that a firm's total logistics costs could be reduced, customer service improved, and interdepartmental conflicts substantially reduced by the coordination of logistics activities, has been accepted in many major corporations. Computers, operations research techniques, and the systems approach brought high-speed processing and the logic of mathematics to the field of logistics and led not only to changes in transportation strategy, inventory control techniques, warehousing location policy, order processing systems, and logistics communication, but also to the desire to manage the costs associated with these functions in an integrated format.

Most of the early obstacles confronting full implementation of the integrated logistics management concept appear to have been removed. The lack of adequate cost data, however, has prevented logistics management

[1] Douglas M. Lambert and John T. Mentzer, "Is Integrated Physical Distribution Management a Reality?" *Journal of Business Logistics* 2, no. 1 (1980), pp. 18–34; and Douglas M. Lambert and Jay U. Sterling, "What Types of Profitability Reports Do Marketing Managers Receive?" *Industrial Marketing Management* 16, no. 4 (1987), pp. 295–303.

from reaching its full potential. In general, accountants have not kept pace with developments in logistics. They have, in fact, shown relatively little interest in the area. Consequently, much of the necessary cost analysis has not been carried out.[2]

Accurate Cost Data Are Required for Integrated Logistics

Accurate cost data are required for successful implementation of the integrated logistics management concept using total cost analysis. They are also required for the management and control of logistics operations.

Total Cost Analysis

Total Cost Analysis Is the Key to Managing Logistics

The key to managing the logistics function is *total cost analysis*.[3] That is, at a given level of customer service, management should minimize total logistical cost rather than attempt to minimize the cost of individual activities. The major shortcoming of a nonintegrative approach to logistics cost analysis is that attempts to reduce specific costs within the logistics function may be less than optimal for the system as a whole, leading to greater total costs.

Total logistics costs do not respond to cost-cutting techniques individually geared to warehouse, transportation, or inventory costs. Reductions in one cost invariably result in increases in one or more of the others. For example, aggregating all finished goods inventory into fewer distribution centers may minimize warehousing costs and increase inventory turnover, but it will lead to increased transportation expense. Similarly, savings resulting from favorable purchase prices on large orders may be entirely offset by greater inventory carrying costs. Thus, to minimize total cost, management must understand the effect of trade-offs within the distribution function.

Cost Trade-Offs Are Essential

Cost trade-offs between and among the various components of the logistics system are essential. Profit can be enhanced, for example, if the reduction in inventory carrying cost is more than the increase in the other functional costs (Figure 15–1), or if improved customer service yields greater overall revenue. If knowledgeable trade-offs are to be made, however, management must be able to account for the costs associated with each component, and to explain how changes in each cost contribute to total costs.

As the cost of logistics increases, the need for accurate accounting for the costs becomes increasingly critical. Since the logistics function is relatively more energy-intensive and labor-intensive than other areas of the firm, its ratio of costs to total company costs has been steadily increasing. Management cannot realize the full potential of logistics cost trade-off analysis until it can fully determine the costs related to separate functional areas and their interaction.

---

[2] Douglas M. Lambert and Howard M. Armitage, "Distribution Costs: The Challenge," *Management Accounting* 60, no. 11 (May 1979), p. 33.

[3] This section is adapted from Lambert and Armitage, pp. 33–34; and Lambert and Sterling, pp. 295–303.

FIGURE 15–1 Cost Trade-Offs Required in a Logistics System

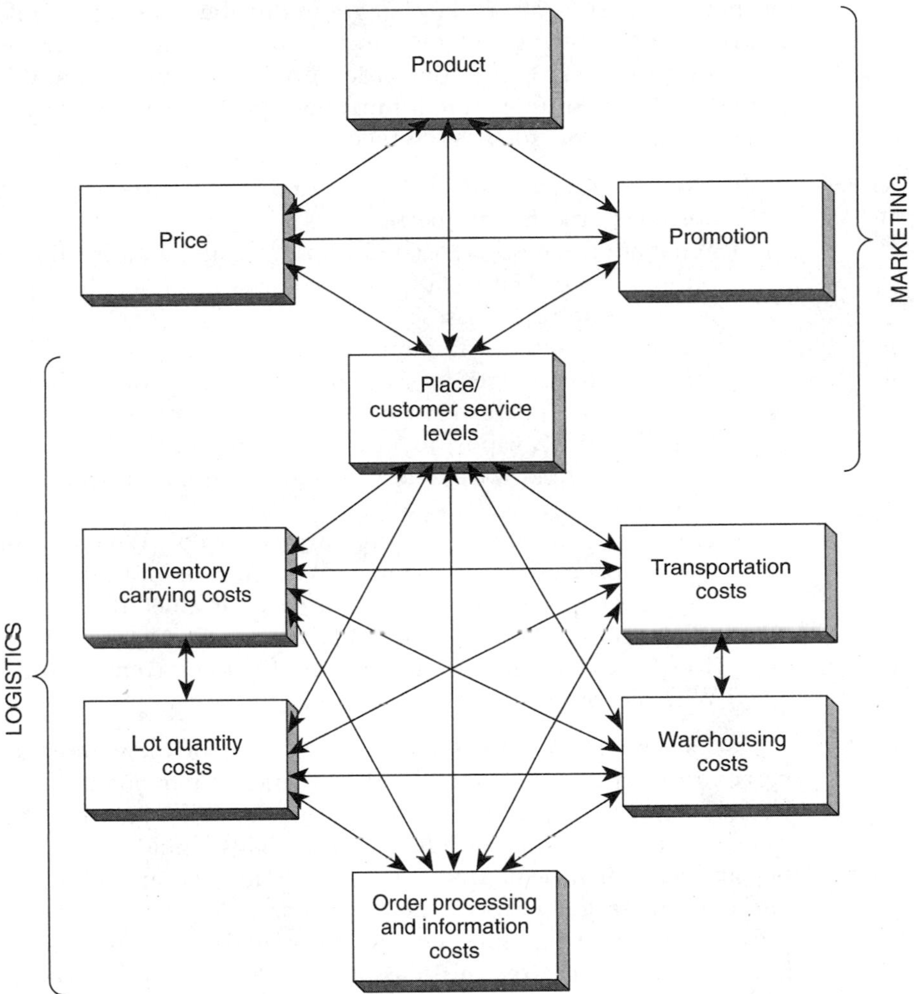

Marketing objective: Allocate resources to the marketing mix to maximize the long-run profitability of the firm.
Logistics objective: Minimize total costs, given the customer service objective, where: Total costs = Transportation costs + Warehousing costs + Order processing and information costs + Lot quantity costs + Inventory carrying costs.

SOURCE: Adapted from Douglas M. Lambert, *The Development of an Inventory Costing Methodology: A Study of the Costs Associated with Holding Inventory* (Chicago: National Council of Physical Distribution Management, 1976), p. 7.

The quality of the accounting data influences management's ability to exploit new markets, take advantage of innovative transportation systems, choose between common carriers and private trucking, increase deliveries or increase inventories, make changes in distribution center configuration, restructure the echelon of inventories, make changes in packaging, and determine to what extent the order processing system should be automated. The accounting system must be capable of providing information to answer questions such as the following:

Many Management Decisions Require Good Cost Data

- How do logistics costs affect contribution by product, by territory, by customer, and by salesperson?
- What are the costs associated with providing additional levels of customer service? What trade-offs are necessary, and what are the incremental benefits or losses?
- What is the optimal amount of inventory? How sensitive is the inventory level to changes in warehousing patterns or to changes in customer service levels? How much does it cost to hold inventory?
- What mix of transport modes/carriers should be used?
- How many field warehouses should be used and where should they be located?
- How many production setups are required? Which plants will be used to produce each product? What are the optimum manufacturing plant capacities based on alternative product mixes and volumes?
- What product packaging alternatives should be used?
- To what extent should the order processing system be automated?
- What distribution channels should be used?

To answer these and other questions, management must know what costs and revenues will change if the logistics system changes. That is, the determination of a product's contribution should be based on how corporate revenues, expenses, and hence profitability would change if the product line were dropped. Any costs or revenues that are unaffected by this decision are irrelevant to the problem. For example, a relevant cost is the public warehouse handling charges associated with a product's sales. An irrelevant cost is the overhead associated with the firm's private trucking fleet.

Only Consider Relevant Costs

Implementation of this approach to decision making is severely hampered by the unavailability of accounting data, or the inability to use the right data when they are available. The best and most sophisticated models are only as good as the accounting input. A number of studies attest to the inadequacies of logistics cost data.[4]

---

[4]See for example David Ray, "Distribution Costing and The Current State of the Art," *International Journal of Physical Distribution* 6, no. 2 (1975), pp. 75–107 at p. 88; Michael Schiff, *Accounting and Control in Physical Distribution Management* (Chicago: National Council of Physi-

Controlling Logistics Activities

Cost Data Are Essential for Control

One of the major reasons for improving the availability of logistics cost data is to control and monitor logistics performance. Without accurate cost data, performance analysis is next to impossible. How can a firm expect to control the cost of shipping a product to a customer if it does not know what the cost should be? How can management determine if distribution center costs are high or low in the absence of performance measurements? What is "good" performance for the order processing function? Are inventory levels satisfactory, too high, or too low? These questions are not the only ones we can ask, but they serve to illustrate the need for accurate cost data.

The following paragraphs describe the importance of a good measurement program for the management and control of logistics:

> If no measurement program exists, the "natural" forces shaping the behavior of busy managers tend to place the emphasis on the negative. Issues only attract management attention when something is "wrong." In this type of situation, there is often little reinforcement of positive results. A *formal* measurement program helps focus attention on the positive and helps improve employee moral. . . . Once a plan has been established, actual results can be measured and compared with the plan to identify variances requiring management attention.[5]

Case Studies

As the cost of logistics continues to rise, the need for management to be able to account for the costs associated with each component becomes increasingly critical.[6] It is also necessary to know how changes in the costs of each component affect total costs and profits. Estimates of logistics costs ranging from 15 percent to 50 percent of total sales are not uncommon, depending on the nature of the company. However, these are at best only educated guesses since they are usually based on costs incorrectly computed by management. From a corporate standpoint, the inability to measure and manage logistics costs leads to missed opportunities and expensive

---

cal Distribution Management, 1971), pp. 4–21; Lambert and Mentzer, "Is Integrated Physical Distribution Management a Reality?" pp. 18–34; Douglas M. Lambert, *The Distribution Channels Decision* (New York: The National Association of Accountants, and Hamilton, Ontario: The Society of Management Accountants of Canada, 1978) pp. 88–91, 102–111; and Douglas M. Lambert, *The Product Abandonment Decision* (New York: The National Association of Accountants, and Hamilton, Ontario: The Society of Management Accountants of Canada, 1985), pp. 98, 127–32.

[5] A. T. Kearney, *Measuring Productivity in Physical Distribution* (Chicago: National Council of Physical Distribution Management, 1978), pp. 18–19.

[6] This material is adapted from Douglas M. Lambert and Howard M. Armitage, "Managing Distribution Costs for Better Profit Performance," *Business* 30, no. 5 (September-October 1980), pp. 46–52. Reprinted by permission from *Business* magazine.

mistakes. The following four actual examples will serve to highlight the problems associated with most logistics accounting systems.

Average Freight Costs Distort Segment Profitability

Case 1—The Effect of Average Freight Costs on Customer/Product Profitability. Freight costs are a major expense in most companies, yet few accounting systems track actual freight costs by customer or by product. When management does try to determine these costs, it usually relies on national averages. These averages, however, do not indicate the actual costs of moving each product to its destination; hence, profitability calculations are erroneous.

For example, management of Company A used a national average freight rate when calculating customer and product profitability. It determined the rate by taking the total corporate transportation bill as a percentage of total sales revenue. It applied the same cost—4 percent of sales—to products moving by common carrier from Chicago to New York and from Chicago to Los Angeles, as well as to deliveries in the Chicago area, where the company used its own vehicles. It used the 4 percent figure for transportation cost regardless of the product being shipped, the size of the shipment, or the distance involved.

The fallacy of this approach is threefold. First, management was unable to determine the profitability of individual products or customers. The averaging process hid the fact that delivery of small quantities and deliveries to distant customers may be highly unprofitable, thereby reducing the overall corporate rate of return. Second, using the same percentage rate for all products ignores the impact of product characteristics such as weight, cube, and distance on freight rates and consequently on product and customer profitability. Finally, management did not know actual delivery costs for customers, which made it more difficult to perform a tradeoff analysis between the cost of the current system and the cost of an alternative system, where carload shipments would go first to a regional warehouse on the West Coast, and then on to the customers in that market by motor carrier. In this company, the allocation of freight costs on a percentage of sales basis led to erroneous profitability figures for customers and products, and lower overall performance.

Separating Fixed and Variable Costs Can Be a Problem

Case 2—Inability to Distinguish between Fixed and Variable Costs. Management of Company B utilized a product reporting statement that deducted manufacturing, logistics, and marketing costs from sales to arrive at a net income for each product. It used the profit statement for making decisions about the acceptability of product performance, the assignment of marketing support, and the deletion of products. The allocation of logistics costs to each product was carried out using ABC analysis, in which A products were allocated a certain amount of logistics costs, B products twice as much as A, and C products three times as much as A. These allocations contained costs that varied with activity, such as warehouse labor, supplies, and freight expenses. They also included costs that remained fixed regardless of activity levels (e.g., corporate allocations, depreciation, and administration costs of the corporate fleet). Several of the company's products, including one that was among the company's top 10 in terms of sales performance, were showing negative profits and were therefore candidates for being discontinued. However, analysis revealed that a large proportion of the total distribution cost, along with approximately 30 percent of the manufacturing cost, was fixed and would not be saved if the products were eliminated. In fact, by discontinuing these products, total corporate profitability would decline, since all of the revenues related to these products would disappear, but all of the costs would not. Although the variable costs and the specifically identifiable fixed costs would be saved, the company would continue to incur the majority of fixed costs—which in this case were substantial—regardless of the product deletions being considered. If the firm discontinued the products, the existing fixed costs would be redistributed to the remaining products, leading to the very real possibility that even more products would appear to be unprofitable.

Most Logistics Costing Systems Rely on Allocations

Case 3—The Pitfalls of Allocation. Most logistics costing systems are in their infancy and rely heavily on allocations to determine the performance of segments such as product, customers, territories, divisions, or functions. In Company C such allocations led to erroneous decision making and loss of corporate profits. The firm was a multidivision corporation that manufactured and sold high-margin pharmaceutical products, as well as a number of lower-margin packaged goods. The company maintained a number of field warehouse locations managed by corporate staff. These climate-controlled facilities were designed for the pharmaceutical business and required security and housekeeping practices far exceeding those necessary for packaged goods. In order to fully utilize the facilities, however, the corporation encouraged nonpharmaceutical divisions to store their products in these distribution centers. The costs of operating the warehouses were primarily fixed, although overtime and/or additional warehouse employees were necessary if the throughput increased. The corporate policy was to allocate costs to user divisions on the basis of the square footage occupied. Due to the pharmaceutical warehousing requirements, this charge was relatively high. Furthermore, the corporate divisions were managed on a decentralized profit center basis. The vice president of logistics in a division that marketed relatively bulky and low-value consumer products realized that similar services could be obtained a lower cost to his division by using a public warehouse. For this reason, he withdrew the division's products from the corporate facilities and began to use public warehouses in these locations. Although the volume of product handled and stored in the corporate distribution centers decreased significantly, the cost savings were minimal in terms of the total costs incurred by these facilities due to the high proportion of fixed costs. Consequently, approximately the same cost was allocated to fewer users, making it even more attractive for the other divisions to change to public warehouses in order to obtain lower rates. The result was higher, not lower, total company warehousing costs. The corporate warehousing costs were primarily fixed. Whether or not the space was fully occupied would not significantly alter these costs. When the nonpharmaceutical divisions moved to public warehouses, the company continued to incur approximately the same total expense for the corporate-owned and operated warehouses, as well as the additional public warehousing charges. In effect, the logistics costing system motivated the divisional logistics managers to act in a manner that was not in the company's best interests, and total costs escalated.

Case 4—Control Deficiencies. Control of costs and motivation of key personnel is critical in every business activity. Logistics is no exception. However, the control concepts successfully utilized by other functional areas have not been widely adopted for logistics activities. Some have argued that logistics is different from other disciplines and cannot be evaluated with the same tools. In most cases, however, the application has never been attempted. A particular case in point is the application of the flexible budgeting concept.

The Application of Control Techniques Is Lacking in Logistics

Company D maintained an annual budget for its branch warehousing costs. These costs consisted of variable and fixed expenses. Each month, the budget was divided by 12 and compared to the actual costs of that month. Differences from the budget were recorded as variances, and management took action on these. However, Company D's sales were seasonal, and some months were far more active than others. During peak periods, the variances were virtually always unfavorable, while during slow months, the variances were favorable. Productivity ratios, on the other hand, gave different results. Productivity ratios were high during peak periods and dropped during slower periods. In such a situation, neither cost control nor employee motivation is being adequately addressed. Dividing the annual budget by 12 and comparing it to actual monthly costs means that management is trying to compare costs at two different activity levels. However, the costs should be the same only if actual monthly activity is equal to $\frac{1}{12}$ of the planned annual activity. A far more acceptable approach is to recognize that a portion of the costs are variable and will rise or fall with the level of output. Flexing the budget to reflect what the costs should have been at the operating activity level experienced permits a true measure of efficiency and productivity, and provides more meaningful evaluations of performance.

Required Logistics Costs Are Generally Unavailable

These examples are by no means unique. A survey of 300 North American firms by Lambert and Mentzer revealed that the individual cost components necessary to implement logistics cost trade-off analysis, such as inventory carrying costs, transportation cost by channel, product or customer, order processing costs, warehousing costs, and production lot quantity costs, were generally unavailable.[7] In fact, not a single firm reported

[7] Lambert and Mentzer, "Is Integrated Physical Distribution Management a Reality?," pp. 18–34.

the availability of all of the logistics cost components. This lack of cost data makes analysis extremely difficult. The logistics costing system in the majority of firms does not lend itself to effective management, if effective management can be defined as the ability to make the right operational and strategic choices. Moreover, it is difficult for management to obtain the data required to cost-justify proposed logistics systems changes.

LIMITATIONS OF CURRENT PROFITABILITY REPORTS

Four Major Shortcomings of Segment Profitability Reports

In addition, research has shown that gross inadequacies exist in the segment profitability reports used by managers in the majority of U.S. corporations.[8] Most segment profitability reports are based on average cost allocations rather than on the direct assignment of costs at the time a transaction occurs. Period costs (e.g., fixed plant overhead and general/administrative costs) are arbitrarily allocated to customers and products using bases such as direct labor hours, sales revenue, or cost of sales. Opportunity costs, to cover investments in inventories and accounts receivable, are not included. Finally, key marketing and distribution cost components are frequently ignored. In fact, only 16 percent of the *Fortune* 1,000 firms surveyed reported having relatively comprehensive and accurate profitability reports, as determined by the cost categories included in these reports and the methods used to assign costs to segments. It is interesting that these firms also reported an average return on assets that was 50 percent higher than that reported by the other 84 percent of the respondents.

Recent work by Kaplan, Cooper, and others has directed attention toward the problem of insufficient accounting information.[9] While identifying the shortcomings of current accounting systems is important, it is critical that firms develop a cost-effective method of assessing the impact of product-, marketing-, and distribution-related decisions on profitability. Cost/revenue systems must recast external financial information into a format that enables managers to control their functional activities and achieve company objectives.

One Culprit Is "Full Cost" Accounting

Many of the problems encountered by manufacturers result from the use of a "full costing" philosophy that allocates all indirect costs (such as overhead and general administrative expenses) to each product or customer group on some arbitrary basis. As a result, many companies use management controls that focus on the wrong targets: direct manufacturing labor or sales volume. Reward systems based on such controls drive behavior toward either simplistic goals that represent only a small fraction of total cost (labor) or single-minded sales efforts (volume). They ignore

---

[8] Lambert and Sterling, "What Types of Profitability Reports Do Marketing Managers Receive?" pp. 295–303.

[9] Robin Cooper and Robert S. Kaplan, "Measure Costs Right: Make the Right Decisions," *Harvard Business Review* 66, no. 5 (September-October 1988), pp. 96–103.

more effective ways to compete in the 1990s, such as emphasizing product quality, on-time delivery, short lead times, rapid product innovations, flexible manufacturing and distribution, and efficient deployment of scarce capital.

Why Accounting Systems Are Inadequate

Unfortunately, most managers do not know the true cost of their company's products or services, how to most effectively reduce expenses, or how to allocate resources to the most profitable business segments because of the following factors:[10]

- Accounting systems are designed to report the aggregate effects of a firm's operations to its stockholders, its creditors, and governmental agencies.
- Accounting costs are computed to provide a historical record of the company's operations. Thus, all of the firm's costs are allocated to the various business segments. Since costs common to multiple segments are allocated, the process is necessarily subjective and arbitrary.
- Accounting systems typically record marketing and logistics costs in aggregated natural accounts. Seldom is an attempt made to attach the costs to functional responsibilities and to individual products or customers. Accounting systems are not capable of identifying these costs at the time transactions are recorded or incurred. When the detail is captured, it is frequently lost because only aggregated data are carried forward to subsequent accounting periods. Once data are aggregated, the only way to disaggregate them is by allocation methods that distort the profitability.
- Profitability reports do not show a segment's contribution to profitability, but rather include fixed costs, joint product/service costs, and corporate overhead costs. Often top management encourages this approach because of the fear that knowledge of variable costs will lead to unrealistically low prices. However, in most cases, prices are set by the marketplace and not on the basis of costs.
- In most standard cost systems, fixed costs are often treated as variable costs, which masks the true behavior of the fixed costs.

SOLVING THE PROBLEM OF INSUFFICIENT COST DATA

Logistics Costs Are Often Grouped into Natural Accounts

One of the difficulties in obtaining logistics costs is that they may be grouped under a series of natural accounts rather than by functions. *Natural accounts* are used to group costs for financial reporting on the firm's income statement and balance sheet. For example, all payments for salaries might be grouped into a salaries account. Whether they apply to produc-

[10] Ibid., pp. 96–103; Thomas S. Dudick, "Why SG&A Doesn't Always Work," *Harvard Business Review* 65, no. 1 (January-February 1987), pp. 30–35; Robert S. Kaplan, "How Cost Accounting Distorts Product Costs," *Management Account,* April 1988, pp. 20–27; John J.

tion, marketing, logistics, or finance, they usually are lumped together and the total shown on the financial statements at the end of the reporting period.[11] Other examples of natural accounts include rent, depreciation, selling expenses, general and administrative expenses, and interest expense. It is entirely possible that in a firm with a strong financial accounting orientation, logistics costs such as warehousing and transportation may not be given separate headings in the natural accounts. Instead they may be lumped into such diverse catchalls as overhead, selling, or general expense. Furthermore, there has been a tendency, particularly in the case of freight, to abandon the accrual-accounting concept so that costs of one period are matched with revenues of another period. This occurs, for instance, when freight bills are charged directly to an expense account as they are paid—regardless of when the orders are recognized as revenue. These conditions make it difficult to determine logistics expenditures, control costs, or perform trade-off analyses.

Accounting Data Must Be Tailored to Meet Needs of Logistics

The challenge is not so much to create new data, since much of it already exists in one form or another, but to tailor the existing data in the accounting system to meet the needs of the logistics function.[12] By improving the availability of logistics cost data, management is in a better position to make both operational and strategic decisions. Abnormal levels of costs can be detected and controlled only if management knows what they ought to be for various levels of activity. As Figure 15–2 shows, logistics performance can be monitored by using standard costs, budgets, productivity standards and/or statistical process control.[13] Other methods of addressing the problem of insufficient cost data include a computerized management information system, activity-based costing, and an automated order processing system.

Standard Costs and Flexible Budgets

Standard Costs and Flexible Budgets Improve Control

Control of costs through predetermined standards and flexible budgets is the most comprehensive type of control system available. A standard can be defined as a benchmark or "norm" for measuring performance. Stan-

Wheatley, "The Allocation Controversy in Marketing Cost Analysis," *University of Washington Business Review* 30, no. 4, (Summer 1971), pp. 61–70; Ford S. Worthy, "Accounting Bores You? Wake Up," *Fortune,* October 12, 1987, pp. 43–50; and Lambert and Sterling, pp. 295–303.

[11] Wilbur S. Wayman, "Harnessing the Corporate Accounting System for Physical Distribution Cost Information," *Distribution System Costing: Concepts and Procedures,* Proceedings of the Fourth Annual James R. Riley Symposium on Business Logistics (Columbus, Ohio: Transportation and Logistics Research Foundation, 1972), p. 35.

[12] We will discuss a system for recording accounting data in the necessary format on p. 607. It is based on the modular data base concept introduced in Chapter 13, pp. 542–44.

[13] The following sections on standard costs, budgets, and productivity standards are adapted from Douglas M. Lambert and Howard M. Armitage, "Managing Distribution Costs for Better Profit Performance," *Business* 30, no. 5 (September-October 1980), pp. 50–51. Reprinted by permission from *Business* magazine.

FIGURE 15–2 Controlling Logistics Activities

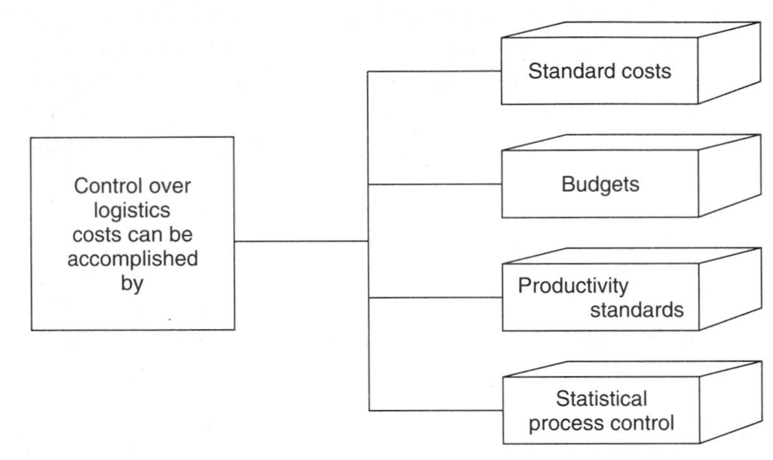

dard costs are what the costs should be if the firm is operating efficiently. Using management by exception, managers direct their attention to variances from standard. A flexible budget is geared to a range of activity. Given the level of activity that occurs, managers can determine what the costs should have been. The use of standard costs represents a direct, effective approach to the logistics costing problem because it attempts to determine what the costs should be, rather than basing future cost predictions on past cost behavior.

A decision to use standard costs requires a systematic review of logistics operations to determine the most effective means of achieving the desired output. Accounting, logistics, and engineering personnel must work together, using regression analysis, time and motion studies, and efficiency studies, so that a series of flexible budgets can be drawn up for various operating levels in different logistics costs centers. Standards can and have been set for such warehouse operations as stock picking, loading, receiving, replenishing, storing, and packing merchandise. In addition, standards have been utilized successfully in order processing, transportation, and even clerical functions. However, the use of standards has not been widespread, due in part to the belief that logistics costs are quite different from those in other areas of the business. While there may be some merit to this argument, logistics activities are, by nature, repetitive operations, and such operations lend themselves to control by standards. A more compelling reason why standard costs have not achieved widespread acceptance is that it is only recently that the importance of logistics cost control has been recognized. However, management accountants and industrial engineers at most firms have a wealth of experience in installing standard costs in the production area, which, with some effort, could be expanded into logistics.

Standard costs for logistics may be more complex to develop because the output measures can be considerably more diverse than in the case of production. For example, in developing a standard for the picking function, it is possible that the eventual control measure could be stated as a standard cost per order, a standard cost per order line, a standard cost per unit shipped, or a standard cost per shipment. Despite the added complexities, work measurement does appear to be increasing in logistics activities.[14] Schiff provided one example of a successful application.[15] The firm used a computerized system with standard charges and routes for 25,000 routes and eight different methods of transportation. Up to 300,000 combinations were possible, and the system was updated regularly. Clerks at any location could obtain from the computer the optimum method of shipment. A monthly computer printout listed the following information by customer:

A Computerized System of Freight Standards

- Destination.
- Standard freight cost to customer.
- Actual freight charges paid for shipments to customer.
- Standard freight to warehouse cost.
- Total freight cost.
- Origin of shipment.
- Sales district office.
- Method of shipment.
- Container used.
- Weight of shipment.
- Variance in excess of a given amount per hundredweight.

Another monthly report listed the deviation from standard freight cost for each customer and the amount of the variance. This system obviously provided the firm with a measure of freight performance. Equally important, the standards provided the means for determining individual customer profitability and identifying opportunities for logistics cost trade-offs. Because this firm used standards as an integral part of its management information system, it could fairly easily determine the impact of a system change—such as an improved, automated order processing system—on transportation costs.

The use of standards as a management control system is depicted in Figure 15-3. As the figure indicates, standards may result from either formal investigation, philosophy/intuition, or both. Lewis and Erickson provided this overview of the use of standards in logistics.

---

[14] See for example Ernst and Whinney, *Transportation Accounting and Control: Guidelines for Distribution and Financial Management* (Chicago: National Council of Physical Distribution Management, and New York: National Association of Accountants, 1983); Ernst and Whinney, *Warehousing Accounting and Control: Guidelines for Distribution and Financial Managers* (Chicago: National Council of Physical Distribution Management, and New York: National Association of Accountants, 1985).

[15] Schiff, *Accounting and Control in Physical Distribution Management,* pp. 4–63 to 4–70.

FIGURE 15–3 The Use of Standards as a Management Control System

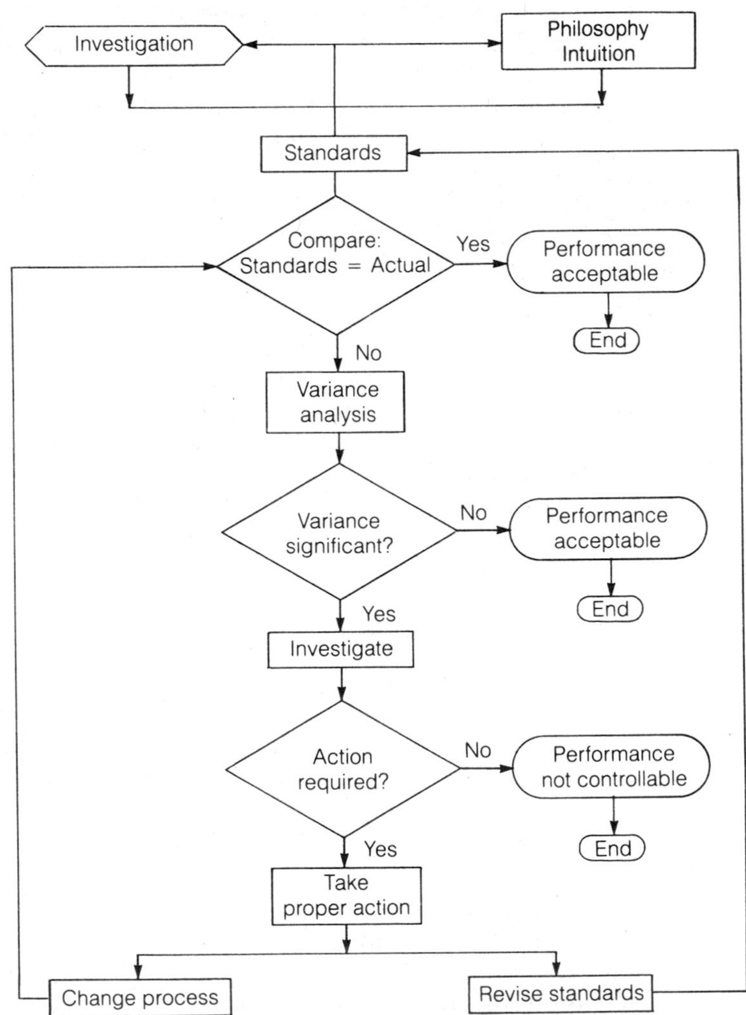

SOURCE: Richard J. Lewis and Leo G. Erickson. "Distribution System Costing: An Overview," in *Distribution System Costing: Concepts and Procedures,* ed. John R. Grabner and William S. Sargent (Columbus, Ohio: Transportation and Logistics Research Foundation, 1972), p. 17A.

Once standards have been set, the firm must compare actual performance with the particular standard to see if it is acceptable. If performance is acceptable, the system is deemed to be under control, and that is the end of the control process. Inherent in this notion is that management operates under the principle of exception—exerting no changes in the system so long as it operates satisfactorily; and the measure of "satisfactory" is found in the standard.

Variances Must Be Analyzed to Identify the Causes

It is highly unlikely that performance will exactly equal standard. Where there is a departure, the procedure is to break the variance down into its component parts to try to ascertain its sources. For example, the standard may be a budgeted amount for transportation in a territory. If the actual exceeds the budget, management would like to see the variance analyzed into separate measures of volume and efficiency. It is impossible to know how to proceed unless the variance is analyzed into meaningful sources.

The next question is whether the observed variance is great enough to be deemed significant. It is possible to handle such a question in strictly statistical terms, setting quality control limits about the standard. This may be done in terms of standard deviations and an acceptable limit established on the down side only or the limit may be on either side of the standard. Thus, in the latter case, if performance exceeds standard, management may decide to raise the standard or reward the performer accordingly. Probably of greater concern are those departures in which performance is below standard.

Much of physical distribution lends itself to measures of statistical significance in departures from standard. However, as with demand-obtaining activities, it is probably more meaningful to judge departures from standards in terms of their *practical* significance. A form of sensitivity analysis goes on here, in which the question is raised: How critical is the departure in its effects on bottom line performance, net profit?

Regardless of how the assessment is made, the variance will be termed either significant or not significant. If it is not significant, performance is judged acceptable and the control process is ended. If significant, the next question is whether action is required.

The variance may be significant but, in analyzing it and explaining it, the departure from standard is not judged controllable. If so, no action may be indicated and the control process terminated. If action is indicated, it will be one of two broad kinds. Either the standard is held to be wrong and must be changed, or the process itself is not producing the results it should and thus must be changed. The feedbacks go up to the appropriate levels. If the process is changed and the standard is held, comparisons are again made. If the standard is changed and the process remains unchanged, the feedback is to the standard. It is possible that both would be changed. Thus, both feedbacks may result from the action phase, and the system cycles through again.[16]

Advantages of Standard Costs

A standard tells management the expected cost of performing selected activities and allows comparisons to be made to determine whether there have been operating inefficiencies. For example, Table 15–1 indicates a re-

[16] Richard J. Lewis and Leo G. Erickson, "Distribution System Costing: An Overview," in *Distribution System Costing: Concepts and Procedures,* ed. John R. Grabner and William S. Sargent (Columbus, Ohio: Transportation and Logistics Research Foundation, 1972), pp. 18–20.

TABLE 15–1 Summary of Warehouse Picking Operation Week of ____________

Items picked during week	14,500
Hours accumulated on picking activities	330
Standard hours allowed for picks performed based on 50 items per hour	290
Variation in hours	40
Standard cost per labor hour	$ 8
Variation in cost due to inefficiency	$320*

*The cost was $320 over budget because of 40 picking hours in excess of the standard number of hours allowed for efficient operation.

port that is useful at the operating level. It shows why the warehouse labor for the picking activity was $320 over budget. The costs of logistics activities can be reported by department, division, function, product group, or total, compared to their standard, and can be included as part of regular weekly or monthly performance reports. Table 15–2 shows a level of aggregation that would be of interest to the firm's president. This report allows the president to see at a glance why targeted net income has not been reached. On the one hand, there is a $3 million difference due to ineffectiveness, which indicates the net income the company has forgone because of its inability to meet its budgeted level of sales. On the other hand, there is also an inefficiency factor of $1.4 million. This factor indicates that at the level of sales actually achieved, the segment-controllable margin should have been $18 million. The difference between $18 million and the actual outcome of $16.6 million is a $1.4 million variation due to inefficiencies within the marketing and logistics functions.

The Appendix to this chapter provides an example of how to develop standard costs and flexible budgets for warehousing.

Budgetary Practices

Control Can Be Achieved Using Budgets

Conceptually, standard costs are generally superior for control purposes. However, sometimes the use of standards is inappropriate. This is particularly true in situations involving essentially nonrepetitive tasks and for which work-unit measurements are difficult to establish. In these situations, control can still be achieved through budgetary practices. However, the extent to which the budget is successful depends on whether individual cost-behavior patterns can be predicted, and whether the budget can be flexed to reflect changes in operating conditions.

Most logistics budgets are static. That is, they are a plan developed for a budgeted level of output. If actual activity happens to be the same as budgeted, management can make a realistic comparison of costs and establish effective control. However, this is seldom the case. Seasonality or internal factors invariably lead to different levels of activity, the efficiency of which can be determined only if the reporting system can compare the

TABLE 15–2 Segmental Analysis Using a Contribution Approach ($000)

		Explanation of Variation from Budget			
	Budget	*Variance Due to Ineffec-tiveness*	*Standard Allowed for Output Level Achieved*	*Variance Due to Ineffi-ciency*	*Actual Results*
Net sales	$90,000	$10,000	$80,000	—	$80,000
Cost of goods sold (variable manufacturing cost)	40,500	4,500	36,000	—	36,000
Manufacturing contribution	$49,500	$ 5,500	$44,000	—	$44,000
Variable marketing and logistics costs (out-of-pocket costs that vary directly with sales to the segment)*	22,500	2,500	20,000	$1,400	21,400
Segment contribution margin	$27,000	$ 3,000	$24,000	$1,400	$22,600
Assignable nonvariable costs (costs incurred specifically for the segment during the period)†	6,000	—	6,000	—	6,000
Segment controllable margin	$21,000	$ 3,000	$18,000	$1,400	$16,600

NOTES: This analysis can be performed for segments such as products, customers, geographic areas, or divisions.
Assumption: Actual sales revenue decreased, a result of lower volume. The average price paid per unit sold remained the same. (If the average price per unit changes then an additional variance—the marketing variance—can be computed.)
Difference in income of $4,400 ($21,000–16,600) between budgeted and actual results can be explained by the following variances:

a. Ineffectiveness—inability to reach target sales objective	$3,000
b. Inefficiency at operating level achieved of $80,000	1,400
	$4,400

*These costs might include: sales commissions, transportation costs, warehouse handling costs, order processing costs, and a charge for accounts receivable.

†These costs might include: salaries, segment-related advertising, bad debts, and inventory carrying costs. The fixed costs associated with corporate-owned and operated facilities would be included if, and only if, the warehouse was solely for this segment of the business.

actual costs with what they should have been at the operating level achieved.

For instance, a firm's warehousing unit may have an estimated or budgeted level of activity of 10,000 line items per week. The actual level of activity, however, may be only 7,500. Comparing the budgeted costs at 10,000 line items against the actual costs at 7,500 leads to the erroneous conclusion that the operation has been efficient, since items such as overtime, temporary help, packing, postage, and order processing are less than budget. A flexible budget, on the other hand, indicates what the costs should have been at the 7,500 line items level of activity, and a true dollar measure of efficiency results.

The key to successful implementation of a flexible budget lies in the analysis of cost behavior patterns. In most firms little of this analysis has been carried out in the logistics function. The expertise of the management accountant and industrial engineer can be invaluable in applying tools such as scatter-diagram techniques and regression analysis to determine the fixed and variable components of costs. These techniques use previous cost data to determine a variable rate per unit of activity and a total fixed cost component. Once this is accomplished, the flexible budget for control becomes a reality. Unlike engineered standards, however, the techniques are based on past cost behavior patterns, which undoubtedly contain inefficiencies. The predicted measure of cost, therefore, may not be a measure of what the activity *should* cost but an estimate of what it *will* cost, based on the results of previous periods.

Productivity Standards

Productivity Ratios

Logistics costs also can be controlled by the use of productivity ratios. These ratios take the form of:

$$\text{Productivity} = \frac{\text{Measure of output}}{\text{Measure of input}}$$

For example, a warehouse operation might make use of such productivity ratios as:

$$\frac{\text{Number of orders shipped this period}}{\text{Number of orders received this period}}$$

$$\frac{\text{Number of orders shipped this period}}{\text{Average number of orders shipped per period}}$$

$$\frac{\text{Number of orders shipped this period}}{\text{Number of direct labor hours worked this period}}$$

Productivity ratios for transportation might include:[17]

$$\frac{\text{Ton-miles transported}}{\text{Total actual transportation cost}}$$

$$\frac{\text{Stops served}}{\text{Total actual transportation cost}}$$

$$\frac{\text{Shipments transported to destination}}{\text{Total actual transportation cost}}$$

The transportation resource inputs for which productivity ratios can be generated include labor, equipment, energy, and cost. Table 15–3 illustrates the specific relationships between these inputs and transportation activities. An X in a cell of the matrix denotes an activity/input combination that can be measured. Table 15–4 illustrates an activity/input matrix for warehousing.

Productivity measures of this type can and have been developed for most logistics activities. In the absence of a standard costing system, they are particularly useful with budgetary practices, flexible budgeting, since

[17] A. T. Kearney, Inc., *Measuring and Improving Productivity in Physical Distribution* (Oak Brook, Ill.: National Council of Physical Distribution Management, 1984), p. 170.

TABLE 15–3 Transportation Activity/Input Matrix

Activities	*Labor*	*Facilities*	*Equipment*	*Energy*	*Overall (cost)*
Transportation strategy development	—	—	—	—	X
Private fleet over-the-road trucking					
Loading	X	—	—	—	X
Line-haul	X	—	—	X	X
Unloading	X	—	—	—	X
Overall	X	—	X	X	X
Private fleet pickup/delivery trucking					
Pretrip	X	—	—	—	X
Stem driving	X	—	—	X	X
On-route driving	X	—	—	X	X
At-stop	X	—	—	—	X
End-of-trip	X	—	—	—	X
Overall	X	—	X	X	X
Purchased transportation operations					
Loading	—	—	—	—	X
Line-haul	—	—	—	—	X
Unloading	—	—	—	—	X
Rail/barge fleet management	—	—	—	—	X
Transportation/traffic management	—	—	—	—	X

SOURCE: A. T. Kearney, Inc., *Measuring and Improving Productivity in Physical Distribution* (Oak Brook, Ill.: National Council of Physical Distribution Management, 1984), p. 144.

they do provide some guidelines on operating efficiencies. Furthermore, such measures are easily understood by management and employees.[18] However, productivity measures are not without their shortcomings:

Three Shortcomings of Productivity Measures

1. Productivity measures are expressed in terms of physical units and actual dollar losses due to inefficiencies, and predictions of future logistics costs cannot be made. This makes it difficult to cost-justify any system changes that will result in improved productivity.

2. The actual productivity measure calculated is seldom compared to a productivity standard. For example, a productivity measure may compare the number of orders shipped this period to the number of direct labor-hours worked this period, but it does not indicate what the relationship *ought* to be. Without work measurement or some form of cost estimation, it is impossible to know what the productivity standard should be at efficient operations.

3. Finally, changes in output levels may in some cases distort measures of productivity. This distortion occurs because the fixed and variable elements are seldom delineated. Consequently, the productivity measure com-

[18] For more information on the development of productivity ratios refer to A. T. Kearney, Inc., *Measuring and Improving Productivity in Physical Distribution;* and Howard M. Armitage, "The Use of Management Accounting Techniques to Improve Productivity Analysis in Distribution Operations," *International Journal of Physical Distribution and Materials Management* 14, no. 1 (1984), pp. 41–51.

TABLE 15–4 Warehouse Activity/Input Matrix

Activities	*Labor*	*Facilities*	*Equipment*	*Energy*	*Financial*	*Overall (cost)*
Company-operated warehousing						
Receiving	X	X	X	—	—	X
Put-away	X	—	X	—	—	X
Storage	—	X	—	X	—	X
Replenishment	X	—	X	—	—	X
Order selection	X	—	X	—	—	X
Checking	X	—	X	—	—	X
Packing and marking	X	X	X	—	—	X
Staging and order consolidation	X	X	X	—	—	X
Shipping	X	X	X	—	—	X
Clerical and administration	X	—	X	—	—	X
Overall	X	X	X	X	X	X
Public warehousing						
Storage	—	—	—	—	—	X
Handling	—	—	—	—	—	X
Consolidation	—	—	—	—	—	X
Administration	—	—	—	—	—	X
Overall	—	—	—	—	—	X

SOURCE: A. T. Kearney, Inc., *Measuring and Improving Productivity in Physical Distribution* (Oak Brook, Ill.: National Council of Physical Distribution Management, 1984), p. 195.

putes utilization, not efficiency. For example, if 100 orders shipped represents full labor utilization and 100 orders were received this period, then productivity as measured by

$$\frac{\text{Number of orders shipped this period}}{\text{Number of orders received this period}}$$

times 100 percent, is 100 percent. However, if 150 orders had been received, and 100 orders shipped, productivity would have been 66.67 percent, even though there was no real drop in either efficiency or productivity.

Statistical Process Control

Statistical Process Control Is Gaining in Popularity

In Japan, there is a high level of sophistication in the use of statistical methods to enhance the quality of products and services.[19] The use of such approaches is increasing in North America with the automobile industry, with high-tech firms, and with many consumer products manufacturers. The output of successful logistics is the level of customer service provided. Although many firms measure the proportion of shipments that arrive on time or the average length of the order cycle from a particular vendor,

[19]This material is adapted from C. John Langley, Jr., "Information-Based Decision Making in Logistics Management," *International Journal of Physical Distribution and Materials Management* 15, no. 7 (1985), pp. 48–52.

further insight into these areas is seldom obtained through the use of statistical process control techniques.

The use of statistical methods offers an alternative to conventional management control processes. Statistical process control (SPC) requires an understanding of the variability of the process itself prior to making management decisions. For example, to analyze delivery times from several vendors, it is necessary to know the mean, or average, time elapsed from the issuance of a purchase order to the receipt of a shipment and the likely variation in delivery times.

Figure 15–4 illustrates the steps of SPC. As with classical approaches to control, the first three steps are:

1. Design system.
2. Establish standards.
3. Perform process.

Once the first three steps are accomplished, SPC requires that the following questions be raised: First, are the measurements "in control"? That is, do they all fall within reasonable proximity of the mean? Second, is the process capable, that is, is the observed variability less in magnitude than a prespecified range? Third, do the measurements meet standards? Only if the answers to these three questions are yes is the process itself said to be in control.

The Control Chart Is Used to Identify Significant Variances

The "control chart" is perhaps the most widely used statistical approach to gain insight into these questions. The control chart permits an examination of process behavior measurements in relation to both upper and lower "control limits." These limits are statistically derived and are used to identify instances where the observed behavior differs significantly from what was expected, and where a problem is likely to exist. The search for explanations can then proceed in an organized efficient manner.

> Figure 15–5 shows two control chart applications which were developed using actual logistics-related data. Part A resulted from an examination of transit time data (in minutes) of shipments traveling between two cities which were 260 miles apart. Once the three out-of-control points (i.e., those located outside the control limits) were identified and isolated, an enquiry was undertaken to determine their causes and assure removal of those causes.
>
> Part B of Figure 15–5 shows the percentages of carrier freight bills which were found by a particular shipper to contain errors. In this particular example the only error percentages which would be of concern are those which are excessively high, and an inspection of Part B shows that only one such point was sufficiently high as to be labeled out-of-control in a statistical sense. In this instance, subsequent investigation resulted in the identification and removal of the cause of the problem at hand.
>
> Although these two examples are relatively simple, any one of a number of activities in logistics management could have been selected for purposes of illustration. Areas having significant applications potential include not only transportation, but warehousing, materials handling, packaging, inventory

FIGURE 15–4 Statistical Process Control (SPC)

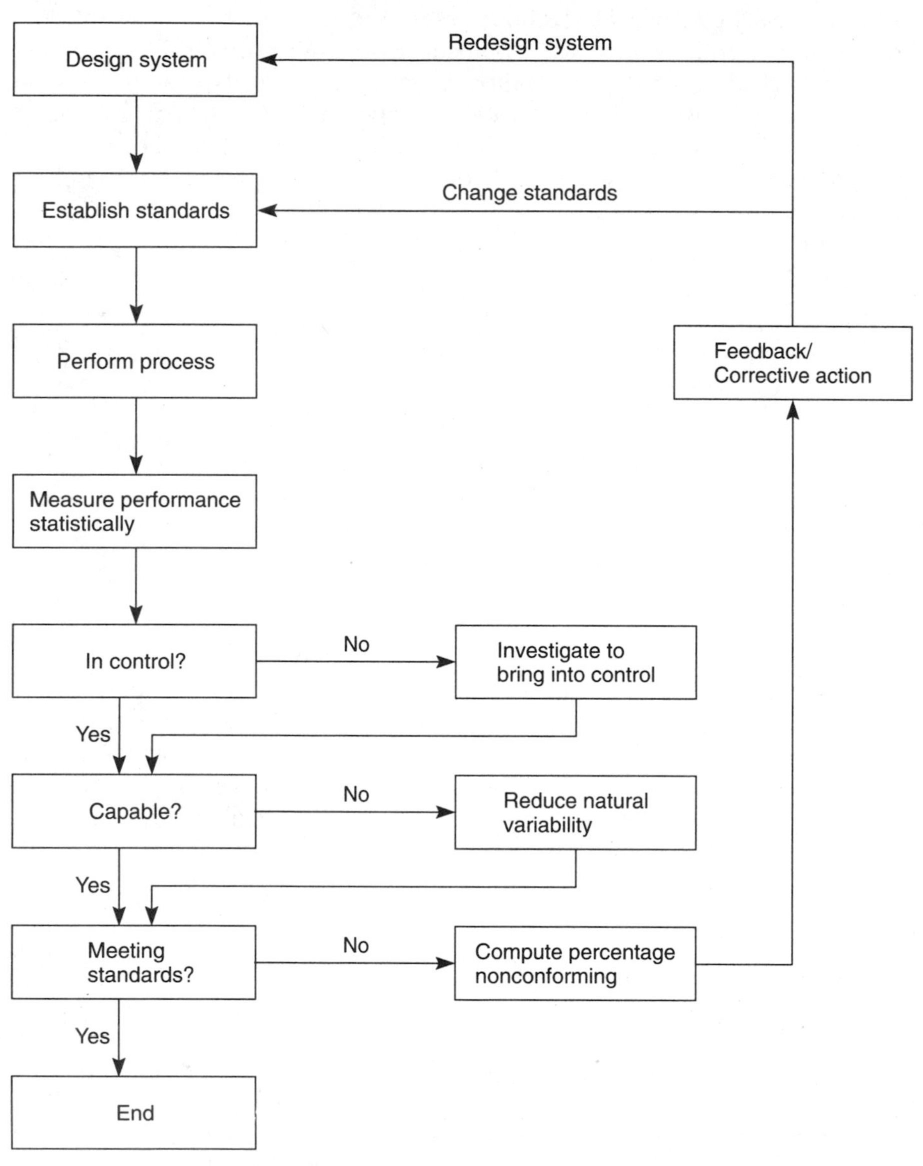

SOURCE: C. John Langley, Jr., "Information-Based Decision Making in Logistics Management," *International Journal of Physical Distribution and Materials Management* 15, no. 7 (1985), p. 50. Copyright MCB University Press Limited.

FIGURE 15–5 Control Chart Examples

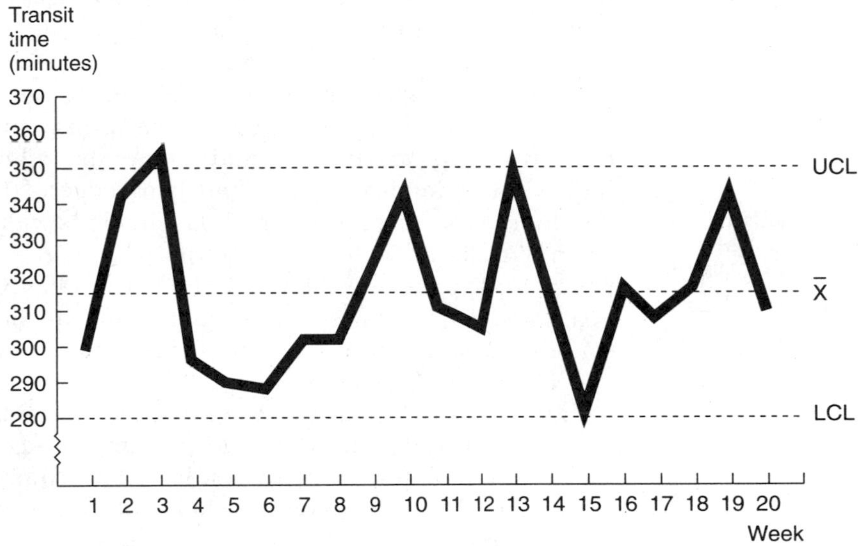

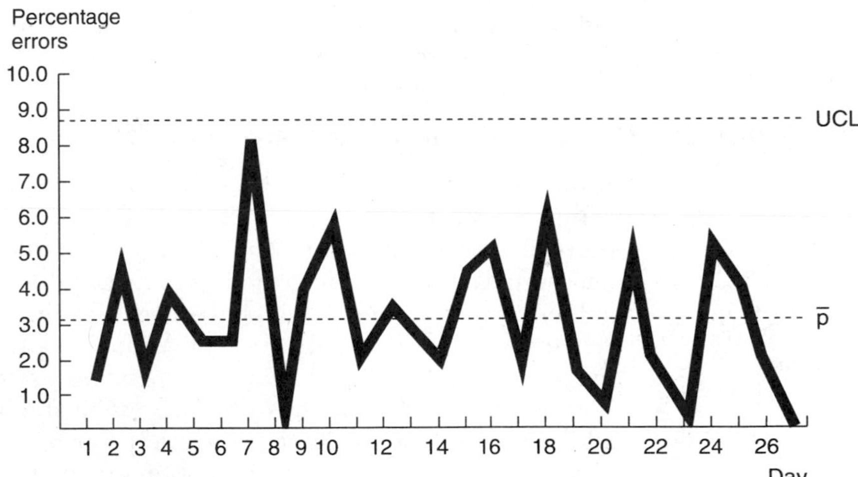

KEY: UCL = Upper control limit.
LCL = Lower control limit.
$\bar{X}$ = Mean (of measurements).
$\bar{p}$ = Mean (of percentages or proportions).

SOURCE: C. John Langley, Jr., "Information-Based Decision Making in Logistics Management," *International Journal of Physical Distribution and Materials Management* 15, no. 7 (1985), p. 51. Copyright MCB University Press Limited.

control, order processing, and customer service. There is strong evidence to suggest that large cost savings can be captured in areas such as these through the appropriate use of statistical methods.[20]

Prerequisites to Success

There are a number of prerequisites to success with SPC. First, it is important to recognize that the use of statistical methods is simply a tool that can assist in improving quality. SPC provides valuable insight into the behavior of the various processes under scrutiny. Second, top management support is necessary for success. The effective use of SPC approaches may involve a cultural change. Successful firms have involvement and commitment from top management and require that all of those involved have a high level of familiarity with and knowledge of the various approaches. Finally, the use of statistical methods should be viewed as a key component of an overall quality management program. Other elements of the quality program may include the establishment of quality policies, the setting of goals and objectives, supervisory training, quality awareness and error cause removal programs, and performance management.

Statistical Methods Must Be Part of an Overall Quality Program

The issue of quality in logistics is frequently addressed in conjunction with the topic of productivity. However, attention has been focused on the identification of specific data and information needs rather than on what to do with the information once it has been acquired. Until more progress is made in this direction, the benefits of improved productivity will continue to represent a largely untapped resource.

Successful implementation of SPC approaches are dependent upon the timely availability of appropriate information. For this reason, SPC provides an opportunity for the logistics and information systems areas to work together to enhance productivity and improve quality.

Logistics Costs and the Corporate Management Information System

Accurate Costs Are Required for Informed Decision Making

While substantial savings can be generated when management is able to compare its actual costs to a set of predetermined standards or budgets, there are even greater opportunities for profit improvement in the area of decision making. If management is to make informed decisions, it must be able to choose between such alternatives as hiring additional common carrier transportation or enlarging the company's private fleet, increasing deliveries or increasing inventories, expanding or consolidating field warehouses, and automating the order processing and information system. The addition or deletion of territories, salespeople, products, or customers requires a knowledge of how well existing segments are currently performing, and how revenues and costs will change with the alternatives under consideration. For this purpose, management needs a data base capable of aggregating data so that it can obtain routine information on individual

[20] Langley, "Information-Based Decision Making," pp. 49–52.

segments such as customers, salespeople, products, territories, or channels of distribution. The system must also be able to store data by fixed and variable components so that the incremental revenues and costs associated with alternative strategies can be developed.

Several types of transactions occur in every business, and each transaction results in the creation of source documents (such as customer orders, shipment bill of lading, sales invoices to customers, and invoices from suppliers/vendors). In addition, companies perform a variety of internal transactions and activities that are documented (e.g., "trip reports" for private fleet activities, salespeople "call reports," and warehouse labor time cards). Other costs may be recognized by means of standard cost systems, engineering time studies, or statistical estimating (e.g., multiple regression techniques). The key for success is that source documents *must* be computerized.

Source Documents Must Be Computerized

The Modular Data Base System

One promising data base is the one we examined in Chapter 13 (Figure 13–10). It is a central storage system in which source documents are fed into the data base in coded form. Inputs can be coded according to function, subfunction, territory, product, revenue or expense, channel, or a host of other possibilities. When combined with the computer, the system is capable of filing large amounts of data and allows rapid aggregation and retrieval of various modules of information for decision analysis.

The modular data base is capable of collecting all of the revenues and costs for every transaction and aggregating them by functional activity (e.g., selling, advertising/promotion, transportation, warehousing, and order processing). This technique is commonly referred to as *responsibility accounting* and is used primarily to develop annual budgets and monthly variance reports by major categories and subcategories of corporate activities, such as manufacturing, research development, marketing/sales, and logistics.

Even though the modular data base concept has been discussed in the literature for more than 20 years, surveys of corporate practices and a review of marketing management texts indicate that there are relatively few integrated operating systems that report segment profits on a timely and accurate basis.[21] Why does this condition exist? Many managers mistakenly feel that the same accounting practices (i.e., the allocation of all costs) used to value inventories and report results to the Internal Revenue Service or Securities and Exchange Commission are required to generate reports for managing the business. Managers may also feel that using only variable and direct fixed costs might encourage suboptimal pricing by salespeople. A separate management accounting system is frequently opposed by accoun-

[21] Douglas M. Lambert and Jay U. Sterling, "Educators are Contributing to Major Deficiencies in Marketing Profitability Reports," *Journal of Marketing Education* 12, no. 3 (Fall 1990), pp. 42–52.

tants. Top management and accountants may feel more comfortable if they can tie the cumulative results of the various segments to total company profit-and-loss data. Managers often fail to recognize the behavioral differences of fixed and variable costs, as well as the distinction between direct and indirect expenses. As a result, they fail to understand the usefulness and purpose of contribution reports. Finally, data processing personnel often discourage the development of such reports by citing the difficulties in creating the data bases and operating systems required to assign direct costs to specific product and market segments. In today's information technology environment, these reasons are no longer valid.

With the information from the modular data base, management is in a position to evaluate the profitability of various segments. In addition, the data base permits the user to simulate trade-off situations and determine the effect of proposed strategic and system changes on total cost.

The Key to Measuring Logistics Performance

The key to measuring logistics performance is an integrated, broad-based computer data file. In order to track an order and its associated costs—for example from origin to receipt by customer—it is necessary to access a number of files in the logistics information system:

- Open orders (for back orders).
- Deleted orders (order history file).
- Shipped manifest (bills of lading).
- Transportation freight bills paid.

With today's data processing capabilities, it is possible to automatically access desired information from these and other necessary files (such as inventory, customer retail feedback data, damage reports/claims, and billing/invoicing files). From these files, a condensed "logistics performance" data base file can be constructed. This will provide all of the necessary information required to measure overall as well as individual activities on a regular basis. What used to take several man years of concerted programming effort and large sums of resources can be developed in a matter of weeks or months using personal computers and standard statistical packages. A major consumer products company uses this approach to construct a series of more than 50 reports using a common "logistics performance file." More than just logistics costs are reported. However, the same data files are used to report financial, customer service, or productivity related reports.

Activity-Based Costing

One method of solving the problem of insufficient cost data that has been receiving increased attention is activity-based costing. Traditional accounting systems in manufacturing firms allocate factory/corporate overhead to products based on direct labor. In the past, this method of allocation may

Activity-Based Costing Requires Identification of Cost Drivers

have resulted in minor distortions. However, product lines and channels have proliferated and overhead costs have increased dramatically, making traditional allocation methods dangerous. Cooper and Kaplan recommend an "activity based system" to examine the demands that are made by particular products (or customers) on indirect resources.[22] They recommend three rules to follow when examining the demands made by individual products on indirect resources:

1. Focus on expensive resources.
2. Emphasize resources whose consumption varies significantly by product and product type.
3. Focus on resources whose demand(s) are uncorrelated with traditional allocation methods such as direct labor or materials cost.[23]

They believe that the process of tracing costs, first from resources to activities and then from activities to specific products (or customers), cannot be done with surgical precision.

But, according to Cooper and Kaplan, it is better to be basically correct with activity-based costing, say within 5 percent or 10 percent of the actual demands a product (or customer) makes on organizational resources, than to be precisely wrong (perhaps by as much as 200 percent) using outdated allocation techniques or including indirect, common costs.

Activity-Based Costing Is Another Method of Allocation

The major shortcoming of activity-based costing is that it is simply another method of allocation, and by definition any method of allocation is arbitrary. The potential problems associated with using activity-based costing for logistics were made very clear in a 1991 article in *Management Accounting*.[24] The article described the use of activity-based costing for marketing and made the claim that physical distribution is the most effective area for application. However, the examples used were simply average costs where selling costs were reported as 5 percent of sales, advertising costs were 40 cents per unit sold, warehousing costs were 10 cents per pound shipped, packing and shipping costs were 20 cents per unit sold, and general office expenses were allocated at $20 per order.[25] Clearly, activity-based costing implemented in this manner represents an average cost system that contains the problems described first in Chapter 3. For example, transportation costs need to be identified by origin and destination zip codes and by shipment size categories before they can be assigned to customers and/or products.

The overriding rule is to *only include, in segment reports, those costs that*

---

[22] Cooper and Kaplan, "Measure Costs Right: Make the Right Decisions," pp. 96–103.

[23] Ibid., p. 98.

[24] Ronald J. Lewis, "Activity-Based Costing for Marketing," *Management Accounting* 73, no. 5 (November 1991), pp. 33–38.

[25] Ibid., p. 35.

Only Revenues and Costs That Will Change with a Decision Are Relevant

would disappear if the revenues of the segment were lost. With this philosophy in mind, we recommend a hybrid system that combines the detailed manufacturing cost structure provided by an *activity-based system* with the marketing and distribution cost components recognized in the *contribution* approach to measure segment profits.

Managers responsible for product and customer business segments need to understand the financial implications of their decisions. Executives must be able to talk the language of accountants, understand the benefits of contribution analysis, recognize the difference between good and bad accounting data, and have the capability of accessing relevant data files on an ongoing basis. The support and active participation by top management, including the chief executive, is necessary since resistance to change is one of the major barriers facing U.S. manufacturers in their quest to be world class.

Segment Contribution Reports Are Required to Manage the Business

Once segment contribution reports are implemented, managers can begin to accurately assess strategic options such as which product lines to drop or whether prices can be raised on inelastic products or reduced on high-volume products. Added emphasis can be placed on those segments that are most profitable. Product lines can be accurately assessed using 80–20 analyses in order to eliminate unprofitable items. The firms that have developed and implemented segment profitability reports have been able to identify products and customers that were either unprofitable or did not meet corporate financial objectives. Ironically, many of these products/customers were previously thought to be profitable, due either to their sales volumes or to manufacturing margins. It is difficult for U.S. firms to compete with foreign competitors even when the U.S. firms have good financial information. It is almost impossible to compete effectively with bad information.

The Role of the Order Processing System

The Order Processing System Can Impact Logistics in Two Major Ways

The order processing system can affect the performance of the logistics function in two major ways. First, the system can improve the quality of the management information system by providing such data as customer names, location of customers, items demanded by customer, sales by customer, sales patterns (when items are ordered), order size, sales by salesperson, and sales data for the company's sales forecasting package.

Second, the customer order is the message that sets the logistics function in motion. The speed and quality of the information provided by the order processing system has a direct impact on the cost and efficiency of the entire logistics process. Slow and erratic communication can lead to lost customers or excessive transportation, inventory, and warehousing costs. It can also bring about possible production inefficiencies because of frequent line changes. Implementation of the latest technology in order processing and communications systems can lead to significant improvements in logistics performance.

COST JUSTIFICATION OF LOGISTICS SYSTEM CHANGES

In Chapter 2 we saw how an integrated approach to the management and control of the logistics function can significantly improve a firm's profitability. However, successful implementation of integrated logistics management depends on total cost analysis. That is, changes in logistics system structure must be cost justified by comparing total costs before and after the change. The availability of accurate cost data is critical for the cost justification of logistics system changes. In order to illustrate how to perform the necessary cost benefit analysis, we will build upon an example first introduced in Chapter 10 (in Figure 10–11) and later described in Chapter 13 (in Figure 13–1). Here is some background on Company XYZ:

A Cost Benefit Analysis

- Financial data for the current year is presented in Figure 15–6.
- Customers mailed orders to the company for processing; the order cycle was 10 days on the average. That is, from the time a customer placed an order until the shipment was received by the customer, an average of 10 days had elapsed. Customers were satisfied with the 10-day order cycle since all major suppliers offered the same terms. However, although the company's average order cycle was 10 days, the range was from 7 to 13 days. Consequently, to avoid stockouts, customers had to plan for the worst possible outcome—a 13-day order cycle.
- The company calculated its inventory carrying costs to be 45 percent of the inventory valued at variable cost delivered to the field warehouse locations.
- The company utilized 10 field warehouse locations for the distribution of its products. Figure 15–7 shows an example of one market area where products were shipped to a public warehouse by rail, and the shipments to customers were by motor carrier.

A study of the company's order processing system revealed that an advanced order entry and processing system would shorten the total order cycle by four days. With the proposed system, customers would telephone their orders to customer service representatives equipped with CRTs. The customer service representative would enter the order on a real-time inventory control system while the customer was still on the telephone. The inventory levels would be reduced by the amount of the purchase, thereby eliminating the problem of two customers being promised delivery of the same stock. In the event of a stockout, product substitution could be arranged, or delivery could be scheduled based on planned production. Con-

Features of the New Order Processing System

FIGURE 15–6 The Strategic Profit Model with Financial Data for Company XYZ—before System Change (financial data in $ millions)

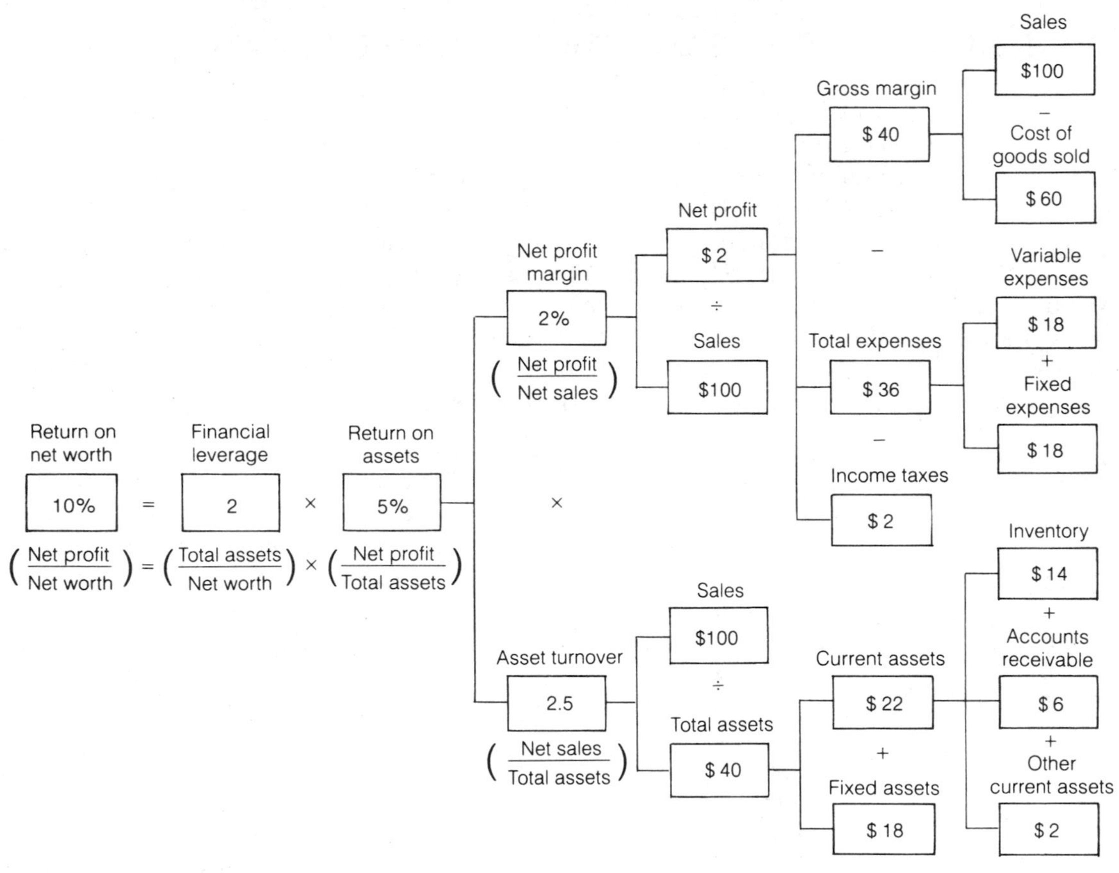

Income taxes are assumed to equal 50 percent of net profit before taxes.

sequently, the proposed system would improve customer service by providing immediate information on inventory availability and by making it possible to arrange for product substitution in case of a stockout. In addition, target delivery dates could be communicated to the customer.

If the estimated annual cost of the proposed order processing system was $300,000 higher than the existing manual system, a cost-benefit analysis would be necessary in order to justify the increased cost.[26] A number

[26] In companies with manual order processing systems, it may be possible to cost justify the proposed system entirely by eliminating excessive costs associated with the current order processing system. Nevertheless, all of the cost savings should be documented in order to fully understand the financial impact of the proposed system.

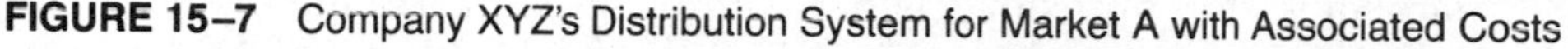

FIGURE 15–7 Company XYZ's Distribution System for Market A with Associated Costs

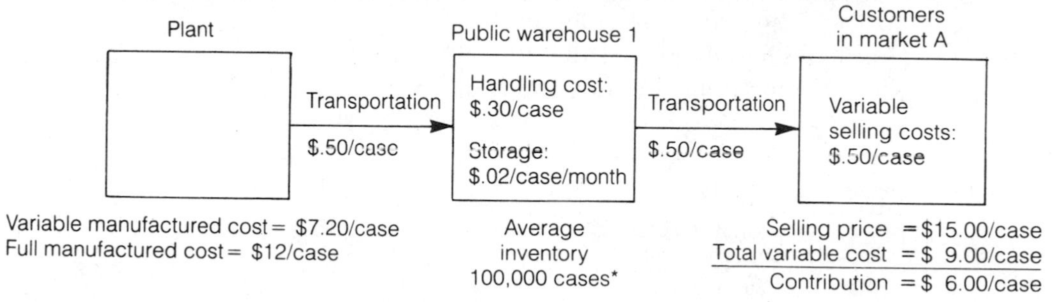

*Average inventory valued at variable cost delivered to the distribution center = ($7.20 + $0.50 + $0.30) × 100,000 = $800,000.

Impact of Reducing Lead Time to Customers

of possibilities exist for cost-benefit analysis, but some are better than others. First, the four-day improvement in order cycle could be passed along to the company's customers by reducing the lead time on orders from 10 to 6 days. The rationale would be that the manufacturer's market share and profitability would increase as a result of the improved customer service. Alternatively, customers of the manufacturer might be willing to pay for the increased service because it would enable them to reduce their inventory levels. The problem with attempting to cost-justify a proposed system change based on either of these outcomes is that the revenue data needed to support the analysis would be difficult to obtain. In addition, the outcomes described above may never be realized because of competitor reactions or other environmental factors.

Impact of Using Order Cycle Reduction Internally

The second alternative is for the manufacturer to use the four-day reduction in order cycle time internally to improve efficiency of the logistics system and thereby reduce its costs. In this case, management could use the cost savings to perform a cost-benefit analysis for the new system. For example, if the company has annual sales of 1,200,000 cases of product in market A, and the additional four days are used for planning, inventory levels in the public warehouse can be decreased to 50,000 cases from 100,000 cases (see Figure 15–7). Since the variable delivered cost of each case of product at the public warehouse is $8.00 ($7.20 variable manufactured cost plus 50 cents per case for transportation and 30 cents per case to move the product into the public warehouse), the reduction in inventory of 50,000 cases represents $400,000. With an inventory carrying cost of 45 percent, which includes a 40 percent pretax cost of money, the inventory reduction will result in an annual savings of $180,000 in inventory carrying costs in market A. The four days will also allow the manufacturer to consolidate some large orders to customers for direct truckload shipment with one or two stop-offs. This will allow the manufacturer to bypass the public warehouse on approximately one third of its annual volume, or 400,000 cases. If the truckload rate, including stop-off charges, was 75 cents per case, the transportation savings per year would be $100,000 [($1.00 − $0.75) × 400,000]. In addition, the company would save the 30 cents per case handling charge on the 400,000 cases; this would create savings of $120,000 in public warehousing costs.

In summary, the annual cost savings in market A, the company's largest market, would be as follows:

Reduced inventory carrying costs	$ 180,000
Reduced transportation costs	100,000
Reduced warehousing costs	120,000
Total annual savings	$ 400,000

When this analysis was repeated for all of the manufacturer's markets, the following total annual savings were calculated:

Reduced inventory carrying costs	$ 936,000
Reduced transportation costs	275,000
Reduced warehousing costs	335,000
Total annual savings	$1,546,000

The analyst would have to deduct from these savings the net annual cost of $300,000 associated with the new system. In addition, the freight consolidation program would make it necessary to carry more inventory at plant locations to cover direct shipments to customers. The associated inventory carrying costs would be $150,000. Additional warehouse handling expenses of $96,000 would also be incurred at plant locations. Therefore, the net savings associated with the new system would be $1 million before taxes, or $500,000 after income taxes. The $500,000 after-tax savings would increase profitability from $2 million to $2.5 million, thereby increasing return on assets from 5 percent to 6.25 percent and return on net worth from 10 percent to 12.5 percent.

In addition to the financial analysis, a number of qualitative—or less easily quantified—benefits can be presented to management. These should not be relied on to justify the system, but should instead supplement the financial analysis—as icing on the cake. The additional benefits should include the following:

Additional Benefits of Using the Time Internally

1. *Customer Service Improvements.* Customer service will be improved basically in two ways. First, the improved communication will allow the customer and the customer service representative to arrange for immediate substitution if a stockout occurs. Or, the representative can provide the customer with a realistic estimated delivery date, if it is necessary to wait for the product to be manufactured. The new system also facilitates postorder inquiries regarding order status.
   Second, the improved communication should reduce the variability

associated with the order cycle time. Recall that the current order cycle of 10 days actually ranged from 7 to 13 days—a variability of 3 days. Reducing order cycle variability by 2 days, to a range of 9 to 11 days, will enable the customers to reduce their safety stocks.

2. *Improved Cash Flow.* The advanced order processing system will result in more accurate and timely invoicing of customers, thereby improving cash flow.
3. *Improved Information.* The advanced order processing will improve information in two major ways. First, sales data will be captured sooner and more reliably, leading to more timely and better information for sales forecasting and production planning. Second, the system can be used as a source of valuable input for the logistics management information system.

A similar analysis can be used to determine the financial impact of purchasing a new forecasting model, an inventory control package, or any other logistics system change.

With a well thought-out financial analysis, the logistics executive will be able to determine the probable profit impact of any proposed system. In the process he or she will contribute to improved productivity in logistics in the United States, thereby raising the standard of living for everyone.

SUMMARY

Accurate cost data are required to achieve least-cost logistics. Successful implementation of integrated logistics management depends on a full knowledge of the costs involved. Cost data are also required to manage logistics operations.

In this chapter we saw how to use logistics costs for decision making and how erroneous decisions result when inaccurate costs are used. We also examined the measurement and control of logistics performance using standard costs and flexible budgets, budgetary practices, and productivity standards. Finally, we discussed how to cost-justify changes in logistics structure using the total cost concept.

In the next chapter we will see how management theory can apply to logistics organization structure, how to evaluate existing logistics structures, and how to develop an effective logistics organization.

SUGGESTED READINGS

ARMITAGE, HOWARD M. "The Use of Management Accounting Techniques to Improve Productivity Analysis in Distribution Operations." *International Journal of Physical Distribution and Materials Management* 14, no. 1 (1984), pp. 41–51.

COOPER, ROBIN. "You Need a New Cost System When . . ." *Harvard Business Review* 67, no. 1 (January-February 1989), pp. 77–82.

COOPER, ROBIN, AND ROBERT S. KAPLAN. "Measure Costs Right: Make the Right Decisions." *Harvard Business Review* 66, no. 5 (September-October, 1988), pp. 96–103.

ERNST AND WHINNEY. *Transportation Accounting and Control: Guidelines for Distribution and Financial Management.* Oak Book, Ill.: National Council of Physical Distribution Management, and New York: National Association of Accountants, 1983.

———. *Warehouse Accounting and Control: Guidelines for Distribution and Financial Managers.* Chicago: National Council of Physical Distribution Management, and New York: National Association of Accountants, 1985.

GRABNER, JOHN R., AND WILLIAM S. SARGENT, eds. "Distribution System Costing: Concepts and Procedures." Proceedings of the Fourth Annual James R. Riley Symposium on Business Logistics, 1972.

KAPLAN, ROBERT S. "One Cost System Isn't Enough." *Harvard Business Review* 66, no. 1 (January-February 1988), pp. 61–66.

———. "How Cost Accounting Distorts Product Costs." *Management Accounting* 70 (April 1988), pp. 20–27.

A. T. KEARNEY, INC. *Measuring and Improving Productivity in Physical Distribution.* Oak Brook, Ill.: National Council of Physical Distribution Management, 1984.

KELLY, KEVIN. "A Bean-Counter's Best Friend." *Business Week* special issue, *The Quality Imperative,* October 25, 1991, pp. 42–43.

LAMBERT, DOUGLAS M., AND JAY U. STERLING. "What Types of Profitability Reports Do Marketing Managers Receive?" *Industrial Marketing Management* 16, no. 4 (1987), pp. 295–303.

MENTZER, JOHN T. AND BRENDA PONSFORD KONRAD. "An Efficiency/Effectiveness Approach to Logistics Performance Analysis." *Journal of Business Logistics* 12, no. 1 (1991), pp. 33–62.

MOSSMAN, FRANK H., W. J. E. CRISSY, AND PAUL M. FISCHER. *Financial Dimensions of Marketing Management.* New York: John Wiley and Sons, 1978.

NOVAK, ROBERT A. "Quality and Control in Logistics: A Process Model." *International Journal of Physical Distribution and Materials Management* 19, no. 11 (1989), pp. 1–44.

ROTH, HAROLD P., AND A. FAYE BORTHICK. "Are You Distorting Costs by Violating ABC Assumptions?" *Management Accounting* 73 (November 1991), pp. 39–42.

TYNDALL, GENE R., AND JOHN R. BUSHER. "Improving the Management of Distribution with Cost and Financial Information." *Journal of Business Logistics* 6, no. 2 (1985), pp. 1–18.

WORTHY, FORD S. "Accounting Bores You? Wake Up." *Fortune* (October 12, 1987), pp. 43, 44, 48–50.

QUESTIONS AND PROBLEMS

1. Why is it so important to have accurate cost data for management of the logistics function?
2. What problems are associated with the use of average cost data for decision making?
3. How does the inability to distinguish between fixed and variable costs hamper good management practice?
4. What are the problems associated with the arbitrary allocation of logistics costs?
5. How do accurate cost data contribute to the motivation of personnel?
6. Why is it difficult to obtain logistics cost data in many firms?
7. Explain the four methods that can be used for controlling logistics activities. What are the advantages and disadvantages of each?
8. What is activity-based costing? What are the advantages of activity-based costing? What are the potential limitations associated with activity-based costing?
9. How can the order processing system improve the quality of the logistics information system?
10. The shipping department of Company A has recently converted to a standard cost system for cost control and performance measurement. For every 1,000 containers packed and shipped, the department expects the following variable cost pattern.

Standard cost of shipping 1,000 containers:	
Materials: 1000 containers at $5	= $ 5,000
20,000 cartons at 20 cents (each container holds 20 cartons)	= 4,000
Labor: 200 hours at $5	= 1,000
Variable overhead (varies with direct labor-hours)	= 200
Total	$10,200

The budgeted level of activity for the previous reporting period was 1,000 containers packed and shipped. The actual results for the period are as follows:

Actual shipments: 1,100 containers	
Materials purchased and used:	
Containers: 1,100 at $5.10	= $ 5,610
Cartons: 22,300 at 22 cents	= 4,906
Labor: 210 hours at $5.00	= 1,050
Variable overhead	= 230
	$11,796

Show the variances due to ineffectiveness and inefficiency for containers, cartons, labor, variable overhead, and for the total variable costs of the shipping department. Explain how your answer provides management with more useful information than would be obtained by simply comparing budgeted figures with actual results.

11. What is the impact on return on net worth of a new order processing sys-

tem, given the following information about the Southland Manufacturing Company:

a. Sales of $200 million.
b. Net profit of $8 million after taxes.
c. Asset turnover of 2.5 times.
d. Financial leverage of 2.
e. Taxes are 50 percent of net income.
f. The new system will provide management with four additional days for planning logistics operations.
g. Inventories will be reduced by $3 million, valued at variable costs delivered to the storage location.
h. The company's inventory carrying cost is 45 percent, which is comprised of a pretax cost of money of 40 percent, and non-cost of money components of 5 percent of the inventory value.
i. Transportation consolidations made possible by the additional planning time will reduce transportation costs by $850,000 per year.
j. Warehousing costs of $200,000 will be eliminated.
k. The new order processing system will cost $300,000 per year more than the existing system.
l. Software costs associated with the new system will increase the first-year costs by $100,000.

12. What percentage increase in sales would be necessary in order to realize the same increase in return on net worth (from your answer to Question 11) that is possible by implementing the new order processing system for Southland Manufacturing Company?

APPENDIX

Developing Standard Costs and Flexible Budgets for Warehousing

The first step is to define operating characteristics. Possible units of measure of activities in warehousing might be: order, case, shipment, SKU, line item, arrival, and/or overpacked carton. The basic elements of this warehouse operation consist of receiving (unloading and clerical), shipping (clerical and order consolidation), stock put-away, stock replenishment, order picking, and overpacking. A description of the process is shown in Figure 15A–1.

All of the basic functions of warehousing are present. A 45-day sample

SOURCE: This material is adapted from Howard M. Armitage and James F. Dickow, "Controlling Distribution with Standard Costs and Flexible Budgets," in *Proceedings of the Seventeenth Annual Conference of the National Council of Physical Distribution Management,* 1979, pp. 116–20.

FIGURE 15A–1 Operating Characteristics

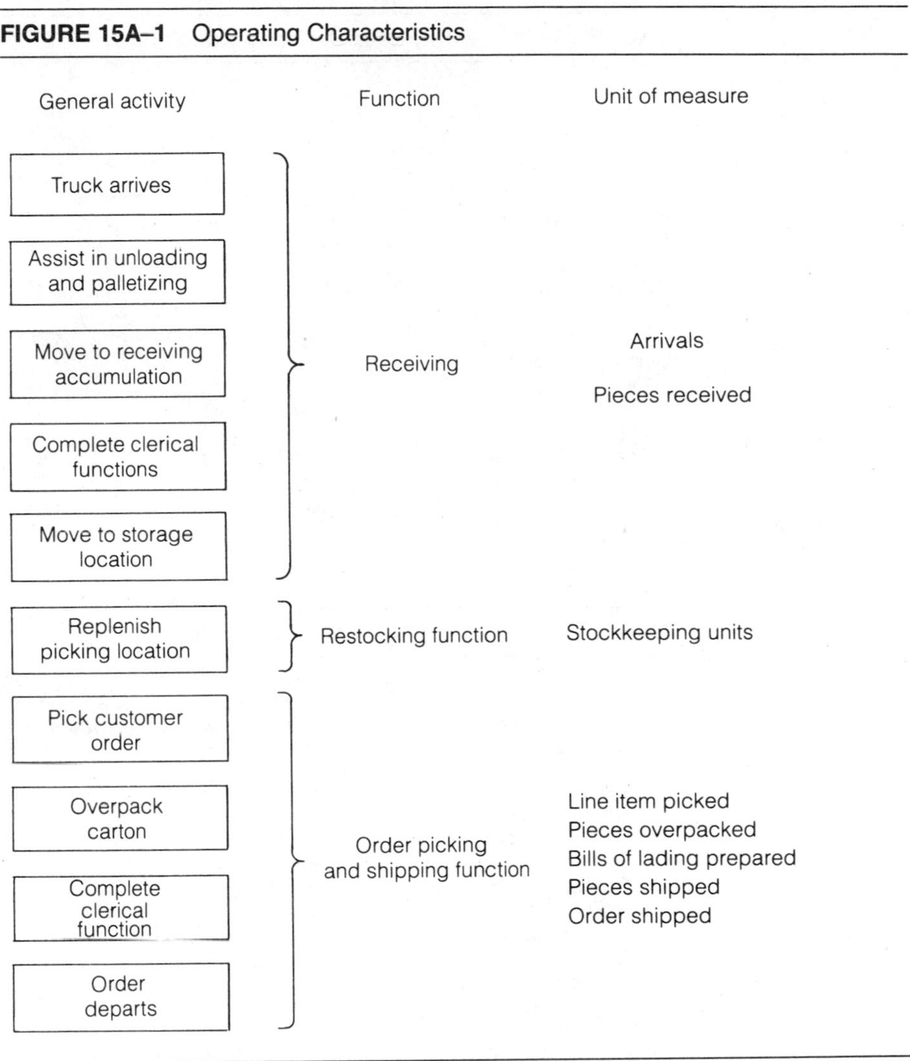

was obtained and data were accumulated for the various important functions of the operation. The results of the sample are shown in Table 15A–1. Also included are the average number of occurrences observed per day and the standard deviation, which is a measure of central tendency or variation around the average. The larger the standard deviation, the more variation there is in day-to-day activity. For instance, the receiving function has higher standard deviations than the order-picking function. This is logical, since receiving activities tend to fluctuate. Shipping, on the other hand, is more consistent, and the standard deviation of the number of lines picked per day is small.

Now that the process has been described—its operating characteristics

TABLE 15A–1 Activity Levels (45-day sample)

Function	*Unit of Measure*	*Average (units of measure per day)*	*Standard Deviation (units of measure per day)*
Receiving functions:			
Arrivals	Arrivals	18	14
Unloaded	Pieces	735	731
Stock put away	Pieces	735	731
Replenishment functions:			
Volume	SKU	200	0
Shipping functions:			
Order picking	Line items	279	72
Overpacking	Pieces	85	37
Orders	Orders	113	31
Freight shipments	Bill of lading	61	14
Small shipments	Pieces	83	24
Load	Pieces	863	198

TABLE 15A–2 Activity Standards—Empirical

Operating Function	*Unit of Measure (per labor-hour)*	*Time Standard (units of measure per labor-hour)*
Warehouse:		
Receiving		
Unload truck	Pieces	250
Check receipts	Pieces	167
Clerical function	Pieces	500
Put-away stock	Pieces	150
Shipping		
Order picking	Line item	30
Order packing	Pieces	22.7
UPS/small shipment	Pieces	100
Freight shipping	Bills of lading	15
Stockkeeping		
Bulk items	Skill	70
QA and shelf items	Skill	50

and activity levels known—the next step is to develop activity standards. These were developed using empirical standards. These standards could have been developed based on industry standards, engineering studies, or historical data, but the empirical method of observing the operation and using judgment to develop estimates was thought to be the most appropriate in this case (see Table 15A–2).

Now that the daily activities, the approximate levels of activity, and knowledge of the process have been determined, this information is used to develop standard costs (see Table 15A–3).

TABLE 15A–3 Standard Costs

Function	Unit of Measure	Daily Activity (units of measure)	Standard Time (units of measure per L-H)	Hourly Rate ($ per L-H)	Standard Cost ($ per unit of measure)
Receiving:					
Unload truck	Pieces	735	250	7.50	3.0¢/Piece
Check receipts	Pieces	735	167	7.50	4.5¢/Piece
Clerical function	Pieces	735	500	7.50	1.5¢/Piece
Put-away stock	Pieces	735	150	7.50	5.0¢/Piece
					14.0¢/Piece
Replenishment:					
Replenish	SKU	200	50	7.50	15.0¢/SKU
Shipping:					
Order picking	Line item	279	30	8.00	26.7¢/Line
Order packing	Pieces	85	23	7.50	32.6¢/Piece
Small shipping	Pieces	83	100	8.00	8.0¢/Piece
Freight shipping	Shipments	61	15	8.25	55.0¢/Shipment

L-H = Labor hour.

TABLE 15A–4 Application to a Flexible Budget

Function	Unit of Measure (U/M)	Standard Cost ($/U/M)	Weekly Summary			
			Activity (U/M)	Std. Cost ($)	Actual Cost ($)	Variance ($)
Receiving	Piece	0.14	4,200	588	800	212 U
Replenishment	SKU	0.15	1,000	150	100	50 F
Shipping:						
Order picking	Line item	0.27	1,430	386	450	64 U
Order packing	Piece	0.33	350	116	100	16 F
Small shipping	Piece	0.08	500	40	25	15 F
Freight shipping	Shipment	0.55	400	220	150	70 F
				1,500	1,625	125 U

The information in Table 15A–3, which includes the standard times and hourly wage rates, allows an incremental cost per unit of measure to be calculated. The unit of measure for each one of the activities might be different, and in this case they are different—that is, piece, SKU, line item, and freight shipment. In some cases it is possible to lump activities together as they are in the receiving function, but this is not possible in every situation. The standard cost per unit of measure is obtained by dividing the labor costs per labor-hour by the estimated standard time.

If this warehousing operation were using flexible budgeting, the standard costs would be used to develop the flexible budget. An example is contained in Table 15A–4.

In this week, 4,200 cases were received, 1,000 stockkeeping units were replenished, etc. These activity levels, when multiplied by the standard cost per unit, gives the total standard cost for each activity. The actual costs incurred during the week also are shown, and variances—favorable or unfavorable—are calculated. For the activity levels achieved during the week, a net unfavorable variance of $125 was calculated. Since this activity level was significantly higher than the average level of activity, the unfavorable variance would have been larger if a fixed budget approach had been used. Developing standard costs and using them to develop a flexible budget gives management a tool to *measure* the *performance* of individuals. The minimization of unfavorable variances is a goal that, when achieved, will yield increased profits.

Chapter 16

Organizing for Effective Logistics

Objectives of This Chapter

To identify how an effective logistics organization can impact a firm

To describe various types of logistics organizational structures

To identify the factors that can influence the effectiveness of a logistics organization

To examine an approach to developing an optimal logistics organization

To identify attributes that can be used to measure organizational effectiveness

INTRODUCTION

In the decade of the 1990s, quality and customer service have become the focus of top management. Embracing the concepts is only the first step, however. A firm must also be able to implement the strategies, plans, and programs to deliver acceptable levels of quality and service to its customers. Logistics and the people that are part of the logistics function play vital roles in that process.

A study by Cleveland Consulting Associates in 1991 highlighted the importance of quality programs in over 200 U.S. and European businesses. In the study, entitled "The State of Quality in Logistics," several barriers to instituting a high-quality program were identified. Interestingly, the top six barriers identified were related to employees and/or organizational issues. They included the following (in order of importance): changing the corporate culture, establishing a common vision throughout the organization, establishing employee ownership of the quality process, gaining senior executive (top-down) commitment, changing management processes, and training and educating employees.[1] Therefore, the roles of individual employees and logistics departments are especially important in strategic logistics management, and each will be explored in this chapter.

Logistics is Developing Rapidly

Logistics executives have seen their discipline develop over the past 30 years from infancy, when the logistics functions were dispersed throughout the organization, to a highly structured, computerized, and large-budget activity. The role of the logistics executive is far different today from what it was 30 years ago and most probably different from what it will be 30 years hence. The next decade promises unprecedented challenges.[2]

The logistics executive has been beset by a multitude of problems, including economic uncertainty, inflation, product and energy shortages, environmentalism and Green Marketing, regulatory constraints, and rising customer demands and expectations. The logistics activity is becoming increasingly more difficult to manage. In this chapter, we will examine the

[1] William R. Read and Mark S. Miller, *The State of Quality in Logistics* (Cleveland, Ohio: Cleveland Consulting Associates, 1991), pp. 12–13.

[2] Dennis R. McDermott and James R. Stock, "A Futures Perspective on Logistics Management: Applying the Project Delphi Technique," *Proceedings of the Eighth Annual Transportation and Logistics Educators Conference,* ed. Robert H. House, 1978, p. 1.

issues of how to organize logistics within the firm as well as how to measure its effectiveness. We will see how important an effective logistics organization is to a firm, and the types of organizational structures that exist. Although no single "ideal" organization structure is appropriate for all companies, we will see how to evaluate various organizational structures and describe the approaches that can be used to develop an effective logistics organization.

IMPORTANCE OF AN EFFECTIVE LOGISTICS ORGANIZATION

An effective and efficient logistics organization is a vital part of a firm's strategic management process: "Companies recognize that their problems, challenges, current efforts, and room for progress do not lie primarily in the area of strategic decision making, but in four other related areas: [organizational] structure, planning process, people, and style."[3] In essence, each can be considered an important strategic resource and a long-term corporate asset.[4]

Many firms have not employed their strategic resources properly. A *Fortune* article claimed that over 90 percent of U.S. businesses had not developed and executed successful corporate strategies.[5] As some have argued, this lack of success may have been due to the lack of a competitive organizational design or structure:

> The challenge of developing such a design can be likened to the challenge facing the general who has prepared a superb campaign strategy and must now design the army that will execute that strategy. Without the correct assembly of different battle units and their support services, the campaign cannot proceed, let alone achieve victory. By design we mean not only the selection of the organization structure but also the design of the support systems, planning systems, and control systems that deliver the strategy via the structure.[6]

Companies Realize Benefits from Reorganizing Logistics Activities

Examples of firms that have been successful in the logistics area include Whirlpool, Johnson & Johnson, Hooker Chemicals, and Nabisco Brands.

Whirlpool Corporation reorganized its logistics activities in late 1971 and established a new position of vice president of distribution. The company estimated savings of more than $10 million a year in logistics costs.[7] The savings resulted from pulling together a number of logistics-related

---

[3] Jacques Horovitz, "New Perspectives on Strategic Management," *The Journal of Business Strategy* 4, no. 3 (Winter 1984), p. 19.

[4] See Milton Lavenstein, "Organizing to Develop Effective Strategy," *The Journal of Business Strategy* 1, no. 3 (Winter 1981), pp. 70–73.

[5] Walter Kiechel III, "Playing by the Rules of the Corporate Strategy Game," *Fortune* 100, no. 6 (September 24, 1979), p. 118.

[6] Ian C. MacMillian and Patricia E. Jones, "Designing Organizations to Compete," *The Journal of Business Strategy* 4, no. 4 (Spring 1984), p. 92.

[7] Thomas J. Murray, "A Powerful New Voice in Management," *Dun's Review* 107, no. 4 (April 1976), p. 71.

activities under a single organizational unit with a reporting relationship to marketing. In addition, Whirlpool placed two traditional marketing activities—sales forecasting and order processing—under logistics control.

In July 1976, Johnson & Johnson Baby Products Company committed itself to reducing its logistics costs by 45 percent.[8] As a result of a logistics system design project, the company was able to achieve a cost savings of 11 percent in 1978. This was partially due to organizational design efficiencies. By 1979 the cost savings were 47 percent, and for the period 1980–1985, the company experienced even larger savings. The cost reductions were achieved through modifications of the firm's organizational structure, customer service levels, storage facilities, and inventory policies.

In 1975, Hooker Chemicals and Plastics Corporation combined its distribution and purchasing functions into a single unit. Hooker created a high-level executive position, director of materials management, to head it. The company reported favorable results in cost reduction, improved levels of customer service, and higher profits.[9] On a larger scale, the 1981 merger of Nabisco and Standard Brands into Nabisco Brands required the combination of two large logistics networks. Integration of the two systems progressed well, and the result was the creation of a much stronger logistics network for the new company.[10] Companies as diverse as Abbott Laboratories, Uniroyal, Rohm and Haas, Eastman Kodak Company, Maremont Corporation, and Mead Johnson and Company have undergone similar changes and achieved much the same results as Johnson & Johnson, Whirlpool, and Hooker.

A Traditional Organization Structure

Traditionally, the various logistics functions were scattered throughout the organization, with no single executive, department, or division responsible for managing the entire distribution process. Such a situation is depicted in Figure 16–1. As Stolle noted:

> Each element of distribution tends to get lost among the other activities of marketing, finance and accounting, and manufacturing. [Figure 16–1] also highlights the inevitable conflict of objectives that results from this organization pattern. Only the president really seeks maximum total company return on investment, and individual objectives of executives in marketing, finance and accounting, and manufacturing often conflict with this overall objective—and with each other.[11]

---

[8] This case example is based on a presentation entitled "Assessing the Organizational Trade-Offs in the Distribution Strategic Planning Process," by Peter H. Soderberg, director of physical distribution and planning, Johnson & Johnson Baby Products Company, at the annual meeting of the National Council of Physical Distribution Management, Houston, Texas, in October, 1979.

[9] Murray, "A Powerful New Voice in Management," p. 70.

[10] See Nicholas J. La Howchic, "Merging the Distribution Operations of Nabisco and Standard Brands, and Customer Service," *Proceedings of the Twenty-Second Annual Conference of the National Council of Physical Distribution Management,* 1984, pp. 179–96.

[11] John F. Stolle, "How to Manage Physical Distribution," *Harvard Business Review* 45, no. 4 (July–August 1967), p. 94.

FIGURE 16–1 Traditional Approach to Logistics Management

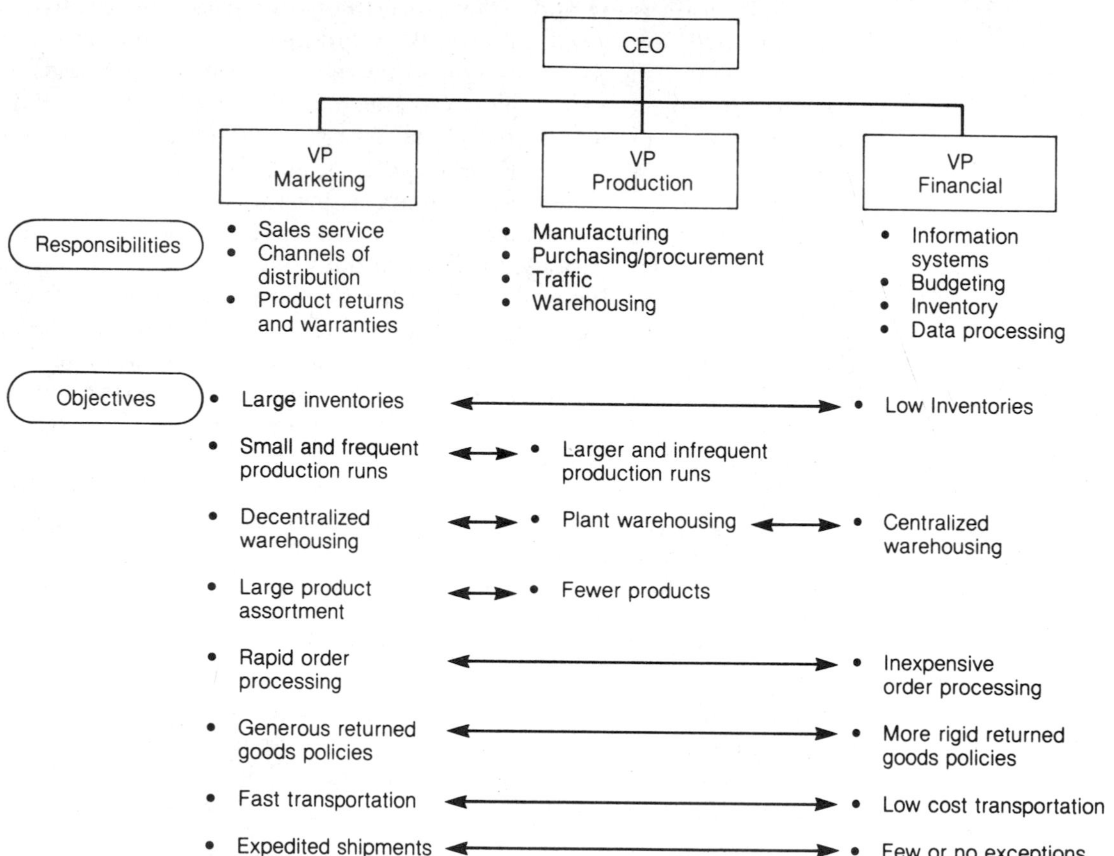

An Integrated Logistics Organization

The lack of an organizational structure that combines the activities of logistics under a single, high-level executive indicates a failure to adopt and implement the integrated logistics management concept (discussed in Chapter 2 of this book).

Since the 1960s, however, there has been a trend toward the integration of many logistics functions under one top-ranking corporate executive. Table 16–1 lists the range of activities over which the logistics executive has had authority. There has been a continual expansion of the logistics executive's span of control to include transportation, warehousing, inventories, order processing, packaging, material handling, forecasting and planning, and purchasing and procurement. Table 16–2 shows a typical job description for the senior logistics executive.

Coordination of the various logistics activities is crucial to the well-

TABLE 16–1 Control Exercised by the Logistics Executive over Selected Logistics Activities

	Percent of Reporting Companies			
Activities	*1966**	*1976†*	*1985‡*	*1990§*
Transportation	89%	94%	97%	98%
Warehousing	70	93	95	97
Inventory control	55	83	81	79
Order processing	43	76	67	61
Packaging	8	70	37	48
Purchasing and procurement	15	58	44	51
Number of reporting companies	47	180	161	216

*From John F. Spencer, "Physical Distribution Management Finds Its Level," *Handling and Shipping* 7, no. 11 (November 1966), pp. 67–69.

†From Bernard J. LaLonde and James F. Robeson, "Profile of the Physical Distribution Executive," in *Proceedings of the Fourteenth Annual Conference of the National Council of Physical Distribution Management*, 1976, pp. 1–23.

‡Data reported are for directors of logistics. From Bernard J. LaLonde and Larry W. Emmelhainz, "Where Do You Fit In?" *Distribution* 8, no. 11 (November 1985), p. 34.

§From James M. Masters and Bernard J. LaLonde, "The 1990 Ohio State University Survey of Career Patterns in Logistics," *Annual Conference Proceedings of the Council of Logistics Management*, Vol. I (1990), pp. 33–52.

being of a firm, as Ronald E. Seger, vice president of A. T. Kearney, Inc., has noted:

> Integrated logistics management—that is, the central control of all logistics-related elements—is a concept whose time has come. . . . Companies are realizing that they can gain a significant competitive advantage by becoming suppliers of the marketplace. Through effective logistics practices during a period of increased energy costs, higher interest rates, and other constraints, these suppliers are improving their positions as effective members of the value-added chain in market fulfillment.[12]

In the next section, we will examine the major organizational types found in business firms.

TYPES OF LOGISTICS ORGANIZATIONAL STRUCTURES

As Collier has emphasized, "Strategic management requires that there be organizational units to which resources can be allocated and which have the capability of carrying out a strategy once agreed to."[13] The specific structure may vary, but even when two companies possess the same out-

[12] Jack W. Farrell, "New Clout for Logistics," *Traffic Management* 24, no. 9 (September 1985), p. 37.

[13] Don Collier, "How to Implement Strategic Plans," *The Journal of Business Strategy* 4, no. 3 (Winter 1984), p. 92.

TABLE 16–2 Job Description of a Typical Senior Logistics Executive

Position: Vice President, Logistics

Overall Responsibility: Management and control of the logistics function and representation of logistics in corporate decision-making processes.

Specific Responsibilities: (partial—example only)

1. Hire, organize, train, and motivate personnel necessary to achieve superior results.
2. Develop annual plans and budgets for CEO approval prior to the commencement of each fiscal year. Develop five-year plans and participate in the annual corporate planning process.
3. Provide direction and leadership to all logistics activities and operations consistent with corporate goals, corporate policies, and annual plans and budgets.
4. Develop and implement more cost-effective approaches to product distribution through improved productivity and optimization of the overall processes.
5. Work with other departments to coordinate activities; thus insuring an economic and efficient logistics process. Provide leadership in developing new approaches to inventory planning, customer service and overall product flow.

Detailed Responsibilities: (partial—example only)

1. Develop annual and five-year plan.
2. Develop annual budget.
3. Authorize budgeted capital expenditures and expenses.
4. Hire and terminate personnel.
5. Authorize new systems whose impact is limited to logistics.
6. Route inbound and outbound freight.
7. Audit and authorize freight bills for payment.
8. Manage private fleet, including service to noncorporate customers.
9. Conduct carrier negotiations.
10. Develop improved systems to manage, operate and control activities.

Other Responsibilities: (partial—example only)

1. Assist in source selection, packaging, and order quantity decisions regarding inbound freight.
2. Assist in inventory planning and customer service decisions, providing alternatives and their cost/impact.
3. Assist in sales forecasting studies providing information as needed on actual shipping patterns and frequencies.

SOURCE: Adapted from David D. Grumhaus, "Organizing the Distribution Function," in *Logistics: Contribution and Control,* ed. Patrick Gallagher, Proceedings of the 1983 Logistics Resource Forum (Cleveland: Leaseway Transportaion Corp., 1983), pp. 70–71.

ward organizational structure, they usually differ in some important area, e.g., personnel quality, capital costs, management style, etc. All organizations are not alike, although they may be similar.[14] For example, the logistics function is often viewed in the same way in many organizations. But as we saw in Chapter 1, they may use many different names to describe it.

Components of a Logistics Organization

Logistics management is that phase of administration responsible for the effective functioning of the overall logistics process. Organizationally, logistics management consists of:

[14] For an interesting discussion of organizational design see Henry Mintzberg, "Organization Design: Fashion or Fit?" *Harvard Business Review* 59, no. 1 (January–February 1981), pp. 103–16.

The top logistics executive in the business unit.

The managers of support services reporting through the logistics organization (such as the logistics controller, manager of logistics systems, manager of logistics engineering) and their respective staffs.

The logistics project services groups, which may or may not fall under one of the previously mentioned support service groups. These may exist as separate staff groups within the logistics organization, or they may be made up of changing groups of line personnel who devote only a portion of their time to staff projects (e.g., planning a new distribution center, designing a new information system).

Field operations management personnel, such as those responsible for distribution centers, the traffic/transportation activities and the private fleet, and their respective line and staff organizations.[15]

Most distribution strategists agree that coordination of the various logistics activities is essential for organizations of all sizes. This is true regardless of the organizational structure.

Manufacturers, wholesalers, and retailers all perform logistics activities but are often organized differently. Manufacturers may use one of three organizational strategies: process-based, market-based, or channel-based. Each of these approaches is described below:

Process-Based Strategy

Process-based [*strategy*] is concerned with managing a broad group of logistics activities as a value-added chain. The emphasis of a process strategy is to achieve efficiency from managing purchasing, manufacturing scheduling, and physical distribution as an integrated system.

Market-Based Strategy

Market-based [*strategy*] is concerned with managing a limited group of logistics activities across a multi-division business or across multiple business units. The logistics organization when following a market-based strategy seeks to: (1) make joint product shipments to customers on behalf of different business units or product groups, and (2) facilitate sales and logistical coordination by a single order-invoice. Often the senior sales and logistics executives report to the same senior manager.

Channel-Based Strategy

Channel-based [*strategy*] focuses on managing logistics activities performed jointly in combination with dealers and distributors. The channel orientation places a great deal of attention on external control. Firms that concentrate on a channel-based strategy typically have significant amounts of finished inventories forward, or downstream, in the distribution channel.[16]

Wholesalers are structured differently from manufacturers because of their position in the channel of distribution and the nature of the activities

---

[15] A. T. Kearney, Inc., *Measuring and Improving Productivity in Physical Distribution* (Oak Brook, Ill.: National Council of Physical Distribution Management, 1984), pp. 303–4.

[16] Donald J. Bowersox, Patricia J. Daugherty, Cornelia L. Dröge, Dale S. Rogers, and Daniel J. Wardlow, *Leading Edge Logistics: Competitive Positioning for the 1990s* (Oak Brook, Ill.: Council of Logistics Management, 1989), pp. 34–35.

they perform. In addition to the traditional wholesaling functions (e.g., transport, storage), a number of value-added services are being done by wholesalers, including light manufacturing and assembly, pricing, order processing, inventory management, logistics system design, and development of promotional materials.[17]

Retailers, because of their direct contact with final customers and the high level of competition they face, often place more emphasis on inventory, warehousing, and customer service activities than do manufacturers. They tend to be more centralized than manufacturers and wholesalers.

> The logistical operations of retailers are geographically focused and highly detailed. Retail distribution warehouses are generally located within one or two days' travel distance from a cluster of store locations. The delivery destinations of retailers' distribution systems are well known, making transportation planning relatively straightforward. Retailers generally ship large numbers of stockkeeping units from their distribution warehouses, creating the need for intricate control systems. The notion of an *inventory pipeline* is critical in retailing due to the high cost of retail space. Proper timing of store deliveries is essential to the maintenance and velocity of store inventory.[18]

Additionally, many retailers are becoming more involved in direct-to-store deliveries from manufacturers and are purchasing many logistics services from third parties rather than performing those activities themselves.

Three Basic Organizational Structures for Logistics

Coordination of the various logistics activities can be achieved in several ways. The basic systems are generally structured utilizing a combination of the following:

1. Strategic versus operational.
2. Centralized versus decentralized.
3. Line versus staff.

Strategic versus operational refers to the level at which logistics activities are positioned within the firm. Strategically, it is important to determine logistics' position in the corporate hierarchy relative to other activities, such as marketing, manufacturing, and finance/accounting. Equally important, however, is the operational structure of the various logistics activities—warehousing, inventory control, order processing, transportation, and others—under the senior logistics executive.

The term *centralized distribution* can reflect a system in which logistics activities are administered at a central location, typically a corporate headquarters, or a system in which operating authority is controlled under a single department or individual. Firms with homogeneous products or markets usually have centralized organizational structures. Centrally pro-

[17] Ibid., p. 37.

[18] Ibid., p. 39.

gramming activities, such as order processing, traffic, or inventory control can result in significant cost savings due to economies of scale. On the other hand, decentralization of logistics activities can be effective for firms with diverse products or markets. Some argue, with justification, that decentralizing logistics activities often leads to higher levels of customer service. With developments in computer technology and information systems, however, it may be possible to deliver high levels of customer service with a centralized logistics activity.

Within the three basic types of organizational structures, logistics activities can be line, staff, or a combination of line and staff.[19] "Many companies are grouping line distribution activities only, thus forming another line function comparable to sales and production. When this is done, one individual is made responsible for 'doing' the distribution job."[20] In the staff organization, the line activities, such as order processing, traffic, and warehousing, are housed under production, marketing, or finance/accounting. The various staff activities assist and coordinate the line functions. The combination of line and staff activities joins these two organizational types, so as to eliminate the shortcomings inherent in systems where line and staff activities are not coordinated.

In the typical staff approach to organization, logistics finds itself in primarily an advisory role. In line organizations, logistics responsibilities are operational; that is, they deal with the management of day-to-day activities. Combinations of line and staff organizations are possible, and most companies are structured in this fashion.

Logistics as a Function

Other organizational approaches are possible. Examples include logistics as a function, logistics as a program, and the matrix organization approach.[21] Figure 16–2 shows the organizational design for logistics as a *function*. Some argue that if a firm treats logistics as a functional area, without regard to other activities, the results will be less than optimal. Logistics is cross-functional and therefore requires a different organizational structure. The functional approach can be considered the antithesis of the systems approach in that:

> The traditional functional view of organizations isolates physical mechanisms, material components, psychosocial effects, political-legal elements, economic constructs, and environmental constraints. Traditionally, each of these elements was optimized, often ignoring the interrelationships among them. But as organizations developed, complex interdependencies evolved, and a holistic approach became necessary to cope with the problems of the organization.[22]

[19] Stolle, "How to Manage Physical Distribution," pp. 96–98.

[20] Ibid., p. 96.

[21] Daniel W. DeHayes, Jr., and Robert L. Taylor, "Making 'Logistics' Work in a Firm," *Business Horizons* 15, no. 3 (June 1972), pp. 41–44.

[22] Ibid., p. 40.

FIGURE 16–2 Organization Design for Logistics as a Function

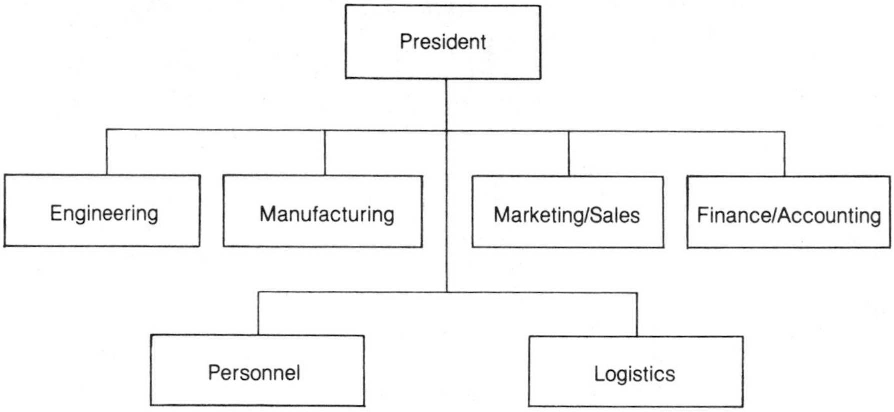

Logistics as a Program

When logistics is organized as a *program* (see Figure 16–3), the distribution activity assumes the role of a program in which the total company participates. Functional areas are subordinate to the program: "Logistics considerations are given paramount importance, and systems cost minimization is equated with organization profit maximization. Demand generation and production processes are considered only in respect to how they contribute to the logistics system."[23]

It can be argued that the optimal logistics organization lies between the two extremes represented by the functional and program approaches. This middle approach has been termed the *matrix organization;* it is shown in Figure 16–4. DeHayes and Taylor described the matrix approach as follows:

Matrix Management

> This type of structure is built around specific programs represented by the horizontal emphasis. Each program manager, such as the logistics program manager, is responsible for his program within established time, cost, quantity, and quality constraints. The line organization (the vertical emphasis) develops from the programs but is now a supporting relationship. . . . Instead of a line-and-staff relationship, there is a web of relationships, all acting and reacting in harmony. The logistics manager can assume his intended role; he becomes the overall coordinator among a whole series of functions.[24]

The matrix management approach requires the coordination of activities across unit lines in the organization. Therefore it is essential that top-level management wholeheartedly support the logistics executive. Even

[23] Ibid., pp. 42–43.

[24] Ibid., pp. 43–44.

FIGURE 16–3 Organization Design for Logistics as a Program

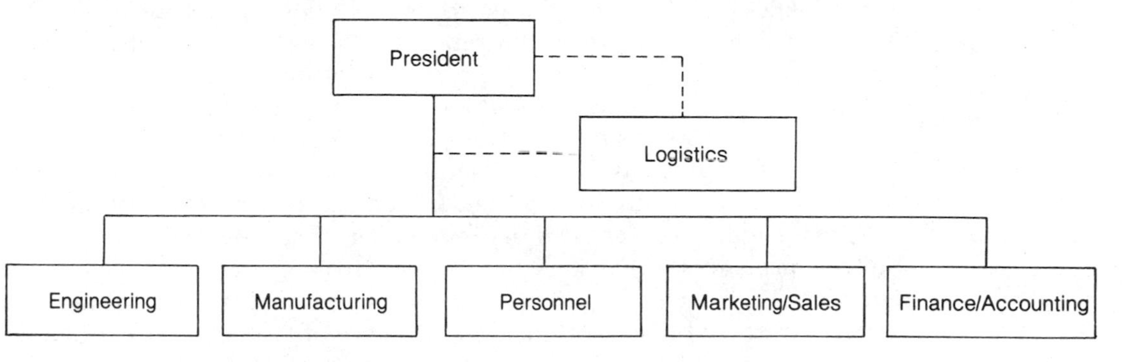

FIGURE 16–4 Logistics in a Matrix Organization

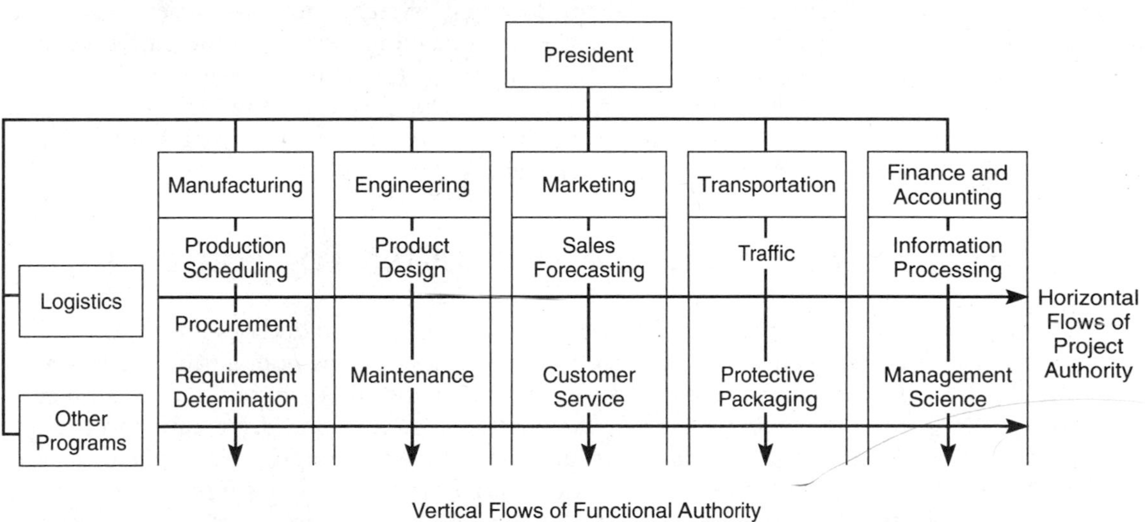

SOURCE: Adapted from Daniel W. DeHayes, Jr., and Robert L. Taylor, "Making 'Logistics' Work in a Firm," *Business Horizons 15*, no. 3 (June 1972), p. 44.

with high-level support, however, the complexities of coordination are difficult to master. For example, any time there are multiple reporting responsibilities, as is common in matrix organizations, problems may arise: "The distribution manager might report to a vice president of distribution but also be responsible to the vice president of marketing where [he/she] contributes to market strategies. It's a teamwork organization."[25] Unfortunately, unless closely supervised, teamwork organizations tend to break down or disintegrate, as spheres of authority and responsibility overlap and come into conflict with one another. In general, matrix organizations "results in a larger corporate staff, more regional offices, and more constraints on local managers."[26] For some industries, matrix organizations can be very effective. High-technology firms are especially suited to organizing in a matrix structure because of the high incidence of task- or project-oriented activities that overlap several functional areas.[27]

What Is the Ideal Organization Structure?

A review of the multitude of organizational types found in companies reveal a variety of structural forms. Firms can be very successful utilizing one or more organizational structures. Which form, however, is optimal for any given company? That is an immensely difficult question to answer. Rather than examining organizational structures of several companies and speculating about "ideal" or "optimal" systems, we need to employ some empirical measures to correlate organizational structure and efficiency/productivity. Obviously, the optimal system for a company is one that maximizes its efficiency and productivity. Diagnostically, the logistics executive must not only determine the firm's organizational structure but also evaluate its performance or effectiveness.

DECISION-MAKING STRATEGIES IN ORGANIZING FOR LOGISTICS

As logistics executives face new challenges in the decades ahead, it will become even more important that logistics systems operate more efficiently. In the face of higher costs of operation and increasing pressures from customers for better service, the logistics organization must evolve and change to meet the challenge. An understanding of the factors that make organizations effective, and knowledge of how these factors interrelate, are the first steps toward developing the optimal system for a firm's customers.

---

[25] James P. Falk, "Organizing for Effective Distribution," in *Proceedings of the Eighteenth Annual Conference of the National Council of Physical Distribution Management,* 1980, p. 185.

[26] Ibid.

[27] For an interesting discussion of how to effectively manage in a matrix organization, see Larry E. Greiner and Virginia E. Schein, "The Paradox of Managing a Project-Oriented Matrix: Establishing Coherence Within Chaos," *Sloan Management Review 22,* no. 2 (Winter 1981), pp. 17–22.

The Logistics Mission Statement[28]

In general, mission statements provide the foundation or basis from which a company develops strategies, plans, and tactics. The mission statement defines the basic purpose of an organization and identifies the parameters under which the firm will operate. Six benefits result from the establishment of a formal written mission statement:

Benefits of Having a Mission Statement

1. To ensure unanimity of purpose within the organization.
2. To provide a basis, or standard, for allocating organizational resources.
3. To establish a general tone or organizational climate.
4. To serve as a focal point for individuals to identify with the organization's purpose and direction, and to deter those who cannot from participating further in the organization's activities.
5. To facilitate the translation of objectives into a work structure involving the assignment of tasks to responsible elements within the organization.
6. To specify organizational purposes and the translation of these purposes into objectives in such a way that cost, time, and performance parameters can be assessed and controlled.[29]

As corporate mission statements serve to provide the starting point for developing corporate goals and objectives, so too will logistics mission statements provide direction for developing business strategies. When combined with a specific set of performance goals and measurement systems, the logistics mission statement can help to eliminate organizational conflicts and provide direction to logistics personnel.[30]

The components of a corporate mission statement or a logistics mission statement will be similar. They will vary in their specific content because the logistics mission statement is only one element of a firm's total corporate mission, but they will both contain similar components. Typically, mission statements will contain eight key components:

Eight Components of a Mission Statement

1. *The specification of target customers and markets.* Who are the firm's customers?
2. *The identification of principal products/services.* What products and/or services does the firm produce?
3. *The specification of geographic domain.* Where are the firm's markets located?

---

[28] This material is based on James R. Stock and Cornelia Dröge, "Logistics Mission Statements: An Appraisal," *Proceedings of the Nineteenth Annual Transportation and Logistics Educators Conference,* James M. Masters and Cynthia L. Coykendale, eds. (Columbus, Ohio: The Ohio State University, 1990), pp. 79–91.

[29] W. R. King and D. I. Cleland, *Strategic Planning and Policy* (New York: Van Nostrand Reinhold, 1979), p. 124.

[30] Frank Yanacek, "The Logic Behind Logistics," *Handling and Shipping Management* 28, no. 8 (August 1987), pp. 30–34.

4. *The identification of core technologies.* What technologies does the firm utilize?
5. *The expression of commitment to survival, growth, and profitability.* What factors does the firm consider important relative to its economic viability?
6. *The specification of key elements in the company philosophy.* What are the basic priorities of the firm?
7. *The identification of the company self-concept.* What are the firm's strengths and weaknesses relative to competition?
8. *The identification of the firm's desired public image.* What is the firm's social responsibility, and what image does it wish to project?[31]

A Comparison of Corporate and Logistics Mission Statements

In a research study examining the logistics mission statements of 88 manufacturers, Stock and Dröge found a number of similarities between corporate and logistics mission statements. Utilizing the eight components previously identified, the following results were reported.[32]

1. *Targeted customers and markets.* The selection of target markets and the development of marketing strategies to reach those segments are vital components of a firm's activities. Within corporate mission statements, mention is often made of customers and markets. An examination of logistics mission statements revealed that 47 percent of firms with formal logistics mission statements included mention of targeted customers and markets. Illustrative of mission statements including such material were the following:

> To deliver quality products to our customers and manufacturing groups in the fastest and most cost effective mode possible. (hospital supply company)
>
> [To] provide integrated logistical support services and facilities to the product groups and field operations units of the division. (communication systems manufacturer)

2. *Principal products/services.* Much like corporate mission statements, more than two-thirds of the firms included discussion of the firm's products and services in their logistics mission statement. In fact, significantly more manufacturers included mention of their principal products and/or services than any other component (70 percent versus 56 percent). Examples of statements that included mention of products/services were the following:

> [To] provide timely and effective services for the storage and commercial movement of all company finished products and of materials and supplies necessary for company operations. (tobacco company)
>
> To deliver our furniture to our customers within six weeks of order, in the most efficient manner possible. (furniture company)

---

[31] John A. Pearce II and Fred David, "Corporate Mission Statements: The Bottom Line," *Academy of Management Executive* 1, no. 2 (1987), p. 109.

[32] Stock and Dröge, "Logistics Mission Statements," pp. 82–84.

3. *Geographic domain.* Typically, firms did not specify locations of their target markets within their logistics mission statements. Only 11 percent included any mention of their competitive markets:

> [To] provide service parts, tools, and test equipment necessary to maintain the company's worldwide installed computer base. (computer manufacturer)

> To sell, produce, and deliver the products of the foods business units in the United States. (conglomerate)

4. *Core technologies.* Few firms (8 percent) included mention of core technologies in their logistics mission statements, which perhaps can be attributed to the fact that manufacturing technologies are distinct from logistics technologies. Even when firms include core technologies relevant to their manufacturing operations (and this is relatively infrequent) in the overall corporate mission statement, they may not include such mention in the logistics mission statement. When they did, however, the following statements were illustrative:

> Integrated distribution network . . . is managed through a single transportation network structure, common information network, effective facilities network, and performance measurement and control. (computer manufacturer)

> To manage . . . a corporate-wide quality transportation network and supporting multidivisional computer systems that will assure the safe delivery of products. (automobile manufacturer)

5. *Survival, growth, and profitability.* Corporate mission statements almost universally include mention of the issues of survival, growth, and profitability. Because some firms may not see any or very little direct correlation between logistics activities and company profits, sales volumes, growth rates, and the like, it was not surprising that only 56 percent of the firms survey included mention of such elements. If logistics is viewed primarily as a way to reduce costs, rather than as a means to improve competitive advantage, corporate management will only see a very indirect linkage existing. At best, management will view logistics from the perspective that lower costs can increase bottom-line profitability but cannot increase sales and, ultimately, profits. Examples of logistics mission statements that included mention of a concern for survival, growth and profitability were:

> [To] provide timely, cost-effective shipment and delivery; to enhance our position . . . and to provide career growth for our employees. (metal products manufacturer)

> To provide a cost-effective distribution system to enhance our competitive position and improve our profits. (food company)

6. *Company philosophy.* One of the noteworthy findings of the analysis of logistics missions statements was the paucity of statements that included any mention of overall company and/or logistics philosophy. Only 9 percent of those firms in the research study included any such statement(s). When logistics mission statements did mention philosophy, they seemed to include the notion that logistics could create competitive advantage for the firm:

> Logistics will be active in the integration and differentiation strategies that produce competitive advantage. (lighting manufacturer)
>
> Our mission is to have the right product at the right place at the right time at the right cost. (building products manufacturer)

7. *Company self-concept.* Did the logistics mission statement include any statements of how the firm viewed itself? Approximately one-third (34 percent) of the respondent firms incorporated mention of self-concept. When they did, statements such as the following were included:

> [To] provide our customers the quality product they need when they desire it so that our service is better than our competitors. (optical manufacturer)
>
> To be the logistics and distribution vendor of choice by exceeding competitive levels of service at lower cost and increased inventory turns. (office systems manufacturer)

8. *Firm's desired public image.* Forty percent of the logistics mission statements identified the firm's desired public image. When firms included mention of public image in their mission statements, only general mention was included. No mention was made of the specific public image the firm was to achieve. Examples included the following statements:

> The goal is to strengthen the company's image, market share, and growth through the excellence of its service and the professionalism of its personnel. (sporting goods manufacturer)
>
> To promote the firm's image, physical distribution is committed to excellence. (pharmaceutical firm)

Firms need a clear statement of purpose in order to develop some optimal combination of logistical activities that must be performed in the day-to-day operations of the enterprise. As stated by George Steiner, "Mission statements . . . provide motivation, general direction, an image, a tone, and a philosophy to guide the enterprise."[33] In sum, the logistics mission statement is an important document to guide the planning, implementation, and control of a firm's logistics activities.

Components of an Optimal Logistics Organization

Many Factors Contribute to Organizational Effectiveness

Many factors can influence the effectiveness of a logistics organization. In general, the factors contributing to organizational effectiveness can be summarized as (1) organizational characteristics, (2) environmental char-

[33] George A. Steiner, *Strategic Planning—What Every Manager Must Know* (Riverside, N.J.: The Free Press, 1979), p. 160.

acteristics, (3) employee characteristics, and (4) managerial policies and practices.[34] Table 16–3 presents some illustrative items within each category.

Structure and Technology

Organizational Characteristics. Structure and technology are the major components of a firm's organizational characteristics. *Structure* refers to the relationships that exist between various functional areas—interfunctional (marketing, finance, operations, manufacturing, logistics) or intrafunctional (warehousing, traffic, purchasing, customer service). The relationships are most often represented by a company's organization chart. Examples of structural variables are decentralization, specialization, formalization, span of control, organization size, and work-unit size. *Technology* "refers to the mechanisms used by an organization to transform raw inputs into finished outputs. Technology can take several forms, including variations in the materials used, and variations in the technical knowledge brought to bear on goal-directed activities."[35]

Environmental Characteristics. The effectiveness of the organization is influenced by factors internal and external to the firm. Internal factors, which are basically controllable by the logistics executive, are known as *organizational climate.* Organizational climate can be defined as follows:

Organizational Climate Defined

> The idea of "organizational climate" appears to refer to an attribute or set of attributes of the work environment. The idea of a "perceived organizational climate" seems ambiguous; one can not be sure whether it implies an attribute of the organization or of the perceiving individual. If it refers to the organization, then measures of perceived organizational climate should be evaluated in terms of the accuracy of the perceptions. If it refers to the individual, then perceived organizational climate may simply be a different name for job satisfaction or employee attitudes.[36]

Organizational climate is related to organizational effectiveness. This is particularly evident when effectiveness is measured on an individual level (e.g., job attitudes, performance, satisfaction, involvement).[37]

External factors, sometimes referred to as uncontrollable elements, include the political and legal, economic, cultural and social, and competitive environments.

---

[34] Richard M. Steers, *Organizational Effectiveness: A Behavioral View* (Santa Monica, Calif.: Goodyear Publishing, 1977), p. 7.

[35] Ibid., pp. 7–8.

[36] R. M. Guion, "A Note on Organizational Climate," *Organizational Behavior and Human Performance* 9, no. 1 (February 1973), pp. 126–46.

[37] See W. R. LaFollette and H. P. Sims, Jr., "Is Satisfaction Redundant with Organizational Climate?" *Organizational Behavior and Human Performance* 13, no. 2 (April 1975), pp. 257–78; G. Litwin and R. Stringer, *Motivation and Organizational Climate* (Cambridge, Mass.: Harvard University Press, 1968); and R. Prichard and B. Karasick, "The Effects of Organizational Climate on Managerial Job Performance and Job Satisfaction," *Organizational Behavior and Human Performance* 9, no. 1 (February 1973), pp. 110–19.

TABLE 16–3 Factors Contributing to Organizational Effectiveness

Organizational Characteristics	*Environmental Characteristics*	*Employee Characteristics*	*Managerial Policies and Practices*
Structure	External	Organizational attachment	Strategic goal setting
Decentralization	Complexity	Attraction	Resource acquisition and utilization
Specialization	Stability	Retention	Creating a performance environment
Formalization	Uncertainty	Commitment	Communication processes
Span of control	Internal (climate)	Job performance	Leadership and decision making
Organization size	Achievement orientation	Motives, goals, and needs	Organization adaptation and innovation
Work-unit size	Employee centeredness	Abilities	
Technology	Reward-punishment orientation	Role clarity	
Operations	Security versus risk		
Materials	Openness versus defensiveness		
Knowledge			

SOURCE: Richard M. Steers, *Organizational Effectiveness: A Behavioral View* (Santa Monica, Calif.: Goodyear Publishing, 1977), p. 8.

People Are Important

Employee Characteristics. The keys to effective organizations are the employees who "fill the boxes" on the organization chart. The ability of individuals to carry out their respective job responsibilities ultimately determines the overall effectiveness of any organization:

> Different employees possess different outlooks, goals, needs, and abilities. These human variations often cause people to behave differently from one another, even when placed in the same work environment. Moreover, these individual differences can have a direct bearing on two important organizational processes that can have a marked impact on effectiveness. These are *organizational attachment,* or the extent to which employees identify with their employer, and individual *job performance.* Without attachment and performance, effectiveness becomes all but impossible.[38]

Managerial Policies and Practices. Policies at the macro (entire company) level determine the overall goal structure of the firm. Policies at the micro (departmental) level influence the individual goals of the various corporate functions, such as warehousing, traffic, order processing, and customer service. Macro and micro policies in turn affect the procedures and practices of the organization. The planning, coordinating, and facilitating of goal-directed activities—which determine organizational effectiveness—depend on the policies and practices adopted by the firm at the macro and micro levels.

Six Factors That Influence Organizational Effectiveness

A number of factors can aid the logistics executive in improving the effectiveness of the organization. Six of the most important factors that have been identified are:

1. Strategic goal setting.
2. Resource acquisition and utilization.

[38] Steers, *Organizational Effectiveness*, p. 9.

3. Performance environment.
4. Communication process.
5. Leadership and decision making.
6. Organizational adaptation and innovation.[39]

Strategic Goal Setting

Strategic goal setting involves the establishment of two clearly defined sets of goals: the overall organization goal(s), and individual employee goals. Both sets must be compatible and aimed at maximizing company/employee effectiveness. For example, the company may have an overall goal to reduce order cycle time by 10 percent, but it is the actions of each employee attempting to improve his or her component of the order cycle that brings about achievement of the goal.

Resource Acquisition and Utilization

Resource acquisition and utilization includes the utilization of human and financial resources, as well as technology, to maximize the achievement of corporate goals and objectives. This involves such things as having properly trained and experienced persons operating the firm's private truck fleet, using the proper storage and retrieval systems for the company's warehouses, and having the capital necessary to take advantage of forward buying opportunities, massing of inventories, and other capital projects.

Performance Environment

The *performance environment* is concerned with having the proper organizational climate that motivates employees to maximize their effectiveness and, subsequently, the effectiveness of the overall logistics function. Strategies that can be utilized to develop a goal-directed performance environment include (1) proper employee selection and placement, (2) training and development programs, (3) task design, and (4) performance evaluation, combined with a reward structure that promotes goal-oriented behavior.[40]

Communication Process

One of the most important factors influencing logistics effectiveness in any organization is the *communication process*. Without good communication, logistics policies and procedures cannot be effectively transmitted throughout the firm, and the feedback of information concerning the success or failure of those policies and procedures cannot take place. Communication flows within the logistics area can be downward (boss-employee), upward (employee-boss), or horizontal (boss-boss or employee-employee). There are a number of ways that communication effectiveness can be improved.[41] Table 16–4 identifies some of the most viable strategies.

Leadership and Decision Making

Comparable to the importance of effective communication in an organization is the quality of *leadership and decision-making* expertise exercised by the senior logistics executive. In many companies the logistics depart-

[39] Ibid., p. 136.

[40] Ibid., p. 142.

[41] For a discussion of employee-boss communication strategies, see Helen L. Richardson, "Communicate through Listening," *Transportation & Distribution* 30, no. 8 (August 1989), pp. 32–33.

TABLE 16–4 Strategies for Improving Communication Effectiveness

Downward communications
1. Job instructions can be presented clearly to employees so they understand more precisely what is expected.
2. Efforts can be made to explain the rationale behind the required tasks to employees so they understand why they are being asked to do something.
3. Management can provide greater feedback concerning the nature and quality of performance, thereby keeping employees "on target."
4. Multiple communication channels can be used to increase the chances that the message is properly received.
5. Important messages can be repeated to insure penetration.
6. In some cases, it is desirable to bypass formal communication channels and go directly to the intended receiver with the message.

Upward communications
1. Upward messages can be screened so only the more relevant aspects are received by top management.
2. Managers can attempt to change the organizational climate so subordinates feel freer to transmit negative as well as positive messages without fear of retribution.
3. Managers can sensitize themselves so they are better able to detect bias and distorted messages from their subordinates.
4. Sometimes it is possible to utilize "distortion-proof" messages, such as providing subordinates with report forms requiring quantified or standardized data.
5. Social distance and status barriers between employees on various levels can be reduced so messages will be more spontaneous.

Horizontal communications
1. Efforts can be made to develop interpersonal skills between group members and departments so greater openness and trust exist.
2. Reward systems can be utilized which reward interdepartmental cooperation and minimize "zero-sum game" situations.
3. Interdepartmental meetings can be used to share information concerning what other departments are involved in.
4. In some cases, the actual design of the organization itself can be changed to provide greater opportunities for interdepartmental contacts (e.g., shifting from a traditional to a matrix organization design).

SOURCE: Richard M. Steers, *Organizational Effectiveness: A Behavioral View* (Santa Monica, Calif.: Goodyear Publishing, 1977), p. 151.

ment or division is a mirror image of the top logistics executive. If the top executive is a highly capable and respected individual, and one who makes thoughtful, logical, and consistent decisions, then the logistics organization that reports to him or her will most likely be highly effective. Conversely, a logistics organization led by an executive who lacks the necessary leadership and decision-making skills usually will not be as efficient.

Organizational Adaptation and Innovation

Finally, *organizational adaptation and innovation* is an important attribute of effective organizations. The environment that surrounds the logistics activity requires constant monitoring. As conditions change, logistics must adapt and innovate to continue to provide an optimal cost-service mix to the firm and its markets. Examples of fluctuating environmental conditions include changes in transportation regulations, service requirements of customers, or degree of competition in the firm's target markets, economic and/or financial shifts in the marketplace, and technological advances in the distribution sector. It is important, however, that adaptation and innovation not be haphazard and unplanned.

An effective organization must also exhibit stability and continuity:

Effective Organizations Exhibit Stability, Continuity, and Adaptability

Management is charged with the responsibility for maintaining a dynamic equilibrium by diagnosing situations and designing adjustments that are most appropriate for coping with current conditions. A dynamic equilibrium for an organization would include the following dimensions:

1. Enough stability to facilitate achievement of current goals.
2. Enough continuity to ensure orderly change in either ends or means.
3. Enough adaptability to react appropriately to external opportunities and demands, as well as changing internal conditions.
4. Enough innovativeness to allow the organization to be proactive (initiate changes) when conditions warrant.[42]

An Approach to Developing an Optimal Logistics Organization[43]

In an address to a group of logistics executives at the 1980 Annual Conference of the National Council of Physical Distribution Management, James P. Falk, director of domestic transportation for Kaiser Aluminum & Chemical Corporation, stated:

> I think it's a fair observation that most [logistics] management organizations, or any others for that matter, *evolve*. The structure is not developed in final form on a piece of paper, then successfully practiced. The distribution manager cannot afford to respond to the special demands of [his/her] interest alone. [He/she] is effective only to the extent [his/her] energy is directed toward company goals and strategies.[44]

Falk identified a rather important organizational truth. Organizations evolve and change; that is, there are probably a variety of good organizational designs for a firm, and over time, a company may have to modify its design or structure to reflect environmental or corporate changes. As an executive attempts to structure a new logistics organizational unit, or perhaps restructure an existing one, he or she should proceed through the following steps or stages:

Steps in Developing a Logistics Organization

1. Research corporate strategy and objectives.
2. Organize functions in a manner compatible with the corporate structure.
3. Define the functions for which the logistics executive is accountable.
4. Know his or her management style.
5. Organize for flexibility.
6. Know the available support systems.

---

[42] Fremont E. Kast and James E. Rosenweig, *Organization and Management: A Systems and Contingency Approach*, 4th ed. (New York: McGraw-Hill, 1985), p. 620.

[43] Much of the material in this section has been developed and adapted from Falk, "Organizing for Effective Distribution," pp. 181–99.

[44] Ibid., p. 186.

7. Understand and plan for human resource allocation so that it compliments both the individual and organization objectives.[45]

Corporate Objectives. Overall corporate strategy and objectives provide the logistics activity with long-term direction. They provide the underlying foundation and guiding light for each functional component of the firm—finance, marketing, production, and logistics. The logistics structure must support the overall corporate strategy and objectives. Therefore, it is imperative that the logistics executive completely understand the role his or her activity will play in carrying out corporate strategy. Furthermore, the logistics organizational structure must be compatible with the primary objectives of the firm.

The Logistics Organizational Structure Resembles the Firm's Corporate Structure

Corporate Structure. The specific organizational structure of the logistics activity is affected by the overall corporate structure. For example, in a highly decentralized organization, the logistics activity is probably structured in a similar fashion. Similarly, if the firm is centralized, then logistics is usually centralized. There are exceptions, but the logistics component of the firm usually closely resembles the overall corporate organization structure. The similarity stems primarily from the inherent advantages—administrative, financial, personnel—that result from organizational uniformity within a firm. Other aspects of overall corporate structure that influence the organization include:

1. Line/staff coordinating responsibility.
2. Reporting relationships.
3. Span of control.

In the area of reporting relationships, logistics will typically report to the marketing group if the firm is a consumer goods company, and to manufacturing/operations/administration if the firm is primarily an industrial goods producer. In many firms with a combination of consumer and industrial goods customers, logistics is often a separate organizational activity reporting directly to the CEO.

Functional Responsibilities. Falk argues, "The question causing more conflicts and problems than any other is a clear definition of the *function* of the [logistics] organization, especially if it is being restructured from other substructures having a traditional responsibility."[46] It is important to have all or most logistics subfunctions housed under a single division or department. Such an organizational structure with full functional responsibility allows the firm to implement the concepts of integrated logistics management and total cost trade-offs. Illustrative of many of the functional responsibilities of the logistics organization are those that were shown in Table 16-1.

[45] Ibid., p. 195.

[46] Ibid., p. 188.

Basic Logistics Functions

An examination of over 100 U.S. companies by Bowersox et al. found that logistics typically had responsibility for outbound transportation, intracompany transportation, warehousing, inbound transportation, materials handling, and inventory management. Because these are basic logistics functions, it is vital that these areas be administered by the senior logistics executive. Other functions, important but not essential to carrying out the logistics mission of the firm, for which logistics often does not have responsibility, include sales forecasting, raw materials inventory, and international distribution activities.[47]

Management Style. Almost as important as the formal structure of the organization is the management style of the senior logistics executive. Many firms have undergone significant changes in such areas as personnel, employee morale, and productivity as a result of a change in top management. Organizational restructuring does not necessarily have to occur. The style or personality of the senior logistics executive, and to a lesser degree his or her lower-level managers, has an influence on the attitudes, motivation, work ethic, and productivity of employees at all levels of the organization. The element of management style is one of those intangibles that can make two companies with identical organizational structures perform at significantly different levels of efficiency, productivity, and profitability. Management style is a vital ingredient to the success of a firm's logistics mission and is one of the primary reasons that many different organizational structures can be equally effective. The key is to possess a "managerial style that is practical, active, sensitive, and flexible, and [that] is based on a philosophy that advocates the generation of many initiatives and the selection and support of the best one(s)."[48]

Flexibility. Any logistics organization must be able to adapt to changes, which inevitably occur. Unresponsive and unadaptable organizations typically lose their effectiveness after a period of time. While it may be difficult to anticipate future changes in the marketplace or the firm, the logistics organization must be receptive to those changes and must respond to them in ways beneficial to the firm.

The Logistics Organization Cannot Exist on Its Own

Support Systems. Due to the nature of the logistics activity, support systems are essential. The logistics organization cannot exist on its own. There must be a variety of support services as well as support specialists available to aid the logistics department or division. As we saw in Chapter 13, a good MIS system, manual or automated, is an important facet of an effective logistics network. Other support services or systems that can be used include legal services, computer systems, administrative services, and financial/accounting services.

---

[47] Bowersox et al., *Leading Edge Logistics,* pp. 74–77.

[48] R. Jeffery Ellis, "Improving Management Response in Turbulent Times," *Sloan Management Review* 23, no. 2 (Winter 1982), p. 3.

Personnel Considerations. Perhaps the most important component of an effective logistics organization is people. It is the people who will ultimately determine how well the company operates. Therefore, it is vital that employees' skills and abilities, pay scales, training programs, selection and retention procedures, and other employee-related policies be considered in the structuring or restructuring of a logistics organization. Other employee aspects must also be considered, however. As Falk has stated:

> We must design our organization so we consider not only *people development,* but individual personalities as well. Show me the theorist who says, "Don't compromise the optimum organization for people consideration" . . . and I'll show you a person who I would like to have managing our competition! We *have* to consider the strengths and weaknesses of our people, and use them where they can contribute most. This is not to say we organize around people . . . the basic organization should *not* be prostituted. It's important, however, to balance organizational structure with strengths and weaknesses of our human resources.[49]

Logistics managers are particularly essential to a successful organization. Productive and efficient employees must be effectively led. Managers must therefore possess certain important qualities or characteristics:

The Qualities of a Good Manager

- Personal integrity/awareness of business ethics.
- Ability to motivate.
- Ability to plan.
- Ability to organize.
- Self-motivation.
- Managerial control.
- Effective oral communication.
- Ability to supervise.
- Problem-solving ability.
- Self-confidence.[50]

Successful organizations are those that blend the optimal combination of organizational structure, planning process, people, and style.

While there is no single best organizational form for a firm's logistics activity, there are benefits to be obtained from examining the organizational structures of successful companies. First, as a purely graphical representation, an organization chart allows a person to view how the many functional areas of the firm relate and how the logistics subfunctions are coordinated. Second, viewing several organization charts of companies in a variety of industries illustrates that there is no single ideal structure. Third, because of the commonality of the logistics activities across industry types, there will be marked similarities in the various organization charts.

---

[49] Falk, "Organizing for Effective Distribution," p. 190.

[50] Paul R. Murphy and Richard F. Poist, "Skill Requirements of Senior-Level Logistics Executives: An Empirical Assessment," *Journal of Business Logistics* 12, no. 2 (1991), pp. 83–87; also see Jonathan L. S. Byrnes and William C. Copacino, "Develop a Powerful Learning Organization," *Transportation & Distribution Presidential Issue 1990* 31, no. 11 (October 1990), pp. 22–25.

Companies have found through experience that certain logistics functions should be structured or organized in certain ways.

Representative organizational charts from four industry groups—chemical manufacturer, consumer and industrial products manufacturer, specialty retail, and mass merchandising—are shown in Figures 16–5 through 16–8. The companies represented are considered to have good logistics organizations by peers within their industries.

Rohm and Haas Company

The Rohm and Haas Company is a $3 billion manufacturer of specialty chemicals, with operations worldwide. Figure 16–5 shows the logistics activity, which was reorganized in 1991 to incorporate all distribution functions under a director of materials management. The company has eight producing locations, five warehouses, and 200 employees in the logistics area. With a 1991 logistics budget of $120 million, Rohm and Haas utilizes all transport modes to ship its chemical products to locations throughout the world.

3M Company

As a $13 billion manufacturer of innovative high-technology products that are produced and sold worldwide, the 3M Company utilizes the organization structure shown in Figure 16–6. With numerous divisions and products, 3M employs approximately 6,000 logistics personnel throughout the world. The company operates nine warehouses or distribution centers in the United States and has 15 sales or order-entry locations.

As evident from the 3M organization chart, some of the functions reporting to logistics include customer service, information systems, transportation, warehousing, and international distribution. Inventory control decisions are made by each warehouse. Overall inventory management decisions (i.e., how much product to stock where and when) are a product division responsibility. With such a structure, 3M is well suited for competing in a global marketplace.

Child World, Inc.

A wholesale/retail operation is somewhat different from a manufacturing enterprise. Child World, Inc., is the second largest toy supermarket chain in the United States, based on net sales. The firm currently operates 153 stores in 28 states in the Northeast, Midwest, and South under the names Child World and Children's Palace. The company offers an assortment of over 18,000 different merchandise items including toys, bicycles, juvenile furniture, electronics, juvenile sporting goods, and outdoor play equipment. The company's merchandising strategy is to offer a broad in-stock selection of these products at competitive prices, with an emphasis on customer service. Its organizational structure is shown in Figure 16-7.

The company distributes merchandise to its stores primarily through six large distribution centers located in Massachusetts, Ohio, Missouri, Indiana, New York, and Texas. The company believes that its large regional distribution centers allow it to maintain the stores' broad in-stock position and to devote more of the stores' square footage to selling space.

Child World ships goods from its distribution centers to its stores using a combination of private carriage and irregular route carriers. The company attempts, where possible, to promote transportation efficiency by

FIGURE 16–5 Rohm and Haas Company

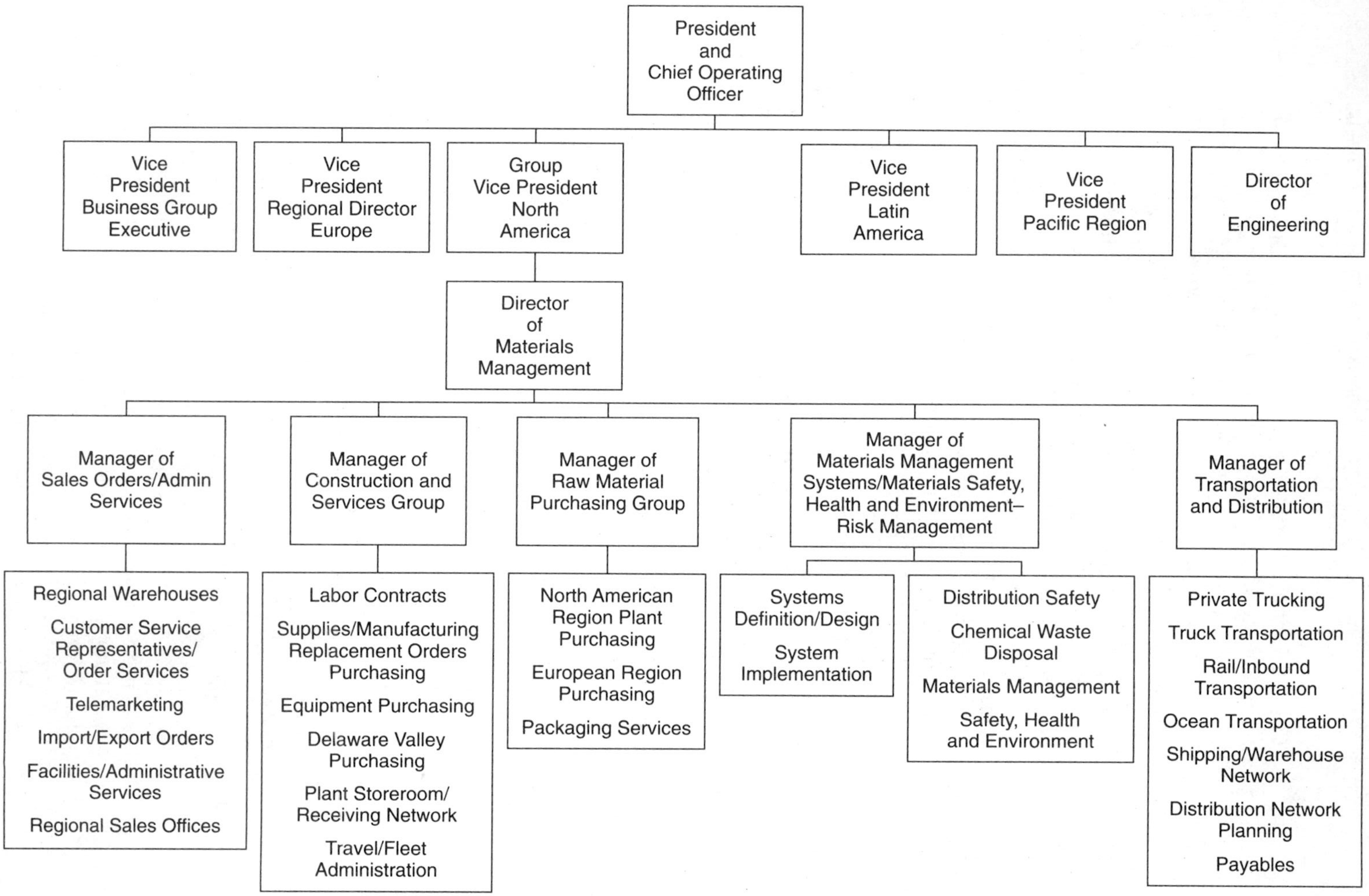

SOURCE: Rohm and Haas Company. Used with permission.

FIGURE 16–6 3M Company

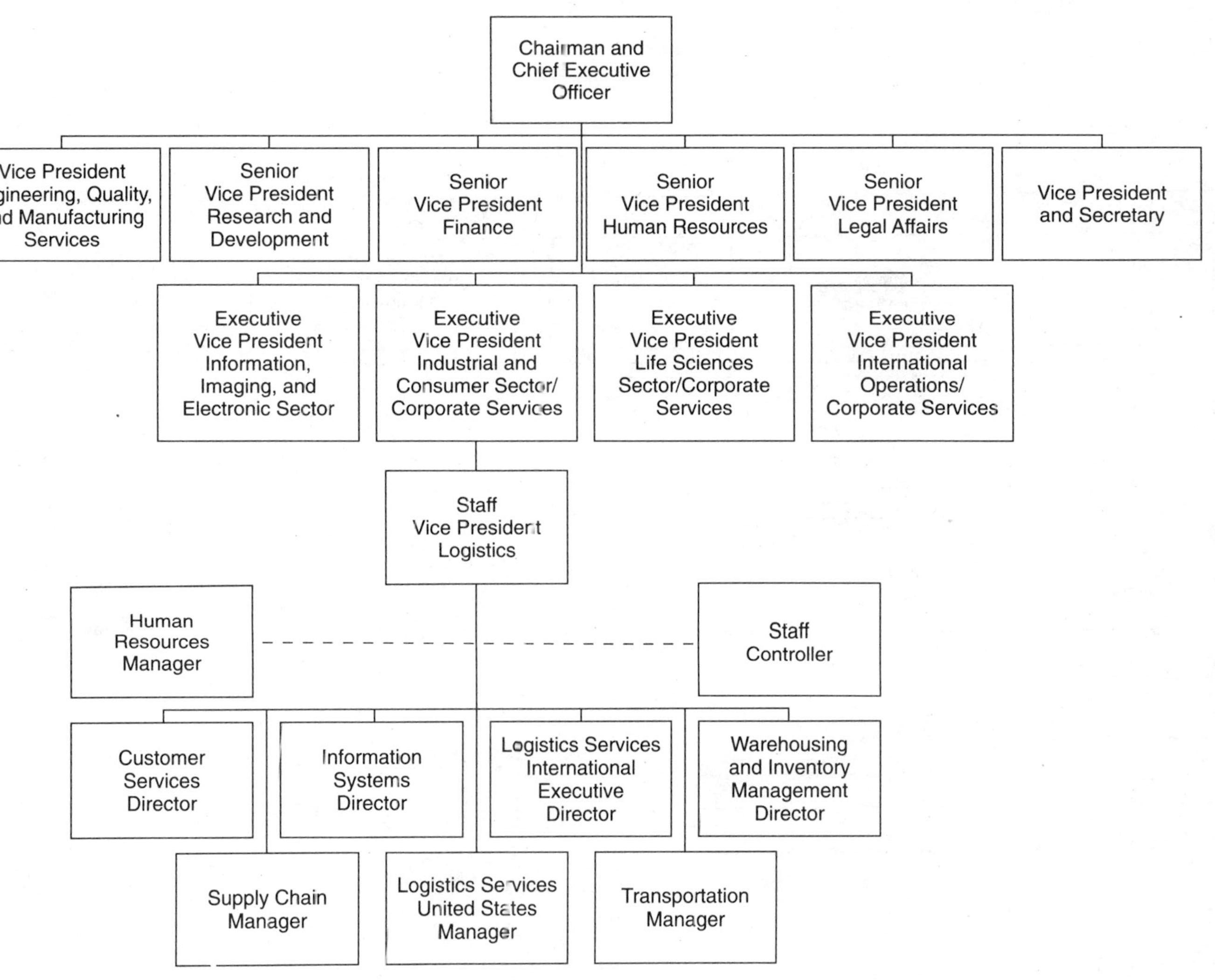

SOURCE: Minnesota Mining & Manufacturing Co. Used with permission.

FIGURE 16–7 Child World, Inc.

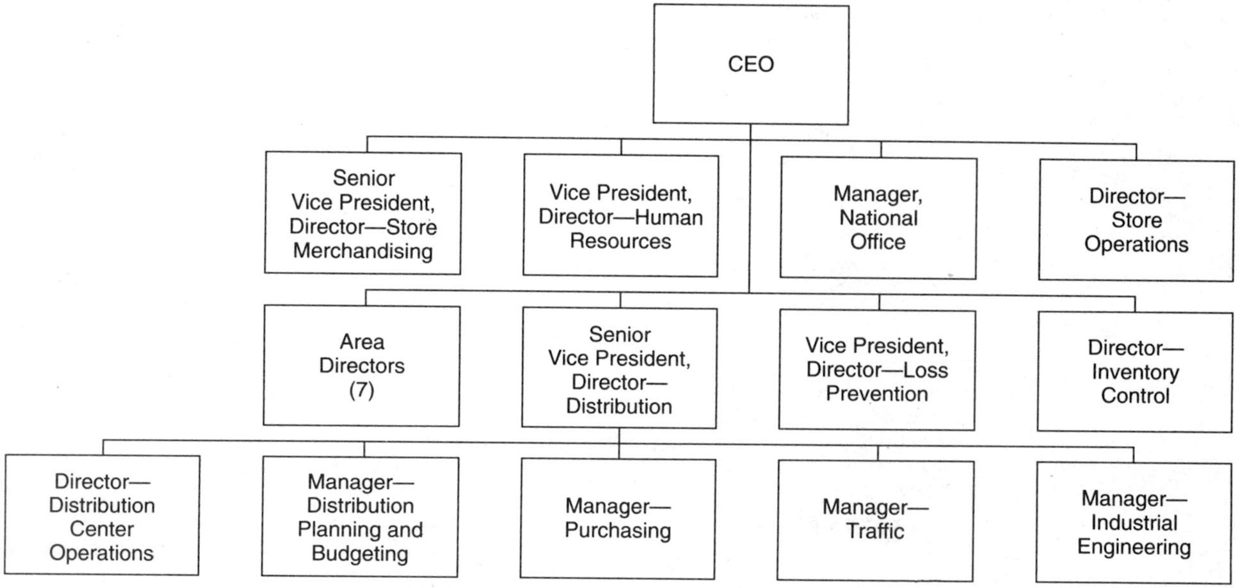

CEO

Senior Vice President, Director—Store Merchandising

Vice President, Director—Human Resources

Manager, National Office

Director—Store Operations

Area Directors (7)

Senior Vice President, Director—Distribution

Vice President, Director—Loss Prevention

Director—Inventory Control

Director—Distribution Center Operations

Manager—Distribution Planning and Budgeting

Manager—Purchasing

Manager—Traffic

Manager—Industrial Engineering

SOURCE: Child World, Inc. Used with permission.

FIGURE 16–8 Target Stores

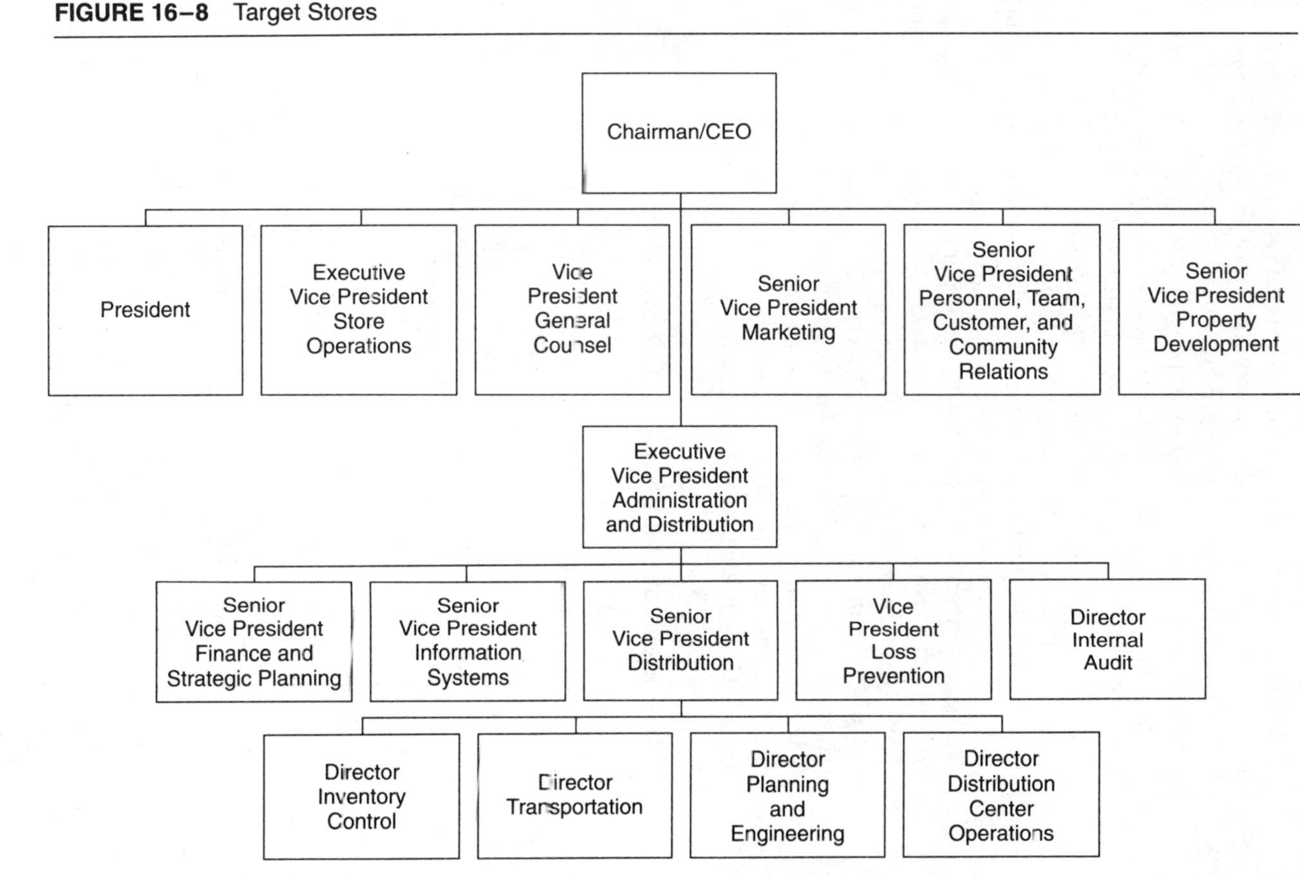

SOURCE: Target Stores, Inc. Used with permission.

backhauling merchandise from vendors on return trips from its retail units. Management has concluded, based on its past experience and current analysis, that utilization of both private carriage and irregular route carriers affords flexibility and economy in distribution.

Target Stores

Target Stores, a division of Dayton Hudson Corporation, is an upscale discount retail store in the United States, with 463 stores located in 32 states. The company is the largest and most successful upscale discounter in the country, with 1990 sales of $8.2 billion. Target employs 3,800 logistics personnel and operates seven regional distribution centers, which encompass over 6.5 million square feet of space.

As evidenced by Figure 16–8, the organization chart for Target varies from operations in such companies as Child World, and is significantly different from those in manufacturing companies such as Rohm and Haas and 3M. Retailers and manufacturers often have different organization structures, reflecting their different markets and customers. However, all of the firms illustrated here are extremely efficient in carrying out their logistics activities, and in each case the senior logistics executive is positioned at a high level in the organization.

Measuring the Effectiveness of the Logistics Organization

Organizational performance can be measured against many criteria. Examples of the multitude of performance dimensions include the following:

There Are Many Dimensions of Effectiveness

1. Flexibility—willingness to tackle unusual problems, try out new ideas.
2. Development—personnel [participation] in training and development.
3. Cohesion—lack of complaints, grievances, conflict.
4. Democratic supervision—subordinate participation in work decisions.
5. Reliability—completion of assignments without checking.
6. Delegation—delegation of responsibility by supervisors.
7. Bargaining—negotiation with other units for favors, cooperation.
8. Results emphasis—results, not procedures, emphasized.
9. Staffing—personnel flexibility among jobs, backups available.
10. Cooperation—responsibilities met and work coordinated with other units.
11. Decentralization—work decisions made at low levels.
12. Conflict—conflict with other units over responsibility and authority.
13. Supervisory backing—supervisors back up subordinates.
14. Planning—waste time avoided through planning and scheduling.
15. Productivity—efficiency of performance within unit.
16. Support—mutual support of supervisors and subordinates.
17. Communication—flow of work information.
18. Initiation—initiate improvements in work methods.
19. Supervisory control—supervisors in control of work progress.[51]

[51] William Weitzel, Thomas A. Mahoney, and Norman F. Crandall, "A Supervisory View of Unit Effectiveness," *California Management Review* 13, no. 4 (Summer 1971), p. 39; copyright

Of course, it is not enough to merely identify the dimensions of organizational effectiveness, although this is a necessary first step. The second step is to prioritize the various effectiveness or performance categories, and to develop specific measuring devices to evaluate the level of effectiveness achieved by the logistics organization. It is vital that management identify the measures of organizational effectiveness it wishes to utilize, and prioritize them. It is impractical in most instances to employ every effectiveness measure in the evaluation process. Time and monetary constraints impede the collection and monitoring of all the data needed for such evaluation. In addition, it is usually sufficient to examine only a portion of the available measures, because patterns or trends are often exhibited very early in the evaluation process. The selection of particular logistics organizational effectiveness measures must depend on a firm's particular characteristics and needs. Perhaps the most difficult process is developing the techniques or procedures needed to measure the effectiveness criteria. In this regard, there are a number of alternatives.

Effectiveness Measures Must Be Prioritized

Cost-to-Sales Ratios

Cost-to-sales ratios are used extensively by business to evaluate organizational effectiveness. As with any measure used by a company, problems exist, especially with regard to which costs to include under the logistics activity. For example: "Were net or gross sales used? What logistics functions were included in the cost total? Were management salaries included? Was inventory carrying cost included? Has there been a change in order mix or service levels?"[52] There are no simple answers to these questions, except to say that all costs that are rightfully logistics costs should be included when computing cost effectiveness measures. If management has adopted and implemented the integrated logistics management concept there is greater likelihood that all relevant costs will be included.

Every measure identified in Table 16–5 must be evaluated against some predetermined standard. The standard may be generated internally—that is, developed within the firm—so as to be compatible with corporate hurdle rates, return on investment percentages, and other financial performance measures. In some instances, logistics performance standards may be externally generated. Many managers believe that the firm's standards should be based on those of other firms within the same industry, or the leaders in other industries with similar characteristics. There are many arguments in favor of this approach, but the major one states that a firm should be most concerned with its position in relation to its competition, and therefore the competition should influence the way management evaluates the firm's effectiveness. After all, in the marketplace customers are indirectly evaluating a firm's level of performance effectiveness through their day-to-day buying decisions. A limitation of this approach is that each competitor

---

1971 by the Regents of the University of California. Reprinted from *California Management Review,* XIII, no. 4, p. 39, by permission of the Regents.

[52] A. T. Kearney, Inc., *Measuring and Improving Productivity in Physical Distribution,* p. 309.

TABLE 16–5 Logistics Management Evaluation Measures

1. Logistics cost as a percent of sales
   a. Compared internally (e.g., among divisions)
   b. Compared externally (between similar companies)
2. Cost of specific logistics functions as a percent of sales or of logistics cost
   a. Compared internally (e.g., among divisions)
   b. Compared externally (between similar companies)
3. Performance
   a. Budget versus actual, expressed in terms of dollars, labor-hours, headcount, or other appropriate measures
   b. Productivity, output compared to input in appropriate terms
      (1) Service provided
      (2) Time (order cycle, invoice cycle)
      (3) On-time dependability
      (4) Customer complaint level
      (5) Errors (invoice, shipping)
   c. Project management within
      (1) Time constraints
      (2) Dollar limitations
      (3) Benefits projected (dollar savings, productivity improvements, etc.)

SOURCE: A. T. Kearney, Inc., *Measuring and Improving Productivity in Physical Distribution* (Oak Brook, Ill.: National Council of Physical Distribution Management, 1984), pp. 307–308.

has a different marketing mix, and perhaps slightly different target markets. One firm may spend substantially more on logistics than another firm, yet realize higher profits and sales. Therefore, direct comparisons between competitors must be approached cautiously.

How Should Logistics Executives Be Evaluated?

One of the areas in which performance measurement is critical is logistics management personnel. Typically, managers are evaluated on three attributes:

1. *Line management ability.* This criterion considers the manager's ability to manage the department's day-to-day operations and meet goals that have been established for productivity, utilization, and all aspects of performance, including budget.
2. *Problem solving ability.* This deals with the ability to diagnose problems within the operation, and identify opportunities for savings, service improvement, or increased return on investment.
3. *Project management ability.* This refers to the ability to structure and manage projects designed to correct problems, improve productivity and achieve improvement benefits.[53]

Firms may employ other measures—for example, the ability to motivate and train employees—but they are not as easily measurable.

Responsibility Charting

Many public and private sector firms have used an approach known as *responsibility charting* to evaluate their managers. Decision making usually involves several participants, and this technique focuses on the decisions

[53] Ibid., p. 305.

being made, the participants themselves, and the types of participation of each person: "When used as a diagnostic technique, there are six steps in responsibility charting: defining the decisions, defining the [participants], defining the types of participation, assigning roles to the [participants] . . . tabulating participant responses, and analyzing results."[54] While the results generated are more qualitative than quantitative, the approach generates a clear picture of how decisions are made and identifies areas of ambiguity and conflict between participants. Once those problems are overcome, the decision process becomes much more efficient and effective. The bottom line is better managers. Specific benefits of responsibility charting include:

1. It forces participants to be concise and to communicate clearly about decisions.
2. It creates a shared vocabulary for describing the types of participation possible in decision making.
3. It establishes an explicit basis for renegotiating responsibilities and roles, if needed.[55]

Four Types of Management Organizations

Another approach was used to measure the effectiveness of logistics organizations in a survey of Council of Logistics Management member firms.[56] A multivariate model of organizational effectiveness, developed by Rensis Likert, was used to examine over 100 manufacturing, retailing, and service firms.[57] Likert identified four management organization systems: exploitive-authoritative (System 1); benevolent-authoritative (System 2); consultative (System 3); and participative group (System 4). Each system has particular measurable characteristics. Likert's multivariate model has been successfully employed, from a general management perspective, in a variety of companies, including Aluminum Company of Canada, Detroit Edison, Dow Chemical, General Electric, Genesco, IBM, Lever Brothers, Sun Oil, and Union Carbide.[58]

In one research study, it was found that companies evaluated their logistics organizations by reviewing data on operating characteristics. The operating characteristics were classified into categories: leadership, motivation, communication, decisions, and goals. The profiles developed from the study are shown in Figure 16–9. Likert has suggested that the profiles be interpreted as follows:

---

[54] Joseph E. McCann and Thomas N. Gilmore, "Diagnosing Organizational Decision Making Through Responsibility Charting," *Sloan Management Review* 24, no. 2 (Winter 1983), p. 5.

[55] Ibid., p. 14.

[56] James R. Stock, "Measuring Distribution Organizational Effectiveness," in *Proceedings of the Tenth Annual Transportation and Logistics Educators Conference,* ed. Bernard J. LaLonde, 1980, pp. 15–25.

[57] See Rensis Likert, *New Patterns in Management* (New York: McGraw-Hill, 1961); and Rensis Likert, *The Human Organization: Its Management and Value* (New York: McGraw-Hill, 1967).

[58] Likert, *The Human Organization,* p. 26.

FIGURE 16–9 Likert Model of Organizational Effectiveness

Operating characteristics	System 1 Exploitive-authoritative	System 2 Benevolent-authoritative	System 3 Consultative	System 4 Participative group
Leadership				
How much confidence is shown in subordinates?				
How free do they feel to talk to superiors about their job?				
Are subordinates' ideas sought and used, if worthy?				
Motivation				
Is predominant use made of 1-fear, 2-threats, 3-punishment, 4-rewards, 5-involvement?				
Where is responsibility for achieving organization's goals?				
Communication				
How much communication is aimed at achieving organization's objectives?				
What is the direction of information flow?				
How is downward communication accepted?				
How accurate is upward communication?				
How well do superiors know problems faced by subordinates?				
Decisions				
At what level are decisions formally made?				
What is the origin of technical and professional knowledge used in decision making?				
Are subordinates involved in decisions related to their work?				
What does decision-making process contribute to motivation?				
Goals				
How are organizational goals established?				
How much covert resistance to goals is present?				
Is there an informal organization resisting the formal one?				
What are cost, productivity, and other control data used for?				

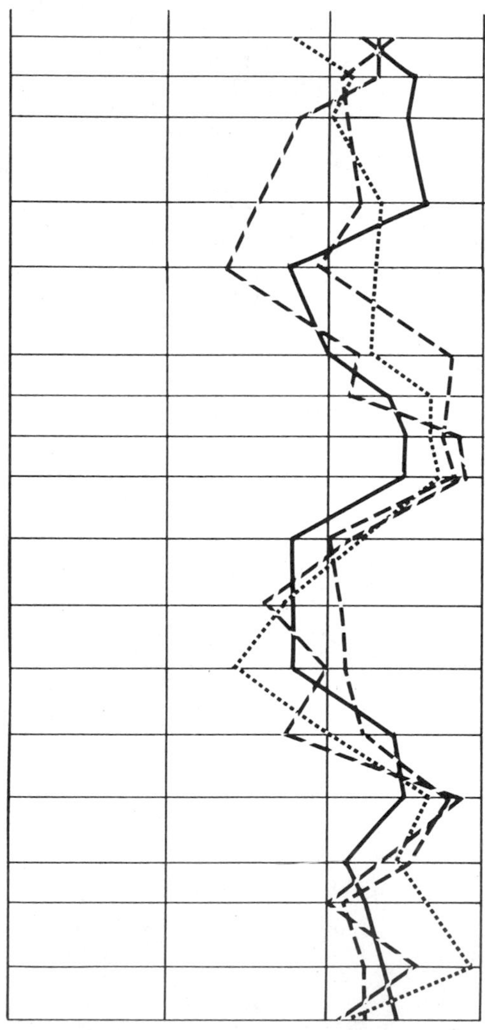

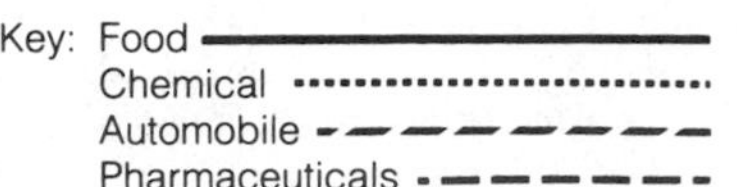

SOURCE: James R. Stock, "Measuring Distribution Organizational Effectiveness," *Proceedings of the Tenth Annual Transportation and Logistics Educators Conference,* ed. Bernard J. La Londe, 1980, p. 22; List of operating characteristics in figure were adapted from *New Patterns in Management* by Rensis Likert. Copyright © 1961, McGraw-Hill Book Company. Used with the permission of McGraw-Hill Book Company.

> Research findings support the perceptions of managers that management systems more to the right—i.e., toward System 4—are more productive and have lower costs and more favorable attitudes than do systems falling more to the left—toward System 1. Those firms . . . where System 4 is used show high productivity, . . . low costs, favorable attitudes, and excellent labor relations. The converse tends to be the case for companies or departments whose management system is well toward System 1. Corresponding relationships are also found with regard to any shifts in the management system. Shifts toward System 4 are accompanied by long-range improvement in productivity, labor relations, costs, and earnings. The long-range consequences of shifts toward System 1 are unfavorable.[59]

The study suggested the possibility of developing effectiveness profiles for companies, based on industry type, company size, location of the firm, and other factors. As a result, management would be able to compare the firm with similar firms and to make improvements where necessary.

Characteristics of Effective Organizations

The same study reviewed the logistics literature and compiled a total of 15 factors that characterized effective organizations. Some of the most widely recognized items included cost efficiency, flexibility, management orientation, employee turnover and morale, communication, coordination, and conflict within the organization.[60] In a fashion similar to that of the Likert model, a profile of organizational effectiveness was developed for firms. Profiles to the right in Figure 16–10 were considered more effective.

After measurement of organizational effectiveness takes place, actions that continue or improve on existing organizational efforts must follow. The landmark 1984 study conducted for the National Council of Physical Distribution Management by A. T. Kearney, Inc., the logistics consulting firm, addressed this issue. Results of the study revealed that firms were using 10 approaches to improve organizational effectiveness. Each is briefly described below:

Ten Ways to Improve Organizational Effectiveness

1. *Organizational change.* Perhaps the most effective means of impacting management productivity is by changing the organization of the logistics function. Organizational changes need not be extensive to be effective. Merely by recognizing the need for an integrated logistics department, many organizations are able either to consolidate farflung activities and thus minimize organizational segmentation, or at least achieve better coordination of all affected activities. Survey interviews indicated that many of the companies which have realized the most significant logistics improvements in recent years are those which have recently undergone substantial reorganization resulting in the creation of a strong central logistics organization. The chemical industry is a notable exception.
2. *MBO programs.* Another useful technique is that of MBO (management by objectives) and goal setting to establish performance standards for various activities.

---

[59] Ibid., p. 46.

[60] Stock, "Measuring Distribution Organizational Effectiveness," p. 17.

FIGURE 16–10 Profile of Logistics Organizational Effectiveness

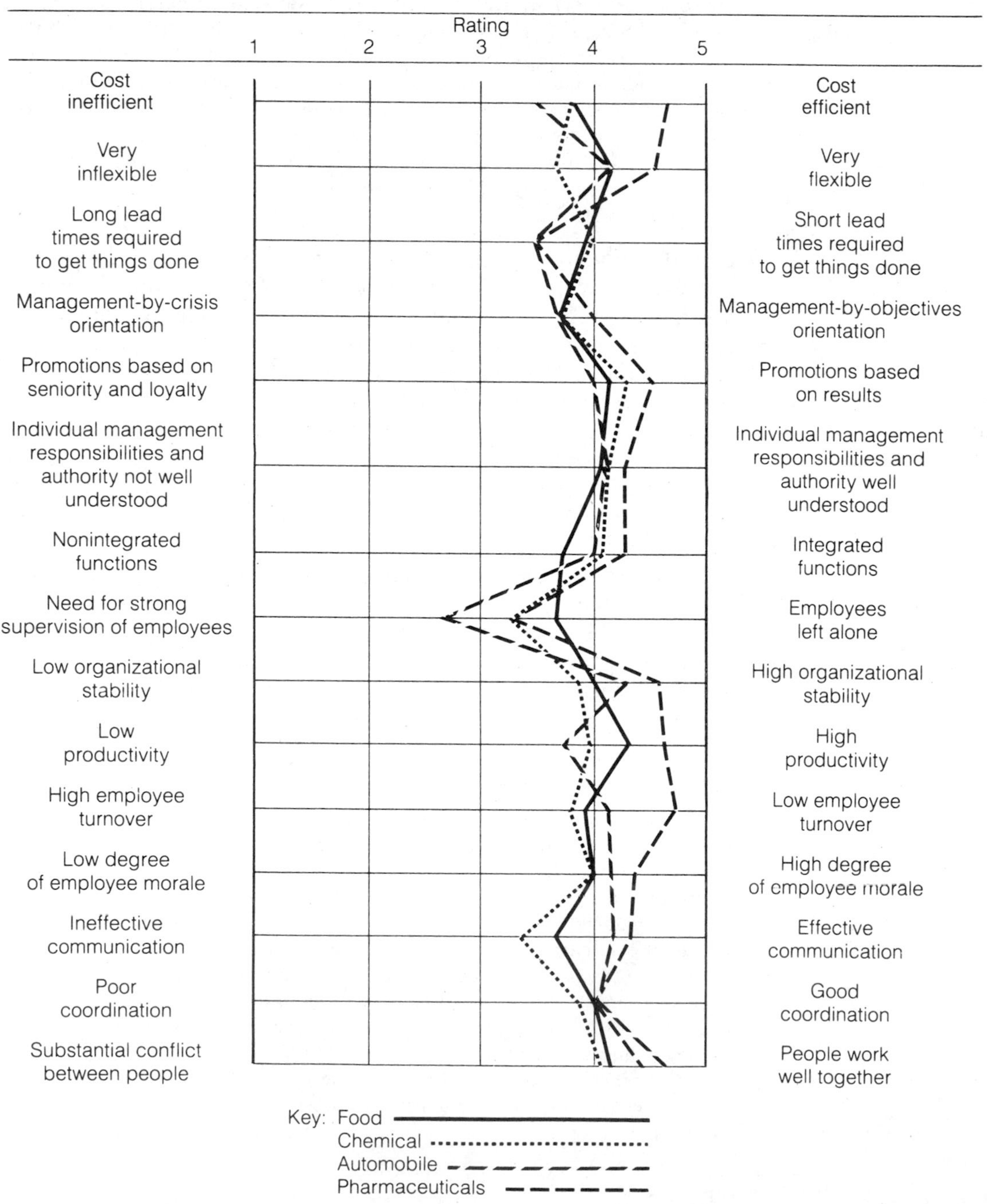

SOURCE: James R. Stock, "Measuring Distribution Organizational Effectiveness," in *Proceedings of the Tenth Annual Transportation and Logistics Educators Conference,* ed. Bernard J. La Londe, 1980, p. 24.

3. *MBX programs.* Once an operation is running relatively smoothly, a management by exception (MBX) program is often implemented. MBX reports exceptional performance to management, identifying only those areas that require attention.

   Responsibility accounting systems are being used with increasing frequency to focus management's attention by reporting only that information which is relevant to the activities under an individual manager's control. The systems effort required to develop a responsibility accounting program is significant, but it can pay off in more effective use of each individual manager's time, allowing them to concentrate only on their own operations.
4. *Systems engineering.* Applications of modern systems engineering techniques to project planning, scheduling, and control has helped to make logistics improvement projects more cost-effective in many companies.
5. *Capital and expenditure management.* Similarly, the development and use of formal capital equipment justification systems has helped ensure that funds are invested in projects which yield the highest return.
6. *Use of computer technology.* Logistics managers are making greatly increased use of computers to handle routine daily tasks so that more management time is available for planning and decision-making activities. More importantly, the computer's ability to handle massive amounts of data has made it an ideal tool for logistics analysis and control. Further, the advent of the personal computer has quite literally brought the power of the computer to a manager's fingertips.
7. *Use of analytical tools.* The use of logistics planning models to answer "what if" questions regarding possible logistics network alternatives is now filtering down to smaller companies. This approach can eliminate a great deal of manual calculation regarding the relative costs and service benefits of various alternative logistics network configurations. It can also provide a wealth of new, useful logistics cost information for firms which previously used manual techniques.
8. *Incentive programs.* In order for an operation to be effective, employees and management must be motivated to excel. Employee motivation through the use of wage incentive systems and other gain-sharing techniques is well known. Some firms are currently developing their managers into improved employee motivators by conducting training programs to improve this aspect of their managerial skills. This type of program, coupled with a feeling of identity and importance on the part of the employees, appears to be the key in effectively motivating the work force and improving productivity.
9. *Personnel/hiring practices.* In addition to upgrading logistics management capabilities through training and other types of development programs, many companies are realizing that the most effective way to get good managers is not to hire bad ones initially. Consequently, exposure of middle and top management personnel to company hiring policies, along with training in how to effectively interview and evaluate, is helping improve overall management quality.
10. *Consolidation of logistics activities across several business units.* Finally, many companies have begun to consolidate logistics activities across business

> units in order to gain economies in areas such as transportation, warehousing, order processing, and logistics engineering, to name a few. This will not work in all companies, and in all situations, but when conditions are right, major improvements in productivity can be made by reduced duplication and greater economies of scale.[61]

If management is to measure the firm's organizational effectiveness, it must employ a variety of factors. In addition, the factors must be measurable, and standards of performance need to be established. Finally, management should compare the firm with others in its industry. It is likely that there is no single ideal organizational structure that every company should adopt. The most logical approach to organizing a firm's logistics activities to maximize its effectiveness is to understand the factors that contribute to organizational performance, and include them in the planning, implementation, and control of the organization.

SUMMARY

In an article entitled "The Driving Force of Successful Organizations," Truskie asked: "What makes some organizations much more successful than their counterparts? Luck? More effective marketing strategies? Superior technology? Greater financial leverage? Perhaps all these, but beyond them, successful organizations possess two common properties, clarity and commitment, that provide the driving force to propel them to the forefront and help keep them there."[62]

It has been said that, "Where there is no vision, the people will perish."[63] Logistics organizations with clear statements of purpose, specific and measurable objectives, strategies and plans for achieving those objectives, and a committed work force undoubtedly achieve higher levels of efficiency.

Logistics organizations must, of necessity, become more cost- and service-efficient. An understanding of the factors that affect a firm's organizational effectiveness, along with strategies to improve the factors that reveal weakness or deficiencies, can help create more efficient logistics systems. Organizational changes form the basis for procedural modifications that can reduce costs or improve service.

In this chapter the importance to a firm of an effective logistics organization was discussed. Many firms have shown significant improvements in their logistics cost/service mix as a result of organizational changes. The

---

[61] Adapted from A. T. Kearney, Inc., *Measuring and Improving Productivity in Physical Distribution,* pp. 311–14. Used by permission of the Council of Logistics Management.

[62] Stanley D. Truskie, "The Driving Force of Successful Organizations," *Business Horizons* 27, no. 4 (July–August 19845), p. 43.

[63] Proverbs 29:18, *The Bible,* King James Translation.

most important ingredient in successful management is integration of all of the logistics activities under a single individual, department, or division.

Logistics organizations are generally structured along the following lines: strategic versus operational, centralized versus decentralized, and line versus staff, in various combinations. There is probably no single ideal organizational structure. However, there are important elements that comprise an effective organization. In general, the factors contributing to organizational effectiveness can be categorized as organizational characteristics, environmental characteristics, employee characteristics, and managerial policies and practices.

A number of approaches can be used to measure the effectiveness of logistics organizations. Each approach requires management to identify the elements that impact effectiveness, and then to evaluate their relative importance. Next, the elements must be measured and performance evaluated. Evaluation requires that standards of performance be established.

With this and the preceding chapters as background, the concepts and principles already learned can be applied to logistics in international markets. This is the subject of Chapter 17.

SUGGESTED READINGS

ALTIER, WILLIAM J. "Task Forces—An Effective Management Tool." *Sloan Management Review* 27, no. 3 (Spring 1986), pp. 69–76.

AYERS, ALLAN F. "Function vs. Form: The Logistics Dilemma." *Transportation & Distribution Presidential Issue 1990* 31, no. 11 (October 1990), pp. 10–14.

BARKS, JOSEPH V., AND JOSEPH VOCINO. "Career Wastelands: The Way Out." *Distribution* 87, no. 3 (March 1988), pp. 28–34.

BEHLING, ORLANDO, AND CHARLES F. RAUCH, JR. "A Functional Perspective on Improving Leadership Effectiveness." *Organizational Dynamics* 13, no. 4 (Spring 1985), pp. 51–61.

BOWERSOX, DONALD J., PATRICIA J. DAUGHERTY, CORNELIA L. DRÖGE, RICHARD N. GERMAIN, AND DALE S. ROGERS. *Logistical Excellence: It's Not Business as Usual* (Burlington, Mass.: Digital Equipment Corporation, 1992).

BOWERSOX, DONALD J., AND PATRICIA J. DAUGHERTY. "Emerging Patterns of Logistical Organization." *Journal of Business Logistics* 8, no. 1 (1987), pp. 46–60.

BOWERSOX, DONALD J., AND CORNELIA DRÖGE. "Similarities in the Organization and Practice of Logistics Management Among Manufacturers, Wholesalers and Retailers." *Journal of Business Logistics* 10, no. 2 (1989), pp. 61–72.

GARDNER, ROY. "The Distribution Executive's Expanding Role Within the Corporation," in *Logistics: Contribution and Control,* ed. Patrick Gallagher, Proceedings of the 1983 Logistics Resource Forum (Cleveland: Leaseway Transportation Co., 1983), pp. 51–57.

GLASKOWSKY, NICHOLAS A., JR. "Collaborative Logistics." *Logistics Spectrum* 23, no. 1 (Spring 1989), pp. 11–15.

GORDON, RICHARD F. "Plateaued Employee Survival Skills." *Logistics Spectrum* 23, no. 1 (Spring 1989), pp. 17–22.

HOSMER, LARUE TONE. "The Importance of Strategic Leadership." *The Journal of Business Strategy* 3, no. 2 (Fall 1982), pp. 47–57.

KOLODNY, HARVEY F. "Managing in a Matrix." *Business Horizons* 24, no. 2 (March-April 1981), pp. 17–24.

LYNCH, JEANNE, AND DAN ORNE. "The Next Elite: Manufacturing Supermanagers." *Management Review* 74, no. 4 (April 1985), pp. 48–51.

MAISTER, D. H. "Organizing for Physical Distribution," *International Journal of Physical Distribution and Materials Management* 8, no. 3 (1977), pp. 147–78.

MCGINNIS, MICHAEL A., AND BERNARD J. LALONDE. "The Physical Distribution Manager and Strategic Planning." *Managerial Planning* 31, no. 5 (March-April 1983), pp. 30–42, 48.

PERSSON, GORAN. "Organization Design Strategies for Business Logistics." *International Journal of Physical Distribution and Materials Management* 8, no. 6 (1978), pp. 287–97.

RICHARDSON, HELEN L. "Vanishing Human Resources." *Transportation & Distribution* 30, no. 12 (November 1989), pp. 18–20.

SHARMAN, GRAHAM. "The Rediscovery of Logistics." *Harvard Business Review* 62, no. 5 (September-October 1984), pp. 71–79.

STEWART, THOMAS A. "The Search for the organization of Tomorrow." *Fortune* 125, no. 10. (May 18, 1992), pp. 92–98.

TOTOKI, AKIRA. "Management Style for Tomorrow's Needs." *Journal of Business Logistics* 11, no. 2 (1990), pp. 1–4.

YANACEK, FRANK. "A Question of Ethics." *Transporation & Distribution* 29, no. 13 (December 1988), pp. 48–50.

QUESTIONS AND PROBLEMS

1. Discuss the relationship between a firm's organizational structure and the integrated logistics management concept.
2. Coordination of the various logistics activities can be achieved in a variety of ways. Within the context of logistics organizational structure, explain each of the following:
   a. Process-based versus market-based versus channel-based strategies.
   b. Strategic versus operational.
   c. Centralized versus decentralized.
   d. Line versus staff.
3. It has been frequently stated that there is no single ideal or optimal logistics organizational structure. Do you think that statement is accurate? Briefly present the arguments for and against such a statement.
4. How do personnel affect the degree of organizational effectiveness and/or productivity of a firm's logistics activity?

5. Identify the role that the communication process has in influencing logistics effectiveness. Discuss several strategies that can be followed to improve downward, upward, and horizontal communication within a firm.
6. Identify how a firm's logistics management can be evaluated on each of the following factors:
   a. Total logistics cost.
   b. Cost-specific logistics functions.
   c. Performance.

Chapter 17

Global Logistics

Objectives of This Chapter

To identify some of the controllable and uncontrollable factors that affect global logistics activities

To describe the major international distribution channel strategies—exporting, licensing, joint ventures, ownership, and importing

To identify the elements involved in managing export shipments

To identify the organizational, financial, and managerial issues that relate to global logistics

INTRODUCTION

As one writer noted, "One of the most important phenomena of the 20th century has been the international expansion of industry. Today, virtually all major firms have a significant and growing presence in business outside their country of origin."[1] Furthermore,

The Trend toward Global Business

> Current business conditions make the distinction between domestic and international distribution unimportant. Successful enterprises have realized that to survive and prosper in the business environment of today and tomorrow, they must go beyond the organizational structures and strategic approaches of the past, and adopt a worldwide, global view of business.[2]

For an ever-growing number of firms, management is defining the marketplace globally. Table 17–1 identifies the world's largest industrial corporations. The companies may be headquartered in Europe, Asia, or North America, but their markets are international in scope. For example, approximately 40 percent of Procter & Gamble's $24 billion annual revenues are generated from international operations. P & G products are sold in 140 countries.[3]

New markets are opening up and existing markets are expanding worldwide. The economies of the industrialized nations have matured; that is, their economic growth rates have slackened; and, as a result, those countries are seeking additional market opportunities abroad. A global financial network has developed that has allowed multinational enterprises to expand their operations.[4] In addition, manufacturers have increased new ma-

---

[1] James E. Leontiades, *Multinational Business Strategy* (Lexington, Mass.: D. C. Heath and Co., 1985), p. 3.

[2] Paul S. Bender, "The Challenge of International Distribution," *International Journal of Physical Distribution and Materials Management* 15, no. 4 (1985), p. 20.

[3] Greg Brown, "Education a Matter of Global Concern, Says P & G's Smale," *Mutual Interest* (December 1990), p. 7.

[4] See David C. Shanks, "Strategic Planning for Global Competition," *The Journal of Business Strategy* 5, no. 3 (Winter 1985), pp. 80–89.

TABLE 17–1 The World's Largest Industrial Corporations (1990)

Rank	*Company*	*Headquarters*	*Industry*	*Sales ($ millions)*
1	General Motors	United States	Motor vehicles and parts	$125,126
2	Royal Dutch/Shell Group	Netherlands/Britain	Petroleum refining	107,204
3	Exxon	United States	Petroleum refining	105,885
4	Ford Motor	United States	Motor vehicles and parts	98,275
5	IBM	United States	Computers, office equipment	69,018
6	Toyota Motor	Japan	Motor vehicles and parts	64,516
7	IRI	Italy	Metals	61,433
8	British Petroleum	Britain	Petroleum refining	59,540
9	Mobil	United States	Petroleum refining	58,770
10	General Electric	United Staets	Electronics	58,414
11	Daimler-Benz	Germany	Motor vehicles and parts	54,259
12	Hitachi	Japan	Electronics	50,686
13	Fiat	Italy	Motor vehicles and parts	47,752
14	Samsung	South Korea	Electronics	45,042
15	Philip Morris	United States	Food	44,323
16	Volkswagen	Germany	Motor vehicles and parts	43,710
17	Matsushita Electric	Japan	Electronics	43,516
18	ENI	Italy	Petroleum refining	41,762
19	Texaco	United States	Petroleum refining	41,235
20	Nissan Motor	Japan	Motor vehicles and parts	40,217
21	Unilever	Netherlands/Britain	Food	39,972
22	E I Du Pont de Nemours	United Staes	Chemicals	39,839
23	Chevron	United States	Petroleum refining	39,262
24	Siemens	Germany	Electronics	39,228
25	Nestlé	Switzerland	Food	33,359
26	Elf Aquitaine	France	Petroleum refining	32,939
27	Chrysler	United States	Motor vehicles and parts	30,868
28	Philips' Gloeilampen-fabrieken	Netherlands	Electronics	30,866
29	Toshiba	Japan	Electronics	30,182
30	Renault	France	Motor vehicles and parts	30,050
31	Peugeot	France	Motor vehicles and parts	29,380
32	BASF	Germany	Chemicals	29,184
33	Amoco	United States	Petroleum refining	28,277
34	Hoechst	Germany	Chemicals	27,750
35	Asea Brown Boveri	Switzerland	Industrial, farm equipment	27,705
36	Boeing	United States	Aerospace	27,595
37	Honda Motor	Japan	Motor vehicles and parts	27,070
38	Alcatel Alsthom	France	Electronics	26,456
39	Bayer	Germany	Chemicals	26,059
40	NEC	Japan	Electronics	24,390
41	Procter & Gamble	United States	Consumer products	24,376
42	Total	France	Petroleum refining	23,590
43	Petroleos de Venezuela	Venezuela	Petroleum refining	23,469
44	Imperial Chemical Industries	Britain	Chemicals	23,348
45	Daewoo	South Korea	Electronics	22,260
46	Occidental Petroleum	United States	Food, mining, crude oil	21,947
47	United Technologies	United States	Aerospace	21,783
48	Thyssen	Germany	Metals	21,491
49	Mitsubishi Electric	Japan	Electronics	21,228
50	Nippon Steel	Japan	Metals	21,156

SOURCE: Adapted from Sara Hammes and Richard S. Teitelbaum, "The World's Biggest Industrial Corporations," *Fortune* 124, no. 3 (July 29, 1991), p. 245.

terial and component acquisitions from other countries (i.e., global sourcing). As a result:

> Major changes are already underway in the international distribution operations of many companies, with even more broad-based ones likely in the future. Deregulation of the U.S. ocean liner companies will create new opportunities for international shippers to redesign existing distribution channels in order to reduce order-cycle days and shipment costs. Further, as the United States continues to shift towards a technology- and service-based economy—implying that we will produce fewer goods domestically and buy more from abroad—it is clear that for many firms international logistics will become a more important part of the physical distribution function.
>
> The increasing importance of international logistics operations to corporations presents both prospects and problems for distribution professionals. On one hand, they will gain stature in their company because of the necessary and close linkage between international product marketing (or sourcing) and logistics—more so than in domestic operations, because of the longer, cross-border supply lines associated with overseas activities. On the other hand, they will face a larger number of more sophisticated logistics problems stemming from the complex nature of overseas distribution operations.[5]

Domestic and International Markets Are Different

In some instances, a firm's international markets may produce more sales than their domestic markets. To support nondomestic markets a company must have a distribution system or network that satisfies the particular requirements of those markets. For example, the distribution systems in the developing countries of Africa, South America, or Asia are characterized by large numbers of intermediaries (middlemen) supplying an even larger number of small retailers. These nations' systems are also marked by inadequate transportation and storage facilities, a large market comprised mainly of unskilled workers, and an absence of distribution support systems. In more highly developed countries, such as Japan, Canada, the United States, and most of Western Europe, the distribution systems are highly sophisticated. A firm entering those countries will find distribution networks that have good transportation systems, high-technology warehousing, a skilled labor force, and a variety of distribution support systems available.

In this chapter we will discuss some of the similarities and differences in the management of logistics in domestic and international environments. We will see how to assess the global logistics environment and how to develop meaningful logistics strategies in that environment.

---

[5] David L. Anderson, "International Logistics Strategies for the Eighties," *Proceedings of the Twenty-Second Annual Conference of the National Council of Physical Distribution Management,* 1984, p. 356.

INTERNATIONAL DISTRIBUTION CHANNEL STRATEGIES

Many factors can influence a company's decision to enter international markets. They include:

Why Does a Firm Enter International Markets?

1. The market potential of world markets.
2. Geographic diversification.
3. Excess production capacity and the advantage of a low-cost position due to experience-curve economies and economies of scale.
4. A product that is near the end of its life cycle in the domestic market that is beginning to generate growth abroad.
5. Overseas markets that can be the source of new products and ideas; companies in foreign markets that can become joint-venture partners, providing capital and market access.[6]

An additional reason for a firm to enter international markets is sourcing of raw materials, component parts, or assemblies. For example, some raw materials, such as petroleum, bauxite, uranium, certain foodstuffs, and other items, are limited geographically in their availability. A firm may locate a facility overseas or import an item for domestic use, and thereby become international in scope.

Companies which enter into the international marketplace have four principle channel strategies available to them:

Four Channel Strategies

- Exporting.
- Licensing.
- Joint ventures.
- Ownership.

There are also several options available within each channel strategy. Figure 17–1 identifies some of the major participants in an international logistics transaction, including product and information flows.

Successful completion of the various logistics activities in the international distribution channel can contribute to the development of global markets in many ways, including:

Offering goods delivered to the customer gives a competitive advantage and sharpens the marketing approach.

Reduced delivery costs if the manufacturer is able to organize consolidated loads.

Door-to-door freight services offer speed and reliability of delivery, and order lead times may be quoted accurately.

The advent of containerization, rapid transit times, specialist freight equip-

---

[6] Vern Terpstra and Ravi Sarathy, *International Marketing*, 5th ed. (Hinsdale, Ill.: Dryden Press, 1991), pp. 12–13.

FIGURE 17–1 Major Participants in an International Logistics Transaction

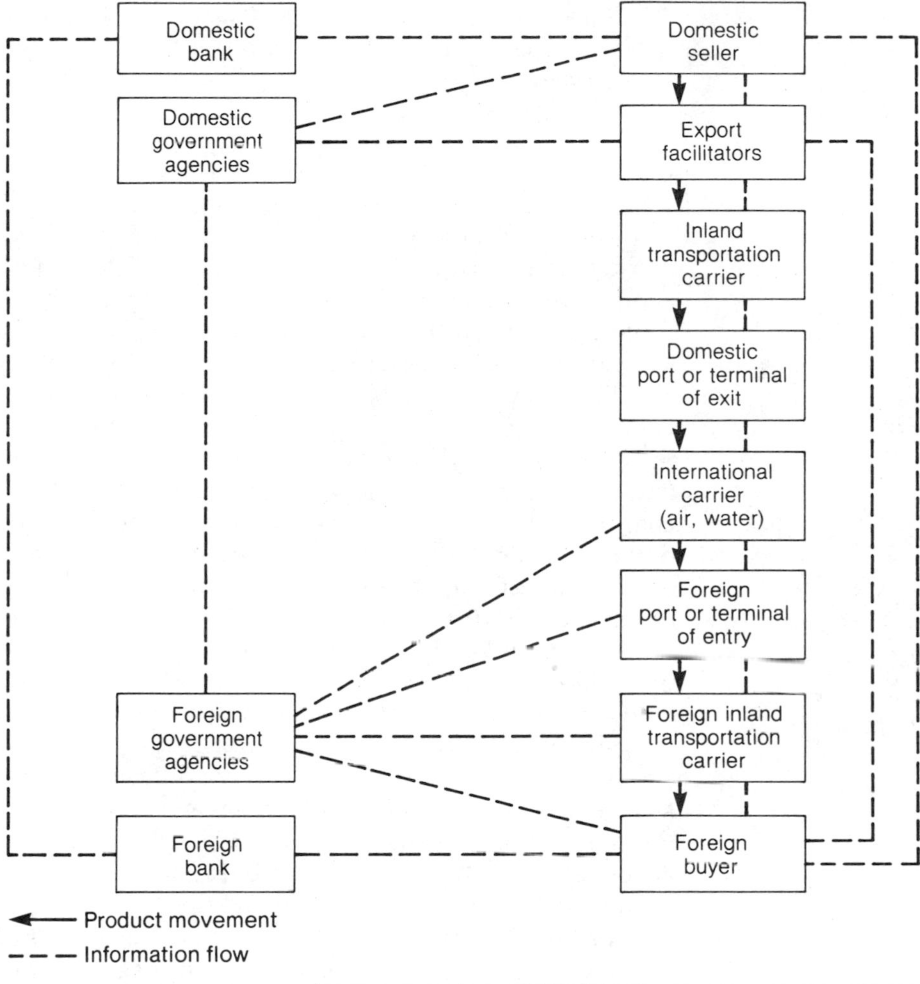

ment (e.g., refrigerated containers), and new freight services has created the opportunity to expand into new world markets which were previously out of reach.

The economies of consolidated freight services have led to the development of marketing activities in overseas countries, based on the influx of product from the domestic base.

Companies may compete for short-term individual export orders, with the confidence that, if they win, they will be able to arrange rapid distribution from the domestic base.

Marketing may now offer, with confidence, a reasonable after-sales service or replacement policy to international markets.

[Inventory]-holding policies in overseas markets may lead to a situation where demand could be considerably stimulated by offering immediate delivery.

Once captured, an overseas market may be held and expanded in the face of intense competition by high levels of customer service offered through distribution services.[7]

Exporting

The most common form of distribution for firms entering international markets is exporting. Exporting requires the least amount of knowledge about foreign markets, because the domestic firm allows an international freight forwarder, distributor, customshouse broker, trading company, or some other organization to carry out the logistics and marketing functions.

Advantages of Exporting

There are many advantages associated with exporting. Typically, the company that exports is able to be more flexible. In addition, exporting involves less risk than other international distribution strategies. For example, no additional production facilities or other fixed assets need to be committed to the foreign market, because the firm produces the product domestically and allows the exporting intermediary to handle distribution of the product abroad. Also, no investment is required to establish a logistics network in the various markets.

Another advantage of exporting is minimal exposure to the political uncertainties of some environments. Without the presence of direct foreign investment, the firm is not concerned with the host country nationalizing its operations. Also, if the foreign market does not meet the firm's profit and/or sales expectations, it is not difficult to withdraw from the market. Perhaps one of the major advantages of exporting is the experience the domestic firm gains: "Private companies may favor exporting either as an initial entry strategy or as the most effective means of continuous servicing. Numerous . . . firms began by exporting, but now they operate their own production and marketing operations abroad. They tested the market by exporting and then employed other strategies to hold or expand it."[8]

Disadvantages of Exporting

Exporting is not without disadvantages. It is sometimes difficult to compete with other firms located in the foreign market. For example, tariffs (taxes assessed on goods entering a market), import quotas (limitations on the amount of goods which can enter a market), or unfavorable currency exchange rates may adversely affect the price or availability of imported goods. In addition, the domestic firm has very little control over the pric-

[7]Alan Slater, "International Marketing: The Role of Physical Distribution Management," *International Journal of Physical Distribution and Materials Management* 10, no. 4 (1980), pp. 166–67.

[8]Ruel Kahler and Roland L. Kramer, *International Marketing*, 4th ed. (Cincinnati, Ohio: South-Western Publishing, 1977), p. 80.

ing, promotion, or distribution of its product when it exports. Success in international markets depends to a large degree on the capability of the exporting intermediaries.

Management must recognize that the export process is not as simple as it first appears:

> The export process begins long before the first carton leaves the warehouse. There is market planning, package design, sales negotiation, financial monitoring, banking, insurance, and consular documentation, just to name a few. These preliminary activities are the framework on which an export program hangs, and [the] distribution department should be involved in all of them. Without distribution's participation in various marketing and financial plans, the company risks serious problems.
>
> For instance, if a promised delivery time cannot be met, the company risks a costly default under many standard methods of export financing. Or if insufficient margin has been allowed for export sales because certain costs were overlooked, the company needlessly takes a loss.[9]

A firm involved in exporting often has to deal with a number of intermediaries who provide a variety of exporting services.

Licensing

Kahler and Kramer defined licensing as a "method of foreign operation whereby a firm in one country (the licensor) agrees to permit a company in another country (the licensee) to use the manufacturing, processing, trademark, know-how, technical assistance, merchandising knowledge, or some other skill provided by the licensor."[10] Unlike exporting, licensing allows the domestic firm more control over how the product is distributed, because distribution strategy is usually part of the preliminary discussions. The specific logistics functions are carried out by the licensee using the established distribution systems of the foreign country.

Advantages of Licensing

Licensing does not require large capital outlays. In this way it is similar to exporting in that it is less risky and provides more flexibility than other forms of international marketing. Licensing is a strategy frequently used by small and medium-sized businesses, and can be an excellent approach if the foreign market has high tariff barriers or strict import quotas. The licensor is usually paid a royalty or a percentage of sales by the licensee.

Disadvantages of Licensing

Licensing is not without disadvantages. Although licensing does provide the domestic firm with flexibility, it does not mean that licensing agreements can be terminated quickly. Although the agreement with the licensee may include termination or cancellation provisions, there is usually a time lag between the decision to terminate and the actual date of termination.

---

[9] Thomas A. Foster, "Anatomy of an Export," *Distribution* 79, no. 10 (October 1980), p. 76.

[10] Kahler and Kramer, *International Marketing*, p. 86.

The time lag is typically longer than in an exporting situation. Another drawback—perhaps the most serious—is that the licensee has the potential of becoming a competitor. As licensees develop their own know-how and capabilities, they may end the licensing agreement and compete with the licensor.

> One way of avoiding the danger of strengthening a competitor through a licensing agreement is to ensure that all licensing agreements provide for a cross-technology exchange between the licensor and licensee.
>
> For companies that do decide to license, agreements should anticipate the possibility of extending market participation and, insofar as is possible, keep options and paths open for expanded market participation.[11]

Joint Ventures

Joint Ventures Enable More Control in International Markets

Management may wish to exercise more control over the foreign firm than is available in a licensing agreement. On the other hand, management may not desire to establish a freestanding manufacturing plant or other facility in a foreign market. If so, the joint venture offers a compromise.

The risk is higher and the flexibility is lower to the domestic firm because an equity position is established in the foreign firm. However, the domestic firm is able to provide substantial management input into the channel and distribution strategies of the foreign company due to its financial partnership. This increased management voice does place additional burdens on the domestic firm—namely, it requires a greater knowledge of the international markets the firm is trying to serve.

> A joint venture can be attractive to an international marketer: (1) when it enables a company to utilize the specialized skills of a local partner; (2) when it allows the marketer to gain access to a partner's local distribution system; (3) when a company seeks to enter a market where wholly owned activities are prohibited; and (4) when the firm lacks the capital or personnel capabilities to expand its international activities otherwise.[12]

The joint venture may be the only method of market entry if management wishes to exercise significant control over the distribution of its products. This would be especially true if wholly owned subsidiaries are prohibited by the foreign government. Such restrictions occur frequently in less developed countries (LDCs), which often attempt to promote internal industrial or retail development.[13]

---

[11] Warren J. Keegan, *Multinational Marketing Management,* 3rd ed. (Englewood Cliffs, N.J.: Prentice-Hall, 1984), p. 255.

[12] Philip Cateora, *International Marketing,* 7th ed. (Homewood, Ill.: Richard D. Irwin, 1990), p. 343.

[13] For a discussion of joint ventures in developing countries, see Anthony J. F. O'Reilly, "Establishing Successful Joint Ventures in Developing Nations: A CEO's Perspective," *Columbia Journal of World Business* 23, no. 1 (Spring 1988), pp. 65–71.

Ownership

Foreign Ownership Requires Total Responsibility for Marketing and Logistics

Complete ownership of a foreign subsidiary offers the domestic firm the highest degree of control of its international marketing and logistics strategies. Ownership can occur through acquisition or expansion. Acquisition of a foreign facility can be advantageous because it minimizes the start-up costs—locating and building facilities, hiring employees, and establishing distribution channel relationships.

Ownership of a foreign subsidiary requires the most knowledge of the international market compared to other forms of market entry. The firm is totally responsible for marketing and distributing its product, and cannot have an exporter, licensee, or joint venture assume the responsibility for it.

Direct ownership in the foreign market allows the company to compete more effectively on a price basis, due to the elimination of transportation costs incurred in shipments from domestic plants to foreign points of entry. Customs duties and other import taxes are also eliminated.

There are drawbacks associated with direct ownership. The firm loses flexibility because it has a long-term commitment to the foreign market. Fixed facilities and equipment cannot be disposed of quickly. This is a major disadvantage should the firm decide to withdraw from the market due to sales or profit declines, increased levels of competition, or other adversities.

Another drawback with ownership, especially in politically unstable countries, is the possibility of government nationalization of foreign-owned businesses. Although such events do not occur frequently, management must consider the possibility when entering some international markets.

In general, firms follow more than one market entry strategy. Markets, product lines, economic conditions, and political environments change over time, so it stands to reason that the optimal market entry strategy may also change. Furthermore, a good market entry strategy in one country may not be so good in another.

Formal Procedures are Needed in Evaluating Market-Entry Strategies

For the domestic firm considering the various market entry methods—exporting, licensing, joint venture, ownership—a formal procedure should be established for evaluating each alternative. Each market-entry strategy can be evaluated on a set of management-determined criteria. Each functional area of the firm (e.g., accounting, manufacturing, marketing, logistics) must be involved in establishing the criteria and their evaluation. Only after a complete analysis of each market-entry strategy takes place should a firm decide on a method of international involvement.

Importing

Many firms will also be involved in activities that bring raw materials, parts, components, supplies, and/or finished goods from sources outside the country. This may involve importing, countertrade, and duty drawbacks.

Importing involves the purchase of goods from an overseas source.

Items being imported can be used immediately in the production process or sold directly to customers. They can be transported to other ports of entry, stored in bonded warehouses (where goods are stored until import duties are paid), or placed in a free trade zone (where goods are exempted from customs duties until they are removed for use or sale).

Countertrade

Countertrade is the term that applies to the requirement that a firm import something from a country in which it has sold something else. There is typically an agreement between firms in each country to buy the other company's products or services. At times, if such agreements are not negotiated, it may be difficult to penetrate markets in a particular country.

Duty Drawbacks

Firms that import goods used in manufacturing or that export products that contain imported materials can take advantage of drawbacks. A drawback is a refund of customs duties paid on imported items, often referred to as a duty drawback. As illustrated in Figure 17–2, duty drawbacks involve many steps and can be time-consuming. However, for firms that can take advantage of them, duty drawbacks can result in significant refunds of customs duties.

MANAGING GLOBAL LOGISTICS

Key Questions for Analysis, Planning, and Control of Foreign Markets

Management of a global distribution system is much more complex than that of a purely domestic network. Managers must properly analyze the international environment, plan for it, and develop the correct control procedures to monitor the success or failure of the foreign distribution system. Figure 17–3 identifies some of the questions the international logistics manager must ask—and answer—about the firm's foreign distribution program. The questions can be classified into five categories: (1) environmental analysis, (2) planning, (3) structure, (4) plan implementation, and (5) control of the logistics program.[14]

The overall objective of the process diagrammed in Figure 17–3 is to develop the optimal logistics system for each international target market. It involves examining the various characteristics of the foreign market and developing a set of alternatives or strategies that will fulfill the company's objectives. Given a set of objectives or strategies, management defines the proper organizational and channel structures. Once it establishes specific organizational structures, management implements the distribution system. The final step is to measure and evaluate the performance of the system, and provide feedback to the strategic planning process for purposes of adjustment or modification of the system.

---

[14] Warren J. Keegan, *Multinational Marketing Management*, 3rd ed. (Englewood Cliffs, N.J.: Prentice Hall, 1984), p. 41.

FIGURE 17–2 How Duty Drawback Works

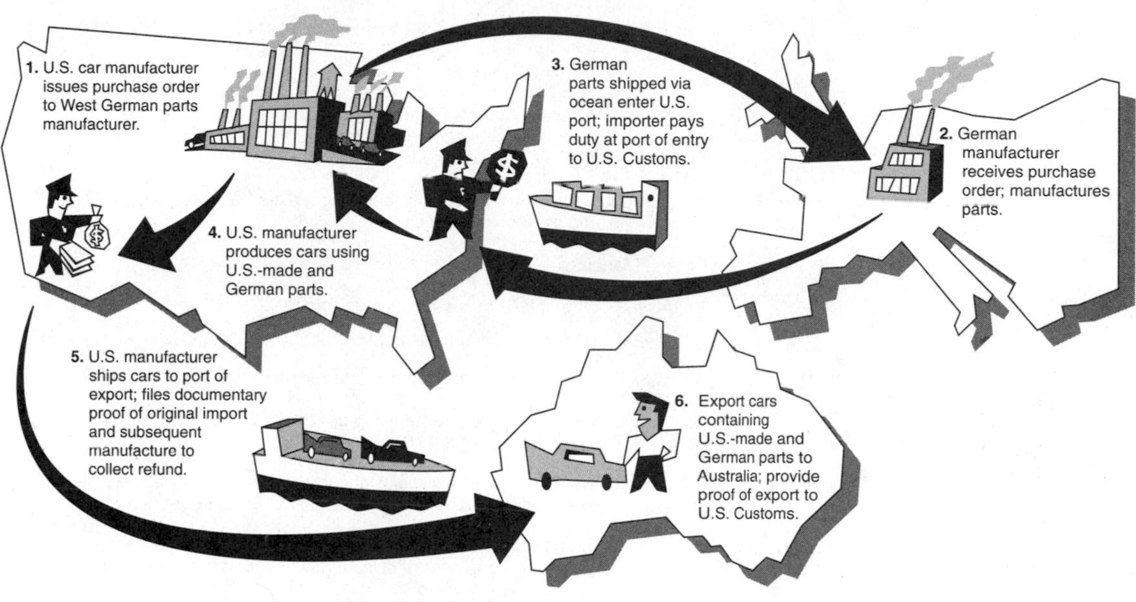

SOURCE: Lisa H. Harrington, "How to Take Advantage of Duty Drawback," *Traffic Management* 28, no. 6 (June 1989), p. 121A.

An integral part of the global logistics management process is cost/service trade-off analysis. Being able to properly identify, evaluate and implement the optimal cost/service mix is always important to the firm and its customers, whether operations are domestic or international. The only difference between the two is in the emphasis placed on each cost and service element.

Some Important Cost and Service Considerations

Some particularly important cost and service considerations involve response times, order completeness, shipping accuracy, and shipment condition.[15] Sales and costs are less sensitive to the longer *response times* in international logistics because customers expect longer and less reliable order-cycle times. There are a number of reasons for these longer, less consistent response times:

The distances involved are much longer.

A substantial fraction of international freight moves by ocean, at a slower speed and with less consistency than land [or air] transportation.

[15] Paul S. Bender, "The International Dimension of Physical Distribution Management," in *The Distribution Handbook*, ed. James F. Robeson and Robert G. House (New York: Free Press, 1985), p. 784.

FIGURE 17–3 The Global Logistics Management Process

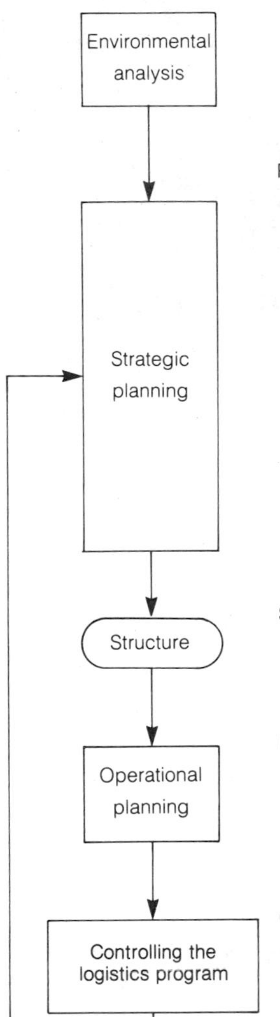

KEY QUESTIONS FOR ANALYSIS, PLANNING AND CONTROL

Environmental analysis

1. What are the unique characteristics of each national market? What characteristics does each market have in common with other national markets?
2. Should the firm cluster national markets for logistics operating and/or planning purposes?

Planning

3. Who should make logistics decisions?
4. What are our major assumptions about target markets? Are they valid?
5. What are the customer service needs of the target markets?
6. What are the characteristics of the logistics systems available to our firm in each target market?
7. What are our firm's major strengths and weaknesses relative to existing and potential competition in each target market?
8. What are our objectives, given the logistics alternatives open to us and our assessment of opportunity, risk and company capability?
9. What is the balance of payments and currency situation in target markets? What will be their impact(s) on our firm's physical distribution system?

Structure

10. How do we structure our logistics organization to optimally achieve our objectives, given our skills and resources? What is the responsibility of each organizational level?

Plan implementation

11. Given our objectives, structure, and our assessment of the market environment, how do we develop effective operational logistics plans? Specifically, what transportation, inventory, packaging, warehousing, and customer service strategies do we have for each target market?

Controlling the logistics program

12. How do we measure and monitor plan performance? What steps should be taken to bring actual and desired results together?

SOURCE: Adapted from Warren J. Keegan, *Multinational Marketing Management,* 3rd ed., p. 41. Copyright 1984. Reprinted by permission of Prentice Hall, Inc., Englewood Cliffs, N.J.

Additional documentation and arrangements that are usually required, such as letters of credit and consular invoices, may take considerable time to complete.[16]

Order completeness is much more important in international logistics, because the costs of back orders and expedited shipments are substantially higher. Processing and shipping costs must be weighed against the cost of improving order completeness. It is more expensive to ship complete orders all of the time, but this higher service level may be justified in view of the costs associated with shipping incomplete or partial orders. A similar logic can be used in the case of *shipping accuracy*. Because of the higher costs associated with shipping errors in international distribution, it is important to maximize the accuracy of both shipment routing and the items that make up a shipment. Once the shipment is made, *shipment condition* becomes important: "This service requirement is very often taken for granted in domestic shipments because of short lead times and minimal need of rehandling. However, it is a major consideration in international systems, not only because of the time and costs needed to replace damaged merchandise, but also because of the significant packaging costs that must be incurred in the first place."[17]

In developing a global logistics strategy, some general guidelines apply. The following list can be useful to firms in almost any international market:

Guidelines for Developing a Global Logistics Strategy

1. Build an international distribution strategy for your products gradually and methodically. Begin by exporting directly to each country, using agents or distributors. Develop company-affiliated sales offices as product awareness gets established. As demand grows, stock inventory at a for-hire warehouse in a centralized location covering several countries. Replenish these inventories with volume shipments. Make scheduled deliveries to customers from the centralized location. Monitor customer service requirements carefully, and make adjustments in deliveries accordingly. Build a company-owned or leased facility when ongoing demand can be forecasted reasonably, and when operating costs can be reduced. From this point on, look for the least cost source for production or procurement, and do not depend on the parent company's resources alone.
2. From a purely distribution point of view, several countries in the world generally offer advantages in terms of customs, transportation and ease of operation. Holland and Singapore are in a class by themselves. Hong Kong is almost as good. If nondistribution factors such as tax moratoriums and low-interest loans are considered, Taiwan and Ireland are popular choices. The list of countries to avoid, on the other hand, is long—too long to include here.

[16] Ibid.

[17] Ibid., pp. 784–85.

3. It is generally better to have too few plants and stocking locations than too many. Keeping fixed costs down is the key to profitability. Despite what salespeople say, consolidated transportation can serve a market well, if done properly.
4. Along the same lines, most companies' customer service levels are too high, so they spend more on transportation than they have to. In almost every case, except for spare parts, scheduled deliveries will meet your needs, as long as you constantly monitor service levels.
5. Investment dollars should first be spent on good data and communications systems. A well-integrated communications system can eliminate the need for much of the safety stock, and almost all expedited shipments. A common mistake is to put only major regions or divisions into a communications system, and to leave out the more remote and smaller regions. This approach stifles the growth of smaller markets, and assures that they will always carry high costs.
6. Centralization is often a good strategy because it allows more control over inventories and transportation. It is also more adaptable to computerized systems. Centralization is not always the right strategy, though. Where the market is extremely competitive, where the risk of obsolescence is high, or where the value of the product is extremely high, decentralization is often better.
7. When shipping to the EEC, it is generally better to make a customs clearance immediately. Once the item is officially in the EEC, the customs classification won't change. But if you clear in each country, the classification could be different in every one. Also, the duty is paid on the total landed cost of the item, including transportation. The sooner you pay the duty, the lower the landed cost. There will be no further duty on later transportation. Finally, procedures for handling customs problems vary within the EEC. Some countries, like France and Belgium usually hold the whole "shipment"—usually an entire trailer or container—if there is a problem with even one item. To avoid this snag, document each shipment as separate customs transactions.
8. Within Europe, air freight is rarely necessary. From Holland, France, or Germany, virtually every point in Western Europe can be reached by truck within 24 hours. Two possible exceptions are Italy and parts of Scandinavia. Besides trucking, other modes of transportation are gaining in popularity. Container barges on the Rhine and other major waterways are being used more because costs are often 30 to 50 percent less than truck. Intermodal transportation to Italy is also gaining in popularity.[18]

Managers who approach the global logistics process using the above guidelines, along with good judgment and a determination to succeed, are likely to do well. While the international marketplace may be uncertain, it is certainly manageable, and offers exciting opportunities and challenges to the firm seeking global markets.

---

[18] Thomas A. Foster, "Eight Ways to Be Great" in the article entitled "Planning an International Strategy," *Distribution* 83, no. 10 (October 1984), pp. 12–13.

Organizing for Global Logistics

Proper organization and administration of the logistics function is just as important internationally as it is domestically: "International distribution will continue to become more important in the future, and the firm that begins to devote more time and effort to this area [can potentially be] the eventual leader among its competitors."[19]

When a logistics organization operates globally, "The best type of organization is usually one in which the planning and control functions are centralized and the operations functions are decentralized."[20] In terms of structure, there is typically a middle-management executive in charge of international logistics. Such a manager or director is responsible for an organization structured along the lines of those illustrated in Figure 17–4. Any of the structures shown can be effective. The key concern is that all important international logistics elements be grouped together under a single logistics executive.

Though they may differ structurally, successful global logistics operations do possess some common traits or characteristics. They are:

Successful Global Logistics Operations Are Similar

> The absence of any inherent distinction between the domestic and foreign.
>
> International power balance . . . The firm's domestic operations do not hold a special position of power within the organization.[21]

Only those firms that are truly global or multinational will possess such traits. This is primarily due to the increasing sales and profits generated by international markets, which, after a time, can become a significant part of a company's operations. As companies enter the international marketplace, initially through exporting or licensing, it is likely that domestic operations will hold the balance of power in the firm. Obviously, that is only proper in the early stages of development. As foreign operations grow in sales and profits, and thus in importance, the international component of the business must be given more input into corporate decision making.

Financial Aspects of Global Logistics

A firm that is involved in global logistics faces a financial environment quite different from that of a strictly domestic firm. Whether the company is involved in exporting, licensing, joint ventures, or owns a foreign subsidiary, there are concerns over currency exchange rates, costs of capital, the

---

[19] Richard Lancioni and Martin Christopher, "More Trends in International Distribution," *Distribution* 83, no. 10 (October 1984), p. 60.

[20] Bender, "The International Dimension of Physical Distribution Management," p. 814; also see Lisa H. Harrington, "Dow's Worldwide Distribution: Organized for Profitability," *Traffic Management* 27, no. 12 (December 1988), pp. 33–36.

[21] Leontiades, *Multinational Corporate Strategy*, p. 196.

FIGURE 17–4 Organization of Global Logistics

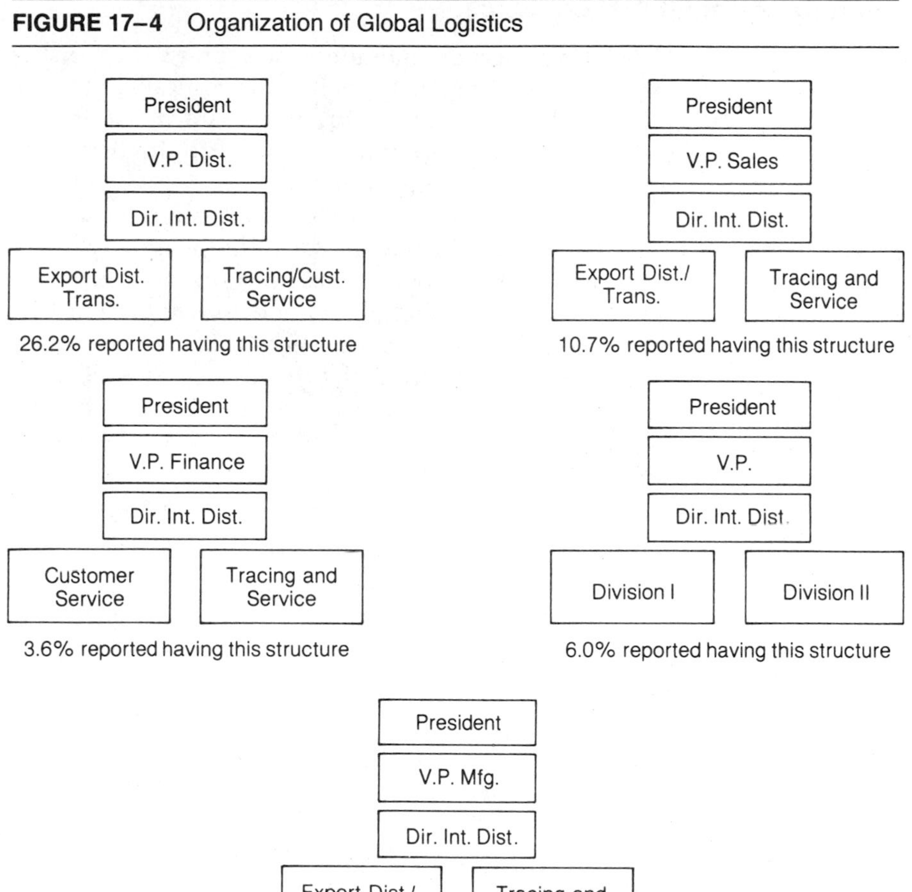

Approximately one third of the responding companies had a director of international distribution. The five organization charts presented here show how this director fits into the corporate structure. The most popular structure has the international distribution director reporting to a vice president of distribution. The least popular has the director reporting to a financial VP. Other structures were almost evenly divided, and had the director of international distribution reporting to a manufacturing, sales/marketing, or administrative VP.

SOURCE: Richard Lancioni and Martin Christopher, "More Trends in International Distribution," *Distribution* 83, no. 10 (October 1984), p. 61.

effects of inflation on logistics decisions and operations, tax structures, and other financial aspects of performing logistics activities in foreign markets.

Financing Is More Critical in Global Logistics

Global logistics activities require financing for working capital, inventory, credit, investment in buildings and equipment, and accommodation of merchandise adjustments that may be necessary. *Working capital* considerations are very important to the international firm:

> Time lags caused by distance and crossing international borders add cost elements to international marketing that make cash-flow planning especially important. Even in a relatively simple transaction, money may be tied up for months while goods are being shipped from one part of the world to another; customs clearance may add days, weeks, or months; payment may be held up while the international payment documents are being transferred from one nation to another; and breakage, commercial dispute, or governmental restrictions can add further delay.[22]

Typically, foreign operations require larger amounts of working capital than domestic operations.

Inventories are also an important aspect of global logistics: "Adequate servicing of overseas markets frequently requires goods to be inventoried in several locations; one company that uses two factory warehouses for the entire United States needed six foreign distribution points that together handled less merchandise than either U.S. outlet.[23] In general, higher levels of inventory are needed to service foreign markets because of longer transit times, greater variability in transit times, port delays, customs delays, and other factors.

Inventory Valuation in International Markets

Additionally, inventories can have a substantial impact on the international firm due to the rapid inflation that exists in some countries. In inflationary economies, it is very important to use the proper inventory accounting procedure because of its impact on company profits. The LIFO (last in-first out) method is probably the most appropriate strategy because the cost of sales is valued closer to the current cost of replacement.[24] On the other hand, the FIFO (first in-first out) method gives a larger profit figure than LIFO because old costs are matched with current revenues. FIFO "fails to correct the data for the depreciation in currency value. FIFO, therefore, gives management a false sense of gain and also an excessive tax liability."[25]

Management of an international firm must weigh the cost trade-offs

[22] Cateora, *International Marketing*, p. 657.

[23] Ibid., p. 658.

[24] At the same time, in periods of inflation, products in inventory will be carried at a much lower value than their current replacement cost.

[25] Endel H. Kolde, *International Business Enterprise*, 2nd ed. (Englewood Cliffs, N.J.: Prentice Hall, 1973), p. 387.

involved in the buildup of inventories, in anticipation of higher costs due to inflation or other factors. The trade-off is between the accumulation of excess inventory and its associated inventory carrying costs and the reduction of carrying costs by holding less inventory, which would require paying higher acquisition costs at a later date.

Capital Budgeting Requires Lots of Information

When management considers direct investment in facilities and logistics networks in the foreign market, the capital budgeting aspects of financial planning become important. Developing an international capital budget would require a great deal of information, including:

1. An assessment of political uncertainties.
2. An economic forecast including the possibilities of inflation.
3. An analysis of the differences in financial costs and risks, with particular reference to
   a. Currency controls.
   b. Exchange rates.
   c. Character of money and capital markets of each country involved.
4. A projection of the impact which any particular investment will have on cash flows.
5. A measurement of capital availability under different alternatives.
6. Methods to compute the cost of capital on the basis of capital-availability estimates.
7. A method for reducing the items in different currencies to a common denominator reflective of the real values involved.[26]

Currency Fluctuations Make Planning Difficult

One aspect of the capital budgeting process that deserves particular mention is the effect of currency exchange fluctuations on logistics operations in exporting. As is the case in domestic operations, customers in the international sector do not tender payment to the shipper until the product is delivered. As previously mentioned, many factors can cause the foreign shipment to take longer to be delivered than a comparable domestic shipment. The exporter must be concerned with exchange rate fluctuations that may occur between the time when the product is shipped, delivered to the consignee, and finally paid for by the customer: "When the price is quoted in the foreign currency, the exporter accepts the risk of exchange fluctuation. Unless steps are taken to protect expected profits, a decline in exchange rates may reduce them or even convert them into loss."[27] Table 17–2 identifies some of the factors which management can use to forecast currency value changes.[28]

---

[26] Ibid., p. 366.

[27] Kahler and Kramer, *International Marketing*, p. 61.

[28] For an interesting discussion of the political and economic risks associated with international business, see William D. Coplin and Michael K. O'Leary, "The 1986 World Political Risk Forecast," *Planning Review* 14, no. 2 (March 1986), pp. 28–38; and Asayehgn Desta, "Assessing Political Risk in Less Developed Countries," *The Journal of Business Strategy* 5, no. 4 (Spring 1985), pp. 40–53.

TABLE 17–2 Elements in Forecasting Currency Value Changes

Economic

1. Balance of Payments:
   a. Current account. Trade surplus or deficit for goods, services, investment income and payments, and so on.
   b. Capital account. Surplus or deficit of demand for short- and long-term financial instruments.
2. Nominal and real interest rates.
3. Domestic inflation.
4. Monetary and fiscal policies.
5. Estimate of international competitiveness, present and future.
6. Foreign exchange reserves.
7. Attractiveness of country currency and assets, both financial and real.
8. Government controls and incentives.
9. Importance of currency in world finance and trade.

Political Factors

10. Philosophies of political party and leaders.
11. Proximity of elections or change in leadership.

Expectative or Psychological Factors

12. Expectations and opinions of analysts, traders, bankers, economists, and businesspeople.
13. Forward exchange market prices.

The Bottom Line

The bottom line for all of the above factors is that foreign exchange rates are determined by transactions which reflect the sum total of all of the motives, reasons, and beliefs behind currency supply and demand. The intersection of the supply and the demand *is* the rate.

SOURCE: Warren J. Keegan, *Global Marketing Management,* 4th ed., ©1989. p. 221. Reprinted by permission of Prentice Hall, Inc., Englewood Cliffs, N.J.

Letters of Credit

To ensure that international customers pay for products shipped to them, *letters of credit* are often issued. A letter of credit is a document issued by a bank on behalf of a buyer that authorizes payment for merchandise received. Payments are made to the seller by the bank rather than by the buyer. Figure 17–5 shows how a letter of credit works. "Although it might appear to be more the concern of the corporate financial department, it is crucial that logistics managers involved in international trade understand how letters of credit work. If they misinterpret information or fail to diligently follow the shipping instructions contained in the document, it could jeopardize the company's chances of receiving payment for the goods shipped."[29]

The Global Marketplace

All forms of entry into the international marketplace require an awareness of the variables that can affect a firm's distribution system. Some of these factors can be controlled by logistics executives. Others, unhappily, are not subject to control, but must still be addressed and dealt with in any inter-

[29] James Aaron Cooke, "What You Should Know about Letters of Credit," *Traffic Management* 29, no. 9 (September 1990), pp. 44–45.

FIGURE 17–5 How a Letter of Credit Works

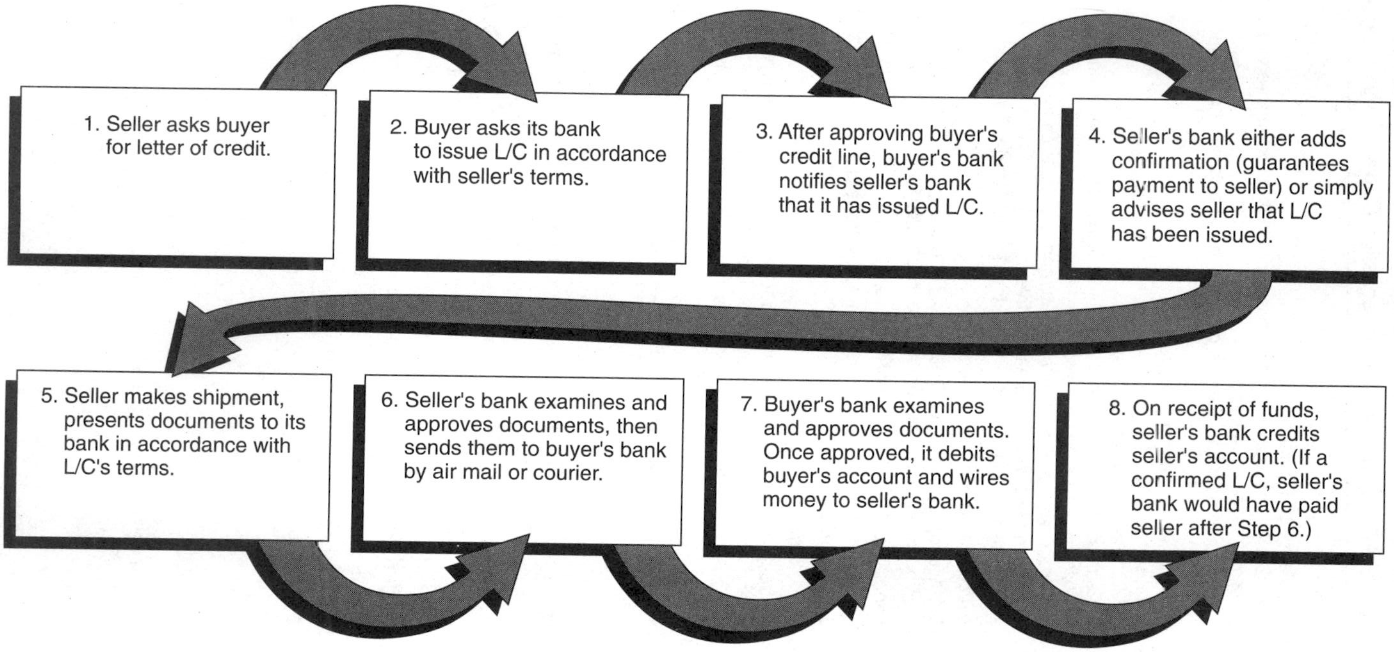

SOURCE: Adapted from James Aaron Cooke, "What You Should Know about Letters of Credit," *Traffic Management* 29, no. 9 (September 1990), pp. 44–45.

national marketing undertaking. Figure 17–6 shows the environment in which the logistics executive operates.

Uncontrollable Elements. Anything that affects the logistics strategy of the international firm, yet is not under the direct control and authority of the logistics manager, is an uncontrollable element. The major uncontrollable elements or environments include the political and legal systems of the foreign markets, economic conditions, the degree of competition in each market, the level of distribution technology available or accessible, the geographic structure of the foreign market, and the social and cultural norms of the various target markets.

An uncontrollable environment is characterized by uncertainty and, many times, volatility. The logistics executive must make decisions within such an environment—cost trade-offs, customer service levels, and pricing, for example. Some of the cost trade-offs involved between the political and economic environments and various logistics activities are listed below.

Examples of International Cost Trade-Offs

Political versus Transportation	Shipping component parts instead of finished product may result in a lower duty but higher transportation costs.
Political versus Warehousing	Using a bonded warehouse instead of a private warehouse may result in higher customs supervision costs but lower overhead costs for storage.
Political versus Inventory	Shipping component parts instead of finished product may result in a lower duty but higher inventory carrying costs due to the higher value of finished goods.
Political versus Packaging	The use of more distribution management time and cost to reduce red tape and customs entry time for perishable products may allow the products to be shipped with less protective packaging.
Political versus Communications	The use of more distribution management time and cost to reduce customs time, thereby increasing service to a foreign warehouse, may reduce the number of back orders that need to be processed.
Economic versus Transportation	Paying higher export broker costs to source raw materials from a nationalistic government experiencing real exchange rate depreciation may result in lower real cost (value) of raw materials, and therefore lower transportation insurance costs.
Economic versus Warehousing	A central warehouse site in a European Economic Community (Common Market) country may have a higher exchange rate (lower cost of money/more purchasing

FIGURE 17–6 The Global Logistics Environment

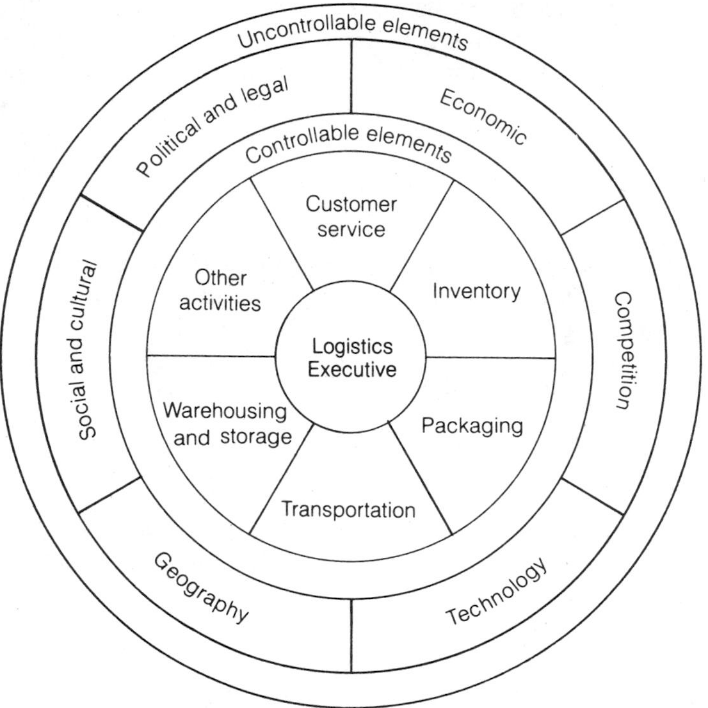

	power), but higher private warehouse construction overhead and operating costs than another country.
Economic versus Inventory	Paying higher customshouse broker fees to speed customs entry may result in lower order-cycle times and inventory carrying costs.
Economic versus Packaging	Paying higher prices for a freight forwarder with lower damage rates may allow the firm to reduce packaging costs.
Economic versus Communications	Incurring higher export distribution costs because of the influence of commercial bribery may result in lower international documentation preparation time and costs.[30]

[30] Robert Lorin Cook and James R. Burley, "A Framework for Evaluating International Physical Distribution Strategies," *International Journal of Physical Distribution and Materials Management* 15, no. 4 (1985), pp. 29–30.

Such trade-offs are only a few of the many that the logistics executive must evaluate.

Firms are experiencing increasing competitive pressures from many sources. In the United States, manufacturers in a variety of industries have found themselves at a competitive disadvantage compared to their Asian and European counterparts. For example, the market for microwave ovens, a product invented in the United States in 1945 and introduced commercially to consumers in 1955, has been taken over by Japanese manufacturers. Within the past decade, the domestic market share for U.S.-made computers dropped from 94 percent to 66 percent. Similar trends have been evident in semiconductors (90 percent to 67 percent), machine tools (77 percent to 54 percent), apparel (86 percent to 74 percent), industrial machinery (95 percent to 83 percent), household appliances (92 percent to 81 percent), and telephone equipment (95 percent to 81 percent).[31] According to *Fortune* magazine, an even more startling statistic was that during the first four months of 1990, 300,000 American flags were imported into the United States from Taiwan and elsewhere.[32]

Remaining Competitive Internationally

U.S. manufacturers have attempted to respond in several ways—manufacturing, research and development, and marketing (including logistics). Senior executives in businesses facing Japanese competition identified a number of steps they had taken to remain competitive, including (1) improving the quality of service to customers, and (2) adopting more aggressive marketing tactics and strategies.[33] Each is related to logistics.

It is beyond the scope of this chapter to examine in detail each of the various uncontrollable factors in the global marketplace. A number of international marketing textbooks address these elements.[34] It is sufficient to say that the uncontrollable elements affect the actions of the logistics executive and must be considered in the planning, implementation, and control of the firm's global distribution network.

Controllable Elements. When a firm becomes involved in international operations, the scope of the logistics executive's responsibilities often expands to include international distribution activities. Although the logistics executive may have full international responsibility, others within the or-

---

[31] Edmund Faltermayer, "Is 'Made in U.S.A.' Fading Away?" *Fortune* 122, no. 7 (September 24, 1990), pp. 62–64.

[32] Ibid., p. 62.

[33] Stuart E. Jackson, "BW/Harris Poll: Sure, Japan Is a Problem—But Not Mine," *Business Week* 2909 (August 26, 1985), p. 68.

[34] See Gerald Albaum, Jesper Strandskov, Edwin Duerr, and Laurence Dowd, *International Marketing and Export Management* (Reading, Mass.: Addison-Wesley Publishing Co., 1989); Edward W. Cundiff and Marye Tharp Hilger, *Marketing in the International Environment,* 2nd ed. (Englewood Cliffs, N.J.: Prentice Hall, 1988); Philip R. Cateora, *International Marketing,* 7th ed. (Homewood, Ill.: Richard D. Irwin, 1990); and Michael R. Czinkota and Ilkka A. Ronkainen, *International Marketing,* 2nd ed. (Hinsdale, Ill.: Dryden Press, 1990).

ganization probably have some involvement. A 1991 survey by the Council of Logistics Management found that approximately 60 percent of all logistics executives polled had direct responsibility for their company's international distribution operations.[35] However, almost all had at least partial responsibility.

Management of a firm involved in international distribution must try to administer the logistics components to minimize cost and provide an acceptable level of service to its customers. However, a firm's cost/service mix will vary in international markets. For example, logistics costs as a percentage of sales are much higher in Japan and the United States than in Australia or in the United Kingdom.[36] Managers involved in international distribution—especially in those firms that own foreign subsidiaries—should be aware of the variety of differences between the administration of domestic and foreign logistics activities.

Logistics Costs Will Be Different in International Markets

When all factors are considered, international distribution is generally more expensive than domestic distribution. Increased shipping distances, documentation costs, the larger inventory levels required, longer order cycle times, and other factors combine to increase the expense of international distribution. For firms involved internationally, logistics costs usually vary as follows:

8 to 10 percent of the delivered price for trade within a continent (e.g., Europe, North America).

20 to 30 percent of the delivered price for trade between continents (e.g., Europe to South America).

30 to 35 percent for shipments requiring movement between and within continents.[37]

Customer service strategies. In general, a firm can provide a higher level of service to its domestic customers than to its foreign customers. This is primarily caused by the distances products must be transported and delays due to customs procedures. The same consistency of service that a firm is able to provide its domestic customers cannot be easily achieved internationally. Because international transportation movements tend to be longer and can involve several different types of carriers, multiple transfers and handlings, and the crossing of a number of international boundaries, time-in-transit often varies significantly from one shipment to the next. As

---

[35] Bernard J. La Londe, James M. Masters, and Terrance L. Pohlen, "The 1991 Ohio State University Survey of Career Patterns in Logistics," *Proceedings of the Annual Conference of the Council of Logistics Management,* vol. I, 1991, p. 55.

[36] See Peter Gilmour, *Managing Distribution in Australia in the Mid-1980s,* Graduate School of Management, Macquarie University, North Ryde, New South Wales, 1985, p. 21; Peter Gilmour and P. J. Rimmer, "Business Logistics in the Pacific Basin," *Columbia Journal of World Business* 11, no. 1 (Spring 1976), p. 65; and *Survey of Distribution Costs,* (London, England: The Centre for Physical Distribution Management, 1985).

[37] Slater, "International Marketing," pp. 167–68; also see Francis J. Quinn, "Mapping Out an International Strategy," *Traffic Management* 24, no. 10 (October 1985), pp. 43–49.

a result, firms tend to require larger amounts of inventory to meet safety and cycle stock requirements.

Customer Service Is Viewed Differently in International Markets

In some cases, customer service levels may be higher in international markets, especially if the firm has a facility in the foreign market. For example, in Japan, the order cycle time is generally shorter than in the United States. Because of the geographical differences between the two countries, the physical facilities of many wholesalers and retailers, and financial considerations, the majority of all consumer goods orders in Japan can be delivered in 24 hours or less. For that reason, many international firms operate owned facilities in foreign markets in order to compete effectively on a customer service basis.

The cost of providing a specified level of customer service often varies between countries. A company must examine the service requirements of customers in each foreign market and develop a logistics package that best serves each area. Because of competition, specific customer needs, and other factors, a firm may have to incur higher logistics costs. This will necessarily result in lower profits for the firm. Such a decision requires a complete analysis of the situation by top management.

Subaru Expands Internationally

Subaru of America (SOA) is an example of a company that was able to gain competitive advantage internationally by improving its level of customer service: "(SOA) upgraded service levels by restructuring its international and domestic distribution network. In the process, the automaker saved thousands of dollars in freight costs and improved warehouse productivity by 50 percent."[38] On a larger scale, Subaru was able to maintain its position within the industry as a firm with a topflight parts and vehicle support effort. An indication of that success in the marketplace was revealed in a nationwide American survey that placed Subaru second only to Mercedes-Benz in maintaining "customer satisfaction with the cars they owned."[39]

Inventory strategies. Inventory control is particularly important to the international company. It requires an awareness that international and domestic inventory management systems differ in several respects:

It Costs More to Carry Inventories in Other Countries

> International systems usually have more inventory points at more levels between suppliers and customers; thus multilevel inventory systems are more complex and more common than in domestic systems.
>
> In-transit inventories can be substantially higher than for a domestic operation with similar sales volume. This results from the larger number of locations and levels involved, and longer transportation times.[40]

---

[38] Lisa Harrington, "Customer Service Puts Subaru on Fast Track," *Traffic Management* 24, no. 10 (October 1985), p. 76.

[39] Ibid., p. 84.

[40] Bender, "The International Dimension of Physical Distribution Management," pp. 785–86.

Depending on the length of transit and delays that can occur in international product movements, a firm may have to supply its distributors or other foreign intermediaries with higher than normal levels of inventory. A typical firm will have 25 to 30 percent of its assets in inventory. Firms engaged in international marketing often have inventories that comprise 50 percent or more of their assets. For high-value products, the inventory carrying costs as well as the amount of accounts receivable outstanding can be extremely high.

In markets where the firm's products are sold at the retail level, the shopping patterns of the population can be very important in determining inventory strategies. Companies in the United States can usually exercise greater control over their inventories because they can influence the amount of product ordered by their customers through discounts. This may not be a viable strategy in some international markets.

Since conditions may vary in foreign markets, it is important for the firm to develop inventory policies and control procedures that are appropriate for each market area.

Package Design Is Important

Packaging. "Among the major factors involved in designing the package are transportation and handling, climate, pilferage, freight rates, customs duties, and most important, the customer's requirements. The greater number of handlings goods are subjected to, the greater the possibility of damage. International trade may require several such handlings.[41] In general, the rates of damage and loss in international traffic movements are higher than in domestic movements. Therefore, the international shipper must be much more concerned with the protective aspect of the package than his or her domestic counterpart.

The bottom line of all international packaging decisions is that the item should arrive at its destination in an undamaged condition. Logistics executives can help to ensure that goods arrive safely at their international destinations by following some basic guidelines, namely:

Minimizing Damage through Packaging

1. Know the merchandise.
2. Analyze the transportation environment and pack for the toughest leg of the journey.
3. Know the supplier.
4. Determine packaging regulations applicable in the country of origin, on each of the carriers, and at the port of entry.
5. Arrange for prompt pickup at point of entry.[42]

---

[41] Kahler and Kramer, *International Marketing*, p. 80.

[42] Betsy Haggerty, "How to Package Goods for International Transportation," *Inbound Logistics* 5, no. 4 (October 1985), p. 25; also see David A. Clancy, "Develop a Global Package," *Transportation and Distribution* 31, no. 10 (October 1990), pp. 34–36.

In order to facilitate product handling and protect the product during movement and storage, many firms have turned to the use of containers. Containers are widely used in international logistics, especially when water movements are part of the transport network. Many companies have adopted standard container sizes (8' × 8' × 10', 20', 30', or 40') that allow for intermodal movements. The use of standardized material handling equipment has also become commonplace.

Containers Facilitate International Shipments

The advantages of containers are numerous:

Costs due to loss or damage are reduced because of the protective nature of the container.

Labor costs in freight handling are reduced due to the increased use of automated material handling equipment.

Containers are more easily stored and transported than other types of shipments, which results in lower warehousing and transportation costs.

Containers are available in a variety of sizes, many of which are standardized for intermodal use.

Containers are able to serve as temporary storage facilities at ports and terminals where warehousing space may be limited.

On the other hand, containerization is not without disadvantages. The major problem with the use of containers is that container ports or terminals may not be available in certain parts of the world. Even when such facilities exist, they may be so overburdened with inbound and outbound cargo that long delays occur. The next major problem associated with containerization is the large capital expenditure required to initiate a container-based transportation network. Significant capital outlays for port and terminal facilities, material handling equipment, specialized transport equipment, and the containers themselves are necessary before a firm can utilize containerization.

Labeling Considerations

Related to the packaging component of global logistics is labeling. From a cost standpoint, labeling is a relatively minor aspect of international logistics. However, accurate labeling is essential to the timely and efficient movement of products across international borders. Important issues relating to labeling include content, language, color, and location on the package.

Other activities. Each of the activities or functions of logistics must be performed in the international market. The difference between the domestic and foreign market is not *whether* the logistics activity should be performed, but rather *how* each activity should be carried out.

International Sourcing

One such activity where differences occur is in the sourcing of materials. Firms traditionally obtained raw materials, parts, supplies and components from domestic sources. In recent years, however, there has been an

FIGURE 17–7 Xerox's European Pipeline

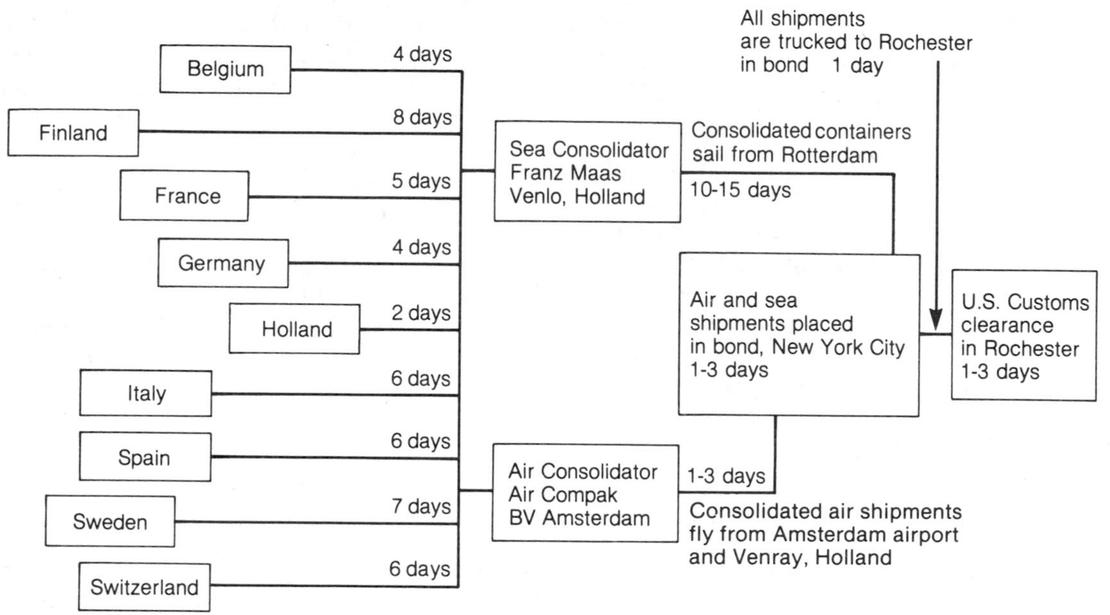

Xerox's European pipeline extends from suppliers in the Old World to U.S. Customs clearance in Rochester, N.Y. Shipments from Belgium (upper left of chart), for example, take an average of four days to be transported to and consolidated in Holland. Most goods are then transported via ocean to the United States, a 10 to 15 day trip. Goods are placed in bond in New York City and trucked to Rochester, where they clear customs. Total in-transit time, six weeks when Xerox began sourcing in Europe, has been lowered to five weeks and will soon be reduced to four weeks.

SOURCE: Jim Curley, "Can You Copy Xerox's Success?" *Inbound Logistics* 15, no. 4 (October 1985), p. 17. © Copyright 1985. Reprinted from *Inbound Logistics* with permission of the publisher.

accelerating trend toward international sourcing. For example, Xerox Corporation's Reprographic Business Group sources 35 to 40 percent of its parts from Europe, the Far East, and Latin America.[43]

Xerox's European Pipeline

Although Xerox employed a Just-in-Time (JIT) approach, it found that foreign sourcing provided significant cost savings in many instances (30 to 40 percent) and that deliveries could be controlled just as rigidly as if all suppliers were domestic. In Europe, Xerox purchased parts directly from the European supplier, using a network as shown in Figure 17–7.

Results were positive. In addition to cost savings, "Inventory from all sources [was] down to about one month's worth, on average more than a

[43] Jim Curley, "Can You Copy Xerox's Success?" *Inbound Logistics* 5, no. 4 (October 1985), p. 16.

FIGURE 17–8 Logistics Information Clearinghouse (LICH)

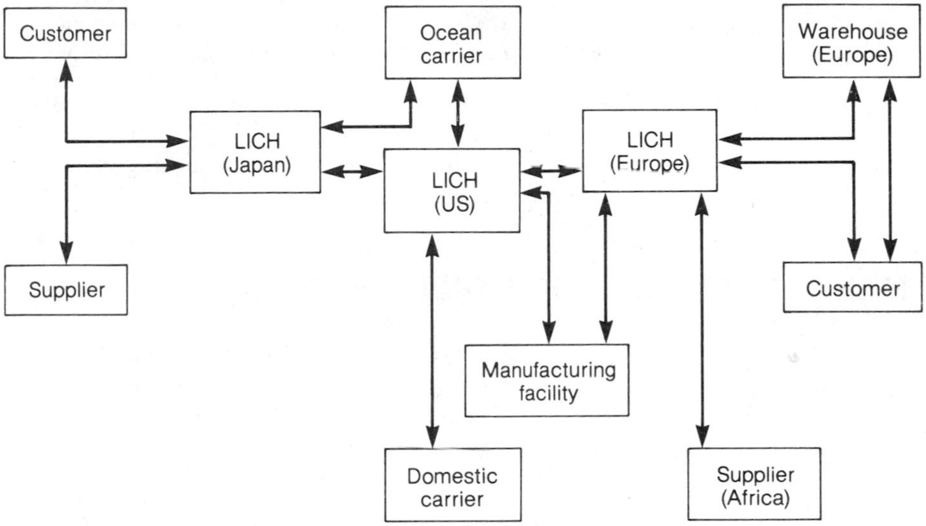

SOURCE: David L. Anderson, "International Logistics Strategies for the Eighties," *Proceedings of the Twenty-Second Annual Conference of the National Council of Physical Distribution Management,* 1984, p. 368. Used by permission of the Council of Logistics Management.

50 percent decrease in the past three years, even with offshore sourcing, which increased significantly in the same period.[44]

The concepts of *integrated logistics management* and *cost trade-off analysis* are still very important in international logistics. However, the relative importance of each logistics component may vary from market to market, as may the costs incurred in carrying out each activity. This results in different cost/service equations for each international market.

Logistics Information Clearinghouse

The best advice for the executive whose company is entering into international logistics for the first time is to obtain as much information about business conditions and operating procedures in each market, from as many data sources as possible. There are various secondary and primary information sources, although as logistics systems become more complex, monitoring systems similar to the clearinghouse system shown in Figure 17–8 will be necessary.

The overall importance of product flow information, coupled with the high costs of maintaining individual carrier- or shipper-based control systems, will

[44] Ibid.

result in the development of logistics information clearinghouses. Like the automated clearinghouses already used by the world banking system to transfer funds and checks among participating banks, the logistics information clearinghouse (LICH) system would provide multicarrier and intermediary shipment information to a shipper at any global location, 24 hours a day.[45]

Each of the logistics activities of a company must be performed, although the task may be completed by one or more members of the international channel of distribution. The specific entities involved depend on the channel strategy selected.

MANAGEMENT OF THE EXPORT SHIPMENT

There are many facilitators or organizations that are involved in the exporting activity. The types of organizations utilized most extensively are:

Types of Export Facilitators

1. Export distributor.
2. Customshouse broker.
3. International freight forwarder.
4. Trading company.

Other facilitators are also used, including export brokers, export merchants, foreign purchasing agents, and others, but their use is to a much lesser degree than those organizations listed above.

Export Facilitators

A firm involved in exporting for the first time would likely use an export distributor, customshouse broker, international freight forwarder, or trading company.

Export Distributor. A company involved in international markets often utilizes the services of an export distributor. An export distributor (1) is located in the foreign market; (2) buys on his or her own account; (3) is responsible for the sale of the product; and (4) has a continuing contractual relationship with the domestic firm.[46]

The distributor frequently is granted exclusive rights to a specific territory. He or she may refrain from handling the products of competing manufacturers, or may sell goods of other manufacturers to the same outlets.

---

[45] Anderson, "International Logistics Strategies for the Eighties," pp. 367–68. For an example of how Unisys Corp. utilizes automated information systems to link its worldwide operations, see Lisa H. Harrington, "Traveling the Global Data Highway," *Traffic Management* 29, no. 4 (April 1990), pp. 38–42.

[46] Randolph E. Ross, "Selection of the Overseas Distributor: An Empirical Framework," *International Journal of Physical Distribution* 3, no. 1 (Autumn 1972), p. 83.

Functions Performed by an Export Distributor

The following functions are often performed by the distributor:

1. Obtaining and maintaining agreed-on levels of channel and sales effort.
2. Obtaining import business and handling the arrangements for customs clearance.
3. Obtaining the necessary foreign exchange for payment to the supplier.
4. Maintaining necessary government relations.
5. Maintaining inventories.
6. Providing warehouse facilities.
7. Performing, or overseeing, the inland freight and delivery functions.
8. Performing break-bulk operations.

To these can be added an additional number of functions that the distributor may perform alone, or in cooperation with the supplier:

1. Extending credit to channel intermediaries and final customers.
2. Gathering and transmitting market information.
3. Planning and operating advertising and sales promotion programs.
4. Maintaining stocks of parts, etc., and providing postsale servicing.[47]

Customshouse Broker. The customshouse broker performs two critical functions: (1) facilitating product movement through customs and (2) handling the necessary documentation that must accompany international shipments.

The Customshouse Broker Is a Documentation Specialist

For many firms, the task of handling the many documents and forms that accompany an international shipments can be overwhelming. Coupled with the variety of customs procedures, restrictions, and requirements that differ in each country, the job of facilitating export shipments across international borders requires a specialist—the customshouse broker. In general, if a company is exporting to a number of countries with different import requirements or if the company has a large number of items in its product line (e.g., automotive parts, electronic components, food products), a customshouse broker should be a part of the firm's international distribution network.

Selecting a Customhouse Broker

When selecting a customshouse broker a number of factors should be considered. Typical of the most important questions or issues that should be addressed are the following:

1. Does the broker specialize in certain commodities and/or shipping methods?
2. How long has the broker been in business?

[47] Ibid., pp. 83–84.

3. What resources does the broker have to ensure speedy clearance and delivery of your products?
4. How does the broker advise his or her clients of delays in handling or clearance?
5. What assistance does the broker offer in terms of records maintenance?
6. Does the broker have computerized or electronic data interchange (EDI) systems that can expedite document preparation and transmittal and/or expedite customs clearance? What information can it provide?[48]

International Freight Forwarder. International freight forwarders serve an important role in the export distribution strategies of many firms. They "can handle the movement of goods from the site of production to the customer's location. They have an intimate knowledge of the transportation alternatives and can handle documentation responsibilities."[49] International forwarders:

Services Provided by International Freight Forwarders

1. Prepare government-required export declarations.
2. Make cargo-space bookings.
3. Provide for transportation from the exporter to final destination.
4. Prepare and process air waybills and bills of lading.
5. Prepare consular documents in the languages of the countries to which the goods are shipped, and provide for certification.
6. Provide for warehouse storage when necessary.
7. Arrange for insurance upon request.
8. Prepare and send shipping notices to banks, shippers, or consignees as required.
9. Complete shipping documents and send them to shippers, banks, or consignees as directed.
10. Provide general assistance on export traffic matters.[50]

Nearly every international company utilizes the services of an international freight forwarder: "Even in large companies with active export departments capable of handling documentation, a forwarder is usually involved in coordination duties at the port or at the destination."[51]

Trading Company. Most trading companies are primarily involved in exporting, with some in the import business as well. "The export trading

[48] *Freight Facts* (New York: Port Authority of New York and New Jersey, 1989), pp. 28–29.

[49] Ibid., p. 9.

[50] F. R. Lineaweaver, Jr., "The Role of the Export Traffic Manager," *Distribution Worldwide* 72, no. 10 (October 1973), p. 46.

[51] Thomas A. Foster, "Freight Forwarders: The Export Experts," *Distribution* 79, no. 3 (March 1980), p. 38.

company finds buyers for goods or services and takes care of all or most of the export arrangements, including documentation, inland and over-seas transportation, and foreign government requirements."[52]

Export Trading Company Act

In the United States, export trading companies became more important as a result of legislation enacted in 1982. The Export Trading Company Act[53] allowed financial institutions (e.g., banks and bank holding companies) to own or participate in export trading companies. That affiliation helped to minimize cash flow, terms of payment, credit, and other financial problems related to exporting. In addition, the act allowed trading companies to export services as well as goods. Specifically, the act defined export trade services to include:

> . . . consulting, international market research, advertising, marketing, insurance, product research and design, legal assistance, transportation, including trade documentation and freight forwarding, communication and processing of foreign orders to and for exporters and foreign purchasers, warehousing, foreign exchange, financing, and taking title to goods, when provided in order to facilitate the export of goods or services.[54]

Trading companies will continue to be widely used in the future as a result of the Export Trading Company Act.

Documentation

Examples of Export Documents

"To most [logistics] managers, exporting means international transportation. In reality, the most important part of exporting is the planning, negotiating, and paperwork that takes place before the first pound of freight is shipped. The [logistics] manager has to know this side of exporting as well."[55] International documentation is much more complex than domestic documentation because each country has its own specifications and requirements. Absolute accuracy is required; errors may result in delayed shipments or penalties. It is beyond the scope of this textbook to examine in detail the multitude of export documents that exist. However, some of the more widely used items are listed below.

1. **Air waybill.** *Issued by:* Airline, consolidator. *Purpose:* Each airline has its own air waybill form, but format and numbering system have been standardized by airline industry to allow computerization. Like the ocean bill of lading, serves as contract of carriage between shipper and carrier.

---

[52] Evelyn A. Thomchick and Lisa Rosenbaum, "The Role of U.S. Export Trading Companies in International Logistics," *Journal of Business Logistics* 5, no. 2 (1984), p. 86.

[53] See the Export Trading Company Act of 1982, PLB.L No. 97–290.

[54] Ibid.

[55] Foster, "Anatomy of an Export," p. 75.

2. **Certificate of origin.** *Issued by:* Exporter or freight forwarder on exporter's behalf. *Purpose:* Required by some countries to certify origin of product components. Used for statistical research or for assessing duties, particularly under trade agreements.
3. **Commercial invoice.** *Issued by:* Seller of goods. *Purpose:* Invoice against which payment is made. Required for clearing goods through customs at destination.
4. **Dock receipt (D/R).** *Issued by:* Exporter or freight forwarder on exporter's behalf. *Purpose:* No standard form, but must include shipment description, physical details, and shipping information. Used by both shipper and carrier to verify shipment particulars, condition, and delivery to carrier.
5. **Ocean bill of lading (B/L).** *Issued by:* Steamship line. *Purpose:* Each carrier has its own bill of lading form. Serves as contract of carriage between carrier and shipper, spelling out legal responsibilities and liability limits for all parties to the shipment. The B/L also can be used to transfer title to the goods to a party named in the document. Specifies shipment details, such as number of pieces, weight, destination, etc.
6. **Packing list.** *Issued by:* Exporter. *Purpose:* Provides detailed information of contents of each individual package in shipment. Customs authorities at destination use information during clearance and inspection procedures. Also invaluable when filing claims for damage or shortage.
7. **Shipper's export declaration (SED).** *Issued by:* Exporter or freight forwarder on exporter's behalf. *Purpose:* Required by federal law for any commodity with value over $2,500 or any shipment requiring validated export license.
8. **Sight, time drafts.** *Issued by:* Exporter or freight forwarder on exporter's behalf. *Purpose:* Request for payment from foreign buyer. Instructs buyer's bank to collect payment; when collected, it [the bank] releases shipping documents to buyer. Buyer's bank then remits to seller's bank. Sight drafts are payable on receipt at buyer's bank. Time drafts extend credit; foreign bank releases documents immediately but collects payment later.
9. **Validated export license.** *Issued by:* U.S. Department of Commerce. *Purpose:* Required for commodities deemed important to national security, foreign-policy objectives, or protecting domestic supplies of strategic materials. Constitutes permission to export a specific product to a specific party.[56]

---

[56]"Ten Key Trade Documents," *Traffic Management* 29, no. 9 (September 1990), pp. 53 and 55.

Terms of Trade

Who Pays the Freight?

Closely related to the actual documents used in the export process are the terms of shipment or terms of trade. The terms of shipment are much more important in international shipping than in domestic shipping because of the uncertainties and control problems that accompany foreign traffic movements. "For this reason, negotiating the final terms of sale is probably the most important part of an export deal. These terms of sale determine who is responsible for the various stages of delivery, who bears what risks, and who pays for the various elements of transportation."[57] A summary of the most commonly used terms of shipment in exporting from the United States is shown below and in Table 17–4. Foreign-based exports use the same or similar terminology.

Ex Origin: Origin should be identified as factory, plant, etc. Seller bears costs and risks until buyer is obligated to take delivery. Buyer pays for documents, must take delivery when specified, and must pay for any export taxes.

FOB (Free on Board) Inland Carrier: Seller arranges for loading on railcars, truck, etc. Seller provides a clean bill of lading and is responsible for loss or damage until goods have been placed on inland vehicle.

FOB Vessel U.S. Port: The price quoted covers all expenses involved in delivery of goods upon the vessel designated at the port named. Buyer must give seller adequate notice of sailing date, name of ship, berth, etc. Buyer bears additional costs resulting from vessel being late or absent.

FAS (Free Alongside) Vessel U.S. Port: Similar to FOB vessel, but certain additional port charges for the seller, such as heavy lift may apply. The buyer is responsible for loss or damage while goods are on a lighter (small barge) or within reach of the loading device. Loading costs are also the responsibility of the buyer.

FOB Vessel Foreign Port: The price quoted includes all transportation costs to the point where goods are off-loaded in the destination country. Seller is responsible for insurance to this point. The buyer assumes risk as soon as the vessel is at the foreign port.

FOB Inland Destination: The price quoted includes all costs involved in getting the goods to the named inland point in the country of importation.

C & F (Cost and Freight): The price quoted includes all transportation to the point of destination. Seller also pays export taxes and similar

[57] Foster, "Anatomy of an Export," p. 76.

TABLE 17–4 Who's Responsible for Costs under Various Terms?

Cost Items/Terms	*FOB (Free on Board) Inland Carrier at Factory*	*FOB (Free on Board) Inland Carrier at Point of Shipment*	*FAS (Free Alongside) Vessel or Plane at Port of Shipment*	*CIF (Cost, Insurance, Freight) at Port of Destination*
Export packing*	Buyer	Seller	Seller	Seller
Inland freight	Buyer	Seller	Seller	Seller
Port charges	Buyer	Buyer	Seller	Seller
Forwarder's fee	Buyer	Buyer	Buyer	Seller
Consular fee	Buyer	Buyer	Buyer	Buyer†
Loading on vessel or plane	Buyer	Buyer	Buyer	Seller
Ocean freight	Buyer	Buyer	Buyer	Seller
Cargo insurance	Buyer	Buyer	Buyer	Seller
Customs duties	Buyer	Buyer	Buyer	Buyer
Ownership of goods passes	When goods onboard an inland carrier (truck, rail, etc.) or in hands of inland carrier	When goods unloaded by inland carrier	When goods alongside carrier, in hands of air or ocean carrier	When goods on board air or ocean carrier *at port of shipment*

*Who absorbs export packing? This charge should be clearly agreed on. Charges are sometimes controversial.

†The seller has responsibility to arrange for consular invoices (and other documents requested by buyer's government). According to official definitions, buyer pays fees, but sometimes as a matter of practice, seller includes in quotations.

SOURCE: Philip R. Cateora, *International Marketing,* 7th ed. (Homewood, Ill.: Richard D. Irwin, 1990), p. 640.

fees. The buyer pays the cost of certificates of origin, consular invoices, or other documents required for importation to the buyer's country. The seller must prove these, but at the buyer's expense. The buyer is responsible for all insurance from the point of vessel loading.

CIF (Cost, Insurance, and Freight): The price quoted under these terms includes the cost of goods, transportation, and marine insurance. The seller pays all taxes or fees, as well as marine and war risk insurance. Buyer pays for any certificates or consular documents required for importation. Although seller pays for insurance, buyer assumes all risk after seller has delivered the goods to the carrier.[58]

Free Trade Zones

Free trade zones (FTZs), sometimes referred to as foreign trade zones, are areas where companies may ship products to postpone or reduce customs duties or taxes. Products remaining in the FTZ are not subject to duties or taxes until they are reshipped out of the zone into the country of destination. Within the FTZ, firms often process, assemble, sort, and repackage the product before reshipment.

Benefits of Free Trade Zones

> In situations where goods are imported into the United States to be combined with American-made goods and reexported, the importer or exporter can avoid payment of U.S. import duties on the foreign portion and eliminate the complications of applying for a "drawback," that is, a request for a refund from the government of 99 percent of the duties paid on imports later reexported. Other benefits for companies utilizing foreign-trade zones include: (1) lower insurance costs due to the greater security required in FTZs; (2) more working capital since duties are deferred until goods leave the zone; (3) the opportunity to stockpile products when quotas are filled or while waiting for ideal market conditions; (4) significant savings on goods or materials rejected, damaged, or scrapped for which no duties are assessed; and (5) exemption from paying duties on labor and overhead costs which are excluded in determining the value of the goods when incurred in a FTZ.[59]

While there are potentially many benefits in using a FTZ, most FTZs are underutilized, with space going to waste.[60] The facilities, services offered, and quality of FTZ management vary significantly. Management wishing to utilize a FTZ will have to explore each zone individually in order to determine their potential usefulness.[61]

---

[58] Ibid., pp. 76–77. For a definition of these and other import/export terms, see "Export/Import Terms You Need to Know," *Traffic Management* 29, no. 9 (September 1990), pp. 37–41.

[59] Cateora, *International Marketing*, p. 635.

[60] "International Merchandising," *Inbound Traffic Guide* 3, no. 3 (July-August 1983), p. 14.

[61] For an examination of the role of FTZs in global marketing see, Patriya S. Tansuhaj and James W. Gentry, "Firm Differences in Perceptions of the Facilitating Role of Foreign Trade Zones in Global Marketing and Logistics," *Journal of International Business Studies*, Spring

GLOBAL MARKET OPPORTUNITIES

Europe

Significant developments are occurring in Western Europe with the creation of a single European market. Referred to as "Europe 1992," the creation of a unified market comprised of over 324 million people promises to have dramatic influences on business and commerce, not only in Europe but also throughout the world.

Commenting on the differences between Europe and the United States, and the implications of those differences on logistics, an international logistics consultant stated:

> Demographically and geographically Europe is much more compact than North America. . . . Almost 85 percent of the population of 324 million is within a *five hundred mile radius*. Therefore the pattern of transport and distribution is different in Europe to that of the USA. In particular, only 1 percent of inter-European freight is intermodal.[62]

Within Europe, logistics presently operates much differently compared to how it will operate after Europe 1992. According to a European study conducted by the consulting firm A. T. Kearney, the characteristics of present-day European logistics operations are as follows:

Characteristics of European Logistics Operations

1. There is extensive warehousing—one warehouse in every country.
2. Shipping to your own company is the normal way of doing business—60 percent of motor transportation is own-account, with the exception of that in Germany.
3. Inventory consists of small amounts, widely dispersed.
4. There is regional focus of management.
5. Use of sophisticated methods and approaches is limited.
6. Circuitous routing of vehicles occurs frequently.
7. Logistics costs are higher than necessary.
8. Service levels exhibit high variability.[63]

Additionally, customs delays at European borders can be considerable. For example, customs requires 7.74 hours from Germany to Italy, but from Italy to Germany the time required is 4.90 hours. For goods moving from Germany to the Netherlands, the time required for customs is only 1.43 hours, but for movements from the United Kingdom to Italy, customs re-

---

1987, pp. 19–33; also see Wade Ferguson, "Using Foreign Trade Zones to Reduce Costs," *International Journal of Physical Distribution and Materials Management* 17, no. 1 (1987), pp. 47–53.

[62] Stephen Byrne, "European Partnerships," *Proceedings of the Annual Conference of the Council of Logistics Management,* vol. II, 1990, p. 287.

[63] Ibid., p. 288; also see *Logistics Productivity: The Competitive Edge in Europe*, management report prepared by A. T. Kearney, Inc., 1987.

quires 9.75 hours.[64] On the average, trucks spend approximately 30 percent of their transit time awaiting customs clearances.[65]

Other characteristics of the pre-Europe-1992 logistics environment include a highly fragmented motor carrier (or road hauler) industry comprised of small firms, rail systems that provide reasonable levels of service but that are financially weak, a strong and dominating freight forwarder industry, highly competitive intercoastal shipping and inland barge operations, and the presence of few transportation companies that are prepared to operate in a unified European marketplace.[66]

Impacts of Europe 1992

Logistics executives believe that Europe 1992 will bring about substantial changes in the marketing, manufacturing, and distribution strategies of firms selling products in Europe. The anticipated changes will occur in five major areas: manufacturing, transportation, distribution channels, administration, and organization.[67]

Manufacturing. Many firms have traditionally established plants in each country, but with the economic unification of Europe, single plants can be established that can service multiple countries. With larger plants, it is likely that greater economies of scale can be realized. This will have a variety of effects on logistics activities carried out in the channel of distribution due to the larger amounts of product being produced. If firms maintain several plant locations, the focused factory concept could be implemented, with each plant specializing in one or a few product lines.

Deregulation of European Transportation

Transportation. Accompanying Europe 1992 will be the deregulation of transportation, particularly motor transport.

> Until recently, the growth of accompanied services outwards from the UK was inhibited by a lack of international haulage permits. Most European countries only grant entry to foreign hauliers in possession of either a *bilateral* or *multilateral permit*. (These permits are not required by own-account operators moving their own traffic.) Each bilateral permit enables a haulier to make a single journey from his home country to, or through, one other country, while a multilateral one allows him to make an unlimited number of journeys between his home country and any other EC country during a twelve-month period. Bilateral permits are more freely available for movements to some countries than to others. The supply of permits for West Germany, Italy and Spain, for ex-

---

[64] James Cooper, Michael Browne, and Melvyn Peters, "Logistics Performance in Europe: The Challenge of 1992," *The International Journal of Logistics Management* 1, no. 1 (1990), p. 33.

[65] Shawn Tully, "Europe Gets Ready for 1992," *Fortune* 120, no. 3 (February 1, 1988), p. 83.

[66] Manfred Tuerks and Justin F. Zubrod, "Transport Changes Advance Europe's Single Market," *Europe-1992* (May 24, 1989); appeared in *The Emerging Europe: Approaching the Single Market*, management report prepared by A. T. Kearney, Inc., 1990, pp. 32–39.

[67] Material presented in the following sections relative to these five areas of change have been adapted from Alan Braitwaite, "Achieving Outstanding Logistics Performance in Europe post-1992," a paper presented at the Annual Conference of the Council of Logistics Management, October 1991.

ample, has fallen well short of British hauliers' demands. This has impeded the growth of accompanied haulage to these countries and favoured the movement of unaccompanied trailers, which do not require permits.[68]

With a single European market, the transport industry should experience financial improvement. Freight consolidation opportunities should increase due to many factors, including deregulation, more optimal routing and scheduling opportunities, and the development of Pan-European (across Europe) services. Additionally, the channel tunnel, called the "Chunnel," will link the United Kingdom with the rest of Europe and facilitate motor transport between England and France.

Distribution Channels. Within the European channel of distribution, there will be a decline in the use of channel intermediaries. With a single European market, separate channels will not be required for each country. Likely, larger wholesalers and distributors will develop. Vertical integration will also occur, and direct marketing and distribution will increase. The result will be less inventory within the system and a lowering of channel wide logistics costs.

Administration. The removal of customs procedures will result in greater efficiencies in transportation, packaging, and labeling. Technology improvements can be implemented throughout Europe instead of within individual countries. More centralization of order processing, inventory control, warehousing, and computer technology can occur with a unified Europe.

Organization. Organizational changes will be significant in Europe after 1992. As a result of the centralization trend mentioned previously, coupled with organizational structures that recognize national boundaries to a lesser extent, pervasive changes will occur in all industries.

> This will be a bigger change than might appear at first sight to an American audience. This is pretty much the way you [American firms] operate. But in Europe the country style organisation is part of the culture and the directors have ownership and technical authority over their facilities. Headcount is a measure of prestige and status. This is turn has proved to be a major barrier to downsizing and adjusting to demand.[69]

In sum, the competitive situation in Europe will intensify. The penalties for poor performance will be greater, but the rewards much higher for those firms that are able to effectively implement optimal manufacturing, marketing and logistics strategies in a unified European economy.

---

[68] Alan C. McKinnon, *Physical Distribution Systems* (London: Routledge, 1989), p. 225.

[69] Braitwaite, "Achieving Outstanding Logistics Performance in Europe post-1992," p. 11.

The Commonwealth of Independent States/Eastern Europe

During the early 1990s, significant changes took place in the Soviet Union (much of which reorganized itself into the Commonwealth of Independent States) and throughout Eastern Europe. The fall of the Berlin Wall, which had symbolized the separation of Eastern and Western Europe; the merging of East and West Germany into a unified Germany; political freedom in Poland, Hungary, and Czechoslovakia; and the independence movements of many of the republics in the former Soviet Union (e.g., the Baltic states, Georgia) have reshaped political and commercial boundaries in Europe and Asia.

Since 1989, significant U.S. investment in Eastern Europe and the Commonwealth of Independent States (CIS) has occurred. Pepsi has invested $1 billion in the CIS; General Electric and General Motors invested over $150 million each in Hungary; and Coca Cola invested $140 million in Germany.[70]

Opportunities and Challenges of the CIS and Eastern Europe

A study of Eastern Europe by A. T. Kearney, Inc., the international logistics consulting firm, identified the tremendous opportunities and challenges facing companies interested in entering that market. Not including the CIS, the market potential of Eastern Europe has been estimated at over $1 trillion.[71] However, the attractiveness of individual markets within Eastern Europe will vary significantly and will be dependent on several factors, including the following:

1. Degree of indebtedness.
2. Development of the banking system.
3. Level of productivity.
4. Quality of the work force.
5. Condition of the infrastructure.
6. State of technology.
7. Depth of managerial skills.
8. Supply of production materials.
9. Profit repatriation regulations.[72]

Evaluations of several of the Eastern European countries and the CIS (the former Soviet Union) are shown in Table 17–5. As indicated in the table, Germany offers the greatest opportunities, and the CIS the worst. Of course, the items in the table are equally weighted. If a company felt that some criteria were more important than others, those factors could be

[70] Web Bryant, "Biggest Deals in the East Bloc," *USA Today* (May 1, 1990), p. 1B.

[71] *The Iron Curtain Rises: Investiment Opportunities in East Central Europe*, management report prepared by A. T. Kearney, Inc., January 1991, p. 3.

[72] Ibid., p. 6.

TABLE 17–5 Evaluating the Opportunities in Eastern Europe

Factor	*German Democratic Republic*	*Hungary*	*Federal Republic of Germany*	*Poland*	*Soviet Union*	*Yugoslavia*	*Bulgaria*	*Romania*
Indebtness	5	2	3	1	1	3	3	4
Banking system	5	4	4	3	1	4	2	2
Productivity	4	3	3	3	1	3	2	2
Labor force	5	4	5	3	1	3	2	2
Infrastructure	4	4	4	2	1	4	2	2
Technology	5	4	3	2	2	3	2	1
Managerial skills	4	3	4	3	3	3	1	2
Supply of production material	4	4	3	3	1	4	1	1
Profit repatriation	5	4	3	2	1	4	2	2
Total	41	32	32	22	12	31	17	18

Situation: 1 = very bad; 2 = bad; 3 = medium; 4 = good; 5 = very good; relative to Eastern Europe.

SOURCE: *The Iron Curtain Rises: Investment Opportunities in East Central Europe,* management report by A. T. Kearney, Inc., January 1991, p. 7. Reprinted by permission, A. T. Kearney, Inc.

AUTHOR'S NOTE: This table was prepared before the unification of the German Democratic Republic (East Germany) with the Federal Republic of Germany (West Germany) and the breakup of the Soviet Union.

given greater weights. If that were done, it is possible that the countries offering the greatest opportunities could change from that as shown.

From a logistics perspective, the CIS and Eastern Europe offer special challenges. Most businesspeople traveling to those areas recognize the poor transportation infrastructures resulting from decades of Communist rule. The concepts of customer satisfaction and customer service are unknown except in a very few instances. Sophisticated logistics techniques and the use of computerized order processing and information systems are impossible in most areas.

However, because of the immense opportunities, many firms will decide that the benefits outweigh the costs. It will be a slow process, but the firms that penetrate the markets of Eastern Europe and the CIS will gain competitive advantage over those firms that wait.

The Pacific Rim/China

In the fall of 1990, *Fortune* magazine published a special issue entitled "Asia: Mega-Market of the 1990's." An advertisement in that issue by the California Department of Commerce stated that the Pacific Basin was a $4 trillion market growing at $5 billion per week.[73] Some statistics indicate the rising importance of the Pacific region:

[73] Advertisement by the California Department of Commerce in a special issue of *Fortune* 122, no. 8 (Fall 1990), inside front cover.

- Steel consumption is higher in the Pacific Rim region than in the United States and in Europe.
- Within two years, Asia's demand for semiconductors will exceed that of the European Community (EC).
- By the end of the 1990s, the Pacific Rim economies will be bigger in total than those of the EC and about the same as those of North America.
- Asia is the world's best market for cars, telecommunications equipment, paint, and many other products.
- Asian manufacturers, excluding Japan, have captured 25 percent of the world's market for personal computers.[74]

Pacific Rim Countries Have Different Logistics Systems

Firms involved in importing from or exporting to the Pacific Rim region, those outsourcing materials from the region, and those interested in entering markets in that part of the globe recognize that differences in economics, politics, and culture greatly influence business activities in specific Asian countries. Ranging from the affluence of Japan to the poverty of Indonesia and China, the region offers a myriad of immense problems and significant opportunities for companies.

Firms marketing products to Japan, South Korea, Hong Kong, and other industrialized areas of the Pacific Rim will find logistics environments that are similar to those found in North America and the European Community. While cultures and politics are different, transportation infrastructures are developed, a variety of warehousing options exist, the use of automated systems is widespread, and customer service concepts are understood and accepted by logistics service providers.[75]

Such cannot be said for underdeveloped countries of the Pacific Rim and Asia, such as China. In China, most logistics activities are handled by the government. The economy is characterized by materials shortages, planned distribution by the government, and a dual pricing system (planned prices and market prices).[76] Logistically, China can be described as follows:

> The technological level of logistics is still relatively low in China and only a small number of materials enterprises have computers. The 10,000 such enterprises under the government departments had only 1,200 computers at the end of 1987. The computers are mostly used to compile statistics and are not connected to form a network in the service of transactions. There are also only

---

[74] Louis Kraar, "The Rising Power of the Pacific," Special Issue of *Fortune* 122, no. 8 (Fall 1990), pp. 8–9.

[75] See "The Art of Distribution in Japan," *Traffic Management* 28, no. 12 (December 1989), pp. 75A-79A; and Paul S. Bender, "Japan's Distribution Revolution," *Traffic Management* 29, no. 4 (April 1990), p. 61.

[76] Sun Yao-jun and Li Kening, "Materials Distribution and its Reform in China," *Asia Pacific International Journal of Business Logistics* 1, no. 2 (1988), pp. 8–9.

> about 30 automated warehouses in China. The management of materials remains at a relatively low level on industrial enterprises. Advanced management methods, such as MRP, MRPII, and DRP, are not widely known.[77]

Firms penetrating the Chinese market will find great difficulties logistically. Conditions are changing for the better, much as in Eastern Europe and the CIS. However, the process will be very slow, requiring great patience both managerially and financially. Involvement in countries like China will not show significant payback for many years, and firms will not be able to utilize the same financial criteria in evaluating Chinese logistics efficiencies as in other parts of the world.

MAQUILADORA OPERATIONS

Many firms throughout the world have become involved in global manufacturing; that is, they have manufacturing facilities located in various parts of the world. When firms have multiple plant locations, they face different logistics constraints and opportunities.

Global Manufacturing Has Many Advantages

The major advantage of producing products throughout the world is that a firm has greater opportunities to reduce the costs of production, especially the labor component.

> Many opportunities for production sharing currently exist and are actively taken advantage of by global manufacturers. While American manufacturers have traditionally focused on the Pacific Basin countries when establishing production sharing facilities, they are increasingly active in setting up production sharing facilities in the Caribbean Basin, Mexico, South America, and even in some European countries. Similarly, Japanese firms have taken advantage of low-cost labor in other Pacific Basin countries and have recently begun establishing a presence in Mexico. Likewise, European companies have set up many production facilities in Mexico and are beginning to take advantage of the new production opportunities that are becoming available in Eastern Europe.[78]

Maquiladora Defined

An example of production sharing is the "maquiladora," or twin plant (also known as in-bond manufacturing), operation. Companies from throughout the world "set up assembly and manufacturing facilities along the Mexican side of the U.S.-Mexican border. The production sharing aspects . . . are encouraged by special tariff provisions that reduce the duties that would normally be assessed on materials that flow across the border."[79]

From a logistics perspective, maquiladora operations affect the costs of performing various logistics activities. Generally, costs for documentation,

---

[77] Ibid., p. 11.

[78] Stanley E. Fawcett, "Logistics and Manufacturing Issues in Maquiladora Operations," *International Journal of Physical Distribution and Logistics Management* 20, no. 4 (1990), p. 13, © MCB University Press Limited.

[79] Ibid.

inventory, sourcing, and transportation are higher in maquiladoras than in domestic-only operations. Order processing, packaging, and warehousing costs tend to be the same or slightly lower in maquiladoras.[80] Therefore, the logistics executive will often see logistics costs increase when the firm is involved in maquiladora operations. In total, however, because of the significantly lower labor costs in manufacturing, the total cost to the firm will be lower.

The logistics, as well as manufacturing, implications of maquiladoras need to be considered by any firm planning the establishment of twin plant operations. Over 1,600 U.S. firms utilize maquiladora operations in Mexico, and that number is increasing each year.[81] As international sourcing and manufacturing options are evaluated by firms in their search to gain competitive advantage, the maquiladora operation will continue to be a viable option for many companies.

SUMMARY

More and more companies are expanding their operations into the international sector. As firms locate and service customer markets in various countries, they must establish logistics systems to provide the products and services demanded. While the components of a global logistics system may be the same as in a domestic system, the management and administration of the international network can be vastly different.

To be a global company, management must be able to coordinate a complex set of activities—marketing, production, financing, procurement—so that least total cost logistics is realized. This will allow the firm to achieve maximum market impact and competitive advantage in its international target markets.

In this chapter we examined some of the reasons firms expand into global markets. Companies that do so have four principle strategies available: exporting, licensing, joint ventures, and ownership. As part of the exporting process, we discussed the specific roles of the export distributor, customshouse broker, international freight forwarder, and trading company. In addition, we looked at the importance of documentation and the use of free trade zones.

The international logistics manager must administer the various logistics components in a marketplace characterized by a number of uncontrollable elements—political and legal, economic, competitive, technological,

---

[80] Ibid., p. 17; also see U.S. International Trade Commission, *The U.S.-Mexican Border Industrialization Program: Use and Economic Impact of TSUS Items 806.3 and 807.0* (Washington, D.C.: Government Printing Office, January 1988), p. 500.

[81] "Double-Stacks Head South of the Border," *Traffic Management* 29, no. 6 (June 1990), p. 19.

geographical, and social and cultural. Within the uncontrollable environment the manager attempts to optimize the firm's cost/service mix. A number of differences exist between countries in administering logistics activities.

We examined the financial aspects of global logistics. Since logistics management is concerned with the costs associated with supplying a given level of service to foreign customers, it is important to recognize the factors which influence the costs of carrying out the process.

Some global market opportunities for companies in various regions of the world—Europe, the CIS (the former Soviet Union)/Eastern Europe, the Pacific Rim/China—were identified and discussed. In addition to identifying some of the opportunities within each of those world regions, we presented the many challenges or disadvantages facing firms attempting to penetrate those markets.

Finally, maquiladora, or twin plant, operations were examined, with emphasis given to the logistics implications of U.S. firms locating assembly and manufacturing facilities in Mexico.

With the first 17 chapters as background, we are now ready to develop an overall strategic logistics plan for a firm. This is the topic of the final chapter of this book, Chapter 18.

SUGGESTED READINGS

BOVET, D. "Logistics Strategies for Europe in the '90s." *Planning Review* 19, no. 4 (July/August 1991), pp. 12–18.

COPACINO, WILLIAM C., AND FRANK F. BRITT. "Perspectives on Global Logistics." *The International Journal of Logistics Management* 2, no. 1 (1991), pp. 35–41.

DEMPSEY, WILLIAM, AND RICHARD A. LANCIONI. "How to Improve Your International Customer Service." *Management Decision* 28, no. 3 (1990), pp. 35–38.

"Europe 1992: A Special Report." *Transportation & Distribution* 31, no. 2 (February 1990), pp. 17–38.

FAWCETT, STANLEY E., AND LAURA M. BIROU. "Exploring the Logistics Interface between Global and JIT Sourcing." *International Journal of Physical Distribution and Logistics Management* 22, no. 1 (1992), pp. 3–14.

GARREAU, ALAIN, ROBERT LIEB, AND ROBERT MILLEN. "JIT and Corporate Transport: An International Comparison." *International Journal of Physical Distibution and Logistics Management* 21, no. 1 (1991), pp. 42–47.

GILMORE, JAMES H. "Designing a Distribution Strategy for Canada." *CCA White Paper* published by Cleveland Consulting Associates, undated, 12 pages.

GILMOUR, PETER. *The Management of Distribution: An Australian Framework*, 2d ed., Melbourne, Australia: Longman Chesire Pty Limited, 1987, 302 pages.

HAGGERTY, BETSY. "How to Package Goods for International Transportation." *Inbound Logistics* 5, no. 4 (October 1985), pp. 21–26.

HAMEL, GARY, AND C. K. PRAHALAD. "Do You Really Have a Global Strategy?" *Harvard Business Review* 63, no. 4 (July-August 1985), pp. 139–48.

JONAS, NORMAN. "The Hollow Corporation." *Business Week* 2935 (March 3, 1986), pp. 56–59.

KOGUT, BRUCE. "Designing Global Strategies: Comparative and Competitive Value-Added Chains." *Sloan Management Review* 26, no. 4 (Summer 1985), pp. 15–28.

LIONEL-MARIE, HERVE. "Shipping Overseas." *Logistics Spectrum* 23, no. 1 (Spring 1989), pp. 41–44.

LOUTER, PIETER J., COK OUWERKERK, AND BEN A. BAKKER. "An Inquiry Into Successful Exporting." *European Journal of Marketing* 25, no. 6 (1991), pp. 7–23.

MACDONALD, MITCHELL E. "Who Does What in International Shipping." *Traffic Management* 30, no. 9 (September 1991), pp. 38–40.

MCDANIEL, WILLIAM R., AND EDGAR W. KOSSACK. "The Financial Benefits of Users of Foreign-Trade Zones." *Columbia Journal of World Business* 18, no. 3 (Fall 1983), pp. 33–41.

MCKEON, JOSEPH E. "Outsourcing Begins In-House." *Transportation & Distribution* 32, no. 9 (September 1991), pp. 24–28.

RINEHART, LLOYD M. "Global Logistics Partnership Negotiation." *International Journal of Physical Distribution and Logistics Management* 22, no. 1 (1992), pp. 27–34.

ROBERTS, JOHN H. "Formulating and Implementing a Global Logistics Strategy." *The International Journal of Logistics Management* 1, no. 2 (1990), pp. 53–58.

SAMIEE, SAEED, AND KENDALL ROTH. "The Influence of Global Marketing Standardization on Performance." *Journal of Marketing* 56, no. 2 (April 1992), pp. 1–17.

TERPSTRA, VERN. "The Chinese Look to World Markets." *International Marketing Review* 5, no. 2 (Summer 1988), pp. 7–19.

U.S. DEPARTMENT OF COMMERCE. *A Basic Guide to Exporting*. Washington, D.C.: U.S. Government Printing Office, September 1986, 148 pages.

VAN DER HOOP, HANS. "Europhobia or Europhoria?" *Distribution* 87, no. 10 (October 1988), pp. 38–46.

VOORHEES, ROY DALE, AND JOHN I. COPPETT. "Logistics and Strategy in Global War and Worldwide Trade." *Logistics Spectrum* 22, no. 4 (Winter 1988), pp. 27–31.

WIGGIN, PETER. "Europe, All Together." *Sky Magazine* 20, no. 6 (June 1991), pp. 10–19.

WOOD, DONALD F. "Toward a Channels Theory of International Logistics." *Proceedings of the Eighteenth Annual Transportation and Logistics Educators Conference*, eds. James M. Masters and Cynthia L. Coykendale, 1989, pp. 98–113.

WORTZEL, HEIDI VERNON. "The Logistics of Distribution in China." *International Journal of Physical Distribution and Materials Management* 15, no. 5 (1985), pp. 51–60.

ZINN, WALTER, AND ROBERT E. GROSSE. "Barriers to Globalization: Is Global Distribution Possible?" *The International Journal of Logistics Management* 1, no. 1 (1990), pp. 13–18.

QUESTIONS AND PROBLEMS

1. An increasing number of firms are becoming involved in international marketing. Discuss the factors that would influence a company to enter international markets.
2. Companies which enter into the global marketplace have four principal channel strategies available to them: (*a*) exporting, (*b*) licensing, (*c*) joint ventures, and (*d*) ownership. Briefly discuss each strategy and include the advantages and disadvantages of each alternative.
3. Explain the role each of the following exporting organizations has in global logistics:
   a. Export distributor.
   b. Customshouse broker.
   c. International freight forwarder.
   d. Trading company.
4. Explain how it is usually more difficult for a firm to provide the same level of customer service in its international markets that it provides in its domestic markets.
5. Identify the factors that make the packaging component of the logistics process so much more important in international systems than in domestic logistics systems.
6. Discuss the relative importance of inventories in domestic and global logistics. In your response, consider the financial impact of inventory decisions on the strategic position of the firm.
7. Discuss how "letters of credit" are used in international business transactions and identify why they are important to the logistics executive.
8. Briefly identify the opportunities and challenges facing firms seeking to market products in the following regions:
   a. Europe
   b. The Commonwealth of Independent States (CIS)/Eastern Europe
   c. The Pacific Rim/China

Chapter 18

The Strategic Logistics Plan

Objectives of This Chapter

To show how the logistics audit can be used to formulate logistics objectives and strategy

To show how to develop a strategic logistics plan

To identify future challenges that the logistics professional will face

INTRODUCTION

A number of factors promise to make the 1990s a period of challenge and opportunity for the logistics executive. The high cost associated with logistics activities, the fact that most firms are competing in mature markets, and the concern for customer satisfaction have resulted in increased top management awareness of the importance of logistics in attaining corporate profit objectives. In addition, globalization of supply sources, production, demand, and competition has led to increased interest in logistics on the part of top management. The challenges and opportunities for the logistics professional have never been greater. In order to successfully meet these challenges and capitalize on the opportunities, logistics executives must become involved in the strategic planning process. In this chapter we will look at the importance of the logistics audit and trace the development of a strategic logistics plan. In addition, future challenges that the logistics executive will face will be identified and explored.

WHAT IS STRATEGIC PLANNING?

Cooper, Innis, and Dickson defined strategic planning as follows:

> The process of identifying the long-term goals of the entity (where we want to be) and the broad steps necessary to achieve these goals over a long-term horizon (how to get there), incorporating the concerns and future expectations of the major stakeholders.[1]

The mission statement and strategic plan provide direction and control for tactical plans and daily operations. The company's management may decide that the long-term goal is to achieve a sustainable competitive advantage by focusing on customer requirements and capitalizing on opportunities in the marketplace. "The strategic plan should anticipate the service expectations of both current and future customers."[2] The strategic plan-

---

[1] Martha C. Cooper, Daniel E. Innis and Peter Dickson, *Strategic Planning for Logistics* (Oak Brook, Ill.: Council of Logistics Management, 1992), p. 3.

[2] Ibid.

ning process should also include the financial implications of major shifts in strategy and the resources required.

Logistics strategic planning has been defined as follows:

Logistics Strategic Planning Defined

> A unified, comprehensive, and integrated planning process to achieve competitive advantage through increased value and customer service, which results in superior customer satisfaction (where we want to be), by anticipating future demand for logistics services and managing the resources of the entire supply chain (how to get there). This planning is done within the context of the overall corporate goals and plan.[3]

This definition is comprised of three major elements: "(1) the long-term goals (customer satisfaction, competitive advantage, supply chain management); (2) the means to achieving these goals (value, customer service); and (3) the process for achieving these goals (anticipate, manage, relate to company's goals)."[4] The strategic plan covers a period of five or more years.

THE IMPORTANCE OF PLANNING

Strategic Planning Minimizes Risks in a Changing Environment

The development of a strategic plan, along with its continued evaluation and modification, is essential to long-run profitable business development.[5] The rate of change in the business environment increases the risk of business failure or loss of market position for firms whose management has neglected to consider alternative future scenarios. In the absence of planning, managers must spend a disproportionate amount of their time in the role of "fire fighter"—reacting to crises rather than anticipating change and developing strategies to deal with it.

The Operating Plan and the Strategic Plan

There are basically two types of plans: the operating plan, which covers a period of one or two years, and the strategic plan, which covers a period of five or more years. The strategic plan "can be thought of as a set of guideposts which keep the operating plan on the path to meeting objectives. It is the operating plan which must be programmed in fine detail to demonstrate how the objectives will be reached and to justify the expenditures of the . . . budget."[6]

Planning requires that managers evaluate the probability of various scenarios and anticipate possible problems and opportunities. In the process, management's outlook shifts from crisis management, or reacting to changes in the environment, to planning for change. By planning for change, management can anticipate capital requirements and, when nec-

---

[3] Ibid., pp. 4–5.

[4] Ibid., p. 5.

[5] Portions of this section are from Douglas M. Lambert and James R. Stock, "Strategic Planning for Physical Distribution," *Journal of Business Logistics* 3, no. 2(1982), pp. 26–46.

[6] Mark E. Stern, *Marketing Planning: A Systems Approach* (New York: McGraw-Hill, 1966), p. 4.

essary, arrange financing. Consider the case of a manufacturer that has built its entire freight consolidation program around shipments to the more than 2,000 individual stores of a major retail chain. How should marketing react if, in next year's negotiation, the chain wants deliveries made to its distribution centers in return for a price reduction? A number of questions need to be answered. How important is the chain's business to the firm's overall market penetration objectives? Is the business profitable? Will it be profitable if the new conditions are accepted? What will happen to the cost or frequency of deliveries to the firm's other customers if the chain's conditions are accepted? What will happen to the profitability of nonchain accounts? How important are these accounts to the firm's long-run profitability? What is the chain likely to demand in the future? To respond to the retailer's request in a knowledgeable way, management must answer these questions in advance and include logistics in the planning process. The traditional emphasis on sales might cause many managers, when faced with a similar situation, to protect sales volume and accept the chain's conditions without considering the impact on overall corporate profitability.

A major advantage of planning is that managers establish benchmarks, and therefore can measure their progress and take corrective action. Thus, as Stern has stated, "The plan provides a management philosophy, a day-to-day operating guide, and a basis for measuring both individual and total company performance."[7]

THE CORPORATE PLANNING PROCESS

Marketing and Logistics Must Be Closely Coordinated in the Planning Process

The logistics plan is an important component of the overall corporate plan. As we saw in Chapters 1 and 2, marketing and logistics must be closely coordinated in the planning process. The logistics plan is deeply rooted in the marketing plan, which must be based on corporate objectives and strategy. Figure 18–1 provides a useful framework for visualizing logistics planning within the context of the overall corporate planning process, the channel of distribution, and the firm's environment. It illustrates that all planning must take place within the following constraints:

- The political and legal environment.
- The social and economic environment.
- The technological environment.
- The competitive environment.

A number of steps must be performed in the corporate planning process before the strategic logistics plan can be formulated. They include:

[7] Ibid., p. 4.

FIGURE 18–1 A Model for Design, Evaluation, and Modification of a Distribution Channel

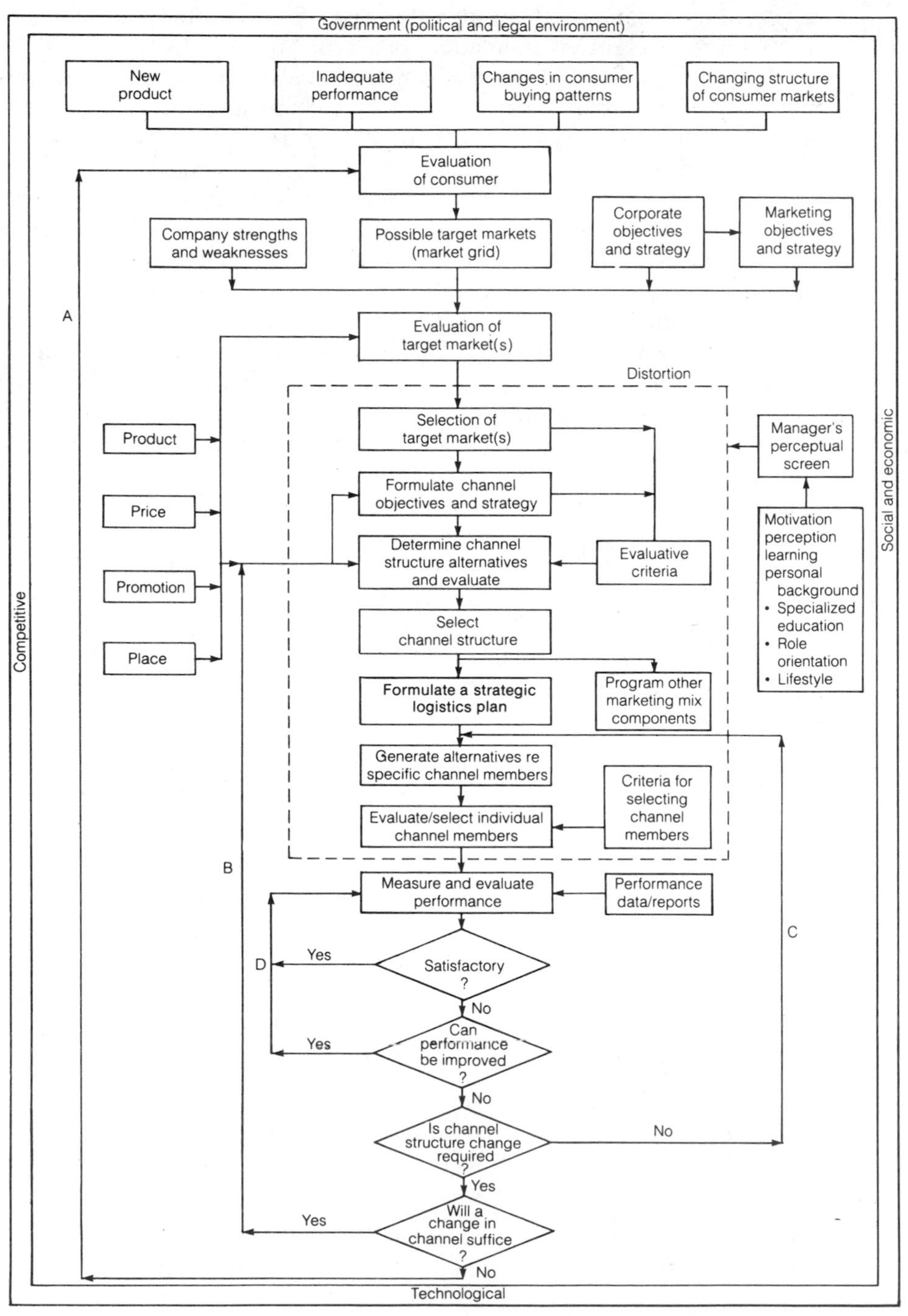

SOURCE: Adapted from Douglas M. Lambert, *The Distribution Channels Decision* (New York: National Association of Accountants, and Hamilton, Ontario: The Society of Management Accountants of Canada, 1978), pp. 44–45, 112–13.

Steps in the Corporate Planning Process

- Evaluation of consumer and/or industrial customer needs.
- Identification of possible target markets.
- Evaluation of target markets.
- Selection of target markets.
- Formulation of channel objectives and strategy.
- Identification and evaluation of channel structure alternatives.
- Selection of the channel structure.

While the example used to illustrate the planning process is a consumer good viewed from the manufacturer's perspective, the model applies equally to other channel participants such as retailers and wholesalers as well as to industrial products and services.

Evaluation of the Consumer and Identification of Potential Target Markets

Evaluation of the consumer can be triggered by one or more of the following: a new product introduction; inadequate performance in terms of market share, sales volume, profitability, and return on investment; changing consumer buying patterns; or the changing structure of consumer markets. At this point, management must determine if it will be possible to satisfy the needs of a large enough segment of customers, the *target market,* to generate the desired rate of return. Meaningful customer groups or segments have to be defined so that the following questions can be answered:

- Who buys or will buy?
- Why do customers buy?
- When do customers buy?
- Where do customers buy?
- What services do they require?
- How do they buy?
- What is the competitive environment in each of these segments?

A competitive analysis by market segment is more meaningful than an overall competitive analysis, since a competitor's strengths and weaknesses usually vary depending on the market segment in question.

Evaluation and Selection of Target Markets

Once identified, potential target markets must be evaluated and target markets selected giving full consideration to company strengths and weaknesses, such as production capabilities, marketing strengths, and financial resources; corporate objectives and strategy; marketing objectives and strategy; environmental considerations; and the marketing mix required for successful market development. Selection of target markets requires a preliminary profitability analysis of the type introduce in Chapter 3 and shown in Table 3–1 (see page 97). The analysis is based on the cost trade-off framework that we have used throughout this text; it is illustrated once

Selection of Target Markets Requires a Preliminary Profitability Analysis

FIGURE 18–2 Cost Trade-Offs Required in Marketing and Logistics

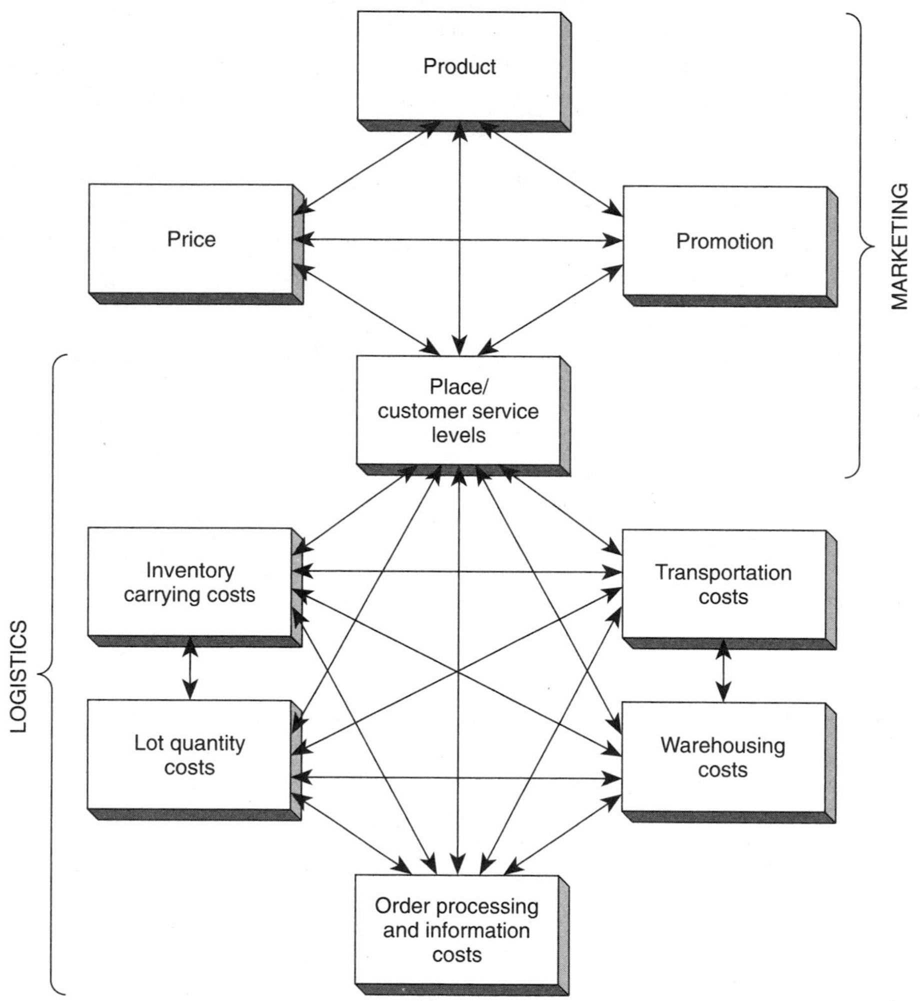

Marketing objective: Allocate resources to the marketing mix to maximize the long-run profitability of the firm.
Logistics objective: Minimize total costs, given the customer service objective, where: Total costs = Transportation costs + Warehousing costs + Order processing and information costs + Lot quantity costs + Inventory carrying costs.

SOURCE: Adapted from Douglas M. Lambert, *The Development of an Inventory Costing Methodology: A Study of the Cost Associated with Holding Inventory* (Chicago: National Council of Physical Distribution Management, 1976), p. 7.

again in Figure 18–2. The total dollars committed to the marketing mix—that is, for product development, promotion, price, and place—influence the ultimate market share, sales volume, and profitability of the firm. The total amount spent on logistics (customer service) is equal to the place expenditure. Management should allocate dollars to the marketing mix and the individual logistics activities in a way that will improve marketing effectiveness and efficiency and result in greater profitability. For example, the decision to use wholesalers to reach retail accounts may lower advertising, selling, and logistics expenditures, but the manufacturer will receive a lower price per unit for its products. The channel of distribution selected by the firm will have a significant impact on its profitability.

The goal is to select target markets that promise to generate the highest net segment margin. Only those costs that would change by adding or dropping a segment should be included in the profitability analysis.

Formulation of Channel Objectives and Strategy

With target markets selected, the next step is to formulate channel objectives and strategy. A channel of distribution can be defined as the collection of organizational units, internal and external to the firm, that perform the functions involved in product marketing. These functions are pervasive; they include buying, selling, transporting, sorting, grading, financing, bearing market risk, and providing marketing information.[8] A firm that performs one or more of the marketing functions becomes a member of the distribution channel.

The Marketing Functions

Channel objectives flow from the firm's marketing objectives. Specific marketing objectives include market coverage objectives and customer service objectives at the retail level that give full consideration to product characteristics that may limit channel alternatives. Channel strategy is the specific plan that management will use to achieve its objectives. For example, consumer advertising can be used to "pull" the product through the channel of distribution, or discounts can be offered in order to encourage wholesalers and retailers to "push" the product to consumers. In addition, management may wish to perform certain functions internally and "spin off" other functions to external channel members. There are a number of potential strategies available. It is important that logistics executive be involved in the formulation of channel objectives and strategy, since logistics costs affect the efficiency of the channel and logistics considerations affect channel effectiveness.

---

[8]Fred E. Clark, *Principles of Marketing* (New York: Macmillan, 1923), p. 11; and Robert Bartels, *Marketing Theory and Metatheory* (Homewood, Ill.: Richard D. Irwin, 1970), pp. 166–75.

Identification and Evaluation of Channel Structure Alternatives

Marketing Functions May Be Performed Internally or Externally

The nature of the channel structure affects the speed and consistency of delivery and communications, the control of the functions' performance, and the cost of operations. In selecting a channel or channels of distribution management may choose to perform all of the marketing functions internally, or it may choose to have one or more of the functions performed by external channel members. A number of alternatives are presumed to be available to the channel designer. However, in most cases not all channel alternatives are known or available when the decisions must be made. In fact, in some instances there may be "an extremely limited choice of types of middlemen."[9] Consequently, the decisions may be less than optimal. Even if management makes the optimal channel decision at a particular time, unforeseen environmental changes may lead to a reevaluation of the decision.

Selection of the Channel Structure

Potential Profitability Is Important When Selecting Channel Structure

Various alternative channel structures should be evaluated in detail, using segment profitability reports in the format introduced in Table 3–1 (page 97). Management should select the alternatives that best satisfy corporate and marketing objectives. Multiple channels may be used to satisfy an objective of national coverage. For example, in some geographic areas the volume of business may permit direct sales to retailers, while in other areas corporate return on investment objectives can be met only when wholesalers or distributors are utilized. Logistics considerations affect both the efficiency and effectiveness of individual channel structures, and must be included in the selection process.

Finally, management must program the various components of the marketing mix. It is at this point that the strategic logistics plan is formulated.

Formulation of the Strategic Logistics Plan

The development of an effective logistics plan depends on several key inputs from marketing, manufacturing, finance/accounting, and logistics.

Marketing Input

Marketing must provide the proposed product, pricing, and promotional strategies for each channel of distribution used. This will include full knowledge of the *product line,* complete with planned product introductions and product deletions; *pricing programs,* including volume discounts and

---

[9] Phillip McVey, "Are Channels of Distribution What the Textbooks Say?" *Journal of Marketing* 24, no. 1 (January 1960), p. 62. See also Douglas M. Lambert, *The Distribution Channels Decision* (New York: National Association of Accountants, and Hamilton, Ontario: The Society of Management Accountants of Canada, 1978).

terms of sale; planned *promotions and sales incentive programs;* forecast *monthly sales volumes* by geographic area, by type of account, and by customer, if available; and, *customer service policies* by type of account and geographic area. The planned customer service policies are especially significant to the logistics strategist, who should be involved in establishing them. Customer service policies should include the following elements on a customer class or geographic area basis: the method of order transmittal, order entry, and order processing; the desired order cycle time; the acceptable level of variability in order cycle time; the level of in-stock availability; policies on expediting and transshipment; and product substitution policies.

Manufacturing Input

Manufacturing should provide a list of production facilities, including manufacturing capabilities and the planned production for each product. When products can be manufactured at more than one plant, logistics and manufacturing must determine where products can be produced most economically, giving full consideration to the sales forecast and the necessary cost trade-offs.

Finance/Accounting Input

Finance/accounting is the source of the cost data required to perform segmental analysis and cost trade-off analysis. In addition, finance/accounting must provide information on corporate hurdle rates and the availability of capital to finance logistics assets such as inventory, facilities, and equipment.

Logistics Input

Logistics must provide information that describes the existing logistics network in terms of product storage locations at plants and in the field; transportation linkages between vendors and plants, plants and distribution centers, and distribution centers and customers; and the operating characteristics of the distribution centers in terms of size, volume, and product mix. In addition, logistics must identify the costs associated with materials flow and storage.

Typically, the costs required from logistics include fixed and variable costs for storage and handling by location; transportation costs by link in the channel of distribution; order processing costs; inventory carrying costs; and purchasing/acquisition costs.

Components of the Strategic Logistics Plan

The strategic logistics plan should consist of the following:[10]

1. A *management overview,* describing the logistics strategy in general terms and its relationship to the other major business functions.
2. A *statement of the logistics objectives* related to cost and service for both products and customers.
3. A *description of the individual customer service, inventory, warehousing,*

[10] Adapted from Robert E. Murray, "Strategic Distribution Planning: Structuring the Plan," *Proceedings of the Eighteenth Annual Conference of the National Council of Physical Distribution Management,* 1980, pp. 220–21.

order processing, and transportation strategies necessary to support the overall plan.

4. An *outline of the major logistics programs or operational plans* described in sufficient detail to document plans, related costs, timing, and their business impact.
5. A *forecast* of the necessary work force and capital requirements.
6. A *logistics financial statement* detailing operating costs, capital requirements, and cash flow.
7. A description of the *business impact of the logistics strategy,* in terms of corporate profits, customer service performance, and the impact on other business functions.

Evaluation and Selection of Individual Logistics Channel Members

Once it establishes the strategic logistics plan, management must develop operational procedures or methods for carrying it out. It is at this stage that management must develop alternatives with respect to individual channel members such as carriers and warehousers. Channel members must be evaluated and those that satisfy the evaluative criteria selected. Criteria for channel member selection and evaluation were discussed in previous chapters of this text, beginning with Chapter 3.

Performance Evaluation and Channel Modification

Performance Measurement Is Critical for Success

Successful implementation of the strategic logistics plan requires that performance be measured on a timely basis and changes made when performance is not satisfactory. Total channel performance should be measured using the profitability analysis framework shown in Table 3–1 (page 97).

When performance is not satisfactory, management must determine whether performance can be improved with existing channel members. If performance can be improved, management must make the required changes and continue to monitor performance (see Loop D in Figure 18–1). If performance cannot be improved with the existing channel participants and a structural change is not required, management should consider alternative channel members and select a replacement(s) (see Loop C in Figure 18–1). If a replacement is not available or a change in the logistics channel structure is required, channel objectives and strategy must be reviewed, and the planning process repeated at that point (see Loop B in Figure 18–1). However, if a change in the logistics structure does not yield the necessary level of performance, management must repeat the entire planning process (see Loop A in Figure 18–1). In any case, the strategic logistics plan should be reevaluated each year to accommodate changes in consumer needs, marketing strategy, the economic environment, the competitive environment, governmental regulation, and available corporate resources.

The logistics planning process is a natural extension of the corporate planning process. The remainder of this chapter is devoted to a detailed discussion of how to develop a strategic logistics plan.

DEVELOPING A STRATEGIC LOGISTICS PLAN

Requirements of a Strategic Logistics Plan

The development of a strategic logistics plan requires the following:[11]

- A thorough understanding and appreciation of corporate strategies and marketing plans, in order to provide sound strategic planning recommendations and move toward a logistics system that balances cost and service effectiveness.
- A customer service study to determine what elements of service are viewed as key, how service is measured, what levels of performance are expected, and how the firm's performance compares to that of specific competitors.
- Identification of the total costs associated with alternative logistics systems to identify the lowest cost network that meets corporate, marketing, and customer requirements.

When overall corporate strategies and marketing plans have been determined, the logistics planner must evaluate basic alternatives and recommend the system configuration that satisfies customer requirements at lowest total cost. Consequently, the process must begin with identifying and documenting customer service goals and strategies. Management can use a customer service survey to determine the specific needs and requirements of the firm's customers—as well as the firm's performance compared to that of competitors. The survey can be supplemented with face-to-face interviews. The plan must consider the specific requirements of customers, competitive service levels, changing environmental conditions, and the amount of service that the company is willing to offer.

In many companies, collecting such information may be a difficult process. It is here that the logistics audit, first described in Chapter 2, can be of significant benefit.

The Logistics Audit[12]

An audit program should be conducted on a routine basis, although the length of time between audits may vary among firms. One reason for the logistics audit is to develop a data base that can be used to evaluate the various components of the logistics operating system in order to identify productivity improvements. Consequently, it is necessary to identify,

[11] Murray, "Strategic Distribution Planning," p. 216.

[12] This section is adapted from Jay U. Sterling and Douglas M. Lambert, "A Methodology for Assessing Logistics Operating Systems," *International Journal of Physical Distribution and Materials Management* 15, no. 6 (1985), pp. 1–44.

collect, and analyze the data that will best describe current costs and customer service levels. When conducting a logistics audit in a manufacturing environment, management should take the following steps:

The Steps that Should Be Taken When Conducting a Logistics Audit

1. A "task force" should be established to assist in the review process.
2. Current corporate strategies and objectives that could affect, or be affected by, logistics must be determined.
3. Key questions should be constructed by the task force to serve as a basis for both internal and external audit interviews, for identifying weaknesses in the current system, and for recommending improvements.
4. Critical variables and measurements that are accurate, reliable, and efficient must be identified and conceptualized by major customer segments.
5. An *external* audit of customer perspectives and requirements should be undertaken to determine the firm's performance, competitive practices and performance, and the specific levels of service required.
6. An *internal audit* of current logistics performance should be conducted. This audit involves two distinct processes:
   a. Personal interviews with representatives from various functions throughout the firm.
   b. Sampling of firm records and transaction data so that the existing operating system can be statistically analyzed and performance accurately described.
7. Cost and service trade-off alternatives must be identified and analyzed.
8. The questions identified in step 3 must be addressed, and improvements and changes to the current system identified and recommended to management,
9. The system that will exist after the recommended changes should be described, and expected performance predicted.

Figure 18–3 summarizes these steps. The process is described in the following sections.

The Logistics Task Force. Firms should use a task force approach because members of the task force are directly involved in the decision-making process and recognize that they are responsible for implementing the recommendations. The task force approach leads to a level of commitment that is not possible when recommended strategies and system changes are proposed by an outside agency, or by an individual within the firm who is not involved in the actual day-to-day operations of the function.

The Task Force Should Include Representatives from Logistics and Other Corporate Functions

Two types of individuals need to be included in the task force: those involved in managing logistics activities such as traffic, warehousing, private fleet operations, customer service, and inventory management; and those representing other corporate functions that regularly interact with logistics. Consequently, representatives from the controller's office, market-

FIGURE 18–3 The Logistics Audit: A Conceptual Model

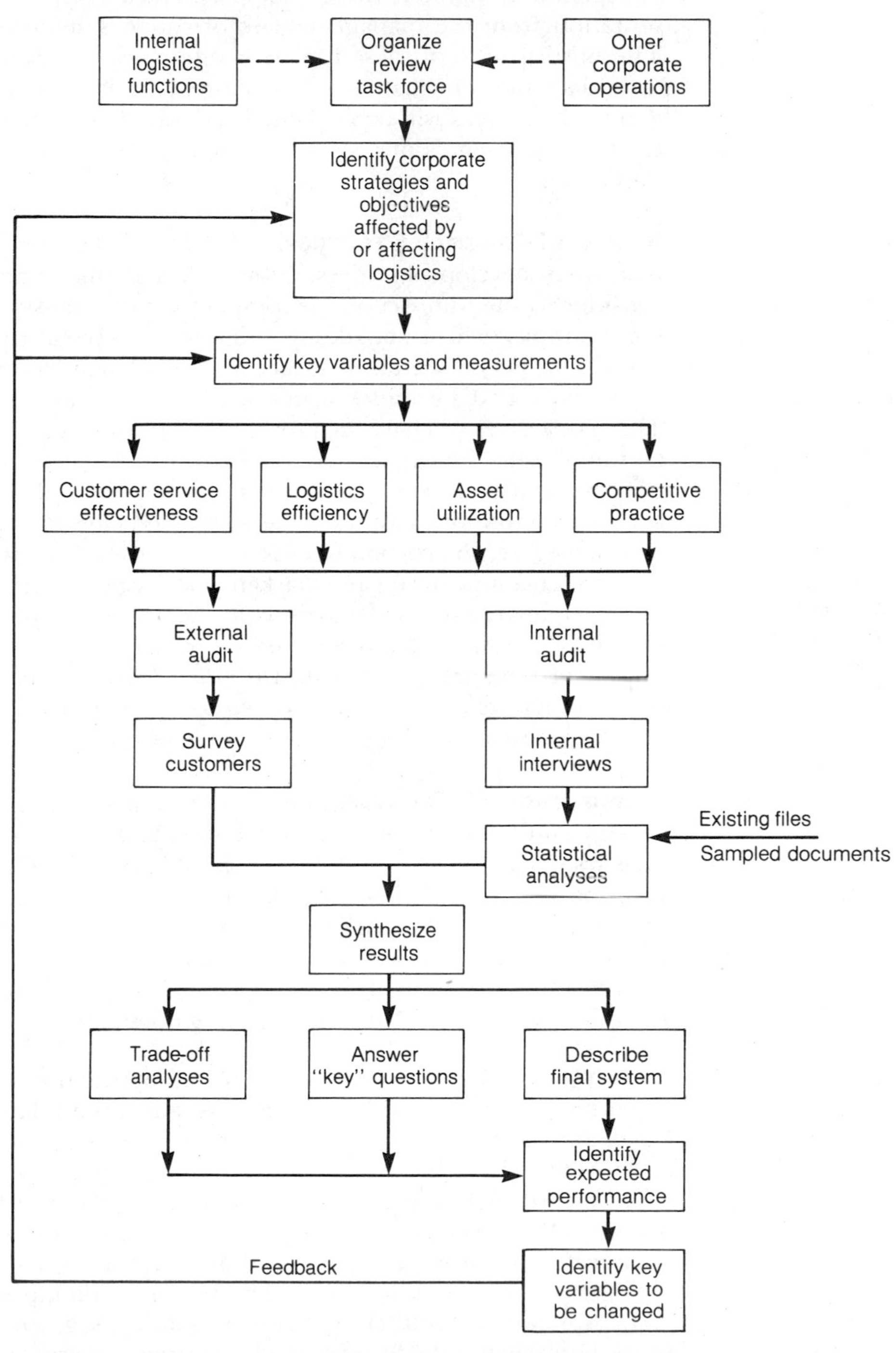

SOURCE: Jay U. Sterling and Douglas M. Lambert, "A Methodology for Assessing Logistics Operating Systems," *International Journal of Physical Distribution and Materials Management* 15, no. 6 (1985), p. 13.

ing/sales, and manufacturing should be asked to participate. Also, representation from the management information systems area is important. The participation of these functions offers several advantages: corporate-wide data and information will be more accessible; cooperation across organizational areas will be facilitated; broader perspectives will evolve; and final recommendations will be more practical and more easily implemented.

Review of Company Strategies. Too frequently, one function of a company may develop objectives, strategies, and operating systems without considering their impact on the company's overall mission and stated goals. For example, a firm may desire to grow 15 percent a year, achieve a 10 percent profit before taxes, target new investment returns at 25 percent after taxes, and introduce a minimum of five new products each year. These objectives will have an impact on every activity and output controlled by the logistics function. It is useless to propose an expanded warehouse network if the projected return (ROI) would be only 10 percent or the additional inventories would decrease profits below the targeted level.

Three Good Reasons for Reviewing Company Strategies

Therefore, the corporate mission, the firm's goals and objectives, and the firm's manufacturing and marketing strategies must be analyzed during the preliminary phases of a logistics audit. This procedure helps to identify (1) critical questions that need to be addressed during subsequent interview phases of the audit; (2) key measurements that will be used to compare current logistics performance with customer requirements; and (3) potential alternative strategies.

Construction of Key Questions. Before attempting to interview customers and internal operating personnel, and before measuring current logistics performance, the task force should prepare a list of questions that, if properly resolved, will enable the company to achieve a distinct competitive advantage in the markets it serves. These questions should be broad in scope, so that they do not restrict the task force's charter. They must consider the corporate mission and goals, and address the individual concerns of top management. The following questions can serve as examples:

- What changes are likely to occur in the structure of each market segment, and how will these changes affect the relative importance of each segment?
- What distribution systems are competitors currently using, and where might the firm gain a differential advantage?
- Will achievement of the company's current order cycle time and fill rate standards make it a leader in its industry?
- What overall customer service strategies should be developed, and how will these differ by customer (market) segment?
- How should the firm respond in a proactive way to the desire of customers to reduce inventories or other costs?

- What order processing system requirements must the company meet in order to lead the industry in responding to customer needs?
- Should the company utilize a centralized or decentralized/regional warehousing network?
- How can the company improve productivity in its warehouses, and what measurements are required?
- How can transportation costs be reduced without adversely influencing customer service levels?
- Are small orders a problem? How is this likely to change in the future, and what strategies should management employ to minimize the associated costs?
- Should the company expand, contract, or retain its current investment in private carriage?
- What are the best cost-reduction opportunities for the firm's logistics operation?
- How can the company's logistics organization best interface with manufacturing, marketing, and finance/accounting organizations?
- Are there opportunities for consolidating logistics operations of the firm's subsidiaries/independent operating divisions?

Identification of Critical Variables. Once the key questions have been identified, the task force can identify specific variables and measurements that, if available, will enable it to successfully answer the questions and begin to restructure the firm's logistics strategies. These variables involve both quantitative and qualitative data, and can be grouped into four broad categories:

Four Categories of Variables Must Be Identified

1. Customer service *effectiveness,* such as:
   - Order cycle time, in total and for each component of the order cycle.
   - Fill rate (percent ordered versus delivered).
   - Order cycle consistency (variance in delivery time).
   - Response capabilities to customer inquiries.
   - Ability to adjust order quantities.
   - Ability to change requested delivery dates.
   - Ability to interact with production schedules.
   - Ability to substitute or back order line items.
2. Logistics *efficiency* (costs) associated with each of the following functional activities:
   - Transportation.
   - Warehousing.
   - Inventory management.
   - Production planning and scheduling.
   - Purchasing.
   - Order entry and order processing.
3. *Utilization* of assets, such as:
   - Inventories.

- Warehousing facilities.
- Private carriage operations.

4. *Competitive practices* and performance with respect to customer service attributes and asset utilization.

External Audit. The external audit may be comprised of a comprehensive mail survey, as described in Chapter 4, or selected in-depth interviews with customers who represent the different market segments served, such as original equipment manufacturers, private-label retailers, wholesalers, or large mass merchant retailers; differences in annual dollar volumes purchased; and geographic location. A primary purpose is to replicate the firm's overall business/product mix. This is accomplished by collecting specific information regarding the interaction between vendor and customer logistics systems, as well as determining the logistics/customer service effectiveness of major competitors. Inquiries should be made concerning both the *current* and *future* competitive environment and customer service requirements. The logistics audit will include a number of basic questions as well as unique industry/situation-specific questions. Table 18–1 provides a sample of the basic inquiries that need to be included in a competitive analysis.

Many of the questions in Table 18–1 can be further segregated by customer segment, made-to-order versus made-to-stock products, channel segments, or product line/product group. Ideally, the identity of the firm should not be disclosed during the interview process, so that objective, industrywide data can be collected. For this reason, the assistance of university researchers or consultants is frequently preferable when conducting a logistics audit. The in-depth interviews may provide enough data to proceed with the development of a logistics strategy, or management may use them as the basis of a comprehensive mail survey of the type described in Chapter 4.

Internal Audit: Personal Interviews. In addition to using the external audit, those analyzing logistics performance should collect information from in-depth interviews with the firm's management. Specifically, formal interview guides need to be prepared for each of the following management functions:

Formal Interview Guides Need to Be Prepared for Each of These Functions

- Customer service/order administration.
- Transportation (inbound and outbound).
- Warehousing operations.
- Inventory management and forecasting.
- Production planning and scheduling.
- Purchasing/procurement.
- Marketing/sales.
- Financial control/accounting.
- Data processing.

TABLE 18–1 Sample Questions in a Competitive Analysis

1. How often do you order products from your major vendors?
2. What are the typical sizes of these orders?
3. What are the typical lead times encountered when replenishing inventories from your major vendors?
4. What percentage of the product ordered is normally delivered by your requested delivery date?
5. What lead time would you prefer?
6. What percentage of your orders are eventually delivered, and how long does it typically take to receive all of your order?
7. What is the current performance by each of your major vendors with respect to order cycle (lead) time and fill rate?
8. If a supplier is unable to commit to an order by your requested "date wanted," what percentage of the time do you:
   a. Cancel your order?
   b. Back order with supplier?
   c. Request substitution?
   d. Back order and also submit to a second source?
9. What percentage of the time do you use the following techniques to transmit orders to your major suppliers:
   a. On-line terminal?
   b. Inward WATS telephone service?
   c. Telephone paid by you?
   d. Mail?
   e. Fax
   f. Hand-deliver to salesperson?
10. Do any of your suppliers use a "scheduled delivery" program? Which one(s)?
11. What percentage of your orders would you classify as emergency (ship as soon as possible)?
12. Do any of your major suppliers furnish you with any of the following written information/reports on a regular basis:
    a. Confirmation notices on orders submitted?
    b. Open order status reports?
    c. Product availability/inventory status data?
    d. Advance notice of shipping information?
13. Do any of your major suppliers offer incentives, such as prepaid freight, quantity discounts, claims handling for damage, or extended payment terms, for ordering in larger quantities?
14. What type of terms do your major suppliers offer? What terms do you prefer?
15. How many supplier sources do you normally use when purchasing your major components/products?
16. What criteria do you use to select suppliers?
17. How has the number of vendors with whom you regularly do business changed in the past three years?
18. How do you anticipate this will change in the future?
19. What are the distinguishing features or services of those suppliers who consistently provide you with desired/satisfactory customer service as compared to those who do not?
20. How have your major suppliers improved their customer service, deliveries, and information with respect to your orders in the past 12 to 18 months?
21. What services would you like suppliers to provide with respect to logistics/customer service that are not presently available to you?
22. What are the normal/published lead times that you provide to *your* customers?
23. What method do your customers use to submit their orders to you?
24. Have you experienced, or are you experiencing, any changes in the ordering characteristics of your customers?
25. Do you have a computerized inventory record-keeping/customer order status system that identifies balance on hand, on order, and on back order by individual items?
26. What are your annual inventory turnovers by SKU, product, and product line?
27. Do you use, or are you contemplating using, a "Just-in-Time/zero inventory" concept in managing your inventories, or when ordering from your major vendors?
28. Do you perform trade-off analysis to weigh the economics of quantity discounts or forward buys against the added inventory carrying costs?
29. Do you attempt to carry different levels of safety stock for fast movers as compared to low-volume items?
30. What has been your average annual growth rate during the *past* five years? What do you anticipate this percentage will be in the *next* five years?
31. Have you made any significant changes in the way you order materials from your major vendors during the past 12 to 18 months?

Sample interview guides are included in Appendixes A through I. They include the most important questions that need to be answered during the internal audit interviews.

Internal Audit: Sampling of Firm's Records. Various types of source documents can serve as a basis for the quantitative phase of a logistics audit. They can be obtained by modifying or extracting data from existing files, or they can be compiled by using sampling techniques. The following represent possible data sources:

Internal Audit: Possible Data Sources

1. Existing files.
   a. Order history and/or open order files.
   b. Bills of lading and/or shipment manifest data files.
   c. Paid transportation freight bills for both inbound and outbound shipments.
   d. Private fleet trip reports.
   e. Warehouse labor time cards or payroll records.
2. Original documents.
   a. Trailer contents of all incoming and outgoing shipments for a selected time span, by origin and destination ZIP codes, contents, weight, trailer cube percentages, and damage condition upon arrival.
   b. Warehouse labor-hours for receiving, put-away, picking, packing, shipping, housecleaning, and stock rearrangement.
   c. Private fleet data, including routes, miles driven, empty miles, trailer cube percentages, shipment weight, and fixed and variable costs incurred.
   d. Freight charges (pro-bills) paid to common, contract, and rail carriers, compiled by commodity codes, actual weight, deficit weight, mode, carrier name, and origin/destination ZIP codes.
   e. Order cycle and fill rate information extracted from individual orders and/or line items shipped and compiled by customer segment, product group, quantities shipped and ordered, date ordered by customer, date received, date inventory committed/reserved, date released to distribution center, date picked, and date shipped.

The source documents outlined above, and a computer-based statistical package, will make it possible to efficiently perform a wide range of analyses. The output reports from this phase of the methodology can be grouped into the following broad categories:

Categories of Reports that Can Be Developed

- The weight, cube, and commodities/product categories of trailers, boxcars, or vans received at, or shipped from, each of the firm's facilities.

- Channel flow and configuration volumes into and out of each company facility.
- Warehouse labor-hours and dollar amounts by company facility and internal activities.
- Geographic dispersions of receipts (origins) and shipments (destinations).
- Where applicable, routes, miles driven, cost/revenue, and composition of trailers transported by private fleet or contract carriage.
- Inbound and outbound freight volumes shipped by, and paid to, common and contract carriers, grouped by mode, individual carrier, geographic area, and weight break categories.
- Order-history data regarding cycle time and service of supply measurements, such as fill rates and on-time delivery.

To facilitate the various analyses, common coding structures should be developed for all source documents. Common codes provide the ability to identify channel movements, as well as applicable logistics costs and key customer service measurements, for segments such as geographic area, company location, product group, customer, channel member, and in total. Any problems in data collection should be fully documented. The following represents a sample of common coding structures:

An Example of a Coding Structure

1. All transactions should include the first three digits of the postal ZIP code(s) involved.
2. A single digit table of transportation modes involved in all shipments can be compiled, such as:
   a. Private fleet.
   b. Contract carrier.
   c. Common carrier.
   d. Local cartage.
   e. Rail.
   f. TOFC.
   g. Air freight.
   h. Air express parcel service.
   i. Broker.
   j. Freight forwarder.
3. Each of the company's shipping and receiving locations should be identified by a unique code.
4. The name of the carrier involved in the shipment should be identified. This can be accomplished by constructing a three- or four-digit cross-reference coding system.
5. Customers should be reviewed so that a logic can be developed to regroup customers into meaningful market segments.
6. Inbound receipts should be classified into a representative range of commodities, such as steel, copper, plastics, motors, packaging, and

returns. A single-digit alpha code has proven to be most useful in this respect.

7. Stock-keeping units (SKUs) should be categorized by:
   a. Fast versus slow movers.
   b. Brand.
   c. Customer group.
   d. Product class/group.

   SKU categorization can often be accomplished by selecting certain fields in the model or stock number, in conjunction with customer number classifications.

Synthesis Process. Once the internal and external audit phases have been completed, it is necessary to identify cost and service trade-off opportunities; address the questions originally constructed in the "key question" phase of the methodology; and describe the recommended strategy, including required changes to the existing measurements in order to accurately report the effectiveness of the logistics system.

If the sampling process is sufficiently comprehensive, it should be possible to perform statistical analyses that will accurately predict the impact of alternative strategies and trade-offs. For example, regression analysis can be used to predict the expected order cycle time, given a range of fill rates. Or, fill rates can be accurately predicted based on the actual level of safety stock. Similarly, shipment costs and transit times can be predicted for shipments of various size or weight. This analysis is useful in determining how long to hold less-than-truckload (LTL) orders at the firm's distribution center for consolidation into truckload (TL) shipments. Likewise, management can use analysis of variance (ANOVA) statistics to identify if various customer, product, or channel segments require or utilize significantly different: order cycle times, fill rates, order sizes, product mixes, expedited/emergency orders, transport modes, made-to-order versus in-stock product, and damage prevention techniques.

All of these data are necessary for the development of an efficient and effective logistics strategy. The previously described analyses make it possible to recommend a strategy that will identify specific changes that need to be made to the current logistics operating system, describe which key variables require adjustment, and provide the firm with a competitive/differential advantage in the marketplace.

The external audit allows management to benchmark the firm's performance relative to that of major competitors on those attributes rated to be most important by customers. Combined with the internal audit, the external audit enables management to identify the key gaps in performance. Then, every effort should be made to identify "world class" practices and processes, regardless of the industry in which they have been successfully implemented, in order to close the gaps and build a competitive advantage over industry rivals.

The Logistics Plan

The Logistics Plan Starts with Customer Service Goals and Strategies

Developing a Logistics Strategy Involves 10 Key Areas

Logistics decisions are generally made hierarchically, but in an iterative manner from strategic (business objectives, marketing strategy, service requirements) to structural (make/buy, number/location/size of facilities, transportation modes, etc.) to functional (site selection, inventory deployment, carrier/vendor selection, etc.) to operational (operating policies, operating control rules, operating procedures, and routing and scheduling). This process is shown in Figure 18–4. Developing a logistics strategy involves the integration of 10 key areas: (1) customer service, (2) channel design, (3) network strategy, (4) warehouse design and operations, (5) transportation management, (6) materials management, (7) information systems, (8) policies and procedures, (9) facilities and equipment, and (10) organization and change management (see Figure 18–5).

10 Corresponding Questions

The corresponding questions representing each of the 10 key areas that are addressed by the logistics strategy include the following:[13]

1. What are the service requirements for each customer segment?
2. How can operational integration be achieved among the various channel members?
3. What is the distribution system that best minimizes costs and provides competitive levels of service?
4. What materials handling/storage technologies will facilitate attaining the service objectives with optimum levels of investment in facilities and equipment?
5. Are there opportunities to reduce transportation costs in both the short term and long term?
6. Can current inventory management procedures support more stringent service demands?
7. What information systems are required to gain maximum efficiency in logistics operations?
8. What changes to operating methods are needed to achieve improved performance?
9. How should we introduce changes to our network and facilities?
10. How should resources be organized to best achieve service and operating objectives?

The answers to these questions in the order illustrated in Figure 18–4 provide the basis for the logistics plan.

---

[13] William C. Copacino, Andersen Consulting, from a presentation at the International Logistics Management and Strategy Seminar, University of North Florida, March 9–11, 1992.

FIGURE 18–4 Making Logistics Decisions

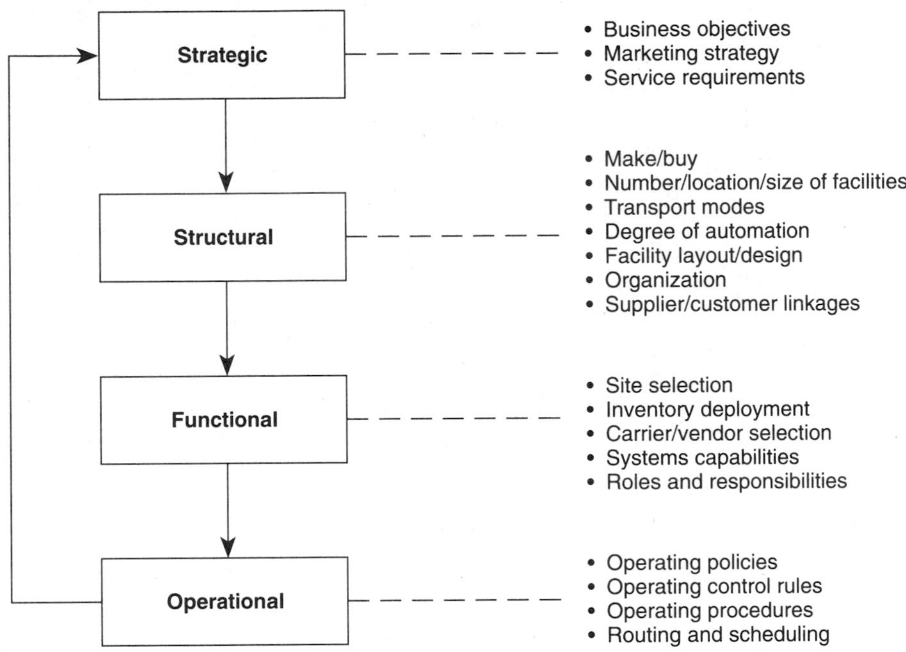

Logistics decisions are generally made hierarchically, but in an iterative manner.

SOURCE: William C. Copacino, Andersen Consulting, from a presentation at the International Logistics Management and Strategy Seminar, University of North Florida, March 9–11, 1992. All rights reserved by the author.

An Industry Example

A strategic logistics plan was developed for a $500 million division of a billion dollar firm that manufactured and distributed industrial products used in the manufacture of home appliances.[14] A major objective was to identify the firm's current customer service performance. The company operated manufacturing and warehousing facilities in the Midwest, Southwest, and West Coast. It sold its product to original equipment manufacturers (OEM) and to wholesalers and retailers.

The company was under growing pressure for local warehousing from OEM customers who were attempting to implement Just-in-Time inventory management concepts in their own firms. Large OEM accounts wanted the firm to place warehouses near their plants in order to reduce lead times. Management was concerned about the effect this decision would have on

[14]This example is adapted from Douglas M. Lambert and Jay U. Sterling, "Developing a Logistics Strategy: A Case Study," unpublished manuscript.

FIGURE 18–5 Logistics Strategy Integrates 10 Key Areas

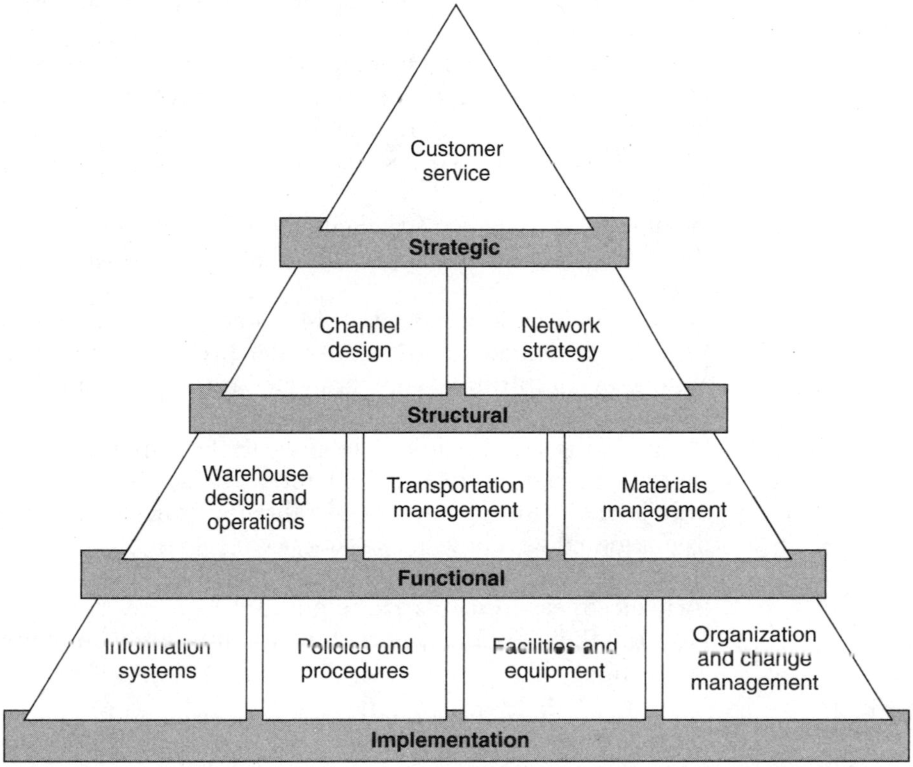

SOURCE: William C. Copacino, Andersen Consulting, from a presentation at the International Logistics Management and Strategy Seminar, University of North Florida, March 9–11, 1992.

the firm's inventory levels and logistics operations. In fact, the increased inventory necessary to provide local warehousing for two large OEM customers would be approximately $2 million.

Initially, management believed that the best way to determine if a regional network of distribution centers was feasible would be to purchase the services of a consulting firm that had a simulation model. However, the cost and time required by this approach proved to be unacceptable.

After initial discussion with the firm's management, the project was refocused into a study of the company's current customer service capabilities, as well as the recommended logistics strategies it should pursue in the future. To facilitate this task, management identified the following key questions:

Key Questions that Must Be Answered

- What changes will likely occur in the structure of trade (consumer) and OEM (industrial) markets?

- How will these changes affect the relative importance of trade and OEM segments of the business?
- What logistics systems are currently used by competitors? Are they likely to change?
- How can a differential advantage be achieved in the marketplace?
- How does the current order processing and information system compare to state-of-the-art information processing technology?
- What customer service system capabilities are required to lead the industry?
- What customer service strategies should be implemented? How will these strategies differ by customer segment, product class, and order size?
- Will an order cycle standard of three weeks lead the industry?
- What is the extent of the small-order problem? How is it likely to change in the future? What strategies are required to deal with this problem?
- What changes are required to proactively respond to Just-in-Time inventory programs or requirements?
- Should the firm implement centralized warehousing or a decentralized/regional warehousing strategy?
- How can distribution center productivity be improved? What performance measurements are required?
- How can the logistics organization best interface with manufacturing and marketing?

In order to answer these questions, an internal audit and an external audit were conducted. The objectives of the internal audit were to quantify the firm's actual performance in key customer service areas such as the order cycle and levels of in-stock availability; and to identify current and potential problems/conflicts between the various logistics operating departments as well as between logistics and other corporate functions such as manufacturing, marketing/sales, and finance/accounting. The goals of the external audit were to identify the elements of customer service that customers used in their evaluation of vendors, and to determine the relative performance of the firm and its competitors.

The Internal Audit

The internal audit was completed in two phases. In the first phase, 7 in-depth interviews were conducted within the customer service, transportation, and warehousing functions, and 11 interviews were conducted with finance/accounting, forecasting, manufacturing, production planning, inventory management, purchasing, and marketing. Comprehensive interview guides were constructed[15] and used in the interviews; all interviews were tape-recorded. After the interviews were completed, the information was synthesized and key comments and issues were summarized.

The second phase of the internal audit was comprised of a two-month

[15] See Appendixes A through G at the end of this chapter.

sample of customer order shipments. This was necessary because the company did not possess an order-history file that contained all of the data required to identify order cycle times, order cycle variability, and fill rates. Orders were tracked through the system from shipment back to receipt of the order. The sample was comprised of all shipments made during the two-month period. For each of the shipments, the firm's records were reviewed to determine the following times:

- Order received until accumulated in customer service.
- Order accumulated until released to distribution center.
- Order released to distribution center until picked at the distribution center.
- Order picked until packed at the distribution center.
- Packed until shipped.

This information was collected by stock class, type of customer, ZIP code, date wanted, date promised, date shipped, weight, shipment location, and mode. The sample may not have been totally representative of annual business, but if a bias existed, management believed it was conservative because more stockouts and longer lead times were likely to occur at other times of the year during peak periods. Since 50 percent of the OEM orders and 75 percent of trade orders were received by mail, a one-week sample of incoming orders was conducted in order to determine order-transmittal times.

The External Audit

The external audit was comprised of in-depth interviews with selected OEM and trade customers. The customers were selected so that they would be representative of the firm's business. The individuals interviewed were told that the interviewers were conducting research on Just-in-Time inventory management systems. Information was collected concerning the methods vendors were using to reduce customer inventories. The interviews were designed to collect specific information with respect to the interaction between vendor and customer logistics systems, as well as the effectiveness of major vendors. Interviewers also asked questions about the current and future competitive environment and customer service requirements.

By matching the output from the internal and external audits, management was able to identify the firm's current performance, customer expectations, and areas that required improvement for the following customer service categories:

- Order cycle time by internal function, as well as for order transmission and outbound transit times.
- Range in order cycle times.
- On-time delivery performance.
- Product shipped versus ordered.
- Split order quantities and frequencies.
- Shipment quantities by size categories (weight).

Based on the audit results and the division's stated mission to "maintain both a leading position in key markets and required profit margins in an environment characterized by increasing competition, rapid technological changes, and increasing emphasis on product quality and service," the following logistics strategy was recommended:

Recommended Logistics Strategy

> Support the division's strategic emphasis by providing dependable lead times for customer orders, high levels of in-stock availability for "A" items, consistency of service on all orders, and responsiveness and flexibility to customers' inquiries and emergency needs in a cost-effective manner. Customer service improvements will be achieved by improving logistics productivity using appropriate state-of-the-art technologies.

It was recommended that the strategy be implemented for "A" items by establishing a three-week order cycle, measured from the time the customer initiated the order to customer receipt of the ordered products. The three-week order cycle was to be accompanied by an in-stock availability standard of 95 percent. That is, customers would receive their orders 95 percent complete within three weeks of order placement and with a high level of on-time performance. The corresponding standard for "B" items was six weeks with 99 percent order completeness.

In order to implement this strategy the following changes were recommended:

Recommended Changes

- Implementation of an automated order processing system.
- Implementation of an inside sales/telemarketing program.
- Modification of current terms of sale for wholesale/retail customers.
- Implementation of formal production and inventory strategies and establishment of procedures and responsibilities between customer service and production planning.
- Revisions in the system used to transmit orders to distribution centers.
- Implementation of a scheduled delivery program.
- Implementation of inbound transportation programs.
- Upgrading of the warehouse management system.
- Design and implementation of integrated performance measurements for logistics.

Estimated Savings

Successful implementation of the recommended changes would make the firm the industry leader in customer service. In addition, the firm would achieve annual cost savings conservatively estimated to be in the range of $2 and $4 million as a result of cost reductions in order entry and order processing; reductions in production downtime; consolidation of outbound freight shipments; consolidation and routing of inbound transportation; productivity improvements in warehouse handling activities and techniques; reductions in raw materials, work-in-process, and finished product inventories; and reductions in overtime at month's end due to changes in payment terms. More optimistic estimates placed the annual savings at $10 million.

Nonquantified Benefits

In addition to quantifiable benefits, the study identified a number of nonquantified opportunities that would enable the firm to achieve further improvements in its ability to serve both trade and OEM customers more effectively. These included:

- Reducing the effort required to schedule production.
- Reducing raw material and work-in-process inventories.
- Reducing administrative costs that resulted from excessive expediting of vendor parts orders.
- Eliminating duplicative efforts with respect to routing and planning warehouse shipments.
- Eliminating customer safety stocks due to shorter and more consistent order cycle times.
- Increasing order quantities due to on-line substitution and more accurate availability information.
- Implementing scheduled deliveries and revised terms of sale, in order to smooth shipment activity.
- Providing more reliable and consistent service to customers.
- Reducing both inbound and outbound damage.
- Reducing transit times for inbound and outbound shipments.
- Improving control over vendor transportation policies.
- Reducing vendor packaging, routing, and timing errors.

Costs to the Firm

The one-time costs associated with achieving these savings and benefits were estimated at $1.3 to $1.5 million. These costs primarily reflected new, on-line, interactive order processing and warehouse management information systems. The firm's out-of-pocket cost for the study was about $30,000.

FUTURE CHALLENGES

In addition to the topics that received considerable attention in the previous chapters of this book, there are two emerging issues that represent significant challenges and at the same time opportunities for the logistics professional during the 1990s: integrated channel management and the green movement.

Integrated Channel Management

Integrated Logistics Must Be Extended to Include Channel Partners

While many firms have been successful at implementing the integrated logistics management concept within the boundaries of their corporation, there are relatively few examples of successful implementation throughout the supply chain. Integrated channel systems of this type have been referred to as "supply chain management," "partnerships," "strategic alliances," and in retailing, "quick response" programs. Typically, *supply chain management* definitions relate to the management of materials flow from sources of supply to consumption and the related information flows. Integration is accomplished by:

1. Recognizing end-user customer service level requirements.
2. Defining where to position inventories along the supply chain, and how much to stock at each point.
3. Developing the appropriate policies and procedures for managing the supply chain as a single entity.[16]

The definitions of supply chain management are not appreciably different from the Council of Logistics Management's definition of logistics provided in Chapter 1.

Partnerships are collaborative relationships where a supplier and customer form strong and extensive social, economic, service, and technical ties over time. The objective of partnerships, which are often referred to as strategic alliances, is to lower costs and/or increase value for the channel, providing benefits to both parties. Drug wholesalers such as Bergen Brunswig and McKesson Corporations represent good examples of the benefits of partnerships. These companies are wholesalers that sold to traditional drugstores that were being displaced by powerful national and regional chains. These wholesalers strengthened the independent pharmacies by developing improved order processing and distribution programs. The result was improved inventory management at the store level and reduced costs of order processing and distribution for the wholesalers. The wholesalers provided the drugstore customers with computerized systems and technology that no store was able to develop on its own. Information technology formed the basis for the partnership.

Logistics partnerships involve subcontracting logistics functions to third-party organizations, capable of managing these logistics activities to high levels of service while reducing long-term asset investment for the host company through the provision of variable service costs.[17] Examples of companies that compete in this arena as third-party providers are Ryder Distribution Resources, Sealand Logistics, TNT, Excel Logistics, and Unit Companies.

Retail *quick response programs* provide a means of integrating the operations of manufacturers and retailers. The most visible example is probably the Wal-Mart and Procter & Gamble Company (P&G) relationship. In an effort to improve its customer service levels to Wal-Mart, P&G sent a 12-

---

[16] Thomas C. Jones and Daniel W. Riley, "Using Inventory for Competitive Advantage through Supply Chain Management," *International Journal of Physical Distribution and Materials Management* 17, no. 2 (1987), p. 97.

[17] John Mostyn, "Distribution Partnerships," *Eurolog* 1, no. 2 (October 1991), p. 7.

person task force to Bentonville, Arkansas, to develop a joint strategy. The results are remarkable support for the benefits of quick response programs:

> "P&G now receives daily data by satellite on Wal-Mart's Pampers sales and forecasts and ships orders automatically. As a result, Wal-Mart can maintain smaller inventories and still cut the number of times it runs out of Pampers. And P&G has gone from a vendor that was maybe the least desirable to deal with to the most desirable to deal with," says a now retired former president of Wal-Mart. The results have been astonishing. Procter's volume at Wal-Mart grew by more than 40%, or by more than $200 million.[18]

Another example of a successful quick response program is the relationship between 3M and Target (a division of Dayton Hudson Corporation).

Integrated Channel Management Includes More than Logistics

Integrated channel management suggests the integration of all channel members' programs and is broader than the traditional logistics orientation of supply chain management. Integrated channel management includes the coordination of all activities between channel members that result in high levels of customer satisfaction for end-users.

Figure 18–6 provides an example of integrated channel management using firms in the apparel industry in the United States. What differentiates this program from most quick response programs is that four levels of the channel (fiber suppliers, fabric manufacturers, apparel manufacturers, and retailers) are included in a system designed to provide higher levels of satisfaction to customers.[19] In the mid-1980s, prior to beginning this program, the apparel industry in the United States lost over $25 billion per year as a result of inefficiencies.[20] Now, when a garment is purchased at a participating retailer, it is bar-code scanned at the checkout counter and the information is shared on a daily basis with other channel members (see Figure 18–6). Each level of the channel then prepares product to replenish the downstream partner. This system has reduced the traditional nine-month fashion cycle to six weeks, and the ultimate goal is two weeks.[21]

The major challenge facing the logistics professional is to determine how to proceed with integrated channel management strategies. There are four major options that are available, and these will vary by the size of the firm wishing to pursue such strategies and the size of that firm's channel

---

[18] Zachary Schiller, "Stalking the New Consumer," *Business Week* 28 (August 1989), p. 62.

[19] *Quick Response in the Apparel Industry* (Boston, Mass.: Harvard Business School, 1990), pp. 1–18.

[20] Robert M. Frazier, "Quick Responses in Soft Lines," *Discount Merchandiser* (January 1986), p. 42.

[21] See *Quick Response in the Apparel Industry*, pp. 1–18; and Janice H. Hammond, "Coordination in Textile and Apparel Channels: A Case for 'Virtual' Integration," *Proceedings of the Twentieth Annual Transportation and Logistics Educators Conference* (Columbus, Ohio: The Ohio State University, 1991), pp. 113–41.

FIGURE 18–6 Integrated Channel Management in the U.S. Apparel Industry

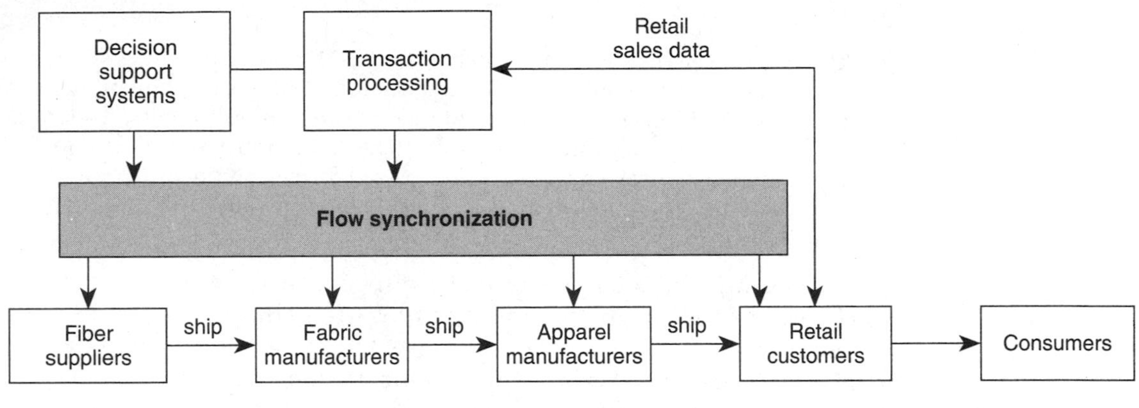

partners.[22] Figure 18–7 illustrates this approach from the manufacturer's perspective as well as that of its channel partners. Four strategies are possible:

Integrated Channel Strategies Management

1. Implement channel integration strategies.
2. Assume channel leadership.
3. Form alliances with channel leader.
4. Focus on selected activities.

Implement Channel Integration Strategies. Integration strategies may include some or all of the following:

- Joint inventory management—channelwide DRP.
- Joint transportation management.
- Production planning based on channel sales and inventory.
- Promotion coordination.
- Full EDI.
- Advance information sharing (POS data, inventory levels, promotion effectiveness).
- Channel inventory visibility.
- Bar coding.
- Automatic replenishment.
- Inbound JIT.
- Reduce stocking locations.
- Modify flows.

[22] This material is adapted from William C. Copacino and Douglas M. Lambert, *Integrated Channel Management*, unpublished manuscript, 1992. Used with permission. All rights reserved by the authors.

- Handling efficiencies.
- Function-to-function meetings.
- Joint problem solving.
- Channel performance metrics.[23]

Channel integration strategies are appropriate when large manufacturers/distributors/retailers deal with other large manufacturers/distributors/retailers.

Assume Channel Leadership. Assumption of channel leadership focuses on strategies that improve profitability for the company and its channel partners by sharing information, providing value-added tools, and implementing productivity improvements. These strategies are appropriate when large firms deal with smaller partners. The goal is to reinforce the firm's dominant position.

Form Alliances with Channel Leader. The strategy for small firms when they deal with large channel partners is to form alliances with the channel leader. The goal is to preempt the stronger channel members from dictating standard policies and procedures that will be costly to the firm. The firm should identify the channel leader's goals and present alternate methods of achieving them.

Focus on Selected Activities. When small firms deal with other small firms, the competition may be larger and more powerful competitive channels. In this situation management should focus on selected activities that build the relationship at low cost and with low levels of investment. Examples might include implementing telephone order entry systems, sharing business plans, and reducing cycle times to increase responsiveness.[24]

The Green Movement

Environmental Considerations are Increasingly Important

During the decades of the 1980s and 1990s, environmental issues, often referred to as the "green marketing revolution," have become much more important to individual consumers; retailers; manufacturers; and governmental bodies at the local, state, federal, and international levels. Issues such as recycling, hazardous wastes, solid-waste disposal, renewable versus nonrenewable resources, and energy conservation have become emotionally charged and politically sensitive topics. Illustrative of the expanded

---

[23] Ibid.

[24] For a good review of time-based competition see George Stalk, Jr., "Time: The Next Source of Competitive Advantage," *Harvard Business Review* 66, no. 4 (July-August, 1988), pp. 41–51; and George Stalk, Philip Evans, and Lawrence E. Shulman, "Competing on Capabilities: The New Rules of Corporate Strategy," *Harvard Business Review* 70, no. 2 (March-April 1992), pp. 57–69.

FIGURE 18–7 Integrated Channel Management Strategies

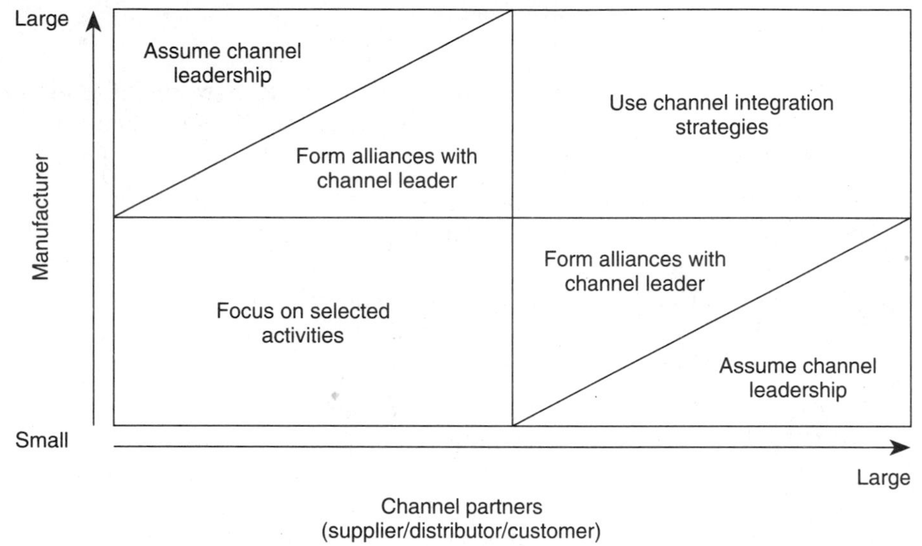

SOURCE: William C. Copacino and Douglas M. Lambert, *Integrated Channel Management,* unpublished manuscript, 1992. Used with permission. All rights reserved by the authors.

environmental awareness on the part of society are the following public opinion survey results of the past few years.[25]

1. A CBS/*New York Times* poll conducted in 1990 stated that 84 percent of Americans believed that pollution was a serious national problem and 74 percent indicated that the environment must be protected regardless of cost (compared to 45 percent who responded in a similar fashion in 1981).[26]
2. A survey performed by Gallup for the American Paper Institute found that
   a. Fifty-four percent of consumers are interested in purchasing products packaged in recycled paper containers.
   b. Seventy percent of consumers would be very likely or fairly likely to purchase products packaged in recycled paper.[27]

---

[25] Several of the examples cited here as well as many others are reported in Richard M. Kashmanian, *Assessing the Environmental Consumer Market* (Research Report for the U.S. Environmental Protection Agency, Contract No. 68-D9-0169, April 1, 1991).

[26] *New York Times*, April 17, 1990, pp. A1 and B10.

c. Approximately 65 percent of consumers say that package recyclability influenced their decision to buy a product. This represented an increase of about 15 percent over a previous study conducted a year earlier. Additionally, 20 percent of the respondents indicated that they would be willing to pay 6–10 cents more for a product in a recyclable package.[28]

Reverse Logistics

"Reverse logistics" concerns such as source reduction/conservation, recycling, substitution, and disposal are major issues that interface with logistics activities such as purchasing and procurement, traffic and transportation, warehousing and storage, and packaging. The process begins with the use of virgin or secondary materials in processing and manufacturing operations. Products are produced and sold to consumer (or industrial) markets. After the products are used by customers, they are disposed of in some fashion. In both consumer and industrial sectors, many of the used products are disposed of as mixed waste; that is, they are not separated into various components, but discharged into the solid-waste stream together. Source separation occurs when waste materials are segregated by source, such as yard waste, paper, cans, jars and bottles, and hazardous waste.

The vast majority of mixed waste ends up in landfills or is incinerated, where the possibility exists that some form of energy recovery may occur. Hazardous wastes are disposed of in approved dump sites or are destroyed. Yard waste, paper, cans, jars, and bottles can be recycled. If collected and sorted, they are processed into flattened cans, compost, densified plastics, and/or baled paper to prepare them for use in various secondary raw materials markets. These reprocessed materials can then be used as inputs into processing and manufacturing. The process continues, with the major objective being to maximize source reduction and recycling.

Life-cycle Analysis

Implicit in the process just described is the notion that firms will utilize life-cycle analysis to make and evaluate product and packaging decisions. Life-cycle analysis involves "cradle-to-grave" evaluation of products and/or packages in order to determine their impact(s) on resources and the environment. From an environmental perspective, the approach is useful because it considers the product throughout its life span, which includes the development of the product through to its ultimate disposal in the solid-waste stream. Examination of reverse logistics using life-cycle analysis must include consideration of the elements of source reduction, recycling, substitution, and disposal.

Green Legislation

For the most part, environmentally related legislation and government initiatives are becoming more strict, more limiting, and less forgiving to

[28] *Packaging*, July 1990, pp. 8–10.

organizations and individuals that harm the environment. In many countries throughout the world, waste disposal, recycling, and environmental pollution are major concerns. In Canada, the Canadian Council of Ministers of the Environment has established a target for reducing waste generation by 50 percent by the year 2000.[29]

In Europe, Italy, Denmark, and Norway are among the countries with environmental/recycling legislation. Germany passed legislation that will ban all corrugated containers, plastic foam materials, wooden pallets, and polyethylene foils from landfill storage and incineration by 1993. Other countries are considering similar solid-waste bans for landfills.

Many countries have attempted to minimize wastes through the use of tax incentives, technical assistance, public information, and other methods. Generally, countries have exhibited a keen interest in waste minimization policies. Their efforts in this area will likely intensify in the near term. As the green movement picks up momentum, logistics executives will necessarily become more involved in reverse logistics activities.

Those firms in which management responds in a proactive manner will find that there are marketing advantages in terms of market share improvements and/or premium prices. In addition, the potential negative affects on profitability will be minimized since high cost, short-term responses will be avoided.

SUMMARY

Three decades have elapsed since the integrated logistics management concept was recognized and the first courses were offered in the area. The emphasis in the years ahead will be on the profitable development of business segments, and the lack of growth in many markets promises to make the logistics function a focal point within North American firms. The challenges and opportunities for the logistics professional have never been greater. The rewards for accepting these challenges and finding creative solutions will be significant. It is our hope that we have presented the material in this text in a manner that will encourage bright young men and women to seek careers within the profession, and will provide present practitioners with a reference source that will help them in their day-to-day management activities.

---

[29] *Waste Paper Recycling in Canada*, Factsheet published by the Office of Waste Management, Environment Canada, June 1991.

SUGGESTED READINGS

BRAITHWAITE, ALAN, AND MARTIN CHRISTOPHER. "Managing the Global Pipeline." *The International Journal of Logistics Management* 2, no. 2 (1991), pp. 55–62.

CAMP, ROBERT C. *Benchmarking: The Search for Industry Best Practices that Lead to Superior Performance*. Milwaukee, Wis.: ASQC Quality Press, 1989.

COOPER, MARTHA C., DANIEL E. INNIS, AND PETER DICKSON, *Strategic Planning for Logistics*. Oak Brook, Ill.: Council of Logistics Management, 1992.

COPACINO, WILLIAM C., AND FRANK F. BRITT. "Perspectives on Global Logistics." *The International Journal of Logistics Management* 2, no. 1 (1991), pp. 35–41.

DAVIS, STANLEY M. *Future Perfect*. Reading, Mass.: Addison-Wesley, 1987.

DAY, GEORGE S. *Strategic Market Planning: The Pursuit of Competitive Advantage*. St. Paul, Minn.: West Publishing, 1984.

HAMMOND, JANICE H. "Coordination in Textile and Apparel Channels: A Case for 'Virtual' Integration." *Proceedings of the Twentieth Annual Transportation and Logistics Educators Conference*. Columbus, Ohio: The Ohio State University, 1991, pp. 113–41.

KANTER, ROSABETH MOSS. *When Giants Learn to Dance*. New York: Simon and Schuster, 1989.

MAGAZINER, IRA C., AND MARK PATINKIN, *The Silent War*. New York: Random House, 1989.

NOVACK, ROBERT A. "Quality and Control in Logistics: A Process Model." *The International Journal of Physical Distribution and Logistics Management* 19, no. 11 (1989), pp. 1–44.

PERSSON, GÖRAN. "Achieving Competitiveness through Logistics." *The International Journal of Logistics Management* 2, no. 1 (1991), pp. 1–11.

PORTER, MICHAEL E. *Competitive Strategy*. New York: The Free Press, 1980.

POWER, CHRISTOPHER, WALECIA KONRAD, ALICE CUNEO, AND JAMES TREECE, "Value Marketing: Quality, Service and Fair Pricing Are the Keys to Selling in the '90s." *Business Week*, November 11, 1991, pp. 132–135, 138, and 140.

Quick Response in the Apparel Industry. Boston, Mass.: Harvard Business School, 1990, pp. 1–18.

SCOTT, CHARLES, AND ROY WESTBROOK, "New Strategic Tools for Supply Chain Management," *The International Journal of Physical Distribution and Logistics Management* 21, no. 1 (1991), pp. 23–33.

STEINER, GEORGE A. *Strategic Planning*. New York: The Free Press, 1979.

STERLING, JAY U., AND DOUGLAS M. LAMBERT. "A Methodology for Assessing Logistics Operating Systems." *International Journal of Physical Distribution and Logistics Management* 15, no. 6 (1985), pp. 3–44.

STOCK, JAMES R. *Reverse Logistics*. Oak Brook, Ill.: Council of Logistics Management, 1992.

VAN AMSTEL, M. J. PLOOS, AND M. F. G. M. VERSTEGEN, "Development of a Total

Logistics Concept: A Method for Improving Logistics Performance" *The International Journal of Logistics Management* 2, no. 2 (1991), pp. 63–73.

VAN AMSTEL, M. J. PLOOS, AND DAVID FARMER. "Controlling the Logistics Pipeline." *The International Journal of Logistics Management* 1, no. 1 (1990), pp. 19–27.

QUESTIONS AND PROBLEMS

1. Why is planning likely to be an important activity for logistics managers in the years ahead?

2. What is the role of the marketing plan in the development of a strategic logistics plan?

3. What do you believe to be the most important elements of the strategic planning process for logistics? Why?

4. Explain the importance of measuring and evaluating the performance of individual channel members.

5. Which of the challenges that face the logistics profession in the coming years do you believe to be the most significant? Why?

6. When describing retail quick rseponse programs, the example of P&G and Wal-Mart was introduced (see page 745). As part of this program, P&G has located 12 people in Bentonville, Arkansas, in order to develop a joint strategy with the large retailer.

a. Should P&G be prepared to do this for all of its customers? Explain.

b. From Wal-Mart's perspective, will every vendor be a candidate for such a program?

c. How should Wal-Mart implement integrated channel management with its vendors?

APPENDIX A
Customer Service/Order Administration Audit

1. Do you have a written customer service policy?
2. Do customers receive a copy of this policy?
3. Can you provide us with a definition of customer service as viewed by your company?
4. Do you provide different levels of customer service by product or customer?
5. Do your customer service standards change?
6. If your company designates a particular area as customer service (or customer relations, distribution services, etc.):
   a. How many people are assigned to the area?
   b. Describe the major responsibilities of these individuals.
   c. To what department does this area report?
   d. If possible, please provide us with all job descriptions that include customer service/customer relations in the title.
7. Relative to your company's order cycle time, how frequently do you monitor the order cycle?
8. Indicate (by circling the appropriate letters from the choices below) which of the following dates are part of your measurement:
   a. Order prepared by customer.
   b. Order received by you.
   c. Order processed and released by customer service.
   d. Order received at D/C.
   e. Order picked and/or packed.
   f. Order shipped by D/C.
   g. Order received by customer.
9. Is order processing centralized in one location or decentralized?
10. On average, how many orders do you process each day, week, month?
11. What is the dollar value of a typical order? Number of line items?
12. What percentage of customer orders are placed by company field salespeople?
13. What percentage of total customer orders are placed by inside salespeople/order clerks who call the customer to get the order?
14. What percentage of total customer orders are placed by customers unaided by either company field or inside salespeople?
15. In terms of methods of order entry: How does each customer group above enter orders? If they use multiple methods, please indicate the percentage of their total entered via each method.
16. How many order entry locations exist in the company?
17. Once received by the firm, does the order taker:
    ______ Fill out a preprinted order form? If yes, ask for a copy.
    ______ Enter the order into the computer via a data terminal off-line?
    ______ Enter the order into the computer via a data terminal on-line?

SOURCE: Appendixes A–G from Jay U. Sterling and Douglas M. Lambert, "A Methodology for Assessing Logistics Operating Systems," *International Journal of Physical Distribution and Materials Management* 15, no. 6 (1985), pp. 29–44, adapted and expanded by the author from Douglas M. Lambert and M. Christine Lewis, "Meaning, Measurement and Implementation of Customer Service," *Proceedings of the Nineteenth Annual Conference of the National Council of Physical Distribution Management,* 1981 (Chicago: National Council of Physical Distribution Management, 1981), pp. 569–95.

Order Entry Methods	*Field Salespeople*		*Customers*		*Inside Sales Order Clerks*	
	Total Company	*This Location*	*Total Company*	*This Location*	*Total Company*	*This Location*
Mail	______%	______%	______%	______%	______%	______%
Telephone (paid by customer)	______	______	______	______	______	______
Free inward WATS telephone	______	______	______	______	______	______
TWX and/or other communication terminal	______	______	______	______	______	______
FAX	______	______	______	______	______	______
Hand-delivered to field sales rep/office	______	______	______	______	______	______
Other (specify)	______	______	______	______	______	______
Total	100%	100%	100%	100%	100%	100%

18. Does the order taker:
    ______ Verify credit?
    ______ Verify inventory availability?
    ______ Assign inventory to the order?
    ______ Make product substitutions?
    ______ Price the order?
    ______ Confirm delivery date?
    ______ Attempt to increase order size to achieve an efficient quantity?
19. Are the following reference files manual or computerized? (Check one)

File	*Manual*	*Computerized*
Customer	______	______
Product model dictionary	______	______
Prices (standard data)	______	______
Prices (special quotes/projects data)	______	______
Promotions	______	______
Inventory balances	______	______
Ship schedules	______	______
Order history	______	______
Bills of lading	______	______
Freight payment data	______	______
Production schedules	______	______
Credit	______	______
Other (please specify)	______	______

20. How are orders processed?
    ______ Batch processed
    ______ Individually processed (on-line, real-time environment)
21. How does the order taker transmit order information to:
    a. Transportation, for determining route, loading sequence, and ship date?
    b. Warehouse, for picking and packing?
22. Do salespeople or customers receive an order acknowledgment?

Sales ______	When? ______	How transmitted? ______
Customers ______	When? ______	How transmitted? ______
Both ______	When? ______	How transmitted? ______
Neither ______		

23. Do you have a single point of contact for customers, or do certain departments handle different types of inquiries/complaints?
24. Do you provide customers with a telephone number? If so, how do you make them aware of it?
25. Do your competitors have an established method of communication for their customers who want to contact them about some aspect of their order after the order has been entered?
26. Do you have a precalculated cost for cutting a customer order?
27. Do you compute a standard cost for a stockout (cost of lost sales)?
28. Do you use a standard cost for a back order?
29. Describe the exact procedures used in assigning transportation routes.
30. How do you determine that you will comply with a customer's request to change to a nonstandard carrier on prepaid shipments?
31. Who determines if an expedite charge will be assessed?
32. What percentage of telephoned orders in require expedited service?
33. What criteria are used to process the following types of orders/order adjustments?
    a. Requests for premium and/or special, nonstandard transport mode.
    b. Revisions/adjustments to production schedules.
    c. Split shipments.
34. Do you attempt to differentiate service to different customers (prioritize)?
35. Has marketing told customer service the service standards it expects for various customers—specific and/or distinct groups of customers?
36. What is (are) the distinguishing feature(s) between "cooperative" and "non-cooperative" customer accounts?
37. How do you view your interface with production planning and scheduling?
38. What data do you provide to production planning?
39. What effort is made to encourage a scheduled delivery program with customers—particularly for those with LTL shipments?
40. How are orders physically transmitted to the distribution center(s)?
41. Please describe the exact procedures followed in sorting/preparing (picking lists) for submission to the distribution center(s).

APPENDIX B

Transportation (Inbound and Outbound) Audit

1. What is the total amount spent annually for transportation?
    a. Inbound shipments from vendors $________
    b. Outbound shipments to customers $________
2. What percentage of your total inbound freight liability is accounted for by the following terms:
    a. Collect (paid by you)?
    b. Prepaid by vendor and included in piece price?
    c. Prepaid by vendor and added to invoice and/or rebilled to you separately?
3. Are outbound transportation costs for finished product allocated to individual marketing groups and/or product lines?

4. What is the basis used to assign outbound transportation costs to products/customers or other meaningful segments (directly from freight bills, or allocated based on sales volume, unit sales volume, or some other basis)?
5. Are the costs applicable to various modes (common carrier and private fleet) accounted for differently?
6. Who selects the modes, routes, and carriers for outbound shipments to customers?
7. Who communicates carrier instructions to warehouses?
8. How frequently are routes and carriers reviewed and selected? At time of order, shipment, or periodically?
9. Is carrier selection for each order based on the size of the shipment?
10. What is the basis used for determining a "preferred carrier"?
11. How do order changes and expedited or "rush" orders affect the mode/route/carrier selection process? Frequency of occurrence?
12. Are inbound orders for raw material and parts reviewed by corporate traffic personnel prior to receipt, in order to:
    a. Determine and communicate least cost mode and carrier to vendor?
    b. Determine opportunities for consolidation of LTL quantities in high-volume metropolitan areas for shipment into factories in truckload increments?
    c. Plan warehouse labor and material handling equipment needs?
    d. Identify "priority" material which will require expedited service to meet scheduled production runs?
    e. Identify candidates for "cover-off" return loads via private fleet?
13. Are outbound LTL customer shipments consolidated to most market areas, and/or is a "scheduled delivery" program utilized to ensure timely, consistent outbound transit times?
14. To what extent, if any, are "commodity rates" negotiated with common carriers, for inbound, outbound, and/or intercompany transfers?
15. If commodity rates currently don't exist, in your opinion could a select group of volume carriers be selected who will agree to the negotiation of exception, commodity, and combination rates?
16. What is the number of carriers with whom you currently do business?
    a. Common ________
    b. Contract ________
    c. Rail ________
17. In your opinion, could this current pool of common/contract carriers be reduced to a workable handful and still realize acceptable service to all geographical areas?
18. If contract carriage is not currently utilized, could a viable contract service be structured to supplement the firm's current transport network in order to further reduce current common carrier costs and improve transit times?
19. Are bills of lading prepared by some type of computerized program?
20. Does a computerized "bill of lading" file exist? If so, what information could be readily accessed to provide planning and performance measurement tools regarding:
    a. Transportation routes, modes, and costs?
    b. Warehouse processing and transit cycle times?
    c. Channel product flow?
    d. Inbound and outbound consolidation?

21. What percentages of total outbound shipments are sent by:
    a. Rail?
    b. Truck?
    c. Will call?
    d. Other (please specify)
22. As a percentage of total product shipped this year, how much product was transhipped?
23. How often do diversions in route occur? Causes? Decision process?
24. What is your procedure for delays in route? Decision process? Communications process? Order tracing capability?
25. Do you backhaul goods? Please explain nature of the backhaul, the scheduling process, economic justification.
26. Are freight charges built into the product's price, or does the customer pay freight separately?
27. Does the customer choose the transport mode? Carrier?
28. How much did you pay in demurrage this year? Causes of demurrage?
29. How much did you pay in detention this year? Causes of detention?
30. What are your terms of sale for outbound shipments to customers?
31. What percentage of the freight bill is attributed to company-operated transportation (private fleet)?
32. What cost categories are included in transportation costs associated with company-operated vehicles?
33. What do you use company-operated vehicles for? Intracompany hauling? Company to customers? Please explain.
34. Regarding management and administration of the private fleet operation:
    a. What are annual miles driven?
    b. What are empty miles driven (miles and percent of total)?
    c. What percentage of inbound and outbound product is shipped via private fleet?
    d. What is the ratio of trailers to tractors? If excessive (greater than 3:1), what are trailers used for?
    e. How are routes configured?
35. Are private fleet trailer movements, usage, and nonusage identified in order to reduce nonproductive uses to a minimum? (Examples: trailers used as storage and duplicative, intercompany transfers.)
36. Are optimum routes and loading techniques developed to maximize utilization of private fleet trailer capacities, minimize empty miles, increase warehouse labor efficiency, and maximize savings versus common carrier modes?
37. Are inbound LTL raw material and parts orders consolidated either in major metropolitan areas, or locally, for delivery in volume to plant sites?

APPENDIX C
Warehouse Operations Audit

1. How many warehouses do you use?
   a. Number ________
   b. Location ________
   c. Total square feet ________
   d. Ceiling height (ft.) ________
2. Do manufacturing and/or traffic personnel contact key vendors for the purpose of scheduling and routing receipts into the appropriate facility?
3. What percentage of raw materials/in-process and finished product inventories move more than once before final disposition?
4. Are there specific firm facilities, product categories, and/or geographical origins/destinations that account for a majority of these duplicate movements?
5. What criteria are used for selecting existing warehouse facilities and sites?
6. What is the company's policy regarding consolidation or relocation of existing facilities?
7. Are warehouse administrative policies, procedures, and financial record keeping uniform throughout the firm? Are they adequate to serve both present and future needs?
8. What costs are included in warehousing expense?
   a. Direct labor
   b. Material handling equipment
   c. Utilities
   d. Administrative salaries
      (1) Clerical
      (2) Management
   e. Fixed depreciation/lease payments for
      (1) Building/facility
      (2) Automated conveyors, etc.
   f. Miscellaneous office supplies and expense
   g. Maintenance
      (1) Building
      (2) Equipment
   h. Data processing
      (1) Terminals
      (2) Central processor
      (3) Lines
      (4) Corporate changes
9. Are the following costs used to measure warehouse performance?
   a. Cost per square foot
   b. Cost per unit
   c. Cost of direct labor per unit
   d. Overtime as a percentage of direct labor
   e. Fixed costs versus variable costs
10. Are systems and/or controls used to manage warehouse activities (in total) and schedule/plan manpower and material handling equipment requirements?

(Circle where used.)
a. Unloading receipts
b. Unpacking
c. Packing
d. Loading trucks
e. Processing returns from customers
f. Processing returns to vendors
g. Put-away into storage
h. Pull orders from storage
i. Writing bill of lading
j. Stock relocation/rearrangement/verification
k. Housekeeping
l. Utility (material handlers)
m. Maintenance

11. What are your total annual warehousing costs?
12. What percentage of total warehousing costs can be attributed to:
    a. In-plant warehouses? ________
    b. Field (private)? ________
    c. Field (public)? ________
13. Are standard costs utilized to expense warehousing costs, such as the following?
    a. Total cost
    b. Direct labor
    c. Material handling equipment
    d. Public warehousing
14. What type of payment arrangement do you have with public warehouse(s) for handling charges? For storage charges?
15. What are the per-unit handling charges at public warehouse(s)? Per-unit storage costs?
16. What techniques and/or system, if any, are used to measure performance of departments within each D/C, as well as individual employees performing direct labor activities?
17. What percentage of trailers received and shipped at each location are less than truckload (LTL), and what are current procedures and tools for consolidation into truckload increments?
18. Is damage a problem? If so, what types of prevention or minimization techniques are utilized?
19. Are shortages and damage recognized, recorded, and accounted for regarding:
    a. Inbound receipts?
    b. Internal D/C activities?
    c. Outbound transit?
    d. Customer receipts?
20. For purchases of raw materials, parts, and/or finished product, are vendors' errors documented and are vendors charged for variances in quantity received versus purchase order, failure to comply with packing and routing instructions, and quality problems? (Circle if yes and explain.)
    a. Raw materials
    b. Work in process
    c. Service parts
    d. Finished product

21. What logic and procedures and/or operating systems are employed to assign receipts to storage locations and extract orders from storage?
22. Is some logic (such as ABC analysis) used to lay out stows and assign products to storage (e.g., fast movers are placed in stows closest to shipping docks)?
23. How are inventories controlled by SKU regarding:
    a. Stow location assignment?
    b. Stow balance on hand?
    c. Preparation of picking lists?
    d. Preparation of bill of lading?
    e. Preparation of packing list?
    f. Preparation of serial number listings?
    g. Identification of slow movers?
        (1) By location
        (2) By SKU
24. How frequently are warehouse inventories physically counted (including periodic test counts)?
25. Are warehouse locations periodically checked for inventory verification?
26. How frequently are warehouse inventories relocated or consolidated?
27. Are orders batch-picked? If so, how are picking lists developed and by whom are they developed?
28. After picking, is a copy of the packing list transmitted to:
    a. Invoicing?
    b. Transportation?
    c. Sales
    d. Customer service?

APPENDIX D
Inventory Management and Forecasting Audit

1. What is your average annual raw material inventory?
    a. Units ________
    b. Delivered cost per unit ________
    c. Annual turns ________
2. What is your average annual finished goods inventory?
    a. Units ________
    b. Variable delivered cost per unit ________
    c. Annual turns ________
3. From how many vendors does your firm purchase raw materials and parts? Where are they located?
4. How frequently do you typically order material (by major commodity category and geographical territory)?

5. Are minimum or fixed quantities used in determining order release quantities on purchase orders (for each major product class)? How are these quantities computed (by computer or manually)?
6. What are average lead times, by product class, for major vendors (from date purchase order is released to vendor until receipt at factories)?
7. Is time-phased, on-order information available on a regular basis? If so, how frequently are these reports published?
8. Are these on-order reports automatically generated from a data processing system? Is the information provided to distribution center personnel?
9. What are purchase order policies with regard to blanket purchase orders (BPOs) with periodic releases; specification of carrier; charge backs (packing/quantity errors, damages/rejects, misroutings, and late deliveries)?
   a. BPOs
   b. Carrier specs
   c. Charge backs
   d. Packing/quantity
   e. Damages/rejects
   f. Misroutings
   g. Late deliveries
10. Describe the exact responsibilities of each of the following corporate functions in the forecasting/production planning/production scheduling/finished goods inventory control process:
   a. Purchasing
   b. Master scheduling
   c. Production (title)
   d. Sales
   e. Marketing
   f. Logistics
   g. Other (describe)
11. Are finished goods inventory level targets established on a regular basis? By whom? And at what level (SKU, product, product line)?
12. What are your standard product availability/service levels, by major product category?

		Percent Available from Current/Future Production	
Category	*Percent Available from Existing Inventory*	*Percent*	*Number of weeks*

13. Who is responsible for establishing product level forecasts? What time frame do these forecasts cover? And how frequently are they compiled?
14. How are inventory levels at the distribution centers (DCs) set? Weeks of supply? Average inventory in units? Variable delivered cost of one unit of product?
15. How is the inventory file updated to reflect new product received and product shipped?
16. With reference to the replenishment of inventory at DCs, how do you know when it is time to order product for the DC? How do you know how much to order? How do you communicate your replenishment need to the plant? Explain.
17. What formal reports are generated regarding inventory?

18. What cost categories do you include in inventory carrying costs?

Cost Category	*Check If Included in Carrying Costs*	*Cost as Percentage of Inventory at Cost*
Cost of money	______	______ %
Taxes	______	______ %
Insurance	______	______ %
Variable storage	______	______ %
Obsolescence	______	______ %
Shrinkage	______	______ %
Damage	______	______ %
Relocation costs	______	______ %
Total carrying costs	______	______ %
Percentage	______	______ %

Average monthly inventory valued at variable costs delivered to the distribution center ______

19. Do financial departments analyze industries to which the firm's products are sold?
20. Describe the statistical forecasting system and its component parts.
21. How frequently are short-range forecasts, by SKU, released to production?
22. Are incoming orders monitored daily from reports generated by the order processing system?
23. Which department determines or sets inventory levels? Are inventory levels based on coverage/fill rate objectives?
24. How are fill rates measured by SKU and category?
25. Are there problems encountered in reviewing daily/weekly order receipt reports from customer service?
26. What types of problems are encountered when forecasting sales to large customers?
27. Are short-range forecasts derived from customer orders? If so, explain the process.
28. What are the major reasons why customers change order quantities and forecasts or request expedited service?
29. Who determines ABC product categories?
30. How many adjustments to your forecast do you average per week?
31. How could forecast accuracy be improved?

APPENDIX E
Production Planning/Scheduling Audit

1. Describe the production scheduling process in detail: steps in the process, inputs (type and source), outputs, all interfaces—where information comes from and goes to, decision points.
2. Describe the exact responsibilities of each of the following corporate functions

in the forecasting/production planning/production scheduling/finished goods inventory control process:

a. Purchasing
b. Production (title)
c. Remote master scheduling
d. Sales
e. Marketing
f. Physical distribution/logistics
g. Forecasting/finance and administration

3. Are there any bottlenecks/problems in exchanging information relevant to production scheduling?
4. How much downtime did you incur this year? Causes? Cost?
5. How long does an average production run take? What is the yield?
6. Does this vary significantly between products and/or customers?
7. Are there any bottlenecks/problems in exchanging information relevant to materials scheduling?
8. How are A, B, and C model categories determined? What criteria are used? Who determines A, B and C categories?
9. Are finished goods inventory level targets established on a regular basis? By whom? And at what level (SKU, product, product line)?
10. What are normal manufacturing lead times, by major product category? How frequently are schedule requirements established?
11. For what period of time, from initial release (establishment of production requirements) for a specific period to actual production, are adjustments permitted (re: additions, deletions, quantity changes, push/pull adjustments)?
12. How frequently and to what extent are changes currently made to production schedules? Who is (are) involved in this decision?
13. What are your standard product availability/service levels, by major product category?
14. Which function(s) are best qualified to make the necessary decisions/trade-offs regarding requests for changes in the production schedule?
15. What percentage of the time are schedules changed during first, second, third week before actual production?
16. What cost savings could be realized if changes were not made in week one, two, or three?
17. What is the typical percentage that line rate is adjusted?
18. What are major causes of reductions in production quantities?
    a. Inventory shortages (record-keeping errors and/or parts do not arrive on time).
    b. Line rate changes (added parts do not arrive in time).
    c. Production changes inside firm periods.
19. What percentage of your production scheduling problems are related to:
    a. A items?
    b. B items?
    c. C items?
20. How frequently are A items typically produced?
21. What customer groups give you the most problems with regard to production changes?
22. What type of reports not presently available would be most beneficial to you?

26. What problems are caused by production changes inside the firm period?
27. What percentage of purchase requisitions (number) are expedited (i.e., requested inside the vendor's stated lead time)?
28. What are the different categories of expedited orders from vendors?
29. What percentage of your requisitions are delivered on time (either standard lead time or negotiated lead time for expedited orders)?
30. How can the percentage of expedited orders be reduced?
31. How do you determine routing instructions and freight terms on requisitions?

APPENDIX F
Marketing/Sales Audit

1. Please describe the marketing/sales organization.
2. Does your division have a formal, written, long-range strategic plan?
   a. If yes, please describe this strategy/plan.
   b. How often is it updated?
   c. Is input provided by organizations outside the marketing division, and does marketing provide input to other divisional plans?
   d. May we have a copy of this plan to review?
3. From a marketer's perspective, what do you believe are your firm's major strengths and weaknesses in each of your major market segments?
   a. Strengths
   b. Weaknesses
4. What percentage of your business is derived from each of the following major market segments?
   a. OEM ________%
   b. Trade/wholesale ________%
   c. Commercial ________%
   d. International ________%
   e. Retail ________%
5. Please describe your role, responsibilities, and function in the forecasting/production planning/scheduling process.
   a. What do you particularly like about the current process?
   b. What do you believe are the weaknesses/shortcomings that you would like corrected? How would you implement these corrections?
   c. How successfully do you believe the current process performs and how could each be improved with regard to:
      (1) Forecast accuracy (please state the actual percent achieved versus your preferred standard)?
      (2) Timing (planned versus actual performance)?
      (3) Lead times/firm periods for major production categories?
      (4) Machine downtime? (Is this a problem?)
      (5) Parts shortages? (Is this a problem?)

(6) Production changes inside the firm X-week period?
(7) Late deliveries of vendor parts?
(8) Shifting demand/order patterns?
(9) Customer service-willingness to meet specific customer needs?
(10) Information system data base?
(11) Use of customer sales to forecast (versus factory shipments to customers)?
(12) Other (describe)?

6. How frequently does your organization intercede on behalf of a customer with customer service regarding:
   a. Adjusting orders?
   b. Reallocating available inventory between competing customers?
   c. Production schedule changes to handle emergency/key orders?
   d. Waivers of freight terms and/or premium freight charges (for expedited shipments)?
   e. Returned goods requests/problems?
   f. Products/orders shipped in error?
   g. Orders damaged in transit to customers (including both visible and concealed damage)?
7. With respect to customer service, what does each of your major customer market segments require in terms of:
   a. Order cycle times (from the time a customer releases an order to receipt of the product)?
   b. Order fill rate (the initial percentage of the order received by the customer's requested delivery date)?
   c. Order completeness percentage (the percentage of the order that the customer eventually receives)?
   d. Order cycle consistency (the variability in the lead time experienced across time as compared to the requested delivery date)?
8. How do you believe the firm is currently performing with respect to each of these measurements, and how could performance be improved?
9. Who establishes the ABC classifications for the products comprising the various product groups/families?
   a. What are the criteria and analytical tools used to determine these assignments?
   b. How do you interface with the other departments in this process?
10. Who is responsible for establishing "terms and conditions of sale" for each of your major market segments, regarding:
    a. Payment period/discounts?
    b. Truckload/quantity discounts?
    c. Freight terms?
    d. Returned goods policies?
    e. Damage and freight terms policies?
11. How effective are your terms in general, and how could each of the above components be improved? In your opinion, is the large volume of business shipped by the DC at month's end a problem? If so, how could it be leveled?
12. What do you perceive to be the major problems of your organization with respect to the activities performed by or in conjunction with logistics? What would you like to see changed with respect to the above stated issues?

13. From a marketer's perspective, what changes do you see occurring in your industry over the next 5 to 10 years with regard to:
    a. Market/market segment growth?
    b. Shifts in demographic and/or geographic characteristics?
    c. Shifts, growth, declines in product groups?
    d. New products/product deletions?
    e. Customer service requirements?
    f. Competitive environment?
    g. Emphasis placed on the individual components of the marketing mix?
14. How do you believe customer service should be organized to better serve customers?
15. Do you provide input to other functions with reference to their divisional long-range plans?
16. Do you receive input from any other area in developing your long-range plans?
17. What are the reasons for any production problems you may encounter?
18. Describe the current and projected five-year marketing environment for each market segment with regard to:
    a. Trade/channel structure
    b. Competitive environment
    c. Product line/mix
    d. Pricing strategies
    e. Promotional programs
    f. Sales/support organization
19. With respect to promotional programs, please describe how you communicate/interface with logistics/customer service regarding:
    a. Timing (including phase in/phase outs)
    b. Coordination of programs between different product managers/customer segment managers
    c. Pricing allowances administration
    d. Inventory requirements to support increased volumes from a promotion program
    e. Special shipment/freight terms
    f. Special payment, dating terms
    g. SKUs to be covered

APPENDIX G
Financial Control/Accounting Audit

1. Are standards established for each function, so that overall performance of the logistics system is measured and compared to these standards?
    a. Customer service
    b. Inventory management
    c. Transportation
    d. Warehousing

e. Order processing
f. Other (describe)

2. What are the components of logistics costs (recognized as such by your firm), and how are they currently captured or otherwise computed?
3. What was your firm's approximate gross sales volume last year?
4. What was the average annual percentage increase in gross sales that your firm experienced over the past five years?
5. What was the after-tax net profit as a percentage of sales for your firm last year?
6. What was the average annual after-tax profit as a percentage of sales that your firm experienced over the past five years?
7. What was the return on net worth for your firm last year?
8. What was the average annual return on net worth that your firm experienced over the past five years?
9. What percentage of your firm's total assets is represented by cash?
10. What percentage of your firm's total assets is represented by inventory (raw, in-process, and finished goods)?
11. What is your average annual inventory turnover rate on finished goods inventories?
12. What percentage of total assets is represented by accounts receivable?
13. What is the firm's minimum acceptable rate of return on new investments (after taxes)?
14. What is your firm's approximate overall market share? (Please include your major business activities).
15. Do you use standard costs in controlling logistics expense?
16. If there is a variance, what corrective actions are initiated, and how frequently?
17. In your opinion, what are specific reports that your firm should compile, on an ongoing basis, to effectively measure the performance of its overall logistics organization, as well as key individual functions?
18. Please describe what, if any, steps, procedures, systems, and so on are currently being employed to:
    a. Set up department standards regarding head count, budgets, and performance measurements.
    b. Secure viable, least cost contract/common carrier services.
    c. Provide management reports/controls.
    d. Minimize use of expensive, duplicative product movements.
    e. Utilize automated freight bill audit and/or payment techniques.

APPENDIX H
Purchasing Audit

1. What is your average investment in raw materials and in-process inventories and turnovers for each major commodity category?
2. From how many vendors does your firm purchase raw materials and parts?
   a. How many vendors account for 80 percent of your purchases?
   b. How has the number of vendors and the amount of business done with your top-volume vendors changed during the past two years?
3. How many vendors do you use for each major category/commodity, and where are they located?

   Commodity Category *Number Used* *Location*

4. How frequently do you typically order material (by major commodity category)?

   Commodity Category *Frequency* *Order Quantity/Weight*

5. Are minimum or fixed quantities used in determining order release quantities on purchase orders (for each major product class)? How are these quantities computed (by computer or manually)?

   Commodity Category *Basis* *How Computed?*

6. What are average lead times, by product class, for major vendors (from date purchase order is released to vendor until receipt at factories)?

   Commodity Category *Average Lead Time*

7. Is time-phased order information for raw materials and parts available on a regular basis? If so, how frequently are these reports published? Describe.
8. Are these recommended order reports automatically generated from a data processing system?
9. What are purchase order policies with regard to the following: blanket orders with periodic releases; specification of carrier; and charge back to vendors (packing/quantity errors, damages/rejects, misroutings, and late deliveries)?
10. What is the typical lead time encountered in replenishing your inventories (days/weeks from time order is placed to times product is received)? Please list by major vendor or product category.
11. What amount of lead time do you require/desire (from order submission to receipt of order)?
    a. Major suppliers ______
    b. Other suppliers ______
12. What percentage of line items you order are normally delivered by the date requested by you? Please list by major vendor or product category.
13. What percentage of your orders would you classify as emergency/ship ASAP orders? Does this vary significantly by vendor and/or product category? (Explain.)

SOURCE: Professor Jay U. Sterling, University of Alabama.

14. If a supplier is unable to commit to an order by the desired "date wanted," what percentage of the time do you:
    a. Cancel the order and seek an alternate supplier? _______%
    b. Back-order with the supplier? _______%
    c. Request substitutions? _______%
    d. Other (please specify)? _______%
15. Does this vary by vendor source? (Explain.)
16. What percentage of your purchase requisitions are expedited (i.e., requested inside the vendor's stated lead time)? _______%
    a. Please describe the different categories of expedited orders from vendors (e.g., orders processed around normal system by phone, request delivery ASAP, small emergency quantities ordered, etc.).
    b. Is the percentage of expedited orders too high?
17. Do you receive periodic reports from your major vendor sources that give you the:
    a. Status of orders? Yes ____ No ____
    b. Availability of individual items? Yes ____ No ____
    c. Recommended stocking balances, by model (based on your inventory levels)? Yes ____ No ____
18. If any answer to question 17 is yes, how do you obtain this information? How frequently do you receive these data?
19. How have your suppliers improved their deliveries and information (orders, etc.) processing systems in the last 12 months?
20. Are you able to determine the availability of product that you would like to order from your major manufacturing source? Yes ____ No ____ If yes, how?
21. If parts/materials are not available, are you able to determine what and when your major manufacturing source will produce the desired products? Yes __ No ____
22. How are you able to communicate with your major manufacturing sources to obtain the above information?
23. What percentage of your parts/materials is received by the following modes of transportation?
    a. Private carriage _______%
    b. Common/contract carrier _______%
    c. UPS _______%
    d. Rail _______%
    e. TOFC (piggyback) _______%
    f. Air express _______%
24. Do you use a scheduled delivery program with any of your suppliers (i.e., order the bulk of your requirements on a regularly scheduled day each week)? If so, with whom? How does program work? How effective is it in helping you to manage your inventories?
25. Do any of your suppliers offer incentives (e.g., prepaid freight, quantity discounts, claims handlings for damage) for ordering in larger quantities? (If so, explain, by supplier.)
26. Do you attempt to carry different levels of safety stock inventories (e.g., fast movers versus low-volume product)? If yes, what type of logic do you use in establishing which product will be maintained in inventory versus ordered only as needed?

27. What are the average days/weeks/months of supply that you typically maintain in your on-hand inventory?
    a. Is this: Too high? ____ Too low? ____
    b. Does this percentage vary by major commodity and/or vendor? (Explain.)
28. Do you perform any type of trade-off analysis to weigh the economies of quantity discounts/forward buys versus the added carrying costs to be incurred?
29. What type of terms do your major suppliers offer?

Vendor	*Commodity*	*Terms*

30. What payment terms would you prefer from your major vendors?
31. Do you regularly measure the performance of your major vendors? (Explain.)
32. How is the performance of the purchasing function measured by your management?
33. What are the major criteria that you use when:
    a. Selecting vendors?
    b. Evaluating performance of vendors?
34. What are the distinguishing features of those vendors/suppliers who consistently provide you with desired/satisfactory customer service versus those who do not?
35. How have your major vendors/suppliers improved their customer service, deliveries, and information with respect to orders over the past 12–18 months?
36. What services would you like vendors/suppliers to provide that presently are not available to you (with respect to logistics/customer service)?
37. Have you made, or are you contemplating making, any changes in the way you order product from your vendors (e.g., stock orders versus made-to-order product, reductions in lead time, higher expected fill rates)?
38. What percentage age of the time do you use the following techniques to transmit orders to your major suppliers?

	Supplier			
Order Transmittal Techniques	*A*	*B*	*C*	*D*
On-line communication terminal	____	____	____	____
Fax	____	____	____	____
Inward WATS	____	____	____	____
Telephone paid by you	____	____	____	____
Mail	____	____	____	____
Hand delivered to sales representative	____	____	____	____
Other (specify)	____	____	____	____
Total	100%	100%	100%	100%

APPENDIX I
General/Senior Management Audit

1. How many product lines do you sell?

Product Line	*Annual Sales*	*Percentage of Your Business*

2. Describe the overall competitive environment in the major industries you serve.
3. What is your overall marketing strategy?
4. Who are your major competitors? What products do they sell? To whom?
5. How do your major competitors distribute their products?
6. Do any of your major competitors offer any unique marketing/distribution services? Explain.
7. Why would your customers purchase products from your competitors rather than from you?
8. What are the estimated market shares in your major markets?
9. Describe the marketing channels (intermediaries and/or retailers) used in the major industries you service.
10. Are your firm's logistics-related strategies identified and/or specified in writing?
    Yes ___ No ___ If yes, please summarize them.
11. How is the physical distribution/logistics function organized?
12. Activities typically associated with distribution/logistics are listed in the table below. For each activity, please indicate with a (✓) whether your firm (it is permissible to check both columns):
    a. Includes these activities/functions in an overall, firmwide, and/or centralized distribution/logistics organization (e.g., corporate).
    b. Includes these activities/functions in a decentralized distribution/logics organization (e.g., divisional or business unit operating group).

Activity	*Included in Decentralized Organization*	*Included in Centralized Organization*	*If Neither, to Whom Do These Activities Report?*
Development of logistics strategies	___	___	___
Logistics audit	___	___	___
System modeling and/or simulation	___	___	___
Logistics performance measurement reports	___	___	___
Accounting/financial reporting systems unique to the logistics organization	___	___	___
Development of customer service strategies	___	___	___
Customer service audit	___	___	___
Development of transportation strategies	___	___	___
Traffic system/network analysis	___	___	___
Private fleet management	___	___	___
Common and/or contract carrier management	___	___	___

SOURCE: Professor Jay U. Sterling, University of Alabama.

Activity	*Included in Decentralized Organization*	*Included in Centralized Organization*	*If Neither, to Whom Do These Activities Report?*
Transportation cost accounting system	______	______	______
Rating/rate books/rate maintenance	______	______	______
Vehicle routing and scheduling	______	______	______
Freight payment/audit system	______	______	______
Transportation claims management	______	______	______
Vehicle dispatching	______	______	______
Vehicle training	______	______	______
Vehicle financing (e.g., lease versus buy)	______	______	______
Development of warehousing strategies	______	______	______
Warehouse site location	______	______	______
Warehouse layout and design	______	______	______
Warehouse space forecast studies	______	______	______
Automated storage and retrieval (AS/AR) systems	______	______	______
Warehouse conveyor systems	______	______	______
Warehouse handling systems design and specification	______	______	______
Warehousing labor management	______	______	______
Warehouse space management	______	______	______
Warehouse stow/slot location record keeping	______	______	______
Warehouse storage and handling rate calculations/negotiations	______	______	______
Public vs. private (company-owned) warehousing analyses	______	______	______
Automated order entry/processing	______	______	______
On-line communication network/systems	______	______	______
Demand forecasting	______	______	______
Official product level forecasting	______	______	______
Inventory deployment to DCs and/or customers	______	______	______
Inventory tracking/record keeping	______	______	______
Distribution requirements planning (DRP) systems	______	______	______
Production planning/scheduling systems	______	______	______
Materials requirements planning (DRP) systems	______	______	______
Energy management	______	______	______
Hazardous materials	______	______	______
Labor management			
Recruitment/placement	______	______	______
Training	______	______	______
Supervision	______	______	______
Incentives	______	______	______
Work measurement/productivity	______	______	______
Safety compliance	______	______	______
Law and industrial relations	______	______	______
International logistics			
U.S. to P.O.E.	______	______	______
Overseas distribution	______	______	______
Data processing (MIS) dedicated and/or assigned to logistics	______	______	______

Activity	*Included in Decentralized Organization*	*Included in Centralized Organization*	*If Neither, to Whom Do These Activities Report?*
Packaging design	________	________	________
Computer aided design and manufacturing (CAD/CAM) systems	________	________	________
Purchasing systems	________	________	________

13. Diagram your company's organizational chart (or provide a photocopy). Show the functions of logistics, marketing, production, purchasing, and top management, or their equivalents. Include any function your company presently defines as customer service (or customer relations, distribution services, etc.). If your company subdivides the logistics activities, show where they report. Show staff responsibility with a dashed line and line responsibility with a solid line. If appropriate, you may describe only a division or subsidiary of your company if most of the corporate functional areas described above are included within it.
14. Are standards established for each logistics function so that overall performance of the logistics system is measured and compared to these standards?
15. Do you have automated files that record distribution-related transactions?
    a. Orders
        Yes ____ No ____ Comments: ______________________________
    b. Bills of lading
        Yes ____No ____ Comments: ______________________________
    c. Freight bills
        Yes ____ No ____ Comments: ______________________________
    d. Inventory by SKU
        Yes ____ No ____ Comments: ______________________________
    e. Warehouse activity
        Yes ____ No ____ Comments: ______________________________
16. In your opinion, what are specific reports that your firm should compile, on an ongoing basis, to effectively measure the performance of its overall logistics organization, as well as key individual functions?

Report	*Key Measurements Included*

17. What kinds of performance data that are not currently available would you like to receive?
18. What problems do you perceive with respect to marketing/production/logistics?
19. Please describe what, if any, steps, procedures, systems, and so on are currently being employed to:
    a. Set up department organizational standards
    b. Secure viable, least cost contract/common carrier services.
    c. Establish efficient warehouse handling and loading procedures.
    d. Provide management reports/controls.
    e. Utilize state-of-the-art logistics concepts and services.
    f. Be responsive to regulatory requirements and changes.
    g. Minimize use of expensive, complex multiple distribution channels.

f. Be responsive to regulatory requirements and changes.
g. Minimize use of expensive, complex multiple distribution channels.
h. Establish customer service standards.
i. Install warehouse manpower planning procedures.
j. Use managed/scheduled shipping programs.
k. Utilize automated freight bill audit and/or payment techniques.
l. Negotiate/implement beneficial freight terms on inbound purchase orders (re: materials and parts).
m. Design and implement on-line order entry systems.
n. Install telephone communications with regard to order entry.
o. Design automated time-phased production and inventory planning programs by SKU and base model.

Cases

1. Horizon Foods Corporation
2. Carlton Electronics
3. RLC Computer Company
4. Giles Laboratories (1992)
5. Favored Blend Coffee Company
6. Hickory Hill Smoked Foods Company
7. Worthing Ski Company
8. Mirror Stainless Steel
9. Flexit International
10. Riverview Distributing Company, Incorporated (1991)
11. SKF
12. Ferle Foods, Inc.

CASE 1
Horizon Foods Corporation

"So, why are we calling this meeting?" Roger Bennett asked. "Are we finally beginning to recognize that we have a distribution problem?" As a newly appointed brand manager, Roger had just been promoted from the sales force and was interested in clearing up some of the problems that had appeared during his customer contacts. "Can we continue to sell our products when we can't tell our customers when our products will be delivered?"

"I think you have guessed the problem" replied Sally Ryan, the production scheduling manager. "We have so many requests for special production runs to supply inventory that we can't seem to plan a decent normal schedule." It seemed that the production scheduling desk had become a crisis center, and there was a continuing series of requests from sales.

Mel Young, the financial director, looked up as they entered the conference room. "Maybe one of you can tell me what's happening out there. I pay some pretty large bills to those public warehouses to store our products. I have had to increase our working capital in order to have enough inventory on hand. Yet we never seem to have enough. Can't we get some kind of control out there?"

Roger spoke first. "Mel, you know how we are organized. We let Production take care of supplying the market, and let Marketing take care of dealing with the customer. My apologies to Sally, but when I was in the field, I was never sure if Production would be able to back me up."

Sally began to burn a little at that last comment. "Roger, I can't blame you because you haven't been in the corporate office very long, but it always seemed to me that Marketing was always a little out of control. You guys wanted everything—the full product line and lots of inventory—but you really couldn't tell me what the customers wanted to buy and when they planned to take it."

* * * * *

Horizon Foods is a relatively small specialty foods processor serving a national market with a broad product line and sales of $300 million per year. They market their products through a network of food brokers who represent the company to retail food chains. Horizon's product lines have focused on ethnic food specialties including salad dressings, sauces for Italian pasta, and condiments such as specialty pickles. They advertise at a low level—about 2 percent of sales, placing most of their promotional efforts

---

This case was written by Professor Philip Schary, College of Business, Oregon State University.

on supporting the brokers with point-of-sale displays and cooperative advertising with local retailers, and couponing for special promotions. Retailers have generally liked Horizon's products because of their high quality. However, they are not alone in this market; there is intense competition for retail shelf space. Competition has become more intense in recent years as other companies are beginning to offer complete product lines which compete directly with Horizon's. The brokers report that there is strong pressure to increase service to retail chain stores. They report that the retail buyers are raising questions about the number of stockouts that they have been recently experiencing. These buyers have occasionally even suggested that they might switch to other brands if service is not improved.

Products are produced in two plants: one in the Central Valley of California at Fresno and the other in Illinois about 60 miles south of Chicago. They buy ingredients from other food suppliers, avoiding the peak seasonal characteristics encountered by food packers. Production takes place in large batch quantities in order to maintain low production costs and assure consistent product quality. As items are packed, they are generally transported to the market in mixed truckload volumes using contract carriers. Product inventories are normally spotted around the country in about 20 public warehouses. The food brokers call on customers and generate orders, which are telexed to these warehouses. These public warehouses then arrange transportation. Horizon's products are packaged and are not considered perishable items. Orders are generally small, amounting to five to six cases per order, or about 150 to 200 pounds at a time. These are then delivered using carriers selected individually by each public warehouse. The costs of delivery are then billed to Horizon. Transportation costs are high, because of these small shipments. Delivery schedules vary by carrier; some provide fast, reliable service, while others have been erratic to the point that customers have commented on poor delivery service. Even though Horizon's two plants are located in agricultural areas, many of the ingredients are shipped over long distances, depending on the season.

Horizon's management is divided into two major departments. One is Marketing and Sales; the other is Production. There are also several smaller staff units for personnel, purchasing, and finance. Production is the oldest of the two. Marketing came in almost as an afterthought and had a difficult time establishing credibility within the company. Production is responsible for scheduling production runs, as well as arranging transportation to and maintaining inventory in the warehouse.

Within Marketing and Sales, two brand managers are responsible for marketing the product line. They are responsible for promotion, product inventory at the public warehouse, providing sales support, and merchandising. There is also a national sales manager who has responsibility for maintaining contact with food brokers, coordinating public warehouses, and arranging for delivery. This split between delivery from production and service from the warehouse has often led to problems in holding enough inventory on many items to meet customer demand.

* * * * *

At that minute the president, Harold Sessions, came in. "I'm glad to see that we are finally getting this problem out in the open. Maybe we can do something about it at last. We need some better control over this product movement process. I chose you people because you seem to have a real interest in doing something about it. Now, how do you suggest that we go about managing it to eliminate some of these problems?"

CASE 2
Carlton Electronics

The marketing director of Carlton Electronics was examining the results of a customer survey concerning the quality of customer service. As he looked through the results, he began to consider possible courses of action that he might take. However, it was not clear in his mind which direction the company should take.

Carlton was a producer of a range of telephone answering machines and related peripherals. They were not a large company, but their reputation as a quality supplier was well established in a fast-changing market. Marketing practices at Carlton had followed a traditional approach in the past, selling mainly through British Telecom. As the telecommunications market changed, Carlton had been forced to keep pace, although they had not taken a position of marketing leadership. First, there had been a wave of new competitors from continental Europe, in which competitive products were offered to customers at slight discounts from Carlton's quoted prices. Carlton had responded, not by matching prices but by investing in an advertising program emphasizing the quality of Carlton products. The next wave of competition, from Japan, was more difficult to deal with. There were some Japanese lines that had become established as equal quality but at a significantly lower price. In addition, there had been a flood of low-priced imports from Southeast Asia which looked as if they were going to take over the consumer market completely.

Carlton's immediate customers fell into three categories: large chain stores, British Telecom, and discount operators. British Telecom had been

---

This case was written by Professor Martin Christopher, Cranfield School of Management, U.K., and Professor Philip Schary, College of Business, Oregon State University, U.S.A.

the basis for Carlton's original markets. However, with the growth of competition through deregulation, Carlton had to rethink its strategy. Within the last few years, new customers had emerged in the form of large chain stores and discount stores. Where British Telecom had previously tended to take the full product line and maintain the established price structure, chain stores tended to be more selective and also to press Carlton for promotional discounts. The discounters were far more aggressive in their dealings with Carlton. They took only high-volume lines but moved these products in significant volumes. They asked for substantial discounts on cumulative quantity purchases. The marketing director believed that these customers used Carlton as bait or leaders to draw in consumers in order to sell them competing lines as soon as they were in the stores. The volume of business with British Telecom had held steady, while that of the chain stores had grown. The promise of future growth, however, lay with the discounters because they were getting a larger share of the consumer business.

Carlton dealt directly with the retail buyers, who as a group were extremely conscious of service by suppliers. There was an attitude which Carlton's salespeople sensed of "What have you done for us lately?" This was obviously most pronounced among the discounters. They tended to operate on weekly order cycles and wanted to manage inventory on a hand-to-mouth basis.

The chain stores followed similar patterns but perhaps not so intensively. Most were on a two-week order cycle and maintained adequate stock levels in their own distribution centers as backup to their stores. They were beginning to inquire about direct ordering from their computers to Carlton's computers, which Carlton was totally unprepared to deal with.

British Telecom was the least aggressive, being the most traditional member of the industry. It ordered in a variety of ways: sometimes using standard order quantities, sometimes on monthly order cycles. Carlton valued British Telecom as a customer because it presented the full product line, which the other customers did not do. Therefore, it could not be pushed aside.

Carlton had commissioned the customer service survey as a means of understanding the customer service problem. No one in the organization had looked at the customer service problem as a whole. Customer complaints had usually come through the sales force, which in turn had passed them on to the sales manager, who in turn referred them to the distribution manager. These complaints referred to a variety of different problems: delivery, credit, representative call frequency. They were hard to pin down in a specific pattern. The marketing director wanted several answers from this survey: Were there specific areas of complaint that stood out? How was Carlton's performance compared to that of the competition? What areas should Carlton try to improve?

The Customer Service Survey

The survey was conducted primarily through direct interviews with a selected number of key customers among chain and discount store buyers. In addition to general comments, questions were asked seeking comparative ratings of Carlton versus major competitors on specific aspects of service. The survey covered several specific aspects of customer service: delivery time, both average and consistency; the quality and knowledge of sales representatives; inventory reliability [fill rate]; communications and order procedures; advertising and promotion; and packaging. The consultants were to report the results of the survey in a form that Carlton could use to take action. The general results of the survey were reported as follows.

Delivery Time. The largest suppliers were about equal in terms of delivery performance. However, as a group they were not equal to the performance of smaller competitors. Carlton's average times were considered to be acceptable, but their performance had slipped in terms of reliability. Customers could not be sure when their orders would arrive. On a local basis, this was caused by Carlton's local delivery dispatching. At a national level, it was due to the performance of the carriers that Carlton was using.

Inventory Reliability. Carlton was again comparable in inventory reliability performance to its major competitors, fulfilling about 80 percent of item demands from stock on hand. Smaller competitors, with their restricted product lines, tended to do better. Carlton's back-order performance was better than average. Customers recognized that back-orders from Carlton would always be filled, even if it took a couple of months. When orders were picked there would be occasional errors, which meant that items once shipped had to be returned. This seemed to lead to considerable confusion on Carlton's part.

Sales Representation. Carlton had very low turnover among its sales representatives, who were well received in the trade. They knew their products and market policies in general. Where they fell down was in dealing with distribution problems, because they had little direct contact with distribution operations. When there was a distribution problem, it seemed to take a long time to get an answer, and then it was not always satisfactory. When orders could not be filled, Carlton did not notify customers, assuming that they understood that products would be delivered when available. The chain and discount buyers, however, noted that they were getting precise indications when their orders would be served and shipped from competitors and found it useful for inventory planning for their own operations.

Orders. Customers expressed considerable annoyance about Carlton's order system. There were frequent errors in recording/filling orders, but there was no confirmation when the order was received. Orders were normally entered by written purchase requests from customers, by sales representatives' order forms, or by telephone requests by customers. When they were received, orders were taken in the sales department and entered in the computer. In the case of documentation, customers expected written confirmation, which some suppliers furnished automatically but others did not.

Advertising and Promotion. Advertising and promotion were not strong points with Carlton. They relied on their retail customers to arrange for special promotions. Most ads for Carlton were corporate, emphasizing product quality in general rather than specific items in the line. This was in direct contrast to the most aggressive competitors, who ran campaigns to push specific products and to support major selling events.

Packaging. Packaging was an important area but involved conflict. Carlton's policy had always been to pack well. Packages were always well labeled. However, some of the chain and discount buyers had begun to use laser bar code scanners and wanted suppliers to adapt their packages to the new system of item identification, requiring preprinted bar codes on a nonreflective surface. Neither Carlton nor the competition had done this yet.

CASE 3
RLC Computer Company

RLC Computer Company is a major electronics manufacturer which produces two categories of high-value, high-technology computers (A and B) and distributes these products from two Midwest production facilities (Detroit and Cincinnati, respectively) to U.S. markets. Since the computers are manufactured at different sites, management's goal is to deliver the products while minimizing the transportation expense. Historically, the firm has utilized daily direct air shipments from each production facility to all major U.S. markets. Exhibit 1 shows the daily demand for each product for the western markets, which are shown on the map in Exhibit 2.

The customer is billed immediately upon receipt of the individual computer shipment. Since a majority of sales are on the basis of delivered cost, the firm assumes the risks of transportation damage and theft, and the cost of financing in-transit inventory. Thus, in addition to minimizing transportation expense, the terms of sale and high product values dictate that the

This case was written by Professor Robert L. Cook, Central Michigan University.

EXHIBIT 1 Average Daily Demand by Product/Market in Units*

Product	*Market*							*Product Total*
	LAX†	*SFO*	*PHX*	*DEN*	*ABQ*	*SLC*	*PDX*	
A	34	23	12	20	8	20	11	128
B	23	21	10	13	4	18	11	100
Market total	57	44	22	33	12	38	22	228

*Each unit weighs 100 pounds and is priced at $100.

†Key to cities: LAX, Los Angeles; SFO, San Francisco; PHX, Phoenix; DEN, Denver; ABQ, Albuquerque; SLC, Salt Lake City; and PDX, Portland (Oregon). Cities in later exhibits are CVG, Cincinnati; and DTW, Detroit.

firm have objectives of (1) maximizing accounts receivable turnover, (2) minimizing damage and theft related to extended transit time and multiple handlings, and (3) minimizing in-transit inventory investment. The firm's desire for a distribution system characterized by high-speed transportation and low in-transit inventory levels has resulted in the following distribution policies or actions:

1. All time lags have been removed from the controllable portion(s) of the order cycle, including order processing.
2. No warehouse facilities are used since they would increase inventories and the potential for damage.
3. Holding product for freight consolidation at production facilities for greater than one day is undesirable because plant storage capacity is limited; delays in billing would decrease accounts receivable turnover, and longer order cycle times would result in unacceptable customer service levels.

Given these assumptions, transportation costs make up a major percentage of the distribution system cost and become the major objective criteria for evaluating alternative distribution system strategies. The objective is to evaluate and identify the consolidation strategy alternative between plants and West Coast markets that results in the lowest total *daily* cost (consolidation cost + transportation cost + cost of lost sales). The case is limited to only one day's units, to limit the number of consolidation alternatives to a manageable number.

With respect to customer service, one-day service for 100 percent of units is the current service level (one-day air transport plant to market and local LTL delivery). The following information on customer requirements was developed from customer interviews:

- Seven-day service is unacceptable to 100 percent of customers.
- Six-day service is unacceptable to 20 percent of customers.
- Five-day service is unacceptable to 5 percent of customers.
- Four-day service is unacceptable to 1 percent of customers.
- Three-day service is unacceptable to .2 percent of customers.

EXHIBIT 2 Major Western Markets

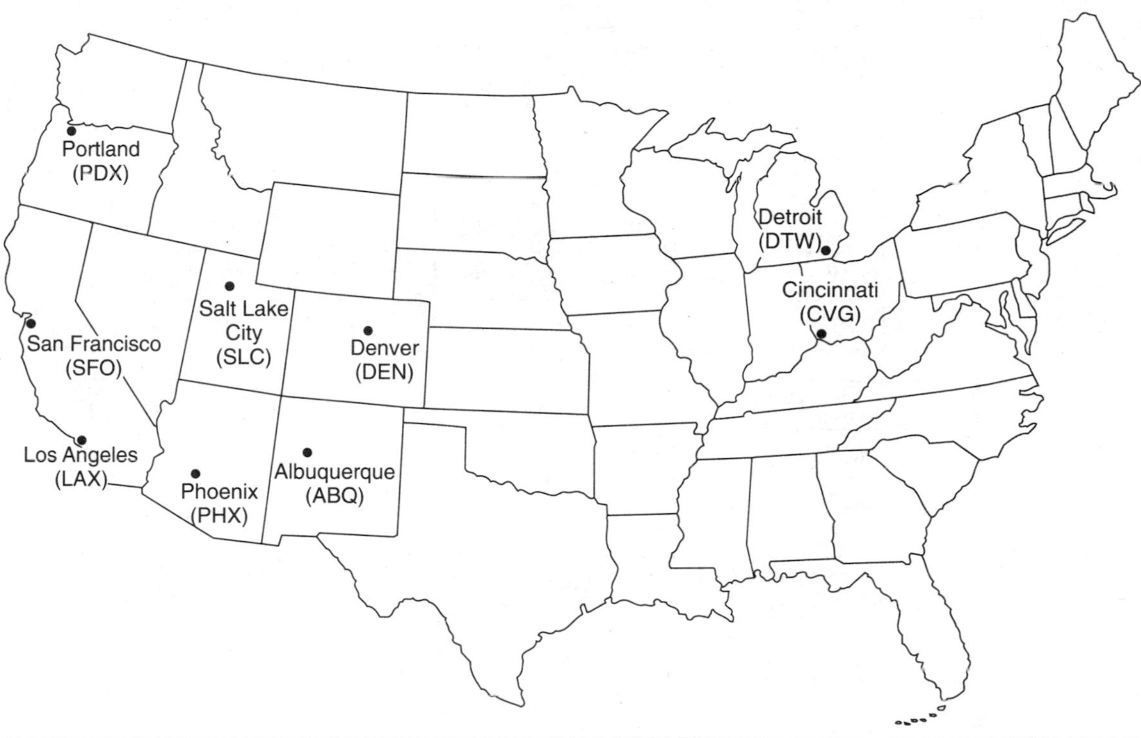

Cost data that were developed included the following:

1. Air freight costs. Exhibit 3 summarizes the air rates from Detroit (DTW) and Cincinnati (CVG) to each city for four weight groups.
2. Truck freight costs. Exhibit 4 depicts the LTL truck rates per 100 pounds between city pairs. Truckload rates are calculated by taking 50 percent of the rates shown in Exhibit 4. Truckload rates may be applied to *all* shipments in a truck that begins at its origin point with 60 or more computers. For example, if the market demand (see Exhibit 1) for Portland (PDX) [22], Salt Lake City (SLC) [38], and Albuquerque (ABQ) [12] were flown to Portland (PDX) and loaded into a truck for delivery, it would be a truckload (72 units) and the truckload rate would apply to all three shipments. In addition, the freight rate (see Exhibit 4) used for each shipment is based on the origin point, that is, Portland (PDX) to Portland (PDX) [$6], Portland (PDX) to Salt Lake City (SLC) [$12], and Portland (PDX) to Albuquerque (ABQ) [$18]. The correct truck freight calculation in this example would be as follows:

.5	[(22 units × $6)	+	(38 × $12)	+	(12 × $18)] = $402.00
(TL)	(PDX to PDX)		(PDX to SLC)		(PDX to ABQ)

EXHIBIT 3 Air Rates in Dollars Per 100 Pounds

100–1,200 Pounds*

From \ To	DTW†	CVG	LAX	SFO	PHX	DEN	ABQ	SLC	PDX
DTW	—	8*	40	43	46	44	48	45	50
CVG	7	—	42	45	46	45	50	44	53

1,201–2,399 Pounds

From \ To	DTW	CVG	LAX	SFO	PHX	DEN	ABQ	SLC	PDX
DTW	—	7	35	38	43	39	46	40	49
CVG	6	—	37	40	44	41	47	41	52

2,400–13,499 Pounds

From \ To	DTW	CVG	LAX	SFO	PHX	DEN	ABQ	SLC	PDX
DTW	—	7	28	30	34	29	37	29	40
CVG	5	—	30	32	36	31	38	33	44

13,500–25,000 Pounds

From \ To	DTW	CVG	LAX	SFO	PHX	DEN	ABQ	SLC	PDX
DTW	—	6	21	23	28	22	30	24	34
CVG	4	—	25	27	30	26	30	26	36

* Each product weighs 100 pounds.
† See Exhibit 1 for identification of cities.

3. Consolidation costs. Each time units are brought together and *sorted* by city, those units involved incur a $1.00 per unit charge. For example, if all Product A and B were shipped consolidated to Portland (PDX) and then sorted by city for delivery, the consolidated costs would be 228 × $1/day.
4. Lost sales. This cost is based on the percentage of customer sales lost due to slow delivery.

Transit time data were as follows:

1. Air transit time:
   One day plant to western city.
   One day Detroit (DTW) to Cincinnati (CVG); or Cincinnati (CVG) to Detroit (DTW).
2. Consolidation transit times:
   One day to customer if any consolidations occur during transit.
3. Truck transit times (see Exhibit 5):
   Unlike truck freight rates, transit times are calculated from city to

EXHIBIT 4 LTL Truck Rates Between Cities (rates per 100 pounds)*

From \ To	DTW†	CVG	LAX	SFO	PHX	DEN	ABQ	SLC	PDX
DTW	6	7	39	38	36	35	38	39	34
CVG	7	6	41	40	37	36	42	43	35
LAX			6	8	9	15	13	11	14
SFO			8	6	12	16	15	12	11
PHX			9	12	6	13	9	11	16
DEN			15	16	13	6	9	10	16
ABQ			13	15	9	9	6	11	18
SLC			11	12	11	10	11	6	12
PDX			14	11	16	16	18	12	6

* Rates are dollars per 100 pounds.
†See Exhibit 1 for identification of cities.

EXHIBIT 5 Truck Transit Time, In Days

From \ To	DTW*	CVG	LAX	SFO	PHX	DEN	ABQ	SLC	PDX
DTW	0	1	9	9	8	6	7	7	9
CVG	1	0	9	9	8	6	7	7	9
LAX			0	1	1	3	2	2	3
SFO			1	0	2	3	3	2	2
PHX			1	2	0	2	1	2	4
DEN			3	3	2	0	1	1	3
ABQ			2	3	1	1	0	2	4
SLC			2	2	2	1	2	0	2
PDX			3	2	4	3	4	2	0

* See Exhibit 1 for identification of cities.

city; same-day delivery can be made *only* in cities where shipments land.

Transit example: All products are flown to Cincinnati (CVG), sorted, and then flown Cincinnati (CVG) to Portland (PDX), where a truckload (Portland (PDX), Salt Lake City (SLC), Albuquerque (ABQ) freight) is routed to Portland (PDX), Salt Lake City (SLC), and Albuquerque (ABQ). A second transit times for the first truck would be:

	Air (DTW to CVG)	*Consolidation*	*CVG to PDX**	*PDX to SLC*	*SLC to ABQ*	*Total Time*
To PDX	1	1	1	—	—	3 days
To SLC	1	1	1	2	—	5 days
To ABQ	1	1	1	2	2	7 days

*Same day delivery.

The transit times for the second truck would be:

	DTW to CVG	*Consolidation*	*CVG to PDX*	*PDX to SFO*	*SFO to LAX*	*Total Time*
To SFO	1	1	1	2	—	5 days
To LAX	1	1	1	2	1	6 days

Flights from each location and the number of trucks at each location are *not* limited. Air and truck capacity is also *not* limited.

CASE 4
Giles Laboratories (1992)

Paul McNaughton, director of distribution services for Giles Laboratories, a wholly owned subsidiary of the worldwide Thurber Pharmaceutical group of companies, was under strong pressure from top management to reduce the number of field warehouses that the company maintained throughout the United States. Top management believed that the company could manage on fewer distribution facilities without hurting sales operations. They were concerned about Giles having more warehouses than the parent company even though the parent carried more products at a higher

This case was made possible by the cooperation of a business firm which remains anonymous. It was written by Albert M. Ladores under the direction of Bernard J. LaLonde of the faculty of Marketing and Logistics, The Ohio State University. Revised 1992 by Douglas M. Lambert.

unit-sales volume. They were also disturbed by the fact that Giles' main competitor had fewer warehouses giving the same national market coverage.

At the beginning of 1992, Giles Laboratories had 37 field warehouses, of which 33 were public. Four warehouses were owned by the parent company, but contractual arrangements with them paralleled those with public warehouses. In addition to the 37 field warehouses, Giles owned four plant warehouses which served the field warehouses and customers located in areas where these plant warehouses were situated.

By March 1992, McNaughton was faced with the decision to phase out the public warehouse at Columbus, Ohio, and serve the customers in the area directly from the main plant warehouse at Indianapolis, Indiana. This meant extending the service area of the Indianapolis facility beyond Dayton, Ohio. The contract with the Columbus warehouse was up for renewal in mid-April.

Thurber Pharmaceuticals

Giles was part of a group of companies that was controlled by Thurber Pharmaceuticals. Although the parent corporation specialized in a variety of prescription drugs, the products of the subsidiary companies ranged from food items to consumer sundries.

Each subsidiary operated as an autonomous corporate entity with its own set of executive officers and was relatively free to set its own policies in marketing, research, and manufacturing activities. Control by Thurber took the form of broad intercorporate policies and close monitoring of significant investment decisions. With the exception of the products of one of the subsidiary companies, an international division supervised the manufacture and marketing of all products in foreign countries.

Background on Giles Laboratories

Product Lines. Giles and its major competitor enjoyed about 75 percent of the nutrient and dietary-food market, with Giles' share of the total market approximately 40 percent.

The company manufactured 35 variations of one basic mixture of raw materials, and product differences were determined primarily by additives and calorie content. Finished products came in both a liquid concentrate and a powder packed in cans of various sizes. The Indianapolis plant, which was the largest and oldest of the company's four plants, produced 25 items of the product line. Each of the other plants manufactured as many as 12 of the products.

Sales Operations. Approximately 90 percent of the company's sales were derived from consumer outlets, the most significant of which were department stores, wholesale drug houses, drug chains, and supermarket chains. The balance was sold directly to hospitals for patient use while recovering from illness. Demand for the company's products was not subject to seasonal variations.

Salespeople concentrated their selling efforts on medical practitioners, hospitals, and the major retail outlets. Their function was to promote product awareness by improving the sales distribution of the product lines and to assist retailers in merchandising. With minor exceptions, they did not act as order takers.

Distribution Organization. Mr. McNaughton, as the company's director of distribution services, reported to the vice president of operations and shared the same rank and status as the comptroller and the director of manufacturing. He had responsibility for four major areas: distribution, operations planning, purchasing, and production planning, each headed by a manager reporting directly to him. The director had control over most of the logistics functions with the exceptions of plant shipping and receiving, which were the responsibility of each plant manager, who reported to the director of manufacturing.

All of the distribution personnel were located at the company's central headquarters in Indianapolis. The coordination of receiving and shipping activities at the plants was accomplished by the plant manager.

Distribution Policies and Practices. Giles Laboratories followed their traditional practice of distributing all products through public warehouses, which was in direct contrast to the parent company's system of ownership and control of warehouses. However, efforts had been initiated by Giles to determine the utility of continuing with its system of dealing exclusively with public warehouses.

Giles currently owned four plant warehouses, dealt with four warehouses owned by the parent company, and, as mentioned, maintained 33 public warehouses specializing in grocery products and servicing other companies in the grocery trade. In no instance did Giles totally occupy the leased space of a specific field warehouse, and individual field warehouse allocation ranged from 3,000 to 100,000 hundredweight. Giles did not share a public warehouse with any of its sister companies.

Most public warehouse rates were negotiated at least every 12 months, and rarely did a contract extend beyond two years. In all cases, a one-shot billing system applied whereby a composite rate for storage and handling was set for every 100 pounds delivered to a warehouse. Accessorial charges for such things as damaged products and telephone expenses were billed separately. The public warehouses would assess a small penalty charge for every hundredweight in excess of the stipulated storage level per month. In plant warehouses, the rule of thumb was to assess storage and handling costs at 1.5 percent per month of the manufactured cost of average monthly inventory which was valued at the full cost of production. Full cost included allocations of overhead and other fixed charges in addition to the direct variable cost of manufacturing, which at Giles represented 80 percent of the full cost.

Top management felt that it was necessary to maintain a 100 percent service level with respect to hospitals. This was a reflection of their belief that hospitals in general had poor inventory management. In actual experience, the achieved customer service level was about 98 percent. Consumer products enjoyed a 96 percent service level, which compared favorably to the target of 98 percent. The distribution manager said that studies were being conducted to determine the optimum service levels considering distribution costs (including the inventory holding costs) and actual service requirements. He explained that prior to 1992, the company did not have a documented inventory carrying cost figure and although a number had been used in plant expansion proposals he was not sure how it had been arrived at. ("Perhaps it was the cost of money at that time applied to the full manufactured cost of the inventory.") However, a study has just been completed by a distribution analyst who had recently completed his M.B.A. degree in the evenings while working at Giles. A memo outlining the results of this study is given as Exhibit 1.

Approximately 60 percent of the shipments to field warehouses were consigned to rail carriers, with the remainder shipped by motor carriers. By policy, the optimum weight for rail shipments was 100,000 pounds. Plant shipments weighing 80,000 pounds and above were shipped by rail, and those below 80,000 pounds were shipped by motor carrier in increments of 40,000 pounds. All plant shipments represented a consolidation of most products, and case packs were closely standardized by size and weight for ease of handling. The rail service from each plant warehouse to public warehouse destination constituted direct point-to-point hauling, and warehouses serving the company had railroad service.

The distribution analyst commented that rail service involved long transit time (a ratio of 6-to-1 time periods versus motor carrier) and a heavy damage toll. However, rail rates for shipments weighing 80,000 pounds and above were in total more favorable than public trucking rates, and the savings more than offset the higher carrying costs and damage burden connected with rail service. Approximately 50 percent of the plant shipments were in the 100,000-pound category.

Shipments from field warehouses to customers were carried by motor carriers at prevailing cartage rates or negotiated contract carrier rates with the exception of a few of the field warehouses which operated their own truck fleets. These customer deliveries were FOB destination. No orders below 15 cases were accepted, and truckload orders (40,000 pounds) were referred to the head office by field warehouse personnel for possible direct service from the nearest plant warehouse. Unit-sales prices for the company's products were quoted at two price break ranges: at 15 to 49 cases, and at 50 cases and over.

EXHIBIT 1

GILES LABORATORIES
INTEROFFICE MEMO

Date: *January 30, 1992*
To: *Mr. Paul McNaughton, Director of Distribution Services*
From: *Wesley Scott, Distribution Analyst*
Subject: *A Documented Inventory Carrying Cost*

The following four basic cost categories must be considered when calculating inventory carrying costs: (1) capital costs, (2) inventory service costs, (3) storage space costs, and (4) inventory risk costs.

The money invested in inventory has a very real cost attached to it. Holding inventory ties up money that could be used for other types of investments. This reasoning holds for internally generated funds as well as those obtained from outside sources. Consequently, the company's opportunity cost of capital should be used in order to accurately reflect the true cost involved.

In order to establish the opportunity cost of capital (the minimum acceptable rate of return on new investments) for Giles Laboratories, the comptroller, Mr. John Munroe, was interviewed. The corporate cost of capital was the charge paid to the parent company, Thurber Pharmaceuticals. Currently, this rate is 10 percent before taxes for working capital. However, due to capital rationing the current hurdle rate on new investments is 30 percent before taxes (15 percent after taxes). The company conducts a postaudit of most projects in order to substantiate the rate of return. This is required by corporate policy, and in the majority of cases the desired return is achieved. Occasionally a 40 percent hurdle rate is employed to ensure that the required corporate rate of 30 percent is realized.

Although it would seem that the 30 percent hurdle rate also should be applied to inventory since in times of capital rationing an investment in inventory precludes other investments at the 30 percent rate, Thurber Pharmaceuticals only requires a 10 percent return on inventory investments. Consequently, 10 percent before taxes is used as the cost of money in this study. However, this is an issue that must be resolved at the top management level.

The opportunity cost of capital should be applied to only the out-of-pocket investment in inventory. This is the direct variable expense incurred up to the point at which the inventory is stored. In other words, it was necessary to obtain the average variable cost of products, FOB the distribution center. The individual cost components and the final carrying cost percentages are shown below.

Inventory Carrying Costs

Cost Component	*Percentage of Inventory Value*
Capital costs	10.00
Inventory service costs	
Taxes	2.50
Insurance	0.26
Warehousing costs	
Public warehouses (recurring storage only)	2.94
Plant warehouses	nil
Inventory risk costs	
Obsolescence	0.30
Shrinkage	0.58
Damage	0.43
Relocation (transshipment) costs	n.a.*
Total	17.01†

*Not available
†Inventory is valued at variable cost FOB the distribution center.

Shipping schedules from plant warehouses to field warehouses were initiated from central headquarters. Supervisors who reported to the distribution manager analyzed warehouse delivery receipts, in-transit stock levels, and bill-of-lading figures that indicated deliveries to customers, in order to initiate corrective action if required. Stocking requirements were determined according to normal usage levels (versus inventory levels) for each field warehouse and were reviewed periodically and changed if required.

Although most communication with public warehouses was by telephone or mail, the company had begun to install direct data-transmission connections with warehouses located in major market areas.

The lead time for processing and consolidating orders was targeted at three days for consumer outlets, but an actual average of five days was experienced. For hospital deliveries, the usual experience was two days compared to a target of one day.

Columbus Warehouse Facts and Data. The Columbus field warehouse was serving the metropolitan area and neighboring municipalities within a 40-mile radius. The outlying areas were being serviced by wholesalers that drew stock from Columbus. The distribution manager estimated that shipments to Columbus would average in excess of 15,000 cases per month for the next year. One-third of the present shipments came from the Michigan plant and were consolidated at 40,000 pounds for shipment at a freight rate of 70 cents per hundredweight. The rest of the shipments were sent out of the Indianapolis plant warehouse in truckload quantities (40,000 pounds) by public motor carrier at a rate of 60 cents per hundredweight. The 60 cents per hundredweight was based on a contract mileage rate of $1.40 per mile for truckload shipments from Indianapolis to Columbus. In this case, motor carrier rates were more favorable than railroad rates. Shipments from Michigan represented products that were not manufactured in Indianapolis.

Mr. McNaughton was reviewing a plan that would phase out the Columbus public warehouse. Michigan shipments would be diverted to Indianapolis and could be expected to be transported at the same freight rate. Indianapolis would then serve Columbus customers by motor carrier under new rates and according to the following schedule:

Percent of Total Weight Shipped	*Cost per Hundredweight*
40% @	$0.60 (TL)
35	1.50 (LTL)
25	2.40 (LTL)

Under the new plan another trucking firm would be contracted to provide local delivery to Columbus customers. This company was willing to offer better rates for LTL shipments and cartage (intracity) rates. Moreover, it had suggested allocating 100 square feet of space at its Columbus terminal for transit storage at no additional expense to Giles Laboratories. The lower cartage rates would result in a small saving to the company. If the contract with the Columbus warehouse was renegotiated, it was estimated that the throughput rate could be fixed at 25 cents per case plus a storage penalty when inventory turns fell below 12 times per annum.

A case of Giles products averaged 25 pounds and had a full manufactured cost of about $18. The selling price to wholesalers and chain retail accounts averaged $24.90 per case. The variable cost of marketing, such as sales commissions, promotional allowances, and local delivery costs, averaged $1.66 per case.

While reviewing the proposal, Mr. McNaughton became aware that total system inventory would decrease in value by $135,000 per annum with the elimination of the Columbus facility. Although this figure represented an intuitive estimate, he felt somewhat encouraged by the fact that it was the consensus among members of his department who had been dealing with distribution since the company started operations. The reduction would be comprised primarily of Indianapolis-produced products.

The phase-out possibility was not without its uncertainties. It was not clear whether additional personnel would be needed to process the orders emanating from the Columbus area. It appeared that the existing system was operating at capacity. There was also the matter of convincing the sales department to lengthen the service time from one day to two or three days. The main competitor was serving Columbus out of Pittsburgh, which is 190 miles northeast of Columbus, while the distance from Indianapolis is 171 miles. Mr. McNaughton has been advised by the president to attempt to phase out at least five field facilities within the year, and the Columbus warehouse was the first to come up for lease renewal.

CASE 5
Favored Blend Coffee Company

The Favored Blend Coffee Company is a prominent manufacturer of coffee sold on a nationwide basis to the consumer and institutional markets. Sales to the consumer market are achieved through wholesalers, chains stores, and other grocery product retailers under the brand name *Favored Blend.*

This case was provided by Donald J. Bowersox of the Graduate School of Business Administration, Michigan State University. The case was updated in 1987.

Sales to the institutional market are achieved by direct account coverage and by the efforts of brokers under the brand name *Best Blend.* With the exception of packaging size and style, the two product lines are identical. Both Favored Blend and Best Blend offer ground and instant coffee in a variety of packages. Both blends are manufactured and distributed in the same production plants and logistics systems.

Until 1985, the Favored Blend Coffee Company prospered and expanded. Sales growth averaged 5 percent annually. Profits, while not increasing in the same proportion as sales, reflected a favorable growth. At the year-end management meeting in 1985, the management group was optimistic about continued growth in both sales and profits. By mid-1987 this optimism had given way to a serious situation. While the sales of Favored Blend's two product lines continued to grow, profits dropped sharply in 1986, and for the first quarter of 1987 a loss was experienced for the first time since 1929. Analysis of the operating figures clearly indicated that increased costs in logistics constituted the major reason for the profit decline. Transportation costs had increased by 4 percent in 1986, as compared to 1985, and warehousing costs were up by 3 percent. Despite a rigorous cost-control program instituted in the last half of 1986, the cost trend had not been reversed during the first quarter of 1987. Year-end finished goods inventory in 1986 was 8 percent higher than in 1985. By the end of the first quarter of 1987, inventory had been forced in line as a result of a reduced production schedule.

In April 1987, Mr. Smith, president and chief executive officer of Favored Blend, called a general management meeting. While the entire group was aware of the fact that a logistics problem existed, the problem reached a new climax when Big Food Chain dropped Favored Blend Coffee from its product line. Mr. Smith had been informed by Big Food Chain's chief executive officer that Big was forced into the decision by alleged poor inventory availability and erratic delivery of orders placed with Favored Blend Coffee. Based upon the apparent inability of Favored Blend's management group to correct the adverse situation, Smith had decided, with the advice of his board of directors, to call in an independent consultant to study and analyze the company and its distribution structure.

At the April meeting Smith presented his decision to retain the services of Able Management Consultants—a firm of logistics specialists. The marketing vice president was in full agreement with the decision. The director of distribution services and the financial vice president were opposed. In their opinion, the problem could be corrected if proper marketing and customer service polices were implemented on a corporatewide basis. They questioned if a so-called high-powered specialist would in fact have sufficient knowledge of food product distribution to conduct a meaningful investigation. At one point in a heated discussion the vice president of manufacturing added to the general argument with the comment, "The last thing we need is some more theory, the last group of so-called experts spent three weeks here and then told us things we already knew and had told them. We need action, not research." After about two hours of discussion, Smith concluded the meeting with the following comment:

> Some of you may be right about consultants, but frankly I feel you're defensive, and the figures just don't support standing by while the situation further deteriorates. I am going to call the head of Able, give him the facts as I know them, and see what he would do if we give him the job.

Case Situation

You are the head of Able Management Consultants. Mr. Smith has reviewed the background of Favored Blend's problem and provided you with the briefing below. Your immediate assignment is to answer questions as instructed at the end of this case.

Smith's Briefing to the Head of Able Management Consultants

In serving its nationwide market, Favored Blend Company operates processing facilities in Philadelphia, New Orleans, and Los Angeles. Each plant supplies a relatively fixed geographical portion of the United States. Operations at each of these fully integrated plants consist of receiving shipments of green coffee from overseas and then blending, roasting, grinding, processing, and packaging the product for customer shipment. As the packaging process is completed, the coffee moves into a shipment either directly to customers or to warehouses throughout the territory of distribution. The production process consists of running a single-size package until estimated weekly requirements are satisfied and then processing other packs in scheduled sequence.

The space devoted to storage and shipping at each plant is small, having been whittled down in recent years by the expansion of space devoted to production facilities for instant coffee. A continuing search for additional space in the plants, on plant property or on property contiguous to the plants, has proven fruitless. As an expedient for making space, the Distribution Services Department has come to favor rail shipments, principally because they find empty boxcars can be used as auxiliary storehouses while being loaded. This added storage space is provided at moderate cost by reason of 48-hour free-time provisions in the demurrage tariff, coupled with the fact that switching is performed at 8:00 A.M. at all plants. As a result, almost three days' loading time is provided on free time before demurrage accrues. Mr. H. J. Speedy, director of distribution services of Favored Blend Coffee Company, is very proud of his accomplishments in this area and has presented the concept several times at industry meetings.

Although coffee consumption in general is fairly predictable, orders from customers tend to be sporadic, so that shipments both direct from the plant and from the warehouses are rather irregular. Attempts have been made at predicting orders; however, the results have not been particularly accurate. The Distribution Services Department has tended to utilize warehouses as outlet valves when the storage problem became burdensome at the plant. In total, 30 public warehouses are utilized by the firm for distribution.

Consequently, though there is a planned supply program, some warehouses have tended to become greatly overstocked, others considerably understocked.

The mixture of Favored Blend and Best Blend products at any single time at any single warehouse often lacks the proper combination of package sizes and grinds. Frequently, cross-hauling between warehouses and emergency shipments from plants has been necessary in order to fill customer orders.

The physical pattern of distribution has been a source of friction between the Marketing and Distribution Services departments for a number of years. In general, it consists of two principal methods:

1. Direct shipments from the plants to the customer in truckload or carload quantities, with less-frequent shipments in LTL quantities.
2. Shipments in carload and truckload quantities to public warehouses located in the market area, with LTL shipments from the warehouse to the customer.

Quantity shipments direct from the plant to customers were at one time of considerable significance and are, in general, lowest cost and most desirable from the Distribution Services Department's standpoint. However, in line with a general trend in business philosophy in recent years toward lower inventory levels, customers have been hesitant to purchase in large enough quantities to warrant delivery in carload and truckload lots. The Distribution Services Department has confronted an increasing demand on the part of customers to order in small lots on an immediate delivery basis, with requested truck delivery. The degree to which this trend has progressed is illustrated by tonnage reports for 1986 in comparison to 1982. In 1982, 80 percent of all coffee, from all locations combined, was shipped to customers by rail, and 20 percent was shipped by truck. By 1986, these figures had reversed.

Mr. Smith has spent considerable time with the Distribution Services and Marketing departments in the attempt to solve the problem of increasing costs. In general, the Distribution Services Department feels that marketing has not instituted realistic price incentives to encourage quantity purchasing and that salespersons allowed customers to unduly dictate terms and routing of shipments. The Marketing Department, in contrast, points to increased competition from private as well as other national branded coffee as the source of the problem. "Competitors provide the service desired by customers, and we have little choice but to try to meet this service if we want the business."

Questions

1. What principles of logistics system design will be helpful to guide Able in approaching a revamping of Favored Blend's operation if they get the assignment? Be specific.
2. Is there sufficient similarity among logistics systems in general to support Mr. Smith's feeling that Able Management Consultants should be capable of handling a food industry assignment? What factors, principles, or general reasons would you as the president of Able present to the management group of Favored Blend to help get the assignment?

3. With 30 warehouses across the nation, why do you feel Favored Blend is constantly faced with the need to cross-haul between warehouses and make emergency shipments to customers from plants? Be as specific as possible regarding current practices that result in poor inventory assortments in individual warehouses.
4. What in your opinion is the total system impact of the Distribution Services Department's policy of using boxcars as warehouses? Keep in mind that both transportation and warehouse costs have recently increased.

CASE 6
Hickory Hill Smoked Foods Company

Hickory Hill is a well-established smoked foods company specializing in smoked turkeys and has been selling its products throughout the northwestern part of the continental United States since 1967. Initially owned and operated by a German immigrant family, the key to the company's success lay in a secret smoking process native to Rhineland, Germany. By 1991, the firm owned 250 retail outlets in addition to 400 franchise arrangements. Though the company sold a variety of turkey products, its competitive strength lay in two main lines of smoked turkeys: Tender Most (1990 sales: $4,350,000) and Golden Best (1990 sales: $6,775,000). The 1991 sales estimates indicate a 15 percent and a 25 percent growth over the 1990 level for the two brands, respectively.

The turkeys were supplied by Kentucky Meadow Turkeys, Inc. The supplier cleaned and smoked the turkeys using the patented process, and provided the necessary industrial packaging for safe shipment to the retail outlets. Hickory Hill coordinated the remaining retailing functions. The cured and packaged turkeys were purchased from the supplier on an FOB origin basis and sold to the retail outlets on an FOB destination basis. Approximately 40 percent of the sales revenue was attributable to direct variable costs for both the brands; and 60 percent of the direct variable costs were estimated to be actual turkey costs (again, for both the brands). These costing percentages were expected to hold for the next few years.

Products

The smoking process employed by Hickory Hill had some unique characteristics which clearly differentiated the company's products from those of its competitors. The Hickory Hill smoked turkeys could be refrigerated for

---

This case was prepared by Rajiv P. Dant, Boston University, and Daniel L. Kurfees, Appalachian State University. Revised 1991 by Jay U. Sterling.

up to 14 days without spoiling. Moreover, they remained fresh and edible for another seven days even without refrigeration. These features, however, did not permit the company to engage in forward buying since the freezer costs were relatively high. Consequently, the company purchased the turkeys from the Kentucky supplier in simple economic order quantities.

Tender Most and Golden Best were sold to retail outlets for $4.00 and $3.50 per pound, respectively. Golden Best sales in 1992, after four successive years of growth, were expected to remain at the 1991 level. However, due to some planned promotions and better positioning in advertising, a 30 percent sales increase was expected for the Tender Most line.

It took an estimated eight days for the railroad freezer cars to bring the smoked turkeys from the supplier's factory to Butte, Montana (Hickory Hill's centralized distribution point), and another two days on average for the commercial trucks to deliver them to the various retail outlets. Tender Most was shipped in the case pack size of 25 pounds, while Golden Best was shipped in 30-pound packs. The inventory carrying costs and the in-transit inventory carrying costs (both expressed as a proportion of the cost of the turkeys) were 30 percent and 25 percent per annum, respectively. The order processing costs were estimated at $20 per order. Hickory Hill paid $8 per hundred pounds shipped for the refrigerated railcars and another $12 per hundred pounds for the commercial trucks (LTL shipments to stores, on a daily basis).

Planning Issues for 1992

From a logistical standpoint, management wanted to examine two issues for the planning year of 1992. In 1991, the company found itself out of stock of Golden Best on several occasions while the fresh goods were in transit. Since Golden Best was their largest selling brand, the company wanted to minimize its cost of lost sales by determining the best reorder point and the best order size. It was estimated that stockout costs approximated $7 per case (in future losses) in addition to the obvious contribution margin losses. The accounting department reviewed the last 50 working days to find the distribution of daily demand from retailers for 1991 (see Exhibit 1).

The current reorder policy was to place fresh orders as soon as the in-hand inventory was down to 1,200 pounds of Golden Best (40 cases). Management wanted to use this information to objectively determine (*a*) the optimal reorder point and, once this was fixed, (*b*) the optimal quantity of cases to order each time.

With respect to the Tender Most brand, management wished to evaluate alternate modes of transportation. Two alternatives were available: (1) the company could stop the use of the freezer cars for delivery up to Butte, Montana, and use company-owned private trucks; or, (2) the company could bypass the railroad and use an air carrier service that would pick up

EXHIBIT 1 Demand for Golden Best during Lead Time, 1991

Demand (in pounds)	*Cases (d) (pounds ÷ 30)*	*Number of Times This Quantity Was Demanded (f)*
5,400 pounds	180 cases	6 times
6,060	202	8
6,720	224	22
7,380	246	8
8,040	268	6
	Total	50

the cases in Kentucky and deliver them directly to the retail outlets. It was decided that if any changeover is economical for the company and the new system (if at all) works well for Tender Most in 1992, in subsequent years, similar feasibility exercises could be carried out for Golden Best.

This reevaluation of transportation modes was triggered by an offer from a new small aircraft company providing cargo shipping at very attractive rates; $10.50 for the first 10 pounds per case for a guaranteed two-day delivery service anywhere in the continental United States; after 10 pounds, each extra pound per case was to be billed at the rate of 50 cents per pound per case. The company-owned truck was expected to cost $1,450 per trip and had a capacity of holding a maximum of 1,290 cases of Tender Most. Each trip was expected to take four days. Since the shipments from the distribution center to the individual retail outlets were relatively small, it was recognized that even if the firm chose the company-owned truck option, the delivery to retailers would still involve the use of commercial trucks.

You have been hired by Hickory Hill as a logistics consultant to carry out the necessary analyses. What are your recommendations? Specifically, you need to answer the following questions.

Questions*

For Golden Best Brand

1. What is the contribution and cost of goods sold (COGS) per case?
2. Compute the projected annual volume, average daily case volume, and EOQ in cases, for 1992.
3. Using the data in Exhibit 1 of the case, compute the standard deviation of sales (σ_s).
4. Assume an average transit time ($\bar{t}$) from Kentucky to Butte, Montana, of 8 days and an average variance in transit (lead) time ($\sigma^2 +$) of 4 days. Compute safety stock requirements (combined effects standard deviation—σ_c) for Golden Best inventories at the Butte, Montana, distribution center that will provide a stock

*In answering the questions, your answers may result in a fraction. You should ask yourself if such a fraction has any real-life interpretation. If **yes,** retain it. If **not,** round it upward, as you would in real life.

protection level of 93.3 percent. (*Use Exhibit 2 when calculating safety stock requirements.*)

5. How much additional inventory would be required and inventory carrying costs incurred if the stock protection level were *raised* to 99 percent? On the other hand, how much could inventories and holding costs be reduced, if the stock protections level were *lowered* to approximately 84 percent?
6. What is the new reorder point, based on your answers to questions 2 and 4?
7. Assume that average inventory consists of the following three components:
   a. Safety stock computed in 4, above.
   b. Average cycle stock inventory.
   c. In-transit inventory (Kentucky to Montana to stores).

   Remember that total costs include inventory carrying costs on the inventory, plus order processing and transportation costs. Further assume that:
   a. Average cycle stock equals ½ of either EOQ or ($\bar{s}$) ($\bar{t}$) [average demand across average lead time], whichever is greater.
   b. There are 360 working days in the year.
   c. Annual case demand equals your computation in 2, above.
   d. The number of order cycles equals annual demand in cases divided by the EOQ.

   Compute the total costs associated with holding inventories.
8. Compute the expected service levels (fill rates) for each of the three stock protection percentages examined in questions 4 and 5 above. Based on this analysis which stock protection level would you recommend, and why?

   The formula for computing fill rate is:

$$\text{Fill rate} = 1 - \frac{I(K)(\sigma_c)}{OQ}$$

Note that OQ = Order quantity (EOQ or demand over lead time, whichever is the largest). Use Exhibit 2 to obtain $I(K)$.

For Tender Most Brand

1. What is the contribution and costs of goods sold (COGS) per case?
2. Compute the projected annual volume, daily case volume, and EOQ in cases, for 1992.
3. What is the total annual logistics cost associated with the current practice of shipping product by rail to Butte and then by commercial trucks to retail outlets? In solving this question assume that annual costs consist of the following components:
   a. Safety stock (assume 550 cases).
   b. Average cycle stock equals ½ of either EOQ or ($\bar{s}$) ($\bar{t}$) [average demand across average lead time], whichever is greater.
   c. In-transit inventory (Kentucky to Montana to stores).
   d. Annual order processing costs.
   e. Transportation from Kentucky to Montana (rail).
   f. Transportation from Montana to stores (truck).

   Consider the following:

EXHIBIT 2 Cumulative Integrals for Standardized Normal Distribution

Standard Deviation (σ) Stock Protection	*Percentage of Stock Protection*	*I(K) Safety Factor*
0	50.00	.3989
.1	53.99	.3509
.2	57.93	.3068
.3	61.80	.2667
.4	65.55	.2304
.5	69.15	.2304
.6	72.58	.1686
.7	75.81	.1428
.8	78.82	.1202
.9	81.60	.1004
1.0	84.14	.0833
1.1	86.44	.0686
1.2	88.50	.0561
1.3	90.32	.0455
1.4	91.93	.0366
1.5	93.32	.0293
1.6	94.53	.0232
1.7	95.55	.0182
1.8	96.41	.0142
1.9	97.13	.0110
2.0	97.73	.0084
2.1	98.22	.0064
2.2	98.61	.0048
2.3	98.93	.0036
2.4	99.19	.0027
2.5	99.38	.0020
2.6	99.54	.0014
2.7	99.66	.0010
2.8	99.75	.0007
2.9	99.82	.0005
3.0	99.87	.0003

option? (Note calculations should recognize the impact that this decision to ship *individual* cases *from* Kentucky *directly* to stores will have on safety stock and cycle stock, as well as in-transit inventories.)

5. Is the private fleet cost of $1,450 per trip a fixed or variable cost? Will this cost change the EOQ formula? If yes, compute a revised EOQ associated with using company owned trucks (private fleet).
6. What will the total annual logistics cost be if the company uses the private fleet option? (Assume that safety stock requirements will be cut from 550 to 279 cases with this option.)
7. Which transportation mode alternative plan should you select, and why?

CASE 7
Worthing Ski Company

Worthing Ski Company is a manufacturer of recreational skis. Started in 1965 by Dan Worthing, an enthusiastic skier, the company encountered rapid growth during the 1970s with the increasing popularity of the sport. By 1984, skis made by Worthing were known for their quality and reliability. The same year, Phil Kennedy was hired as a logistics specialist to professionalize the distribution activities of the company.

Products and Markets in 1985

The company manufactured three brands of skis (Swift Descent, Silver Fleet, and Omni Norge) and sold its products in Austria, Switzerland, and Sweden, in addition to the domestic U.S. market. In terms of the sales revenue, the domestic market was the single largest market and, in 1985, represented 40 percent of total sales. Among the brands, Swift Descent was the best selling model, and represented 42.75 percent of the 1985 sales revenue. Exhibit 1 presents the complete details.

There were substantial differences in the demand pattern for the three brands in different markets. For instance, Omni Norge was the largest seller in Sweden, while Swift Descent was the most popular model in the other three markets. The detailed breakdown is summarized in Exhibit 2. The total sales in 1985 were $10 million for all markets.

All three brands were manufactured out of three chief components: fiberglass, laminates, and steel rims. A close examination of the costing of the brands revealed that direct variable costs were 50 percent of the sales revenue for all three brands. Exhibit 3 shows further details of the costing information on the brands.

Planning Issues for 1986

The prices of fiberglass had been historically unstable and were typically quoted as good for only a few months by Worthing's Houston supplier. The prices of laminates, steel rims, and other components were stable and quoted as good for an entire year by their respective suppliers. All prices typically increased each January. Worthing Ski Company purchased all its ingredients on FOB destination terms, one month's requirements at a time.

A market research study commissioned by the company in 1985 recommended that (from a logistical perspective) the Worthing Ski Company

---

The case was prepared by Rajiv P. Dant, Boston University, and Mark L. Fisher, Appalachian State University.

EXHIBIT 1 1985 Sales Revenue by Market and Brand (percentages)

Markets	*Percent Contributions*	*Brands*	*Percent Contributions*
USA	40.00%	Swift Descent	42.75%
Switzerland	25.00	Silver Fleet	24.00
Austria	20.00	Omni Norge	33.25
Sweden	15.00		
Total	100.00%	Total	100.00%

EXHIBIT 2 1985 Brand Sales by Market (percentages)

	Markets			
Brands	*USA*	*Switzerland*	*Austria*	*Sweden*
Swift Descent	40.00%	45.00%	55.00%	30.00%
Silver Fleet	25.00	20.00	30.00	20.00
Omni Norge	35.00	35.00	15.00	50.00
Total	100.00%	100.00%	100.00%	100.00%

EXHIBIT 3 Costing Information (as percentages of direct variable costs)

	Brands		
Components	*Swift Descent*	*Silver Fleet*	*Omni Norge*
Fiberglass	75.00%	65.00%	70.00%
Laminates	10.00	10.00	10.00
Steel Rims	10.00	10.00	10.00
Others	5.00	15.00	10.00
Totals	100.00%	100.00%	100.00%

should reexamine its credit policy. Specifically, it was suggested that the company should consider the options of extending 30 or 45 days' credit to its distributors. Dan Worthing and Phil Kennedy liked the idea, since they knew that most ski manufacturers extended such credit. Currently, the Worthing Ski Company allowed only 10 days' credit to its distributors. However, it was decided that the idea should be first examined for only one brand in one market. Phil was asked to determine the brand and the market. Dan Worthing put an additional constraint on Phil. He wanted the incremental credit costs fully recovered by the additional sales of the selected brand from the selected market in the same year (i.e., 1986).

Phil realized that the extra credit can be an attractive customer service element to the distributors and, in time, can increase the sales of the company. The sales department provided him with the sales estimates for 1986, as presented in Exhibit 4.

Phil believed that the brand-market segment to which the credit is first

EXHIBIT 4 Expected Increase in Sales in 1986 over 1985 (as percentages of 1985 sales)

	Markets			
Brands	*USA*	*Switzerland*	*Austria*	*Sweden*
Swift Descent	10%	5%	10%	15%
Silver Fleet	5	10	5	5
Omni Norge	10	5	5	5

extended will grow by an additional 5 percent (over the 1985 sales). Phil decided to try out the additional credit policy in the largest brand-market segment first. He asked the accounting manager to provide some estimates of the incremental costs associated with increasing the credit days. Phil was informed that increasing the credit from 10 days to 30 days would cost the company an additional 5 percent of the brand-market segment sales, whereas extending it from 10 days to 45 days would mean an incremental cost of 7.5 percent of the brand-market segment sales.

In 1986, effective January 1, the price of fiberglass is going up by 10 percent. However, any orders placed in December of 1985 would be met at the current 1985 prices. The order processing costs of the firm are substantial, and are estimated at $350 per order. Moreover, since the fiberglass requires special handling and storage facilities, the inventory carrying costs (as a percentage of the cost of fiberglass) amount to approximately 20 percent per annum. Phil also wanted to investigate the feasibility of forward buying the fiberglass, thereby saving the company some money. The Houston supplier of fiberglass informed him that the price increase of 10 percent on January 1, 1986, will hold until September of 1986. No estimates were available about what the prices may be after September.

Game Plan: 1986

Phil has decided to resolve the logistical planning issues for 1986 in the following manner:

A. He decided to develop a classification matrix (in sales dollars) of the three brands and the four markets for an ABC analysis. Such a matrix, he reasoned, would help him to extend credit gradually starting with class A brand-market segments. As a rule of thumb, he decided to classify all brand-market segments with sales of $1 million or more in 1985 to class A; segments with sales between $750,000 to $999,999 in 1985 to class B; segments contributing $500,000 to $749,999 in sales to class C; and the rest to class D.

B. Phil Kennedy has decided to tackle the forward buying issue for fiberglass by a projection for nine months since the price increase expected on January 1, 1986, is only valid until September of 1986. If it were economical for the company to forward purchase the fiberglass, Phil would place the necessary order in December of 1985 to get the fiberglass at the 1985 prices.

Questions

Put yourself in Phil's position and carry out the analyses planned by him. Specifically, you need to do the following. (Caution: When you get a fraction, ask yourself if such a fraction has any real-life interpretation. If **yes,** retain it. If **not,** round it upward or downward as you would in real life.)

1. *a.* Do an ABC analysis table in a matrix form for the 1985 data. The entries in the matrix would be sales dollars. Be sure to show marginal totals for the matrix.

b. Use the classification system selected by Phil to determine which brand-market segments should be classified in classes A, B, C, and D, respectively. You may indicate this within the matrix.

c. Which brand-market segment should Phil select for trying out the extended credit policy?

d. Using the information on incremental costs associated with extending the credit, do a break-even analysis employing the contribution margin approach for the brand-market segment selected by you in answer to question 1*c*. You should assume that *all* the sales expectations will be met and the costing information provided will hold for 1986.

e. Should the credit be extended to 30 days, 45 days, or retained at 10 days?

f. Justify your answer to question 1*e*.

2. *a.* Carry out a nine-month forward-purchase projection for fiberglass for 1986 showing the value of fiberglass required, average inventory values, inventory carrying costs, inventory carrying costs for remaining months, savings in price, savings in order processing costs, and net savings and losses. (Caution: Fiberglass requirements will go up in 1986 as a result of the anticipated sales increases.) You may assume that any orders Phil Kennedy places in December of 1985 for 1986 needs will be delivered to Worthing Ski Company on January 1, 1986, at the 1985 prices.

b. Should the company do a forward purchase of fiberglass? If yes, why and for how many months? If no, why not?

c. Should Phil Kennedy get a raise?

CASE 8
Mirror Stainless Steel

In February, John Bongard, group purchasing manager for Fisher & Paykel Limited, in Auckland, New Zealand, had to select a supplier for the special stainless steel to be used in the company's new line of dishwashers.

Source: Michiel R. Leenders, Harold E. Fearon, and Wilbur B. England, *Purchasing and Materials Management,* 9th ed. (Homewood, Ill.: Richard D. Irwin, 1989), pp. 505–08.

The Range and Dishwasher Division

The Range and Dishwasher Division, one of eight operating divisions of Fisher & Paykel Limited, manufactured mostly dishwashers and electric ranges, 40 percent of which were exported to Australia and 10 percent to the Pacific Islands. Although last year had been a difficult year for the division because of intense competition for electric ranges and low demand for dishwashers, substantial improvements were expected with the recent introduction of the 650 wall oven and 10-minute-cycle dishwasher.

The 10-Minute-Cycle Dishwasher

The new 10-minute-cycle dishwasher incorporated innovative design and manufacturing techniques at a reasonable price. It had been developed over the last two years and introduced at the end of last year. Mass production was scheduled to start by this July. In view of the extremely warm response received from F&P dealers, strong demand was anticipated in both New Zealand and Australia, and plans were made to expand manufacturing capacity.

Mirror Stainless Steel

The old dishwasher used an outdated grade of dull-finish stainless steel in its inside and on its door. With the new dishwasher, F&P marketing people wanted to change to a special mirror-finish, improved-grade stainless steel. Upon investigation, it was discovered that a new high-strength, heat and corrosion resistant alloy existed with the cosmetic attributes favored by marketing. Because of its physical characteristics, the thickness of the steel sheets would be reduced from at least 0.6mm to 0.5mm, with a possibility of further gauge reduction as well. The old dishwasher required between 600 and 700 metric tons of stainless steel per year at a cost of U.S. $1,400 to U.S. $1,500 per metric ton. It was estimated that only 500 to 600 tons of the new material would be required in the first 12 production months.

Watson Steel of America

Watson Steel of America had been the sole supplier of stainless steel for the dishwashers over the last 15 years. John Bongard was very pleased with the price and service offered by this vendor. However, Watson did not produce the special alloy requested and although the company suggested another alloy alternative, it had to be rejected for technical as well as financial reasons.

The Purchasing of the New Stainless Steel

The purchase of the new stainless steel fell under the responsibility of the group purchasing department, since it represented a major purchase involving international sourcing. John Bongard, group purchasing manager, had formed a six-member special committee composed of technical and commercial F&P experts as well as purchasing staff from both the Range and Dishwasher Division and his department to look into the situation. John himself would have the responsibility for the vendor selection and price negotiations. The subsequent physical ordering and day-to-day purchasing operations were the responsibility of the division.

A year ago the committee identified three possible sources for the new stainless steel:

1. Kunder Steel, a large German steel manufacturer which operated in New Zealand through J. T. Hunter, a local agent.
2. Kim Nik Steel, a Korean company dealing through Kiroko Corporation, a trading company, with Paul Dickie as the local agent.
3. The giant Pera Steel Works, which produced this grade of stainless steel in two subsidiaries located in Taiwan and Australia, respectively.

In line with Deming's philosophy adopted by Fisher & Paykel as a whole and for technical production compatibility reasons, single sourcing was the only option considered.

Initially, at the development stage of the new dishwasher and for its market introduction, Kunder Steel had supplied the new stainless steel since J. T. Hunter, its New Zealand agent, happened to have it in stock and there was not time to import it. However, John Bongard had made it very clear to both J. T. Hunter and Kunder Steel that this was a short-term decision and that testing and evaluation for long-term commitment would involve all three identified vendors.

Material Suitability

Over the last two years, all three possible vendors had sent repeated delegations of technical experts, offered advice, checked compatibility of materials, and undergone extensive testing of samples of their stainless steel.

Quality and technical issues were all controlled by the overseas manufacturers as opposed to their local intermediaries.

Although in February the results of testing were not completely finalized, John felt confident that all three suppliers offered viable products, with Kunder Steel the first one in terms of technical preference. Pera's steel from Taiwan was almost equivalent to Kunder's, but Pera preferred to supply the material from Australia, a heavier gauge not suitable at the present time. John felt he could not eliminate the Australian source as a possibility, however, as some technical adjustments could make Pera's steel suitable, and in view of New Zealand's Closer Economic Relations Agreement with Australia. The terms of the agreement allowed duty concessions for New Zealand products exported to Australia in relation to the Australian/New Zealand area content of the products. John was aware of the remote possibility of political pressures to choose the Australian supplier. Pera was also the only one of the three producers that had previous experience with this grade of steel for dishwasher application.

Supply Stability

The long-term stability of supply was one of the factors that most preoccupied John, not only in terms of material availability but also in terms of length of the supply chain or consistency of shipment.

Although the lead time, that is, time from the placement of order to availability from the factory, was similar for all three suppliers, the transit time varied considerably: six to eight weeks from Europe with possibility of delay of two to four weeks; 18 to 20 days from Korea or Taiwan with delays rarely exceeding two or three days; and optimally five days from Australia but with enormous risks of delays due to the bad industrial record of the Australian wharfies. The water between New Zealand and Australia was known as the most expensive water in the world.

Both Korea and Taiwan had direct, regular, and reliable shipping service to New Zealand, their ships typically returning with full cargoes of beef and lamb. Their shipping rates were also substantially lower than Australian ones because of Australian and New Zealand government regulations and high labor costs.

European shipments would make up to a dozen stops at different ports around the world before reaching their New Zealand destination. They also had to pass through the politically unstable Panama or Suez canals to avoid going the long way around South America or South Africa. Occasionally, it even happened that some ships would only go as far as Australia and drop their cargo there, feeling it was "close enough."

John was aware that one way of circumventing the shipping instability problem was to increase the stock levels. But with current New Zealand interest rates fluctuating between 13 and 16 percent for short-term deposits, the costs of servicing inventory were estimated at 20 to 30 percent of the value of the stock.

Price

By February, the data regarding price and terms of payment were available for all three suppliers (see Exhibit 1). These prices included cost, insurance, and freight. As the person responsible for the price negotiations of this purchase for various volumes over a fixed period of time (12 months most likely), John knew that these prices had required extensive bargaining, especially with Kim Nik Steel, the Korean producer, which had become more interested in its market share for this new steel in the New Zealand market than the actual sales volume.

John felt that a decision could not be made without taking into account the long-term trends of the various currencies involved. Exhibit 1 also shows the major international currency movements in relation to the New

EXHIBIT 1 Prices and Terms of Payment

Name	*Terms*	*Price per Metric Ton*
Kunder Steel	90 days BOL*	4,240 DM
Kim Nik Steel	90 days BOL	1,450 US$
Pera Steel—Taiwan	60 days BOL	1,540 US$
Pera Steel—Australia	60 days BOL	1,950 A$

Exchange Rates as of Early February

NZ$1.00 = US$	0.4540
NZ$1.00 = DM	1.4764
NZ$1.00 = A$	0.5926

*Payment due 90 days from the date the bill of lading (BOL) is issued.

Zealand dollar. He felt that the long-term outlook for the New Zealand currency was not good, as he anticipated further relative strengthening of the U.S. dollar against the other currencies.

Relationships with Suppliers

All three vendors considered were financially stable firms of substantial size. Fisher & Paykel had a proven history of good relations with both Kim Nik Steel and Pera Steel Works, which supplied other grades of steel.

The relationship with Kunder was new and had been initiated with the trial purchase of the new stainless steel. John said he had to admit that so far Kunder had performed satisfactorily for F&P and there had been no shipping problems at all.

With these various considerations in mind, John Bongard was trying to assess which of these three vendors made the most sense for a long-term commitment on the part of Fisher & Paykel. With mass production scheduled for July, he knew there was no time to spare.

CASE 9
Flexit International

The Flexit Company manufactures and sells athletic conditioning and sports equipment. Their primary market is for home use, but they received approximately 15 percent of their profits from sales of equipment and spare parts to Aquarius Health Spas, Inc. Home use products are sold

This case was written by Lt. Col. Frederick W. Westfall, USAF, Air Force Institute of Technology. Revised in 1989 by James R. Stock.

through sporting goods stores and larger chain stores such as Kmart, Target, and Wal-Mart.

History

Flexit began business in 1965 as a small manufacturer of exercise equipment and sold their products—weight sets—to schools and gymnasiums. Their product line expanded slowly until the mid-1970s, when the physical fitness craze took off in America. From 1975 until the present, the company expanded both product line and sales territory. They now sell to the continental United States but have never shipped outside that area.

The company president, Mr. Jim Goodbody, is a self-made individual who has always been able to take a direct hand in all company operations. The firm manufactures 100 percent of their products and utilizes motor transportation exclusively for shipments to customers. Flexit has three manufacturing locations. The home office and original plant is located in Ames, Iowa. That facility produces four of the eight Flexit products, including the mainstay of the firm's product line—weight sets. A plant in Oxnard, California, produces two other products (with the largest sales item being a stationary bicycle), and the newest plant in Atlanta, Georgia, manufactures the remaining two products (the fastest growing products in Flexit's product line, rowing machines, are produced here). Products are only produced at one location, so there is no manufacturing overlap between plants. All overall corporate planning activities are carried out by Mr. Goodbody and his staff at the Iowa facility, while product planning activities are performed by the plants.

An International Opportunity

Market research done by an outside research firm in 1987 indicated that a large demand existed in several European countries for home athletic equipment. Existing levels of competition in Europe were less than in the United States. Mr. Goodbody had indicated several times in the past that he would like to enter the European market and eventually become a dominant company there, as well as in the United States. However, because Flexit had no experience in international marketing, an initial determination was made that the optimal form of market entry had to be some form of exporting.

The task of developing an international marketing plan had been given to Mr. Sellem, head of Flexit's marketing operations. Mr. Sellem had been involved with Flexit for several years and before that was a sales representative in the midwestern United States for a large sporting goods company. Like Jim Goodbody, Mr. Sellem had no international experience.

A direct-sales exporting approach was selected by Mr. Goodbody, and so Mr. Sellem and a few of the marketing staff traveled to European countries in 1988 and spoke with a number of wholesalers and retailers about the potential for their products in those markets. After completion of those discussions, Mr. Sellem returned to Ames with a glowing report to Mr. Goodbody. He believed that the market in Europe offered great potential to the company. The decision was made to contact a number of foreign distributors and select one as the means for initially penetrating the European market.

Entering the European Market

Mr. Sellem, in concert with Jim Goodbody, selected Physique, Ltd., as their foreign distributor. Physique was an established distributor, EEC-based, that specialized in sporting goods and exercise equipment in the European Economic Community (EEC), several non-EEC countries, and in many of the Eastern European countries on a limited basis. Flexit gave Physique exclusive rights to the EEC market, and in turn, Physique agreed to provide product and service support, maintain inventories, provide sales efforts for Flexit, handle customs clearances and documentation, obtain the necessary foreign exchange for payments, and coordinate all logistics activities from the U.S. plants of Flexit to locations in the EEC.

The agreements were signed, and Flexit added a second work shift at each of its plants to produce the additional products needed for export. Because of a perceived need to penetrate the European market quickly, Flexit pulled out all the stops and produced the needed items at a record pace. Mr. Goodbody was justifiably proud of the way in which the firm had responded to the added workload and excitedly looked to a future time when the Flexit name would be firmly established in Europe. Mr. Goodbody anticipated that after the first year, 10 percent of Flexit's total production would be sold in the EEC. That forecast was based on no market research but was the result of a consensus of management opinion in both Flexit and Physique, Ltd. Ten percent of Flexit's production would account for approximately $1 million in additional net sales revenue.

Initial Results of the European Operation

Physique reported to Flexit that initial response in Europe to the firm's products had been favorable. In fact, sales in the first three months had exceeded company projections. Extrapolated out for a full year, EEC sales would account for approximately 20 percent of Flexit's total corporate sales volume. Sales breakdowns by product type revealed that weight sets were being sold in slightly fewer numbers than anticipated, rowing machines and stationary bicycles were selling at almost double company projections, and the remaining items in Flexit's line were selling as expected. As a result, Flexit had continued its second shift at its three plants and was concentrating more of its resources on the European market. All seemed to be progressing nicely when suddenly, about five months into the European marketing effort, a telex was received in Ames from Physique, Ltd.

According to the telex, some problems had developed with respect to product quality. Apparently, some defective parts had been used during the production of the products at the plants, and units with those parts were experiencing high levels of product failure. Unfortunately, in the rush to produce the additional products for Europe, Flexit had not had time to test the items prior to shipment. Product quality had never been a problem before, but in the past, Flexit had always tested every item before it left the factory.

Physique had requested an expedited shipment of replacement parts as soon as possible so that the parts would arrive in Europe no later than one week later. However, the inventory of spares at the plants was inadequate to meet Physique's request, so the firm had to drastically revise its production schedules and produce the parts on an emergency basis. In spite of heroic efforts by the firm, the shipments of replacement parts were not made until three weeks after the initial request by Physique. Mr. Goodbody kept his fingers crossed and hoped for the best.

Postscript

It did not take long for the results to come back from Physique. Although the first products that appeared on the heavily promoted EEC market had sold quickly, subsequent sales had fallen off dramatically. Inventories of all Flexit products were at very high levels at all European locations. Product returns were significant, so in addition to the unsold items, inventories of returned merchandise were also at alarming levels. It was the recommendation from Physique that Flexit should let the market "settle down" before continuing their aggressive penetration policy. Mr. Goodbody reluctantly agreed and subsequently curtailed production of products destined for the European market. He thought, however, that the firm had lost a great opportunity and was at a loss to explain what went wrong. Perhaps it was beyond his, or Physique's, control and would have to be chalked up to a combination of bad luck and poor timing.

Questions

1. In light of the results of Flexit's attempt to penetrate the European market, do you believe that the company was wrong in even considering international expansion?
2. What additional information would you like to have had before making the decision to enter the European market?
3. Briefly identify the marketing, production, and logistics decisions that were incorrectly made by Flexit management.
4. What components and considerations should have been part of the international marketing plan developed by Flexit? To assist you, Exhibits 1 and 2 (on the next page) contain information relative to Flexit's corporate goals for the next five years (1989 to 1993) and a brief description of the firm's operating policies and procedures.

EXHIBIT 1 Flexit Corporate Goals for 1989–1993

1. Remain an industry leader in the home physical fitness market in the continental United States.
2. Maintain the existing product line (eight items), concentrating on product improvements rather than new product introductions.
3. Expand the domestic market share from the present level of 38 percent to 50 percent by the end of 1993.
4. Capture a market share of at least 10 percent of the European market (primarily the EEC) by the end of 1993.
5. As a company, continue to be totally self-sufficient but consider alternatives such as off-shore production, importation of related products for sale in the United States, foreign sourcing of parts and other materials, and the establishment of subsidiary operations in the EEC.

EXHIBIT 2 Flexit Operating Policies and Procedures

1. Each plant location is responsible for planning each of its product lines. This includes domestic sales forecasting (based exclusively on a moving average approach), production scheduling, inbound and outbound transportation, and warehousing of all inventories.
2. Raw materials are ordered by each plant and are received by truck shipments.
3. All products are manufactured on-site, each product at a single plant, with production schedules based on sales forecasts made by market planners at the plant.
4. Inbound and outbound distribution activities are totally controlled by each plant. Motor carriage has been the only form of transportation used by the company.
5. The Ames plant will perform all corporate planning, both domestically and internationally. Planning will be accomplished by a committee of the president and the head of Marketing.
6. Each plant will develop its own program of quality control with the objective of having "zero defects." Returned goods resulting from manufacturing defects would be replaced from safety stocks kept at each plant.
7. While customer service is paramount, plants should attempt to minimize inventories. While not adopting the concept completely, Flexit plants will attempt to implement Just-in-Time (JIT) concepts relative to inventories of parts, supplies, work-in-process, and finished goods.

5. Given the present situation, what course(s) of action would you recommend that the company take in the short term? In the long term?

CASE 10
Riverview Distributing Company, Incorporated (1991)

In January 1991, David Rose, president and owner of Riverview Distributing Company, began to wonder if sales to certain types of retail outlets were more profitable to his firm than others. As a rack jobber of housewares, batteries, light bulbs, and home entertainment equipment based in

This information appeared in Donald J. Bowersox, M. Bixby Cooper, Douglas M. Lambert, and Donald A. Taylor, *Management in Marketing Channels* (New York: McGraw-Hill Book Company, 1980), pp. 326–32. Copyright © 1980 by McGraw-Hill, Inc. Used with the permission of McGraw-Hill Book Company. This case was written by Douglas M. Lambert and updated in 1991 by Professor Jay U. Sterling, University of Alabama.

Lansing, Michigan, Rose felt opportunities for continued sales growth in his current lines were very limited. He was planning a sales meeting in late January and was not sure which type of account offered the most profit potential for new business development or which of the company's existing accounts deserved the most attention from the sales force.

Background

Rose opened Riverview Distributing Company in 1978 when he realized that his earnings potential as a ski instructor was low. The first product lines handled by his firm were light bulbs and electrical hardware equipment. His initial success appeared to be due to development of specialized display equipment which presented to customers many different bulbs and hardware items in one place. Previously, most retailers had purchased these products from cash-and-carry wholesalers, but Rose was successful in placing his display units in variety, drug, and grocery stores on a consignment basis. Although Riverview's prices were slightly higher than other wholesalers', the display units and the service provided by his firm were attractive to many retailers. The stores which used Riverview's display units greatly increased their sales in those products.

As the firm continued to grow, several new product lines were added. Because of its success with light bulbs, the firm added a flashlight product line, which ultimately led to the inclusion of batteries for both the photography and flashlight markets. The tremendous growth of transistorized radios and tape recorders further increased demand for batteries. The firm also expanded into the household products field. Kitchen utensils and supplies provided a steady, but not spectacular, source of income.

During 1986 and 1987, Rose decided his firm could distribute radios and tape recorders since it was currently selling batteries for those products. These two products were successful, and other home entertainment equipment was added. By 1991, Riverview's product lines in the home entertainment field included radios, tape recorders, tape players, and stereo components such as speakers, amplifiers, and tuners. The addition of these "brown goods" brought about some changes in the firm's operations. Although each sale had a higher per-unit value than other products, customer financing was required for a longer period of time. Since this merchandise represented the company's fastest growing product line, accounts receivable quadrupled between 1988 and 1990.

The gross profit margins for products distributed by Rose varied considerably. Although tapes and houseware items carried margins of only 10.5 and 16 percent, respectively, batteries and related items contributed much higher margins of 20–25 percent. Rose believed that with increases in sales, his profit margins would also increase because his firm would qualify for volume discounts from suppliers. An examination of Riverview's income statements, shown in Exhibit 1, shows that gross margins in 1988,

EXHIBIT 1

RIVERVIEW DISTRIBUTING CO.
Statement of Income and Retained Earnings
Years Ending December 31, 1988–1990

	1988	*1989*	*1990*
Sales	$520,392	$663,796	$812,937
Opening Inventory	116,894	187,385	261,291
Purchases	$450,377	$558,477	$745,834
	567,271	745,862	1,007,125
Closing Inventory	187,385	261,291	350,000
Total COS	$379,886	$484,571	$657,125
Gross Margin	140,506	179,225	155,812
Operating Expenses:			
Advertising, Travel/Promotion	5,563	6,675	11,237
Truck Expense	6,181	7,881	11,801
Bad Debts	374	408	2,838
Bank Charges/Interest	1,552	2,127	5,609
Depreciation	6,125	6,145	8,265
Insurance	657	1,155	1,449
Legal and Auditing	2,930	3,187	5,053
Utilities	2,385	2,603	3,881
Taxes	2,950	3,442	5,153
Office Supplies	2,831	3,438	6,234
Repairs	827	1,342	609
Salaries:			
Executive	35,000	35,000	35,000
Other	53,754	69,742	87,085
Telephone	1,358	1,594	2,587
	$122,487	$144,739	$186,801
	$18,019	$34,486	$(30,989)
Cash Discounts Earned	1,632	4,822	5,529
Net Income before Taxes	$19,651	$39,308	$(25,410)
Income Taxes	4,912	10,827	—
Net Income	$14,739	$28,481	$(25,410)
Retained Earnings, Beginning of Year	82,764	97,503	125,984
Retained Earnings, End of Year	$97,503	$125,984	$100,574

1989, and 1990 were 27, 27, and 19 percent, respectively. Exhibit 2 contains balance sheets for the three most recent years.

Sales Representatives and Customers

Until 1991, Riverview operated in three sales territories, each covered by a single sales representative. The three territories were designated North, West, and South, with the major cities in each being Lansing, Grand Rapids, and Jackson. In 1990, a fourth territory (East) was added due to a growth in accounts. Its major city was Flint. Each sales representative had full responsibility for maintaining established accounts and opening new accounts in these territories. The sales representatives carried merchandise in a truck, made sales calls, and replenished stock on the spot. They were also responsible for inventory control in the trucks and for accounts receiv-

EXHIBIT 2

RIVERVIEW DISTRIBUTING CO.
Comparative Balance Sheets
Years Ending December 31, 1988–1990

	1988	*1989*	*1990*
Cash	$ 800	$ 9,500	$ 700
Accounts Receivable	44,875	74,895	200,000*
Inventory	187,385	261,291	350,000*
Total Current Assets	$233,060	$345,686	$550,700
Fixed Assets, Less Depreciation	75,797	76,445	91,912
Total Assets	$308,857	422,131	642,612
Bank Loans	$15,000	$22,500	$50,000
Accounts Payable	83,025	157,854	376,948
Accrued Taxes and Insurance	3,329	5,793	5,090
Total Current Liability	$101,354	$186,147	$432,038
Long-Term Loans Due to Directors	100,000	100,000	100,000
Common Stock	10,000	10,000	10,000
Retained Earnings	97,503	125,984	100,574
Total Liabilities and Stockholders' Equity	$308,857	$422,131	$642,612

*Estimated.

able. Sales representatives replenished their inventories from Riverview's office-warehouse location in Lansing. They were compensated on a straight commission basis—8 percent of their net collected sales—and were expected to call on each account at least every 30 days.

Sales representatives were given complete discretion to call on accounts they felt would be potential customers. Informal meetings were held periodically in which Rose discussed the company's plans and encouraged the sales representatives to discuss problems they had with products and/or customers. Through such meetings and with many sales contests, he emphasized the importance of increased sales volume.

An analysis of the company's active customers by type and by route is shown in Exhibit 3. Exhibit 4 shows the sales breakdown by type of account.

Company Growth

Rose and his wife initially assumed all management responsibility for the firm. Mrs. Rose handled office duties until the job became so complex that another person was hired to handle all record keeping. The firm had moved from the basement of the Rose home to an office-warehouse location in Lansing in 1983. As product lines and sales volume grew, Rose hired a warehouse manager who also did some selling in the company's showroom attached to the office.

Objectives

Rose wanted to increase sales because he wanted the firm to make more money. Until 1978 he had been interested primarily in skiing and enjoying

EXHIBIT 3 Analysis of Active Accounts by Type and Route—1990

Type of Account	*Route*				*All Accounts*
	North	*South*	*West*	*East*	
Variety stores	98 accounts: 24 with sales of over $2,000; 16 with sales of less than $200	62 accounts: 21 with sales of over $2,000; 3 with sales of less than $200	41 accounts: 10 with sales of over $2,000; 18 with sales of less than $200	93 accounts: 26 with sales of over $2,000; 12 with sales of less than $200	294 accounts: 81 with sales of over $2,000; 49 with sales of less than $200
Grocery stores	25 4 over $2,000	18 6 over $2,000	12	20	75 10 over $2,000
Drugstores	13 7 over $2,000	10 8 over $2,000	7 2 over $2,000	8 1 over $2,000	38 18 over $2,000
Camera shops	9 1 over $2,000	4	1	13 1 over $2,000	27 2 over $2,000
Discount stores	10 3 over $2,000	1	8 5 over $2,000	10 7 over $2,000	29 12 over $2,000
Hardware stores	10 5 over $2,000*	9 7 over $2,000†	4 2 over $2,000	6 5 over $2,000	29 19 over $2,000
Department stores	7 1 over $2,000	5 1 over $2,000	5 1 over $2,000	4	21 3 over $2,000
Radio/TV/appliance	22 4 over $2,000	10 5 over $2,000	14 3 over $2,000	19 6 over $2,000	65 18 over $2,000
Gas stations/auto supply	27 7 over $2,000	9 2 over $2,000	10 4 over $2,000	34 4 over $2,000	80 17 over $2,000
Miscellaneous	15 2 over $2,000; 5 less than $200	14 3 over $2,000; 4 less than $200	16 5 over $2,000; 5 less than $200	20 1 over $2,000; 8 less than $200	65 11 over $2,000; 22 less than $200
Total accounts	236	142	118	227	723
Sales	$260,953	$175,594	$192,666	$183,724	$812,937
Sales/account	$1,106	$1,237	$1,633	$809	$1,124
New accounts (1990)	50	35	1	72	158

*Includes company's largest account, $11,303.

†Includes company's second largest account, $11,150.

life. But, after Rose married, his father-in-law began to pressure him to build a career. The other members of Mrs. Rose's family had successful professional careers, and Rose was determined to show his father-in-law that he could be just as successful. His objective for Riverview Distributing Company was to achieve a sales volume of $1.5 million by 1995.

The Current Situation

During 1990, accounts receivable had risen to approximately $200,000, and although the year-end inventory count had not yet been made, the book value of inventories was approximately $350,000. Because of this growth, as well as the general overall deterioration of his financial condi-

EXHIBIT 4 Analysis of Accounts by Type of Account for the Year Ended December 31, 1990

Type of Account	Number of Accounts	Cumulative Sales	Percent of Total Sales
		All Routes	
Variety stores	9	$ 37,801	5.72%
	20	82,757	10.18
	36	125,591	15.08
	57	163,400	20.10
	81	203,884	25.08
	116	244,937	30.13
	161	284,690	35.02
	245	325,418	40.03
	294	333,710	41.05
Grocery stores	37	40,891	5.03
	75	47,558	5.85
Drugstores	27	41,053	5.05
	38	43,493	5.35
Camera shops	27	17,072	2.10
Discount stores	12	42,842	5.27
	29	65,521	8.06
Hardware stores	6	39,834	4.90
	29	81,211	9.99
Department stores	21	59,832	7.36
Radio/TV/appliance	12	40,484	4.98
	65	77,148	9.49
Gas stations/auto supply	20	41,785	5.14
	80	67,556	8.31
Miscellaneous	7	13,232	1.63
	65	19,837	2.44
Total	723	$812,937	100.00%

tion, Rose decided to improve his financial management skills by attending a seminar on accounting and finance for wholesalers and retailers conducted by a noted university in the Southeast. This seminar exposed him to several concepts used by accountants to measure the profitability and financial performance of both customer and product line segments, such as the following:

1. Segment contribution margin (sales less variable marketing and distribution costs).
2. Inventory turns and associated costs to carry inventory.
3. GMROI (gross margin return on investments in inventories and accounts receivable).
4. Contribution margin ROI.
5. Earns times turns (gross margin percentage × inventory turnover rate).

EXHIBIT 5 Assorted Data by Product Line

Product	*Vendors' Lead Time*	*Vendors' Payment Terms*	*Riverview's Margin*	*Estimated Average Accounts Receivable*	*Approximate Average Inventory*
Batteries	7–10 days	Net 60 days	25%	$8,000	$28,000
Electrical hardware	2–4 weeks	Net 30 days	28	3,000	9,000
Kitchen utensils	2–4 weeks	2% 10/net 30	16	6,000	20,000
Light bulbs	7–10 days	Net 90 days	18	2,000	14,500
Flashlights	7–10 days	Net 60 days	21	5,000	11,000
Stereo components	Up to 3 months	Net 90 days	22	92,000	160,500
Transistors	Majority 30 days	Net 60 days	18	45,000	60,000
Tapes	10–14 days	Net 60 days	10.5	39,000	47,000

EXHIBIT 6 Percentage of Sales by Account and Product Category

	Batteries	*Electrical Hardware*	*Kitchen Utensils*	*Light Bulbs*	*Flash-lights*	*Stereo Components*	*Transistors*	*Tapes*	*Total*
Variety stores	20%	10%	5%	5%	10%	10%	20%	20%	100%
Grocery stores	35	5	35	15	10	—	—	—	100
Drugstores	10	5	5	5	5	10	35	25	100
Camera shops	65	—	—	—	10	—	—	25	100
Discount stores	10	15	15	15	15	—	—	30	100
Hardware stores	10	35	25	10	20	—	—	—	100
Department stores	10	5	10	10	10	15	15	25	100
Radio/TV/appliance	5	—	—	—	10	35	30	20	100
Gas stations/auto supply	5	—	—	—	10	20	25	40	100
Miscellaneous	5	—	5	5	5	25	30	25	100

As a result of this course, Rose compiled the data in Exhibits 5 and 6 and felt he was now ready to begin his analysis.

Questions

1. What meaningful measurements and ratios should Rose compute as part of his analysis, given the information currently available to him?
2. Which segments of Riverview's business are contributing the most toward corporate overhead and profits?
3. What action should Rose take in order to achieve profitable future growth? For your analysis use an inventory carrying cost of 25 percent and a charge for accounts receivable of 20 percent.
4. What additional information would be useful for the analysis referred to in question 1?

CASE 11
SKF

SKF (Svenska Kullagerfabriken), one of the world's biggest manufacturers of bearings, was established in Sweden in 1907. By 1910, sales offices had been set up in France and Germany and agents had been appointed as far apart as Helsinki and Melbourne. Subsidiary companies had also been set up in the United Kingdom and the United States.

The first U.K. factory opened in 1911, while 1913 saw the opening of the first manufacturing unit in Germany. SKF bought its own steelworks in 1916. The rapid development of the U.S. motor industry led to the setting up of SKF's first manufacturing company in the United States at Hartford, Connecticut, in 1916. Between the two wars there was further expansion of the business, including the purchase of another competitor in the United States and the opening of a second factory in France. World War II brought a halt to the booming expansion, and like other international engineering groups, SKF was placed on a war footing. The task of getting back to normal after five years of war was formidable, although SKF's position was probably no worse than that of other international groups at the same time. The German factories, over which SKF had exercised little control since the 1930s, were largely in ruins. SKF's French installations had also been badly bombed.

Increasing Competition

Competition in the early 1960s was becoming even fiercer. SKF decided to strengthen its Common Market operations. This was partially achieved by the takeover, in 1965 in Italy, of RIV, a bearing manufacturer with 10 local plants and 1 each in Spain and Argentina. After a decade, 67 percent of the Italian bearing market was supplied by RIV-SKF. At the same time, the French SKF company started expanding, partly to meet the needs of its own increasing exports. Two new subsidiaries, Les Applications du Roulement (ADR) and RKS developed satisfactorily, before major interests were taken in La Technique Integrale and Compagnie Generale du Roulement (CGR).

Throughout the 1960s and 1970s, SKF bought up many companies, both inside and outside the bearing business. Despite the diversification of interest, roller bearings still accounted for 70 percent of SKF's business.

In 1973, a corporate audit of SKF's position in the European bearings industry showed them to be a fragmented organization, comprising five largely uncoordinated manufacturing and marketing operations in Sweden, West Germany, the United Kingdom, France, and Italy. SKF had a

---

This case was written by Professor Martin Christopher, Cranfield School of Management, Cranfield, England.

strong position in the market, in part because they had developed a very large product range (50,000 variants) to cater for every need of their customers. Many of these were low-volume products, tailored for the specific requirements of individual customers. Also, the majority of the range was manufactured at all or several of the European locations. This marketing policy necessitated the use of low-volume batch production.

In the early 1970s, SKF came under competitive pressure from a hitherto unknown area, that of Japan. Two of Japan's largest general machinery manufacturers, Fuyo and Sumitomo, poured vast amounts of resources into bearing companies such as Koyo Seiko, Tsubakimoto Precision Products, and many others. This meant that the Japanese manufacturers could pursue an aggressive pricing strategy to penetrate the European market. Using line production, that is, high volumes of each variant, the production costs were much lower than those of SKF. Although the Japanese produced fewer variants—only 10,000 compared to 50,000 of SKF—they were able to sell products of equivalent quality at prices equal to SKF's manufacturing costs.

Question

Discuss the courses of action open to SKF to counter the Japanese competitive threat in Europe.

CASE 12
Ferle Foods, Inc.

It was 7:35 A.M. on November 17, 1986, and the American Airlines 727 had just taken off from New York's LaGuardia Airport enroute to Chicago. In seat 17C was Charlie Sims, AT&T's national account manager on the XYZ Industries account. Charlie found it difficult to contain his excitement. He had been directing a major order processing system study at Ferle Foods, Inc., a subsidiary of XYZ Industries, for the past four months, and the study was now drawing to a close. Bill Belt, the account executive on the Ferle Foods account had called Charlie on Friday with the news that the automated order processing system that the AT&T account team was planning to recommend to management would require a one-time investment for hardware and software of $495,000 and would result in annual

---

This case was adapted by Douglas M. Lambert from material provided by the American Telephone and Telegraph Company, Business Marketing, Market Management Division. It was prepared to illustrate the type of situation the AT&T account executive is likely to face, and any similarity with actual individuals or companies is purely coincidental. Used with permission of American Telephone and Telegraph Company.

savings of $131,000 over the company's existing order processing system. In addition, the proposed system would lead to inventory reductions, transportation consolidations, warehousing cost savings, and customer service improvements. However, dollar amounts still had to be attached to these benefits, and Charlie wanted to assist in the calculations. He hoped that the savings would be large, in excess of $1 million, so that management at XYZ Industries would purchase the proposed system and want similar studies in its other divisions.

XYZ Industries

Ferle Foods was a wholly owned subsidiary of XYZ Industries, a *Fortune* 500 corporation which manufactured and sold a variety of packaged goods products ranging from food items to consumer sundries. Products of the subsidiary companies included food, beverages, disposable plastic containers, toys, clothing, and specialty chemicals.

Each subsidiary operated as a separate corporate entity with its own management team which set policies. However, corporate approval was required for investment decisions involving more than $25,000. Corporate headquarters was placing the subsidiaries under increasing pressure to improve cash flow and return on investment.

Ferle Foods was the most recent acquisition made by XYZ Industries, and, although its sales volume was larger than many of the company's other subsidiaries, its net profit and return on investment were the lowest.

Background: Ferle Foods, Inc.

Ferle Foods manufactured and distributed nationally a full line of canned vegetables, fruits, condiments, and specialty items. The company had manufacturing facilities in Indianapolis, Indiana; Anaheim, California; and Griffin, Georgia. Each plant manufactured some of the product line, but no plant manufactured the complete line.

The Indianapolis plant, which was the largest and oldest, produced 75 percent of the products in the product line, the Anaheim plant produced 50 percent of the product line, and the Griffin plant manufactured about 35 percent of the products.

Ferle Foods had a sales volume of $200 million and profit of $2 million in its most recent year of operations. The company's financial data are summarized in a strategic profit model format in Exhibit 1.

Approximately 90 percent of the company's sales were derived from wholesale grocers and supermarket chains. The balance was sold to institutional accounts. The company marketed its products under the Ferle brand name and also private labeled for major supermarket chains. About 10 percent of the annual sales volume was private label business, but this was increasing.

The company handled between 2,000 and 2,200 orders per month. Ferle brand items, which comprised about 98 percent of the orders, were

EXHIBIT 1 The Strategic Profit Model (Financial data in $ million)

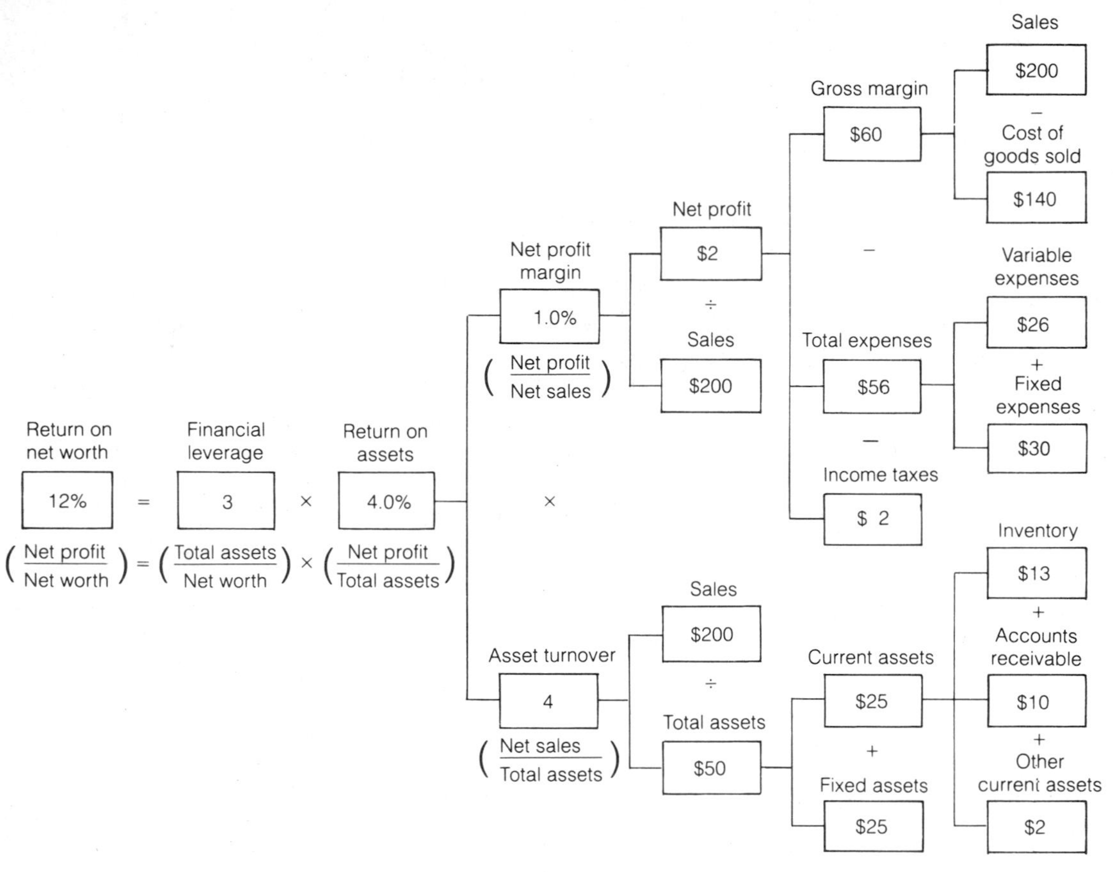

NOTE: Net worth = Shareholder's investment + Retained earnings.

sold to more than 1,000 customers. However, fewer than 50 of these customers represented 75 percent of the business. There were only 40 private label customers, primarily the large supermarket chains, which accounted for almost one half of the Ferle brand business and all of the private label sales.

Price was the single most important method of competing for private label sales, followed by customer service. The private label market was characterized by a large number of small competitors. No advertising was undertaken, and minimal sales effort was required. Generally customers wanted fast deliveries of these items because stockouts on the private label resulted in lost retail sales.

National brands, on the other hand, were a different story. A few large companies dominated this market. Large sales forces and considerable

EXHIBIT 2 Partial Organization Chart

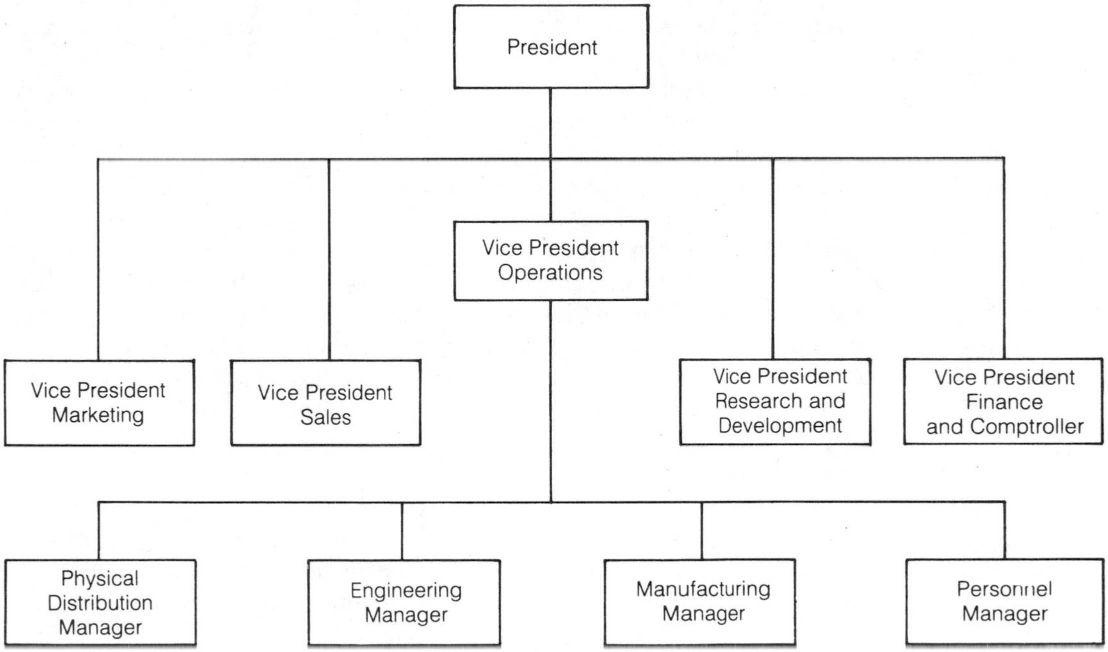

mass advertising and promotional expenditures were the major means of meeting competition. Price was a much less important factor with nationally advertised brands. Ferle Foods employed a sales force of 83 for its nationally advertised Ferle brand products and 1 for the private label business. When stockouts occurred on a national brand item, another national brand was usually given the shelf space.

Orders for Ferle brand products were filled from inventory, and private label products were manufactured on receipt of orders.

Physical Distribution at Ferle Foods. The company's manager of physical distribution reported to the vice president of operations and shared the same rank and status as the manufacturing manager (see Exhibit 2). His areas of responsibilities included warehousing, distribution system design, inventory management, and transportation. All of the physical distribution personnel were located at the company's central headquarters in Chicago.

Ferle currently owned three plant warehouses, which, in addition to serving as distribution centers (DCs) in their respective market areas, restocked field distribution centers. Ferle also used four warehouses owned by the company and maintained three public warehouses specializing in grocery products and servicing other companies in the grocery trade. Customer service levels were set at 95 percent in stock availability, but the company was currently achieving about 90 percent. Although many of Ferle's competitors were providing customers with a 10-day order cycle, Ferle's order cycle averaged 14 days. The locations of the various facilities are summarized in Exhibit 3.

Approximately 60 percent of the shipments to field warehouses were by rail, and the remainder were shipped by motor carriers. All customer shipments were FOB destination. Truckload and carload orders received direct service from the nearest plant warehouse.

Restocking of field warehouses was based on normal usage levels for each location, which were reviewed periodically and changed if required. This enabled the company to react more quickly to changes in the marketplace than would be possible if an order were placed for the economic order quantity whenever the inventory on hand and on order reached a predetermined minimum level (fixed order point, fixed order quantity model). With the current system, orders were placed for inventory transfer when the normal usage indicated that the remaining cycle inventory was equal to the expected demand during the replenishment cycle.

Communication with field warehouses was by telephone, teletype, or mail. Effective communications had been a problem with some of the public warehouses because their teletype terminals were not compatible with Ferle's system. In each case the warehouse operator solved the problem by adding an additional terminal.

Order Processing. All incoming orders were received by the sales/service department in Chicago from the field sales offices. The customer service representatives within sales/service answered customer inquiries about order status and solved customer problems related to damaged merchandise, incorrect shipments, or billing errors. Normally, the sales/service department received 100 orders per day, but this volume could reach 350 per day in peak periods. An organization chart for this department is presented in Exhibit 4. Approximate salary figures for different positions are also indicated.

The procedure for processing orders was as follows:

1. The salespeople either met with or called their customers on a weekly or biweekly basis to get the orders which they called or mailed to a district sales office. When orders were called in, a written confirmation order was sent to the sales office. Orders were transmitted to the company's headquarters via teletype.
2. At the headquarters office, orders were given to clerical personnel who manually looked up all necessary information in the customer's file. The order-writing clerks filled out standard order forms, transcribing directly onto these forms the customers' requested shipping or delivery dates as the dates which would be met by the company.
3. Customer orders were then directed to the sales/service manager,

EXHIBIT 3 Ferle Foods Locations

Headquarters:
Chicago, Illinois

Plants/distribution centers:
Indianapolis, Indiana
Anaheim, California
Griffin, Georgia

Distribution centers:
Elizabeth, New Jersey
Richmond, Virginia*
Kansas City, Missouri*
Dallas, Texas
Denver, Colorado
San Francisco, California
Portland, Oregon*

Sales offices:
Atlanta, Georgia
Hartford, Connecticut
Detroit, Michigan
Chicago, Illinois
Dallas, Texas
Denver, Colorado
San Francisco, California
Long Beach, California
Kansas City, Kansas
Baltimore, Maryland
Seattle, Washington
New York, New York

*Public warehouses.

EXHIBIT 4 Organization Chart—Sales/Service Department

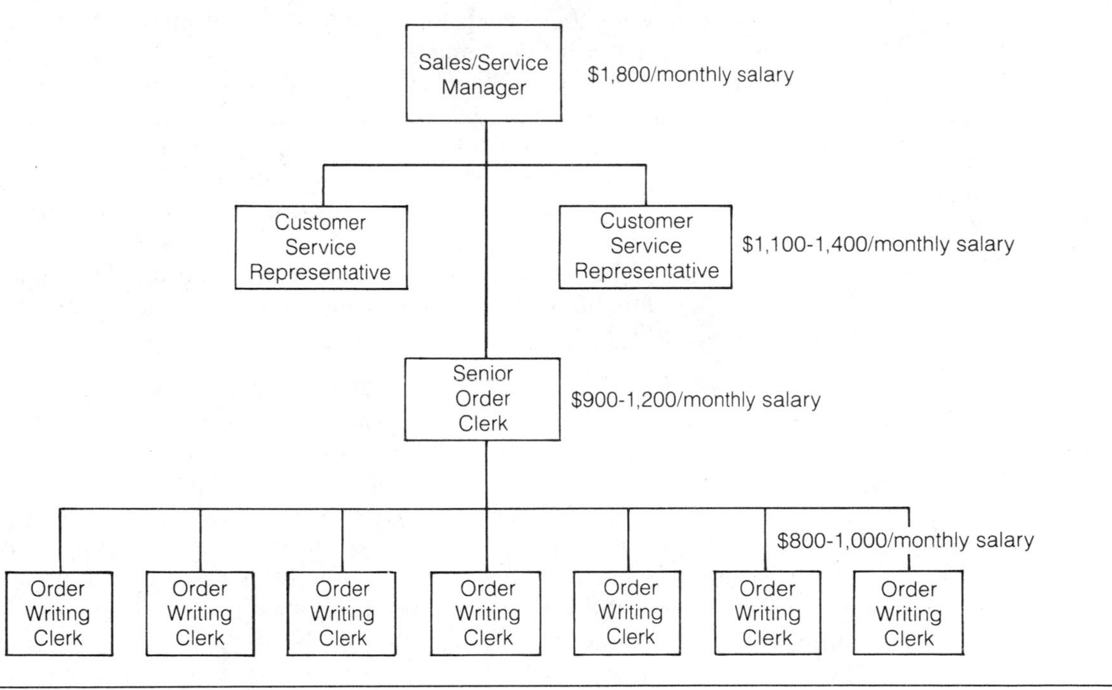

who compiled a log of the number of orders for branded products by truck/rail route and total tonnage by route, distribution center, and total company. The log also indicated the volume of private-label products ordered by plant location. Often, manufacturing managers from plants would call the sales/service manager to get a general idea of the volume of private label product being ordered on a given day. Likewise, distribution center managers called to get the jump on equipment needs, that is, the number of trucks/railcars required. Sometimes transportation needed to urge sales to sell more volume on a particular route to avoid shipping at less-than-truckload (LTL) rates. After entering the order in the log, the orders were directed to the appropriate customer service representatives.

4. The customer service representatives noted the orders in their records and passed them back to the order-writing clerks. The customer service representatives spent about one third of their time actually processing orders and two thirds tracing late orders and resolving customer problems.
5. When the order-writing clerks received the orders, they keypunched them on an IBM key-to-diskette unit.
6. The orders were then batch loaded into the computer, which generated the final order documents.
7. The computer generated picking documents and shipping information, which were sent by teletype to each distribution center. Sales orders for private label products were transmitted to the appropriate plant location for production scheduling.
8. The teletypes at the field warehouse locations received and printed four-part picking and shipping documents. The orders were filled, and a copy of the packing list was mailed to the Chicago headquarters for keypunching. From the packing list, customer invoices were prepared. Bills of lading were prepared at the field warehouses.

A simplified flowchart of the order processing system as described above is presented in Exhibit 5. The order cycle from the customer's point of view is summarized in Exhibit 6. The customer's order cycle time, that is, the time from order placement to receipt of merchandise, ranged from 6 to 22 days and averaged 14 days. However, when order levels increased greatly prior to price changes, the average order cycle time increased. Sometimes individual orders were lost in high-volume periods and did not reappear until after the customers complained about not receiving the shipment. Some of the confusion was due to the high turnover of order clerks, and some was caused by the order clerks' processing the less complicated orders first.

When the district sales offices were busy, orders often would not be transmitted to the Chicago headquarters until written confirmation had been received from the salesperson. The cutoff for the batch processing of orders was 3:00 P.M. each day, and sometimes salespeople would attempt

EXHIBIT 5 Flowchart of Existing Order Processing System for Ferle Brand Sales

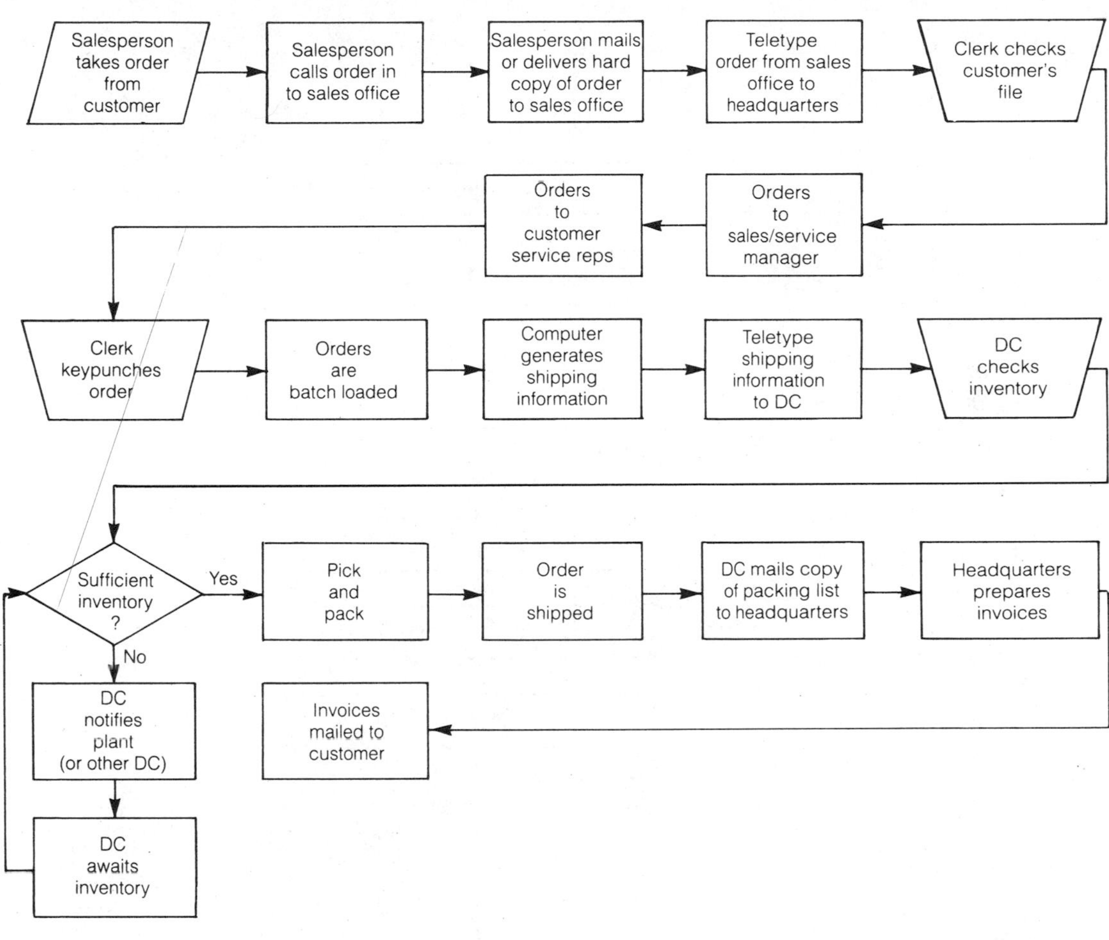

to override the system by telephoning late orders directly to the order-writing clerks for keypunching.

Salespeople did not receive notification that an order had been entered into the system. Nor did they receive notice of product substitutions, shorts, order cancellations, or shipping delays. The changes in individual product pricing were updated monthly and were sent out to the field on Thursdays. Promotions were also updated on Thursdays but did not take effect until the following Monday. Consequently, customers could be quoted incorrect prices or promotion information and be unaware of the discrepancy in prices until their copy of the invoice was received. However, the problem that annoyed customers the most was inconsistent delivery times. Two practices that contributed to this problem were (1) when a stockout occurred,

EXHIBIT 6 Customer's Order Cycle

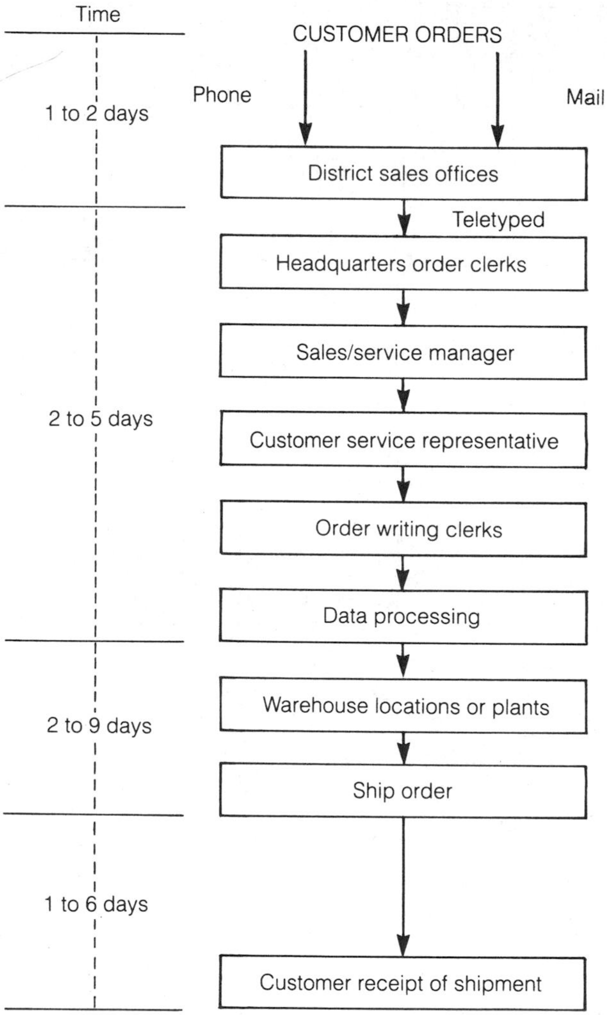

NOTES:

1. The order cycle ranged from 6 to 22 days.
2. The average order cycle was 14 days.

orders were held at the distribution center or plant until the product was available; and (2) the shipping department often held up shipments until a full truckload could be arranged.

Stockouts at the distribution centers occurred in part because there was no system for tracking customer usage by product and, therefore, no established basic inventory levels by product. When an order reached the distribution center, it was discovered that there was not enough inventory to fill the order. As a result, the order was held until the needed inventory arrived. There was no notification to either the customer or the salesperson that the order was waiting to be filled. When the inventory was low, the order was shipped short or held for 100 percent fill, which could delay the order for as long as a week.

Complaint calls usually were made to the district sales offices, but also to field warehouses. When customers were really annoyed, they would call the vice president of sales.

The AT&T Study

During the flight, Charlie Sims reviewed the major findings of the study conducted by the AT&T account team. A good deal of information had been collected, and he wanted to be prepared for his meeting in Chicago.

Excerpt from an interview with a distribution center manager:

There are really many reasons for delivery dates being missed, and not all originate here in the distribution center. Sometimes we do let orders sit because we don't have sufficient inventory to fill them. When that happens, we end up having to fill an inordinate amount of orders in a short period of time, because we are filling the back orders as well as those new orders that are coming in.

Excerpt from an interview with a salesperson:

The price figures we get are mailed from headquarters. They arrive on a weekly basis, usually on Tuesday, but they're effective beginning Monday. Unfortunately, we're frequently not in the office on Tuesday because we're out calling on customers. So we don't see the new prices until at least Tuesday night, and that means that what we've quoted for two days has been wrong. Therefore, orders have to wait to be corrected by the shipping department or the clerks or someone. At any rate, the corrections really are out of our hands. But we hear about errors every day from the customers. They receive their bills and call to tell us we misquoted the price. Another recent problem involves consumer complaints. We hear about these problems through our customers. Ferle prints an address on packages so that consumers can write to the company with complaints.

Excerpt from an interview with an accounts receivable clerk:

Each of the five accounts receivable clerks is assigned to a certain region, and we are in charge of making sure that the accounts are paid on time and that they are invoiced correctly. The job includes cutting the original invoice.

We have to correct any errors that are noted on remittances and then check every other item on the order individually to make sure that it's correct. Essentially, it means redoing the entire order. Let me tell you, it's a time-consuming job. Do you realize each price and promotion has to be looked up by hand? Sometimes, because the invoices are weeks old, we have to go back and check through three or four weeks of summaries to find the applicable unit price or promotion. It can be a slow process. The customers sure let us know when we've made a mistake, too. That is, the customers complain when the price on the invoice is higher than the one originally quoted. I have no idea how many errors are made in the customers' favor; I receive very few inquiries when the price on the invoice is less than the one originally quoted. An invoice can be processed in 10 minutes if everything is straightforward. However, if there are any questions and errors, it could take as much as two hours of an accounts receivable clerk's time as well as delay payment to Ferle by an average of 10 days. It takes an average of 45 minutes to reconcile an invoice. About 2 percent of all invoices require reconciliation. On the average, accounts receivable requiring adjustment contained overcharges equal to 10 percent of the invoice value.

Excerpt from an interview with the vice president of sales:

Consumer inquiries and complaints are handled by our customer service group at headquarters. We receive about 100 letters a month. Consumers today are getting very demanding. They want to know as much about the product as we do! We try to satisfy their curiosity, but it's difficult. Often, we don't even have the information they want.

Safety Stock Calculations. The safety stock required to achieve the desired 95 percent product availability at the Elizabeth, New Jersey, distribution center was calculated by statistically sampling product movement for a representative 25-day period (10 percent sample), as shown in the table below.

Day	*Cases Demanded*	*Day*	*Cases Demanded*	*Day*	*Cases Demanded*
1	900	10	900	18	1,100
2	1,100	11	900	19	1,200
3	1,300	12	800	20	900
4	1,000	13	1,000	21	800
5	700	14	1,200	22	600
6	1,200	15	1,300	23	700
7	1,100	16	1,100	24	800
8	1,400	17	1,000	25	1,000
9	1,000				

Since the safety stock calculation must consider lead time variability as well, a sample of 16 replenishment cycles for the Elizabeth facility was taken.

Replenishment Cycle	*Lead Time in Days*	*Replenishment Cycle*	*Lead Time in Days*	*Replenishment Cycle*	*Lead Time in Days*
1	7	7	6	12	6
2	8	8	9	13	9
3	6	9	8	14	8
4	10	10	5	15	7
5	7	11	7	16	5
6	4				

Because field and plant warehouses were restocked on the basis of the central inventory file at headquarters, shipments were not authorized until two or three days after the inventory level at the warehouse indicated a need for more stock. It was believed that the proposed information system could reduce the average replenishment cycle to the Elizabeth distribution center from seven days to five days and would eliminate two days of variability in the replenishment cycle.

The safety stock levels for the company's other six distribution centers before and after the proposed system change are summarized below:

Distribution Center	*Current Safety Stock*	*Estimated Safety Stock*
Richmond, Virginia	1,875	1,150
Kansas City, Missouri	1,640	1,250
Dallas, Texas	2,400	1,350
Denver, Colorado	1,800	1,000
San Francisco, California	3,850	1,700
Portland, Oregon	2,400	1,400
Totals	13,965	7,850

In addition, it was estimated that inventories at plant warehouse locations could be reduced by a total of approximately 10,000 cases of product.

Inventory Investment Costs. The average variable cost per case of a product delivered to the distribution center had to be calculated for each location. The company used a full standard costing system, and, based on the inventory plan, a weighted-average cost per case was $60.00. The weighted-average variable manufactured cost was 75 percent of the full cost. The transportation cost associated with replenishing the Elizabeth distribution center was approximately $750,000 for the most recent year. Warehouse handling charges for the same period were $125,000. The business year was comprised of 250 days.

Average variable cost figures for the other six field distribution centers used by the company were as follows:

Distribution Center	*Average Variable Cost**
Richmond, Virginia	$50
Kansas City, Missouri	49
Dallas, Texas	51
Denver, Colorado	50
San Francisco, California	49
Portland, Oregon	52

*Per case of product delivered to location.

The inventory carrying cost data collected by the study team are summarized in Exhibit 7.

EXHIBIT 7 Inventory Carrying Costs—Summary of Data Collection Procedure

Cost Category	*Source*	*Explanation*	*Amount (current study)*
1. Cost of money	Comptroller	This represents the cost of having money invested in inventory and the return should be comparable to other investment opportunities	40 percent before taxes
2. Average monthly inventory valued at variable costs delivered to the distribution center	Standard cost data—comptroller's department Freight rates and product specs are from distribution department reports Average monthly inventory in cases from printout received from sales forecasting	Only wants variable costs since fixed costs go on regardless of the amount of products manufactured and stored	$10,140,000 valued at variable cost delivered to the DC. (Variable manufactured cost equaled 75 percent of full manufactured cost. Variable cost FOB the DC averaged 78 percent of full manufactured cost.)
3. Taxes	Bill Johnson of the comptroller's department	Personal property taxes paid on inventory	$116,000
4. Insurance	Bill Johnson	Insurance rate per $100 of inventory (at variable costs)	$5,000
5. Recurring storage (public warehouses and corporate warehouses)	Frank Gardner, distribution operations analyst	This represents the portion of warehousing costs that are related to the volume of inventory stored	$289,000 annually
6. Variable storage (plant warehouses)	Manager, transportation services	Only those costs that are variable with the amount of inventory stored should be included	nil
7. Obsolescence	From distribution department reports	Cost of holding product in inventory beyond its useful life	0.8 percent of inventory
8. Shrinkage	Frank Gardner, from distribution department reports	Requires managerial judgment to determine portion attributable to inventory storage	$128,000 (8 and 9 combined)
9. Damage	Frank Gardner, from distribution department reports	Requires managerial judgment to determine portion attributable to inventory storage	

EXHIBIT 7 *(concluded)*

Cost Category	*Source*	*Explanation*	*Amount (current study)*
10. Relocation costs	Not available	Only relocation costs incurred to avoid obsolescence should be included	Not available

Transportation Consolidations. The company's annual transportation bill was almost $16 million. The transportation manager believed that a distribution information system such as the one described by the study team could enable him to consolidate shipments from distribution centers to customers and in some cases from plant locations to customers. Shipments from plants direct to customers would lead to warehouse handling savings. The savings associated with the number of planning days were estimated as follows:

Number of Planning Days	*Estimated Transportation Cost Savings*	*Estimated Warehousing Cost Savings*
1	$ 100,000	$ 15,000
2	250,000	35,000
3	500,000	75,000
4	900,000	150,000
5	1,250,000	180,000
6 or more	1,400,000	200,000

Current Communication and Data Equipment. The cost of the company's current order processing system and the cost of the system proposed by the AT&T account team are summarized in Exhibit 8. Exhibits 9–11 provide detail on the cost of the current system. The AT&T solution included 800-number service for customer order transmittal and an improved communications network linking headquarters with sales offices, manufacturing facilities, and distribution centers. The cost of the proposed system summarized in Exhibit 8 includes personnel costs and the annual cost of 800-numbers, outward WATS lines, and the communications network. In addition, there would be a one-time cost of $495,000 for hardware and software. Other pertinent information is contained in Exhibit 12.

EXHIBIT 8 Annual Savings in Order Processing Costs Associated with the Proposed Order Entry and Order Processing System

Activity	Annual Cost: Existing System	Annual Cost: Proposed System	Savings Associated with Proposed System
Order processing			
Headquarters	$152,416.50*	$169,455.00	($ 17,038.50)
Sales office	149,832.00†	139,480.00	10,352.00
Distribution centers	246,277.00‡	108,250.00	138,027.00
Total	$548,525.50	$417,185.00	$131,340.50

*From Exhibit 9.

†From Exhibit 10.

‡From Exibit 11.

EXHIBIT 9 Headquarters Costs—Existing System

Activity	Annual Cost	
Order receipt (equipment costs)		
$103 × 12 months		$ 1,236.00
Order processing costs		
Six order clerks		
100 orders at 30 minutes per order		
= 50 hours which is 50 hours ÷ 6 clerks		
= 8.33 hours per clerk per day at $6.40*		
= $53.31 a clerk per day × 250 days		
= $13,328 per year per clerk × 6 clerks	$79,968.00	
Two customer service reps.		
2.5 hours × $8.96 per hour †		
= $22.40 × 250 days		
= $5,600 per year × 2 people	11,200.00	
Sales/service manager at $21,600‡		
75% time reviewing/logging orders		
25% time answering calls	21,600.00	
Senior order clerk at $14,400§		
Job undefined (assume back up)	14,400.00	127,168.00
Paper costs		
Order forms		
100 order forms per day × $0.05 per page × 250 days	$1,250.00	
Logs—sales/service manager		
3 pages per day × $0.05 per page × 250 days	37.50	
Customer service reps		
2 × 9 pages per day × $0.05 per page × 250 days	225.00	1,512.50
Transmission costs		
Distribution centers		
15 minutes × 10 DCs × $.50 per minute × 250 days	$18,750.00	
Plants		
10 minutes × 3 plants × $.50 per minute × 250 days	3,750.00	$22,500.00
Total headquarters cost—existing system		$152,416.50

*6 order clerks at $12,000 per year = $6.40 per hour (usually only 6 of the 7 order clerk positions were filled).

†2 customer-service representatives at $16,800 = $8.96 per hour.

‡1 sales/service manager at $21,600 = $11.52 per hour.

§1 senior clerk at $14,400 = $7.68 per hour.

EXHIBIT 10 Sales Office Costs—Existing System

Activity	*Annual Cost*
Labor (clerk time)	
One clerk is required for each office at $10,000 each	$120,000
Transmission	
100 orders per day × 1 minute each × $0.50 × 250 days	12,500
Paper	
100 orders per day × 2 (salespersons' forms plus clerk's forms) × $0.05 per form × 250 days	2,500
Costs for 12 sales offices	$135,000
Teletype rental ($103 × 12 months × 12)	14,832
Total sales office costs	$149,832

Note: Salesperson expense for DDD (direct distance dialing) to call in orders was not calculated. Also, it was assumed that there was no change in salesperson call time.

EXHIBIT 11 Distribution Center—Existing System

Cost Category	*Annual Cost*
Labor	
Clerks	
One clerk is required at each DC at $15,000 each	$105,000
Clerks (inventory—assume full time)	
Physical inventory inbound and outbound records, transshipments, etc.	
Total salary at $15,000 × 7 DCs	105,000
Paper	
10 order forms per day × $0.05 per form × 250 days × 7 DCs	875
Mail (assumes mailing two envelopes per day)	
Accounts Receivable mail 2.50 per day × 250 × 7 DCs	4,375
Inventory mail 2.50 per day × 250 × 7 DCs	4,375
Teletype machine	
$103 per month × 12 months × 7 DCs	8,652
Telephone	
Inter-DC/plant calls (stockouts, etc.)	
200 calls per month × 15 minutes × $.50 per minute × 12 months	18,000
Total cost for seven distribution centers	$246,277

Assumption: Four company-owned DCs and three public warehouses were treated the same under the assumption that all expenses were billed to the manufacturer either under contract or by separate billing.

EXHIBIT 12 Other Pertinent Information

1. Order forms were purchased in large quantities because Ferle received the best price this way: 20,000 forms cost $1,000. These are four-part forms and are used by salespeople, sales clerks and order-writing clerks at headquarters. Each one fills out a form for every order. The salesperson fills out the form at the customer's place of business and gives one copy to the customer, keeps one, mails one to the sales office, and throws the last copy away. If the order is called in, the sales clerk fills out a form during and after the call. One copy is filed, the others thrown away after the order is teletyped to headquarters. The order-writing clerk at headquarters fills out a form, gives a copy to the sales-service manager, and throws two copies away.
2. Order-writing clerks spent 30 minutes writing, editing, referencing files, and keypunching one order. They reference customer credit files, price lists, and promotional lists.

EXHIBIT 12 *(concluded)*

3. The sales service manager spent 75 percent of his time reviewing and logging orders; the other 25 percent was spent responding to telephone calls from plant and DC managers. Some managers called twice daily, while others never called.
4. The headquarters transmitted picking and shipping information on branded goods to 10 DCs daily at 5:00 P.M. It took 15 minutes per transmission.
5. At the DCs, picking was carried out in a batch format; that is, all the cases of a given product were picked at one time and brought to a staging area. Here orders were assembled and loaded onto trucks or rail cars.
6. Headquarters had to send several documents to each DC: (1) picking lists—one for each storage area; (2) order information for use in staging, sequencing, and loading trucks and rail cars. All documents were sent to a warehouse clerk who sorted them, made copies when necessary, and delivered them to the appropriate personnel. In addition, sales offices teletyped special instructions and product allocation rules to the DCs.
   Following is a description of how these documents were distributed:
   a. Four-part picking lists—taken to the supervisor who filed one copy, gave two copies to three picking supervisors (different picking lists), and threw one copy out. At the end of the night one copy of each of the picking lists was mailed to headquarters, where they were keypunched and entered into the computer to update the inventory file. This file was used to determine replenishment of the DCs and plant warehouses. As mentioned in the text, this caused delays and variability in replenishment cycles and contributed to large safety stock levels and stockouts.
   b. Assembly copies of order—four-part document, one for each order—the clerk takes these to the transportation office for sequencing. A transportation clerk writes a sequence number on each one and makes a log of the orders by sequence and by route. The clerk takes the assembly documents to the supervisor, who gives them to the two assemblers. As an order is assembled, this person records on the form shorts, substitutions, and weight of product being shipped. At the end of the night one copy is sent back to the transportation office, where the bills of lading (BOLs) are prepared (they require tonnage data). The BOLs are sent to the dock and given to truck drivers. The remaining three copies are:
      (1) Sent with the order to the customer.
      (2) Mailed to headquarters for invoice preparation.
      (3) Filed at the DC.
   c. Special instructions and product allocation instructions were first copied by the clerk; then distributed to the supervisor, who gave a copy to picking supervisors, inventory clerk, assemblers, and two or three men loading the trucks and rail cars; and then sent to the transportation department.
7. The cost to mail picking and packing papers was $2.50 per day. Keypunching was accomplished the same day the assembly and picking document arrived at headquarters.
8. Because stockouts occurred often at DCs, they tended to circumvent headquarters by calling direct to plants or other DCs to locate product needed to fill orders. Telephone calls between DCs and plants usually lasted 15 minutes. About 200 calls per month were made for this reason. Ten calls could be placed in just one instance of a stockout. Transshipments did come about as a result, which cost Ferle $500,000 annually in transportation costs alone.
9. The company works 22 days per month. (250 days per year).
10. Salaries at the distribution centers:
   a. Supervisor—$25,000 per year.
   b. Picking supervisor—$22,000 per year.
   c. Transportation manager—$28,000 per year.
   d. Clerks—$15,000 per year.
   e. Assemblers and dock workers—$20,000 per year.
11. Customer service is defined as order fill rate, that is, the number of orders shipped versus the number of orders received (not line-item fill).
12. When stockouts occurred on major products, manufacturing was often required to modify production schedules during the week of production. The manufacturing manager estimated that the cost of these last-minute changes in the production schedule was in excess of $40,000 per month.

Questions

1. Develop a proposal for the Ferle Foods account.
2. Demonstrate the cost justification for the new order processing system.
3. Based upon the information given and upon your proposal, what is the next area that you will pursue with this account?

Company Index

Author Index

Subject Index